STATISTICAL METHODS

Volume Two

SIXTH EDITION

James R. Beatty
San Diego State University

The McGraw-Hill Companies, Inc.
Primis Custom Publishing

New York St. Louis San Francisco Auckland Bogotá
Caracas Lisbon London Madrid Mexico Milan Montreal
New Delhi Paris San Juan Singapore Sydney Tokyo Toronto

McGraw-Hill Higher Education
A Division of The McGraw-Hill Companies

Statistical Methods
Volume Two

McGraw-Hill's Primis Custom Series consists of products that are produced from camera-ready copy. Peer review, class testing, and accuracy are primarily the responsibility of the author(s).

1 2 3 4 5 6 7 8 9 0 DEH DEH 0 9 8 7 6 5 4 3 2 1 0

ISBN 0-07-246126-8

Editor: Barbara Duhon
Cover Design: Maggie Lytle
Printer/Binder: DeHart's Printing Services

Go forth in peace!
Render no one evil for evil!
Be kind to one another!
Practice quality in every
aspect of your life!
Learn for learning's sake!
You will be blessed!

This book is dedicated to Russell and Thelma,
to Kimberly, Lynn, and Susannah,
to Dylan, Mark, and Joe,
to Bethany, Samantha, Sydney, and Noah,
to Brunhilda and Samson,
and especially to Ann. I am truly blessed!

Table of Contents

CHAPTER 12

ONE-WAY ANALYSIS OF VARIANCE

Case Study 12.1

Problem. Hardshell Industries is a large farming complex that has recently received a number of complaints from grocery stores regarding an increase in the quantity of broken eggs per shipment. Robert Gray, Operations Manager of the farm, has been approached by a number of suppliers, each claiming to have "state-of-the-art" egg containers that will minimize egg breakage during shipping. Before signing a long term contract with any one supplier for egg containers, Mr. Gray has decided to evaluate the claims of the three lowest bidders by giving one month contracts to each supplier. At the end of each month, he intends to check with his customers to determine the number of broken eggs received. He plans to randomly assign one summer month to each of the suppliers, and he will examine an equal number of shipments per supplier. The shipments to be examined will also be randomly determined.

Methodology Solution. In the problem described above, Mr. Gray has one variable of interest (the number of broken eggs per shipment) and one classification variable or factor (suppliers of egg containers). He is interested in comparing the number of broken eggs shipped per supplier. We will follow the flowcharts in Figure 12.1 to determine an appropriate methodology for analyzing Case Study 12.1. We enter the flowcharts at ***Start***. Since he wants to compare the central tendencies of broken eggs for the three suppliers, we turn to flowchart 1. We only have one variable of interest (broken eggs); the number of broken eggs is at least interval level; and we are not limited to only one sample. In fact, we have more than two samples, so we turn to flowchart 3. We now confirm that we are seeking a test for comparing central tendencies that satisfies at least one of the following conditions: We have either more than one classification variable, more than two samples, the existence of concomitant variables, or any combination of these. We do not have more than one variable of interest; and we do not have repeated measures on the variable of interest (as each egg is measured only one time) or matched samples. We have only one classification variable (suppliers); we are not using any concomitant variables; and each of the samples of egg shipments per supplier is independent of the shipments of other suppliers. If we have satisfied the assumptions for a one-way analysis of variance (ANOVA) as discussed in this chapter, we will use this procedure. If we do not feel that these assumptions have been satisfied, we have other choices. One alternative would be to modify our data in an effort to satisfy the assumptions for ANOVA, such as making nonlinear transformations on the data (if it would make sense to do so). Another alternative would be to use the Kruskal-Wallis test, which is a nonparametric statistical procedure. Figure 12.1 shows the route taken as described above.

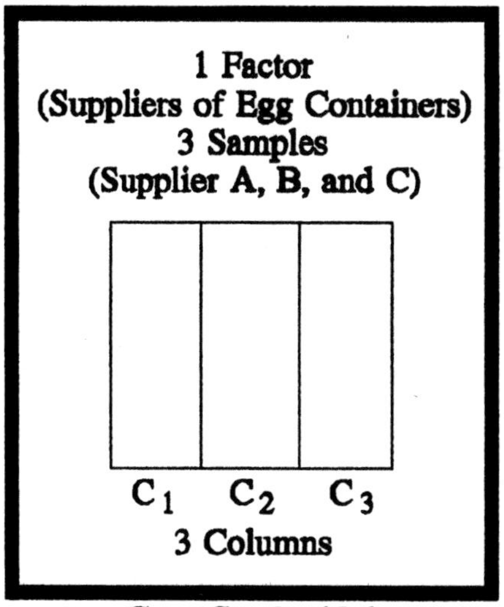

Case Study 12.1

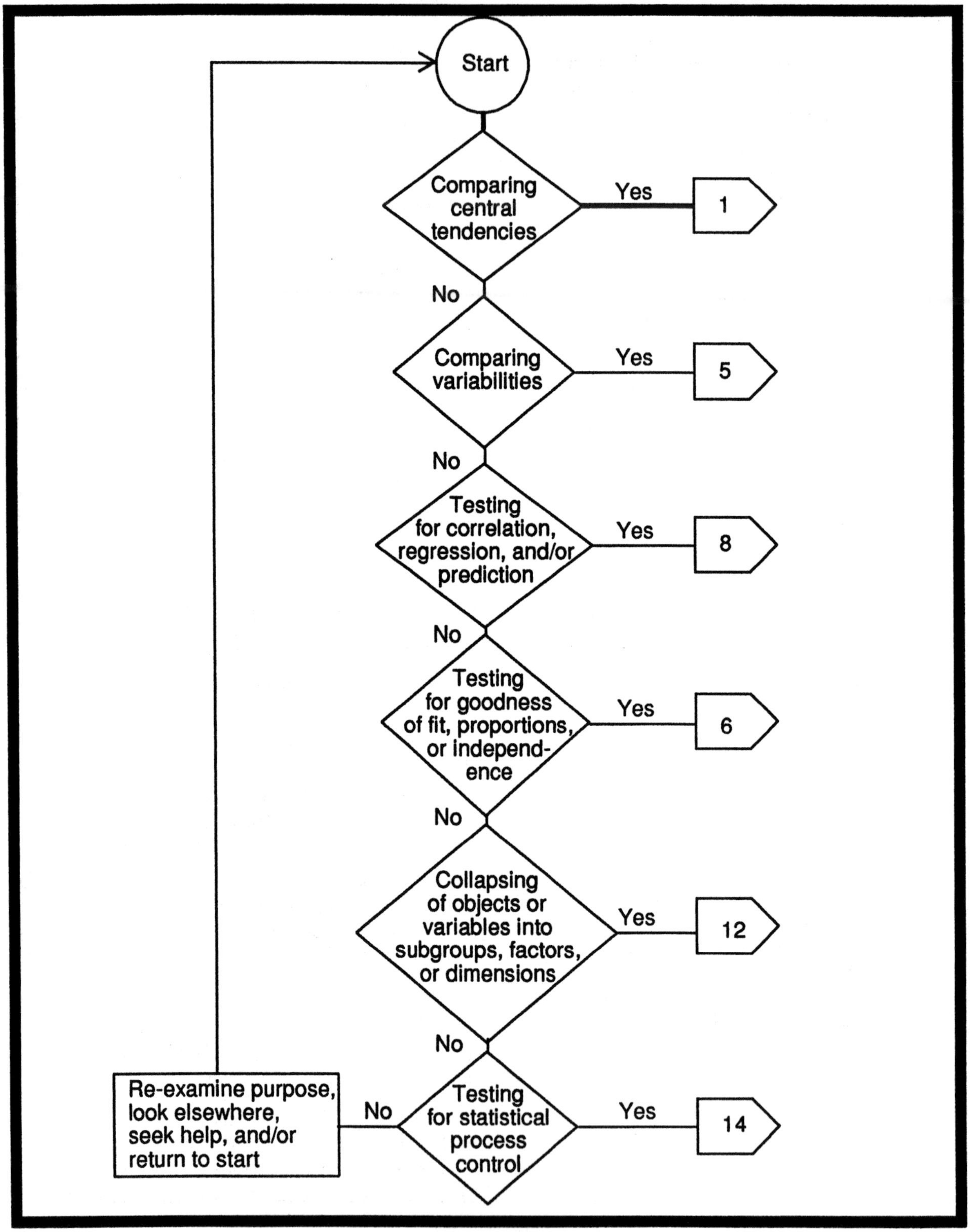

Figure 12.1
Statistical Decision-Making Flowchart for Case Study 12.1

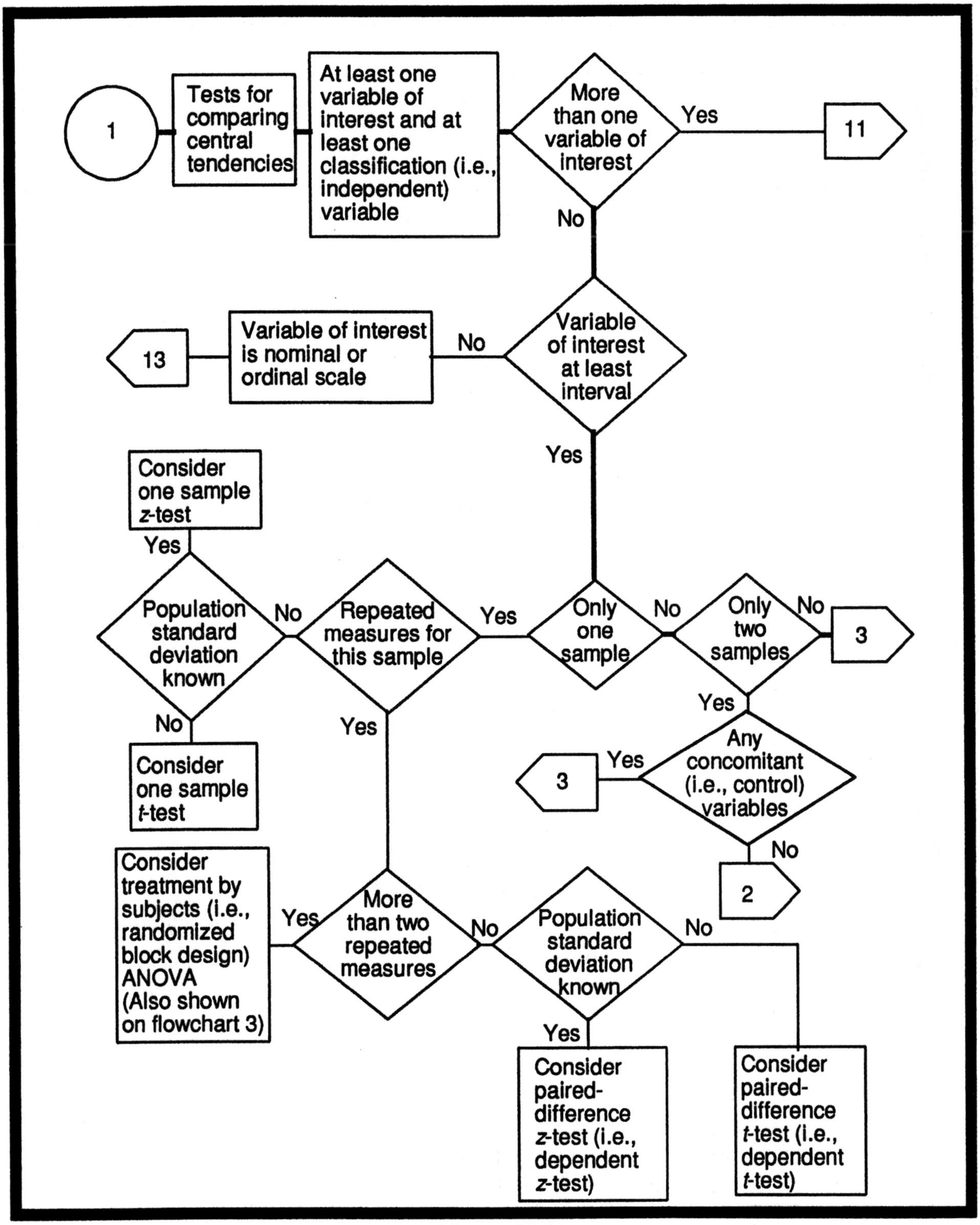

Figure 12.1
Statistical Decision-Making Flowchart for Case Study 12.1
(continued)

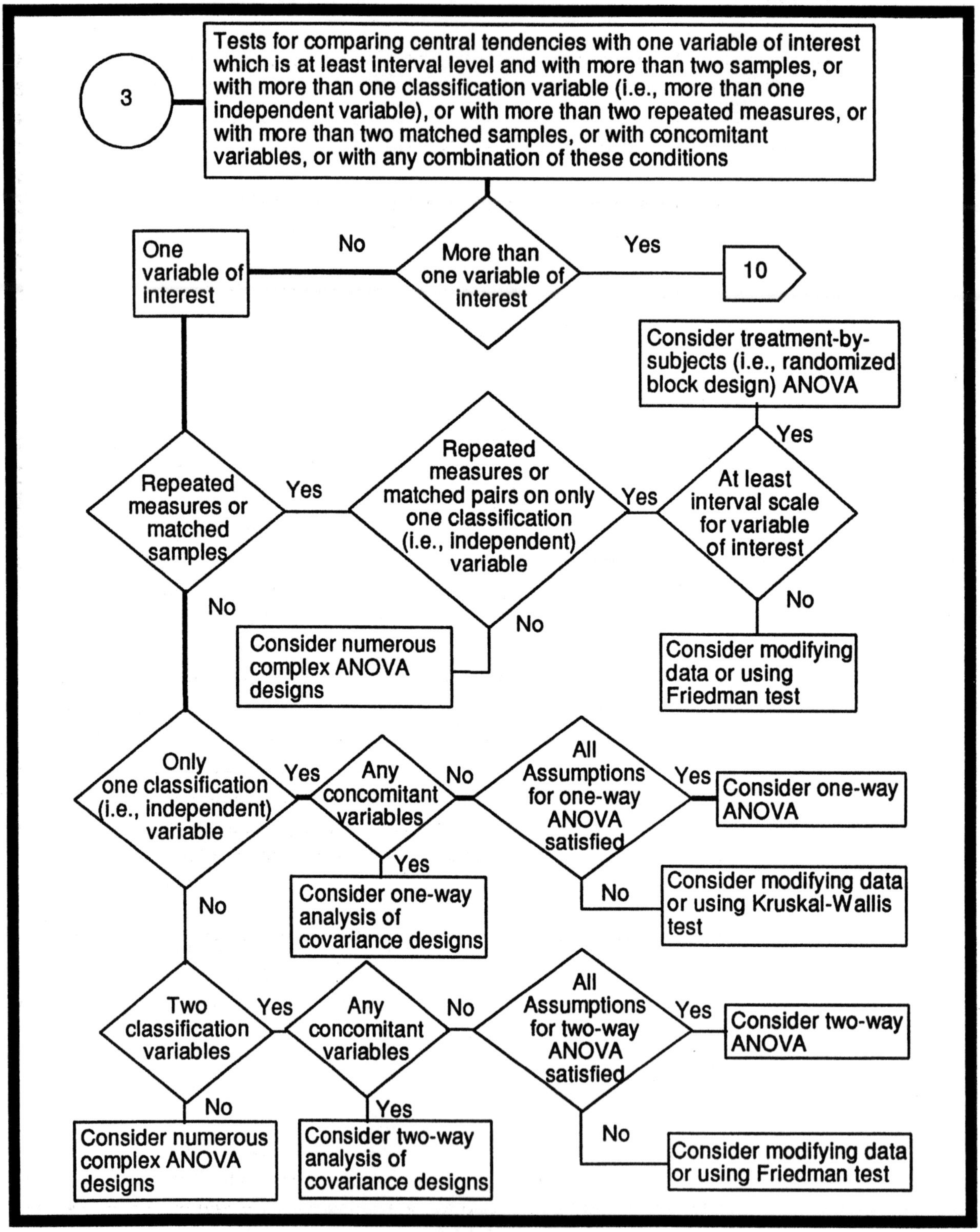

Figure 12.1
Statistical Decision-Making Flowchart for Case Study 12.1
(continued)

Where Are We Going?

Previously, we discussed tests for comparing the mean of a sample with the mean of a population and for comparing two sample means. These tests provide methods for analysis of elementary research problems. However, as we attempt to examine hypotheses and make decisions about situations in our complex world, we often encounter problems that go beyond one or two sample situations. Chapter 12 and Chapter 13 discuss analysis of variance (ANOVA), a family of statistical techniques for analyzing differences among means for two or more samples, using one or more classification variables, using repeated measures on the variable of interest, working with three or more matched samples, and/or using concomitant variables. Chapter 12 will focus on the general concepts of ANOVA, emphasizing one-way ANOVA, while Chapter 13 will focus on several ANOVA designs beyond the one-way model.

Flowcharts and Terminology for Chapter 12

When using the master flowcharts to locate statistical procedures for comparing central tendencies beyond the one-sample and two-sample situations, we begin with ***Start***, immediately advance to flowchart 1, and soon move to flowchart 3, as shown in Figure 12.1. We will concern ourselves with problems that deal with comparing central tendencies of at least interval level data for only one variable of interest; thus, we will utilize flowcharts 1 and 3. Textbooks concerned with multivariate statistics often address situations dealing with more than one variable of interest. Flowchart 11 would be appropriate under such circumstances.

Chapter 12 deals with situations where we have more than two samples but only one classification variable. Chapter 13 deals with situations that have more than one classification variable, or with situations where we have matched more than two samples, or with situations in which we have only one sample but have three or more repeated measures on each case within the sample. As stated above, ANOVA can be used to analyze problems with ***two or more samples***; however, most researchers will use z-tests and t-tests to analyze differences between two samples, while reserving ANOVA for problems with more than two samples.

Methodological concepts and terminology may need clarification before we can determine which of the many analysis of variance designs is appropriate for particular situation. Table 12.1 gives a list of many of the terms associated with analysis of variance. Several of these terms are discussed at the onset to assist in understanding analysis of variance. Specific details associated with these terms and concepts will be addressed later.

Classification Variables

We have made reference to classification variables above and in previous chapters. Classification variables typically refer to nominal or ordinal variables consisting of categories or levels. We are usually interested in the impact of these variables on the variable of interest. For Case Study 12.1 we had one classification variable (the supplier distributing the various egg containers) and three categories of supplier (the three egg container companies). Other examples

Table 12.1
Analysis of Variance Terminology

Analysis of Variance Terminology
1. Classification Variables
2. Classification Variables as Factors, Dimensions, Attributes, or Levels
3. Analysis of Variance Designs
4. Nonparametric Statistical Alternatives
5. Repeated Measures
6. Matched Samples
7. Concomitant Variables

of classification variables include sex, college major, type of company, type of product, type of reward system, type of accounting procedure used, presence or absence of experimental treatment, etc. Classification variables are typically thought of as nominal level variables, since we are usually classifying data (e.g., individuals, companies, organisms, etc.) into discrete categories without regard to rank order. However, classification variables are sometimes ordinal level, as discussed below.

Classification Variables as Factors, Dimensions, Attributes, or Levels

Some textbooks use the word ***factors*** when referring to classification variables. For example, the one-way analysis of variance recommended for Case Study 12.1 can also be referred to as a ***one-factor*** analysis of variance.[1] Other textbooks will refer to classification variables as ***dimensions***. The one-way or one-factor analysis of variance is then referred to as a one-dimensional analysis of variance. When we use analysis of variance to evaluate data for a research design that includes two classification variables, we can refer to the statistical procedure as a two-way analysis of variance, as a two-factor analysis of variance, or as a two-dimensional analysis of variance.

---

[1]The term ***factor*** is also used in regard to ***factor analysis***, where the word has a different connotation. Thus, we will avoid the use of this term when referring to a classification variable in one-way analysis of variance situations.

We may occasionally find the word ***attributes*** used when referring to classification variables. For Case Study 12.1, we are only looking at one particular attribute of the egg containers: the supplier that distributes the egg containers. Therefore, we might refer to the statistical procedure as a one-attribute analysis of variance. If we were to include another attribute of the egg containers, such as type of material used (either cardboard or plastic), we could refer to the statistical procedure as a two-attribute analysis of variance.[2]

Classification variables have also been referred to as ***levels***. However, the present textbook will reserve the use of the word ***levels*** to classification variables that are treated as ordinal level variables. For example, we may be interested in the level of supervision of our subjects (e.g., first level, second level, third level), the level of management, the level of education, the level of training, the level of experience, or the level of heights. As suggested by these examples, such classification variables are ordinal level variables or are being treated as ordinal level (e.g., height of the subject is ratio but could be reclassified as tall, medium, and short).

These terms (classification variables, factors, dimensions, attributes, or levels) have also been referred to as the independent variable(s). In fact, it is not uncommon to refer to the variable of interest as the dependent variable and the variable whose impact we are examining as the independent variable.

Analysis of Variance Designs

As suggested earlier, there are many analysis of variance designs. Chapter 12 will be limited to one-way analysis of variance designs. Chapter 13 will discuss two-way analysis of variance designs and treatment by subjects designs. A brief introduction to three-way analysis of variance will also be given. Analysis of covariance (ANOCOVA) and other ANOVA designs have also been developed to compare means. Such designs are natural extensions of the basic one-way and two-way models. While these designs will not be presented in the present textbook, the reader may want to consult Duncan (1986), Juran and Gryna (1988), Keppel (1991), Kirk (1968), Winer (1971), or a variety of other sources for a discussion of these designs.

Nonparametric Statistical Alternatives

Nonparametric statistical procedures have been mentioned in flowchart 3 and elsewhere as statistical alternatives to the many analysis of variance designs available. If we cannot satisfy certain assumptions for analysis of variance (e.g., interval level measurement) to be discussed shortly, we do not have to terminate our analysis. Alternatives do exist with which to complete

---

[2]Some textbooks, especially in the field of quality control, use the term ***attribute*** to refer to a two-category situation: either the attribute exists or it does not exist. For example, the product is defective or is not defective; the valve switch is on or is not on; the formula includes the chemical or does not include the chemical; the experimental condition is used or is not used.

the analysis. Two such nonparametric alternatives are the Kruskal-Wallis test and the Friedman test. Although these nonparametric techniques are less powerful than traditional analysis of variance techniques, they are often very useful options. Textbooks by Daniel (1978), Noether (1971), Siegel (1956), and others give good discussions of these techniques.

Repeated Measures

Example 12.1. Example 12.1 will be used to illustrate the concept of repeated measures in an analysis of variance design. Suppose that a company has obtained performance data for a set of 50 employees who have been with the company for a period of one year. Their potential performance was evaluated during pre-employment training; it was again evaluated at the end of one month, six months, and twelve months. Identical procedures were used to evaluate performance at each of these four checkpoints. The company now wants to compare the means across each of these four trials.

Following Figure 12.1, we again turn to flowchart 1, where we are soon asked whether we have only one sample. In this example, we do have only one sample, but we also have ***repeated measures*** on the variable of interest since we have observed performance over several time trials. As a dependency exists for performance scores from trial to trial (i.e., performance on trial 2 is somewhat dependent upon trial 1, etc.), this dependency must be accounted for in our statistical analysis. If we have only two repeated measures, we can use the paired differences *t*-test discussed in Chapter 10. However, since we have more than two repeated measures, a treatment by subjects analysis of variance design (T x S ANOVA) would be appropriate to analyze this example. The T x S ANOVA design will be discussed in Chapter 13.[3]

Matched Samples

Example 12.2. Example 12.2 will be used to illustrate the concept of matched samples in an analysis of variance design. Suppose that the above company now wants to compare the performance of employees at four different plants. Although they are interested in comparing average performance across plants, they have a potential problem in their analysis since they may have very different samples from plant to plant. Therefore, they have attempted to match ***similar*** employees from plant to plant on some variable before comparing the results. They have matched an employee in the first plant with an employee at the second, third, and fourth plants on some variable, then matched a second employee at the first plant with similar employees at the other three plants, etc.[4]

---

[3]The term ***trend analysis*** has also been used occasionally to describe this design.

[4]Matching employees across four different plants may be a very difficult task. There are usually limitations in regard to variables which can be used to match individuals. Also, potential samples may be too limited in size to satisfy the necessary criteria for effectively matching employees across plants.

Since the central tendencies for more than two samples are now being compared, Figure 12.1 will now lead us to flowchart 3. Soon a question is asked regarding whether the situation includes either repeated measures or ***matched samples***. For Example 12.2, the employees have been matched over the four plants. The treatment by subjects analysis of variance is again appropriate to analyze the data. A dependency exists in the scores for the matched sets of employees, since every employee is similar with counterparts in three other plants on some matching variable. The designs for Example 12.1 and Example 12.2 are different; but the statistical procedure is the same, since dependencies are being accounted for in both examples.

Concomitant Variables Anocova

Example 12.3. We will use Example 12.3 to illustrate the utilization of concomitant variables in analysis of variance designs. Suppose that a team of industrial psychologists employed by a company is experimenting with three different compensation methods. They want to determine whether these methods have different impacts on employee performance. Since the study is being conducted within an organization instead of within a laboratory setting, they do not have the luxury of randomly sampling and assigning employees to different work activities (i.e., treatment groups) through experimental design. Therefore, the psychologists have decided to use a different method of compensation with each of three existing work segments within their labor pool. They will assign compensation methods to groups by convenience. Of course, employees within these groups must be given the option to continue with the organization-wide compensation program. This option adds to the complexity of the study, since some halo effect may now be influencing the results. Only those who agree to accept the new programs will be included in the data base for the samples to be analyzed. Unfortunately, the three samples differ considerably in regard to the length of time that employees have been with the company. It is not feasible to ***match*** each employee with similar employees across the two other settings on length of time, since time with the company varies considerably from group to group. Instead, the team of psychologists has decided to control for these pre-existing differences among samples by using time with the company as a ***concomitant*** (i.e., control) variable. That is, in the absence of an experimental design that controls for differences in the length of time, they will use length of time as a concomitant variable to made statistical adjustments on the variable of interest.

Since the central tendencies for more than two samples are being compared, Figure 12.1 will again lead us to flowchart 3. Performance is the only variable of interest, there are no repeated measures on the variable of interest, and the three groups have not been matched. There is only one classification variable (type of compensation method), and the psychologists are using a concomitant variable. Analysis of covariance is an appropriate statistical tool for analyzing Example 12.3. ANOCOVA is referred to as a subset of ANOVA in some textbooks and as a multivariate statistical procedure in others. ANOCOVA will not be discussed in the present textbook.

Assumptions for the One-Way Analysis of Variance

Example 12.4. Before discussing the quantitative aspects of analysis of variance, we will examine the assumptions associated with this procedure. In Example 12.4, suppose that four hamburger chains have been aggressively competing for the "quarter-pounder" hamburger market. Each chain has boasted that its hamburgers are bigger than those of the competition. Although the Food and Drug Administration has regulations in regard to weight *before* cooking, consumers are typically interested in the size of the hamburgers *after* cooking. An independent consumer advocacy group wants to determine whether there are any differences in the weights of these hamburgers after they have been cooked and, if so, whether any such differences can be attributed to the hamburger chains. For the sake of the present chapter, we will assume that size is the only criterion for hamburger satisfaction (disregarding taste, appearance, fat content, calories, or other potential criterion variables). Thus, the weight of the hamburgers after cooking is the variable of interest.

Methodology Solution. In this example, the advocacy group wants to compare the central tendencies of the hamburger weights for four independent hamburger chains. To determine a correct statistical procedure for the advocacy group, we should enter Figure 12.1 at ***Start*** and then go to flowchart 1. The only variable of interest is the weight of the hamburgers, which is at least interval level. They are not limited to only one sample; in fact, they have more than two samples (four hamburger chains), which takes us to flowchart 3. We now confirm that they are seeking a test for comparing central tendencies that satisfies at least one of the following conditions: either more than one classification variable, more than two samples, existence of concomitant variables, or any combination of these. They do not have more than one variable of interest; they do not have repeated measures on the variable of interest (as each hamburger is measured only one time); and we do not have matched samples. They have only one classification variable (hamburger chains); they are not using any concomitant variables to statistically control for other variables (e.g., we do not have access to the size of the hamburgers prior to cooking); and the size of each of the hamburgers per chain is independent of sizes of the hamburgers of the other chains. Thus, flowchart 3 leads to the one-way ANOVA design (assuming that the assumptions for this design, to be discussed below, have been satisfied).

Assumptions

The assumptions associated with the one-way analysis of variance are essentially the same as those associated with the two-sample independent *t*-test given in Chapter 10 earlier. These assumptions are listed in Table 12.2. As before, we can perform tests of significance to examine several of these assumptions, and we will have to presume that the other assumptions have been satisfied. Otherwise, we should not perform analysis of variance.

Table 12.2
Assumptions for One-Way Analysis of Variance

1.	The sample data have been randomly and independently selected.
2.	The quality of the data satisfy at least interval level measurement.
3.	The population variances are equal.
4.	The sampling distribution is normal (i.e., the central limit theorem holds).
5.	The sources of squared deviations are additive and independent.
6.	The null hypothesis is true.

Homogeneity of variance

Goal: Reject the Null

Evaluating the Assumptions

Assumption 1. Assumption 1 is that the sample data have been randomly and independently selected. Only those individuals who actually design and carry out the sampling process will know whether Assumption 1 has been satisfied. They have exclusive knowledge of how the data have been collected, and sometimes even they may not know. We cannot test this assumption; we simply must hope that a sound sampling plan has been developed and followed.

Assumption 2. Assumption 2 states that the quality of the data satisfy at least interval level measurement. We must make a judgmental decision as to whether our data have satisfied this assumption. In the present example the level of measurement for the variable of interest is obvious: weight is at least an interval level measurement (actually ratio level). In other situations, the level of measurement may not be as obvious. It was mentioned in Chapter 2 that some statisticians have less concern about issues regarding levels of measurement than others.

Assumption 3. Assumption 3 states that the population variances from which the samples are drawn are equal. This is the assumption that we have referred to as homogeneity of variance. Box (1953) and Norton (1952) reported that the *t*-distribution (which we use in one-sample and two-sample tests of significance) and the *F*-distribution (which we use in analysis of variance tests of significance) are ***robust*** in regard to all but extreme violations of this assumption. However, since several statistical procedures are available to test this assumption and since computer software programs have eliminated the computational labor associated with performing these tests, there is little reason not to evaluate this assumption. Information concerning homogeneity of variance may be of value in its own light for a set of data. Two commonly used methods for testing the assumption of homogeneity of variance with more than two samples are the ***Bartlett chi-square test for homogeneity of variance*** and the ***Hartley*** F_{MAX} ***test***, which were discussed in Chapter 11.

Assumption 4. Assumption 4 is concerned with the satisfaction of the central limit theorem. We know that the central limit theorem will be satisfied if the samples are selected from populations that are normally distributed or are large samples. Various methods have been used to examine this assumption, including goodness of fit tests, tests for skewness and kurtosis, and other techniques, some of which were discussed in Chapter 6. Fortunately, numerous studies (Boneau, 1960; Box, 1954a, 1954b; Lindquist, 1953; Norton, 1952) have suggested that both the t-distribution and the F-distribution are very robust in regard to this assumption as well. They can withstand violations of the assumption of normality without having the probability level for alpha greatly influenced. Therefore, the assumption of normality is often not tested and is sometimes ignored entirely. If we feel that the central limit theorem has not been satisfied, we may want to consider making various transformations on our data or using some nonparametric statistical tool as an alternative to analysis of variance.

Assumption 5. Assumption 5, which states that the sources of squared deviations are additive and independent, is not considered as a major concern to most statisticians. As Keppel stated: "Researchers do not appear to question this assumption of additivity, and little is said [in the literature] · · · about conditions in which the assumption is not tenable or in which a violation of the assumption can be recognized" (1973, p. 77). Therefore, we will not be concerned with this assumption in either Chapter 12 or Chapter 13.

Assumption 6. Assumption 6 states that the population means from which the samples are drawn are equal. Of course, this is the assumption we are usually hoping to reject. As we will soon see, the F-distribution is used to evaluate an analysis of variance. Since the F-distribution is a probability distribution, we know that computed F-values will exceed the critical F-value $\alpha\%$ of the time by chance alone. When we obtain a significantly large F-value, we conclude that the event is either the result of chance or that we have violated at least one of the assumptions associated with the corresponding statistical test. We usually would like to be able to conclude that Assumption 6 regarding equal population means is incorrect!

Procedures for the One-Way Analysis of Variance

Example 12.5. We now present a numerical example so that we can discuss the mathematics of one-way analysis of variance. For Example 12.5, suppose a management scientist has developed the research hypothesis that subordinate perceptions of managers in regard to the initiation of structure differ from industry to industry. This researcher has obtained data for 124 middle level managers, distributed as follows: 31 in the aerospace industry, 29 in high technology, 31 in the mining industry, and 33 in the automotive industry. Each subordinate of these 124 managers was asked to evaluate the leadership of his/her supervisor, using the SBD instrument described in previous chapters. The researcher has computed composite mean scores on initiating structure for each of the 124 managers by averaging the responses of their subordinates on the SBD-IS.

Methodology Solution. The variable of interest for the researcher is the initiating structure dimension of the Supervisory Behavior Description instrument (SBD-IS), based on the computed mean scores (rounded off) for each manager as obtained from his or her set of subordinates. We will again follow Figure 12.1 to determine an appropriate statistical method for analyzing the researcher's data. As always, we enter the flowcharts at ***Start***. Since he wants to compare the central tendencies of SBD-IS scores across the four industries, we immediately turn to flowchart 1. We only have one variable of interest (SBD-IS scores); we are willing to assume that these scores yield at least interval level data; and we are not limited to only one sample. In fact, we have more than two samples, so we turn to flowchart 3. We now confirm that we are seeking a test for comparing central tendencies that satisfies at least one of the following conditions: either more than one classification variable, more than two samples, existence of concomitant variables, or any combination of these. We do not have more than one variable of interest; and we do not have repeated measures on the variable of interest (as each manager has only one mean score on the SBD-IS) or matched samples. We have only one classification variable (type of industry); we are not using any concomitant variables to statistically control for external variables; and each of the samples of managers per industry is independent of the managers from the other industries. If we have satisfied all of the traditional assumptions for a one-way analysis of variance discussed above (e.g., homogeneity of variance, independent and random sampling), we will use a one-way ANOVA. If we do not feel that the assumptions for analysis of variance have been reasonably satisfied, we can transform our data in an attempt to satisfy several of the assumptions; or we can use the Kruskal-Wallis test, a nonparametric statistical procedure.

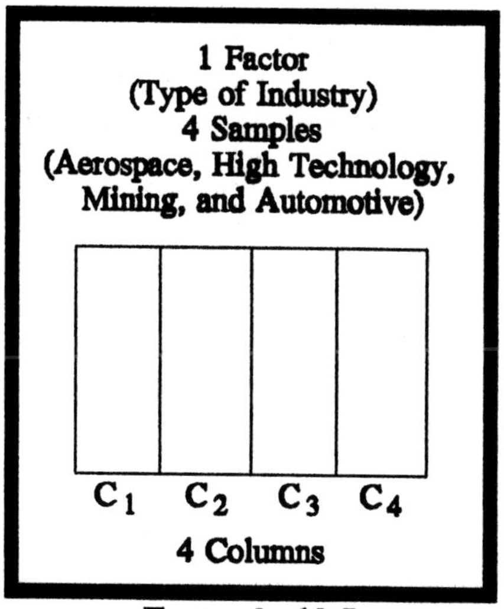

Example 12.5

For the moment, we will assume that the first five assumptions have been satisfied. We will examine these assumptions in more detail later. Table 12.3 contains the initiating structure scores on this leadership instrument for 124 managers for Example 12.5. The table consists of four columns, with each column representing one of the categories of the classification variable.

Table 12.4 gives the sample sizes, means, standard deviations, variances, and sums of squares for the four groups of participants, as well as for all 124 individuals when considered as one group. This ***total*** group is obtained by disregarding group membership for each of the individual participants. The mean for the total group, which we sometimes refer to as the ***grand mean*** and symbolize as $\overline{X}_T$, becomes a weighted average of the four sample means. However, the standard deviation, s_T, the variance, s_T^2, and the sum of squares, $\Sigma (X - \overline{X}_T)^2$, for the total group are ***not*** weighted averages. We will discuss the nature of these values in this chapter and have included them in Table 12.4 because the information about the total group plays such an important role in the computational steps of analysis of variance. Published results of findings usually include only the sample sizes, means, and standard deviations or variances of the samples.

Table 12.3
Sample Data for SBD-IS Scores in Four Industries

Industry 1 *Aerospace*	*Industry 2* *High Technology*	*Industry 3* *Mining*	*Industry 4* *Automotive*
36	42	44	44
44	41	43	44
43	45	44	46
41	43	45	46
40	40	40	47
42	43	47	45
37	46	48	46
39	42	45	43
41	44	46	45
40	44	44	46
43	47	43	47
40	41	42	45
39	42	43	44
41	43	42	48
38	44	45	43
40	45	44	45
39	43	43	49
41	43	41	44
40	42	47	41
40	46	44	43
42	44	46	42
39	43	45	47
41	39	41	48
38	40	45	46
40	41	42	42
39	45	43	44
41	44	44	45
38	43	45	43
39	42	46	45
37		44	47
42		43	45
			46
			44

Table 12.4
Summary Statistics for SBD-IS Scores

Group	*n*	$\overline{X}$	*s*	s^2	$\Sigma (X - \overline{X})^2$
1	31	40.0000	1.8619	3.4667	104.0000
2	29	43.0000	1.9086	3.6428	102.0000
3	31	44.0000	1.8619	3.4667	104.0000
4	33	45.0000	1.8708	3.4999	112.0000
Total	124	43.0323	2.6502	7.0236	863.8710

Problems Associated with Multiple *t*-Tests

One approach for testing the null hypothesis regarding equal means would be to simply compare each sample mean against every other sample mean. For Example 12.5, we could compute two-sample *t*-tests for every possible combination of the 4!/(2! 2!) = 6 different pairings of sample means. However, we do not recommend such an approach. Numerous problems may occur when we compare the mean of sample one with the mean of sample two, then with the mean of sample three, and finally with the mean of sample four in a repeated fashion.

Suppose that sample 1, which was selected from the aerospace industry, is not really representative of that industry by some unfortunate sampling process. If we compare the mean of the first sample with the mean of the second sample, we may not detect any significant differences. If we compare the mean of the first sample with the mean of the third sample, we again may not detect any significant differences. However, if the mean of sample one is not a good estimate of μ_1, and if we make enough comparisons, we may eventually find significant differences even if such differences do not exist in the populations. Keep in mind that we did not re-sample managers from the aerospace industry each time we compared it to another industry. Thus, we have increased the probability of making a Type I error (rejecting the null hypothesis when the null is true). In other words, the probability level for alpha has been increased without our intention, desire, or perhaps our awareness. For a somewhat dated but still lucid explanation, see F. J. McGuigan's textbook, ***Experimental psychology: A methodological approach*** (1968, pp. 238-240).

If we want to hold alpha at the desired level, we need to compare all four sample means simultaneously. Independent *t*-tests can only compare two means at a time. Analysis of variance was designed to compare more than two means simultaneously. Indeed, this is the purpose and the beauty of analysis of variance! It allows us to compare more than two groups simultaneously, without inappropriately influencing the value of alpha.

Frequency Distributions for Example 12.5

Figure 12.2 contains five graphs of frequency distributions, one for each of the four samples of managers and one that was obtained by combining these four samples into one group consisting of all 124 managers. As can be seen in the figure, samples two, three, and four have a considerable amount of overlap, while sample one is to the left of the other three. The graph for the total of the combined groups is a function of the individual groups. As can be seen in Table 12.4, the sum of squares for this combination of all four groups is greater than the sum of the sums of squares for the four groups taken separately. Thus, some factor beyond the dispersion of cases within each individual group must be contributing to the total sum of squares.

In analysis of variance, we are interested in determining whether our samples are very far apart and in determining the likelihood of them being that far apart on the basis of chance alone. To accomplish this task, we will decompose the ***total*** variation into two additive parts: the variation ***within*** the individual groups and the variation ***among*** the individual groups.

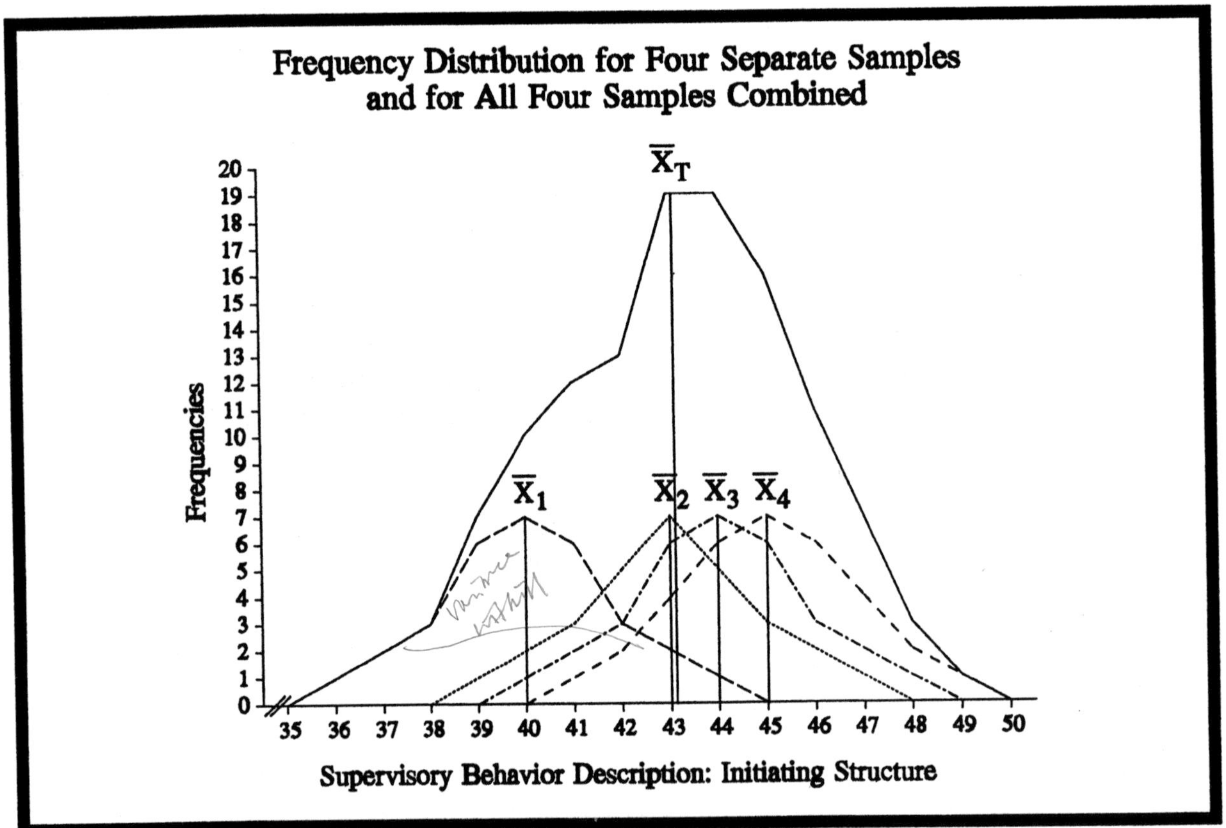

Figure 12.2
Graphs for Four Separate Samples and for the Total

variance is quite same. Same skewness. Kurtosis
Not the same mean
Sum of square

Example 12.5 Represented by Line Segments

Figure 12.3 includes line segments to assist in understanding this decomposition of the total variation into its component parts. The first line segment represents the distance between a particular individual and the total mean ($\overline{X}_T$) for all of the samples combined. We could have used any individual value as an illustration; we randomly selected the 7th person in the 1st group ($X_{7,1}$). This person had an SBD-IS score of 37. The second line segment represents the distance between that person's score ($X_{7,1}$) and their sample mean ($\overline{X}_1$). The third line segment represents the distance between the sample mean ($\overline{X}_1$) and the total mean ($\overline{X}_T$) for all samples combined.

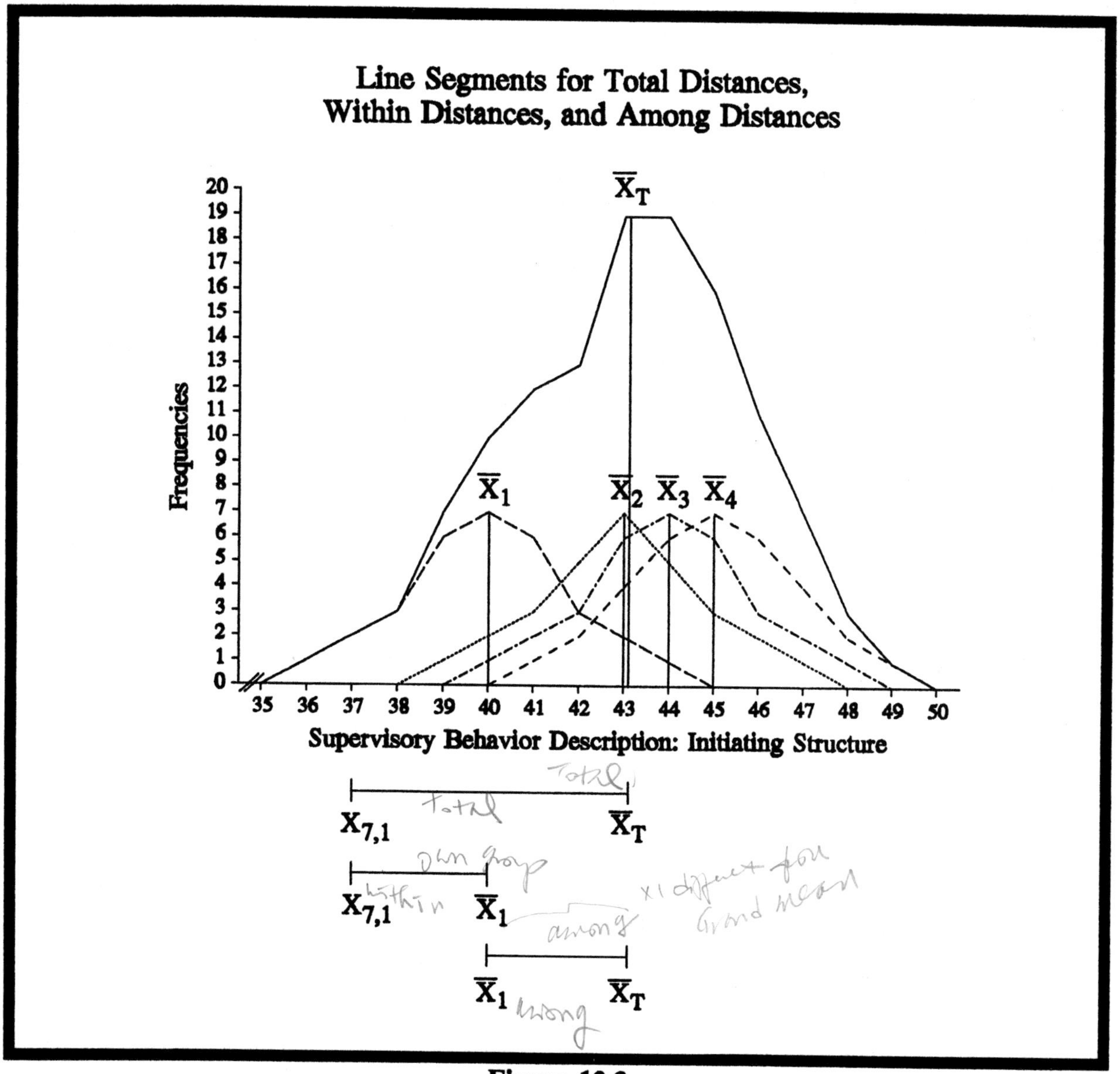

Figure 12.3
Line Segments Representing the Components of Variation

We can now determine that the distance between this individual's score and the mean for the total of all the cases consists of two component parts that are additive. Equation 12.1 shows this relationship:

$$(X_{7,1} - \overline{X}_T) = (X_{7,1} - \overline{X}_1) + (\overline{X}_1 - \overline{X}_T) \quad \textbf{(12.1)}$$

This relationship can be verified by inserting the actual values into Equation 12.1, as follows:

$$(X_{7,1} - \overline{X}_T) = (X_{7,1} - \overline{X}_1) + (\overline{X}_1 - \overline{X}_T)$$

$$(37 - 43.0323) = (37 - 40) + (40 - 43.0323)$$

$$-6.0323 = -6.0323$$

We are not simply interested in the component parts of how only *one* individual value such as $X_{7,1}$ deviates from the grand mean; we are interested in the component parts of how *all* of the individual values deviate from the grand mean. Further, since we are talking about ***analysis of variance***, we are interested in the ***squared deviations*** from the mean. Therefore, we will determine the deviations between each of the individual values and the grand mean, square these deviations, and sum them across all observations in the total set. We will then examine the two component parts that make up this sum of squares for the total. Equation 12.2 gives the ***sum of the squared deviations*** from the grand mean on the left side of the equation and its algebraic decomposition into two terms on the right side of the equation:

$$\sum_{j=1}^{k} \sum_{i=1}^{n_j} (X_{i,j} - \overline{X}_T)^2 = \sum_{j=1}^{k} \sum_{i=1}^{n_j} (X_{i,j} - \overline{X}_j)^2 + \sum_{j=1}^{k} n_j (\overline{X}_j - \overline{X}_T)^2 \quad \textbf{(12.2)}$$

where:

$\overline{X}_T$ = the total mean

$\overline{X}_j$ = the mean of the jth group

X_{ij} = the ith case in the jth group

n_j = the sample size for the jth group

k = the number of groups

Sums of Squares Terms

The three terms in Equation 12.2 are referred to as the sums of squares for total, within, and among, respectively. The among term and the within term are the key components for one-way analysis of variance. Together, they add to the total term, which serves as a check for our computations.

Sums of Squares Total. The term on the left side of Equation 12.2 is the sum of the squared deviations about the grand mean, as now defined in Equation 12.3. We often refer to this term as the ***sum of squares total***, symbolized as SS_T. The SS_T term does not need to be computed and only serves as a check for the computational analysis. However, we will find it very useful to compute this value first anyhow, as will be demonstrated shortly.

$$SS_T = \sum_{j=1}^{k} \sum_{i=1}^{n_j} (X_{i,j} - \overline{X}_T)^2 \qquad (12.3)$$

Sums of Squares Within. The first term to the right of the equal sign in Equation 12.2 is obtained by adding the sums of the squared deviations for all of the individual cases from their own means, as defined in Equation 12.4. Simply stated, this term is the sum of the numerators for each of the sample variances. We refer to it as the ***sum of squares within***, symbolized as SS_W. The SS_W provides us with information about the collective dispersions or variabilities within all groups. We will find it very useful to compute this value second.

$$SS_W = \sum_{j=1}^{k} \sum_{i=1}^{n_j} (X_{i,j} - \overline{X}_j)^2 \qquad (12.4)$$

Sums of Squares Among. The second term to the right of the equal sign in Equation 12.2 is the sum of the squared deviations of each sample mean from the grand mean, after adjusting for sample size. This term is defined in Equation 12.5. This term is sometimes referred to as the ***sum of squares between***, symbolized as SS_B. However, since analysis of variance is typically concerned with three or more groups, we will use the more grammatically correct expression ***sum of squares among***, symbolized as SS_A. If we have already computed SS_T and SS_W, we will find that SS_A is more easily obtained through subtraction than through Equation 12.5, as we will soon discover.

$$SS_A = \sum_{j=1}^{k} n_j \cdot (\overline{X}_j - \overline{X}_T)^2 \qquad (12.5)$$

We have thus decomposed the total variation into two component parts: among variation and within variation. We often express this relationship with an equation that based on the symbolism given for the three sums of squares terms. Equation 12.6 provides this abbreviated expression for Equation 12.2:

$$SS_T = SS_W + SS_A \qquad (12.6)$$

sum of squares / df

Degrees of Freedom

Although the name of the statistical procedure that we are discussing in Chapter 12 is analysis of variance, thus far we have only obtained sums of squares. We know that whenever we computed variances in the past, we divided our sums of squares by the corresponding degrees of freedom. We will use this same approach to obtain total, within, and among variances here. For the total variation, we lose one degree of freedom for our collective data set, so we have $n_T - 1$ degrees of freedom for the total term. For the within variation, we lose a degree of freedom within each of the individual groups; consequently, we have $(n_1 - 1)$, plus $(n_2 - 1)$, · · · , plus $(n_k - 1) = n_T - k$ degrees of freedom for the within term. For the among variation, we use k group means to compute the among sums of squares, so we have $k - 1$ degrees of freedom for the among term. Equation 12.7 gives the degrees of freedom for total, Equation 12.8 gives the degrees of freedom for within, and Equation 12.9 gives the degrees of freedom for among, respectively:

$$df_T = n_T - 1 \tag{12.7}$$

$$df_W = n_T - k \tag{12.8}$$

$$df_A = k - 1 \tag{12.9}$$

where:

df_T = degrees of freedom for the total variance

df_W = degrees of freedom for the within variance

df_A = degrees of freedom for the among variance

The degrees of freedom for these three sources of variation are additive, just as the sums of squares are additive. In other words, the degrees of freedom for among plus the degrees of freedom for within add to the degrees of freedom for total, as shown below:

$$\begin{aligned}(n_T - 1) &= (n_T - k) + (k - 1)\\ &= n_T - k + k - 1\\ &= n_T - 1\end{aligned}$$

Mean Squares

To obtain our appropriate variance terms, we now divide the squared deviation terms by their respective degrees of freedom. In the terminology of analysis of variance, we refer to these variances as ***mean squares***. The notation for the ***mean squares total*** is MS_T; the notation for the ***mean squares within*** is MS_W; and the notation for the ***mean squares among*** is MS_A. Equation 12.10 gives the mean squares total:

$$MS_T = \frac{\sum_{j=1}^{k} \sum_{i=1}^{n_j} (X_{i,j} - \overline{X}_T)^2}{n_T - 1} \tag{12.10}$$

Equation 12.11 gives the mean squares within:

$$MS_W = \frac{\sum_{j=1}^{k} \sum_{i=1}^{n_j} (X_{i,j} - \overline{X}_j)^2}{n_T - k} \tag{12.11}$$

Equation 12.12 gives the mean squares among:

$$MS_A = \frac{\sum_{j=1}^{k} n_j \cdot (\overline{X}_j - \overline{X}_T)^2}{k - 1} \tag{12.12}$$

We know that $SS_T = SS_W + SS_A$ and that $df_T = df_W + df_A$. However, this additive relationship does not hold for the mean squares terms. In other words, $MS_T \neq MS_W + MS_A$. The equality no longer holds because we have divided by degrees of freedom rather than by the actual values (n_T, k, and n_i). As Kerlinger suggested, although this may be unappealing mathematically, it does provide statistical appeal (1973, p. 219). Since the MS_T term is of limited value in research, it is usually not computed anyway. We are primarily concerned with the MS_W and the MS_A terms, for which we shall now make comparisons.

The Omnibus *F*-Test for One-Way ANOVA

We established a format for statistical tests regarding central tendencies in Chapter 9 and Chapter 10, and we will continue to use this same format in Chapter 12. The general form for our statistical test is given in Equation 12.13:

$$\text{Statistic} = \frac{\text{Observed Value vs. Expected Value}}{\text{Chance}} \tag{12.13}$$

For one-way analysis of variance, the observed value in Equation 12.13 is represented by the MS_A. This term is a measure of how much variation we have observed among our sample means. The expected value in Equation 12.13 is represented by the value stated in the null hypothesis, which is typically zero. The chance value is represented by some standard error term.

Standard Error Term. The expected value of the MS_W is the mean of all possible mean square within terms that can be obtained from comparing all possible samples. We know that the expected value of a sample variance obtained from the first population, noted as $E(s_1^2)$, is σ_1^2. That is, if all possible sample variances from the first population are computed from an equation that gives unbiased results, the mean of all these possible sample variances will be equal to the population variance. It also follows that $E(s_2^2) = \sigma_2^2$, $E(s_3^2) = \sigma_3^2, \cdots$, and that $E(s_k^2) = \sigma_k^2$. Since we have pooled the sample variances to obtain the MS_W, and since we have assumed that all of the populations have equal variances, $\sigma_1^2 = \sigma_2^2, \cdots, = \sigma_k^2 = \sigma^2$ (the assumption of homogeneity of variance), the expected value of our pooled variance is $E(MS_W) = \sigma^2$. The mean squares within is an unbiased estimate. It represents our measure of chance in Equation 12.13 and becomes our standard error term for the F-test described below.

Omnibus *F*-Test. We are now ready to compare our observed value to our expected value, relative to our measure of chance. We compare the mean squares among term with the mean squares within term so that we can determine which is having the greater impact on the magnitude of the total variation. Thus, our test statistic is obtained by dividing the MS_A by the MS_W. We refer to this test as an ***omnibus F-test*** for analysis of variance. It is referred to as an omnibus test because it allows for the analysis of many groups being evaluated simultaneously. It is referred to as an F-test in honor of Ronald A. Fisher, who first studied this distribution in 1924. Equation 12.14 gives this F-ratio:

$$F = \frac{MS_A}{MS_W} \qquad \textbf{(12.14)}$$

The Critical *F*-Value for One-Way ANOVA

The computed value of the omnibus F-test must now be compared to some critical value for the F-test. We determine this critical value through the use of the F-distribution given in Appendix C, Table 4. First, we must decide on our desired level of significance; the table in the appendix only includes values for $\alpha = .05$ and $\alpha = .01$. Second, we must decide on the degrees of freedom for the numerator of the F-test. The mean squares among term is used in the numerator of the computed F-value; therefore, the degrees of freedom associated with the numerator of the critical F-value become $df_A = k - 1$. Third, we must decide on the degrees of freedom for the denominator of the F-test. The mean squares within term is used in the denominator of the computed F-value; therefore, the degrees of freedom for the denominator of the critical F-value become $df_W = n_T - k$. We can now locate the critical F-value in our table.

Null Hypothesis

As mentioned earlier, the null hypothesis for the one-way analysis of variance states that all of the population means are equal. Symbolically, the null hypothesis is written as follows:

$H_0: \mu_1 = \mu_2 = \bullet \bullet \bullet = \mu_k$

Alternative Hypothesis

The alternative hypothesis for analysis of variance is more difficult to express than the alternative hypothesis for the *z*-test or the *t*-test. We may be tempted to state this alternative hypothesis as follows: $H_A: \mu_1 \neq \mu_2 \neq \bullet \bullet \bullet \neq \mu_k$. Unfortunately, this statement implies that ***none*** of the means are equal. If we reject the null hypothesis, we cannot conclude that *all* of the means are different; we can only conclude that they are not all equal. Thus, our alternative hypothesis is usually stated in one of the following ways: a) Not all population means are equal; or b) At least two of the population means are not equal. As we can see, the alternative hypothesis cannot be written symbolically as easily as the null hypothesis. Instead, we typically express the alternative hypothesis in words instead of in symbols, as follows:

H_A: Not all μ values are equal

or:

H_A: At least two μ values are not equal

Directionality

Since the numerator of the *F*-test is expected to be greater than or equal to the denominator, the omnibus *F*-test for analysis of variance will be a one-tailed test. If the null hypothesis is true, then the *F*-value should equal 1.00; if the null hypothesis is false, then the *F*-value should be greater than 1.00. It is, of course, possible to obtain an *F*-value less than 1.00, since both MS_A and MS_W are only ***estimates*** of population parameters and since each estimate is independent of the other. However, *F*-values less than one are also very unlikely. When they occur, we still fail to reject the null hypothesis.

ANOVA Table

When performing an analysis of variance to compare the differences among means for several groups, we traditionally report the following set of information in an analysis of variance (ANOVA) table: the sources of variation, the degrees of freedom, the sums of squares, the mean squares, and the computed *F*. This analysis of variance table (with appropriate numerical results replacing the equations) typically follows the format given in Table 12.5.

Table 12.5
One-Way Analysis of Variance Table

Source of Variation	*df*	*Sums of Squares*	*MS*	*F*
Among	$k - 1$	$\sum_{j=1}^{k} n_j \cdot (\overline{X}_j - \overline{X}_T)^2$	$\frac{SS_{AMONG}}{df_{AMONG}}$	$\frac{MS_{AMONG}}{MS_{WITHIN}}$
Within	$n_T - k$	$\sum_{j=1}^{k} \sum_{i=1}^{n_j} (X_{i,j} - \overline{X}_j)^2$	$\frac{SS_{WITHIN}}{df_{WITHIN}}$	
Total	$n_T - 1$	$\sum_{j=1}^{k} \sum_{i=1}^{n_j} (X_{i,j} - \overline{X}_T)^2$		

Fixed Effects Model

The above approach to analysis of variance is often referred to as a ***fixed effects model*** or as a ***one-way analysis of variance***. The term "one-way" is used to indicate that only one grouping variable (i.e., dimension, classification variable, independent variable) is being used in the study. In Example 12.4, hamburger chain was our only classification variable; and with Example 12.5, the type of industry is our only classification variable. Thus, we have one variable of interest (the weight of the hamburger or the SBD-IS score) and one classification variable (hamburger chains or work industries). When more than one grouping variable is involved, we have more than one classification variable. The study is then at least two dimensional; such two dimensional models will be discussed later.

The "fixed effects" term refers to the condition in which only specific groups of interest have been included in the study. We usually do not attempt to account for all possible groups, either existing or hypothetical. Rather, we typically concentrate on a fixed subset of groups. In the hamburger example, more than four hamburger chains exist in the United States or in the world, but the investigation is only concerned with a fixed set of these chains.

Numerical Solution for Example 12.5

Returning to Example 12.5, we will now complete the computations necessary to compare SBD-IS scores across the four populations of interest. That is, we will attempt to determine the likelihood of obtaining samples that deviate as much as these four samples.

Probability Level

The management scientist conducting the study wants to be rather certain of the findings before drawing conclusions about the four populations on the basis of the sample data. Therefore, alpha has been set to .05 ($\alpha = .05$).

Assessment of the Assumptions

Since we have no additional information, we will have to assume that the researcher has randomly and independently selected the data. We will also assume that the data are at least interval level, since the researcher has concluded that the SBD-IS instrument yields at least interval level measurement.

Assumption Regarding the Central Limit Theorem. In regard to the central limit theorem, the four samples have sizes of 31, 29, 31, and 33, respectively; thus, the sample sizes appear to be reasonably adequate to satisfy the central limit theorem. However, if we want to examine this assumption further, we could look at the skewness and kurtosis of each of the four samples, perform goodness of fit tests, or examine other characteristics of the data. An observation of Figure 12.2 reveals that the four samples are symmetric; thus, each of the four samples must have z_{skew} values of 0.00. If we test for kurtosis, we will obtain a z_{kurt} of -.4338,

-.5110, -.4338, and -.5983 for each of the four groups, respectively. Table 12.7, presented later, gives the z-values for skewness and kurtosis as obtained by a computer analysis. While the these values for kurtosis reveal somewhat platykurtic samples, the z-values are not significant at α = .05. As discussed in earlier chapters, our sample sizes are too small to test for the significance of skewness or kurtosis; however, these measures do tend to support our assumption that the central limit theorem has been satisfied.

Assumption Regarding Homogeneity of Variance. In regard to homogeneity of variance, we can test this assumption by using either the ***Bartlett chi-square test for homogeneity of variance*** or the ***Hartley F_{MAX} test.*** We will use the Bartlett chi-square test to examine the following null hypothesis:

H_0: $\sigma_1^2 = \sigma_2^2 = \sigma_3^2 = \sigma_4^2$

Results of the Bartlett Chi-Square Test for Homogeneity of Variance. The Bartlett chi-square test for homogeneity of variance was discussed in Chapter 11; thus, the computational steps will not be shown here. The graph of the chi-square distribution with k - 1 = 3 degrees of freedom is given in Figure 12.4. The computed value for the Bartlett chi-square test is χ^2 = .0238, and the critical cutoff value is χ^2 = 7.8147, with α = .05. Since the computed value is less than the critical value, we fail to reject the null hypothesis. We do not have evidence to cause us to doubt our assumption of homogeneity of variance.

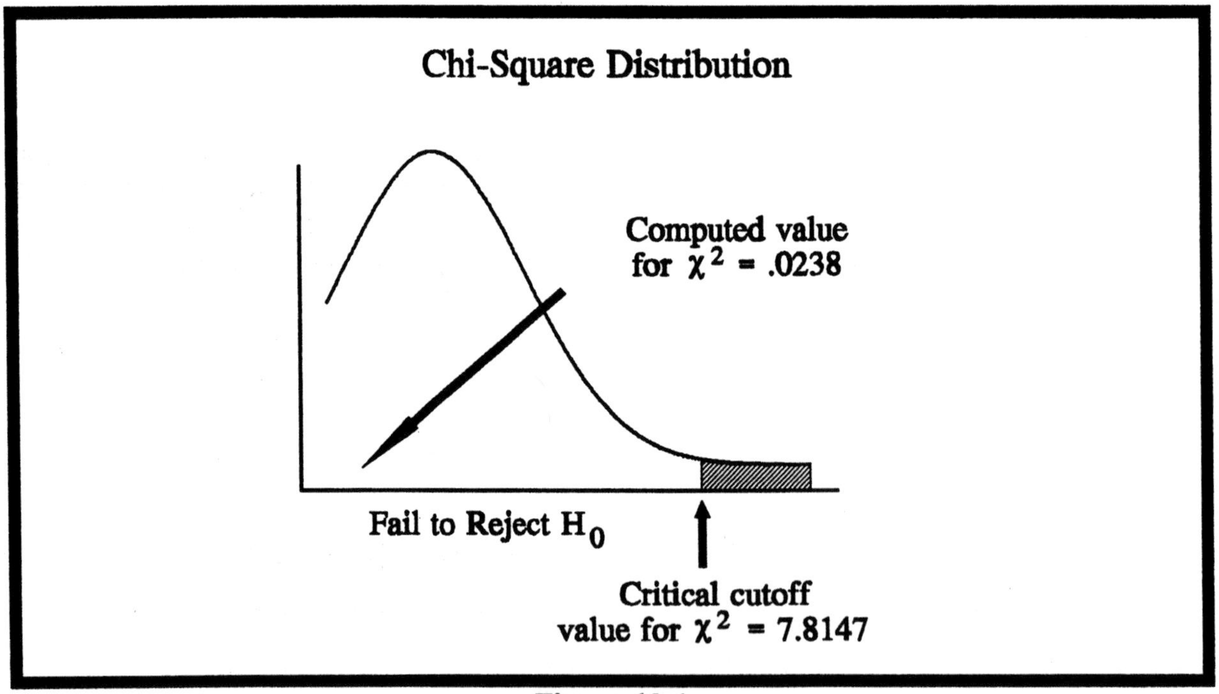

Figure 12.4
Bartlett Chi-Square Test for Homogeneity of Variance

Null Hypothesis Regarding Population Means

We have concluded that the basic assumptions for analysis of variance are satisfied. We can now test the final assumption, which is based on the null hypothesis regarding population means. We are attempting to determine whether middle level managers from the four industries differ on the average in regard to SBD-IS scores. We have assumed that the data yield interval level data. Sample means can be computed and compared in an effort to draw conclusions about population means. Thus, the null hypothesis is stated as follows:

$$H_0: \mu_1 = \mu_2 = \mu_3 = \mu_4$$

Alternative Hypothesis

Based on the null hypothesis given above, the alternative hypothesis becomes:

H_A: Not all μ values are equal

Statistical Test

The appropriate statistical tool for the present problem is the one-way analysis of variance, and the appropriate statistical test of significance is the omnibus *F*-test. The computed *F*-value will be compared to the critical *F*-value, as obtained from the *F*-table.

Computing the Sums of Squares

Sums of Squares Total. We are now ready to perform the analysis of variance. First, we will find the SS_T term. As stated earlier, this term serves as a check on our computations. However, since SS_T is very straightforward to compute, we recommend finding this value first and then using subtraction to find either of the remaining terms. We compute the SS_T term as defined in Equation 12.3 and included in Table 12.5. Manually, we subtract the grand mean from each of the values in the four groups, square, and sum, as follows:

$$SS_T = \sum_{j=1}^{k} \sum_{i=1}^{n_j} (X_{i,j} - \bar{X}_T)^2$$

$$= (36 - 43.0323)^2 + (44 - 43.0323)^2 + \cdots + (42 - 43.0323)^2$$

$$+ (42 - 43.0323)^2 + (41 - 43.0323)^2 + \cdots + (42 - 43.0323)^2$$

$$+ (44 - 43.0323)^2 + (43 - 43.0323)^2 + \cdots + (43 - 43.0323)^2$$

$$+ (44 - 43.0323)^2 + (44 - 43.0323)^2 + \cdots + (44 - 43.0323)^2$$

$$= 863.8710$$

Of course, if we have a scientific calculator with statistical functions or a computer with statistical software and/or spreadsheet functions, there is a much easier way to obtain SS_T. We simply calculate the sample standard deviation for the total set of values (s_T), square this value, and multiply by n_T - 1. We know that this will always give us a sum of squares, since the sum of the squared deviations about any mean is equal to the numerator of the variance for that set of data. Consequently, we can easily obtain SS_T based on the information given previously in Table 12.3 (recognizing that the standard deviations have been rounded to four decimal places), as follows:

$$SS_T = \sum (X - \overline{X}_T)^2$$

$$= (s_T)^2 \cdot (n_T - 1)$$

$$= (2.6502)^2 \cdot (124 - 1)$$

$$= 863.8710 \textit{ (rounded)}$$

Sums of Squares Within. Next, we obtain the SS_W term. Based on the formula defined in Equation 12.4 and included in Table 12.5, we compute SS_W as follows:

$$SS_W = \sum_{j=1}^{k} \sum_{i=1}^{n_j} (X_{i,j} - \overline{X}_j)^2$$

$$= (36 - 40.0)^2 + (44 - 40.0)^2 + \cdots + (42 - 40.0)^2$$

$$+ (42 - 43.0)^2 + (41 - 43.0)^2 + \cdots + (42 - 43.0)^2$$

$$+ (44 - 44.0)^2 + (43 - 44.0)^2 + \cdots + (43 - 44.0)^2$$

$$+ (44 - 45.0)^2 + (44 - 45.0)^2 + \cdots + (44 - 45.0)^2$$

$$= 104.0 + 102.0 + 104.0 + 112.0$$

$$= 422.0$$

If we have already obtained the sample standard deviations for each of the individual samples, as we have done in Table 12.3 for our example, we can simply square each of these sample standard deviations and multiply by the n_j - 1 values that correspond to each sample. Now the SS_W term has been simplified! We only need to obtain the numerators of the variances for each of the individual samples and then sum (or ***pool***) these values across all four of our groups. While verifying our previous approach, we also see that SS_W is more easily computed as follows:

$$SS_W = \sum (X - \overline{X}_1)^2 + \sum (X - \overline{X}_2)^2 + \cdots + \sum (X - \overline{X}_K)^2$$

$$= (s_1)^2 \cdot (n_1 - 1) + (s_2)^2 \cdot (n_2 - 1) + \cdots + (s_K)^2 \cdot (n_K - 1)$$

$$= \sum_{j=1}^{k} (s_j)^2 \cdot (n_j - 1)$$

$$= [(1.8619)^2 \cdot (31 - 1)] + [(1.9086)^2 \cdot (29 - 1)]$$

$$+ [(1.8619)^2 \cdot (31 - 1)] + [(1.8708)^2 \cdot (33 - 1)]$$

$$= 104.0 + 102.0 + 104.0 + 112.0$$

$$= 422.0$$

Sums of Squares Among. Finally, we can obtain SS_A by using the approach defined in Equation 12.5 and included in Table 12.5, as follows:

$$SS_A = \sum_{j=1}^{k} n_j \cdot (\overline{X}_j - \overline{X}_T)^2$$

$$= [(31) \cdot (40.0 - 43.0323)^2] + [(29) \cdot (43.0 - 43.0323)^2]$$

$$+ [(31) \cdot (44.0 - 43.0323)^2] + [(33) \cdot (45.0 - 43.0323)^2]$$

$$= 441.8710$$

However, since we already know SS_T and SS_T, it is much easier to obtain the SS_A term simply through subtraction. Based on our previous results, we can also verify that our new computations are correct. Consequently, we always prefer to compute the SS_A term simply as follows:

$$SS_A = SS_T - SS_W$$

$$= 863.8710 - 422.0000$$

$$= 441.8710$$

Computing the Mean Squares

Mean Squares Among. The mean squares for among is determined by dividing the sums of squares for among by the degrees of freedom for among. Since we have 4 groups, we have 3 degrees of freedom for among. Therefore:

$$MS_A = \frac{SS_A}{df_A}$$

$$= \frac{441.8710}{3}$$

$$= 147.2903$$

Mean Squares Within. The mean squares for within is determined by dividing the sums of squares for within by the degrees of freedom for within. Since we have 124 cases and 4 groups, we have 124 - 4 = 120 degrees of freedom for within. Therefore:

$$MS_W = \frac{SS_W}{df_W}$$

$$= \frac{422.0000}{120}$$

$$= 3.5167$$

***F*-Value.** Finally, the omnibus F-value for the one-way analysis of variance is obtained by dividing the mean squares for among by the mean squares for within. Here, we obtain the following value for F:

$$F = \frac{MS_A}{MS_W}$$

$$= \frac{147.2903}{3.5167}$$

$$= 41.8835$$

We should notice that several terms were rounded when recorded earlier. The actual value of $F = 41.8835$ was computed without rounding in the process.

Results

Table 12.6 gives the results of the one-way analysis of variance. The table includes the sources of variation (among, within, and total), the degrees of freedom, the sums of squares, the mean squares, the computed F-value, and the critical F-value. We are now ready to make our decision for the null hypothesis regarding population means.

Table 12.6
ANOVA Results for Comparing Four Industries on SBD-IS

Source of Variation	*df*	*SS*	*MS*	*Omnibus F*	*Critical F*
Among	3	441.8710	147.2903	41.8835**	2.68
Within	120	422.0000	3.5167		
Total	123	863.8710			

Decision

Based on the above analysis, we have found that the computed omnibus $F = 41.8835$. With alpha set at .05, 3 degrees of freedom in the numerator, and 120 degrees of freedom in the denominator, the critical $F = 2.68$. The computed F-value falls in the region of rejection, and we conclude that at least two of the populations have unequal means. The graph presented in Figure 12.5 verifies these results.

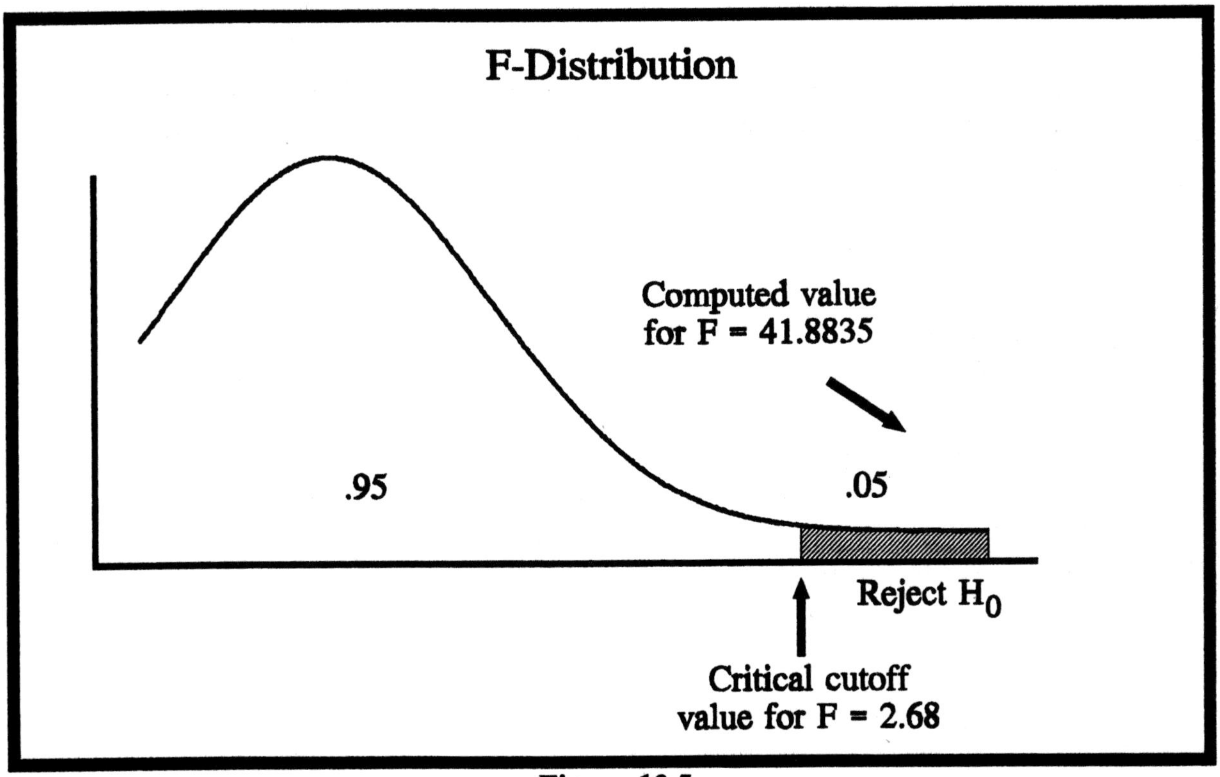

Figure 12.5
Conclusion of the Omnibus *F*-Test

Reporting the Results

There are three standard formats for indicating the decision and the level of significance for our findings. All three approaches are widely used in textbooks, professional reports, and journals. The decision as to which approach to use is primarily one of personal preference. These three approaches are as follows:

Asterisk Approach. The first approach is to place ***one*** asterisk in the ANOVA table beside any statistical value that is significant at the .05 level and ***two*** asterisks beside any value that is significant at the .01 level.

Text Approach. The second approach is to avoid the use of ANOVA tables altogether and to give the results in the text itself. Using this approach for Example 12.5, we would express our findings as follows: F (3, 120) = 41.8835, $p < .01$. The p-value given in this format typically corresponds to the lowest probability level at which the computed statistic is significant based on available tables. The computed F-value of 41.8835 for Example 12.5 is found to be significant at both the .05 and the .01 levels of the F-table; thus, the $p < .01$ statement is used.

Probability Approach. The third approach is to directly determine and report the probability associated with the computed F-value through the use of a computer or a advanced scientific calculator. When such technology is used, we can find both the computed statistic and a *specific* p-value associated with the computed statistic.

The third method of reporting can be misleading. If the degrees of freedom are extremely large, the computed probability may become extremely small. Computer programs will round extremely small computed p-values to zero. As can be seen in the computer generated analysis given in Table 12.7, the p-value for Example 12.5 is $p = .0000$. We know that the probability cannot be equal to zero; it is zero when rounded to four decimal places. Further, when we compute p-values, we may be tempted to make decisions about levels of significance after the fact. Suppose we have determined that $p = .0662$. We might be tempted to conclude: "That is an awfully low probability; I think I should reject the null hypothesis." If we follow classical statistical procedures, we establish an alpha level *a priori* and compare our computed p-value to this established alpha. Otherwise, we might compute the p-value first, then select an alpha value *after the fact*. Under such conditions, we could theoretically always reject the null hypothesis.

Most statistical software packages include a one-way analysis of variance program. Not all of these programs give the same set of statistics and summary data. However, the degrees of freedom, sums of squares, mean squares, F-value, and associated p-value for the analysis of variance should be identical. Table 12.7 gives the results that have been obtained from a computer program written by the present author. This program computes the means, the standard deviations, the z-values associated with the skewness and the kurtosis of each sample, the Bartlett chi-square test for homogeneity of variance, the standard analysis of variance table, and Scheffé ***post hoc*** multiple comparison F-tests. We will now examine these Scheffé post-comparison tests.

Table 12.7
Computer Printout for One-Way Analysis of Variance

Chapter 12 ANOVA Example

Variables of interest:	1
Number of groups:	4
Identification variables to be read (0 if no, 1 if yes):	0
Input data to be printed (0 if no, 1 if yes):	1
Number of cases in group 1:	31
Number of cases in group 2:	29
Number of cases in group 3:	31
Number of cases in group 4:	33

Group	*n*	Mean	Standard Deviation	*z* for Skewness	*z* for Kurtosis
1	31	40.0000	1.8619	.0000	-.4338
2	29	43.0000	1.9086	.0000	-.5110
3	31	44.0000	1.8619	.0000	-.4338
4	33	45.0000	1.8708	.0000	-.5983
Total	124	43.0323	2.6502		

Bartlett Test for Homogeneity of Variance

Chi-quare with 3 *df* =	.0238
One-tailed probability for chi-square =	.9987

critical F = 2.68

ANOVA Table

Source of variation	*df*	*SS*	*MS*	*F*	*Prob.*
Among	3	441.8710	147.2903	41.8835	.0000
Within	120	422.0000	3.5167		
Total	123	863.8710			

Reject Ho

Scheffe *F*-values for Multiple Comparisons

	1	2	3	4
1	.0000	38.3460	70.5213	113.6330
2	.0000	.0000	4.2607 R	17.5569
3	.0000	.0000	.0000	4.5453 R

Scheffé Post-Comparison Tests

Thus far in our analysis of Example 12.5, we have rejected the null hypothesis regarding equal population means. However, we have gained only global information about the four populations; we have not determined ***which*** means are unequal. We recall that the test we just completed was referred to as the ***omnibus*** F-test because it allows for the analysis of many groups simultaneously. With most research, we will be interested in determining not only whether there are differences but also where the differences occur. Therefore, we will want to use post-comparison tests.

Depending upon when the decision was made to perform ***post-comparison*** tests (i.e., before or after observing the results of the omnibus F-test), we will select either an ***a priori*** test or a ***post hoc*** test. The general form of the test to be discussed here was designed by Henry Scheffé (1953; 1959) and is referred to as the Scheffé post-comparison F-test in his honor. It is perhaps the most widely used and one of the most conservative of the ***post hoc*** tests. One form of this test is given in the present section. The Scheffé F-test holds the probability level very close to the level originally specified; thus, it tends to reduce the chance of making a Type I Error.[5] Less conservative tests are available; of course, they may increase the chance of making a Type I Error.

The Scheffé F-test allows us to compare any group against any other group. We can also combine groups into sets so that we can compare one set against another set. In the present example, suppose that we have completed the omnibus F-test and now want to make the following post-comparison tests:

H_0: $\mu_1 = \mu_2$

H_0: $\mu_1 = \mu_3$

H_0: $\mu_1 = \mu_4$

H_0: $\mu_2 = \mu_3$

H_0: $\mu_2 = \mu_4$

H_0: $\mu_3 = \mu_4$

H_0: $\mu_1 = \mu_{2,3,4}$

H_0: $\mu_{1,2} = \mu_{3,4}$

---

[5]Of course, whenever we use a conservative post comparison test, such as the Scheffé F-test, we also run the risk of potentially increasing the chance of making a Type II Error.

The first six of these hypotheses compare the six possible combinations of the groups, taken two at a time. The seventh hypothesis compares group 1 (aerospace) to the other three groups combined. That is, the other three groups are pooled into one group, which is then compared to the first group. In the eighth hypothesis, the data for groups 1 and 2 (aerospace and high technology) are pooled and then compared to the pooled data consisting of groups 3 and 4 (mining and automotive). Equation 12.15 gives the Scheffé post-comparison F-test:

$$\text{Scheffé } F = \frac{(\overline{X}_i - \overline{X}_j)^2}{MS_W \cdot \left(\frac{1}{n_i} + \frac{1}{n_j}\right)} \qquad \textbf{(12.15)}$$

where:

$\overline{X}_i$ = the sample mean for the first group (or the weighted mean of the first of the composite groups) in the comparison

$\overline{X}_j$ = the sample mean for the second group (or the weighted mean of the second of the composite groups) in the comparison

n_i = the sample size for the first group (or the sum of the cases in the first of the composite groups) in the comparison

n_j = the sample size for the second group (or the sum of the cases in the second of the composite groups) in the comparison

MS_W = the mean square within term obtained from the omnibus F-test

To test the first of these post-comparison null hypotheses (H_0: $\mu_1 = \mu_2$) in the present example, the following values are inserted into Equation 12.15:

$$\text{Scheffé } F = \frac{(\overline{X}_i - \overline{X}_j)^2}{MS_W \cdot \left(\frac{1}{n_i} + \frac{1}{n_j}\right)}$$

$$= \frac{(40 - 43)^2}{3.5167 \cdot \left(\frac{1}{31} + \frac{1}{29}\right)}$$

$$= 38.346$$

The Scheffé F-values for the next five null hypotheses can be obtained in a similar manner. They are 70.521, 113.633, 4.261, 17.557, and 4.545, respectively, as shown in the computer printout given in Table 12.7. Hypothesis 7 calls for a comparison of the aerospace industry vs. the three other industries combined. The Scheffé F-value for this hypothesis is computed by comparing the mean for the aerospace industry with the weighted mean for the other three industries. The number of cases in the aerospace industry is 31, and the number of cases in the other three industries combined is 93. We compute this Scheffé F-value as follows:

$$\text{Scheffé } F = \frac{(\bar{X}_i - \bar{X}_j)^2}{MS_W \cdot \left(\frac{1}{n_i} + \frac{1}{n_j}\right)}$$

$$= \frac{(40 - 44.043)^2}{3.5167 \cdot \left(\frac{1}{31} + \frac{1}{93}\right)}$$

$$= 108.068$$

Hypothesis 8 calls for a comparison of the combination of the aerospace and high technology industries vs. the combination of the mining and automotive industries. Following the above procedures, we obtain a Scheffé $F = 82.758$ when testing this hypothesis.

Critical Scheffé *F*-Values

Now that we have computed the Scheffé F-values, we must compare these values against the critical Scheffé F-value. The Scheffé critical F-value is obtained by multiplying the original critical F-value for the omnibus test by a factor of $k - 1$, as shown in Equation 12.16:

$$\text{Critical Scheffé } F = (\text{Omnibus Critical } F) \cdot (k - 1) \tag{12.16}$$

We now determine the critical Scheffé F-value for the post-comparison tests associated with Example 12.5. This critical Scheffé F-value will be the same for all of the post-comparison hypotheses we want to test. Using the same alpha level as set for the omnibus F-test, the critical Scheffé F-value for the present example becomes:

$$\text{Critical Scheffé } F = (\text{Omnibus Critical } F) \cdot (k - 1)$$

$$= (2.68) \cdot (4 - 1)$$

$$= 8.04$$

Six of the eight null hypotheses will be rejected; only hypotheses four and six (H_O: $\mu_2 = \mu_3$ and $\mu_3 = \mu_4$) are not rejected. It appears that sample 1 comes from a population that is different than the other three populations, based on the Scheffé post-comparison F-test.

A Final Look at One-Way ANOVA Procedures

Example 12.6. Before leaving our discussion of the one-way analysis of variance, we will take a final look at ANOVA. We recall that based on the null hypothesis, if we observe no differences among groups in regard to their sample means on the variable of interest, we conclude that the population means are approximately equal. We have assumed during this process that the variances of these groups are approximately equal, or we have at least tested this assumption. With these two thoughts in mind, we will now examine another set of data to further illustrate the logical framework of analysis of variance. In Example 12.6, we will compare four specific departments within an organization in regard to sales. We have obtained data based on a sample of five employees from each department. These 20 employees were hired on the same date. The values given in Table 12.8 represent the number of new accounts secured by these individuals during the first week in August.

Table 12.8
New Accounts Secured During the First Week in August

I	*II*	*III*	*IV*
5	2	3	5
4	1	5	4
2	3	4	3
3	4	2	2
1	5	1	1

Based on this set of data, we find that the sample means are all equal to 3, the grand mean is equal to 3, all sample sizes are 5, and n_T is equal to 20. Since the sample means are all equal, we know that we will fail to reject the null hypothesis regarding the population means. The results of our analysis of variance given in Table 12.9 confirm this conclusion. We also notice that the within variance accounts for all of the total variation in Example 12.6.

Table 12.9
ANOVA Results for New Accounts Secured During the First Week in August

Source of Variation	*df*	*SS*	*MS*	*Omnibus F*	*Critical F*
Among	3	0	0	0	3.24
Within	16	40	2.5		
Total	19	40			

Example 12.7. Example 12.7 represents a revision of the data in Example 12.6. Suppose that the individuals who work in Department IV receive a unique form of training that has not been incorporated into the other three departments. Our data collection has revealed that each of the sample of individuals from Department IV have secured 10 more new accounts during the first week of August than we had previously stated. Table 12.10 includes the new set of data. We are interested in determining whether the unique form of training has resulted in a significant difference among the groups that cannot be accounted for by chance alone.

Table 12.10
New Accounts Secured Based Upon Revised Data

I	*II*	*III*	*IV*
5	2	3	15
4	1	5	14
2	3	4	13
3	4	2	12
1	5	1	11

For Example 12.6, all four samples had equal variances. For Example 12.7, all four samples still have equal variances. The variances for the first three groups have clearly not changed from one situation to another. By adding a constant to each of the values in the sample data from Department IV, the mean has increased by the magnitude of the constant; but the variance has remained the same. Therefore, the sums of squares within has not changed.

While the sums of squares within has remained the same, the sums of squares total has now increased. When we collapse all 20 employees into one group, the total variation has increased. The SS_T is much larger for Example 12.7 than it was for Example 12.6. Since the sums of squares within is exactly the same as it was before, the increase in SS_T must be due to the increase in SS_A. The only change in Example 12.7 is that the employees in Department IV were trained differently than those in Departments I, II, and III. This unique form of training seems to have resulted in a significant difference among the departments, and the *F*-test reflects this difference! A comparison of the two examples should serve to illustrate that analysis of variance has the capability to detect differences in group means when they exist. Table 12.11 provides the ANOVA results for these revised data.

Table 12.11
ANOVA Results for New Accounts Secured Based On Revised Data

Source of Variation	*df*	*SS*	*MS*	*Omnibus F*	*Critical F*
Among	3	375	125.0	50.0	3.24
Within	16	40	2.5		
Total	19	415			

Procedural Flowchart for Performing One-Way ANOVA

Figure 12.6 provides a procedural flowchart for performing the one-way analysis of variance. The flowchart assumes that we have randomly and independently sampled and that our data are at least interval level. If we cannot satisfy the assumption of random and independent sampling, we will have difficulty performing and drawing fair conclusions from any statistical test. If we do not have at least interval level data, we should be considering the use of non-parametric statistical procedures, which will be discussed in a later chapter.

Based on our discussion of analysis of variance, the flowchart first directs us to examine the assumption regarding homogeneity of variance. Two choices for examining this assumption are the Bartlett chi-square test for homogeneity of variance and the Hartley F_{MAX} test. Depending on our results from one of these tests, we will either continue with the analysis of variance or will contemplate other options. If we have to resort to other options, we may want to consider making non-linear transformations upon our data before continuing with the analysis, setting alpha at a more conservative (lower) level, or using a non-parametric statistical procedure. If we have satisfied the assumption of homogeneity of variance, the procedural flowchart directs us to evaluate the assumption that the central limit theorem has been satisfied. To do this, we could plot the sample data and make visual observations, examine the sizes of the samples, evaluate the skewness and kurtosis of the samples, perform a goodness of fit test, or attempt some other form of analysis. If the assumption regarding the central limit theorem has not been satisfied, we will need to consider other, less favorable options. If the assumption is reasonably satisfied, we are now ready to perform the omnibus *F*-test associated with analysis of variance. If our omnibus *F*-test results in our failing to reject the null hypothesis (H_0: $\mu_1 = \mu_2 = \cdots = \mu_k$), we will terminate the analysis of variance. If we reject the null hypothesis regarding equal means, we conclude that not all of the population means are equal. We then may decide to perform post-comparison tests such as the Scheffé post-comparison *F*-test.

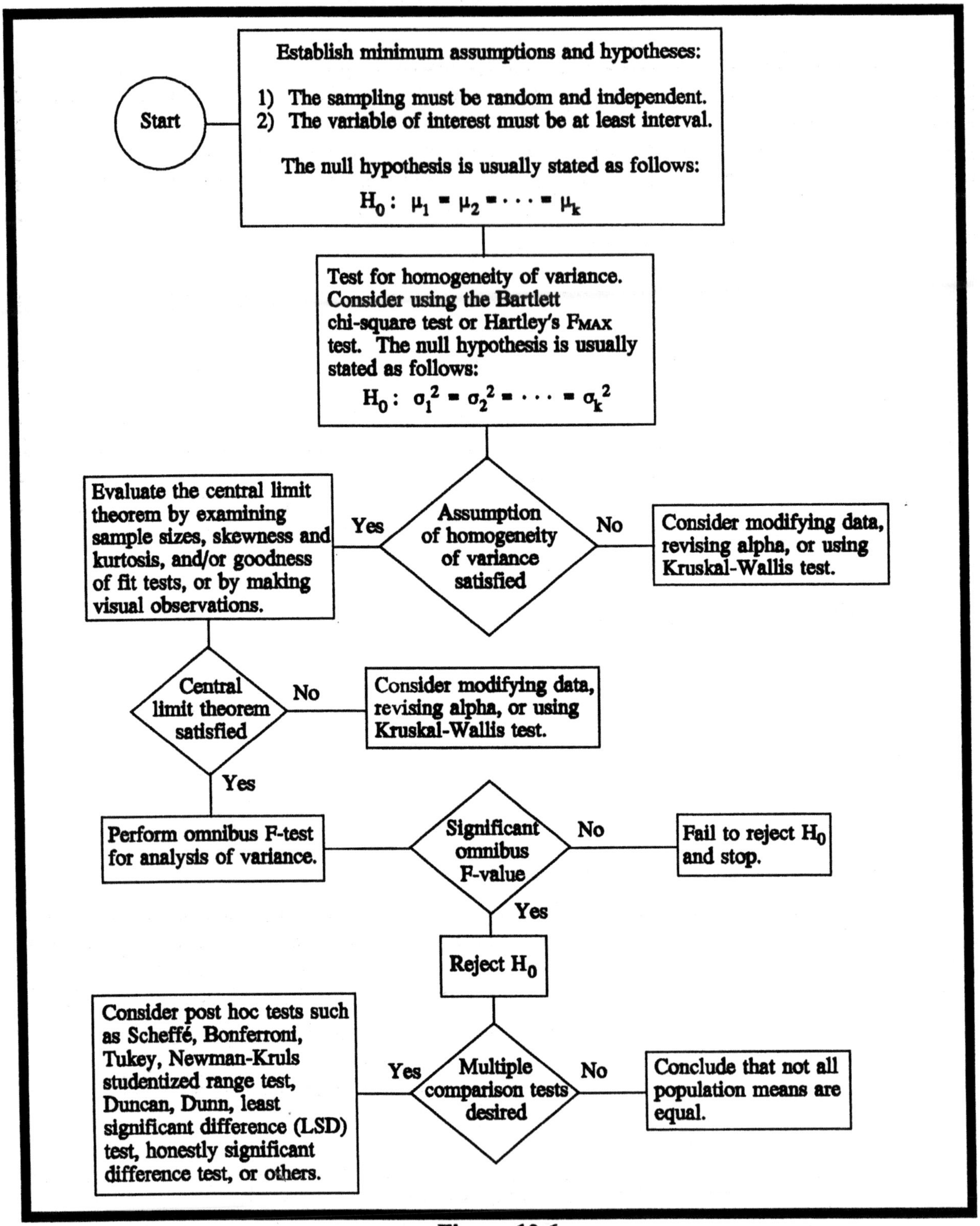

Figure 12.6
Procedural Flowchart for One-Way Analysis of Variance

Linear Models for Analysis of Variance

Analysis of variance is frequently conceptualized in terms of ***linear models***. Viewing analysis of variance as a linear model allows us to examine the impact that various components have on our variable of interest. The differences between each of the individual cases and the grand mean were depicted in Figure 12.3. That illustration demonstrated that individual values may differ from the grand mean as a result of two component parts: differences ***among*** groups and differences ***within*** groups. The "within groups" differences are often referred to as the chance differences or as the error term.

Suppose that we want to determine how well an individual has performed on a task. If we do not have the individual's specific value, we are operating under a ***chance model***. Our best guess for this person would be to guess the average performance score. We know that we probably will not be exactly correct; however, we also know that over the long run, we will make fewer errors if we guess the mean than if we guess any other constant value. This is because the sum of the squared deviations about the mean is a minimum value, as discussed in Chapter 4. We will refer to this chance model as ***Model 0*** (because it contains no classification variable) or as the ***Chance Model***. In this model we express each individual value as a random or chance deviation from its expected value, the population mean. Model 0, or the chance model, is given in Equation 12.17:

$$\textbf{Model 0:}\quad X_i = \mu + \epsilon_i \qquad \textbf{(12.17)}$$

where:

X_i = the individual observation

μ = the population mean

ε_i = the error component, "epsilon"

The error component is a random variable that has a probability distribution assumed to be approximately normal; the mean of the probability distribution for ε is zero (the sum of these errors is zero), and the variance is finite. Since we have expressed the individual value as a linear function of two terms, we now have a linear model. The individual case is a function of the constant effect that results from being a member of the total population and any random error or variation that exists. If every case in the population is identical, which is unlikely, no random error exists. Naturally, the more we can account for, explain away, or reduce the "random" error, the more we will know about the true value of X_i.

The linear model given in Equation 12.17 does not as yet consider any contributions due to classification variables. Yet, analysis of variance is a technique for examining the impact that such contributions have on the differences between X_i and μ. We now expand Model 1 in order to account for group differences. For example, if μ_1 , μ_2 , · · · , μ_k are not all equal to each other and thus are not all equal to **μ**, we know that some portion of the error component must be due to these differences and not just due to random error. ***Model 1***, given in Equation 12.18, includes a component for group differences in our linear model:

$$\text{Model 1:} \quad X_i = \mu + \alpha_j + \epsilon_{i,j} \qquad \textbf{(12.18)}$$

where:

$\alpha_j = \mu - \mu_j$ the contribution of the classification variable (i.e., the deviation of the jth group mean from the grand mean)

Note that $\Sigma\alpha_j$ will equal zero since the sum of the deviations about a mean (μ in this case) will always be zero. Here, we have expressed the individual case as a function of some grand mean for all cases, plus any existing contribution caused by the grouping factor, plus any existing random error. The ***random error*** (ε_i) in the original equation may not have been completely random after all. The one-way analysis of variance has allowed us to extract a source of non-random error from the model, thus further reducing the random error component. By directly comparing the two models, we can see that the value of the error in model 1 must be less than or equal to the value of the error in the chance model. This holds true since the remaining components of the two models are the same. A comparison of the two models follows:

$$\text{Model 0:} \quad X_i = \mu + \epsilon_i$$

$$\text{Model 1:} \quad X_i = \mu + \alpha_j + \epsilon_{i,j}$$

where:

$$X_i = X_{ij}$$

$$\varepsilon_i = \alpha_j + \varepsilon_{i,j}$$

Therefore:

$$\varepsilon_{i,j} \leq \varepsilon_i$$

When discussing linear models, it is common to refer to the variable of interest as the criterion or dependent variable and the classification or grouping variables as the independent variables. We will return to a discussion of linear models in the next chapter. We will see that these linear models can be expanded to include many classification variables, plus interaction terms among all available variables. By taking advantage of additional information gained through the inclusion of more than one classification variable, we may be able to further reduce the error term. Chapter 13 will present several tools for accomplishing this task.

One-Way ANOVA Guidelines for Computations and Decisions

Example 12.8. As the computational process is somewhat lengthy with analysis of variance, the following set of steps are given as an aide in performing the analysis. Example 12.8 gives a very simple example to illustrate these steps. The process begins with an analysis of the problem situation so that the appropriate statistical technique can be determined; this analysis is then followed by the computational procedures.

1. Record all pertinent information:

   A. Variable of interest: __________

   B. Classification variable: __________

   C. Number of categories (i.e., samples, groups): __________

   D. Level of measurement for variable of interest: __________
   (Must be at least interval.)

   E. Alpha: __________

The numerical data for Example 12.8 are given in Table 12.12. The variable of interest and classification variable for this example are defined as follows:

Variable of interest:	Diameter of bolts
Classification variable:	The machines used to make bolts
Number of categories:	3 machines are being evaluated
Level of measurement:	Ratio (diameters have a true, absolute zero)
Alpha:	Arbitrarily set at .05

Table 12.12
Practice Problem Data Base

Machine 1	*Machine 2*	*Machine 3*
12	16	20
14	18	22
13	17	22
	16	24
	18	

The following tables will be helpful in completing the steps of the analysis of variance. These tables are designed for a one-way ANOVA problem with 3 groups. You will want to modify the tables by adding extra rows and columns for ANOVA problems with more than 3 groups.

Summary Statistics

Group	*n*	$\overline{X}$	*s*	s^2	$\Sigma (X - \overline{X})^2$
1					
2					
3					
Total Group					

Bartlett's Chi-Square Test for Homogeneity of Variance = _______

ANOVA Results for Comparing Groups

Source of Variation	*df*	*SS*	*MS*	*Computed Omnibus F*	*Critical Omnibus F*
Among					
Within					
Total					

Scheffé *F*-values for Multiple Comparisons

	1	2	3
1	.0000		
2		.0000	
3			.0000

2. Proceed with the procedural ANOVA flowchart given in Figure 12.6.

3. Make sure the following basic assumptions have been satisfied:

   A. Random and independent sampling

   B. At least interval level data

4. If desired, test the assumption of homogeneity of variance. This assumption states that the variances of the groups are all equal. For Example 12.8, the assumption is written as the following null hypothesis: H_0: $\sigma_1^2 = \sigma_2^2 = \sigma_3^2$. The most common approach for examining this assumption is the Bartlett's chi-square test for homogeneity of variance.

   A. Determine the computed value for Bartlett's chi-square test (often from a computer program). For Example 12.8, the Bartlett's chi-square test for homogeneity of variance is .8900, obtained from a computer analysis.

   B. Draw a picture of the chi-square curve, determine the critical cutoff value from the chi-square table, with k - 1 degrees of freedom. The critical value of chi-square for the present example will be 5.9915. Locate this critical chi-square value on the curve. Shade in the area for alpha, and indicate the "reject H_0" region and the "fail to reject H_0" region. Then, locate the computed value for Bartlett's chi-square on this same curve, as shown in Figure 12.7:

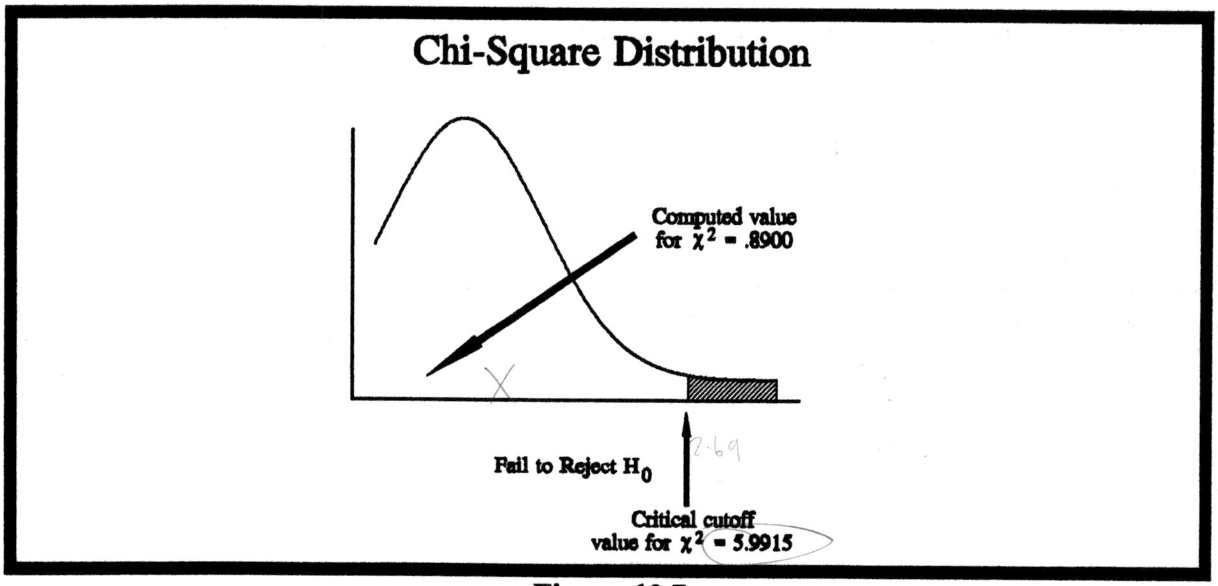

Figure 12.7
Bartlett Chi-Square Test for Homogeneity of Variance

C. Reject or fail to reject the null hypothesis. We usually hope to fail to reject, as we want to have homogeneity of variance, one of the assumptions for analysis of variance. For the present example, we would fail to reject the null hypothesis regarding the variances. This is good news.

D. If the assumption of homogeneity of variance is satisfied, continue.

E. If the assumption of homogeneity of variance is not satisfied, consider making adjustments upon the data (e.g., log transformations) before continuing.

5. Test the assumption that the central limit theorem has been satisfied.

A. The assumption is satisfied if the parent populations are normally distributed.

B. The assumption is generally considered as satisfied if the sample sizes are large enough (usually samples of size 30 are adequate). For the present example, the sample sizes are too small to meet this criterion. We can therefore assume that the parent populations are normal, or we can use some nonparametric statistic, or we can quit. We will assume that the assumption is satisfied and will continue.

6. Establish the null hypothesis regarding the population means:

H_0: $\mu_1 = \mu_2 = \mu_3$

7. Perform the omnibus F-test to evaluate the null hypothesis regarding the population means. The following steps will be helpful to obtain the F-value:

A. Complete a table of summary statistics, as shown in Table 12.13.

Table 12.13
Summary Statistics for Practice Problem

Group	*n*	$\overline{X}$	*s*	s^2	$\Sigma (X - \overline{X})^2$
1	3	13.0000	1.0000	1.0000	2.0000
2	5	17.0000	1.0000	1.0000	4.0000
3	4	22.0000	1.6330	2.6667	8.0000
Total	12	17.6667	3.7739	14.2424	156.6667

B. Find the degrees of freedom for among, within, and total:

$$df_A = k - 1 = 3 - 1 = 2$$

$$df_W = n_T - k = 12 - 3 = 9$$

$$df_T = n_T - 1 = 12 - 1 = 11$$

C. Find the sums of squares for among, within, and total, using the information contained in the table that we have just completed:

$$SS_T = (s_T^2)\cdot(n_T - 1)$$

$$= (3.7739^2)\cdot(12 - 1)$$

$$= 156.6667$$

$$SS_W = (s_1^2)\cdot(n_1 - 1) + (s_2^2)\cdot(n_2 - 1) + (s_3^2)\cdot(n_3 - 1)$$

$$= 2.0000 + 4.0000 + 8.0000$$

$$= 14.0000$$

$$SS_A = SS_T - SS_W$$

$$= 156.6667 - 14.0000$$

$$= 142.6667$$

D. Find the mean squares (variances) for among:

$$MS_A = \frac{SS_A}{df_A}$$

$$= \frac{142.6667}{2}$$

$$= 71.3334$$

E. Find the mean squares (variances) for within:

$$MS_W = \frac{SS_W}{df_W}$$

$$= \frac{14.0000}{9}$$

$$= 1.5556$$

F. Find the omnibus F-value for comparing the results:

$$F = \frac{MS_A}{MS_W}$$

$$= \frac{71.3334}{1.5556}$$

$$= 45.8572$$

G. Complete the Analysis of Variance Table, as shown for Example 12.8 in Table 12.14:

Table 12.14
ANOVA Results for Comparing Three Machines

Source of Variation	*df*	*SS*	*MS*	*Omnibus F*	*Critical F*
Among	2	142.6667	71.3334	45.8572**	4.26
Within	9	14.0000	1.5556		
Total	11	156.6667			

H. Draw the curve. Determine the critical omnibus F-value from the table with k - 1 degrees of freedom in the numerator and n_T - k degrees of freedom in the denominator. For Example 12.8, the critical omnibus F = 4.26. Locate this critical F on the curve, shade in the alpha area, indicate the "reject H_0" and the "fail to reject H_0" regions. Locate the computed omnibus F-value for analysis of variance on the curve, as shown in Figure 12.8:

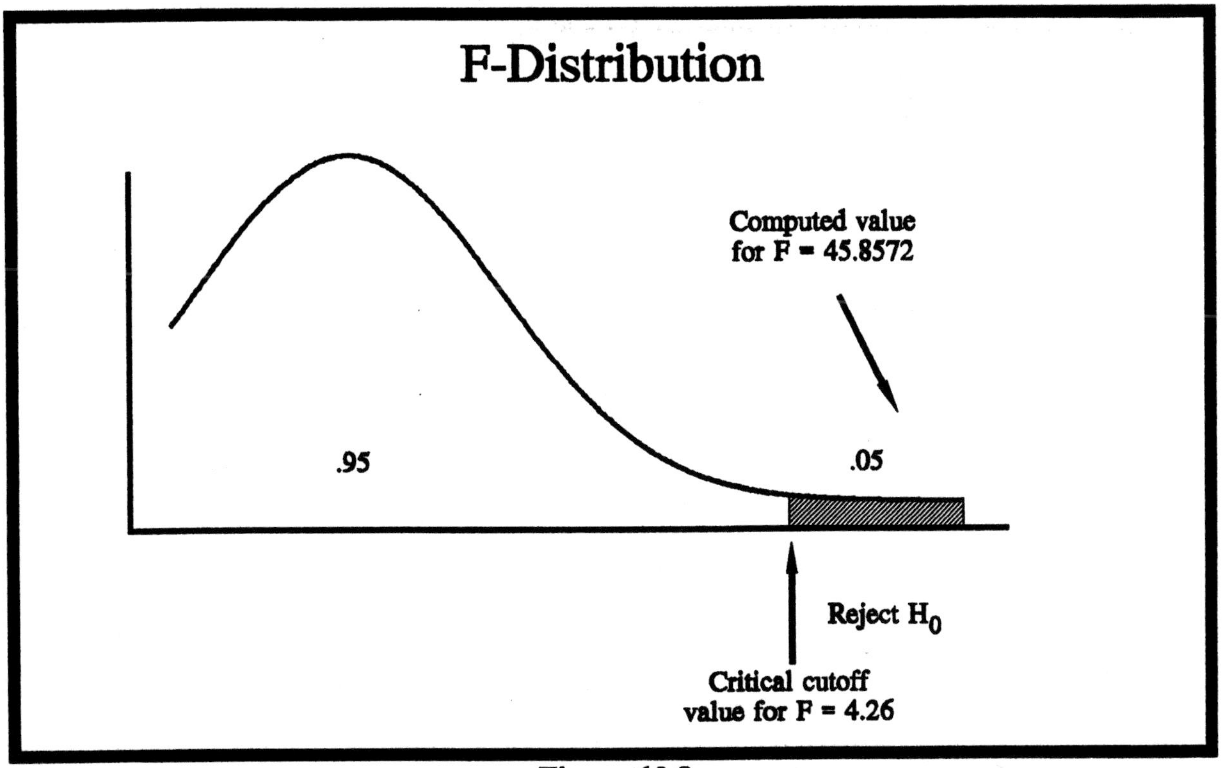

Figure 12.8
Conclusion of the Omnibus *F*-Test

I. Reject or fail to reject. If we fail to reject the null hypothesis, we conclude that there are no significant differences among the population means; and we stop. If we reject the null hypothesis, we conclude that at least two of the population means are not equal. We may then choose to do post-comparison tests, as shown below.

8. If we reject the null hypothesis regarding equal means and we want to determine which means are not equal, we need to perform Scheffé *F*-tests for all desired pairs of means.

A. Decide which groups we want to compare. For Example 12.8, we might want to make all possible paired comparisons, as follows:

H_0: $\mu_1 = \mu_2$ (First of 3 possible Scheffé *F*-tests)

H_0: $\mu_1 = \mu_3$ (Second of 3 possible Scheffé *F*-tests)

H_0: $\mu_2 = \mu_3$ (Third of 3 possible Scheffé *F*-tests)

B. Determine the critical value for the Scheffé F-test by multiplying the omnibus critical F-value by k - 1:

$$\textbf{Critical Scheffé } F = (\textbf{Omnibus Critical } F) \cdot (k - 1)$$

$$= (4.26) \cdot (3 - 1)$$

$$= 8.52$$

C. Compute all desired Scheffé F-value. First, we will test the first of these three null hypotheses:

H_0: $\mu_1 = \mu_2$

$$\text{Scheffé } F = \frac{(\bar{X}_1 - \bar{X}_2)^2}{MS_W \cdot \left(\frac{1}{n_1} + \frac{1}{n_2}\right)}$$

$$= \frac{(13 - 17)^2}{1.5556 \cdot \left(\frac{1}{3} + \frac{1}{5}\right)}$$

$$= 19.286$$

Next, we will test the second of these three null hypotheses:

H_0: $\mu_1 = \mu_3$

$$\text{Scheffé } F = \frac{(\bar{X}_1 - \bar{X}_3)^2}{MS_W \cdot \left(\frac{1}{n_1} + \frac{1}{n_3}\right)}$$

$$= \frac{(13 - 22)^2}{1.5556 \cdot \left(\frac{1}{3} + \frac{1}{4}\right)}$$

$$= 89.265$$

Finally, we will test the third of these three null hypotheses:

H_0: $\mu_2 = \mu_3$

$$\text{Scheffé } F = \frac{(\overline{X}_2 - \overline{X}_3)^2}{MS_W \cdot \left(\frac{1}{n_2} + \frac{1}{n_3}\right)}$$

$$= \frac{(17 - 22)^2}{1.5556 \cdot \left(\frac{1}{5} + \frac{1}{4}\right)}$$

$$= 35.714$$

D. Now we can draw the curve, locate the critical cutoff for the Scheffé *F*-test on the curve, shade in the area for alpha, and indicate the "reject H_0" region and the "fail to reject H_0" region. Then, locate each of the computed Scheffé *F*-values on the curve, as shown in Figure 12.9:

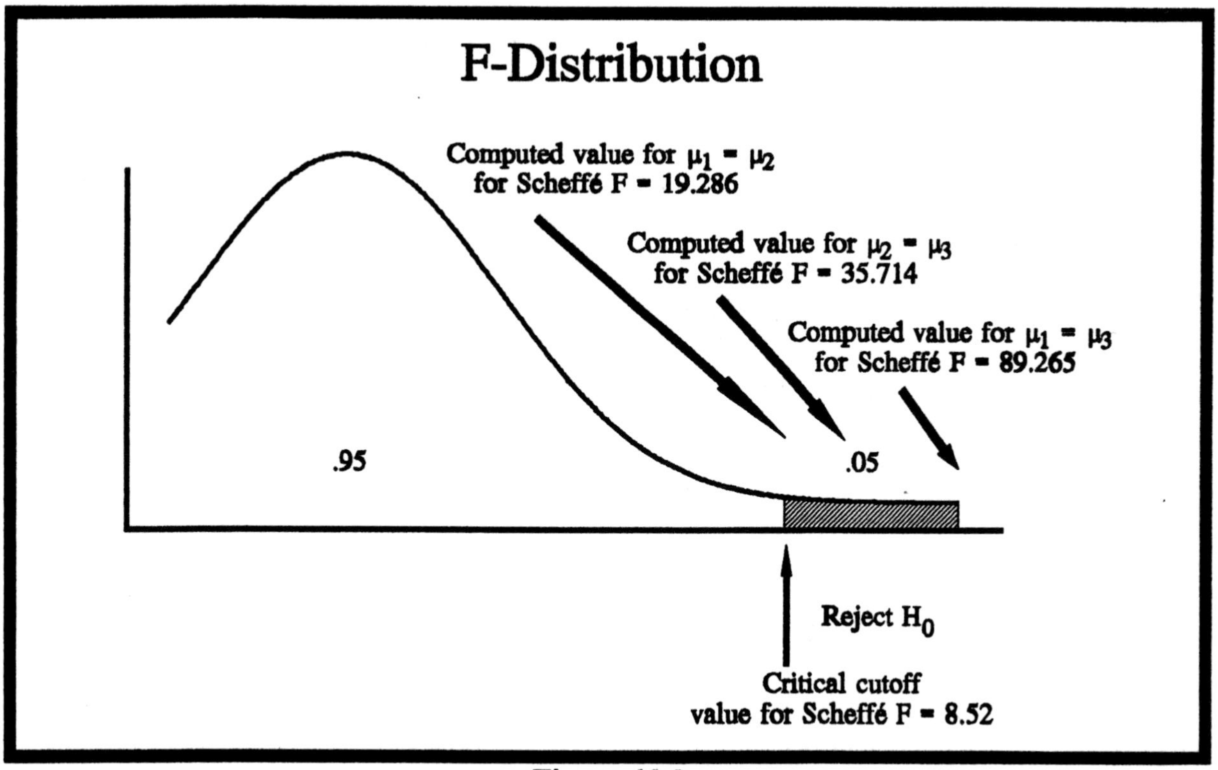

Figure 12.9
Scheffé *F*-Tests

E. Reject or fail to reject for each separate F-test.

F. Draw conclusions. In this example, we would conclude that the average sizes of the bolts produced by machines 1 and 2 are significantly different, that the average sizes of the bolts produced by machines 1 and 3 are significantly different, and that the average sizes of the bolts produced by machines 2 and 3 are significantly different.

References

Boneau, C. A. (1960). The effects of violations of assumptions underlying the *t* test. ***Psychological Bulletin*, *57***, 49-64.

Box, G. E. P. (1953). Non-normality and tests on variance. ***Biometrika*, *40***, 318-335.

Box, G. E. P. (1954a). Some theorems on quadratic forms applied in the study of analysis of variance problems. I. Effect of inequality of variance in the one-way classification. ***Annals of Mathematical Statistics*, *25***, 290-302.

Box, G. E. P. (1954b). Some theorems on quadratic forms applied in the study of analysis of variance problems. II. Effects of inequality of variance and of correlation between errors in the two-way classification. ***Annals of Mathematical Statistics*, *25***, 484-498.

Daniel, W. W. (1978). ***Applied nonparametric statistics***. Boston: Houghton Mifflin.

Duncan, A. J. (1986). ***Quality control and industrial statistics*** (5th ed.). Homewood, IL: Richard D. Irwin.

Juran, J. M., & Gryna, F. M. (1988). ***Juran's Quality Control Handbook*** (4th ed.). New York: McGraw-Hill.

Keppel, G. (1973). ***Design and analysis: a researcher's handbook***. Englewood Cliffs, NJ: Prentice-Hall.

Keppel, G. (1991). ***Design and analysis: a researcher's handbook*** (3rd ed.). Englewood Cliffs, NJ: Prentice-Hall.

Kerlinger, F. N. (1973). ***Foundations of behavioral research*** (2nd ed.). New York: Holt, Rinehart and Winston.

Kirk, R. E. (1968). ***Experimental design: Procedures for the behavioral sciences***. Belmont, CA: Brooks/Cole.

Lindquist, E. F. (1953). ***Design and analysis of experiments in psychology and education***. Boston: Houghton Mifflin.

McGuigan, F. J. (1968). ***Experimental psychology: a methodological approach*** (2nd ed.). Englewood Cliffs, NJ: Prentice-Hall.

Noether, G. E. (1976). ***Introduction to statistics: a nonparametric approach*** (2nd ed.). Boston: Houghton Mifflin.

Norton, D. W. (1952). ***An empirical investigation of some effects of non-normality and heterogeneity of the F-distribution.*** Unpublished doctoral dissertation, State University of Iowa.

Scheffé, H. (1953). A method for judging contrasts in the analysis of variance. ***Biometrika, 40,*** 87-104.

Scheffé, H. (1953). ***The analysis of variance.*** New York: John Wiley & Sons, Inc.

Siegel, S. (1956). ***Nonparametric statistics for the behavioral sciences.*** New York: McGraw-Hill.

Winer, B. J. (1971). ***Statistical principles in experimental design*** (2nd ed.). New York: McGraw-Hill.

Practice Problems
Quick Quiz

Question 1. Fill in all necessary values in the spaces below. Perform the appropriate analyses based on the following information:

Criterion Variable:	Number of New Sales per Salesperson
Classification Variable:	Sales District
Alpha:	.05

Practice Problem Data Base

District I	*District II*	*District III*
25	32	27
24	28	28
22	29	28
27	31	26
26		26
26		

Bartlett's Chi-Square = 1.4043

Question 1. Find the following values:

Summary Statistics

Group	n	$\overline{X}$	s	s^2	$\Sigma (X - \overline{X})^2$
1					
2					
3					
Total					

Question 2. Complete the following ANOVA table:

ANOVA Results for Comparing Three Districts

Source of Variation	***df***	***SS***	***MS***	***Omnibus F***	***Critical F***
Among					
Within					
Total					

Question 3. Formally state the null and alternative hypotheses:

Null hypothesis: ______________________________

Alternative hypothesis: ______________________________

Question 4. Make the necessary decision regarding the null hypothesis:

Decision: Reject H_0 Fail to Reject H_0

Question 5. Give an "English" interpretation of the results:

____

____

____

____

Question 6. Roughly draw a picture of the F-distribution. Include the following in the picture: the curve, the critical F-value, the region of rejection, the region where we fail to reject, and the computed F-value.

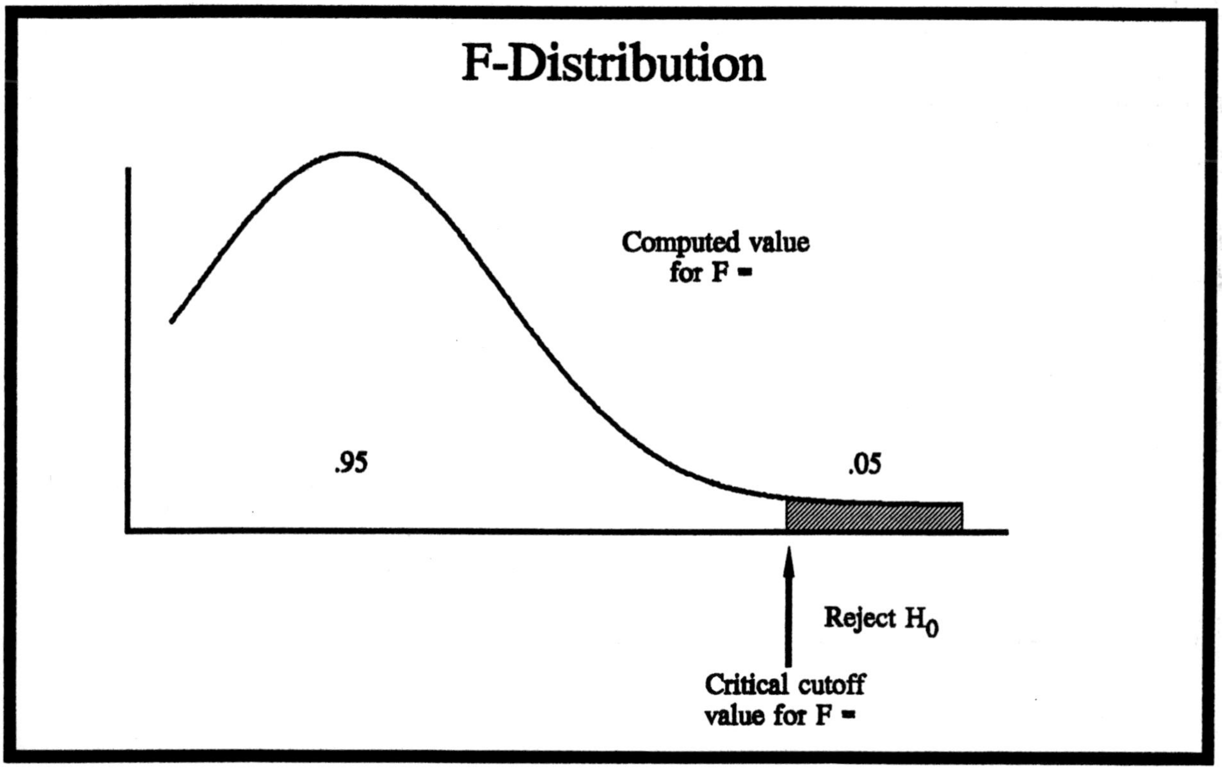

Question 7. Use a Scheffé post-comparison F-test to examine differences between all possible combinations of Districts, taken two at a time. Give the null hypotheses, the computed Scheffé F-values, the critical Scheffé F-value, and the decision (either reject or fail to reject):

Null Hypothesis	Computed Scheffé	Critical F	Decision Scheffé F
H_0: ______	______	______	______
H_0: ______	______	______	______
H_0: ______	______	______	______

Practice Problems
Multiple Choice

Suppose that interval level data have been collected for 5 samples, and we want to draw conclusions about the population means. We have set alpha at .05. We have been given a partially completed ANOVA table, plus some additional information. Use the information given in the tables below to answer the next 10 problems:

ANOVA Table

Source of Variation	df	SS	MS	Omnibus F	Critical F
Among	4	1311.0620	327.7655	30.7851	2.87
Within	20	212.938	10.6469		
Total	24	1514.000			

25

Bartlett's Chi-Square = .9848

Scheffé *F*-values for Multiple Comparisons

	1	2	3	4	5
1	.0000	10.228	0.235	24.430	27.388
2		.0000	13.563	3.943	71.091
3			.0000	29.455	22.551
4				.0000	103.552
5					.0000

1. Which of the following best describes the situation?

A. There are five variables of interest and one classification variable.
B. There is one variable of interest and one classification variable.
C. There is one variable of interest and five classification variables.
D. There is no variable of interest and only one classification variable.
E. There is one variable of interest and no classification variable.

2. Which of the following is not an assumption for analysis of variance when evaluating these data?

A. Homogeneity of variance
B. The central limit theorem holds.
C. Random and independent sampling
D. Interval level data
E. All of the above are assumptions for the analysis of variance.

3. For the preceding data, one of the assumptions has been that of homogeneity of variance. Suppose the researcher wants to test for this assumption. He or she sets the null hypothesis such that: H_0: $\sigma_1^2 = \sigma_2^2 = \sigma_3^2 = \sigma_4^2 = \sigma_5^2$. Which of the following would be consistent with the researcher's findings?

A. Since the computed *F*-value is greater than the tabled *F*-value at $\alpha = .05$, the variances are not equal.
B. Since the computed value of at least 80% of the Scheffé *F*-tests are larger than $F = 2.87$, the variances are not equal.
C. Since the computed value for chi-square is greater than the critical value for chi-square, the null hypothesis will be rejected.
D. Since the computed value for chi-square is greater than the critical value for chi-square, the null hypothesis would not be rejected.
E. Since the computed value for chi-square is less than the critical value for chi-square, the null hypothesis would not be rejected.

4. What are the null and alternative hypotheses regarding the means?

A. H_0: $\overline{X}_1 = \overline{X}_2 = \overline{X}_3 = \overline{X}_4 = \overline{X}_5$; H_A: $\overline{X}_1 \neq \overline{X}_2 \neq \overline{X}_3 \neq \overline{X}_4 \neq \overline{X}_5$
B. H_0: $\mu_1 = \mu_2 = \mu_3 = \mu_4 = \mu_5$; H_A: $\mu_1 \neq \mu_2 \neq \mu_3 \neq \mu_4 \neq \mu_5$
C. H_0: $\mu_1 = \mu_2 = \mu_3 = \mu_4 = \mu_5$; H_A: Not all μs are equal.
D. H_0: $\mu_1 \neq \mu_2 \neq \mu_3 \neq \mu_4 \neq \mu_5$; H_A: All μs are equal.
E. H_0: $\mu_1 = \mu_2 = \mu_3 = \mu_4 = \mu_5$; H_A: All μs are unequal.

5. What is the critical *F*-value for the omnibus *F*-test to evaluate the null hypothesis, stated as H_0: $\mu_1 = \mu_2 = \mu_3 = \mu_4 = \mu_5$?

A. 9.48
B. 4.10
C. 2.34
D. 6.44
E. 2.87

6. What is the computed ratio of the observed variances among the group means to the chance variances within the groups?

A. 2.87
B. 4.43
C. 30.55
D. 9.49
E. .98

7. After computing the omnibus *F*-test, what is the decision regarding the null hypothesis about the means?

A. Reject H_A.
B. Fail to reject H_A.
C. Conclude that all means are unequal.
D. Reject H_0 and conclude that all means are equal.
E. Reject H_0 and conclude that not all five populations have equal means.

8. What is the probability of obtaining an *F*-value equal to or greater than the one computed in the above analysis of variance table, on the basis of chance alone?

A. Somewhere between .20 and .15.
B. Somewhere between .15 and .10.
C. Somewhere between .10 and .05.
D. Somewhere between .05 and .01.
E. Somewhere between .01 and .00.

9. What is the critical cutoff value for making the Scheffé post-comparison *F*-tests for the above data?

A. 8.24
B. 11.48
C. 17.72
D. 2.87
E. 9.49

10. When making post hoc multiple comparison tests using the Scheffé *F*-test, which of the following pairs of means will be found to be significantly different, at $\alpha = .05$?

A. Group 1 vs. Group 2
B. Group 1 vs. Group 3
C. Group 2 vs. Group 4
D. Group 2 vs. Group 3
E. None of the above pairs of groups are significantly different, with alpha set at .05.

11. Suppose that, as an independent investigator, you have been employed by the Consumer Protection Agency to determine whether three major ice cream chains serve scoops of ice cream of equal size or whether the chains differ in terms of the quantity of ice cream served per dip. What statistical procedure will you use to determine whether there are significant differences in the sizes of the scoops?

A. Wilcoxon Matched Pairs Sign Test
B. Friedman test
C. One-way ANOVA
D. Analysis of covariance
E. Multiple *t*-tests

12. Analysis of variance is a statistical procedure designed to analyze:

A. differences among the variances of the groups.
B. differences among the means of the groups.
C. differences among the within terms of the groups.
D. the results of multiple *t*-tests.
E. homogeneity of variance assumptions.

13. One-way analysis of variance is a statistical technique designed to:

A. evaluate situations in which there is more than one independent variable.
B. evaluate situations in which there is more than one dependent variable.
C. evaluate situations in which there is more than one independent variable and more than one dependent variable.
D. evaluate situations in which the independent variable has two or more categories.
E. evaluate situations in which the dependent variable is nominal level and the independent variable is also nominal level.

14. Which of the following is not a true statement?

A. Analysis of variance is useful with two or more groups.
B. When we are comparing two independent groups, the square of the value that we would obtain from a two-sample independent *t*-test will be equal to the *F*-value we would obtain from a one-way analysis of variance.
C. With the two-sample independent *t*-test, there is no need to perform post-comparison tests.
D. With the one-way analysis of variance, the assumptions for homogeneity of variance, normality, and random sampling are the same as for the two-sample independent *t*-test.
E. Analysis of variance should only be used when there are more than two groups.

15. Which of the following statements regarding statistics is most correct?

A. With statistics, you can ***prove*** anything.
B. Statistics and probability are not related topics.
C. If the computed statistic is equal to or greater than the critical value of the statistic, as obtained from the appropriate statistical table, you should fail to reject the null hypothesis.
D. If the computed probability is less than or equal to alpha, you should reject the null hypothesis.
E. All of the above are correct statements.

16. If the mean squares for the within term of a one-way analysis of variance is equal to zero, which of the following statements is true?

A. None of the groups have variance.
B. The means of the groups are all equal.
C. The sums of squares for total must be zero.
D. The degrees of freedom for the within term must be zero.
E. The researcher must have made a mistake.

17. Which of the following regarding one-way analysis of variance is ***not*** a correct statement?

A. The degrees of freedom for within can be obtained by subtracting the degrees of freedom for among from the degrees of freedom for total.
B. The degrees of freedom for within can be determined by subtracting the number of groups (k) from the total number of cases in all groups combined (n_T).
C. The mean square total can be determined by adding the mean square among and the mean square within.
D. The mean square among can be determined by dividing the sums of squares for among by the degrees of freedom for among.
E. All of the above statements regarding one-way analysis of variance are incorrect.

18. Which of the following statements regarding one-way analysis of variance is ***not*** a correct statement?

A. When you have two independent groups of interval level data and you want to compare the means of the two groups, you can use either the independent t-test or the one-way analysis of variance.
B. The Scheffé F-test tends to increase the probability of making a Type II error.
C. All post-comparison tests are designed to reduce the chances of making a Type I error.
D. It is common in research to not bother with testing for the assumption of homogeneity of variance before performing the one-way analysis of variance.
E. If you fail to reject the null hypothesis regarding the omnibus F, you should not perform post-comparison tests.

Suppose that interval level data have been collected for 4 samples, and we want to draw conclusions about the population means. We have set alpha at .05. We have been given a partially completed ANOVA table, plus some additional information. Use the information given in the tables below to answer the next 7 problems:

ANOVA Table

Source of Variation	df	SS	MS	Omnibus F	Critical F
Among	3	82.222	27.407		
Within					
Total	25	168.143			

Bartlett's Chi-Square = .8015

Scheffé *F*-values for Multiple Comparisons

	1	2	3	4
1	.0000	7.2080	0.5640	4.9510
2		.0000	3.8040	20.3600
3			.0000	8.1700
4				.0000

19. Which of the following best describes the situation?

A. There are five variables of interest and one classification variable.
B. There is one variable of interest and one classification variable.
C. There is one variable of interest and five classification variables.
D. There no variable of interest and one classification variable.
E. There is one variable of interest and no classification variable.

20. For the preceding data, one of the assumptions has been that of homogeneity of variance. Suppose the researcher wants to test for this assumption. He or she sets the null hypothesis such that: H_0: $\sigma_1^2 = \sigma_2^2 = \sigma_3^2 = \sigma_4^2$. Which of the following would be consistent with the researcher's findings?

A. Since the computed F-value is greater than the tabled F-value at $\alpha = .05$, the variances are not equal.
B. Since the computed value of at least 80% of the Scheffé F-tests are larger than $F = 3.05$, the variances are not equal.
C. Since the computed value for chi-square is greater than the critical value for chi-square, the null hypothesis will be rejected.
D. Since the computed value for chi-square is greater than the critical value for chi-square, the null hypothesis would not be rejected.
E. Since the computed value for chi-square is less than the critical value for chi-square, the null hypothesis would not be rejected.

21. For the ANOVA data given in this set of problems, what is the computed F-value for the omnibus F-test?

A. 7.017
B. 3.049
C. 8.170
D. 3.906
E. This value cannot be determined on the basis of the limited information given.

22. What conclusions would you make for the data base given for the present set of problems?

A. Since the computed F-value is large, all of the means are significantly different from one another.
B. Since the computed F-value is not greater than the critical F-value, there is no reason to reject the null hypothesis that all means are equal.
C. At least two of the assumptions for the one-way analysis of variance have been violated.
D. The among variance is significantly greater than the within variance for the overall analysis of variance.
E. None of the above would be correct conclusions.

23. What is the ***critical*** value for the Scheffé post-comparison F-test, with α set at .05?

A. 21.05
B. 12.20
C. 20.36
D. 9.15
E. This value cannot be determined on the basis of the limited information given.

24. If you wanted to determine the ***sum*** of the numerators of the variances for each of the groups, you would find that the value would be:

A. 135.356
B. 102.352
C. 85.921
D. 3.906
E. 82.222

25. For which of the following Scheffé post-comparison F-tests would you reject the null hypothesis?

A. H_0: $\mu_1 = \mu_2$
B. H_0: $\mu_1 = \mu_3$
C. H_0: $\mu_1 = \mu_4$
D. H_0: $\mu_2 = \mu_3$
E. H_0: $\mu_2 = \mu_4$

Practice Problems
Written Problems

A well known magazine has been developing differential marketing schemes for four automotive manufacturers. Researchers for the magazine want to determine whether differences exist in the annual incomes of customers of each of the four automotive competitors. Consequently, samples have been collected for each of the sets of customers on a random basis. Annual incomes have been determined for the primary income earner in each household, rounded to the nearest thousand dollars. Alpha is set at .05, and the values below represent the incomes for the four sample sets:

Practice Problem Data Base

Manufacturer A	*Manufacturer B*	*Manufacturer C*	*Manufacturer D*
30000	26000	33000	25000
29000	28000	34000	24000
32000	30000	37000	26000
35000	26000	33000	23000
30000	27000	37000	27000
33000	28000	39000	28000
29000		40000	27000
			25000

1. What are the parameters to be tested?
2. What is the directionality of the test?
3. What is the null hypothesis?
4. What is the alternate hypothesis?
5. What is the appropriate statistical test?
6. What are the results of the statistical test?
7. What is the decision?
8. Suppose you knew that the Bartlett chi-square test for homogeneity of variance is equal to 2.7061. What decision would you make about the null hypothesis that the population variances are equal? What would you then decide about the omnibus *F*-test?

9. What is the critical value for the Scheffé post-comparison F-tests?

10. What are the computed Scheffé F-values for comparing all possible combinations of groups, pairing two groups at a time?

11. What is the computed Scheffé F-value for comparing the combination of groups 1 and 3 vs. groups 2 and 4?

12. What decision should be made about the Scheffé F-values in questions 10 and 11 above?

CHAPTER 13

EXPANDED ANALYSIS OF VARIANCE MODELS

Case Study 13.1

Problem. For some time, Universally Good Distributors (UGD) has received informal feedback that their employees have a negative view of the organization's communication skills. In particular, they have heard rumors that female supervisors are especially dissatisfied with the communication effectiveness of UGD and that field employees feel neglected in terms of communication. In an effort to examine the validity of these rumors, the company has decided to investigate three issues. The first issue is concerned with whether differences exist in the perceptions of male and female first line supervisors regarding organizational communication. The second issue is concerned with whether differences exist in the perceptions of field and shop floor supervisors regarding organizational communication. The third issue is concerned with whether there is any interaction effect between these two variables and organizational communication. They have randomly selected 30 female supervisors with field responsibilities, 30 female supervisors with shop floor responsibilities, 30 male supervisors with field responsibilities, and 30 male supervisors with shop floor responsibilities. They have hired a consulting firm to assess the perceptions of these employees in regard to UGD's communication strengths and weaknesses. The consulting firm claims to have developed a communication questionnaire that is reliable, valid, and yields interval level scores. UGD is now ready to collect and analyze their data.

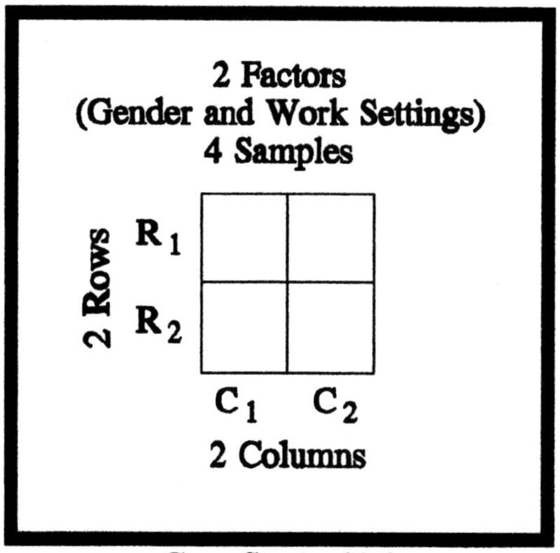

Case Study 13.1

Methodology Solution. The situation in Case Study 13.1 consists of one variable of interest (perceptions of organizational communication) and two classification variables (the gender of the supervisors and their work settings). To determine an appropriate methodology for UGD to analyze their data, we will follow Figure 13.1, which includes relevant flowcharts extracted from the master flowcharts. We enter the flowcharts at ***Start***. Since UGD is interested in comparing the central tendencies for the communication scores of supervisors, we turn to flowchart 1. We only have one variable of interest, and it is being treated as interval scale. We do not have only one or two samples, so we turn to flowchart 3. We again confirm that we have only one variable of interest. We do not have repeated measures on the variable of interest (as each supervisor's perception of organizational communication is measured only one time), and the samples have not been matched. We have more than one classification variable; indeed, we have two classification variables. We are not using any concomitant variables to statistically control for external variables. We are now ready to make our final decision.

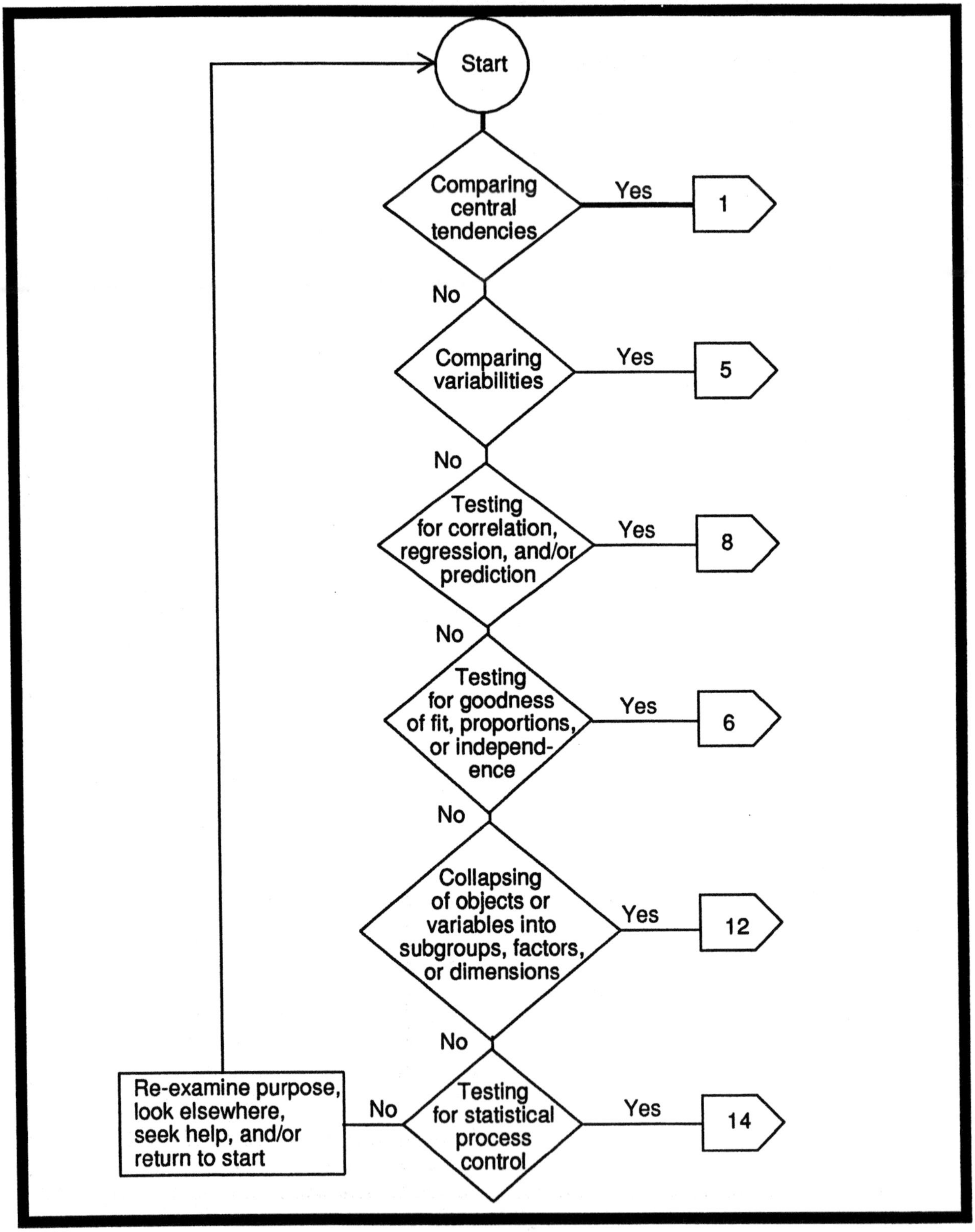

Figure 13.1
Statistical Decision-Making Flowchart for Case Study 13.1

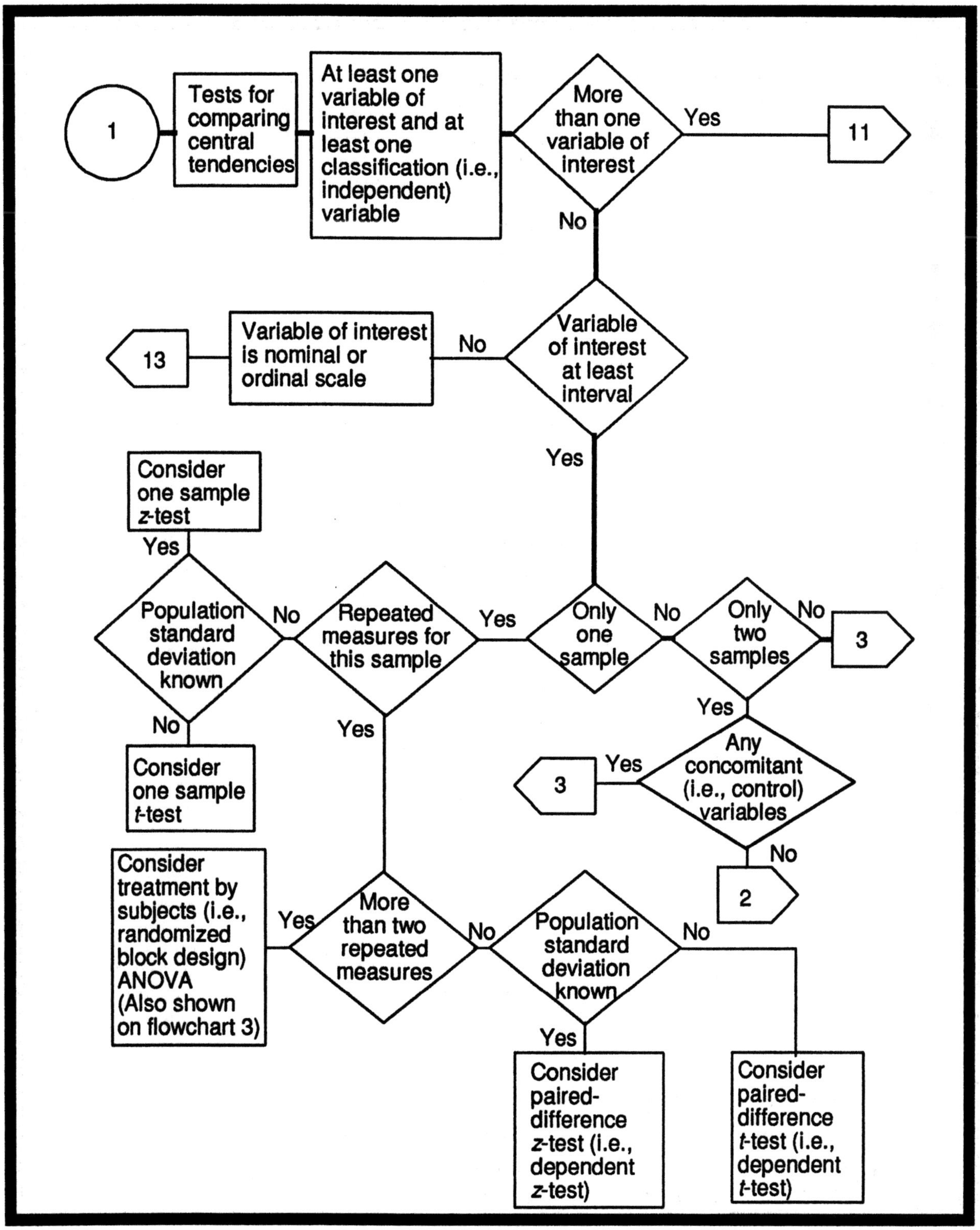

Figure 13.1
Statistical Decision-Making Flowchart for Case Study 13.1 (continued)

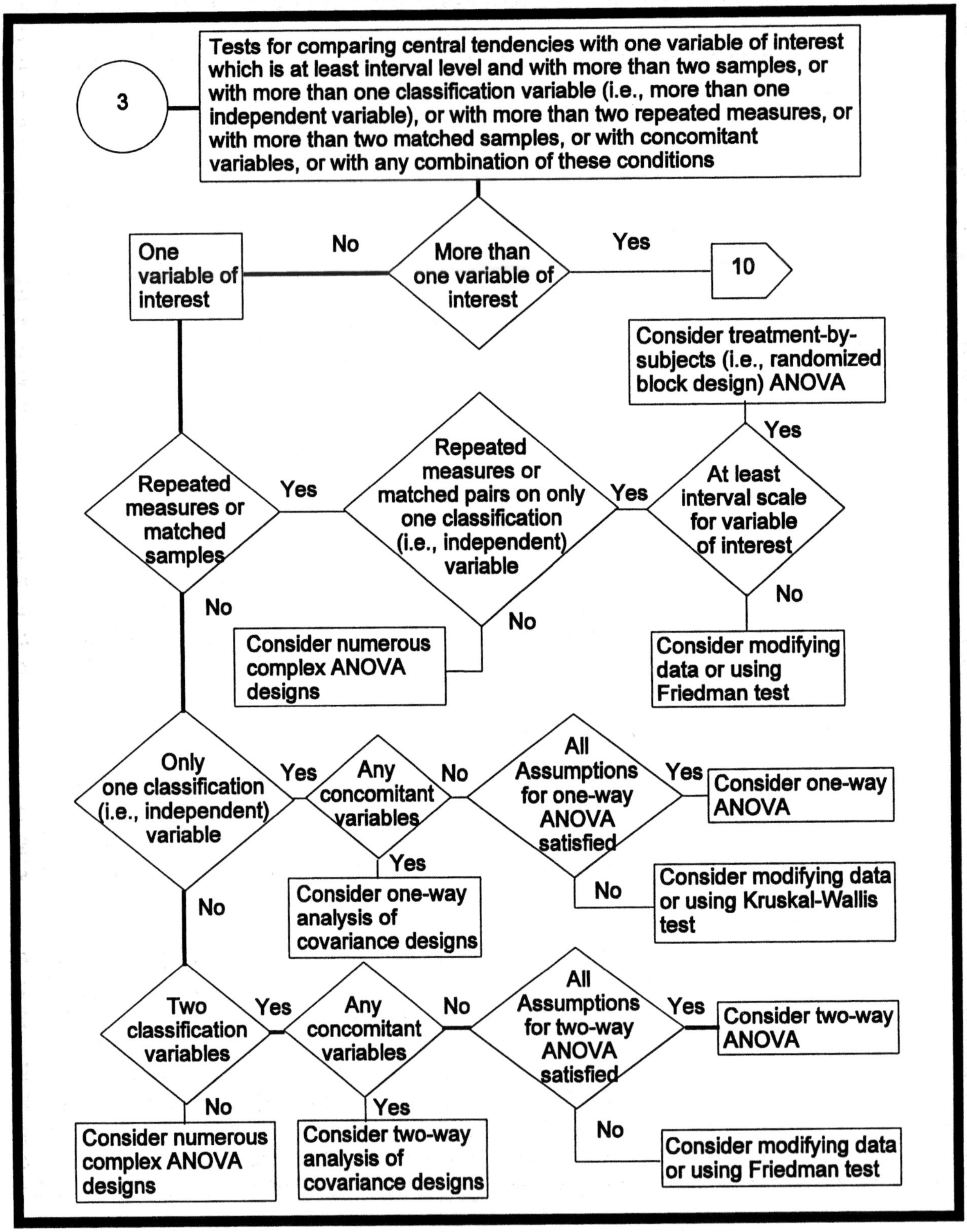

Figure 13.1
Statistical Decision-Making Flowchart for Case Study 13.1
(continued)

If we have satisfied all of the traditional assumptions for analysis of variance (given in Chapter 12) we will use a two-way analysis of variance as our statistical procedure. If we do not feel that these assumptions have been reasonably satisfied, we have other choices. One alternative would be to modify our data in an effort to satisfy the assumptions for ANOVA, such as by making nonlinear transformations on the variable of interest if appropriate. Another alternative would be to use the Friedman test, a nonparametric statistical alternative. Figure 13.1 shows the route taken as described here.

Where are We Going?

As we learned in previous chapters, the knowledge of classification variables can help us to account for individual differences in our variable of interest. Chapter 12 was limited to the use of *one* classification variable. However, we live in a complex world in which problems are seldom one-dimensional. Many variables may potentially impact our variable of interest. Chapter 13 discusses ways of examining situations that require models beyond the simple one-way analysis of variance.

Flowcharts for Chapter 13

Chapter 12 dealt with situations where we had more than two samples but were limited to only one classification variable. Chapter 13 deals with situations in which we have two or three classification variables, or with situations in which we have only one sample but have three or more repeated measures on each case within the sample, or with situations in which we have matched data with more than two samples. Therefore, we begin with ***Start*** and utilize the appropriate flowcharts from the master flowcharts, as given in Figure 13.1.

Fixed, Random, and Mixed Effects Models

In Chapter 12, we pointed out that most one-way analysis of variance studies are based on fixed effects models, although we can have random effects models as well. When using analysis of variance with more than one classification variable or dimension, we may have fixed, random, or mixed effects models.

Two-Factor Fixed Effects Models. As discussed before, the term *fixed effects* refers to the condition in which only specific groups of interest have been included in the study. We usually do not attempt to account for all existing or hypothetical groups. Instead, we are usually interested in looking at only a few selected groups. As an illustration, perhaps an organization wants to compare performance scores for employees in a fixed set of three different work assignments: assembly line workers (ALW), maintenance workers (MW), and security staff (SS). There are many more work categories that could have been compared, but they are only interested in these three. Or perhaps they want to compare performance scores for employees under a fixed set of three different performance programs: behaviorally anchored rating scales (BARS), management-by-objectives (MBO), and total quality management (TQM). There are hypothetically many more performance programs available to be used, but they are only interested in these. As a third alternative, perhaps they want to compare performance scores for employees under *both* of these classification variables simultaneously. The first two situations would be examples of one-dimensional situations with fixed effects. In the third situation, using both variables simultaneously, the two factors have been fixed in regard to the selection of categories within the classification variables; therefore, the model is a *two-factor fixed effects model,* sometimes referred to as a ***Model I*** design. The vast majority of studies that are based on two or more classification variables are of the fixed effects type.

Two-Factor Random Effects Models. If the categories selected in the previous illustration were randomly selected instead of fixed, the appropriate model would be a *two-factor random effects model,* sometimes referred to as a ***Model II*** design. Suppose there are 200 work assignments within the organization, and they have *randomly* selected assembly line workers, maintenance workers, and security staff workers as the three experimental work assignment groups. Further, suppose that the personnel department has developed a list of 20 different performance programs available and have randomly selected three of these for experimental observation: behaviorally anchored rating scales, management-by-objectives, and total quality management. The categories within both classification variables have now been randomly selected; thus, the model is a two-factor random effects model.

Two-Factor Mixed Effects Models. If the categories in one classification variable in the previous illustration were fixed and the categories in the other classification variable were randomly selected, the appropriate model would be a *two-factor mixed effects model,* sometimes referred to as a ***Model III*** design. Again suppose that there are 200 work assignments within the organization, and they have *randomly* selected assembly line workers, maintenance workers, and security staff workers as the three experimental groups. However, suppose that they are *only* interested in behaviorally anchored rating scales, management-by-objectives, and total quality management as our potential performance programs. The categories within the first variable are random, but the categories within the second variable are fixed; thus, the model is a two-factor mixed effects model.

Equal vs. Unequal Cell Sizes

When we design a product or attempt to improve the quality of that product, we often conduct experiments. We can usually specify the number of items that are to be examined or manipulated under each condition across all classification variables. In other words, we can fix the sizes of each of these ***cells***. When we design a study that involves experimentation with human beings or other living organisms, we again want to assign a specified number of subjects to each cell in the design. We usually try to force the cell sizes to be identical or at least proportional across all factors. If the cell sizes are identical or proportional throughout the experimental design, the assumption of additivity for the sources of variation discussed in Chapter 12 will be preserved, and the analysis is rather straightforward. However, many research projects are based on observational studies (i.e., *ex post facto* studies) instead of experimental studies. Under such circumstances, we may be examining data that have been previously collected, and we may not be in a position to assign observations to cells, manipulate data, or otherwise achieve a satisfactory design. Such non-experimental studies seldom have equal cell sizes and usually require a revision in our statistical methods.

If two or more of the factors in an observational study are attribute variables, such as gender, marital status, or job type, equal cell sizes across variables will be extremely difficult to obtain through sampling. Even if the cells are proportional to their corresponding marginals in regard to size, we will have difficulty with the analysis. Proportionality maintains orthogonality among the classification variables, but any ***interaction terms*** that exist among these variables may no longer be independent of the classification variables; thus, the additivity property may not hold. Further, if interrelationships among the classification variables exist, the "non-additivity" of the sources of variation is increased. Several approaches have been suggested for dealing with unequal cell sizes. These approaches are often given as options in computer software packages such as SPSS and others.

TWO-WAY ANALYSIS OF VARIANCE

In the traditional two-way analysis of variance, we have one variable of interest that yields at least interval level measurement and two classification variables that are discrete and nominal (although ordinal variables have also been used as classification variables). Some textbooks refer to any model that has more than one classification variable as a factorial analysis of variance. That is, a two-way analysis of variance is referred to as a two-factor analysis of variance and a three-way analysis of variance is referred to as a three-factor analysis of variance. In general, we find such designs frequently referred to as k-factor designs, where k represents the number of factors.

Example 13.1. We will use a numerical example with fixed effects to better highlight the differences between one-way and two-way designs. For Example 13.1, suppose that the previously mentioned organization is interested in comparing the impacts that behaviorally anchored rating scales, management-by-objectives, and total quality management have on their employees. In addition, the company is interested in determining whether these three programs have different effects on three different work classifications: assembly line workers (ALW), maintenance workers (MW), and members of the security staff (SS). The personnel department has randomly selected 30 employees from each of the three work categories (a fixed effect classification variable) and has randomly subdivided each of the sets of 30 employees into three groups consisting of 10 members each. Ten members of each work category (also a fixed effect classification variable) participated in each of the three performance programs. That is, 10 members of the assembly line group participated in a BARS program, 10 participated in an MBO program, and 10 participated in a TQM program. Similarly, 10 members of the maintenance group participated in BARS, 10 participated in MBO, and 10 participated in TQM. The same conditions follow for the security staff group. After a period of six months, performance appraisal scores were obtained, based on a measure that the personnel staff considered to be at least interval level. Table 13.1 contains the performance scores for these 90 employees.

Table 13.1
Two-Way ANOVA Data

	BARS		*MBO*		*TQM*	
	25	30	35	31	39	32
Assembly Line	27	26	28	29	38	36
Workers	28	29	34	33	37	32
	23	30	28	30	35	34
	27	24	31	32	31	35
	30	28	35	29	35	28
Maintenance	31	29	33	28	27	33
Workers	31	33	34	27	31	32
	27	34	32	32	31	30
	35	30	31	31	34	30
	32	35	31	33	31	24
Security	31	38	30	32	29	30
Staff	34	35	29	28	28	24
	33	38	34	31	27	25
	39	36	27	34	26	27

Methodology Solution. In Example 13.1, the organization wants to compare the central tendencies of various groups of employees in regard to their performance. There is one variable of interest (employee performance) and two classification variables (work type and program type). To determine an appropriate methodology for the organization to analyze their data, we will again follow the flowcharts included in Figure 13.1. As always, we enter the flowcharts at ***Start***. We do not have only one sample, and we do not have only two samples. Therefore, we turn to flowchart 3. Again, we only have one variable of interest; we do not have repeated measures on this variable; and we do not have matched samples. We have two classification variables, but we are not using any concomitant variables. We must now decide whether all of the assumptions for an ANOVA design have been satisfied. If these assumptions (which are similar to the assumptions we examined for a one-way analysis of variance) have been satisfied, we can

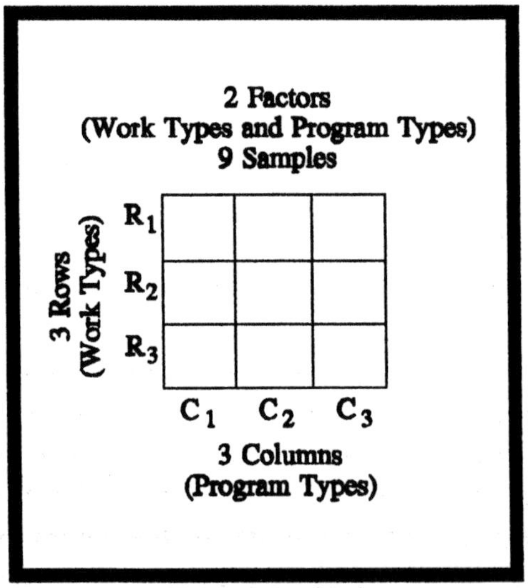

Example 13.1

use a two-way analysis of variance. In regard to the research design, we have two classification variables or factors; therefore, we must have more than two samples. For this example, if rows represent work type and columns represent program type, there are three rows and three columns in our research design. This results in nine cells in the model. We also note that the classification variables are both fixed, since work types were not randomly selected from all possible work classifications in the organization, and the three program types were not randomly selected from a larger set of all possible program types. Summary statistics for this example have been computed and are included in Table 13.2.

Table 13.2
Two-Way ANOVA Data

	BARS	***MBO***	***TQM***	***Row Totals***
Assembly Line Workers	$n_{11} = 10$ $\overline{X}_{11} = 26.9$ $s_{11} = 2.424$	$n_{12} = 10$ $\overline{X}_{12} = 31.1$ $s_{12} = 2.424$	$n_{13} = 10$ $\overline{X}_{13} = 34.9$ $s_{13} = 2.685$	$n_{1.} = 30$ $\overline{X}_{1.} = 30.967$ $s_{1.} = 4.115$
Maintenance Workers	$n_{21} = 10$ $\overline{X}_{21} = 30.8$ $s_{21} = 2.573$	$n_{22} = 10$ $\overline{X}_{22} = 31.2$ $s_{22} = 2.573$	$n_{23} = 10$ $\overline{X}_{23} = 31.1$ $s_{23} = 2.514$	$n_{2.} = 30$ $\overline{X}_{2.} = 31.033$ $s_{2.} = 2.470$
Security Staff	$n_{31} = 10$ $\overline{X}_{31} = 35.1$ $s_{31} = 2.685$	$n_{32} = 10$ $\overline{X}_{32} = 30.9$ $s_{32} = 2.424$	$n_{33} = 10$ $\overline{X}_{33} = 27.1$ $s_{33} = 2.424$	$n_{3.} = 30$ $\overline{X}_{3.} = 31.033$ $s_{3.} = 4.115$
Column Totals	$n_{.1} = 30$ $\overline{X}_{.1} = 30.933$ $s_{.1} = 4.209$	$n_{.2} = 30$ $\overline{X}_{.2} = 31.067$ $s_{.2} = 2.392$	$n_{.3} = 30$ $\overline{X}_{.3} = 31.033$ $s_{.3} = 4.064$	$n_T = 90$ $\overline{X}_T = 31.011$ $s_T = 3.609$

These summary statistics, which are based on the raw data in Table 13.1, will be useful when we conduct a two-way analysis of variance. In order to better understand Table 13.2, we will review the basic rules of summation notation. The first subscript that appears after a symbol, such as the 2 in s_{23}, indicates the row number. The second subscript, such as the 3 in this illustration, indicates the column number. Thus, s_{23} is the standard deviation of the cell that corresponds to row 2 and column 3 (maintenance workers in the TQM program). This standard deviation is equal to 2.514. Appendix E provides a more detailed review of summation notation, if necessary.

There are also three row and three column marginals associated with Table 13.2. The notation for row marginals uses a subscripted number, *followed* by a dot. The dot indicates that we are holding all columns constant while evaluating the overall value for the particular row associated with the first subscript. For example, $s_{3.}$ refers to the standard deviation of the third row, ignoring any column differentiation for the cases in that row. In Example 13.1, the standard deviation for row three is $s_{3.} = 4.115$, the standard deviation for the 30 security staff employees. When the dot appears *before* the number in the subscript notation, we are referring to the overall value for the particular column, while holding the rows constant. For example, $s_{.3}$ refers to the standard deviation of the third column, while ignoring rows. The standard deviation for column three is $s_{.3} = 4.064$.

Before performing the necessary steps for the two-way analysis of variance for Example 13.1, we will illustrate the similarities and differences between one-way ANOVA and two-way ANOVA. First, suppose that the personnel research group for the organization has decided that they only want to compare the means of the 9 cells in Table 13.2 without regard to rows and columns. Under such circumstances, a traditional one-way analysis of variance can be utilized. The results of such a one-way analysis of variance for Example 13.1 are given in Table 13.3.

Table 13.3
One-Way Analysis of Variance Table for Comparing All Cell Means

Source of Variation	*df*	*SS*	*MS*	*F-Value*	*Critical F*
Among	8	641.4889	80.1861	12.5509	2.06
Within	81	517.5000	6.3889		
Total	89	1158.9889			

Note. The critical F-value is based $\alpha = .05$, with 8 and 80 degrees of freedom, as 8 and 81 degrees of freedom are not available in the F-table in Appendix C.

As we can see, there are significant differences among the 9 cell means, with $F(8, 81) = 12.5509, p < .01$.[1] While we can conclude that performance scores differ, our interpretations are limited to differences in the cell means.

[1]The Bartlett chi-square test for homogeneity of variance, which compares the 9 cell variances, yields a value of $\chi^2(8) = .2606, p > .05$. Thus, we do not have reason to suspect that the assumption of homogeneity of variance has been violated. Further, tests for skewness and kurtosis for these same data do not result in significant z-values, giving us no reason to suspect that the central limit theorem does not hold. Of course, these tests for skewness and kurtosis are not very useful when the sample sizes are small.

Instead of simply looking at the 9 cells, suppose that the research group has decided to compare the impact of the three types of training programs on performance, while ignoring the three types of work categories. Table 13.4 consists of summary statistics after collapsing the 9 cells into 3 columns, based on types of training programs. Using the means, standard deviations, and sums of squares generated from this table, we can perform a one-way analysis of variance to simply examine differences in performance scores as a function of types of training programs. The results of this one-way analysis of variance are given in Table 13.5.

Table 13.4
Summary Statistics Based On Program Types as a Single Classification Variable

Row	n	$\overline{X}$	s	s^2	$\Sigma(X - \overline{X})^2$
1	30	30.9333	4.2095	17.7195	513.8667
2	30	31.0667	2.3916	5.7195	165.8667
3	30	31.0333	4.0640	16.5161	478.9667
Total	90	31.0111	3.6086	13.0223	1158.988

Table 13.5
One-Way Analysis of Variance Table for Comparing Program Group Means

Source of Variation	*df*	*SS*	*MS*	*F-Value*	*Critical F*
Among	2	.2889	.1445	.0108	3.11
Within	87	1158.7000	13.3184		
Total	89	1158.9889			

Note. The critical F-value is based $\alpha = .05$, with 2 and 80 degrees of freedom, as 2 and 87 degrees of freedom are not available in the F-table in Appendix C.

As can be seen by an examination of Table 13.5, this one-way ANOVA would lead the personnel department to believe that there are no significant differences among these group means either. They would conclude that the three types of training programs do not result in different performance levels. Yet, we still know that there are differences somewhere!

Now suppose that the research group has decided to compare the impact of the three different work types on performance, while ignoring the various program types. Table 13.6 consists of summary statistics after collapsing the 9 cells into 3 rows, based on common work types. Using the means, standard deviations, and sums of squares generated from this table, we can perform a one-way analysis of variance to simply examine differences in performance scores as a function of the type of work these individuals perform. The results of this one-way analysis of variance are given in Table 13.7.

Table 13.6
Summary Statistics Based On Work Types as a Single Classification Variable

Row	*n*	$\overline{X}$	*s*	s^2	$\Sigma(X - \overline{X})^2$
1	30	30.9667	4.1146	16.9299	490.9667
2	30	31.0333	2.4703	6.1023	176.9667
3	30	31.0333	4.1146	16.9299	490.9667
Total	90	31.0111	3.6086	13.0223	1158.9889

Table 13.7
One-Way Analysis of Variance Table for Comparing Work Group Means

Source of Variation	*df*	*SS*	*MS*	*F-Value*	*Critical F*
Among	2	.0889	.0444	.0033	3.11
Within	87	1158.9000	13.3207		
Total	89	1158.9889			

Note. The critical F-value is based $\alpha = .05$, with 2 and 80 degrees of freedom, as 2 and 87 degrees of freedom are not available in the F-table in Appendix C.

As can be seen by an examination of Table 13.7, this one-way ANOVA would lead the personnel department to believe that there are no significant differences among the means of the work groups. They would conclude that classifying employees into three work types does not result in differences among performance levels. Yet, we still know that there are differences somewhere!

Interaction Among the Classification Variables

An observation of the raw data from Table 13.1 and the one-way ANOVA results given in Table 13.3 suggest that there are considerable differences among the 9 cells. Table 13.2 reveals that the means increase from left to right for the assembly line workers, remain stable for the maintenance workers, and decrease from left to right in regard to the security staff. What we are actually observing is the existence of *interaction* among our variables! We have interaction whenever the cell means differ as a result of the combination of two or more classification variables bringing about a result that cannot be accounted for by the classification variables taken separately. Another way of stating this relationship is that interaction occurs whenever the existence of one of the classification variables brings about different results for different cells within the other classification variable.

When interaction exists, it would be misleading to draw conclusions from the results of a one-way analysis of variance. A major advantage of the two-way analysis of variance over the one-way analysis of variance is that we can actually test for interaction. We can examine whether the whole effect of the two classification variables is more than just the sum of the effects of these variables taken separately.

Linear Models for Identifying Interaction Terms

We introduced the concept of linear models in Chapter 12 as a way of viewing analysis of variance. There, we examined ***Model 0,*** which represented the ***chance model*** where we attempted to determine the variable of interest only from a knowledge of chance. We then examined ***Model 1,*** which included a single variable or factor. We used one-way analysis of variance to determine whether Model 1 was a significant improvement over Model 0, based on the data at hand. In terms of these linear models, we now include the effects of an additional factor or classification variable, along with the impact of an interaction term. Building upon linear Model 0 and Model 1, we now develop ***Model 2.*** This model represents the two-way analysis of variance, as follows:

Model 0: $X = \mu + \varepsilon$

Model 1: $X = \mu + \alpha + \varepsilon$

Model 2: $X = \mu + \alpha + \beta + \alpha\beta + \varepsilon$

where:

μ = the population mean

α = the contribution of the first classification variable

β = the contribution of the second classification variable

$\alpha\beta$ = the contribution of the interaction effect between the first and second variables

ε = the error component, "epsilon"

The subscripts have been omitted to simplify the notation. If the second variable and/or the interaction term contribute to the components of the model, the error term, ε, will be reduced. Since both μ and α have remained the same, the error term in Model 1 has been reduced by the amount of the contribution of either β, $\alpha\beta$, or both in Model 2. We will now determine how to test for the contributions of each of the classification variables, often referred to as the ***main effects*** in a factorial analysis of variance design, as well as for interaction terms.

PROCEDURES FOR THE TWO-WAY ANALYSIS OF VARIANCE

Equations for the two-way analysis of variance model with fixed effects are given in Table 13.8. Equations for the less frequently used random effects and mixed effects models are not included in this textbook. Those equations differ from the equations for the fixed effects model; and, if needed, they can be found in several of the textbooks included in the reference list at the end of this chapter. As given in the table, we can examine sources of variation for *cells*, *columns*, *rows*, *interaction*, *within*, and *total*. The rows (assembly line, maintenance, and security staff for Example 13.1) and the columns (BARS, MBO, and TQM for Example 13.1) represent the *main effects* in the model. If we have significant interaction, we can also test for *simple effects*. The simple effects in a factorial analysis of variance will be discussed later.

As reflected throughout this textbook, decision making based on statistical analysis requires a very systematic approach. Variables have to be identified (e.g., variables of interest and classification variables) and understood (e.g., nominal, ordinal, interval, or ratio); hypotheses need to be established (null and alternative); assumptions should be examined (e.g., normality and homogeneity of variance); a statistical test must be decided on and computed; and, if we reject the null hypothesis, we often will want to perform post comparison tests. With the two-way analysis of variance, we must be even more systematic than before, as we have more sources of variance to examine. Figure 13.2 provides a *logical* flowchart for decision making when using a two-way ANOVA design. However, before we can use this flowchart, we must determine the necessary degrees of freedom, sums of squares, mean squares, computed F-values, and critical F-values related to the set of data being analyzed.

Degrees of Freedom for Two-Way Analysis of Variance

Our first step will be to determine the degrees of freedom for each source of variation. The degrees of freedom for cells, as indicated in Table 13.8, will be equal to the number of cells (k) in the design, minus one (k - 1). The degrees of freedom for rows (r) and columns (c) will be the number of rows minus 1 (r - 1) and the number of columns minus 1 (c - 1), respectively. The degrees of freedom for interaction (r x c) will be the product obtained by multiplying the degrees of freedom for rows times the degrees of freedom for columns [$(r - 1)\cdot(c - 1)$]. Notice that the degrees of freedom for rows, columns, and interaction will always sum to the degrees of freedom for cells, providing a check on our calculations.

The degrees of freedom for the within term will be equal to the number of cases in the total set minus the number of cells in the study (n_T - k). This is similar to the degrees of freedom for within in the one-way ANOVA, except that now we are subtracting by the number of cells instead of by the number of groups.

The degrees of freedom for the total variation is equal to the number of individual cases minus one (n_T - 1), just as it was for the one-way analysis of variance. Notice that the degrees of freedom for cells and for within add to the degrees of freedom for total, providing another check on our calculations.

Table 13.8
Two-Way Analysis of Variance Layout

Source of Variation	*df*	*Sums of Squares*	*MS*	*F*
Cells	$k - 1$	$\sum \sum n_{ij} \cdot (\overline{X}_{ij} - \overline{X}_T)^2$	$\frac{SS_{CELLS}}{df_{CELLS}}$	$\frac{MS_{CELLS}}{MS_W}$
Rows	$r - 1$	$\sum n_{i\cdot} \cdot (\overline{X}_{i\cdot} - \overline{X}_T)^2$	$\frac{SS_{ROWS}}{df_{ROWS}}$	$\frac{MS_{ROWS}}{MS_W}$
Columns	$c - 1$	$\sum n_{\cdot j} \cdot (\overline{X}_{\cdot j} - \overline{X}_T)^2$	$\frac{SS_{COLS}}{df_{COLS}}$	$\frac{MS_{COLS}}{MS_W}$
Interaction	$(r - 1) \cdot (c - 1)$	$\sum n_{ij} \cdot (\overline{X}_{ij} - \overline{X}_{i\cdot} - \overline{X}_{\cdot j} + \overline{X}_T)^2$	$\frac{SS_{R \cdot C}}{df_{R \cdot C}}$	$\frac{MS_{R \cdot C}}{MS_W}$
Within	$n_t - k$	$\sum \sum (X_{ij} - \overline{X}_{ij})^2$	$\frac{SS_W}{df_W}$	
Total	$n_t - 1$	$\sum \sum (X_{ij} - \overline{X}_T)^2$		

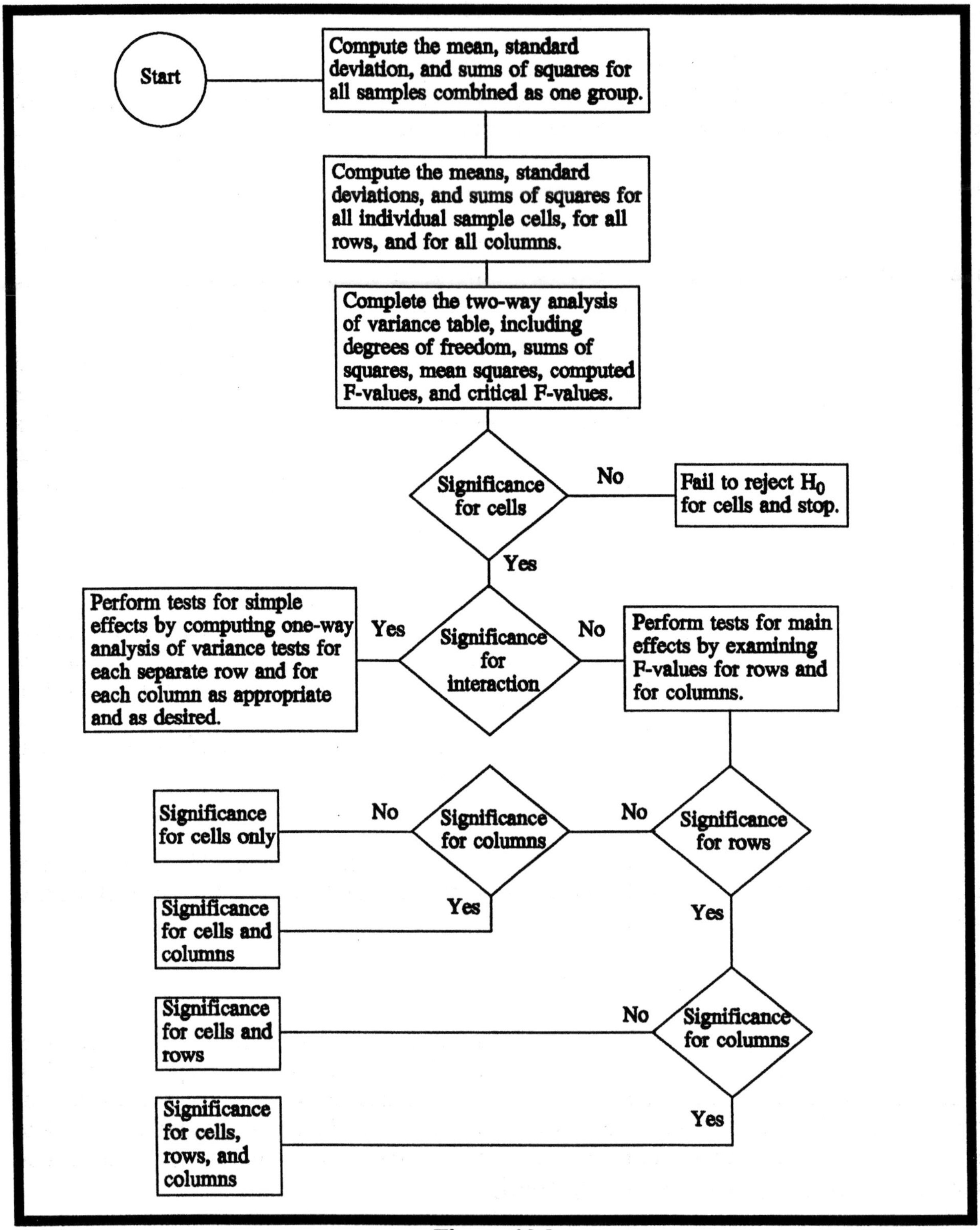

Figure 13.2
Procedural Flowchart for Two-Way Analysis of Variance

Sums of Squares for Two-Way Analysis of Variance

Total Sums of Squares. The total sums of squares is the same as SS_T in the one-way analysis of variance. That is, SS_T is obtained by finding the sum of the squared deviations of each of the individual cases from the grand mean, without regard for rows, columns, or cells. Of course, this is more easily determined if we already have the sample standard deviation for all of our data as one group.

Within Sums of Squares. The within sums of squares is similar to the within term of the one-way analysis of variance; we find the sum of the squared deviations about each of the cell means within each of the individual cells, and then we add these sums across all cells.

Cells Sums of Squares. The cells of the model contain each of the groups that exist within the study, based on combinations of the two classification variables. The sums of squares for *cells* in a two-way analysis of variance is analogous to the sums of squares for *among* in a one-way analysis of variance. Thus, we compute this value by subtracting the grand mean from each of the cell means, squaring the differences, multiplying by the sample sizes, and summing these squared differences over all cells. However, if we have obtained SS_T and SS_W, we know that $SS_T - SS_W = SS_{CELLS}$.

Rows, Columns, and Interaction Sums of Squares. The sums of squares for cells can be decomposed into the sums of squares for rows (SS_{ROWS}), columns (SS_{COLS}), and interaction (SS_{RxC}). Table 13.8 gives the equations for these terms. The three sources of squared deviations add up to the sum of squares for cells. Thus, with a knowledge of this relationship, our actual calculations are easier than Table 13.8 would suggest. If we know any three of these sources (cells, columns, rows, and interaction), we can determine the fourth by addition or subtraction.

Mean Squares

We can now compute mean squares for five sources of variation: cells, rows, columns, interaction, and within. Each of these is obtained by dividing the appropriate sums of squares by its corresponding degrees of freedom.

F-Tests and Their Sequential Analyses

Based on the five mean squares, we can compute four *F*-tests, one for cells, rows, columns, and interaction. The denominator for each of the *F*-tests is the mean squares for within, which is our error term. Therefore, the degrees of freedom associated with the denominator for the four critical *F*-values in the *F*-table will be df_W for each *F*-test. The degrees of freedom associated with the numerators of the critical *F*-values for cells, rows, columns, and interaction are df_{CELLS}, df_{ROWS}, df_{COLS}, and df_{RxC}, respectively.

Although there are four possible *F*-tests that can be made, we seldom perform all of these tests. Following the logical approach given in Figure 13.2, we first test to determine whether we have significant differences among the cell means. If we *do not* find a significant F-value for this test, we should terminate our analysis. Any other analyses may be inaccurate and thus misleading.

If we *do* have significance for cells, we then test for interaction. If we find significance for interaction, we should *not* test for *main effects*. Conclusions regarding significance for rows and/or for columns when interaction exists can be very misleading. Suppose that we find interaction in the present example and also find significant differences for training programs. If we draw conclusions based on the differences for training programs, we are likely to always recommend using the training program that results in the highest performance overall. We would then be disregarding the fact that the particular training program with the highest mean overall may not be the best training program for each individual work type.

When interaction exists, instead of examining differences among the main effects, we should test for differences among the *simple effects*. When we test for simple effects, we compare the means for each of the categories within one of the classification variables with respect to a given category within the other classification variable. In the present example, we could potentially perform six tests for simple effects, as follows:

1. We could compare the means of the three groups of assembly line workers who participated in the three performance programs (BARS, MBO, and TQM).

2. We could compare the means of the three groups of maintenance workers who participated in the three performance programs.

3. We could compare the means of the three groups of security staff workers who participated in the three performance programs.

4. We could compare the means of those who participated in the BARS program across the three work groups.

5. We could compare the means of those who participated in the MBO program across the three work groups.

6. We could compare the means of those who participated in the TQM program across the three work groups.

The number of tests for simple effects that we can perform for a two-way ANOVA will always be equal to the number of rows ***plus*** the number of columns. In this example, we can perform 3 + 3 = 6 tests for simple effects if we desire to do so. Each of these simple effects tests requires separate one-way analyses of variances. Of course, based on the results of the one-way ANOVAs for simple effects, we can also perform Scheffé post-comparison tests for each appropriate situation.

We should only perform the tests for *main effects* when we ***do not*** have significance for interaction. These are the tests that allow us to examine differences among rows and among columns, while the tests for *simple effects* allow us to examine differences within any given row or column.

Results for the Two-Way Analysis of Variance for Example 13.1

We now return to Example 13.1 to complete the two-way analysis of variance. We will use Figure 13.2 to systematically approach the analysis.

Parameters to be Tested. The central tendencies of nine samples are to be compared. We will assume that the performance measure is at least interval level; therefore, we can compute means for each of the nine cells. These cell means, given in Table 13.2, will be compared in an effort to draw conclusions about population means. Based on the results for cell means, we may test for interaction or for main effects.

Probability Level and Directionality. Assuming that the personnel department wants to be rather certain of their conclusions, alpha has been set to .05 ($\alpha = .05$). The test statistic will be one-directional, as discussed in preceding sections.

Null Hypotheses. Instead of one null hypothesis, we now have four null hypotheses, one each for cells, interaction, rows, and columns. These hypotheses are stated as follows:

Cells: H_0: $\mu_{11} = \mu_{12} = \mu_{13} = \mu_{21} = \mu_{22} = \mu_{23} = \mu_{31} = \mu_{32} = \mu_{33}$

Interaction: H_0: $\mu_{ij} - \mu_{i.} - \mu_{.j} + \mu_T = 0$

Rows: H_0: $\mu_{1.} = \mu_{2.} = \mu_{3.}$

Columns: H_0: $\mu_{.1} = \mu_{.2} = \mu_{.3}$

Alternative Hypotheses. For each of the four null hypotheses, we have a corresponding alternative hypothesis. These hypotheses are typically stated in words, as follows:

Cells: H_A: At least two μ_{ij} values are not equal

Interaction: H_A: Not all $\mu_{ij} - \mu_{i.} - \mu_{.j} + \mu_T = 0$

Rows: H_A: At least two $\mu_{i.}$ values for rows are not equal

Columns: H_A: At least two $\mu_{.j}$ values for columns are not equal

Statistical Procedure. An appropriate statistical procedure for the analysis of Example 13.1 is the two-way analysis of variance. Therefore, we need to obtain the necessary sums of squares terms, degrees of freedom, and mean squares so that we can compute the F-tests for cells, interaction, rows, and columns as appropriate.

Computations of Degrees of Freedom

We will now determine all of the appropriate degrees of freedom for Example 13.1. As we know, there is an additive nature to the sums of squares. We also learned that there is an additive nature to the degrees of freedom. While degrees of freedom are much easier to determine than the sums of squares, this additive property for our terms once again serves as a useful check of our work. We should verify that the degrees of freedom are indeed additive after we determine them individually.

Degrees of Freedom for Total. The degrees of freedom for total are equal to $n_T - 1$. Since Example 13.1 has 90 cases, the degrees of freedom for total are as follows:

$$df_T = n_T - 1$$
$$= 90 - 1$$
$$= 89$$

Degrees of Freedom for Within. The degrees of freedom for the within term are equal to $n_T - k$. Since Example 13.1 has 90 cases and 9 cells, the degrees of freedom for within are as follows:

$$df_W = n_T - k$$
$$= 90 - 9$$
$$= 81$$

Degrees of Freedom for Cells. The degrees of freedom for cells are equal to $k - 1$. Since Example 13.1 has 9 cells, the degrees of freedom for cells are as follows:

$$df_{CELLS} = k - 1$$
$$= 9 - 1$$
$$= 8$$

Degrees of Freedom for Rows. The degrees of freedom for rows are equal to $r - 1$. Since Example 13.1 has 3 rows, the degrees of freedom for rows are as follows:

$$df_{ROWS} = r - 1$$
$$= 3 - 1$$
$$= 2$$

Degrees of Freedom for Columns. The degrees of freedom for our columns are equal to c - 1. Since Example 13.1 has 3 columns, the degrees of freedom for columns are as follows:

$$df_{COLS} = c - 1$$

$$= 3 - 1$$

$$= 2$$

Degrees of Freedom for Interaction. The degrees of freedom for interaction are equal to $(r - 1)\cdot(c - 1)$. Since Example 13.1 has 3 rows and 3 columns, the degrees of freedom for interaction are as follows:

$$df_{R \times C} = (r - 1)\cdot(c - 1)$$

$$= (3 - 1)\cdot(3 - 1)$$

$$= (2)\cdot(2)$$

$$= 4$$

Computations of Sums of Squares

Sums of Squares for Total. We are now ready to find the sums of squares for each of the sources of variation. The manual approach for finding the SS_T is as follows:

$$SS_T = \sum \sum (X_{ij} - X_T)^2$$

$$\begin{aligned}
= \quad & (25 - 31.011)^2 + (27 - 31.011)^2 + \cdots + (24 - 31.011)^2 \\
& + (35 - 31.011)^2 + (28 - 31.011)^2 + \cdots + (32 - 31.011)^2 \\
& + (39 - 31.011)^2 + (38 - 31.011)^2 + \cdots + (35 - 31.011)^2 \\
& + (30 - 31.011)^2 + (31 - 31.011)^2 + \cdots + (30 - 31.011)^2 \\
& + (35 - 31.011)^2 + (33 - 31.011)^2 + \cdots + (31 - 31.011)^2 \\
& + (35 - 31.011)^2 + (27 - 31.011)^2 + \cdots + (30 - 31.011)^2 \\
& + (32 - 31.011)^2 + (31 - 31.011)^2 + \cdots + (36 - 31.011)^2 \\
& + (31 - 31.011)^2 + (30 - 31.011)^2 + \cdots + (34 - 31.011)^2 \\
& + (31 - 31.011)^2 + (29 - 31.011)^2 + \cdots + (27 - 31.011)^2 \\
= \quad & 1158.9889
\end{aligned}$$

On the other hand, if we know the sample standard deviation for the entire data set, we simply square the standard deviation and multiply by n_T - 1. This is the easy approach!

Sums of Squares for Within. Next we obtain the SS_W term. Based on the raw value formula given in Table 13.8, we could manually compute SS_W as follows:

$$
\begin{aligned}
SS_W &= \sum \sum (X_{ij} - \bar{X}_{ij})^2 \\
&= (25 - 26.9)^2 + (27 - 26.9)^2 + \cdots + (24 - 26.9)^2 \\
&\quad + (35 - 31.1)^2 + (28 - 31.1)^2 + \cdots + (32 - 31.1)^2 \\
&\quad + (39 - 34.9)^2 + (38 - 34.9)^2 + \cdots + (35 - 34.9)^2 \\
&\quad + (30 - 30.8)^2 + (31 - 30.8)^2 + \cdots + (30 - 30.8)^2 \\
&\quad + (35 - 31.2)^2 + (33 - 31.2)^2 + \cdots + (31 - 31.2)^2 \\
&\quad + (35 - 31.1)^2 + (27 - 31.1)^2 + \cdots + (30 - 31.1)^2 \\
&\quad + (32 - 35.1)^2 + (31 - 35.1)^2 + \cdots + (36 - 35.1)^2 \\
&\quad + (31 - 30.9)^2 + (30 - 30.9)^2 + \cdots + (34 - 30.9)^2 \\
&\quad + (31 - 27.1)^2 + (29 - 27.1)^2 + \cdots + (27 - 27.1)^2 \\
&= 52.9000 + 52.9000 + 64.9000 + 59.6000 + 59.6000 \\
&\quad + 56.9000 + 64.9000 + 52.9000 + 52.9000 \\
&= 517.5000
\end{aligned}
$$

However, if we have already calculated the standard deviations for each of the cells of interest, the SS_W term can be considerably simplified as suggested earlier and as demonstrated in Chapter 12. We only need to sum the numerators of the variances for each of the groups. Since the sample standard deviations are given in Table 13.2, we simply square each of these standard deviations, multiply by the degrees of freedom in each cell, and sum, as follows:

$$
\begin{aligned}
SS_W &= \sum \sum (X_{ij} - \bar{X}_{ij})^2 = \sum \sum (s_{ij})^2 \cdot (n_{ij} - 1) \\
&= (2.424)^2 \cdot (10 - 1) + (2.424)^2 \cdot (10 - 1) + (2.685)^2 \cdot (10 - 1) \\
&\quad + (2.573)^2 \cdot (10 - 1) + (2.573)^2 \cdot (10 - 1) + (2.514)^2 \cdot (10 - 1) \\
&\quad + (2.685)^2 \cdot (10 - 1) + (2.424)^2 \cdot (10 - 1) + (2.424)^2 \cdot (10 - 1) \\
&\quad + 52.9000 + 52.9000 + 64.9000 + 59.6000 + 59.6000 \\
&\quad + 56.9000 + 64.9000 + 52.9000 + 52.9000 \\
&= 517.5000
\end{aligned}
$$

Sums of Squares for Cells. We are now ready to find the sums of squares for cells. Based on the raw value formula given in Table 13.8, we could manually compute the SS_{CELLS} as follows:

$$SS_{CELLS} = \sum \sum n_{ij} \cdot (\bar{X}_{ij} - \bar{X}_T)^2$$

$$= (10) \cdot (26.9 - 31.011)^2 + (10) \cdot (31.1 - 31.011)^2$$

$$+ (10) \cdot (34.9 - 31.011)^2 + (10) \cdot (30.8 - 31.011)^2$$

$$+ (10) \cdot (31.2 - 31.011)^2 + (10) \cdot (31.1 - 31.011)^2$$

$$+ (10) \cdot (35.1 - 31.011)^2 + (10) \cdot (30.9 - 31.011)^2$$

$$+ (10) \cdot (27.1 - 31.011)^2$$

$$= 641.4889$$

However, we should once again take advantage of the additivity properties of ANOVA. If we have already calculated SS_T and SS_W, we can find the difference between these two terms and obtain SS_{CELLS} with a minimum amount of effort, as follows:

$$SS_{CELLS} = SS_T - SS_W$$

$$= 1158.9889 - 517.5000$$

$$= 641.4889$$

We should keep in mind that the means and standard deviations for the rows, columns, and the total will often be rounded. The final results for each equation in Example 13.1 have been obtained via a computer program with maximum decimal place accuracy. Consequently, any manual computation may result in rounding errors that appear to yield different values.

Sums of Squares for Rows. We are now ready to calculate the sums of squares for rows, columns, and interaction. For computational ease, we should calculate rows and columns first, followed by interaction. We will begin with the SS_{ROWS}:

$$SS_{ROWS} = \sum \sum n_{i.} \cdot (\bar{X}_{i.} - \bar{X}_T)^2$$

$$= (30) \cdot (30.967 - 31.011)^2 + (30) \cdot (31.033 - 31.011)^2$$

$$+ (30) \cdot (31.033 - 31.011)^2$$

$$= .0889$$

Sums of Squares for Columns. We again point out that we could have calculated the sums of squares for columns before calculating the sums of squares for rows; the order is not of importance. We calculate the SS_{COLS} in the similar manner:

$$SS_{COLS} = \sum \sum n_{.j} \cdot (\bar{X}_{.j} - \bar{X}_T)^2$$

$$= (30) \cdot (30.933 - 31.011)^2 + (30) \cdot (31.067 - 31.011)^2$$

$$+ (30) \cdot (31.033 - 31.011)^2$$

$$= .2889$$

Sums of Squares for Interaction. We are now ready to calculate the SS_{RxC}. Based on the raw value formula given in Table 13.8, and a knowledge of the row, column, cell, and grand means, we could manually compute the SS_{RxC} as follows:

$$SS_{R \times C} = \sum n_{ij} \cdot (\bar{X}_{ij} - \bar{X}_{i.} - \bar{X}_{.j} + \bar{X}_T)^2$$

$$= (10) \cdot (26.9 - 30.967 - 30.933 + 31.011)^2$$

$$+ (10) \cdot (31.1 - 30.967 - 31.067 + 31.011)^2$$

$$+ (10) \cdot (34.9 - 30.967 - 31.033 + 31.011)^2$$

$$+ (10) \cdot (30.8 - 31.033 - 30.933 + 31.011)^2$$

$$+ (10) \cdot (31.2 - 31.033 - 31.067 + 31.011)^2$$

$$+ (10) \cdot (31.1 - 31.033 - 31.033 + 31.011)^2$$

$$+ (10) \cdot (35.1 - 31.033 - 30.933 + 31.011)^2$$

$$+ (10) \cdot (30.9 - 31.033 - 31.067 + 31.011)^2$$

$$+ (10) \cdot (27.1 - 31.033 - 31.033 + 31.011)^2$$

$$= 641.1111$$

As we can see, the manual approach for calculating the interaction term is very time-consuming. Further, as we increase the number of computational steps, we also increase our chances of making a data entry error. Therefore, we definitely want to take advantage of our rules of additivity here. Since we know that the SS_{CELLS} term is made up of SS_{ROWS}, SS_{COLS}, and SS_{RxC}, we can once again use subtraction to obtain this term, the most difficult of all the sums of squares terms to obtain. Our simplified calculations are as follows:

$$SS_{CELLS} = SS_{ROWS} + SS_{COLS} + SS_{R \times C}$$

$$SS_{R \times C} = SS_{CELLS} - (SS_{ROWS} + SS_{COLS})$$

$$= 641.4889 - (.0889 + .2889)$$

$$= 641.4889 - .3778$$

$$= 641.1111$$

Computations of Mean Squares

As we discussed in Chapter 12, the terminology for analysis of variance is derived from the notion that we are analyzing variances to make decisions about similarities or differences regarding means. Consequently, we must obtain our variances. We also recall that in analysis of variance, we use the terminology of *mean squares* to represent these variance terms. We will obtain each of these mean squares by dividing the sums of squares for each of the sources of variation of concern by its corresponding degrees of freedom.

Mean Squares for Cells. We will begin by determining the mean squares for cells. We obtain this value by dividing the sums of squares for cells by the degrees of freedom for cells:

$$MS_{CELLS} = \frac{SS_{CELLS}}{df_{CELLS}}$$

$$= \frac{641.4889}{8}$$

$$= 80.1861$$

Mean Squares for Within. The mean squares for within is determined by dividing the sums of squares for within by the degrees of freedom for within:

$$MS_W = \frac{SS_W}{df_W}$$

$$= \frac{517.5000}{81}$$

$$= 6.3889$$

Mean Squares for Rows. The mean squares for rows is determined by dividing the sums of squares for rows by the degrees of freedom for rows:

$$MS_{ROWS} = \frac{SS_{ROWS}}{df_{ROWS}}$$

$$= \frac{.0889}{2}$$

$$= .0444$$

Mean Squares for Columns. The mean squares for columns is determined by dividing the sums of squares for columns by the degrees of freedom for columns:

$$MS_{COLS} = \frac{SS_{COLS}}{df_{COLS}}$$

$$= \frac{.2889}{2}$$

$$= .1445$$

Mean Squares for Interaction. The mean squares for interaction is determined by dividing the sums of squares for interaction by the degrees of freedom for interaction:

$$MS_{R \times C} = \frac{SS_{R \times C}}{df_{R \times C}}$$

$$= \frac{641.1111}{4}$$

$$= 160.2778$$

Computations of *F*-Values

Finally, we are ready to obtain the computed *F*-values for cells, interaction, rows, and columns. For the two-way analysis of variance design, we use the within term as our error term or measure of chance. Therefore, the within term becomes the denominator for each of these *F*-values.

***F*-value for Cells.** First, we will calculate the F-value for cells. As indicated, to obtain this value, we divide the mean squares for cells by the mean squares for within. Consequently, we obtain the following *F*-value for cells:

$$F_{CELLS} = \frac{MS_{CELLS}}{MS_W}$$

$$= \frac{80.1861}{6.3889}$$

$$= 12.5509$$

This is the same result as obtained in Table 13.3. As we can see, performing a test for cells with a two-way analysis of variance corresponds to performing an omnibus F-test for a one-way analysis of variance. The groups in the one-way analysis of variance correspond to the cells in a two-way analysis of variance.

F-value for Interaction. Since we have tested for cells and found significance, we continue on by testing for interaction, as suggested by the logical flowchart given in Figure 13.2. The F-value for interaction is obtained by dividing the mean squares for the interaction term by the mean squares for the within term. For this example, we obtain the following F-value:

$$F_{R \times C} = \frac{MS_{R \times C}}{MS_W}$$

$$= \frac{160.2778}{6.3889}$$

$$= 25.0870$$

While there was no way to test for interaction with a one-way analysis of variance, whenever we have more than one factor we can test for such interaction terms. Thus, the two-way ANOVA provides for an additional source of analysis that cannot be accounted for with a one-way analysis of variance. Since there is significant interaction for Example 13.1, we should turn to our tests for simple effects instead of testing for main effects. Only if we ***do not*** have significance for interaction should we test for main effects.

***F*-value for Rows (Main Effects for Rows).** Since we have significance for interaction, there is nothing to be gained by examining the main effects for rows or columns; instead, we might mislead ourselves in the decision-making process. We will discuss the main effects tests for rows and columns here only to *illustrate* these tests. We should not perform them if we have interaction. Having emphasized this caution, if we had needed to test for main effects for rows, we would have calculated the F-value for rows by dividing the mean squares for rows by the mean squares for within. Here, we would have obtained the following F-value:

$$F_{ROWS} = \frac{MS_{ROWS}}{MS_W}$$

$$= \frac{.0444}{6.3889}$$

$$= .0070$$

This is *not* the same result as obtained in Table 13.7. Thus, testing for rows with a two-way analysis of variance does not correspond to the omnibus F-test for a one-way analysis of variance. In other words, if we use the rows in the two-way ANOVA (without regard to columns) as the groups in a one-way ANOVA design, we get different results. This is because we have been able to reduce the error term, MS_W, by removing two other sources of variation (i.e., columns and interaction) from the within term. As indicated earlier, a major advantage of two-way analysis of variance is the reduction of the error term, giving us a more *powerful* statistical test.

***F*-value for Columns (Main Effects for Columns).** If we had needed to test for main effects for columns, we would have calculated this F-value by dividing the mean squares for columns by the mean squares for within. Here, we would have obtained the following F-value:

$$F_{COLS} = \frac{MS_{COLS}}{MS_W}$$

$$= \frac{.1445}{6.3889}$$

$$= .0226$$

Again, this F-value is *not* the same as the one obtained in Table 13.5. As with rows, testing for columns with a two-way analysis of variance does not correspond to the omnibus F-test for a one-way analysis of variance. In other words, if we use the columns in the two-way ANOVA (without regard to rows) as the groups in a one-way ANOVA design, we get different results. As before, this is because we have been able to reduce the error term.

Summary of Results

Table 13.9 presents the results of the two-way analysis of variance, following the procedures that we have discussed. Included in the table are the F-values for cells, rows, columns, and interaction. As stated earlier, we would not even test for rows and columns since we have interaction.

Decision

Based on the two-way analysis of variance, we have a computed $F(8, 81) = 12.5509$, $p < .05$ for cells. (This F-value is also $< .01$.) We reject the null hypothesis and conclude that at least two of the cells come from populations with unequal means. Next, we test for interaction and obtain a computed $F(4, 81) = 25.0870$, $p < .05$. (This F-value is $< .01$, too.) We now know that we have significance for cells and for interaction. Following the logical flowchart given in Figure 13.2, we will not test for the main effects of rows or columns. Instead, we will test for simple effects.

Table 13.9
Two-Way Analysis of Variance Table with Work Classifications and Training Factors

Source of Variation	*df*	*SS*	*MS*	*F-Value*	*Critical F*
Cells	8	641.4889	80.1861	12.5509	2.06
Rows (Work Classifications)	2	.0889	.0444	.0070	3.11
Columns (Training Programs)	2	.2889	.1445	.0226	3.11
Interaction	4	641.1111	160.2778	25.0870	2.49
Within	81	517.5000	6.3889		
Total	89	1158.9889			

Note. The critical F-values are based on $\alpha = .05$, with 80 degrees of freedom in the denominator, as 81 degrees of freedom are not available in the F-table in Appendix C.

Tests for Simple Effects

Tests for simple effects are one-way ANOVAs for specific cells within any of the rows or columns desired. We could consider any or all of six possible one-way ANOVAs for simple effects. For example, we may want to evaluate the performance scores for assembly line workers. A one-way ANOVA would allow us to determine whether significant differences exist for the three samples of assembly line workers, each involved in a different training program. We may also want to perform a one-way ANOVA for the maintenance workers across the three training programs and a one-way ANOVA for the security staff in the same manner. Thus, we could perform three one-way ANOVAs, or tests for simple effects, for this factor.

Further, we could evaluate the performance scores for all those who participated in the BARS program by comparing the means of the three work groups across the BARS category. We could also perform a one-way ANOVA for the three work groups across the MBO category and a one-way ANOVA for these same groups across the TQM program. This gives us three more potential tests for simple effects. An easy way to conceptualize these simple effects tests is to ***explode*** the original design. That is, if we have significance for interaction, we should explode the 3 × 3 matrix for Example 13.1 into six separate one-way layouts as illustrated in Figure 13.3.

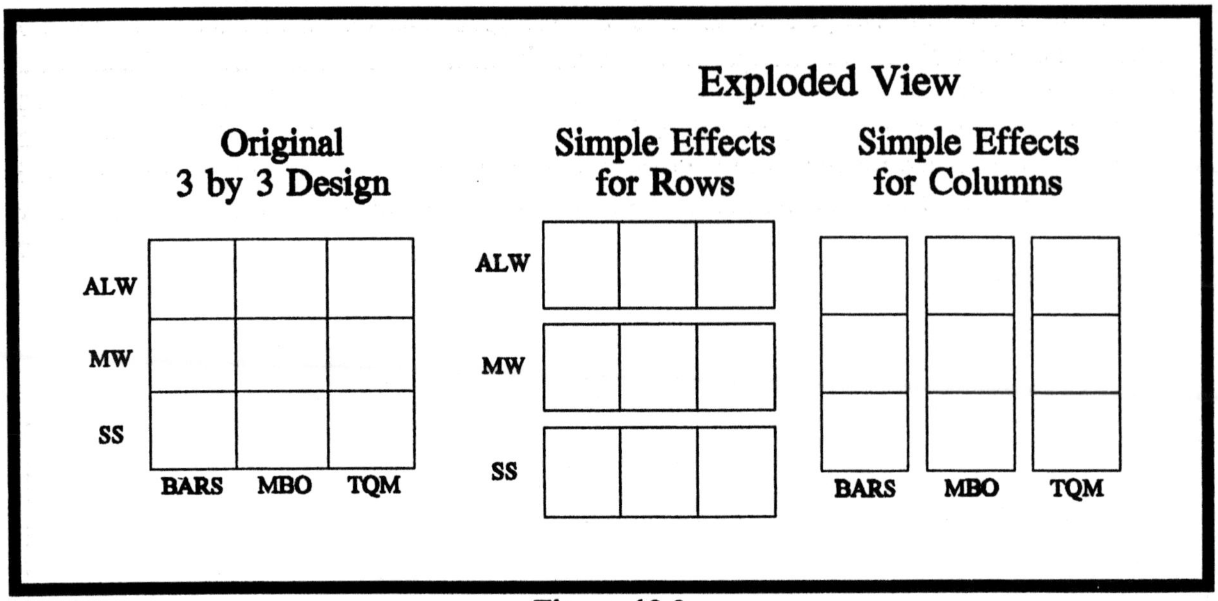

Figure 13.3
Original 3 × 3 Design and Exploded Views

Most statistical software packages include a two-way ANOVA program. Although not all give the same set of statistics and summary data, the *F*-test results for the analysis of variance should be identical. Table 13.10 gives the results obtained from a computer program written by the present author[2]. This printout includes the matrix of cell sizes, the matrix of means, the matrix of standard deviations, and the standard two-way analysis of variance table. As we can see, the two-way ANOVA table agrees with the results previously calculated. The program also generates probability values, or *p*-values, that eliminate the need for looking up critical *F*-values in the *F*-table. As we can see, the probability of obtaining an *F*-value of 12.5509 or greater for cells is very low, with a *p*-value of .0000, rounded to four decimal places. We find the same results when we test for interaction.

Table 13.10 also includes Scheffé *post hoc* multiple comparison *F*-tests for analyzing both the main effects and simple effects. Since there is significant interaction, the Scheffé tests for the main effects will be ignored, and we turn to the six possible tests for simple effects. We find that there is a significant difference among the means for row 1 (assembly line workers) across the three training programs and a significant difference among the means for row 3 (security staff) across these same training programs. We also find that there is a significant difference among the means for column 1 (BARS) across the three types of work classifications and a significant difference among the means for column 3 (TQM) across these same work classifications. We should also note that it might be useful to compute pairwise Scheffé tests for these significant rows and columns.

---

[2]This program is referred to as JRB50.

When we performed a one-way analysis of variance on program types as shown in Table 13.5 and a one-way analysis of variance on work groups as shown in Table 13.7, we did not separate out each of the sub-groups as we would do with the tests for simple effects. That is, when analyzing programs earlier, we *collapsed* all levels of work groups into one work group and used only one dimension: program types. This approach was presented only to illustrate the differences between one-way and two-way analysis of variance. We would *not* do this in actual practice. Instead, we would only look at one category of one dimension at a time (e.g., assembly line workers), evaluating the impact of the other dimension (e.g., program type) on the criterion variable (e.g., performance).

Table 13.10
Computer-Generated Results for Two-Way ANOVA

JRB50 VERSION 2.0---TWO-WAY ANALYSIS OF VARIANCE:
REVISED JANUARY 3, 1997.
COPYRIGHT (C) 1997 BY JAMES R. BEATTY.

MATRIX OF CELL SIZES

	1	2	3	
1	10	10	10	30
2	10	10	10	30
3	10	10	10	30
	30	30	30	90

MATRIX OF MEANS

	1	2	3	
1	26.9000	31.1000	34.9000	30.9667
2	30.8000	31.2000	31.1000	31.0333
3	35.1000	30.9000	27.1000	31.0333
	30.9333	31.0667	31.0333	31.0111

MATRIX OF STANDARD DEVIATIONS

	1	2	3	
1	2.4244	2.4244	2.6854	4.1146
2	2.5734	2.5734	2.5144	2.4703
3	2.6854	2.4244	2.4244	4.1146
	4.2095	2.3916	4.0640	3.6086

ANALYSIS OF VARIANCE TABLE

SOURCE OF VARIATION	DF	SUM OF SQUARES	MEAN SQUARE	F	PROB
CELLS	8	641.4889	80.1861	12.5509	.0000
ROWS	2	.0889	.0444	.0070	.9936
COLUMNS	2	.2889	.1444	.0226	.9784
INTERACTION	4	641.1111	160.2778	25.0870	.0000
WITHIN	81	517.5000	6.3889		
TOTAL	89	1158.9890			

Significant $p < .05$ or $p < .01$

Table 13.10
Two-Way ANOVA Printout---Continued

```
MATRIX OF SCHEFFE F VALUES FOR MAIN EFFECTS FOR ROWS
  (EVALUATE THESE ONLY IF THERE IS NO INTERACTION):
  ROW I VS. ROW I+1 (SEE UPPER-RIGHT TRIANGLE OF MATRIX).

COMPARE THESE VALUES TO THE CRITICAL VALUE, DETERMINED AS FOLLOWS:
  POST COMPARISON MAIN EFFECTS SCHEFFE F FOR ROWS =
  (DF FOR ROWS) TIMES (MAIN EFFECTS CRITICAL F FOR ROWS).

              ROW NUMBER

        1           2           3

  1     .0000       .0104       .0104
  2     .0104       .0000       .0000
  3     .0104       .0000       .0000

MATRIX OF SCHEFFE F VALUES FOR MAIN EFFECTS FOR COLUMNS
  (EVALUATE THESE ONLY IF THERE IS NO INTERACTION):
  COLUMN I VS. COLUMN I+1 (SEE UPPER-RIGHT TRIANGLE OF MATRIX).

COMPARE THESE VALUES TO THE CRITICAL VALUE, DETERMINED AS FOLLOWS:
  POST COMPARISON MAIN EFFECTS SCHEFFE F FOR COLUMNS =
  (DF FOR COLUMNS) TIMES (MAIN EFFECTS CRITICAL F FOR COLUMNS).

             COLUMN NUMBER

        1           2           3

  1     .0000       .0417       .0235
  2     .0417       .0000       .0026
  3     .0235       .0026       .0000

SIMPLE MAIN EFFECTS F TESTS FOR EACH ROW (ONE-WAY ANOVAS)
  (EVALUATE THESE F-VALUES ONLY IF THERE IS INTERACTION):

SIMPLE MAIN EFFECTS FOR ROW  1:  F (  2,    81) =    25.0644  P = .0000
                                 MS(A) =    160.1334  MS(W) =       6.3889

SIMPLE MAIN EFFECTS FOR ROW  2:  F (  2,    81) =      .0678  P = .9341
                                 MS(A) =       .4333  MS(W) =       6.3889

SIMPLE MAIN EFFECTS FOR ROW  3:  F (  2,    81) =    25.0643  P = .0000
                                 MS(A) =    160.1333  MS(W) =       6.3889

SIMPLE MAIN EFFECTS F TESTS FOR EACH COLUMN (ONE-WAY ANOVAS)
  (EVALUATE THESE F-VALUES ONLY IF THERE IS INTERACTION):

SIMPLE MAIN EFFECTS FOR COLUMN  1:  F (  2,    81) =    26.3322  P = .0000
                                    MS(A) =    168.2333  MS(W) =       6.3889

SIMPLE MAIN EFFECTS FOR COLUMN  2:  F (  2,    81) =      .0365  P = .9645
                                    MS(A) =       .2333  MS(W) =       6.3889

SIMPLE MAIN EFFECTS FOR COLUMN  3:  F (  2,    81) =    23.8122  P = .0000
                                    MS(A) =    152.1334  MS(W) =       6.3889

ADDITIONAL SCHEFFE PAIR-WISE COMPARISONS CAN BE MADE.  SET THE FOLLOWING:
  DF (NUMERATOR) = CELLS - 1
  DF (DENOMINATOR) = N - CELLS
  DETERMINE THE CRITICAL SCHEFFE F AS FOLLOWS:
  (CELLS - 1) TIMES (OMNIBUS F FOR CELLS).
```

A helpful approach for examining the interaction among variables is to plot the means of each of the sets of groups. A graph of these means will give a rough indication of whether we have interaction or not. That is, if we observe that the lines are not *parallel,* we have an indication that interaction exists. By parallel, we mean that the graphs of the means remain approximately equidistant apart at various points along the graph. Figure 13.4 and Figure 13.5 graph the results for the present data. Figure 13.4 represents the graph of means for work classifications across programs, while Figure 13.5 represents the graph of means for programs across work classifications.

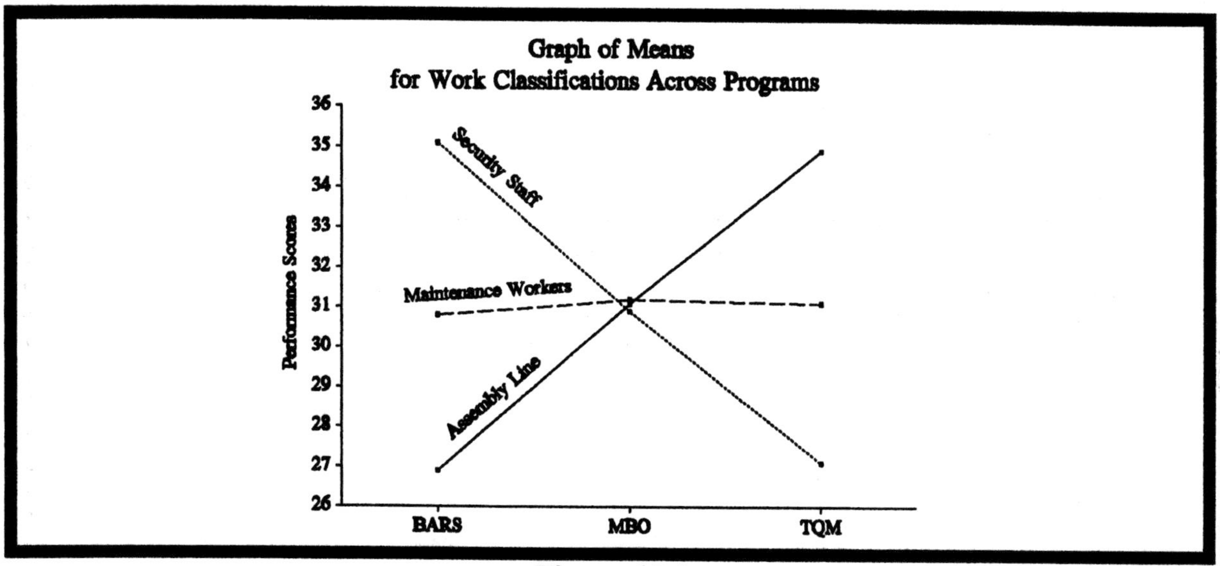

Figure 13.4
Graph of Means for Work Classifications Across Programs

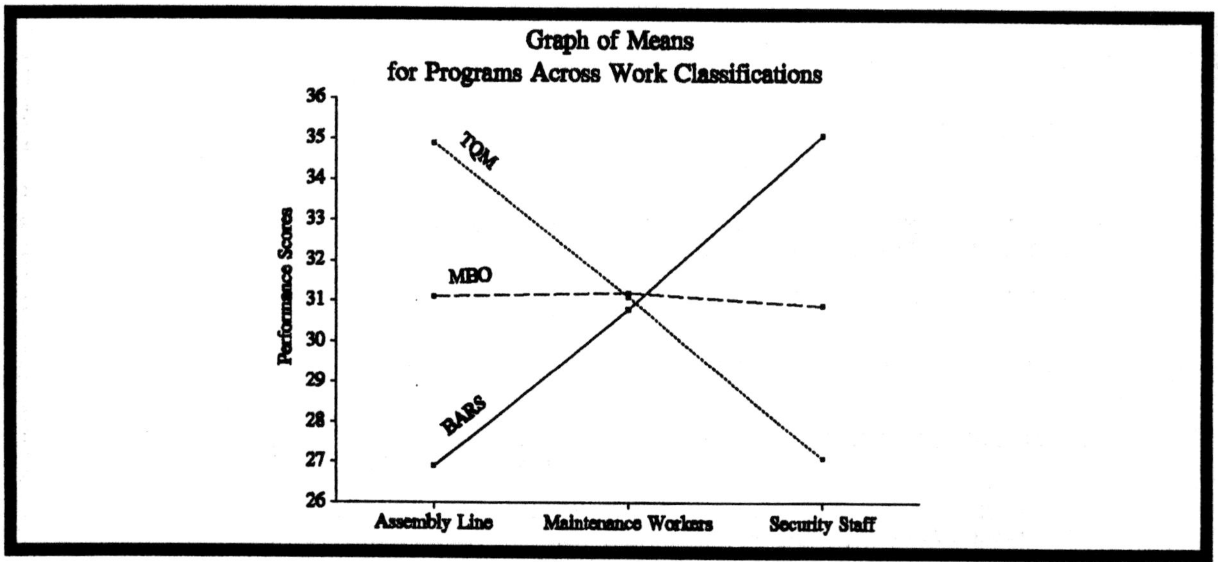

Figure 13.5
Graph of Means for Programs Across Work Classifications

It should be clear from Figure 13.4 that only the means for the maintenance group are stable across programs. Since none of the three programs result in significantly higher performance for this work group (as can be confirmed using the one-way ANOVA for simple effects), the company might simply choose to use the least expensive of the three programs.

The means for the assembly line workers are low for the BARS program, moderate for the MBO program, and high for the TQM program. The company may wish to have this work group involved in TQM activities. On the other hand, the means for the security staff are high for the BARS program, moderate for the MBO program, and low for the TQM program. Perhaps this group should be using BARS in their work situation.

An examination of Figure 13.5 reveals that only the MBO program resulted in consistent means across all three work classifications. The means for those participating in the BARS program were low for assembly line workers, moderate for maintenance workers, and high for the security staff. The means for those participating in the TQM programs were high for assembly line workers, moderate for maintenance workers, and low for the security staff. Again, it is clear from an observation of the graph that the three lines are not "parallel," indicating that interaction has occurred.

TWO-WAY ANALYSIS OF VARIANCE WITHOUT INTERACTION

We have seen the importance of testing for interaction with the two-way ANOVA. When interaction does exist, accounting for it will greatly reduce the error term in our linear model. Further, if we do not account for it when it does exist, we may interpret the main effects of the rows and columns inappropriately. However, interaction does not always occur. When we do not have interaction, we will want to carefully examine the main effects of the two classification variables.

Example 13.2. To illustrate the two-way analysis of variance fixed-effects model with no interaction, suppose that the health department of an organization has been concerned with the absenteeism rates of its employees. Numerous research findings have indicated that smoking has had an impact on absenteeism in that the rates are higher for those who smoke than for those who do not smoke. Other research findings have indicated that planned exercise programs also have an effect on absenteeism. Therefore, our hypothetical company has decided to determine whether absenteeism is a function of smoking and/or exercise programs for their organization. The variable of interest is absenteeism, which is at least interval level. The classification variables are smoking and exercise programs. Based on the absenteeism records reported for the 180 cases, a raw data matrix has been developed.

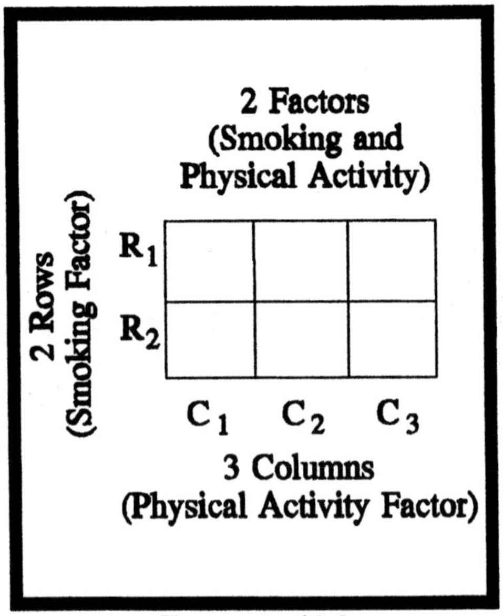

Example 13.2

These raw data values are included in Table 13.11. Based on the raw values in Table 13.11, we can compute the necessary values to compile summary statistics, including means and standard deviations. These summary statistics are given in Table 13.12.

Table 13.11
Two-Way ANOVA Data: Smoking Characteristics and Exercise Programs

	Runners			*Recreation*			*No Exercise*		
	11	8	11	12	8	9	18	12	12
	12	10	10	9	12	11	16	18	15
	13	7	10	13	10	10	15	15	15
	11	9	12	9	9	11	17	18	14
	10	10	10	8	10	10	15	13	15
Smokers	8	12	9	11	8	9	15	17	15
	10	11	8	12	7	12	14	16	14
	8	10	11	11	10	10	15	17	13
	9	9	10	10	8	10	13	15	12
	10	12	9	11	11	9	15	16	15
	5	2	8	8	5	8	9	10	10
	8	5	6	7	4	7	10	12	11
	5	4	5	6	3	6	12	9	9
	4	5	6	5	2	5	11	8	12
	2	3	5	4	5	3	9	10	10
Non-smokers	6	5	3	7	5	7	10	11	11
	5	3	7	6	4	6	8	11	9
	4	7	5	5	3	5	10	10	12
	7	6	4	5	5	5	8	8	10
	5	5	5	2	3	4	11	10	9

Smoking is a nominal, two category variable, consisting of those who smoke and those who do not smoke. Exercise is a nominal, three category variable, consisting of those who have participated in a company-sponsored running program, those who have participated in a company-sponsored recreational sports program for at least six months, and those who have not followed any regular exercise program at all. The two-way analysis of variance for fixed effects is therefore an appropriate statistical technique for this study.

Table 13.12
Two-Way ANOVA Summary Statistics: Smoking and Exercise

	Runners	*Recreation*	*No Exercise*	*Row Totals*
	$n_{11} = 30$	$n_{12} = 30$	$n_{13} = 30$	$n_{1.} = 90$
Smokers	$\overline{X}_{11} = 10$	$\overline{X}_{12} = 10$	$\overline{X}_{13} = 15$	$\overline{X}_{1.} = 11.67$
	$s_{11} = 1.44$	$s_{12} = 1.46$	$s_{13} = 1.71$	$s_{1.} = 2.82$
	$n_{21} = 30$	$n_{22} = 30$	$n_{23} = 30$	$n_{2.} = 90$
Non-smokers	$\overline{X}_{21} = 5$	$\overline{X}_{22} = 5$	$\overline{X}_{23} = 10$	$\overline{X}_{2.} = 6.67$
	$s_{21} = 1.53$	$s_{22} = 1.62$	$s_{23} = 1.23$	$s_{2.} = 2.78$
	$n_{.1} = 60$	$n_{.2} = 60$	$n_{.3} = 60$	$n_T = 180$
Column	$\overline{X}_{.1} = 7.5$	$\overline{X}_{.2} = 7.5$	$\overline{X}_{.3} = 12.5$	$\overline{X}_T = 9.17$
Totals	$s_{.1} = 2.92$	$s_{.2} = 2.95$	$s_{.3} = 2.92$	$s_T = 3.75$

Results for the Two-Way Analysis of Variance for Example 13.2

We now complete the analysis of Example 13.2 through the use of two-way analysis of variance. Again, we will follow the flowchart given in Figure 13.2 in order to have a systematic approach to the analysis.

Parameters to be Tested. The central tendencies of six samples are to be compared. We know that absenteeism is at least interval level data; therefore, we have computed means for each of the six cells. These cell means, given in Table 13.12, will be compared in an effort to draw conclusions about population means. Based on the results for cell means, we may test for interaction or for main effects.

Probability Level and Directionality. Assuming that the health department of the organization wants to be rather certain of their conclusions, alpha has been set to .05 ($\alpha = .05$). The test statistic will be one-directional, as discussed in the preceding section.

Null Hypothesis. Again, we have four null hypotheses, one each for cells, interaction, rows, and columns. These hypotheses are stated as follows:

Cells: H_0: $\mu_{11} = \mu_{12} = \mu_{13} = \mu_{21} = \mu_{22} = \mu_{23}$

Interaction: H_0: $\mu_{ij} - \mu_{i.} - \mu_{.j} + \mu_T = 0$

Rows: H$_0$: $\mu_{1\cdot} = \mu_{2\cdot}$

Columns: H$_0$: $\mu_{\cdot 1} = \mu_{\cdot 2} = \mu_{\cdot 3}$

Alternative Hypothesis. For each of the four null hypotheses, we have a corresponding alternative hypothesis. These hypotheses are typically stated in words, as follows:

Cells: H_A: At least two μ_{ij} values are not equal

Interaction: H_A: Not all $\mu_{ij} - \mu_{i\cdot} - \mu_{\cdot j} + \mu_T = 0$

Rows: H_A: $\mu_{1\cdot} \neq \mu_{2\cdot}$

Columns: H_A: At least two $\mu_{\cdot j}$ values for columns are not equal

Statistical Procedure. The appropriate statistical test for the present problem is the two-way analysis of variance and its related *F*-test.

Results. Table 13.13 presents the results of the two-way analysis of variance, following the procedures given here. Figure 13.7 presents a graph of the means for smoking across the programs classification factor, while Figure 13.8 presents a graph of the means for programs across the smoking classification factor.

Table 13.13
Two-Way Analysis of Variance Table for Smoking and Exercise

Source of Variation	*df*	*SS*	*MS*	*F-Value*	*Critical F*
Cells	5	2125.00	425.00	187.69	2.27
Rows (Smoking)	1	1125.00	1125.00	496.83	3.90
Columns (Exercise)	2	1000.00	500.00	220.81	3.06
Interaction	2	.00	.00	.00	3.06
Within	174	394.00	2.26		
Total	179	2519.00			

Note. The critical *F*-values are based on $\alpha = .05$, with 150 degrees of freedom in the denominator, as 174 degrees of freedom are not available in the *F*-table in Appendix C.

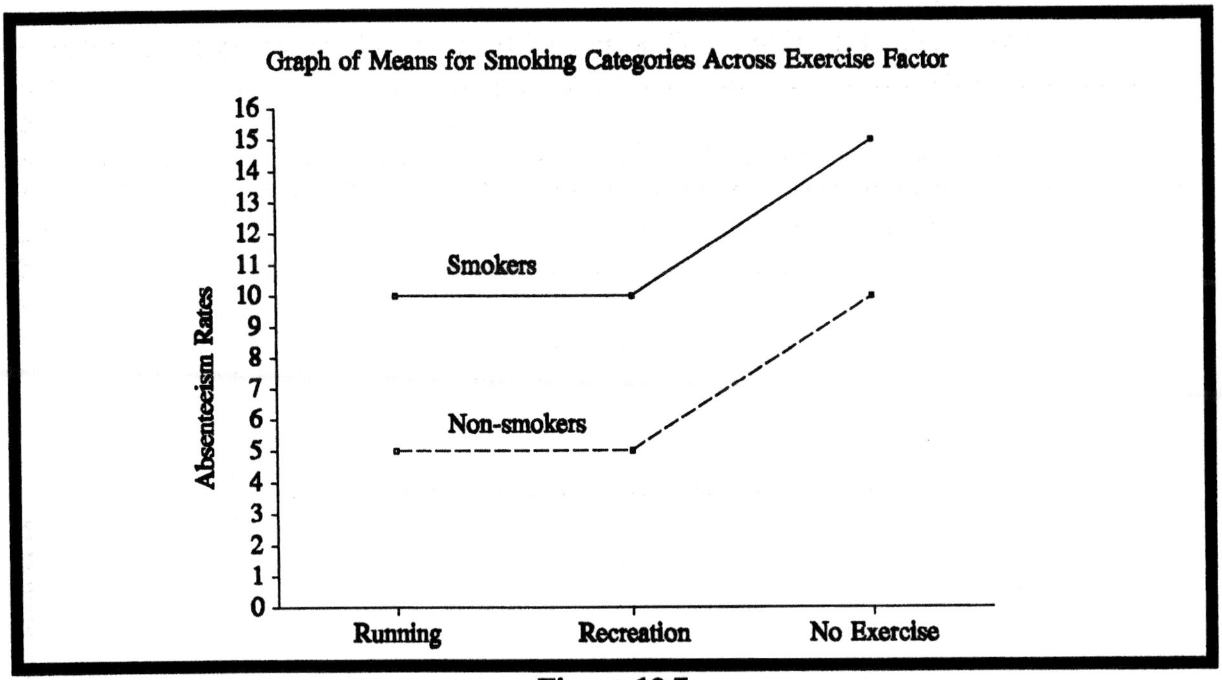

Figure 13.7
Graph of Means for Smoking Categories Across Exercise Factor

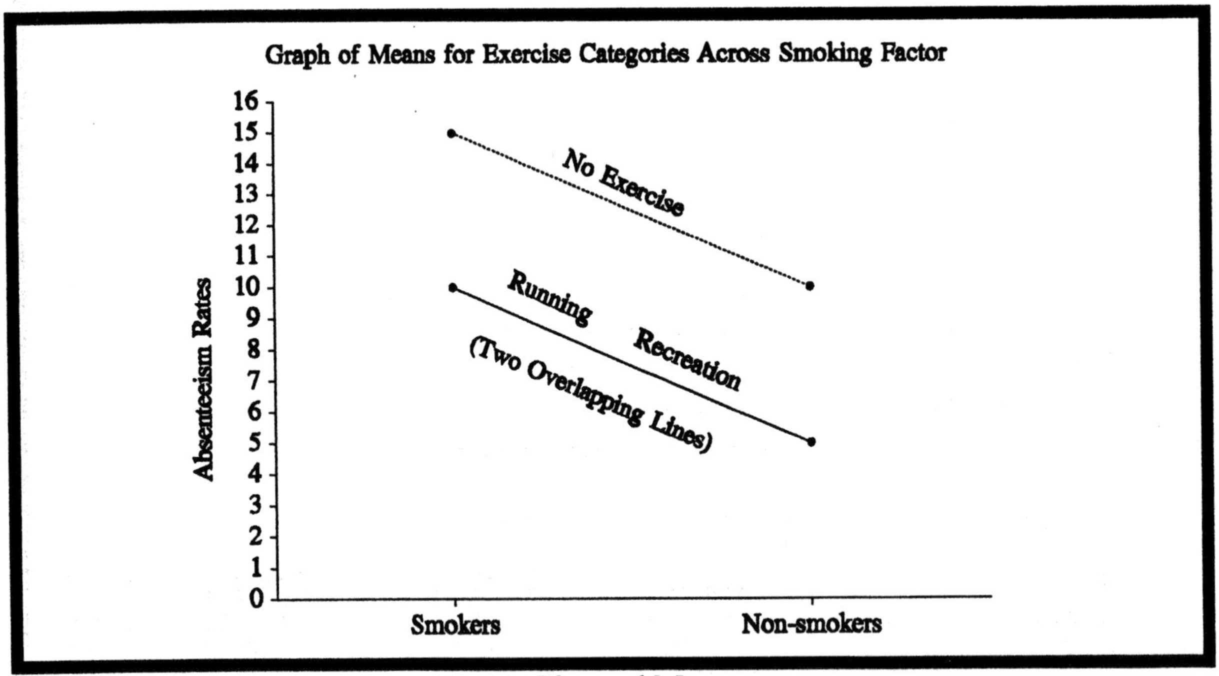

Figure 13.8
Graph of Means for Exercise Categories Across Smoking Factor

Decision. Based on the two-way analysis of variance and the computer printout given in Table 13.14, we find that $F(5, 174) = 187.69$, $p < .01$ for cells. We reject the null hypothesis and conclude that at least two of the cells come from populations with unequal means. When testing for interaction, we obtain a computed $F(2, 174) = 0.00$, $p > .01$. Therefore, we have significance for cells but not for interaction. Next, we test for main effects, evaluating both the rows and columns. The computed value for rows is $F(1, 174) = 496.83$, $p < .01$, indicating that smokers have a significantly greater absenteeism rate than do nonsmokers, based on these data. The computed value for columns is $F(2, 174) = 220.81$, $p < .01$. Therefore, we also conclude that the absenteeism rates of at least two different conditions of exercise are significantly different. The Scheffé tests included in Table 13.14 reveal which columns are significantly different. Since there are only two rows, no post comparison tests are necessary for rows.

Table 13.14
Computer Printout for Two-Way ANOVA with No Interaction

JRB50 VERSION 2.0---TWO-WAY ANALYSIS OF VARIANCE:
REVISED JANUARY 3, 1997.
COPYRIGHT (C) 1997 BY JAMES R. BEATTY.

MATRIX OF CELL SIZES

	1	2	3	
1	30	30	30	90
2	30	30	30	90
	60	60	60	180

MATRIX OF MEANS

	1	2	3	
1	10.0000	10.0000	15.0000	11.6667
2	5.0000	5.0000	10.0000	6.6667
	7.5000	7.5000	12.5000	9.1667

MATRIX OF STANDARD DEVIATIONS

	1	2	3	
1	1.4384	1.4622	1.7019	2.8165
2	1.5313	1.6189	1.2318	2.7803
	2.9198	2.9487	2.9198	3.7513

ANALYSIS OF VARIANCE TABLE

SOURCE OF VARIATION	DF	SUM OF SQUARES	MEAN SQUARE	F	PROB
CELLS	5	2125.0000	425.0000	187.6904	.0000
ROWS	1	1125.0000	1125.0000	496.8275	.0000
COLUMNS	2	1000.0000	500.0000	220.8122	.0000
INTERACTION	2	.0000	.0000	.0000	.9999
WITHIN	174	394.0000	2.2644		
TOTAL	179	2518.9990			

Table 13.14

Computer Printout for Two-Way ANOVA with No Interaction---Continued

```
MATRIX OF SCHEFFE F VALUES FOR MAIN EFFECTS FOR ROWS
  (EVALUATE THESE ONLY IF THERE IS NO INTERACTION):
  ROW I VS. ROW I+1 (SEE UPPER-RIGHT TRIANGLE OF MATRIX).

COMPARE THESE VALUES TO THE CRITICAL VALUE, DETERMINED AS FOLLOWS:
  POST COMPARISON MAIN EFFECTS SCHEFFE F FOR ROWS =
  (DF FOR ROWS) TIMES (MAIN EFFECTS CRITICAL F FOR ROWS).

          ROW NUMBER

         1         2

  1      .0000  496.8275
  2  496.8275      .0000

MATRIX OF SCHEFFE F VALUES FOR MAIN EFFECTS FOR COLUMNS
  (EVALUATE THESE ONLY IF THERE IS NO INTERACTION):
  COLUMN I VS. COLUMN I+1 (SEE UPPER-RIGHT TRIANGLE OF MATRIX).

COMPARE THESE VALUES TO THE CRITICAL VALUE, DETERMINED AS FOLLOWS:
  POST COMPARISON MAIN EFFECTS SCHEFFE F FOR COLUMNS =
  (DF FOR COLUMNS) TIMES (MAIN EFFECTS CRITICAL F FOR COLUMNS).

              COLUMN NUMBER

         1         2         3

  1      .0000      .0000  331.2183
  2      .0000      .0000  331.2183
  3  331.2183  331.2183      .0000

SIMPLE MAIN EFFECTS F TESTS FOR EACH ROW (ONE-WAY ANOVAS)
  (EVALUATE THESE F-VALUES ONLY IF THERE IS INTERACTION):

SIMPLE MAIN EFFECTS FOR ROW  1:  F (  2,   174) =   110.4061   P = .0000
                                 MS(A) =     250.0000   MS(W) =      2.2644

SIMPLE MAIN EFFECTS FOR ROW  2:  F (  2,   174) =   110.4061   P = .0000
                                 MS(A) =     250.0000   MS(W) =      2.2644

SIMPLE MAIN EFFECTS F TESTS FOR EACH COLUMN (ONE-WAY ANOVAS)
  (EVALUATE THESE F-VALUES ONLY IF THERE IS INTERACTION):

SIMPLE MAIN EFFECTS FOR COLUMN  1:  F (  1,   174) =   165.6091   P = .0000
                                    MS(A) =     375.0000   MS(W) =      2.2644

SIMPLE MAIN EFFECTS FOR COLUMN  2:  F (  1,   174) =   165.6091   P = .0000
                                    MS(A) =     375.0000   MS(W) =      2.2644

SIMPLE MAIN EFFECTS FOR COLUMN  3:  F (  1,   174) =   165.6091   P = .0000
                                    MS(A) =     375.0000   MS(W) =      2.2644

ADDITIONAL SCHEFFE PAIR-WISE COMPARISONS CAN BE MADE.  SET THE FOLLOWING:
  DF (NUMERATOR) = CELLS - 1
  DF (DENOMINATOR) = N - CELLS
  DETERMINE THE CRITICAL SCHEFFE F AS FOLLOWS:
  (CELLS - 1) TIMES (OMNIBUS F FOR CELLS).
```

THREE-WAY ANALYSIS OF VARIANCE

While space does not permit a complete discussion here, we certainly can go well beyond one-way and two-way analysis of variance designs. For example, three-way analysis of variance is not an uncommon research design. Such higher order experimental designs are primarily limited by time, money, the ability to control or manipulate variables, and the availability of data. Mathematically speaking, there is nothing to prevent us from performing studies that extend well beyond three-way analysis of variance. Unfortunately, the ***interpretation*** of results based on such higher order designs becomes difficult because we have many interaction terms.

Model 3 given here represents the three-way analysis of variance. Notice that this model includes all of the components that were used in Models 0, 1, and 2 discussed earlier, plus several additional components:

Model 0: $X = \mu + \varepsilon$

Model 1: $X = \mu + \alpha + \varepsilon$

Model 2: $X = \mu + \alpha + \beta + \alpha\beta + \varepsilon$

Model 3: $X = \mu + \alpha + \beta + \alpha\beta + \Delta + \alpha\Delta + \beta\Delta + \alpha\beta\Delta + \varepsilon$

where:

α = the contribution of the first classification variable

β = the contribution of the second classification variable

Δ = the contribution of the third classification variable

$\alpha\beta$ = the contribution of the interaction effect between the first two variables

$\alpha\Delta$ = the contribution of the interaction effect between the first and third variables

$\beta\Delta$ = the contribution of the interaction effect between the second and third variables

$\alpha\beta\Delta$ = the contribution of the interaction effect among all three variables

Suppose that we have designed an experiment that consists of 3 rows, 3 columns, and 2 slabs. The graphic representation of this design is given in Figure 13.9. There would be 3 one-way terms, 2 two-way terms, and 1 three-way term. The contributions of μ, α, β, and $\alpha\beta$ would be the same in Model 3 as they were in Model 2. If the new variable and/or any of its interactions with the first, second, and/or first ***and*** second variables are significant, then the error term, ε, would be even further reduced. If we ever have access to all factors that contribute to the variable of interest, this error term can be completely eliminated. Unfortunately, we seldom have access to all possible information; instead, we strive to minimize the error term as much as possible.

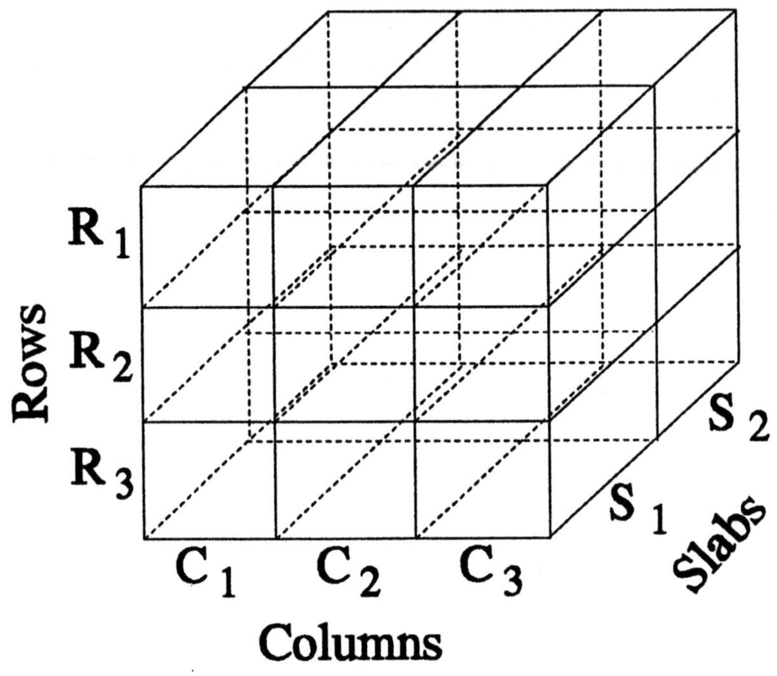

Figure 13.9
Three-Way Analysis Layout

Quantitatively speaking, we can always extend our models well beyond one, two, or three-way analysis of variance. Table 13.15 gives the number of main effects and interaction terms associated with analysis of variance models, from a complete one-way model through a complete six-way model, along with a portion of a fifteen-way model. As we can see from the table, there is a mathematical progression for the total number of terms in the model. The progression is accomplished by simply doubling the last number and then adding 1 to this value. There will always be $2^N - 1$ terms in any model. We can also use Pascal's triangle to determine these values.

These models are often referred to as ***full factorial designs*** because they include all possible components. Practically speaking, as stated many times before, we will always be limited by time, money, data availability, conceptual complications, and interpretation difficulties. In fact, Taguchi (1987, chap. 6), one of the leading researchers and consultants in the design of experiments, seldom considered interaction terms in his own experimental designs, especially those beyond two-way interactions; and Schmidt and Launsby (1994, chap. 1), stated that the interaction terms are seldom important or significant.

Taguchi further recommended using two-category classification variables whenever possible to minimize the complexities of the design. The final column in Table 13.15 includes the *level* name (such as L_8) for these designs when they conform to the two-category Taguchi format. He also encouraged pooling interaction terms into the error term and only examining one-way and two-way terms whenever possible. If interaction terms are significant, they are frequently very difficult to conceptualize and evaluate. Therefore, we often use what are referred to as ***fractional factorial designs***, and we only examine a fraction of the $2^N - 1$ terms in the full model. If we carefully plan our design of experiments, we will be able to focus on more than one or two factors simultaneously (the main effects) and can ignore many of the higher order interaction terms. We must sometimes be willing to give something up (in this case, the higher order interaction terms) in order to look at more classification variables (more main effects) simultaneously. This tradeoff will save us time and money, but we will not be analyzing the complete design. We have to hope that the tradeoff is worthwhile.

Table 13.15
Number of Main Effects and Interaction Terms Associated with Various Models

	Sources of Variation							
Type of Analysis of Variance Model	***Main Effects Terms***	***2-Way Terms***	***3-Way Terms***	***4-Way Terms***	***5-Way Terms***	***6-Way Terms***	***Total Terms in Model***	***"Taguchi" Models (with two categories each)***
One-Way Model	1	0	0	0	0	0	1	not factorial
Two-Way Model	2	1	0	0	0	0	3	L_4
Three-Way Model	3	3	1	0	0	0	7	L_8
Four-Way Model	4	6	4	1	0	0	15	L_{16}
Five-Way Model	5	10	10	5	1	0	31	L_{32}
Six-Way Model	6	15	20	15	6	1	63	L_{64}
.								
.								
.								
Fifteen-Way Model	15	105	455	1365	3003	etc.	32,767	$L_{32,768}$

Case Study 13.2

Problem. Independent Consumers Services (ICS) is a public, nonprofit consumer advocate organization located in a large metropolitan area. ICS continually receives inquiries from consumers wanting to know which grocery chain has the lowest prices overall. More recently, however, they have been receiving complaints that the prices at one particular grocery chain vary greatly from grocery store to grocery store. Those complaining feel that the chain is unfairly pricing products based on socioeconomic differences in the various regions of the city. In order to investigate this concern, ICS has decided to compare the prices of three stores owned by the chain, each store being located in a different socioeconomic region of the city. They have selected a number of items representative of a typical market basket of goods. They now wish to determine whether the average price for this market basket differs significantly from location to location.

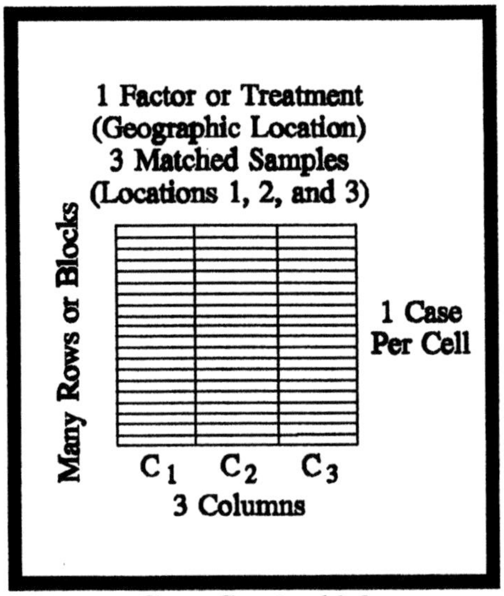

Case Study 13.2

Methodology Solution. In Case Study 13.2, Independent Consumers Services has one criterion variable (prices of goods) and one classification variable (socioeconomic region). ICS is interested in comparing the prices in these three locations. We will now follow the path indicated in the subset of master flowcharts presented at the onset of this chapter. To determine an appropriate methodology for ICS to use in analyzing their data, we enter the master flowcharts at *Start*. Since they wish to compare the central tendencies of prices for the three regions, we immediately turn to flowchart 1. We only have one variable of interest (prices of goods); prices are at least interval scale (in fact, they are ratio); and we do not have only one sample, as we have three stores. We do not have more than one classification variable; but we have more than two samples, so we turn to flowchart 3. We again confirm that we are seeking a test for comparing central tendencies that satisfies at least one of the following conditions: either more than one classification variable, more than two samples, existence of concomitant variables, or any combination of these. We do not have more than one variable of interest, but we do have matched samples (as we have matched identical items and determined the prices of these items across all three stores). We are now ready to make our final decision. We are not using any concomitant variables to statistically control for external variables, so we eliminate the use of analysis of covariance. We decide to use a ***treatment-by-subjects design*** for the analysis of variance, also referred to as a ***randomized blocks design***. We will view the three locations of the chain as the "treatments" and the various items in the market baskets as the "subjects." Figure 13.10 shows the route taken as described here. The relevant flowcharts for Case Study 13.2 have been extracted from the master flowcharts and juxtaposed here for simplification.

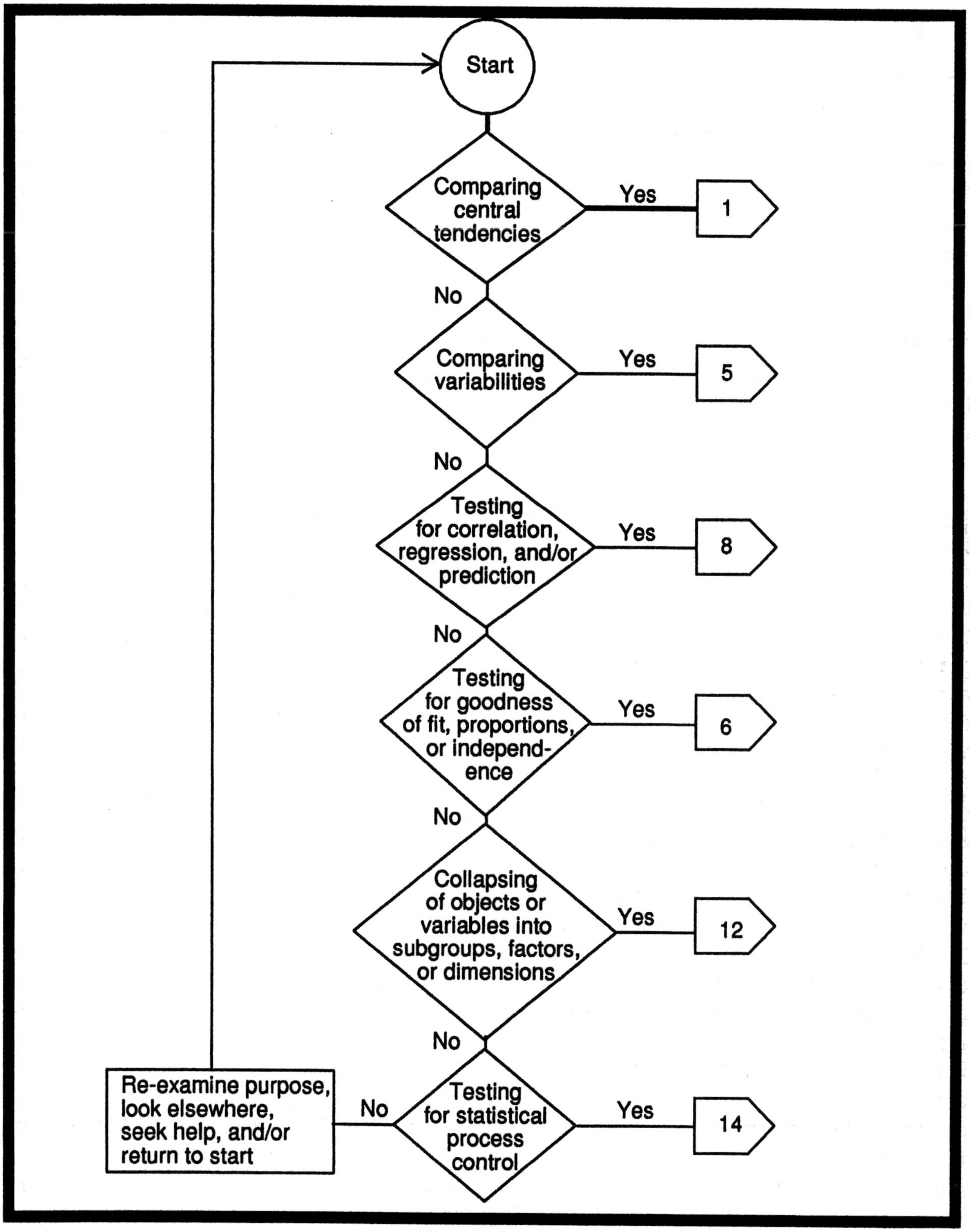

Figure 13.10
Statistical Decision-Making Flowchart for Case Study 13.2

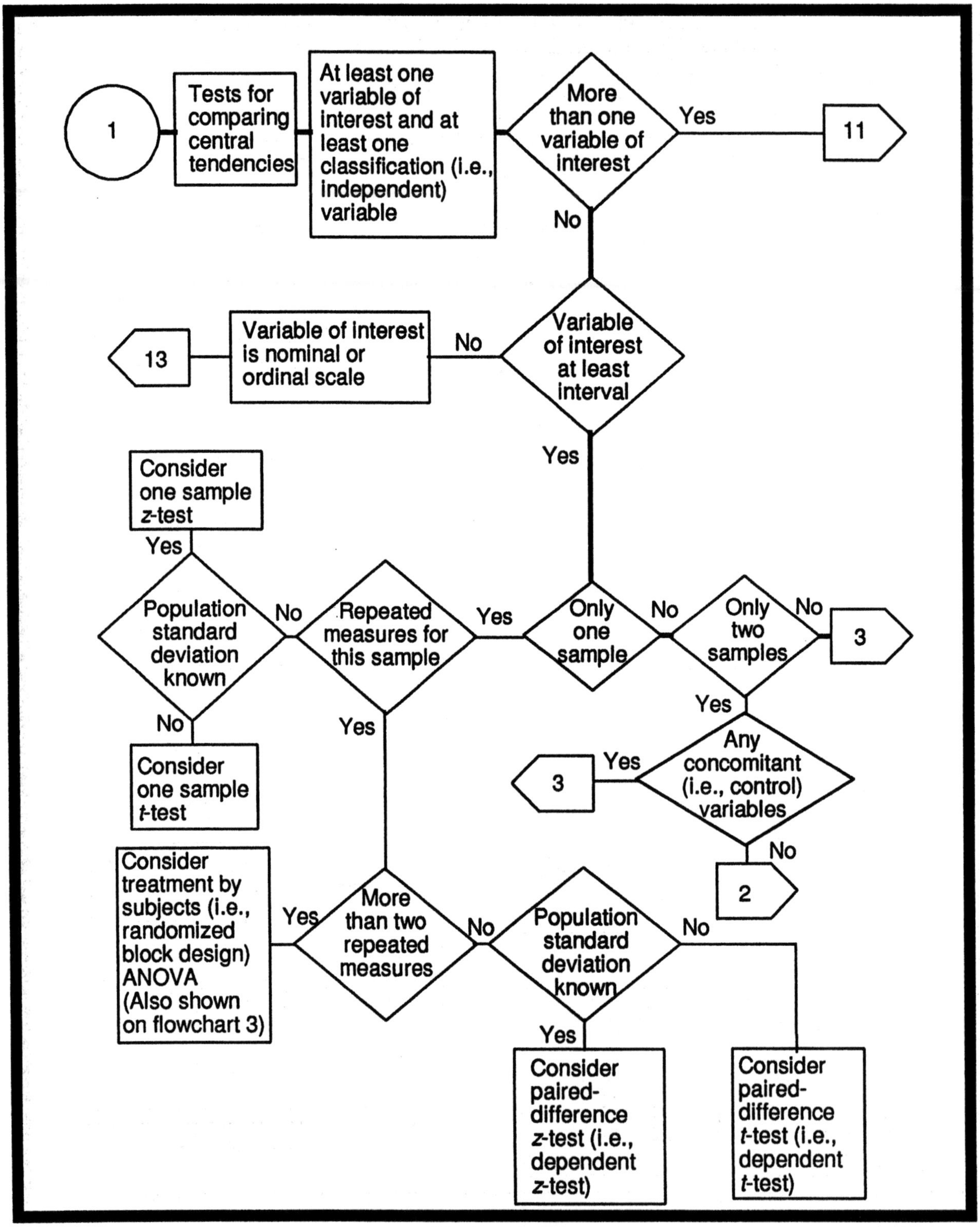

Figure 13.10
Statistical Decision-Making Flowchart for Case Study 13.2
(continued)

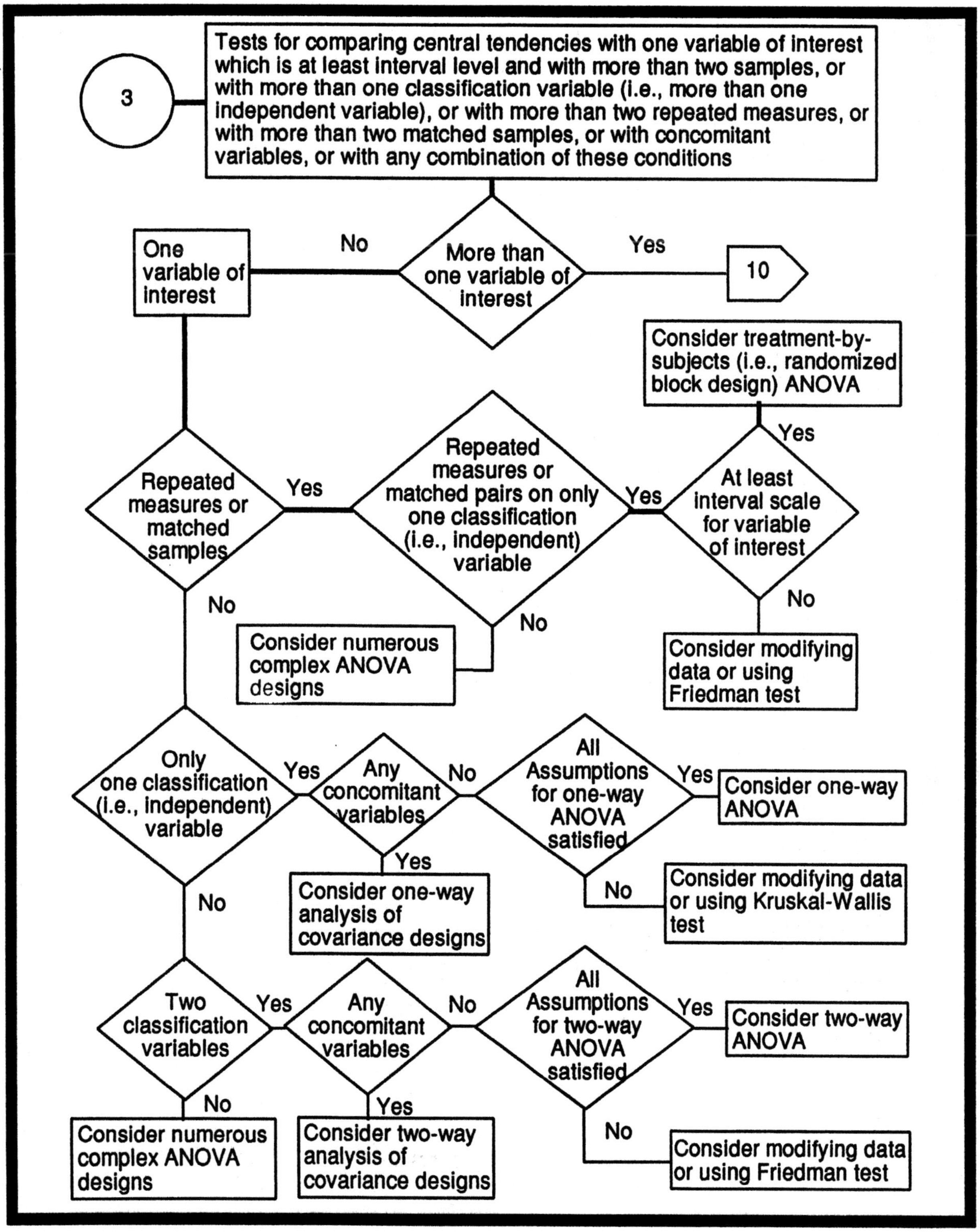

Figure 13.10
Statistical Decision-Making Flowchart for Case Study 13.2
(continued)

Terminology. At the onset of this chapter, we introduced the concepts of having repeated measures of the criterion variable over several trials or having matched data for three or more groups. For example, perhaps we are trying to assess employee improvement over time and have measures of each individual's performance after one month, three months, and six months. Or perhaps we are interested in observing their performance under three different compensation conditions, where we have obtained measures of each individual's performance under different conditions. In both of these examples, we have repeated measures of the same individuals under different circumstances. As a third example, perhaps we want to determine whether three different types of roofs bring about different returns on investment; yet, we also know that housing prices vary from geographic location to location. Thus, we need to match three comparable houses that differ only in the types of roofs of interest. Here, we do not have repeated measures of the same houses; rather, we have matched comparable houses across locations.

We should notice that we could view the situation as a one sample problem with repeated measures, since we have only one sample of products for which we are comparing prices across three stores. Using the flowcharts, we would then have not turned to flowchart 3; instead, we would have continued on with flowchart 1. Yet, we would still have determined that the treatment by subjects design would be appropriate, as it also appears in flowchart 1. However, we actually have three identical tubes of toothpaste, three identical loaves of bread, etc. Therefore, it seems more appropriate to view the situation as one with matched samples. Either way, we would still use the treatment by subjects design, as the methodological concept is the same.

Suppose that we only have two measures on each individual or item in our set; or suppose that we have matched every individual or item within our set with one other "identical" (as identical as possible) individual or item. If so, we could use either the dependent *t*-test or the treatment-by-subjects approach to compare the means of the repeated measures or matched pairs. When we have more than two measures or more than two matchings, we must turn to more complex statistical models. To locate the appropriate model for the first two examples in the previous paragraph we begin with ***Start*** in the master flowcharts and advance to flowchart 1. We have only one criterion variable (performance), and it is at least interval level. We have one sample of employees, with repeated measures for each employee. If we have only two repeated measures, we could use the dependent *t*-test; if we have three or more repeated measures, we would use the *treatment-by-subjects* analysis of variance. As noted earlier, some textbooks refer to this model as a form of the *randomized blocks design*, as each of the blocks (rows or subjects) are randomly ordered in the layout. Others refer to it as a *trend analysis* (Edwards, 1960, chap. 14), and still others refer to it as a *repeated measures design.*

In the roofing example just mentioned, we wanted to determine whether three types of roofs differ in returns on investment, and we matched comparable houses across locations. Again, we begin with ***Start*** in the master flowcharts and turn to flowchart 1. We have only one criterion variable (prices), and it is at least interval level. We have three samples of roofs, so we have more than one sample. We have only one classification variable (types of roofs), but we have more than two samples; thus, we turn to flowchart 3. We are soon asked whether we have matched samples on the variable of interest, to which we answer positively. An analysis of variance design using treatment-by-subjects (T x S) would be appropriate to examine problems such as this one.

Example 13.3. As an example, suppose that we have measured the need for achievement on three different occasions for 25 middle level managers. The first of these three measures was obtained during pre-selection screening, the second was obtained after the managers had participated in a motivation seminar, and the third was obtained six months after the seminar. Thus, we have repeated measures of the same individuals (subjects) over three different time periods (e.g., treatments). Table 13.16 gives the raw scores for these 25 employees.

Table 13.16
Achievement Scores Over Three Different Time Intervals

Employee Number	*Period 1*	*Period 2*	*Period 3*	*Employee Means*	*Employee Std. Dev.*
1.	13	15	19	15.6667	3.0551
2.	9	13	19	13.6667	5.0332
3.	17	15	19	17.0000	2.0000
4.	19	17	18	18.0000	1.0000
5.	16	17	22	18.3333	3.2146
6.	13	13	19	15.0000	3.4641
7.	16	18	24	19.3333	4.1633
8.	22	23	26	23.6667	2.0817
9.	20	20	22	20.6667	1.1547
10.	19	21	18	19.3333	1.5275
11.	16	19	18	17.6667	1.5275
12.	20	23	24	22.3333	2.0817
13.	20	20	21	20.3333	0.5774
14.	25	24	21	23.3333	2.0817
15.	20	19	23	20.6667	2.0817
16.	8	19	21	16.0000	7.0000
17.	12	14	13	13.0000	1.0000
18.	15	14	16	15.0000	1.0000
19.	19	19	17	18.3333	1.1547
20.	13	18	23	18.0000	5.0000
21.	20	21	26	22.3333	3.2146
22.	15	17	20	17.3333	2.5166
23.	16	17	17	16.6667	0.5774
24.	21	24	24	23.0000	1.7321
25.	18	15	16	16.3333	1.5275
Column Means	16.8800	18.2000	20.2400	*Total Mean* =	18.4400
Column Std. Dev.	4.0448	3.3166	3.3076	*Std. Dev.* =	3.7892

Table 13.16 also includes the means and standard deviations for each employee across all three periods, the means and standard deviations for each period, and the total mean and total standard deviation for all 75 observations. Table 13.17 gives summary statistics for these data, including column means, column standard deviations, column sums of squares, and the number of cases in each column. Since we are really not interested in comparing the means of one individual employee vs. another, a summary statistics table based on employee scores over the three time periods has not been created, although the values for such a table could easily be created obtained from Table 13.16. We should recognize that the format of Table 13.17 is the same as the format that we used for a one-way analysis of variance.

The layout of the data in Table 13.16 can be viewed as a two-dimensional table with 25 rows and 3 columns, allowing us to compute 75 cell means. However, since each of the cells includes only one case, the mean of each cell is the same as the value in each cell. When we have only one case per cell, we have no variance within each cell. Therefore, we have no sums of squares for within, and our sums of squares for cells will be the same as the sums of squares for total. The two-way analysis of variance model will now have to be revised to accommodate the situation in which we have no within term. We must create a new layout for this analysis of variance design. Table 13.18 gives the general analysis of variance layout for this treatment-by-subjects model.

Table 13.17
Summary Statistics Based On Achievement Scores Over Three Time Periods

Period	n	$\overline{X}$	s	s^2	$\Sigma(X - \overline{X})^2$
1	25	16.88	4.0447	16.3600	392.64
2	25	18.20	3.3166	11.0000	264.00
3	25	20.24	3.3076	10.9400	262.56
Total	75	18.44	3.7892	14.3578	1062.48

An observation of Table 13.18 reveals that the sources of variation previously labeled as cells and within have been dropped from the layout. We only need to compute the sums of squares for columns, rows, interaction, and total in our new design. Further, since $SS_T = SS_{ROWS} + SS_{COLS} + SS_{RxC}$, we can easily obtain the interaction term. Without the knowledge of this relationship, the interaction term would be extremely difficult and time-consuming to compute. Fortunately, all we need to do is add the sums of squares for rows and columns and then subtract this amount from the sums of squares for total. The difference between these two values represents the sums of squares for interaction. Since we have no within term, we use the interaction term as our measure of chance (our error term) when we compute the *F*-values for rows and columns.

Table 13.18
Treatment-by-Subjects Analysis of Variance Layout

Source of Variation	*df*	*Sums of Squares*	*MS*	*F*
Rows	$r - 1$	$\sum n_{i.} \cdot (\overline{X}_{i.} - \overline{X}_T)^2$	$\frac{SS_{ROWS}}{df_{ROWS}}$	$\frac{MS_{ROWS}}{MS_{R \times C}}$
Columns	$c - 1$	$\sum n_{.j} \cdot (\overline{X}_{.j} - \overline{X}_T)^2$	$\frac{SS_{COLS}}{df_{COLS}}$	$\frac{MS_{COLS}}{MS_{R \times C}}$
Interaction	$(r - 1) \cdot (c - 1)$	$\sum n_{ij} \cdot (\overline{X}_{ij} - \overline{X}_{i.} - \overline{X}_{.j} + \overline{X}_T)^2$	$\frac{SS_{R \cdot C}}{df_{R \cdot C}}$	
Total	$n_t - 1$	$\sum \sum (X_{ij} - \overline{X}_T)^2$		

Results for the Treatment-by-Subjects Analysis of Variance for Example 13.3

We are now ready to complete the treatment-by-subjects analysis of variance for Example 13.3. We will establish the parameters to be tested, set our probability level, determine the null and alternative hypotheses, settle on the appropriate statistical test, and then calculate all necessary values, and make the decision.

Parameters to be Tested. The central tendencies of three samples (the sets of data for three time periods, represented by the columns in Table 13.16) are to be compared in order to examine the central tendencies of the corresponding populations. We will assume that the achievement scores are at least interval level; therefore, we can compute means for each of the columns. These column means, given in Table 13.16 and again in Table 13.17, will be compared in an effort to draw conclusions about population means. We may also be interested in comparing the central tendencies of the 25 employees, as represented by the rows of Table 13.16. However, a comparison of the row means will simply tell us whether our sample of employees is homogeneous or heterogeneous. We typically expect to have rather heterogeneous scores among employees.

Probability Level and Directionality. Assuming that the personnel department wants to be rather certain of their conclusions, alpha has been set to .05 ($\alpha = .05$). Once again, the test statistic will be non-directional, but the area of rejection will fall in one tail, as discussed in preceding sections.

Null Hypotheses. Instead of one null hypothesis as in a one-way analysis of variance, or four null hypotheses as in a two-way analysis of variance, we now have two potential null hypotheses, one for rows and one for columns. These hypotheses are stated as follows:

Rows: H_0: $\mu_{1.} = \mu_{2.} = \mu_{3.} = \cdots = \mu_{25.}$

Columns: H_0: $\mu_{.1} = \mu_{.2} = \mu_{.3}$

Alternative Hypotheses. For each of the these two null hypotheses, we have a corresponding alternative hypothesis. These hypotheses are typically stated in words, as follows:

Rows: H_A: At least two $\mu_{i.}$ values for rows are not equal

Columns: H_A: At least two $\mu_{.j}$ values for columns are not equal

Statistical Procedure. An appropriate statistical procedure for the analysis of Example 13.3 is the treatment-by-subjects analysis of variance. Therefore, we need to obtain the necessary sums of squares terms, degrees of freedom, and mean squares so that we can compute the *F*-tests for rows and columns.

Computations

Sums of Squares for Total. Since the interaction term is the most difficult sums of squares term to compute in a treatment-by-subjects design (requiring 75 separate calculations for a 25 by 3 problem), we will determine the SS_T term first so that we can use subtraction to obtain the interaction term later. Based on the raw data formula given in Table 13.18, we can compute SS_T as follows:

$$SS_T = \sum \sum (X_{ij} - X_T)^2$$

$$= (13 - 18.44)^2 + (15 - 18.44)^2 + (19 - 18.44)^2$$

$$+ (9 - 18.44)^2 + (13 - 18.44)^2 + (19 - 18.44)^2$$

$$+ \cdots + (18 - 18.44)^2 + (15 - 18.44)^2 + (16 - 18.44)^2$$

$$= 1062.48$$

Of course, since Table 13.16 also gives the total variance, we could have more easily obtained the SS_T term by obtaining the numerator of this total variance. That is:

$$s_T^2 = \frac{\sum (X_{ij} - \overline{X}_T)^2}{n_T - 1}$$

$$\sum (X_{ij} - \overline{X}_T)^2 = (s_T^2) \cdot (n_T - 1)$$

$$= (14.3578) \cdot (75 - 1)$$

$$= 1062.48$$

We have obtained the same results using either approach. Consequently, we have verified that our calculation is correct for the sums of squares total. This always serves as a good check for our manual calculations.

Sums of Squares for Rows. We are now ready to calculate the sums of squares for rows, columns, and interaction. These calculations can be performed in any order. We will begin with the SS_{ROWS}:

$$SS_{ROWS} = \sum \sum n_{i.} \cdot (\overline{X}_{i.} - \overline{X}_T)^2$$

$$= (3) \cdot (15.6667 - 18.44)^2 + (3) \cdot (13.6667 - 18.44)^2$$

$$+ \cdot \cdot \cdot + (3) \cdot (16.3333 - 18.44)^2$$

$$= 657.1467$$

Sums of Squares for Columns. Next, we calculate the SS_{COLS} in a similar manner:

$$SS_{COLS} = \sum \sum n_{.j} \cdot (\overline{X}_{.j} - \overline{X}_T)^2$$

$$= (25) \cdot (16.88 - 18.44)^2 + (25) \cdot (18.20 - 18.44)^2$$

$$+ (25) \cdot (20.24 - 18.44)^2$$

$$= 143.2800$$

Sums of Squares for Interaction. Next, we calculate the SS_{RxC}. One approach is to use the raw data based on the equation given in Table 13.18 to obtain SS_{RxC}. As stated earlier, this will require 75 calculations, as follows:

$$SS_{R\times C} = \sum n_{ij}\cdot(\overline{X}_{ij} - \overline{X}_{i\cdot} - \overline{X}_{\cdot j} + \overline{X}_T)^2$$

$$= (1)\cdot(13 - 15.6667 - 16.88 + 18.44)^2$$

$$+ (1)\cdot(15 - 15.6667 - 18.20 + 18.44)^2$$

$$+ (1)\cdot(19 - 15.6667 - 20.24 + 18.44)^2$$

$$+ (1)\cdot(\ 9 - 13.6667 - 16.88 + 18.44)^2$$

$$+ \cdots + (1)\cdot(16 - 16.3333 - 20.24 + 18.44)^2$$

$$= 262.0533$$

However, it was stated earlier that $SS_T = SS_{ROWS} + SS_{COLS} + SS_{RxC}$ in the treatment-by-subjects design. Therefore, it is much easier to compute the interaction term from a knowledge of this relationship. We first add the sums of squares for rows and columns and then subtract this amount from the sums of squares for total. These calculations are confirmed as follows:

$$SS_T = SS_{ROWS} + SS_{COLS} + SS_{R\times C}$$

$$SS_{R\times C} = SS_T - (SS_{ROWS} + SS_{COLS})$$

$$= 1062.4800 - (657.1467 + 143.2800)$$

$$= 1062.4800 - 800.4267$$

$$= 262.0533$$

Mean Squares for Rows. The mean squares for rows is determined by dividing the sums of squares for rows by the degrees of freedom for rows. Since we have 25 rows, we have 24 degrees of freedom for rows. Therefore:

$$MS_{ROWS} = \frac{SS_{ROWS}}{df_{ROWS}}$$

$$= \frac{657.1467}{24}$$

$$= 27.38$$

Mean Squares for Columns. The mean squares for columns is determined by dividing the sums of squares for columns by the degrees of freedom for columns. Since we have 3 columns, we have 2 degrees of freedom for columns. Therefore:

$$MS_{COLS} = \frac{SS_{COLS}}{df_{COLS}}$$

$$= \frac{143.2800}{2}$$

$$= 71.64$$

Mean Squares for Interaction. The mean squares for interaction is determined by dividing the sums of squares for interaction by the degrees of freedom for interaction. Since we have 25 rows and 3 columns, we have (25 - 1)·(3 - 1) = (24)·(2) = 48 degrees of freedom for interaction. Therefore:

$$MS_{R \times C} = \frac{SS_{R \times C}}{df_{R \times C}}$$

$$= \frac{262.0533}{48}$$

$$= 5.46$$

F-value for Rows. Next, we calculate the F-value for rows by dividing the mean squares for rows by the mean squares for interaction. Here, we obtain the following F-value:

$$F_{ROWS} = \frac{MS_{ROWS}}{MS_{R \times C}}$$

$$= \frac{27.38}{5.46}$$

$$= 5.02$$

F-value for Columns. Next, we calculate the F-value for columns by dividing the mean squares for columns by the mean squares for interaction. Here, we obtain the following F-value:

$$F_{COLS} = \frac{MS_{COLS}}{MS_{R \times C}}$$

$$= \frac{71.64}{5.46}$$

$$= 13.12$$

Results and Decisions. Table 13.19 summarizes the results of each of these computations. The rows represent variation for cases, while the columns represent variation for periods. Based on Table 13.19, we conclude that there are significant differences among the column means, with $F(2, 48) = 13.12, p < .01$. Post comparison tests could be used to examine whether the means are significantly different from trials 1 to 2, 1 to 3, and 2 to 3. These tests are similar to the ones discussed earlier.[3]

Table 13.19
Treatment-by-Subjects ANOVA Table for Achievement Scores over Three Periods

Source of Variation	*df*	*SS*	*MS*	*F-Value*	*Critical F*
Rows (Employees)	24	657.1467	27.58	5.02	1.75
Columns (Time Periods)	2	143.2800	71.64	13.12	3.19
Interaction	48	262.0533	5.46		
Total	74	1062.4800			

We also notice from Table 13.19 that we have significant differences for the rows. This finding simply means that there are differences among the employees in regard to their need for achievement. We did not expect our sample to consist of managers with the same need for achievement; it is the comparison of column means that is of interest in most studies.

Treatment-by-Subjects with More Than One Factor

Example 13.3 was concerned with repeated measures of one group of cases over several trials or the matching of cases for two or more groups. We discovered that this treatment-by-subjects model was just a special form of the two-way analysis of variance. If we have repeated measures (or matched cases) of one group of cases over two factors, we will have a *Treatment A by Treatment B by Subjects* analysis of variance, usually denoted as follows: A x B x S. This design is sometimes referred to as a *completely repeated measures design with two factors* (Keppel, 1973, pp. 423-433) or as a *two-factor within-subjects design* (Keppel, 1991, chap. 21). It is also referred to as a *treatment-by-treatment-by-subjects* design (Bruning & Kintz, 1968, pp. 18-19). As the treatment-by-subjects design is equivalent to a two-way ANOVA with one subject per cell, the A x B x S design is equivalent to a three-way ANOVA with one subject per cell. Thus far with the T x S and the A x B x S designs, we have assumed that we only have *one* group of cases. That is, we have not divided our rows into subsets of groups. We could do this as well.

---

[3]It should be noted that if we had only two repeated measures, we could have used the dependent *t*-test, also referred to as the paired differences *t*-test. The results of a *t*-test from that approach, when squared, will be identical to the *F*-test for columns described here.

Summary

If we are interested in comparing several groups of cases (such as assembly line managers, maintenance managers, and security staff managers) over repeated measures of the criterion variable, we can use other extensions of the general treatment-by-subjects design. The following terminology has been used to describe such designs: a two-factor mixed design with repeated measures on one factor (Bruning & Kintz, 1968, pp. 54-61) or a trend analysis for trial means with different treatments (Edwards, 1960, pp. 227-232). Duncan (1986), Juran and Gryna (1988), (Keppel (1973; 1991), Kirk (1968), Taguchi and Wu (1978), and Winer (1971) also offer excellent discussions of these and other complex research designs. As can be seen, an endless number of ANOVA designs exist. We have only scratched the surface of analysis of variance in this chapter!

References

Anderson, V. L., & MeLean, R. A. (1974). ***Design of experiments: a realistic approach.*** New York: Marcel Dekker.

Bruning, J. L., & Kintz, B. L. (1968). ***Computational handbook of statistics.*** Glenview, IL: Scott, Foresman and Company.

Christensen, R. (1987). ***Plane answers to complex questions: the theory of linear models.*** New York: Springer-Verlag.

Collyer, C. E., & Enns, J. T. (1986). ***Analysis of variance: the basic designs.*** Chicago: Nelson-Hall.

Duncan, A. J. (1986). ***Quality control and industrial statistics*** (5th ed.). Homewood, IL: Richard D. Irwin.

Edwards, A. L. (1960). ***Experimental design in psychological research*** (rev. ed.). New York: Holt, Rinehart and Winston.

Fisher, L., & McDonald, J. (1978). ***Fixed effects analysis of variance.*** New York: Academic Press.

Huitema, B. E. (1980). ***The analysis of covariance and alternatives.*** New York: John Wiley & Sons.

Juran, J. M., & Gryna, F. M. (1988). ***Juran's Quality Control Handbook*** (4th ed.). New York: McGraw-Hill.

Keppel, G. (1973). ***Design and analysis: a researcher's handbook.*** Englewood Cliffs, NJ: Prentice-Hall.

Keppel, G. (1991). ***Design and analysis: a researcher's handbook*** (3rd ed.). Englewood Cliffs, NJ: Prentice-Hall.

Keppel, G. & Saufley, W. H., Jr. (1980). ***Introduction to design and analysis: a student's handbook.*** San Francisco: W. H. Freeman and Co.

Kirk, R. E. (1968). ***Experimental design: Procedures for the behavioral sciences.*** Belmont, CA: Brooks/Cole.

Schmidt, S. R. & Launsby, R. G. (1994). ***Understanding industrial designed experiments*** (4th ed.). Colorado Springs: Air Academy Press.

Taguchi, G. (1987). ***System of experimental design: Engineering methods to optimize quality and minimize costs*** (Vols. 1-2). (L. W. Tung, Trans.). Joint publishers: White Plains, NY: UNIPUB/Kraus International Publications; and Dearborn, MI: Supplier Institute, Inc.

Taguchi, G., & Wu, Y. (1978). ***Introduction to off-line quality control.*** Central Japan Quality Control Association. (also available from The American Supplier Institute, Detroit, MI.)

Winer, B. J. (1971). ***Statistical principles in experimental design*** (2nd ed.). New York: McGraw-Hill.

Practice Problems
Quick Quiz

Fill in all necessary values in the spaces below. Perform the appropriate analysis based on the following information:

Criterion Variable:	Number of New Dealers of Automobiles
Classification Variables:	Geographic Location and Make of Automobiles
Alpha:	.05

Raw Data for Two-Way ANOVA

	Mercury	*Chrysler*	*Buick*
California	10 9 8	15 16 17	12 14 16
New York	10 12 14	14 13 15	14 12 16

Question 1. Find the following values:

Summary Statistics

Group	*n*	$\overline{X}$	*s*	s^2	$\Sigma (X - \overline{X})^2$
Cell 1, 1					
Cell 1, 2					
Cell 1, 3					
Cell 2, 1					
Cell 2, 2					
Cell 2, 3					
Row 1					
Row 2					
Column 1					
Column 2					
Column 3					
Total					

Question 2. Complete the following ANOVA table:

Analysis of Variance Table

Source of Variation	***df***	***SS***	***MS***	***F-Value***	***Critical F***
Cells					
Rows (Location)					
Columns (Make)					
Interaction					
Within					
Total					

Question 3. Formally state the null hypotheses:

Null hypothesis for cells: ____________________

Null hypothesis for interaction: ____________________

Null hypothesis for rows: ____________________

Null hypothesis for columns: ____________________

Question 4. Make the appropriate decision regarding each of the following null hypotheses:

Hypothesis for cells:	reject	fail to reject	do not evaluate
Hypothesis for interaction:	reject	fail to reject	do not evaluate
Hypothesis for rows:	reject	fail to reject	do not evaluate
Hypothesis for columns:	reject	fail to reject	do not evaluate

Question 5. Give an "English" interpretation of the results:

____

____

Practice Problems
Multiple Choice

Suppose we have collected ratio level data for 80 people. We know three characteristics for each of these 80 people: their criterion score, their gender, and their marital status (either married or not married). Use the data obtained from the table given below to answer the next 15 questions regarding two-way analysis of variance. Assume that alpha has been set at .05 for all hypotheses related to these data and that each cell in the data matrix has the same number of cases.

Analysis of Variance Table

Source of Variation	*df*	*SS*	*MS*	*F-Value*	*Critical F*
Cells			453.33		
Rows (gender)		0.00			
Columns (marital status)		80.00			
Interaction		1280.00			
Within					
Total	79	4020.00			

1. Which of the following best describes the situation?

   A. There are 5 variables of interest and two classification variables.
   B. There is one variable of interest and two classification variables.
   C. There is one variable of interest and four classification variables.
   D. There no variable of interest and two classification variables.
   E. There is one variable of interest and no classification variable.

2. What are the null and alternative hypotheses regarding the cell means?

   A. $H_0: \overline{X}_{11} = \overline{X}_{12} = \overline{X}_{21} = \overline{X}_{22}$ $H_A: \overline{X}_{11} \neq \overline{X}_{12} \neq \overline{X}_{21} \neq \overline{X}_{22}$
   B. $H_0: \mu_{11} = \mu_{12} = \mu_{21} = \mu_{22}$ $H_A: \mu_{11} \neq \mu_{12} \neq \mu_{21} \neq \mu_{22}$
   C. $H_0: \mu_{11} = \mu_{12} = \mu_{21} = \mu_{22}$ H_A: Not all cell μs are equal.
   D. $H_0: \mu_{11} \neq \mu_{12} \neq \mu_{21} \neq \mu_{22}$ H_A: All cell μs are equal.
   E. $H_0: \mu_{11} = \mu_{12} = \mu_{21} = \mu_{22}$ H_A: All cell μs are unequal.

3. How many cases will we assume that each cell contains?

A. 20
B. 80
C. 40
D. 25
E. 10

4. How many categories exist for each classification variable here?

A. 3 by 3
B. 3 by 2
C. 20 by 20
D. 2 by 2
E. Impossible to determine from the information given.

5. What is the grand mean for the data associated with the present problem?

A. 17.00
B. 12.95
C. 453.33
D. 80.00
E. Impossible to determine from the information given.

6. How many degrees of freedom do we have for cells, rows, columns, interaction, within, and total, respectively?

A. 1, 1, 1, 1, 76, and 79
B. 4, 2, 2, 1, 76, and 79
C. 3, 2, 3, 1, 76, and 79
D. 3, 1, 1, 1, 76, and 79
E. 4, 2, 2, 1, 70, and 79

7. Based on this information, what is the critical value for determining whether the cell means are equal? Use the degrees of freedom closest to those available in the appropriate table, without increasing the chances of making a Type I error.

A. 2.76
B. 2.74
C. 4.00
D. 5.29
E. 12.95

8. What is the mean square for the within term?

A. 24.79
B. 35.00
C. 2660.00
D. 4020.00
E. 50.89

9. What decision should be made regarding the *F*-test for cells?

A. There are no differences among cell means.
B. Reject H_0! Based on the observed data, we conclude that there are significant differences among the population cell means.
C. Two cell means are equal, and two cell means are not equal.
D. Fail to reject the null hypothesis.
E. Reject H_0, and conclude that there are no differences among cell means.

10. What is the probability of obtaining an *F*-value equal to or greater than the one computed for comparing the cell means in the analysis of variance table, on the basis of chance alone?

A. Somewhere between .20 and .15.
B. Somewhere between .15 and .10.
C. Somewhere between .10 and .05.
D. Somewhere between .05 and .01.
E. Somewhere between .01 and .00.

11. What is the mean square for interaction for this set of data?

A. The mean square for interaction cannot be determined from the amount of information given.
B. The mean square for interaction does not exist in a two-way analysis of variance problem.
C. 1280.00
D. 36.57
E. 2660.00

12. Now that you have rejected for cells (you did reject, hopefully), what test should be performed next?

A. Test for interaction
B. Test for rows
C. Test for columns
D. Test for main effects
E. Test for simple effects

13. What conclusion should you make regarding the interaction between rows and columns in regard to the contribution that any such interaction makes in regard to the criterion variable for these data?

A. Since the F-ratio for interaction is less than the critical F-ratio, the null hypothesis of no interaction should not be rejected.
B. Since the F-ratio for interaction is greater than the tabled F-ratio, the null hypothesis for interaction should be rejected.
C. Since the F-ratio for interaction is equal to the critical F-ratio, the study should be re-examined.
D. Since the F-ratio for interaction is smaller than the other F-ratios, the null hypothesis for interaction should be rejected.
E. Two of the above are correct answers.

14. Which of the following sets of decisions will be made?

A. Reject the null for cells, rows, columns, and interaction.
B. Reject the null for cells, rows, and columns, but not for interaction.
C. Reject the null for cells, fail to reject for interaction, then test for simple effects.
D. Reject the null for cells and for interaction, then perform the necessary tests for simple effects.
E. Fail to reject any of the hypotheses for cells, rows, columns, or for interaction.

15. Which of the following statements is the ***best*** answer in regard to the present problem?

A. All of the cell means are exactly equal.
B. All row means are less than the grand mean.
C. All column means are exactly equal.
D. The grand mean is the sum of all cell means.
E. None of the above statements are correct.

16. If you test for simple effects for these data, which would be correct?

A. You must fail to reject the null hypothesis for interaction first.
B. You would only examine the simple effects for rows.
C. You would only examine the simple effects for columns.
D. You may need to perform four tests for simple effects.
E. None of the above are correct statements.

17. With a treatment by subjects analysis of variance, which of the following becomes the error term?

A. Cells
B. Columns
C. Rows
D. Interaction
E. Within

18. With a treatment-by-subjects analysis of variance, which of the following is ***not*** equal to SS_T?

A. $SS_{CELLS} + SS_W$
B. $SS_{ROWS} + SS_{COLS} + SS_{RXC} + SS_W$
C. $SS_{ROWS} + SS_{COLS} + SS_{RXC}$
D. SS_{CELLS}
E. SS_W

19. With a four-way analysis of variance, we would have how many sources of variance to consider in our linear model, not counting the μ and ε terms?

A. 12
B. 15
C. 21
D. 9
E. 11

20. Which of the following statements is ***not*** correct?

A. The t-value for the 2-sample independent t-test will be equal to the square root of the F-value for an ANOVA performed on the same data.
B. The t-value for a paired difference test will be equal to the square root of the F-value for columns for a treatment by subjects ANOVA on the same data, with columns representing treatments.
C. A one-sample treatment by subjects ANOVA is the same basic layout as the two-way ANOVA with one cell per case.
D. For a one-way ANOVA, we could have done multiple t-tests and made the exact same conclusions.
E. A three-way ANOVA has the potential for allowing for more reduction in the error term than does a two-way ANOVA.

21. Which of the following can we evaluate using some form of an analysis of variance test?

A. Comparing the means of four groups over one classification variable.
B. Comparing the means of data in which we have repeated measures over several trials.
C. Comparing the means of two factors, in which one factor is fixed and the other is random.
D. Comparing the means of data in which we have three classification variables.
E. All of the above can be evaluated using analysis of variance.

Practice Problems
Written Problems

I. Data were collected for individuals employed at various organizations throughout the United States. These individuals were evaluated in regard to their need for achievement, their perceptions of the climate of their respective organizations, and their commitment to their organizations. Twenty of these individuals were classified as having high need for achievement and as viewing their organizations as "Systems 4" organizations. Another 20 were classified as having a high need for achievement and as viewing their organizations as less than Systems 4 organizations. Twenty more were classified as having a low need for achievement and as viewing their companies as Systems 4 organizations. A final twenty were classified as having a low need for achievement and as viewing their organizations as less than Systems 4 organizations. Organizational commitment was the variable of interest used with these cases, and alpha was set at .05. The following data were collected in regard to organizational commitment:

	High Need for Achievement					***Low Need for Achievement***				
	85	84	95	94	88	90	91	85	97	83
Systems 4	89	92	83	90	85	92	95	89	88	92
Management	88	89	83	88	87	87	94	88	87	92
	97	83	82	98	92	94	85	89	91	87
	79	78	85	74	73	82	81	79	85	84
Not Systems 4	82	84	80	85	81	79	76	78	82	87
Management	78	70	73	86	77	79	76	78	81	82
	80	72	81	85	79	80	74	72	70	80

Use these data to complete the two-way ANOVA table given on the next page. Then answer the associated questions.

A. First, complete the two-way analysis of variance table.

Analysis of Variance Table

Source of Variation	*df*	*SS*	*MS*	*F-Value*	*Critical F*
Cells					
Rows (management climate)					
Columns (need for achievement)					
Interaction					
Within					
Total					

B. Now, determine the critical *F*-value for evaluating whether the cell means are equal, then make a decision regarding the null hypothesis for cells.

C. Determine the critical *F*-value for evaluating the interaction term, then make a decision regarding the null hypothesis for interaction.

D. Based on the decision made in question three above, what is the next step in the two-way analysis of variance?

E. What is the final decision regarding the data for this problem?

II. Based on the information given in the table below, complete the two-way analysis of variance summary table. Set alpha equal to .05 when determining the critical F-values in the F-table.

	Method 1	*Method 2*	*Method 3*	*Row Totals*
Group A	$n_{11} = 5$ $\overline{X}_{11} = 40$ $s_{11}^2 = 4.00$	$n_{12} = 5$ $\overline{X}_{12} = 36$ $s_{12}^2 = 5.00$	$n_{13} = 5$ $\overline{X}_{13} = 34$ $s_{13}^2 = 3.00$	$n_{1.} = 15$ $\overline{X}_{1.} = 36.67$
Group B	$n_{21} = 5$ $\overline{X}_{21} = 36$ $s_{21}^2 = 6.00$	$n_{22} = 5$ $\overline{X}_{22} = 51$ $s_{22}^2 = 7.00$	$n_{23} = 5$ $\overline{X}_{23} = 35$ $s_{23}^2 = 4.00$	$n_{2.} = 15$ $\overline{X}_{2.} = 40.67$
Group C	$n_{31} = 5$ $\overline{X}_{31} = 34$ $s_{31}^2 = 5.00$	$n_{32} = 5$ $\overline{X}_{32} = 48$ $s_{32}^2 = 5.00$	$n_{33} = 5$ $\overline{X}_{33} = 50$ $s_{33}^2 = 6.00$	$n_{3.} = 15$ $\overline{X}_{3.} = 44.00$
Column Totals	$n_{.1} = 15$ $\overline{X}_{.1} = 36.67$	$n_{.2} = 15$ $\overline{X}_{.2} = 45.00$	$n_{.3} = 15$ $\overline{X}_{.3} = 39.67$	$n_T = 45$ $\overline{X}_T = 40.446$

Analysis of Variance Table

Source of Variation	*df*	*SS*	*MS*	*F-Value*	*Critical F*
Cells					
Rows (Groups)					
Columns (Methods)					
Interaction					
Within					
Total					

III. Based on the raw values for the two-factor, 2 by 3 analysis of variance fixed design given in the table, compute the necessary values for the analysis of variance table. Set $\alpha = .05$ when determining the critical F-values.

Raw Data for Two-Way ANOVA

	Method I	***Method II***	***Method III***
Group A	44 47 45	42 43 42	55 56 54
Group B	40 38 37	48 47 45	49 48 48

Analysis of Variance Table

Source of Variation	***df***	***SS***	***MS***	***F-Value***	***Critical F***
Cells					
Rows (Groups)					
Columns (Methods)					
Interaction					
Within					
Total					

IV. Below are data that have been collected for a set of 10 individuals. Each person has been measured over three different time periods, using the same method of measurement. Complete the treatment by subjects analysis of variance table for these data. Set $\alpha = .05$ when determining the critical F-values in the F-table.

Employee	*Period 1*	*Period 2*	*Period 3*
1.	30	10	50
2.	40	50	30
3.	20	40	20
4.	25	30	40
5.	60	60	80
6.	40	30	20
7.	30	40	50
8.	20	30	10
9.	70	60	65
10.	90	95	85

Analysis of Variance Table

Source of Variation	*df*	*SS*	*MS*	*F-Value*	*Critical F*
Rows (Subjects)					
Columns (Treatments)					
Interaction					
Total					

V. Suppose that your company produces the same number of parts each day. You have subcontracted with two suppliers for a component that is an essential element to your product. You have three different conditions in which you manufacture your product. You have begun to notice an increase in defective products and hope to identify potential causes to this increase in defects. You have collected the following data, based on random sampling of days:

		Conditions		
		I	*II*	*III*
Suppliers	*A*	15 14 12 21	17 18 21 19	14 12 18 11
	B	19 18 15 16	24 18 15 16	17 16 10 14

A. Compute the necessary values to complete the following table for this two-factor, 2-by-3 fixed effects analysis of variance design.

Summary Statistics

Group	*n*	$\overline{X}$	*s*	s^2	$\Sigma (X - \overline{X})^2$
Cell 1, 1					
Cell 1, 2					
Cell 1, 3					
Cell 2, 1					
Cell 2, 2					
Cell 2, 3					
Row 1					
Row 2					
Column 1					
Column 2					
Column 3					
Total					

B. Convert your findings from the previous table into a format that reflects the cells, rows, columns, and total in a 2-by-3 design, using the following table.

	Condition I	*Condition II*	*Condition III*	*Row Totals*
Supplier A	n_{11} = $\overline{X}_{11}$ = s_{11} =	n_{12} = $\overline{X}_{12}$ = s_{12} =	n_{13} = $\overline{X}_{13}$ = s_{13} =	$n_{1.}$ = $\overline{X}_{1.}$ = $s_{1.}$ =
Supplier B	n_{21} = $\overline{X}_{21}$ = s_{21} =	n_{22} = $\overline{X}_{22}$ = s_{22} =	n_{23} = $\overline{X}_{23}$ = s_{23} =	$n_{2.}$ = $\overline{X}_{2.}$ = $s_{2.}$ =
Column Totals	$n_{.1}$ = $\overline{X}_{.1}$ = $s_{.1}$ =	$n_{.2}$ = $\overline{X}_{.2}$ = $s_{.2}$ =	$n_{.3}$ = $\overline{X}_{.3}$ = $s_{.3}$ =	n_T = $\overline{X}_T$ = s_T =

C. Now set $\alpha = .05$ and complete the two-way analysis of variance table.

Analysis of Variance Table

Source of Variation	*df*	*SS*	*MS*	*F-Value*	*Critical F*
Cells					
Rows (Groups)					
Columns (Methods)					
Interaction					
Within					
Total					

VI. A consumer advocate group has been asked to examine whether one chain of groceries offers lower prices than its two major competitors, as advertised. The advocate group has collected data for a sample of 20 products sold by a representative store from each of the three chains. The stores selected were within one block of one another. The selection of the products to be used in the study was random. The data listed below represent the prices for these products at the three stores. Conduct the appropriate analysis of variance, with $\alpha = .05$.

Product	*Chain A*	*Chain B*	*Chain C*
Cooked Shrimp	$7.99	$7.49	$7.29
Hillshire Sausage	2.39	2.55	2.67
Butterball Tom Turkey	0.69	0.79	0.74
Star-Kist Tuna	1.59	1.50	1.35
Veggie Mix	1.39	1.35	1.49
Fresh Limes	0.10	0.10	0.18
Van Camp's Pork and Beans	0.45	0.49	0.44
Pepsi 6 Pack	0.99	1.09	1.89
Fleischmann's Margarine	1.29	1.19	1.15
Quaker Oatmeal	1.49	1.39	1.57
MJB Coffee	3.99	3.49	2.35
Rojo's Salsa	2.39	2.49	1.79
Sour Cream	1.09	1.09	1.09
Hershey's Pudding	1.99	1.85	1.99
Hormel Chili	1.09	1.15	1.17
Lay's Potato Chips	0.89	0.85	1.51
Hotdog Buns	0.69	0.69	0.87
Bar S Jumbo Franks	0.69	0.79	0.99
TreeSweet Orange Juice	1.99	1.89	1.59
Cremora Coffee Creamer	1.99	1.89	2.39
Total Costs	35.17	34.12	34.51
Means	1.76	1.71	1.73

CHAPTER 14

CHI-SQUARE TESTS

Case Study 14.1

Problem. The Executive Oversight Committee at Bayview Hospital had received a staff complaint that the number of beds available for patient assignment was unevenly distributed across the four main wings of the new patient assignment floor. Hospital staff stationed in the northwest wing complained that even though each wing of this floor had the same number of beds, this wing was excessively and disproportionately utilized relative to the other three wings. They requested that more staff be assigned to their wing or that they receive a pay differential to compensate for their excess work. Personnel in the other wings countered that the northwest employees had made an incorrect conclusion, that any observed differences were simply due to chance circumstances, and that all four wings were equally understaffed. In an effort to determine whether occupancy was evenly distributed across all four wings, the Oversight Committee reviewed occupancy data for the past 180 days. They determined the number of beds that were in daily use over that time period. Based on these data, they tabulated a frequency count of 1720 for the northwest wing for those 180 days, a frequency count of 1440 for the northeast wing during the same time period, a count of 1520 for the southwest wing, and a count of 1580 for the southeast wing. Simple observation suggested that the occupancy across the four wings was not evenly distributed.

Northwest	Northeast	Southwest	Southeast
1565	1565	1565	1565
1720	1440	1520	1580

Figure 14.1
Case Study 14.1

Methodology Solution. For the problem described in Case Study 14.1, the hospital is concerned with the distribution of bed occupancies across four different wings of the same floor. While a simple observation of the results might be useful in some circumstances, a more scientific approach is usually desirable for making sound decisions based on sample data. This is especially true when the investigator wants to determine whether the results are statistically significantly different from results that could have been obtained by chance alone. The beds were occupied for a total of 6260 times during the 180 day period. If they were perfectly evenly occupied across the four wings, the patient count should have been 6260 ÷ 4 = 1565 per wing. Thus, the hospital needs to determine an appropriate statistical test for examining whether the *observed distribution* is significantly different than the *expected distribution*. Using the master flowcharts to locate such a test, as indicated in Figure 14.2, we begin at ***Start***. The hospital is not comparing central tendencies, comparing variabilities, or testing for correlation/regression. Instead, the Oversight Committee wants to determine how **good** the observed distribution (1720, 1440, 1520, and 1580) **fits** the expected distribution (1565, 1565, 1565, and 1565), as illustrated in Figure 14.1. Therefore, we should turn to flowchart 6.

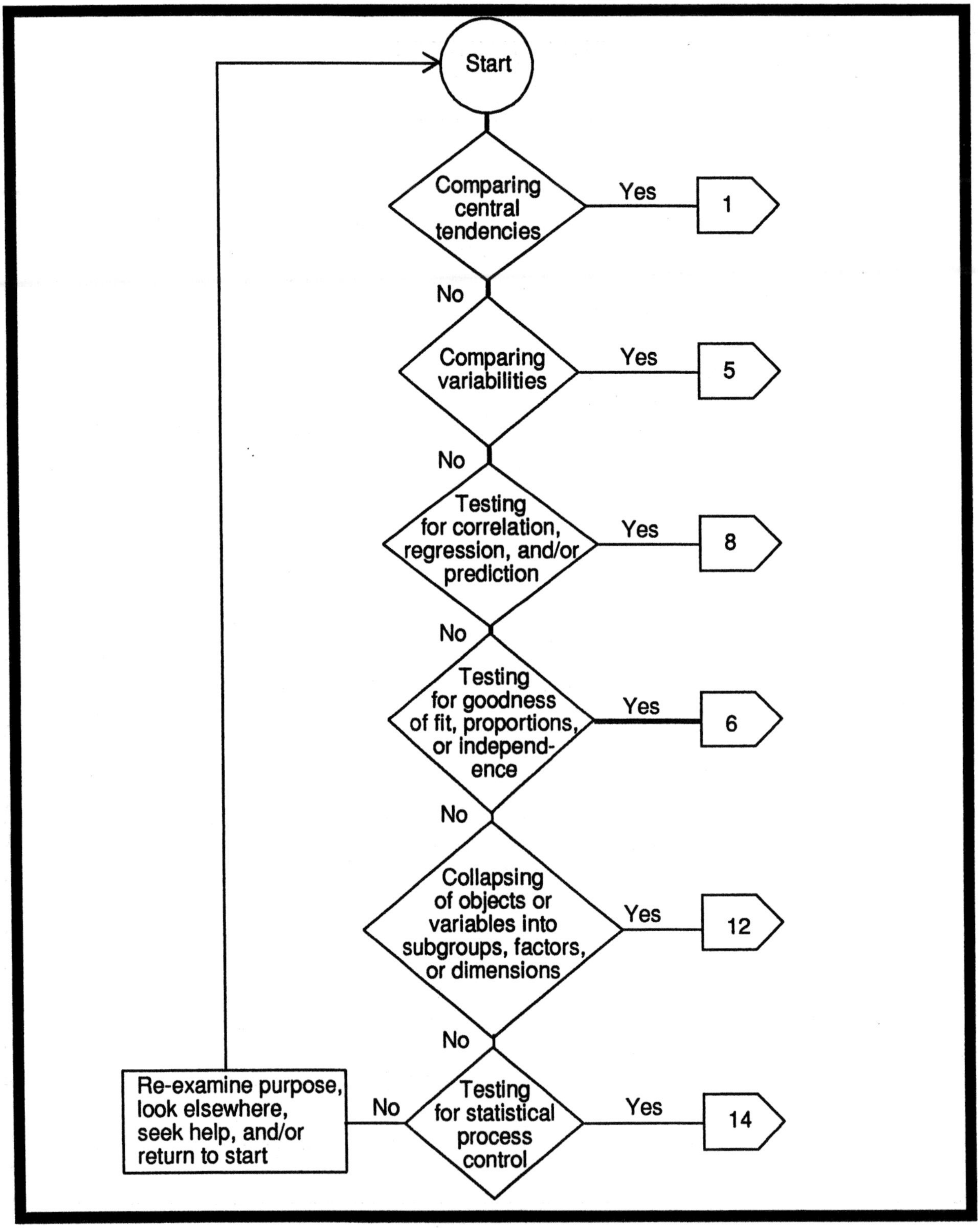

Figure 14.2
Statistical Decision-Making Flowchart for Case Study 14.1

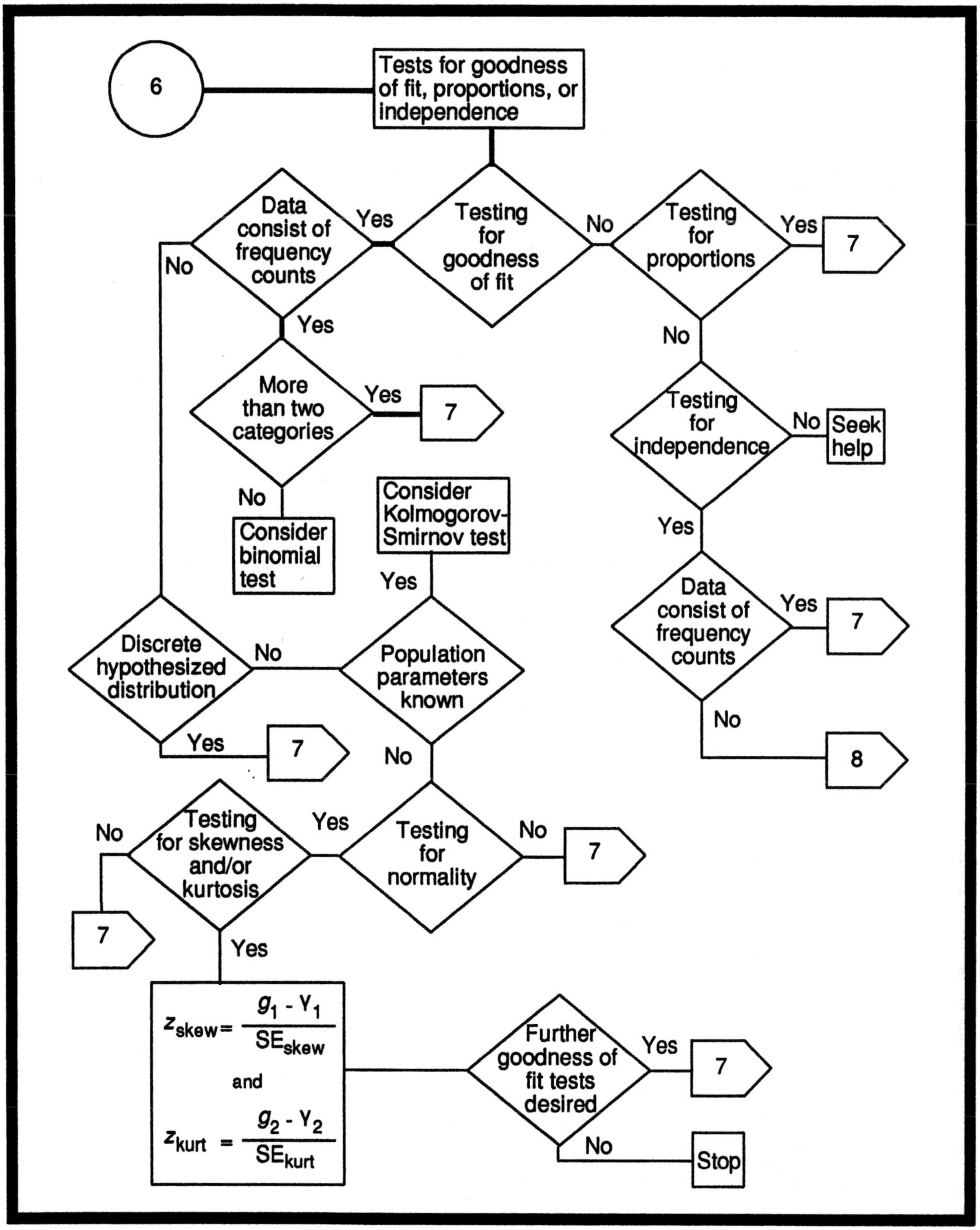

Figure 14.2
Statistical Decision-Making Flowchart for Case Study 14.1
(continued)

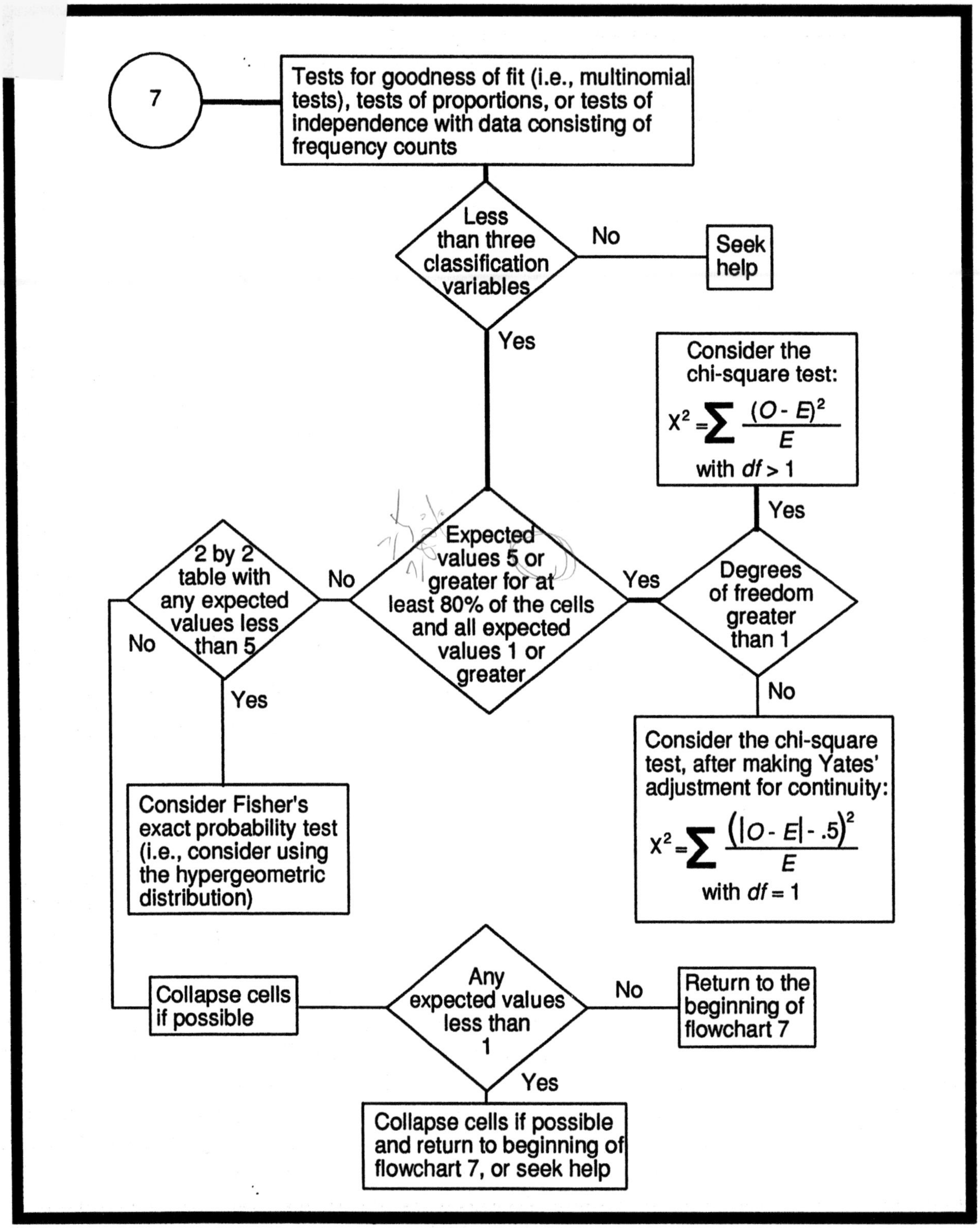

Figure 14.2
Statistical Decision-Making Flowchart for Case Study 14.1
(continued)

We are searching for a **goodness of fit** test, we know that the data consist of frequency counts (the bed occupancies for each of the wings), and we know there are more than two categories in our classification variable (since there are four wings). Consequently, we should turn to flowchart 7. There are less than three classification variables (since wing location is the only such variable). The expected values are five or greater for at least 80% of the cells (actually, the expected values are 1565 in all four cells), and all of these expected values are one or greater. Since there are four cells, the degrees of freedom are greater than one. (As will be discussed shortly, $df = 4 - 1 = 3$ for Case Study 14.1). Therefore, the chi-square test for goodness of fit is an appropriate statistical test.

Where Are We Going?

Chapters 9, 10, 12, and 13 primarily focused on statistical tests for comparing means, while Chapter 11 focused on statistical tests for comparing variances. The statistical tools presented in those chapters require the satisfaction of a number of assumptions, including random and independent sampling, the central limit theorem, at least interval level data, and sometimes other assumptions. However, we learned that when these assumptions cannot be satisfied, we need to look elsewhere for alternative statistical tests. Further, we might not always be interested in comparing central tendencies or variabilities. Instead, we might be interested in testing for correlation, regression, and/or making predictions, in testing for goodness of fit, proportions, or independence, in collapsing of objects or variables into subgroups, factors, or dimensions, or in testing for statistical process control. In Chapter 14, we will address tests for *goodness of fit*, *proportions*, and *independence*. As we will discover, the chi-square distribution is a useful distribution for performing many of these tests. The chi-square distribution was introduced in Chapter 11, along with the chi-square table that is included in Table 3 of Appendix C. While the mathematics of this distribution are somewhat complex, the chi-square table is very easy to use, as are most of the chi-square tests that are associated with the distribution.

CHI-SQUARE TESTS FOR GOODNESS OF FIT

Example 14.1. Whenever we are comparing an observed distribution of data to an expected distribution for these same data, we are examining how well the observed distribution *fits* the expected distribution. Example 14.1 further illustrates this concept. In this example, we are interested in results obtained from tossing one coin repeatedly. Based on the assumption that this is a fair coin, we expect the probability of obtaining a head in any random toss to be the same as the probability of obtaining a tail. The null hypothesis is stated as follows: H_0: $P = Q$. We have now conducted an experiment by tossing the coin 40 times, which yielded 10 heads and 30 tails. Based on our null hypothesis, we expected results to be closer to 20 heads and 20 tails. We now want to determine whether the results of our observed distribution (10 and 30) are significantly different than our expected distribution (20 and 20). Based on the binomial, we can easily determine that the probability of obtaining more than 10 heads but less than 30 heads is .997779. Thus, the probability of obtaining 10 or less heads or 20 or more heads is .002221. If we have set alpha at .05 for a two-tailed test, we would reject the null hypothesis and conclude that the coin does not *appear* to be fair, since .002221 is less than .05. In other words, we would conclude that the observed distribution does not do a good job of fitting the expected distribution.

The binomial distribution worked well for Example 14.1, and there is no need to search for any other form of statistical test in this situation. However, in situations such as the one in Case Study 14.1, we cannot use the binomial equation because we have more than two categories. Instead, we must use a ***multinomial*** equation. For Case Study 14.1, under the assumption of random events, the null hypothesis is written as follows: H_0: $P_1 = P_2 = P_3 = P_4$. The null states that the probabilities (i.e., the proportions, percentages, or frequency counts) for bed occupancies in all four wings of the fifth floor of the hospital are equal. Thus, the appropriate distribution for evaluating Case Study 14.1 is the ***multinomial distribution***, frequently referred to in statistical terminology as a ***goodness of fit test***. Quantitatively, the multinomial can be very difficult to use. The formula for the multinomial is defined by Equation 14.1:

$$\text{Multinomial} = \left(\frac{N!}{n_1! \cdot n_2! \cdots n_k!} \right) \cdot p_1^{n_1} \cdot p_2^{n_2} \cdots p_k^{n_k} \qquad \textbf{(14.1)}$$

As we can see, this equation is an extension of the binomial. However, the number of parameters has increased, along with the computational labor. We learned in Chapter 7 that we are usually interested in some *cumulative* probability (similar to determining the area in one tail of a probability distribution), further complicating the calculation process. Thus, we are seeking a good *approximation* for the multinomial test. As we are about to discover, the ***chi-square distribution*** provides such an approximation.

Procedures for the Chi-Square Goodness of Fit Test (Multinomial Test)

It was pointed out in Chapter 11 that the chi-square distribution is a continuous distribution. However, situations such as the ones in Case Study 14.1 and Example 14.1 are based on discrete data. In Chapter 7, we learned that even though the binomial distribution is a discrete distribution, we can use the normal distribution to make very close approximations to the binomial under appropriate situations. A similar situation is true for the multinomial distribution. We can use the chi-square distribution to make very good approximations to the multinomial under appropriate situations.

Determining the Computed Value for Chi-Square

Unlike the calculations for the multinomial distribution, the calculations for the chi-square test for goodness of fit are straightforward. We simply find the differences between the observed values and the expected values, square these differences, divide the squared differences by the expected values, and sum the results across all cells (i.e., across all categories). The general form of the chi-square test is given in Equation 14.2.

$$\chi^2 = \sum_{i=1}^{k} \frac{(O_i - E_i)^2}{E_i} \tag{14.2}$$

where:

k = number of cells

O_i = Observed value for the ith cell

E_i = Expected value for the ith cell

Determining the Expected Values

While the observed values are generated by the data we have collected, the expected values are based on the shape of the distribution stated in the null hypothesis. For example, we hypothesize under the null that the distribution is uniformly distributed, normally distributed, follows a Poisson distribution, or follows some known distribution unique to a particular population. Thus, the pattern of expected values differ from situation to situation. However, the *sum of the expected values must always be the same as the sum of the observed values.* Expected values for three of the most common goodness of fit tests will now be described.

Expected Values for Uniform Distributions: Case Study 14.1 Revisited. If the null hypothesis states that the values are ***evenly distributed***, we should expect to find the same number of observations in each cell. If there are 6260 observations and four cells, as in Case Study 14.1, and if the null is true, we should expect to find one-fourth of these observations to occur in each cell. Therefore, each cell value should be 1565. Some authors refer to this application of the chi-square test as a goodness of fit test against a ***uniform distribution***, while others refer to it as a chi-square test against a ***rectangular distribution***.

Expected Values for Known Distributions: Example 14.2. Occasionally, we will want to compare our observed values against some known distribution or population, where that distribution is ***not rectangular***. For Example 14.2, suppose an automotive trade magazine has published a report on the distribution of non-commercial vehicles sold within the United States during the past five years. They have segmented the classification variable into six categories: passenger cars, utility vehicles, minivans, trucks, sports cars, and luxury cars. A marketing research firm has now been contracted to determine the distribution of vehicle sales in the regional area so that regional sales can be compared with national sales. If the null hypothesis is that regional sales conform to national sales, we should expect the regional distribution of sales to closely approximate the national distribution. To further illustrate, suppose the trade magazine reported that 30% of the vehicles purchased during that time period were minivans. If the marketing research firm has collected sample data based on 2000 buyers of new vehicles, we should expect 30% of these 2000 buyers (600 individuals) to have purchased minivans. We determine the expected values for the other five categories in a similar manner.

Expected Values for Normal Distributions. One of the most common applications of the chi-square goodness of fit test is to examine whether the observed distribution is approximately normal. Generating a theoretical normal distribution to represent our expected values requires considerable time and effort. The theoretical distribution must have the same number of cells, the same mean, and the same standard deviation as the original distribution in order to make such a comparison. Rather than discussing this process now, we will reserve a separate section later in this chapter for the description and illustration of the chi-square test for goodness of fit against a normal distribution.

Determining the Critical Value for Chi-Square

As with other test statistics, the critical value for the chi-square distribution is based on the desired alpha level and the degrees of freedom for the particular scenario. Since we *square* the differences between the observed values and the expected values in our calculation process, all of our chi-square values will be zero or positive. We are usually interested in the far right end of the chi-square distribution, although we can obtain areas for the far left end of the distribution as well.

Determining the Degrees of Freedom

The degrees of freedom for the chi-square test for goodness of fit depend on the nature of the expected distribution. As noted earlier, there are many potential expected distributions. The degrees of freedom for several of these distributions are defined here.

Degrees of Freedom for Uniform Distributions. If the expected distribution is assumed under the null hypothesis to be rectangular (i.e., uniformly or evenly distributed) and if no other conditions are placed on the expected distribution except than that it has the same number of values (observations) distributed evenly across the same number of categories (cells), the degrees of freedom are equal to $k - 1$, where k represents the number of categories or cells.

Degrees of Freedom for Known Distributions. If the expected distribution is based on some known distribution and there are no other constraints placed on the distribution, the degrees of freedom are $k - 1$.

Degrees of Freedom for Normal Distributions. If the null hypothesis states that the expected distribution is normal, more constraints are placed on the expected distribution. These constraints result in fewer degrees of freedom. When we force our expected distribution to be normal, we require the expected distribution to have the same mean and standard deviation as the observed distribution. Therefore, the degrees of freedom for a chi-square test for goodness of fit against a normal distribution are $k - 3$.

Degrees of Freedom for Poisson Distributions. If the expected distribution is assumed under the null hypothesis to follow a Poisson distribution, only one additional constraint must be placed on the expected distribution. This is because the mean and the variance are equal for the Poisson distribution. Therefore, the degrees of freedom for a chi-square goodness of fit test against a Poisson distribution become $k - 2$.

Example 14.3: Chi-Square Goodness of Fit Test Against a Rectangular Distribution

We now illustrate the use of the chi-square goodness of fit test, beginning with an application that compares an observed distribution to an expected rectangular distribution. In Example 14.3, a toy manufacturer had been receiving complaints in regard to the life span of batteries that the company packages with one of its battery-operated toys. The quality analyst assigned to investigate the problem designed an experiment. He ordered an equal number of batteries from each of five different suppliers, assigned random numbers to a shipment of Model 72A electronic toys, and had the batteries installed in these toys. His first thought was to let each toy run until the battery had completely discharged, record the length of time each battery ran, and then compare the mean run times across all five suppliers, using analysis of variance. However, he did not have enough time or testing space available to examine each battery until the point of failure, so he decided to run each Model 72A for a fixed amount of time. Before running the experiment, he defined his null and alternative hypotheses as follows:

Null Hypothesis: Defective batteries are evenly distributed across the five suppliers.

Alternative Hypothesis: Defective batteries are not evenly distributed across the five suppliers.

Observed Values. He conducted his experiment, created a tally sheet, kept track of the number of batteries per supplier that failed during the time period, and placed the discharged batteries in a large storage bin. At the conclusion of this experiment, he developed a table based on his obtained results, as shown in Table 14.1.

Table 14.1
Observed Distribution for Defective Batteries

Supplier A	Supplier B	Supplier C	Supplier D	Supplier E
72	57	18	85	68

Expected Values. As can be determined from Table 14.1, the storage bin contained a total of 300 discharged batteries at the conclusion of the experiment. If the null hypothesis is true, one-fifth of the batteries in the bin should be from Supplier A, one-fifth should be from Supplier B, and so on, such that each of the expected values for this distribution should be 60.

Table of Observed and Expected Values. We now expand Table 14.1 to include both the observed and expected values, as illustrated in Table 14.2. This table conforms to the traditional format for displaying the results of a chi-square analysis, with the observed values located in each of the cells and the expected values located in the upper right-hand corners of the corresponding cells.

Table 14.2
Observed and Expected Distributions for Defective Batteries

	Supplier A	Supplier B	Supplier C	Supplier D	Supplier E
Expected	60	60	60	60	60
Observed	72	57	18	85	68

Statistical Test. As determined from the flowcharts, an appropriate statistical test for the present problem is the chi-square goodness of fit test. In this particular case, it is a chi-square goodness of fit test against a rectangular distribution.

Probability Level. The quality analyst set the probability level at $\alpha = .05$.

Degrees of Freedom. There are five suppliers; therefore, $k = 5$. The corresponding degrees of freedom are determined as follows: $df = k - 1 = 5 - 1 = 4$.

Critical Value. Since this is a chi-square test, we locate the critical value from the chi-square table given in Table 3 of Appendix C. With $\alpha = .05$ and $df = 4$, the critical value is 9.4877.

Drawing the Picture. We are now ready to draw a picture of the appropriate probability distribution associated with this test and to identify the regions where we reject and fail to reject H_0. Figure 14.3 gives these two regions, as determined by the critical cutoff value.

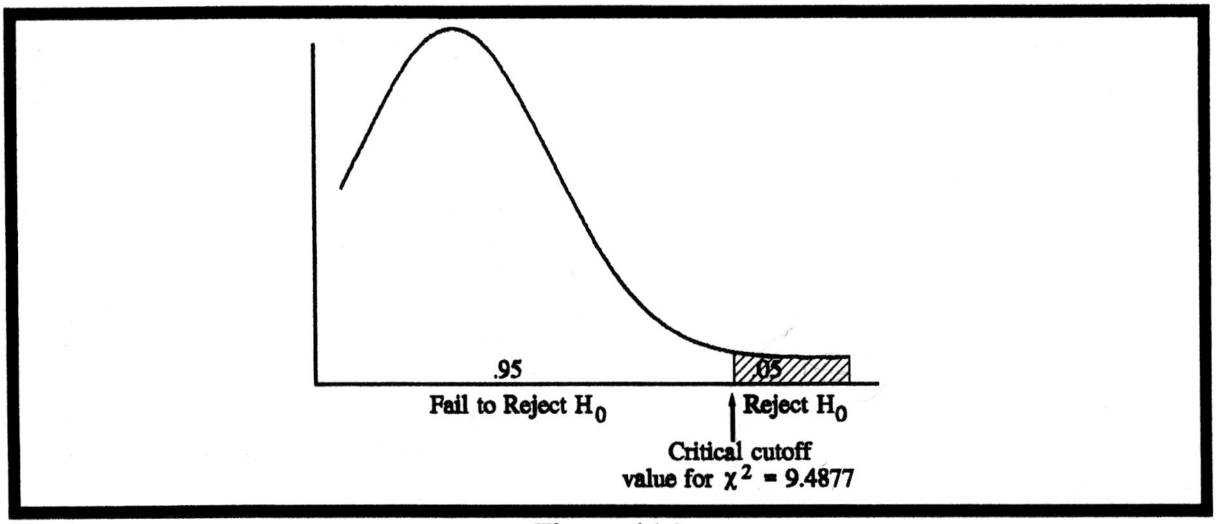

Figure 14.3
Decision-Making Regions for Defective Batteries

Results. For Example 14.3, we know both the observed values and the expected values. Therefore, we are ready to determine the computed value for the chi-square test. Based on Equation 14.2, the computed value is obtained as follows:

C19

$$\chi^2 = \sum_{i=1}^{5} \frac{(O_i - E_i)^2}{E_i}$$

$$= \frac{(72 - 60)^2}{60} + \frac{(57 - 60)^2}{60} + \frac{(18 - 60)^2}{60} + \frac{(85 - 60)^2}{60} + \frac{(68 - 60)^2}{60}$$

$$= 2.4 + .15 + 29.4 + 10.42 + 1.0667$$

$$= 43.4367$$

Decision. Since the computed value of chi-square (43.4367) falls to the right of the critical value (9.4877), the quality analyst should reject the null hypothesis and conclude that defective batteries are not evenly distributed across the five suppliers.

Conclusion. The quality analyst appears to have reason to believe that some suppliers provide better batteries than others.

Example 14.4: Chi-Square Goodness of Fit Test Against a Known Distribution

Our next application of the chi-square goodness of fit test is to compare some observed distribution against a known distribution. For Example 14.4, a study conducted 10 years ago examined the color preferences of first time car buyers. The distribution of color preferences for the individuals participating in that study was as follows: white (20%), black (25%), red (20%), blue (15%), green (10%), and other (10%). An identical study was more recently performed in order to determine whether color preferences have changed during the past 10 years. The new survey examined the preferences for 240 first time buyers. The researchers established their null and alternative hypotheses as follows:

Null Hypothesis: The color preferences of first time new car buyers today are no different than they were 10 years ago.

Alternative Hypothesis: The color preferences of first time new car buyers today are different than they were 10 years ago.

Observed Values. The results of the more recent survey of color preferences found that 31 of the first time buyers preferred white, 64 preferred black, 55 preferred red, 45 preferred green, and 20 preferred some other color.

Expected Values. Based on the null hypothesis, we would expect the distribution of buyers in the new survey to be proportional to those in the original study. Since the new study is based on 240 participants, we would expect 20%, or 48 of these participants to prefer white cars. We would also expect that 25%, or 60 of them to prefer black cars, and so forth.

Table of Observed and Expected Values. The observed and expected values are given in Table 14.3.

Table 14.3
Observed and Expected Distributions for Automobile Color Preferences

	White	Black	Red	Blue	Green	Other
Expected	48	60	48	36	24	24
Observed	31	64	55	25	45	20

Statistical Test. As determined from the flowcharts, an appropriate statistical test for the present problem is the chi-square goodness of fit test. In this particular case, it is a chi-square goodness of fit test against a known distribution.

Probability Level. The research team set the probability level at $\alpha = .05$.

Degrees of Freedom. There are six automobile colors; therefore, $df = k - 1 = 6 - 1 = 5$.

Critical Value. With $\alpha = .05$ and $df = 5$, the critical value is 11.0705.

Drawing the Picture. We again draw a picture of the appropriate probability distribution associated with this test and identify the regions where we reject or fail to reject H_0. Figure 14.4 gives these two regions, based on a critical cutoff value of 11.0705

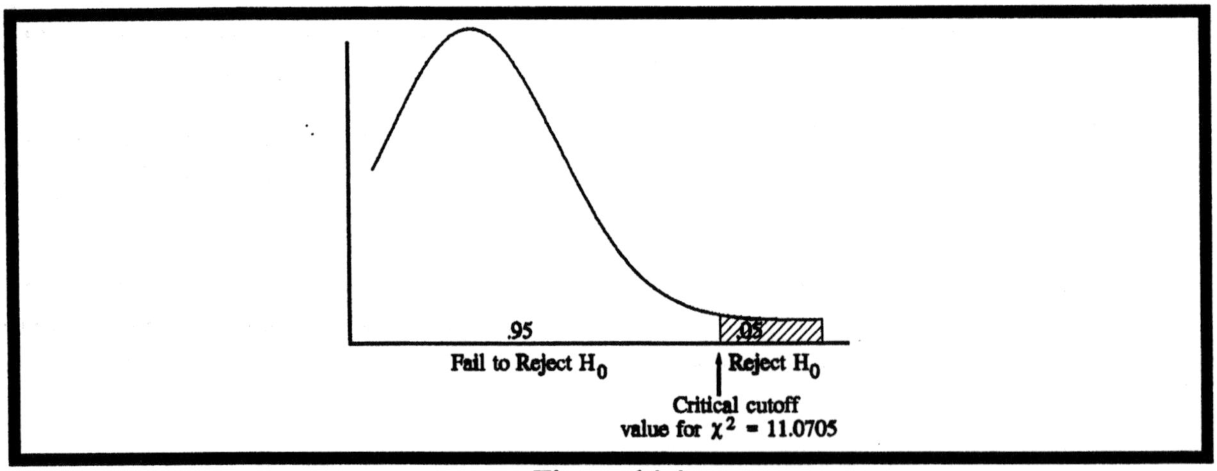

Figure 14.4
Decision-Making Regions for Automobile Color Preferences

Results. We have determined the observed and expected values for Example 14.4. We are now ready to determine the computed value for the chi-square test. Based on Equation 14.2, the computed value is obtained as follows:

$$\chi^2 = \sum_{i=1}^{6} \frac{(O_i - E_i)^2}{E_i}$$

$$= \frac{(31 - 48)^2}{48} + \frac{(64 - 60)^2}{60} + \frac{(55 - 48)^2}{48} + \frac{(25 - 36)^2}{36} + \frac{(45 - 24)^2}{24} + \frac{(20 - 24)^2}{24}$$

$$= 6.02 + .27 + 1.02 + 3.36 + 18.38 + .67$$

$$= 29.71 \ (\textit{rounded})$$

Decision. Since $29.71 > 11.0705$, the researchers should reject H_0.

Conclusion. The researchers have reason to conclude that the color preferences of current first time new car buyers are different than they were 10 years ago. In fact, they have reason to believe that certain colors are more popular and others are less popular. Dealers may want to consider such information when submitting future automobile orders.

Example 14.5: Chi-Square Goodness of Fit Test Against a Normal Distribution

Our next application of the chi-square goodness of fit test is to compare some observed distribution against an expected normal distribution. For Example 14.5 (which corresponds to Example 6.2 in Chapter 6), data were collected regarding the time necessary for data entry technicians to input a specific unit of coded information into a census data base. A group of skilled employees entered a total of 446 units of data regarding several characteristics of households. The seconds necessary for these employees to complete each of the units of entry were recorded, as measured from the onset of the first keystroke to the completion of the final keystroke.

Null Hypothesis: The amount of time necessary for data entry technicians to input a specific unit of coded information into a census data base is normally distributed.

Alternative Hypothesis: The amount of time necessary for data entry technicians to input a specific unit of coded information into a census data base is not normally distributed.

Observed Values. The amounts of time required to enter each of the records for the 446 forms have been tabulated into a frequency distribution, as given in Table 14.4. Time to complete the task is a continuous variable, and these times are rounded to the nearest whole number. The times range from a minimum of 18 seconds to a maximum of 40 seconds. The mean time is 29 seconds, and the standard deviation is 3.4906. Only 1 of the 446 records took 18 seconds, 1 took 19 seconds, 2 took 20 seconds, etc., as can be seen in the first two columns of Table 14.4. The second column (*f*) represents the *observed frequencies* for this distribution.

Table 14.4
Observed Values, Along with Expected Values Assuming a Normal Distribution

X	*f*	*RLL*	*RUL*	*z for RLL*	*z for RUL*	*Area in tail for RLL*	*Area in tail for RUL*	*Area Between z-values*	*Expected Values (Area × N)*	$\frac{(O_i - E_i)^2}{E_i}$
18	1	17.5	18.5		-3.0081		0.0013	0.0013	0.5863	0.2919
19	1	18.5	19.5	-3.0081	-2.7216	0.0013	0.0032	0.0019	0.8625	0.0219
20	2	19.5	20.5	-2.7216	-2.4351	0.0032	0.0074	0.0042	1.8710	0.0089
21	4	20.5	21.5	-2.4351	-2.1486	0.0074	0.0158	0.0084	3.7412	0.0179
22	6	21.5	22.5	-2.1486	-1.8621	0.0158	0.0313	0.0155	6.8949	0.1161
23	11	22.5	23.5	-1.8621	-1.5757	0.0313	0.0576	0.0263	11.7123	0.0433
24	17	23.5	24.5	-1.5757	-1.2892	0.0576	0.0987	0.0411	18.3379	0.0976
25	26	24.5	25.5	-1.2892	-1.0027	0.0987	0.1580	0.0593	26.4639	0.0081
26	35	25.5	26.5	-1.0027	-0.7162	0.1580	0.2369	0.0789	35.2012	0.0012
27	44	26.5	27.5	-0.7162	-0.4297	0.2369	0.3337	0.0968	43.1580	0.0164
28	50	27.5	28.5	-0.4297	-0.1432	0.3337	0.4430	0.1094	48.7710	0.0310
29	52	28.5	29.5	-0.1432	0.1432	0.4430	0.4430	0.1139	50.7998	0.0284
30	50	29.5	30.5	0.1432	0.4297	0.4430	0.3337	0.1094	48.7710	0.0310
31	44	30.5	31.5	0.4297	0.7162	0.3337	0.2369	0.0968	43.1580	0.0164
32	35	31.5	32.5	0.7162	1.0027	0.2369	0.1580	0.0789	35.2012	0.0012
33	26	32.5	33.5	1.0027	1.2892	0.1580	0.0987	0.0593	26.4639	0.0081
34	17	33.5	34.5	1.2892	1.5757	0.0987	0.0576	0.0411	18.3379	0.0976
35	11	34.5	35.5	1.5757	1.8621	0.0576	0.0313	0.0263	11.7123	0.0433
36	6	35.5	36.5	1.8621	2.1486	0.0313	0.0158	0.0155	6.8949	0.1161
37	4	36.5	37.5	2.1486	2.4351	0.0158	0.0074	0.0084	3.7412	0.0179
38	2	37.5	38.5	2.4351	2.7216	0.0074	0.0032	0.0042	1.8710	0.0089
39	1	38.5	39.5	2.7216	3.0081	0.0032	0.0013	0.0019	0.8625	0.0219
40	1	39.5	40.5	3.0081		0.0013		0.0013	0.5863	0.2919
Column Sums	**446**							**1.0000**	**446.0000 (rounded)**	**1.3371**

Expected Values. The null hypothesis states that time to enter census records is normally distributed. To obtain the expected values necessary for the chi-square test, we must determine the number of records expected for any given time, based upon the normal distribution. The observed values were rounded to integers when recording the data, but the normal distribution is continuous. Therefore, we must develop **intervals** for each **category** of observed values and find associated **areas** under the normal curve. We followed this same approach in Chapter 7 when we used the normal distribution to approximate the binomial distribution. For example, if a record requiring 33 seconds is input, we assume that it took somewhere between 32.5 and 33.5 seconds to complete the task, thus creating an interval that has width. Once we have developed intervals for all possible categories of observations, we can determine areas under the normal distribution. The necessary steps are as follows:

Step 1: Determine the mean and standard deviation for the distribution of observed values.

Step 2: Determine the real lower limits *(RLL)* and real upper limits *(RUL)* for each of the observed times.

Step 3: Determine z-values for each of the *RLL*s and *RUL*s.

Step 4: Determine the area under the normal distribution that falls between each of the z-values corresponding to the *RLL*s and *RUL*s. This process usually requires determining the areas associated with the tails of the normal distribution for each value, subtracting the smaller area from the larger area, and thus obtaining the areas between them.

Step 5: Determine the expected values by multiplying each of the corresponding areas times the total number of observed values.

Table 14.4 includes each of these steps. As an illustration, 26 of the 446 records required somewhere between 32.5 and 33.5 seconds to input. The corresponding z-value for the real lower limit is $z = (32.5 - 29) \div 3.4906 = 1.0027$, and the corresponding z-value for the real upper limit is $z = (33.5 - 29) \div 3.4906 = 1.2892$. The area in the tail for a z-value of 1.0027 is approximately .1580, while the area in the tail for a z-value of 1.2892 is approximately .0987. The difference between these two areas in the tails is .0593. In other words, if the distribution is perfectly normal, we would expect 5.93% of the observations to fall within the interval of 32.5 to 33.5 The expected value is obtained as follows: $446 \times .0593 = 26.4478$, rounded.[1]

[1]The value given in Table 14.4 for the illustrated cell is more accurately recorded as 26.4639. The table was created from a spreadsheet and yields greater accuracy, since values were not rounded from step to step. When looking up z-values in Table 1 of Appendix C, these z-values must be rounded two decimal places. Spreadsheets do not require rounding to obtain areas.

Statistical Test. As determined from the flowcharts, an appropriate statistical test for the present problem is the chi-square goodness of fit test. In this particular case, it is a chi-square goodness of fit test against an expected normal distribution.

Probability Level. The census director has set the probability level at $\alpha = .05$.

Degrees of Freedom. There are 23 categories or cells of time periods, ranging from 18 to 40. The expected distribution was forced to be centered around the same mean and to have the same amount of variability as the observed distribution. Therefore, three constraints were forced on the expected distribution: the number of cells, the mean, and the standard deviation. The degrees of freedom are determined as follows: $df = k - 3 = 23 - 3 = 20$.

Critical Value. With $\alpha = .05$ and $df = 20$, the critical value is 31.4104.

Drawing the Picture. We now draw a picture of the appropriate probability distribution associated with this test and identify the regions where we reject or fail to reject H_0. Figure 14.5 gives these two regions, as determined by the critical cutoff value.[2]

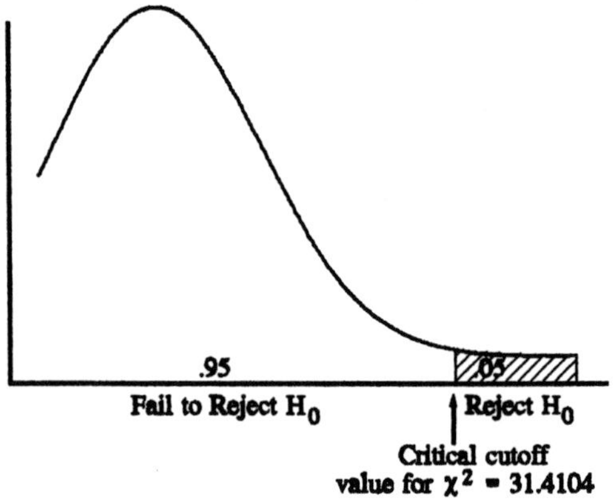

Figure 14.5
Decision-Making Regions for Automobile Color Preferences

Results. Since we know the observed and expected values for Example 14.5, we can now determine the computed value for the chi-square test. The final column of Table 14.4 is based on Equation 14.2 and gives the individual calculations for each category. Summing this column, we obtain $\chi^2 = 1.3371$. The manual calculations are as follows:

---

[2]For simplification, we have used the same general drawing for the chi-square distribution in each of our examples. However, for this particular example, the actual chi-square curve is much less positively skewed and much more normally distributed than the one shown in Figure 14.5, since the degrees of freedom are now much greater. A discussion of the shapes of chi-square distributions is given in Chapter 11.

$$\chi^2 = \sum_{i=1}^{5} \frac{(O_i - E_i)^2}{E_i}$$

$$= \frac{(1 - .5863)^2}{.5863} + \frac{(1 - .8625)^2}{.8625} + \frac{(2 - 1.8710)^2}{1.8710} + \cdots + \frac{(1 - .5863)^2}{.5863}$$

$$= .2919 + .0219 + .0089 + \cdots + .2919$$

$$= 1.3371$$

Decision. Since 1.3371 < 31.4104, the computed chi-square value falls to the left of the critical chi-square cutoff value. The census director should fail to reject the null hypothesis. There is no reason to suspect that the distribution is not normal.

Conclusion. The census director may want to think of data entry time as being normally distributed when staffing data entry technicians in the future. As can be seen from Figure 14.6, the observed distribution is very similar to the expected distribution, reflecting a very strong *goodness of fit.*

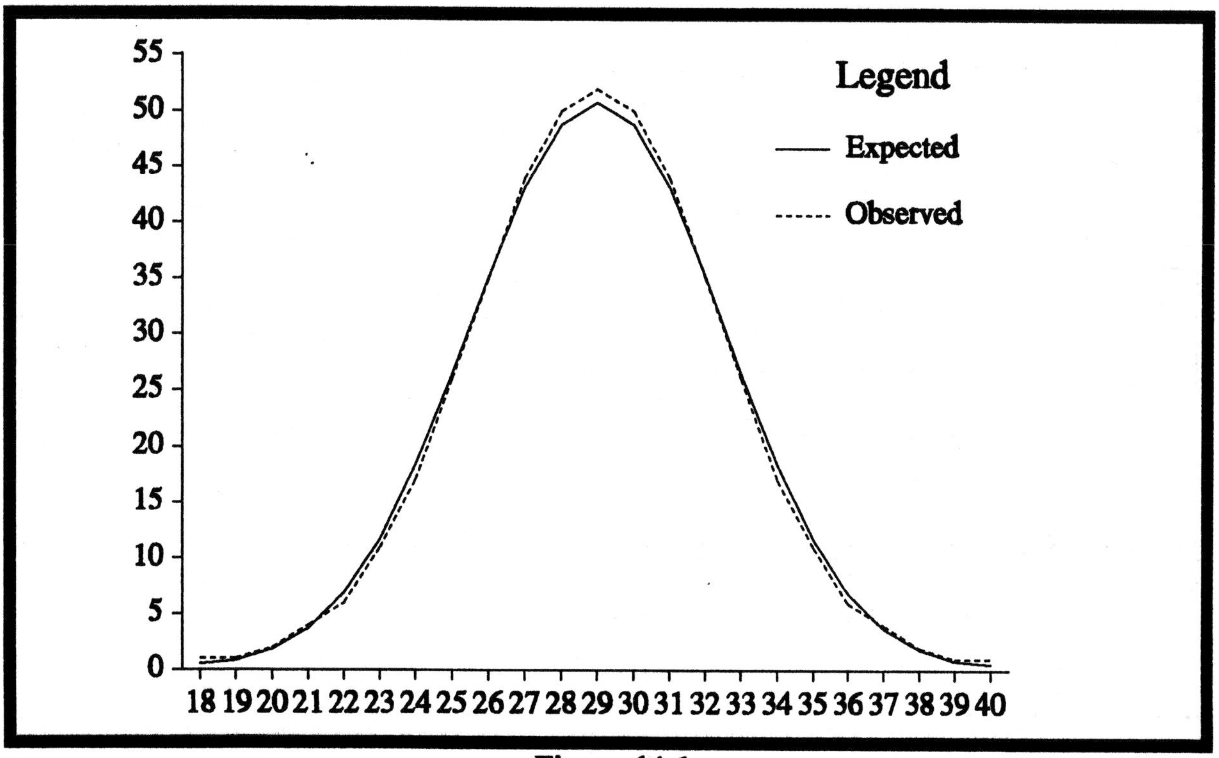

Figure 14.6
Graph of Observed Distribution vs. Expected Normal Distribution

TESTS OF INDEPENDENCE
(Also Referred to as Tests of Association)

As noted before, the chi-square distribution has many applications. In addition to the situations discussed in Chapters 11, 12, 13, and the previous section of this chapter, we can use chi-square to determine whether two or more variables are independent of one-another. There are many different tests of ***independence*** or ***association***, and they are partially a function of the types of variables available. As one illustration, we might want to determine whether two quantitative variables of at least interval level scale (such as seniority and pay) ***correlate*** with each other. Any measurement of such a correlation is a measure of the independence or dependence of the two variables. Chapters 15, 16, and 17 will discuss such measures of correlation and regression in detail. As another illustration, we might want to determine whether two qualitative variables of no more than ordinal scale (such as gender and organizational level) correlate with each other. Under these conditions, we use such terms as *independence* or *association* instead of *correlation*, although all of these illustrations are examining **relationships** among variables. Chapter 14 will now discuss tests of independence among qualitative variables. We will turn to other measures of relationships for more quantitative variables in later chapters.

Procedures for the Chi-Square Tests of Independence (Tests of Association)

Several points need to be discussed before illustrating the use of tests of independence for qualitative data. First, while we can examine the independence of *two or more* variables, the level of computational effort rapidly increases as we examine *more than two* qualitative variables. Second, the tests we use for examining relationships have a number of assumptions or requirements that must be satisfied in order for the tests to be valid. For example, if we are using the chi-square distribution to test for independence, the *expected values* must satisfy certain minimum requirements for cell sizes. When the expected values are not large enough, we may need to resort to collapsing cells in an effort to resolve this problem. Third, we need to determine which variables are our *primary* variables and which are our *secondary* variables. Otherwise, if we need to collapse cells, we might collapse the wrong ones. Fourth, if we are using continuous distributions such as the chi-square distribution or the normal distribution to approximate relationships among discrete variables, we must remember that such approximations become less accurate as the degrees of freedom decrease. We will discuss these and other concerns in the next few sections.

Example 14.6: Test of Independence Between Two Nominal Variables

The marketing department for a calculator manufacturer is interested in determining whether there is any relationship between the type of calculator purchased by customers and the professions of these customers. The manufacturer produces five different models of calculators, all selling for approximately the same list price. However, each calculator has different features. One of their retail outlets has agreed to survey customers at the time of purchase to determine their intended use of the calculators. The principal researcher initially grouped these applications into three categories: business, science, and other applications. However, the retailer noted that most of its customers were either in business-oriented or science-oriented professions. The retailer agreed to record data only for customers who fell into one of these two categories.

For Example 14.6, the marketing department is concerned with whether the types of calculators purchased by customers and the professions of these customers are independent. Returning to Figure 14.2, we begin at ***Start***. The marketing department is not comparing central tendencies, comparing variabilities, or testing for correlation/regression. Instead, they want to test for independence. Therefore, we turn to flowchart 6. They are not searching for a goodness of fit test or a test for proportions; instead, as noted, they want to test for independence. The data consist of frequency counts (the number of customers that fall into each of the intersecting categories), so we turn to flowchart 7. We know that there are two classification variables. Their **primary** classification variable (i.e., their variable of interest) is the type of calculator. Their **secondary** classification variable is the intended use of the calculators, as measured by the professions of the customers. The expected values have not as yet been determined. However, once this determination is made, if the expected values are five or greater for at least 80% of the cells, and if all of these expected values are one or greater, and if we have more than one degree of freedom, we will use the same chi-square test that we used in the previous section. The application of the chi-square distribution may be different, but the test equation is the same!

In summary, the independence of two nominal level variables is to be examined. The primary variable, the one with which the researcher is most concerned, is the type of calculator, consists of five categories. The secondary variable is the intended application for the calculators, and it consists of two categories. Thus, the format of this study is a 2×5 design, consisting of a total of 10 cells. The values recorded within the cells are the sums of the frequency counts for each cell. The marketing researcher established the null and alternative hypotheses as follows:

Null Hypothesis: Customer calculator purchase decisions are independent of intended calculator applications.

Alternative Hypothesis: Customer calculator purchase decisions are not independent of intended calculator applications.

Observed Values. The results of the customer survey are given in Table 14.5. With tests of independence or association, these tables are often referred to as *cross-tabulation tables* or *contingency tables.*

Table 14.5
Observed Values: Professional Applications and Calculator Models

	Model A	Model B	Model C	Model D	Model E	
Business	85	15	10	18	12	140
Science	35	32	30	25	18	140
	120	47	40	43	30	280

Expected Values for Tests of Independence. Based on the null hypothesis, we expect the two variables to be independent of one another. As discussed in Chapter 5, if the two variables are independent, the proportion of Model A calculators purchased for business purposes should be the same as the proportion of all other calculators purchased for business purposes. The row marginal count (*RM*) for business purchases is 140, the column marginal count (*CM*) for Model A calculators is 120, and the total count (*T*) for all calculator purchased is 280. Therefore, the expected value for the corresponding cell ($EV_{1,1}$) is determined as follows: $EV_{1,1} = (RM_1) \times (CM_1 \div T) = (120) \times (140 \div 280) = 60$. Thus, we would expect 60 of the Model A calculators to have been purchased for business purposes. Using Equation 5.18 from Chapter 5 for determining such values, we also obtain the expected values for the remaining nine cells. For example, the expected value for Model C calculators purchased for scientific applications ($EV_{2,3}$) is 20, obtained as follows:

$$EV_{2,3} = \frac{(RM_2)\cdot(CM_3)}{T}$$

$$= \frac{140 \cdot 40}{280}$$

$$= 20$$

Table of Observed and Expected Values. The contingency table that includes both the expected values and the observed values is given in Table 14.6.

Table 14.6
Observed and Expected Values: Professional Applications and Calculator Models

	Model A	Model B	Model C	Model D	Model E	
Business (expected)	60	23.5	20	21.5	15	
Business (observed)	85	15	10	18	12	140
Science (expected)	60	23.5	20	21.5	15	
Science (observed)	35	32	30	25	18	140
	120	47	40	43	30	280

Statistical Test. As determined from the flowcharts, an appropriate statistical test for the present problem is the chi-square test of independence.

Probability Level. The marketing researcher set the probability level at $\alpha = .05$.

Degrees of Freedom for a Contingency Table. Equation 5.10 of Chapter 5 yields the degrees of freedom for a contingency table. These degrees of freedom are again defined as follows: $df = (rows - 1) \times (columns - 1)$. For Example 14.6, there are 2 rows and 5 columns; therefore, $df = (r - 1) \times (c - 1) = (2 - 1) \times (5 - 1) = 1 \times 4 = 4$.

Critical Value. With $\alpha = .05$ and $df = 4$, the critical value is 9.4877.

Results. Returning to Flowchart 7 of the master flowcharts, we can now determine that the expected values are five or greater for at least 80% of the cells and that all of the expected values are one or greater. We also know that our degrees of freedom are greater than one. Thus, we conclude that the computed value for the chi-square test should be based on Equation 14.2. The computed value is 39.3218, obtained as follows:

$$\chi^2 = \sum_{i=1}^{10} \frac{(O_i - E_i)^2}{E_i}$$

$$= \frac{(85 - 60)^2}{60} + \frac{(15 - 23.5)^2}{23.5} + \frac{(10 - 20)^2}{20} + \frac{(18 - 21.5)^2}{21.5} + \frac{(12 - 15)^2}{15}$$

$$+ \frac{(35 - 60)^2}{60} + \frac{(32 - 23.5)^2}{23.5} + \frac{(30 - 20)^2}{20} + \frac{(25 - 21.5)^2}{21.5} + \frac{(18 - 15)^2}{15}$$

$$= 10.4167 + 3.0745 + 5.0000 + 0.5698 + 0.6000$$

$$+ 10.4167 + 3.0745 + 5.0000 + 0.5698 + 0.6000$$

$$= 39.3218$$

Decision. Since 39.3218 > 9.4877, the chi-square value falls in the region of rejection. The marketing researcher should reject the null hypothesis.

Conclusion. The marketing department has reason to believe that customer calculator purchase decisions are not independent of intended calculator applications. They should examine the professional demographics of the targeted geographic area as a part of their marketing strategy.

Example 14.7: Test of Independence Requiring Collapsing of Cells

Example 14.7 provides an illustration of the need for collapsing cells. In this example, the sales department for an automobile dealership is interested in determining whether there is any relationship between customer color preferences for automobiles and the marital status of those customers. If they discover that the two variables are not independent, the sales department plans to use this information to guide them in their future sales strategies and stock orders. Their **primary** variable, the one with which they are the most concerned, is the color of automobiles purchased. They have some control over this variable, as they can determine what colors to stock at their various locations. The preponderance of car colors they have stocked on their lots in the past have been white, black, red, blue, and yellow.

The **secondary** variable is the marital status of their customers. They have very little, if any, control over this variable. Marital status is grouped into five categories: single, married, divorced, separated, and other. Thus, the initial format of this study is a 5 × 5 design, consisting of a total of 25 cells. The research analysis team has established the following null and alternative hypotheses:

Null Hypothesis: Customer color preferences are independent of marital status.

Alternative Hypothesis: Customer color preferences are not independent of marital status.

Table of Observed and Expected Values. They have now collected data for a sample of 262 recent purchases. The marital status of these customers and the colors of the automobiles they purchased have been tabulated. They have developed a contingency table that includes both the observed values and the expected values, as shown in Table 14.7.

Table 14.7
Observed and Expected Values: Color Preferences and Marital Status

	Single	Married	Divorced	Separated	Other	
White	15 (23.82)	40 (26.55)	6 (7.44)	2 (3.72)	2 (3.47)	65
Black	25 (23.45)	30 (26.14)	7 (7.33)	1 (3.66)	1 (3.42)	64
Red	45 (28.21)	20 (31.45)	8 (8.82)	2 (4.41)	2 (4.12)	77
Blue	5 (9.89)	5 (11.03)	4 (3.09)	8 (1.55)	5 (1.44)	27
Yellow	6 (10.63)	12 (11.84)	5 (3.32)	2 (1.66)	4 (1.55)	29
	96	107	30	15	14	262

Collapsing Cells. Returning to Flowchart 7 of the master flowcharts, we know that for Example 14.7 there are less than three classification variables. However, the expected values are not five or greater for at least 80% of the cells (although all of the expected values are one or greater); in fact, only 13 of the 25 expected values (52%) are five or greater. The chi-square test does not conform well to the chi-square distribution under such limitations. We must resolve this issue before applying the chi-square test. If we had a 2 × 2 design, we might consider using the Fisher's exact probability test, which will be discussed later in this chapter. However, we have a 5 × 5 table and must now collapse cells.

When we collapse cells, we combine observations in one category with observations in another category. By doing so, we lose our ability to differentiate among the categories. Unless we have anticipated such a potential problem before collecting data and therefore have collected an adequate amount of data in each category, it is not uncommon to have to collapse cells.

Arbitrary Decisions for Collapsing Cells. The cells to be collapsed are determined by arbitrary decisions. Cells that do not have adequate sizes in regard to their *expected* values are problematic; they are potential candidates for collapsing. We must keep in mind which variables are the *primary* variables and which variables are the *secondary* variables. We should avoid collapsing categories of the primary variable, as this would greatly limit our study. For Example 14.7, we would not want to collapse any of the colors into one common color. Not only would this not make much sense; it also would not allow us to make any decisions about the combined colors. Instead, we collapse categories within the secondary variable. Here, we should collapse the "divorced," "separated," and "other" categories into one combined category and refer to it as "other." The three resulting categories for marital status, "married," "single," and "other," make intuitive sense. Alternatively, it would not make as much sense to collapse "married" with "single" or with some other category of the secondary variable. Such a collapsing of categories would not allow us to make interpretative conclusions. Further, if we collapsed "married" with "single," we still would not have resolved our initial concern that the expected values must be five or greater for at least 80% of the cells. Consequently, we collapse the "divorced," "separated," and "other" categories into one combined category, as shown in Table 14.8.

Table 14.8
Observed and Expected Values After Collapsing Cells

	Single (Observed)	Single (Expected)	Married (Observed)	Married (Expected)	Other (Observed)	Other (Expected)	Total
White	15	23.82	40	26.55	10	14.64	65
Black	25	23.45	30	26.14	9	14.41	64
Red	45	28.21	20	31.45	12	17.34	77
Blue	5	9.89	5	11.03	17	6.08	27
Yellow	6	10.63	12	11.84	11	6.53	29
	96		107		59		262

Statistical Test. After collapsing cells, the chi-square test of independence becomes an appropriate statistical test for Example 14.7.

Probability Level. The research analysis team set the probability level at $\alpha = .05$.

Degrees of Freedom. The degrees of freedom are now based on the collapsed contingency table. The original 5×5 design has been reduced to a 5×3 design. Therefore, $df = (r - 1) \times (c - 1) = (5 - 1) \times (3 - 1) = 4 \times 2 = 8$.

Critical Value. With $\alpha = .05$ and $df = 8$, the critical value is 15.5073.

Results. Returning to Flowchart 7 of the master flowcharts, we now have satisfied the requirements that the expected values are five or greater for at least 80% of the cells and that all of the expected values are one or greater. Our degrees of freedom are greater than one. Consequently, we conclude that the computed value for the chi-square test should be based on Equation 14.2. The computed chi-square for these 15 cells is 60.46, determined as follows:

$$\chi^2 = \sum_{i=1}^{15} \frac{(O_i - E_i)^2}{E_i}$$

$$= \frac{(15 - 23.82)^2}{23.82} + \frac{(40 - 26.55)^2}{26.55} + \cdots + \frac{(11 - 6.53)^2}{6.53}$$

$$= 60.46$$

Decision. Since $60.46 > 15.5073$, the chi-square value falls in the region of rejection.

Conclusion. The team has reason to believe that customer color preferences are not independent of marital status. Therefore, they might want to examine the demographics associated with the geographic locations of their dealerships. For example, if they find that a dealership is located in an area that caters to single individuals, such as near a military base, they might want to stock colors of cars differently than if the dealership was located in some other area.

Example 14.8: Test of Independence with $df = 1$ and with All Expected Values ≥ 5

As noted before, there are exact methods for determining the probabilities for goodness of fit tests and tests of independence. Depending on the situation, one approach is the binomial distribution, another is the multinomial distribution, another is the hypergeometric distribution, and still another is the multivariate hypergeometric distribution. Unfortunately, the computational process necessary for determining cumulative probabilities from these distributions can be very time-consuming. Most of these distributions had been identified long before the advent of calculators and computers, and statisticians were constantly in search of easier ways to approximate their related probabilities. As we learned, the chi-square is one such approximation. The accuracy of this test as an approximation increases as the degrees of freedom increase. However, when we have only one degree of freedom, the chi-square test defined in Equation 14.2 may be quite inaccurate.

In 1934, Frank Yates developed a continuity correction factor that serves to increase the accuracy of the chi-square test when used to approximate the binomial and the hypergeometric distributions. Since the binomial only has two categories, it can be thought of as a goodness of fit test with one degree of freedom. Since the format of the hypergeometric distribution is based on two variables, each with two categories, it can be thought of as a test of independence for a 2 × 2 table with one degree of freedom. Yates' adjustment factor provides a good correction for continuity in either situation. His "corrected" chi-square test is defined in Equation 14.3:

$$\chi^2 = \sum_{i=1}^{k} \frac{(|O_i - E_i| - .5)^2}{E_i} \tag{14.3}$$

Example 14.8. For Example 14.8, a microbrewery and its adjoining bar are located near a university. The brewmaster has hypothesized that the type of beer (regular vs. light) preferred by college students is a function of gender. The bar has been promoting Saturday nights as "Ladies' Night" in an attempt to increase female patronage. If the brewmaster's motivated hypothesis is correct, the microbrewery will want to change its production ratio of regular vs. light beer in preparation for those occasions. The brewmaster has thus established the following null and alternative hypotheses:

Null Hypothesis: The type of beer preferred is independent of gender.

Alternative Hypothesis: The type of beer preferred is not independent of gender.

Table of Observed and Expected Values. The brewmaster randomly sampled the beer orders of 68 male and 52 female college students for four consecutive Saturday nights. He then developed a contingency table that includes both the observed values and the expected values, as shown in Table 14.9.

Table 14.9
Test of Independence with *df* = 1 and with All Expected Values ≥ 5

	Regular (Observed)	Regular (Expected)	Light (Observed)	Light (Expected)	
Males	48	39.6667	20	28.3333	68
Females	22	30.3333	30	21.6667	52
	70		50		120

Statistical Test. Returning to Flowchart 7 of the master flowcharts, we know that for Example 14.8 there are less than three classification variables. The expected values are five or greater for at least 80% of the cells, and all of the expected values are one or greater. We have only one degree of freedom, so we should apply Yates' correction factor to the chi-square test.

Probability Level. The brewmaster has set the probability level at $\alpha = .05$.

Degrees of Freedom. There are 2 rows and 3 columns. Therefore, $df = (r - 1) \times (c - 1) = (2 - 1) \times (2 - 1) = 1 \times 1 = 1$.

Critical Value. With $\alpha = .05$ and $df = 1$, the critical value is 3.8415.

Results. We will use Equation 14.3 to obtain the computed chi-square value, based on Yates' continuity correction factor. The computed chi-square is 8.5676, determined as follows:

$$\chi^2 = \sum_{i=1}^{k} \frac{(|O_i - E_i| - .5)^2}{E_i}$$

$$= \frac{(|48 - 39.6667| - .5)^2}{39.6667} + \frac{(|20 - 28.3333| - .5)^2}{28.3333}$$

$$+ \frac{(|22 - 30.3333| - .5)^2}{30.3333} + \frac{(|30 - 21.6667| - .5)^2}{21.6667}$$

$$= \mathbf{8.5676}$$

Decision. Since 8.5676 > 3.8415, the chi-square value falls in the region of rejection.

Conclusion. Beer preference appears to be dependent on gender. The microbrewery may want to change its light/regular beer production ratio prior to Ladies' Night events. Females appear to prefer light beer, while males appear to prefer regular beer.

Example 14.9: Test of Independence with *df* = 1 and Not All Expected Values ≥ 5

Occasionally, we will find that we do not have at least 80% of the expected values equal to or greater than five; yet, we cannot meaningfully collapse cells. For example, with a 2 × 2 contingency table, if we were to collapse any categories, we would only have one classification variable remaining and could not perform a test of independence. On the other hand, if we ignored the problem and used the chi-square test of independence (with or without Yates' correction factor), the chi-square distribution would no longer provide an adequate approximation. Example 14.9 illustrates such a situation. Sill, Lee, Boyze, Inc. (SLB), a supplier to Blake Manufacturing, complained that Blake had not been treating them fairly in competitive bidding for new work. SLB argued that their success rate in joint projects with Blake was better than that of SLB's three major competitors. After considerable discussion, Blake agreed to make records available to SLB for analysis. Over the past two years, 32 joint projects had been completed between Blake and its suppliers in this product line. The data, as given in Table 14.10, show that SLB had partnered with Blake on 8 occasions, while the competitors had partnered with Blake on 24 occasions. The data also indicated that 16 of the 32 projects had been identified by Blake as being successful without rework, while 16 had been identified as requiring rework. The resulting contingency table reveals that two of the expected values in the 2 × 2 table are less than five. Under such circumstances, the chi-square test does not provide optimal results. Instead of approximating probabilities, we should use the hypergeometric distribution described in Chapter 7 to obtain more accurate probabilities. The hypergeometric distribution is often referred to as ***Fisher's Exact Probability Test.***

Hypothesis Testing. The null and alternative hypotheses for Example 14.9 are defined as follows:

Null Hypothesis: Project success (as measured by minimal rework) is independent of business partnerships.

Alternative Hypothesis: Project success (as measured by minimal rework) is not independent of business partnerships.

Table of Observed and Expected Values. Of the 32 projects completed, 16 required no rework, 16 required rework, 8 were conducted with SLB, and 24 were conducted with competitors of SLB. The cross-tabulations in Table 14.10 include both the observed and expected values for Example 14.9.

Table 14.10
First Scenario: SLB Rework Required Once

	No Rework Required (Observed)	No Rework Required (Expected)	Rework Required (Observed)	Rework Required (Expected)	
SLB, Inc.	1	4	7	4	8
Competitors	15	12	9	12	24
	16		16		32

Statistical Test. As determined from Flowchart 7 of the master flowcharts, Fisher's exact probability test, based on the hypergeometric distribution, is an appropriate tool for this scenario.

Probability Level. Blake and SLB agreed to use $\alpha = .05$ as a mutually acceptable cutoff point for significance.

Degrees of Freedom. Degrees of freedom are not of concern when using the hypergeometric distribution.

Critical Value. Fisher's exact probability test yields a probability instead of a statistical value. Thus, the results can be compared directly to alpha. The critical value is simply $\alpha = .05$.

Results: Part One. Only one of the eight joint projects with SLB required rework. We use Equation 7.10 from Chapter 7 to calculate the probability that exactly one SLB project required rework when the marginal values are fixed at 16 not needing rework, 16 needing rework, 8 partnerships with SLB, and 24 partnerships with competitors. The probability for this scenario is .017402, based on the hypergeometric distribution as follows:

$$p = \frac{\binom{16}{1} \cdot \binom{16}{7}}{\binom{32}{8}}$$

$$= \frac{(16)\cdot(11{,}440)}{10{,}518{,}300}$$

$$= .017402$$

Results: Part Two. As with most statistical tests, we want to determine the *cumulative* probability for *something or less*. If none of the SLB joint projects required rework, that would be a better scenario than one requiring rework. Thus, our next step is to determine the probability that none required rework. The resulting contingency table for this scenario is given in Table 14.11.

Table 14.11
Second Scenario: No SLB Rework Required

	No Rework Required	Rework Required	
SLB, Inc.	4 0	4 8	8
Competitors	12 16	12 8	24
	16	16	32

Applying the hypergeometric distribution equation for this second scenario, a probability of .001224 is obtained, as follows:

$$p = \frac{\binom{16}{0} \cdot \binom{16}{8}}{\binom{32}{8}}$$

$$= \frac{(1)\cdot(12{,}870)}{10{,}518{,}300}$$

$$= .001224$$

Decision. We now sum our results and make our decision. The probability that one or less SLB project needed rework under the conditions of independent events is .017402 + .001224 = .018626. Since .018626 is < .05, we conclude that the two events are not independent.

Conclusion. It appears that there is a relationship between supplier and successful results. On the basis of minimal rework, Sill, Lee, Boyze, Inc., is a significantly better business partner than the other competitors. While other factors such as cost, on time delivery, long-term durability of the results, shipping, general business cooperation, etc., still need to be considered, it certainly appears that continued business partnerships with SLB should be considered and perhaps even increased.

Summary

Example 14.1 Revisited. Before concluding this chapter on tests of goodness of fit and tests of independence, we will revisit Example 14.1. In that example, a coin was tossed 40 times, yielding 10 heads and 30 tails. The probability of obtaining 10 or less heads or 20 or more heads was found to be .0022, based on the binomial distribution. If we had used the general format of the chi-square goodness of fit test to approximate this binomial, we would have obtained $\chi^2 = 10.0$. Using a spreadsheet (or using calculus to integrate the area under the chi-square distribution), we can determine that the probability corresponding to this chi-square value is .0016. However, since $df = 2 - 1 = 1$, we should apply Yates' correction factor when using the chi-square test to approximate the actual value. Based on Yates' correction for continuity, we would have obtained $\chi^2 = 9.0250$. A spreadsheet (or integrating) will allow us to determine that this revised chi-square yields a corresponding probability value of .0027, which is a better approximation. Table 14.12 gives computed probability values for various combinations of heads and tails for this same experiment. We can see that using Yates' correction factor yields consistently better results, especially as the number of heads and tails get closer to one-another.

Table 14.12
Comparison of Binomial vs. Chi-Square (with and without Yates' Correction)

Number of Heads	Number of Tails	Exact Binomial Prob.	χ^2 value with Yates	χ^2 value without Yates	χ^2 Prob. with Yates	χ^2 Prob. without Yates	Error with Yates correction	Error without Yates correction
10	30	0.0022	9.0250	10.0000	0.0027	0.0016	-0.0005	0.0006
12	28	0.0166	5.6250	6.4000	0.0177	0.0114	-0.0011	0.0052
15	25	0.1539	2.0250	2.5000	0.1547	0.1138	-0.0008	0.0401
18	22	0.6358	0.2250	0.4000	0.6353	0.5271	0.0005	0.1087
19	21	0.8746	0.0250	0.1000	0.8744	0.7518	0.0002	0.1228

In conclusion, we should use the binomial and the hypergeometric distributions instead of the chi-square distribution whenever practical. If they are not practical and $df = 1$, we should use chi-square as an approximation; and we should apply Yates' correction factor to improve the approximation. If $df > 1$, the binomial is inappropriate; and the hypergeometric and multinomial distributions become rather labor intensive. Under such circumstances, the chi-square test becomes a very practical solution and yields a good approximation, without need for any adjustments.

References

Bradley, J. V. (1968). ***Distribution-free statistical tests.*** Englewood Cliffs, NJ: Prentice-Hall.

Conover, W. J. (1971). ***Practical nonparametric statistics.*** New York: John Wiley & Sons, Inc.

Mosteller, F., & Rourke, R. E. K. (1973). ***Sturdy statistics: nonparametrics and order statistics.*** Reading, MA: Addison-Wesley.

Siegel, S. (1956). ***Nonparametric statistics for the behavioral sciences.*** New York: McGraw-Hill.

Yates, F. K. (1934). Contingency tables involving small numbers and the χ^2 test. ***Journal of the Royal Statistical Society, 1***, 217-235.

Practice Problems
Quick Quiz

1. Returning to Case Study 1.1, the Process Action Team at Navitech collected data regarding faulty products. They had access to records for 400 parts produced by their manufacturing process over the past six-month period. They determined that the products were tagged as being defective due to one of the following factors: temperature variation, excessive pressure, poor torque, faulty material, and operator error. Prior to developing a Pareto diagram to further examine these factors, they had speculated that none of these factors contributed to faulty products any more than the other factors. Answer the following questions in regard to this problem.

   A. How many classification variables are there?

   B. What is the level of measurement for their variable/variables?

   C. What are their expected values?

   D. What is their null hypothesis?

   E. How many degrees of freedom do they have?

   F. What is an appropriate statistical tool for addressing their concern?

2. The marketing department of an art museum has been attempting to increase the number of visitors they have from outside the local geographic area. Past surveys have indicated that 50% of their visitors reside in the county where the museum is located, 25% come from other counties within the same state, 15% come from other states within the United States, and 10% come from another country. Recently, the museum changed the format of their featured exhibits, their marketing strategy for these exhibits, and their advertizing approach. Then, during the next three featured events, they polled 1000 visitors and determined their home locations, based on these same four categories. They are interested in determining whether their marketing strategy has resulted in changes relative to the distribution of visitors obtained before the new strategy was implemented. Answer the following questions in regard to this problem.

   A. How many classification variables are there?

   B. What is the level of measurement for their variable/variables?

   C. What are their expected values?

   D. What is their null hypothesis?

   E. How many degrees of freedom do they have?

   F. What is an appropriate statistical tool for addressing their concern?

3. The emergency room of a hospital wanted to determine whether job-related accidents are related to type of job. They monitored such accidents for a period of time and coded them into the following categories: broken bones, sprains, cuts, stiffness in joints, dizziness, and others. They categorized the patients into types of work performed: manual labor, office work, management, and other. Their data base consisted of frequency counts for all possible groupings. Answer the following questions in regard to this problem.

   A. How many classification variables are there?

   B. What is the level of measurement for their variable/variables?

   C. What is their null hypothesis?

   D. How many cells do they have?

   E. How many degrees of freedom do they have?

   F. What is an appropriate statistical tool for addressing their concern?

4. A consultant with expertise in quality evaluation and quality awards has been retained to examine the success of a program designed for training national quality examiners. Ten trained and experienced examiners and eight untrained but experienced examiners were asked to evaluate a hypothetical company for which a lengthy case study had been developed. The consultant then evaluated these 18 individuals as either being successful or unsuccessful in their evaluation of the company. Twelve were rated as successful, while six were rated as unsuccessful. Answer the following questions in regard to this problem.

   A. How many classification variables are there?

   B. What is the level of measurement for their variable/variables?

   C. What is their null hypothesis?

   D. How many cells do they have?

   E. How many degrees of freedom do they have?

   F. What is an appropriate statistical tool for addressing their concern?

Practice Problems
Multiple Choice

1. Which of the following is **not** a true statement?

   A. The normal distribution is a continuous distribution.
   B. The chi-square distribution is a continuous distribution.
   C. The hypergeometric distribution is a discrete distribution.
   D. The binomial distributions is a discrete distribution.
   E. The observed frequencies in a contingency table represent a continuous distribution.

2. Regarding degrees of freedom and various chi-square tests, which of the following is a correct statement?

   A. The degrees of freedom for a chi-square test against a rectangular distribution equal k - 1.
   B. The degrees of freedom for a chi-square test against a Poisson distribution equal k - 2.
   C. The degrees of freedom for a chi-square test against a normal distribution equal k - 3.
   D. The degrees of freedom for a chi-square test of independence equal $(r - 1) \times (c - 1)$.
   E. All of the above are correct.

3. When testing a five-category distribution of frequency counts against a hypothesized rectangular distribution, which of the following is **not** a correct statement about the expected values for each category?

   A. All of the expected values will be the same.
   B. All of the expected values will be equal to $.2 \times N$, where N represents the number of observations.
   C. All of the expected values must be one or greater in order to use the chi-square test.
   D. All of the expected values must be five or greater in order to use the chi-square test.
   E. There will be four degrees of freedom when determining the expected values.

4. Which of the following is **not** a discrete distribution?

   A. The hypergeometric distribution.
   B. The binomial distribution.
   C. The chi-square distribution.
   D. The Fisher's exact probability test.
   E. The observed values in a test of association.

5. Which of the following is **not** a true statement regarding the use of the chi-square distribution when testing for goodness of fit or for independence?

   A. With any chi-square test, at least 80% of the *observed* values should be five or greater.
   B. When performing a chi-square goodness of fit test against a normal distribution, there will be k - 3 degrees of freedom.
   C. When performing a chi-square goodness of fit test against a uniform distribution, there will be k - 1 degrees of freedom.
   D. When performing a chi-square test of independence or goodness of fit, all of the *expected* cell values should be at least one and at least 80% should be five or greater.
   E. To perform a chi-square test with only one degree of freedom, you should find the absolute difference between the observed and expected cell values, subtract .5 from these differences, square each of the results, divide each by its corresponding expected value, and sum over all cells.

6. Which of the following would **not** be useful in determining whether a distribution is approximately *normal* in shape?

   A. Chi-square goodness of fit test against an expected normal distribution.
   B. Various measures of skewness.
   C. Various measures of kurtosis.
   D. A comparison of the mean, median, and mode.
   E. All of the above would be useful in determining whether the shape of the distribution is approximately normal.

7. Which of the following is **not** a correct statement.

   A. Fisher's exact probability test is the same as the hypergeometric distribution.
   B. Yates' correction factor should be used whenever performing a test of independence.
   C. The chi-square distribution can be used to approximate a binomial distribution.
   D. The chi-square goodness of fit test can be used to approximate a multinomial distribution.
   E. Tests of independence are also known as tests for association.

8. When performing a chi-square test of independence, the primary variable (as opposed a secondary variable) is:

   A. the variable over which we have no control.
   B. the variable we should collapse when we do not have adequate expected values.
   C. the variable with which we have primary concern.
   D. the variable that always is represented by the rows instead of the columns.
   E. the variable that is the easiest to measure.

9. Which of the following is **not** a correct statement regarding the chi-square distribution?

A. When we have a two-by-two frequency table, when we do not have expected values of five or greater in all four of the cells, and when we are testing for independence, we should use the Fisher exact probability test instead of the chi-square test of independence.
B. When we do not have expected values of at least one for all the cells and when at least 80% of the expected values for our cells are at least five or greater, we must collapse cells before utilizing the chi-square test of independence.
C. The chi-square distribution is a discrete distribution.
D. The chi-square distribution is useful for testing the goodness of fit when comparing an observed distribution against some expected distribution.
E. The chi-square distribution is useful when testing whether two nominal level variables are independent.

10. Suppose that you have obtained a computed chi-square value of 29.65 when comparing an observed distribution against a theoretical normal distribution. There are 18 categories. With alpha set at .01, what is the critical cutoff value for this test?

A. 30.5780
B. 33.4087
C. 5.2294
D. 24.9958
E. 13.2361

11. Suppose that you have computed a chi-square value of 29.65 for comparing an observed distribution versus a theoretical normal distribution. There are 18 categories. With alpha set at .01, what decision would you make?

A. Reject the null hypothesis.
B. Fail to reject the null hypothesis.
C. Assume that the distribution is rectangular.
D. Assume that the distribution is nearly rectangular.
E. Assume that the distribution is shaped in a Poisson fashion.

12. Which of the following would give information concerning the independence or dependence of variables?

A. $P(B) = P(B/A)$
B. $P(A) = P(A/B)$
C. Knowledge of the expected values for all of $(A_i \cap B_j)$.
D. Performing a chi-square test for independence.
E. All of the above would be useful for determining whether the variables are independent or dependent.

13. Suppose it has been suggested that students are evenly distributed in regard to five majors within the College of Business Administration. You are now enrolled in an upper division class required for all five business majors and open only to business majors. Based on your experience, it appears that there are more students in certain majors and less in others. You have decided to examine the original assumption, using data obtained from your class of 120 students. Which of the following statements is the most correct?

A. You have four degrees of freedom.
B. Your null hypothesis is that business majors are not evenly distributed.
C. You should perform an analysis of variance, since the data are at least interval.
D. Based on your class of 120 students, you do not have enough data to test the null hypothesis.
E. The computed value of chi-square is 9.4877.

14. Suppose that you have hypothesized under the null that eye color is uniformly distributed for students in room 222. To test this hypothesis, you have collected sample data from 72 students who participated in a survey. You have thus obtained the following distribution:

Distribution of Eye Color

Brown	Blue	Green	Hazel	Other
24	24	12	9	3

With alpha set at .05, what is the computed value of chi-square, the critical value of chi-square, and the decision you should make regarding the distribution of eye colors for students in room 222?

A. The computed value is 14.45, the critical value is 9.4877, and we conclude that eye color is not uniformly distributed.
B. The computed value is 8.25, the critical value is 9.4877, and we conclude that eye color is uniformly distributed.
C. The computed value is 24.25, the critical value is 9.4877, and we conclude that eye color is uniformly distributed.
D. The computed value is 16.85, the critical value is 11.0705, and we conclude that eye color is not uniformly distributed.
E. The computed value is 24.25, the critical value is 9.4877, and we conclude that eye color is not uniformly distributed.

15. Suppose you have collected frequency data for the 200 students in your class. You found that 73 students completed a lower division statistics course in the mathematics department at your university, 52 students completed their lower division statistics course in the economics department at your university, and 75 students completed a lower division statistics course at a junior college before enrolling in the present course. You also determined their present standing in the course, arbitrarily grouped into two categories: successful (if they have a grade of A, B, or C) and unsuccessful (if they have a grade of D or F). The table of cross-tabulations is given below:

Contingency Table: Grades vs. Lower Division Requirement Location

	Mathematics	Economics	Junior College	
Successful	58	40	40	
Unsuccessful	15	12	35	
	73	52	75	200

With alpha set at .05, perform a test to examine whether the two variables are independent.

A. With a computed chi-square value of 13.86 and a critical value of 5.9915, we reject the null hypothesis. Thus, we have reason to doubt whether the two variables are independent.
B. With a computed chi-square value of 13.86 and a critical value of 3.8415, we reject the null hypothesis. Thus, we have reason to doubt whether the two variables are independent.
C. With a computed chi-square value of 3.8792 and a critical value of 5.9915, we fail to reject the null hypothesis. Thus, we have reason to doubt that the two variables are independent.
D. With a computed chi-square value of 5.9915 and a critical value of 13.86, we fail to reject the null hypothesis. Thus, we have no reason to doubt that the two variables are independent.
E. With a computed chi-square value of 3.8792 and a critical value of 5.9915, we fail to reject the null hypothesis. Thus, we have no reason to doubt that the two variables are independent.

16. Suppose you have hypothesized under the null that the distribution of eye colors for this semester's class is the same as it was for last semester's class. Last semester, you collected data for 72 students and determined that 24 had brown eyes, 24 had blue eyes, 12 had green eyes, 9 had hazel eyes, and 3 indicated some other color of eyes. This semester, you have determined that eye color is distributed as given in the following table:

Distribution of Eye Colors

Brown	Blue	Green	Hazel	Other
60	38	22	27	3

Based on this information and with alpha set at .05, what are the computed and critical values for this chi-square goodness of fit test, and what is the decision which you would make when comparing this semester's distribution with next semester's?

A. The computed value is 4.85, the critical value is 9.4877, and we conclude that the distribution of eye color for this semester is not significantly different than it was for last semester.
B. The computed value is 19.78, the critical value is 9.4877, and we conclude that the distribution of eye color for this semester is significantly different than it was for last semester.
C. The computed value is 10.56, the critical value is 9.4877, and we conclude that the distribution of eye color for this semester is significantly different than it was for last semester.
D. The computed value is 6.89, the critical value is 9.4877, and we fail to reject the null hypothesis.
E. Since the computed and critical values are identical, we cannot make any conclusions.

Practice Problems
Written Problems

1. A new shopping center is opening in a major city. The manager of this center has hired a marketing agency to investigate food preferences of potential customers so that he can make appropriate vendor selection decisions that will result in an appealing food mall. The researchers have surveyed 216 customers based upon a stratified random sample of potential patrons. The manager of the mall wants to determine whether there is a clear cut preference for various types of food or whether food preferences are evenly distributed among the population of potential customers in this geographic location. The following distribution of data has been collected:

Distribution of Food Preferences

Italian	Mexican	Chinese	Greek	Other	None
32	63	48	27	16	30

With alpha set at .05, perform a multinomial test to determine whether food preferences of these customers fit a rectangular distribution. Answer each of the following questions:

A. What are the expected values? (Answer this by inserting them into the empty boxes above.)

B. How many degrees of freedom exist in this example? __________

C. What is the critical chi-square value? __________

D. What is the computed chi-square value? __________

E. What is the appropriate decision regarding the null hypothesis? __________

F. Using the graph below, locate the computed and critical values for chi-square.

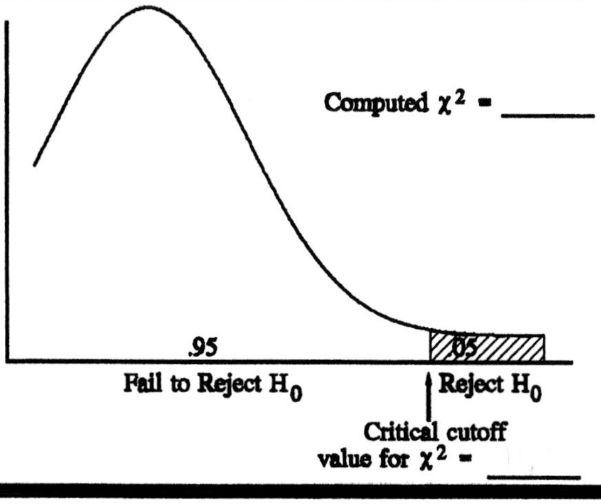

2. As a research project, a student decided to examine whether the religious affiliation of students enrolled in a large section of a general education class at a major university in the United States coincided with that of the general U.S. population. Through an investigation of demographic information available in the campus library, the student determined that the distribution of religious affiliations within the general U.S. population, for those reporting a religious affiliation, was as follows: 54% Protestant, 37% Roman Catholic, 5% Jewish, and 4% Other. The student then polled the members of the class. Based upon the 134 students who responded to the survey and identified a religious affiliation, the following distribution was obtained:

Distribution of Religious Affiliation

Protestant	Roman Catholic	Jewish	Other
51	44	9	30

With alpha set at .05, perform a one-dimensional, multinomial test to determine whether the religious affiliation of these students fits the religious affiliation of the general U.S. population. Answer each of the following questions:

A. What are the expected values? (Answer this by inserting them into the empty boxes above.)

B. How many degrees of freedom exist in this example? __________

C. What is the critical chi-square value? __________

D. What is the computed chi-square value? __________

E. What is the appropriate decision regarding the null hypothesis? __________

3. Pressures levels were recorded for 124 aerosol cans, as selected through a stratified sampling plan. The investigator now wants to determine whether the distribution is approximately normal. Find the mean and standard deviation, fill in the columns, and answer the following questions:

Distribution of Pressure in Aerosol Cans

X	*f*	*RLL*	*RUL*	*z / RLL*	*z / RUL*	*Area*	*Observed Values*	*Expected Values*	$\frac{(O - E)^2}{E}$
24	2								
25	2								
26	5								
27	8								
28	16								
29	15								
30	12								
31	9								
32	21								
33	14								
34	6								
35	6								
36	5								
37	1								
38	0								
39	2								

A. What is the mean for this sample of 124 aerosol cans? __________

B. What is the standard deviation for this sample of 124 aerosol cans? __________

C. How many degrees of freedom are associated with this problem? __________

D. What is the critical chi-square value? __________

E. What is the computed chi-square value? __________

F. What is the null hypothesis? __________

G. What is the appropriate decision regarding the null hypothesis? __________

4. A manufacturer of binoculars is interested in determining whether there is a relationship between the type of binoculars preferred and the intended use of the binoculars. A sample of 300 consumers were asked how they use their binoculars (viewing sports events, viewing nature, or all purpose viewing) and which model of binoculars they prefer among the four models offered by the manufacturer. The motivated hypothesis is that there is a relationship between these two classification variables. The following contingency table has been developed, based upon these 300 consumers:

Usage of Binoculars

	Sports	Nature	All Purpose
Model A	45	12	10
Model B	13	52	29
Model C	23	27	50
Model D	15	14	10

With alpha set at .01, perform the appropriate test to determine whether these two classification variables are related. Answer each of the following questions:

A. What are the expected values? (Answer this by inserting them into the empty boxes above.)

B. How many degrees of freedom are associated with this problem? ____________

C. What is the critical chi-square value? ____________

D. What is the computed chi-square value? ____________

E. What is the appropriate decision regarding the null hypothesis? ____________

5. A TQM professional wanted to determine whether various potential problems that result in poor quality are more prevalent in some industries than others. The researcher contacted quality experts in various industries, including health, manufacturing, service, education, and other industries that he collapsed into one category. He then asked these managers to evaluate the frequency of problems that were associated with four traditional sources of problems: materials, machines, methods, and human resources. A total of 292 situations were evaluated by the managers in this sample. He hopes to reject the null hypothesis, which states that there is no relationship between type of industry and source of problem. The following contingency table has been developed, based upon these 292 consumers:

Quality Problems

	Materials	Machines	Methods	Human Resources
Health	10	20	35	5
Manu-facturing	25	29	48	8
Service	20	3	29	15
Education	4	4	10	5
Other	3	5	12	2

With alpha set at .10, perform the appropriate test to determine whether these two classification variables are related. Answer each of the following questions:

A. What are the expected values?

B. Do these expected values satisfy all of requirements for expected values? ____________

C. Which variable is the primary variable? ____________

D. Which variable is the secondary variable? ____________

E. Which categories should be collapsed? ____________

F. After collapsing the cells, create a revised table of observed and expected values.

G. How many degrees of freedom are now associated with this problem? ________

H. What is the critical chi-square value? ________

I. What is the computed chi-square value? ________

J. What is the appropriate decision regarding the null hypothesis? ________

6. As a potential television sponsor of football games, AvidFan Shoes wants do determine whether there are differences in the educational backgrounds of fans who watch college football and those who watch professional football. The null hypothesis is that there is there is no relationship between the level of education of the viewers and type of football they prefer to view. Level of education has been divided into two categories: those who have attended college and those who have not attended college. A sample of 600 football fans were interviewed; half of these fans had attended college and half had not. They were then asked which type of football they preferred to watch on television: college football or professional football. The results of the survey yielded the following contingency table:

Football Preferences

	Attended College	**No College Attendance**
Preferred College Football	150	98
Preferred Professional Football	150	202

Alpha has been set at .05, and you would like to conduct a test for independence between the two variables. Answer each of the following questions:

A. What are the expected values?

B. How many degrees of freedom are associated with this problem? ________

C. What is the critical chi-square value? ________

D. What is the computed chi-square value before adjusting for degrees of freedom? ________

E. What is the computed chi-square value after using Yates' correction factor to adjust for the degrees of freedom? ________

F. What is the appropriate decision regarding the null hypothesis? ________

7. A group of applicants to a medical school argued that admission to the school was dependent upon whether or not applicants had connections with important alumni of the school. They sought to challenge the medical school regarding its admission policies, but they wanted to examine their claim before pursuing it any further. They obtained data from 21 applicants and developed the following contingency table:

Medical School Admission Decisions

	Admitted	Not Admitted
No Connections	3	9
Connections	7	2

Conduct the appropriate statistical analysis for these data, based upon the null hypothesis that admission to medical school and connections with important alumni are unrelated. Assume that all other characteristics (age, gender, ethnic background, grade point average, etc.) for those admitted and those not admitted are the same. Alpha is set at .05. Answer each of the following questions:

A. What is the appropriate statistical test for performing this analysis? ____________

B. What is the probability that only 2 of those not admitted had connections with important alumni based upon the configuration of this contingency table and the assumption that the two classification variables are indeed independent of one-another? ____________

C. What is the probability that 2 or less of those not admitted had connections with important alumni based upon the configuration of this contingency table and the assumption that the two classification variables are indeed independent of one-another? ____________

D. What is the appropriate decision regarding the null hypothesis? ____________

CHAPTER 15

CORRELATION

Case Study 15.1

Problem. The Rockville Police Department (RPD) would like to identify a predictor variable that they can use to make better staffing decisions concerning the number of patrol officers necessary for any given night shift. They know that violent domestic activity typically increases during the summer months of the year. Officers have long suspected that there is a direct relationship between daytime temperature and nighttime violent domestic activity. These officers have learned to anticipate that they will be very busy responding to nighttime calls if daytime temperatures have been high. The RPD wants to verify that there is indeed a relationship between temperature and violent domestic activities. In order to examine such a relationship, dispatchers have been asked to collect noontime temperature data in central Rockville, along with frequency data for emergency 911 violent domestic activity calls during the night shifts of these same days. If they conclude that these variables are related, they will attempt to develop a model for predicting the frequency of responses and then modify their existing staffing formula to take noontime temperatures into account. The RPD knows that other factors also have an impact upon violent domestic activity, including economic conditions, political circumstances, sporting events, days of the week, and other activities. For example, an increase in violent domestic activity can be predicted several days or even several weeks in advance of championship basketball games. However, the RPD is seeking an improved staffing formula that adjusts for immediate fluctuations in environmental conditions.

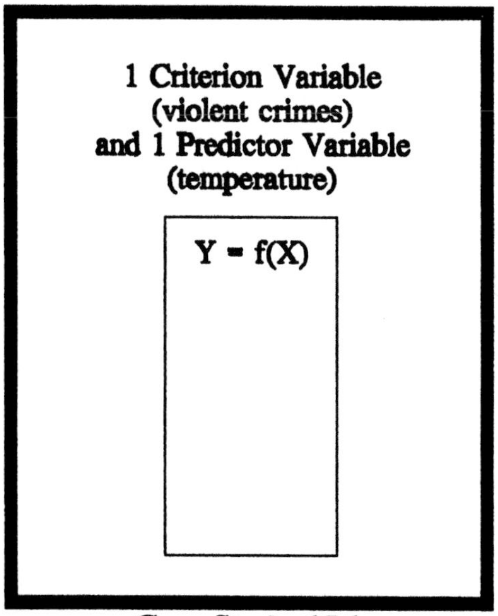

Case Study 15.1

Methodology Solution. The case studies and examples in Chapter 9 through Chapter 14 consisted of one variable of interest that was at least interval level and one or more factors or classification variables that were either nominal or ordinal level. However, Case Study 15.1 consists of two variables that are *both* at least interval level. The variable of interest consists of the number of violent domestic activity calls received during the night shifts, while the other variable consists of noontime temperatures. It would be inappropriate to refer to temperature as a classification variable, since it is not a nominal or ordinal level measure. Instead, we refer to it as a predictor variable. We will follow Figure 15.1, which includes relevant flowcharts from the master flowcharts, to determine an appropriate statistical approach for analyzing Case Study 15.1. We enter the flowcharts at ***Start***. We are not comparing central tendencies, since we do not have subdivisions or groups from which to compute central tendencies. We are not interested in comparing variabilities, either. We are interested in examining the relationship between temperatures and violent domestic activity calls based on correlation, regression, and prediction. Therefore, we will turn to flowchart 8.

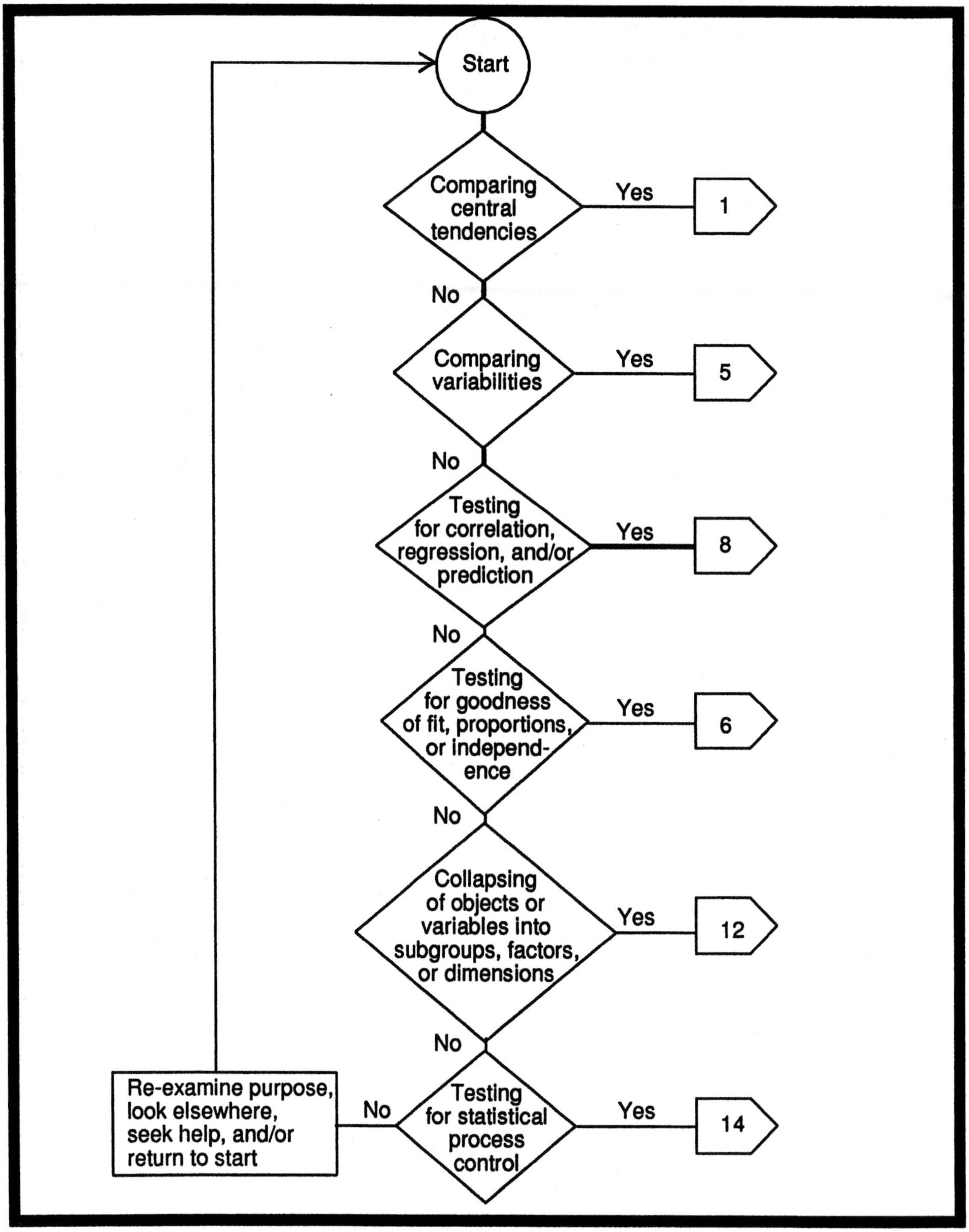

Figure 15.1
Statistical Decision-Making Flowchart for Case Study 15.1

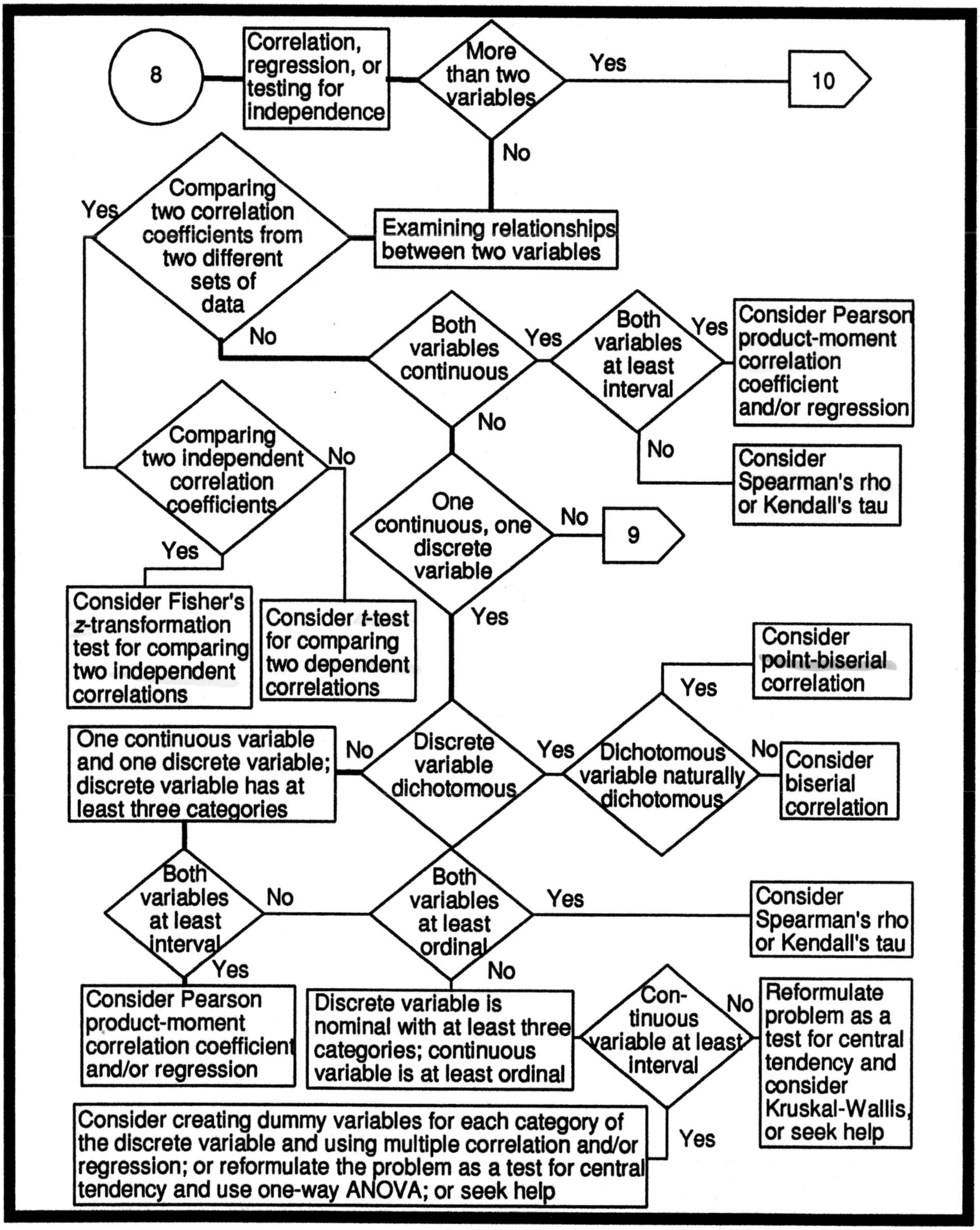

Figure 15.1
Statistical Decision-Making Flowchart for Case Study 15.1
(continued)

Following these flowcharts, we realize that we do not have more than two variables; and we are not comparing two correlation coefficients from two different sets of data, since we only have one set of sample data. Temperature is continuous, and the number of violent domestic activity calls is discrete. (As we shall see, whether the variables are discrete or continuous will not result in a different statistical procedure for this example.) The number of calls is not dichotomous; instead this variable consists of many categories. Finally, both variables are at least interval. We conclude that we should consider using the Pearson product-moment correlation coefficient to examine the relationship between the two variables. If there *is* a significant correlation between these two variables, we should then consider using regression to develop a prediction model. The bold lines in Figure 15.1 show the route taken in the flowcharts. In terms of the research design, we will examine the relationship between one predictor variable and one criterion variable. In terms of the PDCA cycle, we will continue to follow the systematic and orderly approach discussed in Chapter 1, as illustrated in Figure 15.2. In the *plan* stage, we identify the variable of interest and then identify the critical factor or factors related to the problem. In the *do* stage, we plot the data points whenever possible and determine an appropriate mathematical model for evaluating our data. In the *check* stage, we implement the mathematical or analytical model, compute various values, and analyze the findings. Finally, in the *act* stage, we present our findings, make recommendations, and take appropriate actions.

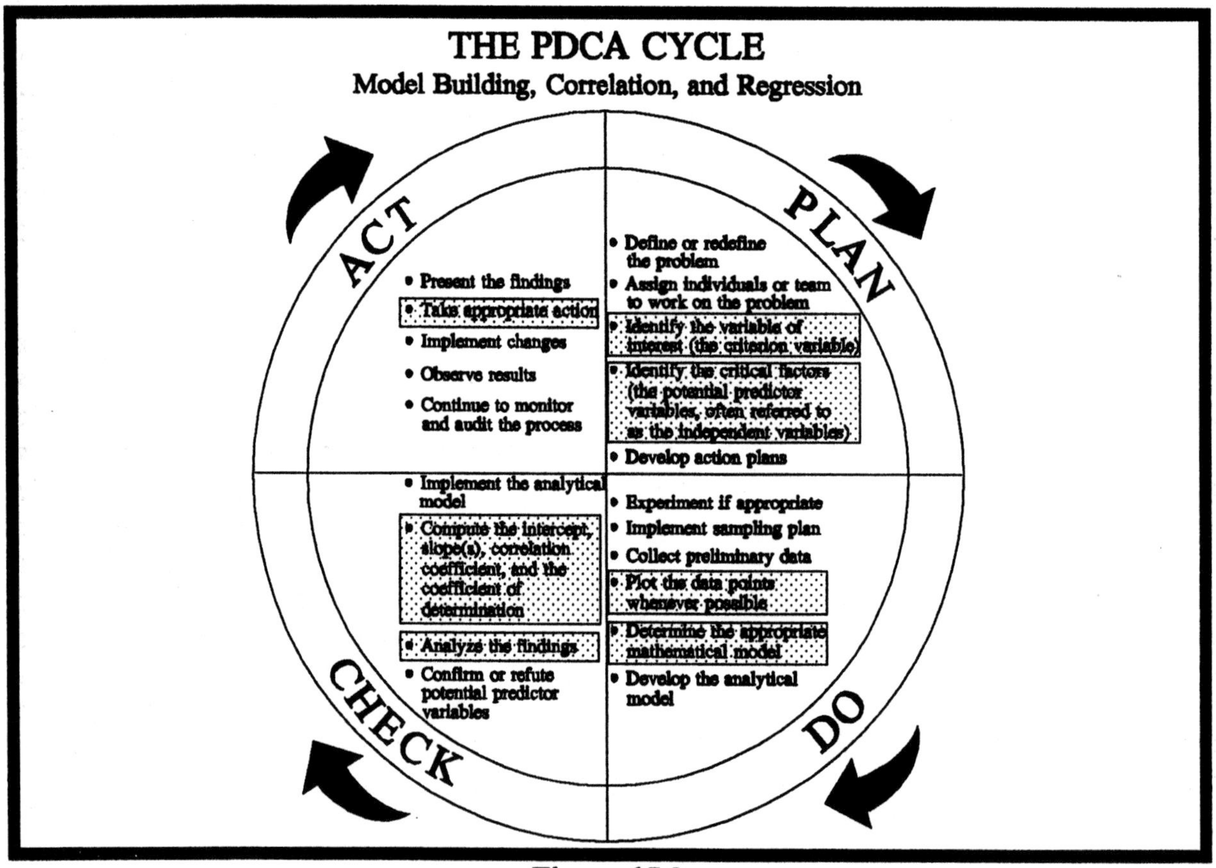

Figure 15.2
The PDCA Cycle As Related to Correlation and Regression

Where Have We Been and Where Are We Going?

Prior to this chapter, we have concentrated on statistical tools for examining situations in which the *variable of interest* was our only interval or ratio level variable. The *other* variable or variables were treated as classification variables or factors. We determined the mean and the standard deviation for the *variable of interest*, and we examined the shape of its frequency distribution. We then attempted to determine whether the mean was big or small, why it was big or small, whether there was very much variation about the mean, and, if so, why the values varied so much. We used the classification variables to help explain the variable of interest by comparing the means of the various categories across these classification variables. If we only had one classification variable, we used *z*-tests, *t*-tests, or one-way analysis of variance, depending upon whether the population variances were known or unknown and whether we had one, two, or more than two categories within the classification variable. Whenever we had more than one classification variable, we found it necessary to use some form of factorial analysis of variance, such as a one-way, two-way, or three-way ANOVA, or perhaps a treatment-by-subjects design. Throughout Chapter 9 to Chapter 14, these *other* variables were either nominal or ordinal level. They were usually referred to as classification variables, although we noted in Chapter 8 and elsewhere that they can also be referred to as dimensions, factors, attribute variables, independent variables, or predictor variables. It is now important to remember that these *other* variables can also be at least interval scale. If so, they usually consist of many categories and will not be referred to as classification variables. Instead, we will refer to them as predictor or independent variables. Chapter 15 discusses statistical procedures that are appropriate for analyzing the relationship between the variable of interest (i.e., the *criterion* or *dependent variable*) and one other variable (i.e., the *predictor* or *independent variable*); Chapter 16 discusses the use of regression to make prediction decisions based on such relationships; and Chapter 17 discusses correlation and regression for situations in which we have one variable of interest and more than one predictor variable—in other words, *multiple regression.*

Returning to Case Study 15.1, the number of calls regarding violent domestic activity is the variable of interest or criterion variable and temperature is the predictor variable. We *could* consider temperature as a classification variable containing many categories. However, if we perform an analysis with number of calls as the criterion variable and temperature as a classification variable, we have an infinite number of categories, one for each possible temperature. We could force temperature to consist of *two* categories by placing all temperatures below some arbitrary point, perhaps 80°, into one group and all temperatures above that point into another group. We could then perform a two-sample independent *t*-test to compare the means of the number of violent domestic activity calls for these two groups of temperatures, as suggested in Figure 15.3.A. Alternatively, we could group temperatures together into a number of arbitrarily defined categories such as 70° or less, 71°-80°, 81°-90°, and 91° or greater. This approach would result in *four* groups, and we could perform a one-way ANOVA to compare the means of these four groups, as suggested in Figure 15.3.B.

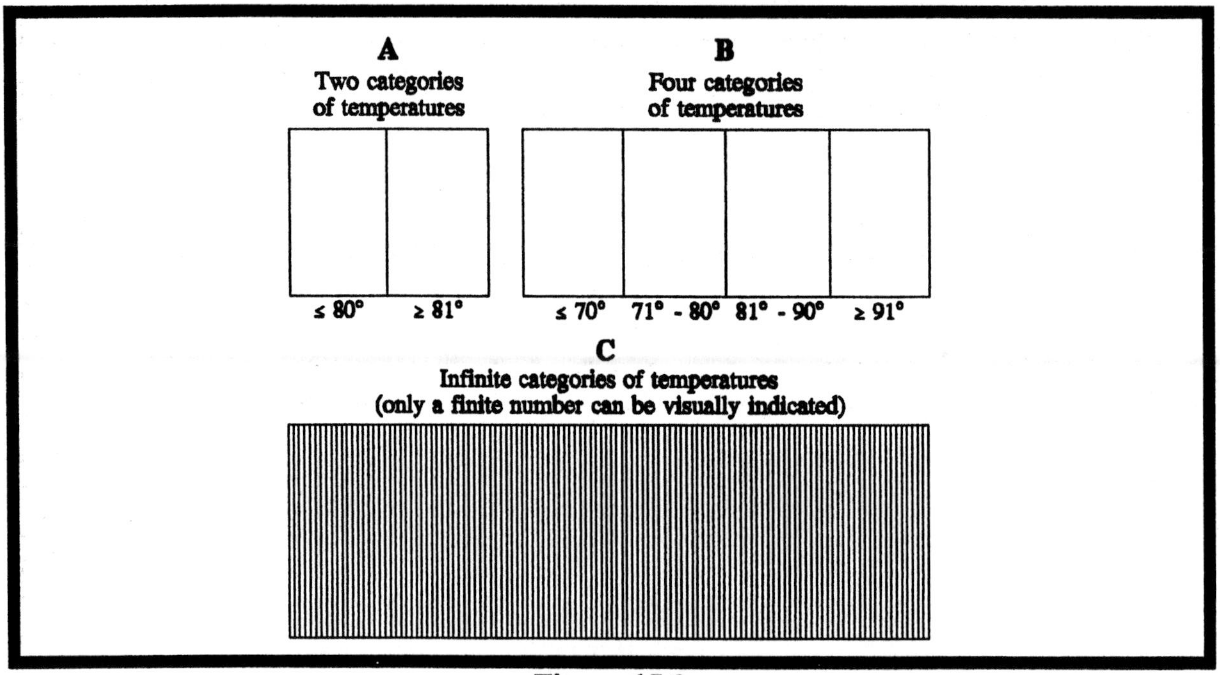

Figure 15.3
Two Categories, Four Categories, and Infinite Categories

With either of these approaches, the newly created categories have been reduced to ordinal level data at best; and we have lost a great deal of information in the process. For example, there is a considerable, perhaps even significant, amount of variation between 81° and 90° that might be related to variation in the number of violent domestic activities. Information contained in such additional variation will go untapped if we use the two sample independent *t*-test or the one-way analysis of variance to analyze the data. The graph in Figure 15.3.C suggests that temperature consists of many, many categories---in fact, an infinite number of categories. If all such categories were included in the illustration, Figure 15.3.C would appear to be a solid mass consisting of an infinite number of lines. It is not practical to treat temperature as consisting of many, many categories. Instead, we will use correlation and regression analysis to take full advantage of the additional information contained in such variable. By using these tools, we can make better decisions, increase our ability to identify and understand relationships, and enhance our ability to predict.

Historical Perspective

Throughout history, a knowledge of relationships among variables has been used to make predictions into the future. Although the methods of our ancestors were not as sophisticated as ours, ancient civilizations were often able to predict future events based on past occurrences. Fishing conditions, droughts, temperature variations, crop production, soil quality, availability of game for food, military strategies, and other concerns were estimated from an awareness of existing relationships among variables. Sometimes these relationships were determined through guesswork or superstition; other times they were based on more scientific approaches. Therefore, predictions ranged from very inaccurate to very accurate. As mathematics, statistics, and scientific technology advanced, quantitative methods were discovered that increased the understanding of relationships between variables and improved the ability to make accurate predictions.

As discussed in Appendix K, the concepts of correlation and regression were specifically advanced as a result of studies conducted by Sir Francis Galton in the Anthropometric Laboratory in England. Galton was comparing the heights of offsprings to the heights of their parents. In order to understand the relationships between these two variables, he converted the pairs of data to z-scores. He then plotted the results and noted that the heights of the offsprings did not increase as rapidly as the heights of their parents. He referred to this phenomenon as *the law of filial regression*, since the heights of the offsprings tended to "regress toward the mean." In order to measure the degree of relationship among these and other variables in some quantitative manner, he developed a value, r, that he referred to as the index of co-relation, to describe the phenomenon he had discovered. Galton then asked James Douglas Hamilton Dickson to develop a more mathematically based equation, and the results were later published as an appendix to one of Galton's papers. Dickson's coefficient was further advanced by Karl Pearson, who is responsible for the present mathematical state of the correlation coefficient and who became Galton's esteemed successor at the Anthropometric Laboratory. The r-value is often formally referred to as the *Pearson product-moment correlation coefficient* in his honor. Although there are several techniques available for measuring relationships among variables, this is the most commonly used method. Other approaches are either special forms of the Pearson product-moment correlation coefficient and are algebraically equivalent to it or are measures only appropriate under unique situations. Chapter 15 focuses on these correlation coefficients, while Chapter 16 and Chapter 17 focus on the concepts of prediction and regression. In other words, we first determine whether there is a relationship; then, if there is a relationship, we use the knowledge of this relationship to make predictions based on bivariate or multiple regression.

Conceptualizing Relationships and Correlation Coefficients

Most readers are familiar with the use of entrance examinations and previous grade point averages (GPA) as admission requirements for college, based on the assumption that there is a relationship between examination scores, GPA, and potential for academic success. In a similar manner, companies use pre-employment variables as a part of the selection process to estimate potential performance for job applicants. In the financial world, indices have been used by economic forecasters to estimate fluctuations in the economy. Corporate planners have used present market conditions to predict the future growth of the industry. Engineers have used measures of relative humidity to predict tolerance levels of products. Nutritionists have used the amount of oil in cookies to predict the amount of cholesterol per cookie after baking. Manufacturers have used the diameter of a sheath to predict its relative strength. Obtaining accurate measures of relationships among variables such as these is of major importance to decision makers. In fact, people in all walks of life are regularly affected by the results of forecasts, predictions, and scientific conclusions.

Example 15.1. For Example 15.1, our variable of interest is customer satisfaction. As suggested in Table 15.1, a chain of relationships may exist between this criterion variable and a number of other variables. We know that customer satisfaction will be related, at least in part, to product lifetime. Product lifetime will in turn be a function of other variables, including employee performance, the quality of materials used to make the product, the quality of the machinery, and the process used to produce the product. Each of these variables will be related to still other variables. Employee performance is a function of the quality of the employees that have been hired, the company reward systems, the quality of employee training, their knowledge of the job, their attitude, commitment, and motivation, the skills of their immediate supervisors, and their orientation toward teamwork. The quality of the employees hired may be a function of their performance on some pre-employment selection tool and the ability of that tool to differentiate between potentially successful and unsuccessful employees. The company reward system may be based on company growth, employee performance, and market conditions. Finally, company growth is a function of customer satisfaction, market conditions, and economic conditions. The chain of relationships has now gone full circle.

Table 15.1
Chain of Relationships

	Variables of Interest	*Predictor Variables*
1.	Customer satisfaction	Product lifetime
2.	Product lifetime	Employee performance, quality of materials, quality of machinery, and the process itself
3.	Employee performance	Company reward system, training, knowledge, attitude, commitment, motivation, the skills of immediate supervisors, and team orientation
4.	Company reward system	Company growth, employee performance, and market conditions
5.	Company growth	Customer satisfaction, market conditions, and economic conditions

Correlation

The word ***correlate*** consists of two terms: ***co*** and ***relate***. When we want to know if two variables are related, we want to determine whether they go together. That is, are they correlated? The correlation coefficient is a numerical measure of that relationship. In this and most statistics textbooks, the population correlation coefficient is symbolized by the Greek letter ρ (rho) and the sample correlation is symbolized by the Roman letter r. All correlation coefficients must fall within the range of -1.00 to +1.00. The sign associated with this coefficient indicates the direction of the relationship---either positive or negative. A zero correlation coefficient suggests that no predictable relationship exists between the variables. We will discuss the calculation of these correlations and methods for determining whether they are statistically significant very soon.

Example 15.2: Positive Correlation. For Example 15.2, suppose we want to examine the relationship between the heights and weights of a group of 100 people who range in age from 5 to 25. We would expect to find a *positive* correlation between these two variables. That is, we would expect to find that taller people will generally weigh more than shorter people, especially since our sample includes both children and adults. Although the relationship between height and weight is not perfect (i.e., we cannot perfectly predict weight from height), a positive relationship definitely exists. Height and weight should *correlate positively.*

Example 15.3: Negative Correlation. For Example 15.3, suppose we want to examine the relationship between employee satisfaction and company grievance rates. This is an example of a *negative* relationship. As employee satisfaction increases, the number of grievances filed by employees typically decreases in most companies. Again, the relationship is not perfect, but a negative relationship does exist. Employee satisfaction and grievance rates should *correlate negatively.*

Example 15.4: No Correlation. For Example 15.4, suppose we examine the relationship between heights of adult males and the length of time these adults have been employed by the company. We do not expect to find a meaningful relationship between these two variables. In fact, we would be surprised to find any relationship. The absence of a relationship is reflected by a near-zero correlation. Heights of adult males and their length of time with the company should have approximately *zero correlation.*

As we can see, a variety of possible relationships may exist. Before we make decisions about such relationships, we should ask ourselves a series of basic questions, as suggested in Table 15.2. First, we will want to determine whether a ***relationship does in fact exist.*** We usually calculate a correlation coefficient to make this decision, and we should determine whether this correlation is statistically significant before continuing with our analysis. Second, if such a relationship exists, we will want to determine whether this relationship is ***perfect.*** The existence of perfect relationships will be very obvious when they exist. They are uncommon in the physical sciences, somewhat unusual in business, and quite rare in the behavioral sciences. Third, if a relationship exists, we will want to determine whether the relationship follows a ***linear or nonlinear*** pattern. Plotting our data will be helpful in recognizing linear and nonlinear trends. Fourth, if a linear relationship exists, we will need to determine whether the direction of that relationship is ***positive or negative.*** The sign of the correlation coefficient will provide information about this concern. After we examine these four issues and make appropriate decisions regarding the strength and nature of our relationships, we can develop regression equations from which to make predictions. At that point, we can apply the bivariate regression models discussed in Chapter 16 or the multiple regression models discussed in Chapter 17.

Table 15.2
Initial Considerations for Examining Relationships

1. Is there a relationship?
2. If there is a relationship, is it perfect?
3. If there is a relationship, is it linear or nonlinear?
4. If there is a linear relationship, is the directionality positive or negative?
5. If there is a relationship, is it statistically significant?

Visual Representations of Relationships

Pictorial representations are often helpful for conceptualizing the nature of relationships. First, we will use Venn diagrams to examine the nature of relationships from the perspective of shared variance. Second, we will create frequency distributions for each variable taken separately. Third, we will plot our paired data in the form of scatter diagrams.

Example 15.5: A Picture of a Perfect Positive Relationship. Example 15.5 illustrates a perfect positive correlation. Suppose we want to determine whether there is a relationship between the ages of 10 people hired by our company ten years ago and their ages ten years later. Table 15.3 gives their ages over both time periods. The mean for this sample ten years ago was 34.1, and the standard deviation was 7.61. The mean for these same people based on current data is 44.1, and the standard deviation is still at 7.61. These findings should not be too surprising! Assuming that our employees have provided honest and accurate information and are all still living, each of these individuals will have aged by a constant amount of 10 years.

Table 15.3
Relationship Between Ages Taken 10 Years Apart

Person	*X* *Ages 10 Years Ago*	*Y* *Current Age*
1	44	54
2	24	34
3	26	36
4	28	38
5	30	40
6	31	41
7	34	44
8	46	56
9	38	48
10	40	50

We can see from the data in Table 15.3 that we have variation within our sample of employees, since not all individuals are the exact same age. We also see that the variation ten years later is identical to the initial variation in age. The factors that contribute to the variation in the *X*-variable are the same factors that contribute to the variation in the *Y*-variable. Thus, we have a perfect positive correlation. Figure 15.4 displays this relationship in a Venn diagram.

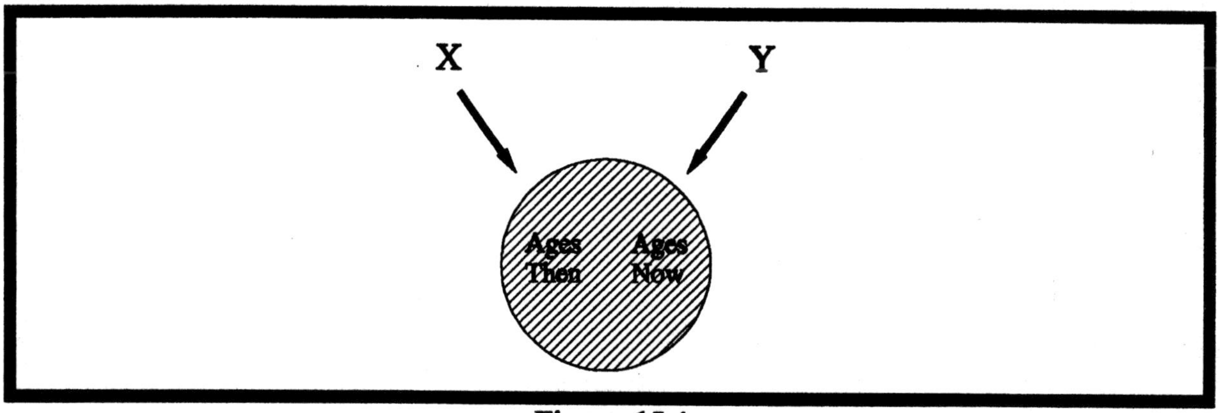

Figure 15.4
Venn Diagram for Employee Ages Assessed 10 Years Apart

The Venn diagram illustrates that the two variables occupy the exact same space in our diagram. The two variables overlap perfectly, and the picture gives the appearance that only one circle exists! It should not be too surprising to find that these two variables correlate perfectly with one another, since the shared variance is 100%. Therefore, 100% of the variation in the *Y*-variable can be explained by a knowledge of the *X*-variable. We will discuss the concept of the *percent of variation explained*, or explained variance, in Chapter 16.

Example 15.6: A Picture of No Relationship. Example 15.6 gives an illustration of the absence of any correlation. Suppose that we are attempting to determine whether a relationship exists between the number of hits collected per week in baseball games played in the National League during a 10-week period and the total number of sales receipts per week at a major department store during the same 10-week time period. These data have been recorded in Table 15.4. The sample mean for the number of hits, the *X*-variable, is 630.0, while the sample mean for the number of sales receipts, the *Y*-variable, is 550.1. An examination of these two variables reveals that each variable has variance about its respective mean. The standard deviation for the number of hits recorded per week is 211.00, while the standard deviation for the number of weekly sales receipts over the 10-week period is 105.41.

Did we expect to find a relationship between these two variables? We might speculate that if there are many hits during a week, baseball fans may be in a very good mood and may celebrate by shopping, perhaps for baseball equipment. If so, we might expect a positive correlation. Alternatively, we may speculate that if baseball is extremely exciting during a particular week, fans might spend more time listing to baseball on radio, watching games on television, or going to the ballpark instead of going shopping. In this case, we might expect a

Table 15.4
Relationship Between Hits and Sales Receipts

Week Number	*X* *Number of Hits per Week in National League*	*Y* *Number of Weekly Sales*
1	492	591
2	644	339
3	566	504
4	430	712
5	848	620
6	894	464
7	368	490
8	974	644
9	636	572
10	448	565

negative correlation. Realistically, however, most of us would be surprised if we found *any* meaningful relationship between the two variables. We would tend to expect that hits and sales receipts in department stores will not correlate.

Figure 15.5 presents a Venn diagram illustrating how these two variables co-relate, or do not co-relate as is the case in this example. The *X*-circle represents the variable regarding hits, while the *Y*-circle represents the variable regarding sales. When we draw these two circles, the first one drawn can be located anywhere within the Venn diagram. Once the first circle is located, the second one becomes fixed in regard to its spatial relationship to the other. Each circle represents 100% of the variation associated with its respective variable.[1] As can be seen in Figure 15.5, the two circles do not overlap. That is, although each variable has variation within its own set of numbers, there is no common or shared variance among the two variables. None of the variation in the number of sales can be attributed to the variation in the number of hits. Thus, there is no ***covariance***, or common variance, between the two variables. The two variables do not relate to each other, and the correlation is zero[2].

---

[1]Since correlation coefficients are based upon the standardization of raw data, the two circles are the same size. As we know, all standardized distributions have means of zero and standard deviations of one. Thus, when the two variables are converted to standard form, the variances are equal.

[2]Computational equations for the correlation coefficient and the covariance will be presented shortly.

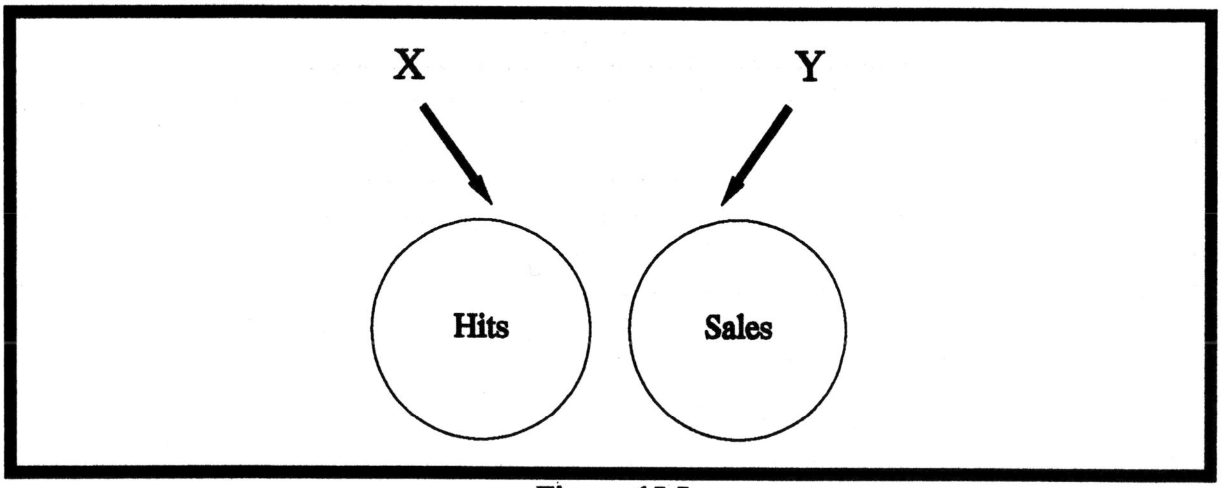

Figure 15.5
Hitting Productivity and Weekly Sales

Example 15.7: A Picture of a Positive but not Perfect Relationship. Example 15.7 gives an illustration of a positive but not perfect relationship. Suppose that we want to examine the relationship between job performance and percent pay increase. Data have been collected for a set of 10 employees. The *X*-variable is their job performance based on a 20-point rating scale, with 20 being the highest possible performance score. The *Y*-variable is the percent pay increase given to these employees after their performance evaluations. Table 15.5 gives a listing of the data for this example.

Table 15.5
Relationship Between Performance and Percent Pay Increase

Employee	*X* *Job Performance*	*Y* *Percent Pay Increase*
1	14	5%
2	10	2%
3	9	1%
4	11	3%
5	17	9%
6	15	7%
7	15	10%
8	16	8%
9	18	10%
10	17	5%

The mean performance score for this sample of employees is 14.2, while the standard deviation for performance scores is 3.16. The mean percent pay increase for these same 10 employees is 6%, while the standard deviation for pay increase is 3.30%. The Venn diagram given in Figure 15.6 indicates that these variables do not perfectly overlap, as in Example 15.5.

Yet, they are not completely independent of one another, as in Example 15.6. There does appear to be a considerable amount of overlap, common variance, or covariance among the variables. A large percentage of the variation in pay increase, perhaps as much as 75% based on visual observation, can be accounted for by a knowledge of the variation in employees' performance scores. This percent will soon be identified as r^2. It is sometimes abbreviated as ***RSQ***, and it is often referred to as the ***coefficient of determination***. Computational approaches for *r* and *RSQ* will be discussed in detail in Chapter 15, Chapter 16, and again in Chapter 17. As can be seen by a comparison of the Venn diagrams in Figure 15.4, Figure 15.5, and Figure 15.6, the more closely the variables are related, the more common variance they share. As the relationship between our variables increases, the overlap in variance increases.

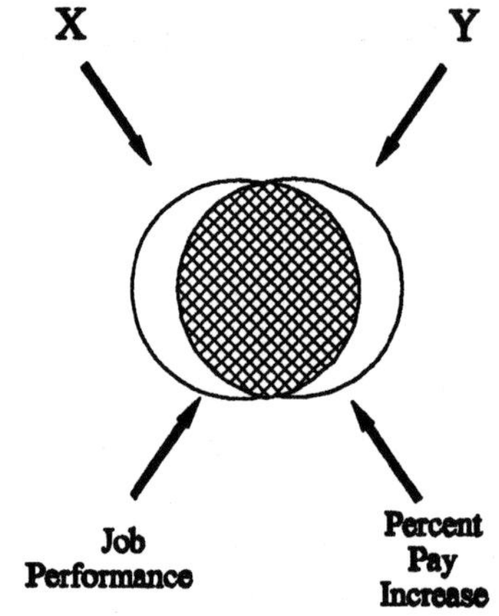

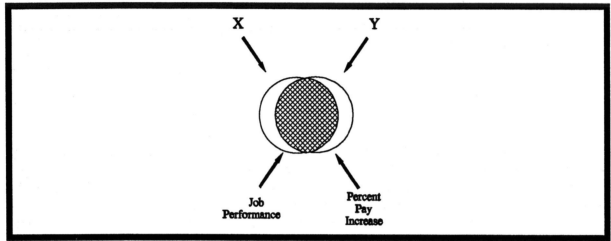

Figure 15.6
Job Performance and Percent Pay Increase

Frequency Distributions and Scatter Diagrams

The relationship between two variables can also be visualized by examining the frequency distributions of the *X*-variable and the *Y*-variable taken separately, and then by examining their shared frequency distribution. We will use a ***scatter diagram*** to represent this shared distribution.

Example 15.5 Revisited. For Example 15.5, we found that the mean age for the 10 employees was 34.1, based on their ages at the time they were hired. None of these individuals had a recorded age of exactly 34.1; thus, we would make errors if we used 34.1 to estimate each individual's age. Further, no two employees were the exact same age at that date, so we have variation in their ages. Figure 15.7 gives a frequency distribution for the *X*-variable, illustrating that deviations exist about the mean age. As usual, when we create frequency distributions we put the raw values on the horizontal axis and the frequencies on the vertical axis. Figure 15.8 gives a frequency distribution for the *Y*-variable, based on the ages of these same employees at the end of the 10-year period. The mean is now 10 years greater, while the standard deviation is the same as before. In the previous paragraph, we noted that the usual practice is to locate the raw values on the horizontal axis and the frequencies on the vertical axis. However, we will ***reverse*** this practice for the *Y*-variable in the present illustrations. This will allow us to better understand bivariate relationships. In Figure 15.8, the raw values are located on the vertical axis and the frequencies are located on the horizontal axis.

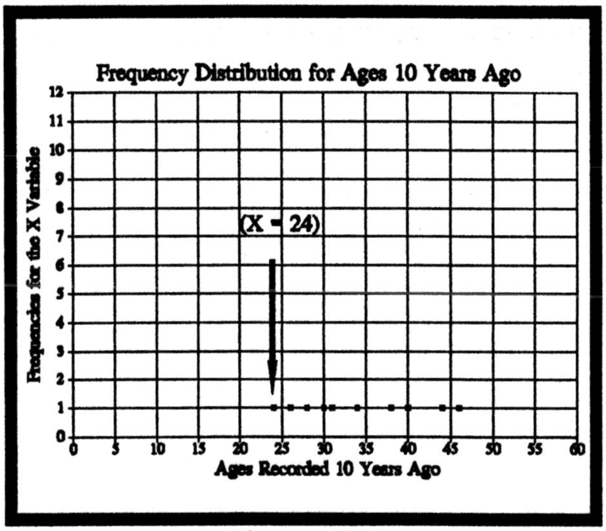

Figure 15.7
Frequency Distribution 10 Years Ago

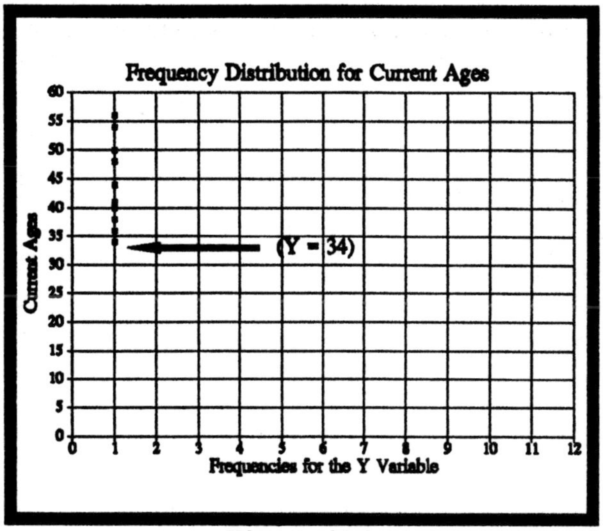

Figure 15.8
Frequency Distribution Now

If we combine Figure 15.7 with Figure 15.8, we can develop a shared frequency distribution or scatter diagram based on the two variables taken together. This scatter diagram, as shown in Figure 15.9, allows us to graphically observe the *bivariate relationship* between the two variables. For example, the second person in the set of data can be located in two-dimensional space. This person was 24 years of age at the hiring date; 10 years later, this same person is 34. First, we locate this person on Figure 15.7; second, we locate the same person on Figure 15.8. Third, we locate a point for these paired values as illustrated in Figure 15.9. This point is at the intersection of 24 on the X-variable and 34 on the Y-variable. In the same manner, we locate the remaining nine employees on our scatter diagram in Figure 15.9.

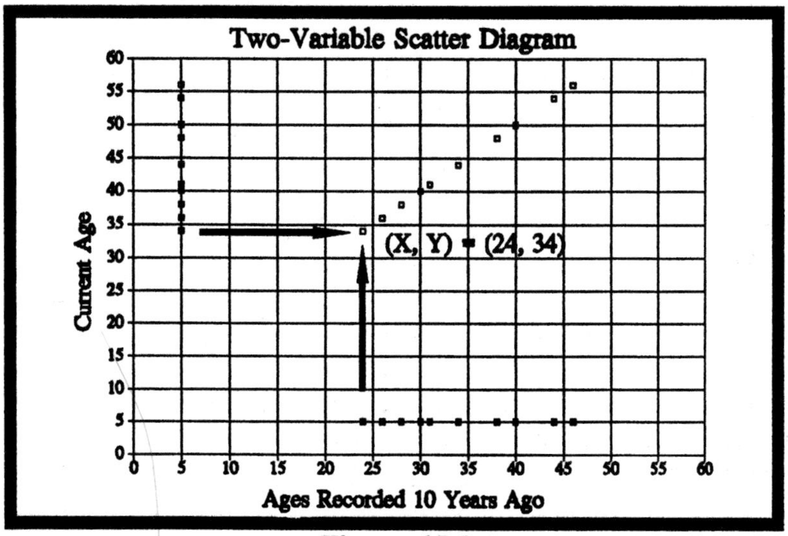

Figure 15.9
Two-Variable Scatter Diagram for Ages Then and Now

Figure 15.9 provides a clear presentation of the relationship between the two variables. All of the values fall in a perfect straight line, and none of the points deviate from this line. Although we have variation about the mean for the *Y*-variable and variation about the mean for the *X*-variable, we have no variation about this bivariate straight line. A one-to-one relationship exists in our graph; for every one year that we move over on the *X*-axis, we move up one year on the *Y*-axis. In Chapter 16, we will determine that this line has a slope of 1 and an intercept of 10. For the present chapter, we simply conclude that with Example 15.5 we can account for 100% of the variation in the *Y*-variable by knowing the variation in the *X*-variable. This is consistent with the conclusions we made earlier based on the Venn diagram for this example.

Example 15.6 Revisited. We knew that there was a perfect relationship between the two variables in Example 15.5. They had perfectly overlapping variance, and we could account for 100% of the variation in the *Y*-variable by a knowledge of the variation in the *X*-variable. However, such relationships are rarely so obvious, and we can almost never explain 100% of the variation of one variable from a knowledge of another variable. Example 15.6 illustrates just the opposite circumstance. As we found in Figure 15.5, there was no common variance between the weekly number of hits and number of sales receipts. Figure 15.10, Figure 15.11, and Figure 15.12 demonstrate that although the same approach is followed for graphing these two variables as was used with Example 15.5, we certainly do not obtain perfect results. In fact, when we combine the information available about the *X*-variable and the *Y*-variable and plot the paired data points on a scatter diagram such as shown in Figure 15.12, we do not recognize any clear relationship between the two variables. The points do not fall in a straight line; therefore, we will have variation about any straight line that we might attempt to use to describe these data. We will also have a considerable amount of error in our prediction. For now, we will simply state that the line of best fit for Example 15.6 has a slope of 0 and an intercept of 550.1. In Chapter 16 we will present equations for determining the slope and intercept for such lines.

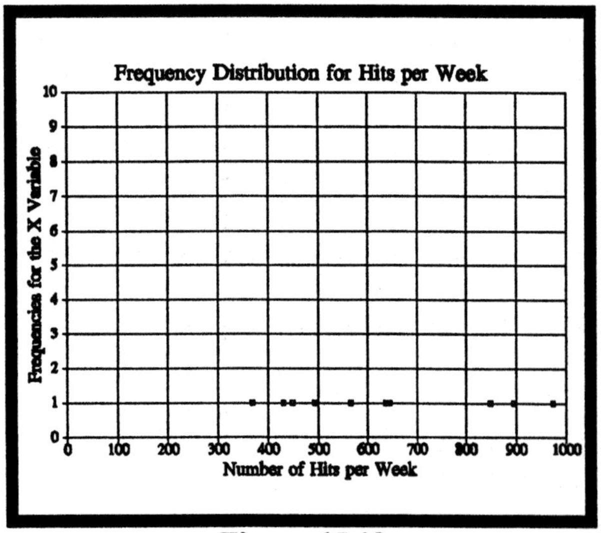

Figure 15.10
Frequency Distribution for Hits

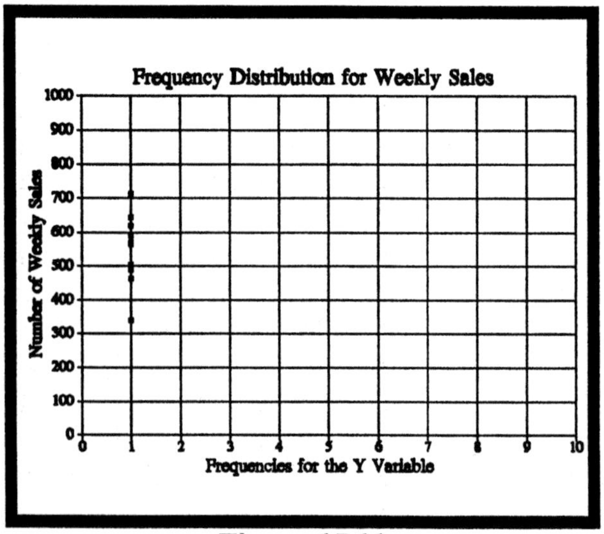

Figure 15.11
Frequency Distribution for Sales

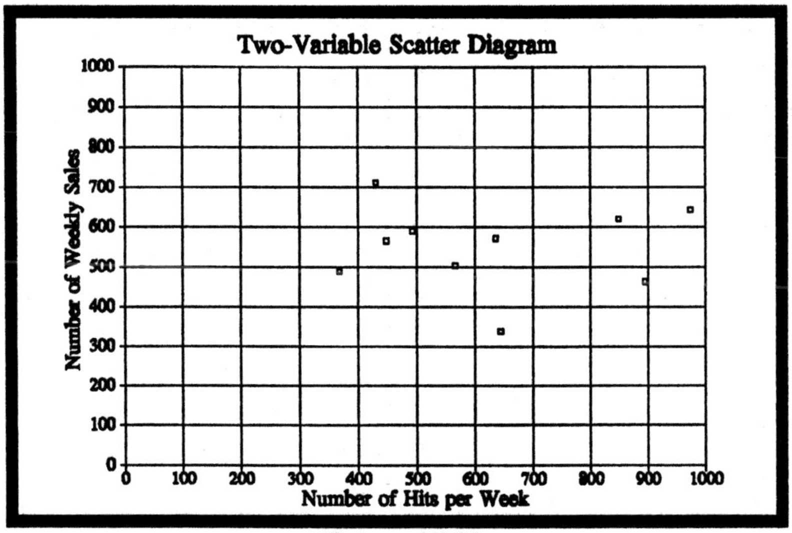

Figure 15.12
Two-Variable Scatter Diagram for Sales and Hits

Example 15.7 Revisited. Returning to Example 15.7, we find a less dramatic graphical representation. We do not have a perfect relationship as we had with Example 15.5, and we do not have a completely chance relationship as we had with Example 15.6. Instead, we find that the percent pay increase variable has *some* covariance, or shared variance, with performance scores. We again observe that we have variance about the mean for performance scores, as illustrated in Figure 15.13, and we have variance about the mean for percent pay increase, as illustrated in Figure 15.14. When the two figures are combined to create Figure 15.15, a ***linear trend*** appears but not a perfect pattern. The 10 data points do not fall on a straight line as they did in Example 15.5; thus, there is no perfect relationship.

However, unlike Example 15.6, many of the points do appear to be related in Example 15.7, as illustrated in Figure 15.6 and confirmed in Figure 15.15. If we cover up several of the unusual cases (perhaps the outliers or special causes), the trend becomes even more obvious. For example, the seventh person had a performance score of 15 and a pay increase of 10%; could this be the boss's son? On the other hand, the tenth person had a performance score of 17 but a pay increase of only 5%; could this be the boss's former son-in-law? Are there special causes associated with these two individuals? Without the inclusion of these two cases, a much stronger trend would be apparent. With the inclusion of these two observations, we know that other variables must be contributing to percent pay increase in addition to performance. In fact, an observation of the graphical relationship between these two variables gives us an opportunity to observe the existence of cases that do not conform to the typical trend of the data. For now, we will simply state that the line of best fit for Example 15.7 has a slope of .09 and an intercept of 6.84. We will discuss the ***slope*** and the ***intercept*** in great detail in Chapter 16, at which time we will determine equations for computing these values.

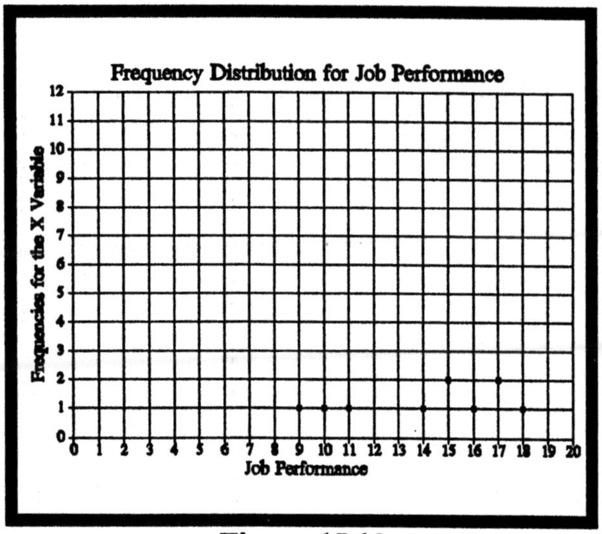

Figure 15.13
Frequency Distribution for Performance

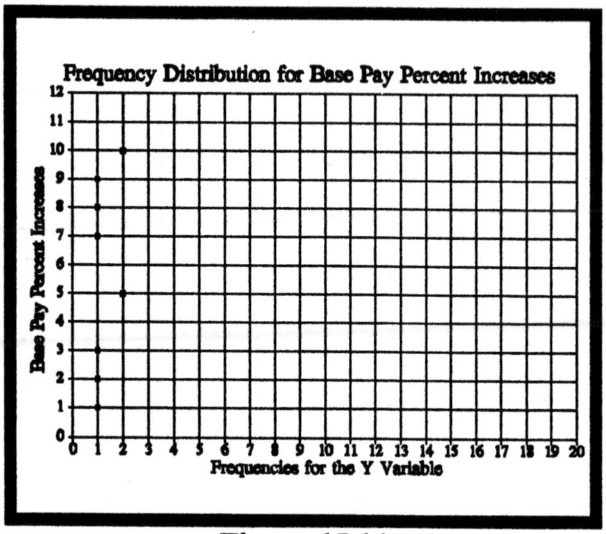

Figure 15.14
Frequency Distribution for Pay Increases

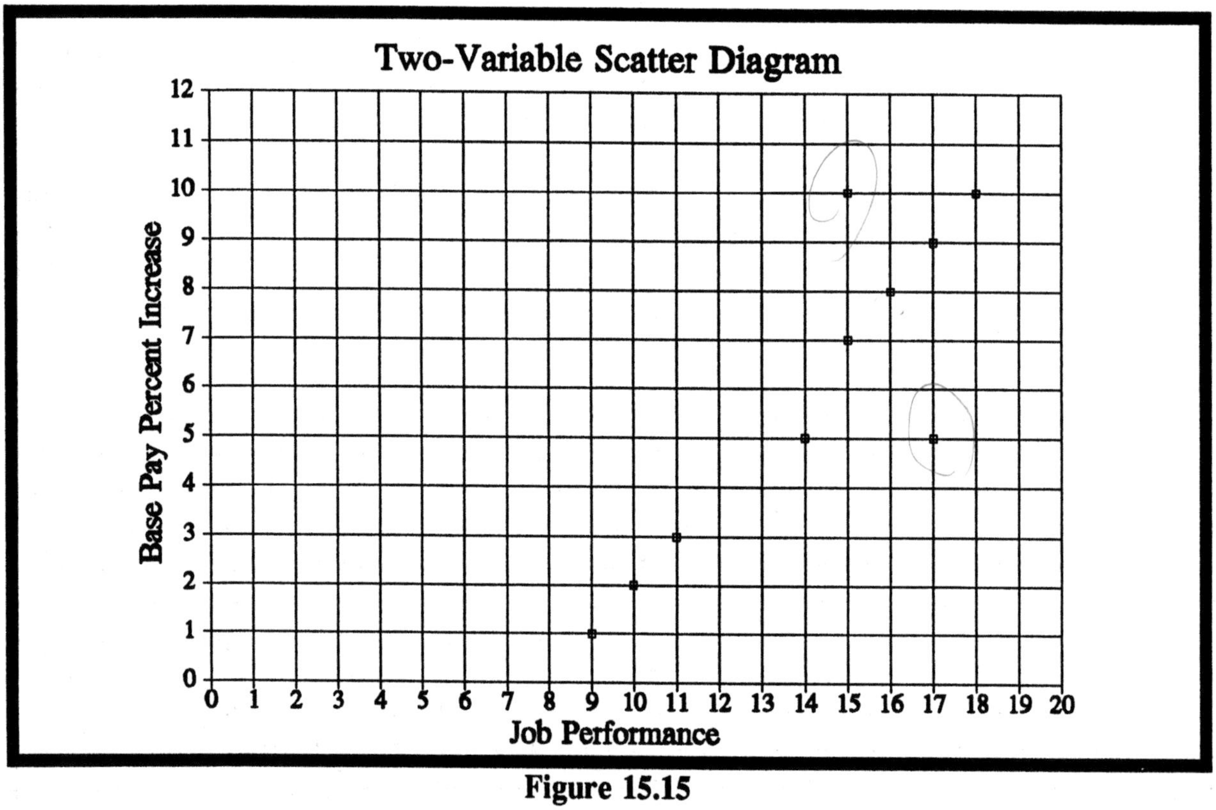

Figure 15.15
Two-Variable Scatter Diagram:
Performance and Percent Pay Increases

Interpreting Scatter Diagrams

The relationship between variables is often plotted on two-dimensional graph paper in the form of scatter diagrams, such as those used in Figure 15.9, Figure 15.12, and Figure 15.15. These scatter diagrams consist of data points that are located according to the coordinates for each observation on the X-axis and Y-axis. When we write mathematical expressions in the form of relationships, we usually state that the Y-variable is a function of the X-variable; thus, the expression becomes: $Y = f(X)$. Bivariate mathematical relationships such as these are graphed by placing the X-variable on the ***abscissa***, or the horizontal axis, and the Y-variable on the ***ordinate***, or the vertical axis. Following this tradition with correlation and regression analysis, we locate the independent, or predictor variable, on the X-axis and the dependent, or criterion variable, on the Y-axis.

Figure 15.16 illustrates examples of six different types of plots. Figure 15.16.A gives an example of a perfect positive correlation. Notice that the data points extend from the lower left to the upper right portion of the graph to form a perfect straight line, as did Figure 15.9. On the other hand, Figure 15.16.B is an example of a perfect negative relationship. Here, the data points extend from upper left to lower right, again forming a perfect straight line. This time the line falls in the opposite direction. The slope for Figure 15.16.A is positive, while the slope for Figure 15.16.B is negative, as we will discuss in Chapter 16. If a perfect relationship exists between the two variables, we can make errorless predictions about the existing set of Y-values from a knowledge of the X-values. As stated earlier, we seldom work with variables that have perfect relationships, especially in business and the behavioral sciences.

Figure 15.16.C is an example of a high positive but not perfect relationship. While this figure follows the same general pattern as Figure 15.16.A, the values do not fall in a perfect straight line. Conversely, Figure 15.16.D is an example of a high negative but not perfect relationship. Again, this figure follows the same general pattern as Figure 15.16.B, but the values do not fall in a perfect negative straight line.

Figure 15.16.E is an example of the absence of any relationship between the two variables. This is the type of graph we might expect when the relationship between the variables is simply due to chance, with no discernable pattern. Finally, Figure 15.16.F is an example of a nonlinear relationship. As we can see, the pattern for these data points increases from lower left to upper right at the onset of the graph. However, we notice that the pattern reverses itself about half way through the graph, decreasing from upper left to lower right as we move along the X-axis. This is an example of a ***parabola***. Such relationships are not completely uncommon in data analysis, and we need to be aware of the existence of nonlinear patterns or trends when they exist. We will state an important practical rule here, and we will repeat it numerous times later: The best way to recognize a pattern among the data points is to ***plot the data***. In the past, creating manual plots was very time-consuming. However, with access to a spreadsheet such as Excel, Lotus 1-2-3, PlanPerfect, or Quattro, or with access to some computer software package such as SAS, SPSS, Execustat, or Statgraphics, we can quickly plot our data. Thus, there is little excuse for not plotting points at the onset of our exploratory data analysis!

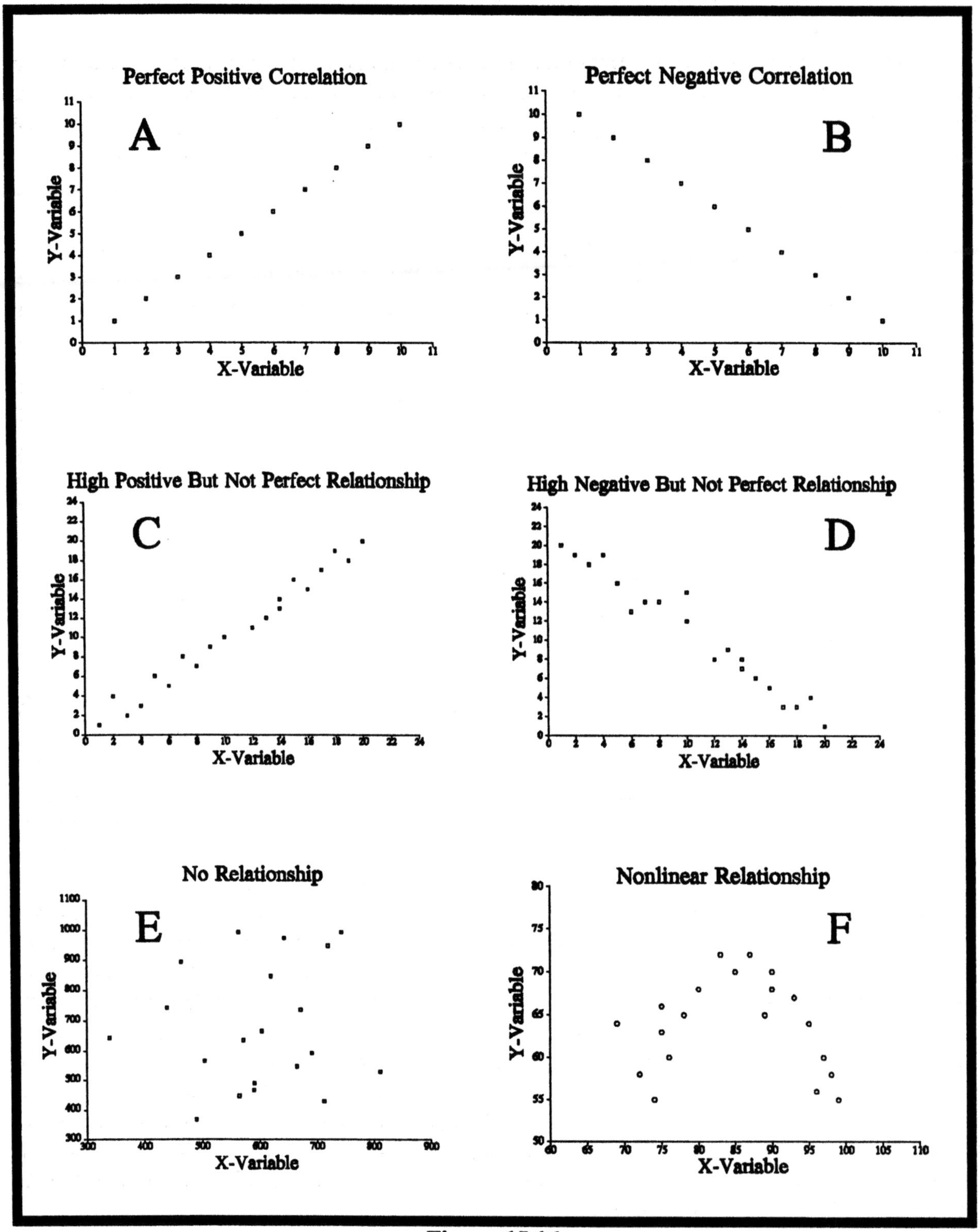

Figure 15.16
Various Plots for Scatter Diagrams

Cautions and Pitfalls When Examining Relationships

We have much to gain by examining the relationships among variables. However, the discovery of such a relationship sometimes leads us to overzealous interpretations of our findings and erroneous conclusions. Consequently, we offer four cautions regarding pitfalls to avoid when examining relationships, as included in Table 15.6 and discussed in the following pages.

Table 15.6
Cautions and Pitfalls

1. A strong correlation does not necessarily imply a ***cause-and-effect*** relationship.

2. Not all relationships are ***linear***. We must consider the possibility of ***nonlinear*** relationships as well.

3. Our conclusions are limited by the ***range restrictions*** of our data.

4. ***Sample size limitations*** reduce the accuracy of our conclusions.

Cause-and-Effect

Our first caution is that just because two variables are related, we cannot automatically conclude that there is a cause-and-effect relationship between these variables. One variable does not necessarily *cause* occurrences or changes in the other variable. Statistically speaking, a correlation coefficient that approaches ±1.00 does not necessarily mean that a cause-and-effect relationship exists. In fact, fluctuations in both variables may be caused by fluctuations in other variables that have not been considered by our model. For example, the volume of cocaine sold in the United States has increased over time, and the salaries of teachers have increased over the same time period. These two variables are highly correlated in a positive direction; yet, we should not conclude that one variable necessarily causes changes in the other variable to occur. As a second example, we know that the ratio of female to male accountants has increased over the past 20 years. During this same time period, there has been a gradual depletion of the ozone layer. Does this imply that an increase in female accountants has resulted in a decrease in the ozone layer? While these two variables are highly correlated in a negative direction, it would be preposterous to draw such a conclusion. As a more obvious example, there is a very high positive correlation between the length of our left arm and the length of our right arm. However, the length of one arm is not caused by the length of the other arm. Genetics and nutrition contribute to this relationship; therefore, these variables must be included in any model used to explain the nature of this relationship.

Linear vs. Nonlinear Relationships

Our second caution is that we cannot generally assume that all relationships follow a linear pattern. It is certainly possible that the X-variable and the Y-variable are related in some nonlinear manner. Although the present chapter will be primarily concerned with linear models, we must always be aware of the possibility of a nonlinear, or *curvilinear*, relationship. As stated earlier, one way to detect linear or nonlinear relationships is to plot the points.

Example 15.8. We will use Example 15.8 to illustrate a nonlinear pattern. Suppose that we have examined the relationship between productivity levels and temperatures in the work environment at a particular plant. Our findings may suggest that productivity is very low at the low ends of the temperature range (e.g., 30°), gradually increases to maximum productivity at more optimal work temperatures (e.g., 68° to 72°), and then gradually decreases as the work environment continues to get hotter and hotter. Clearly, the relationship between the two variables is nonlinear. If we plot the data on two-dimensional graph paper, the scatter diagram may appear as given in Figure 15.17.

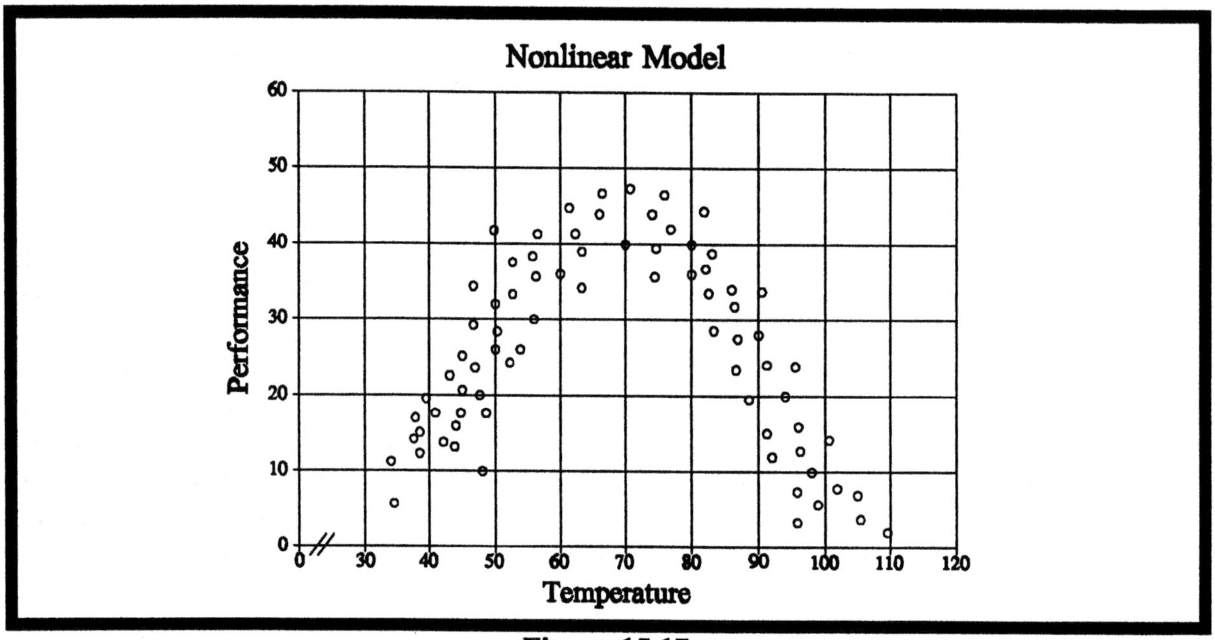

Figure 15.17
Nonlinear Relationship between Temperature and Performance

If we had only collected data for temperatures ranging between 30° and 70°, as illustrated in Figure 15.18, we would have concluded that there is a strong positive relationship between the temperature of the work environment and productivity. We would also have drawn an incorrect conclusion. Similarly, if we had only collected data for temperatures ranging between 70° and 110°, as illustrated in Figure 15.19, we would have incorrectly concluded that there is a strong negative relationship between the two variables. By looking at the entire picture, we can see that a curvilinear relationship exists. If we had plotted a straight line through the entire data set, we would have obtained an inadequate fit. Plotting the points whenever possible will help us recognize and understand the relationships between variables.

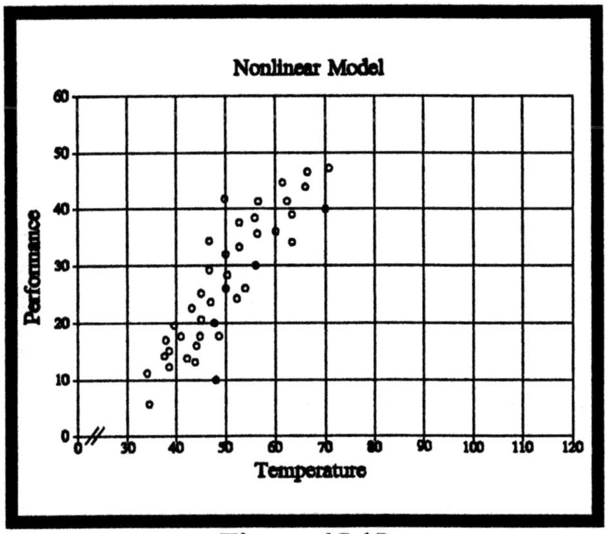

Figure 15.18
Low to Moderate Temperatures Only

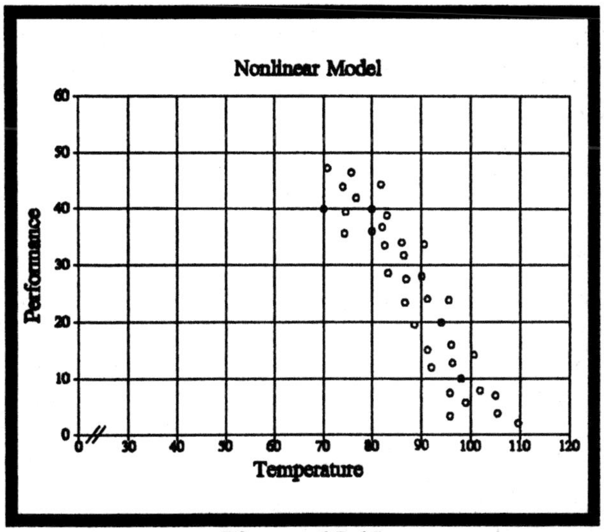

Figure 15.19
Moderate to High Temperatures

Range Restrictions

Our third caution is that any interpretation we make regarding the relationship between variables should be tempered by the range restriction for the data points used to develop this model. As an illustration, suppose that we want to examine the relationship between hourly wages and length of time with the organization. We have collected data for a sample of new employees who have only been with the company for between 0 and 6 months. The relationship that exists between the two variables for this sample of employees may not hold for all employees within the company. The range of time these employees have been with the company is considerably limited relative to the length of time that the majority of employees have been with the company. Conclusions based on such limited data may well be erroneous.

We will return to Example 15.8 to illustrate the range restriction limitation graphically. Suppose that we had only collected data for temperatures ranging from 30° to 72° in that example, as shown in Figure 15.18. We now want to predict the productivity level of employees when the temperature approaches 100°. Based on the limited range of data employed in Figure 15.18, we might have predicted that productivity would increase to approximately 70 productivity points. However, if we had collected a broader range of data, such as shown in Figure 15.17, we would have seen that productivity considerably diminished when temperatures actually were approaching 100°, perhaps to as low as 5 or 10 productivity points!

Sample Size Limitations

Our fourth caution is that sample size can strongly influence our conclusions about population data. This should not be surprising, as we have emphasized the importance of adequate sampling throughout this textbook. If we have very few data points, our correlation usually overestimates the relationship between the variables in the population. One widely accepted rule of thumb is to always have *at least* 10 cases for every predictor variable used, plus an additional 10 cases for the model. If we are trying to predict the Y-variable from a knowledge of one X-variable, we should have at least $10 + 10 = 20$ cases. If we are trying to predict the Y-variable from a knowledge of two variables (as discussed in Chapter 17), we should have at least $20 + 10 = 30$ cases. If we are trying to predict Y from the knowledge of six variables, we should have at least $60 + 10 = 70$ cases. In other words, we should have at least 10 cases for every predictor variable we intend to use in the model, plus 10 additional cases. We call this the ***10 plus 10 for the pot*** rule.

Example 15.9. We will use Example 15.9 to illustrate the potential consequences of sample size limitations. The human resources department of an organization is interested in improving their employee selection process. They have developed a selection instrument designed to measure potential ability to perform a specified task, and they administered this instrument to a group of employees during the hiring process. Later, they evaluated the performance of all of these same employees on this task. Figure 15.20 is a scatter diagram showing the relationship between these two variables. As we can see, there appears to be a positive, somewhat linear relationship between assessment scores and performance.

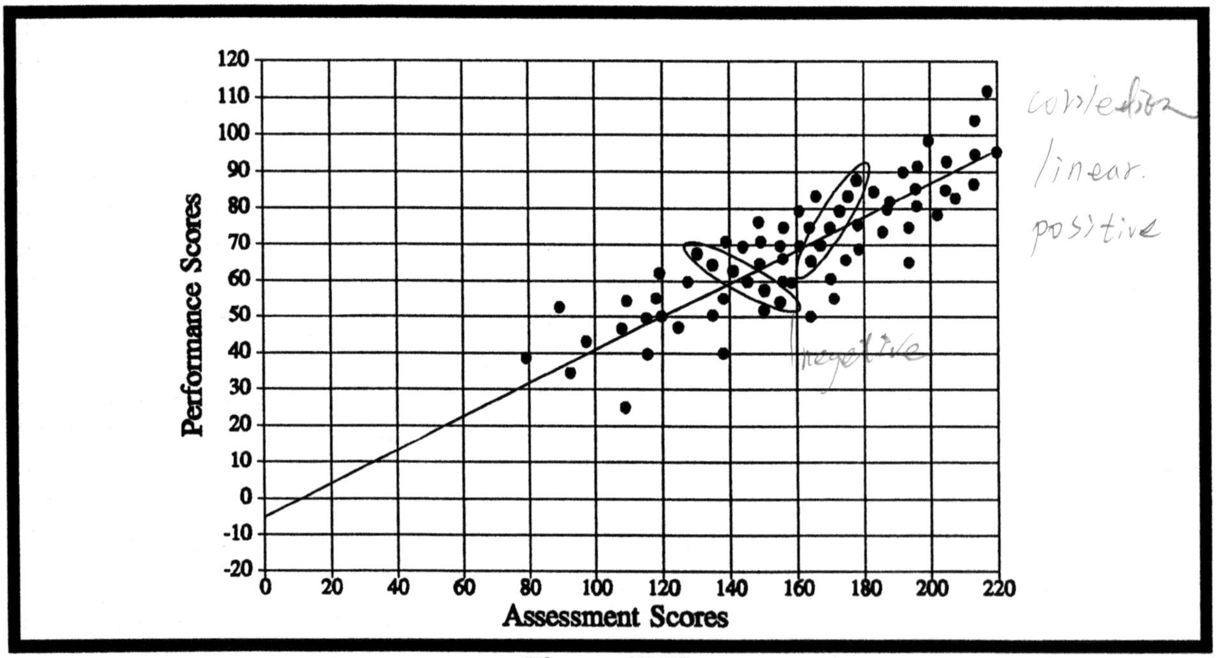

Figure 15.20
Errors Due to Sampling

Now suppose that the human resources department had only examined a small sample of these employees instead of the entire population. Their small sample consists of the set of six individuals included in the lower left ellipsis of Figure 15.20. As we can see, this sample would have resulted in a completely different conclusion. If this had been our sample, we would have concluded that assessment scores and performance are negatively related. Consequently, for those who score poorly on the assessment instrument, we might predict good future performance on the task; and we would have made many hiring errors. On the other hand, if our sample consists of the six individuals included in the upper right ellipsis, we see that the points almost fall in a perfect straight line. We would have again made an incorrect conclusion, feeling that this relationship is almost perfect. Of course, if we had taken a large sample, perhaps 20 data points, these mistaken interpretations would not have occurred.

Examining Relationships through Correlation Coefficients

There are many types of coefficients that have been developed to assess correlations among variables. Correlation coefficients that measure the relationship between two variables are referred to as ***bivariate*** or ***simple*** correlations. Correlation coefficients that measure the relationship between one criterion variable and *more than one* predictor variable are referred to as ***multivariate*** or ***multiple*** correlations. While the equations and computational requirements of multiple correlation are more complex than those for bivariate correlation, the basic concepts are the same. The bivariate model provides a natural step toward understanding multivariate models. While there are various forms of correlation coefficients available for various types of data (depending on the levels of measurement, whether the data are discrete or continuous, and other characteristics), we will concentrate on the most widely used correlation coefficient, the Pearson product moment correlation coefficient. We will simply refer to this term as the correlation coefficient and symbolize it as r, which is consistent with most textbooks, scientific calculators, and computer software.

Example 15.10. We are now ready to calculate correlation coefficients and determine whether they are statistically significant. We will use Example 15.10 to illustrate these calculations throughout the remainder of this chapter. The example is based on a set of six salespersons working within an organization. We should immediately recognize that the small sample size should give us cause for concern, as mentioned in Table 15.6. However, we will use this example to minimize calculations in the example. The company wants to determine whether employee performance on the job is related to performance on a pre-selection assessment tool that was administered to these employees six months prior to their first performance appraisal. Specifically, the company is interested in determining whether the selection tool and future performance on the job are correlated. The independent or predictor variable, X, is the set of assessment scores, based on a multiple choice screening test regarding knowledge of the company's sales strategy. The dependent or criterion variable, Y, is the set of job performance scores, based on the number of new accounts acquired by each employee by the end of the first six months on the job. Pairs of values for the two measures have been collected, as given in Table 15.7. We are now challenged with selecting an appropriate correlation coefficient for evaluating this relationship.

Table 15.7
Selection Scores vs. Number of New Accounts

Employee Number	*X* *Selection Score*	*Y* *Number of New Accounts*
1	11	10
2	8	10
3	8	9
4	5	6
5	2	5
6	2	2

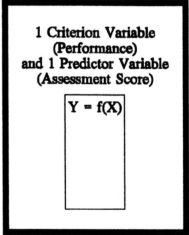

1 Criterion Variable (Performance) and 1 Predictor Variable (Assessment Score)

Y = f(X)

Example 15.10

Methodology Solution. We will follow Figure 15.21 to determine an appropriate statistical approach for analyzing Example 15.10. We enter the flowcharts at ***Start***. We are not comparing central tendencies, since we do not have subdivisions or groups from which to compute central tendencies; and we are not interested in comparing variabilities. We are interested in examining for correlation, regression, and prediction. Therefore, we will turn to flowchart 8. We do not have more than two variables; and we are not comparing two correlation coefficients from two different sets of data. Assessment scores are discrete because they are based on multiple-choice test questions. Performance is also discrete, because it is based on the number of new accounts acquired. Consequently, we turn to flowchart 9. We confirm that we are examining relationships between two discrete variables. We do not have two dichotomous variables; in fact, neither variable is dichotomous. As confirmed earlier, both variables are discrete; each variable also has at least three categories. Finally, both variables are at least interval scale. We conclude that we should consider using the Pearson product-moment correlation coefficient to examine the relationship between the two variables. If there is a significant correlation, we should then consider using regression to develop a prediction model.

It should be pointed out that at times we will use the same technique with discrete or continuous data. However, we should at least attempt to thoroughly understand our data before beginning any formal analysis. This is especially true if we have dichotomous data or if we do not have at least interval level data. Under such circumstances, we may need to consider other correlation coefficients, such as Spearman's rho, the point-biserial correlation coefficient, or the phi coefficient, or several non-Pearsonian correlation coefficients. Several of these coefficients will be discussed at the conclusion of this chapter.

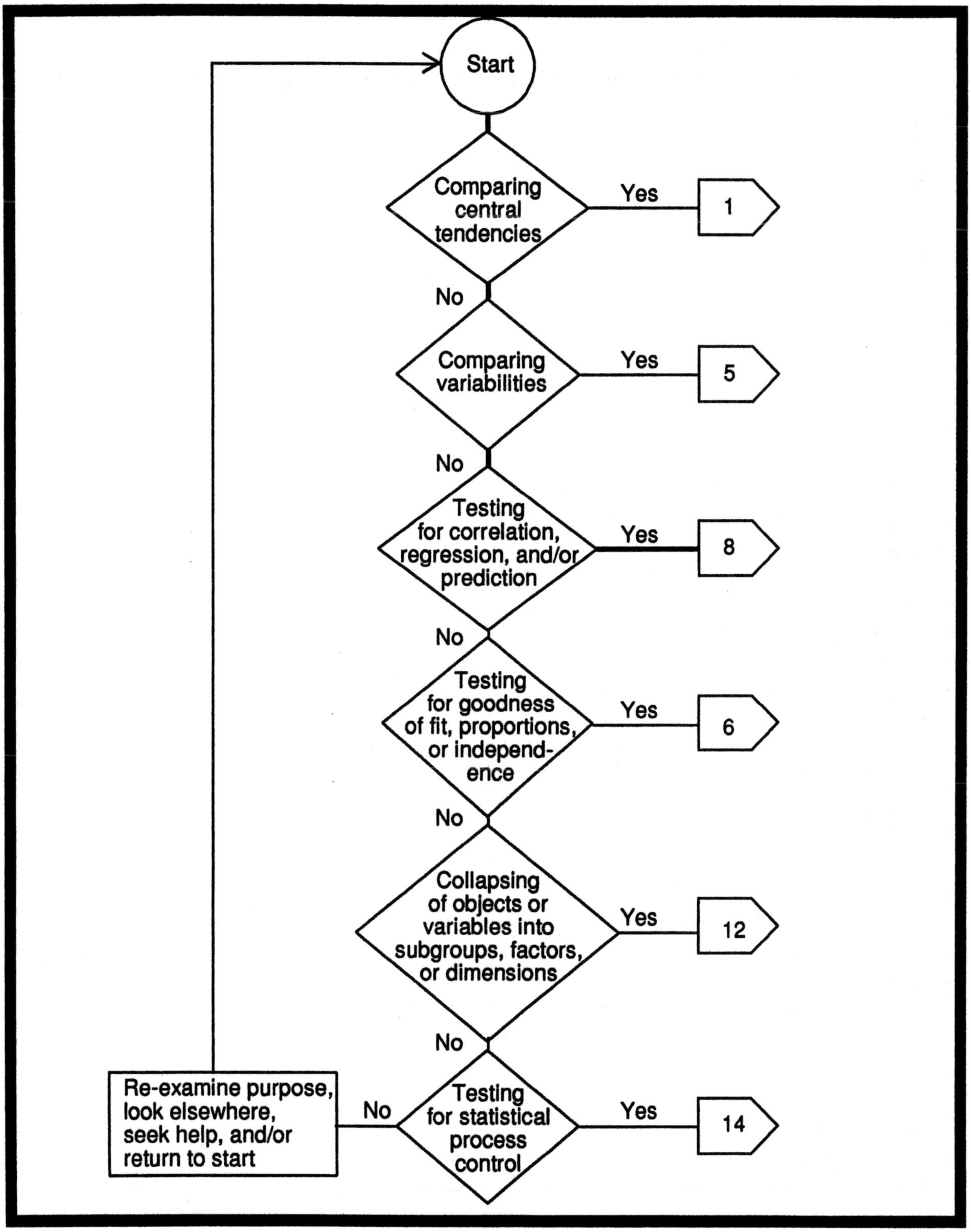

Figure 15.21
Statistical Decision-Making Flowchart for Example 15.10

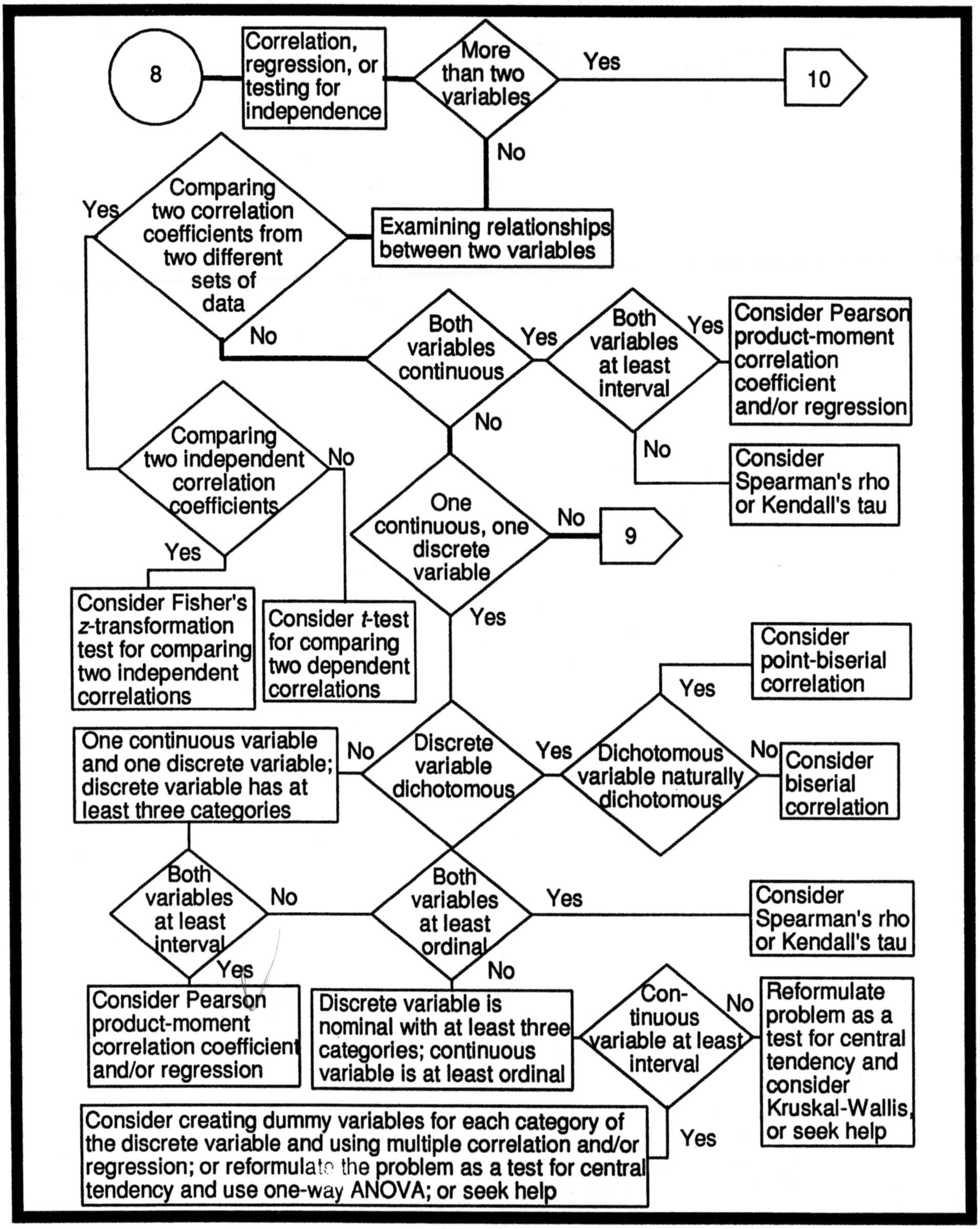

Figure 15.21
Statistical Decision-Making Flowchart for Example 15.10
(continued)

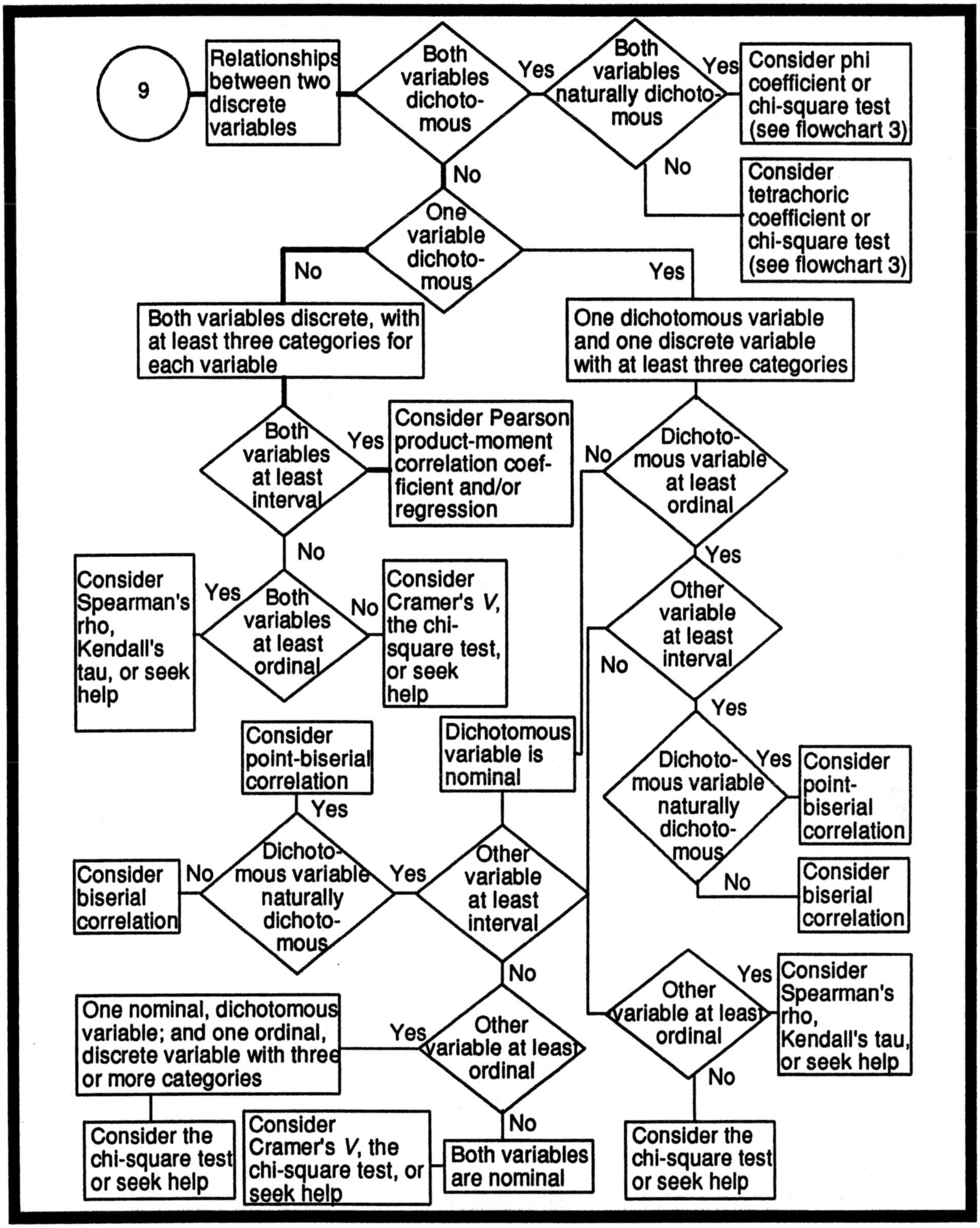

Figure 15.21
Statistical Decision-Making Flowchart for Example 15.10
(continued)

Correlation Coefficients and Related Terms

We will begin our discussion of the computational aspects of correlation and regression by defining the correlation coefficient and the covariance. We will then define a statistical test for determining whether the correlation coefficient is statistically significant. We will also define a confidence interval for the correlation coefficient.

Correlation Coefficient

Basic Equation for the Correlation Coefficient. The value of the correlation coefficient can be obtained through various formulas. Equation 15.1 gives the basic equation for determining the correlation between two sets of sample data:

$$r = \frac{\sum [(X - \overline{X})\cdot(Y - \overline{Y})]}{\sqrt{\sum (X - \overline{X})^2 \cdot \sum (Y - \overline{Y})^2}} \qquad \textbf{(15.1)}$$

We can see that this equation is directly related to variances and standard deviations. The first term under the square root symbol in the denominator of this correlation coefficient equation, $\Sigma(X - \overline{X})^2$, represents the numerator of the variance for the X-variable, while the second term in the denominator, $\Sigma(Y - \overline{Y})^2$, represents the numerator of the variance for the Y-variable. The term in the numerator of this correlation coefficient equation, $\Sigma\,[(X - \overline{X})\cdot(Y - \overline{Y})]$ represents the numerator of the ***covariance*** term. Thus, the correlation coefficient is simply a ratio of the *covariance* of the two variables to the variances of the two variables taken separately.

Computational Equation for the Correlation Coefficient. If we do not have access to a scientific calculator or a computer, we will find that Equation 15.1 is not very "user friendly." Under such circumstances, we may prefer to work with a formula that is computationally more convenient. Equation 15.2 is algebraically equivalent to Equation 15.1, and it provides us with an appropriate formula for obtaining the sample correlation coefficient when we do not have access to a good calculator or computer:

$$r = \frac{\sum X\cdot Y - \frac{(\sum X)\cdot(\sum Y)}{n}}{\sqrt{\left(\sum X^2 - \frac{(\sum X)^2}{n}\right)\cdot\left(\sum Y^2 - \frac{(\sum Y)^2}{n}\right)}} \qquad \textbf{(15.2)}$$

While this formula is perhaps easier to use, it does not appear to be "user friendly." Both of these equations are adequate, and both are troublesome to compute. This textbook makes the assumption that the reader has access to a scientific calculator with built-in functions for computing the means, standard deviations, correlation, slope, intercept, and other useful measures and will not need to calculate these values manually. Therefore, Equation 15.1 will be emphasized, thus preserving the sums of squares format used throughout this book.

Covariance

The covariance between any pair of variables is a measure of how the two variables vary together, or co-vary. While it is directly related to the correlation coefficient, the covariance also has value in its own right. We will find that there are numerous applications for this term. The sample covariance is defined by Equation 15.3:

$$cov = \frac{\sum [(X - \bar{X})\cdot(Y - \bar{Y})]}{n - 1} \qquad (15.3)$$

Correlation Defined by the Covariance and the Two Variances

Returning to Equation 15.1, we can now observe a direct relationship between the covariance of the two variables and the variance for each variable taken separately. The correlation coefficient is obtained by dividing the covariance between the two variables by the square root of the product of the two variable variances. Since all three components of the basic correlation coefficient equation are direct measures of variability, we sometimes define the correlation in variance-covariance terms. Consequently, the sample correlation coefficient can be stated in terms of Equation 15.4:

$$r = \frac{cov}{\sqrt{s_X^2 \cdot s_Y^2}} \qquad (15.4)$$

Covariance as Derived from the Correlation Coefficient and the Two Variances

Having expressed the correlation coefficient in variance-covariance terms, we can develop an straightforward equation for finding the covariance. If we know the values for r, s_x^2, and s_y^2, we can algebraically redefine Equation 15.4 in terms of the covariance, substitute these values into Equation 15.4, take the appropriate square roots, and solve for the covariance, as given in Equation 15.5:

$$cov = (r)\cdot(s_X)\cdot(s_Y) \qquad (15.5)$$

Returning to the sample data given in Table 15.7 for Example 15.10, we will now find the correlation between the assessment tool that was administered to these employees and the number of new accounts acquired by each of these employees by the end of the six month period. The set of test scores represents the independent variable, predictor variable, or X-variable. The number of new accounts acquired represents the dependent variable, criterion variable, or Y-variable. The necessary values for computing the correlation coefficient based on Equation 15.1 are given in Table 15.8, while the necessary values for computing this correlation based on Equation 15.2 are given in Table 15.9.

Table 15.8
Finding the Correlation Coefficient with the Basic Equation

	Column Number						
	(1)	(2)	(3)	(4)	(5)	(6)	(2)
Case	X	Y	$(X - \overline{X})$	$(X - \overline{X})^2$	$(Y - \overline{Y})$	$(Y - \overline{Y})^2$	$(X - \overline{X})\cdot(Y - \overline{Y})$
1.	11	10	5	25	3	9	15
2.	8	10	2	4	3	9	6
3.	8	9	2	4	2	4	4
4.	5	6	-1	1	-1	1	1
5.	2	5	-4	16	-2	4	8
6.	2	2	-4	16	-5	25	20
Σ	36	42	0	66	0	52	54

First, we will calculate the sample correlation coefficient between the assessment tool and the number of new accounts for these six individuals, based on Equation 15.1. We can obtain the three necessary sums for this equation from the bottom row of Table 15.8. The numerator of the variance for the X-variable, or $\Sigma(X - \overline{X})^2$, is 66, while the numerator of the variance for the Y-variable, or $\Sigma(Y - \overline{Y})^2$, is 52. The numerator of the covariance between these two variables, or $\Sigma\,[(X - \overline{X})\cdot(Y - \overline{Y})]$, is 54. If we insert each of these values into Equation 15.1, we will obtain the correlation coefficient, or r, as follows:

$$r = \frac{\sum\,[(X - \overline{X})\cdot(Y - \overline{Y})]}{\sqrt{\sum (X - \overline{X})^2 \cdot \sum (Y - \overline{Y})^2}}$$

variance X   variance Y

$$= \frac{54}{\sqrt{66 \cdot 52}}$$

$$= \frac{54}{58.5833}$$

$$= .9218$$

M = 0.8182
B = 2.0909

Table 15.9
Finding the Correlation Coefficient with the Computational Equation

	Column Number				
	(1)	(2)	(3)	(4)	(5)
Case	*X*	*Y*	X^2	Y^2	*XY*
1.	11	10	121	100	110
2.	8	10	64	100	80
3.	8	9	64	81	72
4.	5	6	25	36	30
5.	2	5	4	25	10
6.	2	2	4	4	4
Σ	36	42	282	346	306

Next, we will calculate the sample correlation coefficient between these same two variables based on Equation 15.2. We obtain the five necessary sums for this equation from the bottom row of Table 15.9. Again inserting the values into our equation, we will obtain the correlation coefficient as follows:

$$r = \frac{\sum X \cdot Y - \frac{(\sum X) \cdot (\sum Y)}{n}}{\sqrt{\left(\sum X^2 - \frac{(\sum X)^2}{n}\right) \cdot \left(\sum Y^2 - \frac{(\sum Y)^2}{n}\right)}}$$

$$= \frac{306 - \frac{(36 \cdot 42)}{6}}{\sqrt{\left(282 - \frac{(36)^2}{6}\right) \cdot \left(346 - \frac{(42)^2}{6}\right)}}$$

$$= \frac{54.0000}{58.5833}$$

$$= .9218$$

$S_x^2 = \frac{\Sigma (x - \bar{x})^2}{n-1}$

$S_y^2 = \frac{\Sigma (y - \bar{y})^2}{n-1}$

$cov = \frac{\Sigma [(x - \bar{x})(y - \bar{y})]}{n-1}$

Finally, we will compute the correlation coefficient for this sample using Equation 15.4. Since we know the numerators of the two variances and the numerator of the covariance, as given in Table 15.8, we divide each of these values by *n* - 1. When we divide 66 by 5, we obtain s_X^2 = 13.2; when we divide 52 by 5, we obtain s_Y^2 = 10.4; and when we divide 54 by 5, we obtain *cov* = 10.8. Inserting these values into Equation 15.4, we again obtain the correlation coefficient:

$$r = \frac{cov}{\sqrt{s_X^2 \cdot s_Y^2}}$$

$$= \frac{10.8}{\sqrt{(13.2) \cdot (10.4)}}$$

$$= \frac{10.8}{11.7167}$$

$$= .9218$$

As we can see, we have obtained $r = .9218$ based on all three approaches. Once we have computed the necessary values, as obtained for Equation 15.1 or Equation 15.4 in Table 15.8, or for Equation 15.2 from Table 15.9, we have completed all of the lengthy computations; we simply insert these values into the equation of our choice and compute the correlation coefficient. Hopefully, however, we will have access to a scientific calculator or computer so that we do not have to perform these manual calculations.

Based on the previous computations, we can now also confirm that the covariance between the two variables is 10.8. We will use Equation 15.5 to verify this conclusion. With the knowledge of r, s_X, and s_Y, we obtain the same value for the covariance term as obtained earlier:

$$cov = (r) \cdot (s_X) \cdot (s_Y)$$

$$= (.9218) \cdot (3.6332) \cdot (3.2249)$$

$$= 10.8 \textit{ (rounded)}$$

We can also determine the correlation coefficients for Examples 15.5, 15.6, and 15.7, based on any of these same approaches. As we will recall, there was no common variance between the two variables in Example 15.6. If we compute the covariance for that example, we will obtain a value of zero. If we compute the correlation coefficient for this example, we will confirm that the relationship between the two variables, as measured by this coefficient, is zero. For Example 15.5, we obtain a correlation coefficient of 1.00, as suggested by the Venn diagram in Figure 15.4 or by the scatter diagram in Figure 15.9. Finally, for Example 15.7, we obtain a correlation coefficient of .8644. This coefficient supports the notion of a high positive but not perfect correlation between the two variables of performance and pay, as suggested by Figure 15.15.

Significance of the Correlation Coefficient

Naturally, we want to interpret the meaning of the r-value. Is it a "big" value, and how big is "big"? To answer these questions, we must put the r-value into some relative perspective. We know that in absolute terms, our computed r-value cannot be bigger than 1.00. But is our observed r-value bigger than we expected it to be? In order to answer this question, we need to compare the r-value, in a relative sense, to some hypothesized or known value. We now define a test for the significance of the correlation coefficient.

The t-Test for the Significance of the Correlation Coefficient. There are several appropriate methods for determining the significance of a correlation coefficient. In this chapter we will use the t-test to determine statistical significance; in later chapters we will also use the F-test to determine the significance of our correlation and regression analysis. When we use the t-test, we convert the r-value to a t-value so that we can compare it to some critical t-value. Based on the same logic as before for establishing test statistics, the sample r-value is our observed value, the population ρ-value is our expected value, and the *standard error of the correlation* (SE_{CORR}) is our estimate of chance. Equation 15.6 defines the general format of the t-test:

$$Statistic = \frac{Observed\ Value\ vs.\ Expected\ Value}{Chance}$$

$$t = \frac{r - \rho}{SE_{corr}} \qquad (15.6)$$

Standard Error of the Correlation Coefficient. As with other standard error terms, the standard error of the correlation coefficient is the standard deviation of the sampling distribution of correlation coefficients. This standard error term is defined by Equation 15.7:

$$SEcorr = \sqrt{\frac{1 - r^2}{n - 2}} \qquad (15.7)$$

Revised t-Test for the Significance of the Correlation Coefficient. We now revise the t-test for the significance of the correlation, as defined by Equation 15.6, by inserting the standard error of the correlation coefficient as defined in Equation 15.7, to obtain the complete t-test. Equation 15.8 gives the general format of this t-test:

$$t = \frac{r - \rho}{\sqrt{\frac{1 - r^2}{n - 2}}} \qquad (15.8)$$

Example 15.10 Revisited

We will use Equation 15.8 to determine the significance of the computed r-value. As usual, we must determine the population parameter to be tested, the desired probability level for alpha, the directionality of the test, the null and alternative hypotheses, the appropriate statistical test, the degrees of freedom for that test, the critical cutoff value, the results of the test, and the appropriate decision.

Parameter to be Tested. As with other statistical tests, the sample statistic, r, is compared to the expected value for the population parameter, ρ. Once this comparison has been made, we will determine the probability associated with the difference between our observed and expected values. Typically, the null hypothesis states that there is no relationship between the two variables (i.e., H_0: $\rho = 0.00$). However, we may at times want to hypothesize that the population correlation coefficient is equal to some non-zero value. Further, our test can be a one-tailed test or a two-tailed test. With exploratory data analysis for which no prior information is available, we typically use two-tailed tests and make no assumption regarding the direction of the relationship.

Probability Level and Directionality. We will assume that the company researcher has set $\alpha = .05$. As stated in the previous paragraph, the test will be two-directional, as no prior information exists about the relationship between these two variables.

Null Hypothesis. For Example 15.10, the null hypothesis states that there is no relationship between the two variables. Formally stated, the null hypothesis becomes:

H_0: $\rho = 0.00$

Alternative Hypothesis. Since the company is in the early stages of exploratory data analysis, the alternative hypothesis will not state a specific direction for any existing relationship. Thus, we will perform a two-tailed test. The alternative hypothesis is formally stated as follows:

H_A: $\rho \neq 0.00$

Statistical Test. The appropriate statistical test for examining the strength of this correlation coefficient is the t-test for correlations. We can either convert our correlation coefficient to a t-value and evaluate the significance of that t-value against a critical t-value as found in Table 2 of Appendix C; or we can obtain a critical r-value from Table 5 of Appendix C (to be discussed shortly), and determine whether our computed r-value exceeds the value in the table. We will first perform the t-test for the significance of a correlation coefficient.

Degrees of Freedom. There are $df = n - 2$ degrees of freedom associated with the t-test for examining the significance of a bivariate correlation coefficient.

Critical Value. Since we have decided on a *t*-test, set α at .05, determined that the *df* = 6 - 2 = 4, and selected a two-directional test, we find that the critical cutoff value becomes *t* = ±2.776. This critical value was obtained from the *t*-table in Table 2 of Appendix C.

Drawing the Picture. We now draw a picture of the *t*-distribution as it applies to Example 15.10. We identify the regions where we will either reject or fail to reject H_0. Figure 15.22 gives these two regions, as determined by the two critical cutoff values.

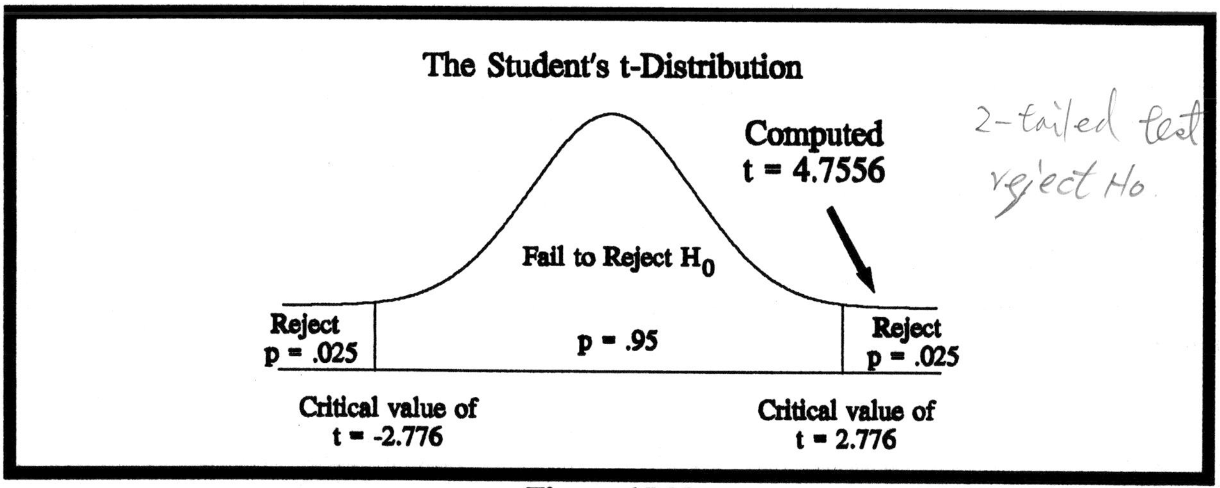

Figure 15.22
Testing the Significance of a Correlation Using Student's *t* Distribution

Results. Based on the formula given in Equation 15.8, we now convert the *r*-value to a *t*-value, as follows:

$$t = \frac{r - \rho}{\sqrt{\dfrac{1 - r^2}{n - 2}}}$$

t = 2.776
r = 0.8114

$$= \frac{.9218 - .0000}{\sqrt{\dfrac{1 - .9218^2}{6 - 2}}}$$

$$= \frac{.9218 - .0000}{\sqrt{\dfrac{1 - .8497}{4}}}$$

$$= \frac{.9218}{.1938}$$

$$= 4.7556$$

Decision. Based on the results of this two-tailed t-test, we find that the computed value is greater than the critical value; therefore, we reject the null hypothesis and support the alternative hypothesis. In terms of probabilities, obtaining a sample correlation of $r = .9218$ by chance from a population that has a correlation coefficient of $\rho = 0.00$ is less than .05.

Conclusion. There appears to be a relationship between the assessment scores and the number of new accounts acquired after six months on the job. This conclusion is consistent with the graph given in Figure 15.22. Based on this decision, the company may want to consider using the assessment instrument as a predictor of account acquisitions. However, due to the size of the sample, a final decision should be withheld until additional data become available for validating these preliminary findings.

Converting t-Values to r-Values

As we know, we can obtain a critical t-value based on the sample size, alpha, and the directionality of the test. If we know the critical t-value and the sample size, we can also obtain a *critical r-value.* We solve for the critical r-value through the use of algebra. This solution is given in Equation 15.9:

$$r = \frac{t}{\sqrt{n - 2 + t^2}} \qquad \textbf{(15.9)}$$

Equation 15.9 tells us how unusual any r-value must be to obtain statistical significance at specified levels of alpha and predetermined sample sizes. For Example 15.10, the critical r-value is determined as follows:

$$\begin{aligned} r &= \frac{t}{\sqrt{n - 2 + t^2}} \\ &= \frac{2.776}{\sqrt{6 - 2 + 2.776^2}} \\ &= \pm.8114 \end{aligned}$$

We conclude that with $\alpha = .05$, $df = 4$, and a two-tailed test, we will need to obtain a correlation coefficient at least as unusual as ±.8114 before we have statistical significance. Since the computed correlation coefficient ($r = .9218$) exceeds the upper boundary of these critical cutoff values (.9218 > .8114), we reject the null hypothesis. Figure 15.23 locates this observed r-value on the r-distribution. We now have an alternative approach to performing a t-test. This approach allows us to determine how unusual the r-value has to be to achieve statistical significance, even before we collect data. Moreover, the entire t-distribution can be converted into an r-distribution, as given in Table 5 of Appendix C. We use this table to quickly determine the r-value necessary for statistical significance under various scenarios.

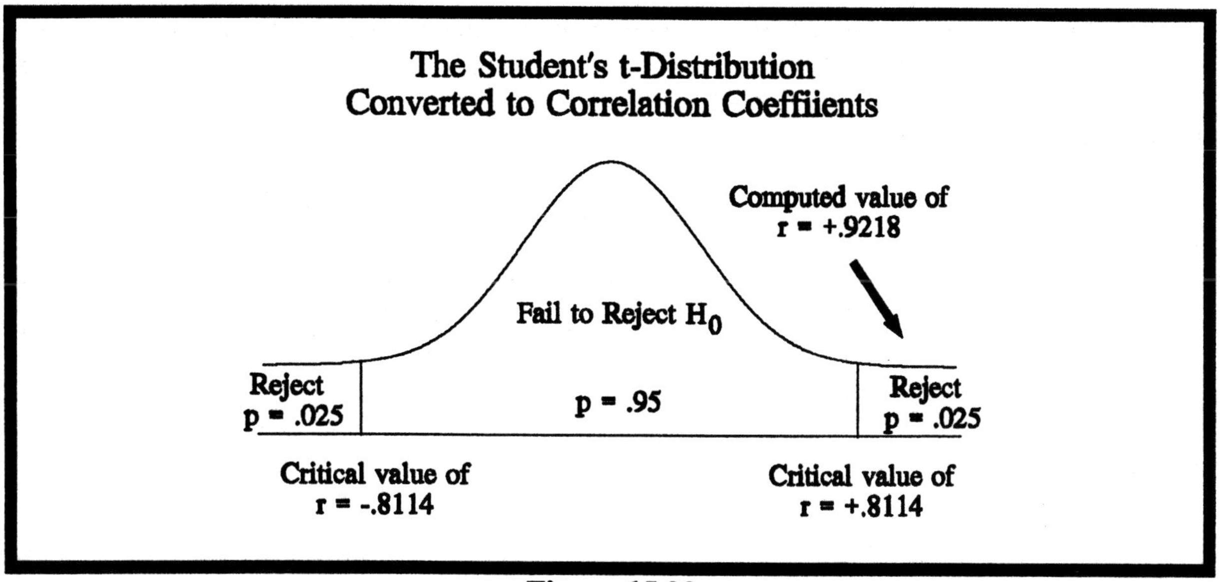

Figure 15.23
Testing the Significance of a Correlation Using a Critical *r*-Table

As another illustration of the use of the critical *r*-value, suppose that we know we are going to collect data for 20 observations. If we set our confidence level at 95%, we need to achieve an *r*-value as unusual as ±.4438 to reject the null hypothesis. This value can be obtained in Table 5 of Appendix C or through the use of Equation 15.9, as follows:

$$r = \frac{t}{\sqrt{n - 2 + t^2}}$$

$$= \frac{2.101}{\sqrt{20 - 2 + 2.101^2}}$$

$$= \pm .4438$$

Confidence Intervals for ρ

If we have obtained a correlation coefficient based on sample data, we might also want to develop a confidence interval for the population correlation coefficient based on the sample value. Unfortunately, as the population correlation coefficient approaches ±1.00, the sampling distribution of correlation coefficients becomes increasingly skewed. Under such circumstances, our confidence intervals lack symmetry. To resolve this problem, Ronald A. Fisher developed a method for obtaining appropriate non-symmetric confidence intervals. First, we transform the observed sample *r*-value into a *z*-value referred to as Fisher's *z*-statistic. Second, we develop a symmetric interval about the transformed *z*-statistic. Third, we convert the lower and upper boundaries of this symmetric interval back to correlation coefficients. Our resulting confidence interval will be symmetric only when *r* = 0.00.

Converting *r* to Fisher's *z*. Our first step toward developing a confidence interval for the correlation coefficient is to convert the *r*-value to a Fisher's *z*-value. This is accomplished through the use of Equation 15.10:

$$z_r = \frac{1}{2} \cdot [\ln(1 + r) - \ln(1 - r)] \qquad \textbf{(15.10)}$$

Converting *r* to Fisher's *z* through Table 6 of Appendix C. While Equation 15.10 gives us the appropriate converted Fisher's *z*-value, it requires the use of natural logs. If we want to avoid such calculations, we can use Table 6 of Appendix C. This table consists of Fisher's *z*-values for correlation coefficients ranging from 0.000 to ±1.000, in increments of .001. We will demonstrate the use of this table shortly.

Confidence Intervals for Fisher's *z*. Our second step is to develop a confidence interval for Fisher's *z*-value. This confidence interval, like most confidence intervals, is derived from an observed value plus or minus a critical value times a standard deviation or standard error. In this case, the observed value is Fisher's *z*-value, the critical value is a *z*-value obtained from the standard normal table (for example, 1.96 or 2.58), and the standard deviation is the standard error of the Fisher's *z*-distribution. The lower and upper boundaries for this confidence interval are defined by Equation 15.11:

$$z_r - (z_{\alpha/2}) \cdot (\sigma_{z_r}) \leq z_\rho \leq z_r + (z_{\alpha/2}) \cdot (\sigma_{z_r}) \qquad \textbf{(15.11)}$$

The Standard Error for Fisher's *z*. The standard error term in Equation 15.11 is symbolized as σ_{z_r}. Equation 15.12 defines this standard error term:

$$\sigma_{z_r} = \frac{1}{\sqrt{n - 3}} \qquad \textbf{(15.12)}$$

Converting Fisher's *z* Back to *r*. Our third step is to convert the lower and upper boundaries of the confidence interval, as obtained by Equation 15.11, back to *r*-values through the use of Equation 15.14:

$$r = \frac{e^{2 \cdot z_r} - 1}{e^{2 \cdot z_r} + 1} \qquad \textbf{(15.13)}$$

where:

e = 2.71828, the base for the natural log system

Converting Fisher's *z* Back to *r* through Table 6 of Appendix C. As before, rather than manually calculating these transformed values with Equation 15.13, we can utilize Table 6 of Appendix C to obtain these values. This time, however, we search inside the *body of the table* to locate the Fisher's z-value. Once we have found this value, or at least the closest available value, we move to the outside boundaries of the table to determine the appropriate r-values.

Example 15.10 Again Revisited

We will follow these steps to develop a 95% confidence interval for the ρ-value associated with Example 15.10. We obtained a correlation coefficient of $r = +.9218$ for this example earlier. Our first step toward developing the desired confidence interval is to convert the observed r-value into a z-value, based on Equation 15.10:

$$z_r = \frac{1}{2} \cdot [\ln(1 + r) - \ln(1 - r)]$$

$$= \frac{1}{2} \cdot [\ln(1 + .9218) - \ln(1 - .9218)]$$

$$= \frac{1}{2} \cdot [\ln 1.9218 - \ln .0782]$$

$$= \frac{1}{2} \cdot [(.65326) - (-2.54848)]$$

$$= \frac{1}{2} \cdot 3.20175$$

$$= 1.60087$$

Our second step is to determine the lower and upper boundaries for this confidence interval, based on the computed z-value obtained in the previous step. We use Equation 15.11 to obtain these boundaries:

$$z_r - (z_{\alpha/2}) \cdot (\sigma_{z_r}) \leq z_\rho \leq z_r + (z_{\alpha/2}) \cdot (\sigma_{z_r})$$

$$1.60087 - (1.96) \cdot (.57735) \leq z_\rho \leq 1.60087 + (1.96) \cdot (.57735)$$

$$.46926 \leq z_\rho \leq 2.73248$$

As we see, our lower boundary is .46926, while our upper boundary is 2.73248. We emphasize that these two values are boundaries for Fisher's z-values, not for r-values. Therefore, our third step is to convert these lower and upper Fisher's z-values back to lower and upper r-values. We will use Equation 15.13 and illustrate the manual calculations of these boundaries. We will then use values obtained in Table 6 of Appendix C to verify these results. We begin by converting the lower value, .46926, to an r-value as follows:

$$r = \frac{e^{2 \cdot z_r} - 1}{e^{2 \cdot z_r} + 1}$$

$$= \frac{e^{(2) \cdot (.46926)} - 1}{e^{(2) \cdot (.46926)} + 1}$$

$$= \frac{e^{.93852} - 1}{e^{.93852} + 1}$$

$$= \frac{1.5562}{3.5562}$$

$$= .43760$$

In the same manner, we use Equation 15.13 to convert the upper value, 2.73248, to an r-value as follows:

$$r = \frac{e^{2 \cdot z_r} - 1}{e^{2 \cdot z_r} + 1}$$

$$= \frac{e^{(2) \cdot (2.73248)} - 1}{e^{(2) \cdot (2.73248)} + 1}$$

$$= \frac{e^{5.46496} - 1}{e^{5.46496} + 1}$$

$$= \frac{235.2664}{237.2664}$$

$$= .99157$$

Final Solution for the Confidence Interval. We have now completed the conversion process based on Fisher's z-transformation and have obtained a 95% confidence interval for the population correlation coefficient for Example 15.10. We conclude that our confidence interval is bounded as follows:

$$.43760 \leq \rho \leq .99157$$

As noted earlier, instead of relying on Equation 15.13, we could use Table 6 of Appendix C and avoid the manual calculations. Since we can seldom find the exact value in the body of the table, we use the closest value we can find. For example, we cannot find the lower value of .46926 in the table, but we can find .4698. This value corresponds to an r-value of .438. We also cannot find the upper value of 2.73248, but we can find 2.7587. This value corresponds to an r-value of .992. As we can see, the values found in Table 6 of Appendix C provide us with lower and upper boundaries for our confidence interval that are accurate to three decimal places; and using the tables requires considerably less effort!

Conclusions Regarding the Confidence Interval. Since our sample statistic is relatively high (i.e, .9218 is approaching +1.00), we know that the range of potential sample correlations falling between .9218 and +1.00 is more limited than the range of potential sample correlations that can fall below .9218. When we develop a confidence interval based on a sample correlation that greatly deviates from zero, our sampling distribution becomes skewed. If the population correlation is near +1.00, as in Example 15.10, the sampling distribution of the correlations will be highly negatively skewed. When we use a sample *r*-value to develop that confidence interval, the sample *r*-value tends to overestimate the population correlation coefficient, especially with small samples. The Fisher's *z* transformation process provides us with a more reliable confidence interval. We should also notice that the range for this confidence interval is quite large. This is a direct result of having a small sample. We cannot have too much confidence in our results if they are based on only six observations!

This entire conversion process, from an *r*-value to a Fisher's *z*-value, to lower and upper bounds for Fisher's *z*-value, and then to lower and upper bounds for the final confidence interval for the *r*-value, is illustrated in Figure 15.24.

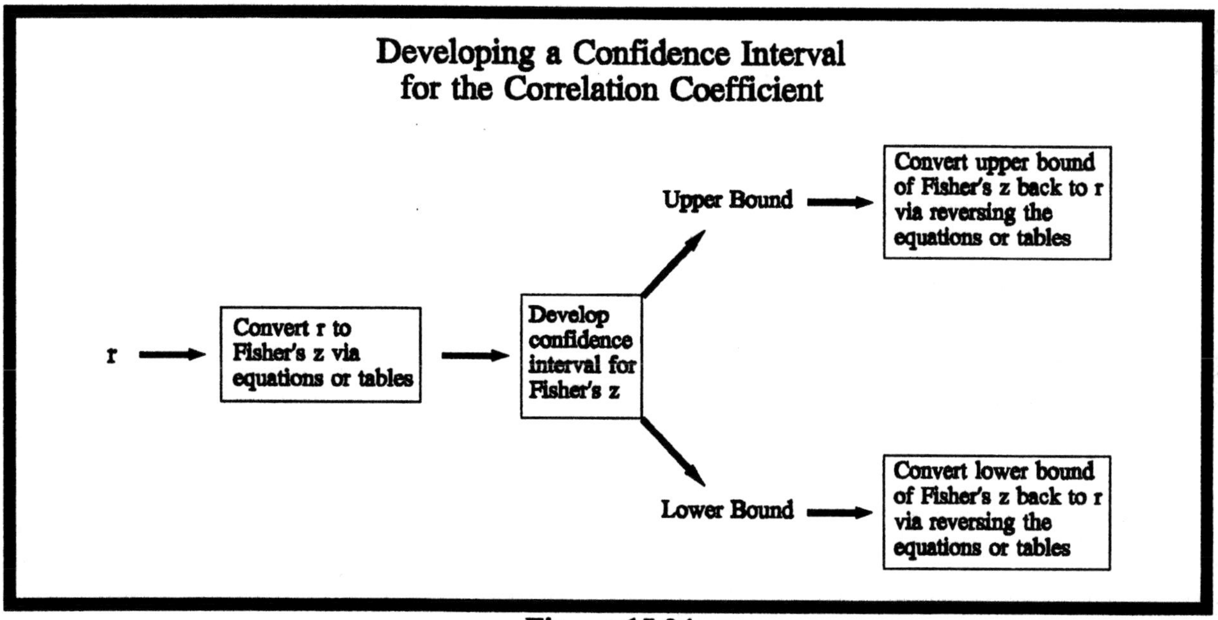

Figure 15.24
Developing Confidence Intervals for *r*

Comparing Two Independent Correlation Coefficients

Sometimes we compare correlation coefficients between two variables collected from two independent samples. That is, we compare r_1, which represents the correlation between two variables collected from the first sample, with r_2, which represents the correlation between these same two variables collected from the second sample. We find that Fisher's *z*-transformation is a helpful tool for making such comparisons.

Example 15.11. Jenner, Omens, and Beatty (1985) collected data for a sample of 74 US managers employed at US-owned, US-based banks. They also collected data for a sample of 22 US managers employed at Japanese-owned, US-based banks. Correlation coefficients were obtained for each sample in order to examine the relationship between organizational commitment scores and scores that measure perceived differences between managers and their immediate supervisors. The correlation between commitment scores and perceived differences for managers in the Japanese-owned banks was .487, while the correlation between these same two scores for managers in the US-owned banks was .095. The researchers then investigated the null hypothesis that these two variables have the same relationship across the two groups.

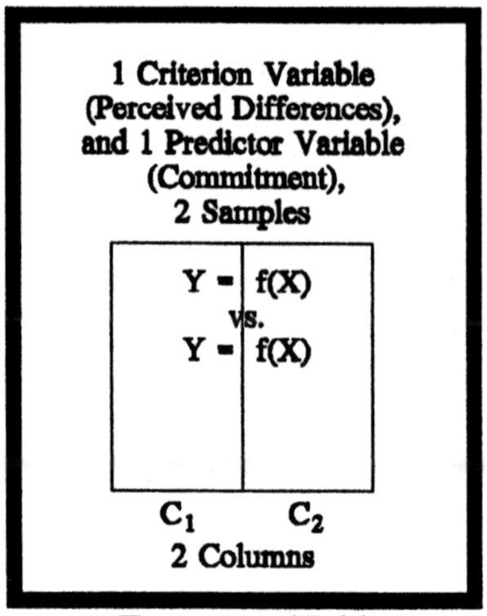

Example 15.11

Methodology Solution. We will use the flowcharts in Figure 15.1, with one modification, to determine an appropriate statistical test for Example 15.11. We enter the flowcharts at ***Start***. We are not comparing central tendencies or variabilities. Instead, we are examining for correlation, regression, and prediction; thus, we turn to flowchart 8. Since both samples are based on the same bivariate model, we do not have more than two variables. We want to compare two correlation coefficients from two different sets of data, and these correlations are from two independent samples. Therefore, we conclude that we should consider using the Fisher's *z* transformation test for comparing the two independent correlations.

The null hypothesis for Example 15.11 is that the two samples come from the same population. As always, we must assume that the two correlations are representative estimates of the corresponding population correlation coefficients between these two variables, based on appropriate sampling procedures. The null and alternative hypotheses are formally stated as follows:

H_0: $\rho_1 = \rho_2$

H_A: $\rho_1 \neq \rho_2$

where:

ρ_1 = the correlation coefficient for the population from which r_1 was obtained

ρ_2 = the correlation coefficient for the population from which r_2 was obtained

Fisher's *z* for Two Independent Correlations. As determined through the flowcharts, the appropriate statistical test for comparing these correlations is the Fisher's *z* transformation test for two independent correlations. This *z*-test is defined by Equation 15.14:

$$z = \frac{z_{r_1} - z_{r_2}}{\sqrt{\frac{1}{n_1 - 3} + \frac{1}{n_2 - 3}}} \qquad \textbf{(15.14)}$$

where:

z_{r_1} = Fisher's z-statistic for the first correlation coefficient

z_{r_2} = Fisher's z-statistic for the second correlation coefficient

n_1 = the number of cases in the first sample

n_2 = the number of cases in the second sample

We are now ready to use Equation 15.14 to determine whether the two independent correlation coefficients are significantly different. This will be a two-directional test, based on the null and alternative hypotheses for Example 15.11; and alpha has been set at .05. First, we convert the two separate correlations to Fisher's z-values. For the first sample, r_1 = .487 and Fisher's z = .53212. For the second sample, r_2 = .095 and Fisher's z = .09529. We insert these values into the Fisher's z-test to compare the two transformed sample z-values. The results of this z-test are as follows:

$$z = \frac{z_{r_1} - z_{r_2}}{\sqrt{\frac{1}{n_1 - 3} + \frac{1}{n_2 - 3}}}$$

$$= \frac{.53212 - .09529}{\sqrt{\frac{1}{74 - 3} + \frac{1}{22 - 3}}}$$

$$= \frac{.53212 - .09529}{\sqrt{.01408 + .05263}}$$

$$= \frac{.43683}{.25829}$$

$$= 1.69122$$

Since the computed z-value of 1.6912 falls between our two critical z-values of ±1.96, we fail to reject the null hypothesis. We conclude that the two correlations are not significantly different.

Other Forms of Correlation Coefficients

There are three special forms of the Pearson product-moment correlation coefficient that are commonly used: ***Spearman's rho***, the ***point-biserial correlation coefficient***, and the ***phi coefficient***. All three can be derived from the previously described *r*-value through algebra, and all three have different focuses.

Spearman's Rho

In our discussion of correlation coefficients, we have assumed that both the *X*-variable and *Y*-variable are at least interval measures. If we are unwilling to assume that these variables are at least interval but are willing to view them as ordinal measures, we often convert the data into rank order values and analyze the *rankings* instead of the original values. If the original data are rank order values in the first place, the process is simplified.

Examining Spearman's Rho. We use Spearman's rho to analyze the relationship between these rank order values. This correlation coefficient is appropriate for ordinal level data and is a special form of the Pearson product-moment correlation coefficient. It is widely used to measure relationships between ordinal level data. The power $(1 - \beta)$ for this *nonparametric* statistic is less than the power of its *parametric* counterpart for situations with identical sample sizes. Equation 15.15 gives the formula for Spearman's rho:

$$\text{Spearman's rho} = 1 - \left[\frac{(6)\cdot(\Sigma d^2)}{(n)\cdot(n^2 - 1)}\right] \qquad \textbf{(15.15)}$$

where:

n = the number of pairs of data

Σd^2 = the sum of the squared differences between the pairs of ranked values

Steps and Guidelines for Converting to Rank Order Values. In order to use Spearman's rho, each of the original performance scores in Example 15.10 must be converted to rank-order values. Since this conversion process can be somewhat confusing, we recommend that the assignment of the rank order values follow the steps and guidelines given below:

1. The original pairings for the data must *remain intact*. Each appropriate rank-order value assigned to the original *X*-value should be located adjacent to the appropriate rank-order value assigned to the original *Y*-value.

2. Assign a rank value for each case, with the highest original number receiving the smallest rank and the smallest number receiving the highest rank.

3. If ties exist among the numbers, the same rank-order value should be given to each of the tied values. For example, suppose the *Y*-variable consists of the following values, listed in descending order: 20, 18, 18, 17, 15, 13, 13, 13, 11, and 10. If we assign rank-ordered numbers to the original values, the first value (20) will receive a ranking of 1. The second and third values (18 and 18) are tied; therefore, they will each

receive a rank-order value of 2.5, which is the average of 2 and 3. The fourth value will receive a ranking of 4, and the fifth value will receive a ranking of 5. The sixth, seventh, and eighth values are tied; therefore, they will each receive a ranking of 7, which is the average of 6, 7, and 8. The ninth value will receive a ranking of 9, and the tenth value will receive a ranking of 10.

4. The sum of the rankings must be equal to $[(n)\cdot(n + 1)]/2$. If the sum of the rankings does not equal $[(n)\cdot(n + 1)]/2$, we have made an error in our ranking process.

Example 15.12. Example 15.12 illustrates the use of Spearman's rho. Performance data have been collected for 20 employees over two evaluation periods. The performance scores are based on a rating scale developed by the company, and these scores are given in Table 15.10. The supervisor wants to determine whether performance scores correlate over the two time periods, but she feels that these subjective ratings should not be treated as if they are at least interval scale. We will use the master flowcharts to determine an appropriate procedure for analyzing these data. Beginning at ***Start***, we go directly to the correlation, regression, and/or prediction decision point and turn to flowchart 8. We are examining the relationship between two variables; we are not comparing two correlation coefficients from two different sets of data; both variables come from underlying continuous distributions; and neither variable is interval level. Therefore, we should consider using either *Spearman's rho* or *Kendall's tau*.

Table 15.10
Converting Performance Scores to Rank-Ordered Data

	Raw Values		*Rank Orders*		*Differences*	
Case	*X*	*Y*	*X*	*Y*	*d*	d^2
1	25	32	8.0	6.0	2.0	4.00
2	30	26	2.0	10.0	-8.0	64.00
3	23	27	12.0	8.0	4.0	16.00
4	16	26	18.0	10.0	8.0	64.00
5	13	26	19.5	10.0	9.5	90.25
6	32	34	1.0	3.0	-2.0	4.00
7	20	24	15.0	12.5	2.5	6.25
8	24	33	10.5	4.5	6.0	36.00
9	27	29	4.5	7.0	-2.5	6.25
10	27	24	4.5	12.5	-8.0	64.00
11	22	21	13.0	17.5	-4.5	20.25
12	27	22	4.5	16.0	-11.5	132.25
13	25	33	8.0	4.5	3.5	12.25
14	25	40	8.0	1.0	7.0	49.00
15	21	23	14.0	14.5	-0.5	0.25
16	13	21	19.5	17.5	2.0	4.00
17	24	23	10.5	14.5	-4.0	16.00
18	27	35	4.5	2.0	2.5	6.25
19	17	17	17.0	19.0	-2.0	4.00
20	18	14	16.0	20.0	-4.0	16.00
Σ	456	530	210.0	210.0	0.0	**615.00**

Both of these statistical procedures are designed to evaluate the relationships between rank order variables. Although there are advantages, disadvantages, and subtle differences associated with each of these two statistical procedures, they usually lead to similar decisions in regard to hypothesis testing. Spearman's rho is more widely used in practice; thus, it is presented here.

Calculating Spearman's Rho. Along with the original performance scores, Table 15.10 also includes the rank order values that have been assigned to each of the original numbers, the differences between each pair of rank-order values, the squares of these differences, and the sums of these respective columns. As can be seen, the sums of the ranks for the X-variable and for the Y-variable are both 210, agreeing with $[(20)\cdot(20 + 1)]/2 = 210$. The sum of the differences in the ranks is $\Sigma d = 0$, again as expected. Finally, the sum of the squared differences in the ranks is $\Sigma d^2 = 615$. We now compute Spearman's rho using Equation 15.15 and the values given in Table 15.10:

$$\text{Spearman's rho} = 1 - \left[\frac{(6)\cdot(\Sigma d^2)}{(n)\cdot(n^2 - 1)}\right]$$

$$= 1 - \left[\frac{(6)\cdot(615)}{(20)\cdot(20^2 - 1)}\right]$$

$$= .5376$$

As we see, we have obtained a Spearman's rho of +.5376 for Example 15.12. We need to compare this computed value to a critical value for our test statistic. Disagreement exists regarding the calculation of the standard error term for Spearman's rho, and different estimates have been computed for critical values of Spearman's rho. Table 7 of Appendix C includes critical values for Spearman's rho based on commonly accepted values for selected values of n. Using this table, we find that with $n = 20$, a two-tailed test, and $\alpha = .05$, the critical cutoff point is $\pm .450$. Figure 15.26 shows that the computed value falls in the region of rejection. Thus, we reject H_0 and conclude that the pairs of performance scores are significantly correlated.

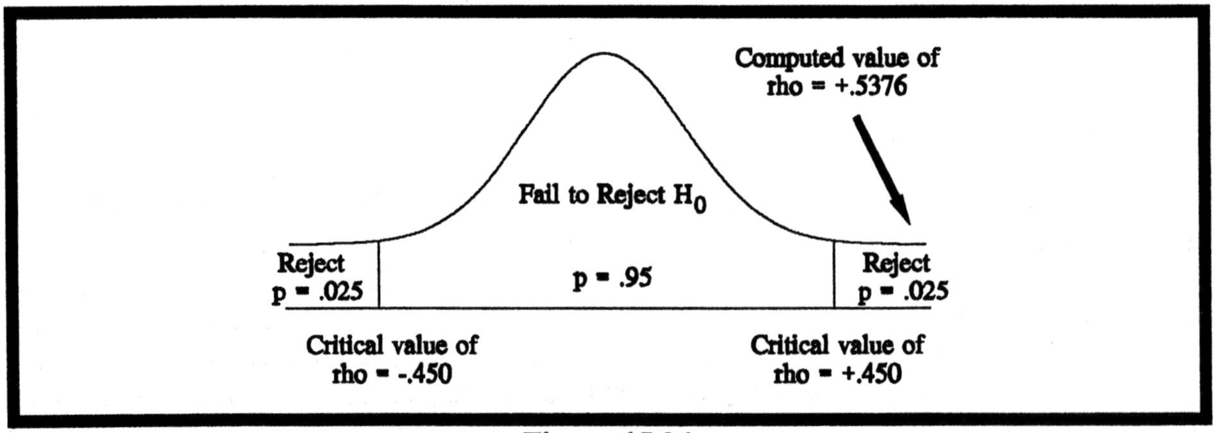

Figure 15.26
Testing the Significance of Spearman's rho

Point-biserial

The *point-biserial correlation coefficient* is also algebraically equivalent to the Pearson product-moment correlation coefficient. It is an appropriate measure of relationships when one of the two variables is at least interval level, while the other variable is naturally dichotomous (although some would specify that the interval level variable should also be continuous). Variables are naturally dichotomous if the cases naturally fall into one of two categories and have not been forced into a such a dichotomy. For example, the dichotomy of male vs. female represents a natural two-category variable. On the other hand, the dichotomy of height based on two categories (tall vs. short) represents a forced two-category variable. The variable has been generated from a naturally continuous variable, and some arbitrary decision must be made regarding the cutoff point to be used to separate these two groups.

Equation for the Point-Biserial Correlation Coefficient. The formula for computing the point-biserial correlation coefficient is based on the means of the two groups on the variable of interest, the standard deviation of these two groups combined (using the population standard deviation format), and the proportion of the total number of cases that belong to each group. This formula is given in Equation 15.16:

$$r_{pbi} = \frac{\overline{X}_1 - \overline{X}_0}{\sigma_T} \cdot \sqrt{p \cdot q} \qquad \textbf{(15.16)}$$

where:

$\overline{X}_1$ = the mean of the first group (coded here as 1)

$\overline{X}_0$ = the mean of the second group (coded here as 0)

σ_T = the standard deviation of the combined set of values, using the formula for the *population* standard deviation

p = the proportion of cases in the first group

q = the proportion of cases in the second group

Example 15.13. A class action suit was filed in a major metropolitan city, charging gender discrimination. The suit was filed against an organization, and it specified that they were giving preferential hiring treatment to males in regard to a particular job. In support of their claim, the plaintiffs proposed that males actually performed less efficiently on this job than females. The plaintiffs compiled data regarding the amount of elapsed time current job incumbents required to assemble the product related to that job. They collected data for both male and female employees under identical conditions. They wanted to examine whether an individual's performance on a specific task was a function of his or her gender.

We will again use our master flowcharts to determine the appropriate statistical procedure to analyze Example 15.13. We begin at ***Start***, go directly to the correlation, regression, and/or prediction decision point, and turn to flowchart 8. We are examining the relationship between two variables, but now only one of the variables (time) has an underlying distribution that is continuous. The second variable (gender) is discrete and dichotomous. In fact, it is naturally dichotomous. Thus, we should consider using the point-biserial correlation coefficient as an appropriate method for examining this relationship. Table 15.11 displays the values submitted by the plaintiffs in their suit.

Table 15.11
Assembly Times for Males and Females

Case Number	***Gender***	***Gender Code***	***Elapsed Time***
1.	male	1	95
2.	female	0	78
3.	male	1	92
4.	male	1	87
5.	male	1	102
6.	female	0	87
7.	female	0	78
8.	male	1	82
9.	female	0	98
10.	male	1	103
11.	male	1	87
12.	female	0	79
13.	male	1	89
14.	female	0	68
15.	female	0	78
16.	female	0	75
17.	male	1	88
18.	female	0	82
19.	male	1	91
20.	female	0	66

Notice that Table 15.11 includes a coded variable of ones and zeros. This coded variable is sometimes referred to as a dummy variable. The value of 1 has been assigned to indicate membership in the first group (males), and the value of 0 indicates membership in the second group (females). These dummy codings are entirely arbitrary; we could have used 1 and 2, 5 and 10, or any other two-number coding. Further, the coding is not necessary for the computation of the point-biserial correlation coefficient; but it will be helpful in understanding the relationship between this coefficient and the regular Pearson product-moment coefficient discussed at the onset of this chapter. The *sign* of the point-biserial correlation is a function of this coding decision; yet, the nature of the relationship will not change. We can examine the means of the two groups to clarify the direction of the relationship.

We now compute the point-biserial correlation coefficient for Example 15.13 to determine whether the elapsed time in assembling the parts is a function of the gender of the individual. Using the data presented in Table 15.11 and the formula for the point-biserial correlation coefficient given in Equation 15.16, the following coefficient is obtained:

$$r_{pbi} = \frac{\overline{X}_1 - \overline{X}_0}{\sigma_T} \cdot \sqrt{p \cdot q}$$

$$= \frac{91.60 - 78.90}{9.8837} \cdot \sqrt{(.5) \cdot (.5)}$$

$$= .64$$

In order to determine whether is a significant correlation, this coefficient is converted to a t-value in the same manner as before. Since the plaintiffs suggested that males perform more slowly than females on the task, a one-tailed test is appropriate. The computed t-value that corresponds to this r-value is +3.55, which is significant at $\alpha = .01$ for a one-tailed test.

The conclusion was that the test supported the plaintiff's charge that the coefficient is significantly greater than zero. However, we need to verify that the results are in the hypothesized direction. We can examine the means to answer to this question. Whenever the mean of the first group is greater than the mean of the second group, the correlation coefficient will be a positive value. In this case, the mean of the males is greater than the mean of the females; consequently, the correlation is positive, as is the computed t-value. We conclude that based on these sample data males have higher elapsed times than females. The plaintiff was able to win their case based on these findings and other supporting factors.

As stated earlier, the point-biserial correlation coefficient is just a special form of the Pearson product-moment correlation coefficient. In fact, if we compute a correlation coefficient between the two columns (gender code and elapsed time) in Table 15.11 in the usual manner, we will obtain $r = .64$. Although the point-biserial is commonly used in the literature as a method for computing the correlation between one variable that is naturally dichotomous and another variable that is continuous and at least interval level, either approach would be satisfactory, and the traditional approach is built into most scientific calculators!

We make one further observation regarding the point-biserial correlation coefficient. For Example 15.13, we could have used a two-sample independent t-test to compare the means. We will find that such a t-test results in a t-value of +3.55, exactly the same as the t-value obtained by converting the point-biserial to a t-value. Either test would have been appropriate, illustrating the point that research questions can often be formulated from several perspectives!

Phi Coefficient

The phi coefficient is an appropriate form of the Pearsonian correlation coefficient when *both* of the variables are naturally dichotomous, or when both can be generated from naturally dichotomous data. This correlation coefficient is also algebraically equivalent to the traditional Pearson product-moment correlation coefficient.

We find that the easiest way to perform such a test is to display our data in a two-by-two contingency table, similar to those we use with chi-square tests of independence, with the Fisher exact probability test for independence, and with the hypergeometric distribution. The rows represent one variable, while the columns represent the other variable. Since each variable is dichotomous, there will be two rows and two columns. We make arbitrary decisions about which of the two rows represents which of the categories in this variable, and we make the same arbitrary decision regarding columns. We emphasize that these are *arbitrary* decisions. As with the point-biserial correlation, the *sign* of the phi coefficient will be a direct function of these decisions. Only the sign of the computed value will be affected, not the numerical value of the correlation. As long as we understand the coding that we used and the nature of the relationship, we can make the correct interpretation about the direction of the observed relationship. Table 15.12 presents a format for this two-by-two matrix layout.

Table 15.12
Cells for a Two-by-Two Contingency Table

	Variable 1		
Variable 2	a	b	a + b
	c	d	c + d
	a + c	b + d	n

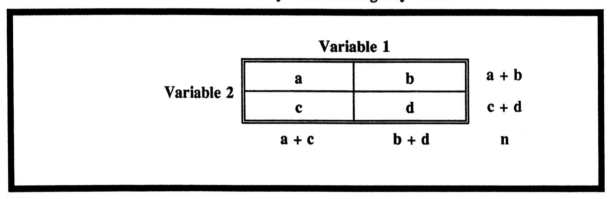

Equation for the Phi Correlation Coefficient. Our equation for the phi coefficient is derived from this two-by-two table. To compute the phi coefficient, we will use Equation 15.17, based on the symbolism given in Table 15.12:

$$r_{phi} = \frac{c \cdot b - a \cdot d}{\sqrt{(a + b) \cdot (a + c) \cdot (b + d) \cdot (c + d)}} \qquad (15.17)$$

Example 15.14. As an example of the use of the phi coefficient, suppose that we have collected records for a sample of 20 organizations. Half of the organizations are from the wholesale industry, while half are from the retail industry. We have also obtained bankruptcy information for these same organizations. Table 15.13 provides a summary of these findings.

Table 15.13
Bankruptcy Cases for Wholesale and Retail Businesses

Case Number	*Bankruptcy Filed*	*Industry Type*	*Bankruptcy Code*	*Industry Code*
1.	yes	wholesale	1	1
2.	yes	retail	1	0
3.	no	wholesale	0	1
4.	no	retail	0	0
5.	yes	wholesale	1	1
6.	yes	retail	1	0
7.	no	wholesale	0	1
8.	no	retail	0	0
9.	yes	retail	1	0
10.	yes	retail	1	0
11.	no	wholesale	0	1
12.	no	wholesale	0	1
13.	yes	wholesale	1	1
14.	yes	retail	1	0
15.	no	wholesale	0	1
16.	no	retail	0	0
17.	yes	retail	1	0
18.	yes	retail	1	0
19.	no	wholesale	0	1
20.	no	wholesale	0	1

Our master flowcharts again lead us directly to the correlation, regression, and/or prediction decision point, where we turn to flowchart 8. We are examining the relationship between two variables, and both variables are discrete; therefore, we turn to flowchart 9. Both variables are dichotomous, and both are naturally dichotomous. Consequently, we should consider using the phi coefficient.

Based on the findings presented in Table 15.13, we develop a two-by-two contingency table to examine the relationship between the two sets of variables. Table 15.14 quantifies and summarizes the values that appear in Table 15.13. This contingency table is much more revealing than the list of nominal information in Table 15.13 for Example 15.14.

Table 15.14
Two-by-Two Contingency Table for Bankruptcy and Industry

	Bankruptcy Filed	Bankruptcy Not Filed	
Wholesale	3	7	10
Retail	7	3	10
	10	10	20

The values of *a, b, c, d,* and *n,* respectively, are 3, 7, 7, 3, and 20 for our example. We insert these values into Equation 15.17 and solve for the phi coefficient as follows:

$$r_{phi} = \frac{c \cdot b - a \cdot d}{\sqrt{(a + b) \cdot (a + c) \cdot (b + d) \cdot (c + d)}}$$

$$= \frac{7 \cdot 7 - 3 \cdot 3}{\sqrt{(3 + 7) \cdot (3 + 7) \cdot (7 + 3) \cdot (7 + 3)}}$$

$$= .40$$

We have concluded that $r = .40$ for Example 15.14. We can convert this *r*-value to a *t*-value and determine the significance of the correlation coefficient in the normal way. The computed *t*-value corresponding to the *r*-value is 1.85, which is not significant at $\alpha = .05$ for a two-tailed test. We do not have sufficient sample data to conclude that bankruptcy status and type of industry (wholesale or retail) are related.

Once again, we point out that the phi coefficient is also a special form of the Pearson product-moment correlation coefficient. If we compute a correlation coefficient between the two columns (bankruptcy code and industry code) in the usual manner, we will obtain an *r*-value of .40. As with the point-biserial coefficient, the signs might differ depending on the way we coded the data; however, the nature of the relationship does not change. Although the phi coefficient is also commonly used in the literature, either approach would be satisfactory.

Non-Pearsonian Correlation Coefficients

There are many other coefficients that have been developed to measure relationships between variables. Three commonly used coefficients are ***Kendall's tau***, the ***biserial coefficient***, and the ***tetrachoric coefficient***. These correlation coefficients are not members of the family of Pearson product-moment correlation coefficients. Kendall's tau is very different from Spearman's rho, although both are frequently used in similar situations dealing with rank-ordered data. The biserial coefficient is used when one variable is at least interval and continuous and the other is arbitrarily dichotomous. In the same manner, the tetrachoric coefficient may be used when both variables are arbitrarily dichotomous instead of naturally dichotomous. Variables are arbitrarily dichotomous if they are naturally continuous but have been reformatted into two categories. For example, the distribution of height is continuous and at least interval level; however, if we classify people into one of two categories (tall or short), we have arbitrarily converted a continuous variable into a dichotomous variable. Guilford (1965), Nunnally (1978), and Nunnally and Bernstein (1994, chap. 4) have provided excellent discussions on these measures of relationships, and they are still recommended readings today. Table 15.15 compares and contrasts the Pearsonian and non-Pearsonian correlation coefficients under various scenarios.

Table 15.15
Various Types of Correlation Coefficients

Situations	One Variable	Other Variable	Type of Pearson Product-Moment Correlation	Type of Alternative Correlation Coefficient
1	Nominal and dichotomous	Nominal and dichotomous	Phi	Tetrachoric
2	Ordinal	Ordinal	Spearman's rho	Kendall's tau
3	At least interval	Nominal and dichotomous	Point Biserial	Biserial
4	At least interval	At least interval	Traditional correlation coefficient	None widely accepted

References

Guilford, J. P. (1965). ***Fundamental statistics in psychology and education*** (4th ed.). New York: McGraw-Hill.

Jenner, S. R., Omens, A. E., & Beatty, J. R. (1985, October). ***Intercultural perceptions and organizational commitment in United States subsidiaries of Japanese multinational corporations.*** Paper presented at the meeting of the Academy of International Business, New York, NY.

Nunnally, J. C. (1978). ***Psychometric theory*** (2nd ed.). New York: McGraw-Hill.

Nunnally, J. C., & Bernstein, I. H. (1994). ***Psychometric theory*** (3rd ed.). New York: McGraw-Hill.

1-10

Practice Problems
Multiple Choice

The following 15 questions are based on a sample of 25 observations across two variables. The first variable consists of the number of days since a high volume printer has been adjusted, while the second variable consists of the number of paper jams in that printer. The table below gives the results of that survey.

Adjustments vs. Paper Jams

Observation Number	Hours Since Adjustment X	Number of Paper Jams Y
1	9	15
2	10	19
3	10	21
4	12	17
5	10	18
6	10	16
7	10	18
8	12	21
9	12	17
10	12	18
11	17	25
12	9	13
13	13	12
14	14	19
15	13	25
16	10	11
17	13	26
18	5	14
19	18	23
20	8	16
21	13	22
22	17	25
23	9	24
24	11	15
25	19	25
	296	475

M = 11.84   M = 19

S 3.2873   S = 4.5

$\Sigma(X-\bar{X})^2 = 259.36$ $\Sigma(Y-\bar{Y})^2 = 486$

1. Which of the following is the most reasonable statement?

   A. The number of hours since last adjustment represents the variable of interest.
   B. The number of paper jams represents the predictor variable.
   C. The number of hours since last adjustment represents the criterion variable.
   D. The number of paper jams represents the dependent variable.
   E. The number of hours since last adjustment represents the Y-variable.

2. What is the covariance between the X-variable and the Y-variable?

   A. 4.65
   B. 2.69
   C. 9.55
   D. 9.29
   E. 1.41

3. What is the sample variance for the X-variable?

   A. 6.66
   B. 12.43
   C. 10.81
   D. 2.45
   E. 20.25

4. What is the sum of the squared deviations about the mean for the Y-variable?

   A. 242.63
   B. 259.36
   C. 486.00
   D. 5847.00
   E. 233.88

5. What is the correlation between the X-variable and Y-variable?

   A. .63
   B. .14
   C. .98
   D. .09
   E. .78

6. What is the standard error of the correlation coefficient?

A. 0.9252
B. 9.3423
C. .1623
D. .8768
E. .4028

.1619

7. What is the computed t-value for testing the significance of the correlation coefficient?

A. 0.30
B. 2.67
C. 1.17
D. 5.42
E. 3.87

8. What is the critical t-value for testing the significance of the correlation coefficient, with $\alpha = .05$ for a two-tailed test?

A. ±2.069
B. ±2.262
C. ±2.228
D. ±1.860
E. ±3.355

±2.0687

9. What decision will you make regarding the correlation coefficient?

A. Fail to reject the null hypothesis, since the r-value is not significantly greater than 0.00.
B. Fail to reject the null hypothesis, since the r-value is large.
C. Reject the null hypothesis, and conclude that there is no relationship between the two variables.
D. Fail to reject the null, as the probability for the t-value is greater than alpha.
E. Reject the null hypothesis, and conclude that there is a significant relationship between the number of hours since last adjustment and the number of paper jams.

10. How big would this r-value need to be to achieve statistical significance with $\alpha = .05$ for a two-tailed test?

A. ±.341
B. ±.396
C. ±.355
D. ±.784
E. ±.648

±0.3961

11. What is the Fisher's z-value that corresponds to the correlation coefficient for the two variables based on these 25 managers?

A. 0.6281
B. 0.0000
C. 0.7383
D. 1.1562
E. 1.9600

12. Determine the standard error for Fisher's z-value for the current data.

A. 0.2132
B. 0.1623
C. 0.1185
D. 0.9215
E. 2.5817

13. Develop a symmetric 95% confidence interval for Fisher's z-value.

A. $0.3099 \le z_r \le 0.8198$
B. $0.3204 \le z_r \le 1.1562$
C. $0.2102 \le z_r \le 1.0460$
D. $0.0000 \le z_r \le 1.1562$
E. $0.1602 \le z_r \le 0.5781$

14. Develop an asymmetric 95% confidence interval for the correlation coefficient.

A. $0.3099 \le \rho \le 0.8198$
B. $0.3204 \le \rho \le 1.1562$
C. $0.2102 \le \rho \le 1.0460$
D. $0.0000 \le \rho \le 1.1562$
E. $0.1602 \le \rho \le 0.5781$

15. Suppose that this study was also performed for 30 observations from a printer manufactured by another company. The correlation coefficient between these same two variables for the second printer was $r = .80$. With $\alpha = .05$ for a two-tailed test, determine whether the current correlation is significantly different from the correlation obtained for the original printer.

A. With a computed Fisher's $t = 2.872$ and a critical Fisher's $t = \pm 2.021$, we fail to reject the null hypothesis.
B. With a computed Fisher's $z = -0.5985$ and a critical Fisher's $z = \pm 1.96$, we fail to reject the null hypothesis.
C. With a computed Fisher's $z = 1.68$ and a critical Fisher's $z = \pm 2.021$, we fail to reject the null hypothesis.
D. With a computed Fisher's $z = 2.1869$ and a critical Fisher's $z = \pm 2.021$, we fail to reject the null hypothesis.
E. With a computed Fisher's $z = -1.2546$ and a critical Fisher's $z = \pm 1.96$, we fail to reject the null hypothesis.

The next 15 questions are based on a sample of 10 production workers who were enrolled in a training program in statistical process control. They completed a test designed to evaluate their perceptions of their mathematics knowledge. They also were asked to evaluate their anxiety toward statistics on a 10-point scale, where 10 represents very high anxiety. The motivated hypothesis is that poor perceptions of mathematics knowledge leads to high statistics anxiety. The table below gives the results of that survey.

Observation Number	Self-Perception of Math Knowledge	Anxiety toward Statistics
1	45	10
2	48	8
3	57	9
4	58	7
5	65	5
6	69	4
7	72	4
8	72	2
9	83	3
10	88	2

16. Which of the following is the most reasonable statement?

A. Self-perception of math knowledge represents the variable of interest.
B. Anxiety toward statistics represents the predictor variable.
C. Anxiety toward statistics represents the criterion variable.
D. Self-perception of math knowledge represents the dependent variable.
E. Anxiety toward statistics represents the X-variable.

17. What is the covariance between the X-variable and the Y-variable?

A. -37.4222
B. 4.4273
C. -.91741
D. 37.4222
E. .9214

18. What is the sample variance for the Y-variable?

A. 14.000
B. 4.4273
C. 2.9136
D. 37.4222
E. 8.4889

19. What is the sum of the squared deviations about the mean for the Y-variable?

A. .9214
B. 0.00
C. 1764.1
D. 5847.00
E. 76.4

20. What is the correlation between the X-variable and Y-variable?

A. -.9174
B. -.1452
C. +.8416
D. -.0951
E. -.7882

21. What is the standard error of the correlation coefficient?

A. .9252
B. .1407
C. .1623
D. .8768
E. .4028

22. What is the computed *t*-value for testing the significance of the correlation coefficient?

A. -2.306
B. -2.67
C. -6.52
D. -5.42
E. -3.87

23. What is the critical *t*-value for testing the significance of the correlation coefficient, with $\alpha = .05$ for a two-tailed test?

A. ±2.069
B. ±2.262
C. -2.306
D. ±2.306
E. ±1.960

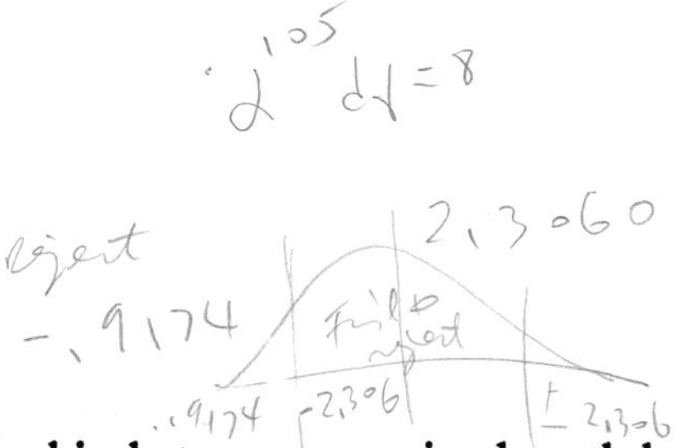

24. What decision will you make regarding the relationship between perceived math knowledge and anxiety toward statistics based on this correlation?

A. Fail to reject the null hypothesis, since the *r*-value is not significantly greater than 0.00.
B. Fail to reject the null hypothesis, since the *r*-value is large.
C. Reject the null hypothesis, and conclude that there is no relationship between the two variables.
D. Fail to reject the null, as the probability for the *t*-value is greater than alpha.
E. Reject the null hypothesis, and conclude that there is a significant relationship between self-perception of math knowledge and anxiety toward statistics.

25. How big would this *r*-value need to be to achieve statistical significance with $\alpha = .05$ for a two-tailed test?

A. ±.341
B. -.396
C. -.355
D. ±.632
E. +.632

26. Suppose that the training director was convinced that both of the variables were only ordinal level at best. Therefore, the director decided to perform a less powerful test. What would be the appropriate test to use under such conditions?

A. Spearman's rho
B. Kendall's rho
C. The biserial correlation
D. The point-biserial correlation
E. The phi coefficient

27. The director has now converted all the values for each variable into rank order data. What is the value of Σd^2 value after making this conversion?

A. 55.0
B. 330.0
C. 318.5
D. 450.5
E. 210.0

28. What is the value of Spearman's rho for these data?

A. -.9172
B. -.9303
C. -.8554
D. -.7251
E. -.5084

29. What is the critical value for Spearman's rho in this example, with $\alpha = .05$ for a two-tailed test?

A. ±.648
B. ±.564
C. ±.738
D. ±.456
E. ±.746

30. What decision will you make regarding the relationship between perceived math knowledge and anxiety toward statistics based on Spearman's rho?

A. Fail to reject the null hypothesis, since the *r*-value is not significantly greater than 0.00.
B. Fail to reject the null hypothesis, since the *r*-value is large.
C. Reject the null hypothesis, and conclude that there is no relationship between the two variables.
D. Fail to reject the null, as the probability for the *t*-value is greater than alpha.
E. Reject the null hypothesis, and conclude that there is a significant relationship between self-perception of math knowledge and anxiety toward statistics.

A researcher collected salary data for entry level assistant professors at 18 business schools. He also determined whether these schools offered a doctoral program and whether they were nationally accredited by the American Assembly of Collegiate Schools of Business (AACSB). The table below gives the results of that survey.

Adjustments vs. Paper Jams

School Code Number	AACSB Accredited	Doctoral Program	Faculty Salary
1.	Yes	Yes	43,000
2.	Yes	No	33,000
3.	No	Yes	40,000
4.	No	No	28,000
5.	Yes	No	29,000
6.	No	Yes	38,000
7.	Yes	Yes	47,000
8.	No	No	26,000
9.	Yes	No	27,000
10.	Yes	Yes	35,000
11.	Yes	No	30,000
12.	No	Yes	31,000
13.	Yes	No	27,000
14.	No	No	27,000
15.	Yes	No	29,000
16.	No	No	26,000
17.	Yes	No	32,000
18.	No	No	34,000

31. If we want to determine whether a relationship exists between salary and accreditation, what would be the most appropriate statistical procedure?

A. Spearman's rho
B. Point-biserial correlation coefficient
C. Phi coefficient
D. Biserial correlation coefficient
E. Kendall's tau

32. If we want to determine whether a relationship exists between accreditation and the existence of doctoral programs, which of the following would be the most appropriate statistical procedure?

A. Tetrachoric coefficient
B. Point-biserial correlation coefficient
C. Phi coefficient
D. Biserial correlation coefficient
E. Kendall's tau

33. Compute a point-biserial correlation coefficient between the variables of AACSB accreditation and salary. What value do you obtain for this correlation coefficient?

A. .16
B. .45
C. .10
D. .98
E. .24

34. Compute a phi coefficient between the variables of AACSB accreditation and the existence of doctoral programs. What value would you obtain for this correlation coefficient?

A. .08
B. .23
C. .92
D. .25
E. .50

CHAPTER 16

BIVARIATE REGRESSION

Case Study 16.1

Problem. The Compensation and Benefits Committee of General Fluids recently completed a series of organizational planning and strategy meetings. Their organization has experienced unparalleled growth in the past 10 years, and they want to make adjustments in their salary administration to meet the needs of their changing organization. Many new jobs have been created, others have been phased out, while still others have been completely redesigned. Job descriptions are in need of revision; and in some cases, they are nonexistent. Consequently, the committee has decided to perform a thorough job analysis, develop a current set of job descriptions, conduct job evaluations for each position, establish the worth of each job on a point factor system, and determine comparable pay rates in the competitive market. In other words, they intend to completely redesign their salary structure. They have relied on outside consultants to guide them through the development of their salary administration plan in the past. They now feel that they have enough staff to develop their own program with minimal outside assistance, as they employ a number of new, well-qualified compensation specialists. Many of these individuals are certified in compensation and benefits, and they have gained insight into quantitative methods for designing salary structures. The committee plans to develop a policy line from which they can determine appropriate and competitive pay. They will identify benchmark jobs based on job worth, participate in a number of salary surveys, match their benchmark jobs with comparable jobs in these surveys, determine the market pay for these jobs, and develop a policy line. They know that they will not find matches for all jobs, and they realize that they may have to adjust this policy line. However, they feel that this approach will improve their position in the competitive market.

Methodology Solution. The committee in Case Study 16.1 wants to develop a policy line so that they will have a guideline for determining pay. This policy line is based on the philosophy that pay should be related to job worth. The model consists of two variables that are both at least interval level. Market-based pay is the variable of interest, the dependent variable, or the criterion variable. Values for this variable will be obtained from salary surveys. Job worth is the independent or predictor variable, and values for this variable will be obtained through a complete job analysis and job evaluation. We will follow Figure 16.1 to determine an appropriate statistical approach for analyzing Case Study 16.1. We enter the flowcharts at *Start*. We are not comparing central tendencies, and we are not interested in comparing variabilities. Instead, we

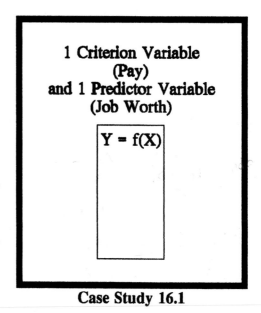

1 Criterion Variable (Pay) and 1 Predictor Variable (Job Worth)

$Y = f(X)$

Case Study 16.1

are interested in examining the relationship between job worth and market-based pay through correlation, regression, and prediction. Therefore, we turn to flowchart 8. We do not have more than two variables; and we are not comparing two correlation coefficients from two different sets of data, since we only have one sample. Job worth is continuous, and market-based pay is discrete. Pay is not dichotomous, and it consists of many categories. Finally, both variables are at least interval. We conclude that we should consider using the Pearson product-moment correlation coefficient to examine the relationship between the two variables. If there is a significant correlation, a policy line can be developed. The policy line will be based on a mathematical model, expressed in terms of pay as a function of job worth. This line can also be used to determine pay for jobs that do not have matches in the salary surveys, using regression analysis. The bold lines in Figure 16.1 show the route taken in the flowcharts.

Where Have We Been and Where Are We Going?

The previous chapter emphasized methods for measuring relationships between pairs of variables. Correlation coefficients were computed and then tested against chance in order to determine whether the observed relationships were statistically significant. Whereas correlation is a *passive* tool primarily concerned with measuring the strength of relationships, regression is an *active* tool. It provides a method for making predictions into the future, building models, examining the contributions of variables to these models, and evaluating whether the observed relationships have *practical* significance as well as statistical significance. We might say that correlation is concerned with establishing relationships, while regression is concerned with understanding and applying these relationships.

The term "regression" comes from the word "regress." We are regressing a set of Y-values onto a set of X-values to determine a mathematical equation that describes the relationship between these variables. If a significant relationship exists, as established by evaluating the correlation coefficient, we can use this mathematical relationship to improve our predictions. The mathematical equation associated with this relationship is referred to as a *regression equation.* Most regression models are derived from linear equations based on straight lines. However, we can also develop nonlinear equations for making predictions. Both types of models are presented in this chapter.

Example 16.1. We will continue to use Example 15.10, as described in Chapter 15, to demonstrate the relationship between correlation and regression. For convenience, we now refer to this illustration as Example 16.1. As we recall, the criterion variable is represented by the number of new accounts that salespersons acquired during their first six months on the job, and the predictor variable is represented by their scores on a pre-selection test instrument. In Chapter 15, we determined that the correlation between these two variables is $r = .9218$ and that this correlation coefficient is statistically significant. Now that we have established a measure of the relationship between these two variables, we will use bivariate regression to build on these concepts, especially with regard to predictability.

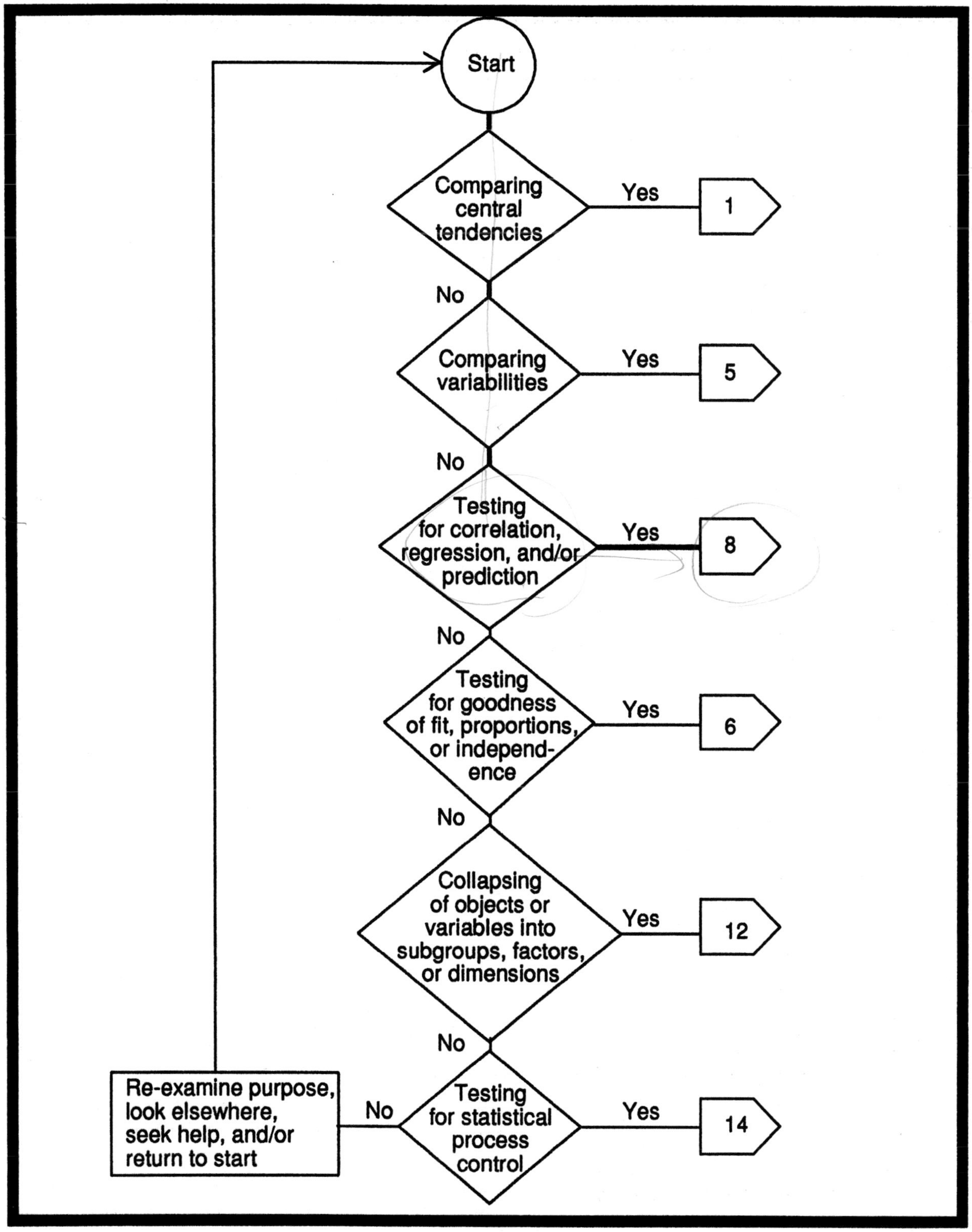

Figure 16.1
Statistical Decision-Making Flowchart for Case Study 16.1

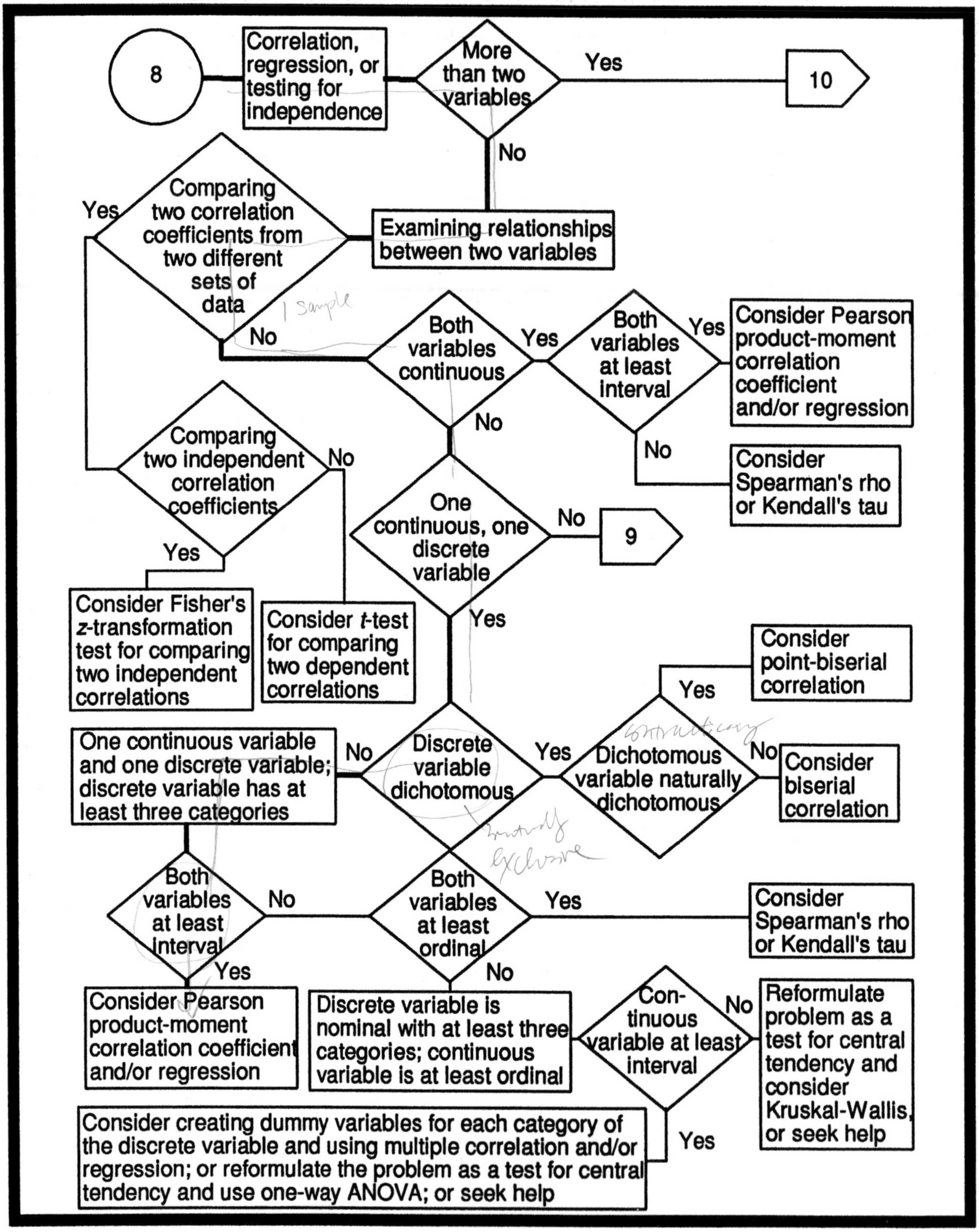

Figure 16.1
Statistical Decision-Making Flowchart for Case Study 16.1
(continued)

In order to explore the concepts of prediction and regression, we will temporarily imagine that someone has given us the list of performance scores for our six employees; but we do not know which scores belong to which individuals. Further, suppose that we have not been given any information about their pre-selection test scores yet. All we know is that the Y-values are 10, 10, 9, 6, 5, and 2. We will further imagine that these six employees are waiting outside our office door. We ask them to enter, one at a time. We would like to be able to predict their performance scores in advance of their entrance as accurately as possible, based on our limited information. What values should we guess for each of their performance scores, assuming that we will not know whether our guesses are correct until the entire process has been completed?

One reasonable approach would be to guess the *same* value (some constant value) for each and every individual, with the hope that we will be as close as possible over our set of guesses. Following this logic, we might choose to guess 10 each time, knowing that we will be exactly correct 33% percent of the time since two of the six values are 10s. This guess would give us a better success rate than if we had decided to guess 2, 5, 6, or 9 every time. Of course, we also know that we will be wrong 67% of the time. If we use 10 as our constant guess, we have selected the *mode*.

Generally speaking, it is not necessary to be *exactly* right in all of our guesses. Besides, guessing the mode may cause us to be very far off on the remaining cases, especially if the distribution is very skewed or very platykurtic. In the present example, we would not need to guess the *exact* rating for these salespersons on their six month performance reviews. We would usually be satisfied to be able to predict whether performances will be high, average, or inadequate. We do, however, want to make estimates that are closer to the actual values than can be obtained by randomly guessing under chance alone. If we guess the mode in each case, find the amount of error we have made, square the errors, and then sum the squares over the six employees, we will find that the sum of the squared errors about this constant is: $\Sigma(Y - \text{Mode})^2 = (10 - 10)^2 + (10 - 10)^2 + (9 - 10)^2 + (6 - 10)^2 + (5 - 10)^2 + (2 - 10)^2 = 106$. We will refer to this value as an ***error sum of squares***. Although we are using a systematic strategy, we find that we have much room for improvement.

An alternative approach might be to use the ***median*** as our constant, guessing 7.5 for each employee. Following the same method described above, we can predict that each salesperson falls at the median performance, subtract this median from each Y-value, determine the amount of error we have made after guessing the median, square these errors, and sum them over the six observations. The sum of the squared errors about this constant, the median, is: $\Sigma(Y - \text{Median})^2 = (10 - 7.5)^2 + (10 - 7.5)^2 + (9 - 7.5)^2 + (6 - 7.5)^2 + (5 - 7.5)^2 + (2 - 7.5)^2 = 53.5$. In this example, we have reduced our amount of error by using the median instead of the mode.

However, we learned in Chapter 3 and Chapter 4 that the sum of the squared deviations about the *mean* is a minimum value. If we guess the *mean* performance score for each employee, find the errors we have made with these guesses, square the errors, and sum these squares, we will obtain an error sum of squares equal to $\Sigma(Y - \text{Mean})^2 = (10 - 7)^2 + (10 - 7)^2 + (9 - 7)^2 + (6 - 7)^2 + (5 - 7)^2 + (2 - 7)^2 = 52$. Although we will not be exactly correct in *any* of our guesses, we have considerably less error now than we did before. We have an error value of 52 when using the mean as our constant, as compared to an error value of 106 based on the mode and an error of 53.5 based on the median.

Since the error sum of squares obtained from guessing the mean is less than our error sum of squares obtained from guessing any other constant value, we conclude that, over the long run, the worst we can do under *chance* is to guess the mean for each employee. Thus, if we knew the mean six-month performance score for a population of existing salespersons, and if our sample is representative of that population, we might simply predict that each new applicant will be an "average" employee, as implied in Figure 16.2. We have drawn a line across the graph corresponding to a value of 7 on the Y-axis. This line is used to indicate that $\overline{Y}$ has been used for each of our predictions. This line intersects the Y-axis at 7 (in other words, at $\overline{Y}$) and has a slope of zero, since it runs parallel to the X-axis.

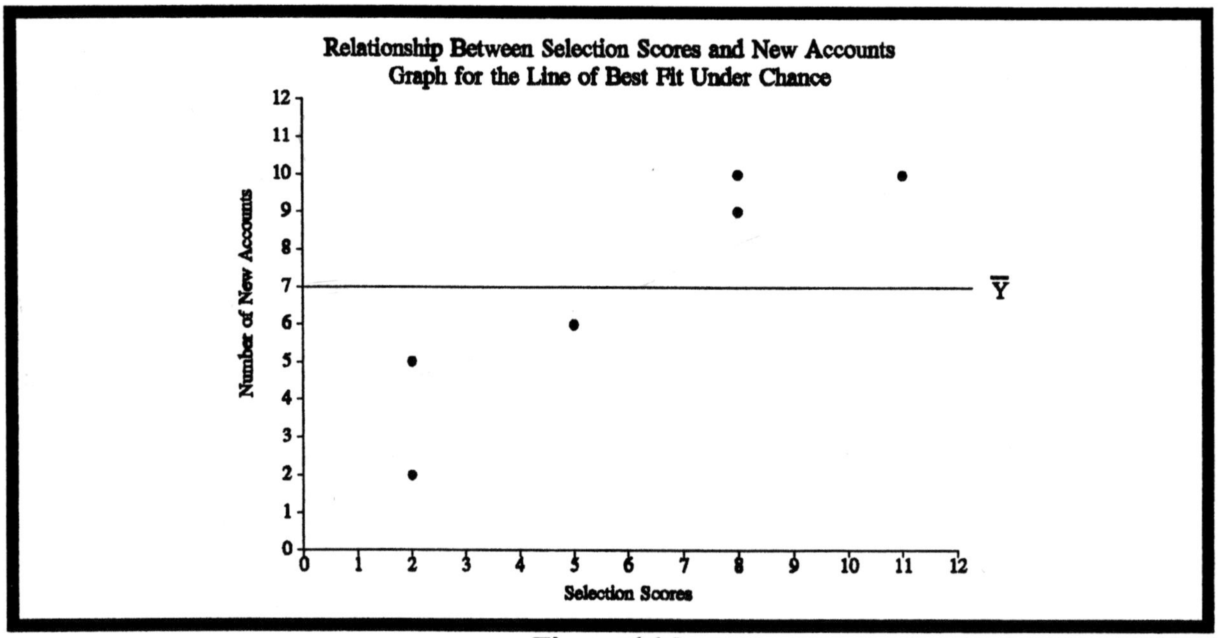

Figure 16.2
Graph of the Line of Best Fit Under the Chance Model

The Line of Best Fit

We are now ready to use the information provided by the X-variable to see if we can improve upon our prediction of the Y-variable. Our approach will be to *regress* the Y-variable onto the X-variable in an effort to make predictions which will have *less* error than we would obtain from chance alone. We will develop a ***line of best fit*** from which to predict the Y-values. Thus far, we are only concerned with linear relationship; therefore, we will only be concerned with straight lines at this point. We know from mathematics that a straight line is defined by Equation 16.1:

$$Y = a + b \cdot X \qquad (16.1)$$

where:

a = the intercept (the point at which the line crosses the Y-axis)

b = the slope of the line

Equation 16.1 is often referred to as a ***deterministic model***, based on the notion that the Y-variable is a direct function of the X-variable, expressing a perfect relationship. If the Y-variable is not perfectly related to the X-variable, then the model will contain an error term, e, as given in Equation 16.2:

$$Y = a + b \cdot X + e \qquad (16.2)$$

This error term represents the difference between our actual value and the value that we predict through our regression equation. The value that we predict is referred to as Y-prime and symbolized as Y'. The error term is defined in Equation 16.3:

$$e = Y - Y' \qquad (16.3)$$

Since we usually employ sample data (as in the present example) to draw inferences about populations, we need to compute values for the sample intercept and the sample slope in an effort to estimate the population values for these two terms. Equation 16.4 gives the deterministic linear model for the straight line, defined in terms of population parameters:

$$Y = \alpha + \beta \cdot X + \epsilon \qquad (16.4)$$

where:

α = the population parameter for the intercept

β = the population parameter for the slope

ε = the error term

The more common and practical expression for the regression relationship is the ***probabilistic model***, which allows for error. This model, again expressed in terms of population parameters, is given in Equation 16.5:

$$Y' = \alpha + \beta \cdot X \qquad (16.5)$$

The Basic Regression Equation for Predicting Under Uncertainty

The Key Regression Equation. If we replace α with a and β with b in Equation 16.5, we will have the probabilistic model based on sample data. This is the key regression equation that we will use for prediction. We use this probabilistic model rather than the deterministic model because we are almost always exploring our data under conditions of uncertainty. Equation 16.6 gives the sample probabilistic linear model:

$$Y' = a + b \cdot X \tag{16.6}$$

Figure 16.3 illustrates the amount of error that we have made when predicting Y from Y', using chance. The equation for the line is as follows: $Y' = a + bX = 7 + 0X$. As we can see, although the line represents our best guess under chance, we still have considerable error in our linear model. We would like to reduce this error as much as possible by using our knowledge of the X-variable to predict the Y-variable.

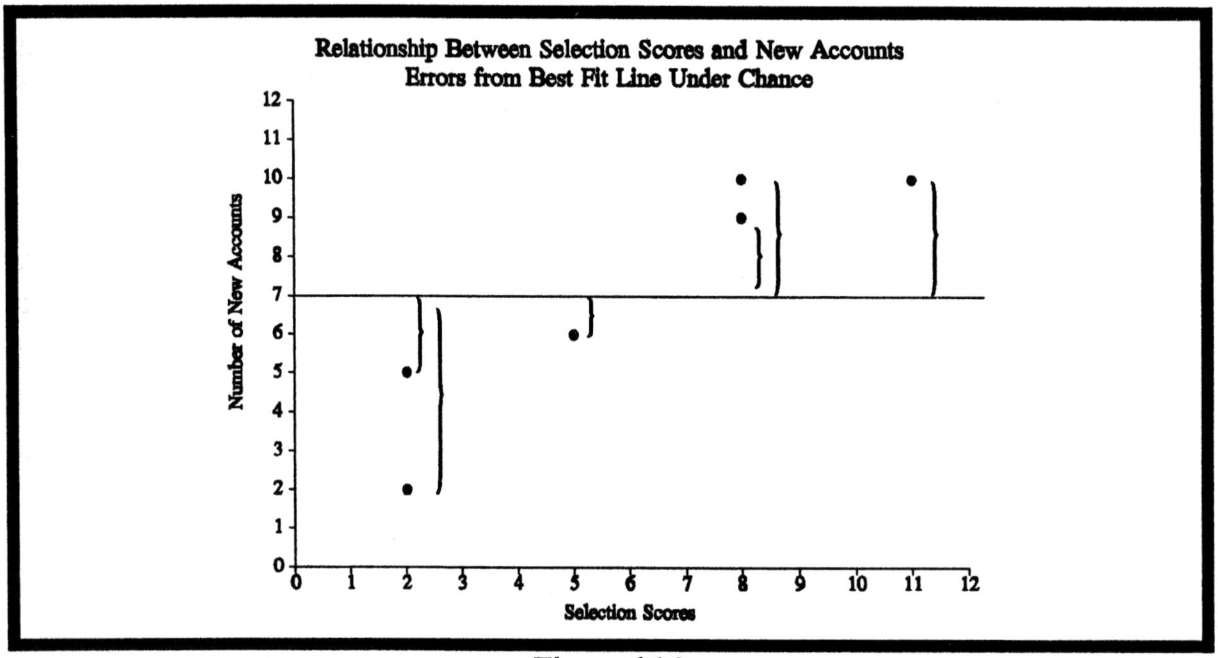

Figure 16.3
Errors from Best Fit Line Under Chance

Minimizing Error with the Objective Function

If we take advantage of our knowledge of the predictor variable, such as pre-selection test scores in Example 16.1, perhaps we can minimize our errors in guessing values for the Y-variable, such as performance scores. In order to improve our prediction, we need to determine values for a and b when predicting the Y-variable from a knowledge of the X-variable, instead of predicting the Y-variable simply from a knowledge of chance. Our ***objective function***, then, is to minimize the error we will make in our predictions when using all available information. That is, we want to minimize Equation 16.7:

$$\Sigma(Y - Y')^2 \qquad (16.7)$$

We now replace the Y'-value that appears in Equation 16.7 with the formula given for Y' in Equation 16.6. This substitution results in Equation 16.8:

$$\Sigma(Y - Y')^2 = \Sigma[Y - (a + b \cdot X)]^2 \qquad (16.8)$$

We simplify Equation 16.8 so that we can develop the error sum of squares expression in terms of a solvable objective function. Equation 16.9 now defines our error sum of squares in terms of a slope and an intercept:

$$\Sigma(Y - Y')^2 = \Sigma(Y - a - b \cdot X)^2 \qquad (16.9)$$

Mathematically speaking, our final task is to use either algebra or calculus to solve for the values of a and b such that $\Sigma(Y - Y')^2$ is a minimum value. We will not include these proofs in our discussion; instead, we will simply present the basic equations for the slope and intercept that guarantee that $\Sigma(Y - Y')^2$ is a minimum value.

Determining the Slope

The slope of a line represents the number of units we shift (move up or down) on the Y-axis for each unit we go over (move to the left or right) on the X-axis. We sometimes refer to this relationship as a measure of the "rise to the run," an expression having its roots in carpentry. The rise of the roof of a building is the vertical distance from the base of the roof to the apex of the roof, while the run is the horizontal distance from the edge of the base of the roof to a point directly below the apex. In regression, the rise is the increase on the Y-axis, and the run is the increase on the X-axis. Therefore, the slope of the line is the ratio of the change in Y-values relative to the change in X-values.

Case Study 16.1 Revisited. Suppose that the compensation and benefits committee has established an initial pay structure for a set of 12 jobs based on comparable market-based pay. They have performed a job evaluation for these positions and have determined their worth in terms of evaluation points. They have also conducted a salary survey and have decided to set the midpoints of those jobs near the 75th percentile for jobs with corresponding evaluation points in the market arena. They do not expect the increments for equivalent market jobs to be perfectly constant. Therefore, they have decided to use a constant dollar increase from midpoint to midpoint in order to smooth out their structure for aesthetic purposes. They set the midpoint of their bottom job at \$1875 per month and the midpoint of their top job at \$6235 per month. They have determined the constant dollar progression based on the following approach:

$$\text{Increment} = \frac{(\text{Midpoint}_{\text{HIGH}} - \text{Midpoint}_{\text{LOW}})}{N-1}$$

$$= \frac{\$6235 - \$1875}{12 - 1}$$

$$= \$396.36$$

This constant increment from midpoint to midpoint has been rounded to the nearest dollar. The midpoints for their new pay structure are given in Table 16.1, along with their corresponding job evaluation points, which range from 150 to 700 points across the 12 jobs.[1]

Table 16.1
Pay Grade vs. Monthly Pay

Job Evaluation Points	Monthly Pay Midpoints
150	1875
200	2271
250	2668
300	3064
350	3460
400	3857
450	4253
500	4650
550	5046
600	5442
650	5839
700	6235

[1]Applications of regression in compensation are also discussed by J. R. Beatty in Chapter 13, "Statistical Analysis in Compensation: Model Building, Correlation, and Regression," in ***Compensation Guide*** (W. A. Caldwell, ed.), published in 1994 by Warren Gorham Lamont and revised in 1996. Other chapters of that guide discuss the pros and cons of matching structure pay to various percentiles, establishing constant increments from midpoint to midpoint, and methods for establishing such increments (e.g., constant dollar increments vs. constant percent increments). The current example is designed to explain the bivariate regression model, not to serve as a model for establishing pay structures. A constant dollar progression has been selected for illustration purposes only. A constant percent progression may be preferred.

An examination of the data in Table 16.1 will quickly confirm that we have variation within the evaluation points of our 12 jobs, since not all jobs are worth the same points. The table also confirms that there is variation among our midpoints throughout the structure. Thus far, the variation in monthly pay for these 12 jobs has been consistently and completely determined by the variation in the job evaluation points. We have a ***perfect positive relationship*** between the two variables!

If our model is perfect, as is the case when correlating the evaluation points and monthly pay midpoints for Case Study 16.1, determining the slope is very easy. We simply select any two data points and calculate the ratio of rise to run for these two points. For example, suppose we select the highest paying job and the sixth-highest paying job in our list of 12 jobs to obtain this ratio, as illustrated in Figure 16.4. We will let X_2 represent 700 and Y_2 represent 6235; therefore, $(X_2, Y_2) = (700, 6235)$. We will let X_1 represent 450 and Y_1 represent 4253; therefore, $(X_1, Y_1) = (450, 4253)$. Consequently:

$$\begin{aligned} \textit{Slope} &= \frac{(\textit{change in Y-values})}{(\textit{change in X-values})} \\ &= \frac{\textit{rise}}{\textit{run}} \\ &= \frac{Y_2 - Y_1}{X_2 - X_1} \\ &= \frac{6235 - 4253}{700 - 450} \\ &= \frac{1982}{250} \\ &= 7.928 \end{aligned}$$

We know that since these two variables are perfectly correlated in Case Study 16.1, we have a perfect linear model. Therefore, this same ratio of rise to run is constant across all 12 data points. We can insert any two data points into this equation and obtain a slope of 7.928 each time, except for differences due to rounding from dollars and cents to whole dollars. Theoretically, we know that there are an infinite number of possible points that can appear along this line. Any point that satisfies the regression equation, which has a constant slope and intercept for the linear model, will fall on this line.

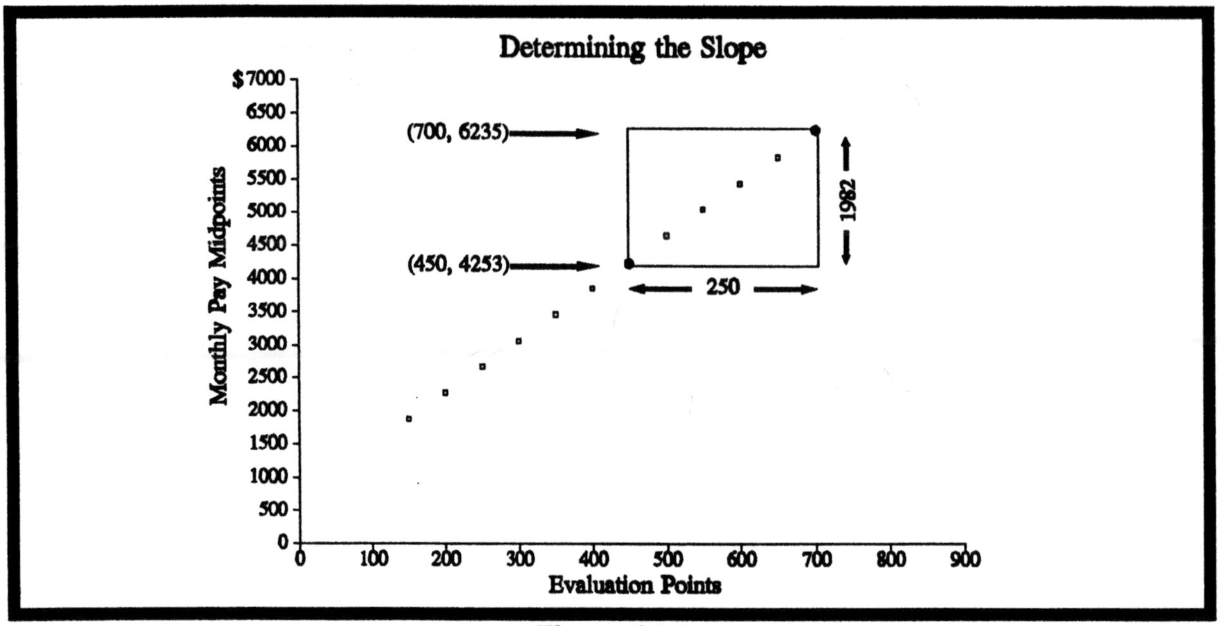

Figure 16.4
Changes in Y-Values Relative to Changes in X-Values

On the other hand, we should not always expect to find a perfect relationship between variables. Instead, we will be interested in locating the ***line of best fit*** through the data points. Unless we have a perfect relationship, this line will not go through ***all*** of the data points. However, we want it to fall as close as possible to these points over the long run. We develop the line of best fit based on the ***method of least squares***, as given earlier in Equation 16.9. That is, we determine a line such that the sum of the squared deviations between the actual Y-values and the Y'-values represented by the line is a minimum value.

Basic Equation for the Slope. The basic equation for the slope of the regression line, based on this method of least squares, is given in Equation 16.10:

$$b = \frac{\sum [(X - \overline{X}) \cdot (Y - \overline{Y})]}{\sum (X - \overline{X})^2} \qquad \textbf{(16.10)}$$

We should recognize that a similarity exists among this equation for the slope, the equation presented in Chapter 15 for the correlation coefficient, and the equation for the covariance. The numerators of all three equations are identical. We should also recognize that the denominator of Equation 16.10 is simply the numerator of the variance for the X-variable. In other words, the slope of the line is simply a ratio of the covariance between the two variables to the variance for the X-variable taken separately. When we are working with raw data, we sometimes refer to this value as the ***raw weight*** for the slope in the regression model. We will return to Example 16.1 to illustrate the calculation of the slope. Table 16.2 includes all the necessary components for determining this value.

Table 16.2
Calculations Associated with the Basic Equations

	Column Number						
	(1)	(2)	(3)	(4)	(5)	(6)	(2)
Case	X	Y	$(X - \bar{X})$	$(X - \bar{X})^2$	$(Y - \bar{Y})$	$(Y - \bar{Y})^2$	$(X - \bar{X}) \cdot (Y - \bar{Y})$
1.	11	10	5	25	3	9	15
2.	8	10	2	4	3	9	6
3.	8	9	2	4	2	4	4
4.	5	6	-1	1	-1	1	1
5.	2	5	-4	16	-2	4	8
6.	2	2	-4	16	-5	25	20
Σ	36	42	0	66	0	52	54

Based on Equation 16.10 and the values in Table 16.2, we find that the slope of the line is $b = .8182$ for the relationship between the pre-selection assessment scores and the number of new accounts acquired at the end of six months. This slope was obtained as follows:

$$b = \frac{\sum [(X - \bar{X}) \cdot (Y - \bar{Y})]}{\sum (X - \bar{X})^2}$$

$$= \frac{54}{66}$$

$$= .8182 \text{ (with repeating decimals)}$$

Calculating the Slope from the Correlation and the Standard Deviations. When we conduct studies regarding the relationships between variables, we almost always begin by computing the means and standard deviations for each variable, along with the correlation coefficient. We can find the slope of the line much easier if we already know the standard deviations and correlation coefficient. Equation 16.11 defines this relationship:

$$b = (r) \cdot \left[\frac{s_y}{s_x}\right] \qquad \textbf{(16.11)}$$

We will use values from Example 16.1 to verify this equation. In Chapter 15 we determined that the correlations was $r = .9218$. Based on the values in Table 16.2, we can determine that the sample standard deviation for the X-variable is $s_X = 3.63318$ and that the standard deviation for the Y-variable is $s_Y = 3.2249$. Consequently, we again determine that the slope of the line is $b = .8182$, as follows:

$$b = (r) \cdot \left[\frac{s_y}{s_x}\right]$$

$$= (.9218) \cdot \left[\frac{3.22490}{3.63318}\right]$$

$$= .8182$$

Before leaving our discussion of the slope, we caution against falling into a common trap when analyzing graphs of regression models. We can easily be fooled by graphs that only show the line and do not show the data points themselves. Under such situations, we may make inappropriate conclusions about the strength of our relationships. Figure 16.5 includes six graphs that illustrate this point. Graphs A, C, and E give the lines for various relationships but do not include the data points. Graphs B, D, and F show these same relationships but also include the data points (the scatter diagram) on the graphs.

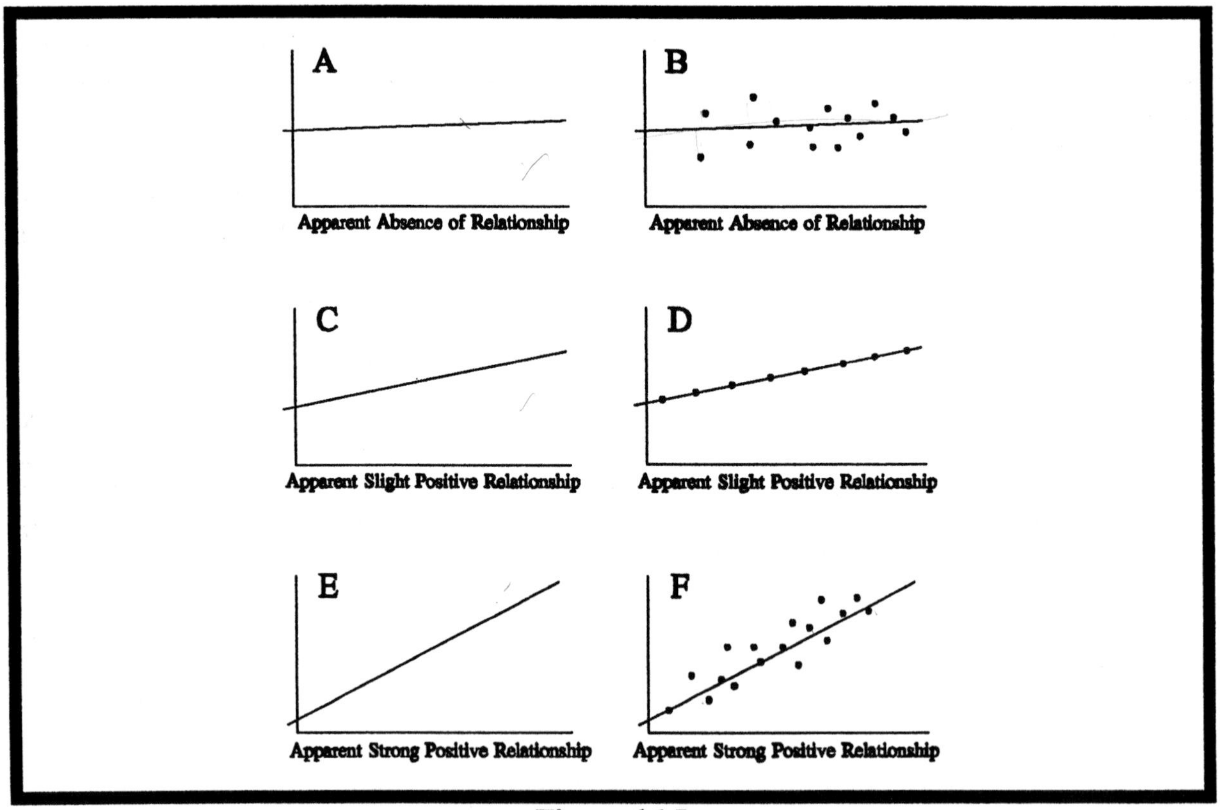

Figure 16.5
Various Examples of Incorrect Perceptions

When comparing graphs *A*, *C*, and *E*, we might jump to the conclusion that graph *E* reveals the strongest relationship between two variables, since the regression line falls at a 45° angle in relationship to the *X*-variable and has a slope of 1.00. However, when we examine graphs *B*, *D*, and *F*, we draw a completely different conclusion. We now see that the variables for graph *C*, as discovered in graph *D*, have an almost perfect relationship. All of the values fall on or very near the line. On the other hand, the variables for graph *E*, as discovered in graph *F*, do not have a perfect relationship after all, since the points vary considerably about the line. Although we tend to think that a regression line that falls at 45° angle relative to our graph and has slope of 1.00 reflects a perfect relationship with a correlation coefficient of 1.00, this is not a true conclusion. We can only draw conclusions about the relationship between the two variables from an observation of the line *after* converting all of the values to *z*-scores, as discussed in the next section.

Determining the Standard Weight for the Slope

As discussed above, we can only draw observational conclusions and make comparative statements about relationships if we have transformed all of our data to *z*-scores. If we have made such transformations, the slope will be equal to the correlation coefficient for the bivariate situation. Comparisons can then be made because we have standardized all the data, such that the two variables now have the same means and standard deviations. We know that a set of *z*-scores always have means equal to 0.00 and the standard deviations equal to 1.00. If both variables have been transformed to *z*-values, both variables will have identical means and standard deviations.

***z*-Weights.** When the data have been converted to *z*-scores, the slope between the two variables is referred to as a *z*-weight. Some textbooks will also refer to this value as a beta weight or ß-weight. However, since we have adopted the policy of using Greek letters to represent population parameters, we prefer to reserve the use of ß for representing the population parameter for the slope. Therefore, we will refer to the standardized slope as the *z*-weight.

The *z*-weight can easily be calculated for the bivariate model without transforming each of the individual *X*-values and *Y*-values to *z*-values and then recomputing the slope. If we know the raw weight for the slope (b), the standard deviation for the *X*-variable (s_X), and the standard deviation for the *Y*-variable (s_Y), Equation 16.12 will save us a considerable amount of time when determining the *z*-weight:

$$z = \frac{b \cdot s_X}{s_Y} \qquad \textbf{(16.12)}$$

Determining the Intercept

Once we have determined the slope of the line, we can obtain the ***intercept***, sometimes referred to as the ***regression constant***. As stated earlier, the intercept corresponds to the point at which the line of best fit crosses, or intersects, the Y-axis. In other words, the intercept represents a value along the Y-variable that corresponds to a value of zero on the X-variable. Although we have no job worth zero evaluation points in Case Study 16.1, we can imagine from an observation of Figure 16.4 that the line would cross the Y-axis at a point somewhere near 685. In other words, a job worth zero points would have a pay rate set at $685. Naturally, we would not expect to pay for a job with no worth. We should notice that although the intercept is important and helps to define our line, we may never have any values falling at the intercept in reality. For Case Study 16.1, such values would fall well beyond our range of data, violating one of the cautions we mentioned in Chapter 15.

In order to determine the intercept with mathematical precision, we need to have a more precise approach than simply drawing the line. The calculation of the intercept can be derived from the means of the two variables and the slope. Based on these three values, the intercept is defined by Equation 16.13:

$$a = \overline{Y} - b \cdot \overline{X} \qquad \textbf{(16.13)}$$

We will now determine the intercept for Case Study 16.1 through our mathematical equation instead of through a graphical observation. The intercept for the line of best fit, as shown in Figure 16.4 for Case Study 16.1, is determined as follows:

$$a = \overline{Y} - b \cdot \overline{X}$$

$$= 4055 - (7.928) \cdot (425)$$

$$= 685.73 \text{ (\textit{the slope has been rounded})}$$

We will also calculate the intercept for Example 16.1. Since we know the values for the slope and the two means, we can use Equation 16.13 to solve for the intercept:

$$a = \overline{Y} - b \cdot \overline{X}$$

$$= 7 - (.8182) \cdot 6$$

$$= 2.0909 \text{ (\textit{with repeating decimals})}$$

We should also notice that if we convert all of the raw values to z-values, as we discussed in regard to the slope, the intercept will become equal to zero. We can easily verify this statement. As we know, standardizing a set of values to z-scores results in transforming the means to zero. If both means in Equation 16.13 are equal to zero, the intercept must also be equal to zero. Consequently, the bivariate regression line for standardized data will have a slope that is equal to the correlation coefficient and an intercept equal to zero. It will always pass through the origin.

Plotting the Line of Best Fit

Now we are ready to plot the line of best fit for Example 16.1. In order to locate the least squares line on our graph, we must first determine two points. One easy point is the intercept. In the present example, we have found that this value is 2.0909. An approach for locating a second easy point is to choose one of the large values for the *X*-variable, one that is located near the right end of the graph. We insert that value into our equation for the regression line, and obtain a *Y'*-value. For the present example, we have arbitrarily selected an *X*-value of 12. Inserting 12 into our prediction equation, we obtain a *Y'*-value of 11.90909, as follows:

$$Y' = a + b \cdot X$$

$$= 2.0909 + (.8182) \cdot (12)$$

$$= 11.90909 \text{ (\textit{with repeating decimals})}$$

We now have two data points (0, 2.0909) and (12, 11.90909), through which we can draw a straight line, as illustrated in Figure 16.6. We notice that this line of best fit is much closer to the data points than the line of best fit under the chance model illustrated in Figure 16.2. However, our new line still does not perfectly capture all of the points. This is consistent with the conclusions we have made thus far; the two variables have a high, positive, but not perfect relationship.

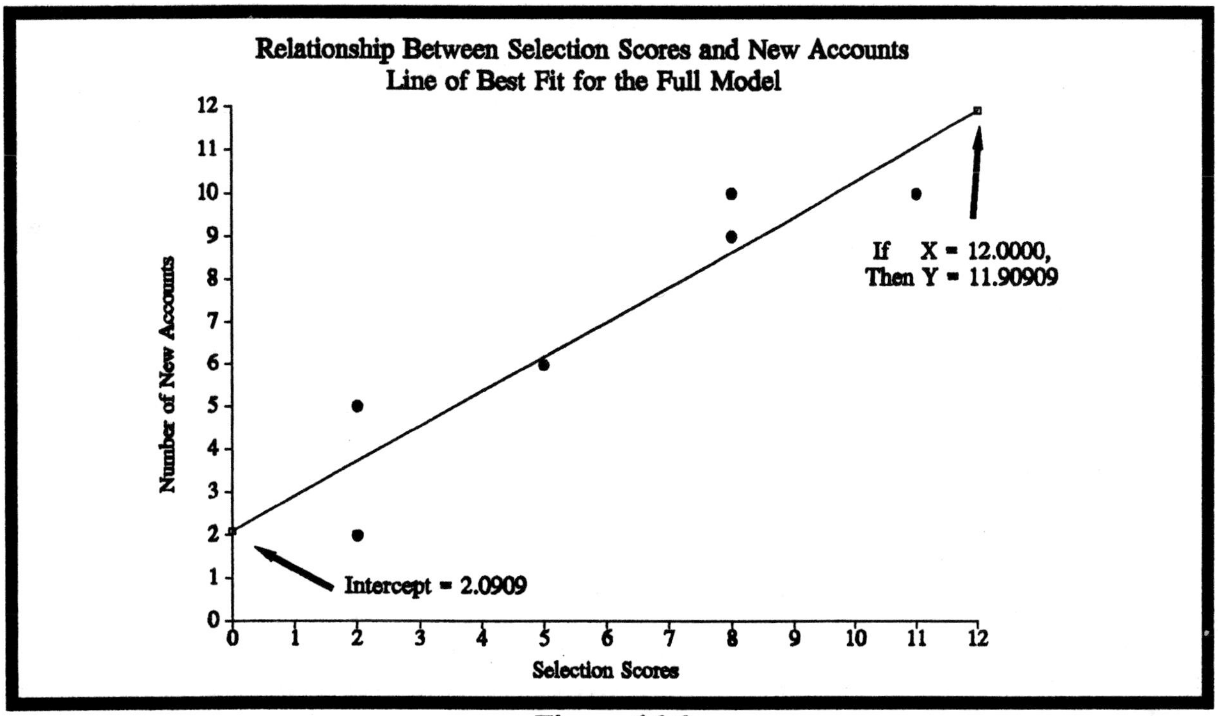

Figure 16.6
Line of Best Fit for the Full Model

Figure 16.7 indicates the amount of error that we have made in our predictions. As we can see, the distances depicted in this figure, when squared and summed, will be considerably less than the comparable distances depicted in Figure 16.3

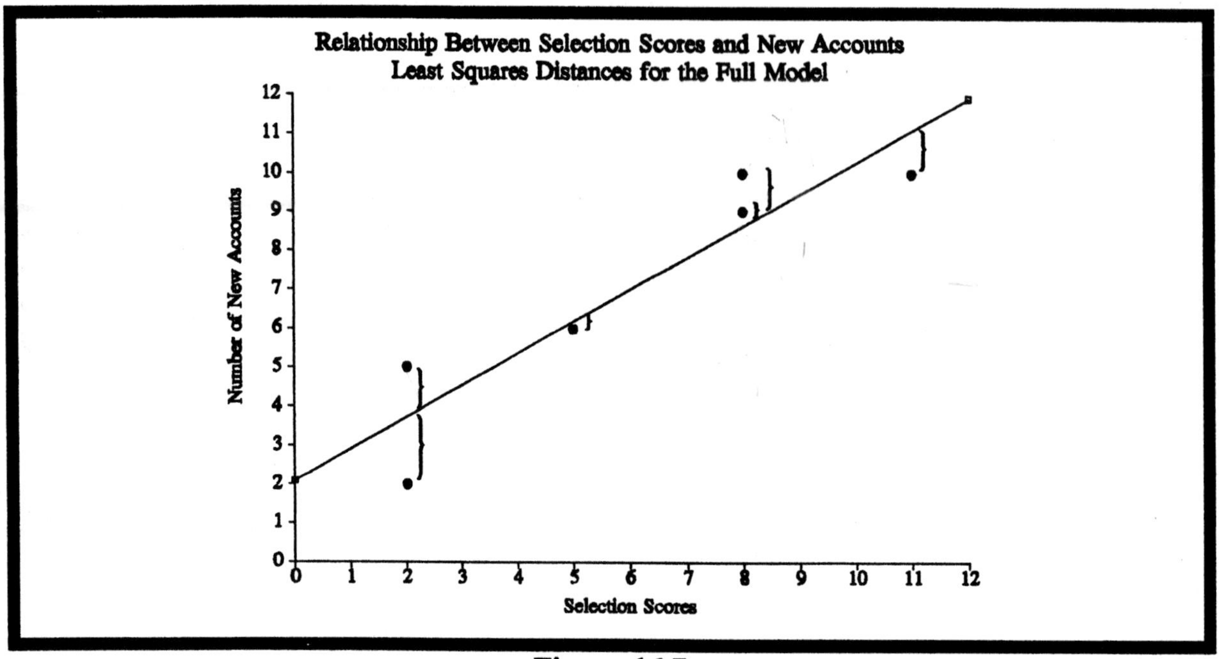

Figure 16.7
Graph for the Line of Best Fit Under the Full Model

Another point that could have been used to draw the line is the location at which the means for the X-variable and the Y-variable intersect. The coordinates for that point are 6 and 7 in Example 16.1. The intersection of the two means will ***always*** fall on the regression line. However, since the means usually include decimal values in real world situations, it is not always an easy value to locate on graph paper. It is usually easier to select an integer value for X that appears far to the right, such as we have done here, and then solve for the corresponding Y'-value. The Y-coordinate for the predicted value may contain decimals (such as in the present example, with Y' equal to 11.90909); however, the X-coordinate will not, assuming that we have selected an integer for the X-value.

Terminology Note: a vs. b_0 and b vs. b_1

We have been using a to represent the regression constant or intercept and b to represent the regression slope. This notation is consistent with most discussions of bivariate regression models. However, when we discuss multiple regression, we will have more than one X-variable and will thus have more than one slope in our model. Slopes in multiple regression are usually subscripted such that b_1 represents the slope for the first X-variable, b_2 represents the slope for the second X-variable, and so forth. Rather than using a to represent the regression constant in multiple regression, b_0 is traditionally used instead.

Models, Residuals, and Error Terms

A regression model is a statement that describes the relationship to be examined between variables. The model is usually stated in a form such as $Y = f(X)$. That is, the Y-variable is a function of the X-variable. There are basically three types of models that we examine: full models, chance models, and restricted models.

Full Models

As mentioned in previous discussions, the concept of regression is based on minimizing the error sum of squares about the best fit line. We have presented the equations for the slope and the intercept for accomplishing this task for the bivariate model. This regression model uses all available information regarding the X-variable to predict values for the Y-variable. We will refer to this model as the ***full model***, and abbreviate it as ***FM***. In the bivariate case, the full model is the same as the model given in Equation 16.6. In other words:

Full Model: $Y' = a + b \cdot X$

For Example 16.1, the full model has been determined to be $Y' = 2.0909 + (.8182) \cdot X$. This is our key regression equation, the one from which we can make predictions.

Chance Models

Whenever we eliminate *all* available predictor variables from our full model, we have created a ***chance model*** and abbreviate it as ***CH***. The chance model does not consist of any predictor variables. Thus, the slope for the chance model that we use as our weighting factor for the X-variable becomes zero:

Chance Model: $Y' = a + 0 \cdot X$

Since the slope of the chance model is zero, we always predict the same Y'-value. This constant value is simply the mean for the Y-variable. Returning to Figure 16.2 for Example 16.1, we intuitively discovered that the chance model is $Y' = 7 + (0) \cdot X$. The slope of the chance model is 0, while the intercept is equal to 7, the mean for the Y-variable.

Restricted Models

A ***restricted model***, abbreviated as ***RM***, is a model that lacks a variable or set of variables included in the full model. The restricted model is a subset of the full model, with one or more predictor variables eliminated from the full model. Since Chapter 16 is only concerned with bivariate regression, there is only one predictor variable that can be eliminated from the full model. Thus, in the bivariate situation, the only possible restricted model is the chance model. In multiple regression, there can be many restricted models; the chance model is then only one of a number of possible restricted models in such situations.

Restricted models are often compared to full models. As we drop variables out of the full model (i.e., as we create restricted models), we can test to see whether we have lost a significant amount of information as a result of the removal of those variables. Such comparisons will become a major part of our discussion when we turn to multiple regression.

Residual Values

After determining our least squares equation for the full model, we may compute the predicted values for the *Y*-variable and find out how accurately these estimates approximate the actual *Y*-values. In other words, we can determine just how badly have we erred in our predictions. We can also determine whether this amount of error is significantly less than the error that would be associated with the chance model.

Returning to Figure 16.7, the graph indicates the distances between each actual data point, (X, Y), and a point that we obtained through the regression equation, (X, Y'). We could attempt to measure the distances between the *Y*-values and the Y'-values to compute the errors in our prediction. Such a measurement process would require more preciseness than we are able to obtain with a ruler or other measurement device. In fact, we probably would not even want to perform this task, due to the tediousness of measuring distances. Instead of physically measuring these errors, we usually compute the error values for each of the individual cases based on our prediction equation. In order to do this, we insert each *X*-value into the full model equation, obtain the corresponding Y'-values, compute the differences between the *Y*-values and the Y'-values, and square these differences. Table 16.3 gives the errors $(Y - Y' = e)$, which are often referred to as the ***residuals***. The table also gives the squares of these errors and the sums of each of the columns.

Table 16.3
Table of Residuals for Example 16.1

Case	*X*	*Y*	Y'	$(Y - Y')$	$(Y - Y')^2$
1	11	10	11.09091	-1.09091	1.19008
2	8	10	8.63636	1.36364	1.85951
3	8	9	8.63636	.36364	.13223
4	5	6	6.18182	-.18182	.03306
5	2	5	3.72727	1.27273	1.61984
6	2	2	3.72727	-1.72727	2.98346
Σ	36	42	42.00000	0.00000	7.81818

An examination of Table 16.3 reveals some interesting findings. For example, we notice that the sum of the predicted values for Y is equal to the sum of the actual Y-values. Although the mathematical proof will not be presented here, these two sums always equal one another. We also note that the sum of the residuals is equal to zero. Again without presenting the proof, the sum of these errors in prediction will always be equal to zero. Consequently, the *mean* of the residuals is zero. We will discuss several assumptions regarding regression at the conclusion of this chapter. We mention one assumptions at this time: The mean of the residuals is equal to zero. (Such assumptions for regression will be presented later.) Finally, we note that since the sum of the Y'-values is the same as the sum of the Y-values, the mean of the predicted values will be equal to the mean for the actual values.

Error Terms

In regression, we are concerned with two error terms: the error sum of squares for the full model and the error sum of squares for the chance model. Each of these error terms simply represents the sum of the squared errors about a particular regression line.

Error Sum of Squares: ESS_{FM}. We have referred to error sum of squares throughout this section and elsewhere and have emphasized methodology for minimizing these terms. Whenever we develop a full regression model, the error sum of squares associated with this model is referred to as the "error sum of squares-full model," or ESS_{FM}. This value is defined in Equation 16.14:

$$ESS_{FM} = \Sigma(Y - Y')^2 \qquad \textbf{(16.14)}$$

For Example 16.1, the ESS_{FM} is 7.81818. This value is the sum of the squared residuals given in Table 16.3.

Error Sum of Squares: ESS_{CH}. The error sum of squares that is obtained for the chance model is referred to as the "error sum of squares-chance," or ESS_{CH}. Under the chance model, the constant term, a, is equal to the mean for the Y-variable. Thus, the error term for chance is equal to the numerator of the variance for the Y-variable, as shown in Equation 16.15:

$$ESS_{CH} = \Sigma(Y - \bar{Y})^2 \qquad \textbf{(16.15)}$$

For Example 16.1, the $ESS_{CH} = 52$. This sum of squares term should be very familiar to us by now. We previously determined that the numerator of the variance for the Y-variable in Example 16.1 is 52.

Error Sum of Squares: ESS_{RM}. The error sum of squares obtained for the restricted model is referred to as the "error sum of squares-restricted model," or ESS_{RM}. For Chapter 16, this error term will always be equal to ESS_{CH}. The only restriction we can place on the bivariate model is to eliminate the X-variable, thus reducing the full model down to the chance model. However, when we turn to multiple regression in Chapter 17, we will have many X-variables and can create many restricted models, in addition to the chance model. For Example 16.1, the ESS_{RM} is equal to 52, since it is the same value as ESS_{CH}.

The Coefficient of Determination (*RSQ*)

The correlation coefficient is useful in measuring the degree of the relationship between two variables, in measuring the direction of that relationship, and in testing for statistical significance. Yet, it sometimes lacks practical or relevant significance. Another term has been prominently used in statistics and research that has more practical value. This term is the square of the correlation coefficient, R^2, also symbolized as r^2, or simply as ***RSQ***. The value of *RSQ* is also referred to as the ***coefficient of determination***. Although *RSQ* can easily be computed for bivariate regression by simply squaring the *r*-value, insight into the real nature of correlation and regression can be gained if we define this term from a somewhat different approach. To accomplish this, we will return to our variance terms and their related error sums of squares.

As we know, when we are operating under conditions of chance, the best fit model is the chance model, the one based on the mean for the *Y*-variable. The *variance* associated with this chance model is the variance for the *Y*-variable (s_Y^2). If we use a predictor variable to estimate values for the criterion variable instead of completely relying on chance, the *variance* associated with this new model is the variance about the line of best fit. We symbolize this variance as s_{REG}^2, which will soon be defined in Equation 16.21. The variance about the line of best fit will always be less than or equal to the variance about $\overline{Y}$. In other words, when we create a new model by adding a predictor variable to our chance model, the new model will always be at least as good as the chance model, if not better. Our new model cannot get worse than the chance model. That is, the full model cannot have more variance about the best fit line than the amount of variance about $\overline{Y}$. If the predictor variable is in fact related to the criterion variable, we will have *reduced* our variance. The difference between these two variances ($s_Y^2 - s_{REG}^2$) is the amount of variance reduced. We sometimes refer to this as the ***error sum of squares reduced*** and abbreviate it as $\boldsymbol{ESS_{RED}}$.

We can easily compare the amount of variance reduced, based on the difference between these two variances ($s_Y^2 - s_{REG}^2$), to the amount of variance we had to start with under the chance model. This comparison establishes a ratio for the percent reduced, as given in Equation 16.16:

$$\textit{Percent Reduced} = \frac{\dfrac{\Sigma(Y - \overline{Y})^2}{df} - \dfrac{\Sigma(Y - Y')^2}{df}}{\dfrac{\Sigma(Y - \overline{Y})^2}{df}} \qquad \textbf{(16.16)}$$

If we are willing to assume that the degrees of freedom for the chance variance are the same as the degrees of freedom for the variance about our line of best fit[2], we can cancel out these degrees of freedom and convert Equation 16.16 from variance terms to error sums of squares terms, as in Equation 16.17:

$$\textit{Percent Reduced} = \frac{\Sigma(Y - \overline{Y})^2 - \Sigma(Y - Y')^2}{\Sigma(Y - \overline{Y})^2} \qquad (16.17)$$

$$= RSQ$$

This percent is represented by the ***coefficient of determination***. The concept is so fundamental to correlation and regression that we have highlighted its definition in Table 16.4.

Table 16.4
The Coefficient of Determination

The coefficient of determination, or *RSQ*, represents the percent of the variance in the *Y*-variable that can be explained, reduced, eliminated, or otherwise accounted for by a knowledge of the variation in the *X*-variable or set of *X*-variables.

As noted, *RSQ* represents the percent of the variance in the *Y*-variable that can be explained, reduced, eliminated, or otherwise accounted for by a knowledge of the *X*-variable or set of *X*-variables. Since it is a percent, *RSQ* will always range between 0.00 and 1.00. Even though one is simply the square of the other, *RSQ* has a considerable amount of practical value over *r*, the correlation coefficient. With *r*-values, we usually convert them into *t*-values so that we could determine whether they are statistically significant. We need to test for the significance of *RSQ*-values as well. If the *r*-value is significant, its corresponding *RSQ*-value must also be significant. However, just because we have ***statistical significance*** does not mean that we have ***practical significance***. Statistical significance is a necessary but not sufficient condition to have practical significance. *RSQ*, on the other hand, provides us with an opportunity for making practical interpretations regarding our data. We can now determine the ***percent*** of the variance accounted for by the predictor variable or variables that have been included in the full model. This adds an element of *practicality* to correlation and regression, since percents are generally understood by most individuals and can easily be explained to our audience. In fact, *RSQ* has become one of the most widely used and recognized terms in research.

---

[2]The sample degrees of freedom for the chance model are $n - 1$, while the sample degrees of freedom for the regression model are $n - k - 1$. This is only a minor technicality that should not dissuade us from understanding the concept of error reduction.

For Example 16.1, we know that the square of the correlation coefficient is equal to .8497 (rounded). Using Equation 16.17, we can also find the *RSQ* value from the error sums of squares terms. The calculations are as follows:

$$RSQ = \frac{52 - 7.81818}{52}$$

$$= \frac{44.18182}{52}$$

$$= .84965$$

With the use of *RSQ*, we can state that 84.97% of the variance in the *Y*-variable has been reduced or accounted for by a knowledge of the *X*-variable. We gain a more intuitive feeling for the relationship between the two variables by evaluating *RSQ* than is obtained by simply evaluating the correlation coefficient!

RSQ can also be very helpful when we wish to obtain ESS_{FM}, which requires a rather lengthy computational process otherwise. First, if we know the *r*-value, we can easily obtain *RSQ*. Second, if we know *RSQ*, we can use algebra to obtain ESS_{FM}. Based on Equation 16.17, we now derive Equation 16.18:

$$ESS_{FM} = \sum (Y - Y')^2 = [(s_Y)^2 \cdot (n - 1)] - [(s_Y)^2 \cdot (n - 1) \cdot (RSQ)] \qquad (16.18)$$

Thus, if we know the variance of the *Y*-variable, the sample size, and the value of *RSQ*, we can easily determine ESS_{FM}. The standard error of the estimate, to be defined soon, can also be easily obtained on the basis of this approach for obtaining ESS_{FM}.

Coefficient of Non-Determination

Occasionally, we hear about or make reference to the ***coefficient of non-determination***. This coefficient is simply the percent of variance in the *Y*-variable that has *not* been reduced by a knowledge of the *X*-variable or variables. The formula for this coefficient is given in Equation 16.19:

$$\textit{Coefficient of Non-Determination} = 1 - RSQ \qquad (16.19)$$

Applying Equation 16.19 to Example 16.1, we find that the coefficient of non-determination is equal to 1 – .84965 = .15035. In other words, 15.04% of the variation in the *Y*-variable remains unaccounted for from a knowledge of the *X*-variable and may be attributed to other factors.

Coefficient of Alienation

Another coefficient that has sometimes been mentioned in the literature is the ***coefficient of alienation***. Similar to the coefficient of non-determination defined above, this value also provides a measure of the lack of relationship in the regression model. It is simply the square root of the coefficient of non-determination, defined as Equation 16.20:

$$\textit{Coefficient of Alienation} = \sqrt{1 - RSQ} \quad \textbf{(16.20)}$$

Since it is not a squared term, it is usually used in conjunction with the r-value rather than with RSQ. It provides us with a measure of the independence among variables, while the r-value gives us a measure of the dependence of variables (Guilford, 1965, p. 377). For Example 16.1, the coefficient of alienation is the square root of 1 - .84965 = or .38775. This value indicates a degree of independence between the two variables not previously revealed.

Variance about the Regression Line

Now that we have defined ESS_{FM} and RSQ, we are ready to calculate the ***variance about the regression line***. Equation 16.21 defines this value as follows:

$$s_{REG}^2 = \frac{\Sigma(Y - Y')^2}{df} \quad \textbf{(16.21)}$$

where:

s_{REG}^2 = variance about the regression line

$\Sigma(Y - Y')^2 = [(s_y^2)\cdot(n - 1)] - [(s_y^2)\cdot(n - 1)\cdot(r^2)]$

$df = n - k - 1$

n = the number of pairs, cases, data points, or observations

k = the number of predictor variables used in the full model

The variance about the regression line for Example 16.1 is equal to 7.81818 ÷ (6 – 1 – 1) = 1.9545. This variance is not typically used in correlation and regression but is useful in computing the *standard error of the estimate*, a very important term.

Standard Error of the Estimate

The square root of the variance about the regression line is the ***standard error of the estimate***. This term is symbolized as SE_{EST} and is a key term for the remainder of this chapter. It represents the standard deviation for the errors about the line of best fit. The standard error of estimate can be defined by any of the algebraically equivalent formulas given in Equation 16.22:

$$SE_{EST} = \sqrt{\frac{\Sigma(Y - Y')^2}{n - k - 1}}$$

$$= \sqrt{\frac{ESS_{FM}}{n - k - 1}} \qquad (16.22)$$

$$= \sqrt{\frac{[(s_Y^2)\cdot(n - 1)] - [(s_Y^2)\cdot(n - 1)\cdot(r^2)]}{n - k - 1}}$$

As we can tell, although the third form of the standard error of the estimate given in Equation 16.22 appears to be more intimidating, in reality it is actually the easiest one to compute. Assuming that we have input our data into a calculator or computer, we will always know n and k. If we have already determined the standard deviation for the Y-variable and the correlation between the two variables, the standard error of the estimate is quite easily obtained from the third algebraic equivalence in Equation 16.22. We already have all the values needed to use the equation. As stated before, we would prefer to avoid manually calculating the ESS_{FM}, so this should be a pleasant discovery. The standard error of the estimate for Example 16.1 is 1.3981.

The Standard Error as a Standard Deviation. The standard error of estimate can be viewed as the standard deviation about the least squares line. However, the numerator of Equation 16.22 reflects the sum of squares about a varying value, rather than about a constant value. In other words, the squares are summed about the Y'-values rather than about just one value such as the mean for the Y-value. If we think of the regression line as a ***floating mean***, one that changes from point to point depending upon the value of the X-variable, we can better understand the similarity between the standard deviation for the Y-variable and the standard deviation for the line of best fit. As the distances between the predicted Y-values and the actual Y-values decrease, the standard error of estimate decreases. When the predicted values are exactly the same as the actual values, we have no error in our estimate, and the standard error of the estimate is equal to zero.

Tests of Significance and Confidence Intervals

Now that we have determined the basic equations for bivariate correlation and regression, we are ready to perform hypothesis tests regarding slopes, intercepts, and predicted values. As mentioned earlier, with multiple regression we have more than one X-variable and thus more than one slope to represent in our model. Slopes in multiple regression are usually subscripted so that we know which slope corresponds to which variables: b_1 represents the slope for the first X-variable, b_2 represents the slope for the second X-variable, $\cdots$, and b_k represents the slope for the kth X-variable. In regard to intercepts, there is still only one intercept in the multiple regression model, regardless of the number of predictor variables. Traditionally, b_0 is used to represent this regression constant or intercept in multiple regression, instead of using a. Consequently, we will use b_0 and b_1 to represent the intercept and the slope in our bivariate tests of hypotheses regarding slopes and intercepts. We will use β_0 and β_1 to represent the population parameters for the intercept and the slope in these same tests. This notation will be consistent with the necessary notation for multivariate tests that appear in Chapter 17.

Significance of the Slope

Most computer printouts include a test for the significance of the slope in regard to the regression model. Since the slope for the chance model is always zero, we perform this test by comparing the observed regression slope in the full model to a hypothesized slope of zero. The null hypothesis for examining the slope, also referred to as the regression weight, for a bivariate model is that the population slope is equal to zero. That is:

$$H_0: \beta_1 = 0$$

We use the *t*-distribution to test the significance of the slope in the model. Equation 16.23 defines the appropriate *t*-test for this regression weight:

$$t = \frac{b_1 - \beta_1}{SE_{SLOPE}} \qquad \textbf{(16.23)}$$

where:

$$SE_{SLOPE} = \sqrt{\frac{SE_{EST}^2}{\sum (X - \overline{X})^2}} = \sqrt{\frac{SE_{EST}^2}{(s_X^2)\cdot(n - 1)}}$$

SE_{EST}^2 = the standard error of the estimate, squared

$\Sigma(X - \overline{X})^2 = s_X^2 \cdot (n - 1)$

= numerator of the variance for the *X*-variable

$df = n - 2$

For Example 16.1, the numerator of the variance for the *X*-variable is 66, as obtained in Table 16.2; the standard error of the estimate is 1.39805; and the square of the standard error of the estimate is 1.9545. Thus, the standard error of the slope is .1721, rounded. The observed sample slope is .8182, and the expected population slope under the null hypothesis is zero. Consequently, the *t*-test yields a value of $t = 4.7544$. With $\alpha = .05$ for a two-tailed test and $df = 6 - 2 = 4$, the slope is determined to be significantly different from zero. We should point out that the results of this *t*-test are identical to the results for the *t*-test for the correlation coefficient we computed in Chapter 15. We can generalize this conclusion for the bivariate model: The *t*-test for the slope and the *t*-test for the correlation coefficient are identical. Some people prefer to test for the significance of the correlation, while others prefer to test for the significance of the slope. As we can see, the same decision will be made about the regression model based on either approach.

Develop a confidence Interval for the predicted value of Y.
Goal = $Y' - (t_{\alpha/2})(SE_{forecast}) \le Y'' \le Y' + (t_{\alpha/2})(SE_{forecast})$
Needed ① SE estimate $= \sqrt{\frac{\Sigma(Y-Y')^2}{n-k-1}}$

Confidence Intervals for the Slope

Instead of *testing* for the significance of the slope, we sometimes prefer to develop a ***confidence interval*** for this regression weight. This interval is based on the critical t-value (with half of alpha in each tail and with $df = n - 2$), the standard error of the slope, and the observed sample slope. The confidence interval for the population slope, β_1, is given in Equation 16.24:

$$b_1 - (t_{\alpha/2}) \cdot (SE_{SLOPE}) \le \beta_1 \le b_1 + (t_{\alpha/2}) \cdot (SE_{SLOPE}) \qquad (16.24)$$

To illustrate, we will develop a two-tailed, 95% confidence interval for the population slope associated with Example 16.1. This confidence interval appears as follows:

$$b_1 - (t_{\alpha/2}) \cdot (SE_{SLOPE}) \le \beta_1 \le b_1 + (t_{\alpha/2}) \cdot (SE_{SLOPE})$$

$$.8182 - (2.776) \cdot (.1721) \le \beta_1 \le .8182 + (2.776) \cdot (.1721)$$

$$.3404 \le \beta_1 \le 1.2959$$

Significance of the Intercept (i.e., Regression Constant)

We may also want to test the significance of the regression intercept, although this test is far less commonly used. Usually when conducting such a test, we hypothesize that the intercept is equal to some observed value computed from another data base. When we do not have another intercept with which to make a comparison, we may choose to test whether the intercept is significantly different from the intercept we would expect to obtain under chance. We know that with the chance model, the intercept is equal to the mean for the Y-variable. While some computer software programs compare the sample intercept to zero, we do not truly expect the intercept to be equal to zero in the chance model. In any case, we once again develop a t-test to examine the significance of the intercept. This test is defined by Equation 16.25:

$$t = \frac{b_0 - \beta_0}{SE_{INTERCEPT}} \qquad (16.25)$$

where:

$$SE_{INTERCEPT} = SE_{EST} \cdot \sqrt{\frac{1}{n} + \frac{\bar{X}^2}{\sum (X - \bar{X})^2}} = SE_{EST} \cdot \sqrt{\frac{1}{n} + \frac{\bar{X}^2}{s_X^2 \cdot (n - 1)}}$$

and, where:

$$df = n - 2$$

② $\Sigma(Y-Y')^2$
③ RSQ

Returning to the data base in Example 16.1, the observed intercept for the full model is 2.0909, the expected intercept is 7 (if we assume that null hypothesis is testing against a *chance* intercept), and the standard error of the intercept is 1.1798. The computed value for this *t*-test becomes -4.1610, which is also statistically significant.

Confidence Intervals for the Intercept

As with the slope, we may also want to develop a confidence interval for the intercept of the bivariate model. The format for developing this confidence interval about β_0 is given in Equation 16.24:

$$b_0 - (t_{\alpha/2}) \cdot (SE_{INTERCEPT}) \le \beta_0 \le b_0 + (t_{\alpha/2}) \cdot (SE_{INTERCEPT}) \qquad (16.26)$$

Returning to Example 16.1, we will develop a two-tailed, 95% confidence interval for the intercept. This confidence interval is defined as follows:

$$b_0 - (t_{\alpha/2}) \cdot (SE_{INTERCEPT}) \le \beta_0 \le b_0 + (t_{\alpha/2}) \cdot (SE_{INTERCEPT})$$

$$.2.0909 - (2.776) \cdot (1.1798) \le \beta_0 \le 2.0909 + (2.776) \cdot (1.1798)$$

$$-1.1842 \le \beta_0 \le 5.3660$$

Confidence Intervals for the Expected Mean of a Predicted *Y*-Value, Given a Specific Value of *X*

Once we have determined our full model and have established predicted values for the *Y*-variable from our sample data, we often want to generalize these results to a larger population. We do not realistically expect our predicted values to be perfect for our sample values; therefore, we certainly do not expect to make perfect predictions for other data not included in the sample. When we use a regression model that is based on sample data to make predictions and draw conclusions about other data, we usually develop confidence intervals based on the *Y'*-values.

For Example 16.1, the company wants to be able to improve their employee selection process. Therefore, they have attempted to develop a model in which they can use some pre-selection instrument to project into the future. If they find that a strong relationship exists between the two variables, they will use their new model to predict future performance. For example, in the absence of any other information, the company may predict that the set of all new applicants with pre-selection test scores of 11 will have a mean performance rating of 11.09 after six months on the job. They have obtained the value of 11.09 as follows:

$$Y' = 2.0909 + (.8182) \cdot (X)$$

$$= 2.0909 + (.8182) \cdot (11)$$

$$= 11.0909$$

Naturally, they do not expect that all future applicants who have assessment scores of 11 will acquire 11.09 new accounts after their first six months on the job. Therefore, we develop confidence intervals for the ***expected mean*** of the predicted Y-value to obtain a more realistic view of what future performance the company might anticipate for individuals who score an 11 on the assessment test. The confidence interval for the expected mean of a predicted Y-value, given a set of cases receiving a specified X-value, and based on the ***standard error of the expected mean***, is defined by Equation 16.27:

$$Y' - (t_{\alpha/2}) \cdot (SE_{\mu_{Y,X}}) \leq \mu_{Y,X} \leq Y' + (t_{\alpha/2}) \cdot (SE_{\mu_{Y,X}}) \qquad \textbf{(16.27)}$$

where:

$$SE_{\mu_{Y,X}} = SE_{EST} \cdot \sqrt{\frac{1}{n} + \frac{(X - \bar{X})^2}{s_X^2 \cdot (n - 1)}}$$

= **the standard error of the expected mean of a predicted Y'-value**

$\mu_{Y,X}$ = **the expected mean of a predicted Y-value**

For Example 16.1, we need to develop separate confidence intervals for all X-values within the limits of the test scores. Using Equation 16.27 and setting alpha at .05, we can determine lower and upper boundaries for the expected mean. With 95% confidence, we can anticipate that for future employees who earn an 11 on the pre-selection test, the average number of new accounts acquired in six months will fall within the range of 8.22 and 13.96. We would also expect that the average performance score for future employees who earn an 8 on the pre-selection test will fall within a range of 6.79 to 10.49. Table 16.5 presents the standard error terms and the 95% confidence intervals for the 6 cases in our example. Notice that the results for cases 2 and 3 are identical, as are the results for cases 5 and 6. This is because these pairs have the same X-values. Also notice that the standard error terms differ, since several of the values of X-differ. As we can see, we have to compute a different standard error term for each X-value.

Table 16.5
Confidence Intervals for the Expected Means of Predicted *Y*-Values

Case	X	Y	Y'	$SE_{\mu_{Y,X}}$	MIN	MAX
1	11	10	11.09	1.03	8.22	13.96
2	8	10	8.64	0.67	6.79	10.49
3	8	9	8.64	0.67	6.79	10.49
4	5	6	6.18	0.60	4.53	7.84
5	2	5	3.73	0.89	1.25	6.21
6	2	2	3.73	0.89	1.25	6.21

Companies often develop comprehensive tables that include the entire range of possible pre-selection test scores. They can locate the observed X-value in the table and quickly determine an expected range for Y-values. With the availability of spreadsheets, the chore of developing these has been minimized.

Confidence Intervals for a Specific, Individual Predicted *Y*-Value, Given a Specific *X*-Value

In the preceding section confidence intervals were based on determining a range for the mean predicted Y-value for a distribution of specified X-values. However, we are often interested in making a prediction for a ***specific observation***, based on the X-value for that observation. We know that we will have less confidence when attempting to predict for a specified value than when predicting for the average of a group of values. One observation may differ considerably from another, limiting the confidence we have in our prediction for that observation. This is a fundamental concept in statistics, sampling, and measurement theory.

In order to reflect this loss in confidence, we will revise our standard error term related to confidence intervals for individual cases. Our new standard error term, often referred to as the ***standard error of forecast***, differs from our previous standard error term in that we have added a constant value of 1 to the term under the radical. The confidence interval for the specific, individual predicted Y-value, given a set of cases receiving a specified X-value, and based on the standard error of the forecast, is defined by Equation 16.28:

$$Y' - (t_{\alpha/2}) \cdot (SE_{FORECAST}) \leq Y'' \leq Y' + (t_{\alpha/2}) \cdot (SE_{FORECAST}) \qquad \textbf{(16.28)}$$

where:

standard Error of Forecast

$$SE_{FORECAST} = SE_{EST} \cdot \sqrt{1 + \frac{1}{n} + \frac{(X - \bar{X})^2}{(n - 1) \cdot s_X^2}}$$

= the standard error of the forecast

Y'' = the expected individual value of Y', given a predicted Y-value

Based on the format for developing confidence intervals for specified, individual predicted Y-values from given X-values, we can determine the lower and upper boundaries for an entire list of individual X-values. Table 16.6 includes the confidence intervals for each of the individuals in Example 16.1. We again notice that this is a tedious process; however, with the use of a spreadsheet or other computer software we can easily develop ranges for Y-values based on an entire set of possible X-values.

Table 16.6
Confidence Intervals for Specific, Individual Predicted *Y*-Values

Case	*X*	*Y*	*Y'*	$SE_{FORECAST}$	MIN	MAX
1	11	10	11.09	1.74	6.27	15.92
2	8	10	8.64	1.55	4.34	12.94
3	8	9	8.64	1.55	4.34	12.94
4	5	6	6.18	1.52	1.96	10.40
5	2	5	3.73	1.66	-0.88	8.33
6	2	2	3.73	1.66	-0.88	8.33

Our new confidence intervals are wider, since the standard error of the forecast is always bigger than the standard error for the expected mean of a predicted *Y*-value. To illustrate, if the *X*-value in Example 16.1 is 8, our confidence interval for the mean value had boundaries from 6.79 to 10.49. Meanwhile, our confidence interval for the specified, individual value based on $X = 8$ has boundaries from 4.34 to 12.94, as seen in Table 16.6.

When we compute ranges for all possible *X*-values in our predictor variable and plot these ranges on a graph about the regression line, we notice that the outer boundary lines are not parallel with the regression line. In fact, they are said to vary ***hyperbolically*** about the regression line. Figure 16.8 presents a number of confidence intervals for specific, individual *Y*-values, given specific *X*-values. These 95% confidence intervals represent the boundaries for acquired new accounts, based on assessment scores from Example 16.1. The selected *X*-values range from 1 to 11. We notice that boundaries based on *X*-values closer to the mean are smaller than boundaries based on *X*-values further from the mean. If we examine the standard error of the forecast used in Equation 16.28 and the computed values for these standard errors, as given in Table 16.6, we will find an explanation for this phenomenon. As the difference between each observed *X*-value and the $\overline{X}$ decreases, the standard error of the forecast decreases; and, as the difference increases, this error term increases.

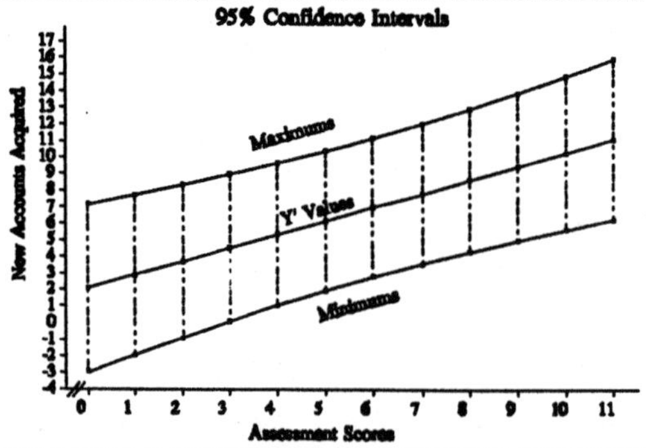

Figure 16.8
Confidence Intervals for Selected *X*-Values

Assumptions for Regression Models

The statistical literature has reported various assumptions in regard to regression models. Most of these assumptions are important only when we are interested in making inferences about populations from our samples or when performing tests of hypotheses. If we are simply interested in the relationships among the variables of interest for the data set used to compute the values, these assumptions are of little concern. Even when we are using our results to make inferences, we find that minor violations in the assumptions will not be critical. This is because most of our tests are robust.

If we assume that our linear model is a fixed model, such as the assumption made for the fixed model in analysis of variance, then the assumptions that we make in regression are quite similar to those for the *t*-test associated with comparing means or for the *F*-test associated with analysis of variance. This is the most common approach for viewing regression analysis---a perspective based on the notion that the *X*-variable consists of a set of fixed values, while the *Y*-variable is randomly distributed about each point along the *X*-axis. The following five assumptions are generally considered as adequate for satisfying the requirements of the model:

1. The error term, epsilon (ε), is independent of (and unrelated to) each of the *X*-variables. Empirically, we can discover that this is true for our sample data by simply computing correlation coefficients between the *e*-terms and the *X*-values for each case. These correlations, $r_{X,e}$, will equal 0.00. Such results, of course, do not mean that the same will hold for the population; this is the assumption that we are making.

   If we wish to test this assumption, we may plot the residuals (the distribution of *e*-values) against the order in which they were obtained. That is, along the *X*-axis of our graph, we number from 1 to *n*, going from left to right. We scale the *Y*-axis such that it spans the range of errors. Usually, we place a residual value of 0.00 at the origin, with negative residual values falling below the *X*-axis and positive residuals falling above the *X*-axis. We then examine our plot to determine whether any pattern has occurred. If the error term is truly independent from *X*, no pattern should emerge, as the graph will appear to be random.

2. The distributions of error terms, epsilons (εs), about the various given points on the regression line corresponding to the *X*-values are normally distributed. This assumption in particular is only important when we are making inferences or testing hypotheses. The theory is that for each fixed *X*-value there is a probability distribution for the *Y*-variable. We then assume that the probability density function of $Y|X$ is normal, with a mean of $\mu_{Y,X}$.

3. The error term, epsilon (ε), is a random variable with a theoretical mean equal to 0.00 and with a finite variance. This assumption is sometimes referred to as the "floating mean" concept, since the regression line represents the mean *Y*-value at any given point for an *X*-value. Our earlier discussion regarding Table 16.3 gave empirical

evidence that the mean of the residuals was equal to 0.00, demonstrating that the model does use the mean as the center of gravity. Of course, the assumption is that when using the weights obtained from the sample data to make predictions for future cases, the mean of the future residuals will also be zero.

4. Any two errors (ε_i and ε_j) are independent of one another, having no covariance, no autocorrelation, no serial correlation. This assumption is most frequently violated when working with time series numbers. We can graphically test this assumption by plotting the residual values against time. If a pattern emerges, we may want to test further for violations of this assumption. One such test is referred to as the Durbin-Watson test.

5. The random variable, epsilon (ε), has a constant variance from point to point about the regression line. This assumption is referred to as ***homoskedasticity*** (which is also sometimes spelled as ***homoscedasticity***). ***Homo*** translates to "the same," while ***skedastic*** translates to "variability." Therefore, if we have satisified the assumption of homoskedasticity, we have the same variabilities from point to point. When this assumption is violated, we have heteroskedasticity. This assumption is equivalent to the assumption of ***homogeneity of variance*** that was discussed in Chapter 10, Chapter 11, and elsewhere. Here, we are assuming that the variance of the distribution of Y-values at any given point along the X-axis is the same as the variance of Y-values at other such points along the X-axis. This assumption can also be examined through a plot of the residuals against the X-values. If the plot tends to "fan" out, the variance is not consistent from point to point, thus indicating heteroskedasticity. Others prefer to plot the error term against the predicted Y-values to examine for homoskedasticity.

We can, in fact, learn much about the nature of our data from various plots. We can plot the X-variable against the Y-variable in the normal fashion. We can also plot the e-term against the X-values, against the order in which the cases were recorded, or against time. We may also want to plot the e-term against the Y-values or against the Y'-values for additional insight. If assumptions 1, 3, 4, and 5 are true, then the intercept, the regression weights, and the predicted Y-values are ***best linear unbiased estimators*** (BLUE), based on the Gauss-Markov theorem.

Properties of Least Squares Estimators

The regression weights described in this chapter are least squares estimators, which means that they have many desirable properties over other contending weights being considered for use in modeling. These properties are basically the same properties that we considered important when determining that, for example, the mean is a better measure of central tendency than the median or the mode, or that the variance is a better measure of variability than the mean deviation, the median deviation, or the semi-interquartile range. Five such properties of these least squares estimators are described here.

1. The sample slopes are ***unbiased*** estimates of the population slopes. That is, the sample slopes do not systematically under estimate or overestimate the population slopes. Over the long run, they will approach the population parameters.

2. The sampling distributions for the slopes will have ***minimum variance***. Therefore, they are ***efficient*** and ***precise*** estimates of their population parameters. Much care was taken to emphasize the importance of developing a "least squares" regression line; that point is highlighted here.

3. The variance of the slope approaches zero as the sample size approaches infinity; therefore, the slope is a ***consistent*** measure. We know that the standard error of the mean decreases as the sample size increases. The same holds true for the standard error of the slope, as can be supported by a simple observation of the equation for that standard error term.

4. The regression weights as estimators use all available information and therefore are ***sufficient*** estimators. No other information will improve upon their ability to function as best estimators.

5. When we substitute the regression weights as estimators for the population parameters in expressions of probability, we maximize the likelihood of the sample. This is referred to as the ***maximum likelihood*** property.

Applications and Summary

Now that we have discussed the concepts of regression, we will apply these concepts with several new examples. These examples will give us an opportunity to verify our understanding of the statistical procedures associated with correlation and regression. First, we will examine a regression model, develop various confidence intervals, and then evaluate the residuals associated with the regression model. Second, we will re-examine the concepts of shared and explained variance, especially through visual interpretations. Third, we will examine a situation in which our data are related but not necessarily in a linear manner.

Example 16.2. In Example 16.2, data have been collected over a period of 23 days by the marketing director of a major law firm. The firm is interested in determining whether the number of new contacts by potential clients fluctuates very much relative to the number of times their advertisement is broadcast on the radio. The marketing director realizes that day of month, word of mouth, and other factors could affect the client base. Therefore, he wants to check for indications of such factors, although he does not have any additional data to examine. The law firm has done very little advertising in the past, and the advertisements are very unobtrusive. Therefore, the director has no reason to suspect that the number of potential clients could decrease as a result of the radio broadcasts. Since he is at the early stages of exploratory data analysis and the cost of these advertisements are reasonable, he is more concerned with making a Type II error than a Type I error. Based on all of these considerations, he has decided to conduct a one-directional test with alpha set at .10.

Using the master flowcharts, we begin at ***Start***. We are not comparing central tendencies or variabilities. Instead, we are interested in correlation, regression, and/or prediction, so we turn to flowchart 8. The marketing director has collected data on the number of times the advertisements were broadcast and the number of contacts made during the same time period; thus, we only have two variables. We are not comparing two correlation coefficients from two different sets of data but are examining the relationship between two discrete variables, which takes us to flowchart 9. We do not have two dichotomous variables; in fact, neither variable is dichotomous. As we have already confirmed, both variables are discrete, and each variable has at least three categories. Finally, both variables are at least interval scale. We conclude that we should consider using the Pearson product-moment correlation coefficient to examine the relationship between the two variables. If there is a significant correlation, we should then consider using regression to develop a prediction model. Descriptive statistics, correlation and regression analysis, the analysis of variance for the regression, and the regression model have been obtained through an ***Excel*** spreadsheet, reorganized, and included in Table 16.7 for Example 16.2.

Table 16.7
Statistics Generated by Excel for Radio Broadcasts and Potential Clients

Descriptive Statistics

Mean	10.9565	80.9565
Standard Error	0.4969	2.6454
Median	11	81
Mode	14	77
Standard Deviation	2.3832	12.6867
Variance	5.6798	160.9526
Kurtosis	0.0964	1.8367
Skewness	-0.6057	-1.0013
Range	9	55
Minimum	5	45
Maximum	14	100
Sum	252	1862
Count	23	23

Correlation Matrix

1.0000	0.3201
0.3201	1.0000

Regression Statistics

Multiple R	.3201
RSQ	.1025
Adjusted R Square	.0598
Standard Error	12.3018
Observations	23

SS **Analysis of Variance**

	df	Sum of Squares	Mean Square	F	Significance F
Regression	1	362.9301	362.9301	2.398196	0.136415
Residual	21	3178.026	151.3346		
Total	22	3540.957			

Regression Model Statistics

	Coefficients	Standard Error	*t* Statistic	*P* Value	Lower 95%	Upper 95%
Intercept	62.283920	12.327470	5.052451	0.0000464	36.64755	87.920300
X_1	1.704245	1.100499	1.548611	0.1357420	-0.58437	3.992858

Reject Ho
>.05

As we can see from the spreadsheet analysis, the standard deviation for the criterion variable is $s_Y = 12.6867$, the standard deviation for the predictor variable is $s_X = 2.3832$, and the correlation between the two variables is $r = .3201$, which converts to a $t = 1.5484$, which has a two-directional probability of $p = .1357$. Since this is a one-directional test, the probability becomes $p = .1357 \div 2 = .0679$ for a one-tailed test. Consequently, we reject the null hypothesis based on the previously specified directionality and alpha level. While we might have made a Type I error, we have not made a Type II error.

Table 16.7 also verifies that the test for the slope does in fact yield the same results as the test for the correlation coefficient when the model is bivariate. The spreadsheet-computed value for the slope is $b_1 = 1.7043$, which is then converted to a $t = 1.5484$. The spreadsheet also includes the two-directional probability associated with the t-test for the slope, yielding a value of $p = .1357$. These results agree with the results for the correlation coefficient.

The spreadsheet also reveals several other interesting facts. We notice that the printout includes an *analysis of variance* table for comparing the regression model to a residual model. We see from the table that the $SS_{RESIDUAL} = 3178.0264$, which we referred to as the SS_{WITHIN} in Chapter 12 and Chapter 13. If we calculate the error sum of squares for the full model, we will also find that the $ESS_{FM} = 3178.0264$. The analysis of variance table indicates that the $SS_{TOTAL} = 3540.9565$. If we calculate the error sum of squares for the chance model, we will also find that the $ESS_{CH} = 3540.9565$. Further, this ANOVA table indicates that the $SS_{REGRESSION} = 362.9301$. If we calculate the error sum of squares reduced, we will find that $ESS_{RED} = ESS_{CH} - ESS_{FM} = 3540.9565 - 3178.0264 = 362.9301$. Finally, the analysis of variance table indicates that the $MS_{RESIDUAL} = 151.3346$. If we calculate the standard error of the estimate, we will find that $(SE_{EST})^2 = (12.3018)^2 = 151.3346$. While we will discuss the remaining values in this spreadsheet in Chapter 17, we can certainly see that there is a direct relationship between regression analysis and analysis of variance! Equation 16.29 directly expresses this relationship:

$$\begin{aligned} RSQ &= \frac{ESS_{CH} - ESS_{FM}}{ESS_{CH}} \\ &= \frac{ESS_{RED}}{ESS_{CH}} \qquad \textbf{(16.29)} \\ &= \frac{SS_A}{SS_T} \end{aligned}$$

This equation shows that the ratio of the among variance to the total variance in ANOVA terms is equivalent to the percent of the variance in the Y-variable accounted for by a knowledge of the predictor variable or variables. This ratio is directly related to ω^2 (omega-squared), a term widely used to summarize analysis of variance tables (Hays, 1963, pp. 325-332).

Table 16.8 includes the data obtained for the 23-day period of concern, along with a number of other values which can be generated from a knowledge of the regression model. The first column consists of the number of new contacts by potential clients, while the second column consists of the number of radio advertisements during the same day. The third column contains the differences between the actual and predicted Y-values, based on the prediction equation. The fourth column contains the squares of these errors; the sixth column contains the standard error terms for the *mean values*; the seventh column contains the confidence intervals for these mean values; and the eighth column contains the standard error of the forecast for each case. Finally, the ninth column consists of the confidence intervals for these specific values.

Table 16.8
Predicted Y-Values and Confidence Intervals for Potential New Clients

Y	X	Y'	e	e^2	$SE_{\bar{Y}_{Y,X}}$	Interval for Mean Value Min to Max	SE_{FORE}	Interval for Individual Value Min to Max
45	9	77.62	-32.62	1064.20	3.3490	70.6562 to 84.5880	12.7495	51.1031 to 104.1411
77	5	70.81	6.19	38.38	7.0391	56.1637 to 85.4465	14.1734	41.3245 to 100.2857
80	12	82.73	-2.73	7.48	2.8104	76.8891 to 88.5805	12.6187	56.4878 to 108.9818
82	14	86.14	-4.14	17.17	4.2188	77.3682 to 94.9183	13.0051	59.0927 to 113.1939
77	14	86.14	-9.14	83.60	4.2188	77.3682 to 94.9183	13.0051	59.0927 to 113.1939
96	12	82.73	13.27	175.97	2.8104	76.8891 to 88.5805	12.6187	56.4878 to 108.9818
83	10	79.33	3.67	13.50	2.7727	73.5591 to 85.0935	12.6104	53.0967 to 105.5559
80	10	79.33	0.67	0.45	2.7727	73.5591 to 85.0935	12.6104	53.0967 to 105.5559
71	8	75.92	-4.92	24.19	4.1432	67.3000 to 84.5356	12.9808	48.9179 to 102.9178
58	8	75.92	-17.92	321.05	4.1432	67.3000 to 84.5356	12.9808	48.9179 to 102.9178
84	13	84.44	-0.44	0.19	3.4113	77.3435 to 91.5346	12.7660	57.8857 to 110.9924
94	10	79.33	14.67	215.32	2.7727	73.5591 to 85.0935	12.6104	53.0967 to 105.5559
81	9	77.62	3.38	11.41	3.3490	70.6562 to 84.5880	12.7495	51.1031 to 104.1411
89	11	81.03	7.97	63.51	2.5655	75.6942 to 86.3669	12.5665	54.8923 to 107.1688
87	8	75.92	11.08	122.81	4.1432	67.3000 to 84.5356	12.9808	48.9179 to 102.9178
70	12	82.73	-12.73	162.18	2.8104	76.8891 to 88.5805	12.6187	56.4878 to 108.9818
76	14	86.14	-10.14	102.89	4.2188	77.3682 to 94.9183	13.0051	59.0927 to 113.1939
90	13	84.44	5.56	30.92	3.4113	77.3435 to 91.5346	12.7660	57.8857 to 110.9924
75	11	81.03	-6.03	36.37	2.5655	75.6942 to 86.3669	12.5665	54.8923 to 107.1688
94	11	81.03	12.97	168.21	2.5655	75.6942 to 86.3669	12.5665	54.8923 to 107.1688
76	13	84.44	-8.44	71.22	3.4113	77.3435 to 91.5346	12.7660	57.8857 to 110.9924
100	14	86.14	13.86	192.01	4.2188	77.3682 to 94.9183	13.0051	59.0927 to 113.1939
97	11	81.03	15.97	255.02	2.5655	75.6942 to 86.3669	12.5665	54.8923 to 107.1688

The *RSQ* for the full model is .1025, meaning that only 10.25% of the variation in the number of new contacts by potential clients can be accounted for by a knowledge of the variation in the number of times their advertisement is broadcast on the radio. Viewing this relationship from another perspective, we find that the coefficient of non-determination is equal to 1 – .1025, or .8975. In other words, 89.75% of the variation in the number of new contacts of potential clients cannot be accounted for by the predictor variable. Although the relationship might have been statistically significant at $\alpha = .10$ for a one-tailed test, it has very little practical significance. As can be seen from Table 16.8, the confidence intervals are rather wide and yield little practical value to the marketing director. For example, during the day in which the advertisement was broadcast 11 times (which was about average), the resulting interval spans from 54.8923 to 107.1688! The marketing director cannot make very conclusive statements based on such results.

We may recall that the marketing director realized that day of the month, word of mouth, and other factors could affect the client base. While he does not have data with which to rule out the influence of such factors in his regression analysis, he can plot the residuals against the order in which the cases were recorded. This might indicate whether there are trends or fluctuations perhaps related to days of the month or other factors. As can be seen from an observation of Figure 16.9, no particular trend is observed, giving no reason to expect autocorrelation or lack of independence of cases.

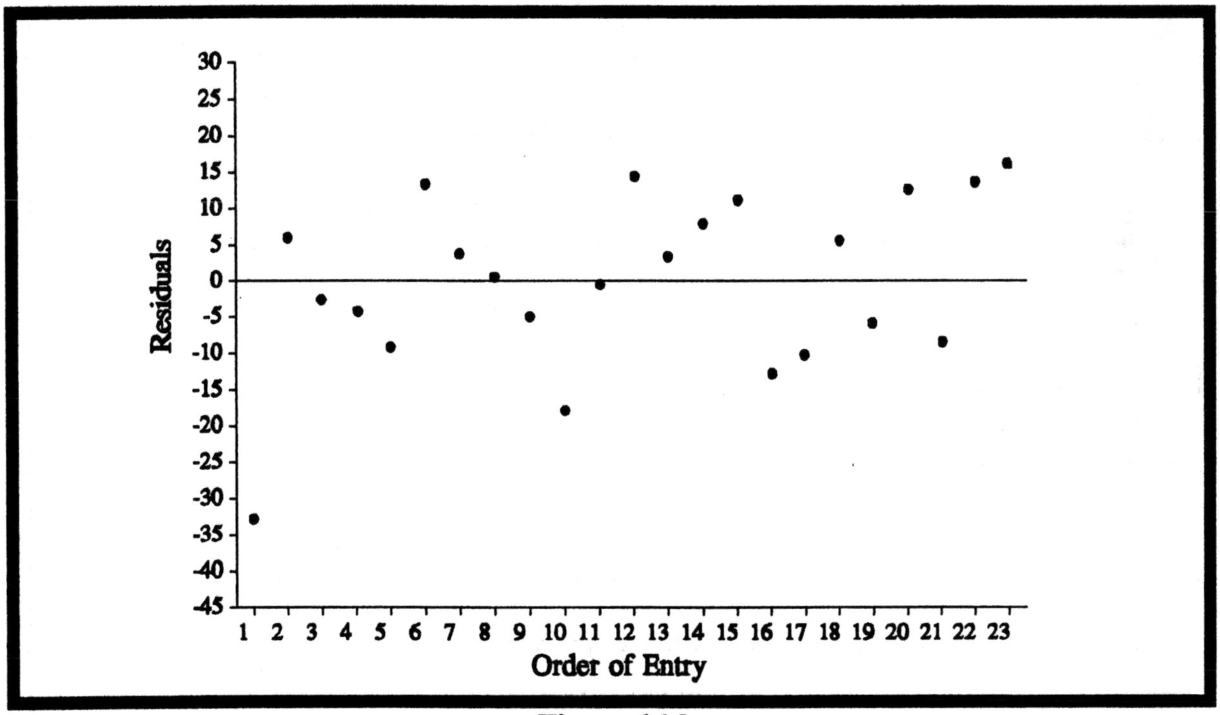

Figure 16.9
Graph of Residuals Plotted Against Order of Entry

Case Study 1.1 Revisited. We now return to Case Study 1.1, which was initially presented in Chapter 1 and further developed in many other chapters of this book. We will recall that the Process Action Team at NaviTech Industries brainstormed, developed a cause-and-effect diagram, and flowcharted their process. Many of the discoveries uncovered by this team have already been addressed. However, another factor that was discussed by the process action team was the reward system within the organization. Team members did not feel that production workers were being fairly compensated for their efforts. Consequently, Mr. Roberts, the Director of Quality, asked the human resources department to investigate this potential problem. The human resources group began their investigation by evaluating the relationship between pay and performance for a sample of 74 welders. They grouped their pay data, a discrete variable, into intervals and appropriately displayed these intervals in the form of a bar graph, as shown in Figure 16.10. They also grouped their performance data into intervals for these same 74 welders. For this investigation, performance was defined as the average number of seconds taken to complete a set of welds, and the welders' averages were determined from a number of observations over time. The team displayed this continuous variable in the form of a histogram. This graph is shown in Figure 16.11.

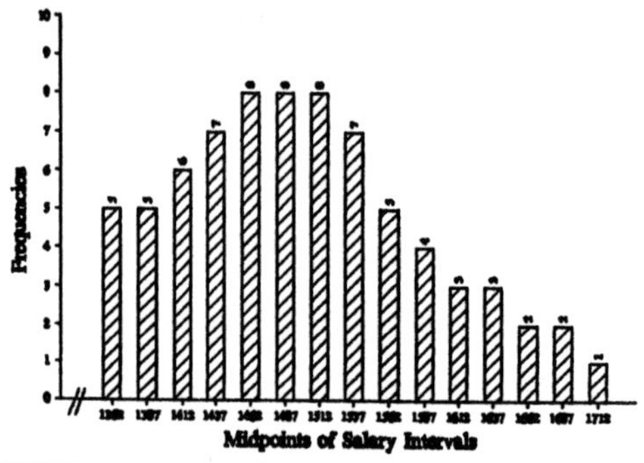

Figure 16.10
Bar Graph for Salaries in Grouped Format

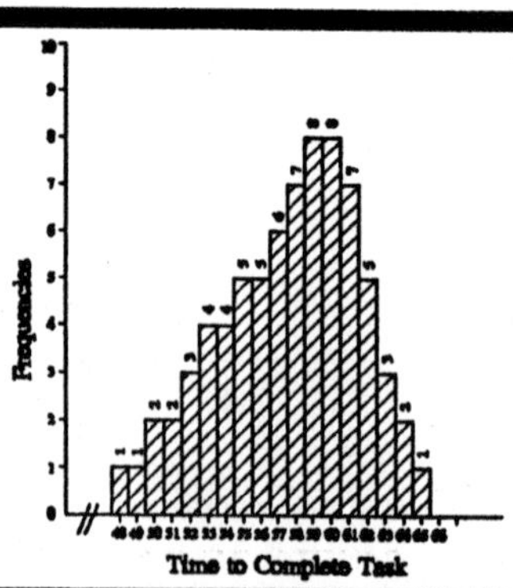

Figure 16.11
Histogram for Time to Complete Task

We will now examine the relationship between the welders' pay and performance. The correlation between these two variables yielded a coefficient of $r = -.8449$. After converting this r-value to a t-value, the test statistic for the correlation produced a $t = -13.40$. This t-value is statistically significant. In other words, the pay for these 74 individuals was significantly correlated to their average number of seconds taken to complete the set of welds. The coefficient of determination, or *RSQ*, is .7138. Thus, they are able to explain 71.38% of the variation in pay from a knowledge performance. They also computed the line of best fit to represent these data, as follows:

$$Y' = a + b \cdot X$$

$$= 2605.0540 - (19.1934) \cdot (X)$$

As we might have expected, there is a strong negative relationship between these two variables. The slope of the line is a negative value, indicating that as the number of seconds required to complete the welding task decreases, the pay of the welders increases. This conclusion is reasonable and suggests that on the basis of this one investigation, pay seems to be fairly distributed to employees. Figure 16.12 allows us to carefully examine this relationship, as well as to examine the concepts of correlation and regression in general.

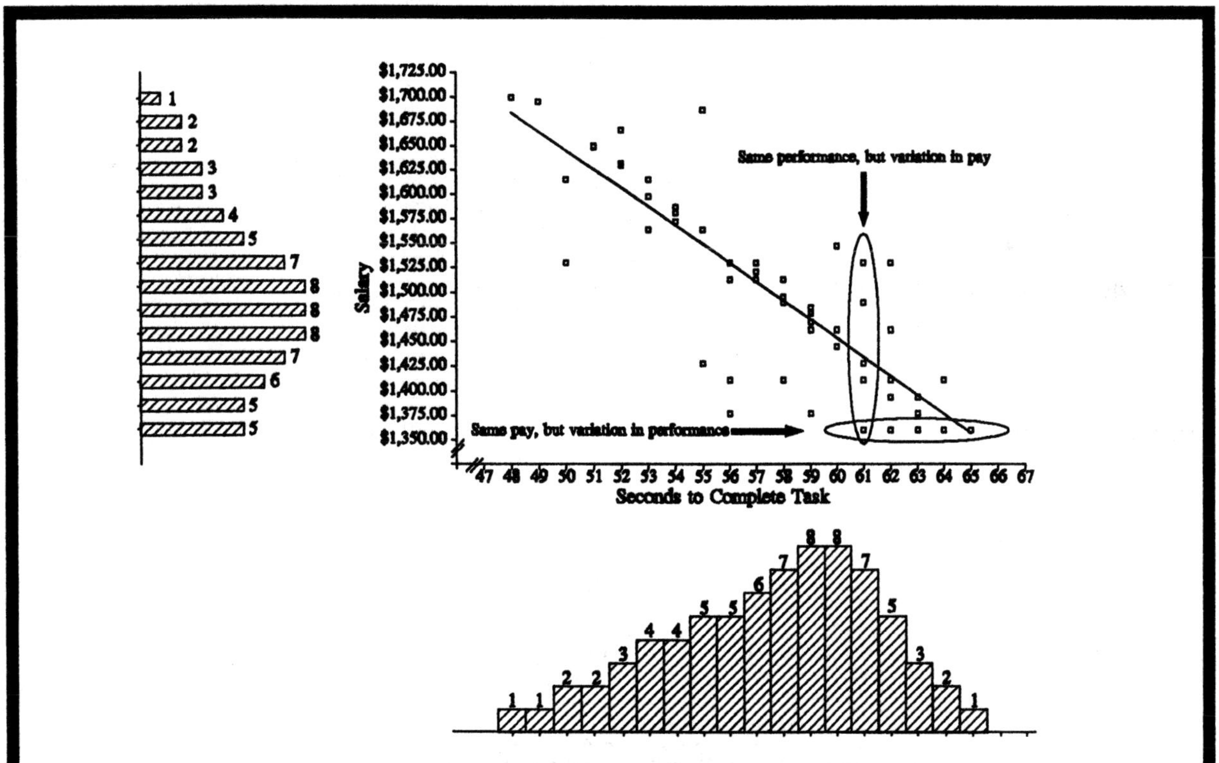

Figure 16.12
Scatter Diagram Using Spreadsheet Defaults

As we can see from Figure 16.12, the scatter diagram has been superimposed with two other graphs: the histogram for seconds to complete the task and the bar graph for welders' pay. The data points in the scatter diagram correspond with each of these frequency distribution graphs. We also notice that default options of the spreadsheet used to create the graph have been used for each variable. That is, neither graph starts at the origin. If they did, the data points on the scatter diagram would have to be located in an extreme corner of the picture, which would also be misleading. On the other hand, we can see that if we extended the line of best fit in this picture, it might appear as if the intercept is approximately $1722. By looking at the regression equation, we know that the intercept is actually $2605.05. We caution here to not be mislead by such default options that can distort reality and result in faulty conclusions.

We can learn something else from Figure 16.12. We have circled the data points for five individuals who required the same amount of time to complete the welding task. We should notice that each of these individuals received different pay. Further, we circled the data points for five individuals who received the same pay but had completely different welding times. This serves to illustrate that we cannot explain 100% of the variation in pay from a knowledge of welding times. Other factors are clearly impacting the pay of these individuals. Bivariate correlation and regression only allow us to explore two variables at a time. When we turn to multiple regression in Chapter 17, we will be able to explore numerous predictor variables simultaneously, along with any interactions that may exist among such predictor variables. For a more detailed discussion on the use of correlation, regression, and multiple regression in compensation analysis, the reader is referred to Chapter 13 of ***Compensation Guide*** (Beatty, 1994b; 1996).

Example 16.3. As our final example, we will illustrate the importance of plotting our points. The engineering department of a local manufacturing firm has been concerned with the fluctuation of waste regarding a precious metal that is used in their manufacturing process. Initially the company was not able to detect any factors that were impacting the amount of waste during the crucial operation. Eventually, they decided to design an experiment whereby they would manipulate various factors and observe any fluctuations in the waste as a result of these manipulations. They found that they could change the temperature in the kiln during this crucial point, but they decided that their ability to control the temperature at the exact moment of impact with any degree of preciseness was limited. They also found that certain chemicals, when mixed with the precious metal, would have an impact on the amount of waste generated. However, the chemicals were very scarce, and they did not want to eliminate their supply of these chemicals at this early stage in their investigation. They also knew that the proper setting of a valve in the system could have a major impact on the results. The valve itself was recalibrated on a daily basis, and the range of settings for the valve were also carefully monitored. Therefore, the project manager decided to manipulate the valve settings and monitor the amount of waste that occurred at each setting. Due to the costs involved in the experiment, she decided to limit the number of observations to 20. She also decided to hold the temperature and the reaction chemicals constant so that they would not distort the impact of the valve settings. Table 16.9 gives the results of her data collection over the set of 20 trials.

Table 16.9
Valve Settings and Grams of Waste

Case Number	Valve Setting	Grams of Waste
1	89	65
2	69	64
3	98	58
4	80	68
5	75	66
6	75	63
7	95	64
8	93	67
9	76	60
10	83	72
11	72	58
12	74	55
13	90	70
14	96	56
15	97	60
16	87	72
17	90	68
18	99	55
19	78	65
20	85	70

The project manager then correlated the valve settings with the amount of waste, as measured in grams. She found that the correlation was $r = -.0849$, and her line of best fit was determined as follows: $Y' = 67.9252 - (.0485)\cdot X$. Needless to say, she was not very happy with her results. The correlation was not significant, and based on *RSQ*, only 0.72% of the variation in waste could be accounted for by a knowledge of the valve settings. However, she was not willing to accept her findings at face value. Based on all of her past experience with the project, she was convinced that these two variables were related. She finally decided to plot her data, as shown in Figure 16.13. As we can see from an observation of this figure, the data clearly are related; however, they are related in a ***nonlinear*** manner! If she had not plotted her data, she may never have made this discovery. She then decided to develop a nonlinear model to capture her data. Figure 16.14 gives a graph of her nonlinear model. The graph appears to be a parabola, based on a quadratic equation. She simply used the X-variable *and* the square of the X-variable as the predictor variables in her new model. While we will rely on multiple regression when we develop models with more than one predictor variable, we point out here that her new model has an *RSQ* of .5701. She is now able to explain 57.01% of the variation in waste by a knowledge of valve settings, and the new model cost her nothing beyond her initial collection of data. She concluded that when the settings are low, the waste is fairly low; when the setting is increased, the waste increases; and when the settings are maximized, the waste once again is low. This is a curvilinear model, requiring the use of multiple regression.

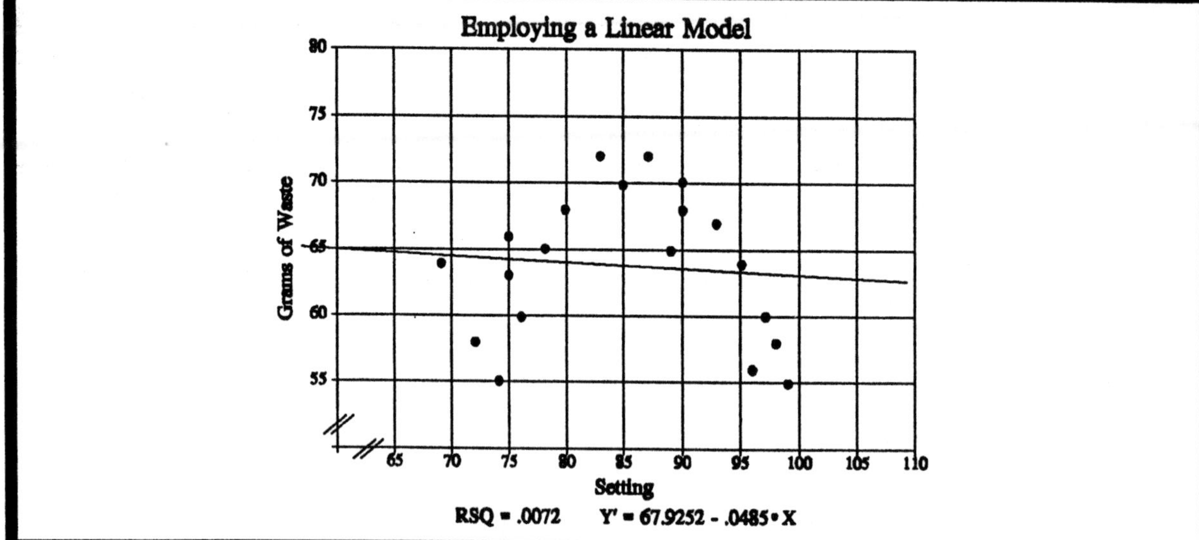

Figure 16.13
Analyzing the Data with a Linear Model

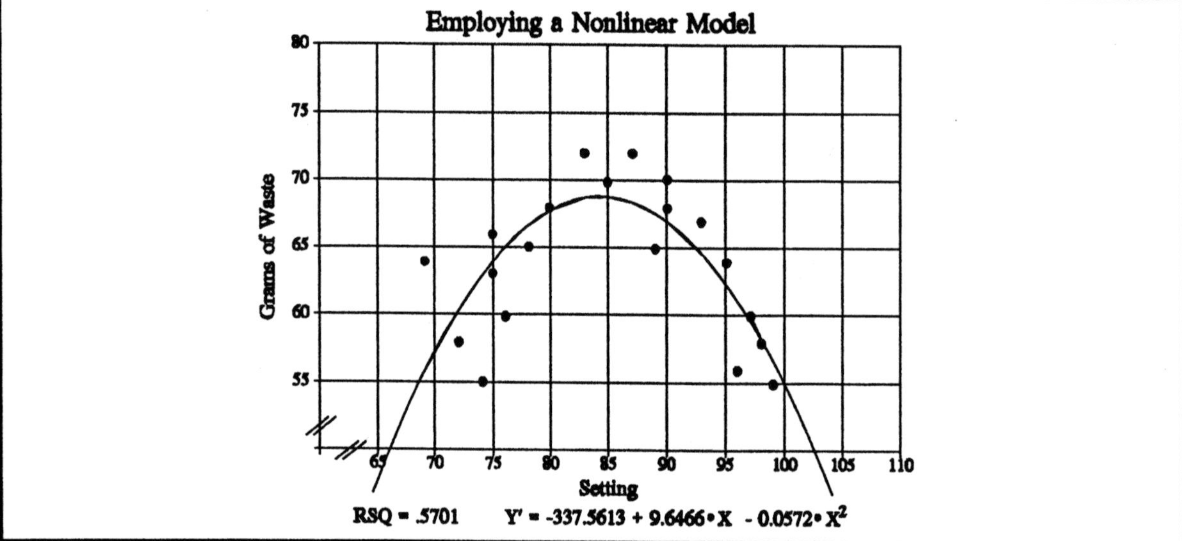

Figure 16.14
Analyzing the Data with a Nonlinear Model

References

Beatty, J. R. (1994b). Statistical analysis in compensation: model building, correlation, and regression. In W. A. Caldwell (Ed.), ***Compensation Guide***, (chap. 13). Boston: Warren Gorham Lamont.

Beatty, J. R. (1996). Statistical analysis in compensation: model building, correlation, and regression. In W. A. Caldwell (Ed.), ***Compensation Guide***, (chap. 13, Rev. ed.). Boston: Warren Gorham Lamont.

Guilford, J. P. (1965). ***Fundamental statistics in psychology and education*** (4th ed.). New York: McGraw-Hill.

Hays, W. L. (1963). ***Statistics for psychologists.*** New York: Holt, Rinehart, and Winston.

Practice Problems
Multiple Choice

The following 15 questions are based on the same sample of 25 observations that appeared in the multiple choice items at the end of Chapter 15. The first variable consists of the number of hours since a high volume printer has been adjusted, while the second variable consists of the number of paper jams in that printer. The table below gives the results of that survey.

Adjustments vs. Paper Jams

Observations	Hours Since Adjustment	Number of Paper Jams
1	9	15
2	10	19
3	10	21
4	12	17
5	10	18
6	10	16
7	10	18
8	12	21
9	12	17
10	12	18
11	17	25
12	9	13
13	13	12
14	14	19
15	13	25
16	10	11
17	13	26
18	5	14
19	18	23
20	8	16
21	13	22
22	17	25
23	9	24
24	11	15
25	19	25

1. What is the numerical value of the slope for the least squares linear regression model that reflects the bivariate relationship for predicting the number of paper jams from a knowledge of the number of hours since the last adjustment?

A. 4.6546
B. 2.6946
C. 9.5562
D. 0.8598
E. 1.4112

2. What is the constant term that must be included in the model to provide the least squares equation for the relationship between the *X*-value and the *Y*-value?

A. 86.6687
B. 12.4346
C. 8.8199
D. 2.4521
E. 51.0657

3. What is the error sum of squares for the model that reflects the line of best fit? This error term is often referred to as the error sum of squares for the full model (ESS_{FM}).

A. 486.0000
B. 4992.9269
C. 294.2626
D. 654.2325
E. 191.7374

4. What is the error sum of squares for the chance model that reflects the line of best fit under the condition that the predictor variable, *X*, is not used?

A. 497.2007
B. 2356.2572
C. 4441.3440
D. 486.0000
E. 294.2626

5. What is the standard error of estimate?

A. 2.4127
B. 16.4826
C. 4.2169
D. 3.5769
E. 6.4546

6. What is the covariance between the two variables?

A. 9.29
B. 2.67
C. 1.17
D. 5.42
E. 1.85

7. What is the percent of the variance in the number of paper jams that can be accounted for by a knowledge of the variation in the hours since adjustment?

A. 2.45%
B. 39.45%
C. 62.81%
D. 60.55%
E. 33.35%

8. If we were to predict the number of paper jams we might have on the printer at any given observation period from a knowledge of chance alone, what would be our best guess?

A. 23.45
B. 19.00
C. 11.84
D. 12.64
E. 43.96

9. If we were to predict the number of paper jams we might have on the printer at any given observation period from a knowledge of chance alone, what would be the slope of our regression line?

A. 00.00
B. 19.00
C. 11.84
D. 12.39
E. 43.96

10. What is the standard error of the slope for the best fit model when using the *X*-variable to predict the *Y*-variable?

A. .341
B. .355
C. .222
D. .784
E. .648

11. What is the t-value that we would compute when testing the significance of the slope against chance?

A. 4.6546
B. 2.6946
C. 3.8712
D. 0.8598
E. 1.4112

12. What is the critical t-value we would find in the table when testing the significance of the slope against chance, with $\alpha = .05$?

A. 2.069
B. 2.080
C. 1.960
D. 1.645
E. 5.057

13. What is the standard error of the regression constant (i.e., the intercept), based on the intercept of the full regression model?

A. .7619
B. 2.7253
C. 94.2626
D. 54.2325
E. 91.7374

14. Based on the full regression model, how many paper jams would you have expected for observation number 5?

A. 19.0000
B. 17.4180
C. 11.8400
D. 6.0000
E. 4.2626

15. Develop a 95% confidence interval for the mean predicted Y-value for all situations in which there had been a 19-hour lapse since last adjustment.

A. $16.9231 \leq \mu_{Y/X} \leq 33.3894$
B. $10.2038 \leq \mu_{Y/X} \leq 30.3736$
C. $9.2699 \leq \mu_{Y/X} \leq 39.9493$
D. $21.5484 \leq \mu_{Y/X} \leq 28.7641$
E. $1.3843 \leq \mu_{Y/X} \leq 8.7266$

16. Suppose that you are going to wait 5 hours before making the next adjustment. How many printer jams can you anticipate having. What would you predict for this situation in regard to the number of paper jams, within a 95% confidence range?

A. $4.9434 \leq Y'' \leq 21.2944$
B. $1.5484 \leq Y'' \leq 8.7641$
C. $8.8990 \leq Y'' \leq 24.2173$
D. $9.6447 \leq Y'' \leq 16.5932$
E. $6.7575 \leq Y'' \leq 56.5478$

Suppose that you have determined the number of miles each of a set of five automobiles has traveled on exactly ten gallons of gas (the *X*-values). You then determined the number of miles each of these same five automobiles has traveled on ten gallons of gas after receiving major tune-ups (the *Y*-values). Based on the circumstances above and the given information below, solve the next 16 problems. Assume that the data are obtained from samples:

Before and After Mileage

Automobiles	Mileage Before Tune-up	Mileage After Tune-up
1	180	238
2	160	217
3	195	245
4	185	240
5	170	228

17. What is the numerical value of the slope for the least squares linear regression model that reflects the bivariate relationship for predicting the *Y*-value from the *X*-value?

A. 89.4932
B. .9814
C. .9627
D. .8096
E. 2.5835

18. What is the constant term that must be included in the model to provide the least squares equation for the relationship between the X-variable and the Y-variable?

A. 26.4710
B. 74.2171
C. 89.4932
D. 98.4926
E. 178.0000

19. What is the error sum of squares for the model that reflects the line of best fit? This error term is often referred to as the error sum of squares for the full model (ESS_{FM}).

A. 184.6754
B. 742.4654
C. 18.7329
D. 263.3027
E. 43.3946

20. What is the error sum of squares for the chance model that reflects the line of best fit under the condition that the X-variable is not used?

A. 294.1037
B. 742.4654
C. 113.1376
D. 497.2000
E. 18.7329

21. What is the standard error of estimate, based on the model for predicting the number of miles traveled after the tune-up from a knowledge of the miles traveled before the tune-up?

A. 18.7329
B. 48.2846
C. .0925
D. 2.4989
E. 3.1826

22. What is the correlation between the number of miles traveled prior to the tune-up and the number of miles traveled after the tune-up?

A. .9810
B. .9623
C. .2348
D. .0000
E. .8207

23. What is the percent of the variance of the miles traveled after the tune-up that can be explained by a knowledge of the variance of the miles traveled before the tune-up?

A. 3.77%
B. 96.23%
C. 98.19%
D. 80.96%
E. 33.35%

24. If we were to predict the number of miles that would be traveled after the tune-up on the basis of chance instead of on the basis of the number of miles traveled before the tune-up, what would be our best guess?

A. 000.0000
B. 233.6000
C. 178.0000
D. 497.0000
E. 89.4932

25. If we were to predict the number of miles that would be traveled after the tune-up on the basis of chance instead of on the basis of the number of miles traveled before the tune-up, what would be the slope of our regression line?

A. 0.0000
B. 2.4842
C. .8096
D. .9810
E. 1.3846

26. What is the standard error of the slope for the best fit model when using the X-variable to predict the Y-variable?

A. .8096
B. .2368
C. .0925
D. .7334
E. .4989

27. What is the *t*-value that we would compute when testing the significance of the full regression model against chance?

A. 3.182
B. 2.394
C. 8.754
D. 1.964
E. 7.472

28. What is the critical *t*-value we would find in the table when testing the significance of the regression model against chance, with $\alpha = .05$?

A. 3.182
B. 2.080
C. 1.960
D. 1.645
E. 2.069

29. What is the standard error of the regression constant, using the intercept of the full regression model?

A. 4820.3658
B. 16.5006
C. 233.6000
D. 89.4932
E. 27.3946

30. Based on the full regression model, how many miles would you have predicted that automobile number one would have traveled after receiving a major tune-up?

A. 238.00
B. 235.22
C. 248.60
D. 233.60
E. 242.48

31. Develop a 95% confidence interval for the mean predicted *Y*-value for automobiles that traveled 180 miles on ten gallons of gas prior to receiving the major tune-up.

A. $219.6000 \leq \mu_{Y/X} \leq 247.6000$
B. $229.2699 \leq \mu_{Y/X} \leq 246.7302$
C. $226.4890 \leq \mu_{Y/X} \leq 243.9493$
D. $231.6148 \leq \mu_{Y/X} \leq 238.8234$
E. $249.4921 \leq \mu_{Y/X} \leq 289.4982$

32. Suppose that you know that an additional automobile, not included in the original study, traveled 180 miles on ten gallons of gas prior to receiving any major tune-up. You know that the automobile then received the tune-up, but you do not know how many miles it traveled on its next ten gallons of gas. What would you predict for this automobile, within a 95% confidence range?

A. $226.4890 \leq Y'' \leq 243.9493$
B. $233.3723 \leq Y'' \leq 234.5867$
C. $210.4846 \leq Y'' \leq 284.6576$
D. $231.6148 \leq Y'' \leq 238.8234$
E. $137.4836 \leq Y'' \leq 357.6745$

33. Which of the following is not a correct way to represent the error sum of squares for the full regression model in the bivariate situation, based on the least squares approach?

A. $\Sigma(Y - Y')^2$
B. $\Sigma[Y - (a + b \cdot X)]^2$
C. $\Sigma(Y - \overline{Y})^2$
D. $\Sigma(Y - a - b \cdot X)^2$
E. $[(s_Y^2) \cdot (n - 1)] - [(s_Y^2) \cdot (n - 1) \cdot (RSQ)]$

34. When testing hypotheses, making inferences, or developing confidence intervals based on the outcomes of regression models, which of the following is **not** one of the conditions usually assumed as holding for the regression model?

A. The random variable ε is normally distributed about various points for the X-variable.
B. Any two errors (ε_i and ε_j) are independent of one another.
C. The random variable ε has a constant variance from point to point along the line.
D. The random variable ε has a mean of zero.
E. All of the above are conditions usually assumed as holding for the model.

35. Which of the following corresponds with the assumption that any two error terms (ε_i and ε_j) are independent of one another?

A. No autocorrelation
B. No serial correlation
C. No covariance among the error terms
D. A Durbin-Watson value that does not fall in the region of rejection
E. All of the above

36. The assumption that the random variable ε has a constant variance from point to point along the least squares regression line implies that the model:

A. has homoskedasticity.
B. consists of best linear unbiased estimators.
C. has no serial correlation.
D. has a standard error of estimate equal to zero.
E. has normal distributions at all points along the regression line.

1-36

CHAPTER 17

MULTIPLE REGRESSION MODELS

Case Study 17.1

Problem. SeaFresh Tuna (SFT) has always been a leader in the industrial fishing industry. It has established a reputation for selling only high quality, toxin-free, flavorful fish that have been caught according to strict animal preservation practices. In the past two years, SFT has become interested in monitoring and reducing the amount of salt penetration in their product. The Food and Drug Administration (FDA) has consistently given SeaFresh positive approval, but the marketing department feels that the company could increase both its market share and its public image if the amount of salt penetration in the fish can be minimized. SeaFresh owns a fleet of tuna boats, and each boat has several wells for storing the catch. From the time the fish have been netted, placed in holding wells for storage while the vessels continue at sea, and transported to the processing plant, many variables may influence the amount of salt penetration per fish. SeaFresh wants to investigate many of these variables to determine whether they can be used to predict the amount of salt penetration.

Unfortunately, SeaFresh cannot design a perfect experiment from which to examine the influence of these variables on salt penetration. Certain variables can be manipulated so that their impact upon the variable of interest can be monitored; however, other variables are unique to the situation and cannot be easily controlled. The brine solution in each well used for storage while the fleet is at sea can be manipulated, as can the temperature of each of the wells. On the other hand, the fleet has less control over the size of the individual fish, the species of the fish captured, or the geographic location of the tuna when captured. Other variables may be controlled to some degree, but there are various costs associated with controlling for these variables. For example, the length of time since capture can be controlled by returning ships to port at various intervals; but this might result in ships returning to port without wells filled to capacity. The condition of the fish after capture can also be controlled, as the crew can be required to handle the tuna more carefully; however, there will be a cost associated with improved handling. The physical location of the fish within the well during storage may also be a factor, but placing various sizes and species of fish in various locations within the wells would be impractical.

SeaFresh has thus decided to randomly select and tag many fish upon capture for future examination. The company can easily record the date of the capture, the size of the fish at the time of capture, its species and condition, the longitude and latitude of the fleet at the time of the catch, the name of the boat, and the number of the well in which the fish were stored. By tagging the fish, SeaFresh can also determine their physical location in the holding well when they are removed upon returning to port. SFT now wants to develop a model with which to predict the amount of salt penetration, based on a knowledge of as many of these variables as possible.

Methodology Solution. In Case Study 17.1, numerous models have potential value. SeaFresh Tuna has decided to examine several of these models and will compare one model against another for further analysis. SeaFresh's first model has one variable of interest (the amount of salt penetration in the fish), and they have decided to examine the relationship between this variable and five predictor variables. The five predictor variables to be used are as follows: a) the brine solution in which the fish have been stored, b) the storage temperature, c) the length of time the fish have been in the well, d) the size of the fish, and e) the physical distance of the fish from the top of the well during storage. To determine an appropriate statistical methodology to analyze this model, we will follow Figure 17.1, which includes relevant flowcharts from the master flowcharts. As indicated in the figure, we enter the flowcharts at START. Since SeaFresh Tuna wishes to predict salt penetration, they are interested in correlation, regression, and prediction; therefore, we turn to flowchart 8. We have more than two variables, so we immediately move on to flowchart 10. We have one variable of interest (i.e., one criterion variable---the amount of salt penetration per fish); salt penetration is at least interval level; and all of the independent variables (i.e., predictor variables) are at least interval level. We conclude that we should consider using multiple regression as an appropriate statistical tool for analyzing this model. The bold lines in Figure 17.1 show the route taken in the flowcharts as described above.

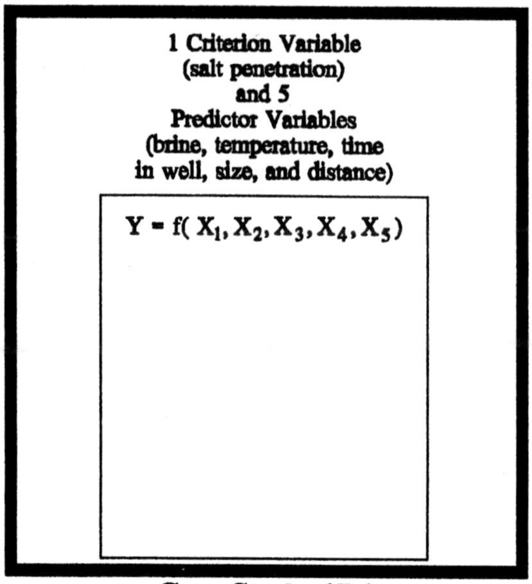

Case Study 17.1

Where Have We Been and Where Are We Going?

The fundamentals of *bivariate* correlation and regression were presented in Chapter 15 and in Chapter 16. These concepts will now be expanded into *multiple* correlation and regression, which are among the most powerful and most useful statistical procedures available for data analysis.

The process of computing weights for multiple regression (i.e., determining the intercept and the slopes) is far more complex than for bivariate regression. The calculations are usually solved with matrix algebra, which will not be discussed in detail in the present textbook. Although some multiple regression models (e.g., those with one variable of interest and with only two predictor variables) can be solved with hand calculators, realistically speaking most multiple regression models are solved through the use of a computer. Statistical software packages and spreadsheets are readily available for this purpose. Once the intercept and the slopes associated with each predictor variable have been determined, the coefficient of determination (*RSQ*), the error sums of squares (*ESS*), and other related terms can be obtained with minimal difficulty. The present textbook assumes that the reader has access to computer software that can be used to generate the various models necessary for performing multiple regression analysis.

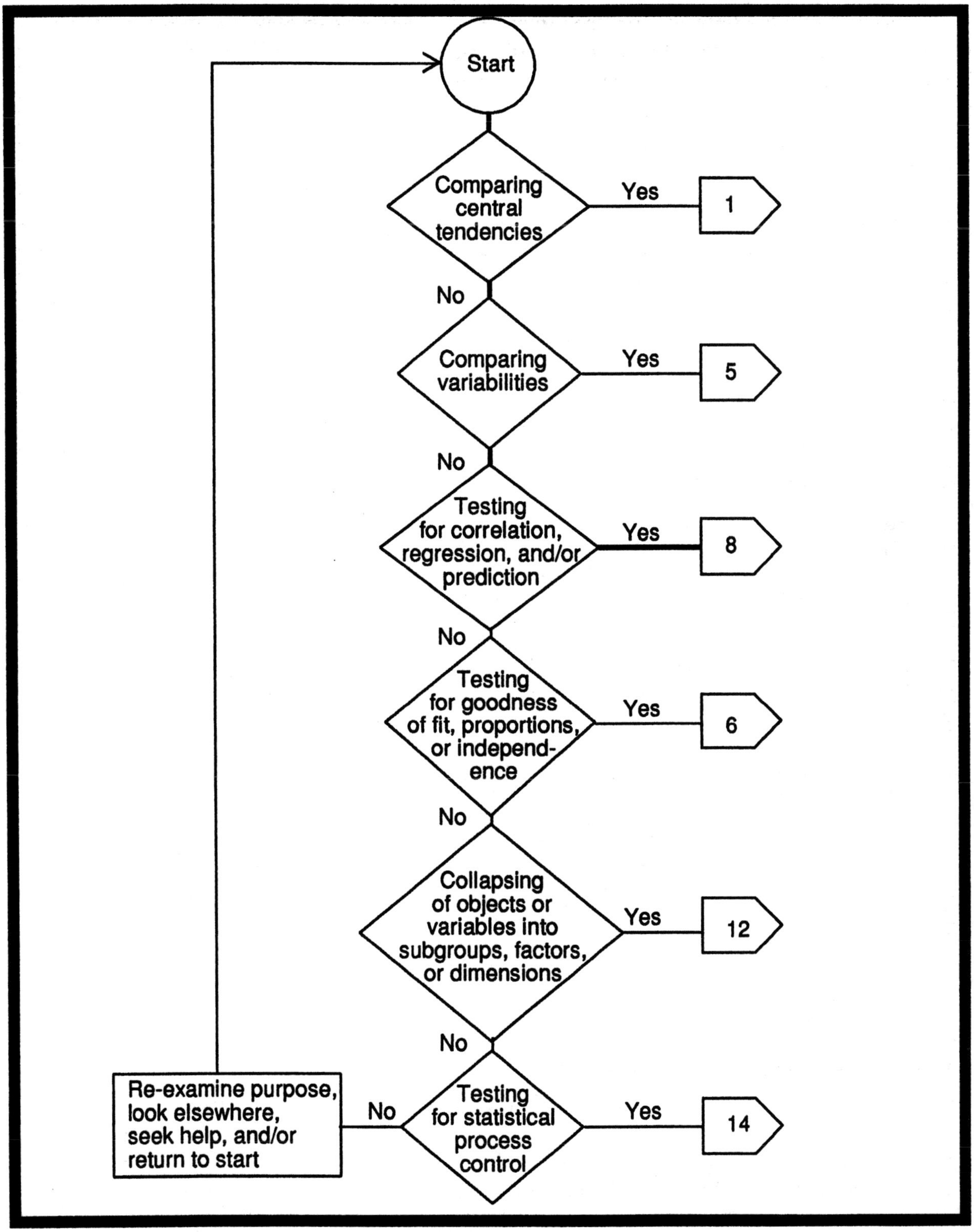

Figure 17.1
Statistical Decision-Making Flowchart for Case Study 17.1

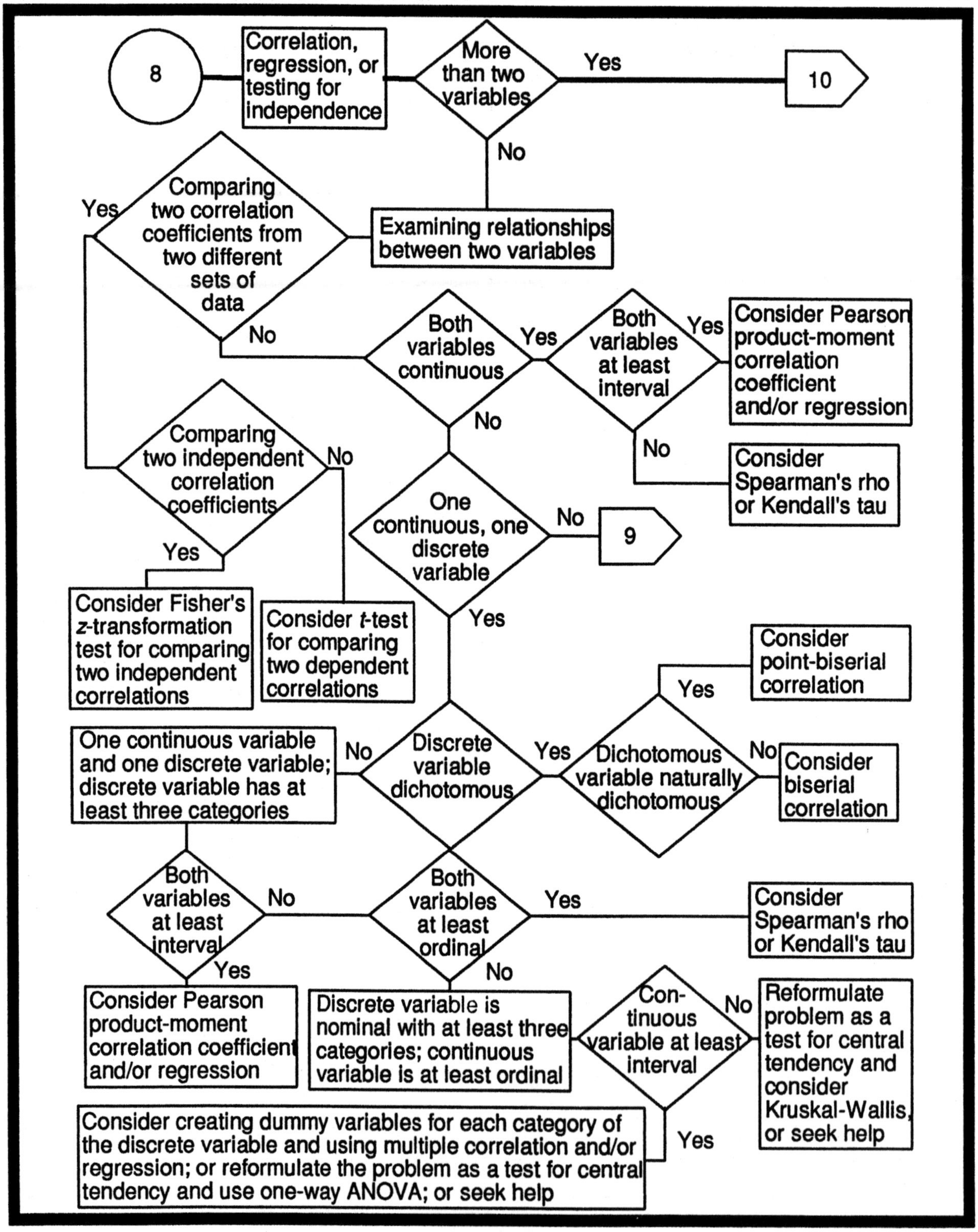

Figure 17.1
Statistical Decision-Making Flowchart for Case Study 17.1
(continued)

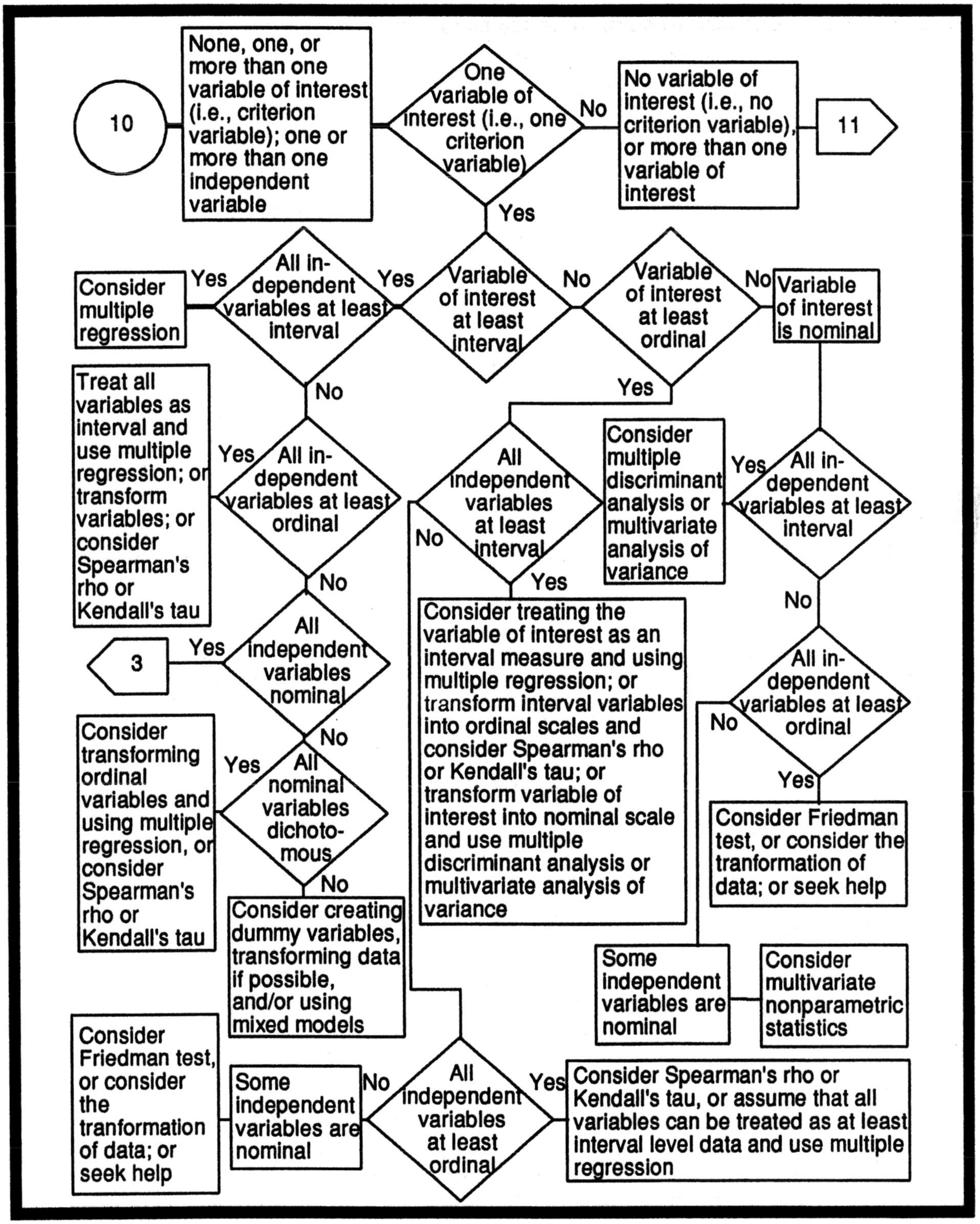

Figure 17.1
Statistical Decision-Making Flowchart for Case Study 17.1 (continued)

Example 17.1. Case Study 17.1 has described a situation for which multiple regression would be appropriate. However, the data base for that case study is too large to provide a simple numerical illustration of the technique. Instead, Example 17.1 will be used to demonstrate the use of multiple regression in model building and data analysis. In this example, data have been collected for 20 individuals who were previously classified as hard-core unemployed and who were selected for participation in a Federally-sponsored job works program. While there were more than 20 participants at the onset of the program, job opportunities, dropout, and other factors associated with attrition caused a reduction in data; a sample of only 20 individuals remained with the program by the end of the 24-month period under observation. Descriptions of all of the variables to be used are given in Table 17.1.

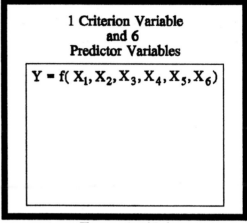

1 Criterion Variable and 6 Predictor Variables

$$Y = f(X_1, X_2, X_3, X_4, X_5, X_6)$$

Example 17.1

Table 17.1
Variable Descriptions for Absenteeism Data

Variable Number	Variable Description
1.	This variable consists of scores on the Consideration dimension of the Supervisory Behavior Description, based upon the employee's evaluation of his or her first level supervisor (SBD-CON-I).
2.	This variable consists of scores on the Initiating Structure dimension of the Supervisory Behavior Description, based upon the employee's evaluation of his or her first level supervisor (SBD-IS-I).
3.	This variable consists of scores on the Consideration dimension of the Supervisory Behavior Description, based upon the employee's evaluation of his or her second level supervisor (SBD-CON-II).
4.	This variable consists of scores on an instrument which was designed to measure the employee's self-esteem (SE).
5.	This variable consists of scores on an instrument which was designed to measure the employee's initiative, as evaluated by his or her immediate supervisor (INIT).
6.	This variable consists of the number of previous jobs the employee has held (JOBS).
7.	This variable consists of the number of days the employee has been absent during the 24-month period of interest (ABS).

Variables 1 through 6 will be used as the predictor variables, while variable 7 (the number of days absent from the job during the 24-month period) will be used as the variable of interest (i.e., the criterion variable). In other words, this study is concerned with developing a model for predicting absenteeism from a knowledge of the six predictor variables. The raw data for Example 17.1 are given in Table 17.2.

Table 17.2
Absenteeism Data for 20 Individuals in a Jobs Works Program

	Unit Vector	Predictor Variables						Criterion Variable
Case	U	X_1	X_2	X_3	X_4	X_5	X_6	Y
1	1	62	31	56	13	7	0	1
2	1	71	24	57	44	6	3	19
3	1	68	38	59	39	4	3	18
4	1	56	62	70	30	7	2	15
5	1	52	54	54	52	7	1	17
6	1	63	33	69	34	2	3	6
7	1	49	49	45	46	1	1	5
8	1	63	22	59	31	7	2	2
9	1	57	44	58	29	6	5	14
10	1	67	33	74	36	4	3	3
11	1	64	26	55	38	6	2	10
12	1	16	80	48	37	6	1	8
13	1	68	37	59	38	4	0	17
14	1	54	54	56	40	6	0	14
15	1	61	46	57	37	7	3	16
16	1	60	42	55	37	4	2	16
17	1	63	34	49	34	5	2	17
18	1	58	41	73	46	4	5	6
19	1	54	56	56	41	3	1	10
20	1	39	57	59	41	5	1	9

As we did with Case Study 17.1, we will use our flowcharts to determine the appropriate statistical tool for analyzing Example 17.1. We know that the situation involves correlation, regression, and/or prediction, so we turn to flowchart 8. We have more than two variables, so we immediately turn to flowchart 10. We have one variable of interest (absenteeism), and it is at least interval level. We will arbitrarily assume that all six of the predictor variables are at least interval scale also. We conclude that multiple regression is an appropriate statistical tool for analyzing this problem.

As we can see from Table 17.2, our data base contains three components. The first component consists of a column of *ones* and is often referred to as the *unit vector*. The second component consists of six columns, with each column representing one of the predictor variables. The third component consists of a column that represents the criterion variable. We use the first component to help us mathematically determine the constant term (i.e., the intercept) in our regression model. We do *not* need to *input* this unit vector into most statistical software programs or spreadsheets, as it is usually built into software packages that compute regression models. We have included this column of ones in Table 17.2 to remind us that if we were to manually determine the regression weights through matrix algebra, we would have to add this additional vector to our data matrix. As stated earlier, matrix algebra is the mathematical approach employed by most statistical software programs.

A brief explanation of the above process is necessary. In a bivariate regression model, we determine two regression weights: one slope and one intercept. In a multiple regression model, we determine more than two regression weights: one slope for *each* predictor variable we use and one intercept. When we use matrix algebra to solve for our regression equation, we need to multiply each regression weight by a corresponding vector (i.e., we need to multiply each regression weight by a corresponding column in the data matrix). Since the intercept does not correspond with an existing column in the matrix, we create the unit vector as a column to correspond with the intercept. We know that whenever a value is multiplied by 1 (such as with the elements of the unit vector), the product will always be equal to the original value. We now have a vector associated with each of the regression weights and can use matrix algebra with conformable data. Since matrix algebra is extremely time consuming, we avoid this tedious process by relying on computer software for determining the weights in our regression equation.

Means, Standard Deviations, and the Intercorrelation Matrix

Means and Standard Deviations. At the onset of our analysis, we usually will want to determine the means and standard deviations for each of our variables. The means and standard deviations for the six predictor variables and for the criterion variable associated with Example 17.1 are given in Table 17.3. As we can see, after a period of 24 months the participants averaged 11.15 days of absenteeism, with a standard deviation of 5.85145.

Intercorrelation Matrix. Based on the data given in Table 17.2, we can also develop an *intercorrelation matrix*, as shown in Table 17.4. The intercorrelation matrix consists of 7 rows and 7 columns, with ones down the principal diagonal. Each of the off-diagonal elements consist of *bivariate* correlations between pairs of variables. An examination of Table 17.4 reveals that this intercorrelation matrix is *square* and *symmetric*. For example, if we wish to determine the bivariate correlation between variable 4 (a predictor variable) and variable 7 (the criterion variable), we can look down the 7th column of the matrix or across the 7th row of the matrix. The element located at the intersection of row 7 and column 4 ($r_{7,4}$ = .34654) is the correlation between these two variables; similarly, the element located at the intersection of row 4 and column 7 ($r_{4,7}$ = .34654) is this same correlation.

Table 17.3
Means and Standard Deviations for Absenteeism Data

Variable Number	Means	Standard Deviations
X_1	57.25000	12.26409
X_2	43.15000	14.44509
X_3	58.40000	7.76226
X_4	37.15000	8.03463
X_5	5.05000	1.76143
X_6	2.00000	1.45095
Y	11.15000	5.85145

Table 17.4
Intercorrelations for Absenteeism Data

	1	2	3	4	5	6	7
1	1.00000	-.85050	.37098	-.15423	-.05177	.28690	.19527
2	-.85050	1.00000	-.21414	.23379	.03485	-.27874	.11741
3	.37098	-.21414	1.00000	-.10481	-.04388	.49068	-.21808
4	-.15423	.23379	-.10481	1.00000	-.32410	.07223	.34654
5	-.05177	.03485	-.04388	-.32410	1.00000	-.06178	.19328
6	.28690	-.27874	.49068	.07223	-.06178	1.00000	.05579
7	.19527	.11741	-.21808	.34654	.19328	.05579	1.00000

Components of the Intercorrelation Matrix

When the variables have been arranged such that the variable to the far right is the criterion variable, the intercorrelation matrix consists of four quadrants, as illustrated in Figure 17.2. For the present example, the upper-left quadrant of the intercorrelation matrix is a 6 by 6 square and symmetric matrix. This quadrant is often referred to as the **R**-matrix, as it consists of the intercorrelations among all of the *predictor* variables. The upper-right quadrant of the intercorrelation matrix contains a 6 by 1 *column* matrix consisting of the correlations between each of the predictor variables and the criterion variable. These correlations are often referred to as ***validities***; and the column matrix is referred to as the **V**-matrix (where **V** stands for validity). Finally, the lower-left quadrant of the intercorrelation matrix is a 1 by 6 row matrix and is identical to the **V**-matrix for columns, except that it is a *row* matrix. The lower-right hand quadrant is a 1 by 1 matrix; it contains the correlation between the *Y*-variable and itself. Since each variable always correlates perfectly with itself, this value will be equal to 1.00.

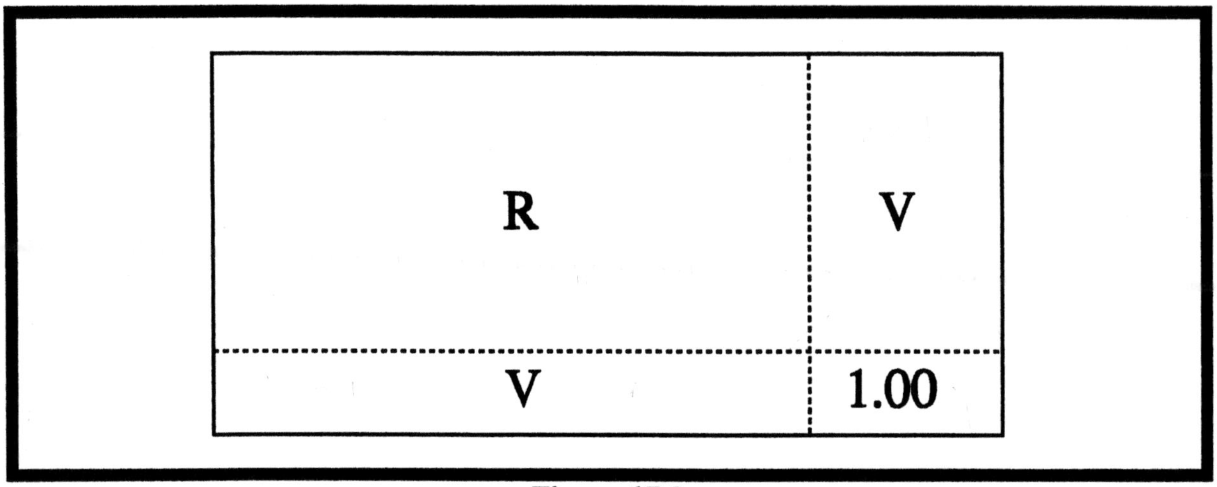

Figure 17.2
Components of the Intercorrelation Matrix

Alternative Multiple Regression Methods

There are many alternative methods that may be used to generate multiple regression models. Regardless of which multiple regression method is selected, *the full model will always be the same.* The full model is the model that is based on the inclusion of *all* of the predictor variables. This model will yield one unique set of regression weights, one unique ESS_{FM}, and one unique *RSQ*.

Spreadsheet Method. Spreadsheets such as *Excel*, *Lotus 1-2-3*, and *Quattro* often have multiple regression capabilities. These spreadsheets typically have built-in functions that compute the overall *RSQ*, the regression weights, and other values related to the full model. However, if models that are supplementary to the full model are desired, they must each be generated separately. Statistical software packages such as *BMD*, *Execustat*, *Minitab*, *SAS*, *SPSS*, *SSP*, *Statgraphics*, and *TSP* (none of which rely on the spreadsheet approach) often use analytical approaches that yield numerous intermediate models in addition to the full model.

Backward Elimination Method. A second method for analyzing the criterion variable is to compute the full model first and then to eliminate variables from that model, based on some user-defined objective or on some computer-defined objective function. This approach is often referred to as the *backward elimination method.* Variables may be eliminated from the full model in a particular sequence as specified by the researcher based on his or her knowledge and judgment (e.g., eliminate one variable at a time, eliminate variables pair-wise or in clusters, etc.); or they may be eliminated on the basis of some computer default value, as determined by the numerical contributions each of the predictor variables is making to the full model.

All-Possible-Combinations Method. A third method is to determine all possible models in a forward-moving, step-by-step fashion. The first step in this method is to determine the variable that has the highest correlation with the criterion variable. The second step is to examine all possible combinations of predictor variables, taken two at a time, in an effort to determine the one combination of predictor variables that yields the highest possible two-variable model *RSQ*. The third step is to examine all possible combinations of variables taken three at a time and then to select the three-variable model that yields the highest *RSQ*. The process continues until all possible variables have been entered into the model, at which point the unique *RSQ* for the full model is obtained. This approach is sometimes referred to as the *all-possible-combinations method.* At first glance, it might appear that this method will allow us to observe the "best" two variable model, the "best" three variable model, etc. However, analyzing intermediate steps based on such an approach takes too much advantage of chance, often leads to conclusions that may be relevant only to the data at hand, and is not recommended.

Stepwise Regression Method. A fourth widely used method for generating the final full model is *stepwise regression.* The traditional approach to this procedure is to first determine the variable that has the highest correlation with the criterion variable, just as was done in the initial step of the all-possible-combinations method. The next step, however, is to select a second variable that, *when used in combination with the initial predictor variable,* will result in a greater increase in *RSQ* than any other combination that *also includes* the previous variable. The third step is to select a third variable that, when used in combination with the first two selected variables, will result in a greater increase in *RSQ* than any other combination that also includes the first two selected variables. The process continues by adding another variable to those that have already been entered into the previous model, based on this same criterion of maximizing *RSQ*. Step-by-step, other variables are added to previous models until the full model, is finally obtained.[1] As we will discuss in more detail later, caution is advised when analyzing the intermediate steps obtained through use of the stepwise regression method.

Flowchart Regression Method. A fifth method for analyzing data through multiple regression is sometimes referred to as the flowchart regression method. This method is based on our own conceptualization of the situation, rather than letting the computer develop arbitrary models for us. For example, we may have developed a series of hypotheses in advance that we want to test. We would most likely begin by comparing the full model to the chance model. We could then continue by comparing the full model to various restricted models in which *subgroups* of variables have been omitted. This gives us an opportunity to test an hypothesis about this *set* of variables. As an illustration, perhaps in Example 17.1 we have hypothesized that the three leadership variables do not contribute to the full model as a group. We can

---

[1]There are several variations available for the stepwise model. One is to establish a requirement whereby the increase in *RSQ* must be of a particular magnitude; otherwise, the process is discontinued. Another variation of stepwise regression is to delete certain variables at various steps along the way if they no longer satisfy some established requirement for remaining in the model.

compare the full model based on all six predictor variables to a restricted model that excludes these leadership variables (i.e., SBD-CON-I, SBD-IS-I, and SBD-CON-II). We may have also hypothesized that the non-leadership variables (i.e., SE, INIT, and JOBS) collectively do not contribute to the full model. We could develop a flowchart that depicts such comparisons prior to any computational analysis and then methodically test these hypotheses. Such an approach often provides a very useful and logical technique for analyzing data.

Any of the above methods *may* be used. The decision as to which method *should* be used depends in part on the extent to which a logical approach has been developed, the software available, the number of predictor variables available, the ratio of cases to variables, the amount of time that is required to collect variables, and the cost of each variable. For example, if we have a satisfactory ratio of cases to variables and if time and expense are not of concern, we may only want to look at the final step of the model and ignore all of the intermediate steps along the way. On the other hand, if we are searching for variables to eliminate in future analyses due to cost and time factors, we might want to consider establishing some rule regarding which variables should be entered into or deleted from the model in an *a priori* fashion. There are numerous issues related to identifying important variables in regard to their contributions to the full model. Several of these issues will be discussed later on in this chapter.

STEPWISE REGRESSION WITH EXAMPLE 17.1

While any of these approaches will do, we have chosen to use stepwise regression to illustrate multiple regression. The data for the six predictor variables and the criterion variable were input into a stepwise regression program entitled JRB04. The calling program incorporates a number of subroutines originally developed by IBM, many of which were later modified by the current author. Results will be given for each intermediate model as well as for the full model obtained in the final step. It is now worth paraphrasing an earlier statement: *All of the above approaches will lead to the same final full regression model.* Examining intermediate steps in the learning process here will serve to bring attention to numerous issues, including problems created by multicollinearity among the predictor variables, limitations due to sample size, and other issues that may result in making unwarranted conclusions. However, the full model will receive the bulk of our attention.

Step 1 of the Stepwise Regression for Example 17.1

As can be seen in Table 17.4, self-esteem has the highest absolute correlation (i.e., highest validity) with absenteeism. Therefore, variable 4 will be the first variable to be entered into the traditional stepwise model. Table 17.5 includes a computer printout generated for step 1 in the analysis. The printout gives results consistent with our expectations. The first variable entered into the model is indeed variable 4; the absolute value of the correlation coefficient based on step 1 is $r = .3465$; and the RSQ for the full model (the model based only on variable 4 at this point) is $RSQ = .1201$.

Table 17.5
Step 1 for Absenteeism Data

```
SELECTION NUMBER  1

THE FOLLOWING SELECTION CARD WAS READ:   1111113

DEPENDENT VARIABLE............. 7
NUMBER OF VARIABLES FORCED.... 6
NUMBER OF VARIABLES DELETED... 0

STEP  1

FIRST VARIABLE ENTERED:     4

ERROR SUM OF SQUARES FOR RESTRICTED MODEL (CHANCE MODEL)                    650.5499
ERROR SUM OF SQUARES FOR FULL MODEL (INCLUSIVE THROUGH THIS STEP)           572.4273
ERROR SUM OF SQUARES REDUCED (EXPLAINED)                                     78.1226

FOR 1 VARIABLE ENTERED
  RSQ FOR FULL MODEL                                                          .1201
  ABSOLUTE VALUE OF BIVARIATE CORRELATION COEFFICIENT (R)                     .3465
  RSQ ADJUSTED FOR DEGREES OF FREEDOM                                         .0712

  F-VALUE FOR COMPARING THIS FULL MODEL
  WITH THE RESTRICTED (CHANCE) MODEL                                         2.4566
       DF FOR THE FULL MODEL =                                 2
       DF FOR THE CHANCE MODEL =                               1
       DF FOR THE NUMERATOR OF THE F-TEST =       2 -  1 =     1
       DF FOR THE DENOMINATOR OF THE F-TEST =    20 -  2 =    18
       PROBABILITY ASSOCIATED WITH THE F-TEST =                               .1312

  STANDARD ERROR OF ESTIMATE                                                 5.6393
  STANDARD ERROR ADJUSTED FOR DEGREES OF FREEDOM                             5.7938

 VARIABLE       RAW       STANDARD    STD. ERROR OF   COMPUTED      PROB.
  NUMBER      WEIGHTS     WEIGHTS       THE SLOPE     T-VALUES      FOR T
    4          .2524       .3465          .1610        1.5673       .1312
 INTERCEPT    1.7743

 VARIABLE     UNIQUE       PROB.      RESTRICTED     USEFUL-      ABS PART
  NUMBER     F-VALUES      FOR F      MODEL RSQ       NESS          CORR
    4         2.4566       .1312        .0000         .1201         .3465
```

Scatter Diagram for Step 1

Figure 17.3 gives a plot of the data points corresponding to variable 4 and variable 7 on a two-dimensional plane. The line of best fit for this model is also included in the graph. The intercept and slope for the line are given in the computer printout under the column labeled *Raw Weights* near the bottom of Table 17.5. The intercept (i.e., the constant term) is 1.7743, while the raw weight for variable 4 (i.e., the slope for variable 4) is .2524. Therefore, the regression line becomes $Y' = 1.7743 + (.2524) \cdot X_4$.

We can evaluate the accuracy of this linear model by examining any of the 20 cases. For example, the fifth employee had a self-esteem score of $X_4 = 52$ and had missed $Y = 17$ days of work, as found in Table 17.2. Using our bivariate regression model, we would predict that this person had missed 14.8991 ≈ 15 days of work. We have underestimated his or her absenteeism

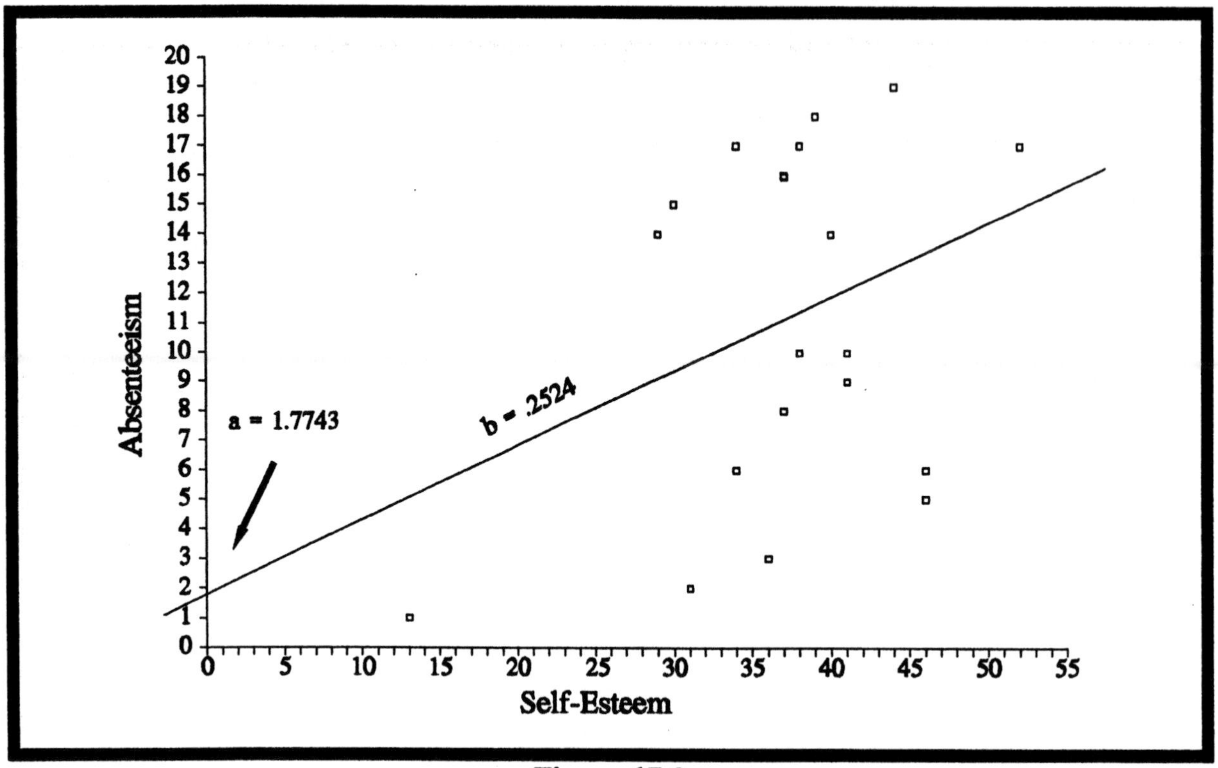

Figure 17.3
Regression Line for Predicting Absenteeism from Self-Esteem

by approximately 3 days. Examining each of the other individuals in a similar manner, we visually conclude that the model does not provide much of an improvement over chance alone. However, we also know that we should not simply rely on visual observation; instead, we should verify this conclusion through use of a test of significance such as the *t*-test discussed earlier.

The *t*-Test for the Correlation Coefficient in Step 1

We can evaluate the first step of the model by converting the *r*-value to a *t*-value and comparing this computed *t*-value to a critical *t*-value. The *t*-test yields the following results:

$$t = \frac{r - \rho}{\sqrt{\frac{1 - r^2}{n - 2}}}$$

$$= \frac{.3465 - .0000}{\sqrt{\frac{1 - (.3465)^2}{20 - 2}}}$$

$$= 1.5673$$

r → t

Based on a two-tailed test, 18 degrees of freedom, and alpha set at .05, the critical *t*-value is 2.101. As we can see from Figure 17.4, we fail to reject the null hypothesis. Therefore, we conclude that the relationship between absenteeism and self-esteem is not statistically significant. Since the absolute correlation between variable 4 and variable 7 is greater than the absolute correlation between any other predictor variable and variable 7, we can also conclude that *none* of the variables correlate significantly with the criterion variable. If our knowledge of correlation and regression is limited to the *bivariate* models discussed in Chapter 15 and Chapter 16, we would have to stop our analysis. However, a knowledge of *multiple* correlation and regression will allow us to continue with the analysis in search for more useful information!

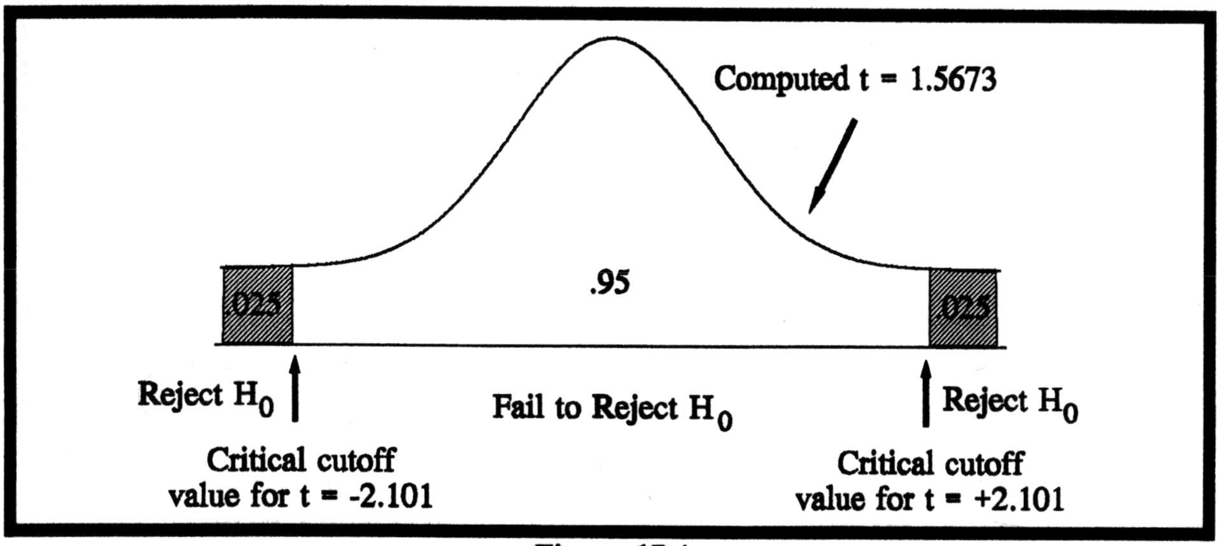

Figure 17.4
The *t*-Test for the Significance of the Bivariate Correlation

Error Terms, *RSQ*, and Absolute *r* for Step 1

Before turning to step 2 in the stepwise process, we will examine a few additional values obtained from the computer printout given in Table 17.5. This will allow us to become familiar with terminology and typical output values obtained through many statistical packages and spreadsheets that have multiple regression options. As we examine steps 2 through 6 in the process, we will find many useful tools for regression analysis.

Error Sum of Squares for Restricted Model (Chance Model). After listing the options chosen by the user in regard to the dependent variable, the number of variables forced into the model, and the number of variables deleted from the model, the computer printout in Table 17.5 gives the *Error Sum of Squares for Restricted Model (Chance Model).* The ESS_{CH} is always equal to the numerator of the variance for the *Y*-variable. In this example, ESS_{CH} = 650.5499, determined as follows:

$$ESS_{CH} = \Sigma(Y - \overline{Y})^2$$
$$= (s_Y)^2 \cdot (n - 1)$$
$$= (5.85145)^2 \cdot (20 - 1)$$
$$= 650.5499$$

Error Sum of Squares for Full Model (Inclusive Through this Step). Next, the printout gives the *Error Sum of Squares for Full Model (inclusive through this step).* As we know, the ESS_{FM} is obtained by finding the sum of the squared distances between each individual's actual absenteeism (Y) and her or his estimated absenteeism (Y'). For our current full model (which has only one predictor variable in the equation at this step), $ESS_{FM} = 572.4254$, calculated as follows:

$$ESS_{FM} = \Sigma(Y - Y')^2$$
$$= [(s_Y)^2 \cdot (n - 1)] - [(s_Y)^2 \cdot (n - 1) \cdot (r^2)]$$
$$= [(5.85145)^2 \cdot (20 - 1)] - [(5.85145)^2 \cdot (20 - 1) \cdot (.34654)^2]$$
$$= 572.4254$$

Error Sum of Squares Reduced (Explained). Based on the difference between the error sum of squares for the chance model and the error sum of squares for the full model, we can determine the *Error Sum of Squares Reduced (Explained)* at this step of the regression analysis. The $ESS_{RED} = ESS_{CH} - ESS_{FM} = 650.5499 - 572.4273 = 78.1226$, as shown by the computations below, except for round-off error:

$$ESS_{RED} = ESS_{CH} - ESS_{FM}$$
$$= \Sigma(Y - \overline{Y})^2 - \Sigma(Y - Y')^2$$
$$= 650.5499 - 572.4254$$
$$= 78.1245$$

***RSQ* for Full Model.** The *RSQ* for the full model is given next on the printout. This term is simply the square of the bivariate correlation coefficient, as discussed in Chapter 15 and Chapter 16. Here, $RSQ = .1201$.

Absolute Value of Bivariate Correlation Coefficient (*r*). The absolute value of the bivariate correlation coefficient is simply the absolute value of the correlation between the Y-variable and the first X-variable entered into the model. In this example, $r = .3465$. In a multiple regression program, the r-values in the first and subsequent steps are given in absolute terms, since the matrix algebra approach for obtaining the solution is based on computing the *RSQ* first. Since *RSQ* cannot be negative, the r-value is reported in the absolute sense.

RSQ Adjusted for Degrees of Freedom

Another value that commonly appears in most multiple regression printouts is the *RSQ Adjusted for Degrees of Freedom*, sometimes referred to as the *RSQ Adjusted for Shrinkage*. As pointed out by Cooley and Lohnes (1971, chap. 3), the regression weights and the *RSQ* itself capitalize on sampling error, especially when the sample size is small. This problem becomes compounded as the number of predictor variables increases, especially when the sample size remains relatively small. In Chapter 15, we emphasized the use of the *10 per X-variable, plus 10 for the pot rule* as a guideline for avoiding excessive overfit of the regression model. It is often impossible to satisfy this rule due to the cost of data collection, the time required to collect additional data, or the sheer lack of data availability. For example, by step 6 in the present situation we would need at least 70 cases in order to realistically evaluate the weights and the *RSQ*. Further, even with a "10 to 1 ratio, plus 10 for the pot," there may still be an overfit!

Statisticians (e.g., Cohen & Cohen, 1983, chap. 3; Kerlinger, 1973, p. 618; McNemar, 1962; Nunnally & Bernstein, 1994, chap. 5) have recommended various forms of a *shrinkage formula* to estimate what the value of *RSQ* might have been if a larger sampling condition had occurred. While such an adjustment is by no means an adequate replacement for using larger samples whenever possible or for cross-validating the original *RSQ* findings with future data, its usage is advised in situations in which the inadequacy of data is a problem. This shrinkage formula adjusts the *RSQ* based on the degrees of freedom, as given in Equation 17.1:

$$RSQ_{ADJ} = 1 - \left[(1 - RSQ_{FM}) \cdot \left(\frac{n - 1}{n - k - 1} \right) \right] \qquad (17.1)$$

where:

RSQ_{ADJ} = *RSQ* after adjusting for the degrees of freedom

RSQ_{FM} = *RSQ* for the full model

n = the number of cases used in the analysis

k = the number of predictor variables in the full model

Table 17.6 gives the amount of overfit estimated by this adjustment factor for *RSQ* values from .2000 to 1.0000, in increments of .1000. This table is based on $k = 1$ predictor variable and samples sizes ranging from $n = 10$ to $n = 200$. It is a subset of Appendix C, Table 11, which gives adjusted *RSQ* values for predictor variables ranging from $k = 1$ to $k = 50$, with samples sizes ranging from $n = 10$ to $n = 200$. As can be determined from the table presented here, the amount of overfit is much greater for small values of *RSQ* than for large values of *RSQ*. For example, if we use a "5 to 1 ratio, plus 5 for the pot" [resulting in a sample size determined as $n = ((5) \cdot (1)) + (5) = 10$], and if the computed *RSQ* is .2000, the RSQ_{ADJ} becomes .1000. If the computed *RSQ* is .9000, the RSQ_{ADJ} becomes .8875.

Table 17.6
Estimated *RSQ* Shrinkage Values with 1 Predictor Variable

Estimated *RSQ* Shrinkage Values
With 1 Predictor Variable

Shrinkage Based Upon Various *n* to 1 Ratios, Plus *n* for the Pot

			Observed *RSQ* Values								
ratio	***n***	***k***	**0.2000**	**0.3000**	**0.4000**	**0.5000**	**0.6000**	**0.7000**	**0.8000**	**0.9000**	**1.0000**
5	10	1	0.1000	0.2125	0.3250	0.4375	0.5500	0.6625	0.7750	0.8875	1.0000
10	20	1	0.1556	0.2611	0.3667	0.4722	0.5778	0.6833	0.7889	0.8944	1.0000
20	40	1	0.1789	0.2816	0.3842	0.4868	0.5895	0.6921	0.7947	0.8974	1.0000
25	50	1	0.1833	0.2854	0.3875	0.4896	0.5917	0.6938	0.7958	0.8979	1.0000
30	60	1	0.1862	0.2879	0.3897	0.4914	0.5931	0.6948	0.7966	0.8983	1.0000
40	80	1	0.1897	0.2910	0.3923	0.4936	0.5949	0.6962	0.7974	0.8987	1.0000
50	100	1	0.1918	0.2929	0.3939	0.4949	0.5959	0.6969	0.7980	0.8990	1.0000
100	200	1	0.1960	0.2965	0.3970	0.4975	0.5980	0.6985	0.7990	0.8995	1.0000

Table 17.6 also illustrates that even with a "10 to 1 ratio, plus 10 for the pot" [resulting in a sample size of $n = ((10) \cdot (1)) + (10) = 20$], we still have an overfit. For example, if the computed *RSQ* is .2000, the RSQ_{ADJ} becomes .1556. On the other hand, for the same computed *RSQ* of .2000, with a "100 to 1 ratio, plus 100 for the pot" (i.e., with $n = 200$), the RSQ_{ADJ} becomes .1960. Obviously, as the ratio of cases to predictors increases, the overfit becomes smaller.

In Example 17.1, the *RSQ* obtained for step 1 was .1201. The RSQ_{ADJ}, or shrunken *RSQ*, becomes .0712, as follows:

$$RSQ_{ADJ} = 1 - \left[(1 - RSQ_{FM}) \cdot \left(\frac{n - 1}{n - k - 1} \right) \right]$$

$$= 1 - \left[(1 \quad .1201) \cdot \left(\frac{20 - 1}{20 - 1 - 1} \right) \right]$$

$$= .0712$$

Even though we have satisfied the "10 to 1 ratio, plus 10 for the pot" rule in step 1, we notice that we still have an overfit. The small computed *RSQ* (.1201) and the minimal ratio of cases to predictor variables (10 to 1, plus 10) both contribute to the difference between the computed *RSQ* and the adjusted *RSQ*. Overfits such as this one become even greater issues in later steps of stepwise regression and all-possible-combinations regression models. We must also remember that the RSQ_{ADJ} is simply an *estimate* of what the actual *RSQ might* have been without the overfit. This estimate is based on a mathematical adjustment; it will never replace the need for taking an adequate sample size in the first place. We shall return to this discussion of the shrunken *RSQ* when we explore the additional steps.

The *F*-Test for the Regression Model

Most multiple regression printouts, including the one in Table 17.5, give the *F-Test for the Regression Model.* Although the *t*-test for the two-variable model can be used for testing the strength of the correlation coefficient used in the first step, its applications are limited to bivariate models. We need a test that is appropriate for examining *all* regression models, regardless of the number of predictor variables used: the *F*-test. Some statisticians and many computer programs refer to this test as the *F-test for the significance of the regression*, while others refer to it as the *F-test for analysis of variance.* We should not be disturbed by the use of analysis of variance terminology, as analysis of variance and regression are directly related. The *F*-test for the significance of the regression is given by Equation 17.2:

$$F = \frac{(RSQ_{FM} - RSQ_{RM}) \;/\; (df_{FM} - df_{RM})}{(1 - RSQ_{FM}) \;/\; (n - df_{FM})} \qquad (17.2)$$

where:

RSQ_{FM} = *RSQ* for the full model

RSQ_{RM} = *RSQ* for the restricted model

df_{FM} = degrees of freedom for the full model

df_{RM} = degrees of freedom for the restricted model

This *F*-test always compares one model to another model. The first model is the full model, while the second model is the restricted model. Later on, we will have numerous models and will want to perform a number of different *F*-tests. Presently, we have only two models available for comparison and can only perform one *F*-test now.

Symbolism for the Intercept, the Unit Vector, and the Slope. Our full and restricted models for the current analysis are given in Table 17.7. As we can see from the table, our full model is based on an intercept, a slope, and a value for the 4th predictor variable, self-esteem. We use b_0 instead of a as our symbol for the intercept and b_4 instead of b to indicate the specific slope. We also include the unit vector, U; and we use a subscript with the X-variable, X_4, to indicate the specific predictor variable used in the model. This symbolism is in keeping with traditional multiple regression notation. Since our restricted model has no predictor variables, it is equal to the chance model and is based on the mean for the criterion variable, $\overline{Y}$.

Table 17.7
Comparing Models for Step 1

Model	*Function*	*Equation*
Full Model	Absenteeism = f(self-esteem)	$Y' = b_0 \cdot U + b_4 \cdot X_4$
Restricted Model	Absenteeism = f(chance)	$Y' = b \cdot U = \overline{Y}$

Regression Model Degrees of Freedom. The degrees of freedom for any regression model correspond to the number of *linearly independent predictor variables* associated with the model. Predictor variables are linearly independent of each other if none of them are identical and if none of them can be perfectly reproduced by any linear combination of the other predictor variables. In other words, we cannot have any *redundant* information. Most computer programs and spreadsheets rely on matrix algebra to perform the regression analysis. These programs will examine for any linear dependencies among the predictor variables. If dependencies are detected, an error message is usually generated; if none are detected, the program will give the complete results. The degrees of freedom for any model that contains no redundancies is defined by Equation 17.3:

$$df \text{ (for any model)} = k + 1 \qquad \textbf{(17.3)}$$

where:

k = the number of linearly independent predictor variables in the model

Degrees of Freedom for the Chance Model. We know that the chance model has no predictor variables. Since the degrees of freedom for *any* model are defined as $df = k + 1$, the chance model will have $df = k + 1 = 0 + 1 = 1$ degree of freedom. This degree of freedom is based on the intercept for the chance model, which is always equal to $\overline{Y}$, as implied in Table 17.7.

Degrees of Freedom for the Full Model (Step 1). The full model generated in the first step of a regression analysis always has one predictor variable, or $k = 1$. Therefore, the model associated with the first step always has $df = k + 1 = 1 + 1 = 2$. One degree of freedom is based on the regression weight (i.e., the slope) associated with the predictor variable used in step 1.

The other degree of freedom is based on the intercept (i.e., the constant term) associated with the unit vector for this model.

Degrees of Freedom for the Full Model (Subsequent Steps). Unless there are redundancies among our predictor variables, a new variable will be entered into the model at each successive step in the stepwise process. A new regression weight will also be added to each successive regression model. Therefore, the next step will have one more degree of freedom than the previous step. If there are any *linearly dependent* predictor variables, the degrees of freedom will not increase. This is because we are not adding any new information to the model that cannot be accounted for by the other predictor variables already in the model. As stated earlier, computer programs usually give error messages under such circumstances. In the first step of any regression model, there cannot be any redundancies because there is only one predictor variable.

We will now compute the F-test for the significance of the regression for step 1 in Example 17.1. We know that $RSQ_{FM} = .1201$, $RSQ_{RM} = .0000$, $n = 20$, $k = 1$, $df_{FM} = 2$, and $df_{RM} = 1$. Therefore, the F-value is obtained as follows:

$$F = \frac{(RSQ_{FM} - RSQ_{RM}) \; / \; (df_{FM} - df_{RM})}{(1 - RSQ_{FM}) \quad / \quad (n - df_{FM})}$$

$$= \frac{(.1201 - .0000) \; / \; (2 - 1)}{(1 - .1201) \; / \; (20 - 2)}$$

$$= 2.4566$$

Degrees of Freedom for the Numerator of the F-Test. Now that we have determined the computed F-value, we need to determine whether it is a significant F-value. Therefore, we need to determine the critical F-value from the F-table. To find this value, we must determine the degrees of freedom associated with the numerator and with the denominator of the F-test. The degrees of freedom for the numerator of the F-test are defined by Equation 17.4:

$$df_{NUM} = df_{FM} - df_{RM} \qquad (17.4)$$

Degrees of Freedom for the Denominator of the F-Test. The degrees of freedom for the denominator of the F-test are given in Equation 17.5:

$$df_{DENOM} = n - df_{FM} \qquad (17.5)$$

For Example 17.1, we find that the $df_{NUM} = 1$, the $df_{DENOM} = 18$, and the critical F-value is $F(1, 18) = 4.41$, with $\alpha = .05$. Therefore, we fail to reject the null hypothesis, as shown in Figure 17.5. We have again confirmed that based on the present data and the current example, self-esteem is not a significant predictor of absenteeism.

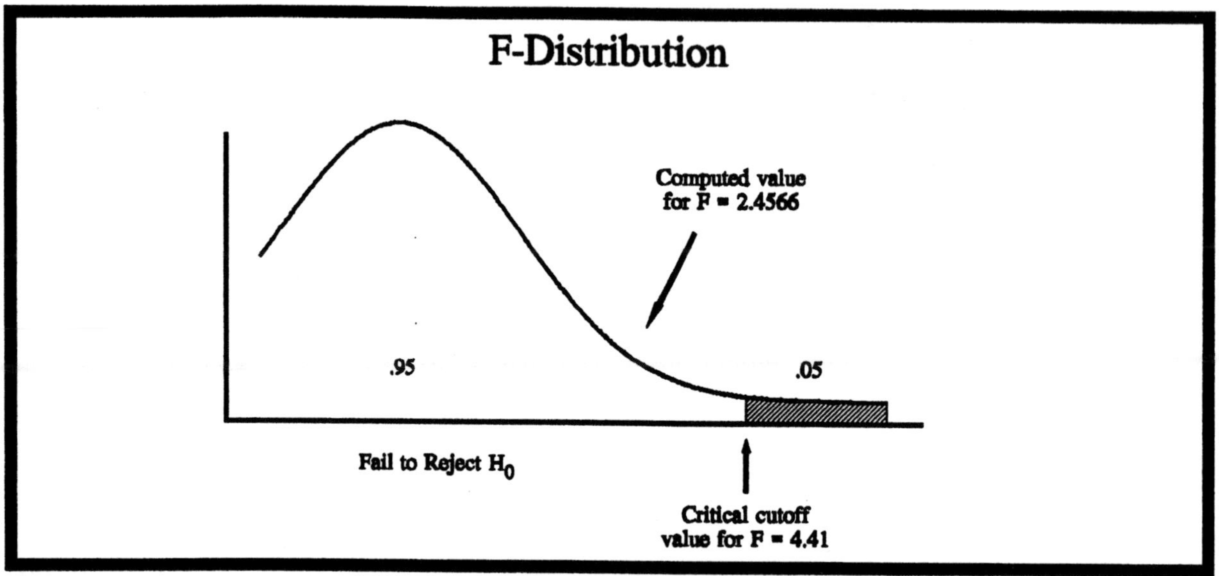

Figure 17.5
***F*-Test for the Significance of the Regression in Step 1**

Comparing the *t*-Test and the *F*-Test in the Bivariate Model. A comparison between the *t*-test presented earlier and the *F*-test above reveals several interesting facts. When we performed the *F*-test, we were concerned with both the degrees of freedom in the numerator and the degrees of freedom in the denominator. When we performed the *t*-test, we were only concerned with degrees of freedom. We did not mention whether these degrees of freedom were associated with a numerator or a denominator. In fact, with the *t*-test we always have 1 degree of freedom associated with the numerator; therefore, we do not have need for an expanded table that includes degrees of freedom for both the numerator and the denominator such as we do with the *F*-table. We only need to determine the degrees of freedom for the denominator. In our present example, there are 18 degrees of freedom for the denominator of the *F*-test, the same as with the *t*-test. A comparison of the results of the two tests sheds additional light. The square of the critical *t*-value is equal to the critical *F*-value; that is, $t^2 = F$, since $(2.101)^2 = 4.41$. Further, the square of the computed *t*-value is equal to the computed *F*-value; that is, $t^2 = (1.5673)^2 = 2.4566 = F$. Whenever we have only 1 degree of freedom associated with the numerator, we can use either approach and draw identical conclusions. If we have more than 1 degree of freedom in the numerator, we must use the *F*-test and the *F*-distribution.

Standard Error of Estimate for the Model

Standard Error of Estimate. The computer printout also includes the standard error of the estimate and the standard error of the estimate adjusted for degrees of freedom. As we recall, the standard error of estimate represents the standard deviation of the errors about the line of best fit. Based on $ESS_{FM} = \Sigma(Y - Y')^2$, and the equation for the standard error of the estimate given in Chapter 16, we determine the SE_{EST} for step 1 of Example 17.1 as follows:

$$SE_{EST} = \sqrt{\frac{\Sigma(Y - Y')^2}{n - k - 1}}$$

$$= \sqrt{\frac{572.4273}{20 - 1 - 1}}$$

$$= \sqrt{\frac{572.4273}{18}}$$

$$= \sqrt{31.8015}$$

$$= 5.6393$$

Standard Error of Estimate Adjusted for Degrees of Freedom. As was the case with *RSQ*, the standard error of the estimate is influenced by the ratio of the number of predictor variables to the number of data points. If the calculated value of *RSQ* becomes an *overfit* due to an inadequate number of observations, the calculated standard error of the estimate becomes an *underfit*. Consequently, we need to revise our standard error term. The *Standard Error of Estimate Adjusted for Degrees of Freedom* is used for this purpose. It is symbolized here as $SE_{EST,\,ADJ}$, and it is often referred to as the *Standard Error of the Estimate Adjusted for Shrinkage*. The formula for the $SE_{EST,\,ADJ}$ is given in Equation 17.6:

$$SE_{EST,ADJ} = SE_{EST} \cdot \sqrt{\left(\frac{n - 1}{n - k - 1}\right)} \qquad (17.6)$$

For the absenteeism data, the standard error of estimate after adjusting for degrees of freedom is 5.7938, as follows:

$$SE_{EST,ADJ} = SE_{EST} \cdot \sqrt{\left(\frac{n - 1}{n - k - 1}\right)}$$

$$= 5.6393 \cdot \sqrt{\left(\frac{20 - 1}{20 - 1 - 1}\right)}$$

$$= 5.6393 \cdot \sqrt{\frac{19}{18}}$$

$$= 5.6393 \cdot 1.0274$$

$$= 5.7938$$

Other Components of the Computer Printout

Thus far, we have discussed numerous terms that appear on the printout in Table 17.5, including the error sum of squares for the restricted model, the error sum of squares for the full model, the error sum of squares reduced, the *RSQ* for the full model, the absolute value of the bivariate correlation coefficient, the *RSQ* adjusted for degrees of freedom, the *F*-test for comparing the full model with the restricted (chance) model, the *df* for the full model, the *df* for the chance model, *df* for the numerator of the *F*-test, the *df* for the denominator of the *F*-test, the standard error of estimate, the standard error adjusted for degrees of freedom, the slope, and the intercept. The computer printout includes other terms that will take on considerable importance once we move beyond bivariate regression and into multiple regression. Some of these terms were discussed in Chapter 16: the standard weight for the predictor variable (i.e., the *z*-weight for self-esteem), the standard error of the slope, the computed *t*-value for the slope, and the probability for this *t*-value. Other terms on the printout that were not previously discussed but are relevant to Chapter 17 include the unique *F*-value, the probability for this *F*-value, the restricted model *RSQ*, the usefulness of the variable, and the part correlation associated with the predictor variable. These terms will now be discussed as we explore regression models that are based on *more than one* predictor variable.

Step 2 of the Stepwise Regression for Example 17.1

The next step in the stepwise process is to select a second variable that, *when used in combination with the previous predictor variable*, will result in a greater increase in *RSQ* than any other combination that *also includes* the previously selected predictor variable. Table 17.8 gives the five potential regression models available for step 2, along with their *RSQ*s. The manual solutions for these models are usually performed through matrix algebra, a very tedious and time consuming process. Fortunately, a stepwise computer program saves us from having to compute each model separately; it determines the best two-variable model for us. As we can see from Table 17.8, the model based on the combination of variable 4 and variable 5 yields the highest *RSQ*. The computer results for step 2 of Example 17.1 are presented in Table 17.9.

Table 17.8
Potential Models for Step 2 with Example 17.1

Potential Models for Step 2	*RSQ*
$Y' = f(X_4, X_1)$	.1835
$Y' = f(X_4, X_2)$	.1215
$Y' = f(X_4, X_3)$	.1535
$Y' = f(X_4, X_5)$	.2244
$Y' = f(X_4, X_6)$	.1210

Table 17.9
Step 2 for Absenteeism Data

```
STEP  2

VARIABLES NOW ENTERED:     4  5

ERROR SUM OF SQUARES FOR RESTRICTED MODEL (CHANCE MODEL)                    650.5499
ERROR SUM OF SQUARES FOR FULL MODEL (INCLUSIVE THROUGH THIS STEP)           504.5442
ERROR SUM OF SQUARES REDUCED (EXPLAINED)                                    146.0057

FOR  2 VARIABLES ENTERED
  RSQ FOR FULL MODEL                                                           .2244
  ABSOLUTE VALUE OF MULTIPLE CORRELATION COEFFICIENT (R)                       .4737
  RSQ ADJUSTED FOR DEGREES OF FREEDOM                                          .1332

  F-VALUE FOR COMPARING THIS FULL MODEL
  WITH THE RESTRICTED (CHANCE) MODEL                                          2.4597
       DF FOR THE FULL MODEL =                          3
       DF FOR THE CHANCE MODEL =                        1
       DF FOR THE NUMERATOR OF THE F-TEST =     3 -  1 = 2
       DF FOR THE DENOMINATOR OF THE F-TEST =  20 -  3 = 17
       PROBABILITY ASSOCIATED WITH THE F-TEST =                                .1139

  STANDARD ERROR OF ESTIMATE                                                  5.4479
  STANDARD ERROR ADJUSTED FOR DEGREES OF FREEDOM                              5.7594
```

VARIABLE NUMBER	RAW WEIGHTS	STANDARD WEIGHTS	STD. ERROR OF THE SLOPE	COMPUTED T-VALUES	PROB. FOR T
4	.3330	.4572	.1644	2.0250	.0562
5	1.1343	.3415	.7500	1.5124	.1457
INTERCEPT	-6.9482				

VARIABLE NUMBER	UNIQUE F-VALUES	PROB. FOR F	RESTRICTED MODEL RSQ	USEFUL-NESS	ABS PART CORR
4	4.1006	.0562	.0374	.1871	.4325
5	2.2872	.1457	.1201	.1043	.3230

Table 17.9 reveals that the stepwise program did in fact select variable 5 (initiative) as the next variable to be entered into the model. The regression model based on $Y' = f(X_4, X_5)$ yields the highest *RSQ* of any two-variable model that includes self-esteem as one of these predictor variables. We also see that ESS_{CH} is still equal to 650.5499. However, the ESS_{FM} term has now been reduced from 572.4273 in step 1 to 504.5442 in step 2. As we know from both Table 17.8 and Table 17.9, the *RSQ* for the full model is .2244. Other results include RSQ_{ADJ} = .1332, SE_{EST} = 5.4479, and $SE_{EST,\,ADJ}$ = 5.7594. Further, our prediction equation is no longer a *line*; it is now a *plane* in three-dimensional space. An observation of the values given at the bottom of Table 17.9 reveals that the prediction equation for the two-variable model is equal to $Y' = (-6.9482)\cdot U + (.3330)\cdot X_4 + (1.1343)\cdot X_5$.

We now want to determine whether the *RSQ* for this new full model is statistically significant. We need to examine the following null hypothesis: H_0: $(\rho_{Y\cdot 4,5})^2 = 0.00$. We have 3 degrees of freedom associated with the new full model and 1 degree of freedom associated with the chance model. When we compare this full model to the chance model, we have 3 - 1 = 2 degrees of freedom for the numerator of the test statistic and can no longer perform the *t*-test to compare models. With more than one predictor variable, we must rely exclusively on the F-test given in Equation 17.2. The results of that test are as follows:

$$F = \frac{(RSQ_{FM} - RSQ_{RM}) \;/\; (df_{FM} - df_{RM})}{(1 - RSQ_{FM}) \;/\; (n - df_{FM})}$$

$$= \frac{(.2244 - .0000) \;/\; (3 - 1)}{(1 - .2244) \;/\; (20 - 3)}$$

$$= 2.4597$$

Table 17.9 reveals that $F\ (2,\ 17) = 2.4597$, $p = .1139$. Since this p-value is greater than the selected alpha level of .05, we fail to reject the null hypothesis and conclude that absenteeism cannot be significantly predicted from a knowledge of the combination of self-esteem and initiative. This conclusion is graphically represented by Figure 17.6. Again, we might be tempted to stop at this point, but multiple regression allows us to continue on!

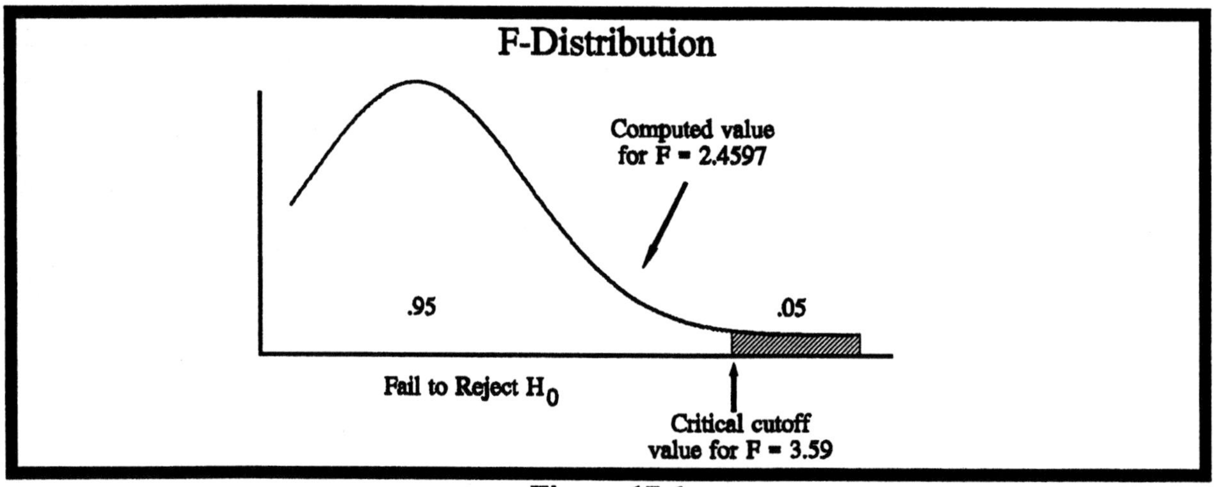

Figure 17.6
F-Test for the Significance of the Regression in Step 2

Multicollinearity

We point out that the stepwise process has not necessarily yielded the highest *RSQ* of *all* possible two-variable models for this set of data. Only the models that include variable 4 as one of the two variables have been examined. There are [6! / (2!·4!)] = 15 possible combinations, and we have examined only five of these possible models. If we were to examine all 15 combinations and select the one that yields the highest *RSQ*, we would be using the *all-possible-combinations method* instead of the stepwise method. As pointed out earlier, the all-possible-combinations method takes too much advantage of chance and often leads us to conclusions that may only be relevant to the current set of data. This method is not recommended because some degree of *multicollinearity* almost always exists in multiple regression models.

An examination of the bivariate correlations given in Table 17.4 will help us to understand the nature of multicollinearity. If we had used the row of validities in the intercorrelation matrix to select our second variable, we would have chosen variable 3 instead of variable 5, as variable 3 has the next highest absolute validity. While such logic holds when the predictor variables are *independent* of one-another (i.e., if the predictor variables are *orthogonal* to each other), such independencies rarely occur in practice. An examination of Table 17.4 reveals that variable 4 is not perfectly *uncorrelated* with the other predictor variables. Therefore, we have multicollinearity among the predictor variables. Such multicollinearity has an impact upon the relationships between the *Y*-variable and any combination of the predictor variables. Under these conditions, we cannot easily anticipate an optimal model. We will discuss the problems associated with multicollinearity in more detail later. Suffice it to say that almost all multiple regression models will be influenced to some degree by multicollinearity and that the all-possible-combinations approach will be more influenced than the stepwise approach.

Graphic Illustrations of the Relationship Between Three Variables

Scatter Diagram. As stated earlier, since we now have two predictor variables and three-dimensional space, our regression line has become a plane, often referred to as a *hyperplane*. Graphically plotting the data points and projecting a hyperplane in three-dimensional space (i.e., in *hyperspace*), is extremely difficult to do manually. With more than two predictor variables (i.e., more than three-dimensional space), plotting and graphing become virtually impossible. Although such graphic representations may be impossible to create, we should at least have an intuitive feeling for the model. Figure 17.7 gives a graphic representation for the 20 data points associated with Example 17.1, without including the hyperplane.

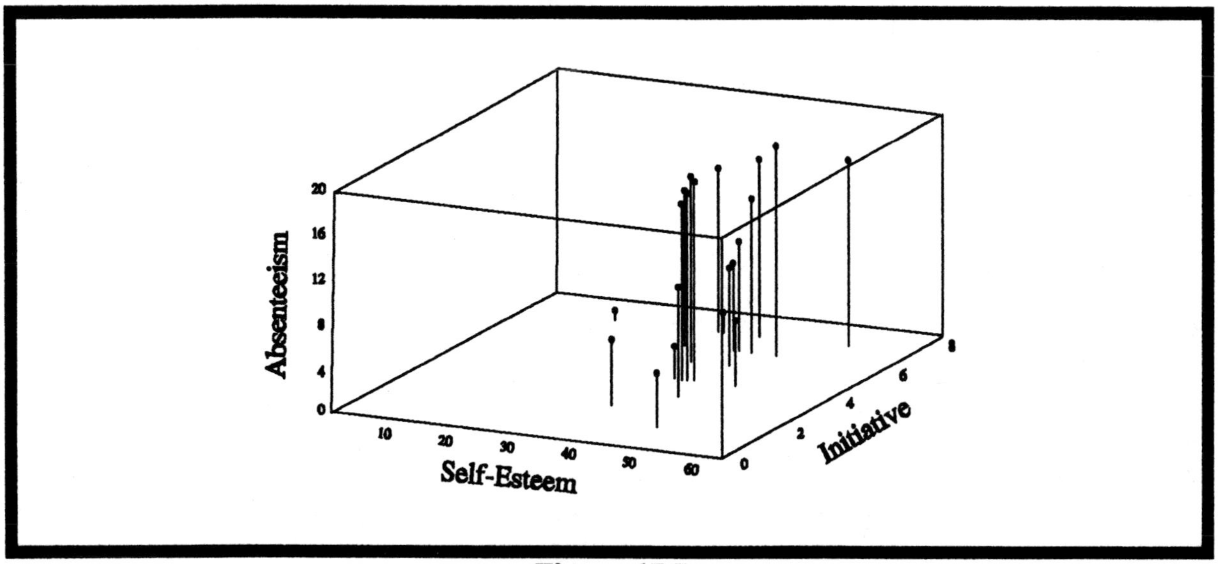

Figure 17.7
Three-Dimensional Graph for Predicting Absenteeism
From Self-Esteem and Initiative

Steps 3, 4, 5, and 6 of the Stepwise Regression for Example 17.1

The next step in the stepwise process is to select a third variable that, when used *in combination* with the first two predictor variables, will result in a greater increase in *RSQ* than any other combination that also includes the previously selected predictor variables. Table 17.10 gives the four potential regression models available for step 3, along with their corresponding *RSQ*s. As before, these *RSQ* values are presented here for pedagogical purposes only. We do not need to compute them manually, since the stepwise computer program will automatically select the model that results in the highest *RSQ*. Table 17.10 reveals that the addition of variable 1 (SBD-CON-I) will provide the highest *RSQ* of any three variable model that also includes the two previously selected variables. The computer results for step 3 of Example 17.1 are presented in Table 17.11.

Table 17.10
Potential Models for Step 3 with Example 17.1

Potential Models for Step 3	*RSQ*
$Y' = f(X_4, X_5, X_1)$	.3077
$Y' = f(X_4, X_5, X_2)$	.2244
$Y' = f(X_4, X_5, X_3)$	.2489
$Y' = f(X_4, X_5, X_6)$	.2264

As we can see from Table 17.11, ESS_{CH} is still equal to 650.5499. However, the ESS_{FM} term has now been reduced from 572.4273 in step 1 to 504.5442 in step 2 to 450.3556 in step 3. As found in Table 17.10 and confirmed in Table 17.11, *RSQ* has now increased to .3077. The RSQ_{ADJ} is now .1779; the SE_{EST} is 5.3054; and the $SE_{EST,\,ADJ}$ is 5.7814. Further, our prediction equation is now a *hyperplane* in four-dimensional space. An observation of the values given in the bottom of Table 17.11 reveals that the prediction equation for the three-variable model is equal to $Y' = (-17.0546)\cdot U + (.3739)\cdot X_4 + (1.2453)\cdot X_5 + (.1402)\cdot X_1$.

We again want to determine whether the *RSQ* for this three-variable full model is statistically significantly greater than the *RSQ* we would have obtained by chance. We now have 4 degrees of freedom associated with the new full model and 1 degree of freedom associated with the chance model. When we compare this full model to the chance model, we have 4 - 1 = 3 degrees of freedom associated with the numerator of the test statistic and 20 - 4 = 16 degrees of freedom associated with the denominator of the test statistic. Thus, we find that $F\ (3, 16) = 2.3708$, $p > .05$. We fail to reject the null hypothesis and conclude that absenteeism cannot be significantly predicted from a knowledge of the combination of self-esteem, initiative, and SBD-CON-II. Again, we may be tempted to stop; however, we will continue with the multiple regression.

Table 17.11
Step 3 for Absenteeism Data

```
STEP  3

VARIABLES NOW ENTERED:     4  5  1

ERROR SUM OF SQUARES FOR RESTRICTED MODEL (CHANCE MODEL)                  650.5499
ERROR SUM OF SQUARES FOR FULL MODEL (INCLUSIVE THROUGH THIS STEP)         450.3556
ERROR SUM OF SQUARES REDUCED (EXPLAINED)                                  200.1943

FOR  3 VARIABLES ENTERED
  RSQ FOR FULL MODEL                                                         .3077
  ABSOLUTE VALUE OF MULTIPLE CORRELATION COEFFICIENT (R)                     .5547
  RSQ ADJUSTED FOR DEGREES OF FREEDOM                                        .1779

  F-VALUE FOR COMPARING THIS FULL MODEL
  WITH THE RESTRICTED (CHANCE) MODEL                                        2.3708
       DF FOR THE FULL MODEL =                               4
       DF FOR THE CHANCE MODEL =                             1
       DF FOR THE NUMERATOR OF THE F-TEST =       4 -  1 =   3
       DF FOR THE DENOMINATOR OF THE F-TEST =    20 -  4 =  16
       PROBABILITY ASSOCIATED WITH THE F-TEST =                              .1081

  STANDARD ERROR OF ESTIMATE                                                5.3054
  STANDARD ERROR ADJUSTED FOR DEGREES OF FREEDOM                            5.7814
```

VARIABLE NUMBER	RAW WEIGHTS	STANDARD WEIGHTS	STD. ERROR OF THE SLOPE	COMPUTED T-VALUES	PROB. FOR T
4	.3739	.5134	.1628	2.2962	.0337
5	1.2453	.3749	.7348	1.6948	.1063
1	.1402	.2939	.1010	1.3875	.1817
INTERCEPT	-17.0546				

VARIABLE NUMBER	UNIQUE F-VALUES	PROB. FOR F	RESTRICTED MODEL RSQ	USEFUL-NESS	ABS PART CORR
4	5.2725	.0337	.0796	.2281	.4776
5	2.8723	.1063	.1835	.1243	.3525
1	1.9252	.1817	.2244	.0833	.2886

Rather than discussing each of the remaining steps separately, we will simply present the possible models available for each new step, along with the results of the stepwise model selected by the computer process in each step. Table 17.12 gives the three potential regression models available for step 4, while Table 17.13 gives the results of this analysis. Table 17.14 gives the two potential regression models available for step 5, while Table 17.15 gives the results of this analysis. Finally, Table 17.16 gives the one possible model available for step 6, and Table 17.17 gives the results of the final full model. As we can see, variable 2 (SBD-IS-I) was the variable added in step 4; variable 3 (SBD-CON-II) was added in step 5; and variable 6 (the number of jobs previously held) was added in step 6.

We will now turn to step 6 in this process and evaluate the results. We will also return to our discussion of the overfit that occurs with each additional step of a stepwise regression model. This issue has become even more important, as the ratio of cases to predictor variables is now 20 to 6, a far cry from the "10 to 1 ratio, plus 10 for the pot" rule.

Table 17.12
Potential Models for Step 4 with Example 17.1

Potential Models for Step 4	*RSQ*
$Y' = f(X_4, X_5, X_1, X_2)$	.5147
$Y' = f(X_4, X_5, X_1, X_3)$	.3846
$Y' = f(X_4, X_5, X_1, X_6)$	.3097

Table 17.13
Step 4 for Absenteeism Data

STEP 4

VARIABLES NOW ENTERED: 4 5 1 2

ERROR SUM OF SQUARES FOR RESTRICTED MODEL (CHANCE MODEL)	650.5499
ERROR SUM OF SQUARES FOR FULL MODEL (INCLUSIVE THROUGH THIS STEP)	315.7123
ERROR SUM OF SQUARES REDUCED (EXPLAINED)	334.8375

FOR 4 VARIABLES ENTERED

RSQ FOR FULL MODEL		.5147
ABSOLUTE VALUE OF MULTIPLE CORRELATION COEFFICIENT (R)		.7174
RSQ ADJUSTED FOR DEGREES OF FREEDOM		.3853
F-VALUE FOR COMPARING THIS FULL MODEL WITH THE RESTRICTED (CHANCE) MODEL		3.9772
DF FOR THE FULL MODEL =	5	
DF FOR THE CHANCE MODEL =	1	
DF FOR THE NUMERATOR OF THE F-TEST = 5 - 1 =	4	
DF FOR THE DENOMINATOR OF THE F-TEST = 20 - 5 =	15	
PROBABILITY ASSOCIATED WITH THE F-TEST =		.0213
STANDARD ERROR OF ESTIMATE		4.5878
STANDARD ERROR ADJUSTED FOR DEGREES OF FREEDOM		5.1633

VARIABLE NUMBER	RAW WEIGHTS	STANDARD WEIGHTS	STD. ERROR OF THE SLOPE	COMPUTED T-VALUES	PROB. FOR T
4	.2999	.4117	.1438	2.0851	.0521
5	1.1599	.3492	.6363	1.8229	.0853
1	.4906	1.0283	.1638	2.9953	.0089
2	.3579	.8836	.1415	2.5293	.0220
INTERCEPT	-49.3798				

VARIABLE NUMBER	UNIQUE F-VALUES	PROB. FOR F	RESTRICTED MODEL RSQ	USEFUL-NESS	ABS PART CORR
4	4.3478	.0521	.3740	.1407	.3751
5	3.3231	.0853	.4072	.1075	.3279
1	8.9716	.0089	.2244	.2903	.5388
2	6.3971	.0220	.3077	.2070	.4549

Table 17.14
Potential Models for Step 5 with Example 17.1

Potential Models for Step 5	*RSQ*
$Y' = f(X_4, X_5, X_1, X_2, X_3)$	.6667
$Y' = f(X_4, X_5, X_1, X_2, X_6)$	.5147

Table 17.15
Step 5 for Absenteeism Data

STEP 5

VARIABLES NOW ENTERED: 4 5 1 2 3

ERROR SUM OF SQUARES FOR RESTRICTED MODEL (CHANCE MODEL)	650.5499
ERROR SUM OF SQUARES FOR FULL MODEL (INCLUSIVE THROUGH THIS STEP)	216.8192
ERROR SUM OF SQUARES REDUCED (EXPLAINED)	433.7307

FOR 5 VARIABLES ENTERED

RSQ FOR FULL MODEL	.6667
ABSOLUTE VALUE OF MULTIPLE CORRELATION COEFFICIENT (R)	.8165
RSQ ADJUSTED FOR DEGREES OF FREEDOM	.5477

F-VALUE FOR COMPARING THIS FULL MODEL WITH THE RESTRICTED (CHANCE) MODEL			5.6012
DF FOR THE FULL MODEL =		6	
DF FOR THE CHANCE MODEL =		1	
DF FOR THE NUMERATOR OF THE F-TEST =	6 - 1 =	5	
DF FOR THE DENOMINATOR OF THE F-TEST =	20 - 6 =	14	
PROBABILITY ASSOCIATED WITH THE F-TEST =			.0051

STANDARD ERROR OF ESTIMATE	3.9354
STANDARD ERROR ADJUSTED FOR DEGREES OF FREEDOM	4.5846

VARIABLE NUMBER	RAW WEIGHTS	STANDARD WEIGHTS	STD. ERROR OF THE SLOPE	COMPUTED T-VALUES	PROB. FOR T
4	.2649	.3637	.1241	2.1339	.0487
5	1.0767	.3241	.5468	1.9690	.0664
1	.6341	1.3290	.1515	4.1841	.0012
2	.4289	1.0588	.1246	3.4425	.0042
3	-.3257	-.4320	.1289	-2.5270	.0230
INTERCEPT	-39.9175				

VARIABLE NUMBER	UNIQUE F-VALUES	PROB. FOR F	RESTRICTED MODEL RSQ	USEFUL-NESS	ABS PART CORR
4	4.5537	.0487	.5583	.1084	.3292
5	3.8769	.0664	.5744	.0923	.3038
1	17.5071	.0012	.2499	.4168	.6456
2	11.8506	.0042	.3846	.2821	.5311
3	6.3855	.0230	.5147	.1520	.3899

Table 17.16
Potential Models for Step 6 with Example 17.1

Potential Models for Step 6	***RSQ***
$Y' = f(X_4, X_5, X_1, X_2, X_3, X_6)$	.7113

Table 17.17
Step 6 for Absenteeism Data

```
STEP  6

VARIABLES NOW ENTERED:    4  5  1  2  3  6

ERROR SUM OF SQUARES FOR RESTRICTED MODEL (CHANCE MODEL)                    650.5499
ERROR SUM OF SQUARES FOR FULL MODEL (INCLUSIVE THROUGH THIS STEP)           187.8424
ERROR SUM OF SQUARES REDUCED (EXPLAINED)                                    462.7075

FOR  6 VARIABLES ENTERED
  RSQ FOR FULL MODEL                                                           .7113
  ABSOLUTE VALUE OF MULTIPLE CORRELATION COEFFICIENT (R)                       .8434
  RSQ ADJUSTED FOR DEGREES OF FREEDOM                                          .5780

  F-VALUE FOR COMPARING THIS FULL MODEL
  WITH THE RESTRICTED (CHANCE) MODEL                                          5.3371
       DF FOR THE FULL MODEL =                                     7
       DF FOR THE CHANCE MODEL =                                   1
       DF FOR THE NUMERATOR OF THE F-TEST =        7 -  1 =        6
       DF FOR THE DENOMINATOR OF THE F-TEST =     20 -  7 =       13
       PROBABILITY ASSOCIATED WITH THE F-TEST =                                .0059

  STANDARD ERROR OF ESTIMATE                                                  3.8012
  STANDARD ERROR ADJUSTED FOR DEGREES OF FREEDOM                              4.5955
```

VARIABLE NUMBER	RAW WEIGHTS	STANDARD WEIGHTS	STD. ERROR OF THE SLOPE	COMPUTED T-VALUES	PROB. FOR T
4	.2293	.3148	.1225	1.8715	.0811
5	1.0547	.3175	.5284	1.9961	.0647
1	.6572	1.3775	.1473	4.4623	.0009
2	.4680	1.1553	.1235	3.7903	.0025
3	-.4217	-.5594	.1418	-2.9748	.0105
6	1.0242	.2540	.7233	1.4161	.1778
INTERCEPT	-37.9372				

VARIABLE NUMBER	UNIQUE F-VALUES	PROB. FOR F	RESTRICTED MODEL RSQ	USEFUL-NESS	ABS PART CORR
4	3.5024	.0811	.6335	.0778	.2789
5	3.9845	.0647	.6228	.0885	.2975
1	19.9121	.0009	.2690	.4423	.6650
2	14.3664	.0025	.3922	.3191	.5649
3	8.8494	.0105	.5147	.1966	.4433
6	2.0054	.1778	.6667	.0445	.2110

Analysis of the Full Model that Includes All Variables

As we can see from step 6 given in Table 17.17, the fullest of our full regression models has an $RSQ = .7113$. We can explain 71.13% of the variance in absenteeism from a knowledge of the variation among the six predictor variables. We also noticed that the *RSQ* has increased from step to step as we have added predictor variables to our model. It must either remain the same or increase; the *RSQ* will never decrease by adding more variables! In order to determine whether the *RSQ* for our full model is significantly better than chance, the following null hypothesis is tested:

$$H_0: (\rho_{Y \cdot 1,2,3,4,5,6})^2 = 0.00$$

We use the *F*-test to evaluate this null hypothesis. Our results are as follows:

$$F = \frac{(RSQ_{FM} - RSQ_{RM}) \,/\, (df_{FM} - df_{RM})}{(1 - RSQ_{FM}) \,/\, (n - df_{FM})}$$

$$= \frac{(.7113 - .0000) \,/\, (7 - 1)}{(1 - .7113) \,/\, (20 - 7)}$$

$$= 5.3371$$

As we can see from Table 17.17, $F\,(6, 13) = 5.3371$, $p = .0059$. We conclude that our full model, the one that is based on all six predictor variables, is statistically significantly greater than the chance model.

We can also compare this full model to various other models that we have obtained along the way. For example, suppose we want to determine whether the *RSQ* for the six-variable model is significantly greater than the *RSQ* for the one-variable model obtained in step 1 of the analysis. We can express the null hypothesis for comparing these two models as follows:

$$H_0: (\rho_{Y \cdot 1,2,3,4,5,6})^2 = (\rho_{Y \cdot 4})^2$$

We will use the six-variable regression model as our full model and the one-variable regression model as the restricted model. Here are the results of this *F*-test:

$$F = \frac{(RSQ_{FM} - RSQ_{RM}) \,/\, (df_{FM} - df_{RM})}{(1 - RSQ_{FM}) \,/\, (n - df_{FM})}$$

$$= \frac{(.7113 - .1201) \,/\, (7 - 2)}{(1 - .7113) \,/\, (20 - 7)}$$

$$= 5.3243$$

Since F (5, 13) = 5.3243, $p < .05$, we reject the null hypothesis and conclude that the RSQ for the fullest model is significantly greater than the RSQ for the restricted model that uses only variable 4. The combination that includes the other five variables is making a significant contribution to the full model. In a similar manner, we can compare our full model to any other model in which one or more predictor variables have been restricted from the full model.

Table 17.17 also reveals that RSQ_{ADJ} = .5780. We should not be surprised with this RSQ, as we have an overfit due to the poor ratio of cases to predictor variables. Although most computer programs do not automatically test the significance of the shrunken RSQ against chance, we can manually compute an F-test for the full model based on the RSQ_{ADJ} as follows:

$$F = \frac{(RSQ_{FM} - RSQ_{RM}) \;/\; (df_{FM} - df_{RM})}{(1 - RSQ_{FM}) \;/\; (n - df_{FM})}$$

$$= \frac{(.5780 - .0000) \;/\; (7 - 1)}{(1 - .5780) \;/\; (20 - 7)}$$

$$= 2.9676$$

Although this computed F-value is not as large as the one obtained before the adjustment for degrees of freedom, we again conclude that the results are statistically significant, as F (6, 13) = 2.9676, $p < .05$. We cannot compare the RSQ_{FM} against the RSQ_{ADJ}, since they represent the same model and have the same seven degrees of freedom.

An observation of Table 11 in Appendix C tells us that if we had an RSQ of .7000 and a "10 to 1 ratio, plus 10 for the pot" [resulting in a sample size determined as n = ((10) · (6)) + (10) = 70], we would have obtained an estimated shrunken RSQ of .6714. With a "20 to 1 ratio, plus 20 for the pot" [resulting in a sample size determined as n = ((20) · (6)) + (20) = 140], an RSQ of .7000 would yield a corresponding estimated shrunken RSQ of .6865, as given in the appendix. Cohen and Cohen (1983, p. 125) suggested that a 40 to 1 ratio "is prudent" for interpreting results of steps in the stepwise regression. However, if we are only going to examine and interpret the final step (i.e., the fullest of the full models), this ratio can be relaxed. We have stated repeatedly that the final step will always be the same regardless of whether the backward regression approach, the all-possible-methods approach, the stepwise approach, or any other approach is used, including commonly used spreadsheet approaches. The current text stresses that *the final step should be examined carefully before evaluating any intermediate steps* obtained in the process. If we are not interested in the intermediate steps and are not trying to use these steps to make decisions about the importance of variables to the models, the RSQ_{ADJ} is not as critical as before.

Table of Residuals

We now have a multiple regression equation for the six-variable model. While we will not attempt to graph this model in seven-dimensional space, we do know that there is an intercept at which the hyperplane crosses the Y-axis. The location of this intercept corresponds to a position at which all of the values of the X-variables are zero. We also know that there are six slopes used as weights for the six predictor variables. The full regression model is as follows:

$$Y' = f(X_1, X_2, X_3, X_4, X_5, X_6)$$

$$= b_0 \cdot U + b_1 \cdot X_1 + b_2 \cdot X_2 + b_3 \cdot X_3 + b_4 \cdot X_4 + b_5 \cdot X_5 + b_6 \cdot X_6$$

$$= (-37.9372) \cdot U + (.6572) \cdot X_1 + (.4680) \cdot X_2 + (-.4217) \cdot X_3$$

$$+ (.2293) \cdot X_4 + (1.0547) \cdot X_5 + (1.0242) \cdot X_6$$

We can use this prediction equation to determine the Y'-values for each of the individuals in the study. For example, suppose we are interested in determining a predicted value for person number 10, based on our full regression model. Returning to Table 17.2 given at the onset of this chapter, we find the following values for this person across variables one through six, respectively: 67, 33, 74, 36, 4, and 3. Inserting these values into the regression model, we obtain a predicted value of $Y' = 5.8826$. Rounded to whole days, we predict that this individual missed approximately six days on the job during the 24-month period, obtained as follows:

$$Y' = b_0 \cdot U + b_1 \cdot X_1 + b_2 \cdot X_2 + b_3 \cdot X_3 + b_4 \cdot X_4 + b_5 \cdot X_5 + b_6 \cdot X_6$$

$$= (-37.9372) \cdot U + (.6572) \cdot X_1 + (.4680) \cdot X_2 + (-.4217) \cdot X_3$$

$$+ (.2293) \cdot X_4 + (1.0547) \cdot X_5 + (1.0242) \cdot X_6$$

$$= (-37.9372) \cdot (1) + (.6572) \cdot (67) + (.4680) \cdot (33) + (-.4217) \cdot (74)$$

$$+ (.2293) \cdot (36) + (1.0547) \cdot (4) + (1.0242) \cdot (3)$$

$$= 5.8826$$

As seen in Table 17.2, this person actually missed only three days on the job during this time period. We have overestimated his or her absenteeism record by $5.8826 - 3 = 2.8826$ days. Of course, we did not really expect to make a perfect prediction. Our RSQ is not perfect, and our ESS_{FM} is not equal to 0.00; therefore, we must anticipate errors in prediction somewhere. On the other hand, if we had predicted this person's absenteeism rate solely on the basis of chance, we would have predicted $\overline{Y} = 11.15$ days of absenteeism, an overestimate of 8.15 days.

Table 17.18, generated from the stepwise regression program, includes the values for Y, Y', $Y - Y'$ (i.e., the residuals, or $Y - Y' = e$), and $(Y - Y')^2$ (i.e., the squares of the residuals) for each of the 20 individuals. As can be seen in Table 17.18, the mean for the original Y-values and the mean for the Y'-values are the same; that is, $\overline{Y} = \overline{Y'} = 11.15$. The mean for the residuals is $\overline{e} = 0$, and the sum of the squares for the residuals is equal to $\Sigma(Y - Y')^2 = ESS_{FM} = 187.84260$ These values provide confirmation for our equations and computations.

Table 17.18
Table of Residuals for Absenteeism Data

TABLE OF RESIDUALS

CASE NO.	Y	Y ESTIMATE	RESIDUAL	RESIDUALS SQUARED
1	1.00000	4.06919	-3.06919	9.41990
2	19.00000	15.41196	3.58804	12.87403
3	18.00000	15.89309	2.10691	4.43909
4	15.00000	14.67617	.32383	.10487
5	17.00000	19.06990	-2.06990	4.28447
6	6.00000	2.79406	3.20594	10.27804
7	5.00000	10.84933	-5.84933	34.21468
8	2.00000	5.42459	-3.42459	11.72782
9	14.00000	13.75833	.24167	.05841
10	3.00000	5.88260	-2.88260	8.30938
11	10.00000	10.19077	-.19077	.03640
12	8.00000	5.61348	2.38652	5.69549
13	17.00000	12.12312	4.87688	23.78394
14	14.00000	14.71082	-.71082	.50526
15	16.00000	18.58545	-2.58545	6.68455
16	16.00000	12.71112	3.28888	10.81670
17	17.00000	13.83592	3.16408	10.01139
18	6.00000	8.47424	-2.47424	6.12187
19	10.00000	13.73612	-3.73612	13.95857
20	9.00000	5.18979	3.81021	14.51774
	Y MEAN	Y ESTIMATE MEAN	RESIDUAL MEAN	ERROR SUM OF SQUARES
	11.15000	11.15000	.00000	187.84260

Interpretation of the Contribution of Predictor Variables

Thus far in our discussion, we have concentrated on developing full models with which to make predictions in regard to the criterion variable. We have not focused on the interpretation, meaning, or importance of the individual predictor variables in these models. Many times our primary concern is to determine which variables are the most important in regard to our models; unfortunately, it is often very difficult to draw conclusions about the importance of variables. This is especially true when we have multicollinearity, where linear dependencies or even *near-dependencies* exist, as discussed in the next few pages.

If we have perfect linear dependencies among the predictor variables, such redundancies will have to be eliminated before a solution can be obtained. In addition to the mathematical problem of solving for regression models when dependencies exist among predictor variables, we do not want to waste time, money, and human resources on variables that do not contribute any additional information to our models beyond what we already know from other variables used in the model. If a variable only reveals information already contained in another variable (or linear combination of a set of other variables), that variable is providing us with no additional information.

The existence of perfect linear dependencies among predictor variables in either experimental or *post hoc* studies is rare. On the other hand, it is not uncommon to have a set of variables that contain near-dependencies. Such near-dependencies exist when relationships among a pair or a combination of predictor variables are strong but not perfect. We may have difficulty recognizing the presence of such dependencies; we may also have difficulty interpreting the relative importance of individual variables in such regression models.

As stated earlier, multiple regression computer software packages that use matrix algebra will give error messages if perfect dependencies exist among the predictor variables. However, error messages are not generated for near-dependencies. Programs have also been developed that use iterative procedures instead of matrix algebra to solve for weights in the presence of perfect dependencies through numerical analysis. Such iterative programs have obvious advantages, but the resulting weights are often somewhat surprising. For example, a zero weight may be arbitrarily assigned to one of the variables. The redundancy is then eliminated and a solution is obtained. However, any one of the variables involved in the redundancy can be assigned a zero weight, making interpretation of the remaining weights impossible.

The following presentation discusses several approaches for examining the importance of the predictor variables. These methods include the examination of various forms of correlation coefficients (e.g., validities, part correlations, partial correlations), various forms of regression weights (e.g., raw weights, standard weights), the usefulness or uniqueness of variables, and other analytic tools. Table 17.19 includes a summary of computed values for these and other terms relative to the full model for Example 17.1. Interested readers are referred to a classic article by Darlington (1968) that provides additional thoughts on these and related topics.

Correlation Coefficients

There are various forms of correlation coefficients associated with multiple regression. Thus far we have concentrated on the multiple correlation coefficient associated with the full model, along with its corresponding *RSQ*. Three other types of correlations that can be useful for interpretation purposes include the validities, the part correlations, and the partial correlations.

Validities. As discussed earlier, the validities are the correlations between the individual predictor variables and the criterion variable. We may refer to these coefficients as *bivariate correlations* or *zero-order correlations*. The validities between the predictor variables and the Y-variable should always be examined. Most stepwise regression programs make the assumption that we will want to include in the full model the variable that does the best job of predicting the Y-variable by itself, at least at the onset. Consequently, the variable with the highest absolute validity is the first variable selected in traditional stepwise models, and it usually remains in the equation throughout the process. Marks (1966) claimed that unless we have an adequate sample size (a minimum of perhaps 200 or more, according to his research), we should not consider regression weights as useful and therefore should stick to conclusions based on the validities themselves. While some feel that such a sample size requirement is perhaps stringent, most agree that under these conditions the validities are more stable than the multiple regression weights.

Table 17.19
Summary of Various Computational Values

Variable Number	*Validities*	*Raw Weights*	*Standard Weights*	*Usefulness*	*Unique F-values*
1	0.1953	0.6572	1.3775	0.4423	19.9121
2	0.1174	0.4680	1.1553	0.3191	14.3664
3	-0.2181	-0.4217	-0.5594	0.1966	8.8494
4	0.3465	0.2293	0.3148	0.0778	3.5024
5	0.1933	1.0547	0.3175	0.0885	3.9845
6	0.0558	1.0242	0.2540	0.0445	2.0054
Variable Number	*Part Correlations*	*Fifth-Order Partials*	*Proportional Values*	*Proportion Over RSQ*	*RSQ_j X as Y*
1	0.6650	0.7778	0.2690	0.3782	0.7669
2	0.5649	0.7245	0.1356	0.1907	0.7609
3	-0.4433	-0.6364	0.1220	0.1715	0.3719
4	0.2789	0.4607	0.1091	0.1534	0.2150
5	0.2975	0.4844	0.0614	0.0863	0.1221
6	0.2110	0.3656	0.0142	0.0199	0.3095

Part Correlations. While the validities may have limited utility beyond bivariate regression, part correlations sometimes provide help in interpreting the importance of the predictor variables to the full model. Part correlations are the bivariate correlations between the *Y*-variable and the "part" of the particular *X*-variable of concern that is uncorrelated with the remaining *X*-variables. Part correlations are sometimes referred to as *semi-partial correlations* because only the part of the intercorrelation between the *predictor* variable of concern and the remaining *predictor* variables has been partialled out. The part of the intercorrelation between the *criterion* variable and the same remaining *predictor* variables *excluding* the predictor variable of concern has *not* been partialled out. Thus, we have only partialled out part of the information; that is, we have "semi-partialled" out the information. When we partial out *both* parts and then correlate the results, we refer to such correlations as *partial correlations*, which we will discuss shortly.

There are several methods for determining the part correlation. We will return to the self-esteem variable in the absenteeism data to illustrate one of these methods. First, we determine the part of the *X*-variable that is unrelated to the other *X*-variables by developing a regression model based on $X_4 = f(X_1, X_2, X_3, X_5, X_6)$. Second, based on this regression model, we obtain the predicted values for each of the cases on the X_4 variable. Third, we subtract these predicted values from the actual X_4 values. The resulting differences are the residuals for X_4. (Notice that we have not as yet used the *Y*-variable anywhere in this process.) These residuals are independent of the remaining X-variables, as can be verified by computing correlations between these residuals and the five other predictor variables. Although the proof will not be given here, the correlations among these residuals and the remaining predictor variables based on this approach are always zero. Finally, we correlate these residuals with the Y-variable to obtain the part correlation. The part correlation between self-esteem and absenteeism is equal to .2789. This value is given in absolute form in step 6, as shown in Table 17.17. It is also given in Table 17.19, which summarizes many of the interpretation methods discussed here. This part correlation is symbolized as follows:

$$r_{Y(4 \cdot 1,2,3,5,6)} = .2789$$

The symbolism implies that we are identifying the part correlation between the Y-variable and a specified predictor variable, after eliminating any intercorrelations among the predictor variable of concern and the remaining predictor variables.

The calculations necessary for determining part correlations can be quite complex without the use of computer software with options for obtaining these values. Fortunately, the *absolute* value of the part correlation can be obtained by finding the ***square root of the usefulness*** of a variable. A variable's usefulness will be defined both qualitatively and quantitatively in upcoming sections. Most computer programs do not report part correlations. A few computer programs, including the one referred to as JRB04 in this chapter, report the *absolute* value of the part correlations. A few others, such as JRB19, report the actual part correlations. Examples of output from JRB19 will be given later.

Partial Correlations. The third type of correlation to be presented here for evaluating the relative importance of predictor variables is the partial correlation coefficient. The partial correlation between a predictor variable and the criterion variable is the correlation between these two variables after eliminating the impact of the remaining predictor variables from *both* of these variables. As we mentioned in our preceding discussion, part correlations are also referred to as semi-partial correlations because we are only taking out the part of the intercorrelations between the predictor variable of interest and the remaining X-variables, not the part of the intercorrelations between the Y-variable and these same remaining X-variables. With partial correlations, we remove the impact of these intercorrelations from both variables. The partial correlations are referred to as *first-order partial correlations* if we partial out the effect of one predictor variable from both the remaining X-variables and the Y-variable, as *second-order partial correlations* if we partial out the effect of two predictor variables from both the remaining X-variables and the Y-variable, as *third-order partial correlations* if we partial out the effect of three predictor variables from both the remaining X-variables and the Y-variable, etc.

We will again return to the self-esteem variable in the absenteeism data to illustrate partial correlations. In this example, we are probably interested in partialing out the effect of five predictor variables when determining each of the individual partial correlations. We would refer to these as *fifth-order partial correlations.* The fifth-order partial correlation between self-esteem and absenteeism is equal to .4607, as given in Table 17.19. This fifth-order partial correlation is symbolized as follows:

$r_{Y,4(\cdot 1,2,3,5,6)} = .4607$

Computing partial correlations for multiple regression models that have many predictor variables is very time-consuming. We first have to obtain the residuals for the Y-variable, based on a regression equation that uses all of our predictor variables except the X-variable of concern. We then have to obtain the residuals for the X-variable of interest, based on a regression equation that uses all of the remaining predictor variables (as was done with the part correlation procedure), and correlate these two sets of residual variables. Using self-esteem as our illustration, the correlation between these sets of residuals is .4607.

Naturally, the bivariate regression equation for these two sets of residual variables has an intercept and a slope. These regression weights for this equation are as follows:

$$(\textit{Residuals}_{Y\cdot 1,2,3,5,6})' = (b_0)\cdot(U) + (b_{4\cdot 1,2,3,5,6})\cdot(\textit{Residuals}_{4\cdot 1,2,3,5,6})$$

$$= (0.00)\cdot(U) + (.2293)\cdot(\textit{Residuals}_{4\cdot 1,2,3,5,6})$$

where:

$(\textit{Residuals}_{Y\cdot 1,2,3,5,6})'$ = $Y - Y' = e$ residual values obtained by predicting absenteeism from predictor variables X_1, X_2, X_3, X_5, and X_6

and, where:

$(\textit{Residuals}_{4\cdot 1,2,3,5,6})$ = $X_4 - X_4' = e$ residual values obtained by predicting self-esteem from predictor variables X_1, X_2, X_3, X_5, and X_6

We can see that the slope in this bivariate equation is the same as our raw regression weight for X_4 in the full regression model, given earlier in Table 17.17 as .2293. This regression weight is also referred to as a partial regression weight, to be discussed shortly. We also notice that the intercept for this bivariate equation is equal to 0.00.

We have obtained a fifth-order partial correlation for one of the six predictor variables. If we want to determine the fifth-order partial correlations for the other predictor variables, we must repeat this process five more times. Without access to a computer program that automatically gives the $(k - 1)^{th}$ order partial correlations, the necessary effort may not be justified. Table 17.20 contains the printout obtained from JRB19, a computer program that does give the $(k - 1)^{th}$ order partial correlations as well as other values not available in many computer programs. As we can see, the fifth-order partial correlation coefficients for predictor variables one through six in Example 17.1 are .77782, .72454, -.63641, .46069, .48435, and .36557, respectively. We will discuss the other values that are included in Table 17.20 later in this chapter.

Table 17.20
Results for the Full Model Based Upon JRB19

REGRESSION RESULTS

RSQ for the Full Model based upon 6 predictor variables	.71126
Absolute Value of the Multiple Correlation Coefficient (R)	.84336
RSQ Adjusted for Degrees of Freedom (Shrunken RSQ)	.57799
Error Sum of Squares for Restricted Model (the Chance Model)	650.55000
Error Sum of Squares for Full Model	187.84260
Error Sum of Squares Reduced (ESS Chance - ESS Full Model)	462.70740
Standard Error of the Estimate	3.80124
Standard Error of the Estimate Adjusted for Degrees of Freedom	4.59548
F-Value for Comparing the Full Model vs. the Chance Model	5.33709
Degrees of Freedom for the Full Model	7
Degrees of Freedom for the Chance Model	1
Degrees of Freedom for the Numerator of the F-Test	6
Degrees of Freedom for the Denominator of the F-Test	13
Probability Associated with the F-Test	.00590

ADDITIONAL VALUES

Predictor Variable Number	Raw Regression Weights	Standard Error of Weights	t-Values for Regression Weights	Prob. for t-Values	Lower 95% Interval	Upper 95% Interval
1	.65725	.14729	4.46229	.00089	.33905	.97545
2	.46801	.12347	3.79030	.00252	.20125	.73476
3	-.42169	.14176	-2.97479	.01046	-.72794	-.11545
4	.22927	.12251	1.87145	.08114	-.03539	.49393
5	1.05474	.52840	1.99611	.06472	-.08680	2.19627
6	1.02423	.72327	1.41612	.17778	-.53829	2.58675
Intercept	-37.93708	13.69617	-3.58400	.00356	-67.52591	-8.34825

Predictor Variable Number	Standard Regression Weights	Restricted Model RSQ	Unique F-values	Prob. for F-Values	Variable Useful-ness	Part Correlation Coefficient
1	1.37753	.26899	19.91203	.00089	.44227	.66503
2	1.15533	.39216	14.36636	.00252	.31909	.56488
3	-.55940	.51470	8.84940	.01046	.19656	-.44334
4	.31481	.63346	3.50234	.08114	.07779	.27891
5	.31750	.62276	3.98444	.06472	.08850	.29749
6	.25397	.66671	2.00540	.17778	.04454	.21105

Predictor Variable Number	Validities (Zero-Order Correlations)	5th Order Partial Correlations	Propor-tional Values	Proportion Divided by RSQFM	RSQ Based Upon this Variable as Y
1	.19527	.77782	.26899	.37819	.76693
2	.11741	.72454	.13564	.19071	.76094
3	-.21808	-.63641	.12199	.17152	.37188
4	.34654	.46069	.10909	.15338	.21506
5	.19328	.48435	.06137	.08628	.12210
6	.05579	.36557	.01417	.01992	.30945
Proportional Sum Check:			.71126	1.00000	

Usefulness/Uniqueness

Perhaps the most practical tool for evaluating the contribution of a predictor variable to the full model is the *usefulness* of that variable. This term has also been referred to as the *uniqueness* of a variable. One simple way to find out whether something is important is to go without it for a while and then decide whether we have missed it! This is true of many factors in life, and it holds true for multiple regression as well. To determine the contribution that a variable makes to a multiple regression model, we can eliminate the variable from the model and then examine the amount of information that has been lost. The difference between the *RSQ* for the full model and the *RSQ* for the model that excludes this predictor variable of concern provides a measure of the information lost. The difference is referred to as the *usefulness* of the variable. We are actually examining the ***unique*** contribution that the variable is making to the full model---the contribution that is not being accounted for by any other variable or combination of variables. As seen in Table 17.17, JRB04 lists each RSQ_{RM} for the individual predictor variables, along with the corresponding unique *F*-values, the probabilities for these *F*-values, and the usefulness of the predictor variables. Each RSQ_{RM} in the printout is the *RSQ* we would obtain if we were to *drop* the corresponding predictor variable from the full model.

For Example 17.1, self-esteem was the most important predictor variable based on examining the bivariate correlations, or validities, discussed earlier. However, this variable is certainly not the most important in regard to its usefulness, or unique contribution, to the full model. As we examine the usefulness of each of these predictor variables, we discover that more information is lost when variable 1 is dropped from the full model than when any other variable is dropped from the model. To obtain the usefulness of a variable, we simply subtract the RSQ_{RM} from the RSQ_{FM}, as defined by Equation 17.7:

$$Usefulness = RSQ_{FM} - RSQ_{RM} \tag{17.7}$$

The unique contribution of variable 4, self-esteem, to the full model is only .0778, which is computed as follows:

$$\begin{aligned} Usefulness &= RSQ_{FM} - RSQ_{RM} \\ &= .7113 - .6335 \\ &= .0778 \end{aligned}$$

On the other hand, the unique contribution of variable 1, SBD-CON, to the full model is .4423, determined as follows:

$$\begin{aligned} Usefulness &= RSQ_{FM} - RSQ_{RM} \\ &= .7113 - .2690 \\ &= .4423 \end{aligned}$$

We can easily test the significance of a variable's usefulness (i.e, its uniqueness or information lost). The null hypothesis regarding the significance of any individual predictor variable to the full model states that the variable does not contribute to the full model. In regard to variable 1, the null hypothesis is expressed as follows:

$$H_0\colon (\rho_{Y \cdot 1,2,3,4,5,6})^2 = (\rho_{Y \cdot 2,3,4,5,6})^2$$

We use the same F-test to evaluate the difference between these two models as we used to compare previous models. Here are the results of this F-test for the usefulness of variable 1:

$$F = \frac{(RSQ_{FM} - RSQ_{RM}) \;/\; (df_{FM} - df_{RM})}{(1 - RSQ_{FM}) \;/\; (n - df_{FM})}$$

$$= \frac{(.7113 - .2690) \;/\; (7 - 6)}{(1 - .7113) \;/\; (20 - 7)}$$

$$= 19.9121 \; (\textit{rounded})$$

As we can see from the above calculation and as confirmed in Table 17.17, variable 1 has a unique F-value equal to 19.9121. With 1 degree of freedom in the numerator, 13 degrees of freedom in the denominator, and α set at .05, the critical F-value for this test is 4.67. Therefore, we conclude that our full model, the one that is based on all six predictor variables, is significantly better than our restricted model, the one that contains five of the six predictor variables but excludes variable 1. This F-test indicates that the excluded variable was making an important contribution to the full model and should not be eliminated.

The *usefulness* of a variable and its *part correlation* are directly related, a fact that simplifies the computation of the part correlation. The usefulness of a variable is equal to the square of the part correlation for that variable, and the square root of a variable's usefulness is equal to the *absolute value* of that variable's part correlation, as shown in Equation 17.8:

$$\textit{Absolute part correlation} = \sqrt{\textit{Usefulness}} = \sqrt{RSQ_{FM} - RSQ_{RM}} \qquad \textbf{(17.8)}$$

The difference between RSQ_{FM} and RSQ_{RM} will always be between zero and one, since RSQ terms are squared values. Therefore, we cannot be certain of the sign of the part correlation when using this approach. For example, the absolute value of the part correlation for variable 3 in Example 17.1 is .4433, as given in Table 17.17; and the actual part correlation for this variable is -.4433, as given in Table 17.20. Since we are usually more interested in the percent of variance explained (i.e., in the RSQ-value) than in the r-value, this is not a major problem. When necessary, the sign of the r-value can be determined by examining the sign of the validity for this variable.

Multiple Regression Weights

As with correlation coefficients, there are several forms of regression weights associated with multiple regression, including raw weights and standard weights. Thus far, we have concentrated on the raw regression weights and their value in predicting the *Y*-values. Standardized regression weights are also important to us and will be discussed here as well.

Raw Weights. The raw weights for multiple regression are the *b*-weights included in the regression equation. These weights have also been referred to as *slopes*, *net regression weights*, *partial regression weights*, *partial regression coefficients*, and simply as *regression coefficients* by various authors in various statistics books.

These raw weights are referred to as *partial* weights because they reflect the expected change in the *Y*-variable for a one-unit increase in the variable being examined, after holding all other predictor variables constant. The partial weights thus provide us with a statistical approach to control for the remaining variables in the model. It might be helpful to view this controlling factor concept from another perspective. In the section regarding part correlations, we discussed the notion of developing a regression model based on using some *X*-variable as the criterion variable and the remaining *X*-variables as the predictor variables. We then discussed obtaining predicted values and the corresponding residual values for this *X*-variable. We stated that these residuals are independent of the remaining *X*-variables. Finally, we noted that the correlation between these residuals and the *Y*-variable is a part correlation. If we were to develop a regression equation based on these two variables, the raw weight for the residuals would be equal to the partial regression coefficient for the full regression model. Thus, we have partialled out the impact of the other predictor variables when looking at the weight of this predictor variable.

As with part and partial correlation coefficients, there are numerous methods for computing partial regression coefficients. When we move beyond bivariate models, such computational procedures become quite complex. The approach discussed in the previous sections is intuitively meaningful but computationally impractical, while other approaches (including matrix algebra approaches) are not intuitively meaningful but are computationally much more practical. We will return to the self-esteem variable and the absenteeism data to illustrate the calculation of a partial regression weight using the current approach. We first obtain predicted values for X_4 based on the following model: $X_4 = f(X_1, X_2, X_3, X_5, X_6)$. We then subtract these values from the actual X_4 values to obtain the residuals. The correlation between this set of residuals and the *Y*-values is $r = .2789$, which we have already determined to be the part correlation. The regression model that expresses the relationship between these two sets of variables (the residuals and the *Y*-values) is as follows:

$$Y' = (b_0)\cdot(U) + (b_{4\cdot1,2,3,5,6})\cdot(\mathit{Residuals}_{4\cdot1,2,3,5,6})$$

$$= (11.15)\cdot(U) + (.2293)\cdot(\mathit{Residuals}_{4\cdot1,2,3,5,6})$$

As we can see from Table 17.17, this regression weight of .2293 is the same as our partial regression weight in multivariate space. The intercept of this bivariate model is equal to $\overline{Y}$. The *standardized* weight (a term that will be discussed in the next section) for this bivariate model is $z_4 = .2789$ and is also equal to the part correlation. We state without proof that these residuals are perfectly independent of the set of *X*-variables. Consequently, the impact of the remaining predictor variables has been eliminated.

These partial regression coefficients are very important in regard to making predictions. They provide us with the weighting factors to be assigned to each of the predictor variables. By knowing these weights and the intercept, we can compare our *Y*′-values to the actual *Y*-values, as we did earlier for individual number 10. We can also use the equation to make predictions for other individuals who were not included in the original data base. For example, suppose that we have a new male for whom we have collected data over the same 6 predictor variables, as follows: 45, 56, 73, 34, 4, and 2, respectively. Assuming that this person remains with the program for the entire 24-month period, we might wonder how many days he will miss during that time period. Based on the full regression model, our prediction would be as follows:

$$Y' = b_0 \cdot U + b_1 \cdot X_1 + b_2 \cdot X_2 + b_3 \cdot X_3 + b_4 \cdot X_4 + b_5 \cdot X_5 + b_6 \cdot X_6$$

$$= (-37.9372) \cdot U + (.6572) \cdot X_1 + (.4680) \cdot X_2 + (-.4217) \cdot X_3$$

$$+ (.2293) \cdot X_4 + (1.0547) \cdot X_5 + (1.0242) \cdot X_6$$

$$= (-37.9372) \cdot (1) + (.6572) \cdot (45) + (.4680) \cdot (56) + (-.4217) \cdot (73)$$

$$+ (.2293) \cdot (34) + (1.0547) \cdot (4) + (1.0242) \cdot (2)$$

$$= 1.1241$$

We have predicted that this person will miss 1.1241 days on the job in the next 24 months, which we would round to approximately one day. If he had received one additional point on the self-esteem scale, our prediction is that he would miss an additional .2293 days on the job. That is, for every 1 unit increase in self-esteem, we would add an additional .2293 to the *Y*′-value. Of course, we will not know how accurate this prediction is until the end of the time period. If we have a valid and reliable model, we can use this estimate to improve the quality of our decision-making process regarding this and other individuals. History continually reminds us that accurate *prediction* is far more important than accurate *postdiction!*

Rather than merely visually examining and speculating about the partial regression coefficients, we can perform a test of significance regarding their contribution to the full model. The null hypothesis for regression weights in multivariate space is that the population slope for the predictor variable of concern is equal to zero. That is:

$$H_0\text{: } \beta_j = 0$$

As with bivariate regression, we use the t-test to compare our observed slope to the slope we expected to obtain under the null hypothesis. Equation 17.9 gives the t-test for the multivariate model:

$$t = \frac{b_j - \beta_j}{SE_{SLOPE_j}} \qquad \textbf{(17.9)}$$

The denominator of this t-test is based on the standard error of the slope for multiple regression. Equation 17.10 gives this standard error term for multivariate models:

$$SE_{SLOPE_j} = \sqrt{\frac{(SE_{EST})^2}{\sum (X - \overline{X}_j)^2 \cdot (1 - RSQ_j)}} \qquad \textbf{(17.10)}$$

where:

$\overline{X}_j$ = mean of the jth predictor variable of concern

RSQ_j = the RSQ that would be obtained when using the jth predictor variable as the criterion variable and using the remaining set of X-variables as predictor variables in a new model. Notice that the original Y-variable is not used in this model.

and, where:

$$df = n - k - 1$$

As an illustration, we will test the significance of the partial regression coefficient for self-esteem in the full model. We have already determined that the raw weight for this variable is .2293, and Table 17.17 reveals that the standard error of the slope for this variable in multivariate space is .1225. Therefore, our t-value is computed as follows:

$$t = \frac{b_j - \beta_j}{SE_{SLOPE_j}}$$

$$= \frac{.2293 - .0000}{.1225}$$

$$= 1.8715 \ (\textit{rounded})$$

The degrees of freedom for this t-test are determined as follows: $df = n - k - 1 = 20 - 6 - 1 = 13$. Since the critical t-value is 2.160 for a two-tailed test, we fail to reject the null hypothesis and conclude that self-esteem is not making a significant contribution to the full model.

Table 17.20 reveals that the computed t-value for examining the significance of any partial regression weight is equal to the square root of the unique F-value for that variable. Further, the corresponding critical t-value is equal to the square root of the critical unique F-value for that variable. Thus, the partial regression weight and the usefulness of a variable are directly related. The usefulness concept seems to have more intuitive appeal for most users than the concept of partialing variables. However, either approach is acceptable.

Computing the Standard Error of the Slope. Hopefully, we will have access to a computer program or spreadsheet that gives the standard errors of the slopes for each of the individual predictor variables. If not, we may need to determine the RSQ_j values in order to obtain these standard errors. As we know, we can develop six separate regression models for Example 17.1 to obtain six RSQ_j values by using each predictor variable separately as a criterion variable and the remaining five X-variables as predictor variables. Rather then generating all of these models, most computer programs use matrix algebra to obtain the standard error terms. First, the individual RSQ_j values are obtained through the use of Equation 17.11:

$$RSQ_j = 1 - \frac{1}{r_{jj}^*} \qquad \textbf{(17.11)}$$

where:

r_{jj}^* = the value located at the intersection of the jth row and j^{th} column along the principal diagonal of the $\mathbf{R}^{-1}$ matrix. The $\mathbf{R}^{-1}$ matrix is the inverse of the **R** matrix that excludes the criterion variable.

Table 17.21 gives the inverse of the **R** matrix for the six predictor variables. Using self-esteem to illustrate, we find the value corresponding to the intersection of the 4th row and 4th column in Table 17.21. Here, r_{44}^* = 1.27398. We then obtain RSQ_4 as follows: RSQ_4 = 1 - (1 / 1.27398) = .2150 (rounded). In other words, the RSQ we would obtain by regressing self-esteem onto the five remaining predictor variables is .2150.

Table 17.21
Inverse Matrix Corresponding to the 6-Predictor Variable R Matrix

	1	**2**	**3**	**4**	**5**	**6**
1	4.29058	3.58735	-.99331	-.31084	-.03012	.27695
2	3.58735	4.18310	-.77410	-.59515	-.15294	.55015
3	-.99331	-.77410	1.59206	.27632	.09010	-.72637
4	-.31084	-.59515	.27632	1.27398	.41245	-.27884
5	-.03012	-.15294	.09010	.41245	1.13908	-.03762
6	.27695	.55015	-.72637	-.27884	-.03762	1.44812

Based on this information, we can verify that for the full regression model, the standard error of the slope for self-esteem is .1225. From Table 17.17, we know that SE_{EST} is 3.8012. From Table 17.3, we know that the standard deviation for self-esteem is 8.03463; therefore, we know that $\Sigma(X - \overline{X}_4)^2 = 8.03463^2 \cdot (20 - 1) = 1226.5503$. We have also learned that RSQ_4 = .2150. Therefore, we obtain the standard error of the slope as follows:

$$SE_{SLOPE_j} = \sqrt{\frac{(SE_{EST})^2}{\sum(X - \overline{X}_j)^2 \cdot (1 - RSQ_j)}}$$

$$= \sqrt{\frac{(3.8012)^2}{[8.03463^2 \cdot (20 - 1)] \cdot (1 - .2150)}}$$

$$= \sqrt{\frac{14.4491}{(1226.5503) \cdot (.7850)}}$$

$$= .1225 \ (\textit{rounded})$$

Limitations of Partial Regression Weights. Unfortunately, the partial regression weights are not as helpful in determining the importance of a predictor variable. Most variables have different units of measure; therefore, one variable will be weighted more heavily than another simply due to the magnitude of that variable. For Example 17.1, the initiative variable is scored on a scale that has a possible range of 1 through 7. On the other hand, the leadership variables are scored on a scale that has a possible range of 20 through 80. If initiative is equally as important as one of the leadership variables in predicting the *Y*-variable, initiative must have a larger weight in order to have the same impact. Consequently, a visual comparison of one raw weight to another may be very misleading. We should convert all of our data to standard scores to adjust for such inequalities in scaling. Standard weights, which are discussed in the next section, are based on this conversion process and are usually given in most standard computer packages that have multiple regression options.

Standard Weights. Standard weights are simply the weights we would obtain if we had converted each of the variables to standard scores. Consequently, these weights are often referred to as *z*-weights. They have also been referred to as *standardized partial regression coefficients* and as *beta weights*. In fact, the term beta weight is quite commonly used. However, β is also commonly used as a symbol for the population parameter for a slope, as discussed in previous chapters. Since we have been following the tradition of using Greek letters to represent our population parameters under the null hypothesis, we will use β_j to symbolize the population slopes. Therefore, we will use the term *z-weight* when referring to standard weights.

The standardized partial regression coefficients are included in Table 17.17 for the six-variable model. Although we do not notice large differences between the raw weights and the standard weights in Example 17.1, in other situations there may be very large differences. The standard weights are based on a common scale of measurement, since standardized values for any variable have a mean of zero and a standard deviation of one.

Computing Standard Weights from Raw Weights. The standard weights are linear transformations of the raw weights. Therefore, rather than actually determining *z*-scores for all values in our data base and then performing a new multiple regression analysis, we will compute the standard weights based on Equation 17.12:

$$z_j = \frac{b_j \cdot s_j}{s_Y} \qquad \textbf{(17.12)}$$

where:

z_j = the standardized weight for the predictor variable of concern

b_j = the raw weight for the predictor variable of concern

s_j = the standard deviation for the predictor variable of concern

s_Y = the standard deviation for the criterion variable

The standard weight for variable 1 in Example 17.1 is β_1 = 1.3775, as we can determine from Table 17.17. Since Table 17.17 also gives the raw regression weights, we can verify this calculation as follows:

$$z_1 = \frac{b_1 \cdot s_1}{s_Y}$$

$$= \frac{(.6572) \cdot (12.26409)}{5.85145}$$

$$= 1.3775 \ (\textit{rounded})$$

Computing Raw Weights from Standard Weights. Conversely, if we want to obtain the raw regression weight for a variable in multivariate space and we know the standardized regression weight, we can obtain the *b*-weight from Equation 17.13:

$$b_j = \frac{z_j \cdot s_Y}{s_j} \qquad \textbf{(17.13)}$$

Returning to the self-esteem variable in Example 17.1, the raw weight for this variable is b_4 = .2293, as given in Table 17.17. Given the standard regression weight, the raw weight can be calculated as follows:

$$b_4 = \frac{z_4 \cdot s_Y}{s_4}$$

$$= \frac{(.3148)\cdot(5.85145)}{8.03463}$$

$$= .2293 \textit{ (rounded)}$$

Computing the Intercept for the Regression Model. In regard to the constant term, it was previously pointed out that the regression line passes through the origin when all of the values have been standardized. Therefore, the constant term is eliminated from the model when using z-weights. On the other hand, if we already know the z-weights and want to convert back to raw form, we must also determine the intercept that corresponds with the raw weights. We first convert the z-weights to b-weights using Equation 17.13; then we obtain the intercept from Equation 17.14:

$$b_0 = \overline{Y} - (b_1 \cdot \overline{X}_1) - (b_2 \cdot \overline{X}_2) - \cdots - (b_k \cdot \overline{X}_k) \qquad \textbf{(17.14)}$$

For the absenteeism data given in Example 17.1, the intercept for the full regression model is computed as follows:

$$b_0 = \overline{Y} - (b_1 \cdot \overline{X}_1) - (b_2 \cdot \overline{X}_2) - (b_3 \cdot \overline{X}_3) - (b_4 \cdot \overline{X}_4) - (b_5 \cdot \overline{X}_5) - (b_k \cdot \overline{X}_k)$$

$$= 11.15 - [(.6572)\cdot(57.25)] - [(.4680)\cdot(43.15)] - [(-.4217)\cdot(58.40)]$$

$$- [(.2293)\cdot(37.15)] - [(1.0547)\cdot(5.05)] - [(1.0242)\cdot(2.00)]$$

$$= -37.9372$$

Summary of Interpretation Methods

The *validities* provide a measure of the relationship between the criterion and the predictor variables, taken one at a time. If we simply want to select one predictor variable and discard the rest, we should use the validities as our decision-making tool. These bivariate correlations are not confounded by the other variables, and we will not be partialing out the influence of external factors.

Both the *part correlations* and *partial correlations* are based on approaches that limit the impact of other variables on the relationship between the designated predictor variable and the criterion variable. Unfortunately, conceptualizing and explaining these revised relationships may not always be practical, especially when we have many predictor variables. In practice, it may be impossible to obtain a true measure of the relationship between the predictor variable and the Y-variable, while eliminating any relationships the Y-variable has with other variables used in the model. In fact, such a relationship may only exist in theory. Efforts have been made to develop such uncontaminated variables through factor analysis, by creating factors that are completely independent of one-another. However, conceptualizing the nature of these mathematically generated factors is often difficult.

The *usefulness* of a variable (i.e., the square of the part correlation) is much easier to conceptualize. In everyday life, whenever we *lose* something we *begin* to understand its value to us. For example, if we wonder whether pay is important as a motivator, we might consider what would happen if we quit paying employees. When people are being paid, pay may seem to have only *relative* importance in their lives. The removal of that pay would, however, have a substantial impact on their attitude and their performance! In regression analysis, the usefulness or *unique* contribution of a variable is the contribution that variable makes to the model that none of the other variables can make. If we drop that variable out of the model and then compute the *RSQ*, we can immediately assess its importance by examining the loss in *RSQ*.

The most important aspect of the *partial regression coefficients* is that they provide a means for making predictions. We cannot determine Y'-values and make predictions without the use of these raw regression weights. On the surface, we cannot examine the importance of each of the predictor variables by an observation of these weights since the predictor variables seldom have the same units of measurement and seldom have equal means and standard deviations. The only way to examine the importance of these weights is through the use of t-tests, which in effect standardize the weights. The *standard weights* eliminate the problem of having to compare weights based on variables with different units of measure.

The *importance* issue regarding variables in multiple regression models must be tempered by at least two key factors: a) multicollinearity and b) the ratio of cases to predictor variables. In light of excessive multicollinearity or inadequate sample size, the results of our regression models may be spurious and may not be supported by future analyses with new data bases. If we hope to interpret the importance of the variables in our regression models, it would be helpful to always select predictor variables that have low intercorrelations. However, we rarely have the opportunity to do so in practice. We analyze what data we have available, and we are limited by sample size and cost. We should always attempt to obtain adequate sample sizes whenever possible. If we cannot, we should at least attempt to validate our findings by replicating the research in the future as new data become available.

As stressed throughout this chapter, interpreting multiple regression results is not always easy. For Example 17.1, we initially concluded that none of the variables were significantly correlated with absenteeism by themselves, as none had significant validities. We later concluded that the *RSQ* for the full model was statistically significant. We initially concluded that certain variables had greater correlations with the criterion variable than others. We later concluded that these same variables were not necessarily as useful as others in regard to the fullest regression model. Table 17.19 summarized a number of these findings for Example 17.1.

We caution that conclusions based on the data given in Example 17.1 may be unwarranted; however, we have discussed several approaches to addressing these issues for the purpose of understanding their values in interpretation. While the *RSQ* for the full model was significant, our ratio of cases to variables was too inadequate to feel very good about the results. This inadequacy resulted in further concern about the findings, and an RSQ_{ADJ} was computed to provide a more realistic estimate of the *RSQ*. Problems of this nature occur frequently in data analysis, and data bases such as the one in the example are expensive to collect and maintain. We also noticed that there is considerable multicollinearity among the predictor variables, making it even more difficult to interpret the results. Again, this is not uncommon in data analysis, as few situations will consist with truly independent predictor variables.

Variable 4 had the highest validity and therefore entered into the model first; yet the validity for this variable was not statistically significant. By the time we reached the final step in the full model, self-esteem was not a very important variable. As given in Table 17.19, the unique *F*-value for self-esteem is 3.5024, which is not statistically significant. On the other hand, variable 1 (SBD-CON) had a very low validity (.1953) but had a very high usefulness value (.4423). It would appear that if we were only going to be able to afford one variable, variable 4 would seem to be the best candidate to use (although it is not statistically significant in this example). On the other hand, if we could afford five of the six variables, we might consider dropping out variable 6 since it is not contributing a significant amount to the full model. We might even consider dropping out variables 4 or 5. However, variable 1 would be the last variable we should consider dropping, due to its significant contribution to the full model. The cost of each of these variables will also be taken into consideration before we make any decisions.

We could consider examining the part correlations, but we discovered that they are directly related to the usefulness of the variables; and the usefulness of the variables is directly related to the significance of the weights. Since the concept of usefulness is easier to understand, this tool is preferred over part correlations or partial regression coefficients when interpreting results. The fifth-order partials might also provide some useful information, but they are often very difficult to obtain. As can be seen in Table 17.19, these fifth-order partial correlations correspond with the part correlations for Example 17.1 in regard to the order of their magnitudes.

Proportional Values. There are several other less frequently used approaches for interpreting the importance of predictor variables. One such approach is to compute the *proportional values* of the variables in regard to their contribution to the full model. These proportional values, also given in Table 17.19, are obtained as shown in Equation 17.15:

$$\textit{Proportional values} = (z\textit{-weights}) \cdot (\textit{validities}) \tag{17.15}$$

The advantage of these proportional values is that they sum to RSQ_{FM}. For Example 17.1, the six "proportional values" sum to $RSQ_{FM} = .7113$. Therefore, if we divide each of these values by RSQ_{FM}, we can obtain a measure of the percent that each predictor variable contributes to the full model. As an illustration, the proportional value of variable 4 is .1091. When we divide that value by .7113, we find that variable 4 represents 15.34% of the total *RSQ*.

Unfortunately, the "proportional value" approach is not very helpful for interpretation purposes. We cannot say that the proportional value or the proportion of the total truly reflects on the percent of variance explained by the variable. When we drop the variable out of the full model, we do not really lose the exact same amount suggested by these proportional values. For example, if we drop out variable 4 from Example 17.1, *RSQ* is reduced to .6335, a drop of .0778, which has traditionally been described as the usefulness of the variable. According to the proportional value approach, this same variable contributes .1091 to the full model *RSQ*, accounting for 15.34% of the full model. As we can see, .7113 - .1091 = .6022, which is not the same as RSQ_{RM} = .6335. The difference between these two results is due in part to interaction between the predictor variable of concern and the other predictor variables. In the traditional usefulness approach, we literally drop a variable from the full model; that is, we eliminate it and *all* of its interaction with other variables. In the proportional value approach, we eliminate only its unique contribution orthogonally. Its interaction with the other variables has not been eliminated. That interaction remains in the model because we have left residual interaction in the model.

Another disadvantage of the "proportional value" approach is that it is possible for one or more of these values to be negative. If either the *z*-weight for the variable or the validity for the variable (but not both) is negative, the "proportional value" will also be negative. Consequently, we might conclude that a negative proportion of the full model *RSQ* is accounted for by a particular predictor variable; this would be a very confusing conclusion. As Cohen and Cohen (1983, p. 90) stated: "Any such interpretation runs into a serious catch—there is nothing in the mathematics that prevents [this value] from being a negative value and a negative proportion of variance hardly makes sense."

Suppressor Variables. We noted earlier that the validity for variable 1 was less than that of several other variables, with r = .19527. The validity for a variable may be zero, near zero, or perhaps even slightly negative, and the variable can still make a significant contribution to the full model. The contribution is usually due to its interaction with other variables in the model. Variables with such characteristics are often referred to as *suppressor* variables. They further confound our ability to immediately recognize the importance of certain predictor variables.

Summary of Terms

We have now discussed the basic sources of variation and weighting factors associated with multiple regression, including correlation coefficients and regression weights. We found that the vocabulary can be very confusing, as the literature is fraught with inconsistencies in terminology. With respect to the coefficients and weights discussed in this textbook, we found more than one term used for every one of them! For example, we discussed four main types of correlations, each of which were referred to by multiple terms: a) bivariate correlations, zero-order correlations, or validities; b) part correlations or semi-partial correlations; c) partial correlations or ordered partial correlations (first order, second order, etc.); and d) usefulness or uniqueness coefficients. The same was true for the two primary types of regression weights: a) raw weights, raw slopes, net regression weights, or partial regression weights; and b) standard weights, standardized partial regression weights, beta weights, or *z*-weights. Hopefully, this discussion will serve as a resource when encountering any of these terms in professional publications.

Model Comparison

We now return to the general concept of model building and model comparison. For Example 17.1, we were able to generate seven different models. We began with a chance model, and progressed through a stepwise process until we concluded with the fullest model, which included six predictor variables. At each step along the way, we compared the full model associated with the particular step of interest against the chance model. At the final step, also compared the full six-variable model against various five-variable restricted models by dropping each variable out of the full model, one at a time, then comparing this new restricted model to the full model. The computer printout was very helpful in this process, since it automatically generated these restricted models, the *unique F*-tests for these models, and the *usefulness* of the corresponding variables in the full model. However, we do not have to be limited to simply comparing full models to chance models or to eliminating one variable at a time and then comparing to the full model.

We will often be interested in comparing a number of models to one another. Under such circumstances, we must always follow one simple rule. We can only compare a pair of models if the full model contains all of the same predictor variables as the restricted model, plus additional predictor variables. This rule is so important that we have highlighted it in Table 17.22.

Table 17.22
Fundamental Rule of Model Comparison

> When comparing two models, the model being used as the full model must always include ***all*** of the same variables that are being used in the restricted model, ***plus*** one or more other variables.

We will use Table 17.23 to illustrate model building and model comparison. Table 17.23 includes a number of variables that have been generated from Example 17.1, along with the original variables. We emphasize, as noted earlier, that the ***sample size is too small*** to provide a meaningful analysis of these data! We use this example only to *illustrate* how to **build** models. As can be seen in Table 17.23, variables 1, 2, 3, 4, 5, and 6 correspond with the predictor variables described in Table 17.1. The original variable 7, the criterion variable, has been moved and now becomes variable 12 (thus remaining the *last* variable in the set). We have generated and inserted five new variables between the original six predictor variables and the criterion variable. New variable 7 was generated by multiplying variable 4 times variable 5 to create an ***interaction term***. Variable 8 was created by squaring variable 6 to create a ***nonlinear*** model. Variables 9, 10, and 11 were created as ***dummy variables***. They were derived from an additional source of information about the participants, their citizenship. The dummy variables associated with citizenship were created by coding each of the participants into one of three citizenship categories: native U.S. citizens, naturalized U.S. citizens, and citizens from a country other than the United States. With 11 variables, the data base should include a minimum of $(11 \times 10) + 10 = 120$ cases; only 20 cases were available for inclusion!

Table 17.23
Original Variables, New (Generated) Variables, and the Criterion Variable

	Original Predictor Variables						*Generated Predictor Variables*					*Criterion Variable*
Case	X_1	X_2	X_3	X_4	X_5	X_6	X_7	X_8	X_9	X_{10}	X_{11}	Y
1	62	31	56	13	7	0	91	0	1	0	0	1
2	71	24	57	44	6	3	264	9	0	1	0	19
3	68	38	59	39	4	3	156	9	1	0	0	18
4	56	62	70	30	7	2	210	4	1	0	0	15
5	52	54	54	52	7	1	364	1	0	1	0	17
6	63	33	69	34	2	3	68	9	0	1	0	6
7	49	49	45	46	1	1	46	1	1	0	0	5
8	63	22	59	31	7	2	217	4	0	0	1	2
9	57	44	58	29	6	5	174	25	1	0	0	14
10	67	33	74	36	4	3	144	9	0	0	1	3
11	64	26	55	38	6	2	228	4	1	0	0	10
12	16	80	48	37	6	1	222	1	0	1	0	8
13	68	37	59	38	4	0	152	0	0	1	0	17
14	54	54	56	40	6	0	240	0	0	0	1	14
15	61	46	57	37	7	3	259	9	0	0	1	16
16	60	42	55	37	4	2	148	4	1	0	0	16
17	63	34	49	34	5	2	170	4	0	0	1	17
18	58	41	73	46	4	5	184	25	0	1	0	6
19	54	56	56	41	3	1	123	1	0	0	1	10
20	39	57	59	41	5	1	205	1	0	1	0	9

Interaction Terms. With multiple regression, as with analysis of variance, we can test for interaction among our variables. Testing for interaction is often quite simple. First, we create a new variable by multiplying one variable times another variable. We then add this new variable to our regression model. If this new variable makes a significant contribution to our model, we know that the two variables interact, because the new term is providing information that we did not know without it. In the present illustration, we created an interaction term by multiplying self-esteem times initiative, as follows: $(X_4) \times (X_5) = X_7$.

Nonlinear Terms. As we discussed in Chapter 16, we can create squared, cubed, and other nonlinear variables so that we can test for more complex relationships among our variables. In fact, multiple regression is an ideal tool for testing nonlinear models, since such variables can easily be generated with the availability of spreadsheets and computer software. Historically, many of the nonlinear models that were *assumed* to hold true in the past have since been verified as indeed nonlinear models with the use of applications of multiple regression.

Dummy Variables. In multiple regression, dummy variables need to be created whenever we have nominal level data. We cannot simply assign a 1 to native U.S. citizens, a 2 to naturalized U.S. citizens, and a 3 to those who do not fall into either of the first two categories and expect such a variable to have meaning. Since citizenship is nominal, numerical order becomes meaningless, as we learned in Chapters 2-4. Under such circumstances, we will generate dummy variables to represent our data. Dummy variables are usually dichotomous and are typically coded as 1s and 0s, although other coding schemes have been used as well. The following system represents the citizenship variable in Example 17.1:

Variable 9: 1 if the person is a native U.S. citizen, 0 otherwise.

Variable 10: 1 if the person is a naturalized U.S. citizen, 0 otherwise.

Variable 11: 1 if the person is not a native or a naturalized U.S. citizen, 0 otherwise.

However, we only need *k* - 1 dummy variables in order to represent the *k* categories in any classification variable. For Example 17.1, we need two dummy variables. The third dummy variable is ***redundant***–it provides no additional information that cannot be obtained from the first two variables. For example, if a person is a member of the third category, he or she will be coded as a 0 in *both* variable 9 and variable 10; therefore, that person's coding is already determined in variable 11 and is *not free to vary*. In fact, we could eliminate *any* of the three dummy variables without losing information. We included all three here only to illustrate the point, but we *cannot* include all three variables in most multiple regression computer analyses. The redundancy usually causes these routines to "bomb" and/or provide error messages. We have arbitrarily eliminated variable 11 for all analyses to avoid such problems.

Model Testing

We will use Table 17.24 to illustrate the process of model building and model comparison. The table includes eight models that have been generated from Example 17.1. Many other multiple regression models could have been generated from the revised data base. Letters have been used to identify the eight models (labeled as models *A*, *B*, *C*, *D*, *E*, *F*, and *G*) so that model numbers would not be confused with variable numbers. As we know, we can learn about the value of a *variable* by dropping it out of the *model* and evaluating the amount of information lost in the process. In a similar manner, we can learn about the significance of a *group of variables* by collectively dropping them out of the model and evaluating the amount of information we have lost. The variable or variables dropped out of the full model (i.e., the ones that we do not include in the restricted model) are the variables under examination. If we drop these variables out and observe that the change in *RSQ* between the full and restricted models is significant, the eliminated variables are making a significant contribution to the full model. Such variables are usually retained in the model. If they are not making significant contributions, we may be able to save ourselves time and money by eliminating them in future analyses.

Table 17.24
Various Models of Interest for Example 17.1

Model Letter	*RSQ*	*df*	*Model*
A	0.8190	9	Y = f(1,2,3,4,5,6,9,10)
B	0.8263	8	Y = f(1,2,3,4,5,6,7)
C	0.7156	8	Y = f(1,2,3,4,5,6,8)
D	0.7113	7	Y = f(1,2,3,4,5,6)
E	0.5171	4	Y = f(1,2,3)
F	0.2821	4	Y = f(4,5,7)
G	0.0098	3	Y = f(9,10)
H	0.0000	1	Y = f(0)

Table 17.24 includes a number of models for Example 17.1, each with variable 12, absenteeism, as the criterion variable. If we know the *RSQ* values associated with these models, we can compare these models and determine whether they are statistically significantly different. The table includes the chance model, the full model, several intermediate models, and several models that are "more full" than the original full model. As can be seen, the original six-variable full model is now identified as *Model D*, the chance model is labeled as *Model H*, and the other models represent new ways of examining the data.

Suppose we are interested in determining whether it is worth our effort to collect data regarding variables 4, 5, and 6 (self-esteem, initiative, and number of previous jobs). We can evaluate this question by generating a new model (*Model E*) and comparing it to the original full model (*Model D*). If there is a significant difference between the *RSQ*s for these two models, we can conclude that the three variables are useful and should not be eliminated; otherwise, we would consider eliminating them, simplifying our model, and saving time and money in future analyses. Table 17.25 gives the results for comparing various models. As we can see, the *RSQ* for *Model D* is .7113, the *RSQ* for *Model E* is .5171, and the *F*-test for comparing these two models is 2.9149. Since this *F*-value is not statistically significant ($p = .0743$), we may want to consider simplifying our model and eliminating variables 4, 5, and 6.

As another illustration, we may want to determine whether the knowledge of citizenship provides any useful information. *Model A* includes the necessary dummy variables to account for this variable, in addition to the original variables. As we can see, if we compare *Model A* to *Model D*, we obtain an $F = 3.2727$, which is not statistically significant. In other words, the citizenship variable is not providing any unique information beyond what we already know about absenteeism.

Table 17.25
***F*-Tests for Comparing Various Models of Interest for Example 17.1**

RSQ	*df*	*Model Letter*	*Model*	*F*	df_N / df_D	*Crit. F*	*Prob.*
.7113	7	*D*	$Y_7 = f(1,2,3,4,5,6)$	2.9149	3	3.41	.0743
.5171	4	*E*	$Y_7 = f(1,2,3)$		13		
RSQ	*df*	*Model Letter*	*Model*	*F*	df_N / df_D	*Crit. F*	*Prob.*
.8190	9	*A*	$Y_7 = f(1,2,3,4,5,6,9,10)$	3.2727	2	3.98	.0767
.7113	7	*D*	$Y_7 = f(1,2,3,4,5,6)$		11		
RSQ	*df*	*Model Letter*	*Model*	*F*	df_N / df_D	*Crit. F*	*Prob.*
.8263	8	*B*	$Y_7 = f(1,2,3,4,5,6,7)$	7.9447	1	4.75	.0155
.7113	7	*D*	$Y_7 = f(1,2,3,4,5,6)$		12		
RSQ	*df*	*Model Letter*	*Model*	*F*	df_N / df_D	*Crit. F*	*Prob.*
.7156	8	*C*	$Y_7 = f(1,2,3,4,5,6,8)$	0.1814	1	4.75	.6777
.7113	7	*D*	$Y_7 = f(1,2,3,4,5,6)$		12		
RSQ	*df*	*Model Letter*	*Model*	*F*	df_N / df_D	*Crit. F*	*Prob.*
.0098	3	*G*	$Y_7 = f(9,10)$	0.0841	2	3.59	.9197
.0000	1	*H*	$Y_7 = f(0)$		17		
RSQ	*df*	*Model Letter*	*Model*	*F*	df_N / df_D	*Crit. F*	*Prob.*
.2821	4	*F*	$Y_7 = f(4,5,7)$	2.0957	3	3.24	.1411
.0000	1	*H*	$Y_7 = f(0)$		16		

When we compare *Model G*, which contains the two citizenship variables, to *Model H* (the chance model), we find that this model is not significantly better than chance, with $F = 0.0841$, $p = .9197$. In other words, we have found that absenteeism is not related to the participants' citizenship alone. We point out that this comparison is comparable to a ***one-way analysis of variance***. If we were to compare the means of the absenteeism scores for the three citizenship categories, we would obtain an *F*-value of precisely .0841, as the two approaches are identical under such circumstances. In fact, many higher order analysis of variance models are often evaluated through the use of multiple regression, due to its more user-friendly format.

Now we will examine the interaction term created by multiplying the self-esteem variable times the initiative variable. *Model B* represents the model that includes the interaction term, along with the original predictor variables. If we compare this model to *Model D*, we obtain an $F = 7.9447$, and a $p = .0155$. We may have discovered some worthwhile information here, as the interaction term is providing some unique information that has not been previously provided. It appears that the combination of scores on self-esteem *and* initiative may be useful in explaining absenteeism. In fact, this variable has a usefulness value of .8263 - .7113 = .1150. In other words, it is accounting for an additional 11.5% of the variance. (Once again, we must remember that these conclusions must be greatly moderated by the fact that we only have 20 cases; we are simply illustrating methods for comparing models.)

Finally, we will examine the nonlinear term that was created by squaring variable 6, which is the number of jobs previously held. A research hypothesis for examining this variable more carefully might be that the number of previous jobs is not a very good predictor in *linear* format because it is limited in its range; the maximum number of jobs previously held by any of these participants was 5. However, the individuals who had as many as five jobs may have an extremely poor work history that might impact their absenteeism in the current situation. Those with more previous jobs could be given an even greater weight through a nonlinear model than through a linear model. Of course, this is just speculation, but the hypothesis can be tested by comparing a nonlinear model to a linear model. *Model C* represents the model that includes the squared term and the original variables. To determine whether the nonlinear term is contributing to *Model C*, we drop it out by comparing *Model C* to *Model D*. As we can see from Table 17.25, this squared term did not make any meaningful contribution to the model, as the difference between these two models is .7156 - .7113 = .0043. The *F*-value is .1814, which is far from being statistically significant. Also, notice that we never compared *Model C* to *Model B*! This would have been a violation of the rule stated in Table 17.22, because *each* model contains a variable that does not appear in the other model.

Alternative Multiple Regression Approaches

We conclude this chapter by briefly examining four approaches that were mentioned at the onset: backward regression analysis, all-possible-combinations analysis, spreadsheet analysis, and flowchart analysis. Each of these approaches has advantages and disadvantages.

Backward Regression Analysis

As stated earlier, one alternative approach to stepwise regression is to compute the full model first and then to eliminate variables from that model, based on some user-defined objective or on some computer-defined objective function. This approach is often referred to as the *backward elimination method.* For the present example, the variables have been eliminated from the full model one variable at a time. The criterion for the sequence of eliminating variables was based on dropping out the variable that contributes the least information at each stage of the process. As we can see from Table 17.26, the first variable to be eliminated was variable 6. After that, variable 5 was eliminated, then variable 4, then 3, and then 2. (It is purely coincidence that the variables removed from the model happen to follow their nominal coding.) As we can see, this is a different sequence than what we had with the forward-moving stepwise method. Our one-variable model in the backward elimination method is variable 1, although this variable did not have the highest validity of the set of variables.

Table 17.26
Results from Using a Backward Regression Model

Backward Regression Models	*RSQ*
$Y' = f(X_1, X_2, X_3, X_4, X_5, X_6)$	.7113
$Y' = f(X_1, X_2, X_3, X_4, X_5)$	.6667
$Y' = f(X_1, X_2, X_3, X_4)$	.5744
$Y' = f(X_1, X_2, X_3)$	.5171
$Y' = f(X_1, X_2)$	.3286
$Y' = f(X_1)$	.0381

All-Possible Combinations Analysis

Another alternative stepwise approach is to compute the best possible model each step along the way. In the first step, we determine the variable that has the highest correlation with the criterion variable. In the second step, we examine all possible combinations of predictor variables, taken two at a time, without regard to the variable used in the first step. The one combination of predictor variables that yields the highest *RSQ* is then selected. This process continues until a model containing all the predictor variables has been obtained. Analyzing intermediate steps based on this approach takes too much advantage of chance and leads to conclusions that may only be relevant to the current set of data. For Example 17.1, there are 6 one-variable models, 15 two-variable models, 20 three-variable models, 15 four-variable models, 6 five-variable models, and 1 six-variable model, for a total of 63 possible models! The opportunities for sampling error have drastically increased. Table 17.27 gives the results of such an approach with Example 6.3. As expected, the one-variable model and the six-variable model are consistent with our earlier findings. However, the intermediate models are considerably different from what we previously calculated. We *strongly* discourage the use of this method!

Table 17.27
Results from Using the All-Possible-Combinations Model

Best All-Possible-Combinations Models	*RSQ*
$Y' = f(X_4)$	.1201
$Y' = f(X_1, X_2)$	.3286
$Y' = f(X_1, X_2, X_3)$	.5171
$Y' = f(X_1, X_2, X_3, X_6)$	.5872
$Y' = f(X_1, X_2, X_3, X_4, X_5)$	.6667
$Y' = f(X_4, X_5, X_1, X_2, X_3, X_6)$	.7113

Spreadsheets

Most sophisticated spreadsheets include options for multiple regression analyses. Figure 17.8 gives the multiple regression output obtained for Example 17.1 using *Excel*. As can be seen, this spreadsheet gives many of the same values included in the final step of the output from JRB04, which is the stepwise computer program used throughout this chapter. Confidence intervals for the slopes and the intercept are included in the *Excel* output; however, the RSQ_{RM} values, unique F-values, usefulness values, part correlations, partial correlations, and several other values are not included. The probabilities associated with the significance of the slopes are very similar to those given by the JRB04 computer program in Table 17.17. The confidence intervals associated with the slopes are very similar to those given by the JRB19 computer program in Table 17.20. Any discrepancies in these probabilities or confidence intervals are due to minor differences in the numerical routines used to calculate the probabilities. On the other hand, the confidence interval associated with the intercept given by Exce differs from the one given by JRB19. For *Excel*, this confidence interval is based on the null hypothesis that $\beta_0 = 0.00$; for JRB19, the confidence interval is based on the null hypothesis that $\beta_I = \overline{Y}$. Identical values have been obtained for RSQ_{FM} using JRB19, *Excel*, and the final step of JRB04. This RSQ_{FM} value also agrees with the RSQ_{FM} obtained from other spreadsheets, including *Quattro* and *Lotus*, and from computer statistical packages including *SAS*, *SPSS*, and *BMD*.

Regression Statistics						
Multiple R	0.84336					
R Square	0.71126					
Adjusted R Square	0.57799					
Standard Error	3.80124					
Observations	20					
Analysis of Variance						
	df	*Sum of Squares*	*Mean Square*	*F*	*Significance F*	
Regression	6	462.70739	77.11790	5.33709	0.00559	
Residual	13	187.84261	14.44943			
Total	19	650.55000				
	Coefficients	*Standard Error*	*t Statistic*	*P-value*	*Lower 95%*	*Upper 95%*
Intercept	-37.93719	13.69617	-2.76991	0.01220	-67.52596	-8.34841
x1	0.65725	0.14729	4.46230	0.00027	0.33905	0.97545
x2	0.46801	0.12347	3.79030	0.00124	0.20125	0.73476
x3	-0.42169	0.14176	-2.97480	0.00778	-0.72794	-0.11545
x4	0.22927	0.12251	1.87146	0.07676	-0.03539	0.49393
x5	1.05474	0.52840	1.99611	0.06046	-0.08679	2.19627
x6	1.02423	0.72327	1.41612	0.17293	-0.53829	2.58675

Figure 17.8
Multiple Regression Results for Absenteeism Data Using Excel

Analysis of Variance and Regression

We stated earlier that there is a direct relationship between analysis of variance and regression. In fact, computer programs and spreadsheets often use analysis of variance terminology when giving the results of a regression analysis. For example, when comparing a full model to a chance model, the F-test is often expressed in terms of the "mean squares among" and the "mean squares within," or in terms of the "mean squares regression" and the "mean squares residual." *Excel* uses the latter terminology, as seen in Figure 17.8. The F-test can thus be based on a comparison of sums of squares such as the "error sum of squares reduced" and the "error sum of squares for the full model," or the "regression sum of squares" and the "residual sum of squares." If we use these terms instead of the *RSQ* terms, two approaches to the F-test can be developed. The first approach is based on the *ESS* notation and the second approach is based on the *SS* notation. Equation 17.16 gives these two approaches and their relationships:

$$F = \frac{(ESS_{CH} - ESS_{FM}) / (df_{FM} - df_{RM})}{(ESS_{FM}) / (n - df_{FM})}$$

$$= \frac{(SS_{TOTAL} - SS_{RESIDUAL}) / (df_{REGRESSION})}{(SS_{RESIDUAL}) / (df_{RESIDUAL})} \qquad (17.16)$$

$$= \frac{MS_{REGRESSION}}{MS_{RESIDUAL}}$$

where:

$$SS_{TOTAL} = ESS_{CH}$$

$$SS_{RESIDUAL} = ESS_{FM}$$

$$SS_{REGRESSION} = ESS_{RED}$$

$$df_{REGRESSION} = df_{FM} - df_{RM}$$

$$df_{RESIDUAL} = n - df_{FM}$$

Inserting the appropriate values using the sums of squares approach, we obtain F = 5.33709, just as we obtained when using the *RSQ* approach. Since the two methods for obtaining the F-value yield identical results, the choice as to which one to use is a matter of personal preference. The values used with the *SS* approach, along with the results, are as follows:

$$F = \frac{(SS_{TOTAL} - SS_{RESIDUAL}) / (df_{REGRESSION})}{(SS_{RESIDUAL}) / (df_{RESIDUAL})}$$

$$= \frac{(650.55000 - 187.84261) / (7 - 1)}{187.84261 / (20 - 7)}$$

$$= \frac{77.11790}{14.44943}$$

$$= 5.33709$$

Flowchart Regression Method

Our final approach is the flowchart regression method. One of the appealing aspects of this method is that it is based on our own conceptualization of the situation, rather than letting the computer develop arbitrary models for us. Suppose that we want to consider the importance of the leadership variables (i.e., SBD-CON-I, SBD-IS-I, and SBD-CON-II). These variables come from a questionnaire, are expensive to collect, and may not always be valid. Therefore, we might want to consider eliminating them from any future study if they do not significantly contribute to the full model. We may also want to consider the block of non-leadership variables (i.e., self-esteem, initiative, and number of previous jobs). Perhaps we have developed a series of hypotheses in advance that we want to test. We begin by comparing the full model to the chance model. If the full model is significant, we continue the analysis by comparing various restricted models against the full model. Figure 17.9 gives an illustration of such an analysis. As can be seen, the two restricted models were compared to the full model. The first heavy line indicates that the route which only includes self-esteem, initiative, and number of jobs should not be pursued since the elimination of the leadership variables resulted in a significant amount of information lost. On the other hand, the route on the left, in which self-esteem, initiative, and number of jobs have been eliminated, did not result in a significant loss of information. These three variables could be eliminated without a significant loss. The flowchart then indicates that the first level supervisor leadership variables should not be eliminated, but we might consider eliminating the second level leadership variable. These decision still require further investigation and arbitrary decisions; however the flowchart approach has considerable intuitive appeal.

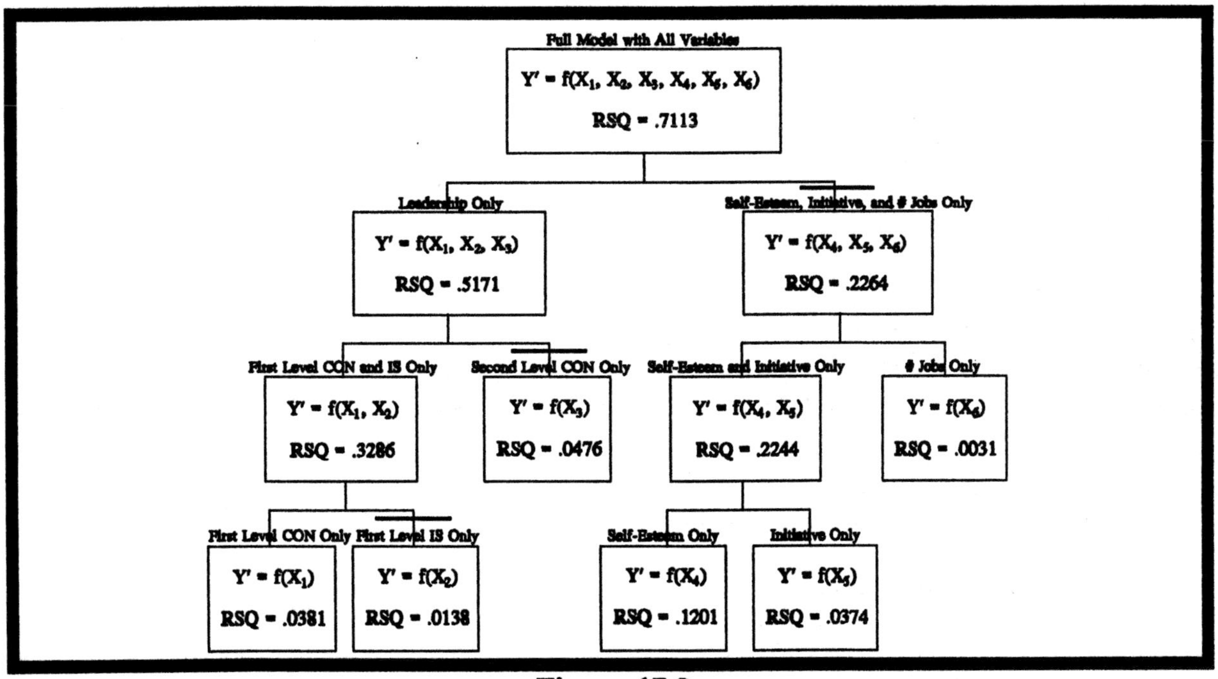

Figure 17.9
Results from Using a Flowchart Regression Model

Multicollinearity Revisited

As we have stated repeatedly throughout this chapter, multicollinearity among the predictor variables is a major concern in multiple regression and other multivariate statistical procedures. This is especially true when we attempt to go beyond making predictions by attempting to *understand* and *interpret* relationships. Interaction among predictor variables can have a significant impact on the *RSQ*, making understanding and interpretation difficult. While there are numerous approaches for addressing the problem of multicollinearity, the following discussion regarding *RSQ* and the standardized regression weights should help to clarify why regression weights cannot be easily interpreted in such situations.

We will begin this discussion by determining the elements of a two-predictor variable model: $Y' = b_0 \cdot U + b_1 \cdot X_1 + b_2 \cdot X_2$. We first recall that *RSQ* is equal to the percent of the variance in the *Y*-variable that can be attributed to the predictor variables. If we convert the *Y*-variable and the set of *X*-variables to standard form (i.e., if we convert all values to *z*-scores), this *RSQ* will now be directly equal to the variance of the predicted *z*-scores. We will state this relationship in terms of an equation. Before doing so, however, we will assume for the moment that we are dealing with population parameters. Our only reason for making this assumption here is to simplify the symbolism and notation. The assumption allows us to use β to symbolize our standardized weights instead of using *z*; otherwise, the multiplication of *z*-weights by *z*-scores becomes extremely confusing in appearance.

Since *RSQ* is equal to the variance of the predicted *z*-scores, we now define *RSQ* in terms of *z*-score variance. Equation 17.17 states this relationship:

$$RSQ = \frac{\Sigma(z_{Y'} - \bar{z}_{Y'})^2}{n} \tag{17.17}$$

Since the mean of a set of *z*-scores always equals zero, we can immediately simplify our relationship, as shown in Equation 17.18:

$$\begin{aligned} RSQ &= \frac{\Sigma(z_{Y'} - \bar{z}_{Y'})^2}{n} \\ &= \frac{\Sigma(z_{Y'})^2}{n} \\ &= \frac{1}{n} \cdot \Sigma(z_{Y'})^2 \\ &= \frac{1}{n} \cdot \Sigma(\beta_1 \cdot z_1 + \beta_2 \cdot z_2)^2 \end{aligned} \tag{17.18}$$

$$= \frac{1}{n} \cdot \Sigma(\beta_1^2 \cdot z_1^2 + 2 \cdot \beta_1 \cdot \beta_2 \cdot z_1 \cdot z_2 + \beta_2^2 \cdot z_2^2)$$

$$= \frac{1}{n} \cdot (\beta_1^2 \cdot \Sigma z_1^2 + 2 \cdot \beta_1 \cdot \beta_2 \cdot \Sigma z_1 \cdot z_2 + \beta_2^2 \cdot \Sigma z_2^2)$$

$$= \beta_1^2 \cdot \frac{\Sigma z_1^2}{n} + 2 \cdot \beta_1 \cdot \beta_2 \cdot \frac{\Sigma z_1 \cdot z_2}{n} + \beta_2^2 \cdot \frac{\Sigma z_2^2}{n}$$

$$= \beta_1^2 \cdot 1 + 2 \cdot \beta_1 \cdot \beta_2 \cdot r_{12} + \beta_2^2 \cdot 1$$

$$= \beta_1^2 + \beta_2^2 + 2 \cdot \beta_1 \cdot \beta_2 \cdot r_{12}$$

Thus, the *RSQ* for the two-predictor variable model is equal to the squared standardized weight of the first variable, plus the squared standardized weight of the second variable, plus 2 times the first standardized weight times the second standardized weight times the correlation coefficient between these two predictor variables. If the two predictor variables are uncorrelated (i.e., independent or orthogonal to one-another), the *RSQ* is equal to the sum of the two squared standardized weights; and the last term in Equation 17.18 would drop out. In most cases, the two predictor variables do correlate to some degree, and the presence of such a relationship generates a separate term for the *RSQ* value. In other words, the existence of multicollinearity creates interaction terms that seriously limit our ability to evaluate the contribution of each variable separately in the full model.

Based on what we have learned from the two-predictor variable model given in Equation 17.18, we can now generalize for other multivariate predictor models. For example, Equation 17.19 gives the relationship between *RSQ* and the standardized weights for a six-predictor variable model, such as the one associated with the full model for the absenteeism data:

$$\begin{aligned} RSQ = {} & \beta_1^2 + \beta_2^2 + \beta_3^2 + \beta_4^2 + \beta_5^2 + \beta_6^2 \\ & + 2 \cdot \beta_1 \cdot \beta_2 \cdot r_{12} + 2 \cdot \beta_1 \cdot \beta_3 \cdot r_{13} + 2 \cdot \beta_1 \cdot \beta_4 \cdot r_{14} \\ & + 2 \cdot \beta_1 \cdot \beta_5 \cdot r_{15} + 2 \cdot \beta_1 \cdot \beta_6 \cdot r_{16} + 2 \cdot \beta_2 \cdot \beta_3 \cdot r_{23} \\ & + 2 \cdot \beta_2 \cdot \beta_4 \cdot r_{24} + 2 \cdot \beta_2 \cdot \beta_5 \cdot r_{25} + 2 \cdot \beta_2 \cdot \beta_6 \cdot r_{26} \\ & + 2 \cdot \beta_3 \cdot \beta_4 \cdot r_{34} + 2 \cdot \beta_3 \cdot \beta_5 \cdot r_{35} + 2 \cdot \beta_3 \cdot \beta_6 \cdot r_{36} \\ & + 2 \cdot \beta_4 \cdot \beta_5 \cdot r_{45} + 2 \cdot \beta_4 \cdot \beta_6 \cdot r_{46} + 2 \cdot \beta_5 \cdot \beta_6 \cdot r_{56} \end{aligned} \tag{17.19}$$

Equation 17.19 clearly illustrates the difficulty in interpreting the standardized weights. The impact that multicollinearity among predictor variables has upon the *RSQ* and thus upon the full model is now very obvious. Only in the complete absence of multicollinearity can we truly interpret the contribution of each predictor variable to the model. On the other hand, if these predictor variables are uncorrelated with one another, we can directly determine the percent each variable contributes to the *RSQ*. We will now discuss two examples that will illustrate these results: one with considerable multicollinearity and one without multicollinearity.

Example 17.2. For Example 17.2, we will examine the ages of a group of 151 middle level managers as a function of work experience and years with the organization. The intercorrelation matrix among these three variables is given in Table 17.28. As we can see, years of work experience correlates with the Y-variable at $r = .84618$, with $r^2 = .7160$. Years with the organization correlates with the Y-variable at $r = .68621$, with $r^2 = .4709$. We should not be surprised to find a high correlation between the two predictor variables also, considering that they both have to do with calendar time; in fact the correlation between years of work experience and years with the organization is $r = .69765$, with and $r^2 = .4867$.

1 Criterion Variable and 2 Predictor Variables

$Y = f(X_1, X_2)$

Example 17.2

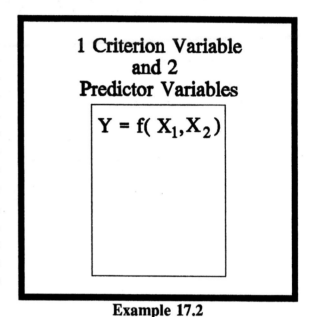

Table 17.28
Intercorrelation Matrix for Work Experience, Years with the Organization, and Age

	X_1	X_2	Y
X_1	1.00000	.69765	.84618
X_2	.69765	1.00000	.68621
Y	.84618	.68621	1.00000

Using multiple regression to examine Y = f(years of work experience and years with the organization), we obtain a full model $RSQ = .7339$, as can be seen in Table 17.29. Since the *RSQ* using our best single predictor variable alone (years of work experience) was .7160, we have increased our *RSQ* by only .0179, which is the usefulness of the years of work experience as a predictor variable in the full model. While this same variable is very useful in the bivariate model, it is not very useful in the full model. We should also point out that for Example 17.2 we have a relatively high ratio of cases (151) to predictor variables ($k + 1 = 3$); therefore, while the increase in *RSQ* is statistically significant, it appears to lack practical significance.

Table 17.29
Results for the Full Model (Step 2) for Highly Correlated Data

```
STEP  2

VARIABLES NOW ENTERED:     1  2

ERROR SUM OF SQUARES FOR RESTRICTED MODEL (CHANCE MODEL)                  8853.2730
ERROR SUM OF SQUARES FOR FULL MODEL (INCLUSIVE THROUGH THIS STEP)         2355.6420
ERROR SUM OF SQUARES REDUCED (EXPLAINED)                                  6497.6310

FOR  2 VARIABLES ENTERED
  RSQ FOR FULL MODEL                                                          .7339
  ABSOLUTE VALUE OF MULTIPLE CORRELATION COEFFICIENT (R)                      .8567
  RSQ ADJUSTED FOR DEGREES OF FREEDOM                                         .7303

  F-VALUE FOR COMPARING THIS FULL MODEL
  WITH THE RESTRICTED (CHANCE) MODEL                                       204.1162
       DF FOR THE FULL MODEL =                                  3
       DF FOR THE CHANCE MODEL =                                1
       DF FOR THE NUMERATOR OF THE F-TEST =        3 -  1 =     2
       DF FOR THE DENOMINATOR OF THE F-TEST =    151 -  3 =   148
       PROBABILITY ASSOCIATED WITH THE F-TEST =                               .0000

  STANDARD ERROR OF ESTIMATE                                                 3.9895
  STANDARD ERROR ADJUSTED FOR DEGREES OF FREEDOM                             4.0164
```

VARIABLE NUMBER	RAW WEIGHTS	STANDARD WEIGHTS	STD. ERROR OF THE SLOPE	COMPUTED T-VALUES	PROB. FOR T
1	.7356	.7159	.0608	12.0958	.0000
2	.2457	.1868	.0778	3.1562	.0023
INTERCEPT	24.0682				

VARIABLE NUMBER	UNIQUE F-VALUES	PROB. FOR F	RESTRICTED MODEL RSQ	USEFUL-NESS	ABS PART CORR
1	146.3081	.0000	.4709	.2630	.5129
2	9.9615	.0023	.7160	.0179	.1338

Both predictor variables have strong correlations with the *Y*-variable and both have strong correlations with each other. Therefore, much of what is being explained by years with the organization is already being accounted for by years of work experience. If we only paid attention to *both* the standard weights ($z = .7159$ for years of work experience and $z = .1868$ for years with the organization), we could easily misinterpret the importance of the variables.

Contrary to Example 17.1, in which the predictor variables had low validities, the predictor variables for Example 17.2 have high validities. The resulting *RSQ* for the full model has not increased substantially from the first step to the second step. We should realize that when the *RSQ* is high at a particular step in the model, the opportunity for increasing *RSQ* in a later step is somewhat limited due to the possible range of any *RSQ* (i.e., $0.00 \leq RSQ \leq 1.00$). On the other hand, when the initial *RSQ* is low, the opportunity for increasing *RSQ* in later steps is not so limited. We should also point out that the multicollinearity among the variables used in Example 17.2 can easily be anticipated due to the nature of the variables. However, multicollinearity is not nearly as obvious in many other analyses, requiring careful investigation and caution.

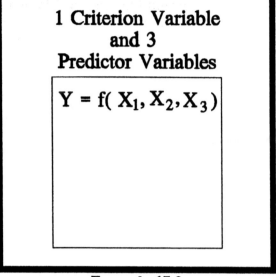

Example 17.3. Example 17.3 consists of one criterion variable and three predictor variables. Here, we are examining a district manager's percent pay increase policy for a number of regional managers. We have access to the number of units sold over a specified work period for each region, the postal zip code numbers for each region, and the attendance records of the subordinates of these regional managers (in terms of subordinate days on the job per work period). The raw data, means, and standard deviations are given in Table 17.30. The intercorrelations for these four variables are given in Table 17.31. For all practical purposes, the bivariate correlations between the pairs of predictor variables are equal to zero. On the other hand, each predictor variable has some correlation with the criterion variable. Units sold correlate with percent pay increase at $r_{Y,1}$ = .75990; postal zip codes for the regions correlate with percent pay increase at $r_{Y,2}$ = .07565; and subordinate attendance records correlate with percent pay increase at $r_{Y,3}$ = .46284. As we might expect, the regional zip code number has a very weak correlation with the percent pay increase.

1 Criterion Variable and 3 Predictor Variables

$$Y = f(X_1, X_2, X_3)$$

Example 17.3

Table 17.30
Raw Data for 10 Regional Managers

Manager Number	*Units Sold*	*Region Zip Code*	*Subordinate Attendance Records*	*Percent Pay Increase*
1	541	43153	5072	6
2	289	50394	5632	3
3	454	46756	5303	5
4	663	40282	5711	9
5	570	60958	5640	5
6	414	63097	4131	2
7	440	36820	5871	3
8	593	67327	4939	8
9	521	50289	5338	5
10	515	40922	2363	2
$\bar{X}$	500.00	49999.80	5000.00	4.80
s	105.46	10541.14	1053.94	2.39

Table 17.31
Results for the Full Model (Step 3) for Highly Uncorrelated Data

Intercorrelation Matrix

	X_1	X_2	X_3	Y
X_1	1.00000	-.00027	.00761	.75991
X_2	-.00027	1.00000	.01569	.07565
X_3	.00761	.01569	1.00000	.46284
Y	.75991	.07565	.46284	1.00000

Multiple Regression Analysis

STEP 3

VARIABLES NOW ENTERED: 1 3 2

ERROR SUM OF SQUARES FOR RESTRICTED MODEL (CHANCE MODEL)	51.6000
ERROR SUM OF SQUARES FOR FULL MODEL (INCLUSIVE THROUGH THIS STEP)	10.9747
ERROR SUM OF SQUARES REDUCED (EXPLAINED)	40.6253

FOR 3 VARIABLES ENTERED

RSQ FOR FULL MODEL	.7873
ABSOLUTE VALUE OF MULTIPLE CORRELATION COEFFICIENT (R)	.8873
RSQ ADJUSTED FOR DEGREES OF FREEDOM	.6810

F-VALUE FOR COMPARING THIS FULL MODEL WITH THE RESTRICTED (CHANCE) MODEL			7.4035
DF FOR THE FULL MODEL =		4	
DF FOR THE CHANCE MODEL =		1	
DF FOR THE NUMERATOR OF THE F-TEST =	4 - 1 =	3	
DF FOR THE DENOMINATOR OF THE F-TEST =	10 - 4 =	6	
PROBABILITY ASSOCIATED WITH THE F-TEST =			.0199

STANDARD ERROR OF ESTIMATE	1.3524
STANDARD ERROR ADJUSTED FOR DEGREES OF FREEDOM	1.6564

VARIABLE NUMBER	RAW WEIGHTS	STANDARD WEIGHTS	STD. ERROR OF THE SLOPE	COMPUTED T-VALUES	PROB. FOR T
1	.0172	.7586	.0043	4.0291	.0073
3	.0010	.4514	.0004	2.3973	.0523
2	.0000	.0829	.0000	.4405	.6762
INTERCEPT	-9.8817				

VARIABLE NUMBER	UNIQUE F-VALUES	PROB. FOR F	RESTRICTED MODEL RSQ	USEFUL-NESS	ABS PART CORR
1	16.2338	.0073	.2119	.5755	.7586
3	5.7471	.0523	.5836	.2037	.4514
2	.1940	.6762	.7804	.0069	.0829

Table 17.31 also gives the multiple regression full model for determining percent pay increase as a function of the number of units sold, the zip code numbers for each region, and the attendance records of the subordinates. This model reveals several very interesting facts. First, an observation of the raw weights might suggest that none of the variables is contributing to the full model (very small raw weights) and that the three predictor variables are of approximately equal importance. However, we have learned that the magnitudes of these raw weights are only

valuable for determining Y'-values and are of minimal use in interpreting the importance of predictor variables.

Second, we notice that the standard regression weights are now identical to the corresponding validities for the three predictor variables (except for roundoff). This relationship will be explained in more detail shortly. We also notice that, as indicated in the discussion of Equation 17.18 and Equation 17.19, when we add the squares of the three standard weights we obtain *RSQ* (rounded). The same is true if we add the squares of the three validities (except for rounding). In the complete absence of multicollinearity of predictor variables, we can very easily interpret the contributions of each of the predictor variables, and the standard weights, the validities, and the part correlations will be identical (again, except for rounding).

Third, if we want to determine the importance of these orthogonal variables in regard to predicting the percent pay increase, our task is now very straightforward. Equation 17.20 gives the total percent of the *RSQ* explained by all three variables:

$$1.0000 = \frac{r_{Y,1}^2}{RSQ_{FM}} + \frac{r_{Y,2}^2}{RSQ_{FM}} + \frac{r_{Y,3}^2}{RSQ_{FM}} \qquad \textbf{(17.20)}$$

Each component part of Equation 17.20 represents the percent of the overall *RSQ* which can be directly attributed to the individual predictor variables. For the present situation, inserting the validities and the *RSQ* into Equation 17.20 yields the following information:

$$1.0000 = \frac{r_{Y,1}^2}{RSQ_{FM}} + \frac{r_{Y,2}^2}{RSQ_{FM}} + \frac{r_{Y,3}^2}{RSQ_{FM}}$$

$$= \frac{.57745}{.78731} + \frac{.00758}{.78731} + \frac{.20347}{.78731}$$

$$= .73344 + .00963 + .25844 \ (\textit{rounded})$$

Thus, 73.34% of the variance of the Y-variable explained by the three predictor variables can be attributed to the number of units sold, 0.96% can be attributed to postal zip codes, and 25.84% can be attributed to attendance records of subordinates. Clearly, postal zip code information was not very useful to the full model.

Finally, we return to the notion of proportional values discussed earlier. We stated that the advantage of these proportional values is that they sum to RSQ_{FM}. For Example 17.3, the three "proportional values" sum to RSQ_{FM} = .78731, as shown in Table 18.1. Dividing each of these proportional values by RSQ_{FM} yields the percent that each predictor variable contributes to the full model. We can now better understand why this relationship was not very helpful when multicollinearity is a problem but is very helpful when we are working with orthogonal data. We should recall that each of the proportional values are equal to the product of the standard weight for the variable times the validity for that same variable. Since the standard weights are equal to the validities for orthogonal data, the proportional values are equal to the squares of the validities. Therefore, the proportional values are now equal to the usefulness of the variables, again as shown in Table 17.32.

Table 17.32
Additional Values for Highly Uncorrelated Data as Obtained from JRB19

Predictor Variable Number	*Raw Regression Weights*	*Standard Error of Weights*	*t-values for Regression Weights*	*Prob. for t-values*	*Lower 95% Interval*	*Upper 95% Interval*
1	.01722	.00427	4.02912	.00726	.00676	.02768
2	.00002	.00004	.44048	.67616	-.00009	.00012
3	.00103	.00043	2.39732	.05226	-.00002	.00207
Intercept	-9.88166	3.72561	-3.94074	.00796	-18.99771	-.76560
Predictor Variable Number	*Standard Regression Weights*	*Restricted Model RSQ*	*Unique F-values*	*Prob. for F-values*	*Variable Usefulness*	*Part Correlation Coefficient*
1	.75864	.21186	16.23378	.00726	.57545	.75859
2	.08294	.78044	.19402	.67616	.00688	.08293
3	.45138	.58359	5.74715	.05226	.20372	.45136
Predictor Variable Number	*Validities (Zero-Order Correlations)*	*2nd Order Partial Correlations*	*Proportional Values*	*Proportion Divided by RSQ_{FM}*	*RSQ Based on this Variable as Y*	
1	.75990	.85448	.57648	.73222	.00013	
2	.08706	.17698	.00722	.00917	.00023	
3	.45108	.69945	.20361	.25861	.00010	
		Proportional Sum Check	.78731	1.00000		

Ridge Regression

Numerous approaches have been offered in an effort to deal with the problem of multicollinearity. One suggestion, as already mentioned, is to select predictor variables whenever possible that have low intercorrelations. Another second suggestion is to generate a new set of predictor variables through the use of factor scores obtained through factor analysis. The shortcoming of this approach is that although such variables are orthogonal to one another, they are often so difficult to interpret that they are not useful in practical applications.

A third suggestion is to increase our sample size whenever possible in order to minimize this impact. We make this suggestion because unique relationships that are peculiar to a small data base may not be generalizable to larger data bases and may lead us to false conclusions. A fourth suggestion is to cross-validate our original regression results, either with a holdout sample or with new data, whenever possible. As pointed out many times before, these latter suggestions may not be practical in many situations due to the cost, time, and effort associated with increasing sample sizes or collecting follow-up data.

A fifth suggestion is to consider *ridge regression.* This statistical tool has been developed in an attempt to provide a "statistical" solution to the problem. Ridge regression adjusts the regression coefficients through a process of developing *bias constants* for adjusting the weights. As a result, the weights are no longer *least squares* weights in the traditional sense. Numerous approaches have been developed for determining these bias constants, and the selection of such constants is arbitrary. Although ridge regression solutions are not appropriate for hypothesis testing, the models can often be useful for prediction.

References

Cohen, J., & Cohen, P. (1983). ***Applied multiple regression/correlation analysis for the behavioral sciences*** (2nd ed.). Hillsdale, NJ: Lawrence Erlbaum Associates.

Cohen, J. (1988). ***Statistical power analysis for the behavioral sciences*** (2nd ed.). Hillsdale, NJ: Lawrence Erlbaum Associates.

Cooley, W. W., & Lohnes, P. R. (1971). ***Multivariate data analysis.*** New York: John Wiley & Sons.

Darlington, R. B. (1968). ***Multiple regression in psychological research and practice.*** New York: John Wiley & Sons.

IBM Corporation. (1970). ***IBM Application program: System/360 Scientific subroutine package (Version III), programmer's manual*** (5th ed.). White Plains, NY: IBM Corporation.

Kerlinger, F. N. (1973). ***Foundations of behavioral research*** (2nd ed.). New York: Holt, Rinehart and Winston.

Marks, M. R. (1966, September). ***Two kinds of regression weights that are better than betas in crossed samples.*** Paper presented at the annual meeting of the American Psychological Association, New York, NY.

McNemar, Q. (1962). ***Psychological statistics*** (3rd ed.). New York: Wiley.

Nunnally, J. C., & Bernstein, I. H. (1994). ***Psychometric theory*** (3nd ed.). New York: McGraw-Hill.

Practice Problems
Multiple Choice

Recall that the means, standard deviations, and bivariate correlation coefficients for the absenteeism data were given at the onset of this chapter. We also found out that the *RSQ* for the full model was .7113. We will need to refer back to these values as we go through the practice problems. Using selected variables from the absenteeism data presented in the chapter, the following multiple regression printout has now been obtained. The predictor variables for this new model are X_1 (SBD-CON-I), X_2 (SBD-IS-I), and X_3 (SBD-CON-II). The *Y*-variable is still absenteeism (ABS). This printout represents the final step for the model. Portions of the printout have been omitted. Answer the next set of problems based on all available information.

```
STEP  3

VARIABLES NOW ENTERED:    3  1  2

ERROR SUM OF SQUARES FOR RESTRICTED MODEL (CHANCE MODEL)                650.5499
ERROR SUM OF SQUARES FOR FULL MODEL (INCLUSIVE THROUGH THIS STEP)       314.1418
ERROR SUM OF SQUARES REDUCED (EXPLAINED)

FOR  3 VARIABLES ENTERED
  RSQ FOR FULL MODEL
  ABSOLUTE VALUE OF MULTIPLE CORRELATION COEFFICIENT (R)                   .7191
  RSQ ADJUSTED FOR DEGREES OF FREEDOM

  F-VALUE FOR COMPARING THIS FULL MODEL
  WITH THE RESTRICTED (CHANCE) MODEL
       DF FOR THE FULL MODEL =                              4
       DF FOR THE CHANCE MODEL =                            1
       DF FOR THE NUMERATOR OF THE F-TEST =      4 -  1 =   3
       DF FOR THE DENOMINATOR OF THE F-TEST =   20 -  4 =  16
       PROBABILITY ASSOCIATED WITH THE F-TEST =                            .0076

  STANDARD ERROR OF ESTIMATE                                              4.4310
  STANDARD ERROR ADJUSTED FOR DEGREES OF FREEDOM

 VARIABLE        RAW        STANDARD    STD. ERROR OF   COMPUTED       PROB.
  NUMBER       WEIGHTS      WEIGHTS       THE SLOPE     T-VALUES       FOR T
    3                       -.4779          .1442       -2.4991        .0225
    1           .6646       1.3930          .1695        3.9223        .0015
    2           .4860                       .1368        3.5536        .0029
INTERCEPT

 VARIABLE       UNIQUE       PROB.       RESTRICTED     USEFUL-      ABS PART
  NUMBER       F-VALUES      FOR F       MODEL RSQ       NESS          CORR
    3           6.2456       .0225         .3286         .1885         .4342
    1                        .0015         .0528         .4643         .6814
    2          12.6278       .0029         .1360         .3811         .6173
```

1. What is the *RSQ* for the full model [$Y' = f(X_1, X_2, X_3)$] when attempting to predict absenteeism from a knowledge of variables 1, 2, and 3?

A. .7191
B. .5171
C. .4603
D. .9912
E. .0586

2. What is the *RSQ* for the $Y' = f(X_1, X_2, X_3)$ model after adjusting for degrees of freedom?

A. .4266
B. .5171
C. .3861
D. .1234
E. .7420

3. What is the computed *F*-value, the critical *F*-value, and the decision in regard to comparing the $Y' = f(X_1, X_2, X_3)$ model against chance, with alpha set at .05?

A. 4.2352, 3.24, reject the null, as the model is significant.
B. 2.6846, 3.24, fail to reject the null.
C. 5.7114, 3.24, reject the null, as the model is significant.
D. 5.7114, 5.29, reject the null, as the model is significant.
E. 4.2352. 5.29, fail to reject the null.

4. What is the computed *F*-value, the critical *F*-value, and the decision in regard to comparing the $Y' = f(X_1, X_2, X_3, X_4, X_5, X_6)$ model given in the chapter against the $Y' = f(X_1, X_2, X_3)$ given here, with alpha set at .05?

A. 2.9149, 3.41, fail to reject the null. In other words, dropping variables 4, 5, and 6 from the full model will result in a significant loss in information.
B. 5.7114, 3.41, reject the null. Do not drop out variables 4, 5, and 6 from the full model.
C. 5.3563, 3.41, reject the null. Do not drop out variables 4, 5, and 6 from the full model.
D. 2.0824, 1.96, reject the null. Do not drop out variables 4, 5, and 6 from the full model.
E. 2.9149, 3.41, fail to reject the null. In other words, dropping variables 4, 5, and 6 from the full model will not result in any significant loss in information.

5. What is the raw weight for variable 3 in the $Y' = f(X_1, X_2, X_3)$ model?

A. .6646
B. .4860
C. -.4779
D. -.3603
E. .5327

6. What is the intercept for the $Y' = f(X_1, X_2, X_3)$ model?

A. -26.83
B. 26.83
C. 27.56
D. 11.15
E. -21.78

7. What is the standard regression weight for variable 2 in the $Y' = f(X_1, X_2, X_3)$ model?

A. -.2351
B. 1.1998
C. 2.6936
D. -.6556
E. .2513

8. What is the unique F-value for variable 1 in regard to the $Y' = f(X_1, X_2, X_3)$ model?

A. 6.24
B. 3.92
C. 15.38
D. 12.62
E. 13.36

9. What is the usefulness of variable 1 in regard to the $Y' = f(X_1, X_2, X_3)$ model?

A. .3619
B. .0528
C. .9472
D. .4643
E. .6814

10. What is the absolute value of the part correlation between variable 2 and Y, based on the $Y' = f(X_1, X_2, X_3)$ model?

A. .2298
B. .0528
C. .3465
D. .4643
E. .6173

11. If you were to eliminate one of the three variables in the $Y' = f(X_1, X_2, X_3)$ model, which one should it most likely *not* be?

A. Variable 1
B. Variable 2
C. Variable 3
D. Variable 4
E. Variable 5

12. What is the computed F-value, the critical F-value, and the decision in regard to comparing the $Y' = f(X_1, X_2, X_3)$ model against chance *after* adjusting *RSQ* for degrees of freedom?

A. 3.9672, 3.24, reject the null.
B. 5.7114, 3.24, reject the null.
C. 3.4532, 3.46, reject the null.
D. 4.5487, 3.24, fail to reject the null.
E. 2.3432, 4.23, fail to reject the null.

Again using selected variables from the absenteeism data, another multiple regression printout has been obtained. This time a model has been developed to predict Y (ABS) from a knowledge of X_4 (SE), X_5 (INIT), and X_6 (NO. JOBS). The following printout represents the final step for the model. Portions of this printout have been omitted. Answer the next set of problems based on all available information.

```
STEP  3

VARIABLES NOW ENTERED:      4  5  6

ERROR SUM OF SQUARES FOR RESTRICTED MODEL (CHANCE MODEL)                650.5499
ERROR SUM OF SQUARES FOR FULL MODEL (INCLUSIVE THROUGH THIS STEP)       503.2842
ERROR SUM OF SQUARES REDUCED (EXPLAINED)

FOR  3 VARIABLES ENTERED
  RSQ FOR FULL MODEL
  ABSOLUTE VALUE OF MULTIPLE CORRELATION COEFFICIENT (R)                   .4758
  RSQ ADJUSTED FOR DEGREES OF FREEDOM

  F-VALUE FOR COMPARING THIS FULL MODEL
  WITH THE RESTRICTED (CHANCE) MODEL
       DF FOR THE FULL MODEL =                                    4
       DF FOR THE CHANCE MODEL =                                  1
       DF FOR THE NUMERATOR OF THE F-TEST =        4 -  1 =       3
       DF FOR THE DENOMINATOR OF THE F-TEST =     20 -  4 =      16
       PROBABILITY ASSOCIATED WITH THE F-TEST =                            .2371

  STANDARD ERROR OF ESTIMATE                                              5.6085
  STANDARD ERROR ADJUSTED FOR DEGREES OF FREEDOM
```

VARIABLE NUMBER	RAW WEIGHTS	STANDARD WEIGHTS	STD. ERROR OF THE SLOPE	COMPUTED T-VALUES	PROB. FOR T
4	0.3311	.4546	.1695	1.9529	.0658
5	1.1406	.3434	.7728	1.4760	.1564
6	.1781		.8898	.2002	.8379
INTERCEPT	-7.2665				

VARIABLE NUMBER	UNIQUE F-VALUES	PROB. FOR F	RESTRICTED MODEL RSQ	USEFUL-NESS	ABS PART CORR
4	3.8139	.0658	.0420	.1844	.4294
5		.1564	.1210	.1054	.3246
6	.0401	.8379	.2244	.0020	.0446

13. What is the *RSQ* for the full model [$Y' = f(X_4, X_5, X_6)$] when attempting to predict absenteeism from a knowledge of variables 4, 5, and 6?

A. .7191
B. .2264
C. .4758
D. .1354
E. .0586

14. What is the *RSQ* for the $Y' = f(X_4, X_5, X_6)$ model after adjusting for degrees of freedom?

A. .0813
B. .4758
C. .2264
D. .1234
E. .7420

15. What is the computed *F*-value, the critical *F*-value, and the decision in regard to comparing the $Y' = f(X_4, X_5, X_6)$ model against chance, with alpha set at .05?

A. 4.2352, 3.24, reject the null, as the model is significant.
B. 2.6846, 3.24, fail to reject the null.
C. 1.5606, 3.24, fail to reject the null.
D. 5.7114, 5.29, reject the null, as the model is significant.
E. 4.2352. 5.29, fail to reject the null.

16. What is the computed *F*-value, the critical *F*-value, and the decision in regard to comparing the $Y' = f(X_1, X_2, X_3, X_4, X_5, X_6)$ model given in the chapter against the $Y' = f(X_4, X_5, X_6)$ given here, with alpha set at .05?

A. 7.2783, 3.41, fail to reject the null. In other words, dropping variables 1, 2, and 3 from the full model will not result in any significant loss in information.
B. 5.7114, 3.41, reject the null. Do not drop out variables 4, 5, and 6 from the full model.
C. 5.3563, 3.41, reject the null. Do not drop out variables 4, 5, and 6 from the full model.
D. 2.0824, 1.96, reject the null. Do not drop out variables 4, 5, and 6 from the full model.
E. 7.2783, 3.41, reject the null. In other words, dropping variables 1, 2, and 3 from the full model will result in a significant loss in information.

17. What is the raw weight for variable 4 in the $Y' = f(X_4, X_5, X_6)$ model?

A. .6646
B. .4860
C. .1781
D. -.3603
E. .3311

18. What is the intercept for the $Y' = f(X_4, X_5, X_6)$ model?

A. -7.2665
B. 6.8329
C. 7.5673
D. 11.1500
E. -5.7665

19. What is the standard regression weight for variable 6 in the $Y' = f(X_4, X_5, X_6)$ model?

A. -.2351
B. .0442
C. .6936
D. .4546
E. .2513

20. What is the unique F-value for variable 5 in regard to the $Y' = f(X_4, X_5, X_6)$ model?

A. 6.24
B. 6.92
C. 2.18
D. 2.62
E. 3.36

21. What is the usefulness of variable 6 in regard to the $Y' = f(X_4, X_5, X_6)$ model?

A. .3619
B. .0447
C. .9472
D. .0020
E. .9553

22. What is the absolute value of the part correlation between variable 5 and Y, based on the $Y' = f(X_4, X_5, X_6)$ model?

A. .8946
B. .0111
C. .5699
D. .3816
E. .3247

23. If you were to eliminate one of the three variables in the $Y' = f(X_4, X_5, X_6)$ model, which one should it most likely *not* be?

A. Variable 4
B. Variable 2
C. Variable 5
D. Variable 3
E. Variable 6

24. What is the computed F-value, the critical F-value, and the decision in regard to comparing the $Y' = f(X_4, X_5, X_6)$ model against chance *after* adjusting *RSQ* for degrees of freedom?

A. .4722, 3.24, fail to reject the null.
B. .6264, 3.24, reject the null.
C. 3.4532, 3.46, reject the null.
D. 7.5487, 3.24, fail to reject the null.
E. 4.3432, 4.23, fail to reject the null.

"End."

Use the following set of information to answer the next set of questions. Data were obtained from a survey of 108 customers of a product sold by a computer software company. The predictor variables include 1) the number of hours the customer used the product per month, 2) the number of directories the customer maintained on his or her computer system, 3) the customer's age, 4) the number of minutes the customer spent modifying the product at the time of installation, 5) the customer's years of computer experience, and 6) the customer's years of formal education. The variable of interest (the Y-variable) is product rating. Assume that alpha is set at .05 for all related questions.

Means and Standard Deviations

Variable Number	*Variable Means*	*Standard Deviations*	*Number of Cases*	*Variable Name*
X_1	78.54630	14.22935	108	Hours product used per month
X_2	51.96296	5.14450	108	Number of directories on system
X_3	42.35185	5.67716	108	Customer's age
X_4	40.87963	8.74639	108	Number of minutes spent modifying
X_5	10.47222	8.00637	108	Customer's years of computer experience
X_6	15.79630	2.01749	108	Customer's years of formal education
Y	6.76852	1.11579	108	Customer's product rating

Intercorrelations for Customer Survey Data

	1	2	3	4	5	6	7
1	1.00000	.07101	.07442	.18263	.09435	-.18361	.52957
2	.07101	1.00000	-.17203	-.10644	.09573	-.02505	.04734
3	.07442	-.17203	1.00000	.07107	.07691	-.04019	.14281
4	.18263	-.10644	.07107	1.00000	.60713	.05050	.62821
5	.09435	.09573	.07691	.60713	1.00000	-.16641	.56263
6	-.18361	-.02505	-.04019	.05050	-.16641	1.00000	-.02945
7	.52957	.04734	.14281	.62821	.56263	-.02945	1.00000

Full Multiple Regression Model

STEP 6

VARIABLES NOW ENTERED: 4 1 5 6 3 2

ERROR SUM OF SQUARES FOR RESTRICTED MODEL (CHANCE MODEL)	133.2130
ERROR SUM OF SQUARES FOR FULL MODEL (INCLUSIVE THROUGH THIS STEP)	47.7445
ERROR SUM OF SQUARES REDUCED (EXPLAINED)	85.4684

FOR 3 VARIABLES ENTERED

RSQ FOR FULL MODEL	.6416
ABSOLUTE VALUE OF MULTIPLE CORRELATION COEFFICIENT (R)	.8010
RSQ ADJUSTED FOR DEGREES OF FREEDOM	

F-VALUE FOR COMPARING THIS FULL MODEL
WITH THE RESTRICTED (CHANCE) MODEL

DF FOR THE FULL MODEL =
DF FOR THE CHANCE MODEL =
DF FOR THE NUMERATOR OF THE F-TEST = - 1 =
DF FOR THE DENOMINATOR OF THE F-TEST = 108 - =
PROBABILITY ASSOCIATED WITH THE F-TEST = .0001

STANDARD ERROR OF ESTIMATE	.6875
STANDARD ERROR ADJUSTED FOR DEGREES OF FREEDOM	

VARIABLE NUMBER	RAW WEIGHTS	STANDARD WEIGHTS	STD. ERROR OF THE SLOPE	COMPUTED T-VALUES	PROB. FOR T
4	.0448	.3510	.0102	4.3844	.0001
1	.0349	.4445	.0049	7.1106	.0000
5	.0437	.3136	.0111	3.9367	.0004
6	.0500	.0904	.0349	1.4339	.1509
3	.0139	.0708	.0120	1.1607	.2470
2	.0081	.0376	.0136	.5994	.5574
INTERCEPT	-.0600				

VARIABLE NUMBER	UNIQUE F-VALUES	PROB. FOR F	RESTRICTED MODEL RSQ	USEFUL-NESS	ABS PART CORR
4		.0001	.5734		
1		.0000	.4622		
5		.0004	.5866		
6		.1509	.6343		
3		.2470	.6368		
2		.5574	.6403		

25. Which of the following is the *best* answer concerning the relationship between the number of hours the product was used per month and product rating, based on these sample data?

A. Product rating appears to be related to the number of hours the product was used per month.
B. Product rating appears to be positively related to the number of hours the product was used per month.
C. Product rating does not appear to be perfectly related to the number of hours the product was used per month.
D. Product rating appears to be more related to the number of hours the product was used per month than to the number of directories the customer maintained on his or her computer system.
E. We can make all of the above statements, based on our sample data.

26. Which of the five choices given below is the *best* answer when testing the significance of the correlation between number of directories on system and customer's age (i.e., X-variables *two* and *three*), after setting alpha = .05?

A. Since the computed t-value for testing the statistical significance of *this* bivariate correlation is -1.798, the correlation is not significant.
B. Since the computed value of F-value for testing the significance of the RSQ for this two-variable model is 3.233, the correlation is not statistically significant.
C. Since the computed correlation coefficient between variables two and three is -.17203 and since the critical r-value for a bivariate correlation coefficient with 106 degrees of freedom is ±.1891 for a two-tailed test, the computed correlation coefficient is not significant.
D. The null hypothesis states that the population correlation coefficient (rho) is equal to zero. We should fail to reject this hypothesis.
E. All of the above are true statements.

27. On the basis of the present sample, which variable would be the best predictor of product rating if you were only able to use one variable?

A. Hours product used per month
B. Number of directories on system
C. Customer's age
D. Number of minutes spent modifying
E. Years with the company

28. If *product rating* is our variable of interest and we wish to use the first six variables in a multiple regression model to predict product rating, *at least* how many cases should we have before we begin to feel reasonably comfortable about drawing conclusions based on the present data?

A. 40
B. 50
C. 30
D. 60
E. 70

29. If *product rating* is our variable of interest and we wish to use the first six variables in a multiple regression model to predict product rating, which of the following is the computed F-value that would be obtained when this regression model is compared against chance?

A. 35.3378
B. 22.6937
C. 41.2349
D. 12.4391
E. 30.1347

30. If *product rating* is our variable of interest and we wish to use the first six variables in a multiple regression model to predict product rating, which of the following is the critical value for F-value obtained from the F-table when the comparing this regression model to the chance model, with alpha set at .05? If you cannot find the necessary degrees of freedom in the table, use the degrees of freedom that are the closest to what you need *without going over the actual degrees of freedom.*

A. 3.45
B. 2.19
C. 2.98
D. 2.17
E. 2.18

31. Using the fullest regression model given by the multiple regression program to predict product rating, $Y' = f(X_1, X_2, X_3, X_4, X_5, X_6)$, what percent of the variance in Y can be accounted for by a knowledge of the variance in the set of X-variables?

A. 54.23%
B. 61.32%
C. 64.16%
D. 82.47%
E. 75.21%

32. Suppose that it is very difficult for the customers to determine the number of hours they used the product per month. Therefore, you have decided to evaluate the unique contribution of this variable to the full model in order to determine whether you can eliminate this variable without losing a significant amount of information. First, perform the necessary F-test to make this decision. Then, which of the following is the best answer?

A. The unique F-value is 23.5656 and the critical F-value is approximately 3.94. Therefore, the number of hours they used the product each month is making a unique contribution to the full model and should not be eliminated.
B. The unique F-value is 50.5664 and the critical F-value is approximately 3.94. Therefore, the number of hours they used the product each month is making a unique contribution to the full model and should not be eliminated.
C. The unique F-value is 42.6576 and the critical F-value is approximately 3.00. Therefore, the number of hours they used the product each month is making a unique contribution to the full model and should not be eliminated.
D. The unique F-value is 53.6327 and the critical F-value is approximately 2.57. Therefore, the number of hours they used the product each month is making a unique contribution to the full model and should not be eliminated.
E. The unique F-value is 3.3755 and the critical F-value is approximately 3.94. Therefore, the number of hours they used the product each month is not making a unique contribution to the full model and can be eliminated.

33. In regard to the full model, what is the *usefulness* of the number of hours they used the product each month?

A. .1794
B. .4236
C. .3268
D. .4314
E. .7334

34. Suppose that all of the variables are very expensive to collect and maintain in our data base. If we are willing to eliminate *one* of these variables, which one would it be based on its contribution to the full model?

A. The number of directories the customer maintained on his or her computer system
B. The customer's age
C. The number of minutes the customer spent modifying the product at the time of installation
D. The customer's years of computer experience
E. The customer's years of formal education

35. Suppose that a new customer who did not participate in the survey had the following values on the respective predictor variables: $X_1 = 85$, $X_2 = 55$, $X_3 = 45$, $X_4 = 40$, $X_5 = 10$, $X_6 = 16$. Based on the fullest model and using all six predictor variables, approximately what rating would you estimate that this individual would give the product?

A. 7
B. 12
C. 5
D. 3
E. 9

Practice Problems
Conceptual Questions

The following correlation matrix was generated from the absenteeism data given in this chapter. Variables 1 through 7 correspond with the intercorrelation matrix for the original set of data, as given at the onset of this chapter. Variable 8 represents the Y' variable, variable 9 represents the residuals based on $e = Y - Y'$, and variable 10 represents the squares of these residuals based on $e^2 = (Y - Y')^2$.

Absenteeism Correlation Matrix with Generated Variables

		1	2	3	4	5	6	7	8	9	10		
		X_1	X_2	X_3	X_4	X_5	X_6	Y	Y'	e	e^2	Mean	S.D.
1	X_1	1.00	-.85	.37	-.15	-.05	.29	.20	.23	.00	.00	57.25	11.95
2	X_2	-.85	1.00	-.21	.23	.03	-.28	.12	.14	.00	-.10	43.15	14.08
3	X_3	.37	-.21	1.00	-.10	-.04	.49	-.22	-.26	.00	-.32	58.40	7.57
4	X_4	-.15	.23	-.10	1.00	-.32	.07	.35	.41	.00	.21	37.15	7.83
5	X_5	-.05	.03	-.04	-.32	1.00	-.06	.19	.23	.00	-.63	5.05	1.72
6	X_6	.29	-.28	.49	.07	-.06	1.00	.06	.07	.00	-.34	2.00	1.41
7	Y	.20	.12	-.22	.35	.19	.06	1.00	.84	.54	-.20	11.15	5.70
8	Y'	.23	.14	-.26	.41	.23	.07	.84	1.00	.00	-.18	11.15	4.81
9	e	.00	.00	.00	.00	.00	.00	.54	.00	1.00	-.09	0.00	3.06
10	e^2	.00	-.10	-.32	.21	-.63	-.34	-.20	-.18	-.09	1.00	9.39	8.11

Answer the following set of questions based on this intercorrelation matrix and the information given in this chapter.

1. Why is the mean for variable 9 equal to zero?
2. Why is the mean for variable 8 equal to 11.15?
3. Why are all of the correlation coefficients between variable 9 and variables 1 through 6 equal to zero?
4. Conceptually speaking, what is the square of the correlation between the actual Y-values and the residual values?
5. Conceptually speaking, what is the square of the correlation between Y and Y'?
6. What is the relationship between Y' and the residuals? Why?
7. What is the numerator of the variance for variable 8? Why?
8. What is the numerator of the variance for variable 9? Why?

APPENDIX A

ANSWERS TO PRACTICE PROBLEMS

CHAPTER 1
Quick Quiz
Answers

1. There is no one correct cause-and-effect diagram for analyzing the difficulty a student is having with a particular course. Each individual or team will have a somewhat different diagram. A cause-and-effect diagram for this problem might appear as follows:

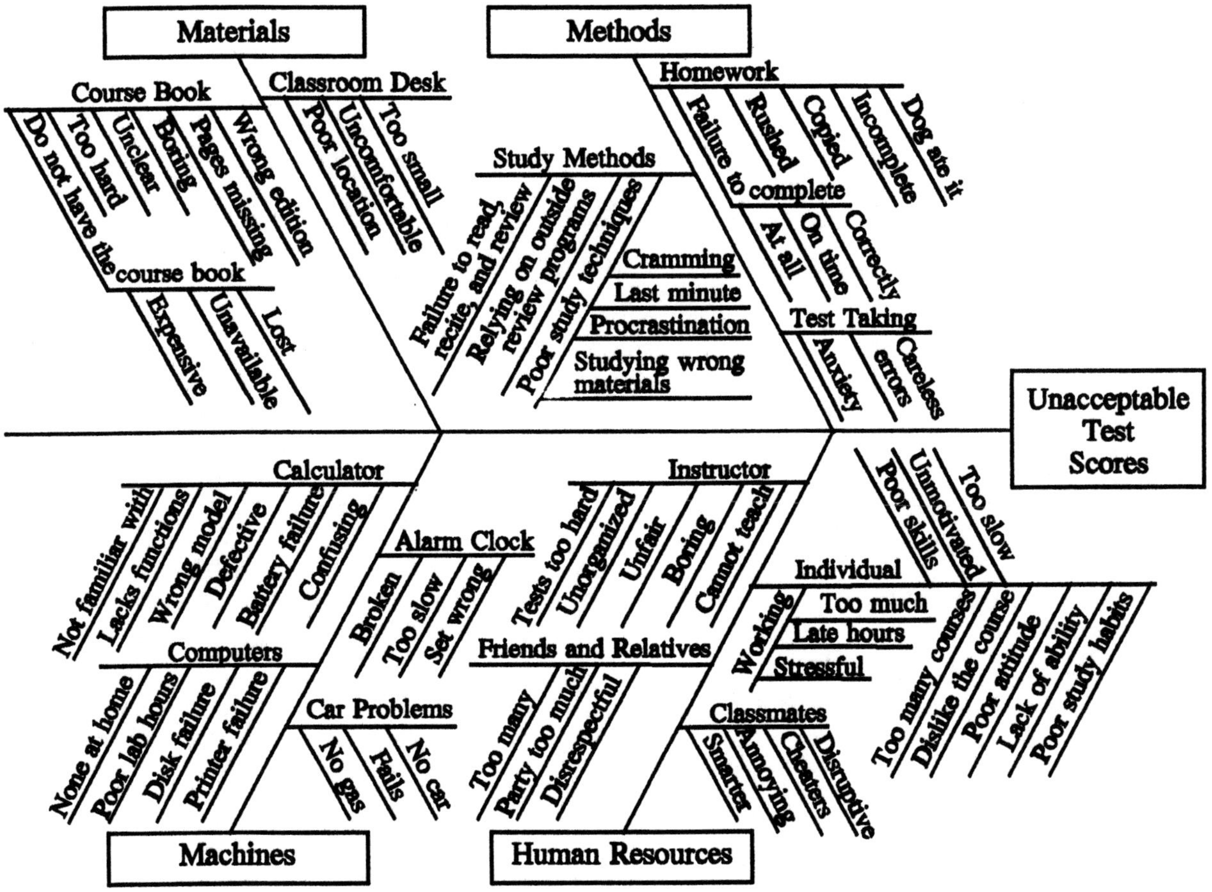

2. As with the cause-and-effect diagram, there is no one correct Pareto diagram that might represent the frequencies of errors. You were given the following categories to evaluate: a) lack of subject knowledge, b) use of incorrect equations, c) making calculation errors, d) lack of calculator knowledge, e) highly difficult items, f) careless errors such as marking the wrong bubble, and g) a general catch-all category labeled as "other." Suppose that your frequency distribution of errors, in respective order of these categories, is as follows: 35, 30, 10, 10, 7, 5, and 3. Then the Pareto diagram would appear as follows:

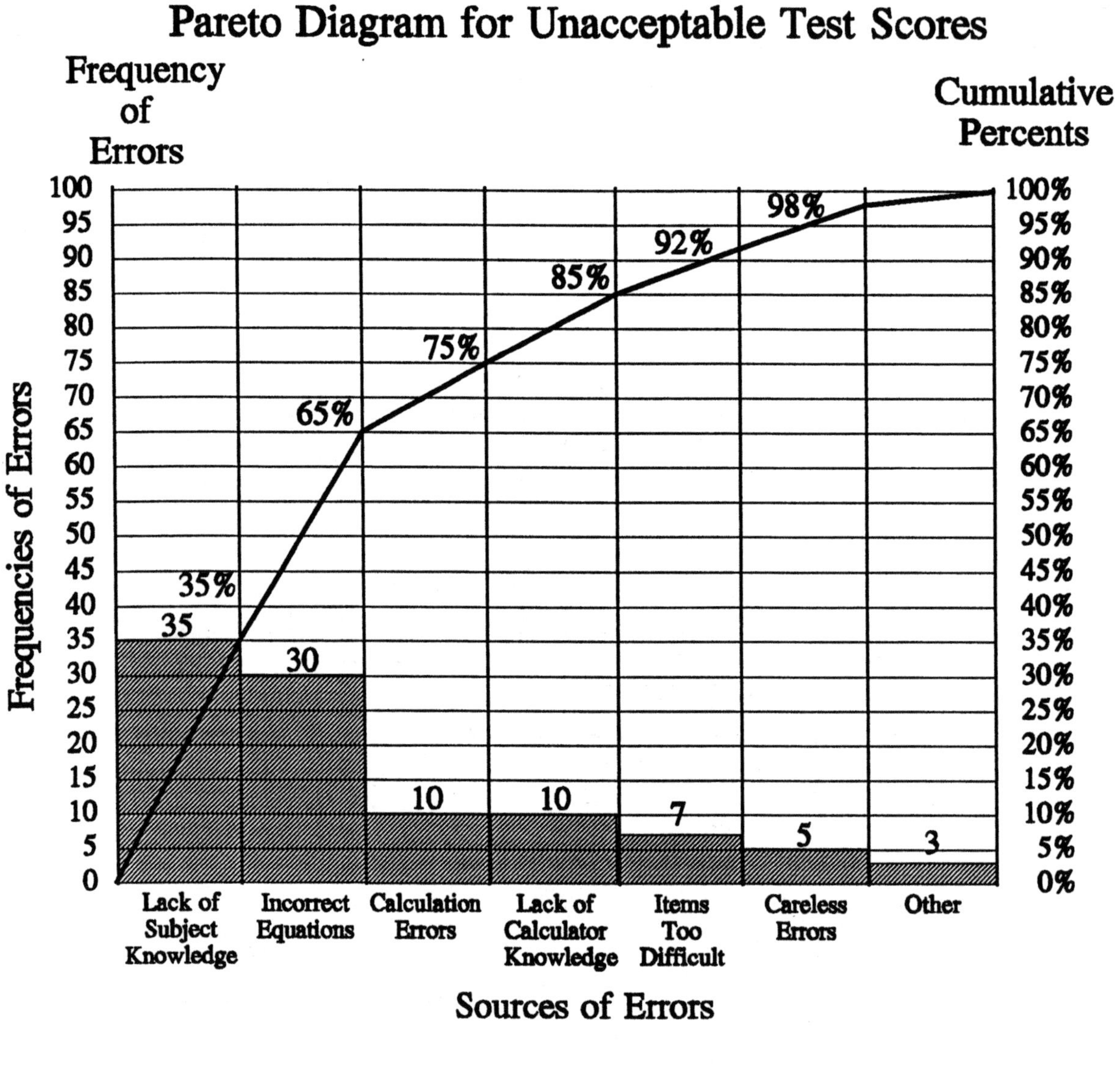

3. As with the cause-and-effect diagram and the Pareto diagram, there is no one correct flowchart that might represent an individual's approach to studying and preparing for examinations in this or in other courses. In fact, different approaches may work better for different courses. A flowchart for one of these courses may appear as follows:

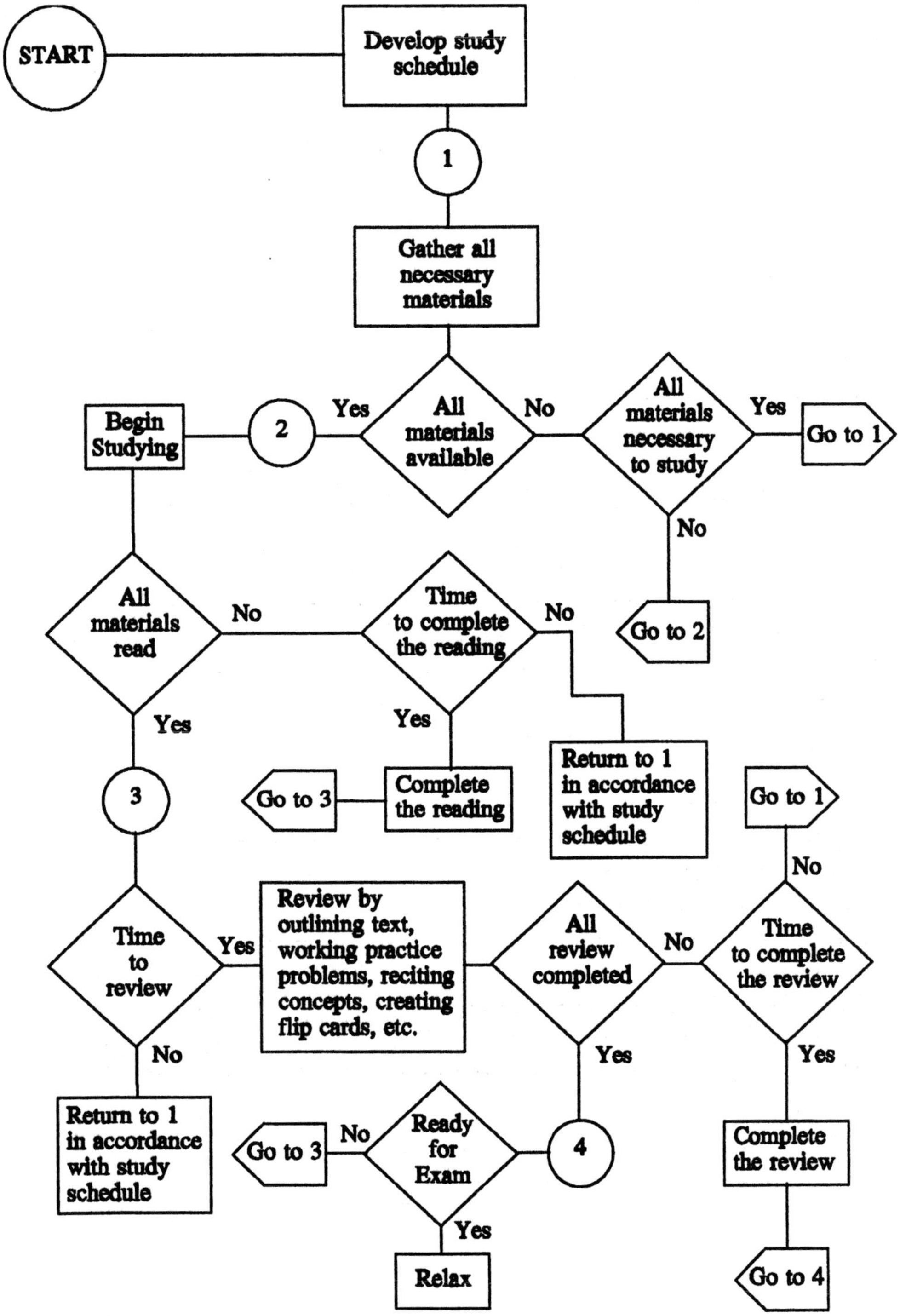

CHAPTER 1
Multiple Choice
Answers

1. D	6. A	11. C	16. E	21. C	26. E
2. D	7. D	12. B	17. A	22. E	
3. E	8. B	13. A	18. D	23. B	
4. A	9. C	14. C	19. A	24. E	
5. C	10. B	15. E	20. D	25. E	

CHAPTER 2
Quick Quiz
Answers

The words used to describe variables do not always mean the same thing to everyone. Therefore, arbitrary decisions will have to be made. The following are reasonable answers for these problems.

1. Number of steps a person is below the CEO (level within the organization)
   (Ordinal; discrete)

2. The measurable degree to which a part does not conform to standards
   (Ratio; continuous)

3. An individual's managerial level within the organization
   (Ordinal; discrete)

4. Number of previous jobs held
   (Ratio; discrete)

5. Number of defective parts observed
   (Ratio; discrete)

6. Degree of customer satisfaction with a product
   (Ordinal; discrete. The *underlying* distribution for customer satisfaction is probably ratio and continuous, but the actual *measurement* of this variable by some arbitrary scale relies on ordinal and discrete values.)

7. Geographic locations of district offices
   (Nominal; discrete)

8. Salaries of branch managers
   (Ratio; discrete)

9. Time necessary to complete a task
(Ratio; continuous)

10. Football jersey numbers
(Nominal; discrete)

11. Social security numbers
(Nominal; discrete)

12. Ages of employees
(Ratio; continuous—even though ages are usually recorded in discrete values, truncated to the nearest whole number, the *underlying* distribution of ages is continuous)

13. Satisfaction regarding service at a restaurant
(Ordinal; discrete. The *underlying* distribution for customer satisfaction at a restaurant is probably ratio and continuous, but the actual *measurement* of this variable by some arbitrary scale relies on ordinal and discrete values.)

14. Gasoline mileage
(Ratio—some of us have found the "true zero" point on this ratio scale when we have run out of gas; continuous)

15. Number of telephone calls received
(Ratio; discrete)

16. Fahrenheit temperature in the room
(Interval; continuous)

17. Anxiety toward statistics as measured on a 10-point scale
(Ordinal; discrete. The *underlying* distribution for most human attitudes is probably ratio and continuous, but the actual *measurement* of this variable is usually obtained through some arbitrary scale that relies on ordinal and discrete values.)

18. Performance evaluation scores for accountant trainees
(Ordinal; discrete. Most performance evaluations are based on some ordinal rating scale, such as 1 = unacceptable, 2 = below standards, 3 = meets standards, 4 = exceeds standards, and 5 = outstanding. The *underlying* distribution for performance is probably ratio and continuous, but the actual *measurement* of this variable is usually obtained through some arbitrary scale that relies on ordinal and discrete values. If the performance for accountant trainees is measured by the number of accounts completed or some other directly measurable unit, it is probably ratio and discrete.)

19. Width of a laser beam
(Ratio; continuous)

20. Thickness of various wafers
(Ratio; continuous)
21. Performance scores
22. Ratio
23. Discrete
24. Probably a population, since the description states "all."
25. Bar graph
26. Test score values
27. Frequencies

28. The graph should be a bar graph, with bars ranging from 32 to 48. Since the lowest value was 32, we did not begin at zero on the *X*-axis. Instead, we used the double slash marks (//) to clearly indicate that we did not begin at the origin of the graph on the *X*-axis.

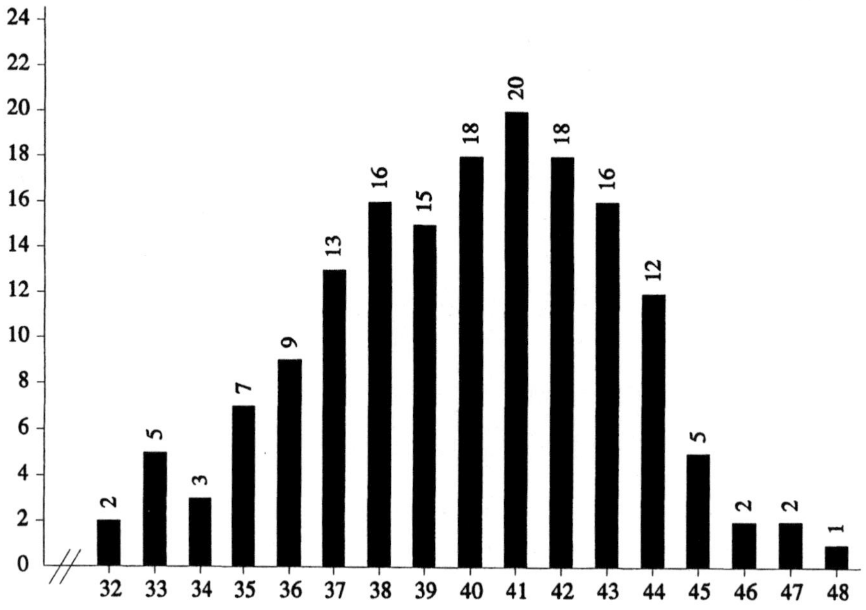

CHAPTER 2
Multiple Choice
Answers

1. C	6. A	11. E	16. D	21. A	26. E
2. D	7. B	12. E	17. B	22. E	
3. A	8. E	13. D	18. E	23. B	
4. E	9. E	14. E	19. C	24. D	
5. E	10. A	15. C	20. C	25. D	

CHAPTER 2
Written Problems
Answers

Frequency Distribution for Welders: Interval Width of 25

LL	*MP*	*UL*	*f*	*f%*	*cf*	*cf%*
1700	1712	1724	1	1%	74	100%
1675	1687	1699	2	3%	73	99%
1650	1662	1674	2	3%	71	96%
1625	1637	1649	3	4%	69	93%
1600	1612	1624	3	4%	66	89%
1575	1587	1599	4	5%	63	85%
1550	1562	1574	5	7%	59	80%
1525	1537	1549	7	9%	54	73%
1500	1512	1524	8	11%	47	64%
1475	1487	1499	8	11%	39	53%
1450	1462	1474	8	11%	31	42%
1425	1437	1449	7	9%	23	31%
1400	1412	1424	6	8%	16	22%
1375	1387	1399	5	7%	10	14%
1350	1362	1374	5	7%	5	7%

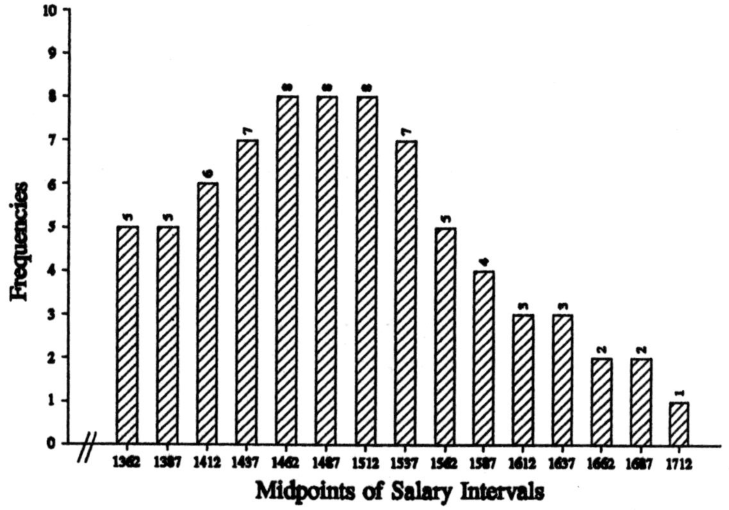

Bar Graph for Salaries in Grouped Format

CHAPTER 3
Numerical Quiz
Answers

1.

A. 29.0000	F. 25.0000
B. 28.9107	G. 28.9119
C. 26.8864	H. 28.8988
D. 30.9091	I. 28.7585
E. 32.8333	J. 28.6032

2. A percentile bar is given below. The mean and the median are approximately equal.

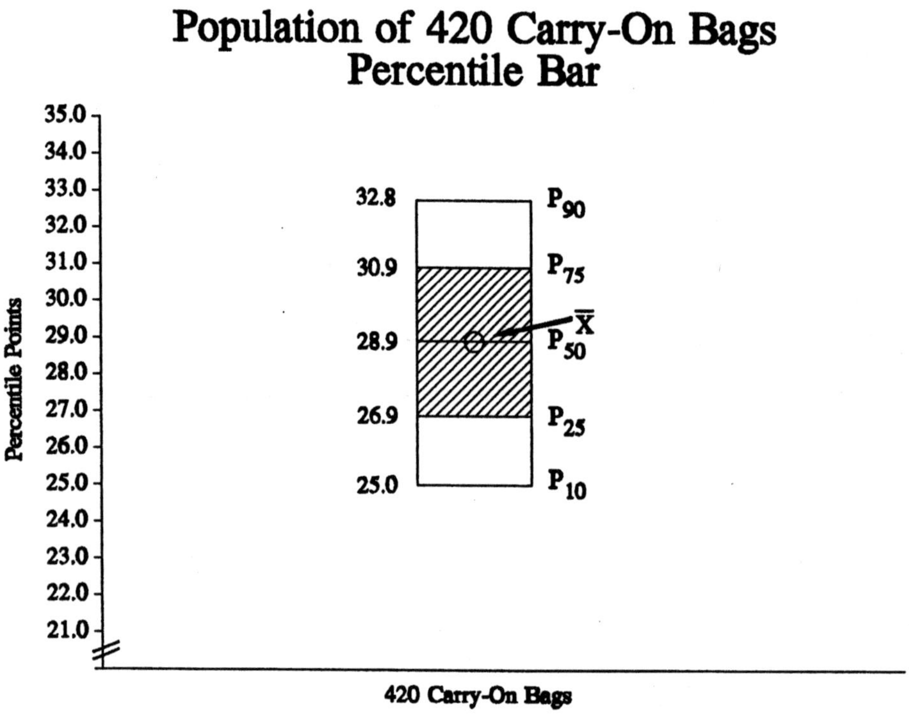

CHAPTER 3
Multiple Choice
Answers

1. C	6. D	11. B
2. A	7. A	12. D
3. B	8. B	13. E
4. C	9. A	14. E
5. A	10. B	15. C

CHAPTER 3
Written Problems
Answers

1. A. time B. ratio C. continuous D. sample
   E. 76.0000 F. 76.3750 G. 77.8148 H. 77.7619
   I. 72.2500 J. 84.7500 K. 77.3637 L. 76.9122

2. A. 75.0000 B. 76.2500 C. 77.7778 D. 77.7143
   E. 72.2500 F. 83.2500 G. 77.3256 H. 76.8756

3. A. days B. ratio C. discrete D. sample
   E. 76.0000 F. 74.5000 G. 73.7222 H. 74.3125
   I. 68.7500 J. 81.0000 K. 72.9209 L. 72.0533

4.

Interval	*MP*	*f*	*cf*
95-99	97	1	54
90-94	92	3	53
85-89	87	5	50
80-84	82	7	45
75-79	77	11	38
70-74	72	11	27
65-69	67	7	16
60-64	62	4	9
55-59	57	1	5
50-54	52	2	4
45-49	47	2	2

A. 72 and 77 B. 74.5000 C. 73.9400 D. 74.5000
E. 67.0000 F. 82.0000 G. 73.0598 H. 72.1017

When finding the mode, the mean, the trimmed mean, the geometric mean, and the harmonic mean for grouped data with an interval width ≠ 1, we make the assumption at all of the values fall at the midpoints of the intervals. When finding percentiles such as q_1, q_2, or q_3, we make the assumption that the values are evenly distributed throughout the intervals. The following steps were followed to obtain the value for q_1:

$$q_1 = p_{25} = \frac{25}{100} \cdot (54 + 1) = 13.75^{th} \text{ value from the bottom}$$

There are 9 values that fall below 65 and 7 values that fall within the interval of 65 to 69. Based on the rules stated in Chapter 3 regarding percentiles for discrete, grouped data with interval widths that are not equal to 1, we assume that these 7 values are distributed within that interval as follows:

Interval	*MP*	*f*	*cf*
69	/	1	16
68	/	1	15
67	///	3	14
66	/	1	11
65	/	1	10

Therefore:

15th observation = 67
14th observation = 67
Difference between 14th and 15th observations = 67 - 67 = 0
Thus: $q_1 = p_{25} = 67 + (.75) \cdot (67 - 67) = 67 + (.75) \cdot (0)$ = 67

The value for q_3 was found as follows:

$$q_3 = p_{75} = \frac{75}{100} \cdot (54 + 1) = 41.25^{th} \text{ value from the bottom}$$

There are 38 values that fall below 80 and 7 values that fall within the interval of 80 to 84. Based on the rules regarding percentiles for discrete, grouped data with interval widths that are not equal to 1, we assume that these values are distributed within that interval as follows:

Interval	*MP*	*f*	*cf*
84	/	1	45
83	/	1	44
82	///	3	43
81	/	1	40
80	/	1	39

Therefore:

42nd observation = 82
41st observation = 82
Difference between 41st and 42nd observations = 82 - 82 = 0
Thus: $q_3 = p_{75} = 82 + (.25) \cdot (82 - 82) = 82 + (.25) \cdot (0)$ = 82

5.

	A.	number of cars	B.	ratio	C.	discrete	D.	sample
	E.	40.0000	F.	40.0000	G.	39.2632	H.	39.5076
	I.	35.0000	J.	43.0000	K.	38.9671	L.	38.6656

6. A. The run chart for these data should appear as follows:

Distances for 40 Drives in Golf:
A Run Chart

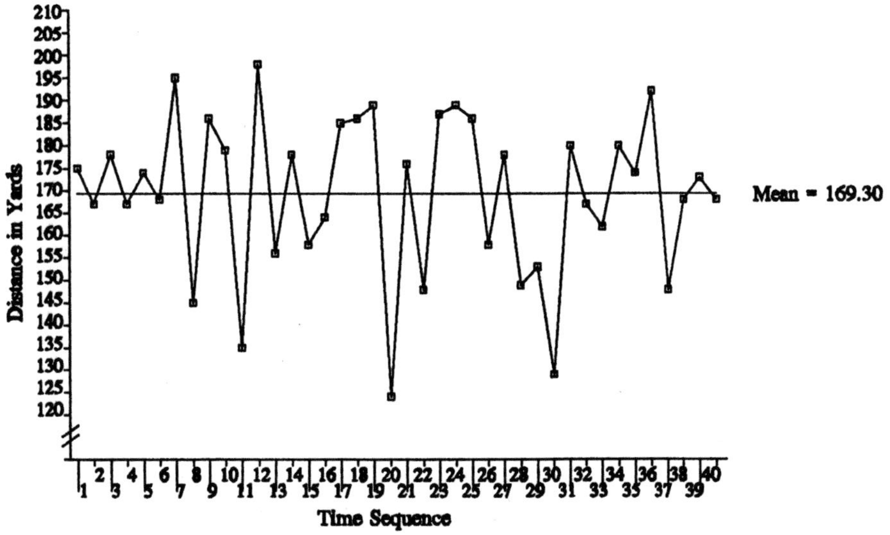

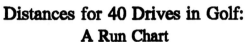

B. The mean distance for these 40 golf balls is 169.30 yards.

C. The center line has been placed on the run chart based on this mean.

D. There does appear to be considerable fluctuation or *variation* about this center line for the golfer. Even without computing any measure of variability, we can look for trends and abnormalities within our data.

E. The run chart suggests that while there is considerable fluctuation, this fluctuation appears to be random in nature. Nowhere do we observe a trend of observations that sequentially appear above the center line or below the center line. We also do not observe an upward or downward trend in any of the sequences. It appears that we can rule out fatigue, since the distances do not decrease over the time period. On the other hand, we do not see an indication of improvement over this period. Since this is a preliminary session before the actual lessons begin, the professional will have an opportunity to view the videotape of the novice over this session. He can look at the position of hands, feet, and other factors during those cases in which the golf balls did not travel a great distance to see if there are any *special causes* of error.

CHAPTER 4
Numerical Quiz
Answers

1. A. $VR =$ .8667
   B. $RG =$ 15.0000
   C. $S\text{-}I\,R =$ 2.0114
   D. $MD =$ 2.3644
   E. $\sigma^2 =$ 8.7803
   F. $\sigma =$ 2.9632
   G. $CV =$ .1025
   H. $SK_P =$ .0012
   I. $SK_Q =$ -.0065
   J. $M_1 =$ 0.0000
   K. $M_2 =$ 8.7803
   L. $M_3 =$ .4760
   M. $M_4 =$ 207.6612
   N. $\gamma_1 =$ .0183
   O. $\gamma_2 =$ -.3064

2. $\mu = 28.9119 + 5 = 33.9119$
   $\sigma = 2.9632$
3. $\mu = (28.9119)\cdot(3) = 86.7357$
   $\sigma = (2.9632)\cdot(3) = 8.8896$
   $M_3 = (.4760)\cdot(3^3) = 12.8520$
   $M_4 = (207.6612)\cdot(3^4) = 16820.5572$
   $\gamma_1 = (M_3)\cdot(c^3) \,/\, (M_2)\cdot(c^2)\cdot(\sqrt{M_2})\cdot(\sqrt{c^2}) = .0183$
   $\gamma_2 = -.3064$
4. $z = 1.7171$
5. Yes. The mean is somewhere between the median and the mode, and the values for SK_P, SK_Q, and γ_1 are not consistent. These peculiarities are probably due to the fact that the interpolation method is used for finding the median, where points have been recorded on a continuous distribution.

CHAPTER 4
Multiple Choice
Answers

1. A	6. C	11. C	16. C
2. E	7. E	12. D	
3. D	8. B	13. A	
4. A	9. A	14. E	
5. C	10. C	15. B	

CHAPTER 4
Written Problems
Answers

1.	A.	0.852	B.	35.000	C.	72.250	D.	84.750
	E.	6.250	F.	6.757	G.	72.849	H.	8.535
2.	A.	0.778	B.	36.000	C.	72.250	D.	83.250
	E.	5.500	F.	6.881	G.	72.583	H.	8.520
3.	A.	112.0912	B.	10.5873	C.	7.9383	D.	6.1250
	E.	-0.2204	F.	49.0000				
4.	A.	121.8946	B.	11.0406	C.	8.6111	D.	7.5000
	E.	-0.1510	F.	54.0000				
5.	A.	22.812	B.	4.776	C.	3.998	D.	4.000
	E.	-0.463	F.	20.000				

6. A. The run chart for these data, with a center line based on a mean of 169.31 yards, and lower and upper lines based on $\overline{X} \pm (2)\cdot s = 169.30 \pm (2)\cdot 17.8458$, should appear as follows:

Distances for 40 Drives in Golf:
A Run Chart

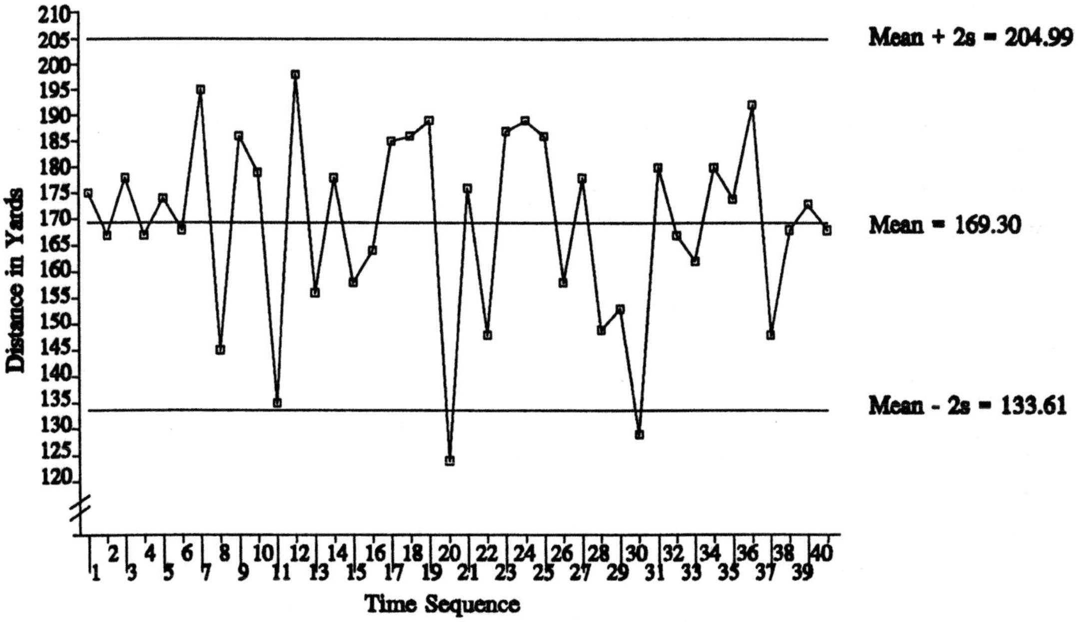

B. The lower 2-sigma line falls at 133.61, and the upper 2-sigma line falls at 204.99. We can now identify abnormalities within our data. We know that at least 75% of the golf balls fall within these two lines. In fact, 38 of the 40 balls (95%) are within these lines.

C. The two exceptions are perhaps outliers which may be the result of special causes rather than common causes. Possibly the balls were defective, the club slipped, the golf tee was placed too low, or the golfer was distracted. If the golfer has taken care to record such conditions as they occur, much can be learned!

7. A. The distribution of performance ratings for upper management given here appears to be negatively skewed, with the majority of employees obtaining very favorable ratings. The mean is to the left of the median and to the left of the mode. Although the underlying distribution of performance may be continuous and ratio scale, this distribution consists of *ratings* of performance. Therefore, the distribution is most likely discrete (since the evaluators could only use integer values of 1, 2, 3, 4, 5, 6, 7, 8, or 9 to rate these upper level managers) and ordinal scale (since the difference between an 8 and a 9 is probably not the same as the difference between a 7 and an 8, etc.).

B. The distribution of performance ratings for production employees given here is bimodal. Eight employees were given ratings of 3, and 8 other employees were given ratings of 8. While the distribution is not symmetric, the skewness is not readily obvious from the graph. The computation of some quantitative measure of skewness would be helpful.

C. The distribution of performance ratings for manufacturing employees given here appears to be somewhat normal. While the distribution is not perfectly symmetric and therefore not perfectly normal, it is quite likely that the supervisor was attempting to conform to the normal distribution while evaluating these employees.

D. The distribution of performance ratings for the entry level employees given here appears to be a rectangular distribution and thus very platykurtic. The distribution is symmetric. It would be quite surprising to find a distribution such as this for the evaluation of employees.

E. Based on this percentile bar, the distribution of weekly salaries for the employees in situation E appears to be positively skewed. The mean is to the right of the median (greater than the median). A comparison of the small distance between P_{25} and P_{50} relative to the large distance between P_{50} and P_{75} also suggests that the distribution is positively skewed. The distribution of weekly salaries is discrete (since employees are paid in monetary quantities that can be counted) and ratio scale (since salary has a true zero).

F. Based on this percentile bar, the distribution of weekly salaries for the employees in situation F appears to be negatively skewed. The mean is to the left of the median (less than the median). A comparison of the large distance between P_{25} and P_{50} relative to the small distance between P_{50} and P_{75} also suggests that the distribution is negatively skewed.

CHAPTER 5
Quick Quiz
Answers

1. 20 (permutations)
2. 1,048,576 or 2^{20} (exponential counting rule)
3. 9.53674316406E13 or 5^{20} (exponential counting rule)
4. A. 28 (combinations)
   B. 6 (combinations)
   C. 16 (multiplication rule)
   D. 6 (combinations)
5. A. 84 (combinations)
   B. 70 (combinations)
6. A. (52!)/(5!)(47!) = 2,598,960
   B. (52!)/(47!) = 311,875,200
   C. (52)(52)(52)(52)(52) = 380,204,032
   D. 40 (with 10 ways of each)
7. (11!) / (2!) (4!) (4!) = 34,650
8. A. .25
   B. .125
   C. .625
   D. .375
9. A. .68
   B. .40
   C. .12
   D. .72
   E. .28
10. A. .40
    B. .10
    C. .46
    D. .60
11. 12
12. 20
13. 4 to 1
14. 2.2451004309E16 (combinations; nothing was stated about order)

CHAPTER 5
Multiple Choice
Answers

1. C	6. C	11. D	16. D	21. E	26. B	31. A
2. B	7. E	12. C	17. D	22. A	27. C	
3. A	8. B	13. A	18. C	23. B	28. D	
4. B	9. C	14. C	19. A	24. E	29. D	
5. E	10. A	15. E	20. D	25. D	30. B	

CHAPTER 5
Written Problems
Answers

1. 64 (the counting rule)
2. 56 (permutations)
3. 28 (combinations)
4. 900,000 (the counting rule)
5. 32 (the counting rule)
6. 12 (the counting rule)
7. 540 (the counting rule)
8. 538,200 (counting rule)
9. A. .4033 or 48/119
   B. .5966 or 71/119
   C. .6974 or 83/119
   D. .1681 or 20/119
   E. .3636 or 20/55
   F. .5625 or 36/64
   G. .1681 or 20/119
   H. .4929 or 35/71
   I. .5833 or 28/48
10. A. .78
    B. 5.50
    C. .50
    D. No, they are dependent.
11. The table is completed as follows:

	A_1	A_2	A_3	
B_1	40	15	5	60
B_2	0	10	30	40
	40	25	35	100

12. .60
13. .60
14. Perhaps. However, they are dependent events even though $P(B_1/A_2) = P(B_1)$.
15. 1.00
16. .75
17. No. They are dependent events.
18. A. 1.00
    B. .00
    C. .60
    D. .40
    E. .14
    F. .86
    G. .40
    H. .00
    I. .15
    J. .10
    K. .05
    L. .30

CHAPTER 6
Quick Quiz
Answers

1. .1587
2. .0668
3. .6827
4. 0
5. .0344
6. .0668
7. 604
8. 336 to 664
9. 567 to ∞
10. 50%
11. -∞ to +433
    and 567 to +∞
12. .1180
13. 3085
14. 7500

CHAPTER 6
Multiple Choice
Answers

1. D	6. B	11. C	16. A
2. A	7. D	12. B	17. E
3. A	8. C	13. E	18. C
4. E	9. E	14. D	
5. A	10. A	15. A	

CHAPTER 6
Written Problems
Answers

1. 0	10. .3085
2. 200000	11. .4796
3. 0	12. .5204
4. 2000	13. .1151
5. -0.5	14. 0
6. 1.7	15. .2743
7. 78.4	16. .6319
8. 57.5	17. 76.7
9. .2119	18. 86.4

CHAPTER 7
Quick Quiz
Answers

1. A. .1029 (binomial)
   B. .8298 (binomial)
   C. .1702 (binomial)
   D. .0059 (binomial)
2. A. .0440 (binomial)
   B. .2501 (binomial)
   C. .8702 (binomial)
   D. .0000 (binomial)
3. .1646 (binomial)
4. A. .00000342 (by calculations; using the table, approximately .0000)
   B. .000000 (binomial)
   C. .4148 (binomial)
   D. .0039 (binomial)
5. A. $\mu = np = 5$
   B. $\sigma = \sqrt{npq} = 1.936$
6. .0059 (based on binomial distribution)
7. .0059 (based on normal approximation, rounding the *z*-values to two decimal places, and using *z*-table in Appendix C)
8. Binomial gives the most precise answer. The normal approximation gives an excellent approximation in this example.
9. A. .1190 (binomial distribution)
   B. .1210 (normal approximation)
10. .0579 (binomial distribution)
11. .0542 (normal approximation)
12. .1719
13. .0009
14. A. .3770
    B. .0917
    C. .8555
15. A. .9672
    B. .0001
    C. .9988
16. A. .9753
    B. .9751
    C. No, as (620)(.00352) is too small
17. A. .000 (to 3 decimals using tables; .0003 to 4 decimals using equation)
    B. .092
    C. .191
    D. .809
18. A. .273
    B. .989
    C. .011
    D. .373
19. A. .135
    B. .036
    C. .045 (where $\lambda = (2)(10) = 20$)
    D. .157 (where $\lambda = (2)(10) = 20$)

20. A. The 2-by-2 contingency table as follows:

	Negative Evaluations	*Positive Evaluations*	
In the Sample	5	5	10
Not in the Sample	0	40	40
	5	45	50

    B. .0001
    C. This is not possible, since only 5 of the 50 employees received negative evaluations.
    D. .3106

CHAPTER 7
Multiple Choice
Answers

1. E	6. B	11. E	16. C	21. B	26. D
2. C	7. B	12. B	17. C	22. A	27. C
3. C	8. A	13. B	18. D	23. B	
4. A	9. B	14. C	19. B	24. E	
5. C	10. B	15. B	20. A	25. E	

CHAPTER 8
Multiple Choice
Answers

1. C	6. A	11. B	16. C	21. E	26. B
2. B	7. C	12. A	17. A	22. B	27. E
3. E	8. B	13. B	18. C	23. C	
4. E	9. A	14. B	19. E	24. E	
5. A	10. D	15. B	20. B	25. B	

CHAPTER 8
Detailed Answers to Multiple Choice Flowchart Problems

1. We want to compare the central tendencies of the two groups, so we turn to flowchart 1. We have only one variable of interest (Religiosity scores), and it is to be viewed as ordinal. We now turn to flowchart 13. We have only one independent variable (smokers vs. nonsmokers); the variable of interest is ordinal; we are not comparing a sample to a population; we have two samples; and, our two samples are independent of one another. If we have satisfied the assumptions for the Mann-Whitney U, it is an appropriate test to use. Otherwise, we can use the two-sample median test.

2. In this example, our variable of interest is the height of the corn. The variable that we are examining in regard to its impact upon the criterion variable is the quantity of fertilizer used. This latter variable is what we typically call our independent, or predictor variable. We could think of this variable as a classification variable, but we now will have as many categories as we have quantities of fertilizer. We have not limited these quantities to certain groupings but have allowed the amount of fertilizer used to vary throughout the continuous distribution. Therefore, the term "classification variable" seems inappropriate here. As usual, we begin with ***Start***. We are not comparing central tendencies, since we do not have subdivisions or groups from which to draw central tendencies. We are not interested in comparing variabilities, either. We are interested in determining the correlation between the two variables, so we turn to flowchart 8. We do not have more than two variables; both of our variables are continuous; and both of our variables are at least interval scale. Therefore, we can use the Pearson product-moment correlation coefficient to analyze the relationship between height and amount of fertilizer.

3. As in problem 2, we begin with ***Start***, do not want to compare central tendencies, do not want to compare variabilities, but do want to determine the correlation between height (the criterion variable) and fertilizer, depth, and density (independent or predictor variables). We turn to flowchart 8, which immediately asks us if we have more than two variables. Our answer is yes, as we actually have four variables; therefore, we turn to flowchart 10. We only have one criterion variable (height); our criterion variable is at least interval; and all of our independent variables are at least interval. Thus, we can use a multiple regression computer program to determine the multiple correlation between the predictor variables and the criterion variable.

4. Beginning with ***Start***, we turn to flowchart 5 since we are wanting to compare variabilities. We have only one variable of interest (diameter), which is greater than nominal and greater than ordinal. We are not comparing one sample vs. one population, and we are not comparing two samples or paired data. We have three or more samples and therefore can choose between the Bartlett chi-square test for homogeneity of variance and the Hartley F_{MAX} test.

5. Beginning with ***Start***, we turn to flowchart 1 since we are wanting to compare central tendencies. We have only one variable of interest (diameter), and it is at least interval scale. We do not have only one sample, and we do not have only two samples. Thus, we turn to flowchart 3. We have only one variable of interest; we do not have repeated measures on the variable of interest or any matched samples; we have only one classification variable; we do not have any concomitant variables; and, our four samples are independent of one another. If we feel that the necessary assumptions have been satisfied for it, we can use one-way analysis of variance. Otherwise, we can attempt to modify our data and use one-way ANOVA, or we can use the Kruskal-Wallis test, a nonparametric statistic.

6. In this example, we have no criterion variable. Rather, the variables can all be viewed as independent variables. Since we are interested in collapsing objects (i.e., executives) into subsets, we immediately advance from ***Start*** to the diamond that states "collapsing of variables or objects into subsets or dimensions." We then turn to flowchart 12. We are interested in an analysis based on the clustering of objects into subgroups, and thus will be doing some form of profile analysis. We have not predetermined the classification of our groups in any way, and we are not interested in locating these executives on any specified dimensions. Consequently, we can use one of a number of cluster analysis techniques, such as hierarchical grouping. (Only variables we are willing to treat as at least interval level and/or variables that are nominal but dichotomous should be used with most of these techniques. The remaining variables may need to be modified or eliminated from the analysis.)

7. Beginning with ***Start***, we turn to flowchart 1 since we are wanting to compare central tendencies. We have only one variable of interest (softness of skin), which was measured by a judgmental rating scale; therefore, it should probably be considered as ordinal scale. We turn to flowchart 13. We have one classification variable (type of product used), which is ordinal level. We are not comparing a sample vs. a population, but we are comparing paired data (left arms with right arms of the same person). It follows that the samples are not independent of one another. We can now use the Wilcoxon matched-pairs sign test if we have

satisfied the necessary assumptions associated with it, or we can use the sign test which is based on the binomial.

8. We can immediately advance from ***Start*** to the diamond that states "collapsing of variables or objects into subsets or dimensions," since we are interested in collapsing the 20 variables into subsets of dimensions. We turn to flowchart 12. We are not interested in clustering of *objects* into subgroups; rather, we are interested in clustering of *variables* into subsets. We have determined that all variables are at least interval scale, so we can perform a factor analysis to examine the dimensions of the instrument.

9. Beginning with ***Start***, we turn to flowchart 5 since we are wanting to compare variabilities. We have only one variable of interest (perception scores). The perception scores have been determined to be greater than nominal scale but not greater than ordinal scale. Therefore, we have several techniques that we may wish to examine in regard to their appropriateness: the Siegel-Tukey test, Freund-Ansari test, Mood test, or the Westenberg interquartile range test.

10. For this example, the variable of interest (i.e., criterion variable) is the number of new customers secured over the past 120 days. We enter the flowcharts at ***Start***. Since we are interested in comparing central tendencies, we turn to flowchart 1. There is only one variable of interest (number of new customers), and this criterion variable is at least interval scale. We do not have only one sample, but we do have only two samples (males and females). Thus, we turn to flowchart 2. The population variances from which the samples were drawn are unknown, and we do not have independent samples (since we have matched each male with a comparable female). Therefore, we can use the dependent *t*-test if we feel that the assumptions for this test have been reasonably satisfied. Otherwise, we can attempt to modify our data through some nonlinear transformations or other adjustments and return to the dependent *t*-test; or we can consider nonparametric statistical tests, such as the Wilcoxon matched pairs sign test or just the sign test itself.

11. We immediately advance from ***Start*** to the diamond that states "collapsing of variables or objects into subsets or dimensions," since we are interested in collapsing the 30 items into subsets of dimensions. Thus, we turn to flowchart 12. This time we are not interested in clustering of *objects* into subgroups; rather, we are interested in clustering of *variables* into subsets. If we are willing to assume that the items are at least interval level, we can perform a factor analysis to examine the dimensions of the instrument.

12. We know that we want to determine a correlation, so we turn directly from ***Start*** to flowchart 8. We have two variables. The number of customers entering the stores is discrete, and having filed for bankruptcy or not is also discrete. Therefore, we turn to flowchart 9. Bankruptcy is a dichotomous (i.e., two category) variable, while the number of customers is not. We therefore have one dichotomous variable and one discrete variable with at least three categories. The dichotomous variable is not at least ordinal, and the other variable is at least interval. The dichotomous variable (bankruptcy) is naturally dichotomous since we have not

artificially forced the stores into either one of the two categories. Therefore, we can use the point-biserial correlation coefficient.

13. Beginning with ***Start***, we know that we are comparing averages so we turn to flowchart 1. We have one variable of interest (salary increases), and our variable of interest yields at least interval level data. We do not have only one sample, or only two samples, so we turn to flowchart 3. Again, we have only one variable of interest. We do not have repeated measures or matched samples. We do not have only one classification variable; instead we have two classification variables: gender and ethnic orientation. We are not using any concomitant variables, since the compensation analyst has already made sure that the employees in the study have approximately the same amount of experience, seniority with the company, and amount of education. If all of our assumptions are satisfied for a two-way analysis of variance, this is our preferred test. Otherwise, we will consider modifying our data or using the Friedman test.

14. As we are testing for statistical process control, we immediately turn to flowchart 14. We have only one variable of interest (scrapped parts), our values are not based on individual observations, as we have recorded daily subgroup statistics over a period of time. Thus, the data follow a sequential pattern. We do not have variable data, as we are not measuring the degree to which a part is bad; we only know whether the part is scrapped or not. Therefore, we have attribute data. We are examining the number of nonconforming parts per subgroup. We do not have a constant sample size from subgroup to subgroup, because the number of parts produced varies from day to day. Consequently, we should consider using a p-chart.

CHAPTER 8
Written Problems

1. Hypothesis Testing: Pregnancy Test

   A. Tamara is not pregnant.

   B. Tamara is pregnant.

   C. See the table on the next page:

DECISION

STATE OF NATURE		FAIL TO REJECT H_0	REJECT H_0	
	H_0 TRUE	Test does not indicate pregnancy when the person is not pregnant.	Test indicates pregnancy when the person is not pregnant.	The person is not pregnant.
	H_0 FALSE	Test does not indicate pregnancy when the person is pregnant.	Test indicates pregnancy when the person is pregnant.	The person is pregnant.
		Do not assume pregnancy.	Assume pregnancy.	

D. Deciding that she is pregnant when she is not pregnant.

E. Deciding that she is not pregnant when she is pregnant.

F. Eventually suffering a major disappointment, telling friends and relatives that she is pregnant, buying baby furniture and baby clothes, and not going on the cruise.

G. Feeling an immediate disappointment, taking the cruise by using the savings, having no savings for baby furniture and baby clothes that are now needed, suffering morning sickness while on the six-month cruise.

H. Many couples would conclude that a Type I Error would be the more serious error in this situation, due to the eventual major disappointment that will occur. With a Type II Error, the couple will eventually discover that their wish has come true. However, either error can be devastating to the couple.

2. Hypothesis Testing: Medical Situation

   A. The drug does not work.

   B. The drug works.

   C. See the table below:

DECISION

STATE OF NATURE	FAIL TO REJECT H_0	REJECT H_0	
H_0 TRUE	CORRECT DECISION Live for 5 more years!	TYPE I ERROR: Die immediately!	The drug does not work.
H_0 FALSE	TYPE II ERROR: Miss out on the cure!	CORRECT DECISION: Illness is cured!	The drug works.
	Do not take the drug.	Take the drug.	

   D. Deciding that the drug will work when the drug does not work.

   E. Deciding that the drug will not work when the drug does work.

   F. Dying immediately instead of living for another 5 years with minimal pain.

   G. Missing out on the cure and dying at the end of 5 years.

   H. Again, this is debatable. Most people would consider that immediate death is a more serious error than missing out on the eventual cure.

3. Hypothesis Testing: Manufacturing Situation

A. The machinery does not work.

B. The machinery works.

C. See the table below:

DECISION

STATE OF NATURE		FAIL TO REJECT H_0	REJECT H_0	
	H_0 TRUE	CORRECT DECISION: Good Move (Net \$30)	TYPE I ERROR: Wasted \$10 M (Net \$20 M)	The machinery does not work.
	H_0 FALSE	TYPE II ERROR: Missed Out (Market Share) (Net \$30 M)	CORRECT DECISION: Good Move (Net \$50 M)	The machinery works.
		Do not buy the machinery.	Buy the machinery.	

D. Deciding that the machinery will work when the machinery does not work.

E. Deciding that the machinery will not work when the machinery does work.

F. Wasting \$10 million of the company's money to buy machinery that does not work. The net profit will be \$20 million.

G. Not spending \$10 million of the company's money. The net profit will be \$30 million for the current year, but the company has missed out on a good deal and an opportunity for additional profit (opportunity loss). Further, suppose that the machinery works and the competition has decided to purchase it; your company may eventually lose market share to the competition.

H. Again, this is debatable. You can get fired for wasting \$10 million of the company's money, but you can also get fired for missing out on the opportunity to make an additional profit and for losing market share. The seriousness of the consequences depends on your company's philosophy, profitability, aggressiveness, and cash flow.

99% 2.58
95% 1.96

CHAPTER 9
Quick Quiz
Answers

1. $237.1 \le \overline{X} \le 262.9$
2. $240.2 \le \overline{X} \le 259.8$
3. $241.8 \le \overline{X} \le 258.2$
4. $242.1 \le \mu \le 267.9$
5. $245.2 \le \mu \le 264.8$
6. Since 2.68 is ≤ 2.831, the sample mean is not considered "unlikely."
7. $76.8958 \le \mu \le 83.1042$
8. All calculations are correct.
9. $t = -2.0755$; critical $t = \pm 2.365$; fail to reject H_0.
10. $t = -2.0755$; critical $t = -1.895$; reject H_0.
11. $t = 2.4214$; critical $t = 1.895$; reject H_0.
12. $4.8848 \le \mu \le 25.115$
13. $8.1631 \le \mu \le 21.8369$
14. $z = -5.00$ (which is a very unlikely z-value)
15. $55.1 \le \mu \le 64.9$
16. With $df = 99$, $35.0395 \le \mu \le 44.9605$
17. .3714
18. .2460
19. $t = 8.35$; reject H_0.
20. $t = -20.327$; reject H_0.

21. $20.3624 \leq \mu_A \leq 21.8376$ (with $df = 94$).

22. $21.5142 \leq \mu_B \leq 22.4858$ (with $df = 160$).

23. The sample means and the sample medians in both groups are very close, giving some intuitive support to the notion that the distributions are fairly symmetric. This gives some confidence to the notion of normality.

24. .3346

CHAPTER 9
Multiple Choice
Answers

1. E	6. C	11. E	16. B
2. B	7. B	12. B	17. C
3. D	8. D	13. D	18. D
4. C	9. A	14. B	
5. A	10. E	15. A	

CHAPTER 9
Written Problems
Answers

1. A. μ
   B. Since alpha has not been stated, we can arbitrarily select any value desired. For the following answers, assume that alpha has been set at .05. The test will be one-directional, as the motivated hypothesis is that the wealthier districts sell less than the other districts.
   C. H_0: $\mu \geq 22.3$
   D. H_A: $\mu < 22.3$
   E. One-sample *z*-test
   F. $z = -5.2191$
   G. Reject the null hypothesis, since the computed value for *z* (-5.2191) is to the left of the critical value of *z* (-1.645). Thus, the wealthier districts appear to have bought significantly fewer potted plants from groceries serviced by the nursery than other districts over Mother's Day.
   H. Since the sample size is 30, we can often assume that the central limit theorem has been satisfied.

2. A. μ
   B. The test is non-directional (i.e., two-tailed), since nothing has been stated as to whether the length might be expected to systematically increase or decrease.
   C. H_0: $\mu = 2.00$
   D. H_A: $\mu \neq 2.00$

E. One-sample t-test
F. $t = .56995$
G. Fail to reject the null hypothesis, since the computed value for t (.56995) is not beyond the critical value of t (±2.064). The average length of the nails is not significantly different than 2.00, with alpha at .05.
H. Although the sample size is only 25, we have been told that the distribution of nails prior to repairs was considered normal. Therefore, we should be able to assume that the central limit theorem has been satisfied.

3. A. μ
B. The test is one-tailed, since they are wanting to determine whether the number of nonconformities has been reduced.
C. H_0: $\mu \geq 25$
D. H_A: $\mu < 25$
E. One-sample t-test
F. $t = -6.1069$
G. Alpha has been set at $\alpha = .05$. Comparing the sample mean (19.08) to the expected mean under the null hypothesis (25), we reject the null. The computed value for t (-6.1069) is to the left of the critical value of t (-1.711). The average number of nonconformities per day appears to have been significantly reduced.
H. Since the sample size is only 25 and since we have not been told that the population distribution is considered normal, we should have some cautions regarding the central limit theorem.

4. A. μ_D, where ***D***ifferences = ***B***efore - ***A***fter
B. The test is one-tailed, since her motivated (alternative) hypothesis was that the prices would drop. That is, she believes that the ***B***efore prices will be greater than the ***A***fter prices.
C. H_0: $\mu_D \leq 0$
D. H_A: $\mu_D > 0$
E. One-sample t-test
F. $t = 5.4004$
G. Alpha has been set at .05. Comparing the observed differences between the pairs of sample values (2.6875) to the expected differences between the pairs of values under the null hypothesis (0) and then dividing by the standard error term (.4977, rounded), we obtain a t-value of 5.4004; therefore, we reject the null. The computed t-value (5.4004) is to the right of the critical t-value (1.753). The average difference in her portfolio of stocks seems to support her motivated hypothesis that the announcement of a potentially explosive political appointment did result in a significant drop in the prices for the population of stocks.
H. Since the sample size is only 16 and since we have not been told that the population distribution of is considered normal, we should have some cautions regarding the central limit theorem.

CHAPTER 10
Quick Quiz
Answers

1. The variable of interest is "remote control station-changing behavior."

2. We have a ratio scale for the number of times a person "flips through the channels."

3. The classification variable is "gender."

4. There are two categories for gender: male and female.

5. The population variances and standard deviations are unknown.

6. Since no effort has been made to match the groups in any way and since there are no repeated measures, we conclude that the two groups are independent.

7. When testing for homogeneity of variance:

   A. Use the *F*-test for homogeneity of variance.
   B. Use $F = 1.72$ as the critical value for the *F*-test for homogeneity of variance. Since this is a two-tailed test with alpha = .05, the critical *F*-value was based on the .025 portion of the *F*-table.
   C. The computed value is $F = 1.5540$.
   D. We should fail to reject the null hypothesis. We have no statistical reason to doubt that we have homogeneity of variance.

8. The sample sizes are both greater than 30, which gives support to the notion that the central limit theorem has been satisfied. Since the sample mean for the first group is equal to the sample median for the first group and since the sample mean for the second group is equal to the sample median for the second group, we also know that the two samples may be reasonably symmetric. This would provide minor support that the populations may be normal.

9. A two-sample independent *t*-test is appropriate for analyzing these data.

10. The null hypothesis is stated as follows: H_0: $\mu_M = \mu_F$
    The alternative hypothesis is stated as follows: H_A: $\mu_M \neq \mu_F$

11. Since we have satisfied the assumption of homogeneity of variance and since the sample sizes are unequal, the pooled standard error of the differences should be used.

12. The pooled standard error of the differences is equal to 1.5706.

13. The computed value for the two-sample independent *t*-test is 5.7302.

14. There are 111 degrees of freedom for this two-sample independent *t*-test.

15. The critical value for the two-sample independent *t*-test is 1.982, with $df = 111$ in the *t*-table.

16. We should reject the null hypothesis. It appears that males "flip the channels" more frequently than females, based on the two samples for this study. Of course, we must realize that there are limitations related to the study that may require additional analysis, including sample size, time of day, programs available, age, and many other factors.

CHAPTER 10
Multiple Choice
Answers

1. A	11. A	21. D	31. D
2. B	12. B	22. B	32. C
3. D	13. D	23. B	33. A
4. E	14. E	24. D	34. B
5. B	15. B	25. C	
6. B	16. B	26. A	
7. A	17. E	27. C	
8. B	18. E	28. B	
9. C	19. C	29. A	
10. D	20. B	30. E	

CHAPTER 10
Written Problems
Answers

1. A. Ratio
   B. Two-sample independent *z*-test
   C. Yes, as the population sizes are finite and known.
   D. H_0: $\mu_1 = \mu_2$ and H_A: $\mu_1 \neq \mu_2$
   E. ±1.96
   F. The computed value is $z = -5.52$. Reject the null hypothesis, since this computed value for the two-sample independent *z*-test falls in the region of rejection. The computed value was obtained as follows:

$$z = \frac{(\overline{X}_1 - \overline{X}_2) - (\mu_1 - \mu_2)}{\sqrt{\left[\left(\frac{\sigma_1^2}{n_1}\right) \cdot \left(\frac{N_1 - n_1}{N_1 - 1}\right)\right] + \left[\left(\frac{\sigma_2^2}{n_2}\right) \cdot \left(\frac{N_2 - n_2}{N_2 - 1}\right)\right]}}$$

$$= \frac{(26 - 30) - (0)}{\sqrt{\left[\left(\frac{2.9631^2}{31}\right) \cdot \left(\frac{420 - 31}{420 - 1}\right)\right] + \left[\left(\frac{2.9631^2}{31}\right) \cdot \left(\frac{420 - 31}{420 - 1}\right)\right]}}$$

$$= -5.52$$

2. A. μ_1 vs. μ_2
   B. The test is non-directional (two-tailed), since nothing has been stated as to whether one form of advertisement is expected to be better than the other.
   C. H_0: $\mu_1 = \mu_2$
   D. H_A: $\mu_1 \neq \mu_2$
   E. Two-sample independent *t*-test
   F. $t = -8.4580$
   G. Reject the null hypothesis, since the computed value for $t = -8.4580$ falls beyond the critical value of $t\ (60) = \pm 2.660$. The number of walk-in customers after newspaper advertisements seems to be less than the number of walk-in customers after radio advertisements, based on these sample data.

3. A. μ_1 vs. μ_2
   B. The test is one-directional, as the motivated hypothesis is that people who read magazine 1 are more liberal than people who read magazine 2.
   C. H_0: $\mu_1 \leq \mu_2$
   D. H_A: $\mu_1 > \mu_2$
   E. Two-sample independent *t*-test
   F. $t = 2.2702$
   G. Reject the null hypothesis, since the computed value for $t = 2.2702$ is to the right of the critical value of $t\ (86) = 1.663$. Those who read magazine 1 appear to be more liberal than those who read magazine 2, based on the data collected.

4. A. μ_1 vs. μ_2
   B. The motivated hypothesis is that the individuals who use Company A's product will have less blemishes than the individuals who use Company B's product. Thus, the test is one-directional.
   C. H_0: $\mu_A \geq \mu_B$
   D. H_A: $\mu_A < \mu_B$
   E. Dependent *t*-test since the data consist of matched-pairs of twins.
   F. $t = -8.8536$ ($r = .9657$)
   G. Reject the null hypothesis, since the computed value for $t = -8.8536$ is to the left of the critical value of $t\ (17) = -2.567$. The treatment seems to have reduced the number of blemishes.

CHAPTER 11
Multiple Choice
Answers

1. C	6. B	11. C
2. E	7. C	12. E
3. A	8. A	13. C
4. C	9. E	14. D
5. D	10. C	15. E

CHAPTER 11
Written Problems
Answers

I. A. Diameters of clip adapters
   B. Ratio level
   C. Chi-square test for comparing a sample variance to a population variance
   D. 8.9065 and 32.8523
   E. 39.4586
   F. Reject the null hypothesis
   G. $.000048 \leq \sigma^2 \leq .000177$
   H. $.0069 \leq \sigma \leq .0133$

II. A. Number of sales
   B. Ratio level
   C. Type of sales approach
   D. No
   E. Independent
   F. The sample sizes are both at least 30. The skewness for each group appears to be within acceptable limits, but the kurtosis for the second group is questionable. With relatively small sample sizes (including sample sizes ≥ n), the tests for skewness and kurtosis are not very reliable. The researcher must hope the parent populations are reasonably normally distributed or may want to consider using some less sophisticated test.
   G. 1. Two-sample independent t-test
      2. -2.002 and + 2.002
      3. .3245
      4. Fail to reject the null hypothesis.
   H. 1. F-test for homogeneity of variance
      2. .48 and 2.10 (with $\alpha \div 2 = .05 \div 2 = .025$ in each tail)
      3. .5027 and 1.98908
      4. Fail to reject the null hypothesis. Remember that the critical values were from the .025 section of the F-table. Therefore, the area in the combined tails is .05. The table provides for a .025 section, allowing the researcher to preserve .05 in the combined tails.

III. 1. Bartlett's χ^2 test for homogeneity of variance
2. 7.8147
3. .7977
4. Fail to reject the null hypothesis

IV. 1. Dependent t-test for homogeneity of variance
2. -2.074 and +2.074
3. 1.1996
4. Fail to reject the null hypothesis

CHAPTER 12
Quick Quiz
Answers

Question 1. The following values should be obtained:

Group	*n*	$\overline{X}$	*s*	s^2	$\Sigma (X - \overline{X})^2$
1	6	25.0000	1.7889	3.2000	16.0000
2	4	30.0000	1.8257	3.3333	10.0000
3	5	27.0000	1.0000	1.0000	4.0000
Total	15	27.0000	2.5355	6.4286	90.0000

Question 2. The following ANOVA table should be completed:

Source of Variation	*df*	*SS*	*MS*	*F*	*Critical F*
Among	2	60.0000	30.0000	12.0000	3.89
Within	12	30.0000	2.5000		
Total	14	90.0000			

Question 3. The null and alternative hypotheses are formally stated as follows:

H_0: $\mu_1 = \mu_2 = \mu_3$

H_A: Not all μ values are equal

Question 4. The following decision is made regarding the null hypothesis:

Decision: Reject H_0

Question 5. Give an "English" interpretation of the results:

Since the computed omnibus *F*-value is greater than the critical F-value, we reject the null hypothesis. Thus, we conclude that at least two of the sales districts have a different number of average sales.

Question 6. Roughly draw a picture of the *F*-distribution. Include the following values in the picture: Critical *F*-value, region of rejection, region of fail to reject, computed *F*-value.

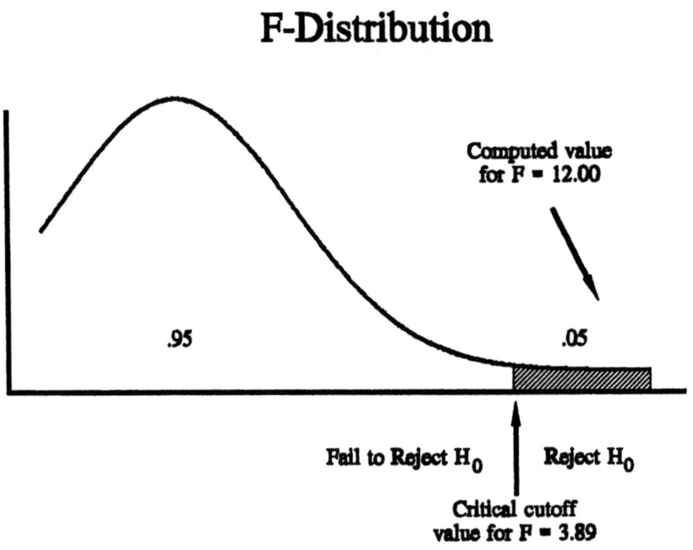

Question 7. Use a Scheffé post-comparison *F*-test to examine differences between all possible combinations of Districts, taken two at a time. Give the null hypotheses, the computed Scheffé *F*-values, the critical Scheffé *F*-value, and the decision (either reject or fail to reject). These values and decisions are shown in the following table:

Scheffé Decision Table

Null Hypothesis	*Computed Scheffé F*	*Critical Scheffé F*	*Decision*
H_0: $\mu_1 = \mu_2$	24.0000	7.78	Reject H_0
H_0: $\mu_1 = \mu_3$	4.3636	7.78	Fail to reject H_0
H_0: $\mu_2 = \mu_3$	8.0000	7.78	Reject H_0

CHAPTER 12
Multiple Choice
Answers

1. B	11. C	21. A
2. E	12. B	22. D
3. E	13. D	23. D
4. C	14. E	24. C
5. E	15. D	25. E
6. C	16. A	
7. E	17. C	
8. E	18. C	
9. B	19. B	
10. D	20. E	

CHAPTER 12
Written Problems
Answers

1. μ_1 vs. μ_2 vs. μ_3 vs. μ_4

2. The test is non-directional, since nothing has been stated as to whether any particular manufacturer attracts higher or lower income earners than another manufacturer.

3. H_0: $\mu_1 = \mu_2 = \mu_3 = \mu_4$

4. H_A: At least two μ values are not equal.

5. One-way analysis of variance, with the related *F*-test.

6. $F = 33.406$

7. Reject the null hypothesis, as the computed value of *F* (33.406) is greater than the critical value of *F* (3.01). It would appear that customers of manufacturer C have significantly greater incomes than those of manufacturer D. Other such comparisons are possible, using post-comparison tests such as the Scheffé or other tests.

8. Fail to reject the null hypothesis for homogeneity of variance. The assumption of homogeneity of variance for the one-way analysis of variance is satisfactory; thus, the omnibus *F*-test appears to be appropriate, based on this particular assumption.

9. 9.03

10. 9.263, 18.904, 24.557, 52.139, 2.604, and 89.226, respectively, for 1 vs. 2, 1 vs. 3, 1. vs. 4, 2 vs. 3, 2 vs. 4, and 3 vs. 4.

11. 78.71

12. Reject the null hypotheses for all except when comparing group 2 vs. 4.

CHAPTER 13
Quick Quiz
Answers

Question 1.

Summary Statistics

Source	*n*	$\overline{X}$	*s*	s^2	$\Sigma(X - \overline{X})^2$
Cell 1,1	3	9.00	1.0000	1.0000	2.0000
Cell 1,2	3	16.00	1.0000	1.0000	2.0000
Cell 1,3	3	14.00	2.0000	4.0000	8.0000
Cell 2,1	3	12.00	2.0000	4.0000	8.0000
Cell 2,2	3	14.00	1.0000	1.0000	2.0000
Cell 2,3	3	14.00	2.0000	4.0000	8.0000
Row 1	9	13.00	3.3541	11.2500	90.0000
Row 2	9	13.33	1.8028	3.2501	26.0000
Column 1	6	10.50	2.1679	4.6998	23.4990
Column 2	6	15.00	1.4142	2.0000	10.0000
Column 3	6	14.00	1.7889	3.2002	16.0010
Total	18	13.17	2.6178	6.8529	116.5000

Question 2.

Analysis of Variance Table

Source of Variation	*df*	*SS*	*MS*	*F-Value*	*Critical F*
Cells	5	86.5000	17.3000	6.9200	3.11
Rows (Location)	1	.5000	.5000	.2000	4.75
Columns (Make)	2	67.0000	33.5000	13.4000	3.89
Interaction	2	19.0000	9.5000	3.8000	3.89
Within	12	30.0000	2.5000		
Total	17	116.5000			

Question 3.

Cells: H_0: $\mu_{11} = \mu_{12} = \mu_{13} = \mu_{21} = \mu_{22} = \mu_{23}$

Interaction: H_0: $\mu_{ij} - \mu_{i.} - \mu_{.j} + \mu_{t} = 0$

Rows: H_0: $\mu_{1.} = \mu_{2.}$

Columns: H_0: $\mu_{.1} = \mu_{.2} = \mu_{.3}$

Question 4.

Hypothesis for cells: reject

Hypothesis for interaction: fail to reject

Hypothesis for rows: fail to reject

Hypothesis for columns: reject

Question 5.

Not all cell means are equal. Since there is no significant interaction (at $\alpha = .05$), we test for rows and columns. There are no significant differences between the row means, but there are significant differences among the column means. During the time period of interest, there apparently were fewer new Mercury dealerships opening than Chrysler or Buick dealerships.

CHAPTER 13
Multiple Choice
Answers

1. B	6. D	11. C	16. D	21. E
2. C	7. B	12. A	17. D	
3. A	8. B	13. B	18. E	
4. D	9. B	14. D	19. B	
5. E	10. E	15. E	20. D	

CHAPTER 13
Written Problems
Answers

Part I.

A. ANOVA Table

ANOVA Table

Source of Variation	*df*	*SS*	*MS*	*Computed F*	*Critical F*
Cells	3	2024.6375	674.8792	34.9500	2.74
Rows	1	2010.0125	2010.0125	104.0925	3.98
Columns	1	9.1125	9.1125	0.4719	3.98
Interaction	1	5.5125	5.5125	0.2855	3.98
Within	76	1467.5500	19.3099		
Total	79	3492.1875			

B. F (3, 60) = 2.76, reject the null hypothesis. Thus, not all cell means are equal.

C. F (1, 60) = 4.00, fail to reject the null hypothesis. Thus, there is not a significant amount of interaction.

D. Since there is no significant interaction, it is now appropriate to test for main effects. We should evaluate the F-values for columns and for rows.

E. The F-tests for cells and for rows are significant. Therefore, we conclude that high commitment scores are related to employee perceptions in regard to whether the organization fits the Systems 4 description.

Part II.

Two-Way ANOVA: Fixed Model

Source of Variation	*df*	*SS*	*MS*	*Computed F*	*Critical F*
Cells	8	2061.1112	257.64	51.53	2.21
Rows	2	404.0890	202.04	40.41	3.26
Columns	2	533.9891	266.99	53.40	3.26
Interaction	4	1123.0331	280.75	56.15	2.63
Within	36	180.0000	5.00		
Total	44	2241.1112			

Part III

Two-Way ANOVA: Fixed Model

Source of Variation	*df*	*SS*	*MS*	*Computed F*	*Critical F*
Cells	5	478.684	95.74	66.49	3.11
Rows	1	43.580	43.58	30.26	4.75
Columns	2	310.373	155.19	107.77	3.89
Interaction	2	124.731	62.38	43.31	3.89
Within	12	17.330	1.44		
Total	17	496.014			

Part IV.
Treatment by Subjects Design

Source of Variation	*df*	*SS*	*MS*	*Computed F*	*Critical F*
Rows	9	13569.89	1507.76	11.72	2.46
Columns	2	35.00	17.50	0.14	3.55
Interaction	18	2315.00	128.61		
Total	29	15919.87			

Part V.A.
Summary Statistics

Group	*n*	$\overline{X}$	*s*	s^2	$\Sigma (X - \overline{X})^2$
Cell 1, 1	4	15.50	3.8730	15.0001	45.0000
Cell 1, 2	4	18.75	1.7078	2.9166	8.7497
Cell 1, 3	4	13.75	3.0957	9.5834	28.7501
Cell 2, 1	4	17.00	1.8257	3.3332	9.9995
Cell 2, 2	4	18.25	4.0311	16.2498	48.7493
Cell 2, 3	4	14.25	3.0957	9.5834	28.7501
Row 1	12	16.00	3.4902	12.1815	133.9965
Row 2	12	16.50	3.3166	10.9998	120.9982
Column 1	8	16.25	2.9155	8.5001	59.5010
Column 2	8	18.50	2.8785	8.2858	58.0003
Column 3	8	14.00	2.8785	8.2858	58.0003
Total	24	16.25	3.3395	11.1523	256.5020

Part V.B.

2-by-3 Layout

	Condition I	*Condition II*	*Condition III*	*Row Totals*
Supplier A	n_{11} = 4 $\overline{X}_{11}$ = 15.50 s_{11} = 3.8730	n_{12} = 4 $\overline{X}_{12}$ = 18.75 s_{12} = 1.7078	n_{13} = 4 $\overline{X}_{13}$ = 13.75 s_{13} = 3.0957	$n_{1.}$ = 12 $\overline{X}_{1.}$ = 16.00 $s_{1.}$ = 3.4902
Supplier B	n_{21} = 4 $\overline{X}_{21}$ = 17.00 s_{21} = 1.8257	n_{22} = 4 $\overline{X}_{22}$ = 18.25 s_{22} = 4.0311	n_{23} = 4 $\overline{X}_{23}$ = 14.25 s_{23} = 3.0957	$n_{2.}$ = 12 $\overline{X}_{2.}$ = 16.50 $s_{2.}$ = 3.3166
Column Totals	$n_{.1}$ = 8 $\overline{X}_{.1}$ = 16.25 $s_{.1}$ = 2.9155	$n_{.2}$ = 8 $\overline{X}_{.2}$ = 18.50 $s_{.2}$ = 2.8785	$n_{.3}$ = 8 $\overline{X}_{.3}$ = 14.00 $s_{.3}$ = 2.8785	n_T = 24 $\overline{X}_T$ = 16.25 s_T = 11.1523

Part V.C.

Analysis of Variance Table

Source of Variation	*df*	*SS*	*MS*	*F-Value*	*Critical F*
Cells	5	86.5000	17.3000	1.8318	2.77
Rows (Groups)	1	1.5000	1.5000	.1588	4.41
Columns (Methods)	2	81.0000	40.5000	4.2882	3.55
Interaction	2	4.0000	2.0000	.2118	3.55
Within	18	170.0000	9.4444		
Total	23	256.5000			

Part VI.
Treatment by Subjects Design

Source of Variation	*df*	*SS*	*MS*	*Computed F*	*Critical F*
Rows	19	139.7915	7.3574	89.6052	1.87
Columns	2	.0282	.0141	.1715	3.24
Interaction	38	3.1202	.0821		
Total	59	142.9398			

CHAPTER 14
Quick Quiz
Answers

1A. 1 classification variable
1B. Nominal
1C. 400 ÷ 5 = 80 for each cell
1D. Faulty products are evenly distributed across the five factors.
1E. k - 1 = 5 - 1 = 4
1F. The chi-square goodness of fit test against a rectangular distribution is appropriate.

2A. 1 classification variable
2B. Nominal
2C. .50 × 1000 = 500; .25 × 1000 = 250; .15 × 1000 = 150; and .10 × 1000 = 100
2D. The home locations of the art museum visitors after the new strategy has been implemented is no different than in the past.
2E. k - 1 = 4 - 1 = 3
2F. The chi-square goodness of fit test against a known distribution is appropriate.

3A. 2 classification variables: types of accidents and type of work
3B. both are nominal
3C. Work-related accidents are independent of job type.
3D. 24 cells
3E. $(r - 1) \times (c - 1) = (4 - 1) \times (6 - 1) = 15$
3F. The chi-square test of independence is appropriate.

4A. 2 classification variable
4B. training is nominal; success is ordinal
4C. Success in as an evaluator is independent of completion of training program.
4D. 4 cells
4E. $(r - 1) \times (c - 1) = (2 - 1) \times (2 - 1) = 1$
4F. Since there are only 18 observations, at least one of the expected values must be less than five. Therefore, the Fisher's exact probability test (based on the hypergeometric distribution) is appropriate.

CHAPTER 14
Multiple Choice
Answers

1. E	6. E	11. B	16. C
2. E	7. B	12. E	
3. D	8. C	13. A	
4. C	9. C	14. E	
5. A	10. A	15. A	

CHAPTER 14
Written Problems
Answers

1. A. Expected values: **Distribution of Food Preferences**

	Italian	Mexican	Chinese	Greek	Other	None
Expected	36	36	36	36	36	36
Observed	32	63	48	27	16	30

B. Degrees of freedom = 5
C. Critical chi-square value = 11.0705
D. Computed chi-square value = 39.0556
E. Decision = Reject H_0
F. Graphic representation: The computed value (39.0556) is to the right of the critical value (11.0705) and falls well into the region of rejection.

2. A. Expected values:

Distribution of Religious Affiliation

	Protestant	Roman Catholic	Jewish	Other
Expected	72.36	49.58	6.70	5.36
Observed	51	44	9	30

These expected values were obtained as follows: Protestant = .54 × 134 = 72.36; Roman Catholic = .37 × 134 = 49.58; Jewish = .05 × 134 = 6.70' and Other = .04 × 134 = 5.36.

B. Degrees of freedom = 3
C. Critical chi-square value = 7.8147
D. Computed chi-square value = 120.9933
E. Decision = Reject H_0

3. Calculation of the expected values:

Distribution of Pressure in Aerosol Cans

X	*f*	*RLL*	*RUL*	*z / RLL*	*z / RUL*	*Area*	*Observed Values*	*Expected Values*	$\frac{(O - E)^2}{E}$
24	2	23.5	24.5		-2.03779	0.02079	2	2.57739	0.12935
25	2	24.5	25.5	-2.03779	-1.71005	0.02284	2	2.83249	0.24468
26	5	25.5	26.5	-1.71005	-1.38231	0.03981	5	4.93639	0.00082
27	8	26.5	27.5	-1.38231	-1.05458	0.06237	8	7.73412	0.00914
28	16	27.5	28.5	-1.05458	-0.72684	0.08785	16	10.89375	2.39346
29	15	28.5	29.5	-0.72684	-0.39910	0.11125	15	13.79466	0.10532
30	12	29.5	30.5	-0.39910	-0.07136	0.12664	12	15.70398	0.87363
31	9	30.5	31.5	-0.07136	0.25638	0.12961	9	16.07225	3.11200
32	21	31.5	32.5	0.25638	0.58411	0.11926	21	14.78806	2.60941
33	14	32.5	33.5	0.58411	0.91185	0.09865	14	12.23241	0.25542
34	6	33.5	34.5	0.91185	1.23959	0.07336	6	9.09660	1.05412
35	6	34.5	35.5	1.23959	1.56733	0.04904	6	6.08153	0.00109
36	5	35.5	36.5	1.56733	1.89507	0.02948	5	3.65518	0.49479
37	1	36.5	37.5	1.89507	2.22280	0.01593	1	1.97499	0.48132
38	0	37.5	38.5	2.22280	2.55054	0.00774	0	0.95935	0.95935
39	2	38.5	39.5	2.55054		0.00538	2	0.66685	2.66522

A. Mean =	30.71774
B. Standard deviation =	3.05122
C. Degrees of freedom =	13
D. Critical Chi-Square =	22.362
E. Computed Chi Square =	15.38910
F. H_0 =	The distribution is normal.
G. Decision =	Fail to reject H_0

4. A. Expected values:

Usage of Binoculars

	Sports	Nature	All Purpose
Model A	45 (21.44)	12 (23.45)	10 (22.11)
Model B	13 (30.08)	52 (32.90)	29 (31.02)
Model C	23 (32.00)	27 (35.00)	50 (33.00)
Model D	15 (12.48)	14 (13.65)	10 (12.87)

B. Degrees of freedom = 6

C. Critical chi-square value = 16.8119

D. Computed chi-square value = 73.3068

E. Decision = Reject H_0

5. A. Expected values:

Quality Problems

	Materials	Machines	Methods	Human Resources
Health	10 (14.86)	20 (14.62)	35 (32.12)	5 (8.39)
Manu-facturing	25 (23.36)	29 (22.98)	48 (50.48)	8 (13.18)
Service	20 (14.23)	3 (14.00)	29 (30.75)	15 (8.03)
Education	4 (4.88)	4 (4.80)	10 (10.55)	5 (2.76)
Other	3 (4.67)	5 (4.60)	12 (10.10)	2 (2.64)

B. No, since only 70% of the cells (14 out of 20) have expected values of 5 or greater.
C. The primary variable is "quality problems."
D. The secondary variable is "industry."
E. We should collapse the "education" and "other" categories of the secondary variable into one category, labeled as "other." We could have make an argument for collapsing "service" with "education" into "service or education," which would have resulted in 13 of the 16 cells (i.e., ≥ 80%) having revised expected values of ≥ 5. However, collapsing "education" and "other" into "other" results in all of the revised expected values being greater than or equal to 5.
F. Revised table of observed and expected values:

Quality Problems

	Materials (Observed)	Materials (Expected)	Machines (Observed)	Machines (Expected)	Methods (Observed)	Methods (Expected)	Human Resources (Observed)	Human Resources (Expected)
Health	10	14.86	20	14.62	35	32.12	5	8.39
Manu-facturing	25	23.36	29	22.98	48	50.48	8	13.18
Service	20	14.23	3	14.00	29	30.75	15	8.03
Other	7	9.56	9	9.40	22	20.65	7	5.39

G. Degrees of freedom = 9
H. Revised critical chi-square value = 14.6837
I. Revised computed chi-square value = 27.4463
J. Decision = Reject H_0

6. A. Expected values:

Football Preferences

	Attended College (Expected)	Attended College (Observed)	No College Attendance (Expected)	No College Attendance (Observed)
Preferred College Football	124	150	124	98
Preferred Professional Football	176	150	176	202

B. Degrees of freedom = 1
C. Critical chi-square value = 3.8415
D. Computed chi-square value before adjusting for degrees of freedom = 18.585
E. Computed chi-square value after using Yates' correction factor to adjust for degrees of freedom = 17.877
F. Decision = Reject H_0

7. A. Appropriate statistical test = Fisher Exact Probability Test (Hypergeometric Distribution)
B. Probability that only 2 of those not admitted had connections with important alumni = .0225
C. Probability that 2 or less of those not admitted had connections with important alumni = .0242
D. Decision = Reject H_0

CHAPTER 15
Multiple Choice
Answers

1.	D	7.	E	13.	B	19.	E	25.	D	31.	B
2.	D	8.	A	14.	A	20.	A	26.	A	32.	C
3.	C	9.	E	15.	E	21.	B	27.	C	33.	A
4.	C	10.	B	16.	C	22.	C	28.	B	34.	A
5.	A	11.	C	17.	A	23.	D	29.	A		
6.	C	12.	A	18.	E	24.	E	30.	E		

CHAPTER 16
Multiple Choice
Answers

1.	D	6.	A	11.	C	16.	A	21.	D
2.	C	7.	B	12.	A	17.	D	22.	A
3.	C	8.	B	13.	B	18.	C	23.	B
4.	D	9.	A	14.	B	19.	C	24.	B
5.	D	10.	C	15.	D	20.	D	25.	A

26.	C	31.	D	36.	A
27.	C	32.	A		
28.	A	33.	C		
29.	B	34.	E		
30.	B	35.	E		

CHAPTER 17
Multiple Choice
Answers

1.	B	7.	B	13.	B	19.	B	25.	E	31.	C
2.	A	8.	C	14.	A	20.	C	26.	E	32.	B
3.	C	9.	D	15.	C	21.	D	27.	D	33.	A
4.	E	10.	E	16.	E	22.	E	28.	E	34.	A
5.	D	11.	A	17.	E	23.	A	29.	E	35.	A
6.	A	12.	A	18.	A	24.	A	30.	B		

CHAPTER 17
Written Problems
Answers

1. Because the sum of the deviations about the best fit line (or hyperplane)is always zero.

2. The mean for Y' is always equal to the mean for Y.

3. Because the residual variable has had the effects of each of these variables eliminated from Y.

4. Using $(.5374)^2$ (since .54 was rounded), we obtain a value of .2887. This gives us the coefficient of alienation.

5. Using $(.8434)^2$ (since .84 was rounded), we obtain an *RSQ* of .7113. This corresponds with the *RSQ* for the full model.

6. 0.00, because the residual variable has had the effects of each of the predictor variables removed and *Y′* is based on these same variables.

7. 464.7074. The numerator of the variance for the *Y′* variable should be equal to the ESS_{RED}.

8. 187.8426. The numerator of the variance for the residual variable should be equal to the ESS_{FM}.

APPENDIX E
Multiple Choice
Answers

1. B	6. D	11. B	16. E
2. B	7. C	12. E	
3. A	8. E	13. E	
4. C	9. D	14. E	
5. B	10. A	15. D	

APPENDIX E
Computational Practice
Answers

I. 1.	21.0	16.	35.5	II. 1.	13	III. 1. $\overline{X}_1$	=	16.1429
2.	27.0	17.	35.5	2.	13			
3.	73.5	18.	22.5	3.	39	$\overline{X}_2$	=	12.5000
4.	48.0	19.	22.5	4.	43			
5.	160.0	20.	3.5	5.	169	$\overline{X}_3$	=	21.1429
6.	17.0	21.	1.8708	6.	169			
7.	17.5	22.	7.1	7.	7	$\overline{X}_4$	=	10.6250
8.	-9.0	23.	2.6646	8.	5			
9.	117.0	24.	+0.9027	9.	38	$\overline{X}_T$	=	15.0357
10.	91.0			10.	21			
11.	157.0			11.	188	2. SS_A	=	463.8750
12.	441.0			12.	3.8333			
13.	729.0			13.	+.6072	SS_W	=	111.0898
14.	17.5			14.	.8077			
15.	17.5			15.	.5000	SS_T	=	574.9648

APPENDIX K
Multiple Choice
Answers

1. A	6. B	11. B	16. E
2. D	7. E	12. D	
3. E	8. C	13. C	
4. E	9. C	14. E	
5. B	10. C	15. D	

APPENDIX B

BIBLIOGRAPHY

BIBLIOGRAPHY

American Compensation Association. (1983). ***1983-1984 salary budget survey***. Scottsdale, AZ: American Compensation Association.

American Compensation Association. (1985, October/November). Salary budget increases continue downward. ***ACA News***, pp. 1, 10.

American Compensation Association. (1987). ***1987-1988 salary budget survey***. Scottsdale, AZ: American Compensation Association.

American Compensation Association. (1994, September). Salary budget survey. ***ACA News***, pp. 1, 18-19.

American Psychological Association. (1983). ***Publication manual of the American Psychological Association*** (3rd ed.). Washington, DC: Author.

American Psychological Association. (1994). ***Publication manual of the American Psychological Association*** (4th ed.). Washington, DC: Author.

Anderson, V. L., & MeLean, R. A. (1974). ***Design of experiments: a realistic approach.*** New York: Marcel Dekker.

Andrews, F. M., Klem, L., Davidson, T. N., O'Malley, P. M., & Rodgers, W. L. (1974). ***A guide for selecting statistical techniques for analyzing social science data.*** Ann Arbor, MI: Survey Research Center, Institute for Social Research.

Augarten, S. (1984). ***Bit by bit.*** New York: Ticknor & Fields.

Bartlett, M. S. (1937). Properties of sufficiency and statistical tests. ***Proceedings of the Royal Society, A901, 160***, 268-282.

Beatty, J. R. (1993). ***Applied multivariate statistics.*** Unpublished manuscript in progress.

Beatty, J. R. (1992). Total quality management and the human resources professional. ***Perspectives in Total Compensation, 3*** (5), 1-6.

Beatty, J. R. (1994a). Statistical analysis in compensation: introductory statistical concepts. In W. A. Caldwell (Ed.), ***Compensation Guide***, (chap. 12). Boston: Warren Gorham Lamont.

Beatty, J. R. (1994b). Statistical analysis in compensation: model building, correlation, and regression. In W. A. Caldwell (Ed.), ***Compensation Guide***, (chap. 13). Boston: Warren Gorham Lamont.

Beatty, J. R. (1996). Statistical analysis in compensation: model building, correlation, and regression. In W. A. Caldwell (Ed.), ***Compensation Guide***, (chap. 13, Rev. ed.). Boston: Warren Gorham Lamont.

Beatty, L. M. (1993). Total quality management: a current bibliography. ***ACA Journal: Perspectives in Compensation and Benefits, 2*** (2), 80-84.

Beatty, R. W., & Beatty, J. R. (1975). Longitudinal study of absenteeism of hard-core unemployed. ***Psychological Reports, 36,*** 395-406.

Bell, E. T. (1956). The Queen of Mathematics. In J. R. Newman (Ed.), ***The world of mathematics*** (pp. 498-515). New York: Simon and Schuster.

Berne, E. (1966). ***Principles of Group Treatment.*** New York: Grove Press, Inc.

Boneau, C. A. (1960). The effects of violations of assumptions underlying the *t* test. ***Psychological Bulletin, 57,*** 49-64.

Box, G. E. P. (1953). Non-normality and tests on variance. ***Biometrika, 40,*** 318-335.

Box, G. E. P. (1954a). Some theorems on quadratic forms applied in the study of analysis of variance problems. I. Effect of inequality of variance in the one-way classification. ***Annals of Mathematical Statistics, 25,*** 290-302.

Box, G. E. P. (1954b). Some theorems on quadratic forms applied in the study of analysis of variance problems. II. Effects of inequality of variance and of correlation between errors in the two-way classification. ***Annals of Mathematical Statistics, 25,*** 484-498.

Bradley, J. V. (1968). ***Distribution-free statistical tests.*** Englewood Cliffs, NJ: Prentice-Hall.

Bruning, J. L., & Kintz, B. L. (1968). ***Computational handbook of statistics.*** Glenview, IL: Scott, Foresman and Company.

Cascio, W. F. (1991). ***Applied psychology in personnel management*** (4rd ed.). Englewood Cliffs, NJ: Prentice-Hall.

Christensen, R. (1987). ***Plane answers to complex questions: the theory of linear models.*** New York: Springer-Verlag.

Cochran. W. G. (1967). Footnote. ***Science, 156,*** 1460-1462.

Cochran. W. G., & Cox, G. M. (1957). ***Experimental designs*** (2nd ed.). New York: John Wiley & Sons.

Cohen, J., & Cohen, P. (1983). ***Applied multiple regression/correlation analysis for the behavioral sciences*** (2nd ed.). Hillsdale, NJ: Lawrence Erlbaum Associates.

Cohen, J. (1988). ***Statistical power analysis for the behavioral sciences*** (2nd ed.). Hillsdale, NJ: Lawrence Erlbaum Associates.

Collyer, C. E., & Enns, J. T. (1986). ***Analysis of variance: the basic designs***. Chicago: Nelson-Hall.

Conover, W. J. (1971). ***Practical nonparametric statistics.*** New York: John Wiley & Sons, Inc.

Cooley, W. W., & Lohnes, P. R. (1971). ***Multivariate data analysis***. New York: John Wiley & Sons.

Crosby, P. B. (1984). ***Quality without tears: the art of hassle-free management.*** New York: McGraw-Hill.

Daniel, W. W. (1978). ***Applied nonparametric statistics.*** Boston: Houghton Mifflin.

Darlington, R. B. (1968). ***Multiple regression in psychological research and practice***. New York: John Wiley & Sons.

Davis, J. H. (1988). ***Quantitative analysis for compensation decision making: Seminar book for Certification Course 3.*** Scottsdale, AZ: American Compensation Association.

Deming, W. E. (1982; 1986). ***Out of the crisis***. Cambridge, MA: Massachusetts Institute of Technology, Center for Advanced Engineering Study.

Deming, W. E. (1993). ***The new economics for industry, government, education.*** Cambridge, MA: Massachusetts Institute of Technology, Center for Advanced Engineering Study.

Dewey, J. (1910). ***How we think.*** Boston: D. C. Heath.

Dixon, W. J. (Ed.). (1975). ***BMD-P: Biomedical computer programs***. Berkeley: University of California Press.

DrawPerfect. (1990). Orem, UT: WordPerfect Corporation.

Dudycha, A. L., & Dudycha, L. W. (1972). Behavioral statistics: An historical perspective. In R. E. Kirk (Ed.), ***Statistical issues: A reader for the behavioral sciences***. Monterey, CA: Brooks/Cole.

Duncan, A. J. (1986). ***Quality control and industrial statistics*** (5th ed.). Homewood, IL: Richard D. Irwin.

Edwards, A. L. (1959). ***Edwards Personal Preference Schedule: Manual, Revised 1959***. New York: The Psychological Corporation.

Edwards, A. L. (1960). ***Experimental design in psychological research*** (rev. ed.). New York: Holt, Rinehart and Winston, Inc.

Ekings, J.D. (1988). Assembly industries. In J. M. Juran & F. M. Gryna (Eds.), ***Juran's Quality Control Handbook*** (4th ed.) (pp. 30.1-30.49). New York: McGraw-Hill.

Feigenbaum, A. V. (1983). ***Total quality control (3rd. ed.).*** New York: McGraw-Hill.

Ferguson, G. A. (1976). ***Statistical analysis in psychology and education*** (4th ed.). New York: McGraw-Hill.

Fisher, L., & McDonald, J. (1978). ***Fixed effects analysis of variance***. New York: Academic Press.

Fisher, R. A. (1924). Proceedings of the International Mathematical Conference, 805.

Fisher, R. A. (1925). ***Statistical methods for research workers.*** Edinburgh: Oliver and Boyd.

Fleishman, E. A. (1969). ***Manual for Leadership Opinion Questionnaire***. Chicago: Science Research Associates.

Glover, J. W. (1926). Requirements for statisticians and their training: Part I--Statistical teaching in American colleges and universities. ***Journal of the American Statistical Association, 21***, 419-424.

Gosset, W. S. (1908). The probable error of the mean. ***Biometrika, 6***, 1-25.

Guilford, J. P. (1954). ***Psychometric methods.*** New York: McGraw-Hill.

Guilford, J. P. (1965). ***Fundamental statistics in psychology and education*** (4th ed.). New York: McGraw-Hill.

Hair, J. F., Jr., Anderson, R. E., Tatham, R. L., & Grablowsky, B. J. (1979). ***Multivariate data analysis: with readings***. Tulsa, OK: Petroleum Publishing Company.

Hall, B. H., & Hall, R. E. (1976). ***TSP: Time series processor. User's manual.*** Boston: Harvard Institute of Economic Research (Harvard Computer Services).

Hankins, F. H. (1968). ***Adolphe Quetelet as statistician.*** New York: AMS Press.

Harshbarger, T. R. (1977). ***Introductory statistics: a decision map*** (2nd ed.). New York: Macmillan.

Hays, W. L. (1963). ***Statistics for psychologists.*** New York: Holt, Rinehart and Winston, Inc.

Hays, W. L., & Winkler, R. L. (1971,). ***Statistics: probability, inference, and decision.*** New York: Holt, Rinehart and Winston, Inc.

Huff, D. (1954). ***How to lie with statistics.*** New York: W. W. Norton & Company.

Huitema, B. E. (1980). ***The analysis of covariance and alternatives.*** New York: John Wiley & Sons.

IBM Corporation. (1970). ***IBM Application program: System/360 Scientific subroutine package (Version III), programmer's manual*** (5th ed.). White Plains, NY: IBM Corporation.

Ishikawa, K. (1976). ***Guide to quality control.*** Toyko: Asian Productivity Organization.

Jenner, S. R., Omens, A. E., & Beatty, J. R. (1985, October). ***Intercultural perceptions and organizational commitment in United States subsidiaries of Japanese multinational corporations.*** Paper presented at the meeting of the Academy of International Business, New York, NY.

Juran, J. M. (1988). The quality function. In J. M. Juran & F. M. Gryna (Eds.), ***Juran's Quality Control Handbook*** (4th ed.) (pp. 2.1-2.13). New York: McGraw-Hill.

Juran, J. M., & Gryna, F. M. (1988). ***Juran's Quality Control Handbook*** (4th ed.). New York: McGraw-Hill.

Keppel, G. (1973). ***Design and analysis: a researcher's handbook.*** Englewood Cliffs, NJ: Prentice-Hall.

Keppel, G. (1991). ***Design and analysis: a researcher's handbook*** (3rd ed.). Englewood Cliffs, NJ: Prentice-Hall.

Keppel, G. & Saufley, W. H., Jr. (1980). ***Introduction to design and analysis: a student's handbook.*** San Francisco: W. H. Freeman and Co.

Kerlinger, F. N. (1973). ***Foundations of behavioral research*** (2nd ed.). New York: Holt, Rinehart and Winston, Inc.

Kirk, R. E. (1968). ***Experimental design: Procedures for the behavioral sciences.*** Belmont, CA: Brooks/Cole.

Kleinbaum, D. G., & Kupper, L. L. (1978). ***Applied regression analysis and other multivariable methods.*** North Scituate, MA: Duxbury.

Likert, R. (1967). ***The human organization: Its management and value.*** New York: McGraw-Hill.

Lindquist, E. F. (1953). ***Design and analysis of experiments in psychology and education.*** Boston: Houghton Mifflin.

Machine of the Year. (1983, January 3). ***Time Magazine, 121***(1), pp. 12-24.

Mann, H. B., & Whitney, D. R. (1947). On a test of whether one of two random variables is stochastically larger than the other. ***Annals of Mathematical Statistics, 18*** 50-60.

Marks, M. R. (1966, September). ***Two kinds of regression weights that are better than betas in crossed samples.*** Paper presented at the annual meeting of the American Psychological Association, New York, NY.

MathPlan. (1985). Orem, UT: SSI Software.

Messina, W. S. (1987). ***Statistical quality control for manufacturing managers.*** New York: John Wiley & Sons.

McGuigan, F. J. (1968). ***Experimental psychology: a methodological approach*** (2nd ed.). Englewood Cliffs, NJ: Prentice-Hall.

McNemar, Q. (1962). ***Psychological statistics*** (3rd ed.). New York: John Wiley & Sons.

Moses, L. E. (1963) Rank tests of dispersion. ***Annals of Mathematical Statistics, 34*** 973-983.

Mosteller, F., & Rourke, R. E. K. (1973). ***Sturdy statistics: nonparametrics and order statistics.*** Reading, MA: Addison-Wesley.

Mowday, R. T., Steers, R. M., & Porter, L. W. (1979). The measurement of organizational commitment. ***Journal of Vocational Behavior, 14***, 224-247.

National Quality Program. (1998). National Institute of Standards and Technology 1998 slide set with speaker notes.

Newman, J. R. (Ed.). (1956). ***The world of mathematics.*** New York: Simon & Schuster.

Nie, N. H., Hull, C. H., Jenkins, J. G., Steinbrenner, K., & Bent, D. H. (1975). ***Statistical package for the social sciences*** (2nd ed.). New York: McGraw-Hill.

Noether, G. E. (1976). ***Introduction to statistics: a nonparametric approach*** (2nd ed.). Boston: Houghton Mifflin.

Norton, D. W. (1952). ***An empirical investigation of some effects of non-normality and heterogeneity of the F-distribution.*** Unpublished doctoral dissertation, State University of Iowa.

Nunnally, J. C. (1978). ***Psychometric theory*** (2nd ed.). New York: McGraw-Hill.

Nunnally, J. C., & Bernstein, I. H. (1994). ***Psychometric theory*** (3nd ed.). New York: McGraw-Hill.

Overall, J. E., & Klett, C. J. (1972). ***Applied multivariate analysis.*** New York: McGraw-Hill.

PlanPerfect (Version 5.0). (1989). Orem, UT: WordPerfect Corporation.

Pearson, E. S. (Ed.). (1978). ***The history of statistics in the 17th and 18th centuries: Against the changing background of intellectual, scientific and religious thought. Lectures by Karl Pearson given at University College London during the academic sessions 1921-1933.*** New York: Macmillan.

Pearson, E. S. (1931). The analysis of variance in cases of non-normal variation. ***Biometrika, 23,*** 114-133.

Pearson, K. (1900). On a criterion that a given system of deviations from the probable in the case of a correlated system of variables is such that it cannot be reasonably supposed to have arisen from random sampling. ***Philosophical Magazine,*** 5th series, ***50,*** 339-357.

Profile of ISO 9000: Handbook of Quality Standards and Compliance. (1992). Needham Heights, MA: Allyn and Bacon.

The Quality Imperative. (1991, October). ***Business Week.***

Ross, W. P. (Ed.). (1955). ***Aristotle: Selections.*** New York: Charles Scribner's Sons.

Salary budget survey results released---increases continue downward. (1985, October/November). ***ACA News,*** pp. 1, 10.

Salary budget survey results released. (1990, September). ***ACA News,*** pp. 1, 8.

Salary budget survey results released. (1991, September). ***ACA News,*** pp. 1, 6.

Salary budget survey. (1994, September). ***ACA News***, pp. 1, 18-19.

Salary budget survey. (1995, September). ***ACA News***, pp. 1.

The San Diego Union. August 7, 1988. 1988 Major League Players' Salaries.

SAS Institute. (1979). ***SAS user's guide***. Raleigh, NC: SAS Institute.

Sasaki, N., & Hutchins, D. (Eds.). (1984). ***The Japanese approach to product quality***. Oxford: Pergamon Press.

Scheffé, H. (1953). A method for judging contrasts in the analysis of variance. ***Biometrika, 40***, 87-104.

Scheffé, H. (1953). ***The analysis of variance.*** New York: John Wiley & Sons, Inc.

Schmidt, S. R. & Launsby, R. G. (1994). ***Understanding industrial designed experiments*** (4th ed.). Colorado Springs: Air Academy Press.

Shea, M. T., & Beatty, J. R. (1983). Measuring Machiavellianism with Mach V: A psychometric investigation. ***Journal of Personality Assessment***, *47*, 509-513.

Sheth, J. N. (1971). The multivariate revolution in marketing research. ***Journal of Marketing***, *35*(1), 13-19.

Siegel, S. (1956). ***Nonparametric statistics for the behavioral sciences***. New York: McGraw-Hill.

Snedecor, G. W., & Cochran, W. G. (1967). ***Statistical Methods*** (2nd. ed.). Ames, IA: The Iowa State University Press.

SuperCalc⁴: User's guide and reference manual (2nd ed.). (1986). San Jose, CA: Computer Associates International, Inc.

Taguchi, G. (1987). ***System of experimental design: Engineering methods to optimize quality and minimize costs*** (Vols. 1-2). (L. W. Tung, Trans.). Joint publishers: White Plains, NY: UNIPUB/Kraus International Publications; and Dearborn, MI: Supplier Institute, Inc.

Taguchi, G., & Wu, Y. (1978). ***Introduction to off-line quality control.*** Central Japan Quality Control Association. (also available from The American Supplier Institute, Detroit, MI.)

Tatsuoka, M. M., & Tiedeman, D. V. (1963). Statistics as an aspect of scientific method in research on teaching. In N. L. Gage (Ed.)., ***Handbook of research on teaching*** (pp. 142-170). Chicago: Rand McNally.

The 1997 Criteria for Performance Excellence: Malcolm Baldrige National Quality Award. (1997). Gaithersburg, MD: United States Department of Commerce, Technology Administration, National Institute of Standards and Technology.

Veldman, D. J. (1967). ***Fortran programming for the behavioral sciences.*** New York: Holt, Rinehart and Winston, Inc.

Walker, H. M. (1929). ***Studies in the history of statistical method.*** Baltimore: The Williams & Wilkins Company.

Walker, H. M., & Lev, J. (1953). ***Statistical inference.*** New York: Holt, Rinehart and Winston, Inc.

Wallace, M. J., & Fay, C. H. (1983). ***Compensation: Theory and practice.*** Kent Publishing Company.

Ward, D. L. (1974 personal communication). ***Transactional Management Inventory.*** Chicago: David L. Ward & Associates and Career Development and Counseling Center.

Ward, J. H., Jr., Hall, K., & Buchhorn, J. (1967). ***PERSUB reference manual.*** (PRL-TR-67-3). (II). Lackland, TX: Personnel Research Laboratory, Aerospace Medical Division, Air Force Systems Command, Lackland Air Force Base.

Ward, J. H., Jr., Buchhorn, J., & Hall, K. (1967). ***Introduction to PERSUB.*** (PRL-TR-67-3). (I). Lackland, TX: Personnel Research Laboratory, Aerospace Medical Division, Air Force Systems Command, Lackland Air Force Base.

Welch, B. L. (1947). The generalization of Student's' problem when several different population variances are involved. ***Biometrika, 34***, 28-35.

Westenberg, J. (1948). Significance test for median and interquartile range in samples from continuous populations of any form. ***Proceedings Koninklijke Nederlandse Akademie van Wetenschappen, 51***, 252-261.

Westergaard, H. (1968). ***Contributions to the history of statistics.*** New York: Agathon Press.

Wilcoxon, F. (1945). Individual comparisons by ranking methods. ***Biometrics, 1***, 80-83.

Winer, B. J. (1971). ***Statistical principles in experimental design*** (2nd ed.). New York: McGraw-Hill.

APPENDIX C

CRITICAL TABLES

2 tail 95%
z=1.96

2 tail 99%
z=2.58

TABLE 1
Values Under the Standard Normal Distribution

Areas Associated with z
for $z = 0.00$ to $z = 0.29$

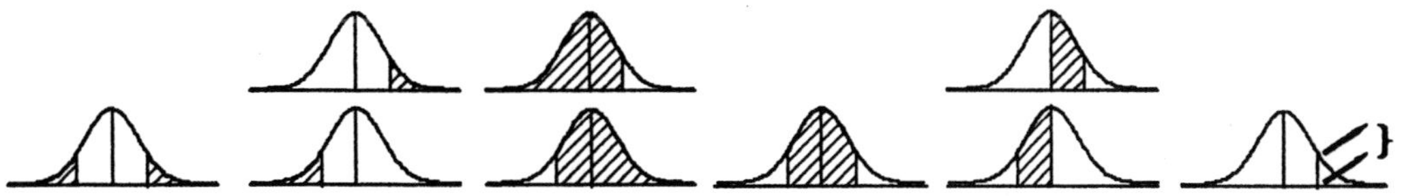

z	2-tail	1-tail	greater	middle	z to mean	ordinate
0.00	1.0000	.5000	.5000	.0000	.0000	.3989
0.01	.9920	.4960	.5040	.0080	.0040	.3989
0.02	.9840	.4920	.5080	.0160	.0080	.3989
0.03	.9761	.4880	.5120	.0239	.0120	.3988
0.04	.9681	.4840	.5160	.0319	.0160	.3986
0.05	.9601	.4801	.5199	.0399	.0199	.3984
0.06	.9522	.4761	.5239	.0478	.0239	.3982
0.07	.9442	.4721	.5279	.0558	.0279	.3980
0.08	.9362	.4681	.5319	.0638	.0319	.3977
0.09	.9283	.4641	.5359	.0717	.0359	.3973
0.10	.9203	.4602	.5398	.0797	.0398	.3970
0.11	.9124	.4562	.5438	.0876	.0438	.3965
0.12	.9045	.4522	.5478	.0955	.0478	.3961
0.13	.8966	.4483	.5517	.1034	.0517	.3956
0.14	.8887	.4443	.5557	.1113	.0557	.3951
0.15	.8808	.4404	.5596	.1192	.0596	.3945
0.16	.8729	.4364	.5636	.1271	.0636	.3939
0.17	.8650	.4325	.5675	.1350	.0675	.3932
0.18	.8572	.4286	.5714	.1428	.0714	.3925
0.19	.8493	.4247	.5753	.1507	.0753	.3918
0.20	.8415	.4207	.5793	.1585	.0793	.3910
0.21	.8337	.4168	.5832	.1663	.0832	.3902
0.22	.8259	.4129	.5871	.1741	.0871	.3894
0.23	.8181	.4090	.5910	.1819	.0910	.3885
0.24	.8103	.4052	.5948	.1897	.0948	.3876
0.25	.8026	.4013	.5987	.1974	.0987	.3867
0.26	.7949	.3974	.6026	.2051	.1026	.3857
0.27	.7872	.3936	.6064	.2128	.1064	.3847
0.28	.7795	.3897	.6103	.2205	.1103	.3836
0.29	.7718	.3859	.6141	.2282	.1141	.3825

Areas Associated with z
for $z = 0.30$ to $z = 0.68$

z	2-tail	1-tail	greater	middle	z to mean	ordinate
0.30	.7642	.3821	.6179	.2358	.1179	.3814
0.31	.7566	.3783	.6217	.2434	.1217	.3802
0.32	.7490	.3745	.6255	.2510	.1255	.3790
0.33	.7414	.3707	.6293	.2586	.1293	.3778
0.34	.7339	.3669	.6331	.2661	.1331	.3765
0.35	.7263	.3632	.6368	.2737	.1368	.3752
0.36	.7188	.3594	.6406	.2812	.1406	.3739
0.37	.7114	.3557	.6443	.2886	.1443	.3725
0.38	.7039	.3520	.6480	.2961	.1480	.3712
0.39	.6965	.3483	.6517	.3035	.1517	.3697
0.40	.6892	.3446	.6554	.3108	.1554	.3683
0.41	.6818	.3409	.6591	.3182	.1591	.3668
0.42	.6745	.3372	.6628	.3255	.1628	.3653
0.43	.6672	.3336	.6664	.3328	.1664	.3637
0.44	.6599	.3300	.6700	.3401	.1700	.3621
0.45	.6527	.3264	.6736	.3473	.1736	.3605
0.46	.6455	.3228	.6772	.3545	.1772	.3589
0.47	.6384	.3192	.6808	.3616	.1808	.3572
0.48	.6312	.3156	.6844	.3688	.1844	.3555
0.49	.6241	.3121	.6879	.3759	.1879	.3538
0.50	.6171	.3085	.6915	.3829	.1915	.3521
0.51	.6101	.3050	.6950	.3899	.1950	.3503
0.52	.6031	.3015	.6985	.3969	.1985	.3485
0.53	.5961	.2981	.7019	.4039	.2019	.3467
0.54	.5892	.2946	.7054	.4108	.2054	.3448
0.55	.5823	.2912	.7088	.4177	.2088	.3429
0.56	.5755	.2877	.7123	.4245	.2123	.3410
0.57	.5687	.2843	.7157	.4313	.2157	.3391
0.58	.5619	.2810	.7190	.4381	.2190	.3372
0.59	.5552	.2776	.7224	.4448	.2224	.3352
0.60	.5485	.2743	.7257	.4515	.2257	.3332
0.61	.5419	.2709	.7291	.4581	.2291	.3312
0.62	.5353	.2676	.7324	.4647	.2324	.3292
0.63	.5287	.2643	.7357	.4713	.2357	.3271
0.64	.5222	.2611	.7389	.4778	.2389	.3251
0.65	.5157	.2578	.7422	.4843	.2422	.3230
0.66	.5093	.2546	.7454	.4907	.2454	.3209
0.67	.5029	.2514	.7486	.4971	.2486	.3187
0.68	.4965	.2483	.7517	.5035	.2517	.3166

Areas Associated with z
for $z = 0.69$ to $z = 1.07$

z	2-tail	1-tail	greater	middle	z to mean	ordinate
0.69	.4902	.2451	.7549	.5098	.2549	.3144
0.70	.4839	.2420	.7580	.5161	.2580	.3123
0.71	.4777	.2389	.7611	.5223	.2611	.3101
0.72	.4715	.2358	.7642	.5285	.2642	.3079
0.73	.4654	.2327	.7673	.5346	.2673	.3056
0.74	.4593	.2296	.7704	.5407	.2704	.3034
0.75	.4533	.2266	.7734	.5467	.2734	.3011
0.76	.4473	.2236	.7764	.5527	.2764	.2989
0.77	.4413	.2206	.7794	.5587	.2794	.2966
0.78	.4354	.2177	.7823	.5646	.2823	.2943
0.79	.4295	.2148	.7852	.5705	.2852	.2920
0.80	.4237	.2119	.7881	.5763	.2881	.2897
0.81	.4179	.2090	.7910	.5821	.2910	.2874
0.82	.4122	.2061	.7939	.5878	.2939	.2850
0.83	.4065	.2033	.7967	.5935	.2967	.2827
0.84	.4009	.2005	.7995	.5991	.2995	.2803
0.85	.3953	.1977	.8023	.6047	.3023	.2780
0.86	.3898	.1949	.8051	.6102	.3051	.2756
0.87	.3843	.1922	.8078	.6157	.3078	.2732
0.88	.3789	.1894	.8106	.6211	.3106	.2709
0.89	.3735	.1867	.8133	.6265	.3133	.2685
0.90	.3681	.1841	.8159	.6319	.3159	.2661
0.91	.3628	.1814	.8186	.6372	.3186	.2637
0.92	.3576	.1788	.8212	.6424	.3212	.2613
0.93	.3524	.1762	.8238	.6476	.3238	.2589
0.94	.3472	.1736	.8264	.6528	.3264	.2565
0.95	.3421	.1711	.8289	.6579	.3289	.2541
0.96	.3371	.1685	.8315	.6629	.3315	.2516
0.97	.3320	.1660	.8340	.6680	.3340	.2492
0.98	.3271	.1635	.8365	.6729	.3365	.2468
0.99	.3222	.1611	.8389	.6778	.3389	.2444
1.00	.3173	.1587	.8413	.6827	.3413	.2420
1.01	.3125	.1562	.8438	.6875	.3438	.2396
1.02	.3077	.1539	.8461	.6923	.3461	.2371
1.03	.3030	.1515	.8485	.6970	.3485	.2347
1.04	.2983	.1492	.8508	.7017	.3508	.2323
1.05	.2937	.1469	.8531	.7063	.3531	.2299
1.06	.2891	.1446	.8554	.7109	.3554	.2275
1.07	.2846	.1423	.8577	.7154	.3577	.2251

Areas Associated with z
for z = 1.08 to z = 1.46

z	2-tail	1-tail	greater	middle	z to mean	ordinate
1.08	.2801	.1401	.8599	.7199	.3599	.2227
1.09	.2757	.1379	.8621	.7243	.3621	.2203
1.10	.2713	.1357	.8643	.7287	.3643	.2179
1.11	.2670	.1335	.8665	.7330	.3665	.2155
1.12	.2627	.1314	.8686	.7373	.3686	.2131
1.13	.2585	.1292	.8708	.7415	.3708	.2107
1.14	.2543	.1271	.8729	.7457	.3729	.2083
1.15	.2501	.1251	.8749	.7499	.3749	.2059
1.16	.2460	.1230	.8770	.7540	.3770	.2036
1.17	.2420	.1210	.8790	.7580	.3790	.2012
1.18	.2380	.1190	.8810	.7620	.3810	.1989
1.19	.2340	.1170	.8830	.7660	.3830	.1965
1.20	.2301	.1151	.8849	.7699	.3849	.1942
1.21	.2263	.1131	.8869	.7737	.3869	.1919
1.22	.2225	.1112	.8888	.7775	.3888	.1895
1.23	.2187	.1093	.8907	.7813	.3907	.1872
1.24	.2150	.1075	.8925	.7850	.3925	.1849
1.25	.2113	.1056	.8944	.7887	.3944	.1826
1.26	.2077	.1038	.8962	.7923	.3962	.1804
1.27	.2041	.1020	.8980	.7959	.3980	.1781
1.28	.2005	.1003	.8997	.7995	.3997	.1758
1.29	.1971	.0985	.9015	.8029	.4015	.1736
1.30	.1936	.0968	.9032	.8064	.4032	.1714
1.31	.1902	.0951	.9049	.8098	.4049	.1691
1.32	.1868	.0934	.9066	.8132	.4066	.1669
1.33	.1835	.0918	.9082	.8165	.4082	.1647
1.34	.1802	.0901	.9099	.8198	.4099	.1626
1.35	.1770	.0885	.9115	.8230	.4115	.1604
1.36	.1738	.0869	.9131	.8262	.4131	.1582
1.37	.1707	.0853	.9147	.8293	.4147	.1561
1.38	.1676	.0838	.9162	.8324	.4162	.1539
1.39	.1645	.0823	.9177	.8355	.4177	.1518
1.40	.1615	.0808	.9192	.8385	.4192	.1497
1.41	.1585	.0793	.9207	.8415	.4207	.1476
1.42	.1556	.0778	.9222	.8444	.4222	.1456
1.43	.1527	.0764	.9236	.8473	.4236	.1435
1.44	.1499	.0749	.9251	.8501	.4251	.1415
1.45	.1471	.0735	.9265	.8529	.4265	.1394
1.46	.1443	.0721	.9279	.8557	.4279	.1374

Areas Associated with z for $z = 1.47$ to $z = 1.85$

z	2-tail	1-tail	greater	middle	z to mean	ordinate
1.47	.1416	.0708	.9292	.8584	.4292	.1354
1.48	.1389	.0694	.9306	.8611	.4306	.1334
1.49	.1362	.0681	.9319	.8638	.4319	.1315
1.50	.1336	.0668	.9332	.8664	.4332	.1295
1.51	.1310	.0655	.9345	.8690	.4345	.1276
1.52	.1285	.0643	.9357	.8715	.4357	.1257
1.53	.1260	.0630	.9370	.8740	.4370	.1238
1.54	.1236	.0618	.9382	.8764	.4382	.1219
1.55	.1211	.0606	.9394	.8789	.4394	.1200
1.56	.1188	.0594	.9406	.8812	.4406	.1182
1.57	.1164	.0582	.9418	.8836	.4418	.1163
1.58	.1141	.0571	.9429	.8859	.4429	.1145
1.59	.1118	.0559	.9441	.8882	.4441	.1127
1.60	.1096	.0548	.9452	.8904	.4452	.1109
1.61	.1074	.0537	.9463	.8926	.4463	.1092
1.62	.1052	.0526	.9474	.8948	.4474	.1074
1.63	.1031	.0516	.9484	.8969	.4484	.1057
1.64	.1010	.0505	.9495	.8990	.4495	.1040
1.65	.0989	.0495	.9505	.9011	.4505	.1023
1.66	.0969	.0485	.9515	.9031	.4515	.1006
1.67	.0949	.0475	.9525	.9051	.4525	.0989
1.68	.0930	.0465	.9535	.9070	.4535	.0973
1.69	.0910	.0455	.9545	.9090	.4545	.0957
1.70	.0891	.0446	.9554	.9109	.4554	.0940
1.71	.0873	.0436	.9564	.9127	.4564	.0925
1.72	.0854	.0427	.9573	.9146	.4573	.0909
1.73	.0836	.0418	.9582	.9164	.4582	.0893
1.74	.0819	.0409	.9591	.9181	.4591	.0878
1.75	.0801	.0401	.9599	.9199	.4599	.0863
1.76	.0784	.0392	.9608	.9216	.4608	.0848
1.77	.0767	.0384	.9616	.9233	.4616	.0833
1.78	.0751	.0375	.9625	.9249	.4625	.0818
1.79	.0735	.0367	.9633	.9265	.4633	.0804
1.80	.0719	.0359	.9641	.9281	.4641	.0790
1.81	.0703	.0351	.9649	.9297	.4649	.0775
1.82	.0688	.0344	.9656	.9312	.4656	.0761
1.83	.0672	.0336	.9664	.9328	.4664	.0748
1.84	.0658	.0329	.9671	.9342	.4671	.0734
1.85	.0643	.0322	.9678	.9357	.4678	.0721

Areas Associated with z for z = 1.86 to z = 2.24

z	2-tail	1-tail	greater	middle	z to mean	ordinate
1.86	.0629	.0314	.9686	.9371	.4686	.0707
1.87	.0615	.0307	.9693	.9385	.4693	.0694
1.88	.0601	.0301	.9699	.9399	.4699	.0681
1.89	.0588	.0294	.9706	.9412	.4706	.0669
1.90	.0574	.0287	.9713	.9426	.4713	.0656
1.91	.0561	.0281	.9719	.9439	.4719	.0644
1.92	.0549	.0274	.9726	.9451	.4726	.0632
1.93	.0536	.0268	.9732	.9464	.4732	.0620
1.94	.0524	.0262	.9738	.9476	.4738	.0608
1.95	.0512	.0256	.9744	.9488	.4744	.0596
1.96	.0500	.0250	.9750	.9500	.4750	.0584
1.97	.0488	.0244	.9756	.9512	.4756	.0573
1.98	.0477	.0239	.9761	.9523	.4761	.0562
1.99	.0466	.0233	.9767	.9534	.4767	.0551
2.00	.0455	.0228	.9772	.9545	.4772	.0540
2.01	.0444	.0222	.9778	.9556	.4778	.0529
2.02	.0434	.0217	.9783	.9566	.4783	.0519
2.03	.0424	.0212	.9788	.9576	.4788	.0508
2.04	.0414	.0207	.9793	.9586	.4793	.0498
2.05	.0404	.0202	.9798	.9596	.4798	.0488
2.06	.0394	.0197	.9803	.9606	.4803	.0478
2.07	.0385	.0192	.9808	.9615	.4808	.0468
2.08	.0375	.0188	.9812	.9625	.4812	.0459
2.09	.0366	.0183	.9817	.9634	.4817	.0449
2.10	.0357	.0179	.9821	.9643	.4821	.0440
2.11	.0349	.0174	.9826	.9651	.4826	.0431
2.12	.0340	.0170	.9830	.9660	.4830	.0422
2.13	.0332	.0166	.9834	.9668	.4834	.0413
2.14	.0324	.0162	.9838	.9676	.4838	.0404
2.15	.0316	.0158	.9842	.9684	.4842	.0396
2.16	.0308	.0154	.9846	.9692	.4846	.0387
2.17	.0300	.0150	.9850	.9700	.4850	.0379
2.18	.0293	.0146	.9854	.9707	.4854	.0371
2.19	.0285	.0143	.9857	.9715	.4857	.0363
2.20	.0278	.0139	.9861	.9722	.4861	.0355
2.21	.0271	.0136	.9864	.9729	.4864	.0347
2.22	.0264	.0132	.9868	.9736	.4868	.0339
2.23	.0257	.0129	.9871	.9743	.4871	.0332
2.24	.0251	.0125	.9875	.9749	.4875	.0325

Areas Associated with z
for $z = 2.25$ to $z = 2.63$

z	2-tail	1-tail	greater	middle	z to mean	ordinate
2.25	.0244	.0122	.9878	.9756	.4878	.0317
2.26	.0238	.0119	.9881	.9762	.4881	.0310
2.27	.0232	.0116	.9884	.9768	.4884	.0303
2.28	.0226	.0113	.9887	.9774	.4887	.0297
2.29	.0220	.0110	.9890	.9780	.4890	.0290
2.30	.0214	.0107	.9893	.9786	.4893	.0283
2.31	.0209	.0104	.9896	.9791	.4896	.0277
2.32	.0203	.0102	.9898	.9797	.4898	.0270
2.33	.0198	.0099	.9901	.9802	.4901	.0264
2.34	.0193	.0096	.9904	.9807	.4904	.0258
2.35	.0188	.0094	.9906	.9812	.4906	.0252
2.36	.0183	.0091	.9909	.9817	.4909	.0246
2.37	.0178	.0089	.9911	.9822	.4911	.0241
2.38	.0173	.0087	.9913	.9827	.4913	.0235
2.39	.0168	.0084	.9916	.9832	.4916	.0229
2.40	.0164	.0082	.9918	.9836	.4918	.0224
2.41	.0160	.0080	.9920	.9840	.4920	.0219
2.42	.0155	.0078	.9922	.9845	.4922	.0213
2.43	.0151	.0075	.9925	.9849	.4925	.0208
2.44	.0147	.0073	.9927	.9853	.4927	.0203
2.45	.0143	.0071	.9929	.9857	.4929	.0198
2.46	.0139	.0069	.9931	.9861	.4931	.0194
2.47	.0135	.0068	.9932	.9865	.4932	.0189
2.48	.0131	.0066	.9934	.9869	.4934	.0184
2.49	.0128	.0064	.9936	.9872	.4936	.0180
2.50	.0124	.0062	.9938	.9876	.4938	.0175
2.51	.0121	.0060	.9940	.9879	.4940	.0171
2.52	.0117	.0059	.9941	.9883	.4941	.0167
2.53	.0114	.0057	.9943	.9886	.4943	.0163
2.54	.0111	.0055	.9945	.9889	.4945	.0158
2.55	.0108	.0054	.9946	.9892	.4946	.0154
2.56	.0105	.0052	.9948	.9895	.4948	.0151
2.57	.0102	.0051	.9949	.9898	.4949	.0147
2.58	.0099	.0049	.9951	.9901	.4951	.0143
2.59	.0096	.0048	.9952	.9904	.4952	.0139
2.60	.0093	.0047	.9953	.9907	.4953	.0136
2.61	.0091	.0045	.9955	.9909	.4955	.0132
2.62	.0088	.0044	.9956	.9912	.4956	.0129
2.63	.0085	.0043	.9957	.9915	.4957	.0126

Areas Associated with z
for $z = 2.64$ to $z = 3.02$

z	2-tail	1-tail	greater	middle	z to mean	ordinate
2.64	.0083	.0041	.9959	.9917	.4959	.0122
2.65	.0080	.0040	.9960	.9920	.4960	.0119
2.66	.0078	.0039	.9961	.9922	.4961	.0116
2.67	.0076	.0038	.9962	.9924	.4962	.0113
2.68	.0074	.0037	.9963	.9926	.4963	.0110
2.69	.0071	.0036	.9964	.9929	.4964	.0107
2.70	.0069	.0035	.9965	.9931	.4965	.0104
2.71	.0067	.0034	.9966	.9933	.4966	.0101
2.72	.0065	.0033	.9967	.9935	.4967	.0099
2.73	.0063	.0032	.9968	.9937	.4968	.0096
2.74	.0061	.0031	.9969	.9939	.4969	.0093
2.75	.0060	.0030	.9970	.9940	.4970	.0091
2.76	.0058	.0029	.9971	.9942	.4971	.0088
2.77	.0056	.0028	.9972	.9944	.4972	.0086
2.78	.0054	.0027	.9973	.9946	.4973	.0084
2.79	.0053	.0026	.9974	.9947	.4974	.0081
2.80	.0051	.0026	.9974	.9949	.4974	.0079
2.81	.0050	.0025	.9975	.9950	.4975	.0077
2.82	.0048	.0024	.9976	.9952	.4976	.0075
2.83	.0047	.0023	.9977	.9953	.4977	.0073
2.84	.0045	.0023	.9977	.9955	.4977	.0071
2.85	.0044	.0022	.9978	.9956	.4978	.0069
2.86	.0042	.0021	.9979	.9958	.4979	.0067
2.87	.0041	.0021	.9979	.9959	.4979	.0065
2.88	.0040	.0020	.9980	.9960	.4980	.0063
2.89	.0039	.0019	.9981	.9961	.4981	.0061
2.90	.0037	.0019	.9981	.9963	.4981	.0060
2.91	.0036	.0018	.9982	.9964	.4982	.0058
2.92	.0035	.0018	.9982	.9965	.4982	.0056
2.93	.0034	.0017	.9983	.9966	.4983	.0055
2.94	.0033	.0016	.9984	.9967	.4984	.0053
2.95	.0032	.0016	.9984	.9968	.4984	.0051
2.96	.0031	.0015	.9985	.9969	.4985	.0050
2.97	.0030	.0015	.9985	.9970	.4985	.0048
2.98	.0029	.0014	.9986	.9971	.4986	.0047
2.99	.0028	.0014	.9986	.9972	.4986	.0046
3.00	.0027	.0013	.9987	.9973	.4987	.0044
3.01	.0026	.0013	.9987	.9974	.4987	.0043
3.02	.0025	.0013	.9987	.9975	.4987	.0042

Areas Associated with z
for $z = 3.03$ to $z = 3.41$

z	2-tail	1-tail	greater	middle	z to mean	ordinate
3.03	.0024	.0012	.9988	.9976	.4988	.0040
3.04	.0024	.0012	.9988	.9976	.4988	.0039
3.05	.0023	.0011	.9989	.9977	.4989	.0038
3.06	.0022	.0011	.9989	.9978	.4989	.0037
3.07	.0021	.0011	.9989	.9979	.4989	.0036
3.08	.0021	.0010	.9990	.9979	.4990	.0035
3.09	.0020	.0010	.9990	.9980	.4990	.0034
3.10	.0019	.0010	.9990	.9981	.4990	.0033
3.11	.0019	.0009	.9991	.9981	.4991	.0032
3.12	.0018	.0009	.9991	.9982	.4991	.0031
3.13	.0017	.0009	.9991	.9983	.4991	.0030
3.14	.0017	.0008	.9992	.9983	.4992	.0029
3.15	.0016	.0008	.9992	.9984	.4992	.0028
3.16	.0016	.0008	.9992	.9984	.4992	.0027
3.17	.0015	.0008	.9992	.9985	.4992	.0026
3.18	.0015	.0007	.9993	.9985	.4993	.0025
3.19	.0014	.0007	.9993	.9986	.4993	.0025
3.20	.0014	.0007	.9993	.9986	.4993	.0024
3.21	.0013	.0007	.9993	.9987	.4993	.0023
3.22	.0013	.0006	.9994	.9987	.4994	.0022
3.23	.0012	.0006	.9994	.9988	.4994	.0022
3.24	.0012	.0006	.9994	.9988	.4994	.0021
3.25	.0012	.0006	.9994	.9988	.4994	.0020
3.26	.0011	.0006	.9994	.9989	.4994	.0020
3.27	.0011	.0005	.9995	.9989	.4995	.0019
3.28	.0010	.0005	.9995	.9990	.4995	.0018
3.29	.0010	.0005	.9995	.9990	.4995	.0018
3.30	.0010	.0005	.9995	.9990	.4995	.0017
3.31	.0009	.0005	.9995	.9991	.4995	.0017
3.32	.0009	.0005	.9995	.9991	.4995	.0016
3.33	.0009	.0004	.9996	.9991	.4996	.0016
3.34	.0008	.0004	.9996	.9992	.4996	.0015
3.35	.0008	.0004	.9996	.9992	.4996	.0015
3.36	.0008	.0004	.9996	.9992	.4996	.0014
3.37	.0008	.0004	.9996	.9992	.4996	.0014
3.38	.0007	.0004	.9996	.9993	.4996	.0013
3.39	.0007	.0003	.9997	.9993	.4997	.0013
3.40	.0007	.0003	.9997	.9993	.4997	.0012
3.41	.0006	.0003	.9997	.9994	.4997	.0012

Areas Associated with z
for $z = 3.42$ to $z = 3.80$

z	2-tail	1-tail	greater	middle	z to mean	ordinate
3.42	.0006	.0003	.9997	.9994	.4997	.0012
3.43	.0006	.0003	.9997	.9994	.4997	.0011
3.44	.0006	.0003	.9997	.9994	.4997	.0011
3.45	.0006	.0003	.9997	.9994	.4997	.0010
3.46	.0005	.0003	.9997	.9995	.4997	.0010
3.47	.0005	.0003	.9997	.9995	.4997	.0010
3.48	.0005	.0003	.9997	.9995	.4997	.0009
3.49	.0005	.0002	.9998	.9995	.4998	.0009
3.50	.0005	.0002	.9998	.9995	.4998	.0009
3.51	.0004	.0002	.9998	.9996	.4998	.0008
3.52	.0004	.0002	.9998	.9996	.4998	.0008
3.53	.0004	.0002	.9998	.9996	.4998	.0008
3.54	.0004	.0002	.9998	.9996	.4998	.0008
3.55	.0004	.0002	.9998	.9996	.4998	.0007
3.56	.0004	.0002	.9998	.9996	.4998	.0007
3.57	.0004	.0002	.9998	.9996	.4998	.0007
3.58	.0003	.0002	.9998	.9997	.4998	.0007
3.59	.0003	.0002	.9998	.9997	.4998	.0006
3.60	.0003	.0002	.9998	.9997	.4998	.0006
3.61	.0003	.0002	.9998	.9997	.4998	.0006
3.62	.0003	.0001	.9999	.9997	.4999	.0006
3.63	.0003	.0001	.9999	.9997	.4999	.0005
3.64	.0003	.0001	.9999	.9997	.4999	.0005
3.65	.0003	.0001	.9999	.9997	.4999	.0005
3.66	.0003	.0001	.9999	.9997	.4999	.0005
3.67	.0002	.0001	.9999	.9998	.4999	.0005
3.68	.0002	.0001	.9999	.9998	.4999	.0005
3.69	.0002	.0001	.9999	.9998	.4999	.0004
3.70	.0002	.0001	.9999	.9998	.4999	.0004
3.71	.0002	.0001	.9999	.9998	.4999	.0004
3.72	.0002	.0001	.9999	.9998	.4999	.0004
3.73	.0002	.0001	.9999	.9998	.4999	.0004
3.74	.0002	.0001	.9999	.9998	.4999	.0004
3.75	.0002	.0001	.9999	.9998	.4999	.0004
3.76	.0002	.0001	.9999	.9998	.4999	.0003
3.77	.0002	.0001	.9999	.9998	.4999	.0003
3.78	.0002	.0001	.9999	.9998	.4999	.0003
3.79	.0002	.0001	.9999	.9998	.4999	.0003
3.80	.0001	.0001	.9999	.9999	.4999	.0003

Areas Associated with z
for $z = 3.81$ to $z = 4.00$

z	2-tail	1-tail	greater	middle	z to mean	ordinate
3.81	.0001	.0001	.9999	.9999	.4999	.0003
3.82	.0001	.0001	.9999	.9999	.4999	.0003
3.83	.0001	.0001	.9999	.9999	.4999	.0003
3.84	.0001	.0001	.9999	.9999	.4999	.0003
3.85	.0001	.0001	.9999	.9999	.4999	.0002
3.86	.0001	.0001	.9999	.9999	.4999	.0002
3.87	.0001	.0001	.9999	.9999	.4999	.0002
3.88	.0001	.0001	.9999	.9999	.4999	.0002
3.89	.0001	.0001	.9999	.9999	.4999	.0002
3.90	.0001	.0000	1.0000	.9999	.5000	.0002
3.91	.0001	.0000	1.0000	.9999	.5000	.0002
3.92	.0001	.0000	1.0000	.9999	.5000	.0002
3.93	.0001	.0000	1.0000	.9999	.5000	.0002
3.94	.0001	.0000	1.0000	.9999	.5000	.0002
3.95	.0001	.0000	1.0000	.9999	.5000	.0002
3.96	.0001	.0000	1.0000	.9999	.5000	.0002
3.97	.0001	.0000	1.0000	.9999	.5000	.0002
3.98	.0001	.0000	1.0000	.9999	.5000	.0001
3.99	.0001	.0000	1.0000	.9999	.5000	.0001
4.00	.0001	.0000	1.0000	.9999	.5000	.0001

TABLE 2
Critical Values for Student's *t*-Distribution

α	.1000	.0500	.0250	.0125	.0100	.0050	.0005
df = 1 to 33			One-Tailed Test				
1	3.0777	6.3137	12.7062	25.4519	31.8210	63.6559	636.5776
2	1.8856	2.9200	4.3027	6.2054	6.9645	9.9250	31.5998
3	1.6377	2.3534	3.1824	4.1765	4.5407	5.8408	12.9244
4	1.5332	2.1318	2.7765	3.4954	3.7469	4.6041	8.6101
5	1.4759	2.0150	2.5706	3.1634	3.3649	4.0321	6.8685
6	1.4398	1.9432	2.4469	2.9687	3.1427	3.7074	5.9587
7	1.4149	1.8946	2.3646	2.8412	2.9979	3.4995	5.4081
8	1.3968	1.8595	2.3060	2.7515	2.8965	3.3554	5.0414
9	1.3830	1.8331	2.2622	2.6850	2.8214	3.2498	4.7809
10	1.3722	1.8125	2.2281	2.6338	2.7638	3.1693	4.5868
11	1.3634	1.7959	2.2010	2.5931	2.7181	3.1058	4.4369
12	1.3562	1.7823	2.1788	2.5600	2.6810	3.0545	4.3178
13	1.3502	1.7709	2.1604	2.5326	2.6503	3.0123	4.2209
14	1.3450	1.7613	2.1448	2.5096	2.6245	2.9768	4.1403
15	1.3406	1.7531	2.1315	2.4899	2.6025	2.9467	4.0728
16	1.3368	1.7459	2.1199	2.4729	2.5835	2.9208	4.0149
17	1.3334	1.7396	2.1098	2.4581	2.5669	2.8982	3.9651
18	1.3304	1.7341	2.1009	2.4450	2.5524	2.8784	3.9217
19	1.3277	1.7291	2.0930	2.4334	2.5395	2.8609	3.8833
20	1.3253	1.7247	2.0860	2.4231	2.5280	2.8453	3.8496
21	1.3232	1.7207	2.0796	2.4138	2.5176	2.8314	3.8193
22	1.3212	1.7171	2.0739	2.4055	2.5083	2.8188	3.7922
23	1.3195	1.7139	2.0687	2.3979	2.4999	2.8073	3.7676
24	1.3178	1.7109	2.0639	2.3910	2.4922	2.7970	3.7454
25	1.3163	1.7081	2.0595	2.3846	2.4851	2.7874	3.7251
26	1.3150	1.7056	2.0555	2.3788	2.4786	2.7787	3.7067
27	1.3137	1.7033	2.0518	2.3734	2.4727	2.7707	3.6895
28	1.3125	1.7011	2.0484	2.3685	2.4671	2.7633	3.6739
29	1.3114	1.6991	2.0452	2.3638	2.4620	2.7564	3.6595
30	1.3104	1.6973	2.0423	2.3596	2.4573	2.7500	3.6460
31	1.3095	1.6955	2.0395	2.3556	2.4528	2.7440	3.6335
32	1.3086	1.6939	2.0369	2.3518	2.4487	2.7385	3.6218
33	1.3077	1.6924	2.0345	2.3483	2.4448	2.7333	3.6109
			Two-Tailed Test				
α	.2000	.1000	.0500	.0250	.0200	.0100	.0010

TABLE 2 (continued)
Critical Values for Student's *t*-Distribution

α	.1000	.0500	.0250	.0125	.0100	.0050	.0005
df = 34 to 66			One-Tailed Test				
34	1.3070	1.6909	2.0322	2.3451	2.4411	2.7284	3.6007
35	1.3062	1.6896	2.0301	2.3420	2.4377	2.7238	3.5911
36	1.3055	1.6883	2.0281	2.3391	2.4345	2.7195	3.5821
37	1.3049	1.6871	2.0262	2.3363	2.4314	2.7154	3.5737
38	1.3042	1.6860	2.0244	2.3337	2.4286	2.7116	3.5657
39	1.3036	1.6849	2.0227	2.3313	2.4258	2.7079	3.5581
40	1.3031	1.6839	2.0211	2.3289	2.4233	2.7045	3.5510
41	1.3025	1.6829	2.0195	2.3267	2.4208	2.7012	3.5443
42	1.3020	1.6820	2.0181	2.3246	2.4185	2.6981	3.5377
43	1.3016	1.6811	2.0167	2.3226	2.4163	2.6951	3.5316
44	1.3011	1.6802	2.0154	2.3207	2.4141	2.6923	3.5258
45	1.3007	1.6794	2.0141	2.3189	2.4121	2.6896	3.5203
46	1.3002	1.6787	2.0129	2.3172	2.4102	2.6870	3.5149
47	1.2998	1.6779	2.0117	2.3155	2.4083	2.6846	3.5099
48	1.2994	1.6772	2.0106	2.3139	2.4066	2.6822	3.5050
49	1.2991	1.6766	2.0096	2.3124	2.4049	2.6800	3.5005
50	1.2987	1.6759	2.0086	2.3109	2.4033	2.6778	3.4960
51	1.2984	1.6753	2.0076	2.3095	2.4017	2.6757	3.4917
52	1.2980	1.6747	2.0066	2.3082	2.4002	2.6737	3.4877
53	1.2977	1.6741	2.0057	2.3069	2.3988	2.6718	3.4837
54	1.2974	1.6736	2.0049	2.3056	2.3974	2.6700	3.4799
55	1.2971	1.6730	2.0040	2.3044	2.3961	2.6682	3.4765
56	1.2969	1.6725	2.0032	2.3033	2.3948	2.6665	3.4730
57	1.2966	1.6720	2.0025	2.3022	2.3936	2.6649	3.4695
58	1.2963	1.6716	2.0017	2.3011	2.3924	2.6633	3.4663
59	1.2961	1.6711	2.0010	2.3000	2.3912	2.6618	3.4632
60	1.2958	1.6706	2.0003	2.2990	2.3901	2.6603	3.4602
61	1.2956	1.6702	1.9996	2.2981	2.3890	2.6589	3.4572
62	1.2954	1.6698	1.9990	2.2971	2.3880	2.6575	3.4545
63	1.2951	1.6694	1.9983	2.2962	2.3870	2.6561	3.4517
64	1.2949	1.6690	1.9977	2.2954	2.3860	2.6549	3.4491
65	1.2947	1.6686	1.9971	2.2945	2.3851	2.6536	3.4466
66	1.2945	1.6683	1.9966	2.2937	2.3842	2.6524	3.4441
			Two-Tailed Test				
α	.2000	.1000	.0500	.0250	.0200	.0100	.0010

TABLE 2 (continued)
Critical Values for Student's *t*-Distribution

α	.1000	.0500	.0250	.0125	.0100	.0050	.0005
df = 67 to 99				One-Tailed Test			
67	1.2943	1.6679	1.9960	2.2929	2.3833	2.6512	3.4418
68	1.2941	1.6676	1.9955	2.2921	2.3824	2.6501	3.4395
69	1.2939	1.6672	1.9949	2.2914	2.3816	2.6490	3.4372
70	1.2938	1.6669	1.9944	2.2906	2.3808	2.6479	3.4350
71	1.2936	1.6666	1.9939	2.2899	2.3800	2.6469	3.4329
72	1.2934	1.6663	1.9935	2.2892	2.3793	2.6458	3.4308
73	1.2933	1.6660	1.9930	2.2886	2.3785	2.6449	3.4289
74	1.2931	1.6657	1.9925	2.2879	2.3778	2.6439	3.4270
75	1.2929	1.6654	1.9921	2.2873	2.3771	2.6430	3.4249
76	1.2928	1.6652	1.9917	2.2867	2.3764	2.6421	3.4232
77	1.2926	1.6649	1.9913	2.2861	2.3758	2.6412	3.4214
78	1.2925	1.6646	1.9908	2.2855	2.3751	2.6403	3.4197
79	1.2924	1.6644	1.9905	2.2849	2.3745	2.6395	3.4180
80	1.2922	1.6641	1.9901	2.2844	2.3739	2.6387	3.4164
81	1.2921	1.6639	1.9897	2.2838	2.3733	2.6379	3.4148
82	1.2920	1.6636	1.9893	2.2833	2.3727	2.6371	3.4132
83	1.2918	1.6634	1.9890	2.2828	2.3721	2.6364	3.4116
84	1.2917	1.6632	1.9886	2.2823	2.3716	2.6356	3.4101
85	1.2916	1.6630	1.9883	2.2818	2.3710	2.6349	3.4086
86	1.2915	1.6628	1.9879	2.2813	2.3705	2.6342	3.4073
87	1.2914	1.6626	1.9876	2.2809	2.3700	2.6335	3.4059
88	1.2912	1.6624	1.9873	2.2804	2.3695	2.6329	3.4046
89	1.2911	1.6622	1.9870	2.2800	2.3690	2.6322	3.4033
90	1.2910	1.6620	1.9867	2.2795	2.3685	2.6316	3.4019
91	1.2909	1.6618	1.9864	2.2791	2.3680	2.6309	3.4006
92	1.2908	1.6616	1.9861	2.2787	2.3676	2.6303	3.3995
93	1.2907	1.6614	1.9858	2.2783	2.3671	2.6297	3.3982
94	1.2906	1.6612	1.9855	2.2779	2.3667	2.6291	3.3970
95	1.2905	1.6611	1.9852	2.2775	2.3662	2.6286	3.3958
96	1.2904	1.6609	1.9850	2.2771	2.3658	2.6280	3.3948
97	1.2903	1.6607	1.9847	2.2767	2.3654	2.6275	3.3937
98	1.2903	1.6606	1.9845	2.2764	2.3650	2.6269	3.3926
99	1.2902	1.6604	1.9842	2.2760	2.3646	2.6264	3.3915
				Two-Tailed Test			
α	.2000	.1000	.0500	.0250	.0200	.0100	.0010

TABLE 2 (continued)
Critical Values for Student's t-Distribution

α	.1000	.0500	.0250	.0125	.0100	.0050	.0005
df = 100 to 132			One-Tailed Test				
100	1.2901	1.6602	1.9840	2.2757	2.3642	2.6259	3.3905
101	1.2900	1.6601	1.9837	2.2753	2.3638	2.6254	3.3894
102	1.2899	1.6599	1.9835	2.2750	2.3635	2.6249	3.3886
103	1.2898	1.6598	1.9833	2.2746	2.3631	2.6244	3.3875
104	1.2897	1.6596	1.9830	2.2743	2.3627	2.6239	3.3865
105	1.2897	1.6595	1.9828	2.2740	2.3624	2.6235	3.3856
106	1.2896	1.6594	1.9826	2.2737	2.3620	2.6230	3.3848
107	1.2895	1.6592	1.9824	2.2734	2.3617	2.6226	3.3838
108	1.2894	1.6591	1.9822	2.2731	2.3614	2.6221	3.3829
109	1.2894	1.6590	1.9820	2.2728	2.3610	2.6217	3.3820
110	1.2893	1.6588	1.9818	2.2725	2.3607	2.6213	3.3811
111	1.2892	1.6587	1.9816	2.2722	2.3604	2.6209	3.3804
112	1.2892	1.6586	1.9814	2.2719	2.3601	2.6204	3.3795
113	1.2891	1.6584	1.9812	2.2717	2.3598	2.6200	3.3787
114	1.2890	1.6583	1.9810	2.2714	2.3595	2.6196	3.3779
115	1.2890	1.6582	1.9808	2.2711	2.3592	2.6193	3.3772
116	1.2889	1.6581	1.9806	2.2709	2.3589	2.6189	3.3763
117	1.2888	1.6580	1.9804	2.2706	2.3586	2.6185	3.3756
118	1.2888	1.6579	1.9803	2.2704	2.3584	2.6181	3.3749
119	1.2887	1.6578	1.9801	2.2701	2.3581	2.6178	3.3742
120	1.2886	1.6576	1.9799	2.2699	2.3578	2.6174	3.3734
121	1.2886	1.6575	1.9798	2.2696	2.3576	2.6171	3.3728
122	1.2885	1.6574	1.9796	2.2694	2.3573	2.6167	3.3721
123	1.2885	1.6573	1.9794	2.2692	2.3570	2.6164	3.3714
124	1.2884	1.6572	1.9793	2.2689	2.3568	2.6161	3.3708
125	1.2884	1.6571	1.9791	2.2687	2.3566	2.6157	3.3701
126	1.2883	1.6570	1.9790	2.2685	2.3563	2.6154	3.3694
127	1.2883	1.6569	1.9788	2.2683	2.3561	2.6151	3.3688
128	1.2882	1.6568	1.9787	2.2681	2.3558	2.6148	3.3682
129	1.2881	1.6568	1.9785	2.2679	2.3556	2.6145	3.3676
130	1.2881	1.6567	1.9784	2.2677	2.3554	2.6142	3.3670
131	1.2880	1.6566	1.9782	2.2675	2.3552	2.6139	3.3663
132	1.2880	1.6565	1.9781	2.2673	2.3549	2.6136	3.3657
			Two-Tailed Test				
α	.2000	.1000	.0500	.0250	.0200	.0100	.0010

TABLE 2 (continued)
Critical Values for Student's *t*-Distribution

α	.1000	.0500	.0250	.0125	.0100	.0050	.0005
df = 133 to 100,000,000				One-Tailed Test			
133	1.2879	1.6564	1.9780	2.2671	2.3547	2.6133	3.3651
134	1.2879	1.6563	1.9778	2.2669	2.3545	2.6130	3.3647
135	1.2879	1.6562	1.9777	2.2667	2.3543	2.6127	3.3641
136	1.2878	1.6561	1.9776	2.2665	2.3541	2.6125	3.3635
137	1.2878	1.6561	1.9774	2.2663	2.3539	2.6122	3.3629
138	1.2877	1.6560	1.9773	2.2661	2.3537	2.6119	3.3624
139	1.2877	1.6559	1.9772	2.2659	2.3535	2.6117	3.3619
140	1.2876	1.6558	1.9771	2.2658	2.3533	2.6114	3.3613
141	1.2876	1.6557	1.9769	2.2656	2.3531	2.6111	3.3609
142	1.2875	1.6557	1.9768	2.2654	2.3529	2.6109	3.3603
143	1.2875	1.6556	1.9767	2.2653	2.3527	2.6106	3.3599
144	1.2875	1.6555	1.9766	2.2651	2.3525	2.6104	3.3595
145	1.2874	1.6554	1.9765	2.2649	2.3523	2.6102	3.3589
146	1.2874	1.6554	1.9763	2.2648	2.3522	2.6099	3.3584
147	1.2873	1.6553	1.9762	2.2646	2.3520	2.6097	3.3580
148	1.2873	1.6552	1.9761	2.2644	2.3518	2.6094	3.3574
149	1.2873	1.6551	1.9760	2.2643	2.3516	2.6092	3.3570
150	1.2872	1.6551	1.9759	2.2641	2.3515	2.6090	3.3565
160	1.2869	1.6544	1.9749	2.2627	2.3499	2.6069	3.3523
170	1.2866	1.6539	1.9740	2.2614	2.3485	2.6051	3.3487
180	1.2863	1.6534	1.9732	2.2603	2.3472	2.6034	3.3453
190	1.2860	1.6529	1.9725	2.2593	2.3461	2.6020	3.3424
200	1.2858	1.6525	1.9719	2.2584	2.3451	2.6006	3.3398
225	1.2853	1.6517	1.9706	2.2565	2.3430	2.5979	3.3343
250	1.2849	1.6510	1.9695	2.2550	2.3414	2.5956	3.3299
275	1.2846	1.6504	1.9686	2.2537	2.3400	2.5938	3.3263
300	1.2844	1.6499	1.9679	2.2527	2.3388	2.5923	3.3232
400	1.2837	1.6487	1.9659	2.2499	2.3357	2.5882	3.3151
500	1.2832	1.6479	1.9647	2.2482	2.3338	2.5857	3.3101
1,000	1.2824	1.6464	1.9623	2.2448	2.3301	2.5807	3.3002
2,000	1.2820	1.6456	1.9612	2.2431	2.3282	2.5783	3.2954
10,000	1.2816	1.6450	1.9602	2.2417	2.3267	2.5763	3.2915
100,000	1.2816	1.6449	1.9600	2.2414	2.3264	2.5759	3.2906
1,000,000	1.2816	1.6449	1.9600	2.2414	2.3264	2.5758	3.2905
100,000,000	1.2816	1.6449	1.9600	2.2414	2.3264	2.5758	3.2905
				Two-Tailed Test			
α	.2000	.1000	.0500	.0250	.0200	.0100	.0010

TABLE 3

Critical Values for the Chi-Square Distribution

Probabilities represent the area to the right of the critical chi-square value.

α	0.9950	0.9900	0.9750	0.9500	0.9000	0.1000	0.0500	0.0250	0.0100	0.0050
df = 1 to 43					Critical Values					
1	0.0000	0.0002	0.0010	0.0039	0.0158	2.7055	3.8415	5.0239	6.6349	7.8794
2	0.0100	0.0201	0.0506	0.1026	0.2107	4.6052	5.9915	7.3778	9.2104	10.5965
3	0.0717	0.1148	0.2158	0.3518	0.5844	6.2514	7.8147	9.3484	11.3449	12.8381
4	0.2070	0.2971	0.4844	0.7107	1.0636	7.7794	9.4877	11.1433	13.2767	14.8602
5	0.4118	0.5543	0.8312	1.1455	1.6103	9.2363	11.0705	12.8325	15.0863	16.7496
6	0.6757	0.8721	1.2373	1.6354	2.2041	10.6446	12.5916	14.4494	16.8119	18.5475
7	0.9893	1.2390	1.6899	2.1673	2.8331	12.0170	14.0671	16.0128	18.4753	20.2777
8	1.3444	1.6465	2.1797	2.7326	3.4895	13.3616	15.5073	17.5345	20.0902	21.9549
9	1.7349	2.0879	2.7004	3.3251	4.1682	14.6837	16.9190	19.0228	21.6660	23.5893
10	2.1558	2.5582	3.2470	3.9403	4.8652	15.9872	18.3070	20.4832	23.2093	25.1881
11	2.6032	3.0535	3.8157	4.5748	5.5778	17.2750	19.6752	21.9200	24.7250	26.7569
12	3.0738	3.5706	4.4038	5.2260	6.3038	18.5493	21.0261	23.3367	26.2170	28.2997
13	3.5650	4.1069	5.0087	5.8919	7.0415	19.8119	22.3620	24.7356	27.6882	29.8193
14	4.0747	4.6604	5.6287	6.5706	7.7895	21.0641	23.6848	26.1189	29.1412	31.3194
15	4.6009	5.2294	6.2621	7.2609	8.5468	22.3071	24.9958	27.4884	30.5780	32.8015
16	5.1422	5.8122	6.9077	7.9616	9.3122	23.5418	26.2962	28.8453	31.9999	34.2671
17	5.6973	6.4077	7.5642	8.6718	10.0852	24.7690	27.5871	30.1910	33.4087	35.7184
18	6.2648	7.0149	8.2307	9.3904	10.8649	25.9894	28.8693	31.5264	34.8052	37.1564
19	6.8439	7.6327	8.9065	10.1170	11.6509	27.2036	30.1435	32.8523	36.1908	38.5821
20	7.4338	8.2604	9.5908	10.8508	12.4426	28.4120	31.4104	34.1696	37.5663	39.9969
21	8.0336	8.8972	10.2829	11.5913	13.2396	29.6151	32.6706	35.4789	38.9322	41.4009
22	8.6427	9.5425	10.9823	12.3380	14.0415	30.8133	33.9245	36.7807	40.2894	42.7957
23	9.2604	10.1957	11.6885	13.0905	14.8480	32.0069	35.1725	38.0756	41.6383	44.1814
24	9.8862	10.8563	12.4011	13.8484	15.6587	33.1962	36.4150	39.3641	42.9798	45.5584
25	10.5196	11.5240	13.1197	14.6114	16.4734	34.3816	37.6525	40.6465	44.3140	46.9280
26	11.1602	12.1982	13.8439	15.3792	17.2919	35.5632	38.8851	41.9231	45.6416	48.2898
27	11.8077	12.8785	14.5734	16.1514	18.1139	36.7412	40.1133	43.1945	46.9628	49.6450
28	12.4613	13.5647	15.3079	16.9279	18.9392	37.9159	41.3372	44.4608	48.2782	50.9936
29	13.1211	14.2564	16.0471	17.7084	19.7677	39.0875	42.5569	45.7223	49.5878	52.3355
30	13.7867	14.9535	16.7908	18.4927	20.5992	40.2560	43.7730	46.9792	50.8922	53.6719
31	14.4577	15.6555	17.5387	19.2806	21.4336	41.4217	44.9853	48.2319	52.1914	55.0025
32	15.1340	16.3622	18.2908	20.0719	22.2706	42.5847	46.1942	49.4804	53.4857	56.3280
33	15.8152	17.0735	19.0467	20.8665	23.1102	43.7452	47.3999	50.7251	54.7754	57.6483
34	16.5013	17.7891	19.8062	21.6643	23.9522	44.9032	48.6024	51.9660	56.0609	58.9637
35	17.1917	18.5089	20.5694	22.4650	24.7966	46.0588	49.8018	53.2033	57.3420	60.2746
36	17.8868	19.2326	21.3359	23.2686	25.6433	47.2122	50.9985	54.4373	58.6192	61.5811
37	18.5859	19.9603	22.1056	24.0749	26.4921	48.3634	52.1923	55.6680	59.8926	62.8832
38	19.2888	20.6914	22.8785	24.8839	27.3430	49.5126	53.3835	56.8955	61.1620	64.1812
39	19.9958	21.4261	23.6543	25.6954	28.1958	50.6598	54.5722	58.1201	62.4281	65.4753
40	20.7066	22.1642	24.4331	26.5093	29.0505	51.8050	55.7585	59.3417	63.6908	66.7660
41	21.4208	22.9056	25.2145	27.3256	29.9071	52.9485	56.9424	60.5606	64.9500	68.0526
42	22.1384	23.6501	25.9987	28.1440	30.7654	54.0902	58.1240	61.7767	66.2063	69.3360
43	22.8596	24.3976	26.7854	28.9647	31.6255	55.2302	59.3035	62.9903	67.4593	70.6157

TABLE 3 (continued)
Critical Values for the Chi-Square Distribution
Probabilities represent the area to the right of the critical chi-square value.

α	0.9950	0.9900	0.9750	0.9500	0.9000	0.1000	0.0500	0.0250	0.0100	0.0050
df = 44 to 86					**Critical Values**					
44	23.5836	25.1480	27.5745	29.7875	32.4871	56.3685	60.4809	64.2014	68.7096	71.8923
45	24.3110	25.9012	28.3662	30.6123	33.3504	57.5053	61.6562	65.4101	69.9569	73.1660
46	25.0413	26.6572	29.1600	31.4390	34.2152	58.6405	62.8296	66.6165	71.2015	74.4367
47	25.7745	27.4158	29.9562	32.2676	35.0814	59.7743	64.0011	67.8206	72.4432	75.7039
48	26.5107	28.1770	30.7545	33.0981	35.9491	60.9066	65.1708	69.0226	73.6826	76.9689
49	27.2494	28.9406	31.5549	33.9303	36.8182	62.0375	66.3387	70.2224	74.9194	78.2306
50	27.9908	29.7067	32.3574	34.7642	37.6886	63.1671	67.5048	71.4202	76.1538	79.4898
51	28.7347	30.4750	33.1618	35.5999	38.5604	64.2954	68.6693	72.6160	77.3860	80.7465
52	29.4811	31.2457	33.9681	36.4371	39.4334	65.4224	69.8322	73.8099	78.6156	82.0006
53	30.2300	32.0185	34.7763	37.2759	40.3076	66.5482	70.9934	75.0019	79.8434	83.2525
54	30.9811	32.7934	35.5863	38.1162	41.1830	67.6728	72.1532	76.1921	81.0688	84.5018
55	31.7349	33.5705	36.3981	38.9581	42.0596	68.7962	73.3115	77.3804	82.2920	85.7491
56	32.4906	34.3495	37.2116	39.8013	42.9373	69.9185	74.4683	78.5671	83.5136	86.9940
57	33.2482	35.1306	38.0267	40.6459	43.8162	71.0397	75.6237	79.7522	84.7327	88.2366
58	34.0085	35.9135	38.8435	41.4920	44.6960	72.1598	76.7778	80.9356	85.9501	89.4770
59	34.7704	36.6982	39.6619	42.3393	45.5769	73.2789	77.9305	82.1174	87.1658	90.7153
60	35.5344	37.4848	40.4817	43.1880	46.4589	74.3970	79.0820	83.2977	88.3794	91.9518
61	36.3005	38.2732	41.3032	44.0379	47.3418	75.5141	80.2321	84.4764	89.5912	93.1862
62	37.0683	39.0633	42.1260	44.8890	48.2257	76.6302	81.3810	85.6537	90.8015	94.4185
63	37.8383	39.8551	42.9503	45.7414	49.1105	77.7454	82.5287	86.8296	92.0099	95.6492
64	38.6097	40.6485	43.7759	46.5949	49.9963	78.8597	83.6752	88.0040	93.2167	96.8779
65	39.3832	41.4436	44.6030	47.4496	50.8829	79.9730	84.8206	89.1772	94.4220	98.1049
66	40.1583	42.2402	45.4314	48.3054	51.7705	81.0855	85.9649	90.3488	95.6256	99.3303
67	40.9349	43.0384	46.2610	49.1623	52.6589	82.1971	87.1080	91.5193	96.8277	100.5538
68	41.7136	43.8380	47.0919	50.0203	53.5481	83.3079	88.2502	92.6885	98.0283	101.7757
69	42.4934	44.6392	47.9241	50.8792	54.4381	84.4179	89.3912	93.8565	99.2274	102.9961
70	43.2753	45.4417	48.7575	51.7393	55.3289	85.5270	90.5313	95.0231	100.4251	104.2148
71	44.0584	46.2456	49.5922	52.6003	56.2206	86.6354	91.6703	96.1887	101.6214	105.4323
72	44.8432	47.0510	50.4279	53.4623	57.1129	87.7431	92.8083	97.3530	102.8163	106.6473
73	45.6291	47.8577	51.2648	54.3253	58.0061	88.8499	93.9453	98.5162	104.0098	107.8619
74	46.4168	48.6657	52.1028	55.1892	58.9000	89.9561	95.0815	99.6784	105.2019	109.0742
75	47.2061	49.4751	52.9419	56.0541	59.7946	91.0615	96.2167	100.8393	106.3929	110.2854
76	47.9964	50.2855	53.7821	56.9198	60.6899	92.1662	97.3510	101.9992	107.5824	111.4954
77	48.7885	51.0973	54.6233	57.7865	61.5859	93.2702	98.4844	103.1581	108.7709	112.7037
78	49.5814	51.9104	55.4656	58.6539	62.4825	94.3735	99.6170	104.3159	109.9582	113.9107
79	50.3760	52.7248	56.3089	59.5223	63.3799	95.4762	100.7486	105.4727	111.1440	115.1163
80	51.1719	53.5400	57.1532	60.3915	64.2778	96.5782	101.8795	106.6285	112.3288	116.3209
81	51.9690	54.3567	57.9984	61.2615	65.1765	97.6796	103.0095	107.7834	113.5123	117.5240
82	52.7672	55.1743	58.8447	62.1323	66.0757	98.7803	104.1387	108.9373	114.6948	118.7261
83	53.5669	55.9930	59.6917	63.0039	66.9756	99.8805	105.2672	110.0902	115.8762	119.9270
84	54.3678	56.8129	60.5398	63.8762	67.8761	100.9800	106.3949	111.2422	117.0566	121.1262
85	55.1695	57.6339	61.3888	64.7494	68.7771	102.0789	107.5217	112.3933	118.2356	122.3244
86	55.9726	58.4559	62.2386	65.6233	69.6788	103.1773	108.6479	113.5436	119.4137	123.5218

TABLE 3 (continued)
Critical Values for the Chi-Square Distribution
Probabilities represent the area to the right of the critical chi-square value.

α	0.9950	0.9900	0.9750	0.9500	0.9000	0.1000	0.0500	0.0250	0.0100	0.0050
df = 87 to 1000					Critical Values					
87	56.7770	59.2791	63.0894	66.4979	70.5810	104.2750	109.7733	114.6929	120.5909	124.7176
88	57.5825	60.1029	63.9409	67.3732	71.4839	105.3723	110.8980	115.8415	121.7672	125.9123
89	58.3888	60.9280	64.7934	68.2493	72.3872	106.4689	112.0220	116.9890	122.9422	127.1060
90	59.1963	61.7540	65.6466	69.1260	73.2911	107.5650	113.1452	118.1359	124.1162	128.2987
91	60.0049	62.5810	66.5007	70.0035	74.1955	108.6606	114.2679	119.2820	125.2893	129.4902
92	60.8146	63.4089	67.3556	70.8816	75.1005	109.7556	115.3898	120.4270	126.4616	130.6812
93	61.6252	64.2380	68.2112	71.7603	76.0059	110.8501	116.5110	121.5714	127.6330	131.8705
94	62.4369	65.0676	69.0676	72.6398	76.9119	111.9442	117.6317	122.7152	128.8032	133.0589
95	63.2495	65.8983	69.9249	73.5198	77.8184	113.0377	118.7516	123.8580	129.9725	134.2466
96	64.0633	66.7300	70.7828	74.4006	78.7254	114.1307	119.8709	125.0001	131.1411	135.4327
97	64.8778	67.5623	71.6415	75.2818	79.6329	115.2232	120.9897	126.1414	132.3089	136.6188
98	65.6935	68.3957	72.5009	76.1638	80.5408	116.3153	122.1077	127.2821	133.4756	137.8030
99	66.5099	69.2299	73.3611	77.0463	81.4492	117.4069	123.2252	128.4219	134.6415	138.9869
100	67.3275	70.0650	74.2219	77.9294	82.3581	118.4980	124.3421	129.5613	135.8069	140.1697
101	68.1459	70.9007	75.0835	78.8132	83.2675	119.5887	125.4584	130.6996	136.9711	141.3509
102	68.9652	71.7373	75.9457	79.6975	84.1773	120.6789	126.5741	131.8375	138.1343	142.5319
103	69.7851	72.5748	76.8086	80.5823	85.0875	121.7686	127.6893	132.9746	139.2973	143.7121
104	70.6062	73.4129	77.6721	81.4678	85.9982	122.8580	128.8039	134.1112	140.4590	144.8914
105	71.4281	74.2521	78.5364	82.3537	86.9093	123.9469	129.9179	135.2470	141.6203	146.0693
106	72.2509	75.0918	79.4013	83.2402	87.8208	125.0353	131.0315	136.3821	142.7803	147.2468
107	73.0743	75.9324	80.2668	84.1273	88.7327	126.1234	132.1444	137.5167	143.9399	148.4237
108	73.8986	76.7737	81.1329	85.0149	89.6451	127.2110	133.2569	138.6506	145.0989	149.5995
109	74.7239	77.6156	81.9997	85.9030	90.5579	128.2983	134.3687	139.7839	146.2568	150.7741
110	75.5498	78.4582	82.8671	86.7916	91.4710	129.3852	135.4802	140.9165	147.4143	151.9482
111	76.3768	79.3017	83.7350	87.6808	92.3846	130.4716	136.5911	142.0486	148.5710	153.1215
112	77.2043	80.1459	84.6036	88.5704	93.2985	131.5576	137.7014	143.1801	149.7269	154.2948
113	78.0328	80.9906	85.4727	89.4605	94.2129	132.6433	138.8113	144.3110	150.8821	155.4666
114	78.8617	81.8362	86.3425	90.3511	95.1276	133.7286	139.9207	145.4413	152.0365	156.6372
115	79.6914	82.6825	87.2128	91.2422	96.0427	134.8135	141.0297	146.5710	153.1904	157.8076
116	80.5222	83.5292	88.0836	92.1338	96.9582	135.8980	142.1382	147.7002	154.3440	158.9772
117	81.3532	84.3768	88.9551	93.0258	97.8740	136.9822	143.2462	148.8288	155.4966	160.1459
118	82.1853	85.2251	89.8270	93.9183	98.7902	138.0660	144.3536	149.9569	156.6483	161.3142
119	83.0179	86.0739	90.6995	94.8113	99.7067	139.1494	145.4607	151.0844	157.7993	162.4814
120	83.8517	86.9233	91.5726	95.7046	100.6236	140.2326	146.5673	152.2113	158.9500	163.6485
125	88.0289	91.1798	95.9458	100.1782	105.2132	145.6429	152.0938	157.8384	164.6939	169.4712
150	109.1423	112.6676	117.9846	122.6918	128.2750	172.5812	179.5806	185.8004	193.2075	198.3599
175	130.5678	134.4379	140.2618	145.4058	151.4933	199.3630	206.8668	213.5236	221.4383	226.9363
200	152.2408	156.4321	162.7280	168.2785	174.8353	226.0210	233.9942	241.0578	249.4452	255.2638
300	240.6631	245.9727	253.9122	260.8781	269.0679	331.7885	341.3951	349.8745	359.9064	366.8439
400	330.9029	337.1552	346.4817	354.6410	364.2074	436.6490	447.6324	457.3056	468.7244	476.6068
500	422.3034	429.3874	439.9360	449.1467	459.9261	540.9303	553.1269	563.8514	576.4931	585.2060
1000	888.5631	898.9124	914.2572	927.5944	943.1326	1057.7240	1074.6794	1089.5307	1106.9690	1118.9475

TABLE 4
Critical Values for the *F*-Distribution
$\alpha = .20$

df_D \ df_N	1	2	3	4	5	6	7	8	9	10	11	12	13	14	15	16	17	18	19
1	9.47	12.00	13.06	13.64	14.01	14.26	14.44	14.58	14.68	14.77	14.84	14.90	14.95	15.00	15.04	15.07	15.10	15.13	15.15
2	3.56	4.00	4.16	4.24	4.28	4.32	4.34	4.36	4.37	4.38	4.39	4.40	4.40	4.41	4.42	4.42	4.42	4.43	4.43
3	2.68	2.89	2.94	2.96	2.97	2.97	2.97	2.98	2.98	2.98	2.98	2.98	2.98	2.98	2.98	2.98	2.98	2.98	2.98
4	2.35	2.47	2.48	2.48	2.48	2.47	2.47	2.47	2.46	2.46	2.46	2.46	2.45	2.45	2.45	2.45	2.45	2.45	2.45
5	2.18	2.26	2.25	2.24	2.23	2.22	2.21	2.20	2.20	2.19	2.19	2.18	2.18	2.18	2.18	2.17	2.17	2.17	2.17
6	2.07	2.13	2.11	2.09	2.08	2.06	2.05	2.04	2.03	2.03	2.02	2.02	2.01	2.01	2.01	2.00	2.00	2.00	2.00
7	2.00	2.04	2.02	1.99	1.97	1.96	1.94	1.93	1.93	1.92	1.91	1.91	1.90	1.90	1.89	1.89	1.89	1.88	1.88
8	1.95	1.98	1.95	1.92	1.90	1.88	1.87	1.86	1.85	1.84	1.83	1.83	1.82	1.82	1.81	1.81	1.80	1.80	1.80
9	1.91	1.93	1.90	1.87	1.85	1.83	1.81	1.80	1.79	1.78	1.77	1.76	1.76	1.75	1.75	1.74	1.74	1.74	1.73
10	1.88	1.90	1.86	1.83	1.80	1.78	1.77	1.75	1.74	1.73	1.72	1.72	1.71	1.70	1.70	1.70	1.69	1.69	1.69
11	1.86	1.87	1.83	1.80	1.77	1.75	1.73	1.72	1.70	1.69	1.69	1.68	1.67	1.67	1.66	1.66	1.65	1.65	1.65
12	1.84	1.85	1.80	1.77	1.74	1.72	1.70	1.69	1.67	1.66	1.65	1.65	1.64	1.63	1.63	1.62	1.62	1.62	1.61
13	1.82	1.83	1.78	1.75	1.72	1.69	1.68	1.66	1.65	1.64	1.63	1.62	1.61	1.61	1.60	1.60	1.59	1.59	1.58
14	1.81	1.81	1.76	1.73	1.70	1.67	1.65	1.64	1.63	1.62	1.61	1.60	1.59	1.58	1.58	1.57	1.57	1.56	1.56
15	1.80	1.80	1.75	1.71	1.68	1.66	1.64	1.62	1.61	1.60	1.59	1.58	1.57	1.56	1.56	1.55	1.55	1.54	1.54
16	1.79	1.78	1.74	1.70	1.67	1.64	1.62	1.61	1.59	1.58	1.57	1.56	1.55	1.55	1.54	1.54	1.53	1.53	1.52
17	1.78	1.77	1.72	1.68	1.65	1.63	1.61	1.59	1.58	1.57	1.56	1.55	1.54	1.53	1.53	1.52	1.52	1.51	1.51
18	1.77	1.76	1.71	1.67	1.64	1.62	1.60	1.58	1.56	1.55	1.54	1.53	1.53	1.52	1.51	1.51	1.50	1.50	1.49
19	1.76	1.75	1.70	1.66	1.63	1.61	1.58	1.57	1.55	1.54	1.53	1.52	1.51	1.51	1.50	1.49	1.49	1.48	1.48
20	1.76	1.75	1.70	1.65	1.62	1.60	1.58	1.56	1.54	1.53	1.52	1.51	1.50	1.50	1.49	1.48	1.48	1.47	1.47
21	1.75	1.74	1.69	1.65	1.61	1.59	1.57	1.55	1.53	1.52	1.51	1.50	1.49	1.49	1.48	1.47	1.47	1.46	1.46
22	1.75	1.73	1.68	1.64	1.61	1.58	1.56	1.54	1.53	1.51	1.50	1.49	1.49	1.48	1.47	1.47	1.46	1.45	1.45
23	1.74	1.73	1.68	1.63	1.60	1.57	1.55	1.53	1.52	1.51	1.50	1.49	1.48	1.47	1.46	1.46	1.45	1.45	1.44
24	1.74	1.72	1.67	1.63	1.59	1.57	1.55	1.53	1.51	1.50	1.49	1.48	1.47	1.46	1.46	1.45	1.44	1.44	1.43
25	1.73	1.72	1.66	1.62	1.59	1.56	1.54	1.52	1.51	1.49	1.48	1.47	1.46	1.46	1.45	1.44	1.44	1.43	1.43
26	1.73	1.71	1.66	1.62	1.58	1.56	1.53	1.52	1.50	1.49	1.48	1.47	1.46	1.45	1.44	1.44	1.43	1.43	1.42
27	1.73	1.71	1.66	1.61	1.58	1.55	1.53	1.51	1.49	1.48	1.47	1.46	1.45	1.44	1.44	1.43	1.42	1.42	1.42
28	1.72	1.71	1.65	1.61	1.57	1.55	1.52	1.51	1.49	1.48	1.47	1.46	1.45	1.44	1.43	1.43	1.42	1.41	1.41
29	1.72	1.70	1.65	1.60	1.57	1.54	1.52	1.50	1.49	1.47	1.46	1.45	1.44	1.43	1.43	1.42	1.41	1.41	1.40
30	1.72	1.70	1.64	1.60	1.57	1.54	1.52	1.50	1.48	1.47	1.46	1.45	1.44	1.43	1.42	1.42	1.41	1.40	1.40
31	1.71	1.70	1.64	1.60	1.56	1.53	1.51	1.49	1.48	1.46	1.45	1.44	1.43	1.42	1.42	1.41	1.41	1.40	1.39
32	1.71	1.69	1.64	1.59	1.56	1.53	1.51	1.49	1.47	1.46	1.45	1.44	1.43	1.42	1.41	1.41	1.40	1.40	1.39

$\alpha = .20$

df_D \ df_N	1	2	3	4	5	6	7	8	9	10	11	12	13	14	15	16	17	18	19
33	1.71	1.69	1.64	1.59	1.56	1.53	1.50	1.49	1.47	1.46	1.44	1.43	1.43	1.42	1.41	1.40	1.40	1.39	1.39
34	1.71	1.69	1.63	1.59	1.55	1.52	1.50	1.48	1.47	1.45	1.44	1.43	1.42	1.41	1.41	1.40	1.39	1.39	1.38
35	1.71	1.69	1.63	1.58	1.55	1.52	1.50	1.48	1.46	1.45	1.44	1.43	1.42	1.41	1.40	1.40	1.39	1.38	1.38
36	1.70	1.68	1.63	1.58	1.55	1.52	1.50	1.48	1.46	1.45	1.43	1.42	1.42	1.41	1.40	1.39	1.39	1.38	1.38
37	1.70	1.68	1.63	1.58	1.54	1.52	1.49	1.47	1.46	1.44	1.43	1.42	1.41	1.40	1.40	1.39	1.38	1.38	1.37
38	1.70	1.68	1.62	1.58	1.54	1.51	1.49	1.47	1.46	1.44	1.43	1.42	1.41	1.40	1.39	1.39	1.38	1.38	1.37
39	1.70	1.68	1.62	1.58	1.54	1.51	1.49	1.47	1.45	1.44	1.43	1.42	1.41	1.40	1.39	1.38	1.38	1.37	1.37
40	1.70	1.68	1.62	1.57	1.54	1.51	1.49	1.47	1.45	1.44	1.42	1.41	1.40	1.40	1.39	1.38	1.38	1.37	1.36
41	1.70	1.67	1.62	1.57	1.54	1.51	1.48	1.46	1.45	1.43	1.42	1.41	1.40	1.39	1.39	1.38	1.37	1.37	1.36
42	1.70	1.67	1.62	1.57	1.53	1.51	1.48	1.46	1.45	1.43	1.42	1.41	1.40	1.39	1.38	1.38	1.37	1.36	1.36
43	1.69	1.67	1.61	1.57	1.53	1.50	1.48	1.46	1.44	1.43	1.42	1.41	1.40	1.39	1.38	1.37	1.37	1.36	1.36
44	1.69	1.67	1.61	1.57	1.53	1.50	1.48	1.46	1.44	1.43	1.42	1.40	1.40	1.39	1.38	1.37	1.37	1.36	1.35
45	1.69	1.67	1.61	1.57	1.53	1.50	1.48	1.46	1.44	1.43	1.41	1.40	1.39	1.38	1.38	1.37	1.36	1.36	1.35
46	1.69	1.67	1.61	1.56	1.53	1.50	1.47	1.46	1.44	1.42	1.41	1.40	1.39	1.38	1.38	1.37	1.36	1.36	1.35
47	1.69	1.67	1.61	1.56	1.53	1.50	1.47	1.45	1.44	1.42	1.41	1.40	1.39	1.38	1.37	1.37	1.36	1.35	1.35
48	1.69	1.66	1.61	1.56	1.52	1.50	1.47	1.45	1.44	1.42	1.41	1.40	1.39	1.38	1.37	1.36	1.36	1.35	1.35
49	1.69	1.66	1.61	1.56	1.52	1.49	1.47	1.45	1.43	1.42	1.41	1.40	1.39	1.38	1.37	1.36	1.36	1.35	1.35
50	1.69	1.66	1.60	1.56	1.52	1.49	1.47	1.45	1.43	1.42	1.41	1.39	1.38	1.38	1.37	1.36	1.35	1.35	1.34
60	1.68	1.65	1.59	1.55	1.51	1.48	1.46	1.44	1.42	1.41	1.39	1.38	1.37	1.36	1.35	1.35	1.34	1.33	1.33
70	1.67	1.65	1.59	1.54	1.50	1.47	1.45	1.43	1.41	1.40	1.38	1.37	1.36	1.35	1.35	1.34	1.33	1.32	1.32
80	1.67	1.64	1.58	1.53	1.50	1.47	1.44	1.42	1.41	1.39	1.38	1.37	1.36	1.35	1.34	1.33	1.32	1.32	1.31
90	1.67	1.64	1.58	1.53	1.49	1.46	1.44	1.42	1.40	1.38	1.37	1.36	1.35	1.34	1.33	1.32	1.32	1.31	1.31
100	1.66	1.64	1.58	1.53	1.49	1.46	1.43	1.41	1.40	1.38	1.37	1.36	1.35	1.34	1.33	1.32	1.31	1.31	1.30
110	1.66	1.63	1.57	1.52	1.49	1.46	1.43	1.41	1.39	1.38	1.36	1.35	1.34	1.33	1.32	1.32	1.31	1.30	1.30
120	1.66	1.63	1.57	1.52	1.48	1.45	1.43	1.41	1.39	1.37	1.36	1.35	1.34	1.33	1.32	1.31	1.31	1.30	1.29
130	1.66	1.63	1.57	1.52	1.48	1.45	1.43	1.41	1.39	1.37	1.36	1.35	1.34	1.33	1.32	1.31	1.30	1.30	1.29
140	1.66	1.63	1.57	1.52	1.48	1.45	1.42	1.40	1.39	1.37	1.36	1.35	1.33	1.32	1.32	1.31	1.30	1.29	1.29
150	1.66	1.63	1.57	1.52	1.48	1.45	1.42	1.40	1.38	1.37	1.36	1.34	1.33	1.32	1.31	1.31	1.30	1.29	1.29
200	1.65	1.62	1.56	1.51	1.47	1.44	1.42	1.40	1.38	1.36	1.35	1.34	1.33	1.32	1.31	1.30	1.29	1.29	1.28
300	1.65	1.62	1.56	1.51	1.47	1.44	1.41	1.39	1.37	1.36	1.34	1.33	1.32	1.31	1.30	1.29	1.29	1.28	1.27
400	1.65	1.62	1.55	1.50	1.47	1.43	1.41	1.39	1.37	1.35	1.34	1.33	1.32	1.31	1.30	1.29	1.28	1.28	1.27
500	1.65	1.61	1.55	1.50	1.46	1.43	1.41	1.39	1.37	1.35	1.34	1.33	1.31	1.30	1.30	1.29	1.28	1.27	1.27
1000	1.64	1.61	1.55	1.50	1.46	1.43	1.40	1.38	1.36	1.35	1.33	1.32	1.31	1.30	1.29	1.28	1.28	1.27	1.26
∞	1.64	1.61	1.55	1.50	1.46	1.43	1.40	1.38	1.36	1.34	1.33	1.32	1.31	1.30	1.29	1.28	1.27	1.26	1.26

$\alpha = .20$

df_D \ df_N	20	21	22	23	24	25	26	27	28	29	30	31	32	33	34	35	36	37	38
1	15.17	15.19	15.21	15.22	15.24	15.25	15.26	15.28	15.29	15.30	15.31	15.31	15.32	15.33	15.34	15.34	15.35	15.36	15.36
2	4.43	4.43	4.44	4.44	4.44	4.44	4.44	4.44	4.45	4.45	4.45	4.45	4.45	4.45	4.45	4.45	4.45	4.45	4.46
3	2.98	2.98	2.98	2.98	2.98	2.98	2.98	2.98	2.98	2.98	2.98	2.98	2.98	2.98	2.98	2.98	2.98	2.98	2.98
4	2.44	2.44	2.44	2.44	2.44	2.44	2.44	2.44	2.44	2.44	2.44	2.44	2.44	2.44	2.44	2.44	2.44	2.44	2.44
5	2.17	2.16	2.16	2.16	2.16	2.16	2.16	2.16	2.16	2.16	2.16	2.16	2.15	2.15	2.15	2.15	2.15	2.15	2.15
6	2.00	1.99	1.99	1.99	1.99	1.99	1.99	1.99	1.98	1.98	1.98	1.98	1.98	1.98	1.98	1.98	1.98	1.98	1.98
7	1.88	1.88	1.88	1.87	1.87	1.87	1.87	1.87	1.87	1.87	1.86	1.86	1.86	1.86	1.86	1.86	1.86	1.86	1.86
8	1.80	1.79	1.79	1.79	1.79	1.79	1.78	1.78	1.78	1.78	1.78	1.78	1.78	1.78	1.77	1.77	1.77	1.77	1.77
9	1.73	1.73	1.73	1.73	1.72	1.72	1.72	1.72	1.72	1.72	1.71	1.71	1.71	1.71	1.71	1.71	1.71	1.71	1.71
10	1.68	1.68	1.68	1.67	1.67	1.67	1.67	1.67	1.67	1.66	1.66	1.66	1.66	1.66	1.66	1.66	1.66	1.66	1.65
11	1.64	1.64	1.64	1.63	1.63	1.63	1.63	1.63	1.62	1.62	1.62	1.62	1.62	1.62	1.62	1.62	1.61	1.61	1.61
12	1.61	1.61	1.60	1.60	1.60	1.60	1.59	1.59	1.59	1.59	1.59	1.59	1.58	1.58	1.58	1.58	1.58	1.58	1.58
13	1.58	1.58	1.58	1.57	1.57	1.57	1.57	1.56	1.56	1.56	1.56	1.56	1.56	1.55	1.55	1.55	1.55	1.55	1.55
14	1.56	1.55	1.55	1.55	1.55	1.54	1.54	1.54	1.54	1.54	1.53	1.53	1.53	1.53	1.53	1.53	1.53	1.52	1.52
15	1.54	1.53	1.53	1.53	1.53	1.52	1.52	1.52	1.52	1.51	1.51	1.51	1.51	1.51	1.51	1.51	1.50	1.50	1.50
16	1.52	1.52	1.51	1.51	1.51	1.50	1.50	1.50	1.50	1.50	1.49	1.49	1.49	1.49	1.49	1.49	1.49	1.48	1.48
17	1.50	1.50	1.50	1.49	1.49	1.49	1.49	1.48	1.48	1.48	1.48	1.48	1.47	1.47	1.47	1.47	1.47	1.47	1.47
18	1.49	1.49	1.48	1.48	1.48	1.47	1.47	1.47	1.47	1.47	1.46	1.46	1.46	1.46	1.46	1.46	1.45	1.45	1.45
19	1.48	1.47	1.47	1.47	1.46	1.46	1.46	1.46	1.45	1.45	1.45	1.45	1.45	1.45	1.44	1.44	1.44	1.44	1.44
20	1.47	1.46	1.46	1.46	1.45	1.45	1.45	1.44	1.44	1.44	1.44	1.44	1.43	1.43	1.43	1.43	1.43	1.43	1.43
21	1.46	1.45	1.45	1.45	1.44	1.44	1.44	1.43	1.43	1.43	1.43	1.43	1.42	1.42	1.42	1.42	1.42	1.42	1.42
22	1.45	1.44	1.44	1.44	1.43	1.43	1.43	1.42	1.42	1.42	1.42	1.42	1.41	1.41	1.41	1.41	1.41	1.41	1.41
23	1.44	1.43	1.43	1.43	1.42	1.42	1.42	1.42	1.41	1.41	1.41	1.41	1.41	1.40	1.40	1.40	1.40	1.40	1.40
24	1.43	1.43	1.42	1.42	1.42	1.41	1.41	1.41	1.41	1.40	1.40	1.40	1.40	1.40	1.39	1.39	1.39	1.39	1.39
25	1.42	1.42	1.42	1.41	1.41	1.41	1.40	1.40	1.40	1.40	1.39	1.39	1.39	1.39	1.39	1.38	1.38	1.38	1.38
26	1.42	1.41	1.41	1.41	1.40	1.40	1.40	1.39	1.39	1.39	1.39	1.39	1.38	1.38	1.38	1.38	1.38	1.37	1.37
27	1.41	1.41	1.40	1.40	1.40	1.39	1.39	1.39	1.39	1.38	1.38	1.38	1.38	1.37	1.37	1.37	1.37	1.37	1.37
28	1.41	1.40	1.40	1.39	1.39	1.39	1.38	1.38	1.38	1.38	1.37	1.37	1.37	1.37	1.37	1.37	1.36	1.36	1.36
29	1.40	1.40	1.39	1.39	1.39	1.38	1.38	1.38	1.37	1.37	1.37	1.37	1.37	1.36	1.36	1.36	1.36	1.36	1.36
30	1.39	1.39	1.39	1.38	1.38	1.38	1.37	1.37	1.37	1.37	1.36	1.36	1.36	1.36	1.36	1.35	1.35	1.35	1.35
31	1.39	1.39	1.38	1.38	1.38	1.37	1.37	1.37	1.36	1.36	1.36	1.36	1.36	1.35	1.35	1.35	1.35	1.35	1.34
32	1.39	1.38	1.38	1.37	1.37	1.37	1.36	1.36	1.36	1.36	1.35	1.35	1.35	1.35	1.35	1.34	1.34	1.34	1.34

$\alpha = .20$

df_D \ df_N	20	21	22	23	24	25	26	27	28	29	30	31	32	33	34	35	36	37	38
33	1.38	1.38	1.37	1.37	1.37	1.36	1.36	1.36	1.36	1.35	1.35	1.35	1.35	1.34	1.34	1.34	1.34	1.34	1.34
34	1.38	1.37	1.37	1.37	1.36	1.36	1.36	1.35	1.35	1.35	1.35	1.34	1.34	1.34	1.34	1.34	1.33	1.33	1.33
35	1.37	1.37	1.37	1.36	1.36	1.36	1.35	1.35	1.35	1.35	1.34	1.34	1.34	1.34	1.33	1.33	1.33	1.33	1.33
36	1.37	1.37	1.36	1.36	1.36	1.35	1.35	1.35	1.34	1.34	1.34	1.34	1.33	1.33	1.33	1.33	1.33	1.33	1.32
37	1.37	1.36	1.36	1.36	1.35	1.35	1.35	1.34	1.34	1.34	1.34	1.33	1.33	1.33	1.33	1.33	1.32	1.32	1.32
38	1.37	1.36	1.36	1.35	1.35	1.35	1.34	1.34	1.34	1.33	1.33	1.33	1.33	1.33	1.32	1.32	1.32	1.32	1.32
39	1.36	1.36	1.35	1.35	1.35	1.34	1.34	1.34	1.33	1.33	1.33	1.33	1.32	1.32	1.32	1.32	1.32	1.32	1.31
40	1.36	1.36	1.35	1.35	1.34	1.34	1.34	1.33	1.33	1.33	1.33	1.32	1.32	1.32	1.32	1.32	1.31	1.31	1.31
41	1.36	1.35	1.35	1.34	1.34	1.34	1.33	1.33	1.33	1.33	1.32	1.32	1.32	1.32	1.31	1.31	1.31	1.31	1.31
42	1.35	1.35	1.35	1.34	1.34	1.34	1.33	1.33	1.33	1.32	1.32	1.32	1.32	1.31	1.31	1.31	1.31	1.31	1.31
43	1.35	1.35	1.34	1.34	1.34	1.33	1.33	1.33	1.32	1.32	1.32	1.32	1.31	1.31	1.31	1.31	1.31	1.30	1.30
44	1.35	1.35	1.34	1.34	1.33	1.33	1.33	1.32	1.32	1.32	1.32	1.31	1.31	1.31	1.31	1.31	1.30	1.30	1.30
45	1.35	1.34	1.34	1.34	1.33	1.33	1.32	1.32	1.32	1.32	1.31	1.31	1.31	1.31	1.30	1.30	1.30	1.30	1.30
46	1.35	1.34	1.34	1.33	1.33	1.33	1.32	1.32	1.32	1.31	1.31	1.31	1.31	1.30	1.30	1.30	1.30	1.30	1.30
47	1.34	1.34	1.33	1.33	1.33	1.32	1.32	1.32	1.31	1.31	1.31	1.31	1.30	1.30	1.30	1.30	1.30	1.29	1.29
48	1.34	1.34	1.33	1.33	1.33	1.32	1.32	1.32	1.31	1.31	1.31	1.30	1.30	1.30	1.30	1.30	1.29	1.29	1.29
49	1.34	1.34	1.33	1.33	1.32	1.32	1.32	1.31	1.31	1.31	1.31	1.30	1.30	1.30	1.30	1.29	1.29	1.29	1.29
50	1.34	1.33	1.33	1.33	1.32	1.32	1.31	1.31	1.31	1.31	1.30	1.30	1.30	1.30	1.29	1.29	1.29	1.29	1.29
60	1.32	1.32	1.31	1.31	1.31	1.30	1.30	1.30	1.29	1.29	1.29	1.29	1.28	1.28	1.28	1.28	1.27	1.27	1.27
70	1.31	1.31	1.30	1.30	1.30	1.29	1.29	1.29	1.28	1.28	1.28	1.27	1.27	1.27	1.27	1.27	1.26	1.26	1.26
80	1.31	1.30	1.30	1.29	1.29	1.28	1.28	1.28	1.27	1.27	1.27	1.27	1.26	1.26	1.26	1.26	1.25	1.25	1.25
90	1.30	1.30	1.29	1.29	1.28	1.28	1.27	1.27	1.27	1.27	1.26	1.26	1.26	1.25	1.25	1.25	1.25	1.25	1.24
100	1.30	1.29	1.29	1.28	1.28	1.27	1.27	1.27	1.26	1.26	1.26	1.25	1.25	1.25	1.25	1.24	1.24	1.24	1.24
110	1.29	1.29	1.28	1.28	1.27	1.27	1.27	1.26	1.26	1.26	1.25	1.25	1.25	1.24	1.24	1.24	1.24	1.24	1.23
120	1.29	1.28	1.28	1.27	1.27	1.27	1.26	1.26	1.26	1.25	1.25	1.25	1.24	1.24	1.24	1.24	1.23	1.23	1.23
130	1.29	1.28	1.28	1.27	1.27	1.26	1.26	1.26	1.25	1.25	1.25	1.24	1.24	1.24	1.24	1.23	1.23	1.23	1.23
140	1.28	1.28	1.27	1.27	1.26	1.26	1.26	1.25	1.25	1.25	1.24	1.24	1.24	1.24	1.23	1.23	1.23	1.23	1.22
150	1.28	1.28	1.27	1.27	1.26	1.26	1.25	1.25	1.25	1.24	1.24	1.24	1.24	1.23	1.23	1.23	1.23	1.22	1.22
200	1.27	1.27	1.26	1.26	1.25	1.25	1.25	1.24	1.24	1.24	1.23	1.23	1.23	1.22	1.22	1.22	1.22	1.21	1.21
300	1.27	1.26	1.26	1.25	1.25	1.24	1.24	1.23	1.23	1.23	1.22	1.22	1.22	1.22	1.21	1.21	1.21	1.21	1.20
400	1.26	1.26	1.25	1.25	1.24	1.24	1.23	1.23	1.23	1.22	1.22	1.22	1.21	1.21	1.21	1.21	1.20	1.20	1.20
500	1.26	1.26	1.25	1.25	1.24	1.24	1.23	1.23	1.22	1.22	1.22	1.22	1.21	1.21	1.21	1.20	1.20	1.20	1.20
1000	1.26	1.25	1.25	1.24	1.24	1.23	1.23	1.22	1.22	1.22	1.21	1.21	1.21	1.20	1.20	1.20	1.20	1.19	1.19
∞	1.25	1.25	1.24	1.24	1.23	1.23	1.22	1.22	1.22	1.21	1.21	1.21	1.20	1.20	1.20	1.19	1.19	1.19	1.19

$\alpha = .20$

df_D \ df_N	39	40	50	60	70	80	90	100	110	120	130	140	150	200	300	400	500	1000	∞
1	15.37	15.37	15.42	15.44	15.46	15.48	15.49	15.50	15.50	15.51	15.52	15.52	15.52	15.54	15.55	15.56	15.56	15.57	15.58
2	4.46	4.46	4.46	4.46	4.47	4.47	4.47	4.47	4.47	4.47	4.47	4.47	4.47	4.48	4.48	4.48	4.48	4.48	4.48
3	2.98	2.98	2.98	2.98	2.98	2.98	2.98	2.98	2.98	2.98	2.98	2.98	2.98	2.98	2.98	2.98	2.98	2.98	2.98
4	2.44	2.44	2.43	2.43	2.43	2.43	2.43	2.43	2.43	2.43	2.43	2.43	2.43	2.43	2.43	2.43	2.43	2.43	2.43
5	2.15	2.15	2.15	2.15	2.14	2.14	2.14	2.14	2.14	2.14	2.14	2.14	2.14	2.14	2.14	2.14	2.14	2.14	2.13
6	1.98	1.98	1.97	1.97	1.97	1.97	1.96	1.96	1.96	1.96	1.96	1.96	1.96	1.96	1.96	1.96	1.96	1.96	1.95
7	1.86	1.86	1.85	1.85	1.85	1.84	1.84	1.84	1.84	1.84	1.84	1.84	1.84	1.84	1.83	1.83	1.83	1.83	1.83
8	1.77	1.77	1.76	1.76	1.76	1.76	1.75	1.75	1.75	1.75	1.75	1.75	1.75	1.75	1.75	1.74	1.74	1.74	1.74
9	1.71	1.70	1.70	1.69	1.69	1.69	1.69	1.69	1.68	1.68	1.68	1.68	1.68	1.68	1.68	1.68	1.68	1.67	1.67
10	1.65	1.65	1.65	1.64	1.64	1.64	1.63	1.63	1.63	1.63	1.63	1.63	1.63	1.63	1.62	1.62	1.62	1.62	1.62
11	1.61	1.61	1.60	1.60	1.60	1.59	1.59	1.59	1.59	1.59	1.59	1.59	1.58	1.58	1.58	1.58	1.58	1.58	1.57
12	1.58	1.58	1.57	1.56	1.56	1.56	1.56	1.55	1.55	1.55	1.55	1.55	1.55	1.55	1.54	1.54	1.54	1.54	1.54
13	1.55	1.55	1.54	1.53	1.53	1.53	1.52	1.52	1.52	1.52	1.52	1.52	1.52	1.51	1.51	1.51	1.51	1.51	1.51
14	1.52	1.52	1.51	1.51	1.50	1.50	1.50	1.50	1.50	1.49	1.49	1.49	1.49	1.49	1.48	1.48	1.48	1.48	1.48
15	1.50	1.50	1.49	1.49	1.48	1.48	1.48	1.47	1.47	1.47	1.47	1.47	1.47	1.46	1.46	1.46	1.46	1.46	1.46
16	1.48	1.48	1.47	1.47	1.46	1.46	1.46	1.45	1.45	1.45	1.45	1.45	1.45	1.44	1.44	1.44	1.44	1.44	1.43
17	1.47	1.46	1.46	1.45	1.44	1.44	1.44	1.44	1.43	1.43	1.43	1.43	1.43	1.43	1.42	1.42	1.42	1.42	1.42
18	1.45	1.45	1.44	1.43	1.43	1.43	1.42	1.42	1.42	1.42	1.42	1.42	1.41	1.41	1.41	1.41	1.40	1.40	1.40
19	1.44	1.44	1.43	1.42	1.42	1.41	1.41	1.41	1.40	1.40	1.40	1.40	1.40	1.40	1.39	1.39	1.39	1.39	1.39
20	1.42	1.42	1.41	1.41	1.40	1.40	1.40	1.39	1.39	1.39	1.39	1.39	1.39	1.38	1.38	1.38	1.38	1.37	1.37
21	1.41	1.41	1.40	1.40	1.39	1.39	1.38	1.38	1.38	1.38	1.38	1.38	1.38	1.37	1.37	1.37	1.36	1.36	1.36
22	1.40	1.40	1.39	1.39	1.38	1.38	1.37	1.37	1.37	1.37	1.37	1.37	1.36	1.36	1.36	1.35	1.35	1.35	1.35
23	1.40	1.39	1.38	1.38	1.37	1.37	1.36	1.36	1.36	1.36	1.36	1.36	1.35	1.35	1.35	1.34	1.34	1.34	1.34
24	1.39	1.39	1.38	1.37	1.36	1.36	1.36	1.35	1.35	1.35	1.35	1.35	1.35	1.34	1.34	1.34	1.33	1.33	1.33
25	1.38	1.38	1.37	1.36	1.35	1.35	1.35	1.35	1.34	1.34	1.34	1.34	1.34	1.33	1.33	1.33	1.33	1.32	1.32
26	1.37	1.37	1.36	1.35	1.35	1.34	1.34	1.34	1.34	1.33	1.33	1.33	1.33	1.33	1.32	1.32	1.32	1.31	1.31
27	1.37	1.36	1.35	1.35	1.34	1.34	1.33	1.33	1.33	1.33	1.32	1.32	1.32	1.32	1.31	1.31	1.31	1.31	1.30
28	1.36	1.36	1.35	1.34	1.33	1.33	1.33	1.32	1.32	1.32	1.32	1.32	1.32	1.31	1.31	1.30	1.30	1.30	1.30
29	1.35	1.35	1.34	1.33	1.33	1.32	1.32	1.32	1.32	1.31	1.31	1.31	1.31	1.30	1.30	1.30	1.30	1.29	1.29
30	1.35	1.35	1.34	1.33	1.32	1.32	1.31	1.31	1.31	1.31	1.31	1.30	1.30	1.30	1.29	1.29	1.29	1.29	1.28
31	1.34	1.34	1.33	1.32	1.32	1.31	1.31	1.31	1.30	1.30	1.30	1.30	1.30	1.29	1.29	1.29	1.28	1.28	1.28
32	1.34	1.34	1.33	1.32	1.31	1.31	1.30	1.30	1.30	1.30	1.29	1.29	1.29	1.29	1.28	1.28	1.28	1.28	1.27

$\alpha = .20$

df_N / df_D	39	40	50	60	70	80	90	100	110	120	130	140	150	200	300	400	500	1000	∞
33	1.33	1.33	1.32	1.31	1.31	1.30	1.30	1.30	1.29	1.29	1.29	1.29	1.29	1.28	1.28	1.27	1.27	1.27	1.27
34	1.33	1.33	1.32	1.31	1.30	1.30	1.29	1.29	1.29	1.29	1.29	1.28	1.28	1.28	1.27	1.27	1.27	1.27	1.26
35	1.33	1.32	1.31	1.30	1.30	1.29	1.29	1.29	1.28	1.28	1.28	1.28	1.28	1.27	1.27	1.27	1.26	1.26	1.26
36	1.32	1.32	1.31	1.30	1.29	1.29	1.29	1.28	1.28	1.28	1.28	1.27	1.27	1.27	1.26	1.26	1.26	1.26	1.25
37	1.32	1.32	1.31	1.30	1.29	1.29	1.28	1.28	1.28	1.27	1.27	1.27	1.27	1.26	1.26	1.26	1.26	1.25	1.25
38	1.32	1.31	1.30	1.29	1.29	1.28	1.28	1.28	1.27	1.27	1.27	1.27	1.27	1.26	1.26	1.25	1.25	1.25	1.24
39	1.31	1.31	1.30	1.29	1.28	1.28	1.27	1.27	1.27	1.27	1.27	1.26	1.26	1.26	1.25	1.25	1.25	1.24	1.24
40	1.31	1.31	1.30	1.29	1.28	1.28	1.27	1.27	1.27	1.26	1.26	1.26	1.26	1.25	1.25	1.25	1.24	1.24	1.24
41	1.31	1.30	1.29	1.28	1.28	1.27	1.27	1.27	1.26	1.26	1.26	1.26	1.26	1.25	1.24	1.24	1.24	1.24	1.23
42	1.30	1.30	1.29	1.28	1.27	1.27	1.27	1.26	1.26	1.26	1.26	1.25	1.25	1.25	1.24	1.24	1.24	1.23	1.23
43	1.30	1.30	1.29	1.28	1.27	1.27	1.26	1.26	1.26	1.25	1.25	1.25	1.25	1.24	1.24	1.24	1.23	1.23	1.23
44	1.30	1.30	1.28	1.28	1.27	1.26	1.26	1.26	1.25	1.25	1.25	1.25	1.25	1.24	1.23	1.23	1.23	1.23	1.22
45	1.30	1.29	1.28	1.27	1.27	1.26	1.26	1.25	1.25	1.25	1.25	1.24	1.24	1.24	1.23	1.23	1.23	1.22	1.22
46	1.29	1.29	1.28	1.27	1.26	1.26	1.25	1.25	1.25	1.25	1.24	1.24	1.24	1.23	1.23	1.23	1.22	1.22	1.22
47	1.29	1.29	1.28	1.27	1.26	1.26	1.25	1.25	1.25	1.24	1.24	1.24	1.24	1.23	1.23	1.22	1.22	1.22	1.21
48	1.29	1.29	1.27	1.27	1.26	1.25	1.25	1.25	1.24	1.24	1.24	1.24	1.24	1.23	1.22	1.22	1.22	1.22	1.21
49	1.29	1.29	1.27	1.26	1.26	1.25	1.25	1.24	1.24	1.24	1.24	1.23	1.23	1.23	1.22	1.22	1.22	1.21	1.21
50	1.29	1.28	1.27	1.26	1.25	1.25	1.24	1.24	1.24	1.24	1.23	1.23	1.23	1.22	1.22	1.22	1.21	1.21	1.21
60	1.27	1.27	1.25	1.24	1.24	1.23	1.23	1.22	1.22	1.22	1.21	1.21	1.21	1.21	1.20	1.20	1.19	1.19	1.18
70	1.26	1.26	1.24	1.23	1.22	1.22	1.21	1.21	1.21	1.20	1.20	1.20	1.20	1.19	1.18	1.18	1.18	1.17	1.17
80	1.25	1.25	1.23	1.22	1.21	1.21	1.20	1.20	1.20	1.19	1.19	1.19	1.19	1.18	1.17	1.17	1.17	1.16	1.16
90	1.24	1.24	1.23	1.21	1.21	1.20	1.19	1.19	1.19	1.18	1.18	1.18	1.18	1.17	1.16	1.16	1.16	1.15	1.15
100	1.24	1.23	1.22	1.21	1.20	1.19	1.19	1.18	1.18	1.18	1.17	1.17	1.17	1.16	1.15	1.15	1.15	1.14	1.14
110	1.23	1.23	1.21	1.20	1.19	1.19	1.18	1.18	1.17	1.17	1.17	1.17	1.16	1.16	1.15	1.14	1.14	1.14	1.13
120	1.23	1.23	1.21	1.20	1.19	1.18	1.18	1.17	1.17	1.17	1.16	1.16	1.16	1.15	1.14	1.14	1.14	1.13	1.12
130	1.22	1.22	1.21	1.20	1.19	1.18	1.17	1.17	1.17	1.16	1.16	1.16	1.15	1.15	1.14	1.13	1.13	1.12	1.12
140	1.22	1.22	1.20	1.19	1.18	1.18	1.17	1.17	1.16	1.16	1.16	1.15	1.15	1.14	1.13	1.13	1.13	1.12	1.11
150	1.22	1.22	1.20	1.19	1.18	1.17	1.17	1.16	1.16	1.16	1.15	1.15	1.15	1.14	1.13	1.13	1.12	1.12	1.11
200	1.21	1.21	1.19	1.18	1.17	1.16	1.16	1.15	1.15	1.14	1.14	1.14	1.14	1.13	1.12	1.11	1.11	1.10	1.09
300	1.20	1.20	1.18	1.17	1.16	1.15	1.15	1.14	1.14	1.13	1.13	1.13	1.12	1.11	1.10	1.10	1.09	1.08	1.07
400	1.20	1.20	1.18	1.16	1.16	1.15	1.14	1.14	1.13	1.13	1.12	1.12	1.12	1.11	1.09	1.09	1.08	1.07	1.06
500	1.19	1.19	1.17	1.16	1.15	1.14	1.14	1.13	1.13	1.12	1.12	1.12	1.11	1.10	1.09	1.08	1.08	1.07	1.06
1000	1.19	1.19	1.17	1.16	1.15	1.14	1.13	1.12	1.12	1.11	1.11	1.11	1.10	1.09	1.08	1.07	1.07	1.05	1.04
∞	1.18	1.18	1.16	1.15	1.14	1.13	1.12	1.12	1.11	1.11	1.10	1.10	1.10	1.08	1.07	1.06	1.05	1.04	1.00

TABLE 4 (continued)
Critical Values for the F-Distribution
$\alpha = .10$

df_D \ df_N	1	2	3	4	5	6	7	8	9	10	11	12	13	14	15	16	17	18	19
1	39.86	49.50	53.59	55.83	57.24	58.20	58.91	59.44	59.86	60.19	60.47	60.71	60.90	61.07	61.22	61.35	61.46	61.57	61.66
2	8.53	9.00	9.16	9.24	9.29	9.33	9.35	9.37	9.38	9.39	9.40	9.41	9.41	9.42	9.42	9.43	9.43	9.44	9.44
3	5.54	5.46	5.39	5.34	5.31	5.28	5.27	5.25	5.24	5.23	5.22	5.22	5.21	5.20	5.20	5.20	5.19	5.19	5.19
4	4.54	4.32	4.19	4.11	4.05	4.01	3.98	3.95	3.94	3.92	3.91	3.90	3.89	3.88	3.87	3.86	3.86	3.85	3.85
5	4.06	3.78	3.62	3.52	3.45	3.40	3.37	3.34	3.32	3.30	3.28	3.27	3.26	3.25	3.24	3.23	3.22	3.22	3.21
6	3.78	3.46	3.29	3.18	3.11	3.05	3.01	2.98	2.96	2.94	2.92	2.90	2.89	2.88	2.87	2.86	2.85	2.85	2.84
7	3.59	3.26	3.07	2.96	2.88	2.83	2.78	2.75	2.72	2.70	2.68	2.67	2.65	2.64	2.63	2.62	2.61	2.61	2.60
8	3.46	3.11	2.92	2.81	2.73	2.67	2.62	2.59	2.56	2.54	2.52	2.50	2.49	2.48	2.46	2.45	2.45	2.44	2.43
9	3.36	3.01	2.81	2.69	2.61	2.55	2.51	2.47	2.44	2.42	2.40	2.38	2.36	2.35	2.34	2.33	2.32	2.31	2.30
10	3.29	2.92	2.73	2.61	2.52	2.46	2.41	2.38	2.35	2.32	2.30	2.28	2.27	2.26	2.24	2.23	2.22	2.22	2.21
11	3.23	2.86	2.66	2.54	2.45	2.39	2.34	2.30	2.27	2.25	2.23	2.21	2.19	2.18	2.17	2.16	2.15	2.14	2.13
12	3.18	2.81	2.61	2.48	2.39	2.33	2.28	2.24	2.21	2.19	2.17	2.15	2.13	2.12	2.10	2.09	2.08	2.08	2.07
13	3.14	2.76	2.56	2.43	2.35	2.28	2.23	2.20	2.16	2.14	2.12	2.10	2.08	2.07	2.05	2.04	2.03	2.02	2.01
14	3.10	2.73	2.52	2.39	2.31	2.24	2.19	2.15	2.12	2.10	2.07	2.05	2.04	2.02	2.01	2.00	1.99	1.98	1.97
15	3.07	2.70	2.49	2.36	2.27	2.21	2.16	2.12	2.09	2.06	2.04	2.02	2.00	1.99	1.97	1.96	1.95	1.94	1.93
16	3.05	2.67	2.46	2.33	2.24	2.18	2.13	2.09	2.06	2.03	2.01	1.99	1.97	1.95	1.94	1.93	1.92	1.91	1.90
17	3.03	2.64	2.44	2.31	2.22	2.15	2.10	2.06	2.03	2.00	1.98	1.96	1.94	1.93	1.91	1.90	1.89	1.88	1.87
18	3.01	2.62	2.42	2.29	2.20	2.13	2.08	2.04	2.00	1.98	1.95	1.93	1.92	1.90	1.89	1.87	1.86	1.85	1.84
19	2.99	2.61	2.40	2.27	2.18	2.11	2.06	2.02	1.98	1.96	1.93	1.91	1.89	1.88	1.86	1.85	1.84	1.83	1.82
20	2.97	2.59	2.38	2.25	2.16	2.09	2.04	2.00	1.96	1.94	1.91	1.89	1.87	1.86	1.84	1.83	1.82	1.81	1.80
21	2.96	2.57	2.36	2.23	2.14	2.08	2.02	1.98	1.95	1.92	1.90	1.87	1.86	1.84	1.83	1.81	1.80	1.79	1.78
22	2.95	2.56	2.35	2.22	2.13	2.06	2.01	1.97	1.93	1.90	1.88	1.86	1.84	1.83	1.81	1.80	1.79	1.78	1.77
23	2.94	2.55	2.34	2.21	2.11	2.05	1.99	1.95	1.92	1.89	1.87	1.84	1.83	1.81	1.80	1.78	1.77	1.76	1.75
24	2.93	2.54	2.33	2.19	2.10	2.04	1.98	1.94	1.91	1.88	1.85	1.83	1.81	1.80	1.78	1.77	1.76	1.75	1.74
25	2.92	2.53	2.32	2.18	2.09	2.02	1.97	1.93	1.89	1.87	1.84	1.82	1.80	1.79	1.77	1.76	1.75	1.74	1.73
26	2.91	2.52	2.31	2.17	2.08	2.01	1.96	1.92	1.88	1.86	1.83	1.81	1.79	1.77	1.76	1.75	1.73	1.72	1.71
27	2.90	2.51	2.30	2.17	2.07	2.00	1.95	1.91	1.87	1.85	1.82	1.80	1.78	1.76	1.75	1.74	1.72	1.71	1.70
28	2.89	2.50	2.29	2.16	2.06	2.00	1.94	1.90	1.87	1.84	1.81	1.79	1.77	1.75	1.74	1.73	1.71	1.70	1.69
29	2.89	2.50	2.28	2.15	2.06	1.99	1.93	1.89	1.86	1.83	1.80	1.78	1.76	1.75	1.73	1.72	1.71	1.69	1.68
30	2.88	2.49	2.28	2.14	2.05	1.98	1.93	1.88	1.85	1.82	1.79	1.77	1.75	1.74	1.72	1.71	1.70	1.69	1.68
31	2.87	2.48	2.27	2.14	2.04	1.97	1.92	1.88	1.84	1.81	1.79	1.77	1.75	1.73	1.71	1.70	1.69	1.68	1.67
32	2.87	2.48	2.26	2.13	2.04	1.97	1.91	1.87	1.83	1.81	1.78	1.76	1.74	1.72	1.71	1.69	1.68	1.67	1.66

$\alpha = .10$

df_D \ df_N	1	2	3	4	5	6	7	8	9	10	11	12	13	14	15	16	17	18	19
33	2.86	2.47	2.26	2.12	2.03	1.96	1.91	1.86	1.83	1.80	1.77	1.75	1.73	1.72	1.70	1.69	1.67	1.66	1.65
34	2.86	2.47	2.25	2.12	2.02	1.96	1.90	1.86	1.82	1.79	1.77	1.75	1.73	1.71	1.69	1.68	1.67	1.66	1.65
35	2.85	2.46	2.25	2.11	2.02	1.95	1.90	1.85	1.82	1.79	1.76	1.74	1.72	1.70	1.69	1.67	1.66	1.65	1.64
36	2.85	2.46	2.24	2.11	2.01	1.94	1.89	1.85	1.81	1.78	1.76	1.73	1.71	1.70	1.68	1.67	1.66	1.65	1.64
37	2.85	2.45	2.24	2.10	2.01	1.94	1.89	1.84	1.81	1.78	1.75	1.73	1.71	1.69	1.68	1.66	1.65	1.64	1.63
38	2.84	2.45	2.23	2.10	2.01	1.94	1.88	1.84	1.80	1.77	1.75	1.72	1.70	1.69	1.67	1.66	1.65	1.63	1.62
39	2.84	2.44	2.23	2.09	2.00	1.93	1.88	1.83	1.80	1.77	1.74	1.72	1.70	1.68	1.67	1.65	1.64	1.63	1.62
40	2.84	2.44	2.23	2.09	2.00	1.93	1.87	1.83	1.79	1.76	1.74	1.71	1.70	1.68	1.66	1.65	1.64	1.62	1.61
41	2.83	2.44	2.22	2.09	1.99	1.92	1.87	1.82	1.79	1.76	1.73	1.71	1.69	1.67	1.66	1.64	1.63	1.62	1.61
42	2.83	2.43	2.22	2.08	1.99	1.92	1.86	1.82	1.78	1.75	1.73	1.71	1.69	1.67	1.65	1.64	1.63	1.62	1.61
43	2.83	2.43	2.22	2.08	1.99	1.92	1.86	1.82	1.78	1.75	1.72	1.70	1.68	1.67	1.65	1.64	1.62	1.61	1.60
44	2.82	2.43	2.21	2.08	1.98	1.91	1.86	1.81	1.78	1.75	1.72	1.70	1.68	1.66	1.65	1.63	1.62	1.61	1.60
45	2.82	2.42	2.21	2.07	1.98	1.91	1.85	1.81	1.77	1.74	1.72	1.70	1.68	1.66	1.64	1.63	1.62	1.60	1.59
46	2.82	2.42	2.21	2.07	1.98	1.91	1.85	1.81	1.77	1.74	1.71	1.69	1.67	1.65	1.64	1.63	1.61	1.60	1.59
47	2.82	2.42	2.20	2.07	1.97	1.90	1.85	1.80	1.77	1.74	1.71	1.69	1.67	1.65	1.64	1.62	1.61	1.60	1.59
48	2.81	2.42	2.20	2.07	1.97	1.90	1.85	1.80	1.77	1.73	1.71	1.69	1.67	1.65	1.63	1.62	1.61	1.59	1.58
49	2.81	2.41	2.20	2.06	1.97	1.90	1.84	1.80	1.76	1.73	1.71	1.68	1.66	1.65	1.63	1.62	1.60	1.59	1.58
50	2.81	2.41	2.20	2.06	1.97	1.90	1.84	1.80	1.76	1.73	1.70	1.68	1.66	1.64	1.63	1.61	1.60	1.59	1.58
60	2.79	2.39	2.18	2.04	1.95	1.87	1.82	1.77	1.74	1.71	1.68	1.66	1.64	1.62	1.60	1.59	1.58	1.56	1.55
70	2.78	2.38	2.16	2.03	1.93	1.86	1.80	1.76	1.72	1.69	1.66	1.64	1.62	1.60	1.59	1.57	1.56	1.55	1.54
80	2.77	2.37	2.15	2.02	1.92	1.85	1.79	1.75	1.71	1.68	1.65	1.63	1.61	1.59	1.57	1.56	1.55	1.53	1.52
90	2.76	2.36	2.15	2.01	1.91	1.84	1.78	1.74	1.70	1.67	1.64	1.62	1.60	1.58	1.56	1.55	1.54	1.52	1.51
100	2.76	2.36	2.14	2.00	1.91	1.83	1.78	1.73	1.69	1.66	1.64	1.61	1.59	1.57	1.56	1.54	1.53	1.52	1.50
110	2.75	2.35	2.13	2.00	1.90	1.83	1.77	1.73	1.69	1.66	1.63	1.61	1.59	1.57	1.55	1.54	1.52	1.51	1.50
120	2.75	2.35	2.13	1.99	1.90	1.82	1.77	1.72	1.68	1.65	1.63	1.60	1.58	1.56	1.55	1.53	1.52	1.50	1.49
130	2.74	2.34	2.13	1.99	1.89	1.82	1.76	1.72	1.68	1.65	1.62	1.60	1.58	1.56	1.54	1.53	1.51	1.50	1.49
140	2.74	2.34	2.12	1.99	1.89	1.82	1.76	1.71	1.68	1.64	1.62	1.59	1.57	1.55	1.54	1.52	1.51	1.50	1.48
150	2.74	2.34	2.12	1.98	1.89	1.81	1.76	1.71	1.67	1.64	1.61	1.59	1.57	1.55	1.53	1.52	1.50	1.49	1.48
200	2.73	2.33	2.11	1.97	1.88	1.80	1.75	1.70	1.66	1.63	1.60	1.58	1.56	1.54	1.52	1.51	1.49	1.48	1.47
300	2.72	2.32	2.10	1.96	1.87	1.79	1.74	1.69	1.65	1.62	1.59	1.57	1.55	1.53	1.51	1.49	1.48	1.47	1.46
400	2.72	2.32	2.10	1.96	1.86	1.79	1.73	1.69	1.65	1.61	1.59	1.56	1.54	1.52	1.50	1.49	1.47	1.46	1.45
500	2.72	2.31	2.09	1.96	1.86	1.79	1.73	1.68	1.64	1.61	1.58	1.56	1.54	1.52	1.50	1.49	1.47	1.46	1.45
1000	2.71	2.31	2.09	1.95	1.85	1.78	1.72	1.68	1.64	1.61	1.58	1.55	1.53	1.51	1.49	1.48	1.46	1.45	1.44
∞	2.71	2.30	2.08	1.94	1.85	1.77	1.72	1.67	1.63	1.60	1.57	1.55	1.52	1.50	1.49	1.47	1.46	1.44	1.43

$\alpha = .10$

df_D \ df_N	20	21	22	23	24	25	26	27	28	29	30	31	32	33	34	35	36	37	38
1	61.74	61.81	61.88	61.94	62.00	62.05	62.10	62.15	62.19	62.23	62.26	62.30	62.33	62.36	62.39	62.42	62.44	62.47	62.49
2	9.44	9.44	9.45	9.45	9.45	9.45	9.45	9.45	9.46	9.46	9.46	9.46	9.46	9.46	9.46	9.46	9.46	9.46	9.46
3	5.18	5.18	5.18	5.18	5.18	5.17	5.17	5.17	5.17	5.17	5.17	5.17	5.17	5.17	5.16	5.16	5.16	5.16	5.16
4	3.84	3.84	3.84	3.83	3.83	3.83	3.83	3.82	3.82	3.82	3.82	3.82	3.81	3.81	3.81	3.81	3.81	3.81	3.81
5	3.21	3.20	3.20	3.19	3.19	3.19	3.18	3.18	3.18	3.18	3.17	3.17	3.17	3.17	3.17	3.16	3.16	3.16	3.16
6	2.84	2.83	2.83	2.82	2.82	2.81	2.81	2.81	2.81	2.80	2.80	2.80	2.80	2.79	2.79	2.79	2.79	2.79	2.78
7	2.59	2.59	2.58	2.58	2.58	2.57	2.57	2.56	2.56	2.56	2.56	2.55	2.55	2.55	2.55	2.54	2.54	2.54	2.54
8	2.42	2.42	2.41	2.41	2.40	2.40	2.40	2.39	2.39	2.39	2.38	2.38	2.38	2.38	2.37	2.37	2.37	2.37	2.36
9	2.30	2.29	2.29	2.28	2.28	2.27	2.27	2.26	2.26	2.26	2.25	2.25	2.25	2.25	2.24	2.24	2.24	2.24	2.24
10	2.20	2.19	2.19	2.18	2.18	2.17	2.17	2.17	2.16	2.16	2.16	2.15	2.15	2.15	2.14	2.14	2.14	2.14	2.14
11	2.12	2.12	2.11	2.11	2.10	2.10	2.09	2.09	2.08	2.08	2.08	2.07	2.07	2.07	2.06	2.06	2.06	2.06	2.06
12	2.06	2.05	2.05	2.04	2.04	2.03	2.03	2.02	2.02	2.01	2.01	2.01	2.01	2.00	2.00	2.00	1.99	1.99	1.99
13	2.01	2.00	1.99	1.99	1.98	1.98	1.97	1.97	1.96	1.96	1.96	1.95	1.95	1.95	1.95	1.94	1.94	1.94	1.94
14	1.96	1.96	1.95	1.94	1.94	1.93	1.93	1.92	1.92	1.92	1.91	1.91	1.91	1.90	1.90	1.90	1.89	1.89	1.89
15	1.92	1.92	1.91	1.90	1.90	1.89	1.89	1.88	1.88	1.88	1.87	1.87	1.87	1.86	1.86	1.86	1.85	1.85	1.85
16	1.89	1.88	1.88	1.87	1.87	1.86	1.86	1.85	1.85	1.84	1.84	1.84	1.83	1.83	1.83	1.82	1.82	1.82	1.82
17	1.86	1.86	1.85	1.84	1.84	1.83	1.83	1.82	1.82	1.81	1.81	1.81	1.80	1.80	1.80	1.79	1.79	1.79	1.79
18	1.84	1.83	1.82	1.82	1.81	1.80	1.80	1.80	1.79	1.79	1.78	1.78	1.78	1.77	1.77	1.77	1.76	1.76	1.76
19	1.81	1.81	1.80	1.79	1.79	1.78	1.78	1.77	1.77	1.76	1.76	1.76	1.75	1.75	1.75	1.74	1.74	1.74	1.73
20	1.79	1.79	1.78	1.77	1.77	1.76	1.76	1.75	1.75	1.74	1.74	1.73	1.73	1.73	1.72	1.72	1.72	1.72	1.71
21	1.78	1.77	1.76	1.75	1.75	1.74	1.74	1.73	1.73	1.72	1.72	1.72	1.71	1.71	1.71	1.70	1.70	1.70	1.69
22	1.76	1.75	1.74	1.74	1.73	1.73	1.72	1.72	1.71	1.71	1.70	1.70	1.69	1.69	1.69	1.68	1.68	1.68	1.68
23	1.74	1.74	1.73	1.72	1.72	1.71	1.70	1.70	1.69	1.69	1.69	1.68	1.68	1.68	1.67	1.67	1.67	1.66	1.66
24	1.73	1.72	1.71	1.71	1.70	1.70	1.69	1.69	1.68	1.68	1.67	1.67	1.66	1.66	1.66	1.65	1.65	1.65	1.65
25	1.72	1.71	1.70	1.70	1.69	1.68	1.68	1.67	1.67	1.66	1.66	1.65	1.65	1.65	1.64	1.64	1.64	1.64	1.63
26	1.71	1.70	1.69	1.68	1.68	1.67	1.67	1.66	1.66	1.65	1.65	1.64	1.64	1.64	1.63	1.63	1.63	1.62	1.62
27	1.70	1.69	1.68	1.67	1.67	1.66	1.65	1.65	1.64	1.64	1.64	1.63	1.63	1.62	1.62	1.62	1.61	1.61	1.61
28	1.69	1.68	1.67	1.66	1.66	1.65	1.64	1.64	1.63	1.63	1.63	1.62	1.62	1.61	1.61	1.61	1.60	1.60	1.60
29	1.68	1.67	1.66	1.65	1.65	1.64	1.63	1.63	1.62	1.62	1.62	1.61	1.61	1.60	1.60	1.60	1.59	1.59	1.59
30	1.67	1.66	1.65	1.64	1.64	1.63	1.63	1.62	1.62	1.61	1.61	1.60	1.60	1.59	1.59	1.59	1.58	1.58	1.58
31	1.66	1.65	1.64	1.64	1.63	1.62	1.62	1.61	1.61	1.60	1.60	1.59	1.59	1.59	1.58	1.58	1.58	1.57	1.57
32	1.65	1.64	1.64	1.63	1.62	1.62	1.61	1.60	1.60	1.59	1.59	1.59	1.58	1.58	1.57	1.57	1.57	1.56	1.56

$\alpha = .10$

df_D \ df_N	20	21	22	23	24	25	26	27	28	29	30	31	32	33	34	35	36	37	38
33	1.64	1.64	1.63	1.62	1.61	1.61	1.60	1.60	1.59	1.59	1.58	1.58	1.57	1.57	1.57	1.56	1.56	1.56	1.55
34	1.64	1.63	1.62	1.61	1.61	1.60	1.60	1.59	1.59	1.58	1.58	1.57	1.57	1.56	1.56	1.56	1.55	1.55	1.55
35	1.63	1.62	1.62	1.61	1.60	1.60	1.59	1.58	1.58	1.57	1.57	1.56	1.56	1.56	1.55	1.55	1.55	1.54	1.54
36	1.63	1.62	1.61	1.60	1.60	1.59	1.58	1.58	1.57	1.57	1.56	1.56	1.55	1.55	1.55	1.54	1.54	1.54	1.53
37	1.62	1.61	1.60	1.60	1.59	1.58	1.58	1.57	1.57	1.56	1.56	1.55	1.55	1.54	1.54	1.54	1.53	1.53	1.53
38	1.61	1.61	1.60	1.59	1.58	1.58	1.57	1.57	1.56	1.56	1.55	1.55	1.54	1.54	1.54	1.53	1.53	1.53	1.52
39	1.61	1.60	1.59	1.59	1.58	1.57	1.57	1.56	1.56	1.55	1.55	1.54	1.54	1.53	1.53	1.53	1.52	1.52	1.52
40	1.61	1.60	1.59	1.58	1.57	1.57	1.56	1.56	1.55	1.55	1.54	1.54	1.53	1.53	1.52	1.52	1.52	1.51	1.51
41	1.60	1.59	1.58	1.58	1.57	1.56	1.56	1.55	1.55	1.54	1.54	1.53	1.53	1.52	1.52	1.52	1.51	1.51	1.51
42	1.60	1.59	1.58	1.57	1.57	1.56	1.55	1.55	1.54	1.54	1.53	1.53	1.52	1.52	1.52	1.51	1.51	1.50	1.50
43	1.59	1.58	1.58	1.57	1.56	1.55	1.55	1.54	1.54	1.53	1.53	1.52	1.52	1.51	1.51	1.51	1.50	1.50	1.50
44	1.59	1.58	1.57	1.56	1.56	1.55	1.54	1.54	1.53	1.53	1.52	1.52	1.51	1.51	1.51	1.50	1.50	1.50	1.49
45	1.58	1.58	1.57	1.56	1.55	1.55	1.54	1.53	1.53	1.52	1.52	1.51	1.51	1.51	1.50	1.50	1.50	1.49	1.49
46	1.58	1.57	1.56	1.56	1.55	1.54	1.54	1.53	1.53	1.52	1.52	1.51	1.51	1.50	1.50	1.50	1.49	1.49	1.48
47	1.58	1.57	1.56	1.55	1.55	1.54	1.53	1.53	1.52	1.52	1.51	1.51	1.50	1.50	1.49	1.49	1.49	1.48	1.48
48	1.57	1.57	1.56	1.55	1.54	1.54	1.53	1.52	1.52	1.51	1.51	1.50	1.50	1.50	1.49	1.49	1.48	1.48	1.48
49	1.57	1.56	1.55	1.55	1.54	1.53	1.53	1.52	1.52	1.51	1.51	1.50	1.50	1.49	1.49	1.48	1.48	1.48	1.47
50	1.57	1.56	1.55	1.54	1.54	1.53	1.52	1.52	1.51	1.51	1.50	1.50	1.49	1.49	1.48	1.48	1.48	1.47	1.47
60	1.54	1.53	1.53	1.52	1.51	1.50	1.50	1.49	1.49	1.48	1.48	1.47	1.47	1.46	1.46	1.45	1.45	1.45	1.44
70	1.53	1.52	1.51	1.50	1.49	1.49	1.48	1.47	1.47	1.46	1.46	1.45	1.45	1.44	1.44	1.43	1.43	1.43	1.42
80	1.51	1.50	1.49	1.49	1.48	1.47	1.47	1.46	1.45	1.45	1.44	1.44	1.43	1.43	1.42	1.42	1.42	1.41	1.41
90	1.50	1.49	1.48	1.48	1.47	1.46	1.45	1.45	1.44	1.44	1.43	1.43	1.42	1.42	1.41	1.41	1.41	1.40	1.40
100	1.49	1.48	1.48	1.47	1.46	1.45	1.45	1.44	1.43	1.43	1.42	1.42	1.41	1.41	1.40	1.40	1.40	1.39	1.39
110	1.49	1.48	1.47	1.46	1.45	1.45	1.44	1.43	1.43	1.42	1.42	1.41	1.41	1.40	1.40	1.39	1.39	1.38	1.38
120	1.48	1.47	1.46	1.46	1.45	1.44	1.43	1.43	1.42	1.41	1.41	1.40	1.40	1.39	1.39	1.39	1.38	1.38	1.37
130	1.48	1.47	1.46	1.45	1.44	1.43	1.43	1.42	1.42	1.41	1.40	1.40	1.39	1.39	1.39	1.38	1.38	1.37	1.37
140	1.47	1.46	1.45	1.45	1.44	1.43	1.42	1.42	1.41	1.41	1.40	1.39	1.39	1.38	1.38	1.38	1.37	1.37	1.36
150	1.47	1.46	1.45	1.44	1.43	1.43	1.42	1.41	1.41	1.40	1.40	1.39	1.39	1.38	1.38	1.37	1.37	1.36	1.36
200	1.46	1.45	1.44	1.43	1.42	1.41	1.41	1.40	1.39	1.39	1.38	1.38	1.37	1.37	1.36	1.36	1.35	1.35	1.35
300	1.45	1.44	1.43	1.42	1.41	1.40	1.39	1.39	1.38	1.37	1.37	1.36	1.36	1.35	1.35	1.34	1.34	1.34	1.33
400	1.44	1.43	1.42	1.41	1.40	1.39	1.39	1.38	1.37	1.37	1.36	1.36	1.35	1.35	1.34	1.34	1.33	1.33	1.32
500	1.44	1.43	1.42	1.41	1.40	1.39	1.38	1.38	1.37	1.36	1.36	1.35	1.35	1.34	1.34	1.33	1.33	1.32	1.32
1000	1.43	1.42	1.41	1.40	1.39	1.38	1.38	1.37	1.36	1.36	1.35	1.34	1.34	1.33	1.33	1.32	1.32	1.32	1.31
∞	1.42	1.41	1.40	1.39	1.38	1.38	1.37	1.36	1.35	1.35	1.34	1.34	1.33	1.33	1.32	1.32	1.31	1.31	1.30

$\alpha = .10$

df_N / df_D	39	40	50	60	70	80	90	100	110	120	130	140	150	200	300	400	500	1000	∞
1	62.51	62.53	62.69	62.79	62.87	62.93	62.97	63.01	63.04	63.06	63.08	63.10	63.11	63.17	63.22	63.25	63.26	63.30	63.33
2	9.47	9.47	9.47	9.47	9.48	9.48	9.48	9.48	9.48	9.48	9.48	9.48	9.48	9.49	9.49	9.49	9.49	9.49	9.49
3	5.16	5.16	5.15	5.15	5.15	5.15	5.15	5.14	5.14	5.14	5.14	5.14	5.14	5.14	5.14	5.14	5.14	5.13	5.13
4	3.80	3.80	3.80	3.79	3.79	3.78	3.78	3.78	3.78	3.78	3.77	3.77	3.77	3.77	3.77	3.77	3.76	3.76	3.76
5	3.16	3.16	3.15	3.14	3.14	3.13	3.13	3.13	3.12	3.12	3.12	3.12	3.12	3.12	3.11	3.11	3.11	3.11	3.11
6	2.78	2.78	2.77	2.76	2.76	2.75	2.75	2.75	2.74	2.74	2.74	2.74	2.74	2.73	2.73	2.73	2.73	2.72	2.72
7	2.54	2.54	2.52	2.51	2.51	2.50	2.50	2.50	2.49	2.49	2.49	2.49	2.49	2.48	2.48	2.48	2.48	2.47	2.47
8	2.36	2.36	2.35	2.34	2.33	2.33	2.32	2.32	2.32	2.32	2.31	2.31	2.31	2.31	2.30	2.30	2.30	2.30	2.29
9	2.23	2.23	2.22	2.21	2.20	2.20	2.19	2.19	2.19	2.18	2.18	2.18	2.18	2.17	2.17	2.17	2.17	2.16	2.16
10	2.13	2.13	2.12	2.11	2.10	2.09	2.09	2.09	2.08	2.08	2.08	2.08	2.08	2.07	2.07	2.06	2.06	2.06	2.06
11	2.05	2.05	2.04	2.03	2.02	2.01	2.01	2.01	2.00	2.00	2.00	2.00	1.99	1.99	1.98	1.98	1.98	1.98	1.97
12	1.99	1.99	1.97	1.96	1.95	1.95	1.94	1.94	1.93	1.93	1.93	1.93	1.93	1.92	1.92	1.91	1.91	1.91	1.90
13	1.93	1.93	1.92	1.90	1.90	1.89	1.89	1.88	1.88	1.88	1.87	1.87	1.87	1.86	1.86	1.86	1.85	1.85	1.85
14	1.89	1.89	1.87	1.86	1.85	1.84	1.84	1.83	1.83	1.83	1.83	1.82	1.82	1.82	1.81	1.81	1.80	1.80	1.80
15	1.85	1.85	1.83	1.82	1.81	1.80	1.80	1.79	1.79	1.79	1.78	1.78	1.78	1.77	1.77	1.76	1.76	1.76	1.76
16	1.81	1.81	1.79	1.78	1.77	1.77	1.76	1.76	1.75	1.75	1.75	1.75	1.74	1.74	1.73	1.73	1.73	1.72	1.72
17	1.78	1.78	1.76	1.75	1.74	1.74	1.73	1.73	1.72	1.72	1.72	1.71	1.71	1.71	1.70	1.70	1.69	1.69	1.69
18	1.76	1.75	1.74	1.72	1.71	1.71	1.70	1.70	1.69	1.69	1.69	1.69	1.68	1.68	1.67	1.67	1.67	1.66	1.66
19	1.73	1.73	1.71	1.70	1.69	1.68	1.68	1.67	1.67	1.67	1.66	1.66	1.66	1.65	1.65	1.64	1.64	1.64	1.63
20	1.71	1.71	1.69	1.68	1.67	1.66	1.65	1.65	1.65	1.64	1.64	1.64	1.64	1.63	1.62	1.62	1.62	1.61	1.61
21	1.69	1.69	1.67	1.66	1.65	1.64	1.63	1.63	1.63	1.62	1.62	1.62	1.62	1.61	1.60	1.60	1.60	1.59	1.59
22	1.67	1.67	1.65	1.64	1.63	1.62	1.62	1.61	1.61	1.60	1.60	1.60	1.60	1.59	1.58	1.58	1.58	1.57	1.57
23	1.66	1.66	1.64	1.62	1.61	1.61	1.60	1.59	1.59	1.59	1.58	1.58	1.58	1.57	1.56	1.56	1.56	1.55	1.55
24	1.64	1.64	1.62	1.61	1.60	1.59	1.58	1.58	1.57	1.57	1.57	1.57	1.56	1.56	1.55	1.54	1.54	1.54	1.53
25	1.63	1.63	1.61	1.59	1.58	1.58	1.57	1.56	1.56	1.56	1.55	1.55	1.55	1.54	1.53	1.53	1.53	1.52	1.52
26	1.62	1.61	1.59	1.58	1.57	1.56	1.56	1.55	1.55	1.54	1.54	1.54	1.54	1.53	1.52	1.52	1.51	1.51	1.50
27	1.61	1.60	1.58	1.57	1.56	1.55	1.54	1.54	1.53	1.53	1.53	1.53	1.52	1.52	1.51	1.50	1.50	1.50	1.49
28	1.60	1.59	1.57	1.56	1.55	1.54	1.53	1.53	1.52	1.52	1.52	1.51	1.51	1.50	1.50	1.49	1.49	1.48	1.48
29	1.59	1.58	1.56	1.55	1.54	1.53	1.52	1.52	1.51	1.51	1.51	1.50	1.50	1.49	1.48	1.48	1.48	1.47	1.47
30	1.58	1.57	1.55	1.54	1.53	1.52	1.51	1.51	1.50	1.50	1.50	1.49	1.49	1.48	1.47	1.47	1.47	1.46	1.46
31	1.57	1.56	1.54	1.53	1.52	1.51	1.50	1.50	1.49	1.49	1.49	1.48	1.48	1.47	1.46	1.46	1.46	1.45	1.45
32	1.56	1.56	1.53	1.52	1.51	1.50	1.49	1.49	1.48	1.48	1.48	1.47	1.47	1.46	1.45	1.45	1.45	1.44	1.44

$\alpha = .10$

df_D \ df_N	39	40	50	60	70	80	90	100	110	120	130	140	150	200	300	400	500	1000	∞
33	1.55	1.55	1.53	1.51	1.50	1.49	1.49	1.48	1.48	1.47	1.47	1.47	1.46	1.46	1.45	1.44	1.44	1.43	1.43
34	1.54	1.54	1.52	1.50	1.49	1.48	1.48	1.47	1.47	1.46	1.46	1.46	1.46	1.45	1.44	1.43	1.43	1.43	1.42
35	1.54	1.53	1.51	1.50	1.49	1.48	1.47	1.47	1.46	1.46	1.45	1.45	1.45	1.44	1.43	1.43	1.42	1.42	1.41
36	1.53	1.53	1.51	1.49	1.48	1.47	1.46	1.46	1.45	1.45	1.45	1.44	1.44	1.43	1.42	1.42	1.42	1.41	1.40
37	1.52	1.52	1.50	1.48	1.47	1.46	1.46	1.45	1.45	1.44	1.44	1.44	1.43	1.43	1.42	1.41	1.41	1.40	1.40
38	1.52	1.52	1.49	1.48	1.47	1.46	1.45	1.45	1.44	1.44	1.43	1.43	1.43	1.42	1.41	1.40	1.40	1.40	1.39
39	1.51	1.51	1.49	1.47	1.46	1.45	1.45	1.44	1.43	1.43	1.43	1.42	1.42	1.41	1.40	1.40	1.40	1.39	1.38
40	1.51	1.51	1.48	1.47	1.46	1.45	1.44	1.43	1.43	1.42	1.42	1.42	1.42	1.41	1.40	1.39	1.39	1.38	1.38
41	1.50	1.50	1.48	1.46	1.45	1.44	1.43	1.43	1.42	1.42	1.42	1.41	1.41	1.40	1.39	1.39	1.38	1.38	1.37
42	1.50	1.50	1.47	1.46	1.45	1.44	1.43	1.42	1.42	1.41	1.41	1.41	1.40	1.40	1.39	1.38	1.38	1.37	1.37
43	1.49	1.49	1.47	1.45	1.44	1.43	1.42	1.42	1.41	1.41	1.41	1.40	1.40	1.39	1.38	1.38	1.37	1.37	1.36
44	1.49	1.49	1.46	1.45	1.44	1.43	1.42	1.41	1.41	1.40	1.40	1.40	1.39	1.39	1.38	1.37	1.37	1.36	1.35
45	1.49	1.48	1.46	1.44	1.43	1.42	1.41	1.41	1.40	1.40	1.40	1.39	1.39	1.38	1.37	1.37	1.36	1.36	1.35
46	1.48	1.48	1.46	1.44	1.43	1.42	1.41	1.40	1.40	1.40	1.39	1.39	1.39	1.38	1.37	1.36	1.36	1.35	1.34
47	1.48	1.48	1.45	1.44	1.42	1.41	1.41	1.40	1.40	1.39	1.39	1.38	1.38	1.37	1.36	1.36	1.35	1.35	1.34
48	1.47	1.47	1.45	1.43	1.42	1.41	1.40	1.40	1.39	1.39	1.38	1.38	1.38	1.37	1.36	1.35	1.35	1.34	1.34
49	1.47	1.47	1.44	1.43	1.42	1.41	1.40	1.39	1.39	1.38	1.38	1.38	1.37	1.36	1.35	1.35	1.34	1.34	1.33
50	1.47	1.46	1.44	1.42	1.41	1.40	1.39	1.39	1.38	1.38	1.38	1.37	1.37	1.36	1.35	1.34	1.34	1.33	1.33
60	1.44	1.44	1.41	1.40	1.38	1.37	1.36	1.36	1.35	1.35	1.34	1.34	1.34	1.33	1.32	1.31	1.31	1.30	1.29
70	1.42	1.42	1.39	1.37	1.36	1.35	1.34	1.34	1.33	1.32	1.32	1.32	1.31	1.30	1.29	1.28	1.28	1.27	1.27
80	1.41	1.40	1.38	1.36	1.34	1.33	1.33	1.32	1.31	1.31	1.30	1.30	1.30	1.28	1.27	1.27	1.26	1.25	1.24
90	1.39	1.39	1.36	1.35	1.33	1.32	1.31	1.30	1.30	1.29	1.29	1.28	1.28	1.27	1.26	1.25	1.25	1.24	1.23
100	1.39	1.38	1.35	1.34	1.32	1.31	1.30	1.29	1.29	1.28	1.28	1.27	1.27	1.26	1.24	1.24	1.23	1.22	1.21
110	1.38	1.37	1.35	1.33	1.31	1.30	1.29	1.28	1.28	1.27	1.27	1.26	1.26	1.25	1.23	1.23	1.22	1.21	1.20
120	1.37	1.37	1.34	1.32	1.31	1.29	1.28	1.28	1.27	1.26	1.26	1.26	1.25	1.24	1.22	1.22	1.21	1.20	1.19
130	1.37	1.36	1.33	1.31	1.30	1.29	1.28	1.27	1.26	1.26	1.25	1.25	1.24	1.23	1.22	1.21	1.20	1.19	1.18
140	1.36	1.36	1.33	1.31	1.29	1.28	1.27	1.26	1.26	1.25	1.25	1.24	1.24	1.22	1.21	1.20	1.20	1.19	1.18
150	1.36	1.35	1.33	1.30	1.29	1.28	1.27	1.26	1.25	1.25	1.24	1.24	1.23	1.22	1.20	1.20	1.19	1.18	1.17
200	1.34	1.34	1.31	1.29	1.27	1.26	1.25	1.24	1.23	1.23	1.22	1.22	1.21	1.20	1.18	1.17	1.17	1.16	1.14
300	1.33	1.32	1.29	1.27	1.26	1.24	1.23	1.22	1.22	1.21	1.20	1.20	1.19	1.18	1.16	1.15	1.14	1.13	1.11
400	1.32	1.32	1.29	1.26	1.25	1.23	1.22	1.21	1.21	1.20	1.19	1.19	1.18	1.17	1.15	1.14	1.13	1.12	1.10
500	1.32	1.31	1.28	1.26	1.24	1.23	1.22	1.21	1.20	1.19	1.19	1.18	1.18	1.16	1.14	1.13	1.12	1.11	1.09
1000	1.31	1.30	1.27	1.25	1.23	1.22	1.21	1.20	1.19	1.18	1.17	1.17	1.16	1.15	1.12	1.11	1.10	1.08	1.06
∞	1.30	1.30	1.26	1.24	1.22	1.21	1.20	1.18	1.18	1.17	1.16	1.16	1.15	1.13	1.11	1.09	1.08	1.06	1.00

TABLE 4 (continued)
Critical Values for the F-Distribution
$\alpha = .05$

df_D \ df_N	1	2	3	4	5	6	7	8	9	10	11	12	13	14	15	16	17	18	19
1	161.45	199.50	215.71	224.58	230.16	233.99	236.77	238.88	240.54	241.88	242.98	243.90	244.69	245.36	245.95	246.47	246.92	247.32	247.69
2	18.51	19.00	19.16	19.25	19.30	19.33	19.35	19.37	19.38	19.40	19.40	19.41	19.42	19.42	19.43	19.43	19.44	19.44	19.44
3	10.13	9.55	9.28	9.12	9.01	8.94	8.89	8.85	8.81	8.79	8.76	8.74	8.73	8.71	8.70	8.69	8.68	8.67	8.67
4	7.71	6.94	6.59	6.39	6.26	6.16	6.09	6.04	6.00	5.96	5.94	5.91	5.89	5.87	5.86	5.84	5.83	5.82	5.81
5	6.61	5.79	5.41	5.19	5.05	4.95	4.88	4.82	4.77	4.74	4.70	4.68	4.66	4.64	4.62	4.60	4.59	4.58	4.57
6	5.99	5.14	4.76	4.53	4.39	4.28	4.21	4.15	4.10	4.06	4.03	4.00	3.98	3.96	3.94	3.92	3.91	3.90	3.88
7	5.59	4.74	4.35	4.12	3.97	3.87	3.79	3.73	3.68	3.64	3.60	3.57	3.55	3.53	3.51	3.49	3.48	3.47	3.46
8	5.32	4.46	4.07	3.84	3.69	3.58	3.50	3.44	3.39	3.35	3.31	3.28	3.26	3.24	3.22	3.20	3.19	3.17	3.16
9	5.12	4.26	3.86	3.63	3.48	3.37	3.29	3.23	3.18	3.14	3.10	3.07	3.05	3.03	3.01	2.99	2.97	2.96	2.95
10	4.96	4.10	3.71	3.48	3.33	3.22	3.14	3.07	3.02	2.98	2.94	2.91	2.89	2.86	2.85	2.83	2.81	2.80	2.79
11	4.84	3.98	3.59	3.36	3.20	3.09	3.01	2.95	2.90	2.85	2.82	2.79	2.76	2.74	2.72	2.70	2.69	2.67	2.66
12	4.75	3.89	3.49	3.26	3.11	3.00	2.91	2.85	2.80	2.75	2.72	2.69	2.66	2.64	2.62	2.60	2.58	2.57	2.56
13	4.67	3.81	3.41	3.18	3.03	2.92	2.83	2.77	2.71	2.67	2.63	2.60	2.58	2.55	2.53	2.51	2.50	2.48	2.47
14	4.60	3.74	3.34	3.11	2.96	2.85	2.76	2.70	2.65	2.60	2.57	2.53	2.51	2.48	2.46	2.44	2.43	2.41	2.40
15	4.54	3.68	3.29	3.06	2.90	2.79	2.71	2.64	2.59	2.54	2.51	2.48	2.45	2.42	2.40	2.38	2.37	2.35	2.34
16	4.49	3.63	3.24	3.01	2.85	2.74	2.66	2.59	2.54	2.49	2.46	2.42	2.40	2.37	2.35	2.33	2.32	2.30	2.29
17	4.45	3.59	3.20	2.96	2.81	2.70	2.61	2.55	2.49	2.45	2.41	2.38	2.35	2.33	2.31	2.29	2.27	2.26	2.24
18	4.41	3.55	3.16	2.93	2.77	2.66	2.58	2.51	2.46	2.41	2.37	2.34	2.31	2.29	2.27	2.25	2.23	2.22	2.20
19	4.38	3.52	3.13	2.90	2.74	2.63	2.54	2.48	2.42	2.38	2.34	2.31	2.28	2.26	2.23	2.21	2.20	2.18	2.17
20	4.35	3.49	3.10	2.87	2.71	2.60	2.51	2.45	2.39	2.35	2.31	2.28	2.25	2.22	2.20	2.18	2.17	2.15	2.14
21	4.32	3.47	3.07	2.84	2.68	2.57	2.49	2.42	2.37	2.32	2.28	2.25	2.22	2.20	2.18	2.16	2.14	2.12	2.11
22	4.30	3.44	3.05	2.82	2.66	2.55	2.46	2.40	2.34	2.30	2.26	2.23	2.20	2.17	2.15	2.13	2.11	2.10	2.08
23	4.28	3.42	3.03	2.80	2.64	2.53	2.44	2.37	2.32	2.27	2.24	2.20	2.18	2.15	2.13	2.11	2.09	2.08	2.06
24	4.26	3.40	3.01	2.78	2.62	2.51	2.42	2.36	2.30	2.25	2.22	2.18	2.15	2.13	2.11	2.09	2.07	2.05	2.04
25	4.24	3.39	2.99	2.76	2.60	2.49	2.40	2.34	2.28	2.24	2.20	2.16	2.14	2.11	2.09	2.07	2.05	2.04	2.02
26	4.23	3.37	2.98	2.74	2.59	2.47	2.39	2.32	2.27	2.22	2.18	2.15	2.12	2.09	2.07	2.05	2.03	2.02	2.00
27	4.21	3.35	2.96	2.73	2.57	2.46	2.37	2.31	2.25	2.20	2.17	2.13	2.10	2.08	2.06	2.04	2.02	2.00	1.99
28	4.20	3.34	2.95	2.71	2.56	2.45	2.36	2.29	2.24	2.19	2.15	2.12	2.09	2.06	2.04	2.02	2.00	1.99	1.97
29	4.18	3.33	2.93	2.70	2.55	2.43	2.35	2.28	2.22	2.18	2.14	2.10	2.08	2.05	2.03	2.01	1.99	1.97	1.96
30	4.17	3.32	2.92	2.69	2.53	2.42	2.33	2.27	2.21	2.16	2.13	2.09	2.06	2.04	2.01	1.99	1.98	1.96	1.95
31	4.16	3.30	2.91	2.68	2.52	2.41	2.32	2.25	2.20	2.15	2.11	2.08	2.05	2.03	2.00	1.98	1.96	1.95	1.93
32	4.15	3.29	2.90	2.67	2.51	2.40	2.31	2.24	2.19	2.14	2.10	2.07	2.04	2.01	1.99	1.97	1.95	1.94	1.92

$\alpha = .05$

df_D \ df_N	1	2	3	4	5	6	7	8	9	10	11	12	13	14	15	16	17	18	19
33	4.14	3.28	2.89	2.66	2.50	2.39	2.30	2.23	2.18	2.13	2.09	2.06	2.03	2.00	1.98	1.96	1.94	1.93	1.91
34	4.13	3.28	2.88	2.65	2.49	2.38	2.29	2.23	2.17	2.12	2.08	2.05	2.02	1.99	1.97	1.95	1.93	1.92	1.90
35	4.12	3.27	2.87	2.64	2.49	2.37	2.29	2.22	2.16	2.11	2.07	2.04	2.01	1.99	1.96	1.94	1.92	1.91	1.89
36	4.11	3.26	2.87	2.63	2.48	2.36	2.28	2.21	2.15	2.11	2.07	2.03	2.00	1.98	1.95	1.93	1.92	1.90	1.88
37	4.11	3.25	2.86	2.63	2.47	2.36	2.27	2.20	2.14	2.10	2.06	2.02	2.00	1.97	1.95	1.93	1.91	1.89	1.88
38	4.10	3.24	2.85	2.62	2.46	2.35	2.26	2.19	2.14	2.09	2.05	2.02	1.99	1.96	1.94	1.92	1.90	1.88	1.87
39	4.09	3.24	2.85	2.61	2.46	2.34	2.26	2.19	2.13	2.08	2.04	2.01	1.98	1.95	1.93	1.91	1.89	1.88	1.86
40	4.08	3.23	2.84	2.61	2.45	2.34	2.25	2.18	2.12	2.08	2.04	2.00	1.97	1.95	1.92	1.90	1.89	1.87	1.85
41	4.08	3.23	2.83	2.60	2.44	2.33	2.24	2.17	2.12	2.07	2.03	2.00	1.97	1.94	1.92	1.90	1.88	1.86	1.85
42	4.07	3.22	2.83	2.59	2.44	2.32	2.24	2.17	2.11	2.06	2.03	1.99	1.96	1.94	1.91	1.89	1.87	1.86	1.84
43	4.07	3.21	2.82	2.59	2.43	2.32	2.23	2.16	2.11	2.06	2.02	1.99	1.96	1.93	1.91	1.89	1.87	1.85	1.83
44	4.06	3.21	2.82	2.58	2.43	2.31	2.23	2.16	2.10	2.05	2.01	1.98	1.95	1.92	1.90	1.88	1.86	1.84	1.83
45	4.06	3.20	2.81	2.58	2.42	2.31	2.22	2.15	2.10	2.05	2.01	1.97	1.94	1.92	1.89	1.87	1.86	1.84	1.82
46	4.05	3.20	2.81	2.57	2.42	2.30	2.22	2.15	2.09	2.04	2.00	1.97	1.94	1.91	1.89	1.87	1.85	1.83	1.82
47	4.05	3.20	2.80	2.57	2.41	2.30	2.21	2.14	2.09	2.04	2.00	1.96	1.93	1.91	1.88	1.86	1.84	1.83	1.81
48	4.04	3.19	2.80	2.57	2.41	2.29	2.21	2.14	2.08	2.03	1.99	1.96	1.93	1.90	1.88	1.86	1.84	1.82	1.81
49	4.04	3.19	2.79	2.56	2.40	2.29	2.20	2.13	2.08	2.03	1.99	1.96	1.93	1.90	1.88	1.85	1.84	1.82	1.80
50	4.03	3.18	2.79	2.56	2.40	2.29	2.20	2.13	2.07	2.03	1.99	1.95	1.92	1.89	1.87	1.85	1.83	1.81	1.80
60	4.00	3.15	2.76	2.53	2.37	2.25	2.17	2.10	2.04	1.99	1.95	1.92	1.89	1.86	1.84	1.82	1.80	1.78	1.76
70	3.98	3.13	2.74	2.50	2.35	2.23	2.14	2.07	2.02	1.97	1.93	1.89	1.86	1.84	1.81	1.79	1.77	1.75	1.74
80	3.96	3.11	2.72	2.49	2.33	2.21	2.13	2.06	2.00	1.95	1.91	1.88	1.84	1.82	1.79	1.77	1.75	1.73	1.72
90	3.95	3.10	2.71	2.47	2.32	2.20	2.11	2.04	1.99	1.94	1.90	1.86	1.83	1.80	1.78	1.76	1.74	1.72	1.70
100	3.94	3.09	2.70	2.46	2.31	2.19	2.10	2.03	1.97	1.93	1.89	1.85	1.82	1.79	1.77	1.75	1.73	1.71	1.69
110	3.93	3.08	2.69	2.45	2.30	2.18	2.09	2.02	1.97	1.92	1.88	1.84	1.81	1.78	1.76	1.74	1.72	1.70	1.68
120	3.92	3.07	2.68	2.45	2.29	2.18	2.09	2.02	1.96	1.91	1.87	1.83	1.80	1.78	1.75	1.73	1.71	1.69	1.67
130	3.91	3.07	2.67	2.44	2.28	2.17	2.08	2.01	1.95	1.90	1.86	1.83	1.80	1.77	1.74	1.72	1.70	1.68	1.67
140	3.91	3.06	2.67	2.44	2.28	2.16	2.08	2.01	1.95	1.90	1.86	1.82	1.79	1.76	1.74	1.72	1.70	1.68	1.66
150	3.90	3.06	2.66	2.43	2.27	2.16	2.07	2.00	1.94	1.89	1.85	1.82	1.79	1.76	1.73	1.71	1.69	1.67	1.66
200	3.89	3.04	2.65	2.42	2.26	2.14	2.06	1.98	1.93	1.88	1.84	1.80	1.77	1.74	1.72	1.69	1.67	1.66	1.64
300	3.87	3.03	2.63	2.40	2.24	2.13	2.04	1.97	1.91	1.86	1.82	1.78	1.75	1.72	1.70	1.68	1.66	1.64	1.62
400	3.86	3.02	2.63	2.39	2.24	2.12	2.03	1.96	1.90	1.85	1.81	1.78	1.74	1.72	1.69	1.67	1.65	1.63	1.61
500	3.86	3.01	2.62	2.39	2.23	2.12	2.03	1.96	1.90	1.85	1.81	1.77	1.74	1.71	1.69	1.66	1.64	1.62	1.61
1000	3.85	3.00	2.61	2.38	2.22	2.11	2.02	1.95	1.89	1.84	1.80	1.76	1.73	1.70	1.68	1.65	1.63	1.61	1.60
∞	3.84	3.00	2.60	2.37	2.21	2.10	2.01	1.94	1.88	1.83	1.79	1.75	1.72	1.69	1.67	1.64	1.62	1.60	1.59

$\alpha = .05$

df_D \ df_N	20	21	22	23	24	25	26	27	28	29	30	31	32	33	34	35	36	37	38
1	248.02	248.31	248.58	248.82	249.05	249.26	249.45	249.63	249.80	249.95	250.10	250.23	250.36	250.47	250.59	250.69	250.79	250.89	250.98
2	19.45	19.45	19.45	19.45	19.45	19.46	19.46	19.46	19.46	19.46	19.46	19.46	19.46	19.47	19.47	19.47	19.47	19.47	19.47
3	8.66	8.65	8.65	8.64	8.64	8.63	8.63	8.63	8.62	8.62	8.62	8.61	8.61	8.61	8.61	8.60	8.60	8.60	8.60
4	5.80	5.79	5.79	5.78	5.77	5.77	5.76	5.76	5.75	5.75	5.75	5.74	5.74	5.74	5.73	5.73	5.73	5.72	5.72
5	4.56	4.55	4.54	4.53	4.53	4.52	4.52	4.51	4.50	4.50	4.50	4.49	4.49	4.48	4.48	4.48	4.47	4.47	4.47
6	3.87	3.86	3.86	3.85	3.84	3.83	3.83	3.82	3.82	3.81	3.81	3.80	3.80	3.80	3.79	3.79	3.79	3.78	3.78
7	3.44	3.43	3.43	3.42	3.41	3.40	3.40	3.39	3.39	3.38	3.38	3.37	3.37	3.36	3.36	3.36	3.35	3.35	3.35
8	3.15	3.14	3.13	3.12	3.12	3.11	3.10	3.10	3.09	3.08	3.08	3.07	3.07	3.07	3.06	3.06	3.06	3.05	3.05
9	2.94	2.93	2.92	2.91	2.90	2.89	2.89	2.88	2.87	2.87	2.86	2.86	2.85	2.85	2.85	2.84	2.84	2.84	2.83
10	2.77	2.76	2.75	2.75	2.74	2.73	2.72	2.72	2.71	2.70	2.70	2.69	2.69	2.69	2.68	2.68	2.67	2.67	2.67
11	2.65	2.64	2.63	2.62	2.61	2.60	2.59	2.59	2.58	2.58	2.57	2.57	2.56	2.56	2.55	2.55	2.54	2.54	2.54
12	2.54	2.53	2.52	2.51	2.51	2.50	2.49	2.48	2.48	2.47	2.47	2.46	2.46	2.45	2.45	2.44	2.44	2.44	2.43
13	2.46	2.45	2.44	2.43	2.42	2.41	2.41	2.40	2.39	2.39	2.38	2.38	2.37	2.37	2.36	2.36	2.35	2.35	2.35
14	2.39	2.38	2.37	2.36	2.35	2.34	2.33	2.33	2.32	2.31	2.31	2.30	2.30	2.29	2.29	2.28	2.28	2.28	2.27
15	2.33	2.32	2.31	2.30	2.29	2.28	2.27	2.27	2.26	2.25	2.25	2.24	2.24	2.23	2.23	2.22	2.22	2.21	2.21
16	2.28	2.26	2.25	2.24	2.24	2.23	2.22	2.21	2.21	2.20	2.19	2.19	2.18	2.18	2.17	2.17	2.17	2.16	2.16
17	2.23	2.22	2.21	2.20	2.19	2.18	2.17	2.17	2.16	2.15	2.15	2.14	2.14	2.13	2.13	2.12	2.12	2.11	2.11
18	2.19	2.18	2.17	2.16	2.15	2.14	2.13	2.13	2.12	2.11	2.11	2.10	2.10	2.09	2.09	2.08	2.08	2.07	2.07
19	2.16	2.14	2.13	2.12	2.11	2.11	2.10	2.09	2.08	2.08	2.07	2.07	2.06	2.06	2.05	2.05	2.04	2.04	2.03
20	2.12	2.11	2.10	2.09	2.08	2.07	2.07	2.06	2.05	2.05	2.04	2.03	2.03	2.02	2.02	2.01	2.01	2.01	2.00
21	2.10	2.08	2.07	2.06	2.05	2.05	2.04	2.03	2.02	2.02	2.01	2.00	2.00	1.99	1.99	1.98	1.98	1.98	1.97
22	2.07	2.06	2.05	2.04	2.03	2.02	2.01	2.00	2.00	1.99	1.98	1.98	1.97	1.97	1.96	1.96	1.95	1.95	1.95
23	2.05	2.04	2.02	2.01	2.01	2.00	1.99	1.98	1.97	1.97	1.96	1.95	1.95	1.94	1.94	1.93	1.93	1.93	1.92
24	2.03	2.01	2.00	1.99	1.98	1.97	1.97	1.96	1.95	1.95	1.94	1.93	1.93	1.92	1.92	1.91	1.91	1.90	1.90
25	2.01	2.00	1.98	1.97	1.96	1.96	1.95	1.94	1.93	1.93	1.92	1.91	1.91	1.90	1.90	1.89	1.89	1.88	1.88
26	1.99	1.98	1.97	1.96	1.95	1.94	1.93	1.92	1.91	1.91	1.90	1.89	1.89	1.88	1.88	1.87	1.87	1.87	1.86
27	1.97	1.96	1.95	1.94	1.93	1.92	1.91	1.90	1.90	1.89	1.88	1.88	1.87	1.87	1.86	1.86	1.85	1.85	1.84
28	1.96	1.95	1.93	1.92	1.91	1.91	1.90	1.89	1.88	1.88	1.87	1.86	1.86	1.85	1.85	1.84	1.84	1.83	1.83
29	1.94	1.93	1.92	1.91	1.90	1.89	1.88	1.88	1.87	1.86	1.85	1.85	1.84	1.84	1.83	1.83	1.82	1.82	1.81
30	1.93	1.92	1.91	1.90	1.89	1.88	1.87	1.86	1.85	1.85	1.84	1.83	1.83	1.82	1.82	1.81	1.81	1.80	1.80
31	1.92	1.91	1.90	1.88	1.88	1.87	1.86	1.85	1.84	1.83	1.83	1.82	1.82	1.81	1.81	1.80	1.80	1.79	1.79
32	1.91	1.90	1.88	1.87	1.86	1.85	1.85	1.84	1.83	1.82	1.82	1.81	1.80	1.80	1.79	1.79	1.78	1.78	1.77

α = .05

df_D \ df_N	20	21	22	23	24	25	26	27	28	29	30	31	32	33	34	35	36	37	38
33	1.90	1.89	1.87	1.86	1.85	1.84	1.83	1.83	1.82	1.81	1.81	1.80	1.79	1.79	1.78	1.78	1.77	1.77	1.76
34	1.89	1.88	1.86	1.85	1.84	1.83	1.82	1.82	1.81	1.80	1.80	1.79	1.78	1.78	1.77	1.77	1.76	1.76	1.75
35	1.88	1.87	1.85	1.84	1.83	1.82	1.82	1.81	1.80	1.79	1.79	1.78	1.77	1.77	1.76	1.76	1.75	1.75	1.74
36	1.87	1.86	1.85	1.83	1.82	1.81	1.81	1.80	1.79	1.78	1.78	1.77	1.76	1.76	1.75	1.75	1.74	1.74	1.73
37	1.86	1.85	1.84	1.83	1.82	1.81	1.80	1.79	1.78	1.77	1.77	1.76	1.76	1.75	1.74	1.74	1.73	1.73	1.73
38	1.85	1.84	1.83	1.82	1.81	1.80	1.79	1.78	1.77	1.77	1.76	1.75	1.75	1.74	1.74	1.73	1.73	1.72	1.72
39	1.85	1.83	1.82	1.81	1.80	1.79	1.78	1.77	1.77	1.76	1.75	1.75	1.74	1.73	1.73	1.72	1.72	1.71	1.71
40	1.84	1.83	1.81	1.80	1.79	1.78	1.77	1.77	1.76	1.75	1.74	1.74	1.73	1.73	1.72	1.72	1.71	1.71	1.70
41	1.83	1.82	1.81	1.80	1.79	1.78	1.77	1.76	1.75	1.74	1.74	1.73	1.72	1.72	1.71	1.71	1.70	1.70	1.69
42	1.83	1.81	1.80	1.79	1.78	1.77	1.76	1.75	1.75	1.74	1.73	1.72	1.72	1.71	1.71	1.70	1.70	1.69	1.69
43	1.82	1.81	1.79	1.78	1.77	1.76	1.75	1.75	1.74	1.73	1.72	1.72	1.71	1.71	1.70	1.70	1.69	1.69	1.68
44	1.81	1.80	1.79	1.78	1.77	1.76	1.75	1.74	1.73	1.73	1.72	1.71	1.71	1.70	1.69	1.69	1.68	1.68	1.67
45	1.81	1.80	1.78	1.77	1.76	1.75	1.74	1.73	1.73	1.72	1.71	1.71	1.70	1.69	1.69	1.68	1.68	1.67	1.67
46	1.80	1.79	1.78	1.77	1.76	1.75	1.74	1.73	1.72	1.71	1.71	1.70	1.69	1.69	1.68	1.68	1.67	1.67	1.66
47	1.80	1.78	1.77	1.76	1.75	1.74	1.73	1.72	1.72	1.71	1.70	1.70	1.69	1.68	1.68	1.67	1.67	1.66	1.66
48	1.79	1.78	1.77	1.76	1.75	1.74	1.73	1.72	1.71	1.70	1.70	1.69	1.68	1.68	1.67	1.67	1.66	1.66	1.65
49	1.79	1.78	1.76	1.75	1.74	1.73	1.72	1.71	1.71	1.70	1.69	1.69	1.68	1.67	1.67	1.66	1.66	1.65	1.65
50	1.78	1.77	1.76	1.75	1.74	1.73	1.72	1.71	1.70	1.69	1.69	1.68	1.67	1.67	1.66	1.66	1.65	1.65	1.64
60	1.75	1.73	1.72	1.71	1.70	1.69	1.68	1.67	1.66	1.66	1.65	1.64	1.64	1.63	1.62	1.62	1.61	1.61	1.60
70	1.72	1.71	1.70	1.68	1.67	1.66	1.65	1.65	1.64	1.63	1.62	1.62	1.61	1.60	1.60	1.59	1.59	1.58	1.58
80	1.70	1.69	1.68	1.67	1.65	1.64	1.63	1.63	1.62	1.61	1.60	1.59	1.59	1.58	1.58	1.57	1.56	1.56	1.55
90	1.69	1.67	1.66	1.65	1.64	1.63	1.62	1.61	1.60	1.59	1.59	1.58	1.57	1.57	1.56	1.55	1.55	1.54	1.54
100	1.68	1.66	1.65	1.64	1.63	1.62	1.61	1.60	1.59	1.58	1.57	1.57	1.56	1.55	1.55	1.54	1.54	1.53	1.52
110	1.67	1.65	1.64	1.63	1.62	1.61	1.60	1.59	1.58	1.57	1.56	1.56	1.55	1.54	1.54	1.53	1.52	1.52	1.51
120	1.66	1.64	1.63	1.62	1.61	1.60	1.59	1.58	1.57	1.56	1.55	1.55	1.54	1.53	1.53	1.52	1.52	1.51	1.50
130	1.65	1.64	1.62	1.61	1.60	1.59	1.58	1.57	1.56	1.55	1.55	1.54	1.53	1.53	1.52	1.51	1.51	1.50	1.50
140	1.65	1.63	1.62	1.61	1.60	1.58	1.57	1.57	1.56	1.55	1.54	1.53	1.53	1.52	1.51	1.51	1.50	1.50	1.49
150	1.64	1.63	1.61	1.60	1.59	1.58	1.57	1.56	1.55	1.54	1.54	1.53	1.52	1.51	1.51	1.50	1.50	1.49	1.49
200	1.62	1.61	1.60	1.58	1.57	1.56	1.55	1.54	1.53	1.52	1.52	1.51	1.50	1.49	1.49	1.48	1.48	1.47	1.47
300	1.61	1.59	1.58	1.57	1.55	1.54	1.53	1.52	1.51	1.51	1.50	1.49	1.48	1.48	1.47	1.46	1.46	1.45	1.45
400	1.60	1.58	1.57	1.56	1.54	1.53	1.52	1.51	1.50	1.50	1.49	1.48	1.47	1.47	1.46	1.45	1.45	1.44	1.44
500	1.59	1.58	1.56	1.55	1.54	1.53	1.52	1.51	1.50	1.49	1.48	1.47	1.47	1.46	1.45	1.45	1.44	1.43	1.43
1000	1.58	1.57	1.55	1.54	1.53	1.52	1.51	1.50	1.49	1.48	1.47	1.46	1.46	1.45	1.44	1.43	1.43	1.42	1.42
∞	1.57	1.56	1.54	1.53	1.52	1.51	1.50	1.49	1.48	1.47	1.46	1.45	1.44	1.44	1.43	1.42	1.42	1.41	1.40

$\alpha = .05$

df_D \ df_N	39	40	50	60	70	80	90	100	110	120	130	140	150	200	300	400	500	1000	∞
1	251.06	251.14	251.77	252.20	252.50	252.72	252.90	253.04	253.16	253.25	253.33	253.41	253.47	253.68	253.89	254.00	254.06	254.19	254.32
2	19.47	19.47	19.48	19.48	19.48	19.48	19.48	19.49	19.49	19.49	19.49	19.49	19.49	19.49	19.49	19.49	19.49	19.49	19.50
3	8.60	8.59	8.58	8.57	8.57	8.56	8.56	8.55	8.55	8.55	8.55	8.55	8.54	8.54	8.54	8.53	8.53	8.53	8.53
4	5.72	5.72	5.70	5.69	5.68	5.67	5.67	5.66	5.66	5.66	5.66	5.65	5.65	5.65	5.64	5.64	5.64	5.63	5.63
5	4.47	4.46	4.44	4.43	4.42	4.41	4.41	4.41	4.40	4.40	4.40	4.39	4.39	4.39	4.38	4.38	4.37	4.37	4.37
6	3.78	3.77	3.75	3.74	3.73	3.72	3.72	3.71	3.71	3.70	3.70	3.70	3.70	3.69	3.68	3.68	3.68	3.67	3.67
7	3.34	3.34	3.32	3.30	3.29	3.29	3.28	3.27	3.27	3.27	3.26	3.26	3.26	3.25	3.24	3.24	3.24	3.23	3.23
8	3.05	3.04	3.02	3.01	2.99	2.99	2.98	2.97	2.97	2.97	2.96	2.96	2.96	2.95	2.94	2.94	2.94	2.93	2.93
9	2.83	2.83	2.80	2.79	2.78	2.77	2.76	2.76	2.75	2.75	2.74	2.74	2.74	2.73	2.72	2.72	2.72	2.71	2.71
10	2.66	2.66	2.64	2.62	2.61	2.60	2.59	2.59	2.58	2.58	2.58	2.57	2.57	2.56	2.55	2.55	2.55	2.54	2.54
11	2.53	2.53	2.51	2.49	2.48	2.47	2.46	2.46	2.45	2.45	2.44	2.44	2.44	2.43	2.42	2.42	2.42	2.41	2.40
12	2.43	2.43	2.40	2.38	2.37	2.36	2.36	2.35	2.34	2.34	2.34	2.33	2.33	2.32	2.31	2.31	2.31	2.30	2.30
13	2.34	2.34	2.31	2.30	2.28	2.27	2.27	2.26	2.26	2.25	2.25	2.25	2.24	2.23	2.23	2.22	2.22	2.21	2.21
14	2.27	2.27	2.24	2.22	2.21	2.20	2.19	2.19	2.18	2.18	2.17	2.17	2.17	2.16	2.15	2.15	2.14	2.14	2.13
15	2.21	2.20	2.18	2.16	2.15	2.14	2.13	2.12	2.12	2.11	2.11	2.11	2.10	2.10	2.09	2.08	2.08	2.07	2.07
16	2.15	2.15	2.12	2.11	2.09	2.08	2.07	2.07	2.06	2.06	2.06	2.05	2.05	2.04	2.03	2.02	2.02	2.02	2.01
17	2.11	2.10	2.08	2.06	2.05	2.03	2.03	2.02	2.02	2.01	2.01	2.00	2.00	1.99	1.98	1.98	1.97	1.97	1.96
18	2.07	2.06	2.04	2.02	2.00	1.99	1.98	1.98	1.97	1.97	1.96	1.96	1.96	1.95	1.94	1.93	1.93	1.92	1.92
19	2.03	2.03	2.00	1.98	1.97	1.96	1.95	1.94	1.93	1.93	1.93	1.92	1.92	1.91	1.90	1.89	1.89	1.88	1.88
20	2.00	1.99	1.97	1.95	1.93	1.92	1.91	1.91	1.90	1.90	1.89	1.89	1.89	1.88	1.86	1.86	1.86	1.85	1.84
21	1.97	1.96	1.94	1.92	1.90	1.89	1.88	1.88	1.87	1.87	1.86	1.86	1.86	1.84	1.83	1.83	1.83	1.82	1.81
22	1.94	1.94	1.91	1.89	1.88	1.86	1.86	1.85	1.84	1.84	1.83	1.83	1.83	1.82	1.81	1.80	1.80	1.79	1.78
23	1.92	1.91	1.88	1.86	1.85	1.84	1.83	1.82	1.82	1.81	1.81	1.81	1.80	1.79	1.78	1.77	1.77	1.76	1.76
24	1.90	1.89	1.86	1.84	1.83	1.82	1.81	1.80	1.79	1.79	1.79	1.78	1.78	1.77	1.76	1.75	1.75	1.74	1.73
25	1.88	1.87	1.84	1.82	1.81	1.80	1.79	1.78	1.77	1.77	1.76	1.76	1.76	1.75	1.73	1.73	1.73	1.72	1.71
26	1.86	1.85	1.82	1.80	1.79	1.78	1.77	1.76	1.75	1.75	1.74	1.74	1.74	1.73	1.71	1.71	1.71	1.70	1.69
27	1.84	1.84	1.81	1.79	1.77	1.76	1.75	1.74	1.74	1.73	1.73	1.72	1.72	1.71	1.70	1.69	1.69	1.68	1.67
28	1.82	1.82	1.79	1.77	1.75	1.74	1.73	1.73	1.72	1.71	1.71	1.71	1.70	1.69	1.68	1.67	1.67	1.66	1.65
29	1.81	1.81	1.77	1.75	1.74	1.73	1.72	1.71	1.70	1.70	1.69	1.69	1.69	1.67	1.66	1.66	1.65	1.65	1.64
30	1.80	1.79	1.76	1.74	1.72	1.71	1.70	1.70	1.69	1.68	1.68	1.68	1.67	1.66	1.65	1.64	1.64	1.63	1.62
31	1.78	1.78	1.75	1.73	1.71	1.70	1.69	1.68	1.68	1.67	1.67	1.66	1.66	1.65	1.63	1.63	1.62	1.62	1.61
32	1.77	1.77	1.74	1.71	1.70	1.69	1.68	1.67	1.66	1.66	1.65	1.65	1.64	1.63	1.62	1.61	1.61	1.60	1.59

$\alpha = .05$

df_D \ df_N	39	40	50	60	70	80	90	100	110	120	130	140	150	200	300	400	500	1000	∞
33	1.76	1.76	1.72	1.70	1.69	1.67	1.66	1.66	1.65	1.64	1.64	1.64	1.63	1.62	1.61	1.60	1.60	1.59	1.58
34	1.75	1.75	1.71	1.69	1.68	1.66	1.65	1.65	1.64	1.63	1.63	1.62	1.62	1.61	1.60	1.59	1.59	1.58	1.57
35	1.74	1.74	1.70	1.68	1.66	1.65	1.64	1.63	1.63	1.62	1.62	1.61	1.61	1.60	1.58	1.58	1.57	1.57	1.56
36	1.73	1.73	1.69	1.67	1.66	1.64	1.63	1.62	1.62	1.61	1.61	1.60	1.60	1.59	1.57	1.57	1.56	1.56	1.55
37	1.72	1.72	1.68	1.66	1.65	1.63	1.62	1.62	1.61	1.60	1.60	1.59	1.59	1.58	1.56	1.56	1.55	1.55	1.54
38	1.71	1.71	1.68	1.65	1.64	1.62	1.61	1.61	1.60	1.59	1.59	1.58	1.58	1.57	1.55	1.55	1.54	1.54	1.53
39	1.70	1.70	1.67	1.65	1.63	1.62	1.61	1.60	1.59	1.58	1.58	1.58	1.57	1.56	1.55	1.54	1.53	1.53	1.52
40	1.70	1.69	1.66	1.64	1.62	1.61	1.60	1.59	1.58	1.58	1.57	1.57	1.56	1.55	1.54	1.53	1.53	1.52	1.51
41	1.69	1.69	1.65	1.63	1.61	1.60	1.59	1.58	1.57	1.57	1.56	1.56	1.56	1.54	1.53	1.52	1.52	1.51	1.50
42	1.68	1.68	1.65	1.62	1.61	1.59	1.58	1.57	1.57	1.56	1.56	1.55	1.55	1.53	1.52	1.51	1.51	1.50	1.49
43	1.68	1.67	1.64	1.62	1.60	1.59	1.58	1.57	1.56	1.55	1.55	1.54	1.54	1.53	1.51	1.51	1.50	1.49	1.48
44	1.67	1.67	1.63	1.61	1.59	1.58	1.57	1.56	1.55	1.55	1.54	1.54	1.53	1.52	1.51	1.50	1.49	1.49	1.48
45	1.66	1.66	1.63	1.60	1.59	1.57	1.56	1.55	1.55	1.54	1.54	1.53	1.53	1.51	1.50	1.49	1.49	1.48	1.47
46	1.66	1.65	1.62	1.60	1.58	1.57	1.56	1.55	1.54	1.53	1.53	1.52	1.52	1.51	1.49	1.49	1.48	1.47	1.46
47	1.65	1.65	1.61	1.59	1.57	1.56	1.55	1.54	1.53	1.53	1.52	1.52	1.51	1.50	1.49	1.48	1.47	1.47	1.46
48	1.65	1.64	1.61	1.59	1.57	1.56	1.54	1.54	1.53	1.52	1.52	1.51	1.51	1.49	1.48	1.47	1.47	1.46	1.45
49	1.64	1.64	1.60	1.58	1.56	1.55	1.54	1.53	1.52	1.52	1.51	1.51	1.50	1.49	1.47	1.47	1.46	1.45	1.44
50	1.64	1.63	1.60	1.58	1.56	1.54	1.53	1.52	1.52	1.51	1.51	1.50	1.50	1.48	1.47	1.46	1.46	1.45	1.44
60	1.60	1.59	1.56	1.53	1.52	1.50	1.49	1.48	1.47	1.47	1.46	1.46	1.45	1.44	1.42	1.41	1.41	1.40	1.39
70	1.57	1.57	1.53	1.50	1.49	1.47	1.46	1.45	1.44	1.44	1.43	1.42	1.42	1.40	1.39	1.38	1.37	1.36	1.35
80	1.55	1.54	1.51	1.48	1.46	1.45	1.44	1.43	1.42	1.41	1.40	1.40	1.39	1.38	1.36	1.35	1.35	1.34	1.32
90	1.53	1.53	1.49	1.46	1.44	1.43	1.42	1.41	1.40	1.39	1.39	1.38	1.38	1.36	1.34	1.33	1.33	1.31	1.30
100	1.52	1.52	1.48	1.45	1.43	1.41	1.40	1.39	1.38	1.38	1.37	1.36	1.36	1.34	1.32	1.31	1.31	1.30	1.28
110	1.51	1.50	1.47	1.44	1.42	1.40	1.39	1.38	1.37	1.36	1.36	1.35	1.35	1.33	1.31	1.30	1.29	1.28	1.27
120	1.50	1.50	1.46	1.43	1.41	1.39	1.38	1.37	1.36	1.35	1.35	1.34	1.33	1.32	1.30	1.29	1.28	1.27	1.25
130	1.49	1.49	1.45	1.42	1.40	1.38	1.37	1.36	1.35	1.34	1.34	1.33	1.32	1.31	1.29	1.28	1.27	1.26	1.24
140	1.49	1.48	1.44	1.41	1.39	1.38	1.36	1.35	1.34	1.33	1.33	1.32	1.32	1.30	1.28	1.27	1.26	1.25	1.23
150	1.48	1.48	1.44	1.41	1.39	1.37	1.36	1.34	1.34	1.33	1.32	1.31	1.31	1.29	1.27	1.26	1.25	1.24	1.22
200	1.46	1.46	1.41	1.39	1.36	1.35	1.33	1.32	1.31	1.30	1.30	1.29	1.28	1.26	1.24	1.23	1.22	1.21	1.19
300	1.44	1.43	1.39	1.36	1.34	1.32	1.31	1.30	1.29	1.28	1.27	1.26	1.26	1.23	1.21	1.20	1.19	1.17	1.15
400	1.43	1.42	1.38	1.35	1.33	1.31	1.30	1.28	1.27	1.26	1.26	1.25	1.24	1.22	1.19	1.18	1.17	1.15	1.13
500	1.42	1.42	1.38	1.35	1.32	1.30	1.29	1.28	1.26	1.26	1.25	1.24	1.23	1.21	1.18	1.17	1.16	1.14	1.11
1000	1.41	1.41	1.36	1.33	1.31	1.29	1.27	1.26	1.25	1.24	1.23	1.22	1.22	1.19	1.16	1.14	1.13	1.11	1.08
∞	1.40	1.39	1.35	1.32	1.29	1.27	1.26	1.24	1.23	1.22	1.21	1.20	1.20	1.17	1.14	1.12	1.11	1.07	1.00

TABLE 4 (continued)
Critical Values for the F-Distribution
$\alpha = .025$

df_D \ df_N	1	2	3	4	5	6	7	8	9	10	11	12	13	14	15	16	17	18	19
1	647.79	799.48	864.15	899.60	921.83	937.11	948.20	956.64	963.28	968.63	973.03	976.72	979.84	982.55	984.87	986.91	988.72	990.35	991.80
2	38.51	39.00	39.17	39.25	39.30	39.33	39.36	39.37	39.39	39.40	39.41	39.41	39.42	39.43	39.43	39.44	39.44	39.44	39.45
3	17.44	16.04	15.44	15.10	14.88	14.73	14.62	14.54	14.47	14.42	14.37	14.34	14.30	14.28	14.25	14.23	14.21	14.20	14.18
4	12.22	10.65	9.98	9.60	9.36	9.20	9.07	8.98	8.90	8.84	8.79	8.75	8.72	8.68	8.66	8.63	8.61	8.59	8.58
5	10.01	8.43	7.76	7.39	7.15	6.98	6.85	6.76	6.68	6.62	6.57	6.52	6.49	6.46	6.43	6.40	6.38	6.36	6.34
6	8.81	7.26	6.60	6.23	5.99	5.82	5.70	5.60	5.52	5.46	5.41	5.37	5.33	5.30	5.27	5.24	5.22	5.20	5.18
7	8.07	6.54	5.89	5.52	5.29	5.12	4.99	4.90	4.82	4.76	4.71	4.67	4.63	4.60	4.57	4.54	4.52	4.50	4.48
8	7.57	6.06	5.42	5.05	4.82	4.65	4.53	4.43	4.36	4.30	4.24	4.20	4.16	4.13	4.10	4.08	4.05	4.03	4.02
9	7.21	5.71	5.08	4.72	4.48	4.32	4.20	4.10	4.03	3.96	3.91	3.87	3.83	3.80	3.77	3.74	3.72	3.70	3.68
10	6.94	5.46	4.83	4.47	4.24	4.07	3.95	3.85	3.78	3.72	3.66	3.62	3.58	3.55	3.52	3.50	3.47	3.45	3.44
11	6.72	5.26	4.63	4.28	4.04	3.88	3.76	3.66	3.59	3.53	3.47	3.43	3.39	3.36	3.33	3.30	3.28	3.26	3.24
12	6.55	5.10	4.47	4.12	3.89	3.73	3.61	3.51	3.44	3.37	3.32	3.28	3.24	3.21	3.18	3.15	3.13	3.11	3.09
13	6.41	4.97	4.35	4.00	3.77	3.60	3.48	3.39	3.31	3.25	3.20	3.15	3.12	3.08	3.05	3.03	3.00	2.98	2.96
14	6.30	4.86	4.24	3.89	3.66	3.50	3.38	3.29	3.21	3.15	3.09	3.05	3.01	2.98	2.95	2.92	2.90	2.88	2.86
15	6.20	4.77	4.15	3.80	3.58	3.41	3.29	3.20	3.12	3.06	3.01	2.96	2.92	2.89	2.86	2.84	2.81	2.79	2.77
16	6.12	4.69	4.08	3.73	3.50	3.34	3.22	3.12	3.05	2.99	2.93	2.89	2.85	2.82	2.79	2.76	2.74	2.72	2.70
17	6.04	4.62	4.01	3.66	3.44	3.28	3.16	3.06	2.98	2.92	2.87	2.82	2.79	2.75	2.72	2.70	2.67	2.65	2.63
18	5.98	4.56	3.95	3.61	3.38	3.22	3.10	3.01	2.93	2.87	2.81	2.77	2.73	2.70	2.67	2.64	2.62	2.60	2.58
19	5.92	4.51	3.90	3.56	3.33	3.17	3.05	2.96	2.88	2.82	2.76	2.72	2.68	2.65	2.62	2.59	2.57	2.55	2.53
20	5.87	4.46	3.86	3.51	3.29	3.13	3.01	2.91	2.84	2.77	2.72	2.68	2.64	2.60	2.57	2.55	2.52	2.50	2.48
21	5.83	4.42	3.82	3.48	3.25	3.09	2.97	2.87	2.80	2.73	2.68	2.64	2.60	2.56	2.53	2.51	2.48	2.46	2.44
22	5.79	4.38	3.78	3.44	3.22	3.05	2.93	2.84	2.76	2.70	2.65	2.60	2.56	2.53	2.50	2.47	2.45	2.43	2.41
23	5.75	4.35	3.75	3.41	3.18	3.02	2.90	2.81	2.73	2.67	2.62	2.57	2.53	2.50	2.47	2.44	2.42	2.39	2.37
24	5.72	4.32	3.72	3.38	3.15	2.99	2.87	2.78	2.70	2.64	2.59	2.54	2.50	2.47	2.44	2.41	2.39	2.36	2.35
25	5.69	4.29	3.69	3.35	3.13	2.97	2.85	2.75	2.68	2.61	2.56	2.51	2.48	2.44	2.41	2.38	2.36	2.34	2.32
26	5.66	4.27	3.67	3.33	3.10	2.94	2.82	2.73	2.65	2.59	2.54	2.49	2.45	2.42	2.39	2.36	2.34	2.31	2.29
27	5.63	4.24	3.65	3.31	3.08	2.92	2.80	2.71	2.63	2.57	2.51	2.47	2.43	2.39	2.36	2.34	2.31	2.29	2.27
28	5.61	4.22	3.63	3.29	3.06	2.90	2.78	2.69	2.61	2.55	2.49	2.45	2.41	2.37	2.34	2.32	2.29	2.27	2.25
29	5.59	4.20	3.61	3.27	3.04	2.88	2.76	2.67	2.59	2.53	2.48	2.43	2.39	2.36	2.32	2.30	2.27	2.25	2.23
30	5.57	4.18	3.59	3.25	3.03	2.87	2.75	2.65	2.57	2.51	2.46	2.41	2.37	2.34	2.31	2.28	2.26	2.23	2.21
31	5.55	4.16	3.57	3.23	3.01	2.85	2.73	2.64	2.56	2.50	2.44	2.40	2.36	2.32	2.29	2.26	2.24	2.22	2.20
32	5.53	4.15	3.56	3.22	3.00	2.84	2.71	2.62	2.54	2.48	2.43	2.38	2.34	2.31	2.28	2.25	2.22	2.20	2.18

$\alpha = .025$

df_D \ df_N	1	2	3	4	5	6	7	8	9	10	11	12	13	14	15	16	17	18	19
33	5.51	4.13	3.54	3.20	2.98	2.82	2.70	2.61	2.53	2.47	2.41	2.37	2.33	2.29	2.26	2.23	2.21	2.19	2.17
34	5.50	4.12	3.53	3.19	2.97	2.81	2.69	2.59	2.52	2.45	2.40	2.35	2.31	2.28	2.25	2.22	2.20	2.17	2.15
35	5.48	4.11	3.52	3.18	2.96	2.80	2.68	2.58	2.50	2.44	2.39	2.34	2.30	2.27	2.23	2.21	2.18	2.16	2.14
36	5.47	4.09	3.50	3.17	2.94	2.78	2.66	2.57	2.49	2.43	2.37	2.33	2.29	2.25	2.22	2.20	2.17	2.15	2.13
37	5.46	4.08	3.49	3.16	2.93	2.77	2.65	2.56	2.48	2.42	2.36	2.32	2.28	2.24	2.21	2.18	2.16	2.14	2.12
38	5.45	4.07	3.48	3.15	2.92	2.76	2.64	2.55	2.47	2.41	2.35	2.31	2.27	2.23	2.20	2.17	2.15	2.13	2.11
39	5.43	4.06	3.47	3.14	2.91	2.75	2.63	2.54	2.46	2.40	2.34	2.30	2.26	2.22	2.19	2.16	2.14	2.12	2.10
40	5.42	4.05	3.46	3.13	2.90	2.74	2.62	2.53	2.45	2.39	2.33	2.29	2.25	2.21	2.18	2.15	2.13	2.11	2.09
41	5.41	4.04	3.45	3.12	2.89	2.74	2.62	2.52	2.44	2.38	2.33	2.28	2.24	2.20	2.17	2.15	2.12	2.10	2.08
42	5.40	4.03	3.45	3.11	2.89	2.73	2.61	2.51	2.43	2.37	2.32	2.27	2.23	2.20	2.16	2.14	2.11	2.09	2.07
43	5.39	4.02	3.44	3.10	2.88	2.72	2.60	2.50	2.43	2.36	2.31	2.26	2.22	2.19	2.16	2.13	2.10	2.08	2.06
44	5.39	4.02	3.43	3.09	2.87	2.71	2.59	2.50	2.42	2.36	2.30	2.26	2.22	2.18	2.15	2.12	2.10	2.07	2.05
45	5.38	4.01	3.42	3.09	2.86	2.70	2.58	2.49	2.41	2.35	2.29	2.25	2.21	2.17	2.14	2.11	2.09	2.07	2.04
46	5.37	4.00	3.42	3.08	2.86	2.70	2.58	2.48	2.41	2.34	2.29	2.24	2.20	2.17	2.13	2.11	2.08	2.06	2.04
47	5.36	3.99	3.41	3.07	2.85	2.69	2.57	2.48	2.40	2.33	2.28	2.23	2.19	2.16	2.13	2.10	2.07	2.05	2.03
48	5.35	3.99	3.40	3.07	2.84	2.69	2.56	2.47	2.39	2.33	2.27	2.23	2.19	2.15	2.12	2.09	2.07	2.05	2.02
49	5.35	3.98	3.40	3.06	2.84	2.68	2.56	2.46	2.39	2.32	2.27	2.22	2.18	2.15	2.11	2.09	2.06	2.04	2.02
50	5.34	3.97	3.39	3.05	2.83	2.67	2.55	2.46	2.38	2.32	2.26	2.22	2.18	2.14	2.11	2.08	2.06	2.03	2.01
60	5.29	3.93	3.34	3.01	2.79	2.63	2.51	2.41	2.33	2.27	2.22	2.17	2.13	2.09	2.06	2.03	2.01	1.98	1.96
70	5.25	3.89	3.31	2.97	2.75	2.59	2.47	2.38	2.30	2.24	2.18	2.14	2.10	2.06	2.03	2.00	1.97	1.95	1.93
80	5.22	3.86	3.28	2.95	2.73	2.57	2.45	2.35	2.28	2.21	2.16	2.11	2.07	2.03	2.00	1.97	1.95	1.92	1.90
90	5.20	3.84	3.26	2.93	2.71	2.55	2.43	2.34	2.26	2.19	2.14	2.09	2.05	2.02	1.98	1.95	1.93	1.91	1.88
100	5.18	3.83	3.25	2.92	2.70	2.54	2.42	2.32	2.24	2.18	2.12	2.08	2.04	2.00	1.97	1.94	1.91	1.89	1.87
110	5.16	3.82	3.24	2.90	2.68	2.53	2.40	2.31	2.23	2.17	2.11	2.07	2.02	1.99	1.96	1.93	1.90	1.88	1.86
120	5.15	3.80	3.23	2.89	2.67	2.52	2.39	2.30	2.22	2.16	2.10	2.05	2.01	1.98	1.94	1.92	1.89	1.87	1.84
130	5.14	3.80	3.22	2.89	2.67	2.51	2.39	2.29	2.21	2.15	2.09	2.05	2.00	1.97	1.94	1.91	1.88	1.86	1.84
140	5.13	3.79	3.21	2.88	2.66	2.50	2.38	2.28	2.21	2.14	2.09	2.04	2.00	1.96	1.93	1.90	1.87	1.85	1.83
150	5.13	3.78	3.20	2.87	2.65	2.49	2.37	2.28	2.20	2.13	2.08	2.03	1.99	1.95	1.92	1.89	1.87	1.84	1.82
200	5.10	3.76	3.18	2.85	2.63	2.47	2.35	2.26	2.18	2.11	2.06	2.01	1.97	1.93	1.90	1.87	1.84	1.82	1.80
300	5.07	3.73	3.16	2.83	2.61	2.45	2.33	2.23	2.16	2.09	2.04	1.99	1.95	1.91	1.88	1.85	1.82	1.80	1.77
400	5.06	3.72	3.15	2.82	2.60	2.44	2.32	2.22	2.15	2.08	2.03	1.98	1.94	1.90	1.87	1.84	1.81	1.79	1.76
500	5.05	3.72	3.14	2.81	2.59	2.43	2.31	2.22	2.14	2.07	2.02	1.97	1.93	1.89	1.86	1.83	1.80	1.78	1.76
1000	5.04	3.70	3.13	2.80	2.58	2.42	2.30	2.20	2.13	2.06	2.01	1.96	1.92	1.88	1.85	1.82	1.79	1.77	1.74
∞	5.02	3.69	3.12	2.79	2.57	2.41	2.29	2.19	2.11	2.05	1.99	1.94	1.90	1.87	1.83	1.80	1.78	1.75	1.73

$\alpha = .025$

df_D \ df_N	20	21	22	23	24	25	26	27	28	29	30	31	32	33	34	35	36	37	38
1	993.08	994.30	995.35	996.34	997.27	998.09	998.84	999.54	1000.2	1000.8	1001.4	1002.0	1002.5	1002.9	1003.4	1003.8	1004.2	1004.6	1005.0
2	39.45	39.45	39.45	39.45	39.46	39.46	39.46	39.46	39.46	39.46	39.46	39.47	39.47	39.47	39.47	39.47	39.47	39.47	39.47
3	14.17	14.16	14.14	14.13	14.12	14.12	14.11	14.10	14.09	14.09	14.08	14.07	14.07	14.06	14.06	14.06	14.05	14.05	14.04
4	8.56	8.55	8.53	8.52	8.51	8.50	8.49	8.48	8.48	8.47	8.46	8.45	8.45	8.44	8.44	8.43	8.43	8.42	8.42
5	6.33	6.31	6.30	6.29	6.28	6.27	6.26	6.25	6.24	6.23	6.23	6.22	6.21	6.21	6.20	6.20	6.19	6.19	6.18
6	5.17	5.15	5.14	5.13	5.12	5.11	5.10	5.09	5.08	5.07	5.07	5.06	5.05	5.05	5.04	5.04	5.03	5.03	5.02
7	4.47	4.45	4.44	4.43	4.41	4.40	4.39	4.39	4.38	4.37	4.36	4.36	4.35	4.34	4.34	4.33	4.33	4.32	4.32
8	4.00	3.98	3.97	3.96	3.95	3.94	3.93	3.92	3.91	3.90	3.89	3.89	3.88	3.87	3.87	3.86	3.86	3.85	3.85
9	3.67	3.65	3.64	3.63	3.61	3.60	3.59	3.58	3.58	3.57	3.56	3.55	3.55	3.54	3.53	3.53	3.52	3.52	3.51
10	3.42	3.40	3.39	3.38	3.37	3.35	3.34	3.34	3.33	3.32	3.31	3.30	3.30	3.29	3.29	3.28	3.27	3.27	3.26
11	3.23	3.21	3.20	3.18	3.17	3.16	3.15	3.14	3.13	3.13	3.12	3.11	3.10	3.10	3.09	3.09	3.08	3.08	3.07
12	3.07	3.06	3.04	3.03	3.02	3.01	3.00	2.99	2.98	2.97	2.96	2.96	2.95	2.94	2.94	2.93	2.93	2.92	2.92
13	2.95	2.93	2.92	2.91	2.89	2.88	2.87	2.86	2.85	2.85	2.84	2.83	2.82	2.82	2.81	2.80	2.80	2.79	2.79
14	2.84	2.83	2.81	2.80	2.79	2.78	2.77	2.76	2.75	2.74	2.73	2.72	2.72	2.71	2.71	2.70	2.69	2.69	2.68
15	2.76	2.74	2.73	2.71	2.70	2.69	2.68	2.67	2.66	2.65	2.64	2.64	2.63	2.62	2.62	2.61	2.60	2.60	2.59
16	2.68	2.67	2.65	2.64	2.63	2.61	2.60	2.59	2.58	2.58	2.57	2.56	2.55	2.55	2.54	2.53	2.53	2.52	2.52
17	2.62	2.60	2.59	2.57	2.56	2.55	2.54	2.53	2.52	2.51	2.50	2.49	2.49	2.48	2.47	2.47	2.46	2.46	2.45
18	2.56	2.54	2.53	2.52	2.50	2.49	2.48	2.47	2.46	2.45	2.44	2.44	2.43	2.42	2.42	2.41	2.40	2.40	2.39
19	2.51	2.49	2.48	2.46	2.45	2.44	2.43	2.42	2.41	2.40	2.39	2.39	2.38	2.37	2.37	2.36	2.35	2.35	2.34
20	2.46	2.45	2.43	2.42	2.41	2.40	2.39	2.38	2.37	2.36	2.35	2.34	2.33	2.33	2.32	2.31	2.31	2.30	2.30
21	2.42	2.41	2.39	2.38	2.37	2.36	2.34	2.33	2.33	2.32	2.31	2.30	2.29	2.29	2.28	2.27	2.27	2.26	2.26
22	2.39	2.37	2.36	2.34	2.33	2.32	2.31	2.30	2.29	2.28	2.27	2.26	2.26	2.25	2.24	2.24	2.23	2.23	2.22
23	2.36	2.34	2.33	2.31	2.30	2.29	2.28	2.27	2.26	2.25	2.24	2.23	2.22	2.22	2.21	2.20	2.20	2.19	2.19
24	2.33	2.31	2.30	2.28	2.27	2.26	2.25	2.24	2.23	2.22	2.21	2.20	2.19	2.19	2.18	2.17	2.17	2.16	2.16
25	2.30	2.28	2.27	2.26	2.24	2.23	2.22	2.21	2.20	2.19	2.18	2.17	2.17	2.16	2.15	2.15	2.14	2.13	2.13
26	2.28	2.26	2.24	2.23	2.22	2.21	2.19	2.18	2.17	2.17	2.16	2.15	2.14	2.13	2.13	2.12	2.11	2.11	2.10
27	2.25	2.24	2.22	2.21	2.19	2.18	2.17	2.16	2.15	2.14	2.13	2.13	2.12	2.11	2.10	2.10	2.09	2.09	2.08
28	2.23	2.22	2.20	2.19	2.17	2.16	2.15	2.14	2.13	2.12	2.11	2.10	2.10	2.09	2.08	2.08	2.07	2.06	2.06
29	2.21	2.20	2.18	2.17	2.15	2.14	2.13	2.12	2.11	2.10	2.09	2.08	2.08	2.07	2.06	2.06	2.05	2.04	2.04
30	2.20	2.18	2.16	2.15	2.14	2.12	2.11	2.10	2.09	2.08	2.07	2.07	2.06	2.05	2.04	2.04	2.03	2.03	2.02
31	2.18	2.16	2.15	2.13	2.12	2.11	2.10	2.08	2.07	2.07	2.06	2.05	2.04	2.03	2.03	2.02	2.01	2.01	2.00
32	2.16	2.15	2.13	2.12	2.10	2.09	2.08	2.07	2.06	2.05	2.04	2.03	2.02	2.02	2.01	2.00	2.00	1.99	1.99

$\alpha = .025$

df_D \ df_N	20	21	22	23	24	25	26	27	28	29	30	31	32	33	34	35	36	37	38
33	2.15	2.13	2.12	2.10	2.09	2.08	2.06	2.05	2.04	2.03	2.03	2.02	2.01	2.00	2.00	1.99	1.98	1.98	1.97
34	2.13	2.12	2.10	2.09	2.07	2.06	2.05	2.04	2.03	2.02	2.01	2.00	2.00	1.99	1.98	1.97	1.97	1.96	1.96
35	2.12	2.10	2.09	2.07	2.06	2.05	2.04	2.03	2.02	2.01	2.00	1.99	1.98	1.97	1.97	1.96	1.95	1.95	1.94
36	2.11	2.09	2.08	2.06	2.05	2.04	2.03	2.01	2.00	2.00	1.99	1.98	1.97	1.96	1.96	1.95	1.94	1.94	1.93
37	2.10	2.08	2.07	2.05	2.04	2.03	2.01	2.00	1.99	1.98	1.97	1.97	1.96	1.95	1.94	1.94	1.93	1.92	1.92
38	2.09	2.07	2.05	2.04	2.03	2.01	2.00	1.99	1.98	1.97	1.96	1.95	1.95	1.94	1.93	1.93	1.92	1.91	1.91
39	2.08	2.06	2.04	2.03	2.02	2.00	1.99	1.98	1.97	1.96	1.95	1.94	1.94	1.93	1.92	1.91	1.91	1.90	1.90
40	2.07	2.05	2.03	2.02	2.01	1.99	1.98	1.97	1.96	1.95	1.94	1.93	1.93	1.92	1.91	1.90	1.90	1.89	1.89
41	2.06	2.04	2.03	2.01	2.00	1.99	1.97	1.96	1.95	1.94	1.93	1.92	1.92	1.91	1.90	1.90	1.89	1.88	1.88
42	2.05	2.03	2.02	2.00	1.99	1.98	1.96	1.95	1.94	1.93	1.92	1.92	1.91	1.90	1.89	1.89	1.88	1.87	1.87
43	2.04	2.02	2.01	1.99	1.98	1.97	1.96	1.95	1.93	1.93	1.92	1.91	1.90	1.89	1.88	1.88	1.87	1.86	1.86
44	2.03	2.02	2.00	1.99	1.97	1.96	1.95	1.94	1.93	1.92	1.91	1.90	1.89	1.88	1.88	1.87	1.86	1.86	1.85
45	2.03	2.01	1.99	1.98	1.96	1.95	1.94	1.93	1.92	1.91	1.90	1.89	1.88	1.88	1.87	1.86	1.85	1.85	1.84
46	2.02	2.00	1.99	1.97	1.96	1.94	1.93	1.92	1.91	1.90	1.89	1.88	1.88	1.87	1.86	1.85	1.85	1.84	1.83
47	2.01	1.99	1.98	1.96	1.95	1.94	1.93	1.91	1.90	1.89	1.89	1.88	1.87	1.86	1.85	1.85	1.84	1.83	1.83
48	2.01	1.99	1.97	1.96	1.94	1.93	1.92	1.91	1.90	1.89	1.88	1.87	1.86	1.85	1.85	1.84	1.83	1.83	1.82
49	2.00	1.98	1.97	1.95	1.94	1.92	1.91	1.90	1.89	1.88	1.87	1.86	1.86	1.85	1.84	1.83	1.83	1.82	1.81
50	1.99	1.98	1.96	1.95	1.93	1.92	1.91	1.90	1.89	1.88	1.87	1.86	1.85	1.84	1.83	1.83	1.82	1.81	1.81
60	1.94	1.93	1.91	1.90	1.88	1.87	1.86	1.85	1.83	1.82	1.82	1.81	1.80	1.79	1.78	1.78	1.77	1.76	1.76
70	1.91	1.89	1.88	1.86	1.85	1.83	1.82	1.81	1.80	1.79	1.78	1.77	1.76	1.75	1.75	1.74	1.73	1.73	1.72
80	1.88	1.87	1.85	1.83	1.82	1.81	1.79	1.78	1.77	1.76	1.75	1.74	1.73	1.73	1.72	1.71	1.70	1.70	1.69
90	1.86	1.85	1.83	1.81	1.80	1.79	1.77	1.76	1.75	1.74	1.73	1.72	1.71	1.71	1.70	1.69	1.68	1.68	1.67
100	1.85	1.83	1.81	1.80	1.78	1.77	1.76	1.75	1.74	1.72	1.71	1.71	1.70	1.69	1.68	1.67	1.67	1.66	1.65
110	1.84	1.82	1.80	1.79	1.77	1.76	1.74	1.73	1.72	1.71	1.70	1.69	1.68	1.67	1.67	1.66	1.65	1.64	1.64
120	1.82	1.81	1.79	1.77	1.76	1.75	1.73	1.72	1.71	1.70	1.69	1.68	1.67	1.66	1.66	1.65	1.64	1.63	1.63
130	1.82	1.80	1.78	1.77	1.75	1.74	1.72	1.71	1.70	1.69	1.68	1.67	1.66	1.65	1.65	1.64	1.63	1.62	1.62
140	1.81	1.79	1.77	1.76	1.74	1.73	1.72	1.70	1.69	1.68	1.67	1.66	1.65	1.65	1.64	1.63	1.62	1.61	1.61
150	1.80	1.78	1.77	1.75	1.74	1.72	1.71	1.70	1.69	1.68	1.67	1.66	1.65	1.64	1.63	1.62	1.61	1.61	1.60
200	1.78	1.76	1.74	1.73	1.71	1.70	1.68	1.67	1.66	1.65	1.64	1.63	1.62	1.61	1.60	1.60	1.59	1.58	1.58
300	1.75	1.74	1.72	1.70	1.69	1.67	1.66	1.65	1.64	1.63	1.62	1.61	1.60	1.59	1.58	1.57	1.56	1.56	1.55
400	1.74	1.72	1.71	1.69	1.68	1.66	1.65	1.64	1.62	1.61	1.60	1.59	1.58	1.57	1.57	1.56	1.55	1.54	1.54
500	1.74	1.72	1.70	1.68	1.67	1.65	1.64	1.63	1.62	1.61	1.60	1.59	1.58	1.57	1.56	1.55	1.54	1.54	1.53
1000	1.72	1.70	1.69	1.67	1.65	1.64	1.63	1.61	1.60	1.59	1.58	1.57	1.56	1.55	1.54	1.54	1.53	1.52	1.51
∞	1.71	1.69	1.67	1.66	1.64	1.63	1.61	1.60	1.59	1.58	1.57	1.56	1.55	1.54	1.53	1.52	1.51	1.50	1.50

α=.05 2 tail → $\alpha = .025$

df_D \ df_N	39	40	50	60	70	80	90	100	110	120	130	140	150	200	300	400	500	1000	∞
1	1005.3	1005.6	1008.1	1009.8	1011.0	1011.9	1012.6	1013.2	1013.6	1014.0	1014.3	1014.6	1014.9	1015.7	1016.5	1017.0	1017.2	1017.8	1018.3
2	39.47	39.47	39.48	39.48	39.48	39.49	39.49	39.49	39.49	39.49	39.49	39.49	39.49	39.49	39.49	39.50	39.50	39.50	39.50
3	14.04	14.04	14.01	13.99	13.98	13.97	13.96	13.96	13.95	13.95	13.94	13.94	13.94	13.93	13.92	13.92	13.91	13.91	13.90
4	8.41	8.41	8.38	8.36	8.35	8.33	8.33	8.32	8.31	8.31	8.31	8.30	8.30	8.29	8.28	8.27	8.27	8.26	8.26
5	6.18	6.18	6.14	6.12	6.11	6.10	6.09	6.08	6.07	6.07	6.07	6.06	6.06	6.05	6.04	6.03	6.03	6.02	6.02
6	5.02	5.01	4.98	4.96	4.94	4.93	4.92	4.92	4.91	4.90	4.90	4.90	4.89	4.88	4.87	4.87	4.86	4.86	4.85
7	4.31	4.31	4.28	4.25	4.24	4.23	4.22	4.21	4.20	4.20	4.19	4.19	4.19	4.18	4.17	4.16	4.16	4.15	4.14
8	3.84	3.84	3.81	3.78	3.77	3.76	3.75	3.74	3.73	3.73	3.72	3.72	3.72	3.70	3.69	3.69	3.68	3.68	3.67
9	3.51	3.51	3.47	3.45	3.43	3.42	3.41	3.40	3.40	3.39	3.39	3.38	3.38	3.37	3.36	3.35	3.35	3.34	3.33
10	3.26	3.26	3.22	3.20	3.18	3.17	3.16	3.15	3.15	3.14	3.14	3.13	3.13	3.12	3.10	3.10	3.09	3.09	3.08
11	3.07	3.06	3.03	3.00	2.99	2.97	2.96	2.96	2.95	2.94	2.94	2.94	2.93	2.92	2.91	2.90	2.90	2.89	2.88
12	2.91	2.91	2.87	2.85	2.83	2.82	2.81	2.80	2.79	2.79	2.78	2.78	2.78	2.76	2.75	2.74	2.74	2.73	2.72
13	2.78	2.78	2.74	2.72	2.70	2.69	2.68	2.67	2.66	2.66	2.65	2.65	2.65	2.63	2.62	2.61	2.61	2.60	2.60
14	2.68	2.67	2.64	2.61	2.60	2.58	2.57	2.56	2.56	2.55	2.55	2.54	2.54	2.53	2.51	2.51	2.50	2.50	2.49
15	2.59	2.59	2.55	2.52	2.51	2.49	2.48	2.47	2.47	2.46	2.46	2.45	2.45	2.44	2.42	2.42	2.41	2.40	2.40
16	2.51	2.51	2.47	2.45	2.43	2.42	2.40	2.40	2.39	2.38	2.38	2.37	2.37	2.36	2.34	2.34	2.33	2.32	2.32
17	2.45	2.44	2.41	2.38	2.36	2.35	2.34	2.33	2.32	2.32	2.31	2.31	2.30	2.29	2.28	2.27	2.26	2.26	2.25
18	2.39	2.38	2.35	2.32	2.30	2.29	2.28	2.27	2.26	2.26	2.25	2.25	2.24	2.23	2.21	2.21	2.20	2.20	2.19
19	2.34	2.33	2.30	2.27	2.25	2.24	2.23	2.22	2.21	2.20	2.20	2.19	2.19	2.18	2.16	2.15	2.15	2.14	2.13
20	2.29	2.29	2.25	2.22	2.20	2.19	2.18	2.17	2.16	2.16	2.15	2.15	2.14	2.13	2.11	2.11	2.10	2.09	2.09
21	2.25	2.25	2.21	2.18	2.16	2.15	2.14	2.13	2.12	2.11	2.11	2.10	2.10	2.09	2.07	2.06	2.06	2.05	2.04
22	2.21	2.21	2.17	2.14	2.13	2.11	2.10	2.09	2.08	2.08	2.07	2.07	2.06	2.05	2.03	2.03	2.02	2.01	2.00
23	2.18	2.18	2.14	2.11	2.09	2.08	2.07	2.06	2.05	2.04	2.04	2.03	2.03	2.01	2.00	1.99	1.99	1.98	1.97
24	2.15	2.15	2.11	2.08	2.06	2.05	2.03	2.02	2.02	2.01	2.00	2.00	2.00	1.98	1.97	1.96	1.95	1.94	1.94
25	2.12	2.12	2.08	2.05	2.03	2.02	2.01	2.00	1.99	1.98	1.98	1.97	1.97	1.95	1.94	1.93	1.92	1.91	1.91
26	2.10	2.09	2.05	2.03	2.01	1.99	1.98	1.97	1.96	1.95	1.95	1.94	1.94	1.92	1.91	1.90	1.90	1.89	1.88
27	2.07	2.07	2.03	2.00	1.98	1.97	1.95	1.94	1.94	1.93	1.92	1.92	1.91	1.90	1.88	1.88	1.87	1.86	1.85
28	2.05	2.05	2.01	1.98	1.96	1.94	1.93	1.92	1.91	1.91	1.90	1.90	1.89	1.88	1.86	1.85	1.85	1.84	1.83
29	2.03	2.03	1.99	1.96	1.94	1.92	1.91	1.90	1.89	1.89	1.88	1.88	1.87	1.86	1.84	1.83	1.83	1.82	1.81
30	2.01	2.01	1.97	1.94	1.92	1.90	1.89	1.88	1.87	1.87	1.86	1.86	1.85	1.84	1.82	1.81	1.81	1.80	1.79
31	2.00	1.99	1.95	1.92	1.90	1.89	1.87	1.86	1.86	1.85	1.84	1.84	1.83	1.82	1.80	1.79	1.79	1.78	1.77
32	1.98	1.98	1.93	1.91	1.88	1.87	1.86	1.85	1.84	1.83	1.82	1.82	1.82	1.80	1.78	1.77	1.77	1.76	1.75

$\alpha = .025$

df_D \ df_N	39	40	50	60	70	80	90	100	110	120	130	140	150	200	300	400	500	1000	∞
33	1.97	1.96	1.92	1.89	1.87	1.85	1.84	1.83	1.82	1.81	1.81	1.80	1.80	1.78	1.77	1.76	1.75	1.74	1.73
34	1.95	1.95	1.90	1.88	1.85	1.84	1.83	1.82	1.81	1.80	1.79	1.79	1.78	1.77	1.75	1.74	1.74	1.73	1.72
35	1.94	1.93	1.89	1.86	1.84	1.82	1.81	1.80	1.79	1.79	1.78	1.77	1.77	1.75	1.74	1.73	1.72	1.71	1.70
36	1.92	1.92	1.88	1.85	1.83	1.81	1.80	1.79	1.78	1.77	1.77	1.76	1.76	1.74	1.72	1.71	1.71	1.70	1.69
37	1.91	1.91	1.87	1.84	1.81	1.80	1.79	1.77	1.77	1.76	1.75	1.75	1.74	1.73	1.71	1.70	1.70	1.68	1.67
38	1.90	1.90	1.85	1.82	1.80	1.79	1.77	1.76	1.75	1.75	1.74	1.73	1.73	1.71	1.70	1.69	1.68	1.67	1.66
39	1.89	1.89	1.84	1.81	1.79	1.78	1.76	1.75	1.74	1.74	1.73	1.72	1.72	1.70	1.68	1.68	1.67	1.66	1.65
40	1.88	1.88	1.83	1.80	1.78	1.76	1.75	1.74	1.73	1.72	1.72	1.71	1.71	1.69	1.67	1.66	1.66	1.65	1.64
41	1.87	1.87	1.82	1.79	1.77	1.75	1.74	1.73	1.72	1.71	1.71	1.70	1.70	1.68	1.66	1.65	1.65	1.64	1.63
42	1.86	1.86	1.81	1.78	1.76	1.74	1.73	1.72	1.71	1.70	1.70	1.69	1.69	1.67	1.65	1.64	1.64	1.63	1.62
43	1.85	1.85	1.80	1.77	1.75	1.74	1.72	1.71	1.70	1.69	1.69	1.68	1.68	1.66	1.64	1.63	1.63	1.62	1.61
44	1.84	1.84	1.80	1.77	1.74	1.73	1.71	1.70	1.69	1.69	1.68	1.67	1.67	1.65	1.63	1.62	1.62	1.61	1.60
45	1.84	1.83	1.79	1.76	1.74	1.72	1.70	1.69	1.68	1.68	1.67	1.66	1.66	1.64	1.62	1.61	1.61	1.60	1.59
46	1.83	1.82	1.78	1.75	1.73	1.71	1.70	1.69	1.68	1.67	1.66	1.66	1.65	1.63	1.62	1.61	1.60	1.59	1.58
47	1.82	1.82	1.77	1.74	1.72	1.70	1.69	1.68	1.67	1.66	1.65	1.65	1.64	1.63	1.61	1.60	1.59	1.58	1.57
48	1.81	1.81	1.77	1.73	1.71	1.69	1.68	1.67	1.66	1.65	1.65	1.64	1.64	1.62	1.60	1.59	1.58	1.57	1.56
49	1.81	1.80	1.76	1.73	1.71	1.69	1.67	1.66	1.65	1.65	1.64	1.63	1.63	1.61	1.59	1.58	1.58	1.56	1.55
50	1.80	1.80	1.75	1.72	1.70	1.68	1.67	1.66	1.65	1.64	1.63	1.63	1.62	1.60	1.58	1.57	1.57	1.56	1.55
60	1.75	1.74	1.70	1.67	1.64	1.63	1.61	1.60	1.59	1.58	1.57	1.57	1.56	1.54	1.52	1.51	1.51	1.49	1.48
70	1.71	1.71	1.66	1.63	1.60	1.59	1.57	1.56	1.55	1.54	1.53	1.53	1.52	1.50	1.48	1.47	1.46	1.45	1.44
80	1.68	1.68	1.63	1.60	1.57	1.55	1.54	1.53	1.52	1.51	1.50	1.49	1.49	1.47	1.45	1.43	1.43	1.41	1.40
90	1.66	1.66	1.61	1.58	1.55	1.53	1.52	1.50	1.49	1.48	1.48	1.47	1.46	1.44	1.42	1.41	1.40	1.39	1.37
100	1.65	1.64	1.59	1.56	1.53	1.51	1.50	1.48	1.47	1.46	1.46	1.45	1.44	1.42	1.40	1.39	1.38	1.36	1.35
110	1.63	1.63	1.58	1.54	1.52	1.50	1.48	1.47	1.46	1.45	1.44	1.43	1.43	1.40	1.38	1.37	1.36	1.34	1.33
120	1.62	1.61	1.56	1.53	1.50	1.48	1.47	1.45	1.44	1.43	1.42	1.42	1.41	1.39	1.36	1.35	1.34	1.33	1.31
130	1.61	1.60	1.55	1.52	1.49	1.47	1.46	1.44	1.43	1.42	1.41	1.41	1.40	1.38	1.35	1.34	1.33	1.31	1.30
140	1.60	1.60	1.55	1.51	1.48	1.46	1.45	1.43	1.42	1.41	1.40	1.39	1.39	1.36	1.34	1.33	1.32	1.30	1.28
150	1.59	1.59	1.54	1.50	1.48	1.45	1.44	1.42	1.41	1.40	1.39	1.39	1.38	1.35	1.33	1.32	1.31	1.29	1.27
200	1.57	1.56	1.51	1.47	1.45	1.42	1.41	1.39	1.38	1.37	1.36	1.35	1.35	1.32	1.29	1.28	1.27	1.25	1.23
300	1.54	1.54	1.48	1.45	1.42	1.39	1.38	1.36	1.35	1.34	1.33	1.32	1.31	1.28	1.25	1.24	1.23	1.21	1.18
400	1.53	1.52	1.47	1.43	1.40	1.38	1.36	1.35	1.33	1.32	1.31	1.30	1.29	1.27	1.23	1.22	1.21	1.18	1.15
500	1.52	1.52	1.46	1.42	1.39	1.37	1.35	1.34	1.32	1.31	1.30	1.29	1.28	1.25	1.22	1.20	1.19	1.17	1.14
1000	1.51	1.50	1.45	1.41	1.38	1.35	1.33	1.32	1.30	1.29	1.28	1.27	1.26	1.23	1.20	1.17	1.16	1.13	1.09
∞	1.49	1.48	1.43	1.39	1.36	1.33	1.31	1.30	1.28	1.27	1.26	1.25	1.24	1.21	1.17	1.14	1.13	1.09	1.00

TABLE 4 (continued)
Critical Values for the *F*-Distribution
$\alpha = .01$

df_D \ df_N	1	2	3	4	5	6	7	8	9	10	11	12	13	14	15	16	17	18	19
1	4052.2	4999.3	5403.5	5624.3	5764.0	5859.0	5928.3	5981.0	6022.4	6055.9	6083.4	6106.7	6125.8	6143.0	6157.0	6170.0	6181.2	6191.4	6200.8
2	98.50	99.00	99.16	99.25	99.30	99.33	99.36	99.38	99.39	99.40	99.41	99.42	99.42	99.43	99.43	99.44	99.44	99.44	99.45
3	34.12	30.82	29.46	28.71	28.24	27.91	27.67	27.49	27.34	27.23	27.13	27.05	26.98	26.92	26.87	26.83	26.79	26.75	26.72
4	21.20	18.00	16.69	15.98	15.52	15.21	14.98	14.80	14.66	14.55	14.45	14.37	14.31	14.25	14.20	14.15	14.11	14.08	14.05
5	16.26	13.27	12.06	11.39	10.97	10.67	10.46	10.29	10.16	10.05	9.96	9.89	9.82	9.77	9.72	9.68	9.64	9.61	9.58
6	13.75	10.92	9.78	9.15	8.75	8.47	8.26	8.10	7.98	7.87	7.79	7.72	7.66	7.60	7.56	7.52	7.48	7.45	7.42
7	12.25	9.55	8.45	7.85	7.46	7.19	6.99	6.84	6.72	6.62	6.54	6.47	6.41	6.36	6.31	6.28	6.24	6.21	6.18
8	11.26	8.65	7.59	7.01	6.63	6.37	6.18	6.03	5.91	5.81	5.73	5.67	5.61	5.56	5.52	5.48	5.44	5.41	5.38
9	10.56	8.02	6.99	6.42	6.06	5.80	5.61	5.47	5.35	5.26	5.18	5.11	5.05	5.01	4.96	4.92	4.89	4.86	4.83
10	10.04	7.56	6.55	5.99	5.64	5.39	5.20	5.06	4.94	4.85	4.77	4.71	4.65	4.60	4.56	4.52	4.49	4.46	4.43
11	9.65	7.21	6.22	5.67	5.32	5.07	4.89	4.74	4.63	4.54	4.46	4.40	4.34	4.29	4.25	4.21	4.18	4.15	4.12
12	9.33	6.93	5.95	5.41	5.06	4.82	4.64	4.50	4.39	4.30	4.22	4.16	4.10	4.05	4.01	3.97	3.94	3.91	3.88
13	9.07	6.70	5.74	5.21	4.86	4.62	4.44	4.30	4.19	4.10	4.02	3.96	3.91	3.86	3.82	3.78	3.75	3.72	3.69
14	8.86	6.51	5.56	5.04	4.69	4.46	4.28	4.14	4.03	3.94	3.86	3.80	3.75	3.70	3.66	3.62	3.59	3.56	3.53
15	8.68	6.36	5.42	4.89	4.56	4.32	4.14	4.00	3.89	3.80	3.73	3.67	3.61	3.56	3.52	3.49	3.45	3.42	3.40
16	8.53	6.23	5.29	4.77	4.44	4.20	4.03	3.89	3.78	3.69	3.62	3.55	3.50	3.45	3.41	3.37	3.34	3.31	3.28
17	8.40	6.11	5.19	4.67	4.34	4.10	3.93	3.79	3.68	3.59	3.52	3.46	3.40	3.35	3.31	3.27	3.24	3.21	3.19
18	8.29	6.01	5.09	4.58	4.25	4.01	3.84	3.71	3.60	3.51	3.43	3.37	3.32	3.27	3.23	3.19	3.16	3.13	3.10
19	8.18	5.93	5.01	4.50	4.17	3.94	3.77	3.63	3.52	3.43	3.36	3.30	3.24	3.19	3.15	3.12	3.08	3.05	3.03
20	8.10	5.85	4.94	4.43	4.10	3.87	3.70	3.56	3.46	3.37	3.29	3.23	3.18	3.13	3.09	3.05	3.02	2.99	2.96
21	8.02	5.78	4.87	4.37	4.04	3.81	3.64	3.51	3.40	3.31	3.24	3.17	3.12	3.07	3.03	2.99	2.96	2.93	2.90
22	7.95	5.72	4.82	4.31	3.99	3.76	3.59	3.45	3.35	3.26	3.18	3.12	3.07	3.02	2.98	2.94	2.91	2.88	2.85
23	7.88	5.66	4.76	4.26	3.94	3.71	3.54	3.41	3.30	3.21	3.14	3.07	3.02	2.97	2.93	2.89	2.86	2.83	2.80
24	7.82	5.61	4.72	4.22	3.90	3.67	3.50	3.36	3.26	3.17	3.09	3.03	2.98	2.93	2.89	2.85	2.82	2.79	2.76
25	7.77	5.57	4.68	4.18	3.85	3.63	3.46	3.32	3.22	3.13	3.06	2.99	2.94	2.89	2.85	2.81	2.78	2.75	2.72
26	7.72	5.53	4.64	4.14	3.82	3.59	3.42	3.29	3.18	3.09	3.02	2.96	2.90	2.86	2.81	2.78	2.75	2.72	2.69
27	7.68	5.49	4.60	4.11	3.78	3.56	3.39	3.26	3.15	3.06	2.99	2.93	2.87	2.82	2.78	2.75	2.71	2.68	2.66
28	7.64	5.45	4.57	4.07	3.75	3.53	3.36	3.23	3.12	3.03	2.96	2.90	2.84	2.79	2.75	2.72	2.68	2.65	2.63
29	7.60	5.42	4.54	4.04	3.73	3.50	3.33	3.20	3.09	3.00	2.93	2.87	2.81	2.77	2.73	2.69	2.66	2.63	2.60
30	7.56	5.39	4.51	4.02	3.70	3.47	3.30	3.17	3.07	2.98	2.91	2.84	2.79	2.74	2.70	2.66	2.63	2.60	2.57
31	7.53	5.36	4.48	3.99	3.67	3.45	3.28	3.15	3.04	2.96	2.88	2.82	2.77	2.72	2.68	2.64	2.61	2.58	2.55
32	7.50	5.34	4.46	3.97	3.65	3.43	3.26	3.13	3.02	2.93	2.86	2.80	2.74	2.70	2.65	2.62	2.58	2.55	2.53

$\alpha = .01$

df_D \ df_N	1	2	3	4	5	6	7	8	9	10	11	12	13	14	15	16	17	18	19
33	7.47	5.31	4.44	3.95	3.63	3.41	3.24	3.11	3.00	2.91	2.84	2.78	2.72	2.68	2.63	2.60	2.56	2.53	2.51
34	7.44	5.29	4.42	3.93	3.61	3.39	3.22	3.09	2.98	2.89	2.82	2.76	2.70	2.66	2.61	2.58	2.54	2.51	2.49
35	7.42	5.27	4.40	3.91	3.59	3.37	3.20	3.07	2.96	2.88	2.80	2.74	2.69	2.64	2.60	2.56	2.53	2.50	2.47
36	7.40	5.25	4.38	3.89	3.57	3.35	3.18	3.05	2.95	2.86	2.79	2.72	2.67	2.62	2.58	2.54	2.51	2.48	2.45
37	7.37	5.23	4.36	3.87	3.56	3.33	3.17	3.04	2.93	2.84	2.77	2.71	2.65	2.61	2.56	2.53	2.49	2.46	2.44
38	7.35	5.21	4.34	3.86	3.54	3.32	3.15	3.02	2.92	2.83	2.75	2.69	2.64	2.59	2.55	2.51	2.48	2.45	2.42
39	7.33	5.19	4.33	3.84	3.53	3.30	3.14	3.01	2.90	2.81	2.74	2.68	2.62	2.58	2.54	2.50	2.46	2.43	2.41
40	7.31	5.18	4.31	3.83	3.51	3.29	3.12	2.99	2.89	2.80	2.73	2.66	2.61	2.56	2.52	2.48	2.45	2.42	2.39
41	7.30	5.16	4.30	3.81	3.50	3.28	3.11	2.98	2.87	2.79	2.71	2.65	2.60	2.55	2.51	2.47	2.44	2.41	2.38
42	7.28	5.15	4.29	3.80	3.49	3.27	3.10	2.97	2.86	2.78	2.70	2.64	2.59	2.54	2.50	2.46	2.43	2.40	2.37
43	7.26	5.14	4.27	3.79	3.48	3.25	3.09	2.96	2.85	2.76	2.69	2.63	2.57	2.53	2.49	2.45	2.41	2.38	2.36
44	7.25	5.12	4.26	3.78	3.47	3.24	3.08	2.95	2.84	2.75	2.68	2.62	2.56	2.52	2.47	2.44	2.40	2.37	2.35
45	7.23	5.11	4.25	3.77	3.45	3.23	3.07	2.94	2.83	2.74	2.67	2.61	2.55	2.51	2.46	2.43	2.39	2.36	2.34
46	7.22	5.10	4.24	3.76	3.44	3.22	3.06	2.93	2.82	2.73	2.66	2.60	2.54	2.50	2.45	2.42	2.38	2.35	2.33
47	7.21	5.09	4.23	3.75	3.43	3.21	3.05	2.92	2.81	2.72	2.65	2.59	2.53	2.49	2.44	2.41	2.37	2.34	2.32
48	7.19	5.08	4.22	3.74	3.43	3.20	3.04	2.91	2.80	2.71	2.64	2.58	2.53	2.48	2.44	2.40	2.37	2.33	2.31
49	7.18	5.07	4.21	3.73	3.42	3.19	3.03	2.90	2.79	2.71	2.63	2.57	2.52	2.47	2.43	2.39	2.36	2.33	2.30
50	7.17	5.06	4.20	3.72	3.41	3.19	3.02	2.89	2.78	2.70	2.63	2.56	2.51	2.46	2.42	2.38	2.35	2.32	2.29
60	7.08	4.98	4.13	3.65	3.34	3.12	2.95	2.82	2.72	2.63	2.56	2.50	2.44	2.39	2.35	2.31	2.28	2.25	2.22
70	7.01	4.92	4.07	3.60	3.29	3.07	2.91	2.78	2.67	2.59	2.51	2.45	2.40	2.35	2.31	2.27	2.23	2.20	2.18
80	6.96	4.88	4.04	3.56	3.26	3.04	2.87	2.74	2.64	2.55	2.48	2.42	2.36	2.31	2.27	2.23	2.20	2.17	2.14
90	6.93	4.85	4.01	3.53	3.23	3.01	2.84	2.72	2.61	2.52	2.45	2.39	2.33	2.29	2.24	2.21	2.17	2.14	2.11
100	6.90	4.82	3.98	3.51	3.21	2.99	2.82	2.69	2.59	2.50	2.43	2.37	2.31	2.27	2.22	2.19	2.15	2.12	2.09
110	6.87	4.80	3.96	3.49	3.19	2.97	2.81	2.68	2.57	2.49	2.41	2.35	2.30	2.25	2.21	2.17	2.13	2.10	2.07
120	6.85	4.79	3.95	3.48	3.17	2.96	2.79	2.66	2.56	2.47	2.40	2.34	2.28	2.23	2.19	2.15	2.12	2.09	2.06
130	6.83	4.77	3.94	3.47	3.16	2.94	2.78	2.65	2.55	2.46	2.39	2.32	2.27	2.22	2.18	2.14	2.11	2.08	2.05
140	6.82	4.76	3.92	3.46	3.15	2.93	2.77	2.64	2.54	2.45	2.38	2.31	2.26	2.21	2.17	2.13	2.10	2.07	2.04
150	6.81	4.75	3.91	3.45	3.14	2.92	2.76	2.63	2.53	2.44	2.37	2.31	2.25	2.20	2.16	2.12	2.09	2.06	2.03
200	6.76	4.71	3.88	3.41	3.11	2.89	2.73	2.60	2.50	2.41	2.34	2.27	2.22	2.17	2.13	2.09	2.06	2.03	2.00
300	6.72	4.68	3.85	3.38	3.08	2.86	2.70	2.57	2.47	2.38	2.31	2.24	2.19	2.14	2.10	2.06	2.03	1.99	1.97
400	6.70	4.66	3.83	3.37	3.06	2.85	2.68	2.56	2.45	2.37	2.29	2.23	2.17	2.13	2.08	2.05	2.01	1.98	1.95
500	6.69	4.65	3.82	3.36	3.05	2.84	2.68	2.55	2.44	2.36	2.28	2.22	2.17	2.12	2.07	2.04	2.00	1.97	1.94
1000	6.66	4.63	3.80	3.34	3.04	2.82	2.66	2.53	2.43	2.34	2.27	2.20	2.15	2.10	2.06	2.02	1.98	1.95	1.92
∞	6.63	4.61	3.78	3.32	3.02	2.80	2.64	2.51	2.41	2.32	2.25	2.18	2.13	2.08	2.04	2.00	1.97	1.93	1.90

α = .01

df_D \ df_N	20	21	22	23	24	25	26	27	28	29	30	31	32	33	34	35	36	37	38
1	6208.7	6216.1	6223.1	6228.7	6234.3	6239.9	6244.5	6249.2	6252.9	6257.1	6260.4	6264.1	6266.9	6270.1	6272.9	6275.3	6278.1	6280.4	6282.7
2	99.45	99.45	99.46	99.46	99.46	99.46	99.46	99.46	99.46	99.46	99.47	99.47	99.47	99.47	99.47	99.47	99.47	99.47	99.47
3	26.69	26.66	26.64	26.62	26.60	26.58	26.56	26.55	26.53	26.52	26.50	26.49	26.48	26.47	26.46	26.45	26.44	26.43	26.43
4	14.02	13.99	13.97	13.95	13.93	13.91	13.89	13.88	13.86	13.85	13.84	13.83	13.81	13.80	13.79	13.79	13.78	13.77	13.76
5	9.55	9.53	9.51	9.49	9.47	9.45	9.43	9.42	9.40	9.39	9.38	9.37	9.36	9.35	9.34	9.33	9.32	9.31	9.31
6	7.40	7.37	7.35	7.33	7.31	7.30	7.28	7.27	7.25	7.24	7.23	7.22	7.21	7.20	7.19	7.18	7.17	7.16	7.16
7	6.16	6.13	6.11	6.09	6.07	6.06	6.04	6.03	6.02	6.00	5.99	5.98	5.97	5.96	5.95	5.94	5.94	5.93	5.92
8	5.36	5.34	5.32	5.30	5.28	5.26	5.25	5.23	5.22	5.21	5.20	5.19	5.18	5.17	5.16	5.15	5.14	5.14	5.13
9	4.81	4.79	4.77	4.75	4.73	4.71	4.70	4.68	4.67	4.66	4.65	4.64	4.63	4.62	4.61	4.60	4.59	4.59	4.58
10	4.41	4.38	4.36	4.34	4.33	4.31	4.30	4.28	4.27	4.26	4.25	4.24	4.23	4.22	4.21	4.20	4.19	4.19	4.18
11	4.10	4.08	4.06	4.04	4.02	4.01	3.99	3.98	3.96	3.95	3.94	3.93	3.92	3.91	3.90	3.89	3.89	3.88	3.87
12	3.86	3.84	3.82	3.80	3.78	3.76	3.75	3.74	3.72	3.71	3.70	3.69	3.68	3.67	3.66	3.65	3.65	3.64	3.63
13	3.66	3.64	3.62	3.60	3.59	3.57	3.56	3.54	3.53	3.52	3.51	3.50	3.49	3.48	3.47	3.46	3.45	3.45	3.44
14	3.51	3.48	3.46	3.44	3.43	3.41	3.40	3.38	3.37	3.36	3.35	3.34	3.33	3.32	3.31	3.30	3.29	3.29	3.28
15	3.37	3.35	3.33	3.31	3.29	3.28	3.26	3.25	3.24	3.23	3.21	3.20	3.19	3.18	3.18	3.17	3.16	3.15	3.15
16	3.26	3.24	3.22	3.20	3.18	3.16	3.15	3.14	3.12	3.11	3.10	3.09	3.08	3.07	3.06	3.05	3.05	3.04	3.03
17	3.16	3.14	3.12	3.10	3.08	3.07	3.05	3.04	3.03	3.01	3.00	2.99	2.98	2.97	2.96	2.96	2.95	2.94	2.93
18	3.08	3.05	3.03	3.02	3.00	2.98	2.97	2.95	2.94	2.93	2.92	2.91	2.90	2.89	2.88	2.87	2.86	2.86	2.85
19	3.00	2.98	2.96	2.94	2.92	2.91	2.89	2.88	2.87	2.86	2.84	2.83	2.82	2.81	2.81	2.80	2.79	2.78	2.77
20	2.94	2.92	2.90	2.88	2.86	2.84	2.83	2.81	2.80	2.79	2.78	2.77	2.76	2.75	2.74	2.73	2.72	2.72	2.71
21	2.88	2.86	2.84	2.82	2.80	2.79	2.77	2.76	2.74	2.73	2.72	2.71	2.70	2.69	2.68	2.67	2.66	2.66	2.65
22	2.83	2.81	2.78	2.77	2.75	2.73	2.72	2.70	2.69	2.68	2.67	2.66	2.65	2.64	2.63	2.62	2.61	2.60	2.60
23	2.78	2.76	2.74	2.72	2.70	2.69	2.67	2.66	2.64	2.63	2.62	2.61	2.60	2.59	2.58	2.57	2.56	2.56	2.55
24	2.74	2.72	2.70	2.68	2.66	2.64	2.63	2.61	2.60	2.59	2.58	2.57	2.56	2.55	2.54	2.53	2.52	2.51	2.51
25	2.70	2.68	2.66	2.64	2.62	2.60	2.59	2.58	2.56	2.55	2.54	2.53	2.52	2.51	2.50	2.49	2.48	2.47	2.47
26	2.66	2.64	2.62	2.60	2.58	2.57	2.55	2.54	2.53	2.51	2.50	2.49	2.48	2.47	2.46	2.45	2.45	2.44	2.43
27	2.63	2.61	2.59	2.57	2.55	2.54	2.52	2.51	2.49	2.48	2.47	2.46	2.45	2.44	2.43	2.42	2.41	2.41	2.40
28	2.60	2.58	2.56	2.54	2.52	2.51	2.49	2.48	2.46	2.45	2.44	2.43	2.42	2.41	2.40	2.39	2.38	2.37	2.37
29	2.57	2.55	2.53	2.51	2.49	2.48	2.46	2.45	2.44	2.42	2.41	2.40	2.39	2.38	2.37	2.36	2.35	2.35	2.34
30	2.55	2.53	2.51	2.49	2.47	2.45	2.44	2.42	2.41	2.40	2.39	2.38	2.36	2.35	2.35	2.34	2.33	2.32	2.31
31	2.52	2.50	2.48	2.46	2.45	2.43	2.41	2.40	2.39	2.37	2.36	2.35	2.34	2.33	2.32	2.31	2.30	2.30	2.29
32	2.50	2.48	2.46	2.44	2.42	2.41	2.39	2.38	2.36	2.35	2.34	2.33	2.32	2.31	2.30	2.29	2.28	2.27	2.27

$\alpha = .01$

df_D \ df_N	20	21	22	23	24	25	26	27	28	29	30	31	32	33	34	35	36	37	38
33	2.48	2.46	2.44	2.42	2.40	2.39	2.37	2.36	2.34	2.33	2.32	2.31	2.30	2.29	2.28	2.27	2.26	2.25	2.25
34	2.46	2.44	2.42	2.40	2.38	2.37	2.35	2.34	2.32	2.31	2.30	2.29	2.28	2.27	2.26	2.25	2.24	2.23	2.23
35	2.44	2.42	2.40	2.38	2.36	2.35	2.33	2.32	2.30	2.29	2.28	2.27	2.26	2.25	2.24	2.23	2.22	2.21	2.21
36	2.43	2.41	2.38	2.37	2.35	2.33	2.32	2.30	2.29	2.28	2.26	2.25	2.24	2.23	2.22	2.21	2.21	2.20	2.19
37	2.41	2.39	2.37	2.35	2.33	2.31	2.30	2.28	2.27	2.26	2.25	2.24	2.23	2.22	2.21	2.20	2.19	2.18	2.17
38	2.40	2.37	2.35	2.33	2.32	2.30	2.28	2.27	2.26	2.24	2.23	2.22	2.21	2.20	2.19	2.18	2.17	2.16	2.16
39	2.38	2.36	2.34	2.32	2.30	2.29	2.27	2.26	2.24	2.23	2.22	2.21	2.20	2.19	2.18	2.17	2.16	2.15	2.14
40	2.37	2.35	2.33	2.31	2.29	2.27	2.26	2.24	2.23	2.22	2.20	2.19	2.18	2.17	2.16	2.15	2.14	2.14	2.13
41	2.36	2.33	2.31	2.29	2.28	2.26	2.24	2.23	2.21	2.20	2.19	2.18	2.17	2.16	2.15	2.14	2.13	2.12	2.12
42	2.34	2.32	2.30	2.28	2.26	2.25	2.23	2.22	2.20	2.19	2.18	2.17	2.16	2.15	2.14	2.13	2.12	2.11	2.10
43	2.33	2.31	2.29	2.27	2.25	2.23	2.22	2.20	2.19	2.18	2.17	2.15	2.14	2.13	2.12	2.12	2.11	2.10	2.09
44	2.32	2.30	2.28	2.26	2.24	2.22	2.21	2.19	2.18	2.17	2.15	2.14	2.13	2.12	2.11	2.10	2.10	2.09	2.08
45	2.31	2.29	2.27	2.25	2.23	2.21	2.20	2.18	2.17	2.16	2.14	2.13	2.12	2.11	2.10	2.09	2.08	2.08	2.07
46	2.30	2.28	2.26	2.24	2.22	2.20	2.19	2.17	2.16	2.15	2.13	2.12	2.11	2.10	2.09	2.08	2.07	2.07	2.06
47	2.29	2.27	2.25	2.23	2.21	2.19	2.18	2.16	2.15	2.14	2.12	2.11	2.10	2.09	2.08	2.07	2.06	2.06	2.05
48	2.28	2.26	2.24	2.22	2.20	2.18	2.17	2.15	2.14	2.13	2.12	2.10	2.09	2.08	2.07	2.06	2.06	2.05	2.04
49	2.27	2.25	2.23	2.21	2.19	2.18	2.16	2.14	2.13	2.12	2.11	2.09	2.08	2.07	2.06	2.05	2.05	2.04	2.03
50	2.27	2.24	2.22	2.20	2.18	2.17	2.15	2.14	2.12	2.11	2.10	2.09	2.08	2.07	2.06	2.05	2.04	2.03	2.02
60	2.20	2.17	2.15	2.13	2.12	2.10	2.08	2.07	2.05	2.04	2.03	2.02	2.01	2.00	1.99	1.98	1.97	1.96	1.95
70	2.15	2.13	2.11	2.09	2.07	2.05	2.03	2.02	2.01	1.99	1.98	1.97	1.96	1.95	1.94	1.93	1.92	1.91	1.90
80	2.12	2.09	2.07	2.05	2.03	2.01	2.00	1.98	1.97	1.96	1.94	1.93	1.92	1.91	1.90	1.89	1.88	1.87	1.86
90	2.09	2.06	2.04	2.02	2.00	1.99	1.97	1.96	1.94	1.93	1.92	1.90	1.89	1.88	1.87	1.86	1.85	1.84	1.84
100	2.07	2.04	2.02	2.00	1.98	1.97	1.95	1.93	1.92	1.91	1.89	1.88	1.87	1.86	1.85	1.84	1.83	1.82	1.81
110	2.05	2.03	2.00	1.98	1.96	1.95	1.93	1.92	1.90	1.89	1.88	1.86	1.85	1.84	1.83	1.82	1.81	1.80	1.79
120	2.03	2.01	1.99	1.97	1.95	1.93	1.92	1.90	1.89	1.87	1.86	1.85	1.84	1.83	1.82	1.81	1.80	1.79	1.78
130	2.02	2.00	1.98	1.96	1.94	1.92	1.90	1.89	1.87	1.86	1.85	1.84	1.82	1.81	1.80	1.79	1.78	1.77	1.77
140	2.01	1.99	1.97	1.95	1.93	1.91	1.89	1.88	1.86	1.85	1.84	1.82	1.81	1.80	1.79	1.78	1.77	1.76	1.75
150	2.00	1.98	1.96	1.94	1.92	1.90	1.88	1.87	1.85	1.84	1.83	1.81	1.80	1.79	1.78	1.77	1.76	1.75	1.74
200	1.97	1.95	1.93	1.90	1.89	1.87	1.85	1.84	1.82	1.81	1.79	1.78	1.77	1.76	1.75	1.74	1.73	1.72	1.71
300	1.94	1.92	1.89	1.87	1.85	1.84	1.82	1.80	1.79	1.77	1.76	1.75	1.74	1.73	1.72	1.70	1.70	1.69	1.68
400	1.92	1.90	1.88	1.86	1.84	1.82	1.80	1.79	1.77	1.76	1.75	1.73	1.72	1.71	1.70	1.69	1.68	1.67	1.66
500	1.92	1.89	1.87	1.85	1.83	1.81	1.79	1.78	1.76	1.75	1.74	1.72	1.71	1.70	1.69	1.68	1.67	1.66	1.65
1000	1.90	1.87	1.85	1.83	1.81	1.79	1.77	1.76	1.74	1.73	1.72	1.70	1.69	1.68	1.67	1.66	1.65	1.64	1.63
∞	1.88	1.85	1.83	1.81	1.79	1.77	1.76	1.74	1.72	1.71	1.70	1.68	1.67	1.66	1.65	1.64	1.63	1.62	1.61

$\alpha = .01$

df_D \ df_N	39	40	50	60	70	80	90	100	110	120	130	140	150	200	300	400	500	1000	∞
1	6284.6	6286.4	6302.3	6313.0	6320.9	6326.5	6330.7	6333.9	6336.7	6339.5	6341.4	6343.2	6344.6	6349.8	6355.4	6358.1	6359.5	6362.8	6365.6
2	99.47	99.48	99.48	99.48	99.48	99.48	99.49	99.49	99.49	99.49	99.49	99.49	99.49	99.49	99.50	99.50	99.50	99.50	99.50
3	26.42	26.41	26.35	26.32	26.29	26.27	26.25	26.24	26.23	26.22	26.21	26.21	26.20	26.18	26.16	26.15	26.15	26.14	26.13
4	13.75	13.75	13.69	13.65	13.63	13.61	13.59	13.58	13.57	13.56	13.55	13.54	13.54	13.52	13.50	13.49	13.49	13.47	13.46
5	9.30	9.29	9.24	9.20	9.18	9.16	9.14	9.13	9.12	9.11	9.10	9.10	9.09	9.08	9.06	9.05	9.04	9.03	9.02
6	7.15	7.14	7.09	7.06	7.03	7.01	7.00	6.99	6.98	6.97	6.96	6.96	6.95	6.93	6.92	6.91	6.90	6.89	6.88
7	5.91	5.91	5.86	5.82	5.80	5.78	5.77	5.75	5.75	5.74	5.73	5.72	5.72	5.70	5.68	5.68	5.67	5.66	5.65
8	5.12	5.12	5.07	5.03	5.01	4.99	4.97	4.96	4.95	4.95	4.94	4.93	4.93	4.91	4.89	4.89	4.88	4.87	4.86
9	4.57	4.57	4.52	4.48	4.46	4.44	4.43	4.41	4.41	4.40	4.39	4.39	4.38	4.36	4.35	4.34	4.33	4.32	4.31
10	4.17	4.17	4.12	4.08	4.06	4.04	4.03	4.01	4.00	4.00	3.99	3.98	3.98	3.96	3.94	3.94	3.93	3.92	3.91
11	3.87	3.86	3.81	3.78	3.75	3.73	3.72	3.71	3.70	3.69	3.68	3.68	3.67	3.66	3.64	3.63	3.62	3.61	3.60
12	3.63	3.62	3.57	3.54	3.51	3.49	3.48	3.47	3.46	3.45	3.44	3.44	3.43	3.41	3.40	3.39	3.38	3.37	3.36
13	3.43	3.43	3.38	3.34	3.32	3.30	3.28	3.27	3.26	3.25	3.25	3.24	3.24	3.22	3.20	3.19	3.19	3.18	3.17
14	3.27	3.27	3.22	3.18	3.16	3.14	3.12	3.11	3.10	3.09	3.09	3.08	3.08	3.06	3.04	3.03	3.03	3.02	3.00
15	3.14	3.13	3.08	3.05	3.02	3.00	2.99	2.98	2.97	2.96	2.95	2.95	2.94	2.92	2.91	2.90	2.89	2.88	2.87
16	3.02	3.02	2.97	2.93	2.91	2.89	2.87	2.86	2.85	2.84	2.84	2.83	2.83	2.81	2.79	2.78	2.78	2.76	2.75
17	2.93	2.92	2.87	2.83	2.81	2.79	2.78	2.76	2.75	2.75	2.74	2.73	2.73	2.71	2.69	2.68	2.68	2.66	2.65
18	2.84	2.84	2.78	2.75	2.72	2.70	2.69	2.68	2.67	2.66	2.65	2.65	2.64	2.62	2.60	2.59	2.59	2.58	2.57
19	2.77	2.76	2.71	2.67	2.65	2.63	2.61	2.60	2.59	2.58	2.58	2.57	2.57	2.55	2.53	2.52	2.51	2.50	2.49
20	2.70	2.69	2.64	2.61	2.58	2.56	2.55	2.54	2.53	2.52	2.51	2.50	2.50	2.48	2.46	2.45	2.44	2.43	2.42
21	2.64	2.64	2.58	2.55	2.52	2.50	2.49	2.48	2.47	2.46	2.45	2.44	2.44	2.42	2.40	2.39	2.38	2.37	2.36
22	2.59	2.58	2.53	2.50	2.47	2.45	2.43	2.42	2.41	2.40	2.40	2.39	2.38	2.36	2.35	2.34	2.33	2.32	2.31
23	2.54	2.54	2.48	2.45	2.42	2.40	2.39	2.37	2.36	2.35	2.35	2.34	2.34	2.32	2.30	2.29	2.28	2.27	2.26
24	2.50	2.49	2.44	2.40	2.38	2.36	2.34	2.33	2.32	2.31	2.30	2.30	2.29	2.27	2.25	2.24	2.24	2.22	2.21
25	2.46	2.45	2.40	2.36	2.34	2.32	2.30	2.29	2.28	2.27	2.26	2.26	2.25	2.23	2.21	2.20	2.19	2.18	2.17
26	2.42	2.42	2.36	2.33	2.30	2.28	2.26	2.25	2.24	2.23	2.23	2.22	2.21	2.19	2.17	2.16	2.16	2.14	2.13
27	2.39	2.38	2.33	2.29	2.27	2.25	2.23	2.22	2.21	2.20	2.19	2.18	2.18	2.16	2.14	2.13	2.12	2.11	2.10
28	2.36	2.35	2.30	2.26	2.24	2.22	2.20	2.19	2.18	2.17	2.16	2.15	2.15	2.13	2.11	2.10	2.09	2.08	2.06
29	2.33	2.33	2.27	2.23	2.21	2.19	2.17	2.16	2.15	2.14	2.13	2.12	2.12	2.10	2.08	2.07	2.06	2.05	2.03
30	2.31	2.30	2.25	2.21	2.18	2.16	2.14	2.13	2.12	2.11	2.10	2.10	2.09	2.07	2.05	2.04	2.03	2.02	2.01
31	2.28	2.27	2.22	2.18	2.16	2.14	2.12	2.11	2.09	2.09	2.08	2.07	2.07	2.04	2.02	2.01	2.01	1.99	1.98
32	2.26	2.25	2.20	2.16	2.13	2.11	2.10	2.08	2.07	2.06	2.05	2.05	2.04	2.02	2.00	1.99	1.98	1.97	1.96

α = .01

df_D \ df_N	39	40	50	60	70	80	90	100	110	120	130	140	150	200	300	400	500	1000	∞
33	2.24	2.23	2.18	2.14	2.11	2.09	2.07	2.06	2.05	2.04	2.03	2.03	2.02	2.00	1.98	1.97	1.96	1.95	1.93
34	2.22	2.21	2.16	2.12	2.09	2.07	2.05	2.04	2.03	2.02	2.01	2.00	2.00	1.98	1.96	1.94	1.94	1.92	1.91
35	2.20	2.19	2.14	2.10	2.07	2.05	2.03	2.02	2.01	2.00	1.99	1.98	1.98	1.96	1.94	1.92	1.92	1.90	1.89
36	2.18	2.18	2.12	2.08	2.05	2.03	2.02	2.00	1.99	1.98	1.97	1.97	1.96	1.94	1.92	1.91	1.90	1.89	1.87
37	2.17	2.16	2.10	2.06	2.04	2.02	2.00	1.98	1.97	1.96	1.96	1.95	1.94	1.92	1.90	1.89	1.88	1.87	1.85
38	2.15	2.14	2.09	2.05	2.02	2.00	1.98	1.97	1.96	1.95	1.94	1.93	1.93	1.90	1.88	1.87	1.86	1.85	1.84
39	2.14	2.13	2.07	2.03	2.01	1.98	1.97	1.95	1.94	1.93	1.92	1.92	1.91	1.89	1.87	1.86	1.85	1.83	1.82
40	2.12	2.11	2.06	2.02	1.99	1.97	1.95	1.94	1.93	1.92	1.91	1.90	1.90	1.87	1.85	1.84	1.83	1.82	1.80
41	2.11	2.10	2.04	2.01	1.98	1.96	1.94	1.92	1.91	1.90	1.89	1.89	1.88	1.86	1.84	1.83	1.82	1.80	1.79
42	2.10	2.09	2.03	1.99	1.96	1.94	1.93	1.91	1.90	1.89	1.88	1.87	1.87	1.85	1.82	1.81	1.80	1.79	1.78
43	2.08	2.08	2.02	1.98	1.95	1.93	1.91	1.90	1.89	1.88	1.87	1.86	1.86	1.83	1.81	1.80	1.79	1.78	1.76
44	2.07	2.07	2.01	1.97	1.94	1.92	1.90	1.89	1.87	1.87	1.86	1.85	1.84	1.82	1.80	1.79	1.78	1.76	1.75
45	2.06	2.05	2.00	1.96	1.93	1.91	1.89	1.88	1.86	1.85	1.84	1.84	1.83	1.81	1.79	1.77	1.77	1.75	1.74
46	2.05	2.04	1.99	1.95	1.92	1.90	1.88	1.86	1.85	1.84	1.83	1.83	1.82	1.80	1.77	1.76	1.76	1.74	1.73
47	2.04	2.03	1.98	1.94	1.91	1.89	1.87	1.85	1.84	1.83	1.82	1.82	1.81	1.79	1.76	1.75	1.74	1.73	1.71
48	2.03	2.02	1.97	1.93	1.90	1.88	1.86	1.84	1.83	1.82	1.81	1.81	1.80	1.78	1.75	1.74	1.73	1.72	1.70
49	2.02	2.02	1.96	1.92	1.89	1.87	1.85	1.83	1.82	1.81	1.80	1.80	1.79	1.77	1.74	1.73	1.72	1.71	1.69
50	2.01	2.01	1.95	1.91	1.88	1.86	1.84	1.82	1.81	1.80	1.79	1.79	1.78	1.76	1.73	1.72	1.71	1.70	1.68
60	1.94	1.94	1.88	1.84	1.81	1.78	1.76	1.75	1.74	1.73	1.72	1.71	1.70	1.68	1.65	1.64	1.63	1.62	1.60
70	1.89	1.89	1.83	1.78	1.75	1.73	1.71	1.70	1.68	1.67	1.66	1.65	1.65	1.62	1.60	1.58	1.57	1.56	1.54
80	1.86	1.85	1.79	1.75	1.71	1.69	1.67	1.65	1.64	1.63	1.62	1.61	1.61	1.58	1.55	1.54	1.53	1.51	1.49
90	1.83	1.82	1.76	1.72	1.68	1.66	1.64	1.62	1.61	1.60	1.59	1.58	1.57	1.55	1.52	1.50	1.49	1.48	1.46
100	1.80	1.80	1.74	1.69	1.66	1.63	1.61	1.60	1.58	1.57	1.56	1.55	1.55	1.52	1.49	1.47	1.47	1.45	1.43
110	1.79	1.78	1.72	1.67	1.64	1.61	1.59	1.58	1.56	1.55	1.54	1.53	1.52	1.50	1.47	1.45	1.44	1.42	1.40
120	1.77	1.76	1.70	1.66	1.62	1.60	1.58	1.56	1.55	1.53	1.52	1.51	1.51	1.48	1.45	1.43	1.42	1.40	1.38
130	1.76	1.75	1.69	1.64	1.61	1.58	1.56	1.54	1.53	1.52	1.51	1.50	1.49	1.46	1.43	1.41	1.40	1.38	1.36
140	1.75	1.74	1.67	1.63	1.60	1.57	1.55	1.53	1.52	1.50	1.49	1.48	1.48	1.45	1.42	1.40	1.39	1.37	1.35
150	1.74	1.73	1.66	1.62	1.59	1.56	1.54	1.52	1.51	1.49	1.48	1.47	1.46	1.43	1.40	1.39	1.38	1.35	1.33
200	1.70	1.69	1.63	1.58	1.55	1.52	1.50	1.48	1.47	1.45	1.44	1.43	1.42	1.39	1.36	1.34	1.33	1.30	1.28
300	1.67	1.66	1.59	1.55	1.51	1.48	1.46	1.44	1.43	1.41	1.40	1.39	1.38	1.35	1.31	1.29	1.28	1.25	1.22
400	1.65	1.64	1.58	1.53	1.49	1.46	1.44	1.42	1.40	1.39	1.38	1.37	1.36	1.32	1.28	1.26	1.25	1.22	1.19
500	1.64	1.63	1.57	1.52	1.48	1.45	1.43	1.41	1.39	1.38	1.36	1.35	1.34	1.31	1.27	1.25	1.23	1.20	1.16
1000	1.62	1.61	1.54	1.50	1.46	1.43	1.40	1.38	1.37	1.35	1.34	1.33	1.32	1.28	1.24	1.21	1.19	1.16	1.11
∞	1.60	1.59	1.52	1.47	1.43	1.40	1.38	1.36	1.34	1.32	1.31	1.30	1.29	1.25	1.20	1.17	1.15	1.11	1.00

perfect line = 1
perfect correlation

TABLE 5
Critical Values for Correlation Coefficients (Note: df = n - 2)

α	.1000	.0500	.0250	.0125	.0100	.0050	.0005
df = 1 to 33			One-Tailed Test				
1	0.9511	0.9877	0.9969	0.9992	0.9995	0.9999	1.0000
2	0.8000	0.9000	0.9500	0.9750	0.9800	0.9900	0.9990
3	0.6870	0.8054	0.8783	0.9237	0.9343	0.9587	0.9911
4	0.6084	0.7293	0.8114	0.8680	0.8822	0.9172	0.9741
5	0.5509	0.6694	0.7545	0.8166	0.8329	0.8745	0.9509
6	0.5067	0.6215	0.7067	0.7713	0.7887	0.8343	0.9249
7	0.4716	0.5822	0.6664	0.7318	0.7498	0.7977	0.8983
8	0.4428	0.5494	0.6319	0.6973	0.7155	0.7646	0.8721
9	0.4187	0.5214	0.6021	0.6669	0.6851	0.7348	0.8470
10	0.3981	0.4973	0.5760	0.6400	0.6581	0.7079	0.8233
11	0.3802	0.4762	0.5529	0.6159	0.6339	0.6835	0.8010
12	0.3646	0.4575	0.5324	0.5943	0.6120	0.6614	0.7800
13	0.3507	0.4409	0.5140	0.5748	0.5923	0.6411	0.7604
14	0.3383	0.4259	0.4973	0.5570	0.5742	0.6226	0.7419
15	0.3271	0.4124	0.4821	0.5408	0.5577	0.6055	0.7247
16	0.3170	0.4000	0.4683	0.5258	0.5425	0.5897	0.7084
17	0.3077	0.3887	0.4555	0.5121	0.5285	0.5751	0.6932
18	0.2992	0.3783	0.4438	0.4993	0.5155	0.5614	0.6788
19	0.2914	0.3687	0.4329	0.4875	0.5034	0.5487	0.6652
20	0.2841	0.3598	0.4227	0.4764	0.4921	0.5368	0.6524
21	0.2774	0.3515	0.4132	0.4660	0.4815	0.5256	0.6402
22	0.2711	0.3438	0.4044	0.4563	0.4716	0.5151	0.6287
23	0.2653	0.3365	0.3961	0.4472	0.4622	0.5052	0.6178
24	0.2598	0.3297	0.3882	0.4386	0.4534	0.4958	0.6074
25	0.2546	0.3233	0.3809	0.4305	0.4451	0.4869	0.5974
26	0.2497	0.3172	0.3739	0.4228	0.4372	0.4785	0.5880
27	0.2451	0.3115	0.3673	0.4155	0.4297	0.4705	0.5789
28	0.2407	0.3061	0.3610	0.4085	0.4226	0.4629	0.5703
29	0.2366	0.3009	0.3550	0.4019	0.4158	0.4556	0.5621
30	0.2327	0.2960	0.3494	0.3956	0.4093	0.4487	0.5541
31	0.2289	0.2913	0.3440	0.3896	0.4032	0.4421	0.5465
32	0.2254	0.2869	0.3388	0.3839	0.3972	0.4357	0.5392
33	0.2220	0.2826	0.3338	0.3784	0.3916	0.4296	0.5322
			Two-Tailed Test				
α	.2000	.1000	.0500	.0250	.0200	.0100	.0010

TABLE 5 (continued)
Critical Values for Correlation Coefficients (Note: df = n - 2)

α	.1000	.0500	.0250	.0125	.0100	.0050	.0005
df = 34 to 66			One-Tailed Test				
34	0.2187	0.2785	0.3291	0.3731	0.3862	0.4238	0.5254
35	0.2156	0.2746	0.3246	0.3681	0.3810	0.4182	0.5189
36	0.2126	0.2709	0.3202	0.3632	0.3760	0.4128	0.5126
37	0.2097	0.2673	0.3160	0.3586	0.3712	0.4076	0.5066
38	0.2070	0.2638	0.3120	0.3541	0.3665	0.4026	0.5007
39	0.2043	0.2605	0.3081	0.3497	0.3621	0.3978	0.4950
40	0.2018	0.2573	0.3044	0.3456	0.3578	0.3932	0.4896
41	0.1993	0.2542	0.3008	0.3415	0.3536	0.3887	0.4843
42	0.1970	0.2512	0.2973	0.3376	0.3496	0.3843	0.4791
43	0.1947	0.2483	0.2940	0.3339	0.3458	0.3801	0.4742
44	0.1925	0.2455	0.2907	0.3302	0.3420	0.3761	0.4693
45	0.1903	0.2429	0.2876	0.3267	0.3384	0.3721	0.4647
46	0.1883	0.2403	0.2845	0.3233	0.3348	0.3683	0.4601
47	0.1863	0.2377	0.2816	0.3200	0.3314	0.3646	0.4557
48	0.1843	0.2353	0.2787	0.3168	0.3281	0.3610	0.4514
49	0.1825	0.2329	0.2759	0.3137	0.3249	0.3575	0.4473
50	0.1806	0.2306	0.2732	0.3106	0.3218	0.3542	0.4432
51	0.1789	0.2284	0.2706	0.3077	0.3188	0.3509	0.4392
52	0.1772	0.2262	0.2681	0.3048	0.3158	0.3477	0.4354
53	0.1755	0.2241	0.2656	0.3021	0.3129	0.3445	0.4317
54	0.1739	0.2221	0.2632	0.2994	0.3102	0.3415	0.4280
55	0.1723	0.2201	0.2609	0.2967	0.3074	0.3385	0.4244
56	0.1708	0.2181	0.2586	0.2942	0.3048	0.3357	0.4210
57	0.1693	0.2162	0.2564	0.2917	0.3022	0.3328	0.4176
58	0.1678	0.2144	0.2542	0.2892	0.2997	0.3301	0.4143
59	0.1664	0.2126	0.2521	0.2869	0.2972	0.3274	0.4110
60	0.1650	0.2108	0.2500	0.2845	0.2948	0.3248	0.4079
61	0.1636	0.2091	0.2480	0.2823	0.2925	0.3223	0.4048
62	0.1623	0.2075	0.2461	0.2801	0.2902	0.3198	0.4018
63	0.1610	0.2058	0.2441	0.2779	0.2880	0.3173	0.3988
64	0.1598	0.2042	0.2423	0.2758	0.2858	0.3150	0.3959
65	0.1586	0.2027	0.2404	0.2737	0.2837	0.3126	0.3931
66	0.1574	0.2012	0.2387	0.2717	0.2816	0.3104	0.3903
			Two-Tailed Test				
α	.2000	.1000	.0500	.0250	.0200	.0100	.0010

TABLE 5 (continued)
Critical Values for Correlation Coefficients (Note: df = n - 2)

α	.1000	.0500	.0250	.0125	.0100	.0050	.0005
df = 67 to 99				One-Tailed Test			
67	0.1562	0.1997	0.2369	0.2697	0.2796	0.3081	0.3876
68	0.1550	0.1982	0.2352	0.2678	0.2776	0.3060	0.3850
69	0.1539	0.1968	0.2335	0.2659	0.2756	0.3038	0.3823
70	0.1528	0.1954	0.2319	0.2641	0.2737	0.3017	0.3798
71	0.1517	0.1940	0.2303	0.2623	0.2718	0.2997	0.3773
72	0.1507	0.1927	0.2287	0.2605	0.2700	0.2977	0.3748
73	0.1497	0.1914	0.2272	0.2587	0.2682	0.2957	0.3724
74	0.1486	0.1901	0.2257	0.2570	0.2664	0.2938	0.3701
75	0.1477	0.1888	0.2242	0.2554	0.2647	0.2919	0.3678
76	0.1467	0.1876	0.2227	0.2537	0.2630	0.2900	0.3655
77	0.1457	0.1864	0.2213	0.2521	0.2613	0.2882	0.3633
78	0.1448	0.1852	0.2199	0.2505	0.2597	0.2864	0.3611
79	0.1439	0.1841	0.2185	0.2490	0.2581	0.2847	0.3589
80	0.1430	0.1829	0.2172	0.2475	0.2565	0.2830	0.3568
81	0.1421	0.1818	0.2159	0.2460	0.2550	0.2813	0.3547
82	0.1412	0.1807	0.2146	0.2445	0.2535	0.2796	0.3527
83	0.1404	0.1796	0.2133	0.2431	0.2520	0.2780	0.3507
84	0.1396	0.1786	0.2120	0.2416	0.2505	0.2764	0.3487
85	0.1387	0.1775	0.2108	0.2402	0.2491	0.2748	0.3468
86	0.1379	0.1765	0.2096	0.2389	0.2477	0.2732	0.3449
87	0.1371	0.1755	0.2084	0.2375	0.2463	0.2717	0.3430
88	0.1364	0.1745	0.2072	0.2362	0.2449	0.2702	0.3412
89	0.1356	0.1735	0.2061	0.2349	0.2435	0.2687	0.3393
90	0.1348	0.1726	0.2050	0.2336	0.2422	0.2673	0.3375
91	0.1341	0.1716	0.2039	0.2324	0.2409	0.2659	0.3358
92	0.1334	0.1707	0.2028	0.2311	0.2396	0.2645	0.3341
93	0.1327	0.1698	0.2017	0.2299	0.2384	0.2631	0.3323
94	0.1320	0.1689	0.2006	0.2287	0.2371	0.2617	0.3307
95	0.1313	0.1680	0.1996	0.2275	0.2359	0.2604	0.3290
96	0.1306	0.1671	0.1986	0.2264	0.2347	0.2591	0.3274
97	0.1299	0.1663	0.1975	0.2252	0.2335	0.2578	0.3258
98	0.1292	0.1654	0.1966	0.2241	0.2324	0.2565	0.3242
99	0.1286	0.1646	0.1956	0.2230	0.2312	0.2552	0.3226
				Two-Tailed Test			
α	.2000	.1000	.0500	.0250	.0200	.0100	.0010

TABLE 5 (continued)
Critical Values for Correlation Coefficients (Note: df = n - 2)

α	.1000	.0500	.0250	.0125	.0100	.0050	.0005
df = 100 to 132				One-Tailed Test			
100	0.1279	0.1638	0.1946	0.2219	0.2301	0.2540	0.3211
101	0.1273	0.1630	0.1937	0.2208	0.2290	0.2528	0.3196
102	0.1267	0.1622	0.1927	0.2197	0.2279	0.2515	0.3181
103	0.1261	0.1614	0.1918	0.2187	0.2268	0.2504	0.3166
104	0.1255	0.1606	0.1909	0.2177	0.2257	0.2492	0.3152
105	0.1249	0.1599	0.1900	0.2166	0.2247	0.2480	0.3137
106	0.1243	0.1591	0.1891	0.2156	0.2236	0.2469	0.3123
107	0.1237	0.1584	0.1882	0.2147	0.2226	0.2458	0.3109
108	0.1231	0.1576	0.1874	0.2137	0.2216	0.2446	0.3095
109	0.1226	0.1569	0.1865	0.2127	0.2206	0.2436	0.3082
110	0.1220	0.1562	0.1857	0.2118	0.2196	0.2425	0.3068
111	0.1215	0.1555	0.1848	0.2108	0.2186	0.2414	0.3055
112	0.1209	0.1548	0.1840	0.2099	0.2177	0.2403	0.3042
113	0.1204	0.1541	0.1832	0.2090	0.2167	0.2393	0.3029
114	0.1199	0.1535	0.1824	0.2081	0.2158	0.2383	0.3016
115	0.1193	0.1528	0.1816	0.2072	0.2149	0.2373	0.3004
116	0.1188	0.1522	0.1809	0.2063	0.2139	0.2363	0.2991
117	0.1183	0.1515	0.1801	0.2054	0.2131	0.2353	0.2979
118	0.1178	0.1509	0.1793	0.2046	0.2122	0.2343	0.2967
119	0.1173	0.1502	0.1786	0.2037	0.2113	0.2333	0.2955
120	0.1168	0.1496	0.1779	0.2029	0.2104	0.2324	0.2943
121	0.1163	0.1490	0.1771	0.2021	0.2096	0.2315	0.2932
122	0.1159	0.1484	0.1764	0.2013	0.2087	0.2305	0.2920
123	0.1154	0.1478	0.1757	0.2005	0.2079	0.2296	0.2908
124	0.1149	0.1472	0.1750	0.1997	0.2071	0.2287	0.2897
125	0.1145	0.1466	0.1743	0.1989	0.2062	0.2278	0.2886
126	0.1140	0.1460	0.1736	0.1981	0.2054	0.2269	0.2875
127	0.1136	0.1455	0.1729	0.1973	0.2046	0.2260	0.2864
128	0.1131	0.1449	0.1723	0.1966	0.2039	0.2252	0.2853
129	0.1127	0.1443	0.1716	0.1958	0.2031	0.2243	0.2843
130	0.1123	0.1438	0.1710	0.1951	0.2023	0.2235	0.2832
131	0.1118	0.1432	0.1703	0.1943	0.2015	0.2226	0.2822
132	0.1114	0.1427	0.1697	0.1936	0.2008	0.2218	0.2811
				Two-Tailed Test			
α	.2000	.1000	.0500	.0250	.0200	.0100	.0010

TABLE 5 (continued)
Critical Values for Correlation Coefficients (Note: df = n - 2)

α	.1000	.0500	.0250	.0125	.0100	.0050	.0005
df = 133 to 100,000,000				One-Tailed Test			
133	0.1110	0.1422	0.1690	0.1929	0.2001	0.2210	0.2801
134	0.1106	0.1416	0.1684	0.1922	0.1993	0.2202	0.2791
135	0.1102	0.1411	0.1678	0.1915	0.1986	0.2194	0.2781
136	0.1098	0.1406	0.1672	0.1908	0.1979	0.2186	0.2771
137	0.1094	0.1401	0.1666	0.1901	0.1972	0.2178	0.2761
138	0.1090	0.1396	0.1660	0.1894	0.1965	0.2170	0.2752
139	0.1086	0.1391	0.1654	0.1887	0.1958	0.2163	0.2742
140	0.1082	0.1386	0.1648	0.1881	0.1951	0.2155	0.2733
141	0.1078	0.1381	0.1642	0.1874	0.1944	0.2148	0.2723
142	0.1074	0.1376	0.1637	0.1868	0.1937	0.2140	0.2714
143	0.1070	0.1371	0.1631	0.1861	0.1930	0.2133	0.2705
144	0.1067	0.1367	0.1625	0.1855	0.1924	0.2126	0.2696
145	0.1063	0.1362	0.1620	0.1848	0.1917	0.2118	0.2687
146	0.1059	0.1357	0.1614	0.1842	0.1911	0.2111	0.2678
147	0.1056	0.1353	0.1609	0.1836	0.1904	0.2104	0.2669
148	0.1052	0.1348	0.1603	0.1830	0.1898	0.2097	0.2660
149	0.1049	0.1344	0.1598	0.1824	0.1892	0.2090	0.2652
150	0.1045	0.1339	0.1593	0.1818	0.1886	0.2084	0.2643
160	0.1012	0.1297	0.1543	0.1761	0.1826	0.2019	0.2562
170	0.0982	0.1258	0.1497	0.1709	0.1773	0.1959	0.2488
180	0.0954	0.1223	0.1455	0.1661	0.1723	0.1905	0.2419
190	0.0929	0.1191	0.1417	0.1617	0.1678	0.1855	0.2357
200	0.0905	0.1161	0.1381	0.1577	0.1636	0.1809	0.2298
225	0.0854	0.1094	0.1303	0.1488	0.1543	0.1707	0.2170
250	0.0810	0.1039	0.1236	0.1412	0.1465	0.1620	0.2061
275	0.0772	0.0990	0.1179	0.1347	0.1397	0.1545	0.1967
300	0.0740	0.0948	0.1129	0.1290	0.1338	0.1480	0.1884
400	0.0641	0.0822	0.0978	0.1118	0.1160	0.1283	0.1635
500	0.0573	0.0735	0.0875	0.1000	0.1038	0.1149	0.1464
1,000	0.0405	0.0520	0.0619	0.0708	0.0735	0.0813	0.1038
2,000	0.0287	0.0368	0.0438	0.0501	0.0520	0.0576	0.0735
10,000	0.0128	0.0164	0.0196	0.0224	0.0233	0.0258	0.0329
100,000	0.0041	0.0052	0.0062	0.0071	0.0074	0.0081	0.0104
1,000,000	0.0013	0.0016	0.0020	0.0022	0.0023	0.0026	0.0033
100,000,000	0.0001	0.0002	0.0002	0.0002	0.0002	0.0003	0.0003
				Two-Tailed Test			
α	.2000	.1000	.0500	.0250	.0200	.0100	.0010

TABLE 6
Fisher's *z* Values: Conversions from *r* to *z* and from *z* to *r*

$$\text{Fisher's } z_r = (1/2)\cdot[(ln\ (1 + r)) - (ln\ (1 - r))]$$

Directions for Using this Conversion Table

Converting from *r* to Fisher's *z*: Find the desired correlation coefficient by using the far left column to obtain the first two decimal values of the correlation coefficient; then use the top row to obtain the third decimal value. (Note that correlation coefficients are given in increments of .0010). The Fisher *z*-value which corresponds to this correlation coefficient is located within the table at the intersection of this column and row. Example: If *r* = .225, then Fisher's *z* = .2289.

Converting from Fisher's *z* to r: Find the desired Fisher's *z* within the body of the table, rounding when necessary. The first two decimal values of the correlation coefficient are then found in the corresponding far left column, while the third decimal value is found in the corresponding top row. Example: If Fisher's *z* = 1.1042, then *r* = .802.

r	0.0000	0.0010	0.0020	0.0030	0.0040	0.0050	0.0060	0.0070	0.0080	0.0090
0.0000	0.0000	0.0010	0.0020	0.0030	0.0040	0.0050	0.0060	0.0070	0.0080	0.0090
0.0100	0.0100	0.0110	0.0120	0.0130	0.0140	0.0150	0.0160	0.0170	0.0180	0.0190
0.0200	0.0200	0.0210	0.0220	0.0230	0.0240	0.0250	0.0260	0.0270	0.0280	0.0290
0.0300	0.0300	0.0310	0.0320	0.0330	0.0340	0.0350	0.0360	0.0370	0.0380	0.0390
0.0400	0.0400	0.0410	0.0420	0.0430	0.0440	0.0450	0.0460	0.0470	0.0480	0.0490
0.0500	0.0500	0.0510	0.0520	0.0530	0.0541	0.0551	0.0561	0.0571	0.0581	0.0591
0.0600	0.0601	0.0611	0.0621	0.0631	0.0641	0.0651	0.0661	0.0671	0.0681	0.0691
0.0700	0.0701	0.0711	0.0721	0.0731	0.0741	0.0751	0.0761	0.0772	0.0782	0.0792
0.0800	0.0802	0.0812	0.0822	0.0832	0.0842	0.0852	0.0862	0.0872	0.0882	0.0892
0.0900	0.0902	0.0913	0.0923	0.0933	0.0943	0.0953	0.0963	0.0973	0.0983	0.0993
0.1000	0.1003	0.1013	0.1024	0.1034	0.1044	0.1054	0.1064	0.1074	0.1084	0.1094
0.1100	0.1104	0.1115	0.1125	0.1135	0.1145	0.1155	0.1165	0.1175	0.1186	0.1196
0.1200	0.1206	0.1216	0.1226	0.1236	0.1246	0.1257	0.1267	0.1277	0.1287	0.1297
0.1300	0.1307	0.1318	0.1328	0.1338	0.1348	0.1358	0.1368	0.1379	0.1389	0.1399
0.1400	0.1409	0.1419	0.1430	0.1440	0.1450	0.1460	0.1471	0.1481	0.1491	0.1501
0.1500	0.1511	0.1522	0.1532	0.1542	0.1552	0.1563	0.1573	0.1583	0.1593	0.1604
0.1600	0.1614	0.1624	0.1634	0.1645	0.1655	0.1665	0.1676	0.1686	0.1696	0.1706
0.1700	0.1717	0.1727	0.1737	0.1748	0.1758	0.1768	0.1779	0.1789	0.1799	0.1809
0.1800	0.1820	0.1830	0.1841	0.1851	0.1861	0.1872	0.1882	0.1892	0.1903	0.1913
0.1900	0.1923	0.1934	0.1944	0.1955	0.1965	0.1975	0.1986	0.1996	0.2007	0.2017
0.2000	0.2027	0.2038	0.2048	0.2059	0.2069	0.2079	0.2090	0.2100	0.2111	0.2121
0.2100	0.2132	0.2142	0.2153	0.2163	0.2174	0.2184	0.2195	0.2205	0.2216	0.2226
0.2200	0.2237	0.2247	0.2258	0.2268	0.2279	0.2289	0.2300	0.2310	0.2321	0.2331

TABLE 6
(continued)

r	0.0000	0.0010	0.0020	0.0030	0.0040	0.0050	0.0060	0.0070	0.0080	0.0090
0.2300	0.2342	0.2352	0.2363	0.2374	0.2384	0.2395	0.2405	0.2416	0.2427	0.2437
0.2400	0.2448	0.2458	0.2469	0.2480	0.2490	0.2501	0.2512	0.2522	0.2533	0.2543
0.2500	0.2554	0.2565	0.2575	0.2586	0.2597	0.2608	0.2618	0.2629	0.2640	0.2650
0.2600	0.2661	0.2672	0.2683	0.2693	0.2704	0.2715	0.2726	0.2736	0.2747	0.2758
0.2700	0.2769	0.2779	0.2790	0.2801	0.2812	0.2823	0.2833	0.2844	0.2855	0.2866
0.2800	0.2877	0.2888	0.2899	0.2909	0.2920	0.2931	0.2942	0.2953	0.2964	0.2975
0.2900	0.2986	0.2997	0.3008	0.3018	0.3029	0.3040	0.3051	0.3062	0.3073	0.3084
0.3000	0.3095	0.3106	0.3117	0.3128	0.3139	0.3150	0.3161	0.3172	0.3183	0.3194
0.3100	0.3205	0.3217	0.3228	0.3239	0.3250	0.3261	0.3272	0.3283	0.3294	0.3305
0.3200	0.3316	0.3328	0.3339	0.3350	0.3361	0.3372	0.3383	0.3395	0.3406	0.3417
0.3300	0.3428	0.3440	0.3451	0.3462	0.3473	0.3484	0.3496	0.3507	0.3518	0.3530
0.3400	0.3541	0.3552	0.3564	0.3575	0.3586	0.3598	0.3609	0.3620	0.3632	0.3643
0.3500	0.3654	0.3666	0.3677	0.3689	0.3700	0.3712	0.3723	0.3734	0.3746	0.3757
0.3600	0.3769	0.3780	0.3792	0.3803	0.3815	0.3826	0.3838	0.3850	0.3861	0.3873
0.3700	0.3884	0.3896	0.3907	0.3919	0.3931	0.3942	0.3954	0.3966	0.3977	0.3989
0.3800	0.4001	0.4012	0.4024	0.4036	0.4047	0.4059	0.4071	0.4083	0.4094	0.4106
0.3900	0.4118	0.4130	0.4142	0.4153	0.4165	0.4177	0.4189	0.4201	0.4213	0.4225
0.4000	0.4236	0.4248	0.4260	0.4272	0.4284	0.4296	0.4308	0.4320	0.4332	0.4344
0.4100	0.4356	0.4368	0.4380	0.4392	0.4404	0.4416	0.4428	0.4441	0.4453	0.4465
0.4200	0.4477	0.4489	0.4501	0.4513	0.4526	0.4538	0.4550	0.4562	0.4574	0.4587
0.4300	0.4599	0.4611	0.4624	0.4636	0.4648	0.4660	0.4673	0.4685	0.4698	0.4710
0.4400	0.4722	0.4735	0.4747	0.4760	0.4772	0.4784	0.4797	0.4809	0.4822	0.4834
0.4500	0.4847	0.4860	0.4872	0.4885	0.4897	0.4910	0.4922	0.4935	0.4948	0.4960
0.4600	0.4973	0.4986	0.4999	0.5011	0.5024	0.5037	0.5049	0.5062	0.5075	0.5088
0.4700	0.5101	0.5114	0.5126	0.5139	0.5152	0.5165	0.5178	0.5191	0.5204	0.5217
0.4800	0.5230	0.5243	0.5256	0.5269	0.5282	0.5295	0.5308	0.5321	0.5334	0.5347
0.4900	0.5361	0.5374	0.5387	0.5400	0.5413	0.5427	0.5440	0.5453	0.5466	0.5480
0.5000	0.5493	0.5506	0.5520	0.5533	0.5547	0.5560	0.5573	0.5587	0.5600	0.5614
0.5100	0.5627	0.5641	0.5654	0.5668	0.5682	0.5695	0.5709	0.5722	0.5736	0.5750
0.5200	0.5763	0.5777	0.5791	0.5805	0.5818	0.5832	0.5846	0.5860	0.5874	0.5888
0.5300	0.5901	0.5915	0.5929	0.5943	0.5957	0.5971	0.5985	0.5999	0.6013	0.6027
0.5400	0.6042	0.6056	0.6070	0.6084	0.6098	0.6112	0.6127	0.6141	0.6155	0.6169
0.5500	0.6184	0.6198	0.6213	0.6227	0.6241	0.6256	0.6270	0.6285	0.6299	0.6314
0.5600	0.6328	0.6343	0.6358	0.6372	0.6387	0.6401	0.6416	0.6431	0.6446	0.6460
0.5700	0.6475	0.6490	0.6505	0.6520	0.6535	0.6550	0.6565	0.6580	0.6595	0.6610
0.5800	0.6625	0.6640	0.6655	0.6670	0.6685	0.6700	0.6716	0.6731	0.6746	0.6761
0.5900	0.6777	0.6792	0.6807	0.6823	0.6838	0.6854	0.6869	0.6885	0.6900	0.6916
0.6000	0.6931	0.6947	0.6963	0.6978	0.6994	0.7010	0.7026	0.7042	0.7057	0.7073
0.6100	0.7089	0.7105	0.7121	0.7137	0.7153	0.7169	0.7185	0.7201	0.7218	0.7234

TABLE 6
(continued)

r	0.0000	0.0010	0.0020	0.0030	0.0040	0.0050	0.0060	0.0070	0.0080	0.0090
0.6200	0.7250	0.7266	0.7283	0.7299	0.7315	0.7332	0.7348	0.7365	0.7381	0.7398
0.6300	0.7414	0.7431	0.7447	0.7464	0.7481	0.7498	0.7514	0.7531	0.7548	0.7565
0.6400	0.7582	0.7599	0.7616	0.7633	0.7650	0.7667	0.7684	0.7701	0.7718	0.7736
0.6500	0.7753	0.7770	0.7788	0.7805	0.7823	0.7840	0.7858	0.7875	0.7893	0.7910
0.6600	0.7928	0.7946	0.7964	0.7981	0.7999	0.8017	0.8035	0.8053	0.8071	0.8089
0.6700	0.8107	0.8126	0.8144	0.8162	0.8180	0.8199	0.8217	0.8236	0.8254	0.8273
0.6800	0.8291	0.8310	0.8328	0.8347	0.8366	0.8385	0.8404	0.8423	0.8441	0.8460
0.6900	0.8480	0.8499	0.8518	0.8537	0.8556	0.8576	0.8595	0.8614	0.8634	0.8653
0.7000	0.8673	0.8693	0.8712	0.8732	0.8752	0.8772	0.8792	0.8812	0.8832	0.8852
0.7100	0.8872	0.8892	0.8912	0.8933	0.8953	0.8973	0.8994	0.9014	0.9035	0.9056
0.7200	0.9076	0.9097	0.9118	0.9139	0.9160	0.9181	0.9202	0.9223	0.9245	0.9266
0.7300	0.9287	0.9309	0.9330	0.9352	0.9373	0.9395	0.9417	0.9439	0.9461	0.9483
0.7400	0.9505	0.9527	0.9549	0.9571	0.9594	0.9616	0.9639	0.9661	0.9684	0.9707
0.7500	0.9730	0.9752	0.9775	0.9798	0.9822	0.9845	0.9868	0.9892	0.9915	0.9939
0.7600	0.9962	0.9986	1.0010	1.0034	1.0058	1.0082	1.0106	1.0130	1.0154	1.0179
0.7700	1.0203	1.0228	1.0253	1.0277	1.0302	1.0327	1.0352	1.0378	1.0403	1.0428
0.7800	1.0454	1.0479	1.0505	1.0531	1.0557	1.0583	1.0609	1.0635	1.0661	1.0688
0.7900	1.0714	1.0741	1.0768	1.0795	1.0822	1.0849	1.0876	1.0903	1.0931	1.0958
0.8000	1.0986	1.1014	1.1042	1.1070	1.1098	1.1127	1.1155	1.1184	1.1212	1.1241
0.8100	1.1270	1.1299	1.1329	1.1358	1.1388	1.1417	1.1447	1.1477	1.1507	1.1538
0.8200	1.1568	1.1599	1.1630	1.1660	1.1692	1.1723	1.1754	1.1786	1.1817	1.1849
0.8300	1.1881	1.1914	1.1946	1.1979	1.2011	1.2044	1.2077	1.2111	1.2144	1.2178
0.8400	1.2212	1.2246	1.2280	1.2315	1.2349	1.2384	1.2419	1.2454	1.2490	1.2526
0.8500	1.2562	1.2598	1.2634	1.2671	1.2707	1.2745	1.2782	1.2819	1.2857	1.2895
0.8600	1.2933	1.2972	1.3011	1.3050	1.3089	1.3129	1.3169	1.3209	1.3249	1.3290
0.8700	1.3331	1.3372	1.3414	1.3456	1.3498	1.3540	1.3583	1.3626	1.3670	1.3714
0.8800	1.3758	1.3802	1.3847	1.3892	1.3938	1.3984	1.4030	1.4077	1.4124	1.4171
0.8900	1.4219	1.4268	1.4316	1.4365	1.4415	1.4465	1.4516	1.4566	1.4618	1.4670
0.9000	1.4722	1.4775	1.4828	1.4882	1.4937	1.4992	1.5047	1.5103	1.5160	1.5217
0.9100	1.5275	1.5334	1.5393	1.5453	1.5513	1.5574	1.5636	1.5698	1.5762	1.5826
0.9200	1.5890	1.5956	1.6022	1.6089	1.6157	1.6226	1.6296	1.6366	1.6438	1.6510
0.9300	1.6584	1.6658	1.6734	1.6811	1.6888	1.6967	1.7047	1.7129	1.7211	1.7295
0.9400	1.7380	1.7467	1.7555	1.7645	1.7736	1.7828	1.7923	1.8019	1.8117	1.8216
0.9500	1.8318	1.8421	1.8527	1.8635	1.8745	1.8857	1.8972	1.9090	1.9210	1.9333
0.9600	1.9459	1.9588	1.9721	1.9857	1.9996	2.0139	2.0287	2.0439	2.0595	2.0756
0.9700	2.0923	2.1095	2.1273	2.1457	2.1649	2.1847	2.2054	2.2269	2.2494	2.2729
0.9800	2.2976	2.3235	2.3507	2.3796	2.4101	2.4427	2.4774	2.5147	2.5550	2.5987
0.9900	2.6467	2.6996	2.7587	2.8257	2.9031	2.9945	3.1063	3.2504	3.4534	3.8002

TABLE 7
Critical Values for Spearman's Rho

α	.050	.025	.010	.005
n	One-Tailed Test			
5	.900	1.000	1.000	----
6	.829	.886	.943	1.000
7	.714	.786	.893	.929
8	.643	.738	.833	.881
9	.600	.683	.783	.833
10	.564	.648	.746	.794
12	.506	.591	.712	.777
14	.456	.544	.645	.715
16	.425	.506	.601	.665
18	.399	.475	.564	.625
20	.377	.450	.534	.591
22	.359	.428	.508	.562
24	.343	.409	.485	.537
26	.329	.392	.465	.515
28	.317	.377	.448	.496
30	.306	.364	.432	.478
	Two-Tailed Test			
α	.100	.050	.020	.010

TABLE 8
Coefficients for the Binomial Distribution

	n											
N	**0**	**1**	**2**	**3**	**4**	**5**	**6**	**7**	**8**	**9**	**10**	**SUM**
1	1	1										2
2	1	2	1									4
3	1	3	3	1								8
4	1	4	6	4	1							16
5	1	5	10	10	5	1						32
6	1	6	15	20	15	6	1					64
7	1	7	21	35	35	21	7	1				128
8	1	8	28	56	70	56	28	8	1			256
9	1	9	36	84	126	126	84	36	9	1		512
10	1	10	45	120	210	252	210	120	45	10	1	1024
11	1	11	55	165	330	462	462	330	165	55	11	2048
12	1	12	66	220	495	792	924	792	495	220	66	4096
13	1	13	78	286	715	1287	1716	1716	1287	715	286	8192
14	1	14	91	364	1001	2002	3003	3432	3003	2002	1001	16384
15	1	15	105	455	1365	3003	5005	6435	6435	5005	3003	32768
16	1	16	120	560	1820	4368	8008	11440	12870	11440	8008	65536
17	1	17	136	680	2380	6188	12376	19448	24310	24310	19448	131072
18	1	18	153	816	3060	8568	18564	31824	43758	48620	43758	262144
19	1	19	171	969	3876	11628	27132	50388	75582	92378	92378	524288
20	1	20	190	1140	4845	15504	38760	77520	125970	167960	184756	1048576

TABLE 9
Cumulative Probabilities under the Binomial Distribution

The cumulative probability binomial table can be used to determine binomial probabilities when $N \leq 30$ and when p ranges from .05 to 1.00, in increments of .05. When $Np \geq 10$ and $Nq \geq 10$ and $N \geq 30$, the normal approximation to the binomial distribution can be used. The following directions are given for the cumulative binomial distribution table.

Situation A: $p \leq .50$

Exactly n out of N	The probability is obtained by subtracting the cumulative probability given for n-1 from the cumulative probability given for n. When n=0, the solution is directly obtained as the probability for n=0.
n or less out of N	The cumulative probability is directly obtained from the table.
Less than n out of N	The cumulative probability is obtained as the cumulative probability for n-1.
n or more out of N	The cumulative probability is obtained by subtracting the cumulative probability for n-1 from 1.00.
More than n out of N	The cumulative probability is obtained by subtracting the cumulative probability for n from 1.00.

Situation B: $p > .50$:
When $p > .50$, look up the value of q instead of p in the table. Then:

Exactly n out of N	The probability is obtained by subtracting the cumulative probability given for N-(n+1) from the cumulative probability given for N-n. When n=N, the solution is directly obtained by letting n=0.
n or less out of N	The cumulative probability is obtained by subtracting the probability given for N-(n+1) from 1.00. When n=N, the cumulative probability is always 1.00.
Less than n out of N	The cumulative probability is obtained by subtracting the cumulative probability for N-n from 1.00.
n or more out of N	The cumulative probability is directly obtained by observing the cumulative probability given for N-n.
More than n out of N	The cumulative probability is directly obtained by observing the cumulative probability for N-(n+1).

Cumulative Probabilities under the Binomial Distribution For Given Values of p

N	n	.05	.10	.15	.20	.25	.30	.35	.40	.45	.50
1	0	.9500	.9000	.8500	.8000	.7500	.7000	.6500	.6000	.5500	.5000
1	1	1.0000	1.0000	1.0000	1.0000	1.0000	1.0000	1.0000	1.0000	1.0000	1.0000

N	n	.05	.10	.15	.20	.25	.30	.35	.40	.45	.50
2	0	.9025	.8100	.7225	.6400	.5625	.4900	.4225	.3600	.3025	.2500
2	1	.9975	.9900	.9775	.9600	.9375	.9100	.8775	.8400	.7975	.7500
2	2	1.0000	1.0000	1.0000	1.0000	1.0000	1.0000	1.0000	1.0000	1.0000	1.0000

N	n	.05	.10	.15	.20	.25	.30	.35	.40	.45	.50
3	0	.8574	.7290	.6141	.5120	.4219	.3430	.2746	.2160	.1664	.1250
3	1	.9928	.9720	.9393	.8960	.8438	.7840	.7183	.6480	.5748	.5000
3	2	.9999	.9990	.9966	.9920	.9844	.9730	.9571	.9360	.9089	.8750
3	3	1.0000	1.0000	1.0000	1.0000	1.0000	1.0000	1.0000	1.0000	1.0000	1.0000

N	n	.05	.10	.15	.20	.25	.30	.35	.40	.45	.50
4	0	.8145	.6561	.5220	.4096	.3164	.2401	.1785	.1296	.0915	.0625
4	1	.9860	.9477	.8905	.8192	.7383	.6517	.5630	.4752	.3910	.3125
4	2	.9995	.9963	.9880	.9728	.9492	.9163	.8735	.8208	.7585	.6875
4	3	1.0000	.9999	.9995	.9984	.9961	.9919	.9850	.9744	.9590	.9375
4	4	1.0000	1.0000	1.0000	1.0000	1.0000	1.0000	1.0000	1.0000	1.0000	1.0000

N	n	.05	.10	.15	.20	.25	.30	.35	.40	.45	.50
5	0	.7738	.5905	.4437	.3277	.2373	.1681	.1160	.0778	.0503	.0313
5	1	.9774	.9185	.8352	.7373	.6328	.5282	.4284	.3370	.2562	.1875
5	2	.9988	.9914	.9734	.9421	.8965	.8369	.7648	.6826	.5931	.5000
5	3	1.0000	.9995	.9978	.9933	.9844	.9692	.9460	.9130	.8688	.8125
5	4	1.0000	1.0000	.9999	.9997	.9990	.9976	.9947	.9898	.9815	.9688
5	5	1.0000	1.0000	1.0000	1.0000	1.0000	1.0000	1.0000	1.0000	1.0000	1.0000

N	n	.05	.10	.15	.20	.25	.30	.35	.40	.45	.50
6	0	.7351	.5314	.3771	.2621	.1780	.1176	.0754	.0467	.0277	.0156
6	1	.9672	.8857	.7765	.6554	.5339	.4202	.3191	.2333	.1636	.1094
6	2	.9978	.9842	.9527	.9011	.8306	.7443	.6471	.5443	.4415	.3438
6	3	.9999	.9987	.9941	.9830	.9624	.9295	.8826	.8208	.7447	.6563

6	4	1.0000	.9999	.9996	.9984	.9954	.9891	.9777	.9590	.9308	.8906
6	5	1.0000	1.0000	1.0000	.9999	.9998	.9993	.9982	.9959	.9917	.9844
6	6	1.0000	1.0000	1.0000	1.0000	1.0000	1.0000	1.0000	1.0000	1.0000	1.0000

N	*n*	.05	.10	.15	.20	.25	.30	.35	.40	.45	.50
7	0	.6983	.4783	.3206	.2097	.1335	.0824	.0490	.0280	.0152	.0078
7	1	.9556	.8503	.7166	.5767	.4449	.3294	.2338	.1586	.1024	.0625
7	2	.9962	.9743	.9262	.8520	.7564	.6471	.5323	.4199	.3164	.2266
7	3	.9998	.9973	.9879	.9667	.9294	.8740	.8002	.7102	.6083	.5000
7	4	1.0000	.9998	.9988	.9953	.9871	.9712	.9444	.9037	.8471	.7734
7	5	1.0000	1.0000	.9999	.9996	.9987	.9962	.9910	.9812	.9643	.9375
7	6	1.0000	1.0000	1.0000	1.0000	.9999	.9998	.9994	.9984	.9963	.9922
7	7	1.0000	1.0000	1.0000	1.0000	1.0000	1.0000	1.0000	1.0000	1.0000	1.0000

N	*n*	.05	.10	.15	.20	.25	.30	.35	.40	.45	.50
8	0	.6634	.4305	.2725	.1678	.1001	.0576	.0319	.0168	.0084	.0039
8	1	.9428	.8131	.6572	.5033	.3671	.2553	.1691	.1064	.0632	.0352
8	2	.9942	.9619	.8948	.7969	.6785	.5518	.4278	.3154	.2201	.1445
8	3	.9996	.9950	.9786	.9437	.8862	.8059	.7064	.5941	.4770	.3633
8	4	1.0000	.9996	.9971	.9896	.9727	.9420	.8939	.8263	.7396	.6367
8	5	1.0000	1.0000	.9998	.9988	.9958	.9887	.9747	.9502	.9115	.8555
8	6	1.0000	1.0000	1.0000	.9999	.9996	.9987	.9964	.9915	.9819	.9648
8	7	1.0000	1.0000	1.0000	1.0000	1.0000	.9999	.9998	.9993	.9983	.9961
8	8	1.0000	1.0000	1.0000	1.0000	1.0000	1.0000	1.0000	1.0000	1.0000	1.0000

N	*n*	.05	.10	.15	.20	.25	.30	.35	.40	.45	.50
9	0	.6302	.3874	.2316	.1342	.0751	.0404	.0207	.0101	.0046	.0020
9	1	.9288	.7748	.5995	.4362	.3003	.1960	.1211	.0705	.0385	.0195
9	2	.9916	.9470	.8591	.7382	.6007	.4628	.3373	.2318	.1495	.0898
9	3	.9994	.9917	.9661	.9144	.8343	.7297	.6089	.4826	.3614	.2539
9	4	1.0000	.9991	.9944	.9804	.9511	.9012	.8283	.7334	.6214	.5000
9	5	1.0000	.9999	.9994	.9969	.9900	.9747	.9464	.9006	.8342	.7461
9	6	1.0000	1.0000	1.0000	.9997	.9987	.9957	.9888	.9750	.9502	.9102
9	7	1.0000	1.0000	1.0000	1.0000	.9999	.9996	.9986	.9962	.9909	.9805
9	8	1.0000	1.0000	1.0000	1.0000	1.0000	1.0000	.9999	.9997	.9992	.9980
9	9	1.0000	1.0000	1.0000	1.0000	1.0000	1.0000	1.0000	1.0000	1.0000	1.0000

N	*n*	.05	.10	.15	.20	.25	.30	.35	.40	.45	.50
10	0	.5987	.3487	.1969	.1074	.0563	.0282	.0135	.0060	.0025	.0010
10	1	.9139	.7361	.5443	.3758	.2440	.1493	.0860	.0464	.0233	.0107

10	2	.9885	.9298	.8202	.6778	.5256	.3828	.2616	.1673	.0996	.0547
10	3	.9990	.9872	.9500	.8791	.7759	.6496	.5138	.3823	.2660	.1719
10	4	.9999	.9984	.9901	.9672	.9219	.8497	.7515	.6331	.5044	.3770
10	5	1.0000	.9999	.9986	.9936	.9803	.9527	.9051	.8338	.7384	.6230
10	6	1.0000	1.0000	.9999	.9991	.9965	.9894	.9740	.9452	.8980	.8281
10	7	1.0000	1.0000	1.0000	.9999	.9996	.9984	.9952	.9877	.9726	.9453
10	8	1.0000	1.0000	1.0000	1.0000	1.0000	.9999	.9995	.9983	.9955	.9893
10	9	1.0000	1.0000	1.0000	1.0000	1.0000	1.0000	1.0000	.9999	.9997	.9990
10	10	1.0000	1.0000	1.0000	1.0000	1.0000	1.0000	1.0000	1.0000	1.0000	1.0000

N	*n*	.05	.10	.15	.20	.25	.30	.35	.40	.45	.50
11	0	.5688	.3138	.1673	.0859	.0422	.0198	.0088	.0036	.0014	.0005
11	1	.8981	.6974	.4922	.3221	.1971	.1130	.0606	.0302	.0139	.0059
11	2	.9848	.9104	.7788	.6174	.4552	.3127	.2001	.1189	.0652	.0327
11	3	.9984	.9815	.9306	.8389	.7133	.5696	.4256	.2963	.1911	.1133
11	4	.9999	.9972	.9841	.9496	.8854	.7897	.6683	.5328	.3971	.2744
11	5	1.0000	.9997	.9973	.9883	.9657	.9218	.8513	.7535	.6331	.5000
11	6	1.0000	1.0000	.9997	.9980	.9924	.9784	.9499	.9006	.8262	.7256
11	7	1.0000	1.0000	1.0000	.9998	.9988	.9957	.9878	.9707	.9390	.8867
11	8	1.0000	1.0000	1.0000	1.0000	.9999	.9994	.9980	.9941	.9852	.9673
11	9	1.0000	1.0000	1.0000	1.0000	1.0000	1.0000	.9998	.9993	.9978	.9941
11	10	1.0000	1.0000	1.0000	1.0000	1.0000	1.0000	1.0000	1.0000	.9998	.9995
11	11	1.0000	1.0000	1.0000	1.0000	1.0000	1.0000	1.0000	1.0000	1.0000	1.0000

N	*n*	.05	.10	.15	.20	.25	.30	.35	.40	.45	.50
12	0	.5404	.2824	.1422	.0687	.0317	.0138	.0057	.0022	.0008	.0002
12	1	.8816	.6590	.4435	.2749	.1584	.0850	.0424	.0196	.0083	.0032
12	2	.9804	.8891	.7358	.5583	.3907	.2528	.1513	.0834	.0421	.0193
12	3	.9978	.9744	.9078	.7946	.6488	.4925	.3467	.2253	.1345	.0730
12	4	.9998	.9957	.9761	.9274	.8424	.7237	.5833	.4382	.3044	.1938
12	5	1.0000	.9995	.9954	.9806	.9456	.8822	.7873	.6652	.5269	.3872
12	6	1.0000	.9999	.9993	.9961	.9857	.9614	.9154	.8418	.7393	.6128
12	7	1.0000	1.0000	.9999	.9994	.9972	.9905	.9745	.9427	.8883	.8062
12	8	1.0000	1.0000	1.0000	.9999	.9996	.9983	.9944	.9847	.9644	.9270
12	9	1.0000	1.0000	1.0000	1.0000	1.0000	.9998	.9992	.9972	.9921	.9807
12	10	1.0000	1.0000	1.0000	1.0000	1.0000	1.0000	.9999	.9997	.9989	.9968
12	11	1.0000	1.0000	1.0000	1.0000	1.0000	1.0000	1.0000	1.0000	.9999	.9998
12	12	1.0000	1.0000	1.0000	1.0000	1.0000	1.0000	1.0000	1.0000	1.0000	1.0000

N	n	.05	.10	.15	.20	.25	.30	.35	.40	.45	.50
13	0	.5133	.2542	.1209	.0550	.0238	.0097	.0037	.0013	.0004	.0001
13	1	.8646	.6213	.3983	.2336	.1267	.0637	.0296	.0126	.0049	.0017
13	2	.9755	.8661	.6920	.5017	.3326	.2025	.1132	.0579	.0269	.0112
13	3	.9969	.9658	.8820	.7473	.5843	.4206	.2783	.1686	.0929	.0461
13	4	.9997	.9935	.9658	.9009	.7940	.6543	.5005	.3530	.2279	.1334
13	5	1.0000	.9991	.9925	.9700	.9198	.8346	.7159	.5744	.4268	.2905
13	6	1.0000	.9999	.9987	.9930	.9757	.9376	.8705	.7712	.6437	.5000
13	7	1.0000	1.0000	.9998	.9988	.9944	.9818	.9538	.9023	.8212	.7095
13	8	1.0000	1.0000	1.0000	.9998	.9990	.9960	.9874	.9679	.9302	.8666
13	9	1.0000	1.0000	1.0000	1.0000	.9999	.9993	.9975	.9922	.9797	.9539
13	10	1.0000	1.0000	1.0000	1.0000	1.0000	.9999	.9997	.9987	.9959	.9888
13	11	1.0000	1.0000	1.0000	1.0000	1.0000	1.0000	1.0000	.9999	.9995	.9983
13	12	1.0000	1.0000	1.0000	1.0000	1.0000	1.0000	1.0000	1.0000	1.0000	.9999
13	13	1.0000	1.0000	1.0000	1.0000	1.0000	1.0000	1.0000	1.0000	1.0000	1.0000

N	n	.05	.10	.15	.20	.25	.30	.35	.40	.45	.50
14	0	.4877	.2288	.1028	.0440	.0178	.0068	.0024	.0008	.0002	.0001
14	1	.8470	.5846	.3567	.1979	.1010	.0475	.0205	.0081	.0029	.0009
14	2	.9699	.8416	.6479	.4481	.2811	.1608	.0839	.0398	.0170	.0065
14	3	.9958	.9559	.8535	.6982	.5213	.3552	.2205	.1243	.0632	.0287
14	4	.9996	.9908	.9533	.8702	.7415	.5842	.4227	.2793	.1672	.0898
14	5	1.0000	.9985	.9885	.9561	.8883	.7805	.6405	.4859	.3373	.2120
14	6	1.0000	.9998	.9978	.9884	.9617	.9067	.8164	.6925	.5461	.3953
14	7	1.0000	1.0000	.9997	.9976	.9897	.9685	.9247	.8499	.7414	.6047
14	8	1.0000	1.0000	1.0000	.9996	.9978	.9917	.9757	.9417	.8811	.7880
14	9	1.0000	1.0000	1.0000	1.0000	.9997	.9983	.9940	.9825	.9574	.9102
14	10	1.0000	1.0000	1.0000	1.0000	1.0000	.9998	.9989	.9961	.9886	.9713
14	11	1.0000	1.0000	1.0000	1.0000	1.0000	1.0000	.9999	.9994	.9978	.9935
14	12	1.0000	1.0000	1.0000	1.0000	1.0000	1.0000	1.0000	.9999	.9997	.9991
14	13	1.0000	1.0000	1.0000	1.0000	1.0000	1.0000	1.0000	1.0000	1.0000	.9999
14	14	1.0000	1.0000	1.0000	1.0000	1.0000	1.0000	1.0000	1.0000	1.0000	1.0000

N	n	.05	.10	.15	.20	.25	.30	.35	.40	.45	.50
15	0	.4633	.2059	.0874	.0352	.0134	.0047	.0016	.0005	.0001	.0000
15	1	.8290	.5490	.3186	.1671	.0802	.0353	.0142	.0052	.0017	.0005
15	2	.9638	.8159	.6042	.3980	.2361	.1268	.0617	.0271	.0107	.0037
15	3	.9945	.9444	.8227	.6482	.4613	.2969	.1727	.0905	.0424	.0176
15	4	.9994	.9873	.9383	.8358	.6865	.5155	.3519	.2173	.1204	.0592
15	5	.9999	.9978	.9832	.9389	.8516	.7216	.5643	.4032	.2608	.1509
15	6	1.0000	.9997	.9964	.9819	.9434	.8689	.7548	.6098	.4522	.3036

15	7	1.0000	1.0000	.9994	.9958	.9827	.9500	.8868	.7869	.6535	.5000
15	8	1.0000	1.0000	.9999	.9992	.9958	.9848	.9578	.9050	.8182	.6964
15	9	1.0000	1.0000	1.0000	.9999	.9992	.9963	.9876	.9662	.9231	.8491
15	10	1.0000	1.0000	1.0000	1.0000	.9999	.9993	.9972	.9907	.9745	.9408
15	11	1.0000	1.0000	1.0000	1.0000	1.0000	.9999	.9995	.9981	.9937	.9824
15	12	1.0000	1.0000	1.0000	1.0000	1.0000	1.0000	.9999	.9997	.9989	.9963
15	13	1.0000	1.0000	1.0000	1.0000	1.0000	1.0000	1.0000	1.0000	.9999	.9995
15	14	1.0000	1.0000	1.0000	1.0000	1.0000	1.0000	1.0000	1.0000	1.0000	1.0000
15	15	1.0000	1.0000	1.0000	1.0000	1.0000	1.0000	1.0000	1.0000	1.0000	1.0000

N	*n*	.05	.10	.15	.20	.25	.30	.35	.40	.45	.50
16	0	.4401	.1853	.0743	.0281	.0100	.0033	.0010	.0003	.0001	.0000
16	1	.8108	.5147	.2839	.1407	.0635	.0261	.0098	.0033	.0010	.0003
16	2	.9571	.7892	.5614	.3518	.1971	.0994	.0451	.0183	.0066	.0021
16	3	.9930	.9316	.7899	.5981	.4050	.2459	.1339	.0651	.0281	.0106
16	4	.9991	.9830	.9209	.7982	.6302	.4499	.2892	.1666	.0853	.0384
16	5	.9999	.9967	.9765	.9183	.8103	.6598	.4900	.3288	.1976	.1051
16	6	1.0000	.9995	.9944	.9733	.9204	.8247	.6881	.5272	.3660	.2272
16	7	1.0000	.9999	.9989	.9930	.9729	.9256	.8406	.7161	.5629	.4018
16	8	1.0000	1.0000	.9998	.9985	.9925	.9743	.9329	.8577	.7441	.5982
16	9	1.0000	1.0000	1.0000	.9998	.9984	.9929	.9771	.9417	.8759	.7728
16	10	1.0000	1.0000	1.0000	1.0000	.9997	.9984	.9938	.9809	.9514	.8949
16	11	1.0000	1.0000	1.0000	1.0000	1.0000	.9997	.9987	.9951	.9851	.9616
16	12	1.0000	1.0000	1.0000	1.0000	1.0000	1.0000	.9998	.9991	.9965	.9894
16	13	1.0000	1.0000	1.0000	1.0000	1.0000	1.0000	1.0000	.9999	.9994	.9979
16	14	1.0000	1.0000	1.0000	1.0000	1.0000	1.0000	1.0000	1.0000	.9999	.9997
16	15	1.0000	1.0000	1.0000	1.0000	1.0000	1.0000	1.0000	1.0000	1.0000	1.0000
16	16	1.0000	1.0000	1.0000	1.0000	1.0000	1.0000	1.0000	1.0000	1.0000	1.0000

N	*n*	.05	.10	.15	.20	.25	.30	.35	.40	.45	.50
17	0	.4181	.1668	.0631	.0225	.0075	.0023	.0007	.0002	.0000	.0000
17	1	.7922	.4818	.2525	.1182	.0501	.0193	.0067	.0021	.0006	.0001
17	2	.9497	.7618	.5198	.3096	.1637	.0774	.0327	.0123	.0041	.0012
17	3	.9912	.9174	.7556	.5489	.3530	.2019	.1028	.0464	.0184	.0064
17	4	.9988	.9779	.9013	.7582	.5739	.3887	.2348	.1260	.0596	.0245
17	5	.9999	.9953	.9681	.8943	.7653	.5968	.4197	.2639	.1471	.0717
17	6	1.0000	.9992	.9917	.9623	.8929	.7752	.6188	.4478	.2902	.1662
17	7	1.0000	.9999	.9983	.9891	.9598	.8954	.7872	.6405	.4743	.3145
17	8	1.0000	1.0000	.9997	.9974	.9876	.9597	.9006	.8011	.6626	.5000
17	9	1.0000	1.0000	1.0000	.9995	.9969	.9873	.9617	.9081	.8166	.6855
17	10	1.0000	1.0000	1.0000	.9999	.9994	.9968	.9880	.9652	.9174	.8338
17	11	1.0000	1.0000	1.0000	1.0000	.9999	.9993	.9970	.9894	.9699	.9283

N	n	.05	.10	.15	.20	.25	.30	.35	.40	.45	.50
17	12	1.0000	1.0000	1.0000	1.0000	1.0000	.9999	.9994	.9975	.9914	.9755
17	13	1.0000	1.0000	1.0000	1.0000	1.0000	1.0000	.9999	.9995	.9981	.9936
17	14	1.0000	1.0000	1.0000	1.0000	1.0000	1.0000	1.0000	.9999	.9997	.9988
17	15	1.0000	1.0000	1.0000	1.0000	1.0000	1.0000	1.0000	1.0000	1.0000	.9999
17	16	1.0000	1.0000	1.0000	1.0000	1.0000	1.0000	1.0000	1.0000	1.0000	1.0000
17	17	1.0000	1.0000	1.0000	1.0000	1.0000	1.0000	1.0000	1.0000	1.0000	1.0000

N	*n*	.05	.10	.15	.20	.25	.30	.35	.40	.45	.50
18	0	.3972	.1501	.0536	.0180	.0056	.0016	.0004	.0001	.0000	.0000
18	1	.7735	.4503	.2241	.0991	.0395	.0142	.0046	.0013	.0003	.0001
18	2	.9419	.7338	.4797	.2713	.1353	.0600	.0236	.0082	.0025	.0007
18	3	.9891	.9018	.7202	.5010	.3057	.1646	.0783	.0328	.0120	.0038
18	4	.9985	.9718	.8794	.7164	.5187	.3327	.1886	.0942	.0411	.0154
18	5	.9998	.9936	.9581	.8671	.7175	.5344	.3550	.2088	.1077	.0481
18	6	1.0000	.9988	.9882	.9487	.8610	.7217	.5491	.3743	.2258	.1189
18	7	1.0000	.9998	.9973	.9837	.9431	.8593	.7283	.5634	.3915	.2403
18	8	1.0000	1.0000	.9995	.9957	.9807	.9404	.8609	.7368	.5778	.4073
18	9	1.0000	1.0000	.9999	.9991	.9946	.9790	.9403	.8653	.7473	.5927
18	10	1.0000	1.0000	1.0000	.9998	.9988	.9939	.9788	.9424	.8720	.7597
18	11	1.0000	1.0000	1.0000	1.0000	.9998	.9986	.9938	.9797	.9463	.8811
18	12	1.0000	1.0000	1.0000	1.0000	1.0000	.9997	.9986	.9942	.9817	.9519
18	13	1.0000	1.0000	1.0000	1.0000	1.0000	1.0000	.9997	.9987	.9951	.9846
18	14	1.0000	1.0000	1.0000	1.0000	1.0000	1.0000	1.0000	.9998	.9990	.9962
18	15	1.0000	1.0000	1.0000	1.0000	1.0000	1.0000	1.0000	1.0000	.9999	.9993
18	16	1.0000	1.0000	1.0000	1.0000	1.0000	1.0000	1.0000	1.0000	1.0000	.9999
18	17	1.0000	1.0000	1.0000	1.0000	1.0000	1.0000	1.0000	1.0000	1.0000	1.0000
18	18	1.0000	1.0000	1.0000	1.0000	1.0000	1.0000	1.0000	1.0000	1.0000	1.0000

N	*n*	.05	.10	.15	.20	.25	.30	.35	.40	.45	.50
19	0	.3774	.1351	.0456	.0144	.0042	.0011	.0003	.0001	.0000	.0000
19	1	.7547	.4203	.1985	.0829	.0310	.0104	.0031	.0008	.0002	.0000
19	2	.9335	.7054	.4413	.2369	.1113	.0462	.0170	.0055	.0015	.0004
19	3	.9868	.8850	.6841	.4551	.2631	.1332	.0591	.0230	.0077	.0022
19	4	.9980	.9648	.8556	.6733	.4654	.2822	.1500	.0696	.0280	.0096
19	5	.9998	.9914	.9463	.8369	.6678	.4739	.2968	.1629	.0777	.0318
19	6	1.0000	.9983	.9837	.9324	.8251	.6655	.4812	.3081	.1727	.0835
19	7	1.0000	.9997	.9959	.9767	.9225	.8180	.6656	.4878	.3169	.1796
19	8	1.0000	1.0000	.9992	.9933	.9713	.9161	.8145	.6675	.4940	.3238
19	9	1.0000	1.0000	.9999	.9984	.9911	.9674	.9125	.8139	.6710	.5000
19	10	1.0000	1.0000	1.0000	.9997	.9977	.9895	.9653	.9115	.8159	.6762
19	11	1.0000	1.0000	1.0000	1.0000	.9995	.9972	.9886	.9648	.9129	.8204
19	12	1.0000	1.0000	1.0000	1.0000	.9999	.9994	.9969	.9884	.9658	.9165

19	13	1.0000	1.0000	1.0000	1.0000	1.0000	.9999	.9993	.9969	.9891	.9682
19	14	1.0000	1.0000	1.0000	1.0000	1.0000	1.0000	.9999	.9994	.9972	.9904
19	15	1.0000	1.0000	1.0000	1.0000	1.0000	1.0000	1.0000	.9999	.9995	.9978
19	16	1.0000	1.0000	1.0000	1.0000	1.0000	1.0000	1.0000	1.0000	.9999	.9996
19	17	1.0000	1.0000	1.0000	1.0000	1.0000	1.0000	1.0000	1.0000	1.0000	1.0000
19	18	1.0000	1.0000	1.0000	1.0000	1.0000	1.0000	1.0000	1.0000	1.0000	1.0000
19	19	1.0000	1.0000	1.0000	1.0000	1.0000	1.0000	1.0000	1.0000	1.0000	1.0000

N	*n*	.05	.10	.15	.20	.25	.30	.35	.40	.45	.50
20	0	.3585	.1216	.0388	.0115	.0032	.0008	.0002	.0000	.0000	.0000
20	1	.7358	.3917	.1756	.0692	.0243	.0076	.0021	.0005	.0001	.0000
20	2	.9245	.6769	.4049	.2061	.0913	.0355	.0121	.0036	.0009	.0002
20	3	.9841	.8670	.6477	.4114	.2252	.1071	.0444	.0160	.0049	.0013
20	4	.9974	.9568	.8298	.6296	.4148	.2375	.1182	.0510	.0189	.0059
20	5	.9997	.9887	.9327	.8042	.6172	.4164	.2454	.1256	.0553	.0207
20	6	1.0000	.9976	.9781	.9133	.7858	.6080	.4166	.2500	.1299	.0577
20	7	1.0000	.9996	.9941	.9679	.8982	.7723	.6010	.4159	.2520	.1316
20	8	1.0000	.9999	.9987	.9900	.9591	.8867	.7624	.5956	.4143	.2517
20	9	1.0000	1.0000	.9998	.9974	.9861	.9520	.8782	.7553	.5914	.4119
20	10	1.0000	1.0000	1.0000	.9994	.9961	.9829	.9468	.8725	.7507	.5881
20	11	1.0000	1.0000	1.0000	.9999	.9991	.9949	.9804	.9435	.8692	.7483
20	12	1.0000	1.0000	1.0000	1.0000	.9998	.9987	.9940	.9790	.9420	.8684
20	13	1.0000	1.0000	1.0000	1.0000	1.0000	.9997	.9985	.9935	.9786	.9423
20	14	1.0000	1.0000	1.0000	1.0000	1.0000	1.0000	.9997	.9984	.9936	.9793
20	15	1.0000	1.0000	1.0000	1.0000	1.0000	1.0000	1.0000	.9997	.9985	.9941
20	16	1.0000	1.0000	1.0000	1.0000	1.0000	1.0000	1.0000	1.0000	.9997	.9987
20	17	1.0000	1.0000	1.0000	1.0000	1.0000	1.0000	1.0000	1.0000	1.0000	.9998
20	18	1.0000	1.0000	1.0000	1.0000	1.0000	1.0000	1.0000	1.0000	1.0000	1.0000
20	19	1.0000	1.0000	1.0000	1.0000	1.0000	1.0000	1.0000	1.0000	1.0000	1.0000
20	20	1.0000	1.0000	1.0000	1.0000	1.0000	1.0000	1.0000	1.0000	1.0000	1.0000

N	*n*	.05	.10	.15	.20	.25	.30	.35	.40	.45	.50
21	0	.3406	.1094	.0329	.0092	.0024	.0006	.0001	.0000	.0000	.0000
21	1	.7170	.3647	.1550	.0576	.0190	.0056	.0014	.0003	.0001	.0000
21	2	.9151	.6484	.3705	.1787	.0745	.0271	.0086	.0024	.0006	.0001
21	3	.9811	.8480	.6113	.3704	.1917	.0856	.0331	.0110	.0031	.0007
21	4	.9968	.9478	.8025	.5860	.3674	.1984	.0924	.0370	.0126	.0036
21	5	.9996	.9856	.9173	.7693	.5666	.3627	.2009	.0957	.0389	.0133
21	6	1.0000	.9967	.9713	.8915	.7436	.5505	.3567	.2002	.0964	.0392
21	7	1.0000	.9994	.9917	.9569	.8701	.7230	.5365	.3495	.1971	.0946
21	8	1.0000	.9999	.9980	.9856	.9439	.8523	.7059	.5237	.3413	.1917
21	9	1.0000	1.0000	.9996	.9959	.9794	.9324	.8377	.6914	.5117	.3318

21	10	1.0000	1.0000	.9999	.9990	.9936	.9736	.9228	.8256	.6790	.5000
21	11	1.0000	1.0000	1.0000	.9998	.9983	.9913	.9687	.9151	.8159	.6682
21	12	1.0000	1.0000	1.0000	1.0000	.9996	.9976	.9892	.9648	.9092	.8083
21	13	1.0000	1.0000	1.0000	1.0000	.9999	.9994	.9969	.9877	.9621	.9054
21	14	1.0000	1.0000	1.0000	1.0000	1.0000	.9999	.9993	.9964	.9868	.9608
21	15	1.0000	1.0000	1.0000	1.0000	1.0000	1.0000	.9999	.9992	.9963	.9867
21	16	1.0000	1.0000	1.0000	1.0000	1.0000	1.0000	1.0000	.9998	.9992	.9964
21	17	1.0000	1.0000	1.0000	1.0000	1.0000	1.0000	1.0000	1.0000	.9999	.9993
21	18	1.0000	1.0000	1.0000	1.0000	1.0000	1.0000	1.0000	1.0000	1.0000	.9999
21	19	1.0000	1.0000	1.0000	1.0000	1.0000	1.0000	1.0000	1.0000	1.0000	1.0000
21	20	1.0000	1.0000	1.0000	1.0000	1.0000	1.0000	1.0000	1.0000	1.0000	1.0000
21	21	1.0000	1.0000	1.0000	1.0000	1.0000	1.0000	1.0000	1.0000	1.0000	1.0000

N	*n*	.05	.10	.15	.20	.25	.30	.35	.40	.45	.50
22	0	.3235	.0985	.0280	.0074	.0018	.0004	.0001	.0000	.0000	.0000
22	1	.6982	.3392	.1367	.0480	.0149	.0041	.0010	.0002	.0000	.0000
22	2	.9052	.6200	.3382	.1545	.0606	.0207	.0061	.0016	.0003	.0001
22	3	.9778	.8281	.5752	.3320	.1624	.0681	.0245	.0076	.0020	.0004
22	4	.9960	.9379	.7738	.5429	.3235	.1645	.0716	.0266	.0083	.0022
22	5	.9994	.9818	.9001	.7326	.5168	.3134	.1629	.0722	.0271	.0085
22	6	.9999	.9956	.9632	.8670	.6994	.4942	.3022	.1584	.0705	.0262
22	7	1.0000	.9991	.9886	.9439	.8385	.6713	.4736	.2898	.1518	.0669
22	8	1.0000	.9999	.9970	.9799	.9254	.8135	.6466	.4540	.2764	.1431
22	9	1.0000	1.0000	.9993	.9939	.9705	.9084	.7916	.6244	.4350	.2617
22	10	1.0000	1.0000	.9999	.9984	.9900	.9613	.8930	.7720	.6037	.4159
22	11	1.0000	1.0000	1.0000	.9997	.9971	.9860	.9526	.8793	.7543	.5841
22	12	1.0000	1.0000	1.0000	.9999	.9993	.9957	.9820	.9449	.8672	.7383
22	13	1.0000	1.0000	1.0000	1.0000	.9999	.9989	.9942	.9785	.9383	.8569
22	14	1.0000	1.0000	1.0000	1.0000	1.0000	.9998	.9984	.9930	.9757	.9331
22	15	1.0000	1.0000	1.0000	1.0000	1.0000	1.0000	.9997	.9981	.9920	.9738
22	16	1.0000	1.0000	1.0000	1.0000	1.0000	1.0000	.9999	.9996	.9979	.9915
22	17	1.0000	1.0000	1.0000	1.0000	1.0000	1.0000	1.0000	.9999	.9995	.9978
22	18	1.0000	1.0000	1.0000	1.0000	1.0000	1.0000	1.0000	1.0000	.9999	.9996
22	19	1.0000	1.0000	1.0000	1.0000	1.0000	1.0000	1.0000	1.0000	1.0000	.9999
22	20	1.0000	1.0000	1.0000	1.0000	1.0000	1.0000	1.0000	1.0000	1.0000	1.0000
22	21	1.0000	1.0000	1.0000	1.0000	1.0000	1.0000	1.0000	1.0000	1.0000	1.0000
22	22	1.0000	1.0000	1.0000	1.0000	1.0000	1.0000	1.0000	1.0000	1.0000	1.0000

N	n	.05	.10	.15	.20	.25	.30	.35	.40	.45	.50
23	0	.3074	.0886	.0238	.0059	.0013	.0003	.0000	.0000	.0000	.0000
23	1	.6794	.3151	.1204	.0398	.0116	.0030	.0007	.0001	.0000	.0000
23	2	.8948	.5920	.3080	.1332	.0492	.0157	.0043	.0010	.0002	.0000
23	3	.9742	.8073	.5396	.2965	.1370	.0538	.0181	.0052	.0012	.0002
23	4	.9951	.9269	.7440	.5007	.2832	.1356	.0551	.0190	.0055	.0013
23	5	.9992	.9774	.8811	.6947	.4685	.2688	.1309	.0540	.0186	.0053
23	6	.9999	.9942	.9537	.8402	.6537	.4399	.2534	.1240	.0510	.0173
23	7	1.0000	.9988	.9848	.9285	.8037	.6181	.4136	.2373	.1152	.0466
23	8	1.0000	.9998	.9958	.9727	.9037	.7709	.5860	.3884	.2203	.1050
23	9	1.0000	1.0000	.9990	.9911	.9592	.8799	.7408	.5562	.3636	.2024
23	10	1.0000	1.0000	.9998	.9975	.9851	.9454	.8575	.7129	.5278	.3388
23	11	1.0000	1.0000	1.0000	.9994	.9954	.9786	.9318	.8364	.6865	.5000
23	12	1.0000	1.0000	1.0000	.9999	.9988	.9928	.9717	.9187	.8164	.6612
23	13	1.0000	1.0000	1.0000	1.0000	.9997	.9979	.9900	.9651	.9063	.7976
23	14	1.0000	1.0000	1.0000	1.0000	.9999	.9995	.9970	.9872	.9589	.8950
23	15	1.0000	1.0000	1.0000	1.0000	1.0000	.9999	.9992	.9960	.9847	.9534
23	16	1.0000	1.0000	1.0000	1.0000	1.0000	1.0000	.9998	.9990	.9952	.9827
23	17	1.0000	1.0000	1.0000	1.0000	1.0000	1.0000	1.0000	.9998	.9988	.9947
23	18	1.0000	1.0000	1.0000	1.0000	1.0000	1.0000	1.0000	1.0000	.9998	.9987
23	19	1.0000	1.0000	1.0000	1.0000	1.0000	1.0000	1.0000	1.0000	1.0000	.9998
23	20	1.0000	1.0000	1.0000	1.0000	1.0000	1.0000	1.0000	1.0000	1.0000	1.0000
23	21	1.0000	1.0000	1.0000	1.0000	1.0000	1.0000	1.0000	1.0000	1.0000	1.0000
23	22	1.0000	1.0000	1.0000	1.0000	1.0000	1.0000	1.0000	1.0000	1.0000	1.0000
23	23	1.0000	1.0000	1.0000	1.0000	1.0000	1.0000	1.0000	1.0000	1.0000	1.0000

N	n	.05	.10	.15	.20	.25	.30	.35	.40	.45	.50
24	0	.2920	.0798	.0202	.0047	.0010	.0002	.0000	.0000	.0000	.0000
24	1	.6608	.2925	.1059	.0331	.0090	.0022	.0005	.0001	.0000	.0000
24	2	.8841	.5643	.2798	.1145	.0398	.0119	.0030	.0007	.0001	.0000
24	3	.9702	.7857	.5049	.2639	.1150	.0424	.0133	.0035	.0008	.0001
24	4	.9940	.9149	.7134	.4599	.2466	.1111	.0422	.0134	.0036	.0008
24	5	.9990	.9723	.8606	.6559	.4222	.2288	.1044	.0400	.0127	.0033
24	6	.9999	.9925	.9428	.8111	.6074	.3886	.2106	.0960	.0364	.0113
24	7	1.0000	.9983	.9801	.9108	.7662	.5647	.3575	.1919	.0863	.0320
24	8	1.0000	.9997	.9941	.9638	.8787	.7250	.5257	.3279	.1730	.0758
24	9	1.0000	.9999	.9985	.9874	.9453	.8472	.6866	.4891	.2991	.1537
24	10	1.0000	1.0000	.9997	.9962	.9787	.9258	.8167	.6502	.4539	.2706
24	11	1.0000	1.0000	.9999	.9990	.9928	.9686	.9058	.7870	.6151	.4194
24	12	1.0000	1.0000	1.0000	.9998	.9979	.9885	.9577	.8857	.7580	.5806
24	13	1.0000	1.0000	1.0000	1.0000	.9995	.9964	.9836	.9465	.8659	.7294
24	14	1.0000	1.0000	1.0000	1.0000	.9999	.9990	.9945	.9783	.9352	.8463

24	15	1.0000	1.0000	1.0000	1.0000	1.0000	.9998	.9984	.9925	.9731	.9242
24	16	1.0000	1.0000	1.0000	1.0000	1.0000	1.0000	.9996	.9978	.9905	.9680
24	17	1.0000	1.0000	1.0000	1.0000	1.0000	1.0000	.9999	.9995	.9972	.9887
24	18	1.0000	1.0000	1.0000	1.0000	1.0000	1.0000	1.0000	.9999	.9993	.9967
24	19	1.0000	1.0000	1.0000	1.0000	1.0000	1.0000	1.0000	1.0000	.9999	.9992
24	20	1.0000	1.0000	1.0000	1.0000	1.0000	1.0000	1.0000	1.0000	1.0000	.9999
24	21	1.0000	1.0000	1.0000	1.0000	1.0000	1.0000	1.0000	1.0000	1.0000	1.0000
24	22	1.0000	1.0000	1.0000	1.0000	1.0000	1.0000	1.0000	1.0000	1.0000	1.0000
24	23	1.0000	1.0000	1.0000	1.0000	1.0000	1.0000	1.0000	1.0000	1.0000	1.0000
24	24	1.0000	1.0000	1.0000	1.0000	1.0000	1.0000	1.0000	1.0000	1.0000	1.0000

N	*n*	.05	.10	.15	.20	.25	.30	.35	.40	.45	.50
25	0	.2774	.0718	.0172	.0038	.0008	.0001	.0000	.0000	.0000	.0000
25	1	.6424	.2712	.0931	.0274	.0070	.0016	.0003	.0001	.0000	.0000
25	2	.8729	.5371	.2537	.0982	.0321	.0090	.0021	.0004	.0001	.0000
25	3	.9659	.7636	.4711	.2340	.0962	.0332	.0097	.0024	.0005	.0001
25	4	.9928	.9020	.6821	.4207	.2137	.0905	.0320	.0095	.0023	.0005
25	5	.9988	.9666	.8385	.6167	.3783	.1935	.0826	.0294	.0086	.0020
25	6	.9998	.9905	.9305	.7800	.5611	.3407	.1734	.0736	.0258	.0073
25	7	1.0000	.9977	.9745	.8909	.7265	.5118	.3061	.1536	.0639	.0216
25	8	1.0000	.9995	.9920	.9532	.8506	.6769	.4668	.2735	.1340	.0539
25	9	1.0000	.9999	.9979	.9827	.9287	.8106	.6303	.4246	.2424	.1148
25	10	1.0000	1.0000	.9995	.9944	.9703	.9022	.7712	.5858	.3843	.2122
25	11	1.0000	1.0000	.9999	.9985	.9893	.9558	.8746	.7323	.5426	.3450
25	12	1.0000	1.0000	1.0000	.9996	.9966	.9825	.9396	.8462	.6937	.5000
25	13	1.0000	1.0000	1.0000	.9999	.9991	.9940	.9745	.9222	.8173	.6550
25	14	1.0000	1.0000	1.0000	1.0000	.9998	.9982	.9907	.9656	.9040	.7878
25	15	1.0000	1.0000	1.0000	1.0000	1.0000	.9995	.9971	.9868	.9560	.8852
25	16	1.0000	1.0000	1.0000	1.0000	1.0000	.9999	.9992	.9957	.9826	.9461
25	17	1.0000	1.0000	1.0000	1.0000	1.0000	1.0000	.9998	.9988	.9942	.9784
25	18	1.0000	1.0000	1.0000	1.0000	1.0000	1.0000	1.0000	.9997	.9984	.9927
25	19	1.0000	1.0000	1.0000	1.0000	1.0000	1.0000	1.0000	.9999	.9996	.9980
25	20	1.0000	1.0000	1.0000	1.0000	1.0000	1.0000	1.0000	1.0000	.9999	.9995
25	21	1.0000	1.0000	1.0000	1.0000	1.0000	1.0000	1.0000	1.0000	1.0000	.9999
25	22	1.0000	1.0000	1.0000	1.0000	1.0000	1.0000	1.0000	1.0000	1.0000	1.0000
25	23	1.0000	1.0000	1.0000	1.0000	1.0000	1.0000	1.0000	1.0000	1.0000	1.0000
25	24	1.0000	1.0000	1.0000	1.0000	1.0000	1.0000	1.0000	1.0000	1.0000	1.0000
25	25	1.0000	1.0000	1.0000	1.0000	1.0000	1.0000	1.0000	1.0000	1.0000	1.0000

N	n	.05	.10	.15	.20	.25	.30	.35	.40	.45	.50
26	0	.2635	.0646	.0146	.0030	.0006	.0001	.0000	.0000	.0000	.0000
26	1	.6241	.2513	.0817	.0227	.0055	.0011	.0002	.0000	.0000	.0000
26	2	.8614	.5105	.2296	.0841	.0258	.0067	.0015	.0003	.0000	.0000
26	3	.9613	.7409	.4385	.2068	.0802	.0260	.0070	.0016	.0003	.0000
26	4	.9915	.8882	.6505	.3833	.1844	.0733	.0242	.0066	.0015	.0003
26	5	.9985	.9601	.8150	.5775	.3371	.1626	.0649	.0214	.0058	.0012
26	6	.9998	.9881	.9167	.7474	.5154	.2965	.1416	.0559	.0180	.0047
26	7	1.0000	.9970	.9679	.8687	.6852	.4605	.2596	.1216	.0467	.0145
26	8	1.0000	.9994	.9894	.9408	.8195	.6274	.4106	.2255	.1024	.0378
26	9	1.0000	.9999	.9970	.9768	.9091	.7705	.5731	.3642	.1936	.0843
26	10	1.0000	1.0000	.9993	.9921	.9599	.8747	.7219	.5213	.3204	.1635
26	11	1.0000	1.0000	.9998	.9977	.9845	.9397	.8384	.6737	.4713	.2786
26	12	1.0000	1.0000	1.0000	.9994	.9948	.9745	.9168	.8007	.6257	.4225
26	13	1.0000	1.0000	1.0000	.9999	.9985	.9906	.9623	.8918	.7617	.5775
26	14	1.0000	1.0000	1.0000	1.0000	.9996	.9970	.9850	.9482	.8650	.7214
26	15	1.0000	1.0000	1.0000	1.0000	.9999	.9991	.9948	.9783	.9326	.8365
26	16	1.0000	1.0000	1.0000	1.0000	1.0000	.9998	.9985	.9921	.9707	.9157
26	17	1.0000	1.0000	1.0000	1.0000	1.0000	1.0000	.9996	.9975	.9890	.9622
26	18	1.0000	1.0000	1.0000	1.0000	1.0000	1.0000	.9999	.9993	.9965	.9855
26	19	1.0000	1.0000	1.0000	1.0000	1.0000	1.0000	1.0000	.9999	.9991	.9953
26	20	1.0000	1.0000	1.0000	1.0000	1.0000	1.0000	1.0000	1.0000	.9998	.9988
26	21	1.0000	1.0000	1.0000	1.0000	1.0000	1.0000	1.0000	1.0000	1.0000	.9997
26	22	1.0000	1.0000	1.0000	1.0000	1.0000	1.0000	1.0000	1.0000	1.0000	1.0000
26	23	1.0000	1.0000	1.0000	1.0000	1.0000	1.0000	1.0000	1.0000	1.0000	1.0000
26	24	1.0000	1.0000	1.0000	1.0000	1.0000	1.0000	1.0000	1.0000	1.0000	1.0000
26	25	1.0000	1.0000	1.0000	1.0000	1.0000	1.0000	1.0000	1.0000	1.0000	1.0000
26	26	1.0000	1.0000	1.0000	1.0000	1.0000	1.0000	1.0000	1.0000	1.0000	1.0000

N	n	.05	.10	.15	.20	.25	.30	.35	.40	.45	.50
27	0	.2503	.0581	.0124	.0024	.0004	.0001	.0000	.0000	.0000	.0000
27	1	.6061	.2326	.0716	.0187	.0042	.0008	.0001	.0000	.0000	.0000
27	2	.8495	.4846	.2074	.0718	.0207	.0051	.0010	.0002	.0000	.0000
27	3	.9563	.7179	.4072	.1823	.0666	.0202	.0051	.0011	.0002	.0000
27	4	.9900	.8734	.6187	.3480	.1583	.0591	.0182	.0046	.0009	.0002
27	5	.9981	.9529	.7903	.5387	.2989	.1358	.0507	.0155	.0038	.0008
27	6	.9997	.9853	.9014	.7134	.4708	.2563	.1148	.0421	.0125	.0030
27	7	1.0000	.9961	.9602	.8444	.6427	.4113	.2183	.0953	.0338	.0096
27	8	1.0000	.9991	.9862	.9263	.7859	.5773	.3577	.1839	.0774	.0261
27	9	1.0000	.9998	.9958	.9696	.8867	.7276	.5162	.3087	.1526	.0610
27	10	1.0000	1.0000	.9989	.9890	.9472	.8434	.6698	.4585	.2633	.1239
27	11	1.0000	1.0000	.9998	.9965	.9784	.9202	.7976	.6127	.4034	.2210

27	12	1.0000	1.0000	1.0000	.9990	.9922	.9641	.8894	.7499	.5562	.3506
27	13	1.0000	1.0000	1.0000	.9998	.9976	.9857	.9464	.8553	.7005	.5000
27	14	1.0000	1.0000	1.0000	1.0000	.9993	.9950	.9771	.9257	.8185	.6494
27	15	1.0000	1.0000	1.0000	1.0000	.9998	.9985	.9914	.9663	.9022	.7790
27	16	1.0000	1.0000	1.0000	1.0000	1.0000	.9996	.9972	.9866	.9536	.8761
27	17	1.0000	1.0000	1.0000	1.0000	1.0000	.9999	.9992	.9954	.9807	.9390
27	18	1.0000	1.0000	1.0000	1.0000	1.0000	1.0000	.9998	.9986	.9931	.9739
27	19	1.0000	1.0000	1.0000	1.0000	1.0000	1.0000	1.0000	.9997	.9979	.9904
27	20	1.0000	1.0000	1.0000	1.0000	1.0000	1.0000	1.0000	.9999	.9995	.9970
27	21	1.0000	1.0000	1.0000	1.0000	1.0000	1.0000	1.0000	1.0000	.9999	.9992
27	22	1.0000	1.0000	1.0000	1.0000	1.0000	1.0000	1.0000	1.0000	1.0000	.9998
27	23	1.0000	1.0000	1.0000	1.0000	1.0000	1.0000	1.0000	1.0000	1.0000	1.0000
27	24	1.0000	1.0000	1.0000	1.0000	1.0000	1.0000	1.0000	1.0000	1.0000	1.0000
27	25	1.0000	1.0000	1.0000	1.0000	1.0000	1.0000	1.0000	1.0000	1.0000	1.0000
27	26	1.0000	1.0000	1.0000	1.0000	1.0000	1.0000	1.0000	1.0000	1.0000	1.0000
27	27	1.0000	1.0000	1.0000	1.0000	1.0000	1.0000	1.0000	1.0000	1.0000	1.0000

N	*n*	.05	.10	.15	.20	.25	.30	.35	.40	.45	.50
28	0	.2378	.0523	.0106	.0019	.0003	.0000	.0000	.0000	.0000	.0000
28	1	.5883	.2152	.0627	.0155	.0033	.0006	.0001	.0000	.0000	.0000
28	2	.8373	.4594	.1871	.0612	.0166	.0038	.0007	.0001	.0000	.0000
28	3	.9509	.6946	.3772	.1602	.0551	.0157	.0037	.0007	.0001	.0000
28	4	.9883	.8579	.5869	.3149	.1354	.0474	.0136	.0032	.0006	.0001
28	5	.9977	.9450	.7646	.5005	.2638	.1128	.0393	.0111	.0025	.0005
28	6	.9996	.9821	.8848	.6784	.4279	.2202	.0923	.0315	.0086	.0019
28	7	1.0000	.9950	.9514	.8182	.5997	.3648	.1821	.0740	.0242	.0063
28	8	1.0000	.9988	.9823	.9100	.7501	.5275	.3089	.1485	.0578	.0178
28	9	1.0000	.9998	.9944	.9609	.8615	.6825	.4607	.2588	.1187	.0436
28	10	1.0000	1.0000	.9985	.9851	.9321	.8087	.6160	.3986	.2135	.0925
28	11	1.0000	1.0000	.9996	.9950	.9706	.8972	.7529	.5510	.3404	.1725
28	12	1.0000	1.0000	.9999	.9985	.9888	.9509	.8572	.6950	.4875	.2858
28	13	1.0000	1.0000	1.0000	.9996	.9962	.9792	.9264	.8132	.6356	.4253
28	14	1.0000	1.0000	1.0000	.9999	.9989	.9923	.9663	.8975	.7654	.5747
28	15	1.0000	1.0000	1.0000	1.0000	.9997	.9975	.9864	.9501	.8645	.7142
28	16	1.0000	1.0000	1.0000	1.0000	.9999	.9993	.9952	.9785	.9304	.8275
28	17	1.0000	1.0000	1.0000	1.0000	1.0000	.9998	.9985	.9919	.9685	.9075
28	18	1.0000	1.0000	1.0000	1.0000	1.0000	1.0000	.9996	.9973	.9875	.9564
28	19	1.0000	1.0000	1.0000	1.0000	1.0000	1.0000	.9999	.9992	.9957	.9822
28	20	1.0000	1.0000	1.0000	1.0000	1.0000	1.0000	1.0000	.9998	.9988	.9937
28	21	1.0000	1.0000	1.0000	1.0000	1.0000	1.0000	1.0000	1.0000	.9997	.9981
28	22	1.0000	1.0000	1.0000	1.0000	1.0000	1.0000	1.0000	1.0000	.9999	.9995
28	23	1.0000	1.0000	1.0000	1.0000	1.0000	1.0000	1.0000	1.0000	1.0000	.9999
28	24	1.0000	1.0000	1.0000	1.0000	1.0000	1.0000	1.0000	1.0000	1.0000	1.0000

N	n	.05	.10	.15	.20	.25	.30	.35	.40	.45	.50
28	25	1.0000	1.0000	1.0000	1.0000	1.0000	1.0000	1.0000	1.0000	1.0000	1.0000
28	26	1.0000	1.0000	1.0000	1.0000	1.0000	1.0000	1.0000	1.0000	1.0000	1.0000
28	27	1.0000	1.0000	1.0000	1.0000	1.0000	1.0000	1.0000	1.0000	1.0000	1.0000
28	28	1.0000	1.0000	1.0000	1.0000	1.0000	1.0000	1.0000	1.0000	1.0000	1.0000

N	*n*	.05	.10	.15	.20	.25	.30	.35	.40	.45	.50
29	0	.2259	.0471	.0090	.0015	.0002	.0000	.0000	.0000	.0000	.0000
29	1	.5708	.1989	.0549	.0128	.0025	.0004	.0001	.0000	.0000	.0000
29	2	.8249	.4350	.1684	.0520	.0133	.0028	.0005	.0001	.0000	.0000
29	3	.9452	.6710	.3487	.1404	.0455	.0121	.0026	.0005	.0001	.0000
29	4	.9864	.8416	.5555	.2839	.1153	.0379	.0101	.0022	.0004	.0001
29	5	.9973	.9363	.7379	.4634	.2317	.0932	.0303	.0080	.0017	.0003
29	6	.9995	.9784	.8667	.6429	.3868	.1880	.0738	.0233	.0059	.0012
29	7	.9999	.9938	.9414	.7903	.5568	.3214	.1507	.0570	.0172	.0041
29	8	1.0000	.9984	.9777	.8916	.7125	.4787	.2645	.1187	.0427	.0121
29	9	1.0000	.9997	.9926	.9507	.8337	.6360	.4076	.2147	.0913	.0307
29	10	1.0000	.9999	.9978	.9803	.9145	.7708	.5617	.3427	.1708	.0680
29	11	1.0000	1.0000	.9995	.9931	.9610	.8706	.7050	.4900	.2833	.1325
29	12	1.0000	1.0000	.9999	.9978	.9842	.9348	.8207	.6374	.4213	.2291
29	13	1.0000	1.0000	1.0000	.9994	.9944	.9707	.9022	.7659	.5689	.3555
29	14	1.0000	1.0000	1.0000	.9999	.9982	.9883	.9524	.8638	.7070	.5000
29	15	1.0000	1.0000	1.0000	1.0000	.9995	.9959	.9794	.9290	.8199	.6445
29	16	1.0000	1.0000	1.0000	1.0000	.9999	.9987	.9921	.9671	.9008	.7709
29	17	1.0000	1.0000	1.0000	1.0000	1.0000	.9997	.9973	.9865	.9514	.8675
29	18	1.0000	1.0000	1.0000	1.0000	1.0000	.9999	.9992	.9951	.9790	.9320
29	19	1.0000	1.0000	1.0000	1.0000	1.0000	1.0000	.9998	.9985	.9920	.9693
29	20	1.0000	1.0000	1.0000	1.0000	1.0000	1.0000	1.0000	.9996	.9974	.9879
29	21	1.0000	1.0000	1.0000	1.0000	1.0000	1.0000	1.0000	.9999	.9993	.9959
29	22	1.0000	1.0000	1.0000	1.0000	1.0000	1.0000	1.0000	1.0000	.9998	.9988
29	23	1.0000	1.0000	1.0000	1.0000	1.0000	1.0000	1.0000	1.0000	1.0000	.9997
29	24	1.0000	1.0000	1.0000	1.0000	1.0000	1.0000	1.0000	1.0000	1.0000	.9999
29	25	1.0000	1.0000	1.0000	1.0000	1.0000	1.0000	1.0000	1.0000	1.0000	1.0000
29	26	1.0000	1.0000	1.0000	1.0000	1.0000	1.0000	1.0000	1.0000	1.0000	1.0000
29	27	1.0000	1.0000	1.0000	1.0000	1.0000	1.0000	1.0000	1.0000	1.0000	1.0000
29	28	1.0000	1.0000	1.0000	1.0000	1.0000	1.0000	1.0000	1.0000	1.0000	1.0000
29	29	1.0000	1.0000	1.0000	1.0000	1.0000	1.0000	1.0000	1.0000	1.0000	1.0000

N	*n*	.05	.10	.15	.20	.25	.30	.35	.40	.45	.50
30	0	.2146	.0424	.0076	.0012	.0002	.0000	.0000	.0000	.0000	.0000
30	1	.5535	.1837	.0480	.0105	.0020	.0003	.0000	.0000	.0000	.0000
30	2	.8122	.4114	.1514	.0442	.0106	.0021	.0003	.0000	.0000	.0000
30	3	.9392	.6474	.3217	.1227	.0374	.0093	.0019	.0003	.0000	.0000
30	4	.9844	.8245	.5245	.2552	.0979	.0302	.0075	.0015	.0002	.0000
30	5	.9967	.9268	.7106	.4275	.2026	.0766	.0233	.0057	.0011	.0002
30	6	.9994	.9742	.8474	.6070	.3481	.1595	.0586	.0172	.0040	.0007
30	7	.9999	.9922	.9302	.7608	.5143	.2814	.1238	.0435	.0121	.0026
30	8	1.0000	.9980	.9722	.8713	.6736	.4315	.2247	.0940	.0312	.0081
30	9	1.0000	.9995	.9903	.9389	.8034	.5888	.3575	.1763	.0694	.0214
30	10	1.0000	.9999	.9971	.9744	.8943	.7304	.5078	.2915	.1350	.0494
30	11	1.0000	1.0000	.9992	.9905	.9493	.8407	.6548	.4311	.2327	.1002
30	12	1.0000	1.0000	.9998	.9969	.9784	.9155	.7802	.5785	.3592	.1808
30	13	1.0000	1.0000	1.0000	.9991	.9918	.9599	.8737	.7145	.5025	.2923
30	14	1.0000	1.0000	1.0000	.9998	.9973	.9831	.9348	.8246	.6448	.4278
30	15	1.0000	1.0000	1.0000	.9999	.9992	.9936	.9699	.9029	.7691	.5722
30	16	1.0000	1.0000	1.0000	1.0000	.9998	.9979	.9876	.9519	.8644	.7077
30	17	1.0000	1.0000	1.0000	1.0000	.9999	.9994	.9955	.9788	.9286	.8192
30	18	1.0000	1.0000	1.0000	1.0000	1.0000	.9998	.9986	.9917	.9666	.8998
30	19	1.0000	1.0000	1.0000	1.0000	1.0000	1.0000	.9996	.9971	.9862	.9506
30	20	1.0000	1.0000	1.0000	1.0000	1.0000	1.0000	.9999	.9991	.9950	.9786
30	21	1.0000	1.0000	1.0000	1.0000	1.0000	1.0000	1.0000	.9998	.9984	.9919
30	22	1.0000	1.0000	1.0000	1.0000	1.0000	1.0000	1.0000	1.0000	.9996	.9974
30	23	1.0000	1.0000	1.0000	1.0000	1.0000	1.0000	1.0000	1.0000	.9999	.9993
30	24	1.0000	1.0000	1.0000	1.0000	1.0000	1.0000	1.0000	1.0000	1.0000	.9998
30	25	1.0000	1.0000	1.0000	1.0000	1.0000	1.0000	1.0000	1.0000	1.0000	1.0000
30	26	1.0000	1.0000	1.0000	1.0000	1.0000	1.0000	1.0000	1.0000	1.0000	1.0000
30	27	1.0000	1.0000	1.0000	1.0000	1.0000	1.0000	1.0000	1.0000	1.0000	1.0000
30	28	1.0000	1.0000	1.0000	1.0000	1.0000	1.0000	1.0000	1.0000	1.0000	1.0000
30	29	1.0000	1.0000	1.0000	1.0000	1.0000	1.0000	1.0000	1.0000	1.0000	1.0000
30	30	1.0000	1.0000	1.0000	1.0000	1.0000	1.0000	1.0000	1.0000	1.0000	1.0000

TABLE 10
Cumulative Probabilities under the Poisson Distribution
For Given Values of λ and x

λ \ x	0	1	2	3	4	5	6	7	8	9	10
0.02	0.980	1.000	1.000	1.000	1.000	1.000	1.000	1.000	1.000	1.000	1.000
0.04	0.961	0.999	1.000	1.000	1.000	1.000	1.000	1.000	1.000	1.000	1.000
0.06	0.942	0.998	1.000	1.000	1.000	1.000	1.000	1.000	1.000	1.000	1.000
0.08	0.923	0.997	1.000	1.000	1.000	1.000	1.000	1.000	1.000	1.000	1.000
0.10	0.905	0.995	1.000	1.000	1.000	1.000	1.000	1.000	1.000	1.000	1.000
0.15	0.861	0.990	0.999	1.000	1.000	1.000	1.000	1.000	1.000	1.000	1.000
0.20	0.819	0.982	0.999	1.000	1.000	1.000	1.000	1.000	1.000	1.000	1.000
0.25	0.779	0.974	0.998	1.000	1.000	1.000	1.000	1.000	1.000	1.000	1.000
0.30	0.741	0.963	0.996	1.000	1.000	1.000	1.000	1.000	1.000	1.000	1.000
0.35	0.705	0.951	0.994	1.000	1.000	1.000	1.000	1.000	1.000	1.000	1.000
0.40	0.670	0.938	0.992	0.999	1.000	1.000	1.000	1.000	1.000	1.000	1.000
0.45	0.638	0.925	0.989	0.999	1.000	1.000	1.000	1.000	1.000	1.000	1.000
0.50	0.607	0.910	0.986	0.998	1.000	1.000	1.000	1.000	1.000	1.000	1.000
0.55	0.577	0.894	0.982	0.998	1.000	1.000	1.000	1.000	1.000	1.000	1.000
0.60	0.549	0.878	0.977	0.997	1.000	1.000	1.000	1.000	1.000	1.000	1.000
0.65	0.522	0.861	0.972	0.996	0.999	1.000	1.000	1.000	1.000	1.000	1.000
0.70	0.497	0.844	0.966	0.994	0.999	1.000	1.000	1.000	1.000	1.000	1.000
0.75	0.472	0.827	0.959	0.993	0.999	1.000	1.000	1.000	1.000	1.000	1.000
0.80	0.449	0.809	0.953	0.991	0.999	1.000	1.000	1.000	1.000	1.000	1.000
0.85	0.427	0.791	0.945	0.989	0.998	1.000	1.000	1.000	1.000	1.000	1.000
0.90	0.407	0.772	0.937	0.987	0.998	1.000	1.000	1.000	1.000	1.000	1.000
0.95	0.387	0.754	0.929	0.984	0.997	1.000	1.000	1.000	1.000	1.000	1.000
1.00	0.368	0.736	0.920	0.981	0.996	0.999	1.000	1.000	1.000	1.000	1.000
1.10	0.333	0.699	0.900	0.974	0.995	0.999	1.000	1.000	1.000	1.000	1.000
1.20	0.301	0.663	0.879	0.966	0.992	0.998	1.000	1.000	1.000	1.000	1.000
1.30	0.273	0.627	0.857	0.957	0.989	0.998	1.000	1.000	1.000	1.000	1.000
1.40	0.247	0.592	0.833	0.946	0.986	0.997	0.999	1.000	1.000	1.000	1.000
1.50	0.223	0.558	0.809	0.934	0.981	0.996	0.999	1.000	1.000	1.000	1.000
1.60	0.202	0.525	0.783	0.921	0.976	0.994	0.999	1.000	1.000	1.000	1.000
1.70	0.183	0.493	0.757	0.907	0.970	0.992	0.998	1.000	1.000	1.000	1.000
1.80	0.165	0.463	0.731	0.891	0.964	0.990	0.997	0.999	1.000	1.000	1.000
1.90	0.150	0.434	0.704	0.875	0.956	0.987	0.997	0.999	1.000	1.000	1.000
2.00	0.135	0.406	0.677	0.857	0.947	0.983	0.995	0.999	1.000	1.000	1.000
2.10	0.122	0.380	0.650	0.839	0.938	0.980	0.994	0.999	1.000	1.000	1.000
2.20	0.111	0.355	0.623	0.819	0.928	0.975	0.993	0.998	1.000	1.000	1.000
2.30	0.100	0.331	0.596	0.799	0.916	0.970	0.991	0.997	0.999	1.000	1.000
2.40	0.091	0.308	0.570	0.779	0.904	0.964	0.988	0.997	0.999	1.000	1.000

λ \ x	0	1	2	3	4	5	6	7	8	9	10
2.50	0.082	0.287	0.544	0.758	0.891	0.958	0.986	0.996	0.999	1.000	1.000
2.60	0.074	0.267	0.518	0.736	0.877	0.951	0.983	0.995	0.999	1.000	1.000
2.70	0.067	0.249	0.494	0.714	0.863	0.943	0.979	0.993	0.998	0.999	1.000
2.80	0.061	0.231	0.469	0.692	0.848	0.935	0.976	0.992	0.998	0.999	1.000
2.90	0.055	0.215	0.446	0.670	0.832	0.926	0.971	0.990	0.997	0.999	1.000
3.00	0.050	0.199	0.423	0.647	0.815	0.916	0.966	0.988	0.996	0.999	1.000
3.10	0.045	0.185	0.401	0.625	0.798	0.906	0.961	0.986	0.995	0.999	1.000
3.20	0.041	0.171	0.380	0.603	0.781	0.895	0.955	0.983	0.994	0.998	1.000
3.30	0.037	0.159	0.359	0.580	0.763	0.883	0.949	0.980	0.993	0.998	0.999
3.40	0.033	0.147	0.340	0.558	0.744	0.871	0.942	0.977	0.992	0.997	0.999
3.50	0.030	0.136	0.321	0.537	0.725	0.858	0.935	0.973	0.990	0.997	0.999
3.60	0.027	0.126	0.303	0.515	0.706	0.844	0.927	0.969	0.988	0.996	0.999
3.70	0.025	0.116	0.285	0.494	0.687	0.830	0.918	0.965	0.986	0.995	0.998
3.80	0.022	0.107	0.269	0.473	0.668	0.816	0.909	0.960	0.984	0.994	0.998
3.90	0.020	0.099	0.253	0.453	0.648	0.801	0.899	0.955	0.981	0.993	0.998
4.00	0.018	0.092	0.238	0.433	0.629	0.785	0.889	0.949	0.979	0.992	0.997
4.10	0.017	0.085	0.224	0.414	0.609	0.769	0.879	0.943	0.976	0.990	0.997
4.20	0.015	0.078	0.210	0.395	0.590	0.753	0.867	0.936	0.972	0.989	0.996
4.30	0.014	0.072	0.197	0.377	0.570	0.737	0.856	0.929	0.968	0.987	0.995
4.40	0.012	0.066	0.185	0.359	0.551	0.720	0.844	0.921	0.964	0.985	0.994
4.50	0.011	0.061	0.174	0.342	0.532	0.703	0.831	0.913	0.960	0.983	0.993
4.60	0.010	0.056	0.163	0.326	0.513	0.686	0.818	0.905	0.955	0.980	0.992
4.70	0.009	0.052	0.152	0.310	0.495	0.668	0.805	0.896	0.950	0.978	0.991
4.80	0.008	0.048	0.143	0.294	0.476	0.651	0.791	0.887	0.944	0.975	0.990
4.90	0.007	0.044	0.133	0.279	0.458	0.634	0.777	0.877	0.938	0.972	0.988
5.00	0.007	0.040	0.125	0.265	0.440	0.616	0.762	0.867	0.932	0.968	0.986
5.10	0.006	0.037	0.116	0.251	0.423	0.598	0.747	0.856	0.925	0.964	0.984
5.20	0.006	0.034	0.109	0.238	0.406	0.581	0.732	0.845	0.918	0.960	0.982
5.30	0.005	0.031	0.102	0.225	0.390	0.563	0.717	0.833	0.911	0.956	0.980
5.40	0.005	0.029	0.095	0.213	0.373	0.546	0.702	0.822	0.903	0.951	0.977
5.50	0.004	0.027	0.088	0.202	0.358	0.529	0.686	0.809	0.894	0.946	0.975
5.60	0.004	0.024	0.082	0.191	0.342	0.512	0.670	0.797	0.886	0.941	0.972
5.70	0.003	0.022	0.077	0.180	0.327	0.495	0.654	0.784	0.877	0.935	0.969
5.80	0.003	0.021	0.072	0.170	0.313	0.478	0.638	0.771	0.867	0.929	0.965
5.90	0.003	0.019	0.067	0.160	0.299	0.462	0.622	0.758	0.857	0.923	0.961
6.00	0.002	0.017	0.062	0.151	0.285	0.446	0.606	0.744	0.847	0.916	0.957
6.10	0.002	0.016	0.058	0.143	0.272	0.430	0.590	0.730	0.837	0.909	0.953
6.20	0.002	0.015	0.054	0.134	0.259	0.414	0.574	0.716	0.826	0.902	0.949
6.30	0.002	0.013	0.050	0.126	0.247	0.399	0.558	0.702	0.815	0.894	0.944
6.40	0.002	0.012	0.046	0.119	0.235	0.384	0.542	0.687	0.803	0.886	0.939
6.50	0.002	0.011	0.043	0.112	0.224	0.369	0.527	0.673	0.792	0.877	0.933

λ \ x	0	1	2	3	4	5	6	7	8	9	10
6.60	0.001	0.010	0.040	0.105	0.213	0.355	0.511	0.658	0.780	0.869	0.927
6.70	0.001	0.009	0.037	0.099	0.202	0.341	0.495	0.643	0.767	0.860	0.921
6.80	0.001	0.009	0.034	0.093	0.192	0.327	0.480	0.628	0.755	0.850	0.915
6.90	0.001	0.008	0.032	0.087	0.182	0.314	0.465	0.614	0.742	0.840	0.908
7.00	0.001	0.007	0.030	0.082	0.173	0.301	0.450	0.599	0.729	0.830	0.901
7.10	0.001	0.007	0.027	0.077	0.164	0.288	0.435	0.584	0.716	0.820	0.894
7.20	0.001	0.006	0.025	0.072	0.156	0.276	0.420	0.569	0.703	0.810	0.887
7.30	0.001	0.006	0.024	0.067	0.147	0.264	0.406	0.554	0.689	0.799	0.879
7.40	0.001	0.005	0.022	0.063	0.140	0.253	0.392	0.539	0.676	0.788	0.871
7.50	0.001	0.005	0.020	0.059	0.132	0.241	0.378	0.525	0.662	0.776	0.862
7.60	0.001	0.004	0.019	0.055	0.125	0.231	0.365	0.510	0.648	0.765	0.854
7.70	0.000	0.004	0.017	0.052	0.118	0.220	0.351	0.496	0.634	0.753	0.845
7.80	0.000	0.004	0.016	0.048	0.112	0.210	0.338	0.481	0.620	0.741	0.835
7.90	0.000	0.003	0.015	0.045	0.106	0.201	0.326	0.467	0.607	0.729	0.826
8.00	0.000	0.003	0.014	0.042	0.100	0.191	0.313	0.453	0.593	0.717	0.816
8.10	0.000	0.003	0.013	0.040	0.094	0.182	0.301	0.439	0.579	0.704	0.806
8.20	0.000	0.003	0.012	0.037	0.089	0.174	0.290	0.425	0.565	0.692	0.796
8.30	0.000	0.002	0.011	0.035	0.084	0.165	0.278	0.412	0.551	0.679	0.785
8.40	0.000	0.002	0.010	0.032	0.079	0.157	0.267	0.399	0.537	0.666	0.774
8.50	0.000	0.002	0.009	0.030	0.074	0.150	0.256	0.386	0.523	0.653	0.763
8.60	0.000	0.002	0.009	0.028	0.070	0.142	0.246	0.373	0.509	0.640	0.752
8.70	0.000	0.002	0.008	0.026	0.066	0.135	0.235	0.360	0.496	0.627	0.741
8.80	0.000	0.001	0.007	0.024	0.062	0.128	0.226	0.348	0.482	0.614	0.729
8.90	0.000	0.001	0.007	0.023	0.058	0.122	0.216	0.336	0.469	0.601	0.718
9.00	0.000	0.001	0.006	0.021	0.055	0.116	0.207	0.324	0.456	0.587	0.706
9.10	0.000	0.001	0.006	0.020	0.052	0.110	0.198	0.312	0.443	0.574	0.694
9.20	0.000	0.001	0.005	0.018	0.049	0.104	0.189	0.301	0.430	0.561	0.682
9.30	0.000	0.001	0.005	0.017	0.046	0.099	0.181	0.290	0.417	0.548	0.670
9.40	0.000	0.001	0.005	0.016	0.043	0.093	0.173	0.279	0.404	0.535	0.658
9.50	0.000	0.001	0.004	0.015	0.040	0.089	0.165	0.269	0.392	0.522	0.645
9.60	0.000	0.001	0.004	0.014	0.038	0.084	0.157	0.258	0.380	0.509	0.633
9.70	0.000	0.001	0.004	0.013	0.035	0.079	0.150	0.248	0.368	0.496	0.621
9.80	0.000	0.001	0.003	0.012	0.033	0.075	0.143	0.239	0.356	0.483	0.608
9.90	0.000	0.001	0.003	0.011	0.031	0.071	0.137	0.229	0.344	0.471	0.596
10.00	0.000	0.000	0.003	0.010	0.029	0.067	0.130	0.220	0.333	0.458	0.583
10.10	0.000	0.000	0.003	0.010	0.027	0.063	0.124	0.211	0.322	0.445	0.571
10.20	0.000	0.000	0.002	0.009	0.026	0.060	0.118	0.203	0.311	0.433	0.558
10.30	0.000	0.000	0.002	0.008	0.024	0.057	0.112	0.194	0.300	0.421	0.546
10.40	0.000	0.000	0.002	0.008	0.023	0.053	0.107	0.186	0.290	0.409	0.533
10.50	0.000	0.000	0.002	0.007	0.021	0.050	0.102	0.179	0.279	0.397	0.521
10.60	0.000	0.000	0.002	0.007	0.020	0.048	0.097	0.171	0.269	0.385	0.508

λ \ x	0	1	2	3	4	5	6	7	8	9	10
10.70	0.000	0.000	0.002	0.006	0.018	0.045	0.092	0.164	0.260	0.374	0.496
10.80	0.000	0.000	0.001	0.006	0.017	0.042	0.087	0.157	0.250	0.363	0.484
10.90	0.000	0.000	0.001	0.005	0.016	0.040	0.083	0.150	0.241	0.351	0.472
11.00	0.000	0.000	0.001	0.005	0.015	0.038	0.079	0.143	0.232	0.341	0.460
11.10	0.000	0.000	0.001	0.005	0.014	0.035	0.075	0.137	0.223	0.330	0.448
11.20	0.000	0.000	0.001	0.004	0.013	0.033	0.071	0.131	0.215	0.319	0.436
11.30	0.000	0.000	0.001	0.004	0.012	0.031	0.067	0.125	0.206	0.309	0.425
11.40	0.000	0.000	0.001	0.004	0.012	0.029	0.064	0.119	0.198	0.299	0.413
11.50	0.000	0.000	0.001	0.003	0.011	0.028	0.060	0.114	0.191	0.289	0.402
11.60	0.000	0.000	0.001	0.003	0.010	0.026	0.057	0.108	0.183	0.279	0.391
11.70	0.000	0.000	0.001	0.003	0.009	0.025	0.054	0.103	0.176	0.270	0.379
11.80	0.000	0.000	0.001	0.003	0.009	0.023	0.051	0.099	0.169	0.260	0.369
11.90	0.000	0.000	0.001	0.002	0.008	0.022	0.048	0.094	0.162	0.251	0.358
12.00	0.000	0.000	0.001	0.002	0.008	0.020	0.046	0.090	0.155	0.242	0.347
12.10	0.000	0.000	0.000	0.002	0.007	0.019	0.043	0.085	0.149	0.234	0.337
12.20	0.000	0.000	0.000	0.002	0.007	0.018	0.041	0.081	0.142	0.225	0.327
12.30	0.000	0.000	0.000	0.002	0.006	0.017	0.039	0.077	0.136	0.217	0.317
12.40	0.000	0.000	0.000	0.002	0.006	0.016	0.037	0.073	0.131	0.209	0.307
12.50	0.000	0.000	0.000	0.002	0.005	0.015	0.035	0.070	0.125	0.201	0.297
12.60	0.000	0.000	0.000	0.001	0.005	0.014	0.033	0.066	0.120	0.194	0.288
12.70	0.000	0.000	0.000	0.001	0.005	0.013	0.031	0.063	0.114	0.187	0.278
12.80	0.000	0.000	0.000	0.001	0.004	0.012	0.029	0.060	0.109	0.179	0.269
12.90	0.000	0.000	0.000	0.001	0.004	0.011	0.027	0.057	0.104	0.173	0.260
13.00	0.000	0.000	0.000	0.001	0.004	0.011	0.026	0.054	0.100	0.166	0.252
13.10	0.000	0.000	0.000	0.001	0.003	0.010	0.024	0.051	0.095	0.159	0.243
13.20	0.000	0.000	0.000	0.001	0.003	0.009	0.023	0.049	0.091	0.153	0.235
13.30	0.000	0.000	0.000	0.001	0.003	0.009	0.022	0.046	0.087	0.147	0.227
13.40	0.000	0.000	0.000	0.001	0.003	0.008	0.020	0.044	0.083	0.141	0.219
13.50	0.000	0.000	0.000	0.001	0.003	0.008	0.019	0.041	0.079	0.135	0.211
13.60	0.000	0.000	0.000	0.001	0.002	0.007	0.018	0.039	0.075	0.130	0.204
13.70	0.000	0.000	0.000	0.001	0.002	0.007	0.017	0.037	0.072	0.124	0.196
13.80	0.000	0.000	0.000	0.001	0.002	0.006	0.016	0.035	0.068	0.119	0.189
13.90	0.000	0.000	0.000	0.001	0.002	0.006	0.015	0.033	0.065	0.114	0.182
14.00	0.000	0.000	0.000	0.000	0.002	0.006	0.014	0.032	0.062	0.109	0.176
14.10	0.000	0.000	0.000	0.000	0.002	0.005	0.013	0.030	0.059	0.105	0.169
14.20	0.000	0.000	0.000	0.000	0.002	0.005	0.013	0.028	0.056	0.100	0.163
14.30	0.000	0.000	0.000	0.000	0.001	0.005	0.012	0.027	0.053	0.096	0.157
14.40	0.000	0.000	0.000	0.000	0.001	0.004	0.011	0.025	0.051	0.092	0.151
14.50	0.000	0.000	0.000	0.000	0.001	0.004	0.010	0.024	0.048	0.088	0.145
14.60	0.000	0.000	0.000	0.000	0.001	0.004	0.010	0.023	0.046	0.084	0.139
14.70	0.000	0.000	0.000	0.000	0.001	0.003	0.009	0.021	0.044	0.080	0.134

λ \ x	0	1	2	3	4	5	6	7	8	9	10
14.80	0.000	0.000	0.000	0.000	0.001	0.003	0.009	0.020	0.042	0.077	0.129
14.90	0.000	0.000	0.000	0.000	0.001	0.003	0.008	0.019	0.039	0.073	0.123
15.00	0.000	0.000	0.000	0.000	0.001	0.003	0.008	0.018	0.037	0.070	0.118
16.00	0.000	0.000	0.000	0.000	0.000	0.001	0.004	0.010	0.022	0.043	0.077
17.00	0.000	0.000	0.000	0.000	0.000	0.001	0.002	0.005	0.013	0.026	0.049
18.00	0.000	0.000	0.000	0.000	0.000	0.000	0.001	0.003	0.007	0.015	0.030
19.00	0.000	0.000	0.000	0.000	0.000	0.000	0.001	0.002	0.004	0.009	0.018
20.00	0.000	0.000	0.000	0.000	0.000	0.000	0.000	0.001	0.002	0.005	0.011
21.00	0.000	0.000	0.000	0.000	0.000	0.000	0.000	0.000	0.001	0.003	0.006
22.00	0.000	0.000	0.000	0.000	0.000	0.000	0.000	0.000	0.001	0.002	0.004
23.00	0.000	0.000	0.000	0.000	0.000	0.000	0.000	0.000	0.000	0.001	0.002
24.00	0.000	0.000	0.000	0.000	0.000	0.000	0.000	0.000	0.000	0.000	0.001
25.00	0.000	0.000	0.000	0.000	0.000	0.000	0.000	0.000	0.000	0.000	0.001
26.00	0.000	0.000	0.000	0.000	0.000	0.000	0.000	0.000	0.000	0.000	0.000
27.00	0.000	0.000	0.000	0.000	0.000	0.000	0.000	0.000	0.000	0.000	0.000
28.00	0.000	0.000	0.000	0.000	0.000	0.000	0.000	0.000	0.000	0.000	0.000
29.00	0.000	0.000	0.000	0.000	0.000	0.000	0.000	0.000	0.000	0.000	0.000
30.00	0.000	0.000	0.000	0.000	0.000	0.000	0.000	0.000	0.000	0.000	0.000

λ \ x	11	12	13	14	15	16	17	18	19	20	21
3.80	0.999	1.000	1.000	1.000	1.000	1.000	1.000	1.000	1.000	1.000	1.000
3.90	0.999	1.000	1.000	1.000	1.000	1.000	1.000	1.000	1.000	1.000	1.000
4.00	0.999	1.000	1.000	1.000	1.000	1.000	1.000	1.000	1.000	1.000	1.000
4.10	0.999	1.000	1.000	1.000	1.000	1.000	1.000	1.000	1.000	1.000	1.000
4.20	0.999	1.000	1.000	1.000	1.000	1.000	1.000	1.000	1.000	1.000	1.000
4.30	0.998	0.999	1.000	1.000	1.000	1.000	1.000	1.000	1.000	1.000	1.000
4.40	0.998	0.999	1.000	1.000	1.000	1.000	1.000	1.000	1.000	1.000	1.000
4.50	0.998	0.999	1.000	1.000	1.000	1.000	1.000	1.000	1.000	1.000	1.000
4.60	0.997	0.999	1.000	1.000	1.000	1.000	1.000	1.000	1.000	1.000	1.000
4.70	0.997	0.999	1.000	1.000	1.000	1.000	1.000	1.000	1.000	1.000	1.000
4.80	0.996	0.999	1.000	1.000	1.000	1.000	1.000	1.000	1.000	1.000	1.000
4.90	0.995	0.998	0.999	1.000	1.000	1.000	1.000	1.000	1.000	1.000	1.000
5.00	0.995	0.998	0.999	1.000	1.000	1.000	1.000	1.000	1.000	1.000	1.000
5.10	0.994	0.998	0.999	1.000	1.000	1.000	1.000	1.000	1.000	1.000	1.000
5.20	0.993	0.997	0.999	1.000	1.000	1.000	1.000	1.000	1.000	1.000	1.000
5.30	0.992	0.997	0.999	1.000	1.000	1.000	1.000	1.000	1.000	1.000	1.000
5.40	0.990	0.996	0.999	1.000	1.000	1.000	1.000	1.000	1.000	1.000	1.000
5.50	0.989	0.996	0.998	0.999	1.000	1.000	1.000	1.000	1.000	1.000	1.000
5.60	0.988	0.995	0.998	0.999	1.000	1.000	1.000	1.000	1.000	1.000	1.000

λ \ x	11	12	13	14	15	16	17	18	19	20	21
5.70	0.986	0.994	0.998	0.999	1.000	1.000	1.000	1.000	1.000	1.000	1.000
5.80	0.984	0.993	0.997	0.999	1.000	1.000	1.000	1.000	1.000	1.000	1.000
5.90	0.982	0.992	0.997	0.999	1.000	1.000	1.000	1.000	1.000	1.000	1.000
6.00	0.980	0.991	0.996	0.999	0.999	1.000	1.000	1.000	1.000	1.000	1.000
6.10	0.978	0.990	0.996	0.998	0.999	1.000	1.000	1.000	1.000	1.000	1.000
6.20	0.975	0.989	0.995	0.998	0.999	1.000	1.000	1.000	1.000	1.000	1.000
6.30	0.972	0.987	0.995	0.998	0.999	1.000	1.000	1.000	1.000	1.000	1.000
6.40	0.969	0.986	0.994	0.997	0.999	1.000	1.000	1.000	1.000	1.000	1.000
6.50	0.966	0.984	0.993	0.997	0.999	1.000	1.000	1.000	1.000	1.000	1.000
6.60	0.963	0.982	0.992	0.997	0.999	0.999	1.000	1.000	1.000	1.000	1.000
6.70	0.959	0.980	0.991	0.996	0.998	0.999	1.000	1.000	1.000	1.000	1.000
6.80	0.955	0.978	0.990	0.996	0.998	0.999	1.000	1.000	1.000	1.000	1.000
6.90	0.951	0.976	0.989	0.995	0.998	0.999	1.000	1.000	1.000	1.000	1.000
7.00	0.947	0.973	0.987	0.994	0.998	0.999	1.000	1.000	1.000	1.000	1.000
7.10	0.942	0.970	0.986	0.994	0.997	0.999	1.000	1.000	1.000	1.000	1.000
7.20	0.937	0.967	0.984	0.993	0.997	0.999	1.000	1.000	1.000	1.000	1.000
7.30	0.932	0.964	0.982	0.992	0.996	0.999	0.999	1.000	1.000	1.000	1.000
7.40	0.926	0.961	0.980	0.991	0.996	0.998	0.999	1.000	1.000	1.000	1.000
7.50	0.921	0.957	0.978	0.990	0.995	0.998	0.999	1.000	1.000	1.000	1.000
7.60	0.915	0.954	0.976	0.989	0.995	0.998	0.999	1.000	1.000	1.000	1.000
7.70	0.909	0.950	0.974	0.987	0.994	0.997	0.999	1.000	1.000	1.000	1.000
7.80	0.902	0.945	0.971	0.986	0.993	0.997	0.999	1.000	1.000	1.000	1.000
7.90	0.895	0.941	0.969	0.984	0.993	0.997	0.999	0.999	1.000	1.000	1.000
8.00	0.888	0.936	0.966	0.983	0.992	0.996	0.998	0.999	1.000	1.000	1.000
8.10	0.881	0.931	0.963	0.981	0.991	0.996	0.998	0.999	1.000	1.000	1.000
8.20	0.873	0.926	0.960	0.979	0.990	0.995	0.998	0.999	1.000	1.000	1.000
8.30	0.865	0.921	0.956	0.977	0.989	0.995	0.998	0.999	1.000	1.000	1.000
8.40	0.857	0.915	0.952	0.975	0.987	0.994	0.997	0.999	1.000	1.000	1.000
8.50	0.849	0.909	0.949	0.973	0.986	0.993	0.997	0.999	0.999	1.000	1.000
8.60	0.840	0.903	0.945	0.970	0.985	0.993	0.997	0.999	0.999	1.000	1.000
8.70	0.831	0.897	0.940	0.967	0.983	0.992	0.996	0.998	0.999	1.000	1.000
8.80	0.822	0.890	0.936	0.965	0.982	0.991	0.996	0.998	0.999	1.000	1.000
8.90	0.813	0.883	0.931	0.962	0.980	0.990	0.995	0.998	0.999	1.000	1.000
9.00	0.803	0.876	0.926	0.959	0.978	0.989	0.995	0.998	0.999	1.000	1.000
9.10	0.793	0.868	0.921	0.955	0.976	0.988	0.994	0.997	0.999	0.999	1.000
9.20	0.783	0.861	0.916	0.952	0.974	0.987	0.993	0.997	0.999	0.999	1.000
9.30	0.773	0.853	0.910	0.948	0.972	0.985	0.993	0.997	0.998	0.999	1.000
9.40	0.763	0.845	0.904	0.944	0.969	0.984	0.992	0.996	0.998	0.999	1.000
9.50	0.752	0.836	0.898	0.940	0.967	0.982	0.991	0.996	0.998	0.999	1.000
9.60	0.741	0.828	0.892	0.936	0.964	0.981	0.990	0.995	0.998	0.999	1.000
9.70	0.730	0.819	0.885	0.931	0.961	0.979	0.989	0.995	0.998	0.999	1.000

λ \ x	11	12	13	14	15	16	17	18	19	20	21
9.80	0.719	0.810	0.879	0.927	0.958	0.977	0.988	0.994	0.997	0.999	0.999
9.90	0.708	0.801	0.872	0.922	0.955	0.975	0.987	0.993	0.997	0.999	0.999
10.00	0.697	0.792	0.864	0.917	0.951	0.973	0.986	0.993	0.997	0.998	0.999
10.10	0.685	0.782	0.857	0.911	0.948	0.971	0.984	0.992	0.996	0.998	0.999
10.20	0.674	0.772	0.849	0.906	0.944	0.968	0.983	0.991	0.996	0.998	0.999
10.30	0.662	0.762	0.842	0.900	0.940	0.966	0.981	0.990	0.995	0.998	0.999
10.40	0.650	0.752	0.834	0.894	0.936	0.963	0.980	0.989	0.995	0.997	0.999
10.50	0.639	0.742	0.825	0.888	0.932	0.960	0.978	0.988	0.994	0.997	0.999
10.60	0.627	0.732	0.817	0.882	0.927	0.957	0.976	0.987	0.994	0.997	0.999
10.70	0.615	0.721	0.808	0.875	0.923	0.954	0.974	0.986	0.993	0.997	0.998
10.80	0.603	0.710	0.799	0.868	0.918	0.951	0.972	0.985	0.992	0.996	0.998
10.90	0.591	0.700	0.790	0.861	0.913	0.948	0.970	0.984	0.992	0.996	0.998
11.00	0.579	0.689	0.781	0.854	0.907	0.944	0.968	0.982	0.991	0.995	0.998
11.10	0.567	0.678	0.772	0.847	0.902	0.940	0.965	0.981	0.990	0.995	0.997
11.20	0.555	0.667	0.762	0.839	0.896	0.936	0.963	0.979	0.989	0.994	0.997
11.30	0.544	0.655	0.753	0.831	0.891	0.932	0.960	0.978	0.988	0.994	0.997
11.40	0.532	0.644	0.743	0.823	0.885	0.928	0.957	0.976	0.987	0.993	0.997
11.50	0.520	0.633	0.733	0.815	0.878	0.924	0.954	0.974	0.986	0.992	0.996
11.60	0.508	0.622	0.723	0.807	0.872	0.919	0.951	0.972	0.984	0.992	0.996
11.70	0.496	0.610	0.713	0.798	0.865	0.914	0.948	0.970	0.983	0.991	0.995
11.80	0.485	0.599	0.702	0.790	0.859	0.909	0.944	0.967	0.982	0.990	0.995
11.90	0.473	0.587	0.692	0.781	0.852	0.904	0.941	0.965	0.980	0.989	0.994
12.00	0.462	0.576	0.682	0.772	0.844	0.899	0.937	0.963	0.979	0.988	0.994
12.10	0.450	0.565	0.671	0.763	0.837	0.893	0.933	0.960	0.977	0.987	0.993
12.20	0.439	0.553	0.660	0.754	0.830	0.887	0.929	0.957	0.975	0.986	0.993
12.30	0.428	0.542	0.650	0.744	0.822	0.882	0.925	0.954	0.973	0.985	0.992
12.40	0.417	0.530	0.639	0.735	0.814	0.876	0.920	0.951	0.971	0.984	0.991
12.50	0.406	0.519	0.628	0.725	0.806	0.869	0.916	0.948	0.969	0.983	0.991
12.60	0.395	0.508	0.617	0.715	0.798	0.863	0.911	0.945	0.967	0.981	0.990
12.70	0.384	0.496	0.606	0.705	0.790	0.856	0.906	0.941	0.965	0.980	0.989
12.80	0.374	0.485	0.595	0.695	0.781	0.850	0.901	0.938	0.963	0.978	0.988
12.90	0.363	0.474	0.584	0.685	0.772	0.843	0.896	0.934	0.960	0.977	0.987
13.00	0.353	0.463	0.573	0.675	0.764	0.835	0.890	0.930	0.957	0.975	0.986
13.10	0.343	0.452	0.562	0.665	0.755	0.828	0.885	0.926	0.955	0.973	0.985
13.20	0.333	0.441	0.551	0.655	0.746	0.821	0.879	0.922	0.952	0.971	0.984
13.30	0.323	0.431	0.540	0.644	0.736	0.813	0.873	0.918	0.949	0.969	0.982
13.40	0.314	0.420	0.529	0.634	0.727	0.805	0.867	0.913	0.945	0.967	0.981
13.50	0.304	0.409	0.518	0.623	0.718	0.798	0.861	0.908	0.942	0.965	0.980
13.60	0.295	0.399	0.507	0.613	0.708	0.789	0.854	0.904	0.939	0.963	0.978
13.70	0.286	0.389	0.497	0.602	0.699	0.781	0.848	0.899	0.935	0.960	0.976
13.80	0.277	0.378	0.486	0.592	0.689	0.773	0.841	0.893	0.931	0.958	0.975

λ \ x	11	12	13	14	15	16	17	18	19	20	21
13.90	0.269	0.368	0.475	0.581	0.679	0.765	0.834	0.888	0.928	0.955	0.973
14.00	0.260	0.358	0.464	0.570	0.669	0.756	0.827	0.883	0.923	0.952	0.971
14.10	0.252	0.349	0.454	0.560	0.659	0.747	0.820	0.877	0.919	0.949	0.969
14.20	0.244	0.339	0.443	0.549	0.649	0.738	0.813	0.871	0.915	0.946	0.967
14.30	0.236	0.330	0.433	0.539	0.639	0.729	0.805	0.865	0.911	0.943	0.965
14.40	0.228	0.320	0.423	0.528	0.629	0.720	0.797	0.859	0.906	0.940	0.963
14.50	0.220	0.311	0.413	0.518	0.619	0.711	0.790	0.853	0.901	0.936	0.960
14.60	0.213	0.302	0.402	0.507	0.609	0.702	0.782	0.847	0.896	0.933	0.958
14.70	0.205	0.293	0.392	0.497	0.599	0.693	0.774	0.840	0.891	0.929	0.955
14.80	0.198	0.285	0.383	0.486	0.589	0.683	0.766	0.833	0.886	0.925	0.953
14.90	0.191	0.276	0.373	0.476	0.578	0.674	0.757	0.826	0.881	0.921	0.950
15.00	0.185	0.268	0.363	0.466	0.568	0.664	0.749	0.819	0.875	0.917	0.947
16.00	0.127	0.193	0.275	0.368	0.467	0.566	0.659	0.742	0.812	0.868	0.911
17.00	0.085	0.135	0.201	0.281	0.371	0.468	0.564	0.655	0.736	0.805	0.861
18.00	0.055	0.092	0.143	0.208	0.287	0.375	0.469	0.562	0.651	0.731	0.799
19.00	0.035	0.061	0.098	0.150	0.215	0.292	0.378	0.469	0.561	0.647	0.725
20.00	0.021	0.039	0.066	0.105	0.157	0.221	0.297	0.381	0.470	0.559	0.644
21.00	0.013	0.025	0.043	0.072	0.111	0.163	0.227	0.302	0.384	0.471	0.558
22.00	0.008	0.015	0.028	0.048	0.077	0.117	0.169	0.232	0.306	0.387	0.472
23.00	0.004	0.009	0.017	0.031	0.052	0.082	0.123	0.175	0.238	0.310	0.389
24.00	0.003	0.005	0.011	0.020	0.034	0.056	0.087	0.128	0.180	0.243	0.314
25.00	0.001	0.003	0.006	0.012	0.022	0.038	0.060	0.092	0.134	0.185	0.247
26.00	0.001	0.002	0.004	0.008	0.014	0.025	0.041	0.065	0.097	0.139	0.190
27.00	0.000	0.001	0.002	0.005	0.009	0.016	0.027	0.044	0.069	0.101	0.144
28.00	0.000	0.001	0.001	0.003	0.005	0.010	0.018	0.030	0.048	0.073	0.106
29.00	0.000	0.000	0.001	0.002	0.003	0.006	0.012	0.020	0.033	0.051	0.077
30.00	0.000	0.000	0.000	0.001	0.002	0.004	0.007	0.013	0.022	0.035	0.054

λ \ x	22	23	24	25	26	27	28	29	30	31	32
10.40	0.999	1.000	1.000	1.000	1.000	1.000	1.000	1.000	1.000	1.000	1.000
10.50	0.999	1.000	1.000	1.000	1.000	1.000	1.000	1.000	1.000	1.000	1.000
10.60	0.999	1.000	1.000	1.000	1.000	1.000	1.000	1.000	1.000	1.000	1.000
10.70	0.999	1.000	1.000	1.000	1.000	1.000	1.000	1.000	1.000	1.000	1.000
10.80	0.999	1.000	1.000	1.000	1.000	1.000	1.000	1.000	1.000	1.000	1.000
10.90	0.999	1.000	1.000	1.000	1.000	1.000	1.000	1.000	1.000	1.000	1.000
11.00	0.999	1.000	1.000	1.000	1.000	1.000	1.000	1.000	1.000	1.000	1.000
11.10	0.999	0.999	1.000	1.000	1.000	1.000	1.000	1.000	1.000	1.000	1.000
11.20	0.999	0.999	1.000	1.000	1.000	1.000	1.000	1.000	1.000	1.000	1.000
11.30	0.999	0.999	1.000	1.000	1.000	1.000	1.000	1.000	1.000	1.000	1.000

λ \ x	22	23	24	25	26	27	28	29	30	31	32
11.40	0.998	0.999	1.000	1.000	1.000	1.000	1.000	1.000	1.000	1.000	1.000
11.50	0.998	0.999	1.000	1.000	1.000	1.000	1.000	1.000	1.000	1.000	1.000
11.60	0.998	0.999	1.000	1.000	1.000	1.000	1.000	1.000	1.000	1.000	1.000
11.70	0.998	0.999	1.000	1.000	1.000	1.000	1.000	1.000	1.000	1.000	1.000
11.80	0.998	0.999	0.999	1.000	1.000	1.000	1.000	1.000	1.000	1.000	1.000
11.90	0.997	0.999	0.999	1.000	1.000	1.000	1.000	1.000	1.000	1.000	1.000
12.00	0.997	0.999	0.999	1.000	1.000	1.000	1.000	1.000	1.000	1.000	1.000
12.10	0.997	0.998	0.999	1.000	1.000	1.000	1.000	1.000	1.000	1.000	1.000
12.20	0.996	0.998	0.999	1.000	1.000	1.000	1.000	1.000	1.000	1.000	1.000
12.30	0.996	0.998	0.999	1.000	1.000	1.000	1.000	1.000	1.000	1.000	1.000
12.40	0.996	0.998	0.999	1.000	1.000	1.000	1.000	1.000	1.000	1.000	1.000
12.50	0.995	0.998	0.999	0.999	1.000	1.000	1.000	1.000	1.000	1.000	1.000
12.60	0.995	0.997	0.999	0.999	1.000	1.000	1.000	1.000	1.000	1.000	1.000
12.70	0.994	0.997	0.999	0.999	1.000	1.000	1.000	1.000	1.000	1.000	1.000
12.80	0.994	0.997	0.998	0.999	1.000	1.000	1.000	1.000	1.000	1.000	1.000
12.90	0.993	0.996	0.998	0.999	1.000	1.000	1.000	1.000	1.000	1.000	1.000
13.00	0.992	0.996	0.998	0.999	1.000	1.000	1.000	1.000	1.000	1.000	1.000
13.10	0.992	0.996	0.998	0.999	0.999	1.000	1.000	1.000	1.000	1.000	1.000
13.20	0.991	0.995	0.998	0.999	0.999	1.000	1.000	1.000	1.000	1.000	1.000
13.30	0.990	0.995	0.997	0.999	0.999	1.000	1.000	1.000	1.000	1.000	1.000
13.40	0.989	0.994	0.997	0.999	0.999	1.000	1.000	1.000	1.000	1.000	1.000
13.50	0.989	0.994	0.997	0.998	0.999	1.000	1.000	1.000	1.000	1.000	1.000
13.60	0.988	0.993	0.996	0.998	0.999	1.000	1.000	1.000	1.000	1.000	1.000
13.70	0.987	0.993	0.996	0.998	0.999	1.000	1.000	1.000	1.000	1.000	1.000
13.80	0.986	0.992	0.996	0.998	0.999	0.999	1.000	1.000	1.000	1.000	1.000
13.90	0.984	0.991	0.995	0.998	0.999	0.999	1.000	1.000	1.000	1.000	1.000
14.00	0.983	0.991	0.995	0.997	0.999	0.999	1.000	1.000	1.000	1.000	1.000
14.10	0.982	0.990	0.995	0.997	0.999	0.999	1.000	1.000	1.000	1.000	1.000
14.20	0.981	0.989	0.994	0.997	0.998	0.999	1.000	1.000	1.000	1.000	1.000
14.30	0.979	0.988	0.994	0.997	0.998	0.999	1.000	1.000	1.000	1.000	1.000
14.40	0.978	0.987	0.993	0.996	0.998	0.999	1.000	1.000	1.000	1.000	1.000
14.50	0.976	0.986	0.992	0.996	0.998	0.999	0.999	1.000	1.000	1.000	1.000
14.60	0.975	0.985	0.992	0.996	0.998	0.999	0.999	1.000	1.000	1.000	1.000
14.70	0.973	0.984	0.991	0.995	0.997	0.999	0.999	1.000	1.000	1.000	1.000
14.80	0.971	0.983	0.990	0.995	0.997	0.999	0.999	1.000	1.000	1.000	1.000
14.90	0.969	0.982	0.990	0.994	0.997	0.998	0.999	1.000	1.000	1.000	1.000
15.00	0.967	0.981	0.989	0.994	0.997	0.998	0.999	1.000	1.000	1.000	1.000
16.00	0.942	0.963	0.978	0.987	0.993	0.996	0.998	0.999	0.999	1.000	1.000
17.00	0.905	0.937	0.959	0.975	0.985	0.991	0.995	0.997	0.999	0.999	1.000
18.00	0.855	0.899	0.932	0.955	0.972	0.983	0.990	0.994	0.997	0.998	0.999
19.00	0.793	0.849	0.893	0.927	0.951	0.969	0.980	0.988	0.993	0.996	0.998

λ \ x	22	23	24	25	26	27	28	29	30	31	32
20.00	0.721	0.787	0.843	0.888	0.922	0.948	0.966	0.978	0.987	0.992	0.995
21.00	0.640	0.716	0.782	0.838	0.883	0.917	0.944	0.963	0.976	0.985	0.991
22.00	0.556	0.637	0.712	0.777	0.832	0.877	0.913	0.940	0.959	0.973	0.983
23.00	0.472	0.555	0.635	0.708	0.772	0.827	0.873	0.908	0.936	0.956	0.971
24.00	0.392	0.473	0.554	0.632	0.704	0.768	0.823	0.868	0.904	0.932	0.953
25.00	0.318	0.394	0.473	0.553	0.629	0.700	0.763	0.818	0.863	0.900	0.929
26.00	0.252	0.321	0.396	0.474	0.552	0.627	0.697	0.759	0.813	0.859	0.896
27.00	0.195	0.256	0.324	0.398	0.474	0.551	0.625	0.693	0.755	0.809	0.855
28.00	0.148	0.200	0.260	0.327	0.400	0.475	0.550	0.623	0.690	0.752	0.805
29.00	0.110	0.153	0.204	0.264	0.330	0.401	0.475	0.549	0.621	0.687	0.748
30.00	0.081	0.115	0.157	0.208	0.267	0.333	0.403	0.476	0.548	0.619	0.685

λ \ x	33	34	35	36	37	38	39	40	41	42	43
19.00	0.999	0.999	1.000	1.000	1.000	1.000	1.000	1.000	1.000	1.000	1.000
20.00	0.997	0.999	0.999	1.000	1.000	1.000	1.000	1.000	1.000	1.000	1.000
21.00	0.994	0.997	0.998	0.999	0.999	1.000	1.000	1.000	1.000	1.000	1.000
22.00	0.989	0.994	0.996	0.998	0.999	0.999	1.000	1.000	1.000	1.000	1.000
23.00	0.981	0.988	0.993	0.996	0.997	0.999	0.999	1.000	1.000	1.000	1.000
24.00	0.969	0.979	0.987	0.992	0.995	0.997	0.998	0.999	0.999	1.000	1.000
25.00	0.950	0.966	0.978	0.985	0.991	0.994	0.997	0.998	0.999	0.999	1.000
26.00	0.925	0.947	0.964	0.976	0.984	0.990	0.994	0.996	0.998	0.999	0.999
27.00	0.892	0.921	0.944	0.961	0.974	0.983	0.989	0.993	0.996	0.997	0.998
28.00	0.850	0.888	0.918	0.941	0.959	0.972	0.981	0.988	0.992	0.995	0.997
29.00	0.801	0.846	0.884	0.914	0.938	0.956	0.970	0.979	0.986	0.991	0.994
30.00	0.744	0.797	0.843	0.880	0.911	0.935	0.954	0.968	0.978	0.985	0.990

λ \ x	44	45	46	47	48	49	50
26.00	1.000	1.000	1.000	1.000	1.000	1.000	1.000
27.00	0.999	0.999	1.000	1.000	1.000	1.000	1.000
28.00	0.998	0.999	0.999	1.000	1.000	1.000	1.000
29.00	0.996	0.998	0.999	0.999	1.000	1.000	1.000
30.00	0.994	0.996	0.998	0.999	0.999	0.999	1.000

TABLE 11
Estimated *RSQ* Shrinkage Values

Shrinkage Based Upon 5 to 1 Ratio Plus 5 for the Pot

		Observed *RSQ* Values								
n	***k***	**0.2000**	**0.3000**	**0.4000**	**0.5000**	**0.6000**	**0.7000**	**0.8000**	**0.9000**	**1.0000**
10	1	0.1000	0.2125	0.3250	0.4375	0.5500	0.6625	0.7750	0.8875	1.0000
15	2	0.0667	0.1833	0.3000	0.4167	0.5333	0.6500	0.7667	0.8833	1.0000
20	3	0.0500	0.1688	0.2875	0.4063	0.5250	0.6438	0.7625	0.8813	1.0000
25	4	0.0400	0.1600	0.2800	0.4000	0.5200	0.6400	0.7600	0.8800	1.0000
30	5	0.0333	0.1542	0.2750	0.3958	0.5167	0.6375	0.7583	0.8792	1.0000
35	6	0.0286	0.1500	0.2714	0.3929	0.5143	0.6357	0.7571	0.8786	1.0000
40	7	0.0250	0.1469	0.2688	0.3906	0.5125	0.6344	0.7563	0.8781	1.0000
45	8	0.0222	0.1444	0.2667	0.3889	0.5111	0.6333	0.7556	0.8778	1.0000
50	9	0.0200	0.1425	0.2650	0.3875	0.5100	0.6325	0.7550	0.8775	1.0000
55	10	0.0182	0.1409	0.2636	0.3864	0.5091	0.6318	0.7545	0.8773	1.0000
105	20	0.0095	0.1333	0.2571	0.3810	0.5048	0.6286	0.7524	0.8762	1.0000
155	30	0.0065	0.1306	0.2548	0.3790	0.5032	0.6274	0.7516	0.8758	1.0000
205	40	0.0049	0.1293	0.2537	0.3780	0.5024	0.6268	0.7512	0.8756	1.0000
255	50	0.0039	0.1284	0.2529	0.3775	0.5020	0.6265	0.7510	0.8755	1.0000

Shrinkage Based Upon 10 to 1 Ratio Plus 10 for the Pot

		Observed *RSQ* Values								
n	***k***	**0.2000**	**0.3000**	**0.4000**	**0.5000**	**0.6000**	**0.7000**	**0.8000**	**0.9000**	**1.0000**
20	1	0.1556	0.2611	0.3667	0.4722	0.5778	0.6833	0.7889	0.8944	1.0000
30	2	0.1407	0.2481	0.3556	0.4630	0.5704	0.6778	0.7852	0.8926	1.0000
40	3	0.1333	0.2417	0.3500	0.4583	0.5667	0.6750	0.7833	0.8917	1.0000
50	4	0.1289	0.2378	0.3467	0.4556	0.5644	0.6733	0.7822	0.8911	1.0000
60	5	0.1259	0.2352	0.3444	0.4537	0.5630	0.6722	0.7815	0.8907	1.0000
70	6	0.1238	0.2333	0.3429	0.4524	0.5619	0.6714	0.7810	0.8905	1.0000
80	7	0.1222	0.2319	0.3417	0.4514	0.5611	0.6708	0.7806	0.8903	1.0000
90	8	0.1210	0.2309	0.3407	0.4506	0.5605	0.6704	0.7802	0.8901	1.0000
100	9	0.1200	0.2300	0.3400	0.4500	0.5600	0.6700	0.7800	0.8900	1.0000
110	10	0.1192	0.2293	0.3394	0.4495	0.5596	0.6697	0.7798	0.8899	1.0000
210	20	0.1153	0.2259	0.3365	0.4471	0.5577	0.6683	0.7788	0.8894	1.0000
310	30	0.1140	0.2247	0.3355	0.4462	0.5570	0.6677	0.7785	0.8892	1.0000
410	40	0.1133	0.2241	0.3350	0.4458	0.5566	0.6675	0.7783	0.8892	1.0000
510	50	0.1129	0.2237	0.3346	0.4455	0.5564	0.6673	0.7782	0.8891	1.0000

Shrinkage Based Upon 20 to 1 Ratio Plus 20 for the Pot

		Observed *RSQ* Values								
n	*k*	0.2000	0.3000	0.4000	0.5000	0.6000	0.7000	0.8000	0.9000	1.0000
40	1	0.1789	0.2816	0.3842	0.4868	0.5895	0.6921	0.7947	0.8974	1.0000
60	2	0.1719	0.2754	0.3789	0.4825	0.5860	0.6895	0.7930	0.8965	1.0000
80	3	0.1684	0.2724	0.3763	0.4803	0.5842	0.6882	0.7921	0.8961	1.0000
100	4	0.1663	0.2705	0.3747	0.4789	0.5832	0.6874	0.7916	0.8958	1.0000
120	5	0.1649	0.2693	0.3737	0.4781	0.5825	0.6868	0.7912	0.8956	1.0000
140	6	0.1639	0.2684	0.3729	0.4774	0.5820	0.6865	0.7910	0.8955	1.0000
160	7	0.1632	0.2678	0.3724	0.4770	0.5816	0.6862	0.7908	0.8954	1.0000
180	8	0.1626	0.2673	0.3719	0.4766	0.5813	0.6860	0.7906	0.8953	1.0000
200	9	0.1621	0.2668	0.3716	0.4763	0.5811	0.6858	0.7905	0.8953	1.0000
220	10	0.1617	0.2665	0.3713	0.4761	0.5809	0.6856	0.7904	0.8952	1.0000
420	20	0.1599	0.2649	0.3699	0.4749	0.5799	0.6850	0.7900	0.8950	1.0000
620	30	0.1593	0.2643	0.3694	0.4745	0.5796	0.6847	0.7898	0.8949	1.0000
820	40	0.1589	0.2641	0.3692	0.4743	0.5795	0.6846	0.7897	0.8949	1.0000
1020	50	0.1587	0.2639	0.3690	0.4742	0.5794	0.6845	0.7897	0.8948	1.0000

Shrinkage Based Upon 25 to 1 Ratio Plus 25 for the Pot

		Observed *RSQ* Values								
n	*k*	0.2000	0.3000	0.4000	0.5000	0.6000	0.7000	0.8000	0.9000	1.0000
50	1	0.1833	0.2854	0.3875	0.4896	0.5917	0.6938	0.7958	0.8979	1.0000
75	2	0.1778	0.2806	0.3833	0.4861	0.5889	0.6917	0.7944	0.8972	1.0000
100	3	0.1750	0.2781	0.3813	0.4844	0.5875	0.6906	0.7938	0.8969	1.0000
125	4	0.1733	0.2767	0.3800	0.4833	0.5867	0.6900	0.7933	0.8967	1.0000
150	5	0.1722	0.2757	0.3792	0.4826	0.5861	0.6896	0.7931	0.8965	1.0000
175	6	0.1714	0.2750	0.3786	0.4821	0.5857	0.6893	0.7929	0.8964	1.0000
200	7	0.1708	0.2745	0.3781	0.4818	0.5854	0.6891	0.7927	0.8964	1.0000
225	8	0.1704	0.2741	0.3778	0.4815	0.5852	0.6889	0.7926	0.8963	1.0000
250	9	0.1700	0.2738	0.3775	0.4813	0.5850	0.6888	0.7925	0.8963	1.0000
275	10	0.1697	0.2735	0.3773	0.4811	0.5848	0.6886	0.7924	0.8962	1.0000
525	20	0.1683	0.2722	0.3762	0.4802	0.5841	0.6881	0.7921	0.8960	1.0000
775	30	0.1677	0.2718	0.3758	0.4798	0.5839	0.6879	0.7919	0.8960	1.0000
1025	40	0.1675	0.2715	0.3756	0.4797	0.5837	0.6878	0.7919	0.8959	1.0000
1275	50	0.1673	0.2714	0.3755	0.4796	0.5837	0.6877	0.7918	0.8959	1.0000

Shrinkage Based Upon 30 to 1 Ratio Plus 30 for the Pot

n	*k*	Observed *RSQ* Values 0.2000	0.3000	0.4000	0.5000	0.6000	0.7000	0.8000	0.9000	1.0000
60	1	0.1862	0.2879	0.3897	0.4914	0.5931	0.6948	0.7966	0.8983	1.0000
90	2	0.1816	0.2839	0.3862	0.4885	0.5908	0.6931	0.7954	0.8977	1.0000
120	3	0.1793	0.2819	0.3845	0.4871	0.5897	0.6922	0.7948	0.8974	1.0000
150	4	0.1779	0.2807	0.3834	0.4862	0.5890	0.6917	0.7945	0.8972	1.0000
180	5	0.1770	0.2799	0.3828	0.4856	0.5885	0.6914	0.7943	0.8971	1.0000
210	6	0.1764	0.2793	0.3823	0.4852	0.5882	0.6911	0.7941	0.8970	1.0000
240	7	0.1759	0.2789	0.3819	0.4849	0.5879	0.6909	0.7940	0.8970	1.0000
270	8	0.1755	0.2785	0.3816	0.4847	0.5877	0.6908	0.7939	0.8969	1.0000
300	9	0.1752	0.2783	0.3814	0.4845	0.5876	0.6907	0.7938	0.8969	1.0000
330	10	0.1749	0.2781	0.3812	0.4843	0.5875	0.6906	0.7937	0.8969	1.0000
630	20	0.1737	0.2770	0.3803	0.4836	0.5869	0.6901	0.7934	0.8967	1.0000
930	30	0.1733	0.2766	0.3800	0.4833	0.5867	0.6900	0.7933	0.8967	1.0000
1230	40	0.1731	0.2765	0.3798	0.4832	0.5865	0.6899	0.7933	0.8966	1.0000
1530	50	0.1730	0.2763	0.3797	0.4831	0.5865	0.6899	0.7932	0.8966	1.0000

Shrinkage Based Upon 40 to 1 Ratio Plus 40 for the Pot

n	*k*	Observed *RSQ* Values 0.2000	0.3000	0.4000	0.5000	0.6000	0.7000	0.8000	0.9000	1.0000
80	1	0.1897	0.2910	0.3923	0.4936	0.5949	0.6962	0.7974	0.8987	1.0000
120	2	0.1863	0.2880	0.3897	0.4915	0.5932	0.6949	0.7966	0.8983	1.0000
160	3	0.1846	0.2865	0.3885	0.4904	0.5923	0.6942	0.7962	0.8981	1.0000
200	4	0.1836	0.2856	0.3877	0.4897	0.5918	0.6938	0.7959	0.8979	1.0000
240	5	0.1829	0.2850	0.3872	0.4893	0.5915	0.6936	0.7957	0.8979	1.0000
280	6	0.1824	0.2846	0.3868	0.4890	0.5912	0.6934	0.7956	0.8978	1.0000
320	7	0.1821	0.2843	0.3865	0.4888	0.5910	0.6933	0.7955	0.8978	1.0000
360	8	0.1818	0.2840	0.3863	0.4886	0.5909	0.6932	0.7954	0.8977	1.0000
400	9	0.1815	0.2838	0.3862	0.4885	0.5908	0.6931	0.7954	0.8977	1.0000
440	10	0.1814	0.2837	0.3860	0.4883	0.5907	0.6930	0.7953	0.8977	1.0000
840	20	0.1805	0.2829	0.3853	0.4878	0.5902	0.6927	0.7951	0.8976	1.0000
1240	30	0.1801	0.2826	0.3851	0.4876	0.5901	0.6926	0.7950	0.8975	1.0000
1640	40	0.1800	0.2825	0.3850	0.4875	0.5900	0.6925	0.7950	0.8975	1.0000
2040	50	0.1799	0.2824	0.3849	0.4874	0.5899	0.6925	0.7950	0.8975	1.0000

Shrinkage Based Upon 50 to 1 Ratio Plus 50 for the Pot

		Observed *RSQ* Values								
n	*k*	**0.2000**	**0.3000**	**0.4000**	**0.5000**	**0.6000**	**0.7000**	**0.8000**	**0.9000**	**1.0000**
100	1	0.1918	0.2929	0.3939	0.4949	0.5959	0.6969	0.7980	0.8990	1.0000
150	2	0.1891	0.2905	0.3918	0.4932	0.5946	0.6959	0.7973	0.8986	1.0000
200	3	0.1878	0.2893	0.3908	0.4923	0.5939	0.6954	0.7969	0.8985	1.0000
250	4	0.1869	0.2886	0.3902	0.4918	0.5935	0.6951	0.7967	0.8984	1.0000
300	5	0.1864	0.2881	0.3898	0.4915	0.5932	0.6949	0.7966	0.8983	1.0000
350	6	0.1860	0.2878	0.3895	0.4913	0.5930	0.6948	0.7965	0.8983	1.0000
400	7	0.1857	0.2875	0.3893	0.4911	0.5929	0.6946	0.7964	0.8982	1.0000
450	8	0.1855	0.2873	0.3891	0.4909	0.5927	0.6946	0.7964	0.8982	1.0000
500	9	0.1853	0.2871	0.3890	0.4908	0.5927	0.6945	0.7963	0.8982	1.0000
550	10	0.1852	0.2870	0.3889	0.4907	0.5926	0.6944	0.7963	0.8981	1.0000
1050	20	0.1845	0.2864	0.3883	0.4903	0.5922	0.6942	0.7961	0.8981	1.0000
1550	30	0.1842	0.2862	0.3882	0.4901	0.5921	0.6941	0.7961	0.8980	1.0000
2050	40	0.1841	0.2861	0.3881	0.4900	0.5920	0.6940	0.7960	0.8980	1.0000
2550	50	0.1840	0.2860	0.3880	0.4900	0.5920	0.6940	0.7960	0.8980	1.0000

Shrinkage Based Upon 100 to 1 Ratio Plus 100 for the Pot

		Observed *RSQ* Values								
n	*k*	**0.2000**	**0.3000**	**0.4000**	**0.5000**	**0.6000**	**0.7000**	**0.8000**	**0.9000**	**1.0000**
200	1	0.1960	0.2965	0.3970	0.4975	0.5980	0.6985	0.7990	0.8995	1.0000
300	2	0.1946	0.2953	0.3960	0.4966	0.5973	0.6980	0.7987	0.8993	1.0000
400	3	0.1939	0.2947	0.3955	0.4962	0.5970	0.6977	0.7985	0.8992	1.0000
500	4	0.1935	0.2943	0.3952	0.4960	0.5968	0.6976	0.7984	0.8992	1.0000
600	5	0.1933	0.2941	0.3949	0.4958	0.5966	0.6975	0.7983	0.8992	1.0000
700	6	0.1931	0.2939	0.3948	0.4957	0.5965	0.6974	0.7983	0.8991	1.0000
800	7	0.1929	0.2938	0.3947	0.4956	0.5965	0.6973	0.7982	0.8991	1.0000
900	8	0.1928	0.2937	0.3946	0.4955	0.5964	0.6973	0.7982	0.8991	1.0000
1000	9	0.1927	0.2936	0.3945	0.4955	0.5964	0.6973	0.7982	0.8991	1.0000
1100	10	0.1927	0.2936	0.3945	0.4954	0.5963	0.6972	0.7982	0.8991	1.0000
2100	20	0.1923	0.2933	0.3942	0.4952	0.5962	0.6971	0.7981	0.8990	1.0000
3100	30	0.1922	0.2932	0.3941	0.4951	0.5961	0.6971	0.7980	0.8990	1.0000
4100	40	0.1921	0.2931	0.3941	0.4951	0.5961	0.6970	0.7980	0.8990	1.0000
5100	50	0.1921	0.2931	0.3941	0.4950	0.5960	0.6970	0.7980	0.8990	1.0000

APPENDIX D

DATA BASE FOR MIDDLE LEVEL MANAGERS

DATA BASE FOR MIDDLE LEVEL MANAGERS

Examples are used throughout the text to assist the reader in understanding and using the concepts discussed. Many of these examples are taken from a data base developed by the author. These data consist of assessment scores and demographic information on 37 variables pertaining to a number of middle level managers employed in several organizations within the southwestern region of the United States. All of the participants functioned in some managerial capacity within their organization, and all had supervisory experience. The variables are briefly described below, followed by summary statistics and the actual values.

Leadership

LOQ-C. Consideration is one of the most commonly discussed dimensions when assessing an individual's leadership style. The consideration scores included in the middle level manager data are based upon the Leadership Opinion Questionnaire (LOQ) (Fleishman, 1969). LOQ-Consideration (LOQ-C) assesses an individual's perception of how he or she should behave in regard to "friendliness," "mutual trust," "two-way communication," "respect," "approachability," "warmth," "emotional support [on the part of the supervisor to the subordinate]," "concern [for the subordinates' needs],' concern for subordinates' "participation" in decision making, "looking out for the welfare of the group," and "keeping the group abreast of new developments."

LOQ-IS. Initiating structure is a second major dimension widely used when assessing an individual's leadership style. The middle level manager data include initiating structure scores (LOQ-IS) also based upon the LOQ. This dimension measures perceptions of desirable behavior associated with the ability to "organize and define group activities," "define expected roles for each member," "to assign tasks," "plan ahead," "establish work procedures," "strive for production," "clarify expectations," "schedule work assignments," and "achieve organizational goals."

Commitment

ORG COM. Organizational commitment (ORG COM) has been defined by Mowday, Steers, and Porter (1979) in terms of "the relative strength of an individual's identification with and involvement in a particular organization . . . characterized by at least three factors: (1) a strong belief in and acceptance of the organization's goals and values; (2) a willingness to exert considerable effort on behalf of the organization; and (3) a strong desire to maintain membership in the organization" (p. 226). As implied, organizational commitment goes beyond "passive loyalty" to the organization. Those who are high in their commitment to the organization actively demonstrate a willingness to go beyond the requirements of their job in order to enhance the good of the organization. An adapted version of the Mowday, Steers, and Porter commitment scale, was created to assess the commitment of the middle level managers. High scores indicate higher commitment to the organization.

Motivation

N-ACH. The need for achievement (N-ACH) was measured by an adaptation of the Edwards Personal Preference Schedule (Edwards, 1959). It assesses an individual's need for achievement, not the actual realization of that need. N-ACH is defined here as doing "one's part, to be successful, to accomplish tasks requiring skill and effort, to be a recognized authority, to accomplish something of great significance, to do a difficult job well, to solve difficult problems and puzzles, to be able to do things better than others, to write a great novel or play" (Edwards, 1959, p. 11). Higher scores on this scale indicate a higher need for achievement.

N-AFF. The need for affiliation (N-AFF) was measured by another adaptation of the Edwards Personal Preference Schedule. It also only assesses an individual's need, not the realization of that need. N-AFF is defined here as a need "to be loyal to friends, to participate in friendly groups, to do things for friends, to form new friendships, to make as many friends as possible, to share things with friends, to do things with friends rather than alone, to form strong attachments, to write letters to friends" (Edwards, p. 11). Higher scores on this scale indicate a higher need for affiliation.

N-DOM. The need for dominance (N-DOM) was measured by a third adaptation of the Edwards Personal Preference Schedule. As above, it only assesses an individual's need, not the realization of that need. N-DOM is defined here as a need "to argue for one's point of view, to be a leader in groups to which one belongs, to be regarded by others as a leader, to be elected or appointed chair[person] of committees, to make group decisions, to settle arguments and disputes between others, to persuade and influence others to do what one wants, to supervise and direct the actions of others, to tell others how to do their jobs" (Edwards, p. 11). Higher scores on the present scale indicate a higher need for dominance.

Transactional Ego States

TMI-P. In the terminology of transactional analysis (TA), there are three primary ego states: Parent, Adult, and Child (Berne, 1966). According to the theory, while an individual must utilize all three ego states in order to function effectively, each ego state has an appropriate time and place. The Parent is one of these three ego states, and it is usually divided into two sub-states: the Critical Parent and the Nurturing Parent. The Critical Parent is prejudicial, punitive, opinionated, evaluative, judgmental, punishing, and insisting, while the Nurturing Parent is warm, supportive, helping, loving, cuddling, protective, and sympathetic. An adaptation of the Transactional Management Inventory (TMI), developed by David Ward (1974), has been used to assess the three ego states for the middle level managers. Higher scores on the Parent scale (TMI-P) indicate higher orientations in the Parent ego state.

TMI-A. According to transactional analysis, the Adult is the ego state which is concerned with gathering information, analyzing data, storing information for long periods of time, evaluating objectively, operating in an unemotional manner, functioning as the decision maker, translating input, adapting to situations, and working on an objective level. It is often described as the computer within the individual, unemotionally processing data. Higher scores on the Adult scale (TMI-A) indicate higher orientations in the Adult ego state.

TMI-C. The Child is the third of the set of three ego states in transactional analysis. As with the Parent, the Child can function in more than one mode: as either the Natural Child, the Adaptive Child, or the Little Professor. The Natural Child is impulsive, fun loving, warm, self-centered, rebellious, cuddly, affectionate, curious, self-indulgent, has temper tantrums, and sometimes is a spoiled brat. The Adaptive Child is complying, withdrawing, procrastinating, conscientious, quiet, and repressed. The Little Professor is intuitive, creative, manipulative, and possesses a remarkable amount of unschooled wisdom. Higher scores on Child scale (TMI-C) indicate higher orientations in the Child ego state.

Machiavellianism

MACH-R. Machiavellianism is a characteristic associated with the philosophy of Machiavelli, as described in ***The Prince*** and elsewhere (Shea & Beatty, 1983). The scale used for assessing Machiavellian scores for the middle level managers, referred to as the Mach-R scale, measures behavior associated with manipulative activity of an individual in interpersonal relations, emotional detachment, the ability to analyze the situation dispassionately and proceed according to strategy, and the absence of a moralistic view of oneself, others, or interpersonal relations. High scores on this scale tend to indicate an increased view that people in general are manipulatable, while low scores tend to correspond with a personal orientation to others as opposed to an impersonal approach.

Validation

VAL-1. The first Validity measure (VAL-1) used here is a 6-item scale designed to recognize an individual's tendency to provide socially desirable responses. The validity of scores for the middle level managers, especially in regard to the MACH-R, should be questioned for those individuals with extremely high scores on this scale. Those who give responses which are perceived as socially desirable on the VAL-1 (resulting in high scores on this scale) may have higher MACH-R scores than indicated.

VAL-2. The second Validity measure (VAL-2) used here is a 3-item scale also designed to recognize an individual's tendency to provide socially desirable responses. The validity of scores for the middle level managers, especially in regard to ORG COM, should be questioned for those individuals with extremely high scores on this scale. Those who give responses which are perceived as socially desirable on the VAL-2 (resulting in high scores on this scale) may have lower ORG COM scores than indicated.

Similiarity with Colleagues

SIM-SUP. The middle level managers were asked to respond to the following statement on a 7-point Likert scale: "My supervisor and I are similar kinds of people." A response of 7 represents "strongly agree," while a response of 1 represents "strongly disagree." This statement will be referred to as similarity with supervisors (SIM-SUP).

SIM-SUB. The middle level managers were also asked to respond to a 7-point Likert scale concerning their similarity with their subordinates (SIM-SUB). They were asked to evaluate the following statement: "My subordinates and I are similar kinds of people." Again, a response of 7 represents "strongly agree," while a response of 1 represents "strongly disagree."

Leadership as Perceived by Subordinates

SBD-C. Another approach in measuring the leadership styles of managers is to assess the perceptions of subordinates in regard to their supervisors. Thus, employees who reported directly to the middle level managers were asked to rate their supervisors on the same list of items which the supervisors had completed. This modified form is referred to here as the Supervisory Behavior Description (SBD). An SBD-Consideration (SBD-C) scale score was obtained for a subset of each of the supervisor's subordinates. Composite scores were then computed by averaging these subordinates' responses.

SBD-IS. The SBD was also used to assess the perceptions of subordinates in regard to their supervisors on the initiating structure dimension. As above, a composite SBD-Initiating Structure (SBD-IS) scale was computed by averaging responses for a subset of each supervisor's subordinates.

Demographic Variables

GENDER. This variable indicates the gender of the person. A 1 indicates that the participant is a male, while a 2 indicates that the individual is a female.

AGE. This variable indicates the age of the person.

MAR STAT. This variable represents the marital status of the participant at the time of completion of the questionnaire. The key for this variable is as follows: (1) single, (2) married, (3) divorced, (4) separated, and (5) widowed.

CHILDREN. This variable represents the number of children each middle level manager had at the time of the survey.

EDUC. Another demographic characteristic obtained for these individuals was their level of education (EDUC). To assist them in the completion of this item, they were advised that 12 years typically represents the completion of a high school diploma, while a bachelor's degree is usually viewed as a 4-year degree (i.e., 16 years of education).

TIME/ORG. This item represents the length of time each middle level manager has been employed by his or her current organization.

TIME/POS. This item represents the length of time each middle level manager has been employed in his or her present position.

WORK EXP. This item represents the total number of years of work experience each middle level manager has had, based upon all full-time work positions.

 # POSIT. The number of positions each person has held over all jobs is labeled here as # POSIT.

 # ORGS. The number of organizations the individual has been employed by over all work experience is labeled here as # ORGS.

JOB TYPE. In an effort to assess their perceptions of their positions, the participants were asked for their current job titles. The following coding scheme was used: (1) manager, (2) professional, (3) clerical, (4) blue collar, (5) Ph.D. scientist and manager, (6) registered engineer, and (9) other.

 # SUBS. This variable represents the maximum number of subordinates each middle level manager has supervised at any one time.

YRS SUP. This variable represents the number of years of supervisory experience completed by the respondents.

RELIGION. The individuals were asked to indicate their religious affiliation, if they had one, based upon the following scale: (1) Protestant, (2) Catholic, (3) Jewish, (4) Moslem, (5) Hindu, (6) Buddhist, (7) Confucian, (8) any religion not listed above, and (9) no religious orientation.

COUNTRY. Each individual was asked to indicate his or her home country. If they were from the United States, they were asked to indicate their home state. The following elaborate coding scheme was used: (002) Canada, (003) Greenland, (004) Mexico, (005) other North American country, (010) Barbados, (011) Belize, (012) Costa Rica, (013) Cuba, (014) Dominican Republic, (015) El Salvador, (016) Grenada, (017) Guatemala, (018) Haiti, (019) Honduras, (020) Jamaica, (021) Nicaragua, (022) Panama, (023) Puerto Rico, (024) Trinidad and Tobago, (025) other Central American or Antilles country, (030) Argentina, (031) Bolivia, (032) Brazil, (033) Chile, (034) Colombia, (035) Ecuador, (036) Falkland Islands, (037) French Guiana, (038) Guyana, (039) Paraguay, (040) Peru, (041) Surinam, (042) Uruguay, (043) Venezuela, (044) other South American country, (050) Denmark, (051) Finland, (052) Iceland, (053) Norway, (054)

Sweden, (055) other Northern European country, (060) Greece, (061) Italy, (062) Portugal, (063) Spain, (064) other Southern European country, (070) Albania, (071) Bulgaria, (072) Czechoslovakia, (073) East Germany, (074) Hungary, (075) Poland, (076) Romania, (077) Soviet Union, (078) Yugoslavia, (079) other Eastern European country, (080) Austria, (081) Belgium, (082) England, (083) France, (084) West Germany, (085) Ireland, (086) Luxembourg, (087) Netherlands, (088) Northern Ireland, (089) Scotland, (090) Switzerland, (091) Wales, (092) other Western European country, (100) Afghanistan, (101) Bahrain, (102) Cyprus, (103) Iran, (104) Iraq, (105) Israel, (106) Jordan, (107) Kuwait, (108) Lebanon, (109) Oman, (110) Qatar, (111) Saudi Arabia, (112) Syria, (113) Turkey, (114) United Arab Emirates, (115) North Yemen, (116) South Yemen, (117) other Middle East country, (120) Bangladesh, (121) Bhutan, (122) India, (123) Nepal, (124) Pakistan, (125) Sri Lanka, (126) other Southern Asian country, (130) Burma, (131) Indonesia, (132) Kampuchea, (133) Laos, (134) Malaysia, (135) Philippines, (136) Singapore, (137) Thailand, (138) Vietnam, (139) other Southeast Asian country, (140) China, (141) Hong Kong, (142) Japan, (143) North Korea, (144) South Korea, (145) Mongolia, (146) Taiwan, (147) other Eastern Asian country, (150) Algeria, (151) Egypt, (152) Libya, (153) Malta, (154) Morocco, (155) Spanish Sahara, (156) Tunisia, (157) other Northern African country, (160) Burundi, (161) Cameroon, (162) Central African Republic, (163) Chad, (164) Republic of Congo, (165) Dahomey, (166) Djibouti, (167) Equatorial Guinea, (168) Ethiopia, (169) Gabon, (170) Gambia, (171) Ghana, (172) Guinea, (173) Ivory Coast, (174) Kenya, (175) Liberia, (176) Mali, (177) Mauritania, (178) Niger, (179) Nigeria, (180) Port Guinea, (181) Rwanda, (182) Senegal, (183) Sierra Leone, (184) Somalia, (185) Sudan, (186) Tanzania, (187) Togo, (188) Uganda, (189) Upper Volta, (190) Zaire, (191) other Central African country, (200) Angola, (201) Botswana, (202) Lesotho, (203) Malagasy Republic, (204) Malawi, (205) Mozambique, (206) Namibia, (207) South Africa, (208) Swaziland, (209) Zambia, (210) Zimbabwe, (211) other Southern African country, (220) American Samoa, (221) Australia, (222) Fiji, (223) Guam, (224) New Zealand, (225) Papua New Guinea, (226) Western Samoa, (227) other Australian or Oceanic country, (901) Alabama, (902) Alaska, (903) Arizona, (904) Arkansas, (905) California, (906) Colorado, (907) Connecticut, (908) Delaware, (909) Florida, (910) Georgia, (911) Hawaii, (912) Idaho, (913) Illinois, (914) Indiana, (915) Iowa, (916) Kansas, (917) Kentucky, (918) Louisiana, (919) Maine, (920) Maryland, (921) Massachusetts, (922) Michigan, (923) Minnesota, (924) Mississippi, (925) Missouri, (926) Montana, (927) Nebraska, (928) Nevada, (929) New Hampshire, (930) New Jersey, (931) New Mexico, (932) New York, (933) North Carolina, (934) North Dakota, (935) Ohio, (936) Oklahoma, (937) Oregon, (938) Pennsylvania, (939) Rhode Island, (940) South Carolina, (941) South Dakota, (942) Tennessee, (943) Texas, (944) Utah, (945) Vermont, (946) Virginia, (947) Washington, (948) West Virginia, (949) Wisconsin, (950) Wyoming, (951) U.S. But unknown, (952) unknown but not U.S., and (953) unknown.

Organizational Climate

The perceived climate within the organization for each of the middle level managers was assessed by using an instrument adapted from Likert's research (1967) on organizations. In his classification scheme, the System 1 approach, often referred to as exploitive, authoritative, or autocratic management, is generally considered the least effective. The System 2 approach, where supervision is paternalistic or benevolent-authoritative, is viewed as a slight improvement upon the System 1 approach. Yet, control is still very strict, and authority is not delegated downward. The System 3 approach moves away from the authoritative style of management to the consultative style of management, where management accepts participative input from employees but retains control of final decisions. Surveys conducted in metropolitan areas of the United States suggest that most companies participating in these surveys fall within the System 3 category. Likert's research has also found that organizations with open communication which flows freely from top to bottom, bottom to top, and horizontally, tend to be the most successful. These organizations usually fit into the System 4 classification, where the team is emphasized, with participative management practiced by supervisors. Such supervisors in System 4 organizations tend to be democratic, give direction, provide for participation, make decisions by consensus and/or by majority, as well as effectively consulting with those concerned with the activities regarding the job.

Each middle level manager was asked to assess leadership characteristics of his or her organization, using items adapted from Likert's organizational climate research described above. Scores on this scale, referred to as **CLI-LEAD**, can range from 1 to 16, where 1 represents an extremely System 1 climate and 16 represents an extremely System 4 climate. The managers were also asked to assess their perceptions of the motivational climate **(CLI-MOT)**, communication format **(CLI-CMMN)**, decision-making orientation **(CLI-DEC)**, goal orientation **(CLI-GOAL)**, and level of control **(CLI-CON)** exhibited within their organizations.

It should be pointed out that not all variables are as useful (from sampling and statistical perspectives) as would be desired. For example, the vast majority of participants classified their JOB TYPE as manager, with a few classifying themselves as professional. Very few responded in any other category. Further, almost all of the participants claimed the United States as their home country; and many of those did not indicate their home state. Also, most of the respondents are Christians (either Protestant or Catholic). Nevertheless, the data base can be used to illustrate many of the concepts discussed.

MIDDLE LEVEL MANAGERS
VARIABLE LABELS

1. LOQ-Consideration
2. LOQ-Initiating Structure
3. Organizational Commitment
4. N-Achievement
5. N-Affiliation
6. N-Dominance
7. TMI-Parent
8. TMI-Adult
9. TMI-Child
10. Mach-R
11. Validity Check-1
12. Validity Check-2
13. Similar to Supervisors
14. Similar to Subordinates
15. Sbd-Consideration
16. Sbd-Initiating Structure
17. Gender
18. Age
19. Marital Status
20. Number of Children
21. Years of Education
22. Time with Organization
23. Time in Position
24. Years of Work Experience
25. Number of Positions Held
26. Number of Organizations Worked for
27. Job Type
28. Number of Subordinates
29. Number of Years of Supervisory Experience
30. Religion
31. Home Country
32. Leadership Climate
33. Motivation Climate
34. Communication Climate
35. Decisions Climate
36. Goals Climate
37. Control Climate

MIDDLE LEVEL MANAGERS
VARIABLE SUMMARIES

Variable Number	*Variable Name*	*Raw Count*	*Sample Mean*	*Sample Variance*	*Sample S.D.*	*Min Value*	*Max Value*
1	LOQ-C	151.00	55.06	35.18	5.93	40.00	69.00
2	LOQ-IS	151.00	47.03	37.05	6.09	34.00	65.00
3	ORG COM	151.00	79.66	195.55	13.98	34.00	103.00
4	N-ACH	151.00	17.93	12.61	3.55	8.00	27.00
5	N-AFF	151.00	12.12	13.03	3.61	4.00	21.00
6	N-DOM	151.00	18.11	18.63	4.32	6.00	26.00
7	TMI-P	151.00	8.46	3.33	1.82	4.00	14.00
8	TMI-A	151.00	11.67	2.28	1.51	7.00	14.00
9	TMI-C	151.00	7.01	2.81	1.68	1.00	11.00
10	MACH-R	151.00	97.26	360.89	19.00	55.00	146.00
11	VAL-1	151.00	19.54	34.74	5.89	6.00	34.00
12	VAL-2	151.00	12.50	12.92	3.59	1.00	20.00
13	SIM-SUP	151.00	3.87	4.22	2.05	1.00	7.00
14	SIM-SUB	151.00	4.60	2.23	1.49	1.00	7.00
15	SBD-C	151.00	51.81	31.41	5.60	37.00	64.00
16	SBD-IS	151.00	42.69	28.50	5.34	29.00	64.00
17	GENDER	151.00	1.21	0.16	0.41	1.00	2.00
18	AGE	151.00	40.44	59.02	7.68	25.00	62.00
19	MAR STAT	151.00	1.98	0.33	0.57	1.00	5.00
20	CHILDREN	151.00	1.41	1.87	1.37	0.00	9.00
21	EDUC	151.00	15.71	3.39	1.84	11.00	22.00
22	TIME/ORG	151.00	10.42	49.39	7.03	0.00	34.00
23	TIME/POS	151.00	2.26	5.17	2.27	0.00	16.00
24	WORK EXP	151.00	19.36	55.90	7.48	3.00	37.00
25	# POSITIONS	151.00	8.00	8.63	2.94	1.00	18.00
26	# ORGS	151.00	3.75	3.08	1.75	1.00	8.00
27	JOB TYPE	151.00	1.64	2.68	1.64	1.00	9.00
28	# SUBS	151.00	57.50	8822.29	93.93	0.00	650.00
29	YRS SUP	151.00	8.68	34.11	5.84	0.00	26.00
30	RELIGION	151.00	3.03	9.27	3.05	1.00	9.00
31	COUNTRY	151.00	888.06	35385.83	188.11	23.00	951.00
32	CLI-LEAD	151.00	11.34	5.19	2.28	4.00	15.00
33	CLI-MOT	151.00	10.39	8.63	2.94	3.00	16.00
34	CLI-CMMN	151.00	10.07	4.44	2.11	6.00	15.00
35	CLI-DEC	151.00	9.66	5.96	2.44	3.00	15.00
36	CLI-GOAL	151.00	9.64	7.17	2.68	3.00	16.00
37	CLI-CON	151.00	9.86	5.72	2.39	4.00	16.00

FREQUENCIES FOR VARIOUS DEMOGRAPHIC CATEGORIES

Gender		*Marital Status*		*Job Type*	
(1) Male	120	(1) Single	22	(1) Manager	103
(2) Female	31	(2) Married	113	(2) Professional	40
		(3) Divorced	14	(3) Clerical	0
		(4) Separated	1	(4) Blue collar	0
		(5) Widowed	1	(5) Ph.D. Scientist and manager	1
				(6) Registered	1
				engineer	1
				(9) Other	6

Religion		*Home Country*		
(1) Protestant	68	(23)	Puerto Rico	1
(2) Catholic	44	(82)	England	2
(3) Jewish	5	(87)	Netherlands	1
(4) Moslem	3	(103)	Iran	1
(5) Hindu	0	(135)	Philippines	1
(6) Buddhist	0	(140)	China	1
(7) Confucian	0	(146)	Taiwan	1
(8) Other	4	(901-999)	USA	143
(9) None	27			

MIDDLE LEVEL MANAGERS

ID	1	2	3	4	5	6	7	8	9	10	11	12	13	14	15	16	17	18	19	20	21	22	23	24	25	26	27	28	29	30	31	32	33	34	35	36	37
1	43	41	45	20	11	23	12	10	8	126	22	10	2	6	48	36	1	62	2	2	16	27	2	36	7	2	1	8	23	1	915	9	9	8	9	9	9
2	48	52	88	18	15	22	14	7	11	118	32	13	3	3	48	38	1	40	2	3	12	5	1	17	10	5	6	6	1	2	135	12	7	10	10	7	10
3	57	46	84	16	15	21	6	14	5	109	29	10	5	5	52	39	1	34	2	0	16	5	3	18	8	5	1	25	5	9	935	13	14	12	13	12	10
4	50	47	66	16	9	20	8	12	7	107	25	11	2	6	51	41	1	57	2	3	20	23	1	26	6	2	1	14	10	1	913	12	12	12	11	9	10
5	52	54	97	14	11	14	9	11	8	103	12	14	2	2	48	48	1	44	2	3	14	21	1	25	6	3	1	300	9	1	905	12	9	11	10	8	7
6	54	53	77	22	14	26	7	13	6	101	15	9	1	6	52	42	1	50	2	3	14	28	1	31	11	2	2	380	25	1	925	5	7	7	5	6	6
7	55	50	99	17	13	19	11	10	8	96	23	16	6	6	53	43	1	45	2	3	12	20	1	26	5	2	1	123	17	1	923	12	12	12	9	10	9
8	61	56	90	10	12	21	5	14	7	92	22	14	1	7	57	44	1	48	2	3	15	22	4	29	8	1	1	400	12	2	950	14	11	13	12	13	11
9	51	53	51	20	10	16	8	12	8	87	16	13	6	4	49	44	1	51	2	3	19	18	1	24	5	2	1	10	16	1	938	8	4	6	4	5	4
10	47	44	73	16	5	8	6	14	4	86	18	11	3	3	48	46	2	38	2	0	16	5	2	19	9	7	9	1	0	2	903	13	10	11	11	9	9
11	57	50	80	17	15	22	8	13	6	82	22	10	1	5	53	42	1	40	2	2	17	9	5	16	9	7	1	15	10	1	922	12	12	11	10	7	8
12	64	44	92	20	13	20	9	12	7	81	19	10	2	5	56	44	1	45	3	4	20	3	3	25	14	2	1	108	24	2	923	11	14	12	13	13	12
13	64	47	59	23	17	21	9	11	7	78	9	15	6	5	55	44	1	34	2	2	17	2	2	11	6	3	1	11	7	1	922	14	13	10	14	12	14
14	54	50	99	12	7	21	8	11	9	72	34	17	5	3	51	44	1	44	2	2	12	25	1	27	5	2	1	188	16	1	949	13	12	13	10	14	13
15	69	52	86	17	11	10	5	14	7	70	31	10	2	5	56	46	1	38	1	0	16	10	2	16	7	4	1	7	4	1	932	13	9	10	11	11	10
16	61	44	82	8	15	18	7	14	3	66	28	16	1	5	54	42	1	44	2	4	16	23	2	28	6	4	1	26	9	1	932	14	15	12	12	13	13
17	56	42	91	15	15	21	9	13	3	65	28	14	6	5	53	40	1	39	2	3	12	11	1	21	13	5	1	28	12	1	935	12	10	12	12	8	12
18	61	50	84	19	12	20	7	12	8	102	21	10	6	6	54	43	2	33	2	0	16	7	1	7	6	3	1	2	1	1	943	8	11	9	9	11	9
19	48	42	86	19	10	13	9	11	8	104	23	13	4	5	51	41	1	43	2	2	14	3	1	17	3	2	1	8	15	2	927	11	13	13	11	10	10
20	58	47	99	18	12	17	11	9	11	88	20	16	6	3	53	44	1	47	2	2	14	17	1	28	14	2	1	63	4	2	901	14	14	11	11	6	11
21	50	51	77	14	12	11	8	12	6	73	20	10	1	6	51	44	2	36	5	0	15	2	2	19	8	4	1	5	8	2	932	14	11	8	8	10	9
22	54	38	66	13	9	8	7	12	8	100	18	12	5	2	50	43	1	38	2	2	14	20	1	25	7	4	1	36	4	2	926	14	15	9	8	8	8
23	61	40	83	18	5	19	10	10	8	96	26	16	4	5	55	44	1	26	1	0	16	1	2	10	6	4	9	60	2	3	907	13	12	10	10	11	11
24	53	44	61	17	17	16	9	10	9	128	17	12	4	4	50	39	1	39	2	2	15	13	1	25	8	6	2	18	3	1	936	10	8	7	7	7	10
25	42	50	76	16	14	14	9	10	10	102	23	14	1	5	47	41	1	41	2	3	18	17	1	19	8	2	1	12	8	1	914	9	7	9	9	9	10
26	55	49	96	20	12	23	8	12	7	82	26	19	3	5	53	42	1	42	2	3	18	1	1	21	8	2	1	150	21	9	932	12	13	11	11	12	11
27	63	48	91	19	10	15	6	13	7	107	20	12	6	2	52	46	1	31	3	0	16	1	0	8	8	3	1	15	1	9	905	11	11	9	10	10	7
28	56	45	84	17	14	18	9	11	8	91	15	12	3	4	51	43	1	60	2	5	19	19	9	30	10	1	9	15	18	2	82	12	10	11	11	12	13
29	59	43	88	26	10	23	8	11	10	128	15	10	6	6	53	43	1	35	1	0	21	0	3	13	4	3	1	25	3	9	938	14	13	12	13	14	12
30	45	54	60	17	7	18	11	10	6	95	18	10	1	6	50	43	2	35	2	0	14	16	1	16	8	1	1	10	5	9	905	8	6	7	5	3	4
31	51	57	83	12	17	14	10	12	5	95	19	12	3	2	49	43	1	42	2	0	16	17	1	19	5	2	1	3	5	2	932	10	9	11	12	10	11
32	52	54	95	19	18	24	9	11	8	80	20	20	7	6	52	41	1	57	2	3	17	10	4	30	10	5	1	40	10	1	925	13	14	11	9	10	11
33	60	58	79	22	12	22	7	13	7	105	25	18	3	5	54	43	1	55	2	9	16	26	4	30	10	2	1	650	24	2	932	12	11	10	10	10	11
34	62	47	78	25	15	24	5	13	8	115	25	9	2	2	53	40	1	34	2	1	16	2	2	12	3	4	1	18	8	9	925	12	8	7	7	8	7
35	61	47	83	19	13	12	8	12	8	90	18	15	7	6	55	44	1	28	1	0	16	1	1	10	14	4	2	65	3	9	942	15	15	14	13	14	14
36	52	54	80	15	18	22	8	13	6	88	16	10	4	4	51	41	1	47	2	3	18	15	5	30	10	4	1	120	20	1	82	10	9	9	8	9	10
37	59	57	94	16	16	22	6	14	4	62	34	19	5	3	52	43	1	50	2	1	15	8	6	27	12	3	1	120	20	9	916	10	9	10	10	11	10
38	56	53	58	19	11	19	9	12	7	98	26	13	1	5	52	45	1	29	3	0	22	5	3	8	6	2	1	10	3	2	932	13	11	12	10	11	10
39	58	35	89	18	14	19	9	12	7	101	18	19	6	6	54	29	1	57	2	4	16	16	10	36	10	6	1	15	20	2	949	13	14	13	11	12	13
40	58	52	61	14	10	13	8	12	7	73	19	12	1	5	59	46	2	30	2	0	16	5	1	9	6	3	2	7	2	9	905	14	14	13	10	11	10
41	49	52	71	23	9	23	9	11	7	99	13	8	7	5	42	46	1	38	2	2	17	12	2	14	7	4	1	90	6	1	913	8	10	9	7	12	11
42	62	47	79	24	10	25	8	12	7	95	18	10	6	3	54	43	1	31	2	3	16	5	2	5	8	2	2	17	3	1	913	15	12	11	11	10	11
43	49	53	78	22	12	21	10	11	7	102	21	9	3	5	38	39	1	31	1	0	16	2	1	9	6	2	1	20	5	9	932	13	5	8	6	5	8
44	55	45	65	15	12	21	8	12	6	69	23	13	1	6	52	33	2	37	3	2	12	7	2	10	15	6	2	8	2	1	905	14	10	11	12	9	13
45	45	45	66	21	10	16	9	11	7	108	14	8	5	5	48	42	1	56	2	1	14	26	1	35	10	5	1	40	9	9	935	10	11	10	9	11	11
46	49	41	58	27	7	21	9	11	8	121	13	7	5	5	55	39	1	41	2	0	18	7	1	18	8	4	1	16	5	1	905	8	4	6	3	8	5
47	53	51	54	21	13	20	11	12	8	127	34	20	1	2	42	41	1	35	2	2	16	2	2	19	10	6	2	5	6	1	905	9	12	8	6	8	10

ID	1	2	3	4	5	6	7	8	9	10	11	12	13	14	15	16	17	18	19	20	21	22	23	24	25	26	27	28	29	30	31	32	33	34	35	36	37
48	56	41	89	22	16	24	8	12	7	107	21	12	2	4	56	41	1	48	2	2	18	1	0	27	12	5	1	15	10	1	921	11	6	6	9	5	7
49	60	45	46	20	15	16	8	11	7	88	26	12	2	1	54	42	2	30	2	0	14	4	1	14	6	5	2	22	6	8	922	13	7	7	9	7	11
50	41	53	76	17	6	22	10	11	6	86	11	12	2	4	47	44	1	48	1	3	13	24	8	24	6	4	1	7	8	2	905	14	12	10	11	3	11
51	54	50	84	17	15	23	8	12	7	79	14	15	6	6	58	51	1	52	2	2	15	28	16	34	9	2	1	85	14	1	905	13	5	10	12	12	12
52	62	53	84	22	4	15	9	12	8	102	17	14	1	1	61	42	1	48	2	1	16	23	5	23	5	1	1	10	8	1	905	13	14	11	11	10	13
53	59	58	87	16	14	10	9	11	8	94	19	11	7	2	53	47	2	58	2	3	17	17	3	20	10	3	1	8	9	1	911	8	12	9	7	10	10
54	54	42	77	23	8	23	9	11	7	110	17	12	7	2	49	43	1	53	2	2	14	6	1	25	6	4	1	14	4	1	87	4	6	9	9	9	7
55	59	58	86	17	8	17	9	12	8	104	15	12	5	4	53	47	2	45	2	3	11	4	2	15	8	3	1	30	8	2	905	14	15	15	9	14	12
56	54	43	94	12	15	19	7	11	5	57	33	18	6	3	51	41	1	60	2	2	18	1	1	30	12	4	1	100	20	1	932	10	12	12	12	12	14
57	42	42	68	15	6	23	9	12	7	121	20	15	5	6	47	41	1	32	2	1	15	4	0	15	7	3	1	20	4	1	932	8	9	9	9	9	9
58	64	42	74	13	19	22	7	11	7	59	15	14	3	5	51	46	1	44	2	2	18	6	1	15	5	4	1	40	10	2	905	13	9	12	10	12	10
59	65	43	68	12	14	18	8	12	8	101	26	19	4	4	55	41	1	45	2	2	18	5	2	30	10	5	2	85	20	2	921	9	10	6	5	8	7
60	47	48	71	17	8	20	10	14	7	110	18	12	1	6	58	44	2	44	2	0	12	9	6	28	10	7	1	25	10	2	930	8	5	8	7	4	7
61	49	38	81	22	17	18	6	13	7	126	12	12	5	5	48	33	1	43	2	2	18	16	5	25	7	4	1	25	20	2	905	9	7	10	12	9	10
62	58	37	86	16	21	19	7	10	4	81	29	16	5	5	59	33	1	30	2	0	16	6	0	6	2	1	2	2	0	8	905	11	11	11	9	7	9
63	55	51	94	14	13	16	12	11	9	112	24	19	6	6	51	39	1	33	2	2	16	0	0	5	4	4	2	2	1	9	146	13	10	12	10	10	11
64	66	53	82	19	10	18	10	8	8	113	10	13	1	2	52	43	1	48	1	3	16	14	4	30	13	6	1	173	12	1	905	13	11	11	12	9	11
65	61	54	67	15	13	15	8	13	7	101	25	14	1	6	61	44	2	30	2	2	14	5	4	10	3	1	2	4	10	8	905	9	9	14	11	11	8
66	54	41	89	21	15	25	8	10	5	101	25	17	5	5	52	41	1	26	1	0	17	4	0	4	4	2	1	11	1	9	913	11	12	9	8	8	11
67	58	40	83	12	12	13	8	10	8	76	9	4	3	3	56	37	1	37	3	0	16	11	2	16	4	3	1	28	5	2	949	12	11	8	10	10	9
68	51	43	98	17	12	18	8	14	6	96	24	15	7	7	51	32	1	38	2	2	14	5	5	16	5	2	2	10	8	1	949	15	16	12	13	9	13
69	54	49	87	19	15	18	8	14	10	136	13	10	6	6	58	33	2	26	2	0	16	2	0	6	5	3	1	4	0	2	927	12	12	10	13	11	12
70	59	48	54	15	14	10	6	11	8	106	14	9	6	4	53	43	1	25	1	0	16	3	3	3	1	1	2	0	0	9	905	7	9	7	4	9	4
71	49	48	87	16	7	22	10	13	8	103	17	13	3	6	60	43	2	30	2	1	14	6	2	15	8	4	9	21	5	1	942	8	5	8	7	7	10
72	55	50	81	15	9	18	9	11	7	118	13	9	5	4	53	39	2	45	2	0	18	17	4	27	10	7	9	9	16	2	913	10	3	8	7	5	7
73	44	39	78	15	8	18	11	12	7	109	23	16	5	5	48	34	1	41	2	2	16	2	1	25	14	6	2	25	8	2	911	13	9	9	10	14	11
74	48	45	81	21	16	17	8	9	6	121	26	15	5	5	40	43	2	34	4	0	17	2	1	6	7	4	2	8	2	2	932	9	9	7	7	8	7
75	58	42	34	18	12	22	8	11	9	100	10	10	3	5	46	37	2	28	3	0	18	1	1	20	14	4	2	25	7	2	905	8	6	8	9	14	9
76	62	37	70	20	20	6	4	9	8	84	20	1	7	6	59	35	2	38	3	1	14	14	2	17	6	2	1	13	3	1	925	12	8	11	10	8	9
77	52	57	65	21	10	20	8	10	6	85	20	12	6	6	55	42	1	40	2	0	15	3	1	13	12	6	1	45	14	2	914	8	9	9	9	8	7
78	57	44	79	21	8	24	7	9	5	66	12	13	4	4	54	43	1	47	2	1	16	15	1	25	10	3	1	11	10	9	905	9	10	7	9	7	9
79	50	42	81	14	11	22	9	13	5	115	15	12	7	6	52	34	1	43	2	2	14	13	2	23	8	6	1	14	2	2	914	13	13	13	14	12	12
80	59	55	103	16	9	21	9	12	9	73	19	15	5	7	48	60	1	37	2	3	16	14	5	19	12	4	1	15	6	1	913	9	10	10	7	8	10
81	55	42	76	19	10	19	12	12	5	118	21	18	5	5	49	39	1	48	2	2	18	18	15	19	4	2	1	22	15	9	140	14	7	8	9	8	10
82	67	46	72	19	11	8	10	10	9	110	10	12	1	2	38	64	2	56	2	0	15	13	4	26	5	3	2	18	10	1	943	10	7	8	5	7	9
83	64	37	63	14	16	9	7	11	8	84	20	14	1	5	60	43	2	36	3	1	19	12	1	20	10	5	2	10	2	2	23	9	10	11	9	13	11
84	53	43	84	13	13	15	7	13	5	98	19	14	6	6	51	41	1	33	2	3	14	12	4	15	10	3	1	19	4	1	917	9	8	8	9	9	13
85	47	49	56	18	10	8	7	9	4	92	15	7	2	3	54	48	1	44	2	2	16	6	1	26	14	2	1	40	19	1	938	9	10	9	7	9	9
86	52	54	90	19	9	19	9	13	5	135	18	9	7	6	60	45	1	26	2	0	16	3	1	3	2	2	2	5	1	2	905	13	12	10	12	10	7
87	51	54	91	17	13	16	9	12	4	87	23	14	7	5	51	50	1	41	2	3	15	7	1	25	14	8	1	90	13	1	913	10	14	13	11	12	11
88	56	44	46	12	9	11	9	12	9	109	23	11	3	3	56	29	1	33	1	0	18	3	3	12	6	4	2	5	6	2	938	10	10	9	8	4	5
89	53	37	69	17	19	20	6	12	6	94	16	8	3	6	40	39	1	37	1	0	17	5	1	15	3	2	2	3	1	9	938	11	12	8	8	12	8
90	61	50	82	22	9	18	10	14	6	82	25	13	2	3	46	48	2	33	2	0	15	11	4	17	9	6	1	42	6	2	905	14	10	8	8	12	11
91	55	37	75	15	6	20	7	12	8	105	19	11	5	6	48	50	1	25	1	0	16	3	3	4	3	2	2	40	2	9	905	11	11	11	8	10	10
92	63	55	101	18	14	16	10	14	8	74	25	16	1	2	52	41	1	42	3	2	16	17	3	19	4	3	5	12	10	8	103	14	15	12	12	11	10
93	57	49	80	24	15	20	10	11	9	124	11	7	6	3	38	49	1	36	2	0	16	6	1	14	11	4	1	26	10	9	938	10	7	9	10	9	8
94	53	48	61	16	9	19	7	8	9	96	9	5	1	5	45	55	1	42	2	0	12	8	2	25	12	5	9	60	20	1	935	10	7	8	4	9	8
95	62	39	96	14	11	17	9	13	7	66	25	19	7	7	56	51	1	34	1	0	13	3	1	8	15	8	1	9	5	2	905	15	9	15	14	16	16

ID	1	2	3	4	5	6	7	8	9	10	11	12	13	14	15	16	17	18	19	20	21	22	23	24	25	26	27	28	29	30	31	32	33	34	35	36	37
96	57	43	94	23	15	19	6	12	5	67	11	10	6	6	60	41	1	51	2	2	15	34	1	37	18	7	1	600	23	1	927	11	12	11	13	11	10
97	60	56	81	21	16	19	7	10	6	108	10	8	6	4	59	48	1	52	1	2	17	22	2	30	10	3	1	34	6	1	930	15	15	12	13	10	10
98	65	40	100	15	21	11	9	13	8	82	31	13	6	4	54	39	2	43	2	4	13	17	4	19	8	5	1	27	9	1	949	14	14	14	15	13	13
99	64	59	86	21	7	20	9	11	7	146	12	12	2	2	40	55	1	51	2	5	20	2	1	27	8	5	2	110	26	1	937	12	8	10	9	11	8
100	59	45	79	15	8	10	10	10	6	103	25	17	2	3	60	41	1	35	2	1	16	3	1	4	4	1	2	10	5	2	906	13	9	6	6	7	11
101	61	39	76	19	14	21	6	11	7	73	24	15	2	2	53	59	1	40	2	1	15	20	2	20	14	1	1	23	8	9	935	13	14	8	9	12	9
102	47	45	79	26	14	15	11	10	8	103	26	13	5	3	48	38	1	41	2	1	16	8	0	18	8	2	1	7	7	1	951	9	10	8	11	9	5
103	59	47	70	16	12	20	8	13	5	120	21	13	3	5	54	41	1	35	2	1	16	6	3	16	6	4	1	56	8	1	951	10	8	10	7	8	10
104	49	52	99	26	9	25	9	12	3	58	21	12	6	5	40	33	2	47	2	2	15	9	1	19	11	7	1	111	14	1	951	13	15	14	11	9	14
105	50	54	52	19	13	14	10	11	10	109	10	11	1	6	56	40	1	40	2	1	16	14	3	21	7	1	1	56	8	1	951	11	8	9	10	8	9
106	52	47	100	16	7	20	7	10	7	94	28	20	1	2	53	37	1	48	2	3	15	14	1	28	7	3	1	219	15	1	951	14	8	8	9	6	7
107	58	54	78	21	12	21	14	13	8	102	18	10	6	5	51	39	1	35	3	1	14	7	3	12	8	4	1	2	5	4	951	12	13	11	8	10	10
108	67	38	61	19	17	15	7	13	8	61	14	5	1	6	57	41	1	33	2	0	17	10	1	14	9	5	1	6	5	2	951	7	6	8	8	5	4
109	60	61	86	23	14	14	10	13	8	112	12	14	6	6	62	37	2	40	2	2	16	12	4	17	7	3	1	127	9	4	951	12	11	10	13	12	13
110	48	49	85	19	18	12	10	12	9	78	15	11	1	6	52	47	1	44	2	1	15	18	3	25	10	1	1	37	9	2	951	11	10	11	7	6	11
111	58	38	97	17	14	14	7	11	7	55	28	16	7	5	56	43	1	39	2	1	14	9	1	17	9	3	1	45	6	1	951	11	13	9	7	9	11
112	53	43	91	22	17	15	11	12	9	116	13	15	6	6	57	41	1	41	2	1	16	11	4	20	8	4	1	3	6	4	951	15	14	12	11	14	12
113	52	41	71	16	8	16	7	9	8	103	11	6	2	2	39	47	2	42	1	0	15	11	0	23	7	5	1	25	7	9	951	12	12	12	12	13	10
114	64	38	91	16	14	17	4	12	7	95	23	18	7	6	50	47	1	35	3	1	18	3	1	15	7	6	1	125	7	1	951	13	14	12	12	14	10
115	54	43	77	15	14	20	11	13	8	119	19	11	4	5	55	37	1	34	1	0	15	9	2	17	7	5	2	3	3	2	951	14	13	13	13	11	12
116	53	45	102	19	13	23	8	10	7	79	25	14	6	6	61	48	1	40	2	1	13	12	1	20	10	1	2	103	8	1	951	14	15	13	13	14	13
117	57	46	68	21	16	17	8	11	7	92	21	13	3	5	54	38	1	39	2	1	17	8	1	16	8	6	1	24	7	2	951	13	11	8	7	9	7
118	52	51	78	21	8	20	8	13	6	119	9	5	6	6	61	43	2	36	1	0	16	12	2	16	7	6	1	43	5	1	951	13	13	13	12	11	11
119	48	47	74	14	17	11	8	14	8	104	15	11	2	5	41	39	1	40	2	1	16	12	2	21	7	7	1	11	6	1	951	11	9	12	11	7	10
120	51	51	91	14	9	21	9	13	6	96	16	8	5	3	45	48	1	42	3	1	13	13	2	22	8	5	2	20	8	2	951	12	12	9	7	10	9
121	49	42	84	18	15	15	7	12	8	94	17	14	5	6	50	41	1	41	2	1	16	12	2	22	8	4	1	78	8	1	951	12	13	11	11	13	12
122	65	48	86	17	14	24	10	9	9	94	16	7	4	1	59	44	1	43	2	1	17	12	1	22	8	4	1	0	7	2	951	12	14	12	8	12	12
123	50	34	74	18	11	22	5	9	6	83	6	8	4	6	54	43	2	44	2	1	15	17	2	27	9	1	2	133	11	9	951	10	12	11	12	13	13
124	48	42	60	19	15	10	9	10	7	113	18	9	2	5	42	42	1	37	2	0	16	8	0	16	7	4	1	5	5	1	951	10	12	12	9	8	13
125	51	41	96	15	11	21	7	11	7	78	23	15	6	6	48	47	1	40	2	1	14	10	1	21	9	3	2	97	8	1	951	14	15	14	14	14	14
126	57	48	83	20	12	20	10	12	8	102	22	13	1	2	52	37	1	44	2	2	16	12	2	23	7	4	2	56	10	1	951	12	6	8	12	11	10
127	58	39	82	23	14	17	8	12	5	100	19	14	1	3	62	46	1	42	2	1	17	13	3	24	8	3	1	66	11	9	951	8	8	7	8	6	7
128	55	54	94	17	9	17	7	11	4	84	20	16	6	6	50	52	1	42	2	2	14	11	2	19	9	3	1	167	12	1	951	12	7	12	9	10	11
129	60	47	95	14	12	23	7	14	4	127	20	16	2	5	62	44	2	51	3	4	14	20	4	31	5	7	1	312	16	2	951	13	13	11	10	6	9
130	54	56	83	21	4	23	9	13	8	136	14	7	5	3	37	54	1	38	2	1	17	6	1	16	6	7	2	46	7	1	951	9	9	9	10	10	12
131	53	53	64	19	14	20	9	11	7	102	18	11	1	6	43	41	1	39	2	1	18	9	2	18	7	2	1	81	10	1	951	11	12	12	10	9	12
132	59	50	95	19	12	17	7	14	6	121	25	17	4	3	64	45	1	39	2	2	16	11	3	20	6	5	1	123	9	9	951	13	12	9	8	8	8
133	54	37	38	22	12	20	5	13	5	106	18	10	3	3	57	43	2	36	1	0	17	9	2	20	7	4	1	16	8	1	951	6	6	8	5	5	5
134	45	46	80	16	9	21	8	13	9	95	16	14	3	6	49	45	1	42	2	2	14	15	3	26	8	2	2	111	11	2	951	8	5	8	6	5	8
135	52	45	72	19	19	20	8	13	8	94	15	11	2	5	54	42	1	42	2	1	16	16	3	26	8	2	1	64	10	1	951	8	4	8	5	5	4
136	53	45	100	16	11	12	12	13	1	78	25	18	4	5	40	41	1	41	2	1	15	6	3	17	9	6	1	8	9	9	951	11	11	11	11	12	10
137	55	51	78	11	15	12	6	7	6	73	23	11	1	6	44	45	2	41	2	1	15	9	0	18	8	1	2	126	10	1	951	7	13	11	12	13	11
138	57	44	90	15	14	17	10	10	7	95	24	9	5	5	52	48	1	34	1	0	14	7	0	13	8	4	2	4	3	1	951	12	12	10	8	11	10
139	50	49	56	14	12	18	12	13	10	103	20	12	6	3	60	36	1	35	1	0	16	13	2	19	8	4	2	1	2	1	951	13	14	12	11	15	11
140	40	54	87	21	7	23	10	14	6	117	18	13	2	4	53	48	1	45	2	1	14	17	3	26	8	6	1	67	10	2	951	12	10	13	12	10	10
141	51	48	68	21	10	22	9	10	5	103	17	6	2	6	54	32	1	37	2	0	15	9	0	16	7	3	2	55	8	1	951	11	8	10	10	9	7
142	54	43	89	15	10	18	7	13	8	98	19	8	5	5	51	39	1	35	1	0	14	9	1	17	6	5	2	42	4	3	951	9	8	9	8	9	10
143	56	34	83	24	15	21	10	12	8	111	20	15	2	5	49	43	2	39	2	1	17	7	2	19	8	5	1	9	8	9	951	13	13	12	14	12	13

ID	1	2	3	4	5	6	7	8	9	10	11	12	13	14	15	16	17	18	19	20	21	22	23	24	25	26	27	28	29	30	31	32	33	34	35	36	37
144	66	65	94	19	15	12	14	12	10	128	15	11	7	7	55	42	1	33	2	1	15	4	3	7	6	3	1	10	3	2	951	15	11	8	8	6	11
145	52	51	85	20	7	17	8	10	9	122	16	11	6	6	50	49	2	36	1	0	16	6	0	13	7	7	1	55	4	2	951	12	15	11	9	6	4
146	47	44	85	21	10	22	9	13	4	103	21	13	3	4	49	41	1	43	2	1	15	11	2	23	8	5	1	45	11	1	951	9	6	7	10	8	11
147	61	44	96	15	8	21	9	12	8	57	31	15	1	5	54	41	1	37	2	1	14	8	1	17	9	4	1	64	8	3	951	14	11	9	13	12	12
148	49	49	92	19	7	26	8	13	6	90	18	11	5	5	50	44	1	42	2	1	14	13	2	23	9	4	2	110	11	3	951	12	10	8	9	12	9
149	56	48	77	11	15	20	8	12	6	78	25	16	3	3	52	43	1	42	2	1	16	12	1	23	9	6	1	31	8	9	951	10	10	11	11	9	10
150	62	40	95	19	16	14	5	13	5	90	25	19	5	5	46	44	1	39	2	2	17	5	2	18	7	5	1	143	11	1	951	12	6	6	13	7	7
151	53	49	95	23	5	16	10	13	8	141	15	15	3	7	54	50	1	36	3	1	16	9	4	17	6	3	2	111	8	3	951	11	13	12	11	12	11

APPENDIX E

SUMMATION NOTATION

and

OTHER MATHEMATICAL OPERATIONS

RULES FOR SUMMATION NOTATION

This appendix discusses summation notation, summation theorems, the use of summations with constants, the order of mathematical operations, and other mathematical operations. All of these concepts are essential for performing statistical and mathematical operations. We will begin with an explanation of the uppercase Greek letter sigma (Σ), which is used to indicate that the mathematical operation of addition, referred to in statistics as *summation*, is to be performed. Sometimes we use letters and/or numbers above and below this summation symbol; when they are included, they serve to indicate the limits of the operation. Equation E.1 illustrates the general form of a summation process:

$$\sum_{i=1}^{n} X_i = X_1 + X_2 + X_3 + \cdots + X_n \qquad \textbf{(E.1)}$$

where:

n = the number of steps in the summation operation, which is usually equal to the size of the data set. Recall that in this text the Roman lowercase n represents the size of the sample, while the Greek uppercase N (*Nu*) represents the size of the population. Also, recall that the uppercase N is identical in the Greek and Roman alphabets.

i = the starting point at which the operation begins (usually set equal to 1)

X_i = the ith element in the data set

Example E.1. In its simplest form, this notation indicates that the values within a variable are to be summed. We begin with the first value, which is denoted as X_1, and end with the last value, which is denoted as X_n. The letter i initially takes on the value given below the Σ sign. We will use Example E.1 to illustrate this summation process. Suppose that the number of defective parts produced per day at one plant have been recorded for a period of 5 consecutive days, as follows: 3, 4, 8, 1, and 7. Here are the results of the summation process:

$$\sum_{i=1}^{n} X_i = \sum_{i=1}^{5} X_i$$

$$= X_1 + X_2 + X_3 + X_4 + X_5$$

$$= 3 + 4 + 8 + 1 + 7$$

$$= 23$$

For Example E.1, we begin with the first X-value; and since n has been defined as 5, we will sum through the 5th X-value. The summation process reveals that there were a total of 23 defective parts observed over the 5-day period of interest.

Although the initial value for i is usually set at 1, as it was in Example E.1, the initial value does not have to be 1. Furthermore, we do not always have to use n as the last value in the notation. In fact, the values that appear above and below the Σ sign can take on any values desired within the range of operations. Suppose that we are only interested in finding the sum of defective parts over the third, fourth, and fifth days for Example E.1. Then, our summation expression would be written and computed as follows:

$$\sum_{i=3}^{5} X_i = X_3 + X_4 + X_5$$

$$= 8 + 1 + 7$$

$$= 16$$

The summation process indicates that there were a total of 16 defective parts observed over the 3-day period of interest. We simply added the defective parts for the last three days.

Another useful but less common application of the summation operation involves an adjustment to the subscript associated with each variate employed in the operation. For example, instead of being concerned with the ith variate of the X-variable, suppose that we are interested in the "ith plus 1" variate in the variable at each stage of the process. Such situations are not uncommon for those who have written computer programs with sophisticated "do loops." As an illustration, we will perform an operation with the data for Example E.1 in which we are only interested in examining the *next* day's results over a period of three days:

$$\sum_{i=1}^{3} X_{i+1} = X_{1+1} + X_{2+1} + X_{3+1}$$

$$= X_2 + X_3 + X_4$$

$$= 4 + 8 + 1$$

$$= 13$$

The summation process reveals that there were a total of 13 defective parts observed over the 3-day period. Keep in mind that we were interested in the sum of the defective parts for the second, third, and fourth days, not the first, second, and third days.

While we have exceptions such as those already illustrated, summation operations *usually* begin with the first value (i.e., $i = 1$) and end with the last value (i.e., the nth value), with consecutive increments of 1. In such cases, we typically simplify our notation to one of those given in Equation E.2:

$$\sum_{i=1}^{n} X_i = \sum X_i \text{, or simply } \sum X \qquad \text{(E.2)}$$

The indicators above and below the Σ sign have been omitted. Whenever the expression is written in this manner, we assume that the operation begins with the first observation and concludes with the last one, without any additional modification.

Multiple Summation Symbols

Example E.2. Occasionally, we will find it necessary to use more than one summation sign in an operation. Although such expressions may appear to be complex, they follow a very specific, exacting procedure. For example, it is not uncommon to use double summation signs with procedures such as analysis of variance (ANOVA), a statistical tool discussed in detail in Chapter 12 and Chapter 13. For Example E.2, suppose that we have randomly sampled 100 tennis balls from each of four different plants (a total of 400 balls). We are interested in determining whether there are significant differences among the weights of the balls from plant to plant. With problems such as this, we may need to subtract the mean of the first group from all of the elements within that group, square these differences, and then sum these squared differences. We may also need to perform this same operation over all four groups. Finally, we may want to sum these four sums. Reasons for wanting to perform such operations are explained in various chapters of this textbook. Equation E.3 represents all of these steps in one expression:

$$\sum_{j=1}^{k} \sum_{i=1}^{n_j} (X_{i,j} - \overline{X}_j)^2 \qquad \text{(E.3)}$$

where:

n_j = the number of operations of the inner summation (e.g, the number of cases in the *j*th group, which can change from group to group)

k = the number of operations of the outer summation (e.g., the number of groups in the study)

$X_{i,j}$ = the *i*th case in the *j*th group

$\overline{X}$ = the mean of the *j*th group

With a double summation operation such as this, we must be careful to follow the process precisely. The inner summation operation proceeds rapidly, while the outer operation proceeds slowly. If i is associated with the inner Σ and j is associated with the outer Σ, the value of i will go from 1 to n_j before the value of j ever changes. Once i becomes equal to n_j, then j becomes 2 and i returns to 1, starting all over. This process continues until i is equal to n_k and j is equal to k. Note that in Example E.2, all four groups consist of 100 cases. Therefore, n_j will be equal to 100 for each group, and i goes from 1 to 100 during each loop of the inner summation operation. The outer summation operation goes from 1 to 4 in this example. The operation, written in detail, is as follows:

$$\sum_{j=1}^{k} \sum_{i=1}^{n_j} (X_{i,j} - \overline{X}_j)^2 = \sum_{j=1}^{4} \sum_{i=1}^{100} (X_{i,j} - \overline{X}_j)^2$$

$$= (X_{1,1} - \overline{X}_1)^2 + (X_{2,1} - \overline{X}_1)^2 + \cdots + (X_{100,1} - \overline{X}_1)^2$$

$$+ (X_{1,2} - \overline{X}_2)^2 + (X_{2,2} - \overline{X}_2)^2 + \cdots + (X_{100,2} - \overline{X}_2)^2$$

$$+ (X_{1,3} - \overline{X}_3)^2 + (X_{2,3} - \overline{X}_3)^2 + \cdots + (X_{100,3} - \overline{X}_3)^2$$

$$+ (X_{1,4} - \overline{X}_4)^2 + (X_{2,4} - \overline{X}_4)^2 + \cdots + (X_{100,4} - \overline{X}_4)^2$$

Example E.3. Thus far, our discussion has been limited to only *one* variable, and we have consistently designated this variable as the X-variable. Example E.3 is based upon *two* variables obtained for a group of 5 employees. The first variable, designated as the X-variable, consists of scores regarding job competency for these employees as obtained from some evaluation instrument. The second variable, designated as the Y-variable, consists of scores regarding job competency for these same employees as obtained through some alternate evaluation instrument. Table E.1 gives the two sets of scores for these 5 people:

Table E.1
Pairs of Job Competency Scores

Case Number	*X Score*	*Y Score*
1	3	5
2	4	7
3	8	4
4	1	8
5	7	9

We may perform numerous operations based upon the two sets of data that we have available for this group of 5 people. For example, suppose that we wish to combine the test scores for the two variables to give a total score for each individual. We may also want to find the sum of the total scores. One way (there are others, as we shall see) of performing this operation and obtaining the necessary result is as follows:

$$\sum_{i=1}^{n} (X_i + Y_i) = \sum_{i=1}^{5} (X_i + Y_i)$$

$$= \sum (X + Y)$$

$$= (X_1 + Y_1) + (X_2 + Y_2) + (X_3 + Y_3) + (X_4 + Y_4) + (X_5 + Y_5)$$

$$= (3 + 5) + (4 + 7) + (8 + 4) + (1 + 8) + (7 + 9)$$

$$= 8 + 11 + 12 + 9 + 16$$

$$= 56$$

Based upon the data used in Example E.3, we now demonstrate another use of the summation notation when we have more than one variable. Suppose that we wish to find the *cross-products* of the two variables over each of the 5 people and then wish to sum this set of products. The summation notation is expressed, simplified, and solved as follows:

$$\sum_{i=1}^{n} (X_i \cdot Y_i) = \sum_{i=1}^{n} X_i \cdot Y_i$$

$$= \sum_{i=1}^{5} X_i \cdot Y_i$$

$$= X_1 \cdot Y_1 + X_2 \cdot Y_2 + X_3 \cdot Y_3 + X_4 \cdot Y_4 + X_5 \cdot Y_5$$

$$= 3 \cdot 5 + 4 \cdot 7 + 8 \cdot 4 + 1 \cdot 8 + 7 \cdot 9$$

$$= 15 + 28 + 32 + 8 + 63$$

$$= 146$$

In the above operation, we first multiplied each X-value by its corresponding Y-value; we then summed across the 5 products. Notice that we did not need to use parentheses, since the order of mathematical operations requires us to multiply first, then add. We will discuss the order of mathematical operations in more detail shortly. We also did not first sum all of the X-values, and then multiply by Y. We know that Y is a variable, not a constant! In other words:

$$\sum_{i=1}^{n} X_i \cdot Y_i \neq \left(\sum_{i=1}^{n} X_i\right) \cdot Y_i$$

$$\neq \left(\sum_{i=1}^{n} X_i\right) \cdot Y$$

If we wish to divide each individual X-value by each individual Y-value, and sum over all 5 operations, we would proceed as follows:

$$\sum_{i=1}^{n} (X_i \,/\, Y_i) = \sum_{i=1}^{n} \frac{X_i}{Y_i}$$

$$= \frac{X_1}{Y_1} + \frac{X_2}{Y_2} + \frac{X_3}{Y_3} + \frac{X_4}{Y_4} + \frac{X_5}{Y_5}$$

$$= \frac{3}{5} + \frac{4}{7} + \frac{8}{4} + \frac{1}{8} + \frac{7}{9}$$

$$= 4.0742$$

In the above operation, we first divided each X-value by its corresponding Y-value; we then summed across all 5 operations. In the below operation, we first sum across all values of the X-variable; we then sum across all values of the Y-variable; finally, we divide the first sum by the second sum. Notice that the two operations do *not* yield the same results:

$$\sum_{i=1}^{n} X_i \,/ \sum_{i=1}^{n} Y_i = \frac{\sum_{i=1}^{n} X_i}{\sum_{i=1}^{n} Y_i}$$

$$= \frac{(3 + 4 + 8 + 1 + 7)}{(5 + 7 + 4 + 8 + 9)}$$

$$= .69697$$

In this textbook, we may use a notation system that refers to all of the variables as X-variables, rather than having to use a different letter of the alphabet for each variable of concern. Using X, Y, Z, etc., has obvious limitations since there are only 26 letters in the alphabet; and some of these letters are often reserved for other purposes. Consequently, an alternative notation system will be helpful. The most common one is based upon numbering (subscripting) the variables as well as numbering the variates within the variables. As we found in Equation E.3, we often use two subscripts associated with the X-variate, rather than just one. We noticed that subscript i stood for the ith case, while the subscript j stood for the jth variable or group (depending upon the situation). If the data are depicted in a table or in a data matrix such as the one in Table E.1, we can think of the first subscript as being associated with the *row* number. The second subscript is then associated with the *column* number. If we were interested in the second observation (represented by row two) of the second variable (represented by column two), we would denote this value as $X_{2,2}$. For the data in Table E.1, the numerical value associated with $X_{2,2}$ would be 7.

Summation Theorems

Now that we have examined the fundamentals of summation notation, we are ready to discuss three basic summation theorems that will result in considerable simplification of many of the computational processes of statistics. The student of statistics must quickly master these theorems, as they are employed frequently in statistical computations.

Theorem 1

The first of these theorems states that if each value of a variable is multiplied by some constant term and then summed, the operation can be performed by summing the values of the variables first, then multiplying the resulting sum by the constant. Theorem 1 is formally stated in Equation E.4:

$$\sum_{i=1}^{n} c \cdot X_i = c \cdot X_1 + c \cdot X_2 + \cdots + c \cdot X_n = c \cdot \sum_{i=1}^{n} X_i \tag{E.4}$$

As an illustration of theorem 1, suppose that the supervisor of the five people in Example E.3 has decided that the first job competency variable should be given a weighting factor of 3 when determining performance scores. He or she could therefore multiply each of the individual values by a constant of $c = 3$. Suppose that the supervisor also wants to determine the sum of the newly created set of numbers. Since it was previously determined that the sum of the original set of values is $3 + 4 + 8 + 1 + 7 = 23$, rather than having to multiply each of these numbers separately by a constant of 3 and then adding the newly created results, the supervisor could simply multiply the original sum by the constant. That is: $3 \cdot 23 = 69$.

Theorem 2

A second summation theorem states that when a constant value is summed over a number of operations (n operations), the expression is equal to the *number* of operations performed times the *constant*. Theorem 2 is stated formally in Equation E.5:

$$\sum_{i=1}^{n} c = c + c + \cdots + c = n \cdot c \tag{E.5}$$

As an example of this theorem, suppose that we wish to find the sum of an operation, where i goes from 1 to 5, and we know that the constant value is equal to 8. We can either add up the constant over five operations (8 + 8 + 8 + 8 + 8 = 40), or we can simply multiply the constant by the number of operations to be performed: $5 \cdot 8 = 40$.

Theorem 3

The third of the summation theorems to be presented here states that the summation of a sum of values is equal to the summation of each of the separate sums. This is the *distributive rule* of algebra; it also holds for summation notation. Specifically, we are distributing the summation sign throughout the expression. This third theorem is stated in Equation E.6:

$$\sum_{i=1}^{n} (X_i + Y_i + Z_i) = \sum_{i=1}^{n} X_i + \sum_{i=1}^{n} Y_i + \sum_{i=1}^{n} Z_i \tag{E.6}$$

It is important to note that for theorem 3, all of the variables (in this case X, Y, and Z) must contain the same number of elements, since i will go from 1 to n for all of the variables. Theorem 3 can be extended over any number of variables.

As an illustration of this theorem, we will return to a problem that we solved for earlier using the data from Example E.3. We previously found that for this example:

$$\sum_{i=1}^{n} (X_i + Y_i) = 56$$

Using theorem 3, we could have first computed the sums of each of the two variables separately. That is, we could have performed the following two operations:

$$\sum_{i=1}^{n} X_i = 23$$

and:

$$\sum_{i=1}^{n} Y_i = 33$$

Using theorem 3, now we add these separate sums:

$$\begin{aligned}\sum_{i=1}^{n} (X_i + Y_i) &= \sum_{i=1}^{n} X_i + \sum_{i=1}^{n} Y_i \\ &= 23 + 33 \\ &= 56\end{aligned}$$

As we see, the result is 23 + 33 = 56, as determined previously. As we can see, this theorem is very useful if we have already computed each of the separate sums in some previous operation.

Constants

When a constant value, such as 6 or 74 or 3.25, is added to or subtracted from each of the values of a variable, or when each of the values of a variable is multiplied by or divided by a constant, a *transformed* variable is obtained. For Example E.3, if we add a constant of 6 to each of the X-values, we have created a transformed variable:

$$\sum_{i=1}^{5} (X_i + 6) = (3 + 6) + (4 + 6) + (8 + 6) + (1 + 6) + (7 + 6)$$

$$= 9 + 10 + 14 + 7 + 13$$

$$= 53$$

The new elements obtained by transforming the original variable are 9, 10, 14, 7, and 13. The sum of the elements of this transformed variable is 53.

We will use the *mean* of a distribution to further illustrate several of these concepts. As stated in Chapter 3, when working with a population, we use the Greek symbol μ to represent the population mean; and when working with a sample, we use $\overline{X}$ to represent the sample mean. The mean is computed as the sum of all the values in the variable, divided by the number of values contained in that variable. For Example E.3, the mean is obtained as follows:

$$\mu = \frac{\sum_{i=1}^{N} X_i}{N}$$

$$= \frac{3 + 4 + 8 + 1 + 7}{5}$$

$$= 4.6$$

For the transformed set of values, the mean of 9 + 10 + 14 + 7 + 13 is 10.6. We notice that this mean is exactly 6 points higher than the original mean. By adding a constant of 6 to the original mean, we have obtained the same result as we would have obtained by adding a constant of 6 to each value in the original distribution and then computing the mean. With the use of our summation theorems, we can easily prove this relationship. First, we express the operation of adding a constant to each of the values and summing as follows:

$$\sum (X_i + c)$$

Then, by using summation theorem 3, we can distribute the summation sign throughout the expression. That is:

$$\sum (X_i + c) = \sum X_i + \sum c$$

Next, we can use summation theorem 2 to simplify the last term in the above expression:

$$\sum c = n \cdot c$$

Therefore:

$$\sum (X_i + c) = \sum X_i + n \cdot c$$

We now have the numerator of the mean for the new variable. All we need to do is divide this numerator by n to obtain the mean of the newly adjusted variable. The adjusted mean becomes:

$$\mu_{\text{adjusted}} = \frac{(\sum X_i) + n \cdot c}{n}$$

$$= \frac{\sum X_i}{n} + \frac{n \cdot c}{n}$$

$$= \mu_{\text{original}} + c$$

It is important to remember that all values computed for a variable are constant values. The number of values (either N or n) within a variable is a constant value; the sum of those values (ΣX) is a constant; the *mean* of the variable (either μ or $\overline{X}$) is a constant value; the *median* of the variable is a constant; the range, the *interquartile range, the variance*, and the *standard deviation* of that variable are constant values, etc. Suppose we encounter an expression such as the following:

$$\sum_{i=1}^{n} \mu$$

We know that μ is a constant and that we are supposed to compute the sum of this constant over n operations. The result can be obtained by employing theorem 2:

$$\sum_{i=1}^{n} \mu = n \cdot \mu$$

Using the *original* X-variable of Example E.3 (not the transformed variable), we find that:

$$\sum_{i=1}^{n} \mu = n \cdot \mu$$

$$= (5) \cdot (4.6)$$

$$= 23$$

This result in turn should tell us that the sum of the mean over n operations is equal to the sum of the values in the variable, since both operations give us a value of 23. The proof of this relationship is easily obtained:

$$\sum \mu = n \cdot \mu \qquad \text{(by theorem 2)}$$

$$= n \cdot \frac{\sum X}{n} \qquad \text{(by substitution for the mean)}$$

$$= \sum X \qquad \text{(by cancellation)}$$

Sum of the Squared Deviations

We will now take a look at another application of the summation theorems and constants. Suppose that we are interested in obtaining the *sum of the squared deviations* about the original mean for the X-variable of Example E.3 and the sum of the squared deviations about the adjusted mean for the transformed X-variable. First, we will calculate the sum of the squared deviations about the original mean:

$$\sum (X - \mu)^2 = (3 - 4.6)^2 + (4 - 4.6)^2 + (8 - 4.6)^2 + (1 - 4.6)^2 + (7 - 4.6)^2$$

$$= 2.56 + .36 + 11.56 + 12.96 + 5.76$$

$$= 33.20$$

Next, we will calculate the sum of the squared deviations about the adjusted mean for the transformed variable:

$$\sum (X - \mu)^2 = (9 - 10.6)^2 + (10 - 10.6)^2 + (14 - 10.6)^2 + (7 - 10.6)^2 + (13 - 10.6)^2$$

$$= 2.56 + .36 + 11.56 + 12.96 + 5.76$$

$$= 33.20$$

The relationship between the two sets of results is obvious; they both sum to 33.20. We can easily confirm that the sum of the squared deviations about the mean for the original data is equal to the sum of the squared deviations about the transformed data. The proof is as follows:

$$\sum (X_{adjusted} - \mu_{adjusted})^2 = \sum [(X_i + c) - (\mu + c)]^2$$

$$= \sum (X_i + c - \mu - c)^2$$

$$= \sum (X_i - \mu)^2$$

We conclude that when we *add* a constant to each value or *subtract* a constant from each value in a distribution, the sum of the squared deviations about the mean of the transformed distribution is exactly the same as the sum of the squared deviations about the original mean. This concept is very important to us in statistics, since the sum of the squared deviations about the mean is a key value in many statistical operations. This sum of squares term is the numerator of the variance, the numerator of the standard deviation, the denominator of the slope for a line, and is a part of the denominator for the correlation coefficient.

Instead of adding or subtracting a constant to each value in a distribution, we sometimes may want to *multiply* or *divide* each value by a constant. The impact of this transformation upon the data will give considerably different results than when adding or subtracting by a constant. For example, if each value is multiplied by a constant, the *mean* of the transformed distribution will be increased by the *product* of that constant. The proof of this impact upon the mean is demonstrated as follows:

$$\frac{\sum c \cdot X}{n} = \frac{c \cdot \sum X}{n}$$

$$= c \cdot \frac{\sum X}{n}$$

$$= c \cdot \mu$$

On the other hand, when each value is multiplied by a constant, the *sum of the squared deviations about the mean* is multiplied by the product of the constant squared times the sum of the squared deviations about the mean:

$$\sum (X_i \cdot c - \mu \cdot c)^2 = \sum [c \cdot (X_i - \mu)]^2$$

$$= c^2 \cdot \sum (X_i - \mu)^2$$

When each value is multiplied by a constant, the variance is multiplied by the square of that constant. In the same manner, the standard deviation is increased by the absolute value of the product of the constant (unsquared) times the original standard deviation. A summary of the results of a few of these operations and their impact upon various constant measures of a distribution is given in Table E.2.

Table E.2
Various Operations with Constants

Distribution Constant	*Mathematical Operation*	*Resulting Value*
ΣX	+ or -	$\Sigma X + n \cdot c$ or $\Sigma X - n \cdot c$
ΣX	x or /	$c \cdot \Sigma X$ or $(1/c) \cdot \Sigma X$
μ	+ or -	$\mu + c$ or $\mu - c$
μ	x or /	$\mu \cdot c$ or μ/c
σ	+ or -	σ
σ	x or /	$\sigma \cdot c$ or σ/c
σ^2	+ or -	σ^2
σ^2	x or /	$\sigma^2 \cdot c^2$ or σ^2/c^2

We will use the *Y*-variable of Example E.3 to review several of these operations with constants. Table E.3 shows that when all of the values of the *Y*-variable are summed, the resulting value is 33. When each of these individual values is increased by a constant amount, the new sum is 48. Thus, the new sum is $n \cdot c = 5 \cdot 3$, or 15 points higher. When each of these individual values is multiplied by 3 (instead of adding 3), the new sum is 99. Thus, the new sum is $\Sigma Y \cdot c = 33 \cdot 3 = 99$; it has been *tripled*. Further, the original mean is 6.6; when we add a constant to each value, the mean is increased to 9.6. This should make logical sense. For example, imagine that these values had represented the ages of a group of 5 children recorded 3 years ago; on average the children would have been 6.6 years of age. Three years later, their average age would have increased to 9.6 years.

Table E.3 also illustrates what happens to the mean when each value has been multiplied by a constant amount. Here, we see that the mean has tripled, as did the sum of the *Y*-values. In statistical operations, we will find that these rules for constant adjustments to the mean, the standard deviation, and other measures are quite useful.

Table E.3
Various Operations on a Variable

Y = the original variable

$c = 3$ = a constant

Y	$Y + c$	$Y \cdot c$
5	$5 + 3 = 8$	$5 \cdot 3 = 15$
7	$7 + 3 = 10$	$7 \cdot 3 = 21$
4	$4 + 3 = 7$	$4 \cdot 3 = 12$
8	$8 + 3 = 11$	$8 \cdot 3 = 24$
9	$9 + 3 = 12$	$9 \cdot 3 = 27$
$\Sigma Y = 33$	$\Sigma(Y + 3) = 48$	$\Sigma(Y \cdot 3) = 99$
	$\Sigma Y + n \cdot c = 48$	$\Sigma Y \cdot c = 99$
	$33 + (5 \cdot 3) = 48$	$33 \cdot 3 = 99$
	$33 + 15 = 48$	

The mean for the original Y-variable:

$= \Sigma Y / N = 33 / 5 = 6.6$

The mean for the Y-variable after adding the constant to each value:

$= \Sigma(Y + c) / N = 48 / 5 = 9.6$

$= \mu_{\text{original}} + c = 6.6 + 3 = 9.6$

The mean for the Y-variable after multiplying each value by the constant:

$= \Sigma(Y \cdot c) / N = 99 / 5 = 19.8$

$= \mu_{\text{original}} \cdot c = 6.6 \cdot 3 = 19.8$

Order of Mathematical Operations

Summation notation follows the same order of operations that is used with traditional mathematical operations. We first solve for operations within parentheses; we then go outside the parentheses to perform the next operation. The three primary forms of operations are exponentiation, multiplication and division, and addition and subtraction. The order of these mathematical operations is given in Table E.4.

Table E.4
Order of Mathematical Operations

1. Perform operations within parentheses first.
2. Perform exponentiation second.
3. Perform multiplication and division third.
4. Perform addition and subtraction last.

Here are several examples that illustrate the rules for simple arithmetic:

$10 \cdot 5 + 2 = (10 \cdot 5) + 2 = 50 + 2 = 52$

$10 \cdot (5 + 2) = 10 \cdot 7 = 70$

$10 + 5 \cdot 2 = 10 + (5 \cdot 2) = 10 + 10 = 20$

$(10 + 5) \cdot 2 = 15 \cdot 2 = 30$

$10 \cdot 5^2 + 2 = 10 \cdot 25 + 2 = 252$

$(10 \cdot 5)^2 + 2 = 50^2 + 2 = 2502$

$10 + 5^2 \cdot 2 = 10 + (25 \cdot 2) = 10 + 50 = 60$

$(10 + 5^2) \cdot 2 = (10 + 25) \cdot 2 = 35 \cdot 2 = 70$

We will use Example E.3 to illustrate summation and the order of operations. Suppose we want to find the sums of the squared deviations *(SS)* from the mean of the *X*-variable in Example E.3. The *SS* can be obtained from either Equation E.7 or Equation E.8 as follows:

$$SS = \sum (X - \bar{X})^2 \quad \text{(E.7)}$$

or:

$$SS = \sum X^2 - \frac{(\sum X)^2}{n} \quad \text{(E.8)}$$

We will illustrate the use of Equation E.8 to find *SS*. We first square each of the five *X* values, then sum these squares. Next, we sum the five *X* values, working within the parentheses. We then square this sum. Next we divide the square of the sum by *n*. Finally, we subtract the result of this division from the *SS* value. For Example E.3, the answer is obtained as follows:

$$\sum X^2 - \frac{(\sum X)^2}{n} = 139 - \frac{(23)^2}{5}$$

$$= 139 - 105.8$$

$$= 33.2$$

Algebraic Proof of the Equivalency of Sums of Squares Equations

We can also use our three summation theorems and our rules for the order of mathematical operations to verify that Equation E.7 and Equation E.8 are algebraically equal. Before the availability of scientific calculators and computers, this was a very important proof, because computing values manually with Equation E.7 was much more time consuming that with Equation E.8. However, Equation E.7 directly represents the mathematical process, while Equation E.8 is simply an algebraic derivation that lacks any intuitive value. Most readers have access to scientific calculators with built-in statistical function keys, including a key for the standard deviation. Since the sums of squares can be easily obtained from the standard deviation, the equations given throughout the present textbook are based upon Equation E.7 instead of Equation E.8. The proof of the equivalency of these two equations, without omitting any steps, is given below:

$$\sum (X - \overline{X})^2 = \sum[(X - \overline{X})\cdot(X - \overline{X})]$$

$$= \sum[X^2 - \overline{X}X - \overline{X}X + \overline{X}^2]$$

$$= \sum[X^2 - 2\overline{X}X + \overline{X}^2]$$

$$= \sum X^2 - \sum 2\overline{X}X + \sum \overline{X}^2$$

$$= \sum X^2 - 2\overline{X}\sum X + \sum \overline{X}^2$$

$$= \sum X^2 - 2\overline{X}\sum X + n\overline{X}^2$$

$$= \sum X^2 - 2\frac{\sum X}{n}\sum X + n\frac{\sum X}{n}\frac{\sum X}{n}$$

$$= \sum X^2 - 2\frac{(\sum X)^2}{n} + \frac{(\sum X)^2}{n}$$

$$= \sum X^2 - \frac{(\sum X)^2}{n}$$

Multiplication Notation

Multiplication notation is very similar to summation notation. We can use multiplication notation when we are calculating the *product* of a set of values, rather than the *summation* of that set of values. Instead of using the uppercase Greek letter sigma (Σ), with multiplication notation we use the uppercase Greek letter *pi* (Π). This symbol is used to indicate that the mathematical operation of multiplication is to be performed. Keep in mind that this is the uppercase *pi* symbol, not the lowercase *pi* (π), where $\pi = 3.1416$. Equation E.9 illustrates the general form of such a multiplication process:

$$\prod_{i=1}^{n} X_i = X_1 \cdot X_2 \cdot X_3 \cdots X_n \qquad \text{(E.9)}$$

where:

$n =$ the number of steps in the multiplication operation

$i =$ the starting point at which the operation begins

$X_i =$ the ith element in the data set

Returning to Example E.1, suppose that we want to determine the product of the five values, instead of their sum. Here are the results of the new process:

$$\prod_{i=1}^{n} X_i = \prod_{i=1}^{5} X_i$$

$$= X_1 \cdot X_2 \cdot X_3 \cdot X_4 \cdot X_5$$

$$= 3 \cdot 4 \cdot 8 \cdot 1 \cdot 7$$

$$= 672$$

The multiplication process reveals that the product of these five values is 672. Obtaining the product of a set of numbers such as this is very useful when calculating the *geometric mean.* We also should note that if any of the values within the variable is equal to zero, the product of these values is also equal to zero.

Practice Problems
Multiple Choice

Solve the following set of problems based upon a population of data consisting of 12, 17, 14, 15, 21, 28, and 19, with a mean of $\mu = 18$.

1. $\sum_{i=1}^{N} X_i = ?$

A. 142
B. 126
C. 625
D. 38
E. 421

2. $\sum X = ?$

A. 142
B. 126
C. 625
D. 38
E. 421

3. $\frac{\sum X}{N} = ?$

A. 18.000
B. 17.000
C. 17.857
D. 23.413
E. 16.453

4. $\sum X^2 = ?$

A. 7822
B. 15625
C. 2440
D. 8750
E. 126

5. $(\sum X)^2 = ?$

A. 7822
B. 15876
C. 2403
D. 8750
E. 126

6. $\sum_{i=2}^{N-1} X_i = ?$

A. 107
B. 113
C. 126
D. 95
E. 49

7. $\sum (X - \mu)^2 = ?$

A. 170.857
B. 146.449
C. 172.000
D. 0.000
E. 542.567

8. $\sum X^2 - \frac{(\sum X)^2}{N} = ?$

A. 170.857
B. 152.194
C. 15527.429
D. 000.000
E. 172.000

9. $$\frac{\sum X^2 - \frac{(\sum X)^2}{N}}{N} = ?$$

A. 70.567
B. 71.011
C. 18.204
D. 24.571
E. 13.235

10. $$\sqrt{\frac{\sum X^2 - \frac{(\sum X)^2}{N}}{N}} = ?$$

A. 4.957
B. 3.456
C. 8.231
D. 9.488
E. 0.000

11. $$\prod_{i=1}^{N} X_i = ?$$

A. 0
B. 478,608,480
C. 126
D. 68,372,640
E. 8,268.775

12. $$\sqrt[N]{\prod_{i=1}^{N} X_i} = ?$$

A. 0
B. 478,608,480
C. 126
D. 68,372,640
E. 17.3779

13. $e^{\frac{\sum_{i=1}^{N} \ln X_i}{N}} = ?$

A. 0
B. 478,608,480
C. 126
D. 68,372,640
E. 17.3779

14. $\sum_{i=1}^{N} \frac{1}{X_i} = ?$

A. 0.0000
B. 0.0079
C. 8.3415
D. 2.5631
E. 0.4162

15. $\frac{\sum \frac{1}{X_i}}{N} = ?$

A. 0.0011
B. 0.0079
C. 0.3415
D. 0.0595
E. 7.0000

16. $\frac{1}{\left(\frac{\sum \frac{1}{X}}{N}\right)} = ?$

A. 0.0011
B. 0.0079
C. 0.3415
D. 0.0595
E. 16.8181

Practice Problems
Computational Practice

I. For the following set of problems, we have collected data for a sample of 6 supervisors. The X variable represents the number of months on the job for each of these supervisors, while the Y variable represents the number of subordinates working for each supervisor. The constant term, c, represents the mean number of months on the job. Use these values to solve the next 24 problems:

$X_1 = 6$	$Y_1 = 8$	$c = 3.5$
$X_2 = 4$	$Y_2 = 6$	
$X_3 = 5$	$Y_3 = 6$	$\overline{X} = 3.5$
$X_4 = 2$	$Y_4 = 4$	
$X_5 = 1$	$Y_5 = 1$	$\overline{Y} = 4.5$
$X_6 = 3$	$Y_6 = 2$	

1. $\Sigma X =$

2. $\Sigma Y =$

3. $\Sigma c \cdot X =$

4. $\Sigma (X + Y) =$

5. $\sum_{j=1}^{2} \sum_{i=1}^{5} (X_i - Y_j)^2 =$

6. $\sum_{i=1}^{4} Y_{i+1} =$

7. $\Sigma (X - c)^2 =$

8. $\sum_{i=1}^{6} (Y_i - 4.5)^3 =$

9. $\Sigma X \cdot Y =$

10. $\Sigma X^2 =$

11. $\Sigma Y^2 =$

12. $(\Sigma X)^2 =$

13. $(\Sigma Y)^2 =$

14. $\Sigma (X - \overline{X})^2 =$

15. $\Sigma X^2 - \dfrac{(\Sigma X)^2}{N} =$

16. $\Sigma (Y - \overline{Y})^2 =$

17. $\Sigma Y^2 - \dfrac{(\Sigma Y)^2}{N} =$

18. $\Sigma (X - \overline{X}) \cdot (Y - \overline{Y}) =$

19. $\Sigma X \cdot Y - \dfrac{(\Sigma X) \cdot (\Sigma Y)}{N} =$

20. $\dfrac{\sum (X - \overline{X})^2}{n - 1} =$

21. $\sqrt{\dfrac{\sum (X - \overline{X})^2}{n - 1}} =$

22. $\dfrac{\sum (Y - \overline{Y})^2}{n - 1} =$

23. $\sqrt{\dfrac{\sum (Y - \overline{Y})^2}{n - 1}} =$

24. $\dfrac{\sum [(X - \overline{X}) \cdot (Y - \overline{Y})]}{\sqrt{\sum (X - \overline{X})^2 \cdot \sum (Y - \overline{Y})^2}} =$

II. For the following set of problems, we have collected data for a sample of 5 shop workers. The X variable represents the placement scores for these workers, while the Y variable represents the performance scores for these same workers after 6 months on the job. Use these values to solve the next 15 problems:

$X_1 = 4$	$Y_1 = 3$
$X_2 = 3$	$Y_2 = 2$
$X_3 = 1$	$Y_3 = 1$
$X_4 = 2$	$Y_4 = 2$
$X_5 = 3$	$Y_5 = 5$

1. $\Sigma X =$
2. $\Sigma Y =$
3. $\Sigma X^2 =$
4. $\Sigma Y^2 =$
5. $(\Sigma X)^2 =$
6. $(\Sigma Y)^2 =$
7. $\Sigma(X - 2)^2 =$
8. $\sum_{i=2}^{4} Y_i =$
9. $\Sigma X \cdot Y =$
10. $\Sigma [(X - 5)(Y - 4)] =$
11. $\Sigma (4X - 2Y)^2 =$
12. $\sum_{i=1}^{3} (X_i / Y_i) =$

13. $$r = \frac{\sum X \cdot Y - \frac{(\sum X) \cdot (\sum Y)}{n}}{\sqrt{\left(\sum X^2 - \frac{(\sum X)^2}{n}\right) \cdot \left(\sum Y^2 - \frac{(\sum Y)^2}{n}\right)}} =$$

14. $$b = \frac{\sum X \cdot Y - \frac{(\sum X) \cdot (\sum Y)}{n}}{\sum X^2 - \frac{(\sum X)^2}{n}} =$$

15. $a = \overline{Y} - b \cdot \overline{X} =$

Note: Use the value for b found in problem # 14 above

III. For the following summation problems, you will need to use the symbols defined below. Keep in mind that there are four samples, each with a different number of cases. The data for the four samples are given in the table below.

Sample Data for 4 Groups

I	II	III	IV
15	11	18	10
14	13	19	9
17	15	22	11
20	11	18	8
15	12	22	12
18	13	24	13
14		25	12
			10

Symbols:

n_j = the number of cases in the *j*th sample

n_t = the total number of cases $(n_1 + n_2 + \cdots + n_j)$ in the samples of interest

k = the number of samples

X_{ij} = the *i*th case in the *j*th sample

$\overline{X}_j$ = the sample mean of the *j*th sample

$\overline{X}_t$ = the grand mean, based upon the collapsing of all samples into one group

1. Find the means of each of the four groups, and find the grand mean:

$\overline{X}_1 =$ $\overline{X}_2 =$ $\overline{X}_3 =$ $\overline{X}_4 =$ $\overline{X}_t =$

2. Find the values of SS_A, SS_W, and SS_T, as defined below:

$$SS_A = \sum_{j=1}^{k} n_j \cdot (\overline{X}_j - \overline{X}_t)^2 =$$

$$SS_W = \sum_{j=1}^{k} \sum_{i=1}^{n_j} (X_{i,j} - \overline{X}_j)^2 =$$

$$SS_T = \sum_{j=1}^{k} \sum_{i=1}^{n_j} (X_{i,j} - \overline{X}_t)^2 =$$

APPENDIX F

FLOWCHARTS FOR STATISTICAL DECISION-MAKING

F

Flowcharts for Statistical Decision-Making

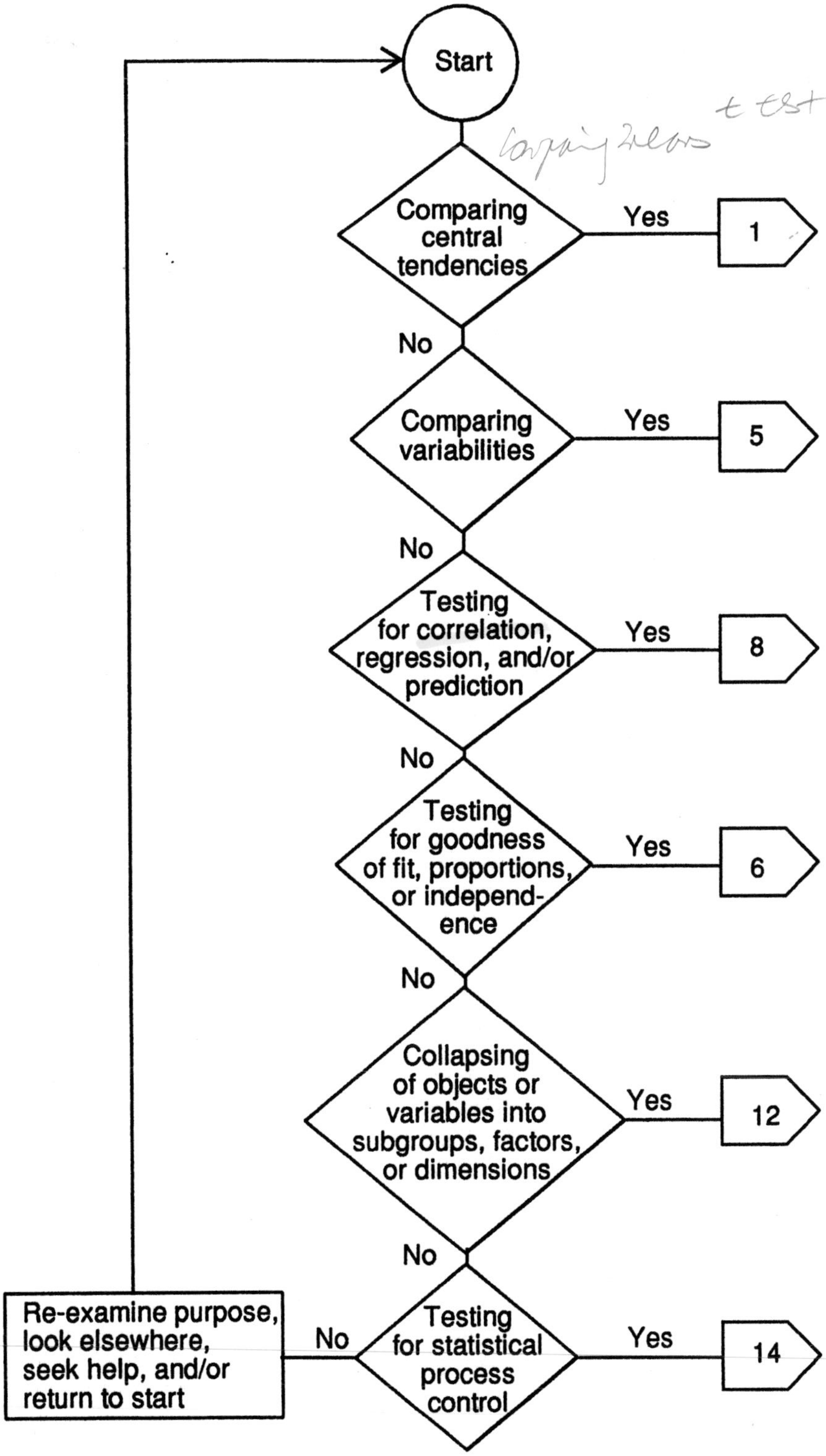

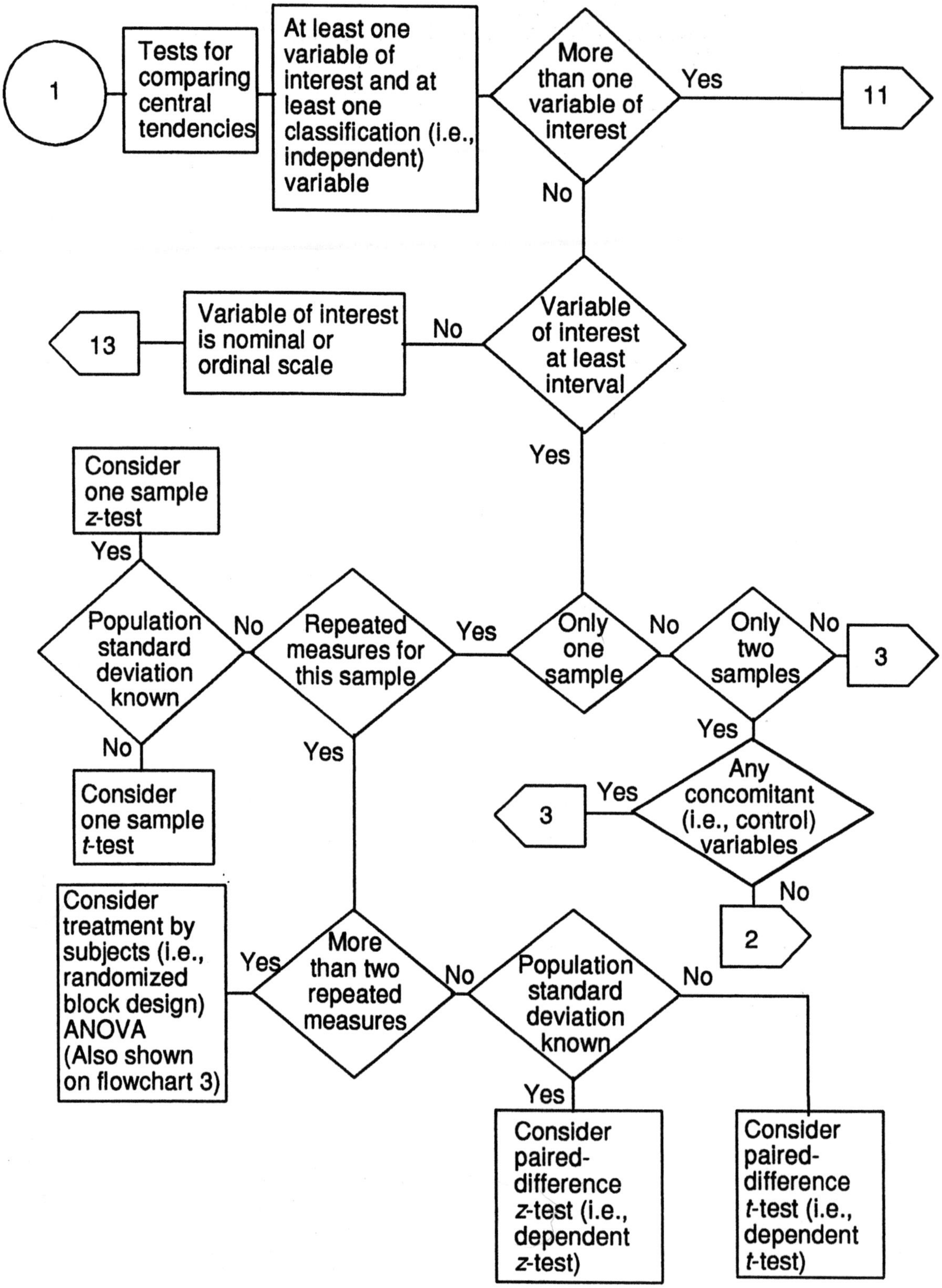
1
Tests for comparing central tendencies
At least one variable of interest and at least one classification (i.e., independent) variable
More than one variable of interest
Yes
11
No
Variable of interest at least interval
No
Variable of interest is nominal or ordinal scale
13
Yes
Only one sample
No
Only two samples
No
3
Yes
Any concomitant (i.e., control) variables
Yes
3
No
2
Yes
Repeated measures for this sample
No
Population standard deviation known
Yes
Consider one sample z-test
No
Consider one sample t-test
Yes
More than two repeated measures
Yes
Consider treatment by subjects (i.e., randomized block design) ANOVA (Also shown on flowchart 3)
No
Population standard deviation known
Yes
Consider paired-difference z-test (i.e., dependent z-test)
No
Consider paired-difference t-test (i.e., dependent t-test)

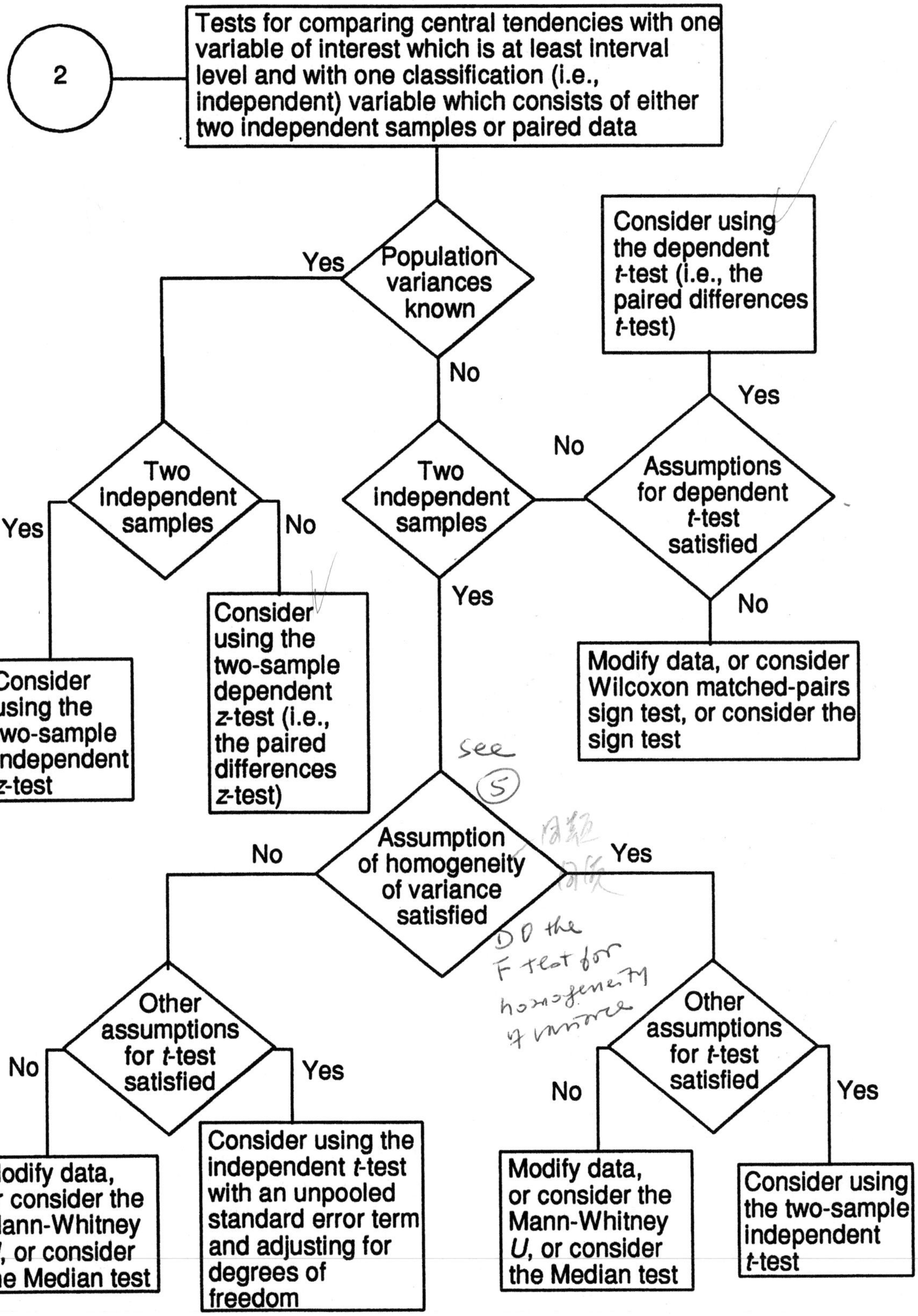
2
Tests for comparing central tendencies with one variable of interest which is at least interval level and with one classification (i.e., independent) variable which consists of either two independent samples or paired data
Population variances known
Yes
No
Two independent samples
Yes
No
Consider using the two-sample independent z-test
Consider using the two-sample dependent z-test (i.e., the paired differences z-test)
Two independent samples
No
Yes
Assumptions for dependent t-test satisfied
Yes
No
Consider using the dependent t-test (i.e., the paired differences t-test)
Modify data, or consider Wilcoxon matched-pairs sign test, or consider the sign test
Assumption of homogeneity of variance satisfied
No
Yes
Other assumptions for t-test satisfied
No
Yes
Modify data, or consider the Mann-Whitney U, or consider the Median test
Consider using the independent t-test with an unpooled standard error term and adjusting for degrees of freedom
Other assumptions for t-test satisfied
No
Yes
Modify data, or consider the Mann-Whitney U, or consider the Median test
Consider using the two-sample independent t-test

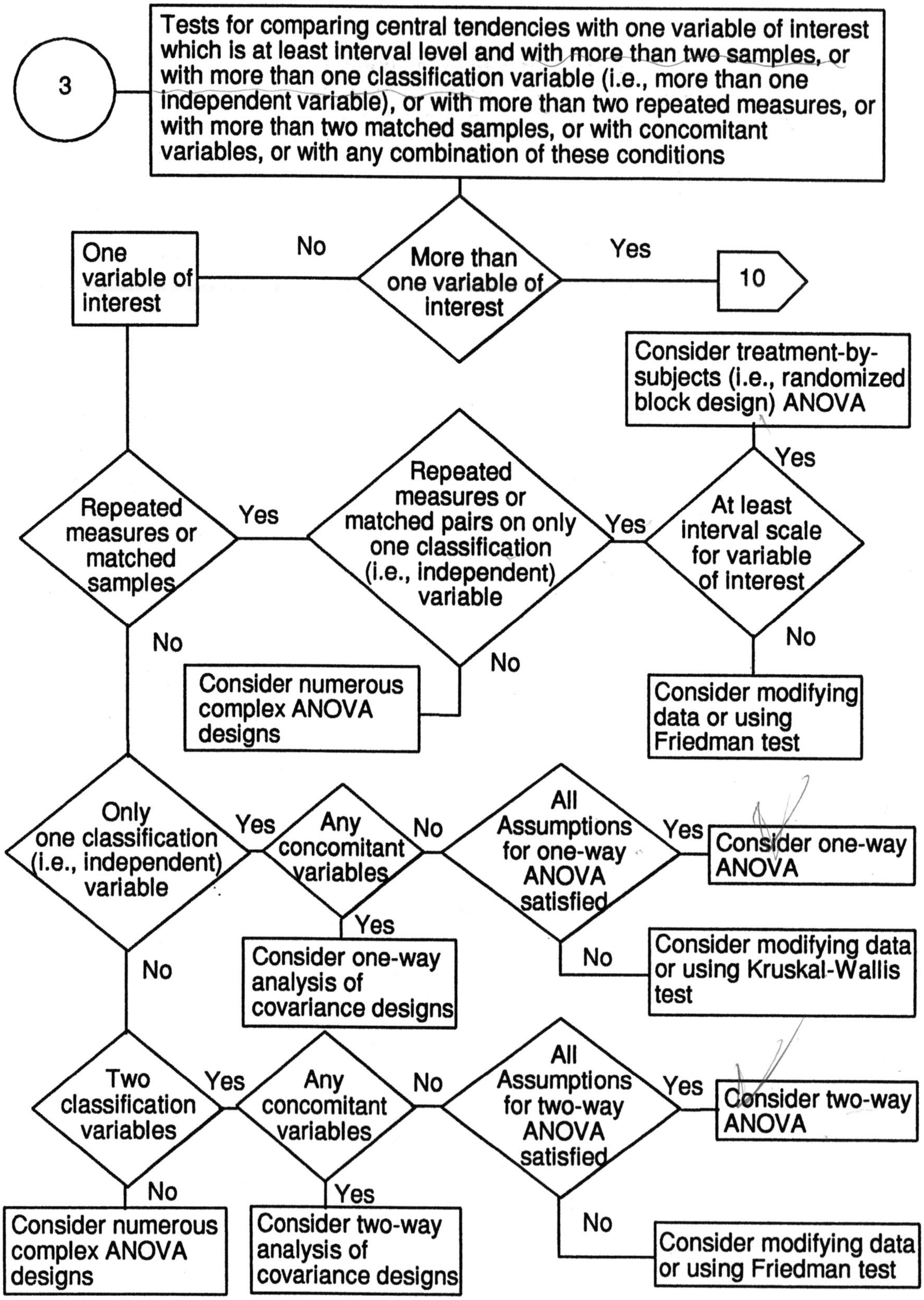
3
Tests for comparing central tendencies with one variable of interest which is at least interval level and with more than two samples, or with more than one classification variable (i.e., more than one independent variable), or with more than two repeated measures, or with more than two matched samples, or with concomitant variables, or with any combination of these conditions
More than one variable of interest
Yes
10
No
One variable of interest
Repeated measures or matched samples
Yes
Repeated measures or matched pairs on only one classification (i.e., independent) variable
Yes
At least interval scale for variable of interest
Yes
Consider treatment-by-subjects (i.e., randomized block design) ANOVA
No
Consider modifying data or using Friedman test
No
Consider numerous complex ANOVA designs
No
Only one classification (i.e., independent) variable
Yes
Any concomitant variables
Yes
Consider one-way analysis of covariance designs
No
All Assumptions for one-way ANOVA satisfied
Yes
Consider one-way ANOVA
No
Consider modifying data or using Kruskal-Wallis test
No
Two classification variables
Yes
Any concomitant variables
Yes
Consider two-way analysis of covariance designs
No
All Assumptions for two-way ANOVA satisfied
Yes
Consider two-way ANOVA
No
Consider modifying data or using Friedman test
No
Consider numerous complex ANOVA designs

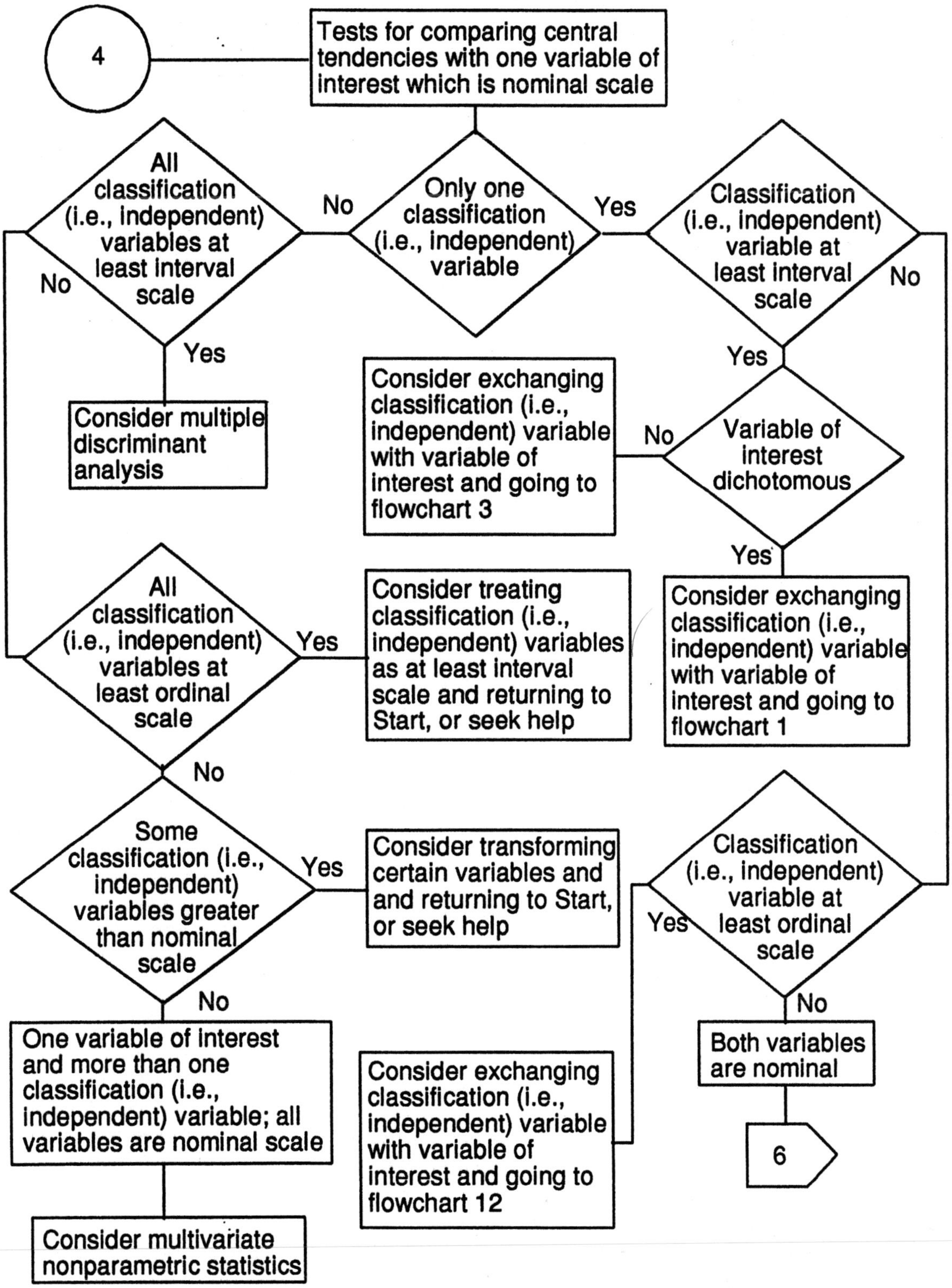
4
Tests for comparing central tendencies with one variable of interest which is nominal scale
Only one classification (i.e., independent) variable
No
All classification (i.e., independent) variables at least interval scale
No
Yes
Consider multiple discriminant analysis
All classification (i.e., independent) variables at least ordinal scale
Yes
Consider treating classification (i.e., independent) variables as at least interval scale and returning to Start, or seek help
No
Some classification (i.e., independent) variables greater than nominal scale
Yes
Consider transforming certain variables and and returning to Start, or seek help
No
One variable of interest and more than one classification (i.e., independent) variable; all variables are nominal scale
Consider multivariate nonparametric statistics
Yes
Classification (i.e., independent) variable at least interval scale
No
Yes
Variable of interest dichotomous
No
Consider exchanging classification (i.e., independent) variable with variable of interest and going to flowchart 3
Yes
Consider exchanging classification (i.e., independent) variable with variable of interest and going to flowchart 1
Classification (i.e., independent) variable at least ordinal scale
Yes
Consider exchanging classification (i.e., independent) variable with variable of interest and going to flowchart 12
No
Both variables are nominal
6

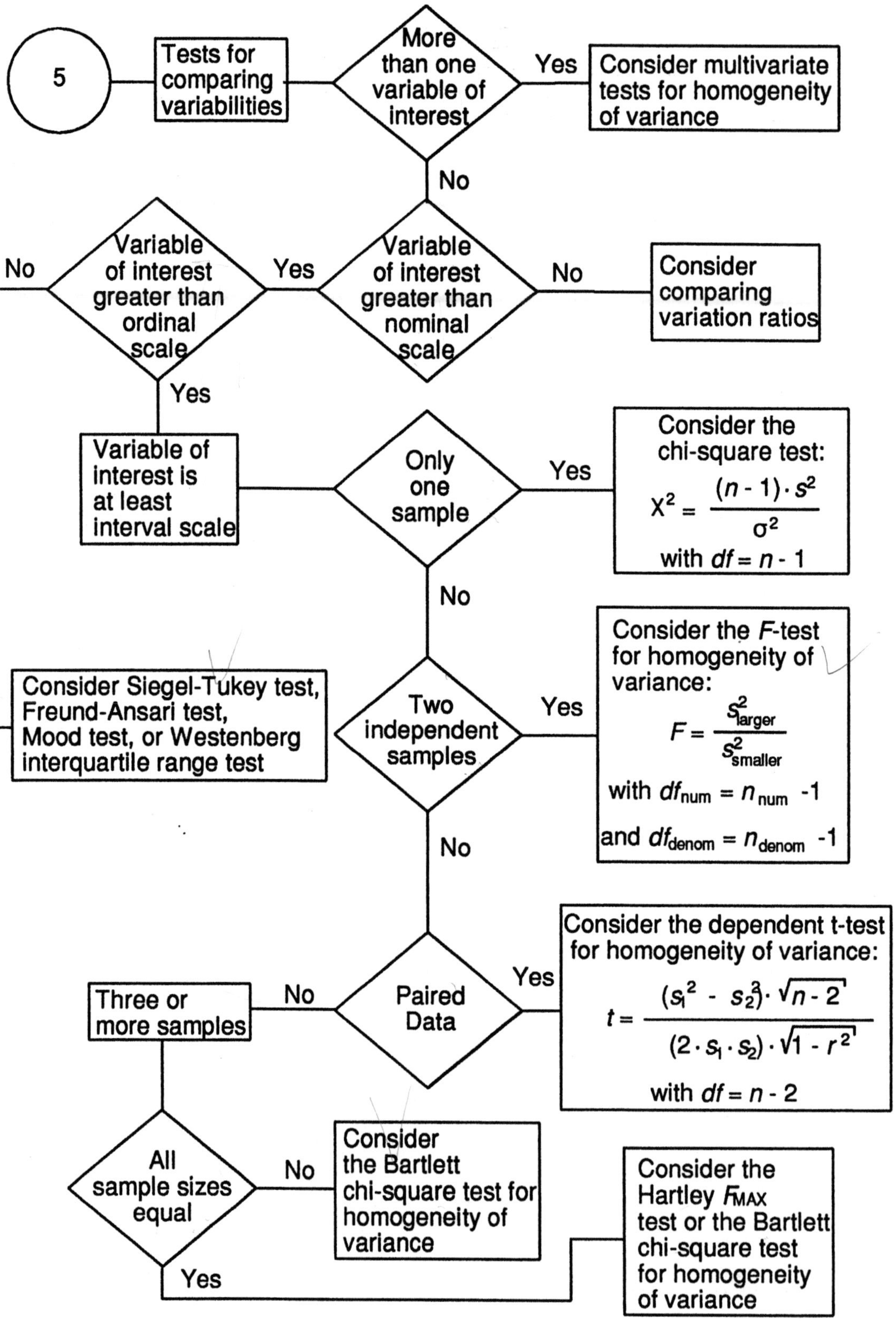
5
Tests for comparing variabilities
More than one variable of interest
Yes
Consider multivariate tests for homogeneity of variance
No
Variable of interest greater than nominal scale
No
Consider comparing variation ratios
Yes
Variable of interest greater than ordinal scale
No
Yes
Variable of interest is at least interval scale
Only one sample
Yes
Consider the chi-square test:
$X^2 = \frac{(n-1) \cdot s^2}{\sigma^2}$
with $df = n - 1$
No
Consider Siegel-Tukey test, Freund-Ansari test, Mood test, or Westenberg interquartile range test
Two independent samples
Yes
Consider the F-test for homogeneity of variance:
$F = \frac{s^2_{larger}}{s^2_{smaller}}$
with $df_{num} = n_{num} - 1$
and $df_{denom} = n_{denom} - 1$
No
Paired Data
Yes
Consider the dependent t-test for homogeneity of variance:
$t = \frac{(s_1^2 - s_2^2) \cdot \sqrt{n-2}}{(2 \cdot s_1 \cdot s_2) \cdot \sqrt{1 - r^2}}$
with $df = n - 2$
No
Three or more samples
All sample sizes equal
No
Consider the Bartlett chi-square test for homogeneity of variance
Yes
Consider the Hartley F_{MAX} test or the Bartlett chi-square test for homogeneity of variance

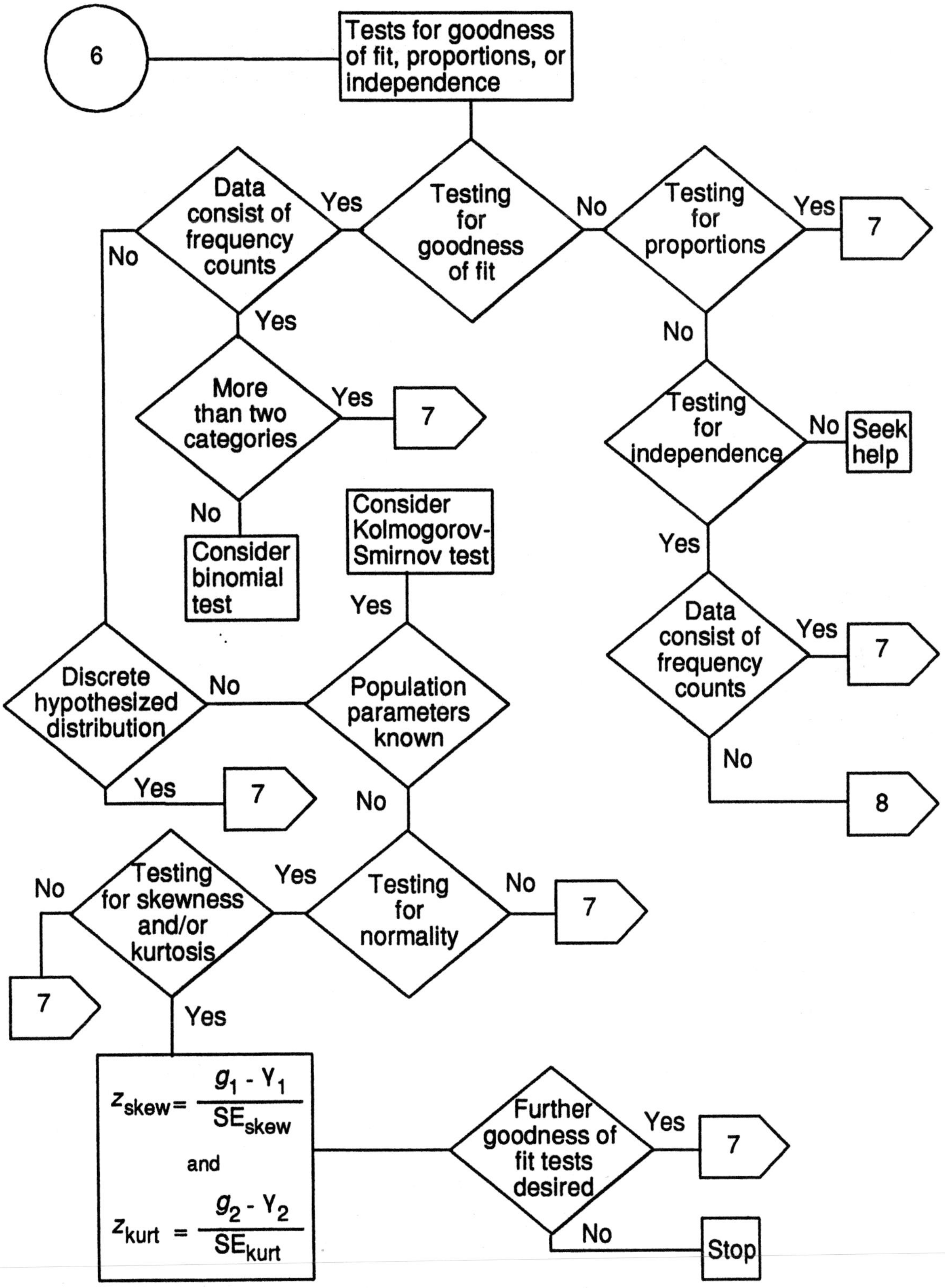
6
Tests for goodness of fit, proportions, or independence
Testing for goodness of fit
Yes
No
Data consist of frequency counts
No
Yes
More than two categories
Yes
7
No
Consider binomial test
Testing for proportions
Yes
7
No
Testing for independence
No
Seek help
Yes
Data consist of frequency counts
Yes
7
No
8
Consider Kolmogorov-Smirnov test
Yes
Discrete hypothesized distribution
No
Population parameters known
Yes
7
No
Testing for normality
No
7
Yes
Testing for skewness and/or kurtosis
No
7
Yes
$z_{skew} = \frac{g_1 - \gamma_1}{SE_{skew}}$
and
$z_{kurt} = \frac{g_2 - \gamma_2}{SE_{kurt}}$
Further goodness of fit tests desired
Yes
7
No
Stop

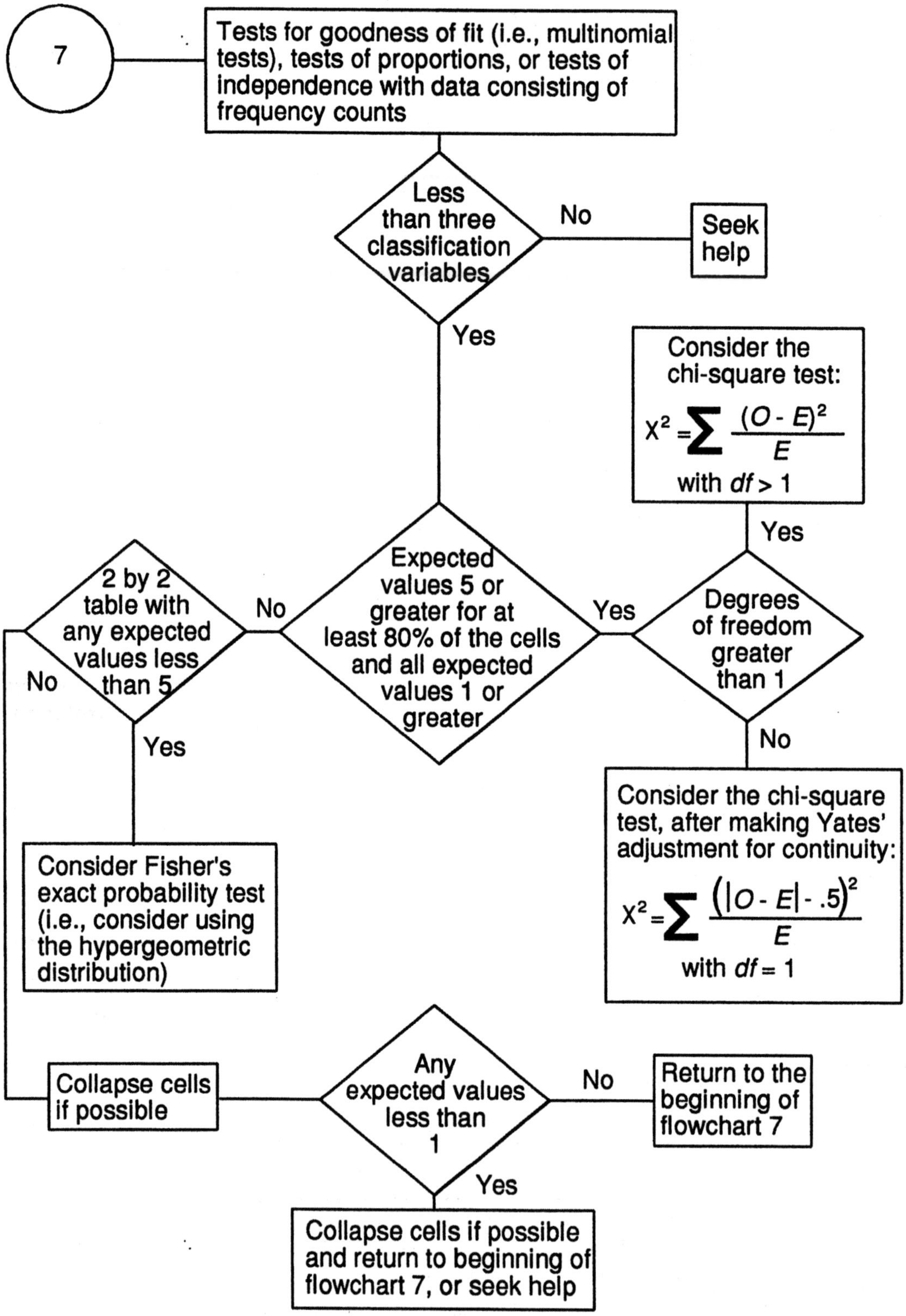

7
Tests for goodness of fit (i.e., multinomial tests), tests of proportions, or tests of independence with data consisting of frequency counts
Less than three classification variables
No
Seek help
Yes
Consider the chi-square test:
$X^2 = \sum \frac{(O - E)^2}{E}$
with $df > 1$
Yes
Expected values 5 or greater for at least 80% of the cells and all expected values 1 or greater
Yes
Degrees of freedom greater than 1
No
Consider the chi-square test, after making Yates' adjustment for continuity:
$X^2 = \sum \frac{(|O - E| - .5)^2}{E}$
with $df = 1$
No
2 by 2 table with any expected values less than 5
No
Yes
Consider Fisher's exact probability test (i.e., consider using the hypergeometric distribution)
Collapse cells if possible
Any expected values less than 1
No
Return to the beginning of flowchart 7
Yes
Collapse cells if possible and return to beginning of flowchart 7, or seek help

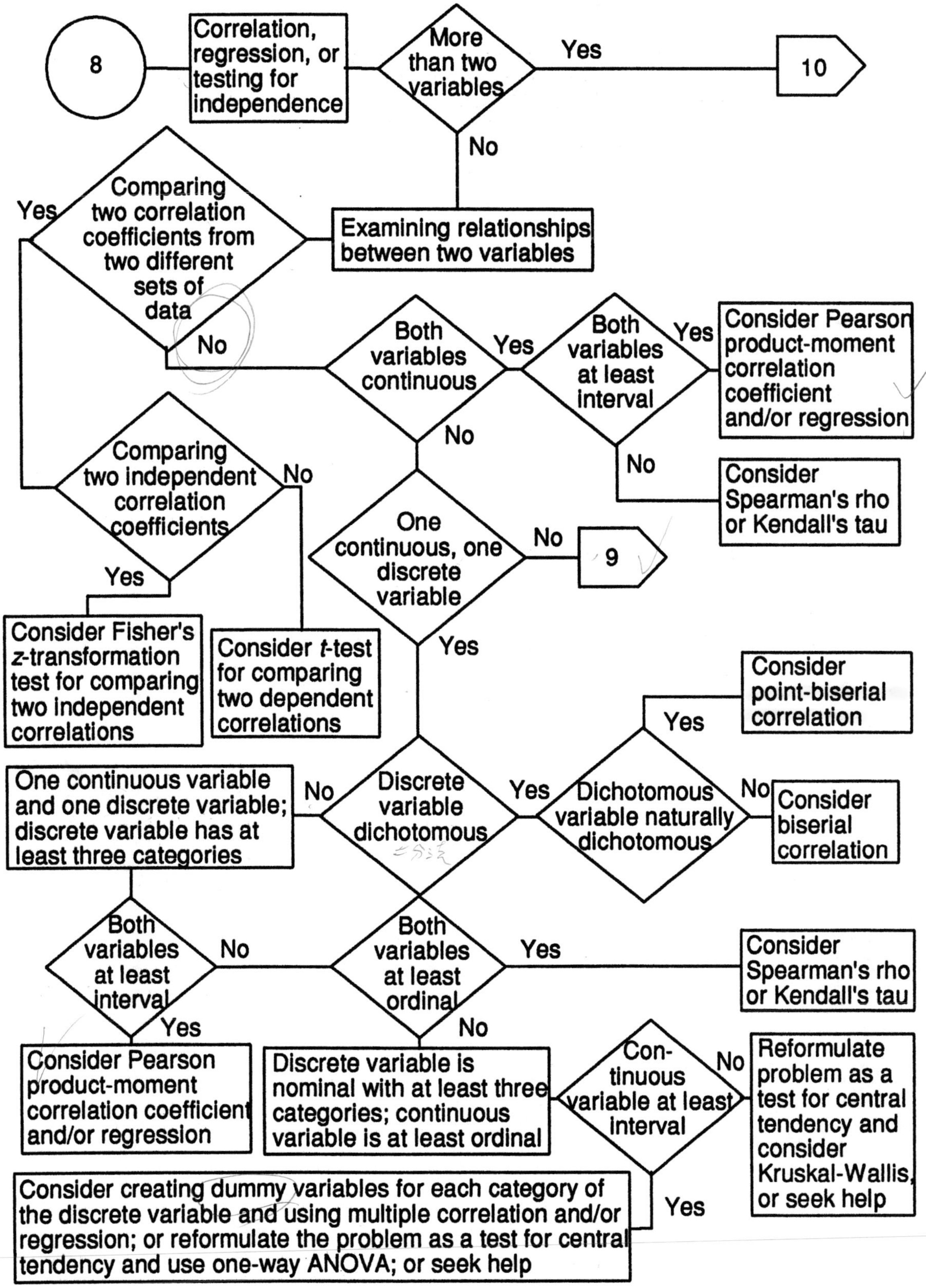
8
Correlation, regression, or testing for independence
More than two variables
Yes
10
No
Examining relationships between two variables
Comparing two correlation coefficients from two different sets of data
Yes
No
Both variables continuous
Yes
Both variables at least interval
Yes
Consider Pearson product-moment correlation coefficient and/or regression
No
Consider Spearman's rho or Kendall's tau
No
Comparing two independent correlation coefficients
No
Yes
One continuous, one discrete variable
No
9
Yes
Consider Fisher's z-transformation test for comparing two independent correlations
Consider t-test for comparing two dependent correlations
Consider point-biserial correlation
Yes
One continuous variable and one discrete variable; discrete variable has at least three categories
No
Discrete variable dichotomous
Yes
Dichotomous variable naturally dichotomous
No
Consider biserial correlation
Both variables at least interval
No
Both variables at least ordinal
Yes
Consider Spearman's rho or Kendall's tau
Yes
No
Consider Pearson product-moment correlation coefficient and/or regression
Discrete variable is nominal with at least three categories; continuous variable is at least ordinal
Con-tinuous variable at least interval
No
Reformulate problem as a test for central tendency and consider Kruskal-Wallis, or seek help
Yes
Consider creating dummy variables for each category of the discrete variable and using multiple correlation and/or regression; or reformulate the problem as a test for central tendency and use one-way ANOVA; or seek help

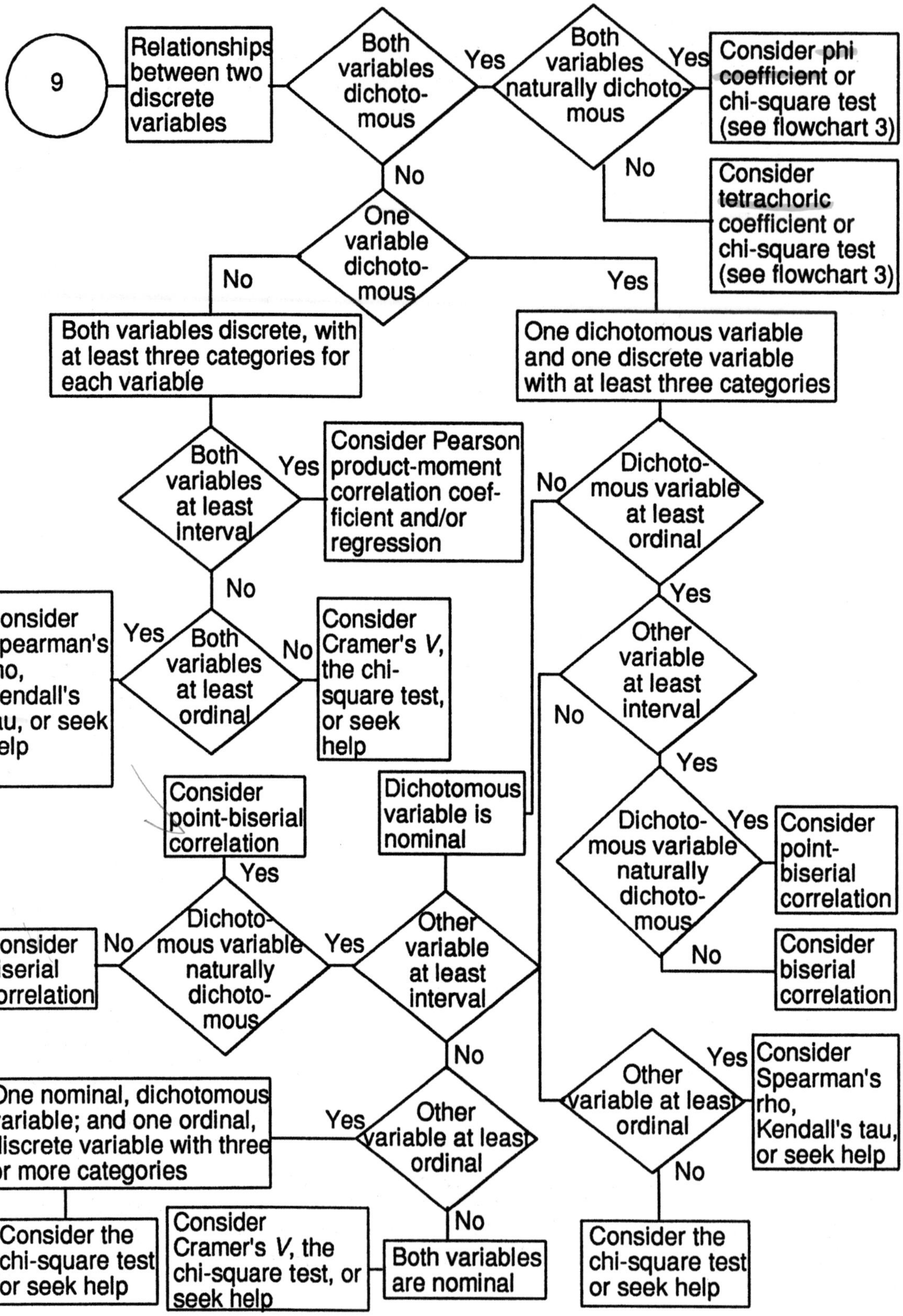
9
Relationships between two discrete variables
Both variables dichotomous
Yes
Both variables naturally dichotomous
Yes
Consider phi coefficient or chi-square test (see flowchart 3)
No
Consider tetrachoric coefficient or chi-square test (see flowchart 3)
No
One variable dichotomous
No
Both variables discrete, with at least three categories for each variable
Yes
One dichotomous variable and one discrete variable with at least three categories
Both variables at least interval
Yes
Consider Pearson product-moment correlation coefficient and/or regression
No
Both variables at least ordinal
Yes
Consider Spearman's rho, Kendall's tau, or seek help
No
Consider Cramer's V, the chi-square test, or seek help
Dichotomous variable at least ordinal
No
Dichotomous variable is nominal
Yes
Other variable at least interval
Yes
Dichotomous variable naturally dichotomous
Yes
Consider point-biserial correlation
No
Consider biserial correlation
No
Other variable at least ordinal
Yes
Consider Spearman's rho, Kendall's tau, or seek help
No
Consider the chi-square test or seek help
Other variable at least interval
Yes
Dichotomous variable naturally dichotomous
Yes
Consider point-biserial correlation
No
Consider biserial correlation
No
Other variable at least ordinal
Yes
One nominal, dichotomous variable; and one ordinal, discrete variable with three or more categories
Consider the chi-square test or seek help
No
Both variables are nominal
Consider Cramer's V, the chi-square test, or seek help

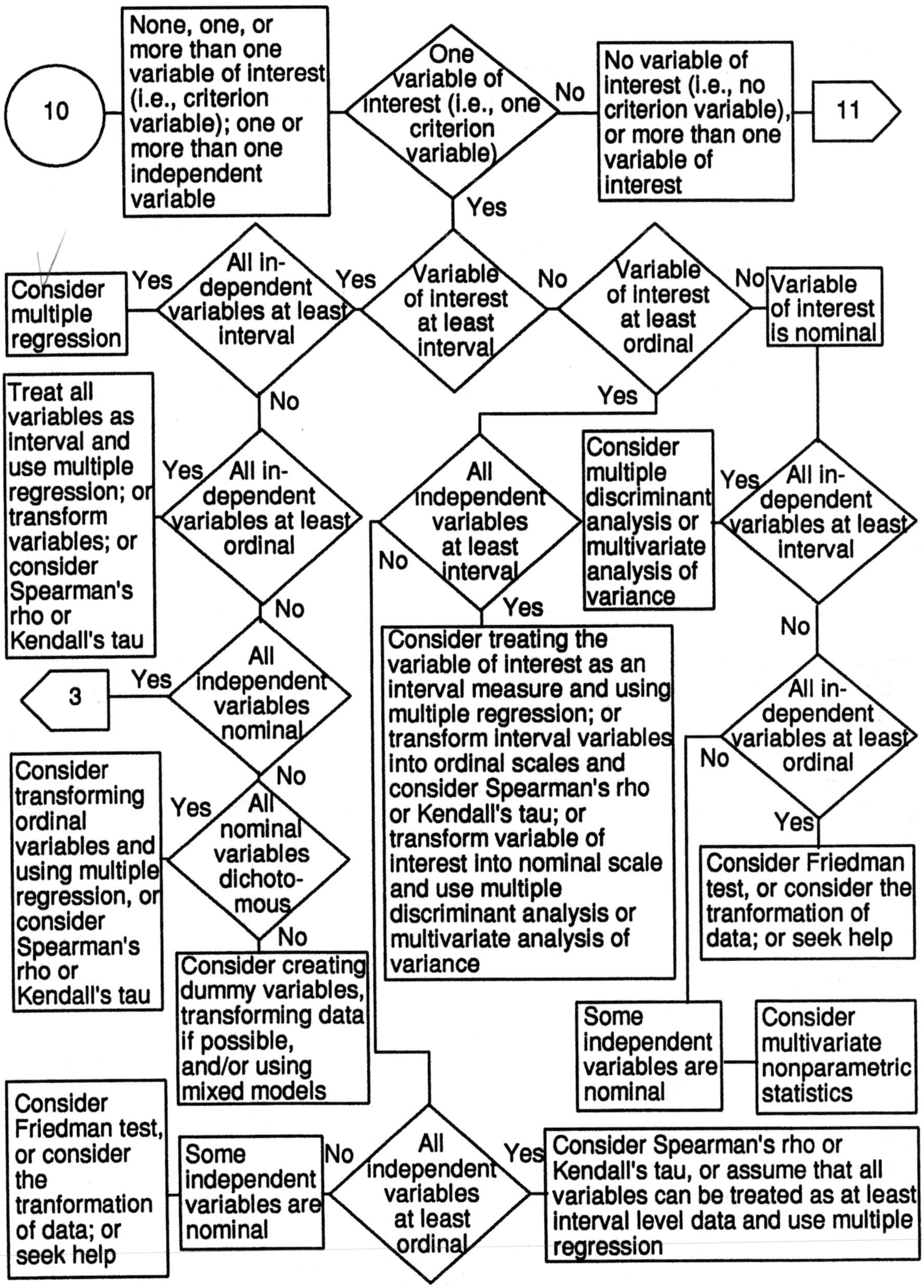
10
None, one, or more than one variable of interest (i.e., criterion variable); one or more than one independent variable
One variable of interest (i.e., one criterion variable)
No
No variable of interest (i.e., no criterion variable), or more than one variable of interest
11
Yes
Consider multiple regression
Yes
All independent variables at least interval
Yes
Variable of interest at least interval
No
Variable of interest at least ordinal
No
Variable of interest is nominal
No
Yes
Treat all variables as interval and use multiple regression; or transform variables; or consider Spearman's rho or Kendall's tau
Yes
All independent variables at least ordinal
All independent variables at least interval
No
Consider multiple discriminant analysis or multivariate analysis of variance
Yes
All independent variables at least interval
No
Yes
No
3
Yes
All independent variables nominal
Consider treating the variable of interest as an interval measure and using multiple regression; or transform interval variables into ordinal scales and consider Spearman's rho or Kendall's tau; or transform variable of interest into nominal scale and use multiple discriminant analysis or multivariate analysis of variance
All independent variables at least ordinal
No
No
Consider transforming ordinal variables and using multiple regression, or consider Spearman's rho or Kendall's tau
Yes
All nominal variables dichotomous
Yes
Consider Friedman test, or consider the tranformation of data; or seek help
No
Consider creating dummy variables, transforming data if possible, and/or using mixed models
Some independent variables are nominal
Consider multivariate nonparametric statistics
Consider Friedman test, or consider the tranformation of data; or seek help
Some independent variables are nominal
No
All independent variables at least ordinal
Yes
Consider Spearman's rho or Kendall's tau, or assume that all variables can be treated as at least interval level data and use multiple regression

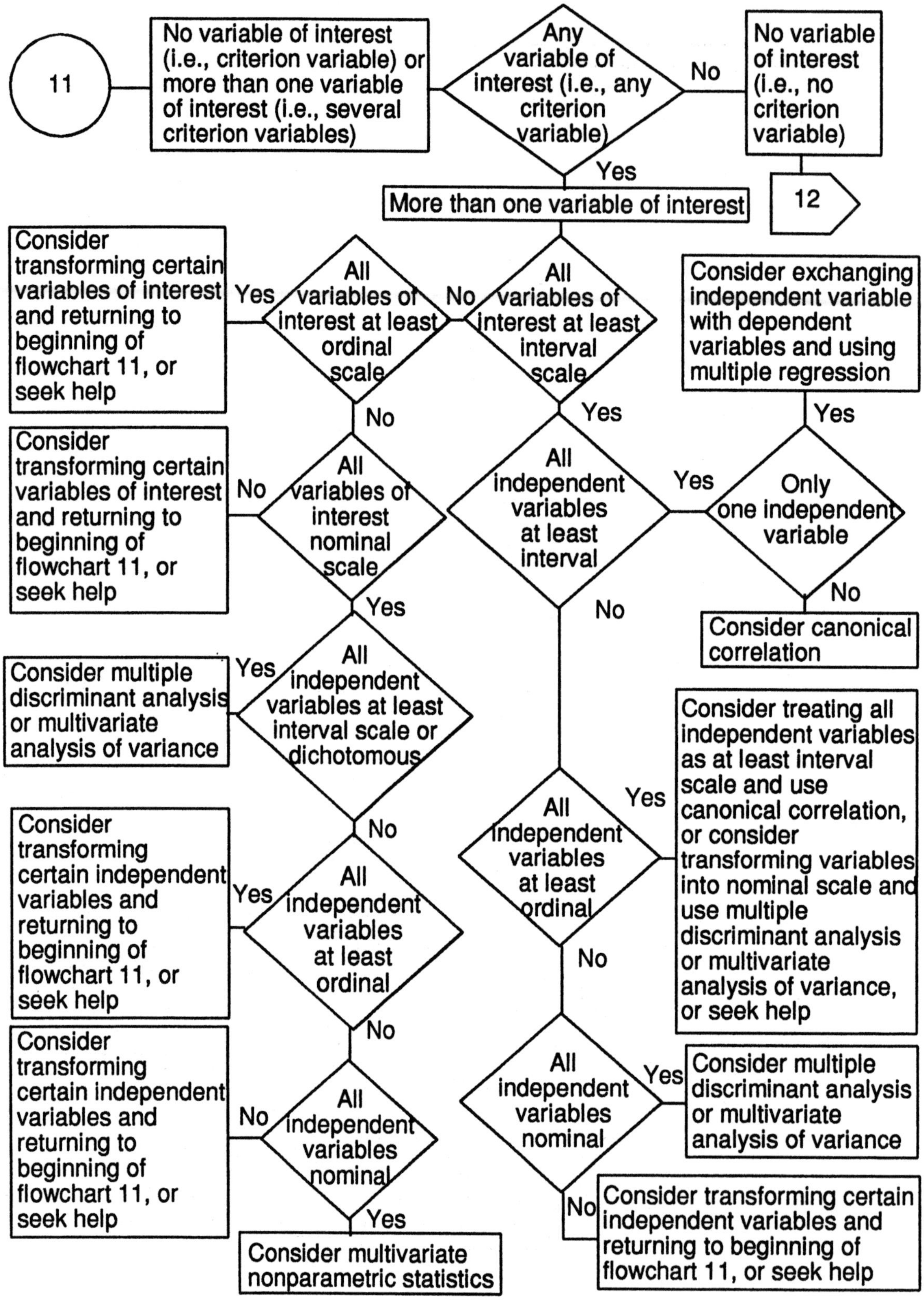
11
No variable of interest (i.e., criterion variable) or more than one variable of interest (i.e., several criterion variables)
Any variable of interest (i.e., any criterion variable)
No
No variable of interest (i.e., no criterion variable)
12
Yes
More than one variable of interest
Consider transforming certain variables of interest and returning to beginning of flowchart 11, or seek help
Yes
All variables of interest at least ordinal scale
No
All variables of interest at least interval scale
Consider exchanging independent variable with dependent variables and using multiple regression
No
Yes
Yes
Consider transforming certain variables of interest and returning to beginning of flowchart 11, or seek help
No
All variables of interest nominal scale
All independent variables at least interval
Yes
Only one independent variable
Yes
No
No
Consider canonical correlation
Consider multiple discriminant analysis or multivariate analysis of variance
Yes
All independent variables at least interval scale or dichotomous
Consider treating all independent variables as at least interval scale and use canonical correlation, or consider transforming variables into nominal scale and use multiple discriminant analysis or multivariate analysis of variance, or seek help
Yes
No
All independent variables at least ordinal
Consider transforming certain independent variables and returning to beginning of flowchart 11, or seek help
Yes
All independent variables at least ordinal
No
No
Consider transforming certain independent variables and returning to beginning of flowchart 11, or seek help
No
All independent variables nominal
All independent variables nominal
Yes
Consider multiple discriminant analysis or multivariate analysis of variance
Yes
No
Consider transforming certain independent variables and returning to beginning of flowchart 11, or seek help
Consider multivariate nonparametric statistics

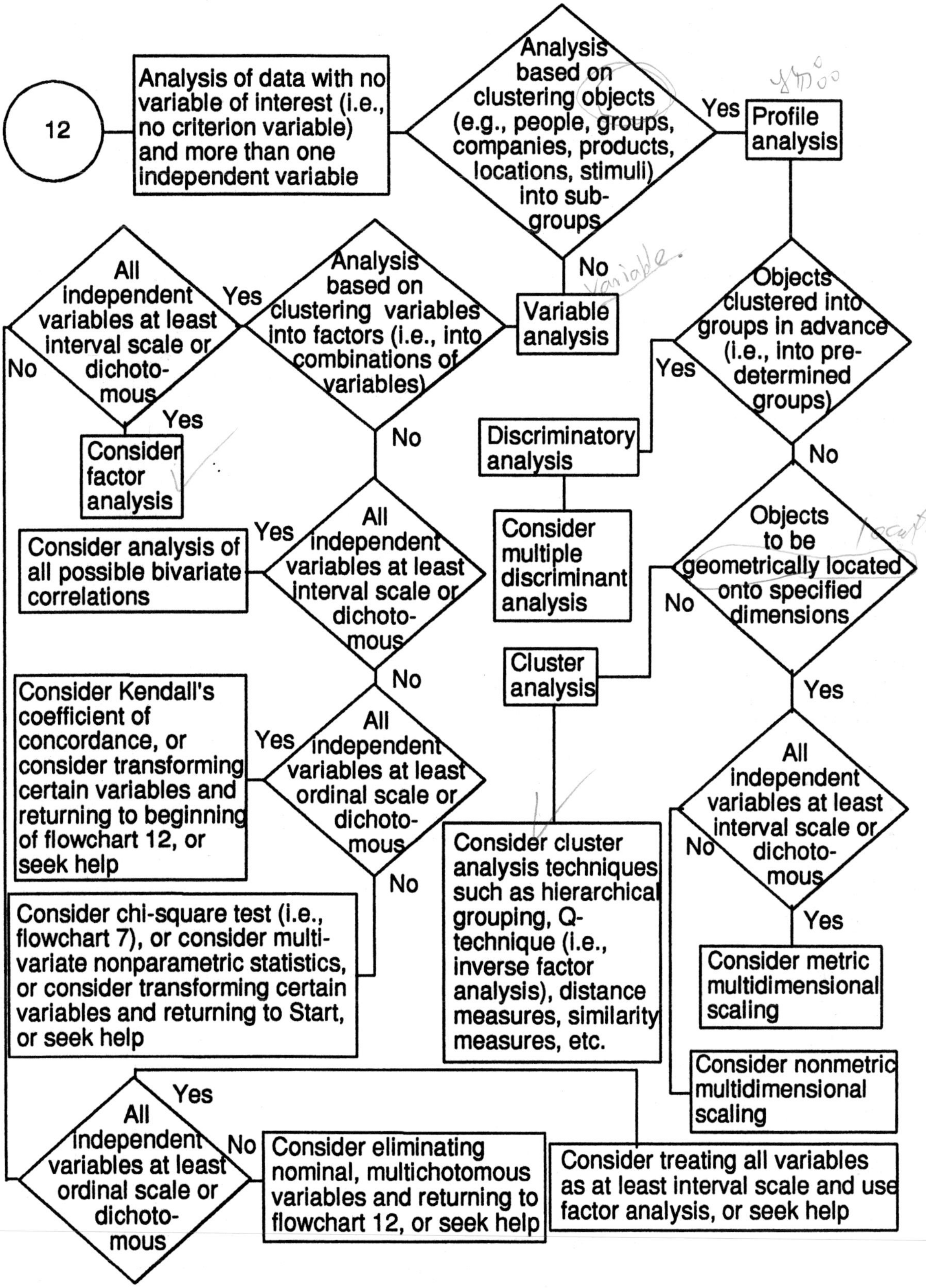
12
Analysis of data with no variable of interest (i.e., no criterion variable) and more than one independent variable
Analysis based on clustering objects (e.g., people, groups, companies, products, locations, stimuli) into sub-groups
Yes
Profile analysis
No
Variable analysis
Analysis based on clustering variables into factors (i.e., into combinations of variables)
Yes
All independent variables at least interval scale or dichotomous
No
Yes
Consider factor analysis
No
All independent variables at least interval scale or dichotomous
Yes
Consider analysis of all possible bivariate correlations
No
All independent variables at least ordinal scale or dichotomous
Yes
Consider Kendall's coefficient of concordance, or consider transforming certain variables and returning to beginning of flowchart 12, or seek help
No
Consider chi-square test (i.e., flowchart 7), or consider multivariate nonparametric statistics, or consider transforming certain variables and returning to Start, or seek help
Objects clustered into groups in advance (i.e., into predetermined groups)
Yes
Discriminatory analysis
Consider multiple discriminant analysis
No
Objects to be geometrically located onto specified dimensions
No
Cluster analysis
Consider cluster analysis techniques such as hierarchical grouping, Q-technique (i.e., inverse factor analysis), distance measures, similarity measures, etc.
Yes
All independent variables at least interval scale or dichotomous
Yes
Consider metric multidimensional scaling
No
Consider nonmetric multidimensional scaling
All independent variables at least ordinal scale or dichotomous
Yes
Consider treating all variables as at least interval scale and use factor analysis, or seek help
No
Consider eliminating nominal, multichotomous variables and returning to flowchart 12, or seek help

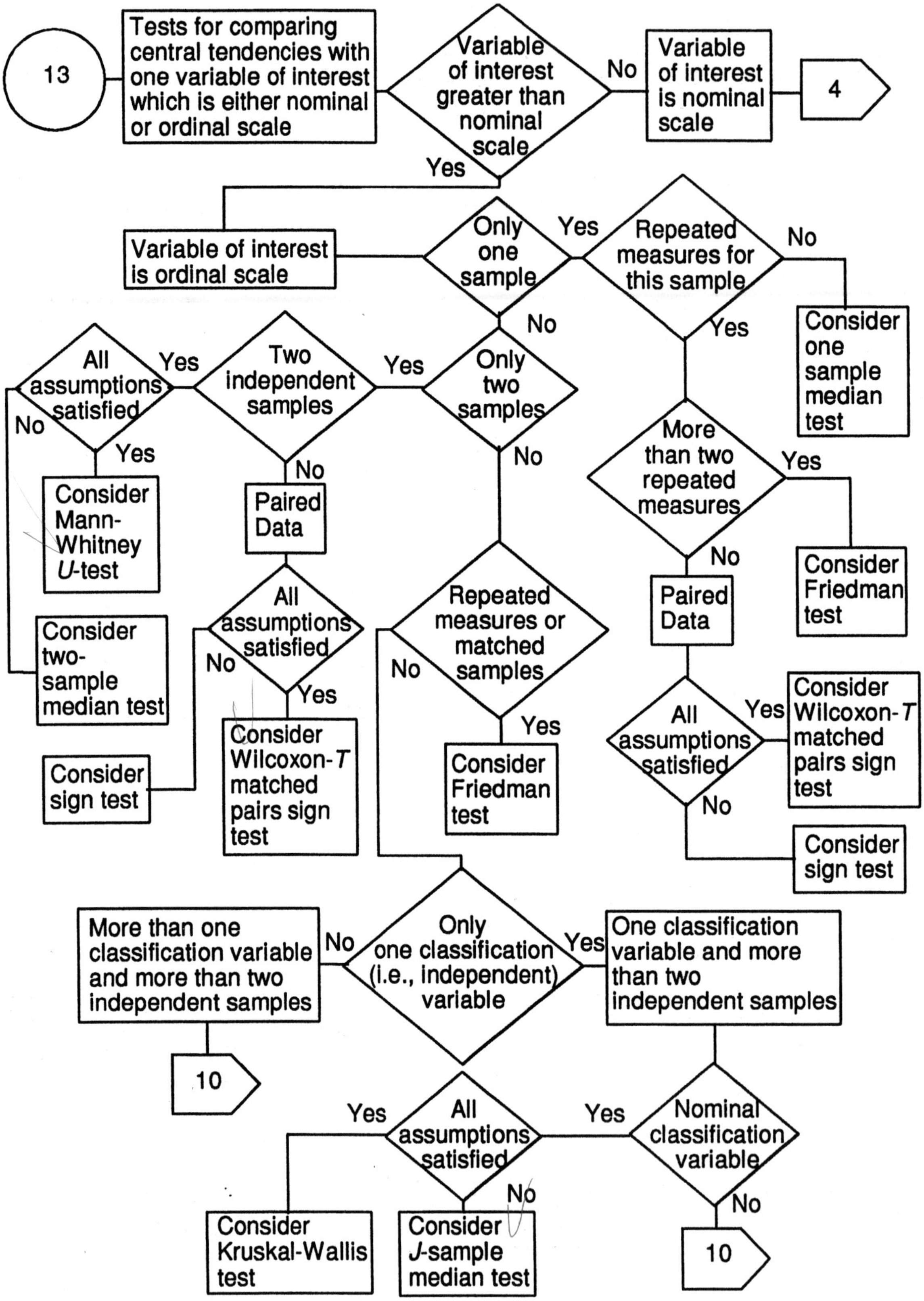
13
Tests for comparing central tendencies with one variable of interest which is either nominal or ordinal scale
Variable of interest greater than nominal scale
No
Variable of interest is nominal scale
4
Yes
Variable of interest is ordinal scale
Only one sample
Yes
Repeated measures for this sample
No
Consider one sample median test
Yes
No
Only two samples
Yes
Two independent samples
Yes
All assumptions satisfied
No
Yes
Consider Mann-Whitney U-test
Consider two-sample median test
No
Paired Data
All assumptions satisfied
No
Yes
Consider sign test
Consider Wilcoxon-T matched pairs sign test
No
Repeated measures or matched samples
No
Yes
Consider Friedman test
More than two repeated measures
Yes
Consider Friedman test
No
Paired Data
All assumptions satisfied
Yes
Consider Wilcoxon-T matched pairs sign test
No
Consider sign test
More than one classification variable and more than two independent samples
No
Only one classification (i.e., independent) variable
Yes
One classification variable and more than two independent samples
10
Yes
All assumptions satisfied
Yes
Nominal classification variable
No
No
Consider Kruskal-Wallis test
Consider J-sample median test
10

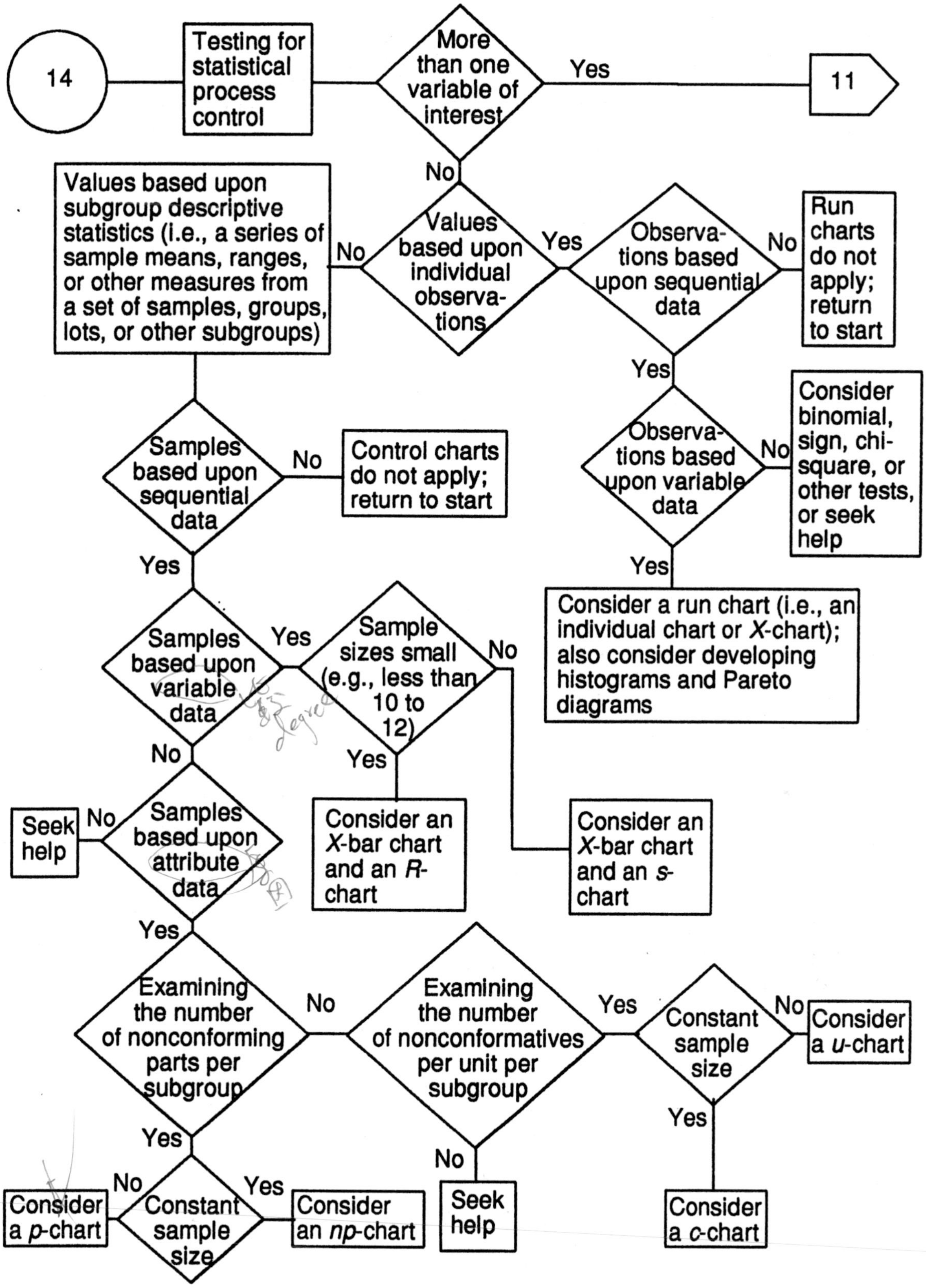
14
Testing for statistical process control
More than one variable of interest
Yes
11
No
Values based upon individual observations
Yes
Observations based upon sequential data
No
Run charts do not apply; return to start
No
Values based upon subgroup descriptive statistics (i.e., a series of sample means, ranges, or other measures from a set of samples, groups, lots, or other subgroups)
Yes
Observations based upon variable data
No
Consider binomial, sign, chi-square, or other tests, or seek help
Yes
Consider a run chart (i.e., an individual chart or X-chart); also consider developing histograms and Pareto diagrams
Samples based upon sequential data
No
Control charts do not apply; return to start
Yes
Samples based upon variable data
Yes
Sample sizes small (e.g., less than 10 to 12)
No
Consider an X-bar chart and an s-chart
Yes
Consider an X-bar chart and an R-chart
No
Samples based upon attribute data
No
Seek help
Yes
Examining the number of nonconforming parts per subgroup
No
Examining the number of nonconformatives per unit per subgroup
Yes
Constant sample size
No
Consider a u-chart
Yes
Consider a c-chart
No
Seek help
Yes
Constant sample size
No
Consider a p-chart
Yes
Consider an np-chart

APPENDIX G

GREEK ALPHABET

GREEK ALPHABET

Greek Letter	*Upper Case Symbol*	*Lower Case Symbol*
Alpha	Α	α
Beta	Β	β
Gamma	Γ	γ
Delta	Δ	δ
Epsilon	Ε	ε
Zeta	Ζ	ζ
Eta	Η	η
Theta	Θ	θ
Iota	Ι	ι
Kappa	Κ	κ
Lambda	Λ	λ
Mu	Μ	μ
Nu	Ν	ν
Xi	Ξ	ξ
Omicron	Ο	ο
Pi	Π	π
Rho	Ρ	ρ
Sigma	Σ	σ
Tau	Τ	τ
Upsilon	Υ	υ
Phi	Φ	φ
Chi	Χ	χ
Psi	Ψ	ψ
Omega	Ω	ω

APPENDIX H

HEWLETT-PACKARD EQUATION-SOLVING ROUTINES

FOR

HP-17B*II* and HP-19B*II* CALCULATORS

HEWLETT PACKARD CALCULATORS:
SETUP INSTRUCTIONS

The Hewlett-Packard HP-17B*II* and HP-19B*II* calculators are two of the most popular business calculators available. If you make a comparison of these calculators, you will find that they are very similar. The HP-17B*II* is more expensive but somewhat easier to handle, while the HP-19B*II* is more expensive, has more features, and is slightly more awkward to handle. The handling issue is a matter of individual preference and comfort. While HP-19B*II* has two sides and opens up like a book, the HP-17B*II* has just one side. This difference gives the HP-19B*II* user the advantage of inputting equations more quickly, but the calculator is not quite as "hand-held." Moving beyond the physical appearance, both calculators have scrolling capabilities that allow you to view values in a list of data during and after the list has been input; you can then correct, add, and delete values and lists as necessary. Both have equation-solver capabilities that allow you to create equations with user-defined menus and store these equations into memory.

Main Menu

The main menu of the calculator has a number of submenus, including **FIN**, **BUS**, **SUM**, **TIME**, and **SOLVE**. The HP-19B*II* calculator also has a **TEXT** submenu. Within this menu, the **SUM** and **SOLVE** menus will be of greatest importance for statistical methods. The **SUM** is used to input the list(s) of data. It allows you to take advantage of various built-in statistical functions such as the total, the mean, median, standard deviation, range, minimum, maximum, and sorting of data from smallest to largest. It also leads you to the **FORECAST** submenu (**FRCST**), which provides tools for correlation, regression, intercepts, slopes, predicted values, nonlinear models, sums of values, sums of squares of values, and sums of cross-products of values. The forecast submenu can also be used for determining means and standard deviations of grouped (weighted) data. They both also have a powerful and relatively user-friendly **SOLVE** menu, where the user can create, edit, revise, and delete equations. The **SOLVE** menu provides you with algebraic solutions of user-supplied equations. It will perform the algebra for you—given all but one term of an algebraic equation, the **SOLVE** menu will compute the remaining, unknown term.

Both calculators have an elaborate **FIN** menu that includes financial functions such as time-value-of-money (TVM), interest conversions, cash flow (both even and uneven), bonds, and depreciation. Both include a **BUS** (business) menu, **TIME** (setting time-of-day, alarms, appointment reminders, etc.), and a **MATH** menu. You have to press the **yellow key**, followed by the **MATH** key to access this menu. The HP-19B*II* has a somewhat more elaborate **MATH** menu, as it includes a **TRIG** submenu with built-in trigonometry functions, as well as a **PROB** submenu that includes a random-number generator, permutations, combinations, and factorials. Fortunately, permutations and combinations can easily and permanently be added to the HP-17B*II* through the use of the equation-solver (**SOLVE**). The HP-19B*II* can also **PLOT** rudimentary scatter diagrams and histograms and has a **TEXT** menu where alphabetical lists, telephone numbers, etc., can be created and maintained.

Setting up your Calculator

Before using the **SUM** menu (where data lists can be created and stored) or **SOLVE** menu (where equations can be created and stored), you may want to follow the steps in one of the next two figures (depending on the model of your calculator) to set it up for easier use. Once you have followed these simple instructions, you will not have to perform this setup process again, unless you accidently delete something or your calculator suffers a memory loss. These are the same concerns you might have with a computer that crashes, with computer-related software needing to be reinstalled.

If you are performing statistical analyses, you will probably have one or more variables to analyze. The following setup guides you through creating "names" for your variable lists in the **SUM** menu. Once these names have been created, you will no longer have to name your variables each time you use the **SUM** menu. Any variable can be input and associated with any named list. The following material will also show you how to delete data from a variable list you have stored by simply clearing the list but not clearing the name of the list. You will learn that you do not want to clear the variable name when you clear the variable list; otherwise, you will have to rename the variable list later. Fortunately, your calculator will prompt you when you are about to clear a variable list or a variable name; be sure to pay attention and take appropriate action at that time (i.e., you probably do not want to clear the variable name).

You can name many variables, and you have considerable flexibility in selecting names for your variables. The step-by-step directions given here provide the necessary instructions for naming and creating four (an arbitrary number) generic variables within your calculator. The generic names chosen here are **VAR1**, **VAR2**, **VAR3**, and **FREQ**, respectively. Any names could have been selected, but these names are easy to remember. Further, many of the equations in the **SOLVE** menu provided in this appendix will access one or more of these variable names. Because of this interrelationship between the **SUM** menu and the **SOLVE** menu, you are ***strongly*** urged to use these ***same*** generic names provided here; and be sure to spell them exactly the same. Otherwise, you may not be able to take advantage of some of the equations described later.

By following the step-by-step directions, you can easily create the names for these four variables in less than five minutes. Later, you may want to add some other variable names (such as VAR4 and VAR5), but you are encouraged not to do so at this time. Be certain that you follow ? if you are using the HP-17B*II* or **Figure H.1** if you are using the HP-19B*II*. The instructions are somewhat different for each model of these two Hewlett-Packard calculators. If you are using the HP-19B*II*, you will find that each letter requires only one keystroke, since the left side of the calculator has keys dedicated to each letter in the alphabet, plus some special characters. If you are using the HP-17B*II*, you are required to use two keystrokes to enter each letter; thus, the process takes slightly longer when using the HP-17B*II*.

Remember that many of the equation-solving routines given later assume that your calculator contains one or more of the following variable names: **VAR1, VAR2, VAR3,** and **FREQ**. When you follow these instructions to create the variable names, you may be curious as to why the instructions lead you to enter these variables in ***reverse order***. You will notice that each time you enter a new name, it is stored to the left of those you have previously named. Therefore, if you enter **FREQ** first, and then enter **VAR3** next, **VAR3** will be stored to the left of **FREQ**. Once you have completed this task, you will find that the names are now given in the desired order of **VAR1, VAR2, VAR3,** and **FREQ**. With the HP-17B*II* calculator, these variables will permanently remain in this order. Unfortunately, with the HP-19B*II*, these names will change positions after various functions are performed. This is not of major concern, but the user will have to remember to look at the menu each time, as you cannot assume the names will always be in the same place as they were the last time they were used.

HP 17B-II SETUP INSTRUCTIONS

[SUM] [GET] [*NEW] [NAME]

Spell out any variable names you wish. I suggest:

[FGHI] [F] [RSTUV] [R] [ABCDE] [E] [NOPQ] [Q] [INPUT]

[GET] (Note that FREQ is now listed.)

[*NEW] [NAME] [RSTUV] [V] [ABCDE] [A] [RSTUV]

[R] [3] [INPUT]

[GET] (Note that VAR3 and FREQ are now listed.)

[*NEW] [NAME] [RSTUV] [V] [ABCDE] [A] [RSTUV]

[R] [2] [INPUT]

[GET] (Note that VAR2, VAR3, and FREQ are now listed.)

[*NEW] [NAME] [RSTUV] [V] [ABCDE] [A] [RSTUV]

[R] [1] [INPUT]

(Notice that the resulting variable names are listed in the following order: VAR1, VAR2, VAR3, and FREQ.)

Figure H.1
Instructions for the HP 17B*II* Calculator

HP 19B-II SETUP INSTRUCTIONS

[SUM] [GET] [*NEW] [NAME]

Spell out any variable names you wish. I suggest:

[F] [R] [E] [Q] [INPUT]

[GET] (Note that FREQ is now listed.)

[*NEW] [NAME] [V] [A] [R] [3] [INPUT]

[GET] (Note that VAR3 and FREQ are now listed.)

[*NEW] [NAME] [V] [A] [R] [2] [INPUT]

[GET] (Note that VAR2, VAR3, and FREQ are now listed.)

[*NEW] [NAME] [V] [A] [R] [1] [INPUT]

(Notice that the resulting variable names are listed in the following order: VAR1, VAR2, VAR3, and FREQ.)

Figure H.2
Instructions for the HP 19B*II* Calculator

Key Words for the Hewlett-Packard Calculators

There are a number of ***key words*** that are unique these calculators. It is important to be aware of these words and associated symbols prior to developing equations for the HP-17B*II* and HP-19B*II* calculators. Many of these key words will be self-explanatory and are consistent with either programming languages (such as FORTRAN and BASIC) and with spreadsheet terminology (such as used in *Excel* and *Quattro*). The following list includes many of these key words, depending upon the model of the calculator: **ITEM, SIZES, COMB, FACT, SQ, SQRT, INV, ABS, LOG, ALOG, LN, EXP, COS, ACOS, SIN, ASIN, TAN, ATAN, GET**, and **LET.** The key words **ITEM** and **SIZES** are important terms used in creating and assessing lists of numbers. The key words **COMB** (for combinations), **FACT** (for factorials), **SQ** (for square), **SQRT** (for square root), and others are related to mathematical functions. Both **GET** and **LET** are key words for using various functions of the equation solver. The following discussion illustrates the use of these calculators. A familiarity with the key words will enhance the understanding, creation, and use of the equation solver and other features of these powerful calculators.

Using the SUM Menu

The **SUM** menu can be used to calculate many statistical functions. It provides separate options for both raw and grouped (weighted) data, yielding both unweighted and weighted values. Illustrations are given for both formats, and you are encouraged to follow these few simple steps to become more comfortable with the format of your calculator. For each illustration, it is assumed that you have created the names for the variables described in the previous sections.

An Illustration of Calculating Statistical Values with Raw Data

Example H-1. For Example H-1, you must have a variable named **VAR1** in your **SUM** menu. For this illustration, suppose you want to find various statistical values for the months of experience of a sample of seven employees. Their months of experience are as follows: 6, 9, 3, 2, 12, 5, and 17. Here are the necessary steps for entering these data into **VAR1** and then for determining several associated statistical values:

1. From the main menu, select the **SUM** option.
2. Press **GET**.
3. Press **VAR1** (which is one of the four variables you named earlier).
4. Clear any old data from within the list for this variable (if necessary) by pressing the **yellow** key, followed by pressing the **INPUT** key. Notice that the "second function" (yellow function) of the input key represents the **CLEAR DATA** feature.
5. Respond to "Clear the list?" by selecting **YES**, since you want to delete any old values you may have previously stored in the **VAR1** list.
6. Respond to "Also clear list name?" by selecting **NO**, since you do not want to have to rename the **VAR1** list later.
7. Input your data, using the values in Example H-1, as follows: 6, 9, 3, 2, 12, 5, and 17. To enter these values, first press 6, then press **INPUT**, then press 9, then press **INPUT**, etc., until all the values are entered. As you observe your screen, you will notice that a running total is given after each number is entered. After you have entered the last number, this running total should sum to 54.
8. If you have the HP-19B*II*, press **CALC**. If you have the HP-17B*II*, press **EXIT**, then press **CALC**.
9. Now you are ready to calculate various statistical values. For example, if you press the key associated with the word **MEAN** on the screen, you will find that the mean is 7.71. If you want to know the full decimal value of this number, you can press the **yellow** key, followed by pressing and <u>holding down</u> the **SHOW** key. Notice that the second function,

or yellow function, of the decimal-point key is the **SHOW** feature. You will find that the mean is 7.71428571429 to full precision. Now let up on the show key, and the value returns to 7.71, or to whatever decimal place precision you have set your calculator to display. The calculator was "fixed" at two decimal places when it was shipped from the factory. You can easily change the number of decimal places displayed at any time, as discussed later.

10. Now press the key associated with the word **STDEV** on the screen, you will find that the sample standard deviation is 5.35 (to two-decimal place precision).

11. You may want to experiment with the other functions of this menu as well. However, you are ***cautioned*** not to press the **SORT** key too quickly or indiscriminately, as you cannot unsort the list once you have pressed this key (i.e., there is no UNDO key or option).

12. Finally, press the **yellow** key, followed by the **EXIT** key. Although you do not have to follow this last step, by using these two keystrokes, you will quickly return to the main menu. Congratulations! You have just become a member of the Yellow Button/Exit club!

An Illustration of Calculating Statistical Values with Grouped (i.e., Weighted) Data

Example H-2. To try Example H-2, you must have already created a variable named **VAR1** and a variable named **FREQ** in your **SUM** menu. The data for this example are based on the weights of all carry-on luggage for the passengers of two wide-bodied airplanes that travel from Los Angeles to New York City. The weights for this continuous distribution of 420 carry-on bags have been *rounded* to the nearest pound. You will need to input the rounded weights of the luggage into **VAR1** and the frequencies associated with each of these corresponding weights into **FREQ**. The values to be input are listed in the following table:

Item Number	VAR1: Luggage Weights	FREQ: Frequencies of Weights
Item (1) =	36	5
Item (2) =	35	9
Item (3) =	34	16
Item (4) =	33	18
Item (5) =	32	31
Item (6) =	31	44
Item (7) =	30	54
Item (8) =	29	56
Item (9) =	28	55
Item (10) =	27	44
Item (11) =	26	34
Item (12) =	25	24
Item (13) =	24	14
Item (14) =	23	10
Item (15) =	22	6

Here are the necessary steps for entering these data into **VAR1** and **FREQ**, and then for determining statistical values based on these weighted data:

1. From the main menu, select the **SUM** option.

2. Press **GET**.

3. Press **VAR1** (which is one of the four variables you named earlier).

4. Clear the list (if necessary) by pressing the **yellow** key, followed by pressing the **INPUT** key. Notice that the second function, or yellow function, of the input key is the **CLEAR DATA** feature.

5. Respond to "Clear the list?" by selecting **YES**, since you want to delete any old values you may have previously stored in the **VAR1** list.

6. Respond to "Also clear list name?" by selecting **NO**, since you do not want to have to rename the **VAR1** list later.

7. Input the 15 groups of luggage weights into **VAR1**. To enter these values, first press 36, then press INPUT, then press 35, then press INPUT, etc., until the entire list of 15 groups of luggage weights are entered. As you observe your screen, you will notice that a running total is given after each number is entered. After you have entered the last number, this running total should sum to 435.

8. If you have the HP-19B*II*, press **GET**. If you have the HP-17B*II*, press **EXIT**, then press **GET**.

9. Now you are ready to enter the frequencies into the **FREQ** list. To enter these values, first press 5, then press INPUT, then press 9, then press INPUT, etc., until the entire list of 15 groups of frequencies are entered. As you observe your screen, you will notice that a running total is given after each number is entered. After you have entered the last number, this running total should sum to 420, since there are 420 bags of luggage.

10. If you have the HP-19B*II*, be certain you are in the ***second*** list (in this case the **FREQ** list), then press **CALC**. If you have the HP-17B*II*, it does not matter which list you are in at the time; simply press **EXIT**, then press **CALC**.

11. If you have the HP-19B*II* and have pressed **CALC**, press the following sequence of keys: **MORE, FRCST, VAR1, LIN, MORE,** and **W.MN.** You will find that the weighted mean is 28.9119, to four-decimal point precision. Next, press **G.SD**. You will find that the grouped standard deviation is 2.9667, again to four-decimal point precision.

12. If you have the HP-17B*II* and have pressed **CALC**, press the following sequence of keys: **MORE, FRCST, VAR1, FREQ,** make sure the word **LINEAR** appears on the screen,

press **MORE,** and **W.MN.** You will find that the weighted mean is 28.9119, to four-decimal point precision. Next, press **G.SD**. You will find that the grouped standard deviation is 2.9667, again to four-decimal point precision.

In review, we will assume you have entered the two columns of values into the two variable lists as described earlier. However, let's also assume that when you entered the data, you decided to check on the means and standard deviations of each of the variables immediately after you finished entering the values for each list separately. That is, suppose that after you had entered all the weights into VAR1, you decided to press **CALC** at that point. You would have obtained a mean of 29 and a sample standard deviation of 4.4721. These values, of course, would not be the mean and standard deviation of the 420 bags of luggage; they would represent the mean and standard deviation of only 15 bags, since the VAR1 list only includes 15 values. Thus, you would have obtained an unweighted mean, since the values are not being weighted by the frequencies. You could have, of course, input all 420 weights into VAR1, but this would take a long time and create additional opportunity for data entry error. Therefore, entering data and frequencies into two variable lists (VAR1 and FREQ), and then using the **FRCST** approach to account for the frequencies would be much easier. It would also yield the weighted mean instead of some unweighted mean.

Setting the Decimal Places

The calculator retains full decimal place precision (usually up to 12 digits), regardless of the decimal places shown on the display. As mentioned earlier, the preset default for decimals is fixed at two places. As an illustration of the calculator's decimal place display, try the following steps: First, press the **DSP** key (for "display"), then press the key associated with the word "**FIX**" shown on the screen. Next, press the number **2**, followed by the **INPUT** key. You have now set your calculator to always display two decimal places. As a demonstration, press **1**, then press ÷, then press **2**, and then press =. The screen now displays 0.50. As another demonstration, press **1**, then press ÷, then press **4**, and then press =. The screen now displays 0.25. Now, press the **DSP** key again, then press the key associated with **FIX**, followed by the number **4**, followed by the **INPUT** key. This time you have set your calculator to display four decimal places. The screen now displays 0.2500.

As another demonstration, press **1**, then press ÷, then press **3**, and then press =. The screen displays 0.3333. Now press the **yellow** key, followed by pressing and holding down the **SHOW** key. You will notice that the display shows 3.33333333333E-1, to the calculator's 12-digit full precision. This example also shows that the calculator has gone into scientific notation. The E-1 at the end of the displayed value indicates that the decimal point needs to be moved one place to the left to give 0.333333333333. If the value had ended with E1 instead of E-1, the decimal would need to be moved one place to the right. Now press the **DSP** key, followed by **FIX**. Next, press the number **2**, followed by the **INPUT** key. You have again set your calculator to display two decimal places. The screen now displays 0.33; however, the actual value of the number is retained to full decimal-place accuracy.

As still another demonstration, press the **DSP** key, followed by the key associate with **ALL** on the screen. Now press **1**, then press ÷, then press **2**, and then press =. The screen displays 0.5, since this is all that is needed to give full decimal accuracy. Next, press **1**, then press ÷, then press

4, and then press =. The screen displays 0.25, since two decimal places are required to give full decimal accuracy. Now, Now press **1**, then press ÷, then press **8**, and then press =. The screen displays 0.125, since three decimal places are required to give full decimal accuracy. Finally, press the **DSP** key again, then press **FIX**, followed by the number **4**, followed by the **INPUT** key. If you leave your calculator set to display four decimal places, it will be useful for many statistical calculations. Remember that the calculator is retaining the values at full decimal place accuracy and is only ***displaying*** the values to four decimal places.

Storing Values into Memory Locations

The HP-17B*II* and HP-19B*II* calculators have 10 memory locations that can be easily accessed from the keyboard. These memory locations correspond to the 10 keys associated with the numbers 0 through 9. For example, to store a value into memory key 7 simply view the number on the screen, then press **STO** (an abbreviation for "store"), and then press 7. To recall a value from memory key 7 simply press **RCL** (an abbreviation for "recall"), and then press 7. This will recall whatever was stored in the number 7 memory location. Follow the same procedure to use the other nine memory locations. There is no need to clear the memory locations; pressing STO, followed by the desired memory location key will ***replace*** whatever was in that location.

Example H-3. Example H-3 consists of two variables. The first of this pair of variables represents assessment scores for a group of sales persons just prior to hiring them, while the second variable represents their performance scores six months after they were hired. The data are given in the accompanying table:

Item Number	VAR1: Assessment	VAR2: Performance
Item (1) =	11	10
Item (2) =	8	10
Item (3) =	8	9
Item (4) =	5	6
Item (5) =	2	5
Item (6) =	2	2

This example will illustrate both the use of the memory locations and an alternative application of the **FRCST** function. We will input the assessment values into **VAR1** and the performance values into **VAR2**, one variable at a time. It is often convenient to perform partial analyses for each variable before entering into the **FRCST** mode so we can determine means, standard deviations, and other values for each variable separately. Following this approach, here are the steps to perform this analysis:

1. From the main menu, select the **SUM** option.

2. Press **GET**.

3. Press **VAR1**.

4. Clear the list (if necessary) by pressing the **yellow** key, followed by pressing the **INPUT** key. Notice that the second function, or yellow function, of the input key is the **CLEAR DATA** feature.

5. Respond to "Clear the list?" by selecting **YES**, since you want to delete any old values you may have previously stored in the **VAR1** list.

6. Respond to "Also clear list name?" by selecting **NO**, since you do not want to have to rename the **VAR1** list later.

7. Input the six assessment score values into **VAR1**.

8. If you have the HP-19B*II*, press **CALC**. If you have the HP-17B*II*, press **EXIT**, then press **CALC**.

9. Press the **MEAN** key. This should yield a value of 6.

10. Press the **STO** key, followed by the 7 key. This will store the mean of the first variable in memory location 7.

11. Press the **STDEV** key. This should yield a value of 3.6332 (to four decimal precision).

12. Press the **STO** key, followed by the 8 key. This will store the sample standard deviation of the first variable in memory location 8.

13. Press the **yellow** key, followed by the + key (the yellow function for the + key is the square key, denoted by $\mathbf{x^2}$. This should yield a value of 13.2000 (to four decimal precision).

14. Press the times (×) key, followed by the number 5, followed by the equal (=) key. (You are using 5, since the degrees of freedom (*df*) for this variable are: *df* = 6 - 1 = 5.) This should yield a value of 66, which represents the ***sum of the squared deviations about the mean*** for the *X*-variable (the one in VAR1), often referred to as the sums of squares ***(SS)***.

15. Press the **STO** key, followed by the 9 key. This will store the sums of squares for the *X*-variable in memory location 9.

16. Now return to the main menu, and select the **SUM** option.

17. Press **GET**.

18. Press **VAR2**.

19. Clear the list (if necessary) by pressing the **yellow** key, followed by pressing the **INPUT** key. Notice that the second function, or yellow function, of the input key is the **CLEAR DATA** feature.

20. Respond to "Clear the list?" by selecting **YES**, since you want to delete any old values you may have previously stored in the **VAR2** list.

21. Respond to "Also clear list name?" by selecting **NO**, since you do not want to have to rename the **VAR2** list later.

22. Input the six performance score values into **VAR2**.

23. If you have the HP-19B*II*, press **CALC**. If you have the HP-17B*II*, press **EXIT**, then press **CALC**.

24. Press the **MEAN** key. This should yield a value of 7.

25. Press the **STO** key, followed by the 4 key. This will store the mean of the second variable in memory location 4.

26. Press the **STDEV** key. This should yield a value of 3.2249 (to four decimal precision).

27. Press the **STO** key, followed by the 5 key. This will store the sample standard deviation of the second variable in memory location 5.

28. Press the **yellow** key, followed by the + key (the yellow function for the + key is the square key, denoted by x^2. This should yield a value of 10.4000 (to four decimal precision).

29. Press the times (×) key, followed by the number 5, followed by the equal (=) key. This should yield a value of 52, which is the sums of squares ***(SS)*** for VAR2.

30. Press the **STO** key, followed by the 6 key. This will store the sums of squares for the *X*-variable in memory location 6.

31. If you have the HP-19B*II*, be certain you are in the ***second*** list (in this case the **VAR2** list), then press **CALC**. If you have the HP-17B*II*, it does not matter which list you are in at the time; simply press **EXIT**, then press **CALC**.

32. If you have the HP-19B*II* and have pressed **CALC** while in VAR2, press the following sequence of keys: **MORE, FRCST, VAR1, LIN, CORR, STO, 1, B, STO, 2, M,** and **STO 3**. If you have the HP-17B*II* and have pressed **CALC** while in either VAR1 or VAR2, press the following sequence of keys: **MORE, FRCST, VAR1, VAR2,** (now make sure you see the word **LINEAR**), **CORR, STO, 1, B, STO, 2, M,** and **STO 3**. You now have calculated the following variables for the ***linear model***: the correlation

Regression Linear B Intercept M = slope

(CORR), intercept (B), and slope (M) and have stored them in memory locations 1, 2, and 3, respectively. You should verify that the correlation is .9218, the intercept is 2.0909, and the intercept is .8182, again to four-decimal point precision.

You may find it useful to visualize where you have stored your values. **Figure H.2** should help you remember where these values have been stored. In this scheme, the top row of values stored in memory corresponds to VAR1, while the middle row of stored values corresponds to VAR2. The first column of memory values for rows one and two corresponds to the respective means, the second column of memory values for rows one and two corresponds to the respective standard deviations, and the third column of memory values for rows one and two corresponds to the respective sums of squares. The third row contains the correlation, intercept, and slope, respectively, regarding the relationship between these two variables. The one remaining memory location has not been used at this point and is now available for storing any temporary values desired. It is referred to as the "junk" key in this scheme, because any stored values in this location are probably only temporary values. This approach avoids having to return to the **SUM** menu if you have forgotten the values you computed earlier. Further, by storing them directly into memory, you will have stored them at full decimal place precision, thus avoiding rounding errors that later may be compounded. Remember, you do not have to clear any of these values; you simply replace them with new values when necessary.

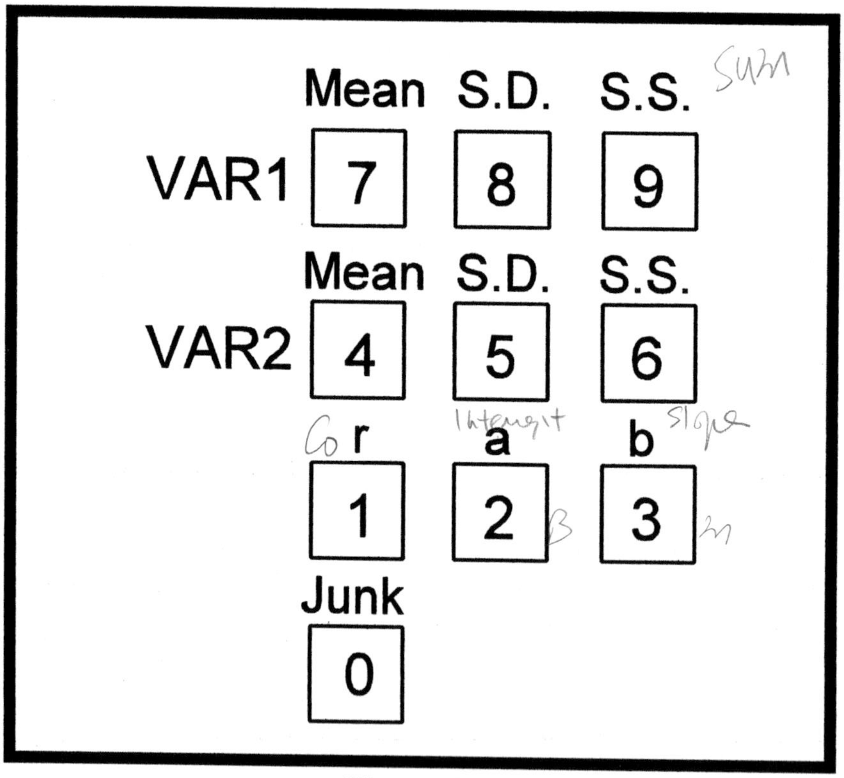

Figure H.3
An Approach for Storing Statistical Values

Using the SOLVE Menu

The **SOLVE** menu can be used in conjunction with the **SUM** menu, or it can be used by itself. You should remember that data lists are only entered into the **SUM** menu lists, while equations are only entered into the **SOLVE** menu. Equations in the **SOLVE** menu can be very brief and simple, or they can be quite complex. In most cases, the equations simply follow the traditional format of basic algebra or summation notation. Summation notation requires a unique format that will be demonstrated in a number of upcoming equations. The first illustrations will be based on very straightforward and common equations.

Illustrations of Statistical Solutions with Hewlett-Packard Calculators

Z-Score.. The *z*-score equation provides for an easy illustration of the use of the **SOLVE** menu. You should recall that the general format for a *z*-score is as follows:

$$z = \frac{(X - \text{Mean})}{\text{Standard Deviation}}$$

As can be seen, the traditional *z*-score equation has four terms: 1) the *z*-value itself, 2) the observed value (*X*), 3) the mean, and 4) the standard deviation. Given any three of these values, the fourth one can easily be obtained, because the HP-17B*II* and the HP-19B*II* have the capacity to solve for the algebra necessary to obtain the unknown value.

You are now ready to create the *z*-score equation in the **SOLVE** menu. If you are using the HP-19B*II* and are at the main menu, press **SOLVE**, and simply begin typing the equation. If you are using the HP-17B*II* and are at the main menu, press **SOLVE**, then NEW, and then begin typing the equation. You may also find it convenient at times to press the DOWNWARD TRIANGLE KEY that appears below the INPUT key until you come to the bottom of the list, or used the UPWARD and DOWNWARD TRIANGLE keys to scroll to a point where you would like to insert your new equation into a list of previously created equations.

You may not want to use such long words as STANDARD DEVIATION and may prefer to abbreviate it as SD (or s, or STDEV, or any other name you want to assign to this component of the equation). Here, we have arbitrarily decided to use the following names for each of the four components in the equation: Z for the *z*-score, X for the observed value, MEAN for the mean value, and SD for the standard deviation value. The equation does not use any calculator-specific terms. The terms Z, X, MEAN, and SD are user-defined and are not unique symbols, words, or names associated with the calculator itself. No equation title has been used to specifically identify the equation (see the next equation for examples of equation titles). You are now ready to enter the new equation into the **SOLVE** menu, arbitrarily written here as follows:

Z=(X-MEAN)÷SD

Once the entire equation has been entered, press INPUT (to save the equation into memory), and then press CALC. Once CALC is pressed, a new menu should appear above the first four keys of the top row (on the menu screen). The new menu should appear as follows:

Z	X	MEAN	SD

Example H-4. Using Example H-4, we will input values for any three of these four names, and solve for the fourth one. In Example H-4, suppose a person has an IQ score (an **X**-value) of 130. Also suppose the **MEAN** of this set of data is 100, and the **SD** is 15. The **Z**-value that corresponds to this **X**-value can now be found. We will assume that you have entered the equation into the **SOLVE** menu and you have now exited the **SOLVE** menu. In fact, suppose you are now in some completely different part of the calculator. To make it easy to get to the desired menu of the calculator, press the **yellow** key, followed by pressing the EXIT key. This will immediately return you to the main menu, from which it is easy to find your way into the other menus. Now take the following steps:

1. From the main menu, select the **SOLVE** option.
2. If there is more than one equation in the **SOLVE** menu, you may have to scroll up or down the list in this menu of equations until the cursor is "pointing" to the desired equation, in this case the **Z-SCORE** equation.
3. Press **CALC**.
4. Input 130, and press **X**.
5. Input 100, and press **MEAN**.
6. Input 15, and press **SD**.
7. Now press **Z**. Your answer should appear on the screen as Z = 2.00. Your calculator may display more or less decimal places, depending on the number of decimals you have set your calculator to display.

Example H-5. Using Example H-5, suppose you want to know what IQ score would be associated with a *z*-score of 3. You can press 3, then press **Z** on the menu. This will register a 3 as your new *z*-score. You can now press **X** on the menu and solve for the IQ score associated with a *z*-score of 3. The resulting answer will yield a value of **Z** = 145.

Quadratic Equation. The next example of an equation that can be created in the **SOLVE** menu is the quadratic equation. This equation yields the value of Y, given any value of X and the values of a, b, and c for the quadratic equation, defined as follows: $Y = aX^2 + bX + c$. Notice, however, that you cannot input lower case letters (such as a, b, and c) into these HP calculators; you must use upper case letters (such as A, B, and C). The equation we will enter into **SOLVE** has been preceded by an equation title, which is not required. However, brief equation titles help identify information about the equation in your equation list. When an equation is preceded by a title (QUADRATIC in this example), which is in turn followed by a colon (:), the title serves to identify the equation but is ignored by the calculator. Only the equation itself is used by the calculator. This equation does not contain any calculator-specific terms. You might have noticed that you have input the equation into the calculator in a slightly different order than the sequential order given in the original equation. We chose to input the equation in this particular order so that Y, X, A, B, and C will appear on the menu in this order, respectively. Otherwise, these values would appear on the menu in the order of Y, A, X, B, and C, which might be somewhat confusing.

QUADRATIC:Y=X^2×A+X×B+C

The menu now appears as follows:

Y	X	A	B	C

Quad Roots. The next two equations give the positive and negative roots for a quadratic equation. They include a term that is a key word to the calculator: **SQRT**. This term is a command that produces the square root of the value in parentheses immediately after the SQRT term. Both of these equations have been preceded by two-part **titles** (QUAD/PLUS and QUAD/MINUS) to help differentiate between the positive and negative forms of the quadratic equation in the equation list. The two-part titles have been separated by a forward slash (/) and are followed by a colon (:). These two-part titles are ignored by the calculator and are arbitrarily created. The two forms of the QUADROOTS equations are as follows:

QUAD/PLUS:X=(1÷(2×A))×(-B+SQRT(B^2-4×A×C))

QUAD/MINUS:X=(1÷(2×A))×(-B-SQRT(B^2-4×A×C))

Population Standard Deviation. Although the HP-17B*II* and the HP-19B*II* calculators have built-in functions in the **SUM** menu to automatically obtain ***sample*** standard deviations, they do not have built-in functions to obtain a ***population*** standard deviation. This shortcoming is easily resolved by creating an equation that will convert the sample standard deviation to a population standard deviation. Here is an equation that will solve for the population standard deviation, given the sample standard deviation and the number of cases in the data set:

POPSD/RAW:POPSD=SQRT(((SAMSD^2)×(N-1))÷N)

Here, **POPSD** represents the population standard deviation, **SAMSD** represents the sample standard deviation, and **N** represents the sample size. Notice that **SAMS** actually appears on the menu instead of SAMSD because SAMSD is too wide for the calculator screen to display above the corresponding key and was automatically truncated by the calculator on the screen (but not within the equation). The equation is still correct and still works properly. The menu on the screen now appears as follows:

POPSD	SAMS	N

You can easily input the sample standard deviation obtained from the **SUM** menu and then input the sample size. If you have already used the **SUM** menu to calculate the sample standard deviation for these data, you may want to store that sample standard deviation into any one of the 10 available memory locations to avoid any potential roundoff problems. For example, if you have calculated the sample standard deviation and it is currently on your screen, press STO 7 to store this value in memory location 7. (Any storage location will do; you may choose to store it under keys 0, 1, 2, 3, 4, 5, 6, 7, 8, or 9.) If you are still in the **SUM** menu, exit to the main menu, and then get into the **SOLVE** menu. Now scroll to the POPSD equation, and press CALC. Your POPSD menu will appear on the screen. You are ready to recall the sample standard deviation value you stored in memory location 7 earlier; therefore, press RCL 7 (or the number where you stored your value) to recall the sample standard deviation. The stored value will appear on your screen and is ready to use as input into the POPSD equation. Press SAMS to input this sample standard deviation into the equation. Next, input the numerical value associated with the size of the data base and press N. Finally, press POPSD to convert the sample standard deviation to a population standard deviation.

Example H-6. For Example H-6, suppose that you have determined that a sample standard deviation is 20 and the size of your data base is 30. You have learned that the data actually represent a population instead of a sample. You want to determine the population standard deviation. The steps for determining this population standard deviation are as follows:

1. From the main menu, select the **SOLVE** option.

2. Find the desired equation in the solve menu. You may have to scroll up or down the list in this menu of equations, especially if you have more than one equation saved. Search through the list of equations until the **POPSD** equation appears.

3. Press **CALC.**

4. Input 20 (or recall the sample standard deviation from memory if you have stored it in some memory location) and press the **SAMS** key (representing **SAMSD).**

5. Input 30 and press **N.**

6. Now press **POPSD,** and your answer should appear as 19.6638. (You may have more or less decimal places, depending upon what options you have selected from your display menu. The default in this example was arbitrarily "fixed" at 4 decimal places.)

Summation Notation and the H-P Equation-Solver

A series of "summation learning equations" will now be presented to help you better understand the summation syntax and capabilities of the Hewlett-Packard HP-17B*II* and HP-19B*II* calculators. You will not necessarily need to store all these equations in your calculator to perform summation tasks, nor will you want to keep all of them in your calculator later. They serve as illustrations of the use of the Σ symbol in the equation-solver. Several of them have very practical applications, however. You may choose to enter these equations into your calculator for practice, knowing you can always delete them when you are finished with them. The following steps are designed with the terminology for the HP-17B*II* and the HP-19B*II* in mind. We will begin with the SUM/LEARN1 equation, as follows:

Learning Equation 1. This equation (which you will probably want to delete later to save calculator memory) can be used to obtain the sum of the values stored in a variable identified as VAR1. To use the equation, you need to input a value for N (the number of observations) and let the calculator determine the SUM. While this sum can easily be determined by simply adding up the values, the equation illustrates the use of Hewlett-Packard notation for summation. Notice that you are *required* to indicate the **subscript** to be associated with the variable (we have arbitrarily chosen to use the letter I), the **starting point** at which the operation begins (we have arbitrarily started at 1, for good reason), the **ending point** at which the operation terminates (we have chosen to end at N), the **increments** for the subscript (we have chosen increments of one), and the **items** to be added. In this equation, we are adding all of the items (as I goes from 1 to N, in increments of 1) that are found in the variable we previously named VAR1. A variable by that exact name must exist in the **SUM** menu of the calculator in order for the equation to be able to access the data identified by that name. Here is the equation:

```
SUM/LEARN1:SUM=Σ(I:1:N:1:(ITEM(VAR1:I)))
```

Your menu should now appear as follows:

SUM	N

Steps for determining the sum of the values in the list entitled VAR1:

1. From the main menu, select the **SUM** option.

2. Press **GET**.

3. Press **VAR1**.

4. Clear the list (if necessary) by pressing the **color-coded key** and the **INPUT** key (which is the second function of the input key, referred to as **CLEAR DATA**).

5. Respond to "Clear the list?" by selecting **YES**.

6. Respond to "Also clear list name?" by selecting **NO**. (Otherwise you will have to re-name the VAR1 list.)

7. Input your data. Try the following values: 6, 9, 3, 2, 12, 5, and 17. This value should sum to 54.

8. Press **EXIT**.

9. Press **EXIT** again. You should be back to the main menu.

10. Press **SOLVE**.

11. If the equation which you have saved and now want to recall does not appear on your screen, use the up/down arrow keys to locate the equation.

12. Once you have found the desired equation (**SUM/LEARN1** in this case), press the **CALC** key.

13. The dedicated keys on your menu should now appear as follows:

SUM	N

14. Press 7 and then press the key under the menu corresponding to **N**.

15. Press the key under the menu corresponding to SUM.

16. You should see the following statement: **SUM=54**

17. Press **EXIT** twice (or **YELLOW KEY and EXIT**) to return to the main menu.

Learning Equation 2. The next equation is similar to Learning Equation 1. However, with this equation you do not need to know or input the value for N (the number of observations). The value of N is determined within the equation, since the statement SIZES(VAR1) represents the size of VAR1, which is the number of values in variable 1, which is N. The purpose of this equation is to illustrate that the value for N (the ending point in the summation process) does not have to be manually input. We can let the calculator determine this value for us. When we use the key word SIZES and indicate the variable name (VAR1 in this example), the calculator looks into VAR1 to determine the number of items included in that variable. As with SUM/LEARN1, you will probably want to delete SUM/LEARN2 after you have had a chance to test the equation and become more familiar with your calculator. This will again allow you to save calculator memory. Here is the equation:

`SUM/LEARN2:SUM=Σ(I:1:SIZES(VAR1):1:(ITEM(VAR1:I)))`

Your menu should now appear as follows:

SUM

Steps for determining the sum of the values in the list entitled VAR1:

1. From the main menu, select the **SUM** option.
2. Press **GET**.
3. Press **VAR1**.
4. Clear the list (if necessary) by pressing the **color-coded key** and the **INPUT** key (which is the second function of the input key, referred to as **CLEAR DATA**).
5. Respond to "Clear the list?" by selecting **YES**.
6. Respond to "Also clear list name?" by selecting **NO**. (Otherwise you will have to re-name the VAR1 list.)
7. Input your data. Try the following values: 6, 9, 3, 2, 12, 5, and 17. This value should sum to 54.
8. Press **EXIT**.
9. Press **EXIT** again. You should be back to the main menu.
10. Press **SOLVE**.
11. If the equation which you have saved and now want to recall does not appear on your screen, use the up/down arrow keys to locate the equation.
12. Once you have found the desired equation (**SUM/LEARN2** in this case), press the **CALC** key.
13. The dedicated keys on your menu should now appear as follows:

SUM

14. Press the key under the menu corresponding to SUM.

15. Press this same key again. (Since you only have one word, term, variable, or character on your menu, you usually have to press this key twice. Pressing it more than twice will continue to yield the same answer).

16. You should see the following statement: **SUM=54**

17. Press **EXIT** twice (or **YELLOW KEY and EXIT)** to return to the main menu.

Learning Equation 3. The next equation illustrates the flexibility of summation notation with these calculators. You may not always want to begin at 1, end at N, or use increments of 1. For example, you may want to eliminate the first three values and the last three values from your variable list before summing them. Rather than deleting them from your variable list, you can skip them through using your notation. This is a very useful equation, and you might consider keeping this equation in your calculator. It will be helpful for finding trimmed means and moving averages. As with the previous learning equations, this equation is based on the assumption that you have placed your data in a variable named VAR1 in the **SUM** menu of your calculator. You now have the flexibility of beginning at any point in the list, ending at any point in the list, and using any increment desired for advancing from value to value. Here is the equation:

SUM/LEARN3:SUM=Σ(I:BEGIN:END:INCRE:(ITEM(VAR1:I)))

Your menu should now appear as follows:

SUM	BEGI	END	INCR

Steps for determining the sum of the values in the list entitled VAR1:

1. From the main menu, select the **SUM** option.

2. Press **GET**.

3. Press **VAR1**.

4. Clear the list (if necessary) by pressing the **color-coded key** and the **INPUT** key (which is the second function of the input key, referred to as **CLEAR DATA**).

5. Respond to "Clear the list?" by selecting **YES**.

6. Respond to "Also clear list name?" by selecting **NO**. (Otherwise you will have to re-name the VAR1 list.)

7. Input your data into VAR1. Suppose you have closed the following number of accounts for the months of January through December, respectively: 42, 37, 21, 42, 25, 62, 74, 69, 50, 40, 39, and 18. These values should sum to 519.

8. Press **EXIT**.

9. Press **EXIT** again. You should be back to the main menu.

10. Press **SOLVE**.

11. If the equation that you have saved and now want to recall does not appear on your screen, use the up/down arrow keys to locate the equation.

12. Once you have found the desired equation (**SUM/LEARN3** in this case), press the **CALC** key.

13. The dedicated keys on your menu should now appear as follows:

SUM	BEGI	END	INCR

14. Press 1 and then press the key under the menu corresponding to **BEGIN**.

15. Press 7 and then press the key under the menu corresponding to **END**.

16. Press 1 and then press the key under the menu corresponding to **INCR**.

17. Press the key under the menu corresponding to SUM.

18. You should see the following statement: **SUM=303**

19. Press **EXIT** twice (or **YELLOW KEY and EXIT**) to return to the main menu.

As another example, if you wanted to only sum the first, third, fifth, seventh, ninth, and eleventh months (every other month), you would press 1, BEGI, 12, END, 2 INCR, and then press SUM. You should see the following statement: **SUM=251.**

As a third example, suppose you only want to find the sum of the accounts closed during the summer months of June, July, and August (months 6, 7, and 8 in your variable list). Simply press 6, BEGI, 8, END, 1, INCR, and then press SUM. You should see the following statement: **SUM=205.** This is the sum for 62, 74, and 69, which correspond to the months of June, July, and August.

As a final example of this equation, suppose you feel that your account results are being distorted too much by the best and worst months. Therefore, you have decided to eliminate those two months from your calculations. Instead of removing them from your variable list, you can simply not use them. To do this, you will need to sort your data. Thus, you need to return to the main menu, then press **SUM, GET, VAR1, CALC, MORE,** and **SORT**. (You may want to scroll through your list to examine the results.) Now return to the main menu once again, press **SOLVE**, **CALC** (assuming that you are still at the same equation in your equation list), 2, BEGI, 11, END, 1, INCR, and then press sum. You should see the following statement: **SUM=427**. You have not included December, which was the lowest month, at 18, and you have not included July, which was the highest, at 74.

Learning Equation 4. You might consider keeping this fourth learning equation in your calculator, as it also is very useful. This equation allows you to determine the sum of the deviations about the mean (or any other value, such as the median), when taken to any power. For example, the sum of the squared deviations about the mean is the numerator of the second moment about the mean (useful for determining the variance of a distribution), the sum of the cubed deviations about the mean is the numerator of the third moment about the mean (useful for determining the skewness of a distribution), and the sum of the deviations about the mean taken to the fourth power is the numerator of the fourth moment about the mean (useful for determining the kurtosis of a distribution). Here is the equation:

```
SUM/LEARN4/DEVIATIONS/ANYPOWER/RAW:SUM=
Σ(I:1:SIZES(VAR1):1:(ITEM(VAR1:I)-CONSTANT)^P)
```

Your menu should now appear as follows:

SUM	CONS	P

Steps for determining the sum of the values in the list entitled VAR1:

1. From the main menu, select the **SUM** option.

2. Press **GET**.

3. Press **VAR1**.

4. Clear the list (if necessary) by pressing the **color-coded key** and the **INPUT** key (which is the second function of the input key, referred to as **CLEAR DATA**).

5. Respond to "Clear the list?" by selecting **YES**.

6. Respond to "Also clear list name?" by selecting **NO**. (Otherwise you will have to re-name the VAR1 list.)

7. Input your data. Try the following values: 6, 9, 3, 2, 12, 5, and 17. This value should sum to 54.

8. Press **CALC**.

9. Press **MEAN**. Depending upon how you have set your decimals, it should now say: **MEAN=7.71428571429**

10. Press **STO** and then **0**.

11. Press **YELLOW KEY and EXIT**.

12. Press **SOLVE**.

13. If the equation which you have saved and now want to recall does not appear on your screen, use the up/down arrow keys to locate the equation.

14. Once you have found the desired equation (**SUM/LEARN4** in this case), press the **CALC** key.

15. The dedicated keys on your menu should now appear as follows:

SUM	CONS	P

16. Press **RCL** and **0**. The screen should say: 7.71428571429

17. Press the key under the menu corresponding to **CONS**.

18. If you want to find the squared differences from this constant value (the sum of the squared differences from the mean in this example), press **2** and then press the key under the menu corresponding to **P**.

19. Press the key under the menu corresponding to SUM.

20. Your screen should now say: **SUM=171.428571428**

21. Press **EXIT** twice (or **YELLOW KEY and EXIT)** to return to the main menu.

Learning Equation 5. This next equation can be used to find the deviations about the mean (or any other value) taken to any power for **grouped** data. The actual values must be in **VAR1** and the frequencies corresponding to each of these values must be in **FREQ**. Here is the equation:

```
SUM/LEARN5/DEVIATIONS/ANYPOWER/GROUP:SUM=
Σ(I:1:SIZES(VAR1):1:(ITEM(VAR1:I)-CONSTANT)
^P×ITEM(FREQ:I))
```

Your menu should now appear as follows:

SUM	CONS	P

If you are using the HP-17B*II*, are at the main menu, want to obtain the sum of the squared deviations from the mean for grouped data, and have already entered your data into VAR1 and FREQ, press the following sequence of keys: **SUM, CALC, MORE, FRCST, VAR1, FREQ (make sure it now says "linear"), MORE, W.MN, STO, 0, YELLOW KEY, EXIT, SOLVE, CALC, RCL 0, CONS, 2, P, SUM**. You now have the sums of squares for your grouped data.

If you are using the HP-19B*II*, are at the main menu, want to obtain the sum of the squared deviations from the mean for grouped data, and have already entered your data into VAR1 and FREQ, press the following sequence of keys: **SUM, GET, FREQ, CALC, MORE, FRCST, VAR1, LIN (for "linear"), MORE, W.MN, STO, 0, YELLOW KEY, EXIT, SOLVE, CALC, RCL 0, CONS, 2, P, SUM**. You now have the sums of squares for your grouped data.

As with the previous equation, you might consider keeping this equation in your calculator. It also allows you to determine the numerators of the second, third, and fourth moments about the mean, useful in calculating the variance, skewness, and kurtosis of a distribution. While the previous equation was designed for raw data, this equation is specifically designed for grouped data.

Learning Equation 6. This next equation can be used to find trimmed means for **grouped** data. The values must be in **VAR1** and the frequencies associated with these values must be in **FREQ**. Before inputting your data into the lists, arrange the values in rank order from highest to lowest. Next, input them in **VAR1** from highest to lowest, and input the corresponding frequencies in **FREQ**. Be certain you have finished all computations with the *original* set of data since you will be deleting part of your data. Here is the equation:

```
SUM/LEARN6/TRIM/GROUP:SUM=Σ(I:BEGIN:END:1:
(ITEM(VAR1:I)×ITEM(FREQ:I)))
```

Your menu should now appear as follows:

SUM	BEGI	END

If you want to find the trimmed mean for grouped data, you will have to make a decision as to how much you want to trim off the bottom and off the top of the list. Once you determine the amount, you can then determine what "rows" of values to eliminate, and which frequencies you will need to adjust. For example, your data base consists of 100 values, and you want to trim 10 values from the top and 10 values from the bottom. Also suppose you have 20 "rows" in your data base, and each row consists of values and frequencies that you have stored in **VAR1** and **FREQ**. Further suppose ITEM(1) in **FREQ** has a value of 2, ITEM(2) in **FREQ** has a value 5, and ITEM(3) in **FREQ** has a value of 9. You need to trim 10 values, so you do not want to include the first and second items in your sum (eliminating the values of 2 and 5) and you want to change the value in ITEM(3) of the **FREQ** list from 9 to 6 (because you need to eliminate a total of 10 items from the top, including 2 of the first item, 5 of the second item, and 3 of the third item). Consequently, you change ITEM(3) in **FREQ** from a 9 to a 6, and then insert 3 for **BEGIN**, to indicate you want to start the sum process with ITEM(3). You follow the same procedure at the bottom of the list, eliminating and revising as necessary to determine where to end and what the numerical rank order value for the appropriate ending **FREQ** needs to be. You then insert that appropriate value into **END**, and then press the **SUM** button. Finally, after determining the sum, you must divide the resulting sum by the number of remaining values (by 80 in this example).

Learning Equation 7. The next learning equation illustrates the use of a double summation process. With double summations, the inside summation operation is faster than the outside summation operation. Suppose you have a list containing 5 values in **VAR1** (4, 5, 7, 9, and 8) and another list containing 3 values in **VAR2** (2, 5, and 3). For some reason you want to subtract the first value of **VAR2** from each of the five values in **VAR1**, square the differences, then subtract the second value of **VAR2** from each of the five values in **VAR1**, square the differences, and finally subtract the third value of **VAR2** from each of the five values in **VAR1**, and square the differences. Here is an equation that will accomplish this task (to any specified power):

```
SUM/LEARN7/DOUBLESUM:SUM=Σ(J:JBEGIN:JEND:1:(Σ(I
:IBEGIN:IEND:1:((ITEM(VAR1:I))-(ITEM(VAR2:J)))^P)))
```

Your menu should now appear as follows:

SUM	JBEG	JEND	IBEG	IEND	P

To perform this operation in the current example, you set **JBEGIN** a 1, **JEND** at 3, **IBEGIN** at 1, **IEND** at 5, and **P** at 2. After pressing SUM, your answer will be 235. If you wanted to take these differences to the third power instead, you would set **P** at 3. After pressing SUM, your answer will now be 1,231. If you want to begin with the second value in **VAR1** and conclude with the fourth value in **VAR1**, and again take the differences to the third power, you would set IBEGIN at 2 and IEND at 4, and press SUM. Your result would be 855.

Learning Equation 8. The next learning equation illustrates the calculation of the numerator of the covariance between two matched variables. This value is often used in conjunction with correlation, regression, and analysis of covariance. In order to determine the covariance or its numerator, two paired variables must be created. Returning to Example H-3 to demonstrate this learning equation, recall that the first variable consists of assessment scores for a group of sales persons just prior to hiring them, while the second variable contains their performance scores six months after they were hired. In order to test this summation learning equation, you will need to input these numbers once again into VAR1 and VAR2 of your calculator, in the corresponding orders:

Item Number	VAR1: Assessment	VAR2: Performance
Item (1) =	11	10
Item (2) =	8	10
Item (3) =	8	9
Item (4) =	5	6
Item (5) =	2	5
Item (6) =	2	2

The numerator of the covariance between these two variables is the sum of the cross-products of the deviations between each paired value and the mean of its corresponding variable. This equation is written as follows:

$$\text{Numerator of the Covariance} = \sum (X - X) \times (Y - \bar{Y})$$

Here is an equation that will determine the numerator of the covariance between these two variables. You must first calculate the means of each of the two variables. The equation relies on the use of both **VAR1** and **VAR2**:

```
SUM/LEARN8/COVAR/NUM:SUM=Σ(I:1:SIZES(VAR1):1:(ITEM(
VAR1:I)-XBAR)×(ITEM(VAR2:I)-YBAR))
```

Your menu should now appear as follows:

SUM	XBAR	YBAR

We will now assume you have calculated the mean for VAR1 (which yields a mean of 6) and have stored it in memory location 7. We will also assume you have calculated the mean for VAR2 (which yields a mean of 7) and have stored it in memory location 4. These storage locations correspond to the scheme for storing means for two variables described earlier. Now press RCL, 7, XBAR, RCL 4, and YBAR. You are now ready to obtain the numerator of the covariance by pressing SUM. This should yield a value of 54.

Useful Equations for the Equation-Solver

The following set of equations will be useful in solving a number of quantitative problems, including basic statistics, basic probability, and advanced statistical analyses. Many of these equations are based on data that must be entered into one or more variables in the calculator. The reference names of the variables being used are VAR1, VAR2, VAR3, or FREQ, depending on the equation. A quick examination of the equation being used will identify the variable or variables being used by the equation. For example, the learning equations calculate sums based on data stored in VAR1 or in the combination of VAR1 and FREQ. Other equations do not refer to any variables at all, and the user simply inserts values for all but one of the terms in the equation. The equation will then solve for the remaining term. *Remember that if the menu for an equation only has one word, term, variable, or character, you should remember to press this key twice. Pressing it more than twice will continue to yield the same answer, but pressing it only once may give an incorrect answer.* First, we will repeat the list of summation learning equations:

SUM/LEARN1:SUM=Σ(I:1:N:1:(ITEM(VAR1:I)))

SUM/LEARN2:SUM=Σ(I:1:SIZES(VAR1):1:(ITEM(VAR1:I)))

SUM/LEARN3:SUM=Σ(I:BEGIN:END:INCRE:(ITEM(VAR1:I)))

**SUM/LEARN4/DEVIATIONS/ANYPOWER/RAW:SUM=
Σ(I:1:SIZES(VAR1):1:(ITEM(VAR1:I)-CONSTANT)^P)**

**SUM/LEARN5/DEVIATIONS/ANYPOWER/GROUP:SUM=
Σ(I:1:SIZES(VAR1):1:(ITEM(VAR1:I)-CONSTANT)
^P×ITEM(FREQ:I))**

**SUM/LEARN6/TRIM/GROUP:SUM=Σ(I:BEGIN:END:1:
(ITEM(VAR1:I)×ITEM(FREQ:I)))**

**SUM/LEARN7/DOUBLESUM:SUM=Σ(J:JBEGIN:JEND:1:(Σ(I:
IBEGIN:IEND:1:((ITEM(VAR1:I))-(ITEM(VAR2:J)))^P)))**

**SUM/LEARN8/COVAR/NUM:SUM=Σ(I:1:SIZES(VAR1):1:
(ITEM(VAR1:I)-XBAR)×(ITEM(VAR2:I)-YBAR))**

Equations for Basic Statistics Such as Central Tendency, Variability, etc.

General Form of a Test Statistic. Many, if not most, statistical tests follow a general format. This general format is based on a comparison of some value we observe with some value we expect to obtain if the null hypothesis is true. We compare the difference between the observed and expected values to some measure of chance variation. This format is appropriate for calculating a *z*-score, for performing a one-sample or two-sample *z*-test, for performing a one-sample or two-sample *t*-test, for determining the significance of a correlation coefficient, and for computing many other statistical tests.

$$\text{Statistic} = \frac{(\text{Observed} - \text{Expected})}{\text{Chance}}$$

The observed value could be an observed *X*-value within a distribution, while the expected value could be the mean of that distribution, and the measure of chance could be the standard deviation. Here is this same equation, now written in a format acceptable to both the HP-17B*II* and the HP-19B*II* calculators:

STATISTIC=(OBSERVED-EXPECTED)÷CHANCE

Determining the Rank Order Position for Percentiles for Discrete Data. In order to determine a percentile for a discrete set of data, the values must be in rank order and must satisfy at least ordinal level measurement. To find the percentile, the rank order position of the desired percentile must be determined. One approach for determining this rank order position is to identify the vth value from the bottom of the list, based on the following equation:

$$v = \left(\frac{x}{100}\right) \times (n + 1)$$

Here is this same equation, again written in a format that is acceptable to both the HP-17B*II* and the HP-19B*II* calculators:

PERC/DISCRETE:V=(X÷100)×(N+1)

In this equation, PERC/DISCRETE represents a brief title, **V** represents the rank order position of the desired percentile, **X** represents the percentile of interest, and **N** represents the number of cases in the data list.

Determining Percentiles for Continuous Data. The following equation is helpful for determining the percentiles for continuous data, either in raw or in grouped format. The resulting percentile value is represented by **PERC**, while **W** represents the constant width of the intervals, **RLL** represents the real lower limit of the interval containing the desired percentile, **X** represents the particular percentile of interest (e.g., if you want to determine the 75th percentile, let X = 75), N represents the number of cases in the set of data, **SBL** represents the sum of the frequencies below the real lower limit, and **SFP** represents the sum of the frequencies in the interval that contains the percentile of interest. Here is the equation for finding the percentile value for continuous data:

$$P_x = RLL + \left(W \times \left(\frac{\left(\left(\left(\frac{X}{100} \right) \times N \right) - SBL \right)}{SFP} \right) \right)$$

Here is this same equation, this time written in a format that is acceptable to both the HP-17B*II* and the HP-19B*II* calculators:

```
PERC/CONT:PERC=RLL+(W×(((X÷100)×N)-SBL)÷SFP))
```

Determining the Geometric Mean for Raw Data. For this equation (as well as for many other equations), the menu generated contains only one term, **GM**. This is because EXP, SIZES, LN, and ITEM are unique key "words" for the Hewlett-Packard calculators, and VAR1 is a user-defined variable name for one of the lists in the **SUM** menu. Consequently, all terms in the equation have been previously determined except for GM. Whenever the menu contains only one term, you should press the key corresponding to that term twice (once to initialize the equation and once to compute the desired value).

```
GM=EXP(Σ(I:1:SIZES(VAR1):1:LN(ITEM(VAR1:I)))
÷SIZES(VAR1))
```

Determining the Geometric Mean for Grouped Data.

```
GMGP=EXP(Σ(I:1:SIZES(VAR1):1:(LN(ITEM(VAR1:I)))
×(ITEM(FREQ:I)))÷Σ(I:1:SIZES(VAR1):1:ITEM(FREQ:I)))
```

Determining the Harmonic Mean for Raw Data.

```
HM=INV(Σ(I:1:SIZES(VAR1):1:INV(ITEM(VAR1:I)))
÷SIZES(VAR1))
```

Determining the Harmonic Mean for Grouped Data.

```
HMGP=Σ(I:1:SIZES(FREQ):1:(ITEM(FREQ:I)))÷
Σ(I:1:SIZES(VAR1):1:(ITEM(FREQ:I))÷(ITEM(VAR1:I)))
```

Determining the Variation Ratio. The variation ratio is one of the few measures of variability appropriate for nominal data. It is based on the frequencies associated with the mode and is only appropriate for unimodal distributions. To determine the variation ratio, input the following equation into the **SOLVE** menu:

```
VR=1 - (FMODE÷N)
```

In this equation, VR represents the variation ratio, FMODE represents the frequency of cases falling at the mode, and N represents the number of cases in the set of data.

Determining the Absolute Deviation about a Constant for Raw Data. This absolute deviation equation can be used to find the mean deviation, the median deviation, or any other absolute deviation average from any given constant value for raw data. After pressing CALC, the following terms will appear above the first two keys: AD and CONSTANT. To find the mean deviation, input the mean as the CONSTANT. Then determine the mean deviation by pressing the AD button. To determine the median deviation, input the median as the CONSTANT, and then determine the median deviation by pressing the AD button.

```
AD=Σ(I:1:SIZES(VAR1):1:(ABS(ITEM(VAR1:I)
-CONSTANT)))÷SIZES(VAR1)
```

Determining the Absolute Deviation about a Constant for Grouped (Weighted) Data. This absolute deviation equation can be used to find the mean deviation, the median deviation, or any other absolute deviation average from any given constant value for grouped (weighted) data. After pressing CALC, the following terms will appear above the first two keys: ADGP and CONSTANT. To find the mean deviation, input the value of the mean as the CONSTANT. Then determine the mean deviation by pushing the AD key. To find the median deviation, input the median instead of the mean and follow the same procedure.

```
ADGP=Σ(I:1:SIZES(VAR1):1:((ABS(ITEM(VAR1:I)
-CONSTANT))×(ITEM(FREQ:I))))÷Σ(I:1:SIZES(VAR1)
:1:ITEM(FREQ:I))
```

Converting from a Sample Standard Deviation to a Population Standard Deviation. Since these HP calculators do not have the population standard deviation built into any menu, you will find it useful to create one for yourself in the **SOLVE** menu. This equation was discussed earlier and is given again here:

```
POPSD=SQRT(((SAMSD^2)×(N-1))÷N)
```

Determining the Sum of Squares (SS) (i.e., the sum of the squared deviations about the mean). There are many ways to determine the sum of the squared deviations about the mean. This concept is essential for many statistical computations, is often abbreviated as *SS*, and for raw data this sum is defined as follows:

$$SS = \sum (X - \overline{X})^2$$

For grouped or weighted data, the frequencies for each of the *X*-values have to be accounted for in the equation. Therefore, the sum of squares for grouped data is defined as follows:

$$SS = \sum f(X - \overline{X})^2$$

Sample SS. The sum of squares for raw data can be obtained by using SUM/LEARN4, while the sum of squares for grouped data can be obtained by using SUM/LEARN5. However, since the sum of the squares is simply the numerator of the variance, this value can be more easily obtained simply by finding the standard deviation, and then solving for the sum of squares. To find the sum of squares for a sample, you can multiply the sample variance times $n - 1$, as follows:

```
SAMPLE/SS:SS=(SAMSD^2)×(N-1)
```

Population SS. To find the sum of squares for a population, you can multiply the population variance times *N*, as follows:

```
POPULATION/SS:SS=(POPSD^2)×(N)
```

Sheppard's Correction Factor to Adjust the Standard Deviation of Grouped Data. In this equation, **SD** represents the standard deviation (either the population or the sample standard deviation), and **W** represents the width of the interval used in the grouping of values into categories or intervals. It should only be used when the constant width of the intervals is greater than 1.

```
SD/SHEPPARD:SDADJ=SQRT(SD^2-(W^2÷12))
```

***Z*-equation for Converting an X-Value to a Z-Value (i.e., *z*-score).** In this equation, **Z** represents the *z*-score, **X** represents the observed value, **MEAN** represents the mean of the data, and **SD** represents the standard deviation of the data.

```
Z=(X-MEAN)÷SD
```

G_1 for Determining the Skewness of a Sample. In this equation, **G1** represents the skewness of the data, **M3** represents the third moment about the mean for the data, and **S** represents the standard deviation for the data.

```
G1/SKEW:G1=M3÷(S^3)
```

G_2 for Determining the Kurtosis of a Sample. In this equation, **G2** represents the kurtosis for the data, **M4** represents the fourth moment about the mean for the data, and **S** represents the standard deviation for the data.

```
G2/KURT:G2=(M4÷(S^4))-3
```

Z_{SKEW} for Determining the *Z*-Value Associated with the Skewness of a Sample. In this equation, **Z** represents the *z*-value associated with the skewness of a sample, **G1** represents the skewness of a sample, **GAMMA1** represents the hypothesized skewness of the associated population, usually set equal to zero under the null hypothesis for skewness, and **N** represents the sample size.

```
Z/SKEW:Z=(G1-GAMMA1)÷(SQRT(6÷N))
```

Z_{KURT} for Determining the *Z*-Value Associated with the Kurtosis of a Sample. In this equation, **Z** represents the *z*-value associated with the kurtosis of a sample, **G2** represents the kurtosis of a sample, **GAMMA2** represents the hypothesized kurtosis of the associated population, usually set equal to zero under the null hypothesis for kurtosis, and **N** represents the sample size.

```
Z/KURT:Z=(G2-GAMMA2)÷(2×(SQRT(6÷N)))
```

Probability and Probability Distributions

PERMUTATIONS
(HP-17B*II* Version)
(Permutations are already built into the HP-19B*II*)

```
NPR:PERM=FACT(N)÷FACT(N-R)
```

COMBINATIONS
(HP-17B*II* Version)
(Combinations are already built into the HP-19B*II*)

```
NCR:COMB=(FACT(N))÷(FACT(R)×FACT(N-R))
```

NORMAL DISTRIBUTION

```
Z/DISTRIBUTION:1÷PROB=((1+.049867347×Z
+.0211410061×Z^2+.0032776263×Z^3+3.80036E-5
×Z^4+4.88906E-5×Z^5+5.383E-6×Z^6)^16)×(2÷TAIL)
```

Input a 1 for "TAIL" if this is a one-tailed test, or input a 2 for "TAIL" if this is a two-tailed test. Then input either the desired probability or the *z*-value and solve for the other. You should remember to only input positive values for *z*.

BINOMIAL DISTRIBUTION
(HP-19B*II* Version)

```
BINOMIAL:PROB=Σ(I:BEGIN:END:1:(COMB(N:I)
×(P^I)×((1-P)^(N-I))))
```

BINOMIAL DISTRIBUTION
(HP-17B*II* Version)

```
BINOMIAL:PROB=Σ(I:BEGIN:END:1:(FACT(N)÷
(FACT(I)×FACT(N-I))×(P^I)×((1-P)^(N-I))))
```

POISSON DISTRIBUTION
(PROBABILITY FOR EXACTLY R OUT OF N)

```
POISSON/EXACT:POIS=(((N×P)^R)×(EXP
(-(N×P))))÷FACT(R)
```

CUMULATIVE POISSON DISTRIBUTION
(PROBABILITY FOR R OR LESS OUT OF N)

```
POISSON/CUMULATIVE:CPOIS=Σ(I:0:R:1:
((((N×P)^I)×(EXP(-N×P))))÷FACT(I))
```

POISSON DISTRIBUTION
(PROBABILITY FOR EXACTLY R OUT OF N)
(With a fixed value for the mean instead of given values for N and P)

```
POISSON/EXACT/LAMBDA:POIS=((LAMBDA^R)
×(EXP(-LAMBDA)))÷FACT(R)
```

CUMULATIVE POISSON DISTRIBUTION
(PROBABILITY FOR R OR LESS OUT OF N)
(With a fixed value for the mean instead of given values for N and P)

```
POISSON/CUM/LAMBDA:CPOIS=Σ(I:0:R:1:
((LAMBDA^I)×(EXP(-LAMBDA)))÷FACT(I))
```

HYPERGEOMETRIC DISTRIBUTION
(HP-19B*II* Version)

```
HYPER:PROB=(COMB(COL1:CELL1)×COMB((NT-COL1)
:(ROW1-CELL1)))÷COMB(NT:ROW1)
```

HYPERGEOMETRIC DISTRIBUTION
(HP-17B*II* Version)

```
HYPER:PROB=((FACT(COL1)÷(FACT(CELL1)×
FACT(COL1-CELL1)))×(FACT(NT-COL1)÷
(FACT(ROW1-CELL1)×FACT((NT-COL1)-(ROW1-CELL1)))))
÷(FACT(NT)÷(FACT(ROW1)×FACT(NT-ROW1)))
```

The menu for the hypergeometric distribution will display the following terms: PROB, COL1, CELL1, NT, and ROW1. The user only needs to input values for column 1 (COL1), row 1 (ROW1), the grand total (NT), and the upper-left cell value (CELL1). By pressing PROB, the exact probability associated with this two-by-two table will be obtained. If another probability table is to be evaluated based upon these same marginal values (i.e., for fixed values of COL1, ROW1, and NT), input a new value for CELL1 and re-compute PROB. Cumulative probabilities can be obtained by adding each of the separate probabilities.

Equations Useful for Comparing Means

OBTAINING THE POOLED STANDARD ERROR OF THE DIFFERENCES BETWEEN TWO INDEPENDENT SAMPLE MEANS (POOLED STANDARD ERROR OF THE DIFFERENCES TERM)

```
SEDIFF/POOLED:SEDIFF=SQRT(((SD1^2×(N1-1)
+SD2^2×(N2-1))÷(N1+N2-2))×((1÷N1)+(1÷N2)))
```

OBTAINING THE UNPOOLED STANDARD ERROR OF THE DIFFERENCES BETWEEN TWO INDEPENDENT SAMPLE MEANS (UNPOOLED STANDARD ERROR OF THE DIFFERENCES TERM)

```
SEDIFF/UNPOOLED:SEDIFF=SQRT((SD1^2÷N1)
+(SD2^2÷N2))
```

OBTAINING THE ADJUSTED DEGREES OF FREEDOM FOR THE TWO-SAMPLE INDEPENDENT *T*-TEST WHEN THE ASSUMPTION OF HOMOGENEITY OF VARIANCE IS NOT MET

```
DF/T/ADJUSTED:DF=(((SD1^2÷N1)+(SD2^2÷N2))^2
÷(((SD1^2÷N1)^2×(1÷(N1+1)))+((SD2^2÷N2)^2
×(1÷(N2+1)))))-2
```

OBTAINING THE STANDARD ERROR OF THE DIFFERENCES BETWEEN THE MEANS OF TWO DEPENDENT SAMPLES (STANDARD ERROR OF THE DIFFERENCES FOR DEPENDENT SAMPLES)

```
SEDIFF/DEPENDENT/T:SEDIFF=SQRT((SD1^2÷N1)
+(SD2^2÷N2)-(2×R×(SD1÷SQRT(N1))×(SD2÷SQRT(N2))))
```

COMPUTING SCHEFFÉ *F*-VALUES FOR POST-COMPARISON TESTS BETWEEN THE MEANS OF TWO SAMPLES

```
SCHEFFE:F=((MI-MJ)^2)÷(MSW×((1÷NI)+(1÷NJ)))
```

Any two means can be compared, two at a time. The first of the pair of means being compared is designated here as MI (for the mean of the ith group) and MJ (for the mean of the jth group). Input the mean of the first group of the pair of means to be compared as MI, and input the mean of the second group of the pair of means as MJ. Input the Mean Square Within value for MSW. This is the value obtained in the ANOVA table. Insert the sample size for the ith group as NI and the sample size for the jth group as NJ. If several groups are to be combined before comparing means, be sure to obtain the weighted mean for each of these combined groups and determine the combined size of these groups.

Equations Useful for Comparing Variances

BARTLETT CHI-SQUARE TEST FOR HOMOGENEITY OF VARIANCE

```
BARTLETT:CHI=(2.30259÷(1+((1÷(3×(K-1)))×
(Σ(I:1:K:1:(1÷(ITEM(VAR1:I)-1)))-(1÷(N-K))))))
×(((N-K)×LOG(MSW))-(Σ(I:1:K:1:((ITEM(VAR1:I)
-1)×(LOG((ITEM(VAR2:I)^2)))))))
```

Before using the Bartlett chi-square test for homogeneity of variance, you must input each of the sample sizes for the **K** groups into VAR1, and each of the ***standard deviations*** for the **K** groups into VAR2. The value of **K** is the number of groups, **N** is the total number of cases in all the **K** groups combined, and **MSW** is the ***Mean Squares Within*** term as obtained through the analysis of variance (ANOVA),

Miscellaneous Equations Useful for Statistical Decisions

DETERMINING NECESSARY SAMPLE SIZES WHEN GIVEN AN ACCEPTABLE ERROR WIDTH

SAMPLE/SIZE:SIZE=(Z×SD÷ERROR)^2

Here, SIZE represents the required sample size, Z represents the critical Z-value, SD represents the standard deviation, and ERROR represents the acceptable width for the band around the mean.

CHI-SQUARE TESTS
(For Tests of Goodness of Fit, Multinomial Tests, Tests of Independence, and Tests Requiring Yates' Correction Factor)

CHI/SQUARE/YATES:CHI=Σ(I:1:SIZES(VAR1):1:(ABS(ITEM(VAR1:I)-ITEM(VAR2:I))-YATES)^2÷ITEM(VAR2:I))

This equation will adjust for Yates' continuity correction factor if desired. When the degrees of freedom for the chi-square test are greater than 1, Yates' correction factor should not be used. Under such circumstances, always set YATES equal to 0. If the degrees of freedom are equal to 1 and you want to adjust for continuity, set YATES equal to .5. Otherwise, set YATES equal to 0 and ignore the correction factor. Note that VAR1 contains the observed values and VAR2 contains the expected values.

Correlation and Regression Equations

STANDARD ERROR OF A CORRELATION COEFFICIENT

SE/CORR:SE=SQRT((1-R^2)÷(N-2))

CONVERTING A CORRELATION COEFFICIENT TO A *t*-VALUE

T/R:T=(R-RHO)÷(SQRT((1-R^2)÷(N-2)))

Note that RHO represents the hypothesized values of the population correlation coefficient, usually assumed to be zero.

COMPUTING THE BIVARIATE COVARIANCE

COVAR=R×SX×SY

CONVERTING A CORRELATION COEFFICIENT TO FISHER'S-*z*
(and converting Fisher's-*z* to a correlation coefficient)

FISHER/Z:Z=(1÷2)×(LN(1+R)-LN(1-R))

OBTAINING THE STANDARD ERROR FOR FISHER'S-*z*

SE/FISHER:SE=1÷SQRT(N-3)

COMPUTING THE ERROR SUM OF SQUARES FOR A REGRESSION MODEL
(Based on for the standard deviation of the *Y*-variable and the size of the data base)

ESS/FM:ESSFM=((SY^2)×(N-1))-((SY^2)×(N-1)×(R^2))

COMPUTING THE BIVARIATE STANDARD ERROR OF ESTIMATE

SE/ESTIMATE:SEE=SQRT(ESSFM÷(N-K-1))

COMPUTING THE BIVARIATE STANDARD ERROR OF THE SLOPE

SE/SLOPE:SESLOPE=SQRT((SEEST^2)÷SSX)
or:
SE/SLOPE:SESLOPE=SQRT((SEEST^2)÷((SX^2)×(N-1)))

COMPUTING THE BIVARIATE STANDARD ERROR OF THE INTERCEPT (THE CONSTANT TERM IN THE REGRESSION EQUATION)

SE/CONSTANT:SECON=SEEST×SQRT((1÷N)+((XBAR^2)÷SSX))

COMPUTING THE BIVARIATE STANDARD ERROR OF THE FORECAST
or for the
STANDARD ERROR OF THE EXPECTED MEAN OF A PREDICTED Y′ VALUE

SE/FORECAST/EXPECTED:SE=SEE×SQRT(FORE+(1÷N)
+((X-XBAR)^2÷((SX^2)×(N-1))))

Note that if the standard error of the forecast is desired, set FORE equal to 1. If the standard error of the expected mean of a predicted Y′ value is desired, set FORE equal to 0.

OBTAINING THE *RSQ* FROM THE ESS_{CH} AND THE ESS_{FM}

RSQ=(ESSCH-ESSFM)÷ESSCH

OBTAINING THE *RSQ* ADJUSTED FOR DEGREES OF FREEDOM

RSQADJ=1-((1-RSQFM)×((N-1)÷(N-K-1)))

OBTAINING AN *F*-VALUE TO TEST THE SIGNIFICANCE OF AN r^2 (RSQ) VALUE

F/RSQ:F=((RSQFM-RSQRM)÷(DFFM-DFRM))÷((1-RSQFM)÷(N-DFFM))

Note that RSQFM represents the r^2 for the full model, RSQRM represents the r^2 for the restricted model, DFFM represents the degrees of freedom for the full model, and DFRM represents the degrees of freedom for the restricted model.

OBTAINING AN *F*-VALUE TO TEST THE SIGNIFICANCE OF AN r^2 (RSQ) VALUE BASED ON ERROR SUM OF SQUARES TERMS

F/ESS:F=((ESSRM-ESSFM)÷(DFFM-DFRM))÷((ESSFM)÷(N-DFFM))

Note that RSQFM represents the r^2 for the full model, RSQRM represents the r^2 for the restricted model, DFFM represents the degrees of freedom for the full model, and DFRM represents the degrees of freedom for the restricted model.

OBTAINING THE STANDARD REGRESSION WEIGHT (*z*-WEIGHT) WHEN THE RAW WEIGHT AND THE STANDARD DEVIATION FOR THE *Y*-VARIABLE ARE KNOWN (OR VICE VERSA)

ZWGT=(RWGT×SDJ)÷(SDY)

Here, ZWGT represents the standard weight (*z*-weight or standard slope), RWGT represents the raw weight (*b*-weight or raw slope), SDJ represents the standard deviation for the predictor variable of interest, and SDJ represents the standard deviation for the criterion variable.

Other Useful Equations

VARIOUS QUADRATIC EQUATIONS

QUADRATIC:Y=X^2×A+X×B+C

QUAD/PLUS:X=(1÷(2×A))×(-B+SQRT(B^2-4×A×C))

QUAD/MINUS:X=(1÷(2×A))×(-B-SQRT(B^2-4×A×C))

COMPUTING THE DETERMINANT FOR A 3 × 3 MATRIX

```
DET3BY3:DET=(ITEM(VAR3:1)×ITEM(VAR3:5)×ITEM(VAR3:9))
-(ITEM(VAR3:1)×ITEM(VAR3:8)×ITEM(VAR3:6))
-(ITEM(VAR3:4)×ITEM(VAR3:2)×ITEM(VAR3:9))
+(ITEM(VAR3:4)×ITEM(VAR3:8)×ITEM(VAR3:3))
+(ITEM(VAR3:7)×ITEM(VAR3:2)×ITEM(VAR3:6))
-(ITEM(VAR3:7)×ITEM(VAR3:5)×ITEM(VAR3:3))
```

Use VAR3 as the name of the variable list called by this equation. If you do not have a variable named VAR3, you must either create one or change VAR3 throughout the equation to a variable name you prefer to use. Enter the elements of the 3 × 3 matrix into this variable list, row-wise. That is, let item 1 correspond to $cell_{1,1}$, let item 2 correspond to $cell_{1,2}$, let item 3 correspond to $cell_{1,3}$, let item 4 correspond to $cell_{2,1}$, let item 5 correspond to $cell_{2,2}$, etc., for the nine items to be input. The DET key will appear on your menu and will be the only named key on your menu for this equation. When using this equation, remember to press the DET key twice.

APPENDIX I

INDEPENDENT STUDY
SAMPLE STUDENT PAPER
WITH APA STYLE MANUAL NOTATIONS

Research Paper Considerations

When reporting research results, the format of the presentation is almost as important as the content of the report. If the report is not well-written, the reader may not be able to follow the content, may lose interest in the report, or perhaps may even lose confidence in the person writing the report. There are many style manuals for report writing. The ***Publication Manual of the American Psychological Association*** is one of the most widely used of these manuals, and it has been adopted by many professional journals in psychology and business administration. The present textbook conforms to this manual whenever possible. In addition to the format and structure recommended by the ***APA Manual***, there are other issues that you should take into consideration before the final draft of the report is submitted. Several of these issues are discussed in the following pages. This appendix also includes a sample paper with hand-written notations regarding correct and incorrect format. The paper is not to be used as an example of a good or bad paper; rather, it is presented in order to highlight various grammatical and structural concerns in formal report writing.

Printing or Typing of the Paper

Whenever possible, papers should be printed from a computer printer via a word processor; if a computer is not available, typed papers are still acceptable today. Handwritten papers are never acceptable. If a less expensive printer is used, you are encouraged to turn off the right justification option, as these printers usually do not provide appropriate spacing between words. If a good printer is available, full justification is often preferred. You should set the margins at approximately 1 1/2 inches (4 cm) from the top, bottom, right, and left side of every page, as specified in the ***APA Manual***.

Spelling, Punctuation, Grammar, Format, Excessive Errors, Citations, and References

General Errors. If the paper consists of excessive spelling errors, grammatical, or punctuation errors, or if it lacks conformity with APA format in regard to citations in the text or in regard to the reference list, the evaluation of the paper often becomes negative before it has been considered in regard to content. A paper with perfect content will not necessarily be an acceptable paper. Always have someone else ***proofread*** the paper before submitting it.

Citations and References. Every citation used in the body of the paper must also be included in the reference list, and every entry in the reference list must have been cited somewhere in the body of the paper. Two examples of references from journals and two references from books are given here for review. Each reference uses proper APA format for the reference list. Note that anything which has been "italicized" could also have been "underlined." It originally was much easier to underline than to italicize when papers were traditionally submitted via typewriters. The following examples demonstrate the APA format to be used in the reference list:

Blake, R. R. & Mouton, J. S. (1964). ***The managerial grid.*** Houston: Gulf Publishing Co.

Keys, J. B. & Miller, T. R. (1984). The Japanese management theory jungle. ***Academy of Management Review, 9***, 342-353.

Ouchi, W. (1981). ***Theory Z: How American business can meet the Japanese challenge.*** Reading, MA: Addison-Wesley.

Triandis, H. C. & Brislin, R. W. (1984). Cross-cultural psychology. ***American Psychologist, 39***, 1006-1016.

Reviewing Journals First. You may find it beneficial to review articles published in scholarly journals prior to beginning your project. The ***Academy of Management Journal***, the ***Journal of Marketing***, ***Decision Sciences***, the ***Journal of Applied Psychology***, the ***Journal of Management***, and the ***Journal of Finance*** are examples of such journals. Not all of these journals follow the APA format, but they will give you a good idea of the traditional approach to scientific writing.

Exceptions to the Formal Guidelines. Certain exceptions to the rules of the ***APA Manual*** may be adopted by the reviewer or journal. For example, student papers typically do not include a "running head," tables are often to be inserted into the body of the paper, and abstracts may or may not be included. A discussion regarding "Material Other than Journal Articles," such as theses, dissertations, and student papers, is included in the Appendix of the ***APA Manual.*** Reading this appendix may be useful.

Commonly Included Sections. Most research papers should include the sections listed below. Each section (except for the introduction) is to be identified by a heading. The headings are to be underlined or italicized and centered above the corresponding sections. Consider using the headings underlined in the examples below. Number the pages of the paper, but do not number the headings. With the exception of the reference list at the end of the paper, you should not start each section on a separate page.

1. A brief *Introduction* to the subject matter, relating a technical base to the topic. This the section of the paper in which most of your references should be cited, and it is often referred to as the "review of the literature." This is the only section that does not have a heading.

2. A description of the *Research Methods*, in which you are to discuss the sample, method of data collection, the research variables and how they are measured, and the statistical methods to be used. Properly identify all variables (e.g., criterion variables, classification variables, etc.).

3. A report of the *Results* of the analysis. Here, you are to describe in words the results of your findings, supported by at least one but no more than two tables (i.e., ANOVA table, table of means, standard deviations, etc.). All tables combined cannot account for more than one page of the paper. Tables are to be properly typed, centered, and lined. They are to appear on separate pages at the conclusion of the paper or in the body of the paper, as determined by the reader and in conjunction with the Appendix of the ***APA Manual.***

4. A brief summary of the *Conclusions* that can be drawn from the findings.

5. A list of the *References*, typed on a separate page.

6. Many papers include tables, figures, footnotes, and other supporting information after the conclusion of the paper. The rules for such materials vary from reviewer to reviewer. While the ***APA Manual*** gives recommendations for papers that are to be submitted to journals, these recommendations may differ from recommendations or requirements of instructors, dissertation and theses committees, non-APA journals, magazines, company guidelines, government outlets for reports, and other publishers. You should consult with the reviewer or check with the reviewer's published guidelines before submitting the written report.

Common Errors on Papers

The following is a list of common errors committed by previous authors in their research reports. Such errors should be avoided at all costs. As noted earlier, all too often a paper is evaluated as unacceptable due to excessive errors in writing, grammar, spelling, punctuation, etc., when the content of the paper might have been very acceptable. At the conclusion of this list is a paper that has been edited, indicating errors and potential problem areas.

1. Spelling, typographical errors, poor copy, generally sloppy appearance of paper.

2. One sentence paragraphs.

3. Leaving a line of print to stand alone at the bottom of one page or at the top of the next page. Such lines are referred to as hanging lines. Word processors often refer to these lines as widows or orphans. It is better to have a small amount of extra space at the bottom of a page than to have hanging lines.

4. Failure to refer to "data" as a plural noun. ***Do*** use the following noun/predicate combination: ***data are.*** ***Do not*** use the following combination: ***data is.***

5. Failure to use generally accepted Greek symbols to represent population parameters when stating hypotheses. (The letters "M," "m,", and "u" are not Greek symbols and therefore ***cannot*** be used to represent the population mean, μ. If you do not have access to the μ symbol, make the symbol by hand.)

6. Failure to conform to prescribed style manual guidelines.
7. Failure to follow the required style manual rules for citations and references.
8. Failure to have a reference in the reference list for all citations in the paper.
9. Failure to use a comma before the conjunction in a series, as stated in the manual.
10. Failure to attend to the rules of seriation as prescribed in the style manual.
11. Sexist use of personal pronouns.
12. Inappropriate use or absence of necessary commas in formal writing.
13. Overuse of "this," "these," "it," etc., without proper referents.
14. Lack of consistency in active vs. passive writing.
15. Lack of consistency in use of first or third person tense.
16. Inappropriate use of past, present, and future tenses.
17. Improper breaking of words (hyphenation) at end of lines of type.
18. Misplaced modifiers.
19. Awkward or confusing sentences.
20. Improper blocking of direct quotations.
21. Failure to have 2 spaces after periods at the end of each sentence.
22. Failure to indent at the beginning of each paragraph.
23. Triteness.
24. Use of contractions in formal writing.
25. Failure to have another person proofread the paper prior to submitting it.
26. Inability to anticipate relevant time factors in order to meet the deadline.
27. Failure to conform to the required length.

Center the title

Perceptual Differences of Leadership Styles Between

Japanese Supervisors and U.S. Subordinates

Use an ampersand when the citation is in parentheses

Double space throughout the paper.

Within the past twenty-five [25] years, the number of studies which [that] compare managerial differences from country to country has substantially increased (e.g., Bass & Burger, 1979; Deming, 1986, 1993; Gruenfeld & MacEachron, 1975). At the heart of these studies is a growing debate between universalists (i.e., "culture free" theorists) and cross-culturalists concerning whether comparative studies of different societies and cultures are theoretically and methodologically possible. The universalists claim that organizational relationships are subject to general laws independent of social context and that there are no real differences in managerial principles governing management practices across different cultures. In contrast, the cross-culturalists believe that management is substantially a function of environmental culture.

Avoid parenthetical material whenever possible

Right justification sometimes results in unnatural spacing.

Oberg (1963) stated that the "ground rules" under which managers operate vary so greatly from country to country that it is hopeless to attempt to find a universal core to managerial behavior. Gonzalez and McMillan (1961), after spending several years as technical consultants in South America, noted that management is highly culture bound and that "our uniquely American philosophy of management is not universally applicable but rather is a special case" (p. 41).

Write out "and" instead of using & when the citation is not in parentheses.

A page number is required for a direct quote.

Recently, controversy has developed concerning whether the Japanese style of management, sometimes referred to as Theory Z by Ouchi (1981), is applicable in the United States and other countries or whether it is culture-bound. Zemke (1981) pointed out that since the very essence of the Japanese style of management is a direct outgrowth of the Japanese culture, it cannot be duplicated in the environment of the United States.

The present study explores the transferability of Japanese leadership styles in an environment in which Japanese and U.S. managers <u>work together</u> on a regular basis in the same organization. They study focuses upon the self-perceptions of senior level Japanese supervisors in regard to how they should behave as leaders; these perceptions are compared to their leadership styles as viewed by their immediate U.S. subordinates.

Only use subheadings if there are more than one section.

Research Methods

Section headings are centered and underlined or italicized.

Data Collection and Samples

The primary sample in this study consisted of participants employed in Japanese-owned retail banks operating in the U.S. Seven such banks agreed to participate by distributing questionnaires to senior level Japanese managers and their immediate U.S. subordinates, who were also upper level managers. All questionnaires were returned anonymously to insure confidentiality and to increase the likelihood of obtaining accurate responses.

Characteristics of Respondents

Use numbers instead of writing out in words, unless the number is at the beginning of the sentence.

"Data" is a plural word. "Datum" is a singular word.

Data were collected for 26 senior level Japanese managers and 34 U.S. upper level managers who reported to these Japanese managers. Although these two groups may appear to be small, the population of senior and upper level managers interacting together as described above is also small, thus limiting the sample sizes. Each of the 34 U.S. respondents reported directly to one of the 26 Japanese managers. The Japanese managers had spent an average of five years in the U.S. at the time the questionnaires were completed, and all were fluent in English.

Measurement Instruments

Many studies have suggested that there are generally two independent leadership styles, often referred to as consideration and initiating structure (Bass, 1981). Numerous instruments are available to assess leadership in regard to these dimensions. The questionnaire which was administered to supervisors in the present study included the Leadership Opinion Questionnaire (LOQ). This instrument assesses self-perceptions of supervisors in regard to how they believe

This word is often misspelled. There are two n's, not one.

they should behave as a leader. The questionnaire which was administered to the subordinates of these supervisors included the identical items given in the LOQ, except that the subordinates were asked to assess how their supervisors performed as leaders. This instrument will be referred to as the Supervisory Behavior Description (SBD) in future discussion.

Write out long phrases or titles the first time they are used, followed by the acronym, then use the acronym in later references.

Statistical Methods

The variable of interest for the present study was the leadership ability of a group of upper level Japanese managers. The classification variable was the method of evaluation. The first method of evaluation was leader self-perception, while the second method was perception of leaders by subordinates. Since differences are generally expected between supervisors' self-perceptions and perceptions of supervisors by their subordinates, regardless of cultural orientations, a comparison base was needed so that conclusions could be drawn from cultural factors after controlling for these expected differences. Data were therefore obtained from comparable samples of bank personnel, using LOQ responses for 22 senior U.S. bank managers and SBD responses from 74 of their immediate upper level U.S. subordinates. The differences in the means for the comparison samples, when contrasting the LOQ-consideration (LOQ-C) with the SBD-consideration (SBD-C) scales, was 55.68 - 51.34 = 4.34 points. The differences in the means for the comparison samples, when contrasting the LOQ-initiating structure (LOQ-IS) with the SBD-initiating structure (SBD-IS) scales, was 50.55 - 44.82 = 5.73 points.

A dependent t-test was preferable, but there was no way to match supervisors with subordinates due to anonymity of responses. Therefore, an independent t-test had to be used. Using the differences between the LOQ and SBD responses obtained from the comparison groups on each of the two dimensions as a control, two null hypotheses were developed. The first one compares the scores of Japanese supervisors on LOQ-C with their scores as perceived by U.S. subordinates on SBD-C, and is stated as follows:

Equations are numbered and located flush to the right margin.

$$H_0: \mu_1 - \mu_2 = 4.34 \qquad (1)$$

The second null hypothesis compares the scores of Japanese supervisors on LOQ-IS with their scores as perceived by U.S. subordinates on SBD-IS, and is stated as follows:

$$H_0: \mu_1 - \mu_2 = 5.73 \qquad (2)$$

Use Greek symbols when appropriate. If the printer does not print Greek letters, make sure the correct symbol is obvious. Do not use the letter "u" for the Greek letter "μ."

Results

Table 1 provides a summary of the sample sizes, means, and standard deviations for these two groups. The results show that the mean LOQ-C score for the Japanese supervisors (55.88) differs from the mean SBD-C score based upon their subordinates perceptions (38.97) by 16.91 points. The results also show that the mean LOQ-IS score for the Japanese supervisors (48.19) differs from the mean SBD-IS score based upon their subordinates' perceptions (42.82) by 5.37 points.

The difference of 16.91 points between the means on consideration after controlling for expected differences (4.34 in this case), was analyzed using the t-test; the results found $t(46) = 4.4530$, $p < .01$. This test used the unpolled standard error of the difference and adjusted for

Statistical results usually give the test (underlined or in italics), followed by the degrees of freedom in parentheses, followed by the value of the statistic, followed by the probability associated with the statistic. The probability is usually set at .10, .05, or .01.

Use brackets for parenthetical material if they already contain parentheses.

degrees of freedom, since a significant difference was found when comparing variances [$F(33, 25) = 5.99$, $p < .01$]. The difference of 5.37 points between the means on initiating structure after controlling for an expected difference (5.73 in this case), was also analyzed using the t-test; the results found $t(58) = -0.1267$, $p > .05$. This test used the pooled standard error of the difference and did not adjusted for degrees of freedom, since a significant difference was not found when comparing variances [$F(33, 25) = 1.94$, $p > .05$]. Thus, the first null hypothesis was rejected, while the second one was not.

also indicate when the probability is not significant.

Table 1

LOQ and SBD Means and Standard Deviations

Insert Tables in the body of the paper if requested to do so. Otherwise, submit them at the end.

Instrument	Size	Mean	S.D.
LOQ-C	26	55.88	6.09
SBD-C	34	38.97	14.91
LOQ-IS	26	48.19	9.00
SBD-IS	34	42.82	12.53

A significant difference was found between the self-perceptions of Japanese supervisors and the way they are perceived by their U.S. subordinates on consideration, even after controlling for expected differences. Significant differences were not found when evaluating initiating structure. When attempting to integrate Japanese supervisors into senior positions of Japanese-owned, U.S.-based banks, cultural challenges appear to exist. U.S.-employees appear to have poor perceptions of their Japanese supervisors on the dimension of consideration, at lease in

wrong word that is not caught by a "spell checker."

comparison to U.S. employees' perception of U.S. supervisors. If intercultural working relationships are to prosper and if a healthy organizational climate is to prevail, action must be taken by the organization. Such action should provide a work environment in which employees perceive an atmosphere of cooperation between partner countries.

References

Both italics and underlines are acceptable. You must use one or the other, but be consistent.

Bass, B. M. (1981). ***Stogdill's handbook of leadership***. New York: Macmillan.

Bass, B. M., & Burger, P. C. (1979). ***Assessment of managers: An international comparison.*** New York: The Free Press.

Use one space after the colon unless it is followed by a complete sentence.

Deming, W. E. (1986). ***Out of the crisis.*** Cambridge, MA: Massachusetts Institute of Technology, Center for Advanced Engineering Study.

Deming, W. E. (1993). ***The new economics for industry, government, education***. Cambridge, MA: Massachusetts Institute of Technology, Center for Advanced Engineering Study.

List all last names of authors first

Gonzalez, R. F., & McMillan, C. (1961). The universality of American management philosophy. ***Journal of the Academy of Management*, *4***, 33-41.

Use ampersands in the reference list.

Gruenfeld, L. W., & MacEachron, A. E. (1975). A cross-national study of cognitive style among managers and technicians. ***International Journal of Psychology*, *10***, 27-55.

Volume numbers are italicized or underlined.

Oberg, W. (1963). Cross-cultural perspectives on management principles. ***Academy of Management Journal*, *6***, 129-143. Capitalize all key words in journal titles.

Ouchi, W. (1981). ***Theory Z: How American business can meet the Japanese challenge.*** Reading, MA: Addison-Wesley.

Use two letter postal service abbreviations.

Zemke, R. (1981). What's good for Japan may not be best for your training department. ***Training*, *18***, 62-65.

The publication date is given immediately after the last author's name.

Use initials, not first names.

Only references actually used in the paper are included in the reference list.

If an article is included in the paper, it must be cited in the reference list.

APPENDIX J

JRB COMPUTER PROGRAMS: MEASUREMENT AND STATISTICS SYSTEMS (MASS)

MASS: MEASUREMENT AND STATISTICS SYSTEMS

Measurement and Statistics Systems (MASS) was originally written by James R. Beatty for use on mainframe computers. ***MASS*** was designed to provide the user with a simple, straightforward, but very powerful set of programs for use in a variety of measurement and statistical situations. Most of these programs handle large data bases. The version that you are currently using was designed by the author specifically for use on a personal computer (PC). The executable programs are written in ***FORTRAN***. They take full advantage of a math coprocessor, and they require that a math coprocessor is present on the PC system being used. You should spend a few minutes examining the capabilities and features of your PC before attempting to use any of the ***MASS*** programs on your system. You should also consider creating several directories on your hard disk for greater convenience and efficiency. While creating these directories is not necessary, you will find it easier to locate files if you create a main directory (entitled ***MASS***) and three subdirectories within the newly created ***MASS*** main directory (entitled JRBEXE, DATA, and RESULTS).

Getting Started: Creating Directories

If you are installing the ***MASS*** system on your own hard disk, perform the following steps in order to create the desired directories. First, obtain a DOS prompt. Second, make sure that your DOS prompt is associated with the hard disk where you wish to install the ***MASS*** programs. Third, make sure that you are in your root directory. (The following set of directions assumes that your hard disk is referred to as the C drive; if this is not correct, you will need to make the necessary adjustments.) You are now ready to create your new directories. Using your keyboard, type the following commands:

```
MD\MASS
MD\MASS\JRBEXE
MD\MASS\DATA
MD\MASS\RESULTS
```

Each of these directories is described below:

MASS This is the name of the main directory. It will contain several subdirectories.

MASS\JRBEXE This is the first of three subdirectories within the MASS main directory. This subdirectory can be used to contain all of the executable JRB programs. You should immediately copy all of your ***MASS*** executable files into this subdirectory. In order to copy these files into the MASS\JRBEXE subdirectory, you may use your DOS copy command, the Windows program manager, a word processor, or any other software that includes file copy capabilities. For example, you may wish to copy the following executable programs into this directory:

JRB28	A basic data analysis statistics program.
JRB51	A chi-square program for goodness of fit tests and tests of independence.
JRB09	A *t*-test program for independent and dependent data.
JRB10	A one-way analysis of variance program.
JRB50	A two-way analysis of variance program, as well as a treatment-by-subjects (i.e., repeated measures or randomized blocks design) program.
JRB04	A stepwise regression program.
JRB19	A matrix algebra regression program.
JRB20	An iterative factor analysis program.
JRB05	A test, survey, or questionnaire analysis program.

MASS\DATA This is the second of three subdirectories within the MASS main directory. This is a good place to store your data files. The data files (with their appropriate title lines, parameter lines, format lines, data, etc.) must be DOS files. You will probably want to create these data files in a word processor, a spreadsheet, or in a DOS editor first. You must make sure that you save a copy of these files in DOS format, as the ***MASS*** programs will only read DOS files.

MASS\RESULTS This is the third of three subdirectories within the MASS main directory. This is a good place to store your results as they are compiled. The results will be DOS files which can be read by most word processors, spreadsheets, and, of course, any DOS editor.

Creating Data Files

Before you can run one of the ***MASS*** programs, you must first create a data file and save it as a DOS file. As stated above, you will probably want to create these data files in a word processor, a spreadsheet, or in a DOS editor. You must then make sure that you save a copy of these files in DOS format, as the ***MASS*** programs will only read DOS files. The columns of data that you have created must correspond exactly with the format statement that you will use to read the data. This agreement is essential for successfully reading the data files. ***A thorough explanation of the use of format statements is included at the conclusion of this appendix.***

As an example, perhaps you are going to use the program entitled JRB04 (a stepwise regression program contained in the ***MASS*** software) to analyze a set of absenteeism data. Perhaps you have created a data file that you refer to as TEST04.ABS. (Any name will do, as long as it conforms to PC-acceptable file names. Although the extension .ABS was suggested here, no extension is necessary.) If your directory drive is a hard disk and is labeled as drive C, you now enter the following command to save this data file in the appropriate subdirectory:

C:\MASS\DATA\TEST04.ABS

As not all data files follow the exact same layout, details for creating data files will be given with the directions of each separate program in the ***MASS*** software package below. In general, however, most of these data files will include three or more lines of information, followed by rows of raw data. In all cases, the first line (the title line) requires the user to give a title to the specific problem being analyzed; this allows the user to differentiate among various output files that may eventually be created. The second line (the parameter line) identifies various parameters of the data (e.g., number of cases, number of variables, etc.). The third or subsequent line is usually a format line; this format line gives instructions to the computer regarding how the data are to be read and where the values are to be found. This format statement is usually followed by the data base. (As stated above and discussed below, the data must conform perfectly with the format statement.) Some programs may have additional required lines.

Executing JRB Programs

If a data file has been created in accordance with the particular program to be used to analyze the data (explained within each program description below), you are now ready to run the program. Based upon the example mentioned above, suppose that you are going to use stepwise regression to analyze a set of absentee data, using the JRB04 program available in the ***MASS*** software. You have created a data file entitled TEST04.ABS and have saved this file in your subdirectory entitled MASS\DATA. In your original setup of the ***MASS*** directories, you also saved an executable file entitled JRB04.EXE in the subdirectory entitled MASS\JRBEXE. To run the executable program, change directories to where your JRB04.EXE executable file is stored, as follows:

CD\MASS\JRBEXE <Then press ENTER.>

Once you are in the proper directory, you are ready to execute the program. At the DOS command prompt, type the following statement:

JRB04 <Then press ENTER.>

You will now be asked for UNIT 1. This is the name of your data file. Your response is to type the name (and location, if necessary) of your data file. Assume that you have named your data file TEST04.ABS (any name will do) and have stored TEST04.ABS in a directory previously named MASS\DATA (a subdirectory of your main directory named MASS). Also assume that your hard disk is labeled as drive C. You simply enter the following statement:

C:\MASS\DATA\TEST04 <Then press ENTER.>

You will now be asked for UNIT 3. This is the name of your output file that will contain the results of your analysis. Your response is either to save the output by giving it a name (and location, if desired) or to have it routed directly to the screen (see below). Most likely you will want to save your newly generated output results in a file that you can read later (through a word processor, spreadsheet, DOS editor file, or other existing package). Suppose you have decided to name your output file TEST04.RES. Again, any name will do; this name might suggest that this file now contains the "results" of the analysis for "test04." (You may have preferred to call it MYSTUFF, or some other name.) You will probably want to store this file in a directory that you are using to contain all of your ***MASS*** results. If you have followed the recommended suggestions above, you have previously created a subdirectory MASS\RESULTS. As discussed above, MASS\RESULTS is a subdirectory of the main directory named MASS. *Remember that if you use the same name for this file as a file name already stored in this directory, the old file will be replaced by the new file---you will not be given the option of renaming the file at that point, so use a unique name!* You now enter the following statement:

C:\MASS\RESULTS\TEST04.RES <Then press ENTER.>

In the unlikely event that you prefer to have the output listed on the screen (be prepared to press the "pause" key, as the output will go by very rapidly), type the following response instead of the one given above:

CON <Then press ENTER.>

The output will be routed directly to the screen for immediate viewing. However, it will not be saved in a file for future use.

After executing the program and saving your output file, you will most likely want to use a word processor to read your file. You may prefer to clean up your output file somewhat, perhaps add tabs, and make other cosmetic changes before printing this file or adding it into some other document. You may also want to select a particular font to satisfy your own particular interests. Keep in mind that the original document was saved as a DOS "text file." If your word processor selects a proportional font, the results file may no longer have straight columns. Tabs are usually needed to create such cosmetically appealing columns. You may prefer to simply print your output using the "courier" font available with most word processors. Courier is not a proportional font and will retain the spacing that you would observe on your screen.

BASIC STATISTICS (JRB28)

The following is a description of the BASIC STATISTICS program. The program provides the following output of information: number of cases, minimum value, maximum value, grand sum, mode, arithmetic mean, harmonic mean, geometric mean, variation ratio, population variance, population standard deviation, sample variance, sample standard deviation, mean deviation, range, coefficient of variation, third moment about the mean, fourth moment about the mean, G_1, G_2, z for skewness, z for kurtosis, probability for skewness, probability for kurtosis, standard error of the mean, standard error for skewness, and the standard error for kurtosis. The program also computes P_{10}, P_{25}, P_{50} (the median), P_{75}, P_{90}, the interquartile range, the median deviation, and the semi-interquartile range using both discrete data rules and continuous data rules, provided that the input data contain no decimals. Input can be based upon raw data files or on frequency distribution data (using the X-values and their corresponding frequency values).

There are several ways that this program can be used. The most common way is to create an input data file, save it as a DOS file on a diskette or in some desired directory of a hard disk, and call upon it at run time. Another method is to create a data file online; however, this approach is very impractical, since the file cannot be edited or saved.

The directions for setting up the data file are as follows:

First line is a title line, using up to 80 characters (i.e., line columns).

Second line is a parameter line. Each parameter uses 5 line columns; they must be right-justified or preceded by zeros. The parameters and their locations on this line are given as follows (with LC representing the corresponding line columns):

LC 1- 5: Insert the number of cases (maximum = 1000).

LC 6-10: Insert the number of variables to be analyzed (maximum = 20). This must be equal to 1 if a frequency distribution (with values and frequencies) is input instead of a list of raw data.

LC 11-15: Insert a 1 if identification labels are to be read for each variable.
Insert a 0 or leave blank if no identification labels are to be read. They cannot be read if the number in LC 6-10 is 1.

LC 16-20: Insert a 0 or leave blank if input values are not to be printed.
Insert a 1 if input values are to be printed.

LC 21-25: Insert a 0 or leave blank if none of the values contain decimals.
Insert a 1 if any of the input values contain decimals. If any of the values contain decimals, P10, P25, P50, P75, P90, the interquartile range, the semi-interquartile range, and the median deviation will not be computed.

LC 26-30: Insert a 0 or leave blank if raw data are being input.
Insert the number of groups (intervals or categories) to be read, if the data are input as grouped data. If grouped data are input, only one variable can be read at a time. (If grouped data are read, the format statement must first read the value associated with the category (the *X*-values) and then the value associated with the frequency for that category (the *F*-values). Use F-format for each of these two variables.)

Next line is a format line. No identification value is read. Up to 4 format lines can be read. Use LC 79-80 to indicate that additional format lines are to be read. Data must be read as one line per case, using F-format for each variable to be read.

If grouped data are read, the format statement must first read the value associated with the category (the *X*-values) and then the value associated with the frequency for that category (the *F*-values). Use F-format for each of these two variables.

Data follow the above lines and must conform to the format line.

Identification labels are read next, if line column 15 of the parameter line is equal to 1. If identification labels are used, they are input as one line per variable. Any or all 80 line columns may be used for each label.

Data may be stacked, unless grouped data are read. If additional sets are to be analyzed, begin next data deck with a new title line, parameter line, etc., following the sequence above for each new data deck.

Here is an example of a data file for analyzing data. The first line is the title line. The second line is a parameter line that indicates there are 20 observations to be read, that 1 variable is to be analyzed, that no identification labels are to be read, that the data are not to be printed, that none of the values contain decimals, and that raw data are being input (rather than frequency data). The third line is the format statement. In this example, we tab over to column 5 and use the F-format to read the values in LC 5-6. The data lines follow.

```
EXAMPLE: SECONDS TO COMPLETE TASK WITH 20 OBSERVATIONS.
   20    1    0    0    0    0
(T5,F2.0)
 1  60
 2  61
 3  55
 4  57
 5  57
 6  51
 7  61
 8  60
 9  58
10  50
11  60
12  59
```

```
13   56
14   52
15   58
16   54
17   60
18   64
19   57
20   59
```

Here is another example of a data file for analyzing data. The first line is the title line. The second line is a parameter line that indicates there are 420 observations to be read, that 1 variable is to be analyzed, that no identification labels are to be read, that the data are to be printed, that none of the values contain decimals, and that frequency data are being input (rather than raw data), with 15 groups (intervals or categories). The third line is the format statement. In this example, we begin with LC 1, read the values in LC 1-2, skip one column, and read the frequencies in LC 4-5. We use the F-format to read both the values and the frequencies. The data lines follow.

```
EXAMPLE: READING GROUPED DATA
00420     1    0    1    0   15
(F2.0,1X,F2.0)
36  5
35  9
34 16
33 18
32 31
31 44
30 54
29 56
28 55
27 44
26 34
25 24
24 14
23 10
22  6
```

Once you have created your data file and saved it as a DOS file, you are ready to run the program. First, change directories to where your JRB28.EXE executable file is stored. If you have stored it in a directory that you have named JRBEXE that is a subdirectory of another directory that you have named MASS, you would type:

CD\MASS\JRBEXE <Then press ENTER.>

Once you are in the proper directory, you are ready to begin running the program. At the DOS command prompt, type the following statement:

JRB28 <Then press ENTER.>

You will now be asked for UNIT 1. This is the name of your data file. Your response is to type the name (and location, if necessary) of your data file. Suppose you have named your data file TEST28 (any name will do) and that you stored TEST28 in a directory you previously named DATA. Further suppose that DATA is a subdirectory of another directory you previously named MASS. You would then type:

C:\MASS\DATA\TEST28 <Then press ENTER.>

You will now be asked for UNIT 3. This is the name of your output file that will contain the results of your analysis. Your response is either to save the output by giving it a name (and location, if necessary) or to have it routed directly to the screen (see below). Most likely you will want to save your newly generated output results in a file that you can read later (through a word processor or DOS editor file). Suppose you have decided to name your output file TEST28.RES (any name will do) and want to store it in a directory that you previously named RESULTS. Further suppose that RESULTS is a subdirectory of another directory you previously named MASS. You would then type:

C:\MASS\RESULTS\TEST28.RES <Then press ENTER.>

In the unlikely event that you prefer to simply have the output listed on the screen (be prepared to press the "pause" key, as the output will go by very rapidly), type the following response instead of the one given above:

CON <Then press ENTER.>

The output will be routed to the screen instead of being saved in a file.

CHI-SQUARE TEST FOR GOODNESS OF FIT AND INDEPENDENCE (JRB51)

The following is a description of the CHI-SQUARE TEST FOR GOODNESS OF FIT AND INDEPENDENCE computer program. For the chi-square test of goodness of fit, observed values can be tested against several assumptions. The default assumption is that the values are evenly (i.e., uniformly or rectangularly) distributed. Under this assumption, the expected values are automatically calculated by the program. The goodness of fit test can also be used to compare observed values against some known distribution, such as the Poisson distribution, the normal distribution, or against some distribution previously recorded. Under such circumstances, these expected values can be read into the data file as expected frequencies or as expected proportions in each cell. When testing against a rectangular distribution or against a known distribution previously recorded, the degrees of freedom will be equal to the number of cells minus 1. When testing against a Poisson distribution, the degrees of freedom will be equal to the number of cells minus 2. When testing against a normal distribution, the degrees of freedom will be equal to the number of cells minus 3. For the chi-square test of independence, the program gives a matrix of observed frequencies, based upon the cross-tabulated frequencies of the two corresponding classification variables. The program also gives a matrix of expected values and a matrix of the percent of cases in each cell.

Under either approach, the program yields the computed value of chi-square, the degrees of freedom, the probability associated with the computed chi-square value, the number of cells, the number of expected values less than 1, the number of expected values greater than or equal to 5, and the percent of the expected values greater than or equal to 5. It advises the user whenever any expected value is less than 1, whenever less than 80% of the expected values are less than 5, and whenever the sum of the observed values differs from the sum of the expected values. If a test of independence is being performed upon a 2 by 2 matrix, the program also computes the chi-square value adjusted by the Yates' correction factor. Finally, the program advises to use the Fisher exact probability test, which is based upon the hypergeometric distribution, whenever a test of independence is being performed for a 2 by 2 matrix with any expected values less than 5.

The directions for setting up the data file are as follows:

First line is a title line, using any or all 80 line columns.

LC 1- 5: Insert a 1 if this is a goodness of fit test against a rectangular distribution. If this option is selected, the expected values will be automatically calculated, using the assumption that they are evenly distributed across all the categories within the classification variable. (No expected values will be input by the user.)

Insert a 2 if this is a goodness of fit test against a Poisson distribution. If this option is selected, the expected values must be input by the user (see directions below), and the degrees of freedom will automatically be set at df = cells - 2. (The expected values must be input by the user---see below.)

Insert a 3 if this is a goodness of fit test against a normal distribution. If this option is selected, the expected values must be input by the user (see directions below), and the degrees of freedom will automatically being set at df = cells - 3. (The expected values must be input by the user---see below.)

Insert a 4 if this is a goodness of fit test against some other known distribution. If this option is selected, the expected values must be input by the user (see directions below), and the degrees of freedom will automatically being set at df = cells - 1. (The expected values must be input by the user---see below.)

Insert a 5 if this is a chi-square test of independence with two classification variables. If this option is selected, the expected values will be automatically calculated, based upon the following equation:

$$\textbf{Expected Value} = \frac{\textbf{Row Marginal x Column Marginal}}{\textbf{Grand Total}}$$

The degrees of freedom will automatically set at (Rows - 1) x (Columns - 1). (No expected values will be input by the user.)

LC 6-10: Insert the number of rows to be input. This must be at least 1.

LC 11-15: Insert the number of columns to be input. This must be at least 1.

LC 16-20: Insert a 0 if the observed values will be input in the form of raw data and have not already been tabulated into cells.
Insert a 1 if the observed values have already been tabulated into cells and are to be input in the form of a matrix of tabulations. This matrix can be an R by 1 matrix, a 1 by C matrix, or an R by C matrix. If this option is selected, the matrix must be input row-wise.

LC 21-25: Insert a 0 if no expected values are input. If no expected values are input, they will automatically be calculated as described above.
Insert a 1 if expected values are input. This option is only available for goodness of fit tests. If the expected values are to be input, they must be input one line per expected value, from the first to the last expected value. Each expected value must begin in line column 1 and must include a decimal.
Insert a 2 if the expected values are input in the form of proportions in each category of the classification variable. This option is only available for goodness of fit tests. If category-proportional values are to be input, they must be input one line per expected value, from the first to the last expected value. Each proportional value must begin in line column 1 and must include a decimal.

Next line is a format line. No identification value is read. Up to 4 format lines can be read. Use lc 79-80 to indicate that additional format lines are to be read. Format statements must conform as follows:

If the observed values are to be input in the form of raw data, they must be input as one line per case, using I-format. The first value corresponds to the row, while the second value corresponds to the column. For example, if the individual row values are located in LC 14 and the individual column values are located in LC 24, the format statement might be as follows:

(T14,I1,T24,I1)

If the observed values have already been tabulated into cells and are to be input in the form of a matrix of tabulations, the matrix must be an r by 1 matrix, a 1 by c matrix, or an r by c matrix. The matrix must be input row-wise, using i-format. Since the matrix is input row-wise, the format statement only needs to account for the locations of the column or columns corresponding to the cells.

For one example, if the study consists of 1 row and 5 columns, with the expected values for the columns located in lc 1-2, 4-5, 7-8, 10-11, and 13-14, the format statement might be as follows:

(I2,1X,I2,1X,I2,1X,I2,1X,I2)

For another example, if the study consists of 5 rows and 1 column, with the expected values for the column located in lc 1-2, the data are still read row-wise. Therefore, the format statement might be as follows:

(I2)

For yet another example, if the study consists of 4 rows and 5 columns, with the expected values for the columns located in lc 1-2, 4-5, 7-8, 10-11, and 13-14, the data are still read row-wise. Therefore, the format statement might be as follows:

(I2,1X,I2,1X,I2,1X,I2,1X,I2)

Of course, this same statement could more simply be written as follows:

(5(I2,1X))

If expected values or expected proportions are to be read (only if this is a goodness of fit test), they are read next, following the format statement. They must be input one line per expected value, from the first to the last expected or proportional value. Each value must begin in line column 1 and must include a decimal.

The raw data or the matrix of cross-tabulations are to be read next.

Data cannot be stacked.

Once you have created your data file and saved it as a DOS file, you are ready to run the program. First, change directories to where your JRB51.EXE executable file is stored. If you have stored it in a directory that you have named JRBEXE that is a subdirectory of another directory that you have named MASS, you would type:

CD\MASS\JRBEXE <Then press ENTER.>

Once you are in the proper directory, you are ready to begin running the program. At the DOS command prompt, type the following statement:

JRB51 <Then press ENTER.>

You will now be asked for UNIT 1. This is the name of your data file. Your response is to type the name (and location, if necessary) of your data file. Suppose you have named your data file TEST51 (any name will do) and that you stored TEST51 in a directory you previously named DATA. Further suppose that DATA is a subdirectory of another directory you previously named MASS. You would then type:

C:\MASS\DATA\TEST51 <Then press ENTER.>

You will now be asked for UNIT 3. This is the name of your output file that will contain the results of your analysis. Your response is either to save the output by giving it a name (and location, if necessary) or to have it routed directly to the screen (see below). Most likely you will want to save your newly generated output results in a file that you can read later (through a word processor or DOS editor file). Suppose you have decided to name your output file TEST51.RES (any name will do) and want to store it in a directory that you previously named RESULTS. Further suppose that RESULTS is a subdirectory of another directory you previously named MASS. You would then type:

C:\MASS\RESULTS\TEST51.RES <Then press ENTER.>

In the unlikely event that you prefer to simply have the output listed on the screen (be prepared to press the "pause" key, as the output will go by very rapidly), type the following response instead of the one given above:

CON <Then press ENTER.>

The output will be routed to the screen instead of being saved in a file.

INDEPENDENT AND DEPENDENT *t*-TEST (JRB09)

The following is a description of the INDEPENDENT AND DEPENDENT *t*-TEST computer program. The program prints the input variable values (if requested), along with means, sum of squares, variances, standard deviations, standard errors of the means, the standard error of the difference (both pooled and unpooled), the adjusted degrees of freedom, the computed *t*-value, the computed *t*-value after adjusting for degrees of freedom, the probability associated with all computed *t*-values, and degrees of freedom for these *t*-values. For independent measures, the computed *F*-test for homogeneity of variance is also performed. For dependent or paired differences data, the computed dependent *t*-value, along with the *r*, and *RSQ* are computed, along with the *t*-test for homogeneity of variance for related measures.

The directions for setting up the data file are as follows:

First line is a title line, using any or all 80 line columns.

Second line is the first of three parameter lines. Each parameter on this line uses 5 columns; they can be right-justified or preceded by zeros. The parameters and their locations on this line are given as follows:

LC 1- 5: Insert a 1 if this is an independent *t*-test (unrelated measures).
Insert a 2 if this is a dependent *t*-test or *t*-test for paired differences. Note: if 2 is selected, the two values must be input in the same line sequence in pairs (first one and then the other value).

LC 6-10: Insert a 1 if the input data are to be printed.
Insert a 0 or leave blank if not.

LC 11-15: Insert the number of codes used to identify the first group. Usually, this will be only one code. However, if several categories are to be combined to form the first group, this is an easy way to combine them. For example, if three categories---perhaps coded as 2, 4, and 6---are to be combined into one group, a value of 3 would be inserted in LC 15. For dependent data, this value must be 1.

LC 16-20: Insert the number of codes used to identify the second group. Usually, this will be only one code. However, if several categories are to be combined to form the second group, this is an easy way to combine them. For example, if four categories---perhaps coded as 1, 3, 5, and 7---are to be combined into one group, a value of 4 would be inserted in LC 20. For dependent data, this value must be 1.

LC 21-25: Insert a 1 if missing data are to be omitted (those with blank or zero values).
Insert a 0 if blank or zero values are to be considered as actual observations to be included in the analysis. This option ensures that for paired data, every value has a pair.

The third and fourth lines are the second and third of three parameter lines. These lines define the coding used for each group (with a maximum of 10 codings for each group). These two parameter lines are not used if dependent data are being analyzed. A line will be read for each of the two groups (for each of the two categories of the classification variable). These lines will identify the sub-categories within each group (if any exist). If there are more than one category in any group, there will be multiple codings. The codes appear in fields of 5, as follows:

Third line is a parameter line (not used with dependent data):

LC 1- 5:	Insert the first code number within the first group.
LC 6-10:	Insert the second code number within the first group.
LC 11-15:	Insert the third code number within the first group.
LC 16-20:	Continue as necessary for up to 10 code numbers for the first group. For paired data, there can only be 1 code number. Therefore, this line is omitted for dependent data.

Fourth line is a parameter line (not used with dependent data):

LC 1- 5:	Insert the first code number within the second group.
LC 6-10:	Insert the second code number within the second group.
LC 11-15:	Insert the third code number within the second group.
LC 16-20:	Continue as necessary for up to 10 code numbers for the second group. For paired data, there can only be 1 code number. Therefore, this line is omitted for dependent data.

For example, suppose we want to compare the means of two independent groups. Perhaps the first group contains categories coded as 2, 4, and 6 in a data file, while the second group contains categories coded as 1, 3, 5, and 7. There will be 3 parameter lines. The first will be the basic parameter line (line two). The second will give the codes for the categories within the first group (line three). The third will give the codes for the categories within the second group (line three). For the above example, the three parameter lines would appear as follows, each beginning in column 1:

0000100001000030000400001	This line indicates that we are analyzing independent data, we want to print the data, first group has 3 categories to be combined, second group has 4 categories to be combined, and zeroes or missing data are to be omitted from the analysis.
000020000400006	This line indicates that the first group consists of data from categories coded as 2, 4, and 6.
00001000030000500007	This line indicates that the second group consists of data from categories coded as 1, 3, 5, and 7).

Next line is a format line. No identification value is read. Up to 4 format lines can be read. Use LC 79-80 to indicate that additional format lines are to be read. Data must be read as one line per case. For independent data, the variable of interest is read first (with F-format), followed by the classification variable (with I-format). A typical format statement for independent data might be as follows:

(T5,F2.0,T10,I2)

With dependent data, the values are read in pairs read from the same line, using F-format. read. A typical format statement for such data might be as follows:

(T5,2F2.0)

The data lines follow the above lines and must conform to the format statement.

Here is an example of a data file for analyzing data. The first line is the title line. The second line is a parameter line that indicates this is to be an independent *t*-test, that the input data are to be printed, that there is only 1 code (only 1 category) for the first group (the married participants), that there are 4 codes (4 categories) used to identify the second group (the single, divorced, separated, or widowed participants), and that missing or blank data are to be ignored. The third line (the second parameter line) indicates that all participants coded as a 2 are to be included in the first group. The fourth line (the third parameter line) indicates that all participants coded as a 1, 3, 4, or 5 are to be included in the second group. The fifth line is the format statement. Here, we first tab over to column 4 and use the F-format to read the variable of interest appearing in LC 4-5. Then we tab over to LC 50 and use the I-format to read the classification variable. The data lines follow.

```
EXAMPLE: LOQ-INIT. STRUCTURE AS V. OF INTEREST; MARITAL STATUS AS CLASSIF. V.
    1    1    1    4    1
    2
    1    3    4    5
(T4,F2.0,T50,I1)
53 56 84 16 15 21  6 14 29 10  5  5 52 39  1 34  2
56 67 66 16  9 20  8 12 25 11  2  6 51 41  1 57  2
51 54 97 14 11 14  9 11 12 14  2  2 48 48  1 44  2
50 43 77 22 14 26  7 13 15  9  1  6 52 42  1 50  4
52 50 99 17 13 19 11 10 23 16  6  6 53 43  1 45  2
62 56 90 10 12 21  5 14 22 14  1  7 57 44  1 48  2
53 49 51 20 10 16  8 12 16 13  6  4 49 44  1 51  3
44 54 73 16  5  8  6 14 18 11  3  3 48 46  2 38  2
55 50 80 17 15 22  8 13 22 10  1  5 53 42  1 40  2
61 44 92 20 13 20  9 12 19 10  2  5 56 44  1 45  3
62 57 59 23 17 21  9 11  9 15  6  5 55 44  1 34  2
53 50 99 12  7 21  8 11 34 17  5  3 51 44  1 44  2
64 48 86 17 11 10  5 14 31 10  2  5 56 46  1 38  1
60 44 82  8 15 18  7 14 28 16  1  5 54 42  1 44  3
56 42 91 15 15 21  9 13 28 14  6  5 53 40  1 39  2
65 50 84 19 12 20  7 12 21 10  6  6 54 43  2 33  2
44 42 86 19 10 13  9 11 23 13  4  5 51 41  1 43  2
53 47 99 18 12 17 11  9 20 16  6  3 53 44  1 47  2
52 51 77 14 12 11  8 12 20 10  1  6 51 44  2 36  5
44 45 81 21 16 17  8  9 26 15  5  5 40 43  2 34  4
```

Here is a second example of a data file for analyzing data. The first line is the title line. The second line is a parameter line that indicates this is to be a dependent *t*-test and that the input data are to be printed. Since we now have dependent data, the next two parameters (the codes) must be set at 1. The parameter line also indicates that missing or blank data are to be ignored. The third line is the format statement. For dependent data, the pairs of data are read from the same line, using F-format; and no classification variable is read. In this example, we read the first of the two values in LC 1-2, skip a column, and read the second of the two values in LC 4-5. The data lines follow.

```
EXAMPLE: STOCKBROKER DATA WITH REPEATED MEASURES
    2    1    1    1    1
(F2.0,1X,F2.0)
22 21
24 23
26 26
25 22
21 20
32 27
45 42
37 35
35 35
37 33
22 21
29 26
63 58
37 34
46 39
52 48
```

Once you have created your data file and saved it as a DOS file, you are ready to run the program. First, change directories to where your JRB09.EXE executable file is stored. If you have stored it in a directory that you have named JRBEXE that is a subdirectory of another directory that you have named MASS, you would type:

CD\MASS\JRBEXE <Then press ENTER.>

Once you are in the proper directory, you are ready to begin running the program. At the DOS command prompt, type the following statement:

JRB09 <Then press ENTER.>

You will now be asked for UNIT 1. This is the name of your data file. Your response is to type the name (and location, if necessary) of your data file. Suppose you have named your data file TEST09 (any name will do) and that you stored TEST09 in a directory you previously named DATA. Further suppose that DATA is a subdirectory of another directory you previously named MASS. You would then type:

C:\MASS\DATA\TEST09 <Then press ENTER.>

You will now be asked for UNIT 3. This is the name of your output file that will contain the results of your analysis. Your response is either to save the output by giving it a name (and location, if necessary) or to have it routed directly to the screen (see below). Most likely you will want to save your newly generated output results in a file that you can read later (through a word processor or DOS editor file). Suppose you have decided to name your output file TEST09.RES (any name will do) and want to store it in a directory that you previously named RESULTS. Further suppose that RESULTS is a subdirectory of another directory you previously named MASS. You would then type:

C:\MASS\RESULTS\TEST09.RES <Then press ENTER.>

In the unlikely event that you prefer to simply have the output listed on the screen (be prepared to press the "pause" key, as the output will go by very rapidly), type the following response instead of the one given above:

CON <Then press ENTER.>

The output will be routed to the screen instead of being saved in a file.

ONE-WAY ANOVA (JRB10)

The following is a description of the ONE-WAY ANOVA computer program. Output includes a listing of the input data (if desired), followed by the means, standard deviations, sample sizes, skewness, and kurtosis of each group used in the analysis. Next, the Bartlett chi-square test for homogeneity of variance is given when k (the number of groups) is greater than two. When k is equal to two, the F-test for homogeneity of variance for independent samples is computed. The probability associated with the appropriate test for homogeneity of variance is also given. After testing for homogeneity of variance (equal variances), the program tests for analysis of variance (equal means). The ANOVA table is printed, including sources of variation, degrees of freedom, sums of squares, mean squares, the computed F-value, and the probability associated with the F-value. In addition, Scheffé post-comparison F-tests are given, comparing every possible combination of k groups taken two at a time.

There are several ways that this program can be used. The most common way is to create an input data file, save it as a DOS file on a diskette or in some desired directory of a hard disk, and call upon it at run time. Another method is to create a data file online; however, this approach is very impractical, since the file cannot be edited or saved.

The following example is used to illustrate how to create the input data file. Suppose we are interested in comparing performance scores for a number of individuals. Our data base consists of a number of people, our variable of interest is monthly salary, and our classification variable is job type. Monthly salaries range from $2000 to $3750 per month. Job type contains 7 categories, coded in this data base as follows: 1 = design engineers, 2 = manufacturing engineers, 3 = sales personnel, 4 = production workers, 5 = chemists, 6 = physicists, and 7 = other. Further suppose that monthly salaries are located in columns 5-8, while job type is located in column 20. Finally, due to a relatively small data base, we do not have very many individuals in the design engineer, manufacturing engineer, chemist, and physicist categories, at least not very many in regard to analysis of variance. We have decided to combine the design engineers and the manufacturing engineers into one category (engineers) and to combine the chemists and the physicists into another category (scientists). Therefore, we now have 5 categories instead of 7: engineers, sales personnel, production workers, scientists, and others. Rather than re-coding these individuals by job type, we will allow the computer program to do this work for us. We will use this example as we define the parameters for JRB10.

The directions for setting up the data file are as follows:

First line is a title line, using any or all 80 line columns.

Second line is the basic parameter line and potentially the first of a number of parameter lines. Each parameter on this basic parameter line uses 5 line columns, and these parameters must be right-justified or preceded by zeros. The parameters and their locations on this line are given as follows:

LC 1- 5: Insert the number of groups (maximum = 14). For the current example, this value will be 5.

LC 6-10: Insert a 1 if input data are to be printed.
Insert a 0 or leave blank otherwise.

LC 11-15: Insert the number of codes used to identify the first group. Usually, this will be only one code. If several categories are to be combined to form the first group, this is an easy way to combine them. For the current example, the first group consists of two types of engineers that we want to combine into one category; they are coded as 1 for design engineer and 2 for manufacturing engineer. Therefore, this parameter will be a 2.

LC 16-20: Insert the number of codes used to identify the second group. Usually, this will be only one code. If several categories are to be combined to form the second group, this is an easy way to combine them. For the current example, the second group consists of sales personnel. Therefore, this parameter will be a 2.

LC 21-25: Insert the number of codes used to identify the third group (if there is a third group). For the current example, the third group consists of production workers. Therefore, this parameter will be a 1.

LC 26-30: Insert the number of codes used to identify the fourth group (if there is a fourth group). For the current example, the fourth group consists two types of scientists combined into one category; they are coded as 5 for chemists and 6 for physicists. Therefore, this parameter will be a 2.

LC 31-35: Insert the number of codes used to identify the fifth group (if there is a fifth group). For the current example, the fifth group consists of the employees categorized as "other." Therefore, this parameter will be a 1.

LC 36-40: Insert the number of codes used to identify the sixth group (if there is a sixth group). For the current example, we only have five groups; therefore, no further parameters are used on this line. We could have used up to 14 parameters, corresponding with up to 14 groups.

LC 41-??: Continue the pattern for up to 14 groups. For the current example, this parameter line appears as follows:

```
Line column location        1         2         3         4
                   1234567890123456789012345678901234567890

Parameter line     000050000100002000010000100002000001
```

Third line is an additional parameter line. There must be an additional parameter line for *every* group in the analysis. The third line is therefore a parameter line that corresponds with the first group. Each parameter on this parameter line uses 5 line columns, and these parameters must be right-justified or preceded by zeros. The parameters and their locations on this line are given as follows:

LC 1- 5: Insert the first code number within the first group.
LC 6-10: Insert the second code number within the first group.
LC 11-15: Insert the third code number within the first group.
LC 16-20: Continue as necessary for up to 10 code numbers for the first group. For the current example, the first group consists of two categories. Design engineers are coded as 1, and manufacturing engineers are coded as 2. Therefore, this parameter line will appear as follows:

```
Line column location        1         2         3         4
                   1234567890123456789012345678901234567890

Parameter line     0000100002
```

Fourth line is an additional parameter line. The fourth line is therefore a parameter line that corresponds with the second group. Each parameter on this parameter line uses 5 line columns, and these parameters must be right-justified or preceded by zeros. The parameters and their locations on this line are given as follows:

LC 1- 5: Insert the first code number within the second group.
LC 6-10: Insert the second code number within the second group.
LC 11-15: Insert the third code number within the second group.
LC 16-20: Continue as necessary for up to 10 code numbers for the second group. For the current example, the second group consists of only one category:

sales personnel. Sales personnel are coded as 3. Therefore, this parameter line has only one parameter and will appear as follows:

```
Line column location              1         2         3         4
                         1234567890123456789012345678901234567890

Parameter line           00003
```

Fifth line is an additional parameter line. The fifth line is therefore a parameter line that corresponds with the third group. Each parameter on this parameter line uses 5 line columns, and these parameters must be right-justified or preceded by zeros. The parameters and their locations on this line are given as follows:

LC 1- 5: Insert the first code number within the third group.
LC 6-10: Insert the second code number within the third group.
LC 11-15: Insert the third code number within the third group.
LC 16-20: Continue as necessary for up to 10 code numbers for the third group. For the current example, the third group consists of only one category: production workers. Production workers are coded as 4. Therefore, this parameter line has only one parameter and will appear as follows:

```
Line column location              1         2         3         4
                         1234567890123456789012345678901234567890

Parameter line           00004
```

Sixth line is an additional parameter line. The sixth line is therefore a parameter line that corresponds with the fourth group. Each parameter on this parameter line uses 5 line columns, and these parameters must be right-justified or preceded by zeros. The parameters and their locations on this line are given as follows:

LC 1- 5: Insert the first code number within the fourth group.
LC 6-10: Insert the second code number within the fourth group.
LC 11-15: Insert the third code number within the fourth group.
LC 16-20: Continue as necessary for up to 10 code numbers for the fourth group. For the current example, the fourth group consists of two categories: chemists and physicists. Chemists are coded as 5, and physicists are coded as 6. Therefore, this parameter line has two parameters and will appear as follows:

```
Line column location              1         2         3         4
                         1234567890123456789012345678901234567890

Parameter line           0000500006
```

Seventh line is an additional parameter line. The seventh line is therefore a parameter line that corresponds with the fifth group. Each parameter on this parameter line uses 5 line columns, and these parameters must be right-justified or preceded by zeros. The parameters and their locations on this line are given as follows:

LC 1- 5:	Insert the first code number within the fifth group.
LC 6-10:	Insert the second code number within the fifth group.
LC 11-15:	Insert the third code number within the fifth group.
LC 16-20:	Continue as necessary for up to 10 code numbers for the fifth group. For the current example, the fifth group consists of only one category: Other. Employees listed as "others" are coded as 7. Therefore, this parameter line has one parameter. It is the last parameter line needed for this example, since there are only five groups. This parameter line will appear as follows:

```
Line column location          1         2         3         4
                     1234567890123456789012345678901234567890

Parameter line       00007
```

Next line is a format line. No identification value is read. Up to 4 format lines can be read. Use LC 79-80 to indicate that additional format lines are to be read. Data must be read as one line per case. The variable of interest is read first (with F-format), followed by the classification variable (with I-format). For the current example, the format statement might be read as follows:

(T5,F4.0,T20,I1)

Data follow the above lines. Data must be read as one data line per case, as there may be more than one variable being read per subject. Two values will be read from this line: a value corresponding to the variable of interest and a value corresponding to the classification variable.

Here is an example of a data file for the current example. The first line is the title line. The second line is a parameter line that indicates there are 5 groups, that the input data are to be printed, that there are 2 codes (2 categories) for the first group (the combined group of design engineers and manufacturing engineers), that there is 1 code (1 category) used to identify the second group (sales personnel), that there is 1 code (1 category) for the third group (the production workers), that there are 2 codes (2 categories) for the fourth group (the combined group of chemists and physicists), and that there is 1 code (1 category) for the fifth group (the "others"). The third line (the second parameter line) indicates that all employees coded as a 1 or as a 2 are to be included in the first group. The fourth line (the third parameter line) indicates that all employees coded as a 3 are to be included in the second group. The fifth line (the fourth parameter line) indicates that all employees coded as a 4 are to be included in the third group. The sixth line (the fifth parameter line) indicates that all employees coded as a 5 or as a 6 are to be included in the fourth group. The seventh line (the sixth parameter line) indicates that all employees coded as a 7 are to be included in the fifth group. The eighth line is the format statement. Here, we first tab over to column 5 and use the F-format to read the variable of interest appearing in LC 5-8. Then we tab over to LC 20 and use the I-format to read the classification variable. The data lines follow.

```
EXAMPLE: ANOVA FOR MONTHLY SALARY VS. JOB TYPE
000050000100002000010000100002000001
0000100002
00003
00004
0000500006
00007
(T5,F4.0,T20,I1)
001 3510           2
002 3700           1
003 2845           4
004 3400           6
005 3025           7
006 2750           3
007 2000           4
008 3425           5
009 3500           5
010 3475           6
011 3375           1
012 3400           1
013 2050           4
014 2700           3
015 3550           5
016 3325           2
017 3075           7
018 3375           1
019 2050           4
020 3475           5
021 2800           3
022 3400           2
023 3500           6
024 2975           7
025 3275           1
026 3300           2
027 3000           7
028 2100           4
029 3350           2
030 3450           6
031 2700           3
```

Once you have created your data file and saved it as a DOS file, you are ready to run the program. First, change directories to where your JRB10.EXE executable file is stored. If you have stored it in a directory that you have named JRBEXE that is a subdirectory of another directory that you have named MASS, your would type:

CD\MASS\JRBEXE <Then press ENTER.>

Once you are in the proper directory, you are ready to begin running the program. At the DOS command prompt, type the following statement:

JRB10 <Then press ENTER.>

You will now be asked for UNIT 1. This is the name of your data file. Your response is to type the name (and location, if necessary) of your data file. Suppose you have named your data file TEST10 (any name will do) and that you stored TEST10 in a directory you previously named DATA. Further suppose that DATA is a subdirectory of another directory you previously named MASS. You would then type:

C:\MASS\DATA\TEST10 <Then press ENTER.>

You will now be asked for UNIT 3. This is the name of your output file that will contain the results of your analysis. Your response is either to save the output by giving it a name (and location, if necessary) or to have it routed directly to the screen (see below). Most likely you will want to save your newly generated output results in a file that you can read later (through a word processor or DOS editor file). Suppose you have decided to name your output file TEST10.RES (any name will do) and want to store it in a directory that you previously named RESULTS. Further suppose that RESULTS is a subdirectory of another directory you previously named MASS. You would then type:

C:\MASS\RESULTS\TEST10.RES <Then press ENTER.>

In the unlikely event that you prefer to simply have the output listed on the screen (be prepared to press the "pause" key, as the output will go by very rapidly), type the following response instead of the one given above:

CON <Then press ENTER.>

The output will be routed to the screen instead of being saved in a file.

TWO-WAY ANALYSIS OF VARIANCE AND TREATMENT-BY-SUBJECTS (JRB50)

The following is a description of the TWO-WAY ANALYSIS OF VARIANCE AND TREATMENT-BY-SUBJECTS ANALYSIS OF VARIANCE computer program. Output includes a listing of the input data (if desired), followed a matrix of means and a matrix of standard deviation for all cells, rows, columns, and totals. The ANOVA table is printed, including sources of variation, degrees of freedom, sums of squares, mean squares, the computed *F*-value, and the probability associated with the *F*-values. In addition, Scheffé post-comparison *F*-tests are given for main effects for rows, for mains effects for columns, for simple effects for rows, and for simple effects for columns.

There are several ways that this program can be used. The most common way is to create an input data file, save it as a DOS file on a diskette or in some desired directory of a hard disk, and call upon it at run time. Another method is to create a data file online; however, this approach is very impractical, since the file cannot be edited or saved.

The directions for setting up the data file are as follows:

First line is a title line, using any or all 80 line columns.

Second line is the parameter line. Each parameter uses 5 line columns, and these parameters must be right-justified or preceded by zeros. The parameters and their locations on this line are given as follows:

LC 1- 5:	Insert a 1 if this is a traditional two-way analysis of variance. Insert a 2 if this a treatment-by-subjects (i.e., a randomized blocks design or an analysis with repeated measures).
LC 6-10:	Insert the number of rows (maximum = 260).
LC 11-15:	Insert the number of columns (maximum = 10).
LC 16-20:	Insert a 1 if input data are to be printed. Insert a 0 or leave blank otherwise.

Third line is a format line. No identification value is read. Up to 4 format lines can be read. Use LC 79-80 to indicate that additional format lines are to be read. Data must be read as one line per case. The variable of interest is read first (with F-format), followed by the classification variables (with I-format), as explained next.

For the traditional two-way analysis of variance:

Values must be input as one line per case. Use F-format to read the values for the variable of interest (the criterion variable). Then, use I-format to read the categories for each of the two classification variables. The ***coding*** for the classification variables must conform to a "1" for row one, a "2" for row two, etc.; followed by a "1" for column one, a "2" for column two, etc. The commonly used 0/1 (zero/one) dummy coding scheme cannot be used here. A row value and a column value must always be read. Thus, the first value corresponds to the variable of interest, the second value corresponds to the row identification, and the third value corresponds to the column identification. For example, if the variable of interest is in LC 1-2, the row identification is in LC 5, and the column identification is in LC 8, the format statement might be as follows:

(F2.0,T5,I1,T8,I1)

For the treatment-by-subjects analysis of variance:

Values must be input as one line per case. Use F-format to read the values for the repeated variable of interest (the criterion variable) in pairs or over the necessary number of trials (columns). Do not use I-format. For example, if the first of a series of repeated measures of the variable of interest is in LC 1-4, the second of this series of repeated measures is in LC 6-9, and the third of this series of repeated measures is in LC 10-13, the format statement might be as follows:

(F4.0,1X,F4.0,1X,F4.0)

Data follow the above lines.

Here is an example of a two-way ANOVA data file with 3 rows and 3 columns. The first line is the title line. The second line is a parameter line that indicates this is a traditional two-way ANOVA (not a treatment-by-subjects ANOVA), that there are 3 rows, that there are 3 columns, and that the input data are to be printed. The third line is the format statement. Here, we use F-format to read the variable of interest located in LC 1-2. We then tab over to LC 5 and use I-format to read the row classification variable located in LC 5. Finally, we tab to LC 8 and use I-format to read the column classification variable located in LC 8. The data lines follow.

```
EXAMPLE: TWO-WAY ANOVA WITH THREE ROWS AND THREE COLUMNS
    1    3    3    1
(F2.0,T5,I1,T8,I1)
25  1  1
27  1  1
28  1  1
23  1  1
27  1  1
35  1  2
28  1  2
34  1  2
28  1  2
31  1  2
39  1  3
38  1  3
37  1  3
35  1  3
31  1  3
30  2  1
31  2  1
31  2  1
27  2  1
35  2  1
35  2  2
33  2  2
34  2  2
32  2  2
31  2  2
35  2  3
27  2  3
31  2  3
31  2  3
34  2  3
32  3  1
31  3  1
34  3  1
33  3  1
39  3  1
31  3  2
```

```
30  3  2
29  3  2
34  3  2
27  3  2
31  3  3
29  3  3
28  3  3
27  3  3
26  3  3
```

Here is another example, this time based upon a treatment-by-subjects ANOVA data file with 20 rows and 3 columns. The first line is the title line. The second line is a parameter line that indicates this is a treatment-by-subjects ANOVA (not a traditional two-way ANOVA), that there are 20 rows, that there are 3 columns, and that the input data are to be printed. The third line is the format statement. Here, we tab to LC 38 and use F-format to read the first measure of the variable of interest (the first column) located in LC 38-41. We then tab over to LC 46 and use F-format to read the second measure of the variable of interest (the second column) located in LC 46-49. Finally, we tab to LC 54 and use F-format to read the third measure of the variable of interest (the third column) located in LC 54-57. The data lines follow.

```
EXAMPLE: TREATMENT BY SUBJECTS FOR GROCERY DATA
    2   20    3    1
(T38,F4.2,T46,F4.2,T54,F4.2)
Cooked Shrimp                     1  7.99     7.49     7.29
Hillshire Sausage                 2  2.39     2.55     2.67
Butterball Tom Turkey             3  0.69     0.79     0.74
Star-Kist Tuna                    4  1.59     1.50     1.35
Veggie Mix                        5  1.39     1.35     1.49
Fresh Limes                       6  0.10     0.10     0.18
Van Camp's Pork and Beans         7  0.45     0.49     0.44
Pepsi 6 Pack                      8  0.99     1.09     1.89
Fleischmann's Margarine           9  1.29     1.19     1.15
Quaker Oatmeal                   10  1.49     1.39     1.57
MJB Coffee                       11  3.99     3.49     2.35
Rojo's Salsa                     12  2.39     2.49     1.79
Sour Cream                       13  1.09     1.09     1.09
Hershey's Pudding                14  1.99     1.85     1.99
Hormel Chili                     15  1.09     1.15     1.17
Lay's Potato Chips               16  0.89     0.85     1.51
Hotdog Buns                      17  0.69     0.69     0.87
Bar S Jumbo Franks               18  0.69     0.79     0.99
TreeSweet Orange Juice           19  1.99     1.89     1.59
Cremora Coffee Creamer           20  1.99     1.89     2.39
```

Once you have created your data file and saved it as a DOS file, you are ready to run the program. First, change directories to where your JRB50.EXE executable file is stored. If you have stored it in a directory that you have named JRBEXE that is a subdirectory of another directory that you have named MASS, your would type:

CD\MASS\JRBEXE <Then press ENTER.>

Once you are in the proper directory, you are ready to begin running the program. At the DOS command prompt, type the following statement:

JRB50 <Then press ENTER.>

You will now be asked for UNIT 1. This is the name of your data file. Your response is to type the name (and location, if necessary) of your data file. Suppose you have named your data file TEST50 (any name will do) and that you stored TEST50 in a directory you previously named DATA. Further suppose that DATA is a subdirectory of another directory you previously named MASS. You would then type:

C:\MASS\DATA\TEST50 <Then press ENTER.>

You will now be asked for UNIT 3. This is the name of your output file that will contain the results of your analysis. Your response is either to save the output by giving it a name (and location, if necessary) or to have it routed directly to the screen (see below). Most likely you will want to save your newly generated output results in a file that you can read later (through a word processor or DOS editor file). Suppose you have decided to name your output file TEST50.RES (any name will do) and want to store it in a directory that you previously named RESULTS. Further suppose that RESULTS is a subdirectory of another directory you previously named MASS. You would then type:

C:\MASS\RESULTS\TEST50.RES <Then press ENTER.>

In the unlikely event that you prefer to simply have the output listed on the screen (be prepared to press the "pause" key, as the output will go by very rapidly), type the following response instead of the one given above:

CON <Then press ENTER.>

The output will be routed to the screen instead of being saved in a file.

STEPWISE REGRESSION (JRB04)

The following is a description of the STEPWISE REGRESSION computer program. The program gives the means, the standard deviations, and the intercorrelation matrix for all of variables being input. It then gives the error sum of squares for the full model, the error sum of squares for the restricted model, and the error sum of squares reduced. It also gives the multiple correlation coefficient, the *RSQ* for the full model, the *RSQ* adjusted for degrees of freedom (sometimes referred to as the *RSQ* adjusted for shrinkage or the shrunken *RSQ*), the F-value for testing the full model against chance, the degrees of freedom for the full model, the degrees of freedom for the chance model, the degrees of freedom for the numerator of the F-test, the degrees of freedom for the denominator of the F-test, the probability for this F-test, the standard error of estimate, the standard error of estimate adjusted for degrees of freedom, the raw weights, the standard beta weights, the standard errors of the slopes, the t-values for the slopes, the unique F-values for each variable when excluded from the full model, the probabilities associated with the unique F-values, the restricted *RSQ*s after dropping each corresponding variable from the full model, the usefulness of each variable, and the part correlation for each variable.

There are several ways that this program can be executed. The most common way is to create an input data file, save it as a DOS file on a diskette or in some desired directory of a hard disk, and call upon it at run time. Perhaps the easiest way of creating such a data file is to use a word processor (e.g., WordPerfect, Word) or a DOS Editor program (e.g., WP Office Editor, IBM-DOS Editor, MS-DOS Editor). Another method is to create a data file online; however, this approach is very impractical, since the file cannot be edited or saved.

The directions for setting up the data file are as follows:

First line is a title line, using up to 80 characters (i.e., line columns).

Second line is a parameter line. Each parameter uses 5 line columns, and these parameters must be right-justified or preceded by zeros. The parameters and their locations on this line are given as follows:

LC 1- 5: Insert the number of cases (maximum = 99999).

LC 6-10: Insert the number of variables read per case (maximum = 50). Note that the number of variables to be read must be at least 3 less than the number of cases for this program to work. (Practically speaking, we hope to have a ratio of at least 10 cases for every predictor variable, plus 10 additional cases for the model.

LC 11-15: Insert the number of regression models to be developed (see below).

LC 16-20: Insert the proportion of the sum of squares used to limit the entering of variables into the regression model. Be sure to insert a decimal in this parameter. Normally, 00.00 should be inserted in these five line columns.

LC 21-25: Insert a 1 if the predicted Y-values and the residuals are to be printed.
Insert a 0 or leave blank if not.

LC 26-30: Insert a 1 if the input data are to be printed.
Insert a 0 or leave blank if not.

For example, suppose that you have collected data for 20 cases, with 7 variables for each case. Further suppose that you want to develop 3 regression models for these data (to be defined later). You do not want to let the computer limit the proportion of the sum of squares used in the regression model; you want to generate the predicted Y-values; and you want to have your original input data included in the output so that you can verify that the data have been read correctly. Your parameter line would appear as follows:

```
Line column location          1         2         3         4
                     1234567890123456789012345678901234567890
                     00020000070000300.000000100001
```

The third line is a format line. This must be in F-format, and it must begin with a left parenthesis and end with a right parenthesis.

For the above example, 7 variables are to be read for each case. Perhaps you have included some 2-digit identification number for each case, followed by the values for each variable. The identification number should not be read; therefore, you want to skip over this number and move to the first data value, which perhaps begins in LC 5. Perhaps this value consists of 2 digits (e.g., 62). Perhaps the second value begins in LC 8 also consists of 2 digits (e.g., 31). The third data value consists of 2 digits (e.g., 56) and begins in LC 11. The fourth data value consists of 2 digits (e.g., 13) and begins in LC 14. The fifth data value consists of 1 digit (e.g., 7) and is in LC 17. The sixth data value consists of 1 digit (e.g., 0) and is in LC 19. The seventh data value consists of 2 digits (e.g., 01) and begins in LC 21. Under this scenario, the data line would appear as follows:

```
Line column location              1         2         3         4
                         1234567890123456789012345678901234567890

Data line                01  62 31 56 13 7 0 01
```

An appropriate format line might appear as follows:

(4X,F2.0,T8,F2.0,T11,F2.0,T14,F2.0,T17,F1.0,T19,F1.0,T21,F2.0)

The data lines follow the above three lines and must conform to the format statement.

The definitions for the regression models follow the data. These model selection lines allow the user to specify the variables to be used and/or omitted in the model. Selection lines specify the dependent (criterion) variable, the independent (predictor) variable(s), and any variables which are not to be included in the model. The following codes define each of these specifications:

CODE	SPECIFICATION
1	Independent variable forced into the model
2	Independent variable deleted from the model
3	Dependent (criterion) variable

The line columns for the selection line(s) correspond with the input variable location numbers for the data. For example, again suppose that 4 variables have been read as input data. You have decided to develop two different models; therefore, you have input 00002 in LC 11-15 of the parameter line. You now need two different selection lines. Perhaps for the first model, you have chosen to use variable 1 as the criterion variable (variable of interest), while variables 2, 3, and 4 are to be used as predictor variables which you want to be forced into the model. The selection line for this model would appear as follows, beginning in line column one and ending in line column four:

3111

Perhaps for the second model, variable 2 is the criterion variable (variable of interest), and variables 3 and 4 are the predictor variables. Further suppose that variable 1 is not to be used at all in this model. The selection line for this model would appear as follows, again beginning in line column one and ending in line column four:

2311

Other selection lines could also follow, depending upon the number used in the third parameter of the parameter line (columns 11-15). The same procedure, as described above, would be used for all selections lines.

Here is an example of a data file for analyzing absenteeism data. The first line is the title line. The second line is a parameter line that indicates there are 20 observations to be read, that there are 7 variables, that there are 3 different regression models to be generated (see the last three lines of the data file), that the cutoff for the proportion point has been set at 00.00, that the predicted values and the residual values are to be printed, and that the input data are to be printed. The format statement skips the first 2 columns, reads 4 consecutive values that consist of 2 columns each, reads 2 consecutive values that consist of 1 column each, and concludes by reading 1 value consisting of 2 columns. The first of the 3 regression models given at the end identifies the first 6 variables as predictor variables and the last variable as the criterion variable. The second of the 3 regression models identifies the first 3 variables as predictor variables, omits the second 3 variables, and identifies the last variable as the criterion variable. The third regression model omits the first 3 variables, identifies the second 3 variables as predictor variables, and identifies the last variable as the criterion variable.

```
EXAMPLE:  ABSENTEE DATA WITH 20 CASES, 7 VARIABLES, 3 MODELS (SEE LAST 3 LINES).
00020000070000300.000000100001
(2X,4F2.0,2F1.0,F2.0)
01623156137001
02712457446319
03683859394318
04566270307215
05525454527117
06633369342306
07494945461105
08632259317202
09574458296514
10673374364303
11642655386210
12168048376108
13683759384017
14545456406014
15614657377316
16604255374216
17633449345217
```

```
18584173464506
19545656413110
20395759415109
1111113
1112223
2221113
```

Once you have created your data file and saved it as a DOS file, you are ready to run the program. First, change directories to where your JRB04.EXE executable file is stored. If you have stored it in a directory that you have named JRBEXE that is a subdirectory of another directory that you have named MASS, your would type:

CD\MASS\JRBEXE <Then press ENTER.>

Once you are in the proper directory, you are ready to begin running the program. At the DOS command prompt, type the following statement:

JRB04 <Then press ENTER.>

You will now be asked for UNIT 1. This is the name of your data file. Your response is to type the name (and location, if necessary) of your data file. Suppose you have named your data file TEST04 (any name will do) and that you stored TEST04 in a directory you previously named DATA. Further suppose that DATA is a subdirectory of another directory you previously named MASS. You would then type:

C:\MASS\DATA\TEST04 <Then press ENTER.>

You will now be asked for UNIT 3. This is the name of your output file that will contain the results of your analysis. Your response is either to save the output by giving it a name (and location, if necessary) or to have it routed directly to the screen (see below). Most likely you will want to save your newly generated output results in a file that you can read later (through a word processor or DOS editor file). Suppose you have decided to name your output file TEST04.RES (any name will do) and want to store it in a directory that you previously named RESULTS. Further suppose that RESULTS is a subdirectory of another directory you previously named MASS. You would then type:

C:\MASS\RESULTS\TEST04.RES <Then press ENTER.>

In the unlikely event that you prefer to simply have the output listed on the screen (be prepared to press the "pause" key, as the output will go by very rapidly), type the following response instead of the one given above:

CON <Then press ENTER.>

The output will be routed to the screen instead of being saved in a file.

MULTIPLE REGRESSION VIA MATRIX ALGEBRA (JRB19)

The following is a description of the MULTIPLE REGRESSION VIA MATRIX ALGEBRA computer program. The program gives the means and the standard deviations for all input variables. It then gives the intercorrelation matrix and the inverse of the intercorrelation matrix for this set of variables. It also gives the determinant of the inverse matrix. The reciprocals of the diagonal elements of the inverse matrix are computed; and the square roots of these reciprocals are given, yielding the coefficients of alienation that result from treating each variable as a criterion variable and treating the remaining variables as predictor variables. Subtracting each of the reciprocals of the diagonal elements of the inverse matrix from 1.00 yields the coefficients of determination (*RSQ*s) when each input variable is treated as a criterion variable and the remaining variables are treated as predictor variables. Next, the program gives the intercorrelation that includes only the predictor variables, the inverse of that intercorrelation matrix, the determinant of that inverse matrix, the reciprocals of the diagonal elements of the inverse of the predictor matrix, the square roots of these reciprocals (the coefficients of alienation for each predictor variable being treated as a criterion variable), and the coefficients of determination when each predictor variable is treated as a criterion variable. The dispersion matrix, consisting of variances and covariances for all of the variables, is then given, followed by the sums of squares and cross-products matrix (*SSCP* matrix), the inverse of the *SSCP* matrix, and the determinant of the *SSCP* matrix.

Next, the program gives the *RSQ* for the full model, the absolute value of the multiple correlation coefficient, the *RSQ* adjusted for degrees of freedom (shrunken *RSQ*), the error sum of squares for the restricted model, the error sum of squares for the full model, the error sum of squares reduced, the standard error of estimate, and the standard error of estimate adjusted for degrees of freedom. It also gives the *F*-value for testing the full model against the chance model, the degrees of freedom for the full model, the degrees of freedom for the chance model, the degrees of freedom for the numerator of the *F*-test, the degrees of freedom for the denominator of the *F*-test, and the probability for this *F*-test. It then gives the raw regression weights, the standard error of the regression weights, the *t*-values for the regression weights, the probabilities for these *t*-values, the confidence intervals for the slopes (based upon 95% confidence intervals), the standard regression weights, the restricted model *RSQ*s after dropping each corresponding variable from the full model, the unique *F*-values for each variable when excluded from the full model, the probabilities associated with the unique *F*-values, the variable usefulness, the part correlation coefficients, the validities (zero-order correlations), the kth-order partial correlations, the proportional values, the proportion divided by the *RSQ* for the full model, and the *RSQ* based upon this variable as a criterion variable. Finally, the table of residuals is given, including the original *Y*-values, the predicted *Y*-values, the residual values, and the squares of the residuals.

There are several ways that this program can be executed. The most common way is to create an input data file, save it as a DOS file on a diskette or in some desired directory of a hard disk, and call upon it at run time. Perhaps the easiest way of creating such a data file is to use a word processor (e.g., WordPerfect, Word) or a DOS Editor program (e.g., WP Office Editor,

IBM-DOS Editor, MS-DOS Editor). Another method is to create a data file online; however, this approach is very impractical, since the file cannot be edited or saved.

The directions for setting up the data file are as follows:

First line is a title line, using up to 80 characters (i.e., line columns).

Second line is a parameter line. Each parameter uses 5 line columns, and these parameters must be right-justified or preceded by zeros. The parameters and their locations on this line are given as follows:

LC 1- 5: Insert the number of cases (maximum = 99999).

LC 6-10: Insert the number of variables read per case (maximum = 50). Note that the number of variables to be read must be at least 3 less than the number of cases for this program to work. (Practically speaking, we hope to have a ratio of at least 10 cases for every predictor variable, plus 10 additional cases for the model.

LC 11-15: Insert a 1 if the input data are to be printed.
Insert a 0 or leave blank if not.

The third line is a format line. This must be in F-format, and it must begin with a left parenthesis and end with a right parenthesis. The format line must first read the set of *X*-variables (i.e., predictor variables), followed by the *Y*-variable (i.e., the criterion variable or variable of interest).

Here is an example of a data file for analyzing absenteeism data. The first line is the title line. The second line is a parameter line that indicates there are 20 observations to be read, that there are 7 variables, and that the input data are to be printed. The format statement tabs to column 5, reads 4 consecutive values that consist of 2 columns each, reads 2 consecutive values that consist of 1 column each, and concludes by reading 1 value consisting of 2 columns.

```
ABSENTEEISM DATA VIA MATRIX ALGEBRA:  FULL MODEL ONLY.
000200000700001
(T5,4F2.0,2F1.0,F2.0)
0101623156137001
0102712457446319
0103683859394318
0104566270307215
0105525454527117
0106633369342306
0107494945461105
0108632259317202
0109574458296514
0110673374364303
0111642655386210
0112168048376108
0113683759384017
```

```
0114545456406014
0115614657377316
0116604255374216
0117633449345217
0118584173464506
0119545656413110
0120395759415109
```

Once you have created your data file and saved it as a DOS file, you are ready to run the program. First, change directories to where your JRB19.EXE executable file is stored. If you have stored it in a directory that you have named JRBEXE that is a subdirectory of another directory that you have named MASS, your would type:

CD\MASS\JRBEXE <Then press ENTER.>

Once you are in the proper directory, you are ready to begin running the program. At the DOS command prompt, type the following statement:

JRB19 <Then press ENTER.>

You will now be asked for UNIT 1. This is the name of your data file. Your response is to type the name (and location, if necessary) of your data file. Suppose you have named your data file TEST19 (any name will do) and that you stored TEST19 in a directory you previously named DATA. Further suppose that DATA is a subdirectory of another directory you previously named MASS. You would then type:

C:\MASS\DATA\TEST19 <Then press ENTER.>

You will now be asked for UNIT 3. This is the name of your output file that will contain the results of your analysis. Your response is either to save the output by giving it a name (and location, if necessary) or to have it routed directly to the screen (see below). Most likely you will want to save your newly generated output results in a file that you can read later (through a word processor or DOS editor file). Suppose you have decided to name your output file TEST19.RES (any name will do) and want to store it in a directory that you previously named RESULTS. Further suppose that RESULTS is a subdirectory of another directory you previously named MASS. You would then type:

C:\MASS\RESULTS\TEST19.RES <Then press ENTER.>

In the unlikely event that you prefer to simply have the output listed on the screen (be prepared to press the "pause" key, as the output will go by very rapidly), type the following response instead of the one given above:

CON <Then press ENTER.>

The output will be routed to the screen instead of being saved in a file.

ITERATIVE FACTOR ANALYSIS (JRB20)

The following is a description of the ITERATIVE FACTOR ANALYSIS program. The program provides the following output of information: the raw data (if desired), the means, standard deviations, number of cases, the unrotated factor matrix based upon the analysis of the set of variables, the eigen values of this unrotated matrix, a varimax rotation of this matrix, the latent roots associated with this varimax solution, the communalities with each solution, and the complexities associated with each variable for each solution. All subsequent factor solutions are based upon a specified number of iterations for the analysis.

There are several ways that this program can be used. The most common way is to create an input data file, save it as a DOS file on a diskette or in some desired directory of a hard disk, and call upon it at run time. Another method is to create a data file online; however, this approach is very impractical, since the file cannot be edited or saved.

The directions for setting up the data file are as follows:

First line is a title line, using up to 80 characters (i.e., line columns).

Second line is a parameter line. Each parameter uses 5 line columns; they must be right-justified or preceded by zeros. The parameters and their locations on this line are given as follows:

LC 1- 5: Insert the number of cases (you may have an unlimited number of cases). There are several other options can be selected to input data into the program, as follows: Insert zeros here if a correlation matrix is to be used (instead of raw data) as input and is to be factor analyzed. The correlation matrix must be square and symmetric. Insert 99999 if a factor matrix is to be input instead of raw data or a correlation matrix. This factor matrix will be further factor analyzed.

LC 6-10: Insert the number of variables to be read per case.

LC 11-15: Insert the maximum number of factors to be extracted.

LC 16-20: Insert the cut off for the eigen values, input in an F-format.

LC 21-25: Insert the number of variables used for factor solution. If zero it will be set equal to the value in LC 6-10.

LC 26-30: Insert some positive value if communalities are input after the correlation matrix; blank or zero otherwise. This value should only be used if a correlation matrix is being input instead of raw data. When the communalities are input, they follow the correlation matrix, and use the same format as used to read the correlation matrix.

LC 31-35: Insert the number of iterations desired. Set equal to zero if the value in LC 1-5 is set to 99999.

LC 36-40: Insert a 1 if the input data are to be printed.
Insert a 0 or leave blank if not.

LC 41-45: Insert a cutoff point for complexity level, using some decimal value between .00 and 1.00. Be sure to include the decimal point. The default is +/- .30.

The third line is a format line. This must be in F-format, and it must begin with a left parenthesis and end with a right parenthesis.

The data, a correlation matrix, or a factor matrix follow, depending upon what is being read as input. See the first parameter in the parameter line. If either a correlation matrix or a factor matrix is input, it must be input row-wise.

Once you have created your data file and saved it as a DOS file, you are ready to run the program. First, change directories to where your JRB20.EXE executable file is stored. If you have stored it in a directory that you have named JRBEXE that is a subdirectory of another directory that you have named MASS, your would type:

CD\MASS\JRBEXE <Then press ENTER.>

Once you are in the proper directory, you are ready to begin running the program. At the DOS command prompt, type the following statement:

JRB20 <Then press ENTER.>

You will now be asked for UNIT 1. This is the name of your data file. Your response is to type the name (and location, if necessary) of your data file. Suppose you have named your data file TEST20 (any name will do) and that you stored TEST20 in a directory you previously named DATA. Further suppose that DATA is a subdirectory of another directory you previously named MASS. You would then type:

C:\MASS\DATA\TEST20 <Then press ENTER.>

You will now be asked for UNIT 3. This is the name of your output file that will contain the results of your analysis. Your response is either to save the output by giving it a name (and location, if necessary) or to have it routed directly to the screen (see below). Most likely you will want to save your newly generated output results in a file that you can read later (through a word processor or DOS editor file). Suppose you have decided to name your output file TEST20.RES (any name will do) and want to store it in a directory that you previously named RESULTS. Further suppose that RESULTS is a subdirectory of another directory you previously named MASS. You would then type:

C:\MASS\RESULTS\TEST20.RES <Then press ENTER.>

In the unlikely event that you prefer to simply have the output listed on the screen (be prepared to press the "pause" key, as the output will go by very rapidly), type the following response instead of the one given above:

CON <Then press ENTER.>

The output will be routed to the screen instead of being saved in a file.

TEST, SURVEY, AND QUESTIONNAIRE ANALYSIS PROGRAM (JRB05)

The following is a description of the TEST, SURVEY, AND QUESTIONNAIRE ANALYSIS computer program. Output includes scores for each participant (including full scale scores and any subscale scores desired), the means, standard deviations, and intercorrelations for all of the scale scores. These values are followed by an item-by-item frequency distribution that includes either frequency counts or percents (whichever is desired), individual item means and standard deviations, individual item values for Q_1, Q_2, Q_3, and individual item semi-interquartile ranges. An item analysis is also given for subscale item-total correlations, subscale item-remainder correlations, full scale item-total correlations, and full scale item-remainder correlations. A reliability coefficient, based upon coefficient alpha, is given for each subscale and for the full scale, along with the standard errors of measurement, the average item-total correlations, and the average item-remainder correlations. Finally, if desired, rank ordering is provided for item means, item medians, item-remainder correlations, and, if a test is being scored, the percent passing each item. Options include test scoring, analyzing up to 20 subscales, directionality reversals, missing data adjustments, addition of a constant to each response, the output of frequency distributions in frequency counts or in percents, and various sorting options. The program is useful for scoring test, for measuring reliability, developing Thurstone scales, or for developing and analyzing Likert scales.

There are several ways that this program can be executed. The most common way is to create an input data file, save it as a DOS file on a diskette or in some desired directory of a hard disk, and call upon it at run time. Perhaps the easiest way of creating such a data file is to use a word processor (e.g., WordPerfect, Word) or a DOS Editor program (e.g., WP Office Editor, IBM-DOS Editor, MS-DOS Editor). Another method is to create a data file online; however, this approach is very impractical, since the file cannot be edited or saved.

The directions for setting up the data file are as follows:

First line is a title line, using up to 80 characters (i.e., line columns).

Second line is a parameter line. Each parameter uses 5 line columns, and these parameters must be right-justified or preceded by zeros. The parameters and their locations on this line are given as follows:

LC 1- 5: Insert the number of items on the test, survey, or questionnaire (maximum = 400).

LC 6-10: Insert a 1 if this is a test to be scored (with an answer key to be input also).
Insert a 0 or leave blank if not.

LC 11-15: Insert the number of subscales within the test, survey, or questionnaire. There can be up to 20 subscales.
Insert a 0 or leave blank if there are no subscales.

LC 16-20: Insert the number of stems per item (i.e., whether it is a 7-point scale, a 5-point scale, etc.) if certain items are to be reversed.
Insert a 0 or leave blank if the item-reversal option is not selected.

LC 21-25: Insert some constant number to be used to replace missing data, if the missing data replacement option is selected. For example, if this is a 7-point scale with 4 as the neutral point, a 4 might be selected as a constant number to be used to replace missing data. This value cannot be greater than 20. (This option is not available for scored data.)
Insert a -1 if missing data are to be omitted (those with blank or zero values). If this option is selected, only the frequency distribution will be given as output.
Insert a 0 if blank or zero values are to be considered as actual observations to be included in the analysis.

LC 26-30: Insert some constant number if a constant is to be added to *every* response. The range of the resulting values must be between 0 and 20. This option cannot be used with the missing data option.
Insert a 0 or leave blank if the constant adjustment option is not selected.

LC 31-35: Insert a 1 if percents are to be given for each category instead of raw frequency counts.
Insert a 0 or leave blank if each category is to be reported in raw frequency counts.

LC 36-40: Insert a 1 if the item means are to be listed in rank order.
Insert a 0 or leave blank otherwise.

LC 41-45: Insert a 1 if the item medians are to be listed in rank order.
Insert a 0 or leave blank otherwise.

LC 46-50: Insert a 1 if the item-remainder correlations are to be listed in rank order.
Insert a 0 or leave blank otherwise.

LC 51-55: Insert a 1 if the items are to be listed in order of percent correct (in the case of a scored test).
Insert a 0 or leave blank otherwise.

The third line is a format line. The format statement must first read the items, using I-format. Then it must read a 16-column field representing some alphanumeric name or other form of identification. If no identification has been created, this portion of the format statement can simply read blank or bogus column data. However, a 4A4 format must be used to read this identification field. For example, if a questionnaire has 30 items in LC 1-30, followed by a person's identification name or code in LC 31-38, the format statement would be as follows:

(30I1,4A4)

Even though the person's name or identification code may be only 8 columns in width, 4A4 (allowing for 16 columns in width) must be used. Up to 4 format lines can be read. Use LC 79-80 to indicate that additional format lines are to be read. Data must be read as one line per case.

The next line is a scoring key line, if this is a test to be scored. The format of this line must be identical to the format of the lines to be scored. If there are no right answers and the instrument is not be scored, this line is simply omitted.

The next line is a subscale key line, if there are subscales to be analyzed. Since there can be up to 20 subscales, the subscale to which the particular item belongs must use 2 line columns. The order of the input of subscale key values corresponds to the order of input of the items. That is, the first subscale key value will correspond to item 1, the second will correspond to item 2, etc. This line (or these lines) begin in LC 1-2 for item 1, LC 3-4 for item 2, etc. Use as many lines as necessary. Only 80 columns can be used per line. Since some items belong to subscales but other items may not, insert zeroes for those items that do not belong to subscales. If there are no subscales, this line is simply omitted. The following is an example of an instrument that has 30 items, some of which fall on one of three subscales and some of which fall on no subscales. This line begins in LC 1 and continues to LC 60:

010101020202030303010101020202030303000000000000000000010203

The next line is an item reversal key, if there are items to be reversed. Beginning with cc 1, insert a 1 if item is to be reversed or 0 if item is not to be reversed. You may have as many item reversal lines as necessary, but only LC 1-80 may be used. The following is an example of a reversal line for a 30 item test. This line begins in LC 1 and continues to LC 30:

100010010000000100101010000000

Here is an example of a data file for analyzing survey evaluating quality. The first line is the title line. The second line is a parameter line that indicates there are 30 items to be read, that this not a test to be scored, that there are 3 subscales, that some of the items are to be reversed and that each item is based upon a 7-point scale, that the missing data option has not been selected, that no constant value is to be added to each and every response, that percents are to be given for each category instead of raw frequency counts, that the item means are not to be listed in rank order, that the item medians are not to be listed in rank order, that the item-remainder correlations are to be listed in rank order, and that the items are not to be listed in order of percent correct (since this is not a scored test). The third line is the format statement, which begins at LC 1 and reads the 30 items with I-format, tabs to LC 31, and then reads the identification codes with the set 4A4 alphanumeric format (even though the identification codes are only 8 columns in length). There is no line for a scoring key, since this not a scored test. The fourth line is a subscale key. Since there are 30 items, 60 columns must be used to read these 30 items (at the required width of 2 columns per item). Here, the first item is in subscale 1, the second item is in subscale 2, the third item is in subscale 1, the fourth item is in subscale 2, the fifth item is in subscale 1, the sixth item is in subscale 3, etc. The fifth line is an item reversal key. It is required since the parameter line indicated that there will be items to be reversed. Here, the first item is not to be reversed, the second, third, and fourth items are to be reversed, etc. The next 30 lines represent the responses and the identification codes for the 30 participants.

```
EXAMPLE: ITEM ANALYSIS OF QUALITY QUESTIONNAIRE WITH 30 ITEMS
   30    0    3    7    0    0    1    0    0    1    0
(30I1,T31,4A4)
010201020103020102010203010201020103020102010203020102010201
011100000011000100011001100110
721116567715676162221661666217BT1256QP
177723371171213437366167232761PT6784TB
744462346757665773514416742256HI6659YN
622263535724462463544665636236SO9393NY
631451175756725771137524735277BO4775NO
721372364747776241122765733127CH4729ER
641442444716753674471612646427ID5112IT
223147725212474153771571145235DE3951MW
711162377723777272311761527117DK1357UP
755672376776713174241616244124DR4571MC
731375166651656271262642655266SD4957BP
723264175724546655446544755576PD1225AZ
743371313647335461143536561136CC3472RT
622264536725545476525653646156WE1000DO
712276753412556462455662324226PK8106WC
711175571755737672217612766377XX4567AS
761166777762774172473464541416DI1234CK
522526675725655274522566435225DE1955ES
```

```
7323654626366476653557567336578MS1957JH
3413632456275463434443741726247GH1961HS
6213524365575345612245436472465C1965BA
7224633557653355611156257752661S1968MS
711174577725755273721742645127NC1973PH
7111565467266565715416523471271EL5112WE
7212656456155663434535362636236MM1931DA
7215724577367574636137547661275M1963AN
```

Once you have created your data file and saved it as a DOS file, you are ready to run the program. First, change directories to where your JRB05.EXE executable file is stored. If you have stored it in a directory that you have named JRBEXE that is a subdirectory of another directory that you have named MASS, your would type:

CD\MASS\JRBEXE <Then press ENTER.>

Once you are in the proper directory, you are ready to begin running the program. At the DOS command prompt, type the following statement:

JRB05 <Then press ENTER.>

You will now be asked for UNIT 1. This is the name of your data file. Your response is to type the name (and location, if necessary) of your data file. Suppose you have named your data file TEST05 (any name will do) and that you stored TEST05 in a directory you previously named DATA. Further suppose that DATA is a subdirectory of another directory you previously named MASS. You would then type:

C:\MASS\DATA\TEST05 <Then press ENTER.>

You will now be asked for UNIT 3. This is the name of your output file that will contain the results of your analysis. Your response is either to save the output by giving it a name (and location, if necessary) or to have it routed directly to the screen (see below). Most likely you will want to save your newly generated output results in a file that you can read later (through a word processor or DOS editor file). Suppose you have decided to name your output file TEST05.RES (any name will do) and want to store it in a directory that you previously named RESULTS. Further suppose that RESULTS is a subdirectory of another directory you previously named MASS. You would then type:

C:\MASS\RESULTS\TEST05.RES <Then press ENTER.>

In the unlikely event that you prefer to simply have the output listed on the screen (be prepared to press the "pause" key, as the output will go by very rapidly), type the following response instead of the one given above:

CON <Then press ENTER.>

The output will be routed to the screen instead of being saved in a file.

WRITING FORMAT STATEMENTS

As stated above, the format of the data base must conform to the format statement included with each file. There are a few basic rules for format statements that you must understand. For example, all format statements must begin with a left parenthesis and end with a right parenthesis. Within this pair of parentheses, you will include directions for reading the data. These directions will be in a specified format or combination of formats, depending upon the program being used.

Certain characters are used in FORTRAN to help identify where the values are to be located within the row of the data base. For example, the letters **T** and **X** help to locate these values within the row, while the symbol "/" indicates that you wish to advance to the next line. These symbols are defined as follows:

T represents "tab":	This symbol, followed by a number, indicates where the particular value is to be located along the row. For example, T10 means that the value is to be located in column 10 of that particular row. Similarly, T20 means that the value is to be located in column 20, and T1 means that the value is to be located in column 1. Tab statements allow you to conveniently move back and forth along the row. You could tab over to column 10 to read the first value, tab further over to column 20 to read the second value, tab back to column 1 to read the third value, etc., in whatever order you prefer to have the values read into the analysis. Tab statements are only required if you need to move about within the data base.
X represents "skip":	This symbol, preceded by a number, indicates the number of columns that you wish to skip to the right from your current location. For example, 10X means that you wish to skip 10 columns to the right of where you are.
/ represents "next line":	Sometimes a row of data is so long that it will require two or more lines. The "/" symbol indicates that you want to advance to the next line so that you can continue to read data for that row.

Other letters are used to identify the "data type" being read. You may be reading floating-point data (**F**-format), integer data (**I**-format), or alphanumeric data (**A**-format). You must specify the data type being used, and this will vary from ***MASS*** program to program, as defined by each specific program in the following pages. These data types are defined as follows:

F-format:	The F-format is referred to as "floating-point" format. This is the most common data type format used in the ***MASS*** programs for reading raw data values. The letter F tells you that this is a

floating-point value. The letter F is then followed by a number, a period, and another number. The first number identifies the width of the data field, while the second number (the one after the period) identifies the number of decimal places to be read. For example, suppose you use the following format statement:

(F5.0)

This statement means that beginning with the first column, the data are to be read with a floating-point format, that each data field consists of (or must accommodate) 5 columns, and that 0 columns contain decimal values.

As another example, you might use the following format statement:

(F6.3)

This statement means that beginning with the first column, the data are to be read with a floating-point format, that each data field consists of (or must accommodate) 6 columns, and that 3 columns contain decimal values.

I-format: The I-format is referred to as "integer" format. This format is sometimes used to read identification numbers, row numbers, or column numbers in the ***MASS*** programs. The letter I tells you that this is an integer value. The letter I is then followed by a number. The number identifies the width of the data field. No decimal values can be read with integer format. For example, suppose you use the following format statement:

(I5)

This statement means that beginning with the first column, the data are to be read with an integer format and that each data field consists of (or must accommodate) 5 columns.

A-format: The A-format is referred to as "alphanumeric" format. This format is not frequently used in the ***MASS*** programs. When used (as specified by the particular program being employed), the alphanumeric format can be used to read alphabetic characters, numbers, or combinations of alpha and numerical characters. The letter A tells you that this is an alphanumeric. The letter A is then followed by a number. The number identifies the width of the data field. For example, suppose you use the following format statement:

(A5)

This statement means that beginning with the first column, the data are to be read with an alphanumeric format and that each data field consists of (or must accommodate) 5 columns.

As an example of the use of several of these format characters, suppose that you have collected absenteeism data for 20 individuals, including values on 7 variables for each individual, and you wish to use the stepwise regression program referred to as JRB04. When you created your data base, perhaps you created 20 rows of information, one for each individual. Maybe you began each row with some 2-digit identification number for the individual, followed by values on each variable for the individual. However, the JRB04 program does not allow for the reading of the identification numbers; you included them in your data base to make it easier to read. Therefore, you want to skip over this number and move to the first data value, which perhaps begins in line column 5 (LC 5). Perhaps this first data value consists of 2 digits (e.g., 62). Perhaps the second value begins in LC 8 and also consists of 2 digits (e.g., 31). The third data value consists of 2 digits (e.g., 56) and begins in LC 11. The fourth data value consists of 2 digits (e.g., 13) and begins in LC 14. The fifth data value consists of 1 digit (e.g., 7) and is in LC 17. The sixth data value consists of 1 digit (e.g., 0) and is in LC 19. The seventh data value consists of 2 digits (e.g., 01) and begins in LC 21. Under this scenario, the data line would appear as follows:

```
Line column location              1         2         3         4
                        123456789012345678901234567890123456789012. . .

First row of data base: 01  62 31 56 13 7 0 01
```

An appropriate format line might appear as follows:

(4X,F2.0,T8,F2.0,T11,F2.0,T14,F2.0,T17,F1.0,T19,F1.0,T21,F2.0)

The above format example illustrates the use of several possible letters available for format statements in this program (X, T, and F). The above is only one of many ways to write the format line for these data. Remember that X allows you to skip columns (in the example above, the first four columns are being skipped), the T allows you to tab to a particular column, and the F indicates that you are using floating-point numbers, which is the common approach in the ***MASS*** programs. (Note that you *must* use the F-format in the JRB04 program to read your data; you cannot use the I-format for integer or A-format for alphanumeric in this program.)

As another example of the use of several of these format characters, suppose that you have collected measurement data for 2500 observations, including measures on 5 different variables. The third variable is the width of the corresponding observation, while the fifth variable is identifying factor pertaining to the condition under which the observation has been produced. You wish to use a two-sample independent *t*-test referred, and JRB09 is appropriate. Perhaps you have 2500 rows of data, and perhaps you began each row with some 2-digit identification number for the observation, followed by values on the 5 variables for the observation. The JRB09 program does not allow for the reading of the identification numbers; you included them in your data base to make it easier to read. This program requires the variable of interest to be read first, using some F-format. This value is then followed by the group membership variable (in this example, the condition under which the observation was produced), using some I-format. Therefore, you want to skip over the identification number, the first variable, and the second variable, and move to the third data value, which contains the width of the corresponding observation and begins in line column (LC) 20. Perhaps the first data value begins in LC 5 and consists of 5 characters, 2 of which are decimal values (e.g., 62.18). The second value begins in LC 11 and consists of 7 characters, 3 of which are decimal values (e.g., 121.316). However, you wish to skip these values and move directly to the third value (the widths of the observations) which consists of 7 characters, 4 of which are decimal values (e.g., 23.1231) and begins in LC 20. The fourth data value consists of 2 digits (e.g., 13) and begins in LC 28; we want to skip this value as well. The fifth value (the identifying factor pertaining to the condition under which the observation has been produced) is a 1 (perhaps it could only be a 1 or a 2, indicating that this observation was produced under condition 1 or 2), and is in LC 35. Under this scenario, the data line would appear as follows:

```
Line column location             1         2         3         4
                        123456789012345678901234567890123456789012. . .

First row of data base: 01  62.18 121.316  23.1231 13     1
```

An appropriate format line might appear as follows:

(T20,F7.4,T35,I1)

APPENDIX K

KNOWLEDGE AND THOUGHT: THE HISTORY OF SCIENCE AND STATISTICS

KNOWLEDGE AND THOUGHT: THE HISTORY OF SCIENCE AND STATISTICS

The present text introduces many concepts in the field of statistical methods, some elementary and some complex. These concepts will be addressed with an emphasis on the relationships among the topics presented. Basic concepts and terminology must logically precede advanced techniques, as users of these tools need to understand the progression from one concept to another. In keeping with such an approach, the present chapter provides a brief history of statistics and related areas to provide the reader with an exposure to the many creative minds that have had an impact on the field.

The science of statistical methods, although relatively young in comparison to other well-defined fields of knowledge, has had a rather lengthy historical development. Ideas have been borrowed from logic, philosophy, mathematics, education, agriculture, psychology, business, economics, sociology, and other disciplines in the process of advancing the field of statistics. Moreover, the relationships have been of a symbiotic nature, since these disciplines have enjoyed continued growth as a result of the increased sophistication of statistical methods.

Ancient Civilizations

In regard to recorded history, the Egyptians provided perhaps the earliest contributions to statistics, as they made practical advancements in both science and mathematics with their understanding and applications of geometry. Meanwhile, across the Mediterranean Sea, Greek philosophers and mathematicians such as Thales (c. 636-546 B.C.), Pythagoras (c. 582-500 B.C.), Democritus (c. 460-370 B.C.), Socrates (c. 470-399 B.C.), Plato (c. 427-347 B.C.), Aristotle (c. 384-322 B.C.), and Euclid (c. 365-300 B.C.) excelled in the areas of logic, abstraction, and theory, thus making contributions to the development of research procedures and, eventually, to probability and statistics. Pythagoras, for example, developed several fundamental geometric straight line relationships that are now important concepts in correlational analysis; he was also familiar with the geometric, harmonic, and arithmetic means, tools that are now widely used in modern statistics. Thales traveled to Egypt and brought their knowledge back to Greece. His approach to teaching, however, was probably more deductive (his major contribution to science) than inductive, contrary to the Egyptian approach (Newman, 1956, p. 14).

Socrates, Plato, and Aristotle were primary contributors in the formulation of ***deductive reasoning*** as a problem-solving technique. In deduction, basic assumptions are made about major and minor premises, and conclusions are then drawn about specific events. The Greek philosophers established syllogisms based on the general premises, and conclusions were deduced by going from the general assumptions to the specific cases. This deductive approach provided a definite structure for the future of scientific investigations and hypothesis testing.

However, incorrect assumptions about the major and minor premises can often lead to errors, incorrect conclusions, or half-truths. Aristotle's writings hinted at another approach to reasoning that has become a part of what is now referred to as the ***scientific method***: the inductive approach to investigation. In ***inductive reasoning***, the problem solver gathers data from specific observations and then draws a general conclusion or principle. In his efforts to advance thought in an orderly manner, Aristotle established the term ***hypothesis***, stating that it is a thesis that "asserts either the existence or the non-existence of a subject" (Ross, 1955, p. 27). Research methodology is now founded on the concept of hypothesis testing.

Unfortunately, after the death of Euclid and other Greek scholars, few theoretical inquiries into science and mathematics were conducted for many centuries; at least, few were recorded in history. In Rome, the center of European civilization following the Greek era, scholars were not interested in science, theory, and abstraction; instead, they excelled in practical applications of existing theory formulated by the earlier Greeks. Much of the more creative thought in mathematics during the next few centuries occurred in India, Arabia, and in the Orient. In fact, during the European medieval period, philosophers were very limited in their opportunities to theorize and make public their findings due to religious dogma and authoritarian rule. Too much science or theory could be an act of heresy, punishable by death! Thus, it was not until the Renaissance period that mathematical interest was rekindled in Europe.

Renaissance Advancements

During the Renaissance, theoretical curiosity was reborn. This intellectual challenge was met throughout the cultural centers of Europe, from Venice to Bologna, from Milan to Rome and Pisa, throughout France, Germany, England, Scotland, Belgium, Switzerland, and elsewhere. Once again an emphasis was placed on the philosophies of the early Greeks. For example, Leonardo da Vinci (1452-1519) explored Aristotelian philosophy, mathematics, and a variety of other disciplines. At the onset of the 1600's, a rapid increase in mathematical discovery began, and the quantitative disciplines enjoyed many new findings for centuries thereafter.

John Napier (1550-1617), a Scottish mathematician who is widely renowned for his development of logarithms, had also recognized a unique arrangement of the coefficients in a set of expanded terms that was to have an impact on the binomial distribution and probability theory in the years to come. England's Sir Francis Bacon (1561-1626) was singularly important in modernizing the inductive method of reasoning and made many other contributions to science and mathematics. Italy's Galileo Galilei (1564-1642) contributed to the areas of precalculus and geometry and helped modernize the scientific method through the interaction of theory with experimentation. Germany's Johann Kepler (1571-1630) presented the principle of continuity, which significantly advanced the concepts of calculus. England's Captain John Graunt (1620-1674) published ***Natural and Political Observations on the London Mortality*** in 1662, just before the Great Plague of London began in 1665. This was the first book on vital statistics in that statistical and probability theory were applied to real world problems. In his history of statistics, Karl Pearson later said that Graunt holds the real claim to the title of Father of Statistics (E. S. Pearson, 1978).

Further advances in mathematics, particularly in calculus, came about through the efforts of Fermat, Newton, and Leibniz. France's Pierre de Fermat (1601-1665) extended the areas of analytic geometry, and number theory; and he contributed to the development of differential calculus. Germany's Gottfried Wilhelm von Leibniz (Leibnitz) (1646-1716) also contributed to the development of differential calculus and is credited by many as being its inventor. He created one of the first calculating machines and developed the binary scale (although the ancient Chinese probably worked with binary systems centuries before). England's Sir Isaac Newton (1642-1727), one of the most brilliant and prolific scholars of all time, also further advanced differential calculus. His discoveries also led to advances in the areas of numerical analysis, interpolation, and integral calculus, all of which helped to advance probability theory. Newton and Leibniz were colleagues and friends for a while; later each accused the other of plagiarism. Considerable debate took place regarding whether Newton or Leibniz first invented differential calculus. As a result of these arguments, much of Leibniz's work was largely ignored in England for many years.

Prior to this period, the laws and axioms of mathematics had not been applied to games of chance. However, with the onset of discoveries that were taking place in the Seventeenth Century, such problems now were of interest to both theoretical and applied mathematicians of the day. Probability and statistics soon began to advance in a manner similar to other areas of mathematics and logic (Guilford, 1954, p. 2). For example, the French mathematician Blaise Pascal (1632-1662) formalized Napier's earlier theories regarding the unique arrangement of the coefficients of a set of terms and developed what is now referred to as Pascal's triangle, an important concept in probability in general and to the binomial in specific. Pascal's personal correspondence with Fermat led to the discovery of the theory of probability also advanced considerable thought in this area (Westergaard, 1968, Ch. 10).

In Holland, Lord Christianus Huygens (1629-1695) was using mathematics and probability for many scientific advancements, especially in regard to motion, gravitation, and astronomy. He also used mathematics to study dice games, developing the first "unique" introduction to probability theory in ***De Ratiociniis in Aleae Ludo*** in 1657. In Switzerland, the Bernoulli family contributed heavily toward theories of probability. Jacques (James or Jacob) Bernoulli (1654-1705) was the oldest of four brilliant brothers. Inspired by Huygens and others, he is generally given credit for the modern theory of combinations and permutations. He was one of the earliest mathematicians to employ the binomial expansion in solving probability problems and was the author of ***Ars Conjectandi*** (1713), a classic in probability theory that included the Law of Large Numbers, or Bernoulli's theorem. The law of large numbers is one of the most important contributions to statistical inference. This law led to the conclusion that the difference between a sample statistic and a population parameter decreases as the size of the sample increases.

The second of these four brothers was Nicholas Bernoulli (1662-1717). He was an artist whose son, Nicholas I (1687-1759), also became a famous mathematician. The third of these brothers was Jean (John) Bernoulli (1667-1748). He further advanced ideas in differential equations, negative numbers, and imaginary numbers. Jean's son Daniel I (1700-1782) and grandson Christopher (1782-1863) also became famous mathematicians. The youngest of the four brothers was Hieronymus Bernoulli (1669-1760), who became a chemist and druggist.

Eighteenth, Nineteenth, and Twentieth Century Advancements

The Eighteenth Century saw continued advancements in probability theory and related distributions. The Académie Royale des Sciences originally was founded in 1666, consisting primarily of scholarly French nobility. However, by the beginning of the Eighteenth Century, this organization began to present membership invitations to prominent international scholars as well as to the French elite. For example, both Newton and Huygens were invited to become members. The Académie survives today as the Institut de France.

One French genius of particular importance, born without wealth or nobility, was Abraham DeMoivre (1667-1754). He, like the Bernoullis, was a Protestant Huguenot. When King Louis XIV revoked the Edit of Nantes in 1685, the Huguenots lost considerable religious freedom. DeMoivre was imprisoned at the age of eighteen, released three years later, and fled to London. He never returned to France and never published his works in French. He became a tutor to children of the wealthy, helped other scholars with their research, and depended on his publications for any source of income. He discovered the *normal distribution* in an effort to provide probabilities for certain scientific observations. He was attempting to find an approximation for the discrete binomial distribution when he discovered this continuous distribution. Since the publication of its equation in 1733 by DeMoivre, it has become the most famous distribution in probability and statistical theory. He also solved gambling problems in the taverns of London, contributed to the random walk theory familiar to those in economics and finance, theorized about the central limit theorem, another fundamental concept in statistics, and discovered the basic concept of the standard deviation. DeMoivre became one of Isaac Newton's closest friends and colleagues, to whom DeMoivre dedicated the classic first modern book on probability theory, ***The Doctrine of Chances***.

Meanwhile, a French nobleman by the name of Pierre Remond de Montmort (1678-1719) travelled throughout Europe, observed games of chance, and wrote on the probabilities associated with these games. Many arguments and accusations of plagiarism developed between Montmort, the nobleman, and DeMoivre, the refugee. Although not the brilliant mathematician that Abraham DeMoivre or Jacques Bernoulli were, Montmort did contribute to the advancement of probability theory.

During this same period, Reverend Thomas Bayes (1702-1761), an English philosopher, mathematician, and minister, advanced certain areas of probability theory, although his findings went unnoticed for many years. Today, one field of statistics, *decision theory*, is often referred to as *Bayesian statistics* in his honor. In Switzerland, Leonhard Euler (1707-1783) a student of the Bernoulli family, made advances in analytic trigonometry, the hypergeometric distribution, and in complex integrals. In Germany, Gottfried Achenwall (1719-1772), sometimes referred to as the Father of Statistical Science (Walker, 1929, p. 32), introduced the term *Statistik* in his writings. However, Karl Pearson later argued that Achenwall "is not really the inventor of the word, and he applied the word to something that is not statistics in the sense now accepted" (E. S. Pearson, 1978, p. 1.). Instead, Achenwall used the word to refer to "statesmanship" or "political economy," a method for determining the political strength of a country. As noted before, Pearson credited Captain John Graunt as being the Father of Statistics.

Another Frenchman, Joseph-Louis LaGrange (1736-1813) contributed to number theory, partial differential equations, and complex multipliers, all of which are important for advanced statistics. Pierre-Simon, Marquis de LaPlace (1749-1827), also of France, made perhaps one of the most significant contributions to probability and statistics of all times by writing a major text on probability theory. He also completed work in the theory of least squares and is credited with developing the normal law of error, concepts that are crucial to students of statistics. Some historians have placed him, along with Newton, as one of the top two scientists of all times (Newman, 1956, p. 1316).

Karl Gauss (1777-1855), a German mathematician, made such contributions to the field of probability that the Gaussian curve, or normal distribution, bears his name. LaPlace had actually worked with the normal distribution 10 years before Gauss; and, as noted earlier, DeMoivre was its real discoverer back in the early 1700's. Gauss also added to the theory of errors, completed some of the earliest work in non-Euclidean geometry and in complex integrals, and employed the median deviation, a statistical procedure used as a measure of the variability of a distribution. (He referred to it as the mean deviation about the middlemost value; the middlemost value, of course, is the median). Simeon Poisson (1781-1840), another French mathematician, discovered a probability distribution directly related to the binomial distribution and to the normal distribution; this distribution is called the Poisson distribution in his honor.

In the social sciences, perhaps the most important forerunner of modern day research is Lambert Adolphe Jules Quetelet (1797-1874), a Belgian mathematician who is sometimes referred to as the Father of Social Science for his investigations of social phenomena. He advanced the areas of probability, descriptive statistics, and data collection for censuses. He also employed the normal distribution to human traits, speculating on the *average* person and on the errors of nature (Hankins, 1968, pp. 60-82). His systematic investigations of individual differences strongly influenced the nature of future studies related to the human organism. He was instrumental in founding the London Statistical Society in 1834, which was incorporated by Royal Charter as the Royal Statistical Society in 1887. He was also the first non-American selected for membership in the American Statistical Association (ASA), which was founded in 1839 (Walker, 1929, pp. 39-40).

The growth of the scientific method of research paralleled the growth of mathematics and science. Advancing from the early beginnings of the Greek scholar Aristotle and the later work of Italy's Galileo, Sir Francis Bacon furthered the inductive method of reasoning, while Descartes made contributions to the deductive method. Charles Darwin (1809-1882) combined elements of both inductive and deductive reasoning in research processes, while two other Englishmen, George Boole (1815-1864) and John Venn (1834-1883), contributed to the method of scientific thought by providing new approaches to problem solving that bear their names: Boolean algebra and Venn diagrams. John Dewey (1859-1952), also an Englishman, provided a major contribution to research in his classic text, ***How We Think***. The two following quotations from that historic work describe the important interaction between induction and deduction in problem solving:

> The inductive movement is toward *discovery* of a binding principle; the deductive toward its *testing* - confirming, refuting, modifying it on the basis of its capacity to interpret isolated details into a unified experience. So far as we conduct each of these processes in the light of the other, we get valid discovery or verified critical thinking. (Dewey, 1910, p. 82)

> This moving back and forth between the observed facts and the conditional idea is kept up till a coherent experience of an object is substituted for the experience of conflicting details - or else the whole matter is given up as a bad job. (Dewey, 1910, p. 83)

Yet, it was not until the work of Darwin, Quetelet, Gustave T. Fechner (1801-1887), and their followers that statistics became a fundamental part of behavioral, social, and scientific research. Darwin, for example, presented studies in evolution in his classic work, ***On the Origin of Species***, in 1859, which developed an interest in the measurement of humankind in many different ways. Gustave Fechner, a German student of medicine, physics, and psychology, published ***Elemente der Psychophysik*** in 1860, marking the beginning of the development of experimental psychology. He has been referred to as both the Father of the New-Psychology and the Father of Psychophysics. He is credited with numerous contributions in the area of statistics, including the development of methods for computing the *median.*

Meanwhile, the person who was to become perhaps the single-most important influence on the discipline of modern statistics, Sir Francis Galton (1822-1911), began to conduct studies in England. Galton, a cousin of Darwin, is often referred to as the Father of Mental Testing. Influenced by Darwin's ***On the Origin of Species***, Galton was trained as a biologist and became interested in eugenics. He was convinced that superior human beings could be developed through proper mating. However, he needed to measure individual differences before a program of eugenics could be undertaken. Thus, he developed the first large scale testing program at his Anthropometric Laboratory in England in 1882. His now famous text, ***Hereditary Genius***, published in 1869, introduced many of the concepts that were to be explored and advanced in this laboratory.

In his efforts to measure individuals, Galton was influenced by the works of an English philosopher, John Locke (1632-1704), who many years earlier had stressed that "all knowledge comes from the *senses*." This philosophy was adopted by many British researchers, and measuring the gifted came about by developing methods of measuring the senses. Most intelligence testing soon was to become centered around a measurement of the senses in the laboratories of the day. Galton's tools of measurement included devices to recognize an individual's sensitivity to tones, devices to measure visual acuity, devices to differentiate among colors, and the Galton whistle, which was constructed to measure the highest tones that humans could hear. He later found that dogs could hear much higher tones, and the whistle soon became widely used as a silent dog whistle.

Galton, who was knighted in 1909, had a tremendous impact upon statistics; his list of contributions to the discipline is voluminous. He advanced the development of percentiles, the median (he was the first to use the word "median," although Fechner had defined the measure earlier), the semi-interquartile range (he introduced the term *semi-interquartile range* in 1889), deciles, ogive curves, and many other statistical tools. His most important contribution was in the area of correlation and regression. Although Auguste Bravais (1811-1863), a Frenchman, worked out the fundamental theorems for correlation in 1846, Galton rapidly advanced the concept. While he was comparing the heights of offsprings to the heights of their parents, he converted all these heights to standard scores (which we also now commonly refer to as *z*-scores) and plotted the results of the conversions. Viewing his graph, he noted that the offsprings' heights did not increase as rapidly as did the parents' heights. In other words, the heights of the offspring tended to "regress toward the mean." He called this the *law of filial regression.* He then formulated a value, *r*, which he referred to as the index of co-relation, to describe the phenomenon he had discovered. Galton then asked James Douglas Hamilton Dickson (1849-1931) to develop a more mathematically based equation; the results were later published as an appendix to one of Galton's papers in 1886. Dickson's coefficient was then further advanced in 1896 by Karl Pearson (1857-1936), who is responsible for the present mathematical state of the correlation coefficient. Francis Ysidro Edgeworth (1845-1926) was the first to refer to the measure as a coefficient of correlation, doing so in a paper he presented in 1892.

Florence Nightingale (1820-1910), the well known English nurse and reformer of hospitals, was also a devout student of statistics. Historians of statistics have often referred to her as the Passionate Statistician. She was an admirer of Quetelet and a supporter and colleague of Galton. Her emphasis on the study of statistics for the improvement of legislation, administration, and institutions in general played an important role in the advancement of statistical training.

In Germany, Wilhelm Wundt (1832-1920) played a key role as a major contributor to the advancement of research, empiricism, and the scientific method. In 1879 at the University of Leipzig, he founded the first experimental laboratory dedicated to the study of psychology. Here, studies related to the structure of consciousness were performed. Wundt emphasized controlled observations under experimental conditions and strongly supported the empirical method. He is referred to as the Father of Experimental Psychology.

In Russia, two mathematicians of particular interest made important contributions to the development of statistics. Pafnuti Lvovich Tchebycheff (Chebyshev or Tchebysheff) (1821-1894) developed a generalization of Bernoulli's theorem that has since become a fundamental tool for statistics. This theorem is referred to as Tchebycheff's theorem or Tchebycheff's inequality. Andrey Andreevich Markov (1856-1922), a student of Tchebycheff also contributed to probability theory, the theory of least squares, and the theory of linear unbiased estimators. He is probably best known for Markov chains.

Karl Pearson, an Englishman who became Galton's successor at the Anthropometric Laboratory, soon became a major force in statistics in the late 1800's and early 1900's. The correlation coefficient now in common use in every scientific discipline is, in fact, referred to as the Pearson product-moment correlation coefficient in his honor. If he had not expanded correlation and regression into areas beyond those initiated by Galton, the tool would have only limited potential. Pearson went on to develop or contribute to the advancement of partial correlation concepts, standardized regression weights, and other measures of relationships such as the correlation ratio, the coefficient of variation, the coefficient of contingency, and the bi-serial coefficient. He also contributed to the advancement of other aspects of statistics, including chi-square tests, the concept of homoscedasticity, measures of kurtosis (platykurtic, mesokurtic, and leptokurtic distributions), moment coefficients, advancements in the standard deviation (he introduced the term *standard deviation* in 1894), and, along with Fechner, applications of the mode. Sometimes he is referred to as the Father of the Science of Statistics. Along with Galton and Walter Frank Raphael Weldon (1860-1906), a British biologist and biometrist, Pearson founded ***Biometrika*** in 1901, the same year that the British Psychological Society was established. This journal soon became one of the most important outlets for scientific papers available, emphasizing mathematical research in psychology, statistics, and the life sciences.

Meanwhile, Alfred Binet (1857-1911) had established the first French psychological laboratory and, with Theodore Simon (1873-1962), developed the Binet-Simon scale in 1909; this instrument has come to be recognized as the first modern individual intelligence test. Revised forms of the tests are still on the market today and are among the major individual intelligence tests available.

In the United States, advancements in statistics and measurement theory were also rapidly developing. The American Statistical Association, which was founded in Boston in 1839, was growing; and meetings of the ASA were held throughout the United States. The ASA currently publishes two leading journals, the ***American Statistician*** and the ***Journal of the American Statistical Association***.

G. Stanley Hall (1844-1924) opened the first psychological laboratory in this country in 1881 and established the first psychological journal in the United States in 1887, the ***American Journal of Psychology***. This journal emphasized statistically sound scientific papers and influenced the concern for sophisticated methodology in future papers. The American Psychological Association was founded in 1892, with Hall as its first president. And in 1917, Hall established another very important journal, the ***Journal of Applied Psychology***. Meanwhile, James McKeen Cattell (1860-1944) was studying in Germany and in 1886 became the first United States student to complete a doctorate in Wundt's new-psychology program.

Wundt had stressed that the purpose of psychology is to form generalizations about the normal human adult mind. Rather than investigating generalizations of normal behavior, Cattell, much to Wundt's dismay, completed his dissertation on individual differences in reaction time. Cattell soon met Galton and became even more convinced of the need to study individual differences. When he returned to the United States, he developed laboratories and statistics courses at both the University of Pennsylvania and at Columbia University. At Columbia, all entering students were given sensory tests of reaction time, pain sensitivity, visual and auditory tests, and others as a part of their admission requirements, an indication of the increasing interest in testing, measurement theory, and statistics. In 1904, Cattell and James Mark Baldwin (1861-1934) founded the ***Psychological Bulletin***, which has remained a most prestigious forum for papers of a statistical or methodological nature. In 1921, he established The Psychological Corporation, which continues as a major test publisher today.

Edward Lee Thorndike (1874-1949), the most famous of Cattell's American students, taught one of the first courses in educational statistics in this country. He advanced the scientific approach to measurement, especially with his studies in the areas of connectionism and the law of effect. Thorndike is often referred to as the Father of Educational Psychology. Louis Madison Terman (1877-1956) was another American interested in the theory and practical applications of measurement. It was under his direction that the Stanford-Binet form of the original Binet-Simon individual intelligence test was developed at Stanford University in 1916. An expert in early childhood intelligence, Terman estimated that if Galton's intelligence could have been tested at childhood with measures later available to Terman, it would have been approximately 200!

Charles Spearman (1863-1945) was another British student and follower of Galton. His major contributions to statistics and measurement theory were in the areas of factor analysis and in the measurement of mental abilities. He suggested that all data could be divided into two types of factors: a general factor, or *g*-factor, and specific factors. This concept is usually referred to as the two-factor theory, although it is typically viewed as a one factor theory, with the set of specific factors explained separately. Because of his significant contributions in the area, he is often referred to as the Father of Factor Analysis. He also developed much of the foundation for the theory of measurement error and developed one of the first reliability coefficient measures.

William Sealy Gosset (1876-1937), a British statistician and student of Pearson, made a major contribution to the field of statistics with a paper he presented in ***Biometrika*** in 1908. He was an employee of the Guinness Brewery in Dublin, Ireland, where security prohibited employees from publishing findings from plant-related research. However, Gosset's work was so significant that the brewery allowed him to publish his findings as long as he used a pseudonym. He chose to use the name *Student* and subsequently published his findings on the now famous Student's *t*-distribution. This probability distribution has come to be one of the major probability distributions in the field of statistics. Gosset also presented concepts related to random sampling experimentation, concepts associated with degrees of freedom for the chi-square tests, the robustness of the z and t distributions, and recommended the use of separate symbolism for sample and population characteristics.

Gosset then influenced another British statistician who was soon to become one of the modern forces in statistics, Ronald Aylmer Fisher (1890-1962). Fisher was a brilliant statistician who was offered the post of chief statistician under Pearson at Galton's laboratory. However, he and Pearson clashed on numerous occasions, and he instead chose to take a position as chief statistician at the Rothamsted Agricultural Station. This was a significant decision for two reasons. First, many of his future studies were based on agricultural data, which led to the introduction of many terms and experimental designs with agricultural connotations (e.g., plot designs). Second, his split with Pearson limited his ability to publish in ***Biometrika***, which was under Pearson's control. However, his work was so important that he easily found audiences and new outlets for his papers. Among his contributions or advancements to existing concepts are the notions of variance (he introduced the term *variance* in 1918), degrees of freedom with the chi-square, the concept of null hypothesis and hypothesis testing in general, small sample testing, analysis of variance, experimental design, properties of estimators, determining exact sampling distributions for r, r^2, and the F-distribution, the Fisher exact probability test, and fiducial probability. In fact, George W. Snedecor (1881-1974) first used the letter F in the F-distribution as a tribute to Fisher. Fisher was knighted in 1952 as a tribute to his many accomplishments. To provide an insight into the man, the quotation below from William G. Cochran (1914-1980), a colleague of both Snedecor and Fisher, is presented from ***Science***:

> He [Fisher] was also unhappy, particularly later in life, at seeing statistics taught essentially as mathematics by professors who overelaborated their notion (in order to make their theorem seem difficult, in his opinion) and who gave the impression that they had never seen any data and would hastily leave the room if someone appeared with data. (1967, p. 1461)

In 1896, perhaps a dozen universities in the United States offered courses in statistics, although courses in probability had been taught in mathematics departments for many years. But by 1925, at least 84 colleges and universities offered one or more courses in statistics. For example, Glover (1926) reported the following distribution for statistics courses offered in universities: mathematics (57 courses in various universities), economics and social sciences (86), schools of business (53), education (34), psychology (12), public health (11), and agriculture (4).

By this time, statistical methods had advanced considerably. Studies in most disciplines, from education to psychology, from economics to business administration, from sociology to anthropology, from history to agriculture, and others soon began to incorporate improved experimental designs and/or better research techniques. In 1936, Egon Sharpe Pearson (1895-1981), son of Karl Pearson, became editor of ***Biometrika*** and also continued in the scientific tradition established by his famous father. He published many articles in collaboration with Karl, but when he met Jerzy Neyman (1894-1981) in 1925, Egon's statistical focus began to take on a new dimension. Neyman, who was born and educated in what is now a part of Russia, later became a citizen of the United States. Both men were strongly influenced by Gosset and by Fisher, and they began to collaborate on what was to become the foundation of the scientific method as we know it today. They stressed the need for the development of specific alternative hypotheses, the establishment of regions of rejection and non-rejection of hypotheses, the need for determining sources of error related to statistical tests, and the importance of the power of statistical tests (Dudycha & Dudycha, 1972, pp. 23-24).

Modern Advancements

Modern statistics has seen the advancement of a wide variety of statistical concepts, including nonparametric statistics, decision theory, econometrics, multivariate statistical analysis, statistical process control, and others. Each of these areas has roots dating back to earlier times, and each will continue to be refined as new advancements and technology prevail.

Nonparametric Statistics. An important area of statistics that began to appear in the literature of the Twentieth Century is that of nonparametric or distribution-free statistics. (Although the two terms are not conceptually the same, they are typically used interchangeably in the literature.) Emphasizing that the researcher's inability to accurately measure often results in the collection of weak levels of measurement and/or a lack of compliance with specific distribution requirements, supporters of the nonparametric movement began to encourage the use of such nonparametric tools. Sidney Siegel (1916-1961) wrote ***Nonparametric Statistics: For the Behavioral Sciences*** in 1956, and it soon became one of the most widely referenced statistics books of all times; it is currently used by many researchers as a basic guideline for nonparametric statistical procedures. Controversy exists over the importance of nonparametric statistics, but it cannot be denied its impact upon statistical methods and research methodology.

Decision Theory. As mentioned earlier, Bayes developed concepts in the Eighteenth Century in regard to probability that would eventually have a marked influence on modern statistics. Although Bayes' accomplishments went either unnoticed, ignored, or incorrectly used for many years, his work now holds a prominent position in statistics today. Bayesian statistics, sometimes referred to as *decision theory*, is often viewed as a counter approach to the more commonly used statistical procedures (i.e., those referred to as *classical statistics*). Most researchers, however, consider Bayesian statistics as an extension of the classical statistics approach.

Econometrics. The field of economics has also been modernized by the advancement of statistics. Jan Tinbergen (1903-), a Dutch economist, and Ragnar Frisch (1895-1973), from Norway, won Nobel Memorial Prizes in Economic Sciences in 1969 for their use of statistical and mathematical models in economics. In fact, Frisch had earlier created the term *econometrics* to refer to the applications of mathematics in economic theory and in empirical research. Paul Samuelson (1915-) of the United States won the Nobel Memorial Prize in Economic Sciences in 1970. He has made contributions in neoclassical price theory, in advanced mathematical analysis, and in linear programming. His textbook, ***Economics: An Introductory Analysis*** was first published in 1948; it soon became a classic standard in colleges and universities. Other prominent U.S. economists have also won the Nobel prize for their work in econometric theory. Russian-born Wassily Leontief (1906-) won the prize in 1973. Herbert Simon (1916-) won the prize in 1978. Simon is also widely recognized in business, psychology, and economics for his considerable contributions in the areas of decision-making, problem-solving, and business psychology. Lawrence Klein (1920-) won the prize in 1980.

Multivariate Statistical Analysis. Multivariate statistical analysis also became quite popular by the Twentieth Century. The early work of LaPlace, Quetelet, Galton, and Pearson led Spearman to advance the movement of factor analysis. His work in turn influenced Sir Godfrey Hilton Thomson (1881-1955), James Clerk Maxwell Garnett (1880-1958), Cyril Burt (1883-1971), Karl Holzinger (1893-1954), and Louis Leon Thurstone (1887-1955), who is generally considered as the major force behind the advancement of modern factor analysis. Thurstone established ***Psychometrika***, a journal dedicated to modern quantitative psychology; he also founded the Psychometric Society in 1935. Raymond B. Cattell (1905-), who received his Ph.D. under Spearman at the University of London, worked as a research associate at Columbia under Thorndike. He then taught at Harvard and later at the University of Illinois, where he became the first president of the Society for Multivariate Experimental Psychology in 1960. His contributions to factor analysis, along with the work of Hans J. Eysenck (1916-), a German who also studied under Spearman and later became a British citizen after the Nazi movement in Germany, have done much to continue research in applied multivariate statistics. Multiple regression became a well established tool, as did canonical correlation, multivariate analysis of variance (MANOVA), and multiple discriminant analysis. Yet, the practical applications of many of these techniques remained dormant until the availability of sophisticated computer technology in the latter half of the century.

Statistical Process Control. Statistical procedures have taken a strong foothold in industrial settings in the Twentieth Century. Walter A. Shewhart (1891-1967) of Bell Telephone Laboratories made the first sketch of a modern control chart for quality control (QC) or statistical process control (SPC) applications in 1924. He published ***Economic Control of Quality of Manufactured Product*** in 1931, which established the standard for statistical methods in SPC. With Shewhart leading the way, the concepts of quality control and statistical process control rapidly advanced. Harold French Dodge (1893-) and Harry G. Romig (1900-), who were colleagues of Shewhart at Bell Laboratories, developed the Dodge-Romig ***Sampling Inspection Tables*** in 1929. They led the way for applying statistical sampling theory to the inspection process. In 1938, W. Edwards Deming (1900-1993), a statistician, persuaded Shewhart to come to Washington, D.C., to teach his concepts at the Department of Agriculture. Deming became immensely involved in statistical quality control and soon became one of the eminent authorities in the field (Messina, 1987, p. 102). Shewhart and Deming worked together on numerous efforts, including the use of statistical quality control in manufacturing plants during World War II.

The American Society for Mechanical Engineers had been established in 1880; the American Society for Testing and Materials had been established in 1898; and the American Standards Association was established in 1918. These three organizations, along with Bell Laboratories and the American National Standards Institute (also established in 1918), initiated standards for quality control and worked to popularize the use of statistics in United States' industry. The American Society for Quality Control was established in 1946 and enjoys a large membership today. Quality had become such an important issue that in 1987 the Malcolm Baldrige National Quality Improvement Act was signed into law by then President Ronald Reagan, establishing an annual United States National Quality Award to "promote quality awareness, to recognize quality achievements of U.S. companies, and to publicize successful quality strategies." This award was modeled after the Deming award, to be discussed shortly.

In addition to Shewhart and Deming, another key player in the development of SPC was Joseph M. Juran (1904-   ). Deming and Juran not only contributed to SPC in the United States; they also had a major impact upon the development of *Japan* as a world leader in quality and productivity!

Japanese Quality Control. At the onset of World War II, the Union of Japanese Science and Engineering (JUSE) was formed to support the Japanese war effort. After the war, Kenichi Koyanagi (deceased 1965), the leader of the JUSE group, was able to hold the organization together to help in the reconstruction of Japan. JUSE invited Deming to Japan in 1950 to assist their statisticians in studies regarding housing and nutrition and to help them to prepare for the 1951 census (Deming, 1986, p. 487). In 1954, Juran was also invited to Japan, where he provided skillful training and insights into statistical process control and management theory. In 1961, the Asian Productivity Organization was established, which has published numerous books and articles in statistical process control and furthered the advancement of SPC in that country.

Deming had such a profound impact upon the Japanese that they invited him back on a regular basis. In 1951, JUSE established the Deming award (commonly referred to as the Deming prize); this prize has become one of the most distinguished awards in industry. Actually, two awards are given annually, one to a company and one to an individual. The prestige of these awards and the Baldrige award can result in millions of dollars in increased business for companies that have won the prize. Deming, Juran, Kaoru Ishikawa (1915-1989), and Genichi Taguchi (1924-   ) have had a major impact upon the modernization of world industry in general and Japanese rise to prominence in specific. Ishikawa's ***Guide to Quality Control*** (1968; 1976) has become a classic in the field of QC. Ishikawa, a winner of the Deming prize, has been referred to as the Father of Quality Control Circles (QCC). The cause-and-effect diagrams (Fishbone diagrams) that are used in problem solving are sometimes referred to as Ishikawa diagrams. The methods developed by Taguchi have begun to challenge the traditional design of experiments and have had an impact upon industrial research.

The Age of Computers

Methods designed to increase and/or simplify computations developed rather slowly since the time of the *abacus*, one of the earliest of the counting tools. Although we think of the abacus as a Chinese tool, it was probably invented in Babylonia, now Iraq, as early as 3000 B.C. (Augarten, 1984, pp. 3-4). The word was derived from the Greek word *abakos*, which means board, tablet, or counting table. The Romans used a counting table or abacus consisting of beads (called *calculi*), which is the plural of *calculus* (or pebble). Thus, we have the origin of the word *calculate*. The Chinese also used a similar form of the abacus, their *suan-pan*; the Japanese used an abacus known as *soroban*; the Russians used one called the *s'choty*. It has also been discovered that the ancient Inca Indians who occupied the land now known as Peru also had a similar counting table; it was known as a *quipu* (Newman, 1956, pp. 456-464).

As noted earlier, Napier developed logarithms in 1614, providing a computational method for solving problems that would otherwise require extensive time and effort. Napier also invented a mechanical calculating device known as *Napier's Bones* in 1617. William Oughtred (1574-1660) invented a form of the slide rule in 1622. Although Pascal is usually given credit for inventing the first mechanical calculator, a relatively unknown German professor by the name of Wilhelm Schickard (1592-1635) actually built the first calculator in 1623. Schickard, a colleague of Kepler, referred to his invention as the *Calculating Clock.* In 1642, Pascal developed a mechanical machine that could add, the world's second adding machine beyond the abacus. This machine came to be known as the *Pascaline*, or simply as the *Pascale.*

Leibniz of Germany then invented a machine, the Stepped Reckoner, which could count, add, subtract, multiply, and divide in 1671 (Augarten, pp. 30-35). Many other attempts were made to develop a practical, accurate calculating machine. Xavier Thomas de Colmar (1785-1870) of France invented the *Arithmometer.* Finally, Charles Babbage (1792-1871), an English mathematician, planned a universal digital machine that he called the *Difference Engine* in 1823. Although the machine was never actually completed, it and the *Analytical Engine*, another of Babbage's efforts that was begun in 1834, were two of the true forerunners of the computer.

In the Twentieth Century real advancements in computational time occurred. Vannevar Bush (1890-1974) led a team of researchers at Massachusetts Institute of Technology's Electrical Engineering Department, working on an analog electrical differential analyzer. The machine was in operation in 1930; however, it soon became obvious that "the future belonged to electronic digital computers" (Augarten, 1984, p. 88). Many scientists and mathematicians soon became interested in advancing computer technology, including George Robert Stibitz (1900-1995), who is credited by many as the father of the modern digital computer. Meanwhile, Konrad Zuse (1910-   ) of Germany rediscovered the ideas of Babbage's Analytical Engine. Zuse decided to build a computer that could theoretically solve *any* equation, one that used a central processing unit, a control unit, a unit for reading input from a punched tape, and an output unit. He also decided to use the binary system instead of the decimal system, saving enormous economy in regard to on/off switches. He developed a set of operating rules for the machine, based on *Boolean algebra* using the three most basic operations: AND, OR, and NOT. He completed his first prototype, the Z1, in 1938 and began on an improved model soon after. In 1941, he built the "first operational general-purpose program-controlled calculator" (Augarten, pp. 89-92). Fortunately for the Allies during World War II, Hitler did not recognize the potential of these computers and did not provide government support. Zuse was permitted to leave Berlin at the end of the war, went to Zurich, established a small computer company, and the German branch of the computer revolution came to an end.

In 1943, the first automatic calculator, *Mark I*, was developed by Howard Hathaway Aiken (1900-1973) of Harvard, with the assistance of International Business Machines (IBM). In 1946, the *Electronic Numerator, Integrator, Analyzer, and Computer (ENIAC)* was built by J. P. Eckert and J. William Mauchley at the University of Pennsylvania. This 30-ton, 8-foot tall machine included 17,000 vacuum tubes and was the world's first programmable computer. Scientists received federal grants to help fund the design and construction of the ENIAC. Years later, much of the ENIAC was on display at the Smithsonian Institution; however, part of it was returned to the University of Pennsylvania in 1996 and restarted with great fanfare to celebrate the 50th anniversary of its development. Amazingly, it packed little more power than one of today's inexpensive calculators.

Although the ENIAC had government support, it was completed too late for the war effort. Through private, government, or public funds, other computers followed shortly thereafter. In 1953 the *Whirlwind I* was built at the Massachusetts Institute of Technology, using the first core memory (Veldman, 1967, p. 4). By 1958, transistors replaced the large vacuum tubes that were used in the earlier machines, and the age of computer technology had begun.

There was also a remarkable growth in the calculator industry during this time period. The development and marketing of the HP-35 by Hewlett-Packard in 1972 signaled the onset of the race for the consumer market in handheld calculators was on. Creativity in the development of such useful tools has been impressive. Complex techniques such as multiple regression can now be obtained through the use of hand calculators, which have remarkable programming capabilities and extensive memory.

Just as the 1970's will be remembered as the decade in which the handheld calculator (sometimes referred to as the pocket calculator) became commonplace, the 1980's will be remembered as the decade in which the personal computer became widely available. Numerous companies entered the market, competing for purchases by individual consumers, small businesses, and large businesses as well. Many entered the market early (e.g., the Osborne and the KayPro personal computers), only to be displaced by larger companies such as IBM and Apple. In fact, at one point advancements in personal computers occurred so rapidly that customers became almost fearful to buy, wondering whether their purchase would be outdated within *months* by new improvements on the horizon. The growth was so rapid and profound that ***Time Magazine***, breaking from its tradition of annually naming a "man of the year," said that for 1982 the man of the year was not a man at all but was a machine! It named the personal computer as "Machine of the Year for 1982" ("Machine of the Year," 1982). Personal computers have now become commonplace in the home, taking their place along side the television and radio!

Perhaps nothing has had such an impact upon the applications of statistical methods as the development of the mainframe computer, the calculator, and the personal computer. The use of statistics has increased at a remarkable rate. Of course, users of these tools could not take advantage of hardware technology without the availability of software. At first, much of the software was awkward and poorly documented. Gradually, textbooks became available that included statistical computer programs as supplements to their discussions of statistical methods, such as Veldman's ***Fortran Programming for the Behavioral Sciences*** (1967), Cooley and Lohnes' ***Multivariate Data Analysis*** (1971), and Overall and Klett's ***Applied Multivariate Analysis*** (1972). However, consumer pressure resulted in the production of software packages that are more *user friendly*. Generalized packages became available that require only a minimum of computer knowledge. A number of highly sophisticated statistical procedures are now available to the general public without a need for programming expertise, including the *Biomedical Computer Programs (BMD-P)*, the *Statistical Package for the Social Sciences (SPSS* and $SPSS^X$*)*, the *Statistical Analysis System (SAS)*, *Minitab*, *Time Series Processor (TSP)*, IBM's

Scientific Subroutine Package (SSP), the *Personnel Subroutines (PERSUB)*, *Epistat*, *SYSTAT*, *IDA*, *Storm*, *MASS*, *MathCAD*, and *Microstat*. Spreadsheets with statistical and graphics software packages are also available, including *Excel*, *Lotus*, *PlanPerfect*, *Quattro*, and *Supercalc*. Examples of other graphics packages include *CorelDraw*, *DrawPerfect*, *Harvard Graphics*, and *Cricket Graph*.

Software packages even exist for the personal calculators. Many have built-in or programmable routines that allow the user to solve systems of simultaneous equations, matrix algebra problems, integration problems, multiple regression problems with limited variables, and other statistical functions. Some even have probability distributions built-in and also plot data.

Professional Societies and Journals

A number of professional associations (some of which have already been cited) were founded that have had a direct impact upon the advancement of statistics and research methods. The Académie Royale des Sciences was founded in 1666 and now continues as the Institut de France. The London Statistical Society (1834) later became the Royal Statistical Society (1887). Others include the American Statistical Association (1839), American Society for Mechanical Engineers (1880), American Psychological Association (1892), American Society for Testing and Materials (1898), British Psychological Society (1901), International Institute of Agriculture (1905), American Standards Association (1918), American National Standards Institute (1918), Econometric Society (1930), Institute of Mathematical Statistics (1935), Psychometric Society (1935), Union of Japanese Science and Engineering (c. 1940), American Society for Quality Control (1946), Society for Multivariate Experimental Psychology (1960), Asian Productivity Organization (1961), and the American Institute for Decision Sciences (1969), which changed its name to the Decision Sciences Institute in 1986 so that its acronym would not be confused with the AIDS virus.

Many of these societies have sponsored important journals, and other journals have developed independently. Below is a representative, although incomplete and ever-changing, list of journals that are dedicated to or typically include articles related to statistics and research methods, along with their library call numbers:

Table 1.1

Journals	Call Numbers
Abstracts of Bioanalytic Technology	QR-1-A32
Administrative Science Quarterly	HD-28-A25
Advances in Applied Probability	QA-273-A34
Allgemeines Statistisches Archiv	HA-1-A4
American Economic Review	HB-1-E26
American Educational Research Journal	L-11-A66
American Journal of Mathematics	QA-1-A51
American Statistical Association Journal	HA-1-A6

American Statistician	HA-1-A614
Analysis Instrumentation	QD-73-A5
Annals of Economic and Social Measurement	H-62-A55
Annals of Mathematical Statistics	HA-1-A8
Annals of Probability	QA-273-A5
Annals of Statistics	QA-276-A64
Applied Statistics	HA-1-A65
Behavior Research Methods and Instrumentation	BF-180-B4
Behavior Science Research	H-1-B452
Biometrics	QH-301-B48
Biometrika	QH-301-B5
British Journal of Mathematical and Statistical Psychology	QH-301-B5
Bulletin of Mathematical Statistics	QA-276-B85
Decision Sciences	HD-69-D4D4
Econometrica	HB-1-E2
Educational and Psychological Measurement	BF-1-E3
Explorations in Economic Research	HC-101-A1-E9
Industrial Research	T-175-I49
Institute of Mathematical Statistics	QA-276-A1I5
Industrial Quality Control	TS-155-A1I6
International Statistical Review	HA-11-I506
Journal of Applied Behavior Analysis	BF-636-A1-J6
Journal of Applied Probability	QA-276-J69
Journal of Business and Economic Statistics	HB-137-J68
Journal of Business Research	HF-5001-J62
Journal of Economic Theory	HB-1-J64
Journal of Educational Measurement	LB-1131-A1N32
Journal of Educational Research	L-11-J815
Journal of Experimental Education	L-11-J77
Journal of Experimental Psychology	BF-1-J6
Journal of Financial and Quantitative Analysis	HG-1-J65
Journal of Functional Analysis	QA-320-J63
Journal of Marketing Research	HF-5415.2-J66
Journal of Mathematical Psychology	BF-1-J657
Journal of Multivariate Psychology	QA-278-J68
Journal of the Operational Research Society	HD-20.5-O22
Journal of Psycholinguistic Research	P-106-J68
Journal of Quality Technology	TS-155-A1J6
Journal of the Royal Statistical Society: Series A (General)	HA-1-R8
Journal of the Royal Statistical Society: Series B (Methodological)	HA-1-R85
Management Science	HD-28-I453
Management Technology	HD-28-M385
Market Research Society Journal	HF-5415-A2-C52

Multivariate Behavioral Research	BF-1-M8
Operations Research	Q-I75-O63
Psychological Bulletin	BF-1-P75
Psychometrika	BF-1-P86
Public Opinion Quarterly	HM-261-A1P8
Quality Progress	TS-155-A1I62
Quality Review Bulletin	RA-972-Q8
Research/Development	T-175-I472
Researcher	Q-4-R42
Research Management	T-175.5-R4
Research Quarterly	GV-201-R4
Review of Economics and Statistics	HA-1-R35
Review of Educational Research	L-11-R35
Sankhya	HA-1-S313
Science	Q-1-S35
Scientific Research	Q-180-A1536
Social Science Research Council	H-62-S7243
Society for Industrial and Applied Mathematics	QA-1-S18
Sociological Methodology	HM-24-S55
Sociological Methods and Research	HM-24-S6
Technometrics	QA-276-T4
Theory and Decision	H-61-T465
Theory of Probability and Its Applications	QA-273-T413

Precautions

Unfortunately, many users of statistical packages such as those cited above suffer from an inadequate training in the fundamental concepts of statistics, let alone the more advanced techniques that are included in these packages. External pressures often cause researchers to go beyond their knowledge, employing a particular statistical method that may not be appropriate and/or necessary. For example, aspiring researchers often perceive professional journals as only accepting articles that include highly advanced statistical analyses of the data (regardless of the nature of the data or the purpose of the study). Such researchers may try to make too much of the data base or unwittingly may employ incorrect statistical methods during the analysis phase of the investigation. The present text stresses the importance of a fundamental background in statistics and forewarns the reader not to fall into the unfortunate trap of simply using available computer packages and/or statistical techniques in the hopes of discovering something *statistically significant*! There are no substitutes for logic, sound methodology, and good experimental design, as research dictates what statistical procedure is to be employed; hopefully, the reader will adhere to such precautions when making decisions in regard to statistical procedures.

References

Augarten, S. (1984). ***Bit by bit.*** New York: Ticknor & Fields.

Bell, E. T. (1956). The Queen of Mathematics. In J. R. Newman (Ed.), ***The world of mathematics*** (pp. 498-515). New York: Simon and Schuster.

Cochran. W. G. (1967). Footnote. ***Science, 156***, 1460-1462.

Cooley, W. W., & Lohnes, P. R. (1971). ***Multivariate data analysis.*** New York: John Wiley & Sons.

Deming, W. E. (1986). ***Out of the crisis.*** Cambridge, MA: MIT Center for Advanced Engineering Study.

Dewey, J. (1910). ***How we think.*** Boston: D. C. Heath.

Dudycha, A. L., & Dudycha, L. W. (1972). Behavioral statistics: An historical perspective. In R. E. Kirk (Ed.), ***Statistical issues: A reader for the behavioral sciences.*** Monterey, CA: Brooks/Cole.

Duncan, A. J. (1986). ***Quality control and industrial statistics.*** Homewood, IL: Richard D. Irwin.

Glover, J. W. (1926). Requirements for statisticians and their training: Part I--Statistical teaching in American colleges and universities. ***Journal of the American Statistical Association, 21***, 419-424.

Guilford, J. P. (1954). ***Psychometric methods.*** New York: McGraw-Hill.

Hankins, F. H. (1968). ***Adolphe Quetelet as statistician.*** New York: AMS Press.

Machine of the Year. (1983, January 3). ***Time Magazine, 121***(1), pp. 12-24.

Messina, W. S. (1987). ***Statistical quality control for manufacturing managers.*** New York: John Wiley & Sons.

Newman, J. R. (Ed.). (1956). ***The world of mathematics.*** New York: Simon & Schuster.

Overall, J. E., & Klett, C. J. (1972). ***Applied multivariate analysis.*** New York: McGraw-Hill.

Pearson, E. S. (Ed.). (1978). ***The history of statistics in the 17th and 18th centuries: Against the changing background of intellectual, scientific and religious thought. Lectures by Karl Pearson given at University College London during the academic sessions 1921-1933.*** New York: Macmillan.

Ross, W. P. (Ed.). (1955). ***Aristotle: Selections.*** New York: Charles Scribner's Sons.

Veldman, D. J. (1967). ***Fortran programming for the behavioral sciences.*** New York: Holt, Rinehart, & Winston.

Walker, H. M. (1929). ***Studies in the history of statistical method.*** Baltimore: The Williams & Wilkins Company.

Westergaard, H. (1968). ***Contributions to the history of statistics.*** New York: Agathon Press.

Practice Problems
Multiple Choice

1. Which of the following countries probably provided us with the earliest contributions in statistics?

   A. Egypt
   B. Greece
   C. Italy
   D. Germany
   E. France

2. During which time period was there the largest void in theoretical inquiries into science and mathematics?

   A. The Renaissance
   B. The rise of the Roman Empire
   C. The rise of the Greek Empire
   D. The European medieval period
   E. The Seventeenth through Twentieth Centuries

3. Which of the following made major contributions to the field of differential calculus?

   A. Pierre de Fermat
   B. Sir Isaac Newton
   C. Gottfried Wilhelm von Leibniz
   D. John Bernoulli
   E. All of the above contributed to the advancement of differential calculus.

4. Which of the following is not a correct pairing of scholar with work?

   A. Captain John Graunt and ***Natural and Political Observations on the London Mortality***
   B. Abraham DeMoivre and ***The Doctrine of Chances***
   C. John Dewey and ***How We Think***
   D. Charles Darwin and ***On the Origin of Species***
   E. All of the above are correct pairings.

5. Which of the following most likely discovered the normal distribution?

   A. Pythagoras
   B. Abraham DeMoivre
   C. Karl Gauss
   D. Karl Pearson
   E. Sir Francis Galton

6. Which of the following is often used synonymously with *decision theory*?

   A. Gaussian statistics
   B. Bayesian statistics
   C. Bernoulli statistics
   D. Pascalian statistics
   E. Boolean statistics

7. Which of the following did not play a role in the development of the correlation coefficient?

   A. Sir Francis Galton
   B. Auguste Bravais
   C. James Douglas Hamilton Dickson
   D. Karl Pearson
   E. All of the above contributed to the development of the correlation coefficient.

8. Who was known as the Passionate Statistician?

   A. Blaise Pascal
   B. Karl Pearson
   C. Florence Nightingale
   D. Dorothea Dix
   E. John Dewey

9. Who developed what is commonly recognized as the first modern individual intelligence test?

   A. Sir Francis Galton
   B. Charles Darwin
   C. Alfred Binet
   D. Wilhelm Wundt
   E. Pafnuti Tchebycheff

10. Who developed the *t*-distribution?

    A. Karl Gauss
    B. Isaac Newton
    C. William Sealy Gosset
    D. Ronald Aylmer Fisher
    E. Charles Spearman

11. Which of the following was said to be so "unhappy, particularly later in life, at seeing statistics taught essentially as mathematics by professors who overelaborated their notion (in order to make their theorem seem difficult, in his opinion) and who gave the impression that they had never seen any data and would hastily leave the room if someone appeared with data"?

A. Karl Pearson
B. Ronald Aylmer Fisher
C. William Sealy Gosset
D. Charles Spearman
E. Edward Lee Thorndike

12. Which of the following is often referred to as the Father of Factor Analysis?

A. Ronald Aylmer Fisher
B. Edward Lee Thorndike
C. James McKeen Cattell
D. Charles Spearman
E. Raymond B. Cattell

13. Which of the following is recognized as the leader in the advancement of quality control?

A. Harold French Dodge
B. Joseph M. Juran
C. Walter A. Shewhart
D. Hans J. Eysenck
E. Charles Babbage

14. Who is usually recognized as primarily responsible for Japan's rapid movement in the areas of quality and productivity?

A. Kaoru Ishikawa
B. Genichi Taguchi
C. Kenichi Koyanagi
D. Joseph M. Juran
E. W. Edwards Deming

15. Which of the following is not credited with developing an early form of a computer?

A. John Napier
B. Gottfried Wilhelm von Leibniz
C. Charles Babbage
D. Aristotle
E. All of the above are known to have developed an early form of a computer.

16. Which of the following is ***not*** a widely used statistical software package designed for analyzing data?

A. Statistical Package for the Social Sciences (SPSS)
B. Statistical Analysis System (SAS)
C. Biomedical Computer Programs (BMD-P)
D. Minitab
E. All of the above are major statistical software packages.

INDEX

Index